ADMINISTRATIVE LAW

CAROLINA ACADEMIC PRESS
Context and Practice Series
Michael Hunter Schwartz
Series Editor

Administrative Law
Richard Henry Seamon

Civil Procedure for All States
Benjamin V. Madison, III

Constitutional Law
David Schwartz and Lori Ringhand

Contracts
Michael Hunter Schwartz and Denise Riebe

Current Issues in Constitutional Litigation
Sarah E. Ricks, with contributions by Evelyn M. Tenenbaum

Employment Discrimination
Susan Grover, Sandra F. Sperino, and Jarod S. Gonzalez

Evidence
Pavel Wonsowicz

International Women's Rights, Equality, and Justice
Christine M. Venter

The Lawyer's Practice
Kris Franklin

Professional Responsibility
Barbara Glesner Fines

Sales
Edith R. Warkentine

ADMINISTRATIVE LAW

A Context and Practice Casebook

Richard Henry Seamon
UNIVERSITY OF IDAHO COLLEGE OF LAW

CAROLINA ACADEMIC PRESS
Durham, North Carolina

ISBN 13: 978-1-59460-676-2
LCCN: 2012948785

Carolina Academic Press
700 Kent Street
Durham, North Carolina 27701
Telephone (919) 489-7486
Fax (919) 493-5668
www.cap-press.com

Printed in the United States of America

To my family: Holly, Maggie, and Pei Tzu

And to my friend, mentor, and the inspiration for this book: John H. Reese

Contents

Part One • Administrative Law Fundamentals

Part Three • Agency Adjudication

List of Diagrams and Figures

Table of Cases

Series Editor's Preface

Welcome to a new type of casebook. Designed by leading experts in law school teaching and learning, Context and Practice casebooks assist law professors and their students to work together to learn, minimize stress, and prepare for the rigors and joys of practicing law. Student learning and preparation for law practice are the guiding ethics of these books.

Why would we depart from the tried and true? Why have we abandoned the legal education model by which we were trained? Because legal education can and must improve.

In Spring 2007, the Carnegie Foundation published *Educating Lawyers: Preparation for the Practice of Law* and the Clinical Legal Education Association published *Best Practices for Legal Education*. Both works reflect in-depth efforts to assess the effectiveness of modern legal education, and both conclude that legal education, as presently practiced, falls quite short of what it can and should be. Both works criticize law professors' rigid adherence to a single teaching technique, the inadequacies of law school assessment mechanisms, and the dearth of law school instruction aimed at teaching law practice skills and inculcating professional values. Finally, the authors of both books express concern that legal education may be harming law students. Recent studies show that law students, in comparison to all other graduate students, have the highest levels of depression, anxiety and substance abuse.

The problems with traditional law school instruction begin with the textbooks law teachers use. Law professors cannot implement *Educating Lawyers* and *Best Practices* using texts designed for the traditional model of legal education. Moreover, even though our understanding of how people learn has grown exponentially in the past 100 years, no law school text to date even purports to have been designed with educational research in mind.

The Context and Practice Series is an effort to offer a genuine alternative. Grounded in learning theory and instructional design and written with *Educating Lawyers* and *Best Practices* in mind, Context and Practice casebooks make it easy for law professors to change.

I welcome reactions, criticisms, and suggestions; my e-mail address is michael.schwartz@washburn.edu. Knowing the author(s) of these books, I know they, too, would appreciate your input; we share a common commitment to student learning. In fact, students, if your professor cares enough about your learning to have adopted this book, I bet s/he would welcome your input, too!

Professor Michael Hunter Schwartz, Series Designer and Editor
Co-Director, Institute for Law Teaching and Learning
Associate Dean for Faculty and Academic Development

Preface

Thank you for opening this book. This preface explains the book's organizing theme, its premises, and its major features.

The book's organizing theme is **power**. Every action by an administrative agency must rest on a valid grant of power and must obey all limits on, and requirements for exercising, that power. Lawyers solve most administrative law problems by identifying and analyzing the laws granting and limiting an agency's power to take some action; and marshalling facts to persuade the agency to exercise its power favorably to the client. When an agency has failed to act within its powers—or failed to obey limits on, or requirements for exercising, those powers—the administrative lawyer must determine what court has power to remedy the agency's failure. The courts' power has special importance because it includes authority to review agency action for abuses of power in the many, many matters as to which agencies have discretion. Besides invoking judicial power, the lawyer may usefully tap other sources of power to control agency action: namely, the executive and legislative branches, and last but not least, the People, who are of course the ultimate source of all this power and the ultimate source of its control.

The book rests on two premises about administrative law. The premises concern (1) the practice of administrative law and (2) preparation for the practice of administrative law:

1. The practice of administrative law mostly involves (a) identifying and analyzing the **laws** (primarily statutes) governing a particular matter involving an administrative agency; (b) identifying and gathering the **facts** relevant to the matter and properly presenting them to the agency (or on behalf of the agency); and (c) identifying and dealing with the **people** in the agency responsible for the matter.

2. To prepare law students for the practice of administrative law, a course on administrative law should systematically (a) introduce students to (i) the variety of **laws** relevant to solving administrative law problems; and (ii) frameworks for analyzing those laws; (b) help students learn to (i) identify what **facts** are relevant to a particular administrative law problem; and (ii) present facts favorable to the client in accordance with legally required procedures; and (c) introduce students to the ways in which authority given to an administrative agency is exercised by ordinary **people** within that agency, and to the ways in which a lawyer may effectively and ethically influence those people's decision making.

These two premises underlie the following features that distinguish this book from traditional casebooks:

A. Rather than excerpting innumerable appellate court opinions, the book excerpts many statutes, agency rules, and other executive-branch material, with the aim of helping students learn to analyze the main ingredients of administrative law.

B.   Rather than focusing on judicial review of agency proceedings, the book focuses on how lawyers can participate in agency proceedings in ways designed to produce outcomes favorable to clients (recognizing that the agency itself may be the lawyer's client). This focus requires careful examination of agency procedures, including procedures for presenting relevant facts and for settling matters or otherwise resolving them informally.

C.   Rather than limiting itself to the inclusion of problems, the book includes many ways of prompting active learning, to prepare students for the self-education process that they must develop to practice administrative law competently. Specifically, Chapter 2 sets out a problem solving framework that provides the architecture for the book and for organizing student learning. Besides that broad framework, the book includes chapter problems at the beginning of each chapter, exercises and graphics within each chapter, and professional development reflection questions at the end of each chapter. All aim to help students organize the material and learn analytic frameworks for solving problems.

The book is meant to be easy for students and teachers to use, especially teachers who are new to the teaching of administrative law or who wish an "off the shelf" product that they do not need to supplement with their own material. Here are the features meant to make the book easy to use:

i.   What you see is what you get. The book has a transparent, logical organization and explicit objectives, and the writing aims to be exceptionally clear.

ii.   This is a not a casebook; it's a course book. The book relies mainly on author-created material, instead of judicial opinions, to teach the law. This minimizes the need to use class time to extract the relevant legal principles from judicial opinions, so that class time can be used instead on other activities, such as discussion of the chapter problems, exercises, graphics, and professional development questions.

iii.   The book's questions generally have answers, and its problems generally have solutions. At least, the answers and solutions are governed by material presented in the book. Complete answers, solutions, and explanations are found in the teacher's manual, which also includes detailed advice for presenting the material on a day-to-day basis.

iv.   The book is clean. It is not cluttered by exhaustive citation of primary law (e.g., case law) or secondary material (e.g., law review articles). The teacher's manual includes citations to selected, additional primary and secondary material where it might be helpful.

v.   The book is progressive. It gets more challenging as students get ready for more challenging material. Thus, the book is organized (A) to present more accessible subjects first, saving less accessible ones for later in the book; and (B) to provide more structure and repetition of key concepts at the beginning of the book than in later chapters, where students are expected to supply their own structure and do their own review of key concepts.

It will help users of this book, and those considering using it, to know two last things. First, the book uses one agency, the Consumer Product Safety Commission (CPSC), to illustrate various administrative law issues throughout the book. Dozens of other agencies are mentioned as well. But the CPSC serves as the "go to" agency, primarily because it regulates a matter with which people are familiar and it has a fairly compact, fairly typical organic statute. Second, almost every chapter begins with at least one chapter problem. The chapter problems have two purposes: (1) to orient students to the material that follows, so they have a sense of what kinds of problems the material can be used to analyze; and (2) to help students review and deepen their understanding of the chapter's material after they have finished studying that material. A teacher can have students skip any or all chapter problems entirely or have students read them only for orientation to the material. Except for a handful of exercises, nothing else in the book depends on students' having read the chapter problems. The exercises, too, are free standing, to give teachers flexibility in how and whether to use them.

I hope you like the book. I welcome your comments, especially your suggestions for improvement. Please email them to me at richard@uidaho.edu. Thank you.

Acknowledgments

I thank the wonderful folks at Carolina Academic Press, including Keith Sipe, Linda Lacy, Tim Colton, Chris Harrow, and Charlsey Rutan.

I thank Michael Hunter Schwartz for inviting me to be part of this pioneering casebook series (even though this is not really a casebook); for his patience with my delay in finishing it; and for his insightful editorial comments. Mostly, I thank him for being so wise, enthusiastic, and inspirational.

I thank four law school colleagues: Dean Don Burnett, for giving me research funding and moral support; Travis Spears, for painstaking research assistance and cite checking; Janis Steffens, for preparing this book's lengthy table of cases and much other editorial assistance; and Ridley Williams, for helping me create this book's graphics and for much other editorial assistance.

I thank student-colleagues who used drafts of this book as their textbook and gave me tons of constructive feedback.

Specifically, the students who took the course in the Spring 2011 semester and helped improve this book are: Brandon Berrett; Katheryn Bilodeau; Jeffrey Bower; Daniel Brady; Dale Braunger; James Browitt; Brandon Brown; Jennifer Brozik; Mark Cecchini Beaver; Kiley Cobb; Ruth Coose; William Reed Cotton; Ryan Crandall; Tanner Crowther; Nita Day; Jason DeLange; Christian Dillman; Elizabeth Dillman; Ryan Dustin; Samuel Eaton; Rainier Elias; Catherine Enright; Theodore Fairchild; Sandy Flores; Mike Griffeath; Kenneth Haack; Gregory Haller; Jameson Hayes; Amanda Herndon; Ted Hobden; Nancy Hurd; Matthew Janz; Paul Jefferies; Andrew Jorgensen; VonDean Renee Karel; Yvonne Ketilsson; Greg Lawson; Scott Lindstrom; Jamal Lyksett; Scott Maisey; Megan Marshall; Traci McCall; Lauren McConnell; John McDevitt; Merete Meador; Vala Metz; Amanda Montalvo; Daniel Mooney; Brian Morris; Evan Muir; Andra Nelson; Johnny O'Barr; Carolyn O'Hara; Christine Olcott; Jennifer Ouellette; Ky Papke; Austin Ross Phillips; Joseph Popplewell; Kartikey Pradhan; Tyler Rice; Casey Riedner; Brandon Ritchie; Aaron Rothrock; Brett Schiller; Brian Schlect; Lisa Schoettger; Ryley Siegner; Matthew Simmons; Esther Sjoren; Jeffrey Slack; James Spencer Smyth; Nolan Sorensen; Christopher Stephens; Steven Stuchlik; Deena Tvinnereim; Matthew VanZeipel; Adam Warr; Jennifer Pleasy Wayas; Mackenzie Jo Welch; Ashley White; Justin Widner; Nolan Wittrock; and Cally Younger.

The students who took the course in the Fall 2011 semester and helped improve this book are: Casi Akerblade; John Anderson; Reed Anderson; Andrew Barton; Katherine Berst; Kimberly Bialock; Josh Bishop; Brittany Ann Bricker; Christopher Brown; Marc Bybee; Joan Callahan; Brian Church; Nathan Cuoio; Patrick Davis; Merritt Decker; Jeremy Deus; Brian Dosch; Jessica Eby; Piper Elmer; Maren Ericson; James Erwin; Tanya Finigan; Adrien Fox; Kristina Fugate; Kale Gans; Anna Garner; Brian Garner; Mark Gawlak; Abigail Germaine; Jane Gordon; Andrew Goshgarian; Monica Gray; Paul Hanes; Katherine Hawkins; Erin Hodgin-Tomlin; Reginald Holmquist; Kirk Houston; Jaclyn Hovda; Alison Hunter; Ryan Hunter; Jayde James; Ryan Jenks; Nathan Jones; Adam Juratovac; Brian

Kanswe; Joslynn Keating; Megan Kernan; Gary Mitchell Kirkham; Michael Kirkham; Shanna Knight; Neal Koskella; Chris Lebens; Ryan Montoya; Phillip Nelsen; Nathan Nielson; Allison Parker; Kristen Pearson; Jacob Pierson; Jessica Pilgrim; Zaida Rivera; Megan Ruble; Micah Runnels; Kurt Schwab; Brian Sheldon; James Storm Shirley; Allen Shoff; Kresten Snow; Rick Sommer; Travis Spears; Rex Steele; Matthew Stucki; Andrew Swanson; Bradley Sweat; Amy Swoboda; Aaron Tribble; Michelle Volkema; Bryan Wheat; Michael Winchester; Erica Wood; and Sarah Wyatt.

Lastly, I thank John H. Reese for writing an administrative law casebook that was ahead of its time and inviting me to participate in its second edition. *See* John H. Reese and Richard H. Seamon, Administrative Law: Principles and Practice (2nd ed. 2003). Whatever virtues this book may have are traceable to John and his work.

ADMINISTRATIVE LAW

PART ONE

Administrative Law Fundamentals

Chapter 1

Welcome to Administrative Law!

Overview

This chapter welcomes you to the field of administrative law and answers frequently asked questions that newcomers to the field often have. As explained in the preface, we begin each chapter with a "chapter problem" to orient you to the material that follows it.

Chapter Problem

Imagine you are a member of your State's legislature. A twelve-year-old girl who lives in the State dies from blood poisoning after getting a tattoo from a local tattoo parlor. People call on the state legislature to do something. Compare and contrast the advantages and disadvantages of the legal system's existing responses, and potential *additional* responses, to this tragic event:

1. Under existing law, the tattoo parlor owner or employees, or both, may be civilly liable to the parents or the child's estate, or both, under the tort law in the State where the city is located. Of course, liability in tort will depend on (1) someone like the parents or the executor of the child's estate filing a lawsuit; and (2) establishing liability by, for example, proof of negligence. A successful civil action could produce an award of money to the estate or the parents, or both.

2. Under existing law, the tattoo parlor owner or employees, or both, may be criminally liable for manslaughter under state law if a prosecutor decides to prosecute and proves criminal liability beyond a reasonable doubt. Proof of manslaughter in many States requires proof of "gross negligence."

3. The State could enact legislation banning tattoo parlors from operating in the State.

4. The State could enact legislation requiring tattoo parlors to get a license from a newly created state agency and to operate subject to random inspections by that agency to ensure compliance with standards to ensure safe and hygienic conditions.

A. What Is This All About?

If you are like this book's author when he began a course on administrative law many years ago, you may be wondering what a course on administrative law is all about. To many people, the term "administrative law" does not mean much (but sounds like it might be boring!). This section will tell you what administrative law is about, in 500 words or so.

Administrative law is the law governing administrative agencies. Administrative agencies are government entities that do the government's work using governmental powers. Administrative agencies collect taxes and collect trash; protect the country against international threats and protect individuals from crime; deliver mail and issue Social Security checks; and grant driver's licenses and licenses to build nuclear power plants. Administrative agencies do all these things, and much more, using an array of powers, including powers that affect the legal rights and duties of individuals and the public—and this is where lawyers come in.

In this book and in a law school course on administrative law, you will learn much more about:

(1) how and why agencies are *created*;

(2) how they *exercise their powers* to carry out their assigned duties; and

(3) how they are *controlled*.

Your study of the *creation* of agencies will primarily be the study of legislation—because most agencies are created by legislation—but will also include learning constitutional limits on the creation of agencies. Your study of agencies' *exercise* of various powers will focus on the procedural requirements for exercising the powers. These procedural requirements come mostly from statutes, but can also come from other sources, including the agency's own procedural rules. Your study of how agencies are *controlled* will focus mostly on judicial review of agency action, in which courts ensure that an agency has acted within the scope of its powers and has followed the required procedures. The organizing theme of all this is power. Students of administrative law learn about agency power and how, as lawyers, to control it.

As you study these matters, you will encounter three features of administrative law. You will benefit from knowing them up front. One feature is that administrative agencies are like snowflakes; no two are exactly alike. This means it is hard—and dangerous—to make generalizations about administrative law. A second feature of administrative law is that, though agencies differ, generalizations about administrative law *are* possible, and are indeed necessary to analyze administrative law problems correctly. There is, after all, a "black letter law" of administrative law. Because of the first feature we mentioned, that black letter law can be elusive. But you can learn it. The third feature of administrative law is that it comes from many sources. Indeed, every source of law is a potential source of administrative law:

- international law

- constitutional law

- legislative enactments (e.g., statutes and ordinances)

- executive-branch material (e.g., agency regulations and executive orders)

- judicial decisions

Administrative law is a sprawling subject because administrative agencies do so many things and administrative law comes from so many sources. You will benefit greatly from taking a law school course on the subject. The course will give you foundational knowledge and skills for analyzing administrative law problems systematically. Indeed, your administrative law course may be one of the most important and useful courses that you take in law school. Welcome!

B. What Are Administrative Agencies?

If you ask an administrative lawyer, "What is an administrative agency?", the lawyer may respond, "Why are you asking?" The lawyer isn't trying to be obnoxious. The lawyer's response reflects that the term "agency" sometimes has a highly technical, specific definition. Let us begin, though, by describing what we mean by administrative agencies in the everyday sense of the term. Then you will see technical definitions.

1. Administrative Agencies in the Everyday Sense

Generally speaking, an administrative agency is simply a government agency that does part of the government's work, using governmental powers. The United States Internal Revenue Service is a federal agency whose job is to collect federal taxes. A local sanitation department is a local agency whose job is to collect trash. Most agencies, like these, have specialized jobs. You won't see a single agency that collects both taxes and trash. Agencies are created (usually by the legislative branch of the national, state, tribal, or local government) with specialized missions, partly so they can become good at what they do.

Although agencies are usually created by the *legislative* branch of government, most agencies are part of the *executive* branch of government. That is because most agencies *execute*—or, to use roughly synonymous terms, they enforce, implement, or administer—the law. The laws that agencies execute are usually statutes enacted by legislatures (with the approval or over the veto of the chief executive). For example, when Congress enacts a law creating a new tax, Congress may assign to the Internal Revenue Service the job of collecting the taxes authorized by the new law. Such a new law creates substantive obligations on the part of the public, and the law at the same time empowers an agency to enforce those substantive obligations. If a state legislature enacts a new law requiring the licensing of tattoo parlors, the law will either have to create a new agency or designate an existing state agency to hand out those licenses and enforce them. Many laws enacted by legislatures would have no effect if there were no agency to execute them.

Diagram 1-1 uses three rectangles to represent the three branches of government. Diagram 1-1 locates the agency within an oval under the "executive" rectangle to indicate that most administrative agencies—and the agencies that we examine in this book—are located in, or associated with, the executive branch. Future diagrams will use these same three rectangles to represent the three branches of government. In particular, Diagram 1-1 illustrates that most executive-branch agencies are created by statutes enacted by the legislative branch, and that those statutes may put substantive duties on members of the public while also empowering agencies to enforce those duties.

Administrative agencies exist at every level of government: federal, state, tribal, and local. At each level, most agencies are considered part of the executive branch of government. These agencies go by different names. Some agencies have the word "Agency" in their

Diagram 1-1. Statutes Creating Legal Duties and Requiring an Agency to Enforce Those Duties

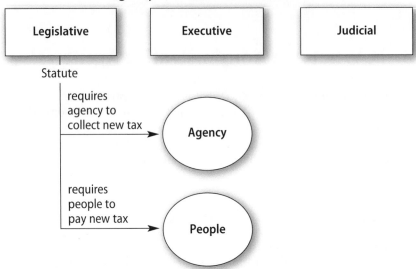

name, like the National Security Agency. Other agencies go by other names, such as Department, Commission, Service, Bureau, and Office.

Exercise: Identifying "Agencies" in the Everyday Sense of That Word

Think of entities with one of these terms in its official name:

- Department
- Commission
- Service
- Bureau
- Office

If you need hints, the federal government has a helpful website that displays a list of federal agencies and has a link to help you identify state, local, and tribal agencies:

> http://www.usa.gov/Agencies/Federal/All_Agencies/index.shtml

---

Federal agencies number in the hundreds. The federal agencies include the cabinet-level executive departments, of which there are currently fifteen. The cabinet-level departments are the Departments of Agriculture, Commerce, Defense, Education, Energy, Health and Human Services, Homeland Security, Housing and Urban Development, Interior, Justice, Labor, State, Transportation, Treasury, and Veterans Affairs. These cabinet-level departments include within them subunits that are themselves agencies. For example, the U.S. Department of Health and Human Services includes the Food and Drug Administration (FDA). The U.S. Department of Agriculture includes the U.S. Forest Service. The U.S. Department of Homeland Security includes the Transportation Security

Administration (TSA). Somewhat like a spider egg, one cabinet-level department may include many smaller agencies.

In addition to the cabinet-level departments and their subparts, federal agencies include other agencies such as the Environmental Protection Agency, the Central Intelligence Agency, and many other entities that aren't part of any cabinet-level Department. Not all of these entities go by the name "agency," either, such as the Social Security Administration.

One set of federal agencies that exists outside of the cabinet-level departments is known as the "independent agencies." Congress can choose to make an agency independent when Congress wants the agency to have insulation from presidential control and other executive-branch centralizing pressures. Independent agencies commonly have these characteristics to give them independence:

- They are headed by multi-person bodies, typically called "commissions."
- No more than a simple majority of the commission's members may come from one political party.
- Agency decisions must be made by a majority vote of a quorum.
- The members of the commission serve staggered terms, and each has a term of office—e.g., six years—that exceeds the President's four-year term.
- They can be removed from office during their term only for good cause, in contrast to the heads of most traditional executive-branch agencies, who can be removed by the President "at will."

See 44 U.S.C. § 3502(5) (2012) (defining "independent regulatory agency" for purposes of Paperwork Reduction Act). Examples of independent agencies include the Consumer Product Safety Commission, the National Labor Relations Board, the Federal Reserve Board, and the Securities and Exchange Commission, to name a few.

Diagram 1-2 is an organizational chart of the federal government. It comes from an official publication called the U.S. Government Manual. Although it is fairly comprehensive, even this official organizational chart does not list all of the agencies in the federal government—perhaps for lack of space. Somewhat mysteriously, for example, it does not include the National Security Agency (?).

Administrative agencies also exist at the state level. Most States have a dozen or more agencies. Many States have their own Department of Agriculture, their own Department of Education, and other agencies responsible for matters similar to those of their federal counterparts. These state agencies execute their respective State's law on the subjects for which they are named. State agencies generally do not administer federal laws, with one major exception. The exception, examined in Chapter 5.B.2, is that some state agencies administer federal law under "cooperative federalism programs." These are programs created by federal law under which States enforce federal laws, usually in exchange for federal money. With that and other, more minor exceptions, state agencies enforce only their own State's laws, just as federal agencies execute only federal laws.

Every State is divided into political subdivisions called counties, cities, parishes, towns, and other things. These subunits often include local agencies. For example, a county may have a sanitation department and a land use agency called something like "the Planning and Zoning Commission." Local governments also have law enforcement agencies, which may be called a police department, a sheriff's office, or a department of public safety.

Like the federal government and the States, Native American tribal governments have agencies to execute the law. Many tribal agencies may have powers and duties similar to those of federal and state agencies, such as law enforcement agencies. Tribal agencies, like

Diagram 1-2. Organizational Chart of the Federal Government

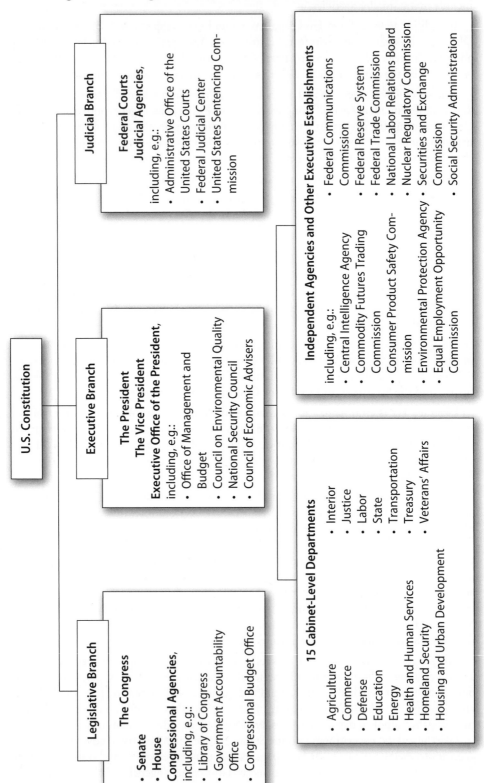

U.S. Constitution

Legislative Branch

The Congress

- **Senate**
- **House**

Congressional Agencies, including, e.g.:
- Library of Congress
- Government Accountability Office
- Congressional Budget Office

Executive Branch

The President
The Vice President
Executive Office of the President, including, e.g.:
- Office of Management and Budget
- Council on Environmental Quality
- National Security Council
- Council of Economic Advisers

15 Cabinet-Level Departments

- Agriculture
- Commerce
- Defense
- Education
- Energy
- Health and Human Services
- Homeland Security
- Housing and Urban Development
- Interior
- Justice
- Labor
- State
- Transportation
- Treasury
- Veterans' Affairs

Independent Agencies and Other Executive Establishments

including, e.g.:
- Central Intelligence Agency
- Commodity Futures Trading Commission
- Consumer Product Safety Commission
- Environmental Protection Agency
- Equal Employment Opportunity Commission
- Federal Communications Commission
- Federal Reserve System
- Federal Trade Commission
- National Labor Relations Board
- Nuclear Regulatory Commission
- Securities and Exchange Commission
- Social Security Administration

Judicial Branch

Federal Courts
Judicial Agencies, including, e.g.:
- Administrative Office of the United States Courts
- Federal Judicial Center
- United States Sentencing Commission

other agencies, are created by law and must exercise their powers within the law. *See, e.g.*, Oneida Tribe of Indians of Wisconsin, Administrative Procedures Act, § 1.2-1(a) (defining "agency" for purposes of the Act), *available at* http://oneida-nsn.gov (follow "Government" link to "Laws and Regulations" link, which has "Code of Laws" listing Administrative Procedures Act).

Consistently with most law school courses on administrative law, this book focuses primarily on federal agencies and secondarily on state agencies. It does not examine tribal agencies or local agencies. Even so, you will see that some principles of administrative law cut across levels of government. Taking a law school course on administrative law helps you, as a lawyer, deal with agencies of all shapes and sizes, at all levels of government.

In short, "administrative agencies," in the everyday sense of the word, are the stuff of which government bureaucracy is made. We encourage you to use the internet or other resources to identify and learn more about governmental entities that interest you and that you believe are "agencies" within the everyday sense of the word. You need a concrete sense of these beasts, as we will study them throughout this book.

2. Technical Definitions of "Agency"

The term "agency" has specialized definitions. The most important such definitions for students and practitioners of administrative law are in administrative procedure acts (APAs). We introduce APAs in Chapter 4, and you will learn about APAs throughout this book. The federal APA prescribes procedures that federal agencies must follow in certain situations. Every State has an APA that prescribes procedures for that State's agencies to follow in certain situations.

The federal APA and most state APAs define the term "agency" broadly, but in ways that may exclude governmental entities that are considered administrative agencies in the everyday sense of the word. The federal APA's definition of agency is set out below. For now just notice that it is detailed and technical:

---

5 U.S.C. § 551. Definitions

For the purpose of this subchapter—

(1) "agency" means each authority of the Government of the United States, whether or not it is within or subject to review by another agency, but does not include—

(A) the Congress;

(B) the courts of the United States;

(C) the governments of the territories or possessions of the United States;

(D) the government of the District of Columbia;

or except as to the requirements of section 552 of this title—

(E) agencies composed of representatives of the parties or of representatives of organizations of the parties to the disputes determined by them;

(F) courts martial and military commissions;

(G) military authority exercised in the field in time of war or in occupied territory; or

(H) functions conferred by sections 1738, 1739, 1743, and 1744 of title 12; chapter 2 of title 41; subchapter II of chapter 471 of title 49; or sections 1884, 1891–1902, and former section 1641(b)(2), of title 50, appendix....

This definition is broad but excludes some governmental entities, including entities that the definition itself refers to as "**agencies**" (5 U.S.C. § 551(1)(E)). This definition matters because, if a government entity falls outside it, that entity usually does not have to follow the procedures prescribed elsewhere in the federal APA (which is referred to as "**this subchapter**" in the definition above). The definition is so important that you will learn more about its scope in Chapter 4. We introduce it now to show you one important, specialized definition of "agency."

Every State defines the term "agency" or "state agency" for purposes of that State's APA. For example, this definition comes from the California Government Code:

Cal. Gov't Code § 11000. Definitions

(a) As used in this title, "state agency" includes every state office, officer, department, division, bureau, board, and commission. As used in any section of this title that is added or amended effective on or after January 1, 1997, "state agency" does not include the California State University unless the section explicitly provides that it applies to the university....

Other state APAs will define the term "agency" or "state agency" differently, depending on what governmental entities that State's legislature intended its APA to cover.

You are seeing these technical definitions now not only to help you learn what an administrative agency is, but also to introduce you to two important, related themes. First, administrative law is predominantly statutory. Most agencies ultimately derive their powers from statutes, and most limitations on those powers come from statutes. Administrative lawyers spend much time finding out what statutes apply to the governmental entity with which they are dealing, and analyzing those statutes. Second, administrative law analysis is highly context-specific. Even so basic a term as "agency" means different things in different settings. You will analyze most administrative law problems by finding and interpreting the particular statutes (and other laws) that apply to the particular problem at hand.

Now you know why an astute lawyer, when asked whether a particular government entity is an "agency" or not, will not answer until the lawyer determines whether the questioner is using the term "agency" in its everyday sense or a technical sense.

C. How Are Administrative Agencies Created?

Most administrative agencies are created by a statute. Thus, most federal agencies trace their existence to a federal statute, and most state (as well as many local) agencies trace their existence to a state statute. In fact, there is a saying in administrative law circles: "Agencies are creatures of statute."

To be totally accurate, though, agencies can be created in any of three ways:

(1) by statute;

(2) by executive-branch action; or

(3) (in the case of some state agencies) by state constitution.

Below you will learn more about the three ways in which agencies are created. Before that, however, notice that the common law, which you study in law school courses such as courses on torts, contracts, and property, is not a source of law that creates agencies. There is no such thing as a "common law" agency.

1. Agencies Created by Statute

Legislatures create agencies, usually one at a time, to deal with a specific matter of public concern or to achieve a specific social objective. For example, Congress created the Department of the Interior to manage certain land owned by the federal government. When a legislature enacts legislation creating an agency, the legislation not only assigns the agency specific *duties*—such as managing public lands. The legislation also typically gives the agency specific *powers* to carry out those duties. The agency then "administers"—or, to use roughly synonymous terms, it executes, enforces, carries out, or implements—the legislation by using its statutorily assigned powers to carry out its statutorily assigned duties.

The statute that creates an agency is known variously as the agency's "organic act" or "organic statute," its "enabling act," its "mandate," or its statutory "charter." These are all simply different names for the statute that created the agency.

An example of an organic act is the Securities Exchange Act of 1934. This is a federal statute, enacted by Congress (with the approval of the President). The 1934 Act created the U.S. Securities and Exchange Commission (SEC). Here is the specific statutory language from the current version of the Act that created the SEC:

---

15 U.S.C. § 78d. Securities and Exchange Commission

(a) Establishment; composition; limitations on commissioners; terms of office

There is hereby established a Securities and Exchange Commission (hereinafter referred to as the "Commission") to be composed of five commissioners to be appointed by the President by and with the advice and consent of the Senate. . . .

Congress enacted the 1934 Act to address misconduct on the stock market. In addition to creating the SEC, the 1934 Act has provisions that give the SEC powers to enforce the Act. One important provision empowers the SEC to issue—or, to use an administrative law synonym, empowers the SEC to "promulgate"—rules specifying what types of conduct are "manipulative and deceptive," and are therefore unlawful, under the Act. 15 U.S.C. § 78j (2012).

Since most agencies are created by statute, the first place to look for an agency's duties and powers is the agency's organic act. The organic act is like a person's DNA. It makes the agency unique. It is an essential source of information for lawyers with matters before the agency. Accordingly, you will learn more in this book about: how to find an agency's organic statute; what kind of information you will typically find in the organic statute; and how to analyze an organic statute.

2. Agencies Created by Executive-Branch Action

Although most agencies are created by statute, some agencies are created instead by executive-branch action. For example, the U.S. Environmental Protection Agency (EPA) was created by a 1970 reorganization plan approved by President Richard Nixon. See Reorganization Plan No. 3 of 1970, *reprinted in* 5 U.S.C. §906 (1988). President Nixon's authority to issue the reorganization plan came from a statute, so in this sense the EPA did have a statutory birth, with the President acting somewhat like a midwife. *See* 5 U.S.C. §906 (2012).

The EPA has power to regulate air and water pollution under the Clean Air and Clean Water Acts, to name just two of the many statutes that EPA is responsible for administering. Though created by executive-branch action, EPA's powers come primarily from federal statutes.

3. State Agencies Created by State Constitution

The U.S. Constitution does not create any federal agencies. In contrast, some state constitutions do create state agencies. For example, the Colorado Constitution creates a "state board of equalization" to ensure that the valuation of taxable property is "just and equalized" among the State's counties. Colo. Const. art. 10, §15(1)(b) (West, Westlaw through amendments adopted through Nov. 2, 2010 election). The significance of an agency's being created by the state constitution is that state statutes cannot alter any constitutional provisions governing the agency (because constitutions are above statutes in the hierarchy of law). Even so, many constitutionally created agencies have statutes elaborating upon their constitutional powers and prescribing procedures for the exercise of those powers.

4. Summary

Most agencies are created by statute; some agencies are created by executive-branch action; and a few state agencies are created by state constitution. Whatever their genesis, most agencies derive their duties and powers primarily from statutes. That is why agencies are called creatures of statute.

D. What Do Administrative Agencies Do, and How Do They Do It?

1. What Administrative Agencies Do

An agency does whatever its creator, usually a legislature, tells it to do. Every agency has a different job. Many agencies, however, do one or more of these things:

    a)   regulate private conduct (including through licensing);

    b)   distribute government benefits; or

    c)   provide public services, manage public land, or manage populations with a special relationship with the government (such as government employees).

Agencies whose main job is to regulate private conduct — e.g., telling people what they can and cannot do — are called "regulatory agencies." Above we mentioned an example of a regulatory agency: the U.S. Securities and Exchange Commission, which regulates the stock market. Other federal regulatory agencies include the EPA and the Nuclear Regulatory Commission. Many States have public utility commissions, which regulate utility companies, and agencies that regulate various professionals, such as doctors and lawyers. Many of these agencies exercise regulatory powers through licensing. For example, state agencies regulate physicians by requiring them to meet certain conditions to get a license to practice, and to adhere to certain rules to avoid losing those licenses or suffering other sanctions.

Some agencies exist mostly to grant government benefits. For example, the U.S. Centers for Medicare and Medicaid Services grant (and deny) Medicare and Medicaid benefits, by which tens of millions of people get free or reduced-cost health care. The U.S. Department of Agriculture gives grants, subsidies, and low-interest loans to farmers. The U.S. Department of Veterans Affairs gives benefits to former members of the armed services. States have agencies — with names such as "Department of Health and Welfare" — that help administer the federal Medicaid program and State-created benefit programs.

Still other agencies have duties and powers associated with: (1) managing public property, such as public parks; (2) providing public services such as water and sewer service and police and fire protection; or (3) managing certain populations that have a special relationship with the government, such as government employees, public school students, and people confined in jails or other state institutions, such as state hospitals for the mentally ill.

Some agencies do all of these things. For example, the U.S. Department of Agriculture (USDA) contains: (1) an agency that licenses businesses that buy or sell animals for laboratory experiments (the Animal and Plant Health Inspection Service); (2) an agency that regulates food safety (the Food Safety and Inspection Service); (3) an agency that distributes what used to be called "food stamps" (the Food and Nutrition Service); and (4) an agency that manages the public forests (the Forest Service). These are only a few of USDA's activities.

Some agencies do other things. For example, the Department of Commerce carries out the decennial census, and the Department of Defense fights wars. Even so, the three activities described above — regulating private sector conduct (including through licensing); granting government benefits; providing public services and managing public property and certain populations (e.g., inmates) — account for much agency activity that concerns lawyers. You will keep encountering these activities in your study of administrative agencies.

2. How Agencies Do What They Do (Types of Agency Powers)

Agencies exercise governmental power. In this country, governmental powers have traditionally been understood as falling into one of three categories: legislative power, executive power, and judicial power. Although most agencies are in the executive branch, many of them receive from their creator not only executive powers but also powers that resemble legislative power and judicial power.

Thus, the legislation creating an agency may empower the agency to exercise (1) the "quasi-legislative" power to issue rules—also known as "regulations"—that operate much like statutes; (2) various executive powers, such as the power to investigate suspected violations of the law; and (3) the "quasi-judicial power" to adjudicate individual cases administratively. For example, the U.S. Environmental Protection Agency has (1) power to make rules (regulations) restricting the amounts of pollutants that companies can discharge into the air and water; (2) power to investigate companies to ensure they are following the rules; and (3) power to decide whether a particular company has violated a particular rule and, if so, whether it should pay a fine or suffer another sanction. The EPA, in short, acts a little like: (1) a legislative body, (2) a police officer, and (3) a judge—all rolled into one! In this way, EPA is typical. Many modern agencies receive from their legislative creator a combination of rulemaking power, executive power, and adjudicative power.

This blending of powers that have ordinarily been associated with separate branches of government has raised concerns under the separation of powers doctrine that the U.S. Constitution and most, if not all, state constitutions contain. The U.S. Supreme Court and most state supreme courts, however, have resolved those concerns in favor of allowing agencies to possess a combination of powers that resemble powers traditionally confided in the separate branches of the government. In this section, you will get an introduction to the types of power that are combined in many modern agencies.

To keep these types of power straight, throughout this book symbols will be used to represent them. They serve as shorthand reminders of the sources and types of government authority that an agency may receive. By thus identifying the types of power, the lawyer gets a better understanding of the interplay among them in specific administrative law contexts. The symbols are quite obvious:

Diagram 1-3. Types of Government Power

Having introduced these symbols, we now go into detail about what agency activities are associated with each category. You will soon see that although we traditionally categorize governmental powers as falling into one of these three categories, many government activities are hard to characterize. In later parts of the book we explore separation of powers principles limiting the powers that can be vested in an agency.

a. Legislative Power—Making Rules with "the Force and Effect of Law"

Many modern agencies get power from a statute to issue (the technical term is "promulgate") rules (also known as "regulations"). This rulemaking power is called a legislative or "quasi-legislative" power because it resembles a legislature's power to enact legislation. When an agency exercises this power, the outcome is called a "legislative rule."

Diagram 1-4. Legislative Power

The U.S. Securities and Exchange Commission (SEC), as mentioned above, is one of many federal agencies with the statutory power to promulgate legislative rules. Here is a provision in the Securities Exchange Act of 1934 granting the SEC the power to make legislative rules, with the relevant language italicized:

---

15 U.S.C. § 78n. Proxies …

(e) Untrue statement of material fact or omission of fact with respect to tender offer

It shall be unlawful for any person to make any untrue statement of a material fact or omit to state any material fact necessary in order to make the statements made, in the light of the circumstances under which they are made, not misleading, or to engage in any fraudulent, deceptive, or manipulative acts or practices, in connection with any tender offer or request or invitation for tenders, or any solicitation of security holders in opposition to or in favor of any such offer, request, or invitation. *The [Securities and Exchange] Commission shall, for the purposes of this subsection, by rules and regulations define, and prescribe means reasonably designed to prevent, such acts and practices as are fraudulent, deceptive, or manipulative....*

Section 78n makes it "unlawful" to engage in certain "fraudulent, deceptive, or manipulative acts" and empowers the SEC to define what acts are "fraudulent, deceptive, or manipulative." Thus, the SEC has power to define unlawful conduct under the Act. Another provision of the Act punishes with fines and imprisonment "willful" violations of § 78n and rules promulgated under it:

---

15 U.S.C. § 78ff. Penalties

(a) Willful violations; false and misleading statements

Any person who willfully violates any provision of this chapter [which includes 15 U.S.C. § 78n] … or any rule or regulation thereunder the violation of which is made unlawful … shall upon conviction be fined not more than $5,000,000, or imprisoned not more than 20 years, or both....

Thus, the SEC can use its legislative rulemaking power to define conduct that a statute punishes with criminal sanctions. That's power!

Not all legislative rules define unlawful conduct. Some legislative rules, for example, establish criteria for getting a government benefit or government license. Agencies with authority to grant government benefits or government licenses often get the power to make legislative rules establishing criteria for receiving the benefits or the license. These rules control people's legal right to the benefits or the license. In this sense the rules make law in much the same way that statutes do.

An agency's power to make legislative rules is often called only a "quasi-legislative" power because it is not identical to the legislative power. For one thing, the source of the two types of power differs. A legislature gets its legislative power from a constitution, whereas an agency gets the power to make legislative rules from the legislature (through a statute). Legislatures can, and do, impose all kinds of conditions and requirements, including procedural requirements, on an agency's exercise of rulemaking power. For another thing, most agency legislative rules are subject to judicial review, to determine if the rule falls within the agency's statutory power. Often, a court can invalidate an agency's legislative rule on grounds that will not invalidate a statute.

Even so, an agency's power to make legislative rules is a power to make law, by making pronouncements that determine legal rights and duties. Agencies use this power extensively. Federal agencies alone issue about 8,000 new rules each year. State and local agencies probably promulgate tens of thousands of rules every year. The number of new legislative rules promulgated by agencies each year far exceeds the number of statutes enacted by legislatures. You will learn more about agency rulemaking in Part Two of this book.

b. Executive Power — Interpreting the Laws to Be Executed; Advising the Public of Those Interpretations; Investigating; and Prosecuting

Diagram 1-5. Executive Power

The task of executing legislation can include many activities. We introduce you to three: (i) interpretation, (ii) investigation, and (iii) prosecution.

(i) Interpretation

An agency charged with executing a law constantly decides how the law applies to various situations. In other words, the agency is constantly *interpreting* the law. Often the laws administered by agencies leave much room for interpretation. Consider the local laws in most jurisdictions that make it illegal to drive at a speed "unsafe under the conditions" or that ban "excessive noise."

The statute administered by an agency may be vague or ambiguous because legislators could not agree on details and therefore omitted the details to gain approval by a legislative majority. For example, it may be easier for a majority to agree to require that employers maintain a "reasonably safe" work place than to agree on particular workplace safety measures. An agency charged with administering the statute must execute the vague and ambiguous parts of the statute as well as the clear and precise parts.

For this reason, whatever its express statutory authority, an agency has implied authority—indeed, it has the duty—to interpret the statute that it is charged with administering. The agency must interpret a statute to decide matters such as (1) the scope of the agency's authority under the statute; (2) the precise meaning of statutory language creating legal rights or imposing legal duties on the public; (3) the legislative goals to be achieved; and (4) the methods that the agency is to use to achieve those goals. It is not necessary for the legislature expressly to authorize the agency to decide these matters, because deciding them is inherent in administering the statute. The U.S. Supreme Court has said of federal statutes, "Interpreting a law enacted by Congress to implement the legislative mandate is the very essence of 'execution' of the law." *Bowsher v. Sy*nar, 478 U.S. 714, 733 (1986). The same is true of state and local laws, which commonly contain vague or ambiguous mandates that state and local agencies must interpret to do their job.

Not only does an agency regularly interpret the legislation that it is responsible for executing; an agency may also announce those interpretations. It may make these announcements for the guidance of the public or the guidance of agency employees, or both. The agency may announce its interpretations on a "retail" level, by giving advice—(say) in an opinion letter—to a particular person or company that wants to know how to obey the law. Alternatively, the agency may announce its interpretations "wholesale," by publishing guidance material for the public in the form of policy statements, guidelines, website material, FAQs, bulletins, or "interpretative rules."

When an agency announces its interpretation of a statute in the exercise of its executive power, the interpretation does not, to use the legal jargon, have "the force and effect of law." In other words, the executive interpretation just reflects the agency's opinion of what the law means. A person affected by the interpretation may be able to challenge it in court. In a court challenge, the court may give deference to the agency's interpretation. The agency does, after all, have primary responsibility for administering the legislation that is being interpreted. Even so, the court will judge for itself whether the agency's executive interpretation is correct. As a practical matter, of course, court challenges take time and money, and they do not earn the agency's friendship. Thus, people who are affected by the agency's executive interpretation may decide that it is wiser to go along with the interpretation or find another way to deal with it, such as by asking the agency to change its mind or by seeking an exemption from the interpretation.

Despite the large practical impact of an agency's exercise of its executive power to interpret legislation, however, such executive interpretations must be distinguished from legislative rules, which were discussed in the last section. You will learn more about the difference between legislative rules and agency guidance material in Part Two of this book.

(ii) Investigations

Many laws administered by agencies prohibit or regulate certain conduct. To execute those laws, agencies must detect conduct that violates the laws. Thus, the legislature may empower an agency to conduct inspections. The legislature may also give the agency other investigative powers, such as the power to issue investigative subpoenas to collect information on suspected violations. In this role, the agency is in effect acting as a police officer or detective. The type of agency investigation that is probably best known is the Internal Revenue Service's audit of people's tax returns.

Similarly, a benefits-granting agency may investigate applicants for benefits to determine eligibility. In addition, the agency may periodically investigate recipients of benefits to determine their continued eligibility.

Investigative activities and other information gathering are typically classified as executive powers.

(iii) Prosecutions

An agency may have the power from its legislative creator not only to investigate but also to prosecute suspected violations of the laws that the agency is responsible for administering. For example, the agency may have power to bring a court action for civil or criminal remedies. Alternatively or additionally, an agency may have authority to commence an adjudicatory proceeding within the agency itself. In an administrative adjudication, one part of the agency acts as a prosecutor — playing the *executive* role of proving a violation — and another part of the agency acts as the judge — playing the quasi-*judicial* role of determining whether a violation has occurred. (The latter, quasi-judicial role is introduced in the next subsection.) The administrative adjudication may end with the agency official who has acted in a quasi-judicial role issuing an order — such as a cease-and-desist order or an order imposing fines — or, instead, the agency official who has acted in a prosecutorial role may negotiate a settlement with its opponent.

This discussion is meant to introduce major types of agency activity that traditionally are classified as "executive" powers. It is not exhaustive. Many other, equally distinctive executive powers exist, such as the power to seize goods and destroy or quarantine them. The wide range of executive powers reflects the variety of laws that agencies are charged with executing.

c. Adjudicatory Power — Deciding Cases

Diagram 1-6. Judicial Power

A statute may give an agency "quasi-judicial" power to decide how the statute itself, or rules that the agency has promulgated under the statute, apply to a particular situation. For example, an environmental agency may have power to decide whether a particular company has violated a particular environmental statute or rule, and, if so, to fine the company. To take another example, an agency may have power to decide whether someone is entitled to government benefits, or a government permit, under the agency's statute and rules. These agency decisions determine the legal rights and duties of individual people and companies, and are final and binding unless set aside by a reviewing court. This power to adjudicate cases administratively, like the quasi-legislative power to make legislative rules, is a power to make law, though, unlike the rulemaking power, it operates on a case-by-case basis.

Agency adjudications vary greatly in the formality of procedures. Suppose, for example, a fifteen-year-old applies for a driver's license in a State where the law requires you to be at least sixteen years old to get a license. In this situation, the agency "adjudication" may consist of an agency employee glancing at the fifteen-year-old's license application form and stamping "denied" on it after ascertaining the applicant's age. Though short on procedure, this is an adjudication; the agency has applied the law to determine the legal rights of an individual. On the other end of the formality spectrum from such "informal adjudications," an agency official known as an "administrative law judge" (ALJ) may hold a trial-like, evidentiary hearing as part of a "formal adjudication" to decide whether to order a business to cease and desist a fraudulent practice. Regardless of formality, agency adjudications determine legal rights of specific people.

An agency's power to adjudicate cases is usually called only a "quasi-judicial" power because it is not identical to the judicial power. Most importantly, most agency adjudicatory decisions are subject to judicial review.

In the United States today, administrative agencies adjudicate many more cases—by orders of magnitude—than do regular courts. This makes agency adjudication an important subject of study. You will learn more about it in Part Three of this book.

d. The Blending of the Three Types of Powers in Many Modern Administrative Agencies

As mentioned above, many modern administrative agencies receive from their legislative creator the powers to (1) make legislative rules; (2) execute those rules as well as the substantive provisions of the statutes that they are responsible for administering; and (3) adjudicate cases administratively, by deciding how their rules and statutes apply in individual cases. The blending of powers can be depicted using the symbols that we have now introduced.

Diagram 1-7. Typical Modern Agency with Blended Powers

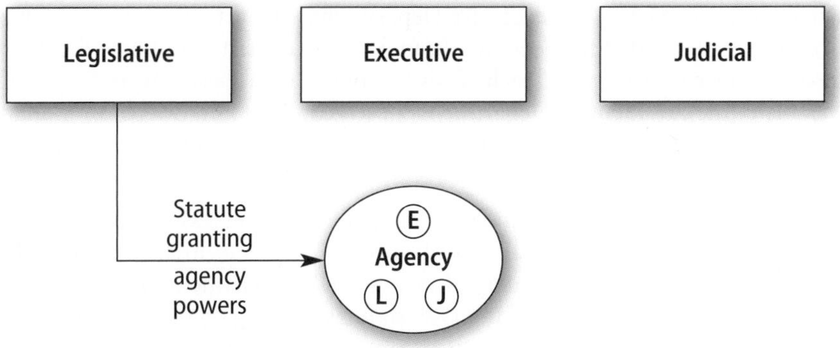

Part of the rationale for allowing agencies to possess a combination of government powers is that their exercise of those powers is subject to control by the legislature, the chief executive, the judicial branch, and the people. These are in addition to the internal controls that shape decision making inside every agency. You will learn more in this book about how these various sources control agency power.

Exercise: Types of Agency Powers

Suppose a state legislature enacted a law that created a state agency to regulate tattoo parlors. Based on the description above of the various types of agency powers—quasi-legislative, executive, and quasi-judicial—please consider these questions:

1. How would you classify the agency's power to issue standards to ensure the hygienic operation of tattoo parlors, such as standards regarding use of tattoo needles?

2. How would you classify the agency's power to inspect a particular tattoo parlor to determine if it is complying with the standards described in question 1?

3. How would you classify the agency's power to hold a trial-type hearing to determine whether a particular tattoo parlor has violated a standard described in question 1, and, if so, to impose a fine?

E. Why Do We Have Administrative Agencies?

The pragmatic answer to that question is: We have them simply because we have always had them. They are essential to the operation of the government.

The framers of the U.S. Constitution anticipated the need for agencies. In Article II of the Constitution, they specified that Congress could empower the President, the courts, or "the Heads of Departments" to appoint "inferior officers." U.S. Const. art. II, § 2, cl. 2. The framers also authorized the President to demand written legal opinions from "the principal Officer in each of the executive Departments." *Id.* art. II, §, 2, cl. 1. Thus, the framers contemplated that the Executive Branch would consist of not only the President, but also "executive Departments," each of which would have a "head," or "principal Officer," answerable to the President. A Department "head" could be empowered by Congress to appoint "inferior officers," presumably to populate that Department. Here we have the seeds of the federal bureaucracy!

In accordance with the framers' understanding, the first Congress created three executive departments in 1789: the Department of Foreign Affairs (which today is called the Department of State), the Department of War (today's Department of Defense), and the Treasury Department. You can find the 1789 statutes creating these three departments in the United States Statutes at Large, which, for 1789, are available on the Library of Congress's website: http://memory.loc.gov/ammem/amlaw/lwsl.html.

Thus, from the beginning the federal government has had agencies filled with employees doing work such as representing the United States in other countries, raising and equipping the armed forces, and collecting taxes to pay for all of this. Each State has its own state agencies to carry out the work of state government. The authority to do this governmental work generally comes from federal and state statutes, as it always has.

Agencies do this work because: Who else is going to do it? The legislative branch enacts legislation and oversees its implementation, but you do not see Members of Congress handing out rifles to soldiers or Social Security checks to retirees. The judicial branch is passive; it awaits parties to present disputes for it to resolve. The President or a Governor serves as chief executive, ultimately responsible that the laws "be faithfully executed," but one person cannot do all the work of federal or state government singlehandedly. The work of government is done by administrative agencies, most of which exist to help the Chief Executive faithfully execute the laws enacted by the legislature.

Administrative agencies are the butt of criticism when they do work that critics believe is no business of the government. The notion that government does not have the right to make private business activity its own business was fostered by widespread acceptance of the economic theories presented in Adam Smith's Wealth of Nations (1776). That work's theme was laissez faire and a market economy free of governmental intrusion. Its philosophy was "that government is best which governs least," to quote Henry David Thoreau's 1849 essay "Civil Disobedience." Henry David Thoreau, *Civil Disobedience, in* Collected Essays & Poems, 203 (Elizabeth Hall Witherell ed., 2001). By and large, federal and state legislatures acted in line with this laissez faire philosophy, making no great effort to intrude government into private economic matters. For the first one hundred years of the United States' existence, faith in the free market maintained the status quo.

By the end of the first one hundred years, there were many who had broken with the faith because they had observed it did not work so well in practice. The reality of less than free markets, less than equal bargaining power, and other inequities, led first to thoughts of and then demands for government intervention into private economic activity. The Congress responded in 1887 by creating the Interstate Commerce Commission (ICC), which is considered the first modern regulatory agency. The ICC was responsible under its organic statute for maintaining "just and reasonable" shipping rates to be charged by the nation's railroads. Government regulation was thereby imposed on private business activity.

Early in the twentieth century, the federal government began regulating things besides railroads, including the production and distribution of food and drugs, maritime shipping, and methods of business competition. With the coming of the Great Depression, faith in the economics of the free market and laissez faire was shattered. During that period, President Franklin Roosevelt promised government intervention into economic affairs to address the imbalances and promote the general public welfare. His New Deal led to extensive governmental regulation of private business activity. Along with the growth of regulatory activity came New Deal programs for the relief of personal economic burdens. Social security programs, public assistance, farm subsidies, and other government benefits programs were enacted. Of course, they were and are implemented by administrative agencies. Attorneys for the private interests wasted no time in mounting legal challenges to the intrusions of government. Those challenges included constitutional attacks on the agencies that caused these intrusions.

By the beginning of World War II, New Deal programs pervaded the private business lives and the personal lives of most Americans. Business regulation included licensing of the professions; control of a person or company's entry into a type of business activity; control of the routes and geographic areas of business activity; control of business rate making; and the policing of business practices. Individual benefits included retirement payments, disability benefits, home loans, health care, welfare, and others. Theoretically, the agency model offered advantages. First, it provided a way for government to respond to free market inequities, yet it was not so threatening (nor as unthinkable) as would be outright nationalization of basic industries. Second, the New Deal faith held that agencies could be and would be repositories of expert knowledge about the problems addressed. That expert knowledge would be brought to bear on the problems in the regulated areas. Analysis would lead to understanding and the design of responses that would bring about corrections—all for the general welfare of the country.

Eighty years after the New Deal, people continue to debate whether there is too much (or not enough) governmental control of everyday life and business. The reality is that, in some forms and settings, government control is more effective than in others. Much depends on whether the legislatures that create and empower agencies properly perceive the problems to be addressed. In any event, debates over the scope and roles of the administrative state are healthy, and lawyers bring important insights to the debate when equipped with an understanding of administrative law. Lawyers also play a major in shaping the law, in this area like others.

F. What Does the Practice of Administrative Law Involve?

Your learning of administrative law will benefit from knowing how lawyers practice administrative law. Lawyers typically practice administrative law on behalf of one of three types of client: (1) private individuals and private businesses; (2) other organizational clients, such as public interest organizations (e.g., the Sierra Club), nongovernmental entities (NGOs), and trade associations (such as the National Association of Manufacturers); or (3) the agency itself. Many administrative lawyers work in more than one of these capacities during their careers.

To cite a few examples of what lawyers do for these clients:

- Regulatory compliance counseling and regulatory assessment: The lawyer may counsel people and companies on how to comply with regulatory statutes and agency rules; or, if the lawyer works for the agency, the lawyer may help the agency assess a regulated entity's compliance with the regulatory statutes and rules. For example, a business owner who wants to start selling goods overseas may hire the lawyer to ensure the owner obeys all applicable regulations.

- Licenses and benefits: The lawyer may help people and companies apply for government licenses (including legally required permits) and benefits. If the lawyer works for a licensing agency, the lawyer may help the agency decide whether to grant, modify, or terminate these licenses and benefits. For example, a lawyer may help a former member of the armed forces apply for veterans' benefits.

- Administrative litigation: The lawyer may represent a client in an administrative or judicial proceeding arising from a dispute with the government about, for example, whether the client has violated a statute or regulation or whether the client has violated a condition for retaining a license or benefits. Alternatively, the lawyer may represent the agency in these disputes. The litigation may begin with a proceeding before the agency and end up in a judicial proceeding. For example, an environmental agency may begin a proceeding to asses a fine against a company that, the agency believes, has polluted a nearby stream.

- Drafting of administrative law material: The lawyer for a private client may influence the drafting of statutes, agency legislative rules, agency interpretative rules and other agency guidance material, and agency case decisions. For example, a lawyer for an environmental organization may draft comments on a proposed regulation that relaxes pollution restrictions on coal-burning power plants.

In short, the practice of administrative law, like the subject itself, is broad and varied. It is also consistently challenging, fun, and productive. OK, we admit that we are biased.

G. Chapter 1 Wrap Up and Look Ahead

Check and consolidate your understanding of this chapter by jotting down or rehearsing in your mind basic answers to these questions:

- What are administrative agencies?
- How are administrative agencies created?
- What do administrative agencies do, and how do they do it?
- Why do we have administrative agencies?
- What does the practice of administrative law involve?

The most important takeaway from this chapter is that, generally, "agencies are creatures of statute." The next chapter explores how to analyze administrative law problems. It also describes the game plan for this book.

Chapter Problem Revisited

Once you have identified the pros and cons of each of the options described in the chapter problem, consider whether you can draw any generalizations about the types of advantages and disadvantages of creating a regulatory agency, such as an agency to license and inspect tattoo parlors.

Professional Development Reflection Question

When you visit a new place, you may think about whether you'd enjoy living there. When you encounter a new area of law as a law student, you will benefit from reflecting on whether you'd enjoy practicing in that area. This book aims to give you some information about what it's like to practice administrative law.

To that end, consider the Chapter Problem. In the scenario that it depicts, lawyers could be involved in at least four capacities. A personal injury lawyer might represent the parents of the child who died after getting a tattoo. A prosecutor might decide whether to file criminal charges against the tattoo parlor. A municipal lawyer may advise the City Council about the legal implications of regulating tattoo parlors. A general practitioner may represent existing or potential future owners of tattoo parlors in the City. Of these four lawyers, the municipal lawyer advising the City Council is considered to be practicing in the area of administrative law—more specifically, in the area of municipal law. Notice, though, that administrative law is also often practiced by general practitioners, such as lawyers who represent small business owners.

You may learn in other law school courses about what it's like to be a general practitioner. You might use your law school course on administrative law to learn more about municipal lawyers.

Indeed, municipal lawyers represent a large, important segment of administrative lawyers. Whether you live in a big city or small town, it has a local government that regularly gets legal advice. The local government may get the advice from a lawyer employed fulltime for the local government, or from lawyers in private practice hired to provide advice as needed, or both. Lest you think municipal law is a sleepy field, in fact municipal lawyers regularly encounter interesting issues, including issues of constitutional law such as whether regulation of tattoo parlors violates the First Amendment's protection of free expression. *See, e.g., Coleman v. City of Mesa*, 265 P.3d 422 (Az. Ct. App. 2011).

And so our question is: Do you think municipal law might interest you? If so, we encourage you to identify one of the lawyers who works for the city or town where you live, and to call her or him to find out more about the practice. If it helps embolden you to make the phone call, you can say that you are doing it as homework for your administrative law course. That is certain to get the conversation off and running!

Chapter 2

Administrative Law Problem Solving; Overview of the Rest of This Book

Overview

Now that you have a sense of what administrative law is, you will begin learning how to do what administrative lawyers do. What they do is solve administrative law problems. This chapter helps you learn a framework for solving many administrative law problems.

Most administrative law problems concern an agency action. For example, the problem may concern an agency's denial of a permit or the agency's issuance of a rule. Broadly speaking, three kinds of legal questions can arise about an agency action:

(1) Has the agency acted under a valid source of power?

(2) If so, has the agency obeyed limits on, and requirements for exercising, that power? (For simplicity's sake, we will often use the term "limits" to mean both limits on, and requirements for exercising, agency power.)

(3) If the agency lacks power to take the action, or has not obeyed limits on that power, what can be done about it?

These questions form a framework addressing three issues:

(1) agency power;

(2) limits on agency power; and

(3) remedies.

This chapter begins to flesh out this three-part framework for analyzing agency action. We will return to this framework in later chapters, as we examine the two important types of agency action—namely, agency rulemaking and agency adjudication—and the most important type of remedy available for improper agency action: judicial review.

Some administrative law problems do not involve affirmative agency action; instead they concern an agency *failure to act*. Suppose, for example, an agency fails to act on application for a permit or fails to issue rules that a statute requires it to issue. Problems involving agency failure to act typically raise three questions:

(1) Does the agency have a legal duty to act?

(2) If so, has the agency breached that duty?

(3) If the agency has a duty to act but has breached it, how can the breach be remedied?

You will encounter many different kinds of agency action and agency inaction throughout this book. But many of the administrative law problems that lawyers are asked to solve involve one of the questions listed above.

This chapter divides into five sections:

A. Types of Agency Action

B. Sources of Agency Power

C. Limits on Agency Power

D. Enforcing Limits on Agency Power

E. Game Plan for the Rest of This Book

Chapter Problem

Suppose you are speaking with a law student who has not taken a course in administrative law. The student has these comments and questions:

1. All I know about administrative agencies is that they seem to control every aspect of our lives. Where exactly do they get all this power?

2. With all of the agencies that exist just in this country, and all the different things that they do, how can you study them in a single law school course. Exactly what agency activities do you study?

3. I've heard agencies described as the "headless fourth branch" of government. Are they really beyond anyone's control?

A. Types of Agency Action

This book focuses on two types of agency action:

• agency rulemaking

• agency adjudication

The book focuses on rulemaking and adjudication because they are the main types of agency actions that can create legal rights and duties and in which lawyers accordingly become involved. In exploring these two activities, we encounter two more subjects:

• agency executive activity, including the announcement of an agency's interpretation of its laws, agency prosecutorial activity, and agency investigations

• agency failure to act

These kinds of agency action and inaction affect legal rights and duties, and thus present problems that administrative lawyers regularly must solve. This book helps you learn how to solve those problems. To do so, the book focuses on (1) how agencies get power—to make rules, adjudicate cases, and gather information; (2) how the law limits these powers; and (3) what can be done when an agency action exceeds those limits. The book also explores situations in which the law imposes duties on agencies to take action and how those duties are enforced.

B. Sources of Agency Power

Agencies are unlike humans and other natural life forms. Agencies have no inherent powers (such as the power to reproduce, thank goodness!). Agencies have no inalienable rights. Agencies are more like Dr. Frankenstein's monster. An agency can only exercise the powers that its creator has given the agency, and a fundamental question often raised by any agency's action is: What is the source of the agency's power to take that action?

Since most agencies are "creatures of statute"—you might say, in other words, that the legislatures are the Dr. Frankensteins—the source of an agency's power is almost always a statute or combination of statutes. True, some state agencies get their power from state constitutions, instead of state statutes. In addition, some federal and state agencies get their powers from executive orders or other executive action taken by the Chief Executive, such as a reorganization plan. Most agencies, however, get most of their powers from statutes.

Moreover, at the federal level, even the Chief Executive's actions must have a constitutional or statutory source of authority. When President Harry Truman issued an executive order authorizing the Secretary of Commerce to seize the nation's steel mills, the U.S. Supreme Court held the order invalid because the President could not justify his order under any statute or constitutional provision. *See Youngstown Sheet & Tube Co. v. Sawyer*, 343 U.S. 579, 587 (1952). Therefore, when a federal agency relies on an executive order or other executive-branch material as a source of power, the question becomes: What is the source of power for the executive order or other executive-branch material? The answer must be a federal statutory or constitutional provision.

The actions of a State's chief executive (Governor) may have to be analyzed differently from the President's, for state governments, unlike the federal government, are not governments of limited, enumerated powers. *See* James Madison, Federalist No. 45, in The Federalist Papers 292 (Clinton Rossiter ed. 1961) ("The powers delegated by the proposed Constitution to the Federal Government, are few and defined. Those which are to remain in the State Governments are numerous and indefinite"). A State's constitution functions as a limitation, not a grant of power. For that reason, that State's government can exercise any governmental powers not denied to it by the state constitution (as long as the exercise of power does not violate federal law). *See, e.g., Woodland v. Mich. Citizens Lobby*, 378 N.W.2d 337, 347 (Mich. 1985) ("State constitutions ... serve as limitations on the otherwise plenary power of state governments"). If a state constitution operates as a limitation on otherwise plenary state governmental power, the branches of state government, including the Governor as head of the executive branch, may have inherent powers. But whatever inherent power a State's *Governor* may have, a state *agency* lacks inherent power and must therefore point to a source of law external to the agency (which may include directives from the Governor) as authority for that agency's actions.

Lawyers sometimes must press an agency persistently and firmly to find out the source of authority the agency claims for its action. A lawyer should not be satisfied when an agency relies solely on its own regulation, or on something else the agency itself has generated, such as a policy manual, as authority for its action. This simply begs the question of the source of authority for that regulation or other agency material. A lawyer should not be put off by agency responses to the effect: "We have always done this; no one has ever questioned our authority to do it before." Indeed, an individual agency official may lose track, or never learn, the supposed source of authority for a longstanding agency practice. A lawyer with a client adversely affected by that practice, however, cannot be satisfied with such ignorance. The lawyer therefore needs strong research skills to identify and analyze all potential sources of authority for the agency action.

If the lawyer does identify a source of power for the agency action, another question arises: Is the source of power valid? Here is an obvious but important principle of administrative law:

If an agency's action rests on an invalid statute, the agency action itself is invalid.

See Oklahoma v. U.S. Civil Serv. Comm'n, 330 U.S. 127, 138 (1947). More specifically, if an agency action rests on an invalid grant of power, the agency action itself is invalid.

Assuming that the agency's grant of power is statutory, as is usually true, why might the statute be invalid? The answer depends on whether the statute is a federal statute or a state statute.

If it is a federal statute, it can be invalid only on one of two grounds: (1) because it violates the U.S. Constitution; or (2) because it has been repealed by a later federal statute.[1] Express repeals are easy to identify. As you may know, a statute can also be impliedly repealed. Repeals by implication are rare, however, partly because of a principle of statutory interpretation providing that "repeal by implication is disfavored." *See, e.g., Tennessee Valley Auth. v. Hill*, 437 U.S. 153, 189–190 (1978). Because repeals are either obvious (if express) or rare (if implied), we do not explore in this book the circumstances under which they occur. We will, however, explore some constitutional limits on statutes that grant agencies various powers.

As for state statutes granting state agencies power, such a state statute is invalid if: (1) it violates the state constitution, the federal constitution, or other valid federal law; (2) if it has been repealed by a later state statute; or (3) if it is preempted by federal law. In addition to studying some federal constitutional limits on statutes granting agencies power, we will examine one area of preemption law important for administrative lawyers. It is known as regulatory preemption.

Suppose the lawyer has determined that there is a valid source of power for the agency action under analysis. A complete analysis must next consider limits on that power. We take up those limits in the next section of this chapter.

Exercise: Determining Whether an Agency Has the Power for Its Action

Many administrative law problems pose the question: "Where does the agency get the power to take this action?" The experienced lawyer keeps that question in mind when analyzing administrative law problems.

1. Based on the discussion above, identify the three potential sources of an agency's power to take an action and identify which of the three is the most common:

    (1) _____

---

1. Federal statutes must also comply with self-executing treaties. See, e.g., Cook v. United States, 288 U.S. 102, 119 (1933). But as discussed later in this chapter, as a practical matter, self-executing treaties and other international agreements seldom if ever limit agency power.

    (2) _____

    (3) _____

2. Based on what you have learned so far in this book, explain why these two types of law *cannot* furnish the ultimate source of power for an agency action (even though they may serve as a source of limits on agency power):

    a.   the agency's own regulations

    b.   the common law

C. Limits on Agency Power

No agency has unfettered power. On the contrary, an agency's power always comes with strings attached. This section discusses limits on agency power. Specifically, you will learn in this section about two ways that many administrative lawyers classify limits on agency power. First, many administrative lawyers distinguish "internal" (or "intrinsic") limits from "external" (or "extrinsic") limits. Second, many administrative lawyers distinguish substantive limits on agency powers from procedural limits on an agency's exercise of power.

Even with all these limits, many agencies have room to make judgment calls about how best to exercise their powers. When applicable laws do not dictate exactly how an agency must act, we say the agency has *discretion*. Agency discretion is an important aspect of administrative law that this section also introduces.

1. Internal Limits vs. External Limits

An internal (or intrinsic) limit on agency power is a limit that comes from the same law granting the power in the first place. Since most agencies get their power from agency-specific legislation, internal limits are those found in the agency legislation upon which the agency bases its action. An external (or extrinsic) limit on agency power comes from someplace other than the agency legislation. Most agency actions are subject to both internal and external limits.

a. Internal (Intrinsic) Limits

Agency legislation empowers an agency to carry out the agency's assigned responsibilities under the legislation. Because the agency's power is tied to its responsibilities, the agency legislation will invariably include limits on the power.

For example, the Consumer Product Safety Act grants the Consumer Product Safety Commission power to regulate "consumer products." This statutory grant of power impliedly precludes the Commission from regulating things that are not "consumer products," such as air pollution. Furthermore, the Act defines the term "consumer product" expressly to exclude certain products, such as tobacco products. *See* 15 U.S.C. § 2052(5) (2012). The definition's exclusions prevent the Commission from exercising power over excluded products. In short, the Consumer Product Safety Act puts internal limits on the regulatory power it grants the Commission.

To see another example of internal limits on agency power, look at the statute below empowering the Secretary of Commerce or the Secretary of Interior to designate a species as endangered. (Such a designation triggers all kinds of legal protections for the species.) To designate a species as endangered, the Secretary must consider certain factors:

---

16 U.S.C. § 1533. Determination of endangered species and threatened species

(a) Generally

(1) The Secretary shall ... determine whether any species is an endangered species or a threatened species because of any of the following factors:

(A) the present or threatened destruction, modification, or curtailment of its habitat or range;

(B) overutilization for commercial, recreational, scientific, or educational purposes;

(C) disease or predation;

(D) the inadequacy of existing regulatory mechanisms; or

(E) other natural or manmade factors affecting its continued existence....

(b) Basis for determinations

(1)(A) The Secretary shall make determinations required by subsection (a) (1) of this section solely on the basis of the best scientific and commercial data available to him after conducting a review of the status of the species and after taking into account those efforts, if any, being made by any State or foreign nation, or any political subdivision of a State or foreign nation, to protect such species, whether by predator control, protection of habitat and food supply, or other conservation practices, within any area under its jurisdiction, or on the high seas....

This provision empowers the Secretary to designate endangered species while limiting that designation power. These internal limits consist of (a) a specification of factors that the Secretary must consider and of (b) the kind of data that the Secretary must consider. If the Secretary ignores those internal limits when designating a species as endangered, the designation may be invalid.

The provision just discussed is not unusual in requiring the agency to consider certain factors and information. This requirement reflects the legislature's desire to give the agency decisionmaking power while also controlling the agency's decisionmaking process. We might add that the provision quoted above is the tip of the iceberg. We quoted above only a small piece of 16 U.S.C. § 1533 (2012). The quoted portion does not include all of the limits that § 1533 alone puts on the Secretary's power to designated endangered species. Moreover, § 1533 is only one of the fifteen provisions that make up the Endangered Species Act (ESA). The lawyer analyzing a designation by the Secretary needs to study the entire ESA for internal limits on the designation power.

b. External (Extrinsic) Limits

The Secretary's power to designate endangered species, like the power of many agencies, is also subject to limits external to the agency legislation. Most importantly to the study of administrative law, the federal Administrative Procedure Act (APA) puts procedural requirements on the process by which the Secretary designates a species as endangered. The federal APA applies to the designation process because it prescribes procedures that an **"agency"** must follow when it engages in **"rule making."** 5 U.S.C. § 551(1) & (5) (2012); *id.* § 553. The Secretary falls within the federal APA's definition of **"agency"** (a term that can include federal officials as well as other federal entities), and the designation process falls within the federal APA's definition of **"rule making."** As a result, the federal APA puts *external* (extrinsic) limits on the Secretary's designation power.

More generally, external limits on an executive-branch agency's powers can come from any source of law:

- foreign and international law
- constitutional law
- statutes
- agency rules, agency case decisions, and other executive-branch material such as executive orders
- judicial opinions interpreting the types of law listed above
- judicial opinions applying judicially devised limits on agency action derived from "equity" and "common law"

We will go into more details about these limits when we examine specific kinds of agency action, such as rulemaking and adjudication.

We will at this point say just a bit more about the first and last sources of external sources of limits listed above.

As to the first: Foreign and international law are generally not studied in law school courses on U.S. administrative law, and they will not be explored in this book. Their absence reflects two main considerations. First, foreign law and international law seldom apply of their own force to actions by U.S. agencies. True, a foreign country's law could conceivably apply to a U.S. agency's action if the agency's action occurred on foreign soil or had a direct effect in a foreign country. But that circumstance will be rare because U.S. laws do not routinely give agencies power to act extraterritorially. *Cf. FTC v. Compagnie de Saint Gobain Pont a Mousson*, 647 F.2d 1345 (D.C. Cir. 1981) (addressing agency's power under agency legislation to serve subpoena in foreign country). Likewise, it is possible for a treaty or other international agreement to apply to a U.S. agency, but in reality international law seldom applies of its own force. For example, a treaty applies domestically only if it is "self-executing," meaning that it "operates of itself without the aid of any legislative provision." *Medellin v. Texas*, 552 U.S. 491, 505 (2008) (internal quotation marks omitted). Some treaties to which the U.S. is a party are self-executing, but most self-executing treaties have little or no relevance for most administrative agencies.

As to the last-listed external limit: In Chapter 1, we said there is no such thing as a "common law" agency. More generally, the common law does not provide a source of power for agencies. Courts have, however, drawn on bodies of judicially created law— both the common law and the law of equity—as a source for *limits* on agency power. Courts have discerned and applied these limits, as you might guess, in lawsuits challenging agency action. We will explore these judge-made limits later in this book.

c. Why Distinguish Internal from External Limits

We said in Chapter 1 that administrative law is a sprawling subject. To practice administrative law effectively, a lawyer must analyze administrative law problems systematically.

Learning the distinction between internal and external limits will help you do so. By doing so, you will remember to look carefully for the limits that may exist in every potential source of power for the agency action under analysis. You will also remember that the search for applicable limits does not end with your examination of the source of power. You must consider other potential sources of limits external to the power-granting law.

2. Substantive vs. Procedural Limits

Another way to think systematically about limits on agency power takes into account two types of limits on agency power: substantive limits and procedural limits. This is a mushier distinction than the internal/external distinction but has some utility.

a. Substantive Limits (or Requirements)

An example of a substantive limit is a limit on the subject matter for which an agency is responsible. Laws invariably limit the subject matter over which the agency has power. The Consumer Product Safety Commission cannot regulate air pollution. The Environmental Protection Agency cannot regulate the stock market. Every State has an agency that licenses doctors. These state medical licensing agencies cannot regulate lawyers. Subject-matter limits on agency power ensure an agency has a defined turf. Agencies usually stay within these bounds, but not always. *See FDA v. Brown & Williamson Tobacco Corp.*, 529 U.S. 120 (2000) (holding that FDA lacked power to regulate cigarettes under statutes as they then existed). And when an agency exceeds legal restrictions on whom and what it can regulate, the agency action may be labeled "*ultra vires*" ("beyond powers").

Some laws substantively limit agency power by requiring the agency to achieve a certain objective or by prohibiting the agency from causing certain results. For example, a federal statute requires the Secretary of Agriculture to regulate the sale of ammonium nitrate "to prevent the misappropriation or use of ammonium nitrate in an act of terrorism." 6 U.S.C. § 488a(a) (2012). Thus, the statute substantively controls the Secretary's regulatory power by requiring the Secretary to prevent a specified, disastrous result. The same statute requires the Secretary to consult with other federal officials "to ensure that the access of agricultural producers to ammonium nitrate is not unduly burdened." *Id.* § 488a(g). Thus, the statute also identifies a beneficial, existing use of ammonium nitrate with which the Secretary must avoid interfering. These provisions control the outcome — the substance — of the Secretary's exercise of power.

The substantive limits that we have described so far are internal, coming from the same statute that grants the agency power. Substantive limits can also come from external sources. For example, the Endangered Species Act generally prohibits federal agencies from taking actions that jeopardize the continued existence of a species that has been designated as endangered. Federal agencies exercise power under their statutes subject to this external, substantive limit that forbids their actions from having a particular result. The U.S. Constitution also puts external, substantive limits on federal and state agencies by, for example, forbidding them from taking action that abridges the freedom of speech.

b. Procedural Limits (or Requirements)

The limits that we have identified so far — restricting whom and what an agency can regulate, what an agency can consider when exercising its power, and what results its exercise of power must achieve and must avoid—might be classified as "substantive" requirements, to distinguish them from "procedural" requirements for agency action. Examples of procedural requirements are:

- a requirement that the agency allow the public to comment on a proposed new agency rule before the agency adopts the final version of the rule

- a requirement that the agency accompany the final version of the new rule with a written explanation of the rationale for the new rule

- a requirement that the agency offer an opportunity for an oral, evidentiary hearing conducted by an administrative law judge before the agency fines a business for violating an agency regulation

- a requirement that the agency provide a written explanation for its denial of any request made to the agency in connection with an agency proceeding

Procedural requirements can be internal or external. In other words, you may find them in the agency legislation, in which case you call them "internal" procedural limits. Alternatively, they may come from an external source. The primary external sources of procedural requirements for agency action are federal and state Administrative Procedure Acts and agency procedural rules. These and other external laws shape the process by which an agency exercises its power. More importantly for lawyers, many of these procedural requirements exist to allow interested members of the public, by participating in the process, to influence the substance of the agency's actions.

c. The Limited Usefulness of Distinguishing Substantive from Procedural Limits

Lawyers and judges and the law itself distinguishes between substance and procedure. Administrative law is no different. For example, the federal Administrative Procedure Act authorizes a court to invalidate agency action if the action has taken place "without observance of *procedure* required by law." 5 U.S.C. § 706(2)(D) (2012) (emphasis added); 2010 Model State APA § 508(a)(3)(B) (authorizing judicial relief if "the agency committed an error of procedure"). To take another example, the Supreme Court has said that an agency's action "may be set aside for any error of law, substantive or procedural." *St. Joseph Stock Yards Co. v. United States*, 298 U.S. 38, 74 (1936). Part of learning administrative law entails learning the distinction between substantive and procedural limits on (or requirements for) agency action.

In learning the distinction, you quickly realize that the distinction is not black and white; there is a gray area. Both the agency legislation and other laws limiting agency power contain limits or requirements that partake of substance and procedure. A prime example consists of requirements that an agency consider certain factors when exercising its power. For example, we reproduced above the portion of 16 U.S.C. § 1533 that requires the Secretary to consider certain factors when deciding whether to designate a species as endangered. This requirement is substantive in the sense that it affects the substance of the Secretary's decision making as well as the ultimate decision. It is also arguably procedural, however, in the sense that it operates during the decisionmaking *process*; it does not exclusively concern the outcome of that process.

In short, lawyers and judges use the substance/procedure distinction in administrative law, as they do in other areas of law. And, as is true in other areas of law, the distinction really refers to a spectrum that runs from the purely procedure—e.g., the requirement to hold a hearing—to the purely substantive—e.g., the requirement that an agency regulate water pollution, not air pollution, while also embracing the quasi-substantive, quasi-procedure—e.g., the requirement that an agency consider specific substantive factors when exercising its power.

Exercise: Types of Limits on Agency Power

In light of the discussion above, please classify the following limits on, or requirements for, agency action as substantive or procedural. If the action partakes of both, say which predominates.

1.   A federal statute requires EPA to set the "lowest achievable emission rate" for certain sources of air pollution in parts of the country. 42 U.S.C. §7501(3) (2012).

2.   A federal statute requires the agency to give parties an opportunity to cross-examine each other's witnesses during a hearing.

3.   A federal statute requires the Secretary of Labor to publish in the Federal Register a "statement of reasons" for any action taken under the Occupational Safety and Health Act of 1970. 29 U.S.C. §655(e) (2012).

4.   The Endangered Species Act requires a federal agency to consult with the Secretary of Commerce or Interior to ensure that the agency's action does not jeopardize the continued existence of any endangered species. 16 U.S.C. §1536 (2012).

5.   A state statute requires the state medical licensing board, when disciplining a physician for violating a rule of the board, to consider the seriousness of the violation and the need to deter future violations by other physicians.

---

3. Agency Discretion

Even with all the legal limits on their power, most agencies have much discretion. By "discretion" in this setting, we mean agency *choice* about how and why to exercise an agency power. Lawyers learn to identify those areas in which an agency has discretion, and learn how to influence the agency's exercise of discretion.

A statute may limit an agency's power but still leave the agency much discretion. Look back, for example, at the statutory provision authorizing the Secretaries of Commerce and Interior to designate endangered species. The provision requires the Secretary to consider certain factors and to consider data of a particular kind and quality. Other statutory provisions requires the Secretary to follow certain procedures when making a designation. The Secretary's authority is hedged about with many statutory restrictions. Even so, the decision whether to designate a particular species as endangered will often require a judgment call about which reasonable minds can differ. In these situations, the Secretary has discretion.

Many statutes on their face grant great discretion. For example, Congress often grants federal agencies power to make all legislative rules "necessary and appropriate" for carrying out their statutory responsibilities. These vague delegations of rulemaking power give agencies great choice in the topics that rules will address and the content of the rules. Similarly, a statute may give an agency great discretion in exercising adjudicatory power or investigative power. Consider the governmental entities that license the practice of law; they typically can determine whether an applicant has the "character and fitness" required for the profession. Talk about discretion!

The existence of discretion does not mean anything goes. If the Secretary of Interior thought it was a close call whether the polar bear should be designated an endangered species, the Secretary could not make the decision based on her or his childhood fear of bears. That way of making the call is an "abuse of discretion." Courts play an important role in ensuring that agencies neither exceed the limits of their powers nor abuse their discretion.

D. Enforcing Limits on Agency Power

Administrative agencies have been described as making up a "Headless Fourth Branch" of government. *FCC v. Fox Television Stations, Inc.*, 556 U.S. 502, 525–526 (2009). That description implies that agencies exist outside and beyond the control of the traditional three branches of government. Agencies *do* wield much power, but they are not beyond control. In this book you will encounter five sources for control of agency action:

(1) the agency itself

(2) the judicial branch

(3) the legislative branch

(4) the executive branch

(5) the people

This section introduces these sources of control, all of which the lawyer may use on behalf of a client with an administrative law problem.

1. The Agency

We put the agency first because of a cardinal rule for the practice of administrative law:

The best place to win your case is in the agency.

If you win your case in the agency, you are usually finished. Success! If you don't win your case in the agency, you face an uphill battle in getting a court or another external source of control to give you victory.

Most agencies want to obey the law but find it easier said than done. The agency may have hundreds or thousands of employees with varying levels of knowledge, competence and diligence. The agency must have a structure and procedures for ensuring its employees obey the law and correcting the inevitable errors. Thus, if a front-line official violates the law — for example, by erroneously denying a person government benefits or a permit — the agency will usually have procedures that enable someone else, typically someone higher up in the agency, to correct the violation.

If you are harmed by an agency official's violation of the law, you are not only smart but also usually required to first seek a remedy within the agency. A lawyer who passes up these internal sources of control is usually making a huge mistake. Most importantly, the lawyer who jumps off the internal agency track and tries to take the matter to court will ordinarily be denied judicial relief (for failure to "exhaust" administrative remedies), and, by the time judicial relief is denied for failure to exhaust administrative remedies, deadlines for seeking administrative remedies may have expired.

In short, the agency itself provides the best means for enforcing legal limits on the agency's own powers. In this book and courses on administrative law, you learn about how agencies operate. More importantly, you learn *how to learn* how an unfamiliar agency operates. This book and courses on administrative law thus pay great attention to administrative agency *procedures*. An administrative lawyer must master these procedures for the same reason an effective trial lawyer must master the trial court's rules of procedure: The merits of a client's case count for little unless they are presented in accordance with legally required procedures.

2. The Judicial Branch

When an agency's final action causes harm or threatens harm to someone, the agency action ordinarily can be challenged in a court. A court will review the agency action to make sure the action itself—and the process that the agency followed when taking the action—were proper. The court may uphold the agency action or strike it down.

In either event, the court may write an opinion explaining why the agency action is invalid or valid. These opinions often interpret the laws applicable to the agency's action. They may also discuss the court's own power to review the agency's decision. These judicial opinions form an important element of administrative law.

Although most agency actions are never reviewed by any court—and those agency actions that are judicially reviewed are usually upheld—judicial review has enormous importance for lawyers because, as a practical matter, the courts are usually the last resort for getting relief from an adverse agency action. Moreover, agencies often shape their conduct to avoid being sued and to maximize their chances of success if they are sued. This is why administrative lawyers must learn about judicial review of agency action, and it is therefore explored in this book and courses on administrative law.

3. The Legislative Branch

The legislative branch exerts control over administrative agencies by enacting statutes creating them in the first place and, in many instances, enacting later statutes modifying the agency's original powers and duties or giving the agency more powers and duties.

The legislature does not simply trust the agency to obey these statutes. Rather, the legislature (often acting through a legislative committee or subcommittee) oversees the agency's activities. One way the legislature does this is by oversight hearings on the agency's operation and its proposed budget. Other means of oversight occur more informally, as legislators contact agency officials, often about complaints from constituents (or their constituents' lawyers).

Throughout this book you will learn about statutory limits on agency power. We will also allude to means by which legislatures enforce these limits and otherwise control agency action.

4. The Executive Branch

Agencies in the executive branch, even so-called independent agencies, are subject to control by the Chief Executive (President or Governor). As discussed above, a chief executive can issue executive orders and similar directives to "take care" that the laws are faithfully executed within the executive branch.

For example, this book discusses several executive orders that apply when federal agencies make rules. These executive orders on rulemaking are actually enforced, not by the President personally, but by (can you guess?) an *agency*—specifically, the Office of Information and Regulatory Affairs (OIRA), which is part of the Office of Management and Budget (OMB). Thus, you have the seemingly unusual arrangement of one agency regulating another agency. Actually, this is not unusual. For example, an agency called the Council on Environmental Quality makes rules for federal agencies about how to comply with the National Environmental Policy Act (NEPA). Wheels within wheels!

In addition to issuing executive orders, a Chief Executive may have power to appoint and remove the head of an agency. The appointment power enables the Chief Executive to select agency heads who share the Chief Executive's policies and priorities. The removal power enables the Chief Executive to ensure agency heads remain accountable to the Chief Executive. And, that is why they call him or her the Chief!

The broader point is that executive-branch agencies are subject to control by forces within the executive branch. Administrative lawyers must know about these sources of control because they may in a particular situation be more effective than other means of control, such as judicial review.

5. The People

We the people have the power to control agency action. We can exercise the power directly—by, for example, giving input directly to agencies and by suing them in court. (You will learn in this book many ways in which members of the public participate in agency activities.) We can also exercise power over agencies indirectly—for example, by electing legislators and chief executives and (in States that elect judges) judges who will create and enforce restrictions on agency actions.

Popular control can ensure that agencies obey the law and respect rights. Lawsuits against agencies or agency officials are a tried-and-true means to that end. *See, e.g., Marbury v. Madison*, 5 U.S. (1 Cranch) 137 (1803); *Youngstown Sheet & Tube Co. v. Sawyer*, 343 U.S. 579 (1952); *Hamdi v. Rumsfeld*, 542 U.S. 507 (2004). Popular control also can influence agency exercises of discretion. For example, public outrage over ABC Corporation's violation of pollution laws can pressure an agency into taking enforcement action against that company. At any one time, the news media usually include a story of misdeeds in the private sector for which inadequate government regulators or regulation takes the blame.

Lawyers play a central role in helping individuals and groups of people control agency action. Indeed, this is one of the highest and best uses for a lawyer.

Summary: How Agencies Are Controlled

The graphic below depicts an agency and the five entities (including the agency itself) that can control the agency's actions.

Diagram 2-1. Types of Control over Administrative Agencies

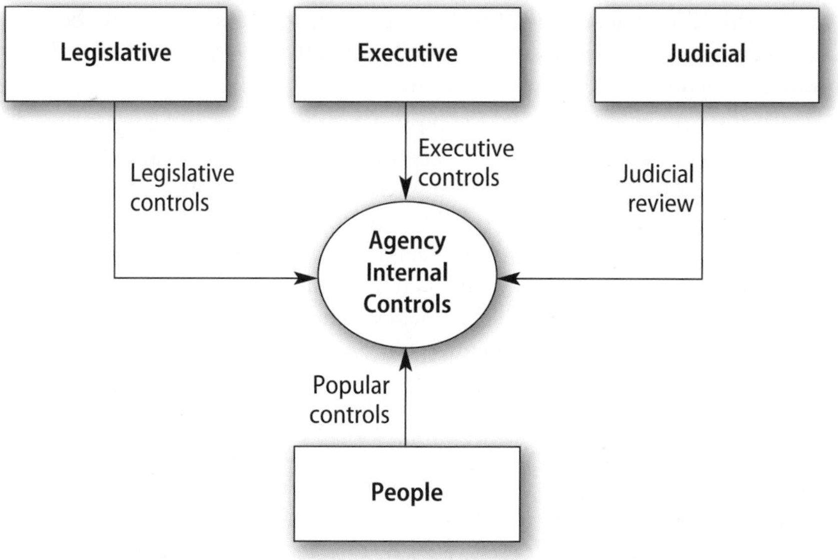

Exercise: Complete the Problem Solving Framework

To help you internalize and remember the framework for analyzing administrative law problems, please complete this outline of it.

1. In taking the action under analysis, has the agency acted under a valid source of power?

    a. Under what source of power did the agency act? There are three possible sources of power for agency action:

        i. _____

        ii. _____ (most common)

        iii. _____

    b. Is the source of power _____ [adjective]?

2. If the agency has acted under a valid source of power, has the agency obeyed limits on, and requirements for exercising, that power? (For simplicity's sake, we use the term "limits" to include requirements.)

    a. Internal limits are: [definition] _____

        i. Internal substantive limits (example: _____)

        ii. Internal procedural limits (example: _____)

    b. External limits are: [definition] _____

    i.   External substantive limits (example: _____)

    ii.   External procedural limits (example: _____)

3.   If the agency lacks power to take the action, or has not obeyed limits on, or requirements for exercising, that power, what can be done about it? List five sources of control and give an example or description of each.

    a. _____

    b. _____

    c. _____

    d. _____

    e. _____

E. Game Plan for the Rest of the Book

This section shows you the game plan for the rest of this book.

This book has four parts:

- Part One: Administrative Law Fundamentals (You are here.)
- Part Two: Agency Rulemaking
- Part Three: Agency Adjudication
- Part Four: Judicial Review of Agency Action

Part One gives you foundational information and introduces you to the fundamental skills for solving administrative law problems. You will use and build upon this information throughout the course. If you think of administrative agencies as a large array of rather unruly animals, you can think of Part One as training you in the basic principles of biology necessary to your study and handling of these critters.

Parts Two and Three examine agency rulemaking and agency adjudication, the main types of agency activity that affect people's legal rights and duties and that lawyers accordingly must learn about. They are as important for administrative lawyers to understand as it is for biologists to understand an animal's metabolic and sensory systems.

Part Four examines when and how courts review agency action. Judicial review provides an especially important form of keeping agencies within legal bounds.

Chapter Problem Revisited

1.   If your personal set of mantras now includes, "Agencies are creatures of statute," you have internalized one of the most important fundamentals of administrative law.

2.   Virtually all law school courses on administrative law study agency rulemaking and agency adjudication. At the same time as we explore these activities in

this book, we suggest you notice how often these activities are the subject of stories in the popular and legal media.

3. Most agency rules, agency adjudications, and other agency actions go unreviewed by courts or any other external source of control. This reality underlies the cardinal rule of administrative law emphasizing the need to win your case in the agency. This reality also lends credence to the notion of agencies as a "headless fourth branch of government." The lawyer's best approach to these admittedly powerful entities is through systematic study of administrative law.

Professional Development Reflection Question

This question concerns habits. You will develop habits in approaching your study of law that you will carry into your practice of law. Therefore, it makes sense to develop good study habits now. Our question is: What habits will you develop specifically for use in learning administrative law as well as you can? We can suggest several that we think will serve most users of this book well:

1. If you are assigned the chapter problems and exercises, really do them; don't gloss over them. Yes, doing them will require you to spend more time on the material than if you don't do them. But doing them is worth it, because you will learn better.

2. Keep a running list of specialized terms, with definitions written in your own words. You will find specialized terms throughout this book. If you only "kind of" learn what a term means, you will lose a lot of information. If you're uncertain what a term means, make sure to find out.

3. Connect what you learn in your administrative law course to (a) your personal experience; (b) your learning in other law school courses; and (c) your career goals. Making these connections helps you learn administrative law better and remember it better. For example, your personal experience is bound to include encounters with agencies like Departments of Motor Vehicles and the U.S. Department of Education (if you've sought federal financial aid). As for other law school courses, courses such as constitutional law and courses in substantive areas dominated by agencies (e.g., environmental law) are bound to be relevant. Finally, consider how you may, as a lawyer, use what you learn in this course. If nothing else, you will learn much in this course about how to read statutes, and that is an essential skill for lawyers in every field.

Chapter 3

Statutory Research and Analysis in Administrative Law

Overview

Statutes are the source of most agencies' powers and most limits on those powers. Consequently, many administrative law problems require you to find all relevant statutes and analyze their applicability to the problem at hand. This chapter introduces you to knowledge and skills for finding and analyzing the statutes applicable to a particular agency.

The sections of this chapter are:

A. Context for Statutory Research and Interpretation in Administrative Law

B. The Three Types of Statutes Governing Administrative Agencies

C. Finding the Agency Legislation

D. Finding Cross-Cutting Statutes

E. Reading the Agency Legislation

F. Chapter 3 Wrap Up and Look Ahead

Chapter Problem

Memorandum

To: Alex Associate

From: Petra Partner

Re: Background Research on Consumer Product Safety Commission

This afternoon I received a call from our longtime client, Shakir Singh, President of Singh Manufacturing, Inc. Mr. Singh called me after being contacted by someone at the Consumer Product Safety Commission (CPSC). I am to meet with Mr. Singh tomorrow. I need your help preparing for that meeting.

All I know about the CPSC is that it regulates consumer products. I assume that one of Singh's products has caught the CPSC's attention. I know that the CPSC can get manufacturers to recall products if the CPSC thinks they pose danger, but I don't know much else about the CPSC's powers. I need you to find and begin to become familiar with the statutes that CPSC administers, including the one that allows for recall of supposedly dangerous consumer products.

I'd appreciate your giving me an overview of the CPSC's powers tomorrow, before my meeting with Mr. Singh. I recommend that you study the agency's website and start to get a sense of the statutes that this agency administers. Between now and then I'll no doubt develop specific questions that I hope you'll be able to answer.

With your help, I believe tomorrow we will be able to secure a new matter for the firm helping a great client. Thank you!

A. Context for Statutory Research and Analysis in Administrative Law

To understand the role of statutory research and interpretation in administrative law, you may benefit from thinking about agencies from the perspective of the legislatures that create them.

Agencies do not sprout up voluntarily as do weeds. They are created, one at a time, usually by a legislature, to address a particular problem or achieve a particular objective—sometimes in response to a specific event: A young person dies because of an unhygienic tattoo parlor (see chapter problem for Chapter 2); a nationwide depression throws millions of people out of work (as occurred in 1929 and led to so many New Deal agencies); or international terrorists fly a plane into a building in the United States (which prompted legislation creating the Department of Homeland Security). You can no doubt think of more recent events that have prompted calls for new government regulation.

After a legislature decides to deal with a problem by creating a new agency, or investing an existing agency with a new set of powers and duties, the legislature must decide what powers and duties the agency should have. Because an agency is typically created—or an existing agency is given new powers and duties—as a response to a particular problem, the legislation enacted should be tailored to effectively addressing that problem. It must be so tailored if the legislative strategy is to be successful. The vagaries of the political process and its legislative compromises, however, may have resulted in less than an optimum match between the problem solving needs and the tools made available to the agency. Also, the problem initially may not have been perceived accurately, and the legislative design for its treatment and correction may be faulty. After all, it is one thing to recognize that a problem exists; it is another thing to design an effective way to deal with it. Of course, in theory, amendments to the agency legislation may be made. But the legislative attention may not be readily recaptured and the needed changes may not be forthcoming or effective when they do come.

Although the typical agency is created by enactment of specific, "organic" legislation that assigns that agency a mission and various powers to carry out that mission, and may be supplemented or modified by later, agency-specific legislation, legislatures also enact laws that apply to multiple agencies, rather than to specific ones. For example, the National Environmental Policy Act (NEPA) requires "*all* agencies of the Federal Government" to prepare environmental impact statements for actions that significantly affect the environment. 42 U.S.C. § 4332(C) (2012) (emphasis added). More importantly for administrative law scholars and practitioners, the federal government and all fifty States have enacted administrative procedure acts (APAs) to provide uniform procedures for agencies to follow.

One of the challenges of learning and practicing administrative law is to determine how broadly applicable legislation, such as NEPA and an APA — which this book will call "cross-cutting" statutes — interact with organic statutes and other agency-specific legislation for purposes of a particular problem. There is no general formula for making this determination; rather, it requires a highly contextual analysis. A central goal of this book is to help you learn frameworks of analysis that allow you to analyze particular administrative law problems systematically and contextually.

B. The Three Types of Statutes Governing Administrative Agencies

As many as three kinds of statutes may control an agency's activities:

(1) The agency's organic act, which is also known as the organic statute, the agency charter, the agency enabling act, the agency enabling statute, or the agency mandate.

(2) Other agency-specific statutes, often enacted after the organic act, that modify, restrict, or add to the agency's existing powers and duties.

(3) Statutes that apply to multiple agencies, which this book calls "cross-cutting statutes."

This book refers to the first two types of statute, collectively, as "the agency statutes" or "the agency legislation" (those phrases being shorter and simpler than the phrase "the organic statutes and other agency-specific statutes"). Below you will learn more about all three types of statute. Analysis of an administrative law problem often requires you to identify all three types, and analyze how they interact in their application to the problem at hand.

1. Agency Organic Statutes

Many, perhaps most, agencies are created by statute and therefore have an organic act. For example, you may remember from Chapter 1 that the U.S. Securities and Exchange Commission was created by the Securities Exchange Act of 1934. Chapter 1 reproduced the small piece of that statute that actually created the SEC, which is reproduced again here:

---

15 U.S.C. §78d. Securities and Exchange Commission

(a) Establishment ...

There is hereby established a Securities and Exchange Commission (hereinafter referred to as the "Commission") to be composed of five commissioners to be appointed by the President by and with the advice and consent of the Senate....

The "hereby established" wording, while legalistic, is helpful for identifying the specific language creating the SEC. Sometimes the generative statutory language is less legalistic, and more understated, as in this provision creating the California Medical Board:

Cal. Bus. & Prof. Code 2001. Medical Board of California

(a) There is in the Department of Consumer Affairs a Medical Board of California that consists of 15 members, seven of whom shall be public members....

The language creating the Consumer Product Safety Commission (CPSC) takes the legalistic tack. *See* 15 U.S.C. § 2053(a) (2012).

Besides creating the agency, the agency's organic act typically establishes the structure of the agency and its duties and powers. As you can see from the excerpts above, both the SEC (a federal agency) and the Medical Board of California (a state agency) are headed by multi-person bodies. An important semantic point worth mentioning here is that "the Securities and Exchange Commission" is the term used to refer to both the five-member group that heads the SEC, as well as the entire agency as a whole, including all 3500 employees. Likewise, the term "Medical Board of California" denotes both the fifteen-member head of the agency and also the agency as a whole, with all of its employees.

Organic acts often have provisions directed, not to the agency, but to the public. For example, the Securities Exchange Act of 1934 makes it "unlawful for any person to make any untrue statement of a material fact ... in connection with any tender offer." 15 U.S.C. § 78n (2012). You need not know what a "tender offer" is to appreciate that this command—which you might call a statutory "thou shalt not"—is addressed to the public. This kind of provision is often called a "substantive provision" because it imposes a legal duty directly on the public. It is not about the operation of the agency, though it is a provision that the SEC is responsible for enforcing. Instead of imposing a legal duty, a statute's substantive provisions may create legal entitlements to licenses or benefits. There are other kinds of substantive provisions, too. The point is simply that an organic statute is not necessarily just about the agency's structure and operations. It often has substantive provisions for the agency to enforce.

2. Other Agency-Specific Statutes

Some agencies administer only one statute, which is typically their organic statute. Other agencies administer many statutes. The U.S. Environmental Protection Agency, for example, administers more than twenty-three major federal statutes, according to its website. http://www.epa.gov/lawsregs/laws/index.html. This simply reflects that once an agency is created to administer a particular statute, the agency often ends up also administering later-enacted statutes on similar subjects requiring similar expertise. To cite another example, the Consumer Product Safety Commission administers its organic act, which is called the Consumer Product Safety Act, plus six other federal statutes.

A lawyer dealing with an agency may have to analyze several of the agency's statutes to analyze a particular agency action. That is because the agency's statutes may overlap. For example, the agency's organic act may have a provision broadly empowering the agency to promulgate all regulations "necessary and proper" to carry out all its statutory responsibilities. Another statute administered by the agency may have a provision empowering the agency to promulgate regulations on a particular subject. The agency might properly rely on both the broadly worded, general grant of rulemaking power and the narrowly worded, specific grant of rulemaking power to support a particular rule. Thus, more than one agency-specific statute may apply to a particular agency's action. *See, e.g., In re Permanent Surface Mining Regulation Litigation (Appeal of Peabody Coal*

Co.), 653 F.2d 514, 525 (D.C. Cir. 1981) (holding that agency's legislative rule was authorized by both a general grant of rulemaking power and a specific one); *see also United States v. Mead*, 533 U.S. 218, 222 (2001) (citing two grants of rulemaking authority relevant to agency's authority to promulgate regulation); *cf. Lubrizol Corp. v. Envt'l Protection Agency*, 562 F.2d 807, 815–820 & 815 n.20 (D.C. Cir. 1977) (holding that neither statute cited by the agency supported its rule). The lawyer therefore must be able to find all pertinent agency legislation, not just the agency's organic statute (if there is one).

3. Cross-Cutting Statutes

In addition to organic statutes and other agency-specific statutes, legislatures enact statutes that apply to multiple agencies. The most important cross-cutting federal statute is the federal Administrative Procedure Act, because it applies to almost all federal agencies and imposes procedural requirements on federal agencies' exercise of important powers. Similarly, the most important cross-cutting statute for each State's agencies will be that State's APA. Even so, federal and state agencies are subject to other cross-cutting statutes, too.

C. Finding the Agency Legislation

Above we identified three kinds of statutes that may govern an administrative law problem. Now we talk about how to find the first two types of statutes, the agency legislation. In this discussion we generally presume you already know what agency you are dealing with, and simply need to find the agency legislation relevant to your problem.

1. Internet

Faced with the research task of finding the agency legislation (as required in the Chapter Problem), your first impulse might be to hop on the internet. That is not a bad first impulse. The internet is a good research tool for certain administrative-law research projects. In particular, the internet is a good place to begin a search for the agency legislation, if you follow two rules:

(1) Rely on a publicly accessible website only if you know it to be trustworthy, and preferably only if it is the agency's official website (as indicated for U.S. agencies by the presence of the extension ".gov" in the website's address).

(2) Do not rely only on a website.

Most federal and state agencies have official websites. An agency's official website often has the statutes that the agency administers. Agencies use various names for the website location of their statutes. For example, the statutes may be found at links or tabs named "laws and regulations," "library," or "legal authority." The CPSC's website puts the agency's statutes behind a tab called "Business." Even when you find the right link to the agency statutes, your research is not done.

You cannot rely exclusively on the agency's website to find the agency's statutes, for three reasons. First, the agency website may not have the agency's statutes at all. Second, the agency website may have a location for the agency's statutes, but it is not complete or up to date. Third, the agency website may not have the version of the statute that governs your research problem. The third problem arises when your problem involves agency action taken under an earlier version of the statute on the website. For these reasons, an agency's website may be a good place to start your research, but it is usually a poor place to stop.

2. Other Resources

a. Federal Agencies

For federal agencies, there are four good print-based resources for research on the agency statutes. These resources are available in most law libraries (often in the reference section). Even if you do not consult these now, you will find it useful to know that such things exist. If you are a hands-on learner, get your hands on these now!

WASHINGTON INFORMATION DIRECTORY: The Washington Information Directory, published yearly by CQ Press, is a good place to start if you don't know what federal agency handles the subject matter that you are dealing with. The Directory identifies which agencies deal with various subjects, such as "Environment and Natural Resources." Its major limitation is that it does not provide citations to agency organic acts or other agency-specific legislation. Fortunately, once you find out what agency you are interested in, the next two sources will help you find the agency legislation.

FEDERAL REGULATORY DIRECTORY: The Federal Regulatory Directory is also published yearly by CQ Press. It provides detailed entries on select government agencies. Each entry lists the agency's organic act and cites other major statutes affecting the agency.

U.S. GOVERNMENT MANUAL: The U.S. Government Manual is published yearly by the U.S. General Printing Office. It cites the agency's organic act and the other statutes that the agency administers. The Manual also depicts the agency's organizational structure—often by providing an organizational chart—and names high-level agency personnel. The U.S. Governmental Manual, unlike the first two sources, is available not only in hard copy but also for free online.

UNITED STATES CODE, GENERAL INDEX: The U.S. Code is the official codification of all federal statutes. The U.S. Code has a general index in which you can find most if not all federal agencies. The tricky thing about the index is that federal agencies are not always listed as major index entries. Sometimes they are subentries. For example, the Consumer Product Safety Commission is listed as a subentry under the entry for "Consumer Protection," and it is referred to only as "Commission." Once you have found the index entry for the agency, however, the entry will ordinarily include a reference to the organic act (though the reference may not use that term) and other statutory provisions that the agency is responsible for administering.

b. State Agencies

Most States lack regulatory directories like the ones that exist for federal agencies. You must often resort to one of three sources:

State agency's official website: As noted above, state agency websites often have the agency statutes, though you will have to do further research to confirm completeness and currency.

State statutory code's general index: Every State has a code of statutes, and every state statutory code has a general index. Like the general index of the U.S. Code, the general index of a state statutory code should include entries for all statutorily created state agencies.

Libraries: Law school libraries and state law libraries often have tools for researching agencies in the State where the law school is located and library personnel who can teach you to use these tools. Never hesitate to ask a librarian; they enjoy this stuff!

3. Timing Is Everything

You must not only find all the relevant statutes but you must also make sure you find the relevant *version* of the statutes.

Sometimes you need the current version of the agency legislation. The "current version" can be a moving target, because statutes are constantly being amended. At the time of this writing, for example, twenty-two bills were pending in Congress that, if enacted, would affect the powers and duties of the Consumer Product Safety Commission. Pending legislation can be found using commercial legal databases. Another good source—and one that is publicly available—is the Library of Congress's THOMAS site, http://thomas.loc.gov/. THOMAS enables you to search for all bills affecting a particular federal agency.

Sometimes, you need a prior version of a statute. Suppose, for example, you find a U.S. Supreme Court case holding that an agency lacked the statutory authority to promulgate a particular rule. That case may address a rule that was promulgated under a statute that was later amended to supply the missing authority. Congress regularly "overrules" U.S. Supreme Court decisions interpreting federal agency legislation statute by amending the legislation. To understand the Supreme Court case, you must know which version of the statute the Court was interpreting. Wouldn't you be embarrassed if you challenged an agency action using judicial precedent that was statutorily overruled!?

Exercise: Finding Agency Legislation

The purpose of this exercise is to have you examine an agency's organic statute. You have two choices.

1. If you have been assigned the chapter problem, find the Consumer Product Safety Commission's organic statute using one of the methods described above.

2. If you have not been assigned the chapter problem, find the organic statute for a federal or state agency of your choice, using one of the above methods.

Once you have found the agency's organic statute, skim it carefully, paying particular attention to the titles of each provision in the statute. The objective of this exercise is to introduce you to the contents and structure of an agency organic statute, in preparation for the upcoming discussion of how to read an agency statute.

D. Finding Cross-Cutting Statutes

There is no single, reliable way to identify all cross-cutting statutes that may apply to a particular agency. The difficulty of identifying the cross-cutting statutes that may apply to a particular agency action is part of the larger challenge of practicing administrative law, given its sprawling nature. Lawyers meet the challenge in several ways.

Many administrative lawyers specialize. They may specialize by limiting their practice to a particular area of administrative law, such as environmental law, labor law, securities law, tax law, immigration law, international trade, land use law, etc. They may specialize by limiting their practice to particular kinds of clients, such as farmers, doctors, the elderly, labor unions, immigrants, environmental protection organizations, oil companies, or securities firms. In this way they gain expertise in comparatively thin slices of administrative law. They have an easier time than generalists keeping up with the law affecting their area of expertise. They mentor lawyers new to their specialty, including lawyers new to the practice of law.

An agency itself can be an important source of information about the range of laws governing it. A phone call or email to the appropriate agency official may save hours in the library. The telephone is one of a lawyer's most important research tools.

Be careful, though, about contacting an agency when you represent a client who has a matter involving that agency. Some contacts may be improper. The American Bar Association's Model Rule of Professional Conduct addressing "Communication with Person Represented by Counsel" states:

> In representing a client, a lawyer shall not communicate about the subject of the representation with a person the lawyer knows to be represented by another lawyer in the matter, unless the lawyer has the consent of the other lawyer or is authorized to do so by law or a court order.

Model Rule of Professional Conduct 4.2. This rule has been adopted in many States to govern lawyers practicing in those States. The rule could be interpreted to prevent you, for example, from directly contacting an agency official whom you are suing on behalf of a client, if that official is being represented by an agency lawyer. The rule's applicability to contacts with governmental entities is complicated, however. An official comment on Rule 4.2 says that a lawyer may contact an agency official "on behalf of a client who is exercising a constitutional or other legal right to communicate with the government." The relevant word in the last sentence is "may." People have a right to petition their government, including government agencies, for redress of grievances, but statutes, agency rules, and Rules of Professional Conduct can put reasonable limits on that right. Most importantly, if your client is a party to a case being adjudicated administratively within an agency, contacting the agency officials who help decide the adjudication may be an improper "ex parte communication." You will learn more about ex parte communications later in this book. The short of it is that, if you are representing a client with a matter involving an agency, make sure before contacting the agency that you know the relevant ground rules.

This does not exhaust the ways to identify all statutes governing an administrative law problem about a particular agency. In administrative law, as in other areas of law, it will pay you to think creatively. For example, perhaps you can get the needed information from someone on the staff of one of the congressional committees with oversight responsibility for the agency. Again, do not forget about the nearest state law library or law school library.

E. Reading the Agency Statutes

Reading a statute is a specialized task because statutes are a specialized form of writing. You cannot read a statute like a short story or novel; statutes do not have much of a plot. You cannot read a statute like a judicial opinion, either; statutes serve a different purpose from judicial opinions.

Agency statutes are a specialized form of statute. Thus, reading agency statutes requires a specialized approach. Fortunately, just about anyone can learn to read an agency statute with the eyes of an administrative lawyer. Even better, it is a skill that you will use throughout your career if it includes administrative law.

The discussion below of reading agency statutes distinguishes between your first readings of an agency statute and re-readings of it. The discussion ends by emphasizing the need to consult other sources, besides the agency statute, to learn about an agency. We encourage you, whether or not you've been assigned the chapter problem for this chapter, to examine the actual text of the statutes that are cited in the discussion below.

1. Reading an Unfamiliar Agency Statute

Reading an unfamiliar agency statute actually requires you to go through the entire statute twice or more. First, you read it to get a lay of the land—to get a sense of its structure and the topics it addresses. Often the best way to do this is by skimming the titles of the provisions. This will give you a general sense of what things are in the statute, and where they are.

Once the experienced administrative lawyer has gotten a lay of the land, the lawyer re-reads the unfamiliar agency statute looking for certain information. Specifically, the lawyer looks for certain categories of information, much like a lawyer reading a judicial opinion looks for certain categories of information named "facts," "issues," "holding," etc. Many administrative lawyers when reading an agency statute look for five categories of information:

a) **Contextual information**, which answers questions such as: What are the purpose and background of this statute? What are its definitions?

b) **Structural information**, which answers questions such as: How does this agency fit into the scheme of government? How is the agency structured internally?

c) Information on **agency duties and powers**

d) Information on **judicial oversight**, which answers the question: What express points of contact exist between the agency and the courts?

e) Information on the **applicability of the APA and other statutes**, which answers the question: How does this agency statute interact with the APA and other statutes?

a. Contextual Information

At the beginning of an agency statute, you often find information on the purpose of the statute; the factual background against which the statute was enacted; and the definitions of terms used in the statute. This information provides contextual information essential for understanding the statute.

Provisions identifying the statute's purpose and factual background are important because they can influence the interpretation of the statute, especially when its applicability to a particular situation is unclear. An example of a statutory provision identifying statutory purposes and findings is in the Consumer Product Safety Commission's organic statute. It is entitled "Congressional Findings and Declaration of Purpose." 15 U.S.C. § 2051 (2012).

Provisions defining terms used in the statute are important because statutes often use common words that have specialized definitions for purposes of the statute. In addition, some terms pop up in many different statutes but have different definitions. For example, as discussed above, the term "agency" may be defined differently in different statutes.

Often, the scope of an agency's power depends on the definition of certain terms. The power of the Consumer Products Safety Commission under its organic statute, for example, depends heavily on the statutory definition of "consumer product." 15 U.S.C. § 2052(a)(5) (2012); *see ASG Indus., Inc. v. CPSC*, 593 F.2d 1323 (D.C. Cir. 1979) (addressing whether products covered by CPSC's safety standard for "architectural glazing material" were "consumer products" that CPSC could regulate).

b. Structural Information

The agency statute may have two types of structural information: information about where the agency fits into the larger scheme of government (external structural information); and information about how the agency is organized internally (internal structural information).

Both kinds of structural information are important to lawyers with matters before an agency. The lawyer must know as much about the agency as possible to deal with it effectively. This is true for the same reason that a lawyer with a litigation matter must know as much as possible about the court, the judge, and the opposing party; and a lawyer seeking legislation must know the key legislators, legislative committees, and legislative staff: Effective advocacy depends on knowing your audience.

The agency's organic statute often includes external structural information. For example, the CPSC's organic statute, the Consumer Product Safety Act, establishes the CPSC as an "independent regulatory commission." 15 U.S.C. § 2053(a) (2012). This information is valuable for lawyers with matters before the CPSC. For instance, it means that most decisions by the CPSC, unlike some decisions of agencies that are part of a larger agency, are not subject to review—and potentially to revision—by an authority higher in the executive-branch food chain. For matters within the CPSC, the buck generally stops at the desks of Commissioners who, as a group, head the agency.

The lawyer also needs information about the internal organization of the agency. Questions about internal organization include: How is the agency headed? Is it headed by one person, or a multi-person body? In either event, how is/are the head(s) of the agency selected? What is her/his/their term of office? How can she/he/they be removed from office? Is the agency broken into subunits (small agencies) according to varying functions? Does it have one central office? Does it have any regional or field offices?

The internal structural information matters because the head of an agency—whether it is one person or a multi-person body—does not personally do all the agency's work. Many agency actions originate at a relatively low level of the agency and work their way up. The lawyer will generally aim to resolve a matter favorably to the client at the lowest level possible but must also know how to appeal to higher authorities if necessary. To do this, the lawyer needs to know the entire agency chain of command as it relates to the particular matter. It can be challenging to find all the appropriate agency officials and to understand their respective powers and responsibilities.

The agency's organic act is usually where you will find structural information. Additional structural information may come from other agency-specific statutes and the agency's own rules, but the organic statute is the place to look first. Thus, for example, a lawyer studying an action taken by the Consumer Product Safety Commission under the Flammable Fabrics Act (15 U.S.C. §§ 1191–1204 (2012)) will want to study not only that Act but also the CPSC's organic statute—the Consumer Product Safety Act (15 U.S.C. §§ 2051–2089 (2012))—for information on the CPSC's structure and other basic information. The organic act is the DNA.

In sum, the agency legislation is the place to begin learning about an agency's organization and leadership. The statute often does not have all the information you need; organizational details will be spelled out in the agency's own organizational regulations and other agency-generated material. If any agency-generated material conflicts with the agency legislation, however, the legislation prevails and for that reason is the place to begin your research.

c. Agency Duties and Powers

An agency statute gives the agency a job to do and powers to do it. It helps to think about powers and duties together because the duties limit the powers, and vice versa. In other words, an agency must exercise its powers to carry out statutory duties. The agency cannot exercise its powers for purposes unrelated to carrying out its statutory duties. By the same token, the agency can carry out its statutory duties using only the powers that it has been given under its statute. The agency cannot exercise powers that the statute has not given it, even if the agency is seeking to further statutory goals.

Administrative lawyers tend to categorize agency powers according to the three traditional categories: legislative, executive, and judicial. Does the agency have the quasi-legislative power to make legislative rules? If so, what matters may the rules address? (In other words, what is the scope of rulemaking power?) Does the agency have executive powers, such as powers of investigation or prosecution? What is the scope of these executive powers? Does the agency have the quasi-judicial power to adjudicate cases? If so, what is the scope of these powers?

The CPSC, like many modern agencies, has powers resembling those traditionally associated with the three separate branches of government. The CPSC's organic statute gives it the "quasi-legislative" power to make rules. The CPSC's rules are called "consumer product safety standards." 15 U.S.C. § 2056 (2012).

Diagram 3-1. Statutory Grant of Legislative (or "Quasi-Legislative") Power

15 U.S.C. § 2056. Consumer product safety standards

(a) Types of requirements

The Commission may promulgate consumer product safety standards in accordance with the provisions of section 2058 of this title ...

The CPSC also has the traditional executive power to investigate for possible violations of the laws it is responsible for administering. The CPSC's investigative powers under its organic statute include the power to inspect places where consumer products are manufactured and the power to make manufacturers keep records. 15 U.S.C. § 2065 (2012).

Diagram 3-2. Statutory Grant of an Executive Type of Power

15 U.S.C. § 2065. Inspection and record-keeping

(a) Inspection

For purposes of implementing this chapter, or rules or orders prescribed under this chapter, officers or employees duly designated by the Commission, upon presenting appropriate credentials and a written notice from the Commission to the owner, operator, or agent in charge, are authorized—

(1) to enter, at reasonable times, (A) any factory, warehouse, or establishment in which consumer products are manufactured or held, in connection with distribution in commerce . . .

The CPSC has the "quasi-judicial" power to determine whether a particular consumer product "presents a substantial product hazard." 15 U.S.C. § 2064(c) (2012). The CPSC may make this determination in an administrative proceeding that may include a trial-like, evidentiary hearing before an administrative law judge employed by the CPSC. If the CPSC determines through such an administrative adjudication that a product presents a substantial hazard, it can order the manufacturer to recall the product and take other steps to protect the public. *Id.* This exercise of quasi-judicial power is depicted in Diagram 3-3.

Examination of the agency's organic statute thus reveals important information about the specific combination of powers that the agency's legislative creator has given it to achieve its statutory mission. The blending of types of power found in the CPSC and typical of other modern agencies is illustrated in Diagram 3-4.

d. Judicial Oversight

When a lawyer reads an agency statute, the lawyer looks for provisions addressing points of contact between the agency and the courts. For example, the agency statute may permit the agency to bring a court action to enjoin a violation of the laws that the agency is responsible for administering, or to seek another type of sanction, such as a civil fine. Alternatively, the agency statute may allow someone adversely affected by agency action to bring a court proceeding to invalidate the agency action. The agency statute may allow other types of judicial proceedings. The Consumer Product Safety

Diagram 3-3. Statutory Grant of Quasi-Judicial Power

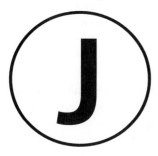

> **15 U.S.C. § 2064. Substantial product hazards . . .**
>
> (c) Public notice of defect or failure to comply; mail notice
>
> (1) If the Commission determines (after affording interested persons, including consumers and consumer organizations, an opportunity for a hearing in accordance with subsection (f) of this section) that notification is required in order to adequately protect the public from such substantial product hazard, or if the Commission, after notifying the manufacturer, determines a product to be an imminently hazardous consumer product and has filed an action under section 2061 of this title, the Commission may order the manufacturer or any distributor or retailer of the product to take any one or more of the following actions: . . .

Diagram 3-4. Organic Act Creating Agency and Granting It a Combination of Powers

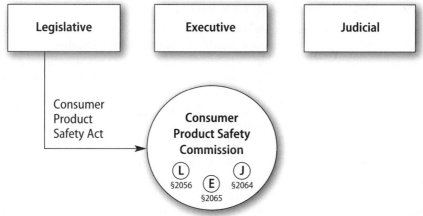

Commission's organic statute illustrates the range of provisions in an agency statute that may trigger judicial involvement.

Two provisions in the CPSC's organic statute authorize the CPSC to be a plaintiff. One provision authorizes the CPSC to file a federal court action to protect the public from an "imminently hazardous consumer product." 15 U.S.C. § 2061(a) (2012). In such an action, the court can order the manufacturer, distributors, or retailers of the product to notify the public and recall the product. *Id.* § 2061(b). The second provision authorizes the CPSC to bring a civil action for up to $15,000,000 in fines for specified "prohibited acts." *Id.* §§ 2068 & 2069 (2012). When the CPSC acts as a plaintiff to enforce the law in courts, it is exercising an executive type of power.

The CPSC's organic statute also authorizes criminal penalties for "prohibited acts." 15 U.S.C. § 2070 (2012). The CPSC does not itself, however, have authority to initiate criminal prosecutions. Instead, like most federal criminal proceedings, prosecutions under the CPSC's organic statute are brought by lawyers in the U.S. Department of Justice (DOJ), working closely with lawyers and other officials from the CPSC. More generally, few federal agencies have power to bring criminal prosecutions. That power is generally vested in DOJ. *See* 28 U.S.C. § 516 (2012). Similarly, most administrative agencies at the state and local level lack prosecutorial authority. The power to prosecute criminal violations of the statutes that they administer typically resides in law enforcement officials such as local prosecutors or a State's attorney general's office.

Two provisions in the CPSC's organic statute authorize private plaintiffs to bring civil actions. Specifically, 15 U.S.C. § 2072 allows suits for money damages to be brought by someone injured by any knowing violation of a consumer product safety rule. *See* 15 U.S.C. § 2072(a) (2012). A separate provision seems designed to authorize civil actions by consumer protection groups. *See id.* § 2073. It authorizes "[a]ny interested person (including any individual or nonprofit, business, or other entity)" to bring a federal court action for "appropriate injunctive relief" against anyone who is violating a consumer product safety rule or a CPSC order relating to a "substantial product hazard." *Id.* These private actions supplement the CPSC's enforcement efforts.

Like many agency statutes, the CPSC's organic statute also provides for the CPSC to be a defendant in some court proceedings. Specifically, the CPSC's organic statute provides for judicial review of the CPSC's rules. 15 U.S.C. §§ 2060 & 2064(j)(2) (2012). This provides for judicial oversight of the CPSC's exercise of its quasi-legislative power.

The agency statute is not the only law that may authorize court proceedings connected with an agency's activities. Most importantly, the federal Administrative Procedure Act (APA) and many state APAs provide a broad right to judicial review of agency action. *See, e.g.*, 5 U.S.C. § 704 (2012) ("Agency action made reviewable by statute and final agency action for which there is no other adequate remedy in a court are subject to judicial review."). Indeed, a central purpose of the federal APA was to ensure that judicial review was available even for agency actions taken under a statute that did not expressly authorize judicial review. The same is true of many state APAs.

Thus, for example, the CPSC's organic statute does not expressly authorize judicial review of CPSC orders requiring a manufacturer to remedy a "substantial product hazard." *See* 15 U.S.C. § 2064 (2012). In this situation, § 704 of the federal APA, quoted in the last paragraph, applies by default to authorize judicial review of such a **final agency action for which there is no other adequate remedy in a court.**" 5 U.S.C. § 704. Thus, the federal APA authorizes judicial oversight of the CPSC's exercise of its quasi-judicial power.

The takeaway from this discussion is that points of contact between the agency and the court can occur under provisions inside, as well as outside, the agency statute. The result is that courts can oversee an agency's exercise of its various powers. Diagram 3-5 illustrates that, typically, judicial oversight of an agency's actions can occur under provisions in the agency legislation or the applicable APA, or both.

e. Applicability of APA and Other Statutes

You have learned that an agency may have duties and powers under more than one agency-specific statute, and that the agency may also be subject to cross-cutting statutes, including an APA. Thus, multiple statutes may bear upon a particular administrative law problem, and the statutes may appear to be inconsistent. That is why administrative law problem solving often requires studying—and reconciling inconsistencies between or among—multiple statutes.

Diagram 3-5. Judicial Oversight of Agency Action

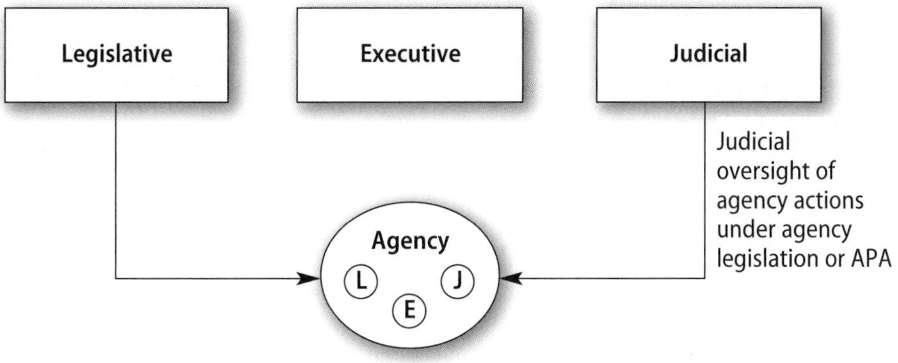

Anticipating this complexity, a lawyer reading an agency statute looks for provisions referring to the APA and other statutes. True, the APA and other statutes may apply even if they are not mentioned in the agency statute. Thus, as discussed above, the APA generally authorizes judicial review of "final agency action" that is not made reviewable by the agency statute. 5 U.S.C. § 704. But sometimes the drafters of the agency statute address the APA's applicability or inapplicability. This is illustrated by the CPSC's organic statute, which addresses the APA's applicability to certain CPSC activities.

As mentioned above, the CPSC can conduct administrative adjudications to determine whether a product presents a "substantial product hazard." 15 U.S.C. § 2064(c). The provision in the organic statute authorizing these administrative adjudications requires the CPSC to provide "an opportunity for a hearing in accordance with section 554 of Title 5." *Id.* § 2064(f). The referenced "section 554 of Title 5" is the provision in the federal APA entitled **"Adjudications."** You must therefore look to both § 554 of the federal APA and the CPSC statute to determine statutory procedures for the CPCS's administrative adjudications on substantial product hazards.

Another provision addressing APA applicability authorizes the CPSC to promulgate "consumer product safety rules":

---

15 U.S.C. § 2058. Procedure for consumer product safety rules ...

(d) Promulgation of rule ...

(2) Consumer product safety rules shall be promulgated in accordance with section 553 of Title 5, except that the Commission shall give interested persons an opportunity for the oral presentation of data, views, or arguments, in addition to

an opportunity to make written submissions. A transcript shall be kept of any oral presentation....

Section 553 of Title 5 is entitled **"Rule making."** Section 553 generally requires an agency to give the public (1) notice that the agency proposes to adopt a rule; and (2) a chance to provide input on the proposed rule. Section 553, standing by itself, allows the agency to limit public input to the filing of written comments. Section 2058(d)(2) above, however, alters the situation for CPSC rules; the CPSC must give members of the public not only a chance to submit written comments but also an opportunity to make "oral presentation[s]." Thus, you must look to both § 553 of the federal APA and the CPSC statute to determine statutory procedures for making CPSC rules.

The CPSC's organic statute, like most agency statutes, refers to other statutes besides the APA. The lawyer reading an agency statute must chase down these cross-references to understand the agency statute completely.

2. Re-Readings of an Agency Statute

Statutes are dense, and agency statutes can be especially dense. The best way to learn the agency legislation is by constantly returning to it to analyze particular problems under it. Lawyers who specialize in working with particular statutes hope to learn the statute so well that they develop instincts about how various problems should be resolved under the statute. This stage is true mastery.

As a student of administrative law, you have the opportunity to learn how to learn about agencies, and part of this challenge entails learning how to learn about an agency by studying its statutes. This introduction should give you a good start.

3. Learning About an Agency from Non-Statutory Sources

Studying the agency legislation lies at the core of learning about an agency, for the agency can act only as authorized by its legislation. But the agency legislation is not the only source of information about the agency. As mentioned, you must also indentify all cross-cutting statutes governing the agency operations.

Besides statutory material, essential information about an agency may be found in these sources:

- the agency's regulations and other agency-generated material that is not codified in regulations, such as agency case decisions, interpretative rulings, press releases, public information guides, etc.;
- other executive-branch material, such as Executive Orders; and
- judicial decisions interpreting the agency's authority.

These are called "primary sources" because, to varying degrees, they constitute actual "law" or official opinions on what the law is.

You can also find important information about an agency in "secondary sources" such as law review articles and commercial publications such as treatises on environmental law, labor law, securities law, and other subjects dominated by administrative agencies. Secondary sources are not "the law" but are instead someone's explanation or commentary on the law. Many lawyers find it useful to start their research into an unfamiliar agency or unfamiliar area of administrative law by examining secondary sources.

The key is finding the most comprehensive and reliable secondary sources. To do that, your best option is your trusty reference librarian or an attorney with experience in the area. Generalized commercial legal databases such as LexisNexis and Westlaw have specialized secondary sources. There is no substitute, however, for word of mouth as a way to find the best secondary sources.

F. Chapter 3 Wrap Up and Look Ahead

This chapter introduced you to the three types of statutes central to administrative law: agency organic statutes, other agency-specific statutes, and cross-cutting statutes. The chapter then discussed how to find these statutes and how to read the first two types, "the agency legislation." The chapter identified the most important type of cross-cutting statute as an Administrative Procedure Act (APA). The next chapter introduces you to APAs.

Chapter Problem Revisited

The partner says he is aware that CPSC can get manufacturers to recall products voluntarily. The statute authorizing the CPSC to order "recalls" of products uses the term "recall" only once, and does so obliquely. *See* 15 U.S.C. § 2064(i) (2012) ("Requirements for recall notices"). What is more, the statute does not refer to voluntary recalls at all. It authorizes the CPSC to require a manufacturer (as well as a distributor and retailer) to take certain actions, including the replacement or repair of a product that "presents a substantial product hazard." 15 U.S.C § 2064(d) (2012). In practice, the CPSC's exercise of this authority is called the power to order "recalls," and, rather than ordering recalls, CPSC in practice almost always gets private companies to recall hazardous items "voluntarily."

Please reflect and jot down notes on what you have learned from reading about, and reading, the CPSC's organic statute.

Professional Development Reflection Question

The chapter problem requires a lawyer to learn about an unfamiliar agency. Even for the simplest agency, there is much to learn. The lawyer confronting an unfamiliar agency may lack confidence in his or her competence to learn enough to represent a client competently. In that situation, the lawyer may—and should—consider Model Rule of Professional Conduct 1.1, entitled "Competence":

A lawyer shall provide competent representation to a client. Competent representation requires the legal knowledge, skill, thoroughness and preparation reasonably necessary for the representation.

Thus, lawyers confronting an unfamiliar problem have a professional responsibility to determine whether they can provide competent representation.

In the chapter problem, Alex Associate must provide competent representation; if Alex fails to do so, Alex cannot blame it on Petra Partner. But that doesn't mean Petra is off the hook; Petra must ensure Alex has the time and resources to develop the needed expertise. For Alex's part, Alex has a responsibility to ask Petra for all resources necessary to enable Alex to provide competent representation.

In this spirit, we ask you to do an imagination exercise. Imagine you are an associate who has received an assignment from a partner under circumstances that cause you seriously to doubt your ability to perform competently. What are tactful approaches you can take to ensure that you satisfy your professional obligation under Rule 1.1 while also maintaining a good relationship with the partner? The idea is to get you used to the idea of using more-experienced lawyers as a valuable source of information and support.

Chapter 4

Administrative Procedure Acts (APAs)

Overview

An administrative agency must obey applicable statutes. The typical agency is subject to both agency-specific statutes and cross-cutting statutes. The most important type of cross-cutting statute—and the star of this chapter—is an administrative procedure act (APA). The federal APA prescribes procedural requirements for most federal agencies. Every State has an APA that prescribes procedural requirements for that State's agencies.

APAs are the most important kind of cross-cutting statute for three reasons:

(1) APAs have broad applicability: The federal APA applies to most federal agencies; and each State's APA applies to most of that State's agencies.

(2) APAs impose procedural requirements for agencies' exercise of the important powers of rulemaking, adjudication, and aspects of agency investigations.

(3) APAs ensure the broad availability of judicial review of agency action.

This chapter introduces you to APAs and to a framework for determining the APA's applicability to a particular administrative law problem. This framework for determining APA applicability fits within the broader framework introduced in Chapter 2. Specifically, the framework for determining APA applicability enables you to determine (under part 2.b.ii of Chapter 2's framework) whether the APA is an external source of procedural requirements for the problem at hand.

This chapter has five sections:

A. The History of APAs

B. The Structure and Purposes of the Federal APA

C. Applicability of APAs

D. The Fundamental Distinction between Rulemaking and Adjudication

E. Chapter 4 Wrap Up and Look Ahead

Chapter Problem

You represent a kennel that raises purebred dogs for sale as pets. The kennel hires you to evaluate the possibility of a successful court challenge to a new federal regulation that increases the kennel's cost of operating. The regulation has been promulgated by the Animal and Plant Health Inspection Service of the U.S. Department of Agriculture under the Animal Welfare Act, 7 U.S.C. §§ 2131–2159 (2012).

Part of your evaluation must include whether the regulation was promulgated using legally required procedures. As part of your procedural analysis, you must determine whether the regulation is subject to the rulemaking procedures required by the federal APA.

1. List the questions that you have to answer, in the proper order, to determine whether the regulation is subject to the rulemaking procedures of the federal APA.

2. Identify what types of law—constitutional law, statutory law, agency rules, or judicial decisions—may bear upon the answer to each question.

3. Your clients fear the regulation could drive them out of business. They ask you, "Is it constitutional for the agency to issue such a regulation without going to court or giving us some kind of right to be heard?" How do you respond?

A. The History of APAs

A central feature of administrative law is that no two agencies are exactly alike. It also used to be true that no two agencies' *procedures* were exactly alike. Then Congress and state legislatures began enacting APAs to achieve more uniformity in agency procedures. By learning about the history of APAs, you will better understand their central importance in modern administrative law.

1. Federal APA

The number and variety of federal agencies exploded during the New Deal (1933–1938). A few years of living with the vast New Deal government apparatus led to concerns about how it operated. For one thing, the procedures for rulemaking varied from agency to agency. For another thing, the procedures for administrative adjudication, in particular, in some ways seemed unfair. For example, the procedures in many agencies allowed a single agency official to act as investigator, prosecutor, and judge of regulatory violations and other weighty matters.

In 1939, President Franklin Roosevelt authorized appointment of a committee to study the administrative procedures used by federal agencies and to make recommendations. The committee was known as the Attorney General's Committee on Administrative Procedure. From 1939–1941, the Committee investigated and produced twenty-seven monographs on agency operations. Its Final Report of 1941 was ultimately to be the basis of the Federal APA. World War II postponed congressional consideration of the Final Report. In 1945, the U.S. Attorney General's office assisted in the drafting and revision of the bill that became the Administrative Procedure Act. Finally, in 1946, the federal Administrative Procedure Act was enacted without a dissenting vote in either House of the Congress.

This unanimity came only after long study and struggle among federal agencies, the private interests regulated by them, and members of Congress. As the Supreme Court described the federal APA, "The Act thus represents a long period of study and strife; it settles long-continued and hard-fought contentions, and enacts a formula upon which opposing social and political forces have come to rest." *Wong Yang Sung v. McGrath*, 339 U.S. 33, 41 (1950).

The federal APA has withstood the test of time. Aside from the amendment of Section 3 of the original Act by the Freedom of Information Act, the original federal APA has gone largely unchanged for the last sixty-plus years. That is why it remains the backbone of federal administrative law.

In 1947, the Attorney General prepared a manual on the federal APA for the guidance of other federal agencies and the public. The Attorney General's Manual said of the federal APA:

> The Act sets a pattern designed to achieve relative uniformity in the administrative machinery of the Federal Government. It effectuates needed reforms in the administrative process and at the same time preserves the effectiveness of the laws which are enforced by the administrative agencies of the Government.

U.S. Dep't of Justice, Attorney General's Manual on the Administrative Procedure Act 5 (1947). This statement captures the Act's objectives of achieving more uniform, fairer procedures, while ensuring the ability of agencies effectively to enforce the laws that they were responsible for administering.

The Attorney General's Manual on the APA remains a useful resource on the meaning of the federal APA. Indeed, the U.S. Supreme Court has often cited the Attorney General's Manual as a helpful guide to interpreting the federal APA. *See, e.g., Shinseki v. Sanders*, 556 U.S. 396, 406 (2009). The lower federal courts also rely on the Attorney General's Manual in interpreting the APA. *See, e.g., Cohen v. United States*, 650 F.3d 717, 738 (D.C. Cir. 2011). Thus, lawyers practicing in or before federal agencies should get to know the Manual. Accordingly, you will find references to it throughout this book. We will sometimes refer to it as the "Attorney General's Manual on the APA," and we will cite it as "AGM ___."

You can find a complete copy of the Attorney General's Manual on the internet here:

Florida State University College of Law, ABA Administrative Procedure Database, Atorney General's Manual on the Administrative Procedure Act, http://www.law.fsu.edu/library/admin/1947cover.html (last visited June 3, 2012).

A print resource reproducing the Manual is published by the American Bar Association's Section on Administrative Law: Federal Administrative Law Sourcebook 39 (William Funk et al. eds., 4th ed. 2008). The Sourcebook also gives citations to the legislative history of the federal APA. Occasionally we will refer to an official compilation of the legislative history of the APA: *Administrative Procedure Act — Legislative History 1944–1946*, S. Doc. No. 248, 79th Cong., 2d Sess. (1946). We cite it as "APA Legislative History."

2. State APAs

A parallel move toward more uniformity and fairness in administrative procedure occurred in the States. In the 1930s state and local governments created more state and local agencies and intruded themselves more into private business and personal lives. The same lack of consistency in agency methods and concern for fair treatment at the hands of these agencies led to development of state administrative procedure legislation. By 1946, the National Conference of Commissioners on Uniform State Laws approved and recommended to the States a Model State Administrative Procedure Act. It was revised in 1961 and, again, in 1981. An updated version of the Model Act was completed in 2010.

The 1961 Model Act was particularly influential. It has provided the basis for the current state APAs in about half the States. We will therefore cite it frequently to show how States deal with various administrative law issues. We will also cite the 1981 and 2010 Model State APAs, because both have influenced (and often reflect) provisions in actual state APAs, and the 2010 Model State APA, in particular, represents what a distinguished group of judges, lawyers, and scholars consider "best practices" for administrative agencies.

The early Model State APAs took many concepts from the federal APA, and those common concepts largely survive in the later model State APAs. States, however, have issues and circumstances to deal with that do not confront the federal government, and every State is different. For those and other reasons, state APAs differ widely among each other and from the federal APA, though you will see commonalities.

State APAs are usually easy to find because they are almost always called the state "administrative procedure act" or "administrative procedure*s* act." Florida State University has a helpful internet site listing all fifty States' APAs. *See* Florida State University College of Law, ABA Administrative Procedure Database, State Resources, State Administrative Procedure Act, www.law.fsu.edu/library/admin/admin3.html (last visited June 3, 2012). If you prefer book-based research, you can find your State's APA in the index to the State's statutory code, probably under "administrative procedure (or procedure*s*) act."

For problems involving a state APA, you are unlikely to find anything comparable to the Attorney General's Manual on the federal APA. For insight into the meaning of a state APA provision, you often must resort to state-court case law interpreting the provision and secondary material such as law review articles and practitioner-oriented, commercial publications. In addition, if the applicable state APA provision is modeled on a provision in one of the Model State APAs, you may wish to consult a multi-volume series called Uniform Laws Annotated. *See* 15 Uniform Laws Annotated: Civil Procedural and Remedial Laws (2000 & Supp. 2011). It has official comments and case annotations from state courts in States that have based their APAs on one of the Model State APAs.

B. The Purposes and Structure of the Federal APA

Now you will learn about the purposes and structure of the federal APA. The objectives of this discussion are:

- to help you begin to get a big-picture understanding of the federal APA as a statutory text; and

- to introduce five important administrative law terms: informal (or notice-and-comment) rulemaking, formal rulemaking, formal adjudication, administrative law judge, and informal adjudication.

The Attorney General's Manual states that the purposes of the federal APA — and the original sections of the Act that serve those purposes — are:

- "To require agencies to keep the public currently informed of their organization, procedures and rules (sec. 3)."

- "To provide for public participation in the rule making process (sec. 4)."

- "To prescribe uniform standards for the conduct of formal rule making (sec. 4(b)) and [formal] adjudicatory proceedings (sec. 5), i.e., proceedings which are required by statute to be made on the record after opportunity for an agency hearing (secs. 7 and 8)."; and

- "To restate the law of judicial review (sec. 10)." AGM 9.

Although the APA has been amended since its enactment in 1946, its basic structure and purposes have stayed the same. Diagram 4-1 is a graphic that was included in the Senate Report on the original APA, enacted in 1946. We have embellished the graphic to identify the sections in Title 5 of the U.S. Code where the current provisions appear.

To understand how the structure of the federal APA relates to its purposes, please review Diagram 4-1 together with the purposes identified in the AGM and quoted above. This exercise will also help you understand how later statutes amending or supplementing the APA fit in with the structure and purposes of the original Act.

One purpose of the APA, served by Section 3 of the original Act, is to ensure that the public gets information on how the government operates. Congress later determined that Section 3 did not adequately serve that purpose and accordingly amended Section 3 of the original Act several times. The first significant amendment was achieved by enactment of the Freedom of Information Act in 1966.

Another purpose of the APA, accomplished by Section 4 of the original Act, is to allow public participation in the rulemaking process. Section 4 applies to most instances in which a federal agency wishes to promulgate a legislative rule. In most such instances, Section 4 requires the agency to publish a notice of its proposed rulemaking and to give the public a chance to submit written comments on the proposed rules. This is called "notice-and-comment" or "informal" rulemaking.

A third purpose of the APA is to prescribe uniform procedures for the conduct of hearings, and the rendering of decisions, in "formal" rulemaking proceedings and "formal" adjudications. As the Attorney General's Manual on the APA explained, formal rulemaking and formal adjudication are "proceedings which are required by statute to be made on the record after opportunity for an agency hearing." AGM 9. In other words, the APA prescribes the hearing and decision making requirements for those instances in which the agency legislation authorizing a particular rule or adjudication requires the agency to base the rule or adjudicatory decision on evidence admitted into the record at a trial-like hearing.

Some required procedures for formal rulemakings are in Section 4, and some required procedures for formal adjudications are in Section 5 of the original APA. More procedural requirements, applicable to the conduct of hearings and the rendering of decisions in both formal rulemaking and formal adjudication, are in Sections 7 and 8 of the original APA, respectively entitled "**Hearings**" and "**Decisions.**" The agency hearings in formal rulemaking and formal adjudication proceedings are usually conducted by officials who used to be called "examiners" and today are called "administrative law judges" (ALJs). The ALJs not only hold hearings in formal rulemakings and adjudications but also make recommended or initial decisions in those proceedings. In short, the defining characteristics of formal rulemaking and formal adjudications are that a statute external to the APA requires an opportunity for a formal hearing, typically conducted by a hearing official today called an ALJ, who both conducts the hearing and also renders a recommended or initial decision based on the record compiled at the hearing.

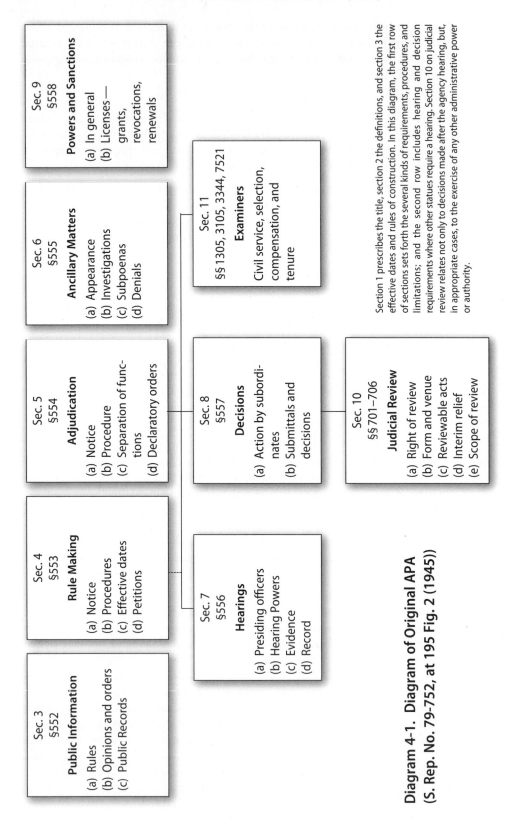

Sec. 3
§552
Public Information
(a) Rules
(b) Opinions and orders
(c) Public Records

Sec. 4
§553
Rule Making
(a) Notice
(b) Procedures
(c) Effective dates
(d) Petitions

Sec. 5
§554
Adjudication
(a) Notice
(b) Procedure
(c) Separation of functions
(d) Declaratory orders

Sec. 6
§555
Ancillary Matters
(a) Appearance
(b) Investigations
(c) Subpoenas
(d) Denials

Sec. 9
§558
Powers and Sanctions
(a) In general
(b) Licenses — grants, revocations, renewals

Sec. 7
§556
Hearings
(a) Presiding officers
(b) Hearing Powers
(c) Evidence
(d) Record

Sec. 8
§557
Decisions
(a) Action by subordinates
(b) Submittals and decisions

Sec. 11
§§ 1305, 3105, 3344, 7521
Examiners
Civil service, selection, compensation, and tenure

Sec. 10
§§ 701–706
Judicial Review
(a) Right of review
(b) Form and venue
(c) Reviewable acts
(d) Interim relief
(e) Scope of review

Section 1 prescribes the title, section 2 the definitions, and section 3 the effective dates and rules of construction. In this diagram, the first row of sections sets forth the several kinds of requirements, procedures, and limitations; and the second row includes hearing and decision requirements where other statues require a hearing. Section 10 on judicial review relates not only to decisions made after the agency hearing, but, in appropriate cases, to the exercise of any other administrative power or authority.

Diagram 4-1. Diagram of Original APA
(S. Rep. No. 79-752, at 195 Fig. 2 (1945))

The hearing officials were the subject of Section 11 of the original APA. Section 11 gave them job protections to ensure their impartiality. These protections are important because, in the federal system, ALJs have always been employees of the agencies for which they hold these formal hearings.

The final stated purpose of the APA is to authorize judicial review of agency action, which was accomplished in Section 10 of the original APA. Section 10 was entitled "**Judicial Review**." It is codified in 5 U.S.C. §§ 701–706 (2012). As noted above, the AGM described Section 10 as restating the existing law of judicial review, much of which had been developed up until that point in case law. Today, administrative lawyers and scholars dispute whether Section 10 merely restated — or instead modified — case law principles of judicial review. In any event, Section 10 governs several aspects of judicial review, including the right to judicial review, the process for obtaining judicial review, and the scope of judicial review.

The two remaining Sections of the original Act depicted in the graphic above deserve mention, for they, too, will be explored later in this book.

Section 6 is called "**Ancillary Matters**" to indicate that it deals with activities that are often incidental, or "ancillary," to an agency's performance of its various functions. Most importantly, Section 6 imposes procedural requirements for two kinds of agency activities that are not systematically addressed elsewhere in the APA: (1) agency investigations, including investigations involving the issuance of agency subpoenas; and (2) agency "informal adjudications." In an informal adjudication, an agency has authority to apply the law in a particular case but is not required, when exercising that authority, to provide an opportunity for a trial-like hearing and is not required to base its decision on the record compiled at such a hearing. When, for example, an agency denies a person's request for a permit after simply reviewing the person's written application, the agency has engaged in informal adjudication.

Section 9 is entitled "**Sanctions and Powers**." It has general provisions about an agency's exercise of powers and provisions specifically about the important agency power of licensing.

In addition to understanding the purposes of the APA, you should keep in mind one thing that the APA does *not* do. With one exception, the APA does not grant *power* to agencies. Rather, it prescribes *procedures* for agencies to follow when they exercise certain powers. To determine whether an agency has power to take an action, you must look outside the APA. You consult the APA, when applicable, to determine whether the agency has followed procedures required for exercising that power. That is why it's called the Administrative *Procedure* Act, not the Administrative *Power* Act.

The exception is in APA § 559, which gives "[e]**ach agency the authority necessary to comply with the requirements of this subchapter through the issuance of rules or otherwise**." 5 U.S.C. § 559. This authorizes agencies to make procedural rules, policies, and orders to ensure that the agency complies with the APA's procedural requirements. So, it is a grant of power — a power to implement APA procedural requirements.

Now is a good time for you to look for the current provisions that correspond to the original sections of the Federal APA depicted in Diagram 4-1. You will find the current provisions of the APA in Title 5 of U.S. Code or in the statutory supplement used in your course. The federal APA's procedural provisions are in the 500s (§§ 551–559); its judicial review provisions are in the 700s (§§ 701–706).

When you look for these provisions, you may encounter other provisions that codify important amendments or additions to the original APA. At this point, you may wish simply to lay your eyes on these amendments and additions, as you will encounter some of them later in the book. For example:

- The public information provisions of Section 3 (5 U.S.C. §552) have been supplemented by the Privacy Act of 1974 and the Government in the Sunshine Act (*id.* §§552a and 552b).

- The rulemaking provisions of Section 4 (5 U.S.C. §553) have been supplemented by later statutes that authorize negotiated rulemaking (*id.* §§561–570), require "regulatory flexibility" analyses of certain rules (id. §§601–612), and require congressional review of most rules (*id.* §§801–808).

- Furthermore, in addition to using rulemaking and adjudication to resolve issues, a federal agency can now use alternative means of dispute resolution, including arbitration. *Id.* §§571–583.

Exercise: Types of Agency Activity Addressed in the Federal APA

Jot down answers to these questions after reviewing what you just read:

1. Under the federal APA, how does the public typically participate in "informal rulemaking"?

2. What distinguishes an *informal* rulemaking proceeding from a *formal* rulemaking proceeding under the federal APA?

3. What is "formal adjudication" for purposes of the federal APA?

4. What do administrative law judges do?

5. What is informal adjudication?

6. What, do you suppose, is the purpose of having uniform procedures for informal rulemaking, formal rulemaking, and formal adjudications?

Diagram 4-2 offers another way to help you learn the structure of the federal APA. Specifically, Diagram 4-2 links the types of power that may be granted to an agency to the APA provisions that may prescribe procedures for the exercise of that power. Do not worry if the diagram does not make sense at this point. You may find it useful to return to this diagram after you have read future chapters examining agency powers and applicable APA procedures in more detail. At that point, the diagram may help you begin to appreciate the big picture.

Diagram 4-2 includes a new term for your administrative law glossary: "hybrid rulemaking." Hybrid rulemaking refers to situations in which the agency legislation that authorizes the agency rule requires the agency to follow the APA's informal rulemaking procedures, with modifications. In that situation, the required rulemaking procedures are a hybrid of APA procedures and procedures required by the agency legislation.

If you'd like to see another graphic depiction of the important information depicted in Diagram 4-2, you can find an excellent one in William R. Andersen, Mastering Administrative Law 68 (2010). Professor Anderson has also created a lesson entitled "Basic

Diagram 4-2. APA Provisions Applicable to Various Agency Activities

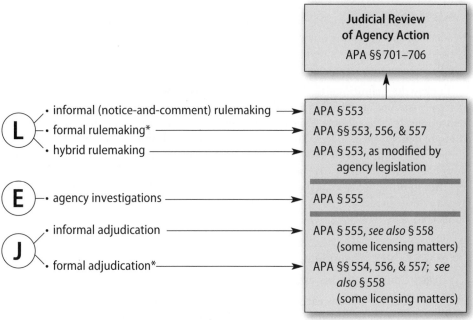

* Applicable when the agency statute authorizing the agency action requires an agency decision "on the record after opportunity for an agency hearing." 5 USC §§ 553(c) & 554(a).

Structure of the Federal Administrative Procedure Act" for the Center for Computer-Assisted Legal Instruction (CALI); this CALI lesson is especially helpful for hands-on students who want a better understanding of the APA's architecture, on which so much administrative law is built.

You have now learned about the purposes and structure of the federal APA. It provides for: (1) public transparency (through its public information provisions); (2) public participation in informal (notice-and-comment) rulemaking proceedings; (3) uniform hearing and decision making requirements for formal rulemaking proceedings and formal adjudications; and (4) judicial review of agency action. These are defining features of modern federal administrative law.

C. General Analysis under an APA

Because of the broad applicability of APAs, when you analyze an administrative law problem, you must always determine whether the APA applies to that problem. The APA is an important, potential external source of procedural requirements for agency action. This section introduces you to the general framework for determining whether the APA applies to a particular agency action.

1. Definitional Section

When you analyze whether and how a statute applies to a problem, you must begin by locating and reviewing any definitional section in the statute. Analysis under an APA is no different. An APA's definitions may resolve, or pose, the main legal issues in a particular administrative law problem.

Review the definitional section of the federal APA, which is reproduced below and currently codified at 5 U.S.C. §551. For now, do not worry about mastering the individual definitions. Instead, review §551 with the objective of becoming familiar with the terms that are defined there. These are key terms in federal administrative law. You will find these terms cropping up, and you will therefore consult these definitions, throughout your course on administrative law and throughout your professional career, if it includes practice in or before federal agencies. Here and throughout this book, we use bold face type to quote the federal APA, to stress its importance and the need for careful attention to its text.

---

5 U.S.C. §551. Definitions

For the purpose of this subchapter—

(1) "agency" means each authority of the Government of the United States, whether or not it is within or subject to review by another agency, but does not include—

   (A) the Congress;

   (B) the courts of the United States;

   (C) the governments of the territories or possessions of the United States;

   (D) the government of the District of Columbia;

or except as to the requirements of section 552 of this title [which codifies the Freedom of Information Act] —

   (E) **agencies composed of representatives of the parties or of representatives of organizations of the parties to the disputes determined by them;**

   (F) **courts martial and military commissions;**

   (G) **military authority exercised in the field in time of war or in occupied territory; or**

   (H) **functions conferred by sections 1738, 1739, 1743, and 1744 of title 12; chapter 2 of title 41; subchapter II of chapter 471 of title 49; or sections 1884, 1891–1902, and former section 1641(b)(2), of title 50, appendix;**

(2) **"person" includes an individual, partnership, corporation, association, or public or private organization other than an agency;**

(3) **"party" includes a person or agency named or admitted as a party, or properly seeking and entitled as of right to be admitted as a party, in an agency proceeding, and a person or agency admitted by an agency as a party for limited purposes;**

(4) **"rule" means the whole or a part of an agency statement of general or particular applicability and future effect designed to implement, interpret,**

or prescribe law or policy or describing the organization, procedure, or practice requirements of an agency and includes the approval or prescription for the future of rates, wages, corporate or financial structures or reorganizations thereof, prices, facilities, appliances, services or allowances therefor or of valuations, costs, or accounting, or practices bearing on any of the foregoing;

(5) "rule making" means agency process for formulating, amending, or repealing a rule;

(6) "order" means the whole or a part of a final disposition, whether affirmative, negative, injunctive, or declaratory in form, of an agency in a matter other than rule making but including licensing;

(7) "adjudication" means agency process for the formulation of an order;

(8) "license" includes the whole or a part of an agency permit, certificate, approval, registration, charter, membership, statutory exemption or other form of permission;

(9) "licensing" includes agency process respecting the grant, renewal, denial, revocation, suspension, annulment, withdrawal, limitation, amendment, modification, or conditioning of a license;

(10) "sanction" includes the whole or a part of an agency —

   (A) prohibition, requirement, limitation, or other condition affecting the freedom of a person;

   (B) withholding of relief;

   (C) imposition of penalty or fine;

   (D) destruction, taking, seizure, or withholding of property;

   (E) assessment of damages, reimbursement, restitution, compensation, costs, charges, or fees;

   (F) requirement, revocation, or suspension of a license; or

   (G) taking other compulsory or restrictive action;

(11) "relief" includes the whole or a part of an agency —

   (A) grant of money, assistance, license, authority, exemption, exception, privilege, or remedy;

   (B) recognition of a claim, right, immunity, privilege, exemption, or exception; or

   (C) taking of other action on the application or petition of, and beneficial to, a person;

(12) "agency proceeding" means an agency process as defined by paragraphs (5), (7), and (9) of this section;

(13) "agency action" includes the whole or a part of an agency rule, order, license, sanction, relief, or the equivalent or denial thereof, or failure to act; and

(14) "ex parte communication" means an oral or written communication not on the public record with respect to which reasonable prior notice to all parties is not given, but it shall not include requests for status reports on any matter or proceeding covered by this subchapter.

2. Applicability of APA to a Problem

The lawyer must always determine whether the federal or state APA applies to the administrative law problem at hand (drawing upon the APA's definitions as needed). If the APA does apply, the lawyer must then analyze how the APA's requirements dovetail with other applicable legal requirements.

Three distinct analyses should be made to determine APA relevance to a particular administrative law problem. Let us summarize them before we delve into each one:

   a.   Does the APA (federal or state) apply to this *agency*?

   b.   If so, does the APA apply in whole or in part to the *agency action* involved in the particular problem under analysis?

   c.   If the APA does apply in whole or in part to the agency action under analysis, how does the APA interact with *other laws* applicable to the problem?

Below we explore each of these three analyses.

a. Does the APA (Federal or State) Apply to This Agency?

The first step is to determine whether the APA applies to the government entity you are dealing with. The federal APA and all state APAs of which we are aware apply only to "agencies," as they define that term. If the entity you're dealing with does *not* fall within the applicable APA's definition of "agency," then the APA will not apply to that entity, except in one situation. That situation is when an otherwise exempt entity is made subject to the APA by the agency legislation. By the same token, if the entity you're dealing with *does* fall within the applicable APA's definition of "agency," then that APA *will* apply to that entity—unless the agency legislation exempts the entity from the APA. It is rare for the agency legislation to address the applicability of the APA to the agency. Usually, if the entity falls outside the applicable APA's definition of "agency," the APA won't apply to that agency, and, if the entity falls within the applicable APA's definition of "agency," the APA will apply to that entity.

(i) APA Definitions of "Agency"

The federal APA defines "**agency**" in § 551(1) to include each "**authority of the Government of the United States,**" with certain exceptions. As defined in the federal APA, the term "**agency**" includes the cabinet-level executive departments, federal independent agencies, and discrete subunits within those departments and independent agencies. The inclusion of subunits is indicated by the portion of the definition of "**agency**" that includes an authority of the United States "**whether or not it is within or subject to review by another agency.**"

The federal APA definition of "**agency**" includes not only artificial entities but also human beings. A federal official can qualify as an "**agency**" under § 551(1) if that official exercises the authority of the United States. At first it might seem odd that a person can be an "**agency**" under the federal APA. Consider, though, that when someone shouts, "Call the authorities!", the person is thinking of human beings with official authority. It also makes sense to include individuals within the APA definition of "**agency**" when you consider that federal statutes often do vest authority in particular officials (referred to by their position). For example, a federal statute addressing pesticide residues on food states, "The Administrator," meaning the Administrator of the Food and Drug Administration, "may issue regulations establishing, modifying, or revoking a tolerance for a pesticide ...

residue in or on a food." 21 U.S.C. § 346a (2012). Because the Administrator (whoever she or he happens to be) is an "**agency**" within the meaning of the federal APA, she or he may have to comply with the federal APA's rulemaking procedures when establishing a tolerance for pesticide residues on a food.

The federal APA's definition of "agency" in § 551(1) does not include all entities with governmental power. Most importantly, the term "**agency**" does not include Congress or the federal courts, including specialized courts such as the U.S. Tax Court. *See Megibow v. Clerk of the U.S. Tax Court*, 432 F.3d 387 (2nd Cir. 2005). Moreover, the U.S. Supreme Court has interpreted the term "**agency**" in § 551(1) not to cover the President, because separation of powers concerns arise if the term is construed to include the President. *Franklin v. Massachusetts*, 505 U.S. 788 (1992). In addition, lower federal courts have interpreted the Freedom of Information Act's (FOIA's) definition of "**agency**," which incorporates § 551's definition of that term, to exclude some entities in the Executive Office of the President. *See, e.g., Citizens for Responsibility & Ethics in Washington v. Office of Admin.*, 566 F.3d 219, 226 (D.C. Cir. 2009) (holding that Office of Administration within Executive Office of the President is not an "agency" for purposes of FOIA). The moral of the story is that you cannot tell whether a federal agency is a federal APA "**agency**" until you examine § 551(1) and, if necessary, case law construing § 551(1).

Even with these exceptions, the federal APA's coverage is comprehensive. It applies to virtually all federal agencies. Of course, by its terms and as a principle of federalism, the federal APA does not apply to any state or local government agency. Instead, state or local entities may be covered by a state (or, in some cases, a local) APA.

We have talked about what an "agency" is. One thing that the term "agency" typically does *not* include — either as a colloquial matter or for purposes of most statutory definitions of the term — is government corporations, such as the Corporation for Public Broadcasting and the Legal Services Corporation, and quasi-governmental entities such as Amtrak. These government corporations and quasi-governmental entities are usually created by statute. The statutes creating them often express the legislature's intention that they not be considered agencies. Here, for example, is the statutory language creating the Corporation for Public Broadcasting:

---

47 U.S.C. § 396. Corporation for Public Broadcasting ...

(b) Establishment of Corporation; application of District of Columbia Nonprofit Corporation Act

There is authorized to be established a nonprofit corporation, to be known as the "Corporation for Public Broadcasting", which will not be an agency or establishment of the United States Government. The Corporation shall be subject to the provisions of this section, and, to the extent consistent with this section, to the District of Columbia Nonprofit Corporation Act....

State APAs vary in how they define the term "agency." The definition of "agency" in state APAs matters for the same reason that it matters under the federal APA: The APA will prescribe procedures for "agencies" to follow. Government entities that fall within the APA definition of "agency" may have to follow those procedures. Other entities ordinarily will not have to do so. In short, the breadth of a state APA's applicability depends primarily on how it defines the term "agency."

To show you an example, the influential 1961 Model State APA defines "agency" to mean:

1961 Model State APA § 1. Definitions

As used in this Act:

(1) "agency" means each state board, commission, department, or officer, other than the legislature or the courts, authorized by law to make rules or determine contested cases....

In administrative law circles, we refer to this as a "functional" definition of "agency." It defines the term agency by reference to whether an entity has power to engage in the functions of making rules or determining contested cases. (The phrase "determine contested cases" means the power to adjudicate cases, such as applications for permits or government benefits, administratively.) This functional definition makes sense because most state APAs prescribe procedures for agency rulemaking and agency adjudication, and have limited relevance for agencies that do not carry out those functions.

(ii) Agency Legislation Addressing the Applicability of the APA to the Agency

Analysis of whether the APA applies to a particular agency cannot end with an examination of the APA's definition of "agency." Instead, the next step is to analyze the agency legislation to learn whether it addresses the applicability of the APA. Thus, to determine whether the APA applies to a particular entity, you have to look beyond the APA's definition of "agency."

The agency legislation may declare that the APA does not apply to this agency. If so, that legislation controls, and the APA drops out of further research as irrelevant. For example, a federal statute says that neither the APA's procedural requirements nor its judicial review provisions apply to the Cost Accounting Standards Board within the Office of Federal Procurement Policy. 41 U.S.C. § 422(g)(3) (2012) ("The functions exercised under this section are excluded from the operation of sections 551, 553 through 559, and 701 through 706 of Title 5."). Even though this Board may be an "**agency**" as defined in federal APA § 551(1), the Board's functions are exempt from the APA. Why? Because Congress said so!

The APA itself reflects that the agency legislation may expressly modify or render altogether inapplicable the APA's requirements to one, some, or all of that agency's actions. Section 559 of the APA says that a statute enacted after the APA (in 1946) may **"supersede or modify"** the APA **"to the extent that [the agency-specific statute] does so expressly."** 5 U.S.C. § 559 (2012).

Similarly, although a state agency may fall within the state APA's definition of "agency," the agency legislation may nonetheless exempt the agency from the state APA. The 2010 Model State APA reflects this principle. It says, "This [act] applies to an agency unless the agency is expressly exempted by a statute of this state." 2010 Model State APA § 103(a).

Instead of exempting an agency from the APA, the agency legislation may make the APA applicable where it does not otherwise apply. Congress can always choose to subject an entity to the federal APA even though the entity does not fall within the federal APA's definition of "**agency**." Congress simply has to make this choice clear in the agency legislation. In principle, the declaration in the agency legislation prevails on the theory that specific legislation controls general legislation where there is a conflict. Besides, § 559 of the federal APA states that the federal APA does not **"limit or repeal additional requirements imposed by statute or otherwise recognized by law."** 5 U.S.C. § 559. This permits Congress in the agency legislation to impose upon a particular governmental entity the procedural requirements of the APA, even though the APA itself, standing alone, does not apply to that entity.

Likewise, a state legislature can subject an agency to the state APA even if the agency would not otherwise fall within the state APA's definition of "agency." For example, the Florida APA addresses this situation in its definition of "agency." The Florida APA defines "agency" to include entities and officials with statewide and regional authority, plus some units of local government (e.g., cities and counties) "to the extent they are expressly made subject to this act by general or special law or existing judicial decisions." Fla. Stat. Ann. § 120.52(1)(c) (West, Westlaw through Apr. 20, 2012). Thus, the Florida APA contemplates that the Florida legislature may decide in other statutes to make the Florida APA applicable to units of local government that would otherwise fall outside the APA (because outside its definition of "agency").

The two-pronged analysis—entailing examination of (1) the APA definition of "agency," including case law construing that definition, and (2) the agency legislation, including case law construing it—has been completed and counsel may predict whether the APA (federal or state) appears to apply to the agency under scrutiny. If not, the APA drops out of the picture as a potential, external source of procedural requirements for the agency action under analysis. If, on the other hand, the APA does apply to the agency involved in the problem at hand, analysis turns to whether the APA applies to the particular agency *action* involved in the problem at hand.

Exercise: Identifying an Agency Subject to the Federal APA

Which of these is an "**agency**" as defined in the federal APA? Assume that this question is governed solely by § 551 and not by any other statute. As necessary, review the text of § 551, which is reproduced above.

1. a private, nonprofit organization that uses grant money from the U.S. Department of Housing and Urban Development to help the homeless

2. a local education agency that is (a) run by a local school board; (b) receives funds from the U.S. Department of Education to educate people with disabilities; and (c) must spend the funds consistently with Department of Education regulations

3. an employee of the U.S. Customs and Immigration Service who has the power under federal law to detain imported goods pending an investigation

4. the Secretary of the U.S. Department of Defense

---

b. If the APA Does Apply to This Agency, Does the APA Apply in Whole or in Part to the Agency Action Involved in the Particular Problem under Analysis?

(i) APA Provisions Addressing Various Agency Activities

Even if the APA generally applies to an agency, the APA may or may not apply to a particular problem involving that agency. The agency may have to comply with the APA when it takes some actions, but not when it takes other actions. Furthermore, an agency action may be subject to some APA requirements but not others.

Take, for example, the APA provision entitled "**Rule making**," APA § 553. Section 553 states that its requirements for agency rulemaking do not apply to rules involving "**a military or foreign affairs function of the United States.**" 5 U.S.C. § 553(a)(1). Section 553 also excludes from its rulemaking requirements matters involving public property, loans, grants, benefits or contracts. 5 U.S.C. § 553(a)(2). Thus, even though an agency such as the U.S. Department of Defense may be generally subject to the APA because it falls within APA § 551(1)'s definition of "**agency**," it does not have to follow § 553 when it makes rules on a military function. Rules on that subject may, however, be subject to other APA provisions, such as the APA §§ 701–706, which authorize judicial review of many types of "**agency action.**" See 5 U.S.C. § 704 (authorizing judicial review of certain agency actions).

As another example of an APA provision not applicable to some agency actions, take the APA provision entitled "**Adjudications,**" 5 U.S.C. § 554. Subsection (a) of § 554 states in relevant part:

---

5 U.S.C. § 554. Adjudications

(a) This section applies, according to the provisions thereof, in every case of adjudication required by statute to be determined on the record after opportunity for an agency hearing, except to the extent that there is involved— ...

(3) proceedings in which decisions rest solely on inspections, tests, or elections....

An agency adjudication covered by § 554 includes an opportunity for a trial-type hearing. But an opportunity for a trial-type hearing is not required in adjudications the outcome of which rests solely on an inspection, test, or election. That makes sense, because those processes don't lend themselves to trial-type hearings, and so § 554 does not apply to adjudications involving them, even when conducted by a governmental entity that falls within the APA's definition of "**agency.**"

In addition to exempting certain agency adjudications, § 554 simply doesn't apply to informal adjudications. Section 554 applies only to an adjudication that is required by statute to be determined exclusively on the basis of an official record, after an opportunity for a trial-type hearing. Many federal agency adjudications occur under agency legislation that doesn't impose those requirements. For example, in the most famous case involving informal adjudication, the U.S. Secretary of Transportation had to decide whether an interstate highway should be built through a municipal park in Memphis, Tennessee, or should instead go around or under the park. *See Citizens to Preserve Overton Park, Inc. v. Volpe,* 401 U.S. 402 (1971). Because the statutes empowering the Secretary to make this decision did not require him to base his decision on the record made at a formal hearing, the APA's formal adjudication provisions did not apply. His decision was therefore an "informal adjudication" and, as such, not subject to § 554.

The federal APA has no provision prescribing specific procedures for informal adjudications by federal agencies. The only two APA provisions that bear on some aspects of some informal adjudications are the provision for "**Ancillary matters,**" § 555, and the provision for "**Imposition of sanctions; determination of applications for licenses; suspension, revocation, and expiration of licenses,**" § 558. Thus, informal adjudication is, for the most part, controlled procedurally by the agency legislation, applicable agency procedural rules, due process of law, and case law.

Let us mention one last type of agency action: namely, an agency's failure to act. The federal APA defines the term **"agency action"** to include certain **"failure[s] to act."** 5 U.S.C. § 551(13). An example of an agency failure to act that falls within the definition of **"agency action"** is an agency's failure to decide whether to grant or deny an application for a government license or government benefits. Such a failure to act can harm someone who needs the license to stay in business or the benefits to stay alive. Yet, as we will discuss in Chapter 29.B.2.b, not all forms of agency inaction qualify as **"failure[s] to act"** as the phrase is used in the federal APA, just as not all forms of agency action qualify as **"agency action"** under the federal APA.

The broader point is that the APA, by its terms, does not apply to all agency actions or agency inaction, even actions taken by **"agenc[ies]"** as that term is defined in the federal APA. The federal APA, like state APAs, prescribes procedures for many important agency activities but not all of them.

(ii) Agency Legislation and Agency Rules Addressing Applicability of APA to the Agency's Activities

As with the analysis of whether the APA applies to the agency involved in a problem, the analysis of whether the APA applies to the agency action associated with a particular problem does not end with examining the APA. The agency legislation may exempt some of the agency's actions from the APA. Conversely, the agency legislation may make the APA applicable to the agency action under analysis even though the APA otherwise does not apply. Furthermore, although an agency cannot exempt itself or any of its activities from the APA, an agency often can subject some of its activities to the APA even though those activities are otherwise exempt from the APA.

An example of agency legislation exempting the agency's rules from the APA's rulemaking requirements is in this statute empowering the Secretary of the U.S. Department of Energy to encourage development and use of wind energy:

---

42 U.S.C. § 9204. Research, development, and demonstration

(a) Areas of knowledge limiting system utilization

The Secretary shall initiate research and development or accelerate existing research and development in areas in which the lack of knowledge limits the widespread utilization of wind energy systems in order to achieve the purposes of this chapter.

(b) Development of system prototypes and improvements ...

The Secretary is authorized to enter into contracts, grants, and cooperative agreements with public and private entities for the purchase, fabrication, installation, and testing to obtain scientific, technological, and economic information from the demonstration of a variety of prototypes of advanced wind energy systems under a variety of circumstances and conditions ...

(d) Other provisions inapplicable

In carrying out the responsibilities under this section, the Secretary is not subject to the requirements of section 553 of Title 5 ... of this title.

Recall that "section 553 of Title 5" is entitled **"Rule making."**

Conversely, the federal Walsh-Healey Act is an example of a statute that makes the APA applicable to certain federal rules that are otherwise exempt from the APA. The Walsh-Healey Act requires companies that contract with the federal government to pay a minimum level of wages to the employees who perform work under that contract. 41 U.S.C. § 35 (2012). The Act also authorizes the Secretary of Labor to adopt regulations for calculating these minimum wages. *Id.* The Act says that, in adopting these minimum-wage regulations for federal contractors, the Secretary must comply with the APA, even though the APA generally exempts from its rulemaking requirements rules relating to "**public ... contracts.**" 5 U.S.C. § 553(a)(1). *See* 41 U.S.C. § 43a. Thus, the Act makes the APA applicable to certain agency rules that would otherwise be exempt from the APA as relating to public contracts.

An agency cannot adopt a rule or policy exempting its activities from the APA. But an agency *can* adopt a rule or policy *subjecting* its activities to the APA, even though those activities would otherwise be exempt from the APA under the APA's own terms. To cite an example, the Department of Agriculture has promulgated a rule subjecting itself to the APA's rulemaking requirements even when it promulgates rules for government benefits and government loans. See 36 Fed. Reg. 13804 (1971). If it had not bound itself to the APA by this rule, the Department of Agriculture could promulgate rules for government benefits and loans without following the APA rulemaking requirements, because rules on government benefits and loans are otherwise exempt from the APA's rulemaking re-quirements, under § 553(a)(2). *See, e.g., Curry v. Block*, 738 F.2d 1556 (11th Cir. 1984) ("[T]he Secretary is bound by his July 24, 1971 pronouncement making the procedural requirements of Section 4 of the Administrative Procedure Act, 5 U.S.C. § 553, applicable to matters relating to 'loans,' and, therefore, the Secretary is so bound in the instant case.").

State APAs often do not follow the federal APA's format. For example, the procedural requirements of a state APA may apply to all agency adjudications—formal and informal. A state APA's provisions prescribing procedures for rulemaking may have exemptions that differ from the rulemaking exemptions of the federal APA. In any event, as true of federal entities, a state governmental entity may be an "agency" for purposes of the state APA, but not all of that agency's activities will be subject to the state APA. For example, the state APA's provisions prescribing rulemaking procedures may exempt rules on certain subjects from their scope, as may the state APA's provisions prescribing adjudication procedures.

Suppose by this point the lawyer has determined that the APA applies to the agency under analysis, and to the agency action under analysis. The question then becomes how the APA interacts with other laws applicable to that agency action.

c. If the APA Does Apply to the Agency Action under Analysis, How Does the APA Interact with Other Laws Applicable to the Problem?

Let us assume that the lawyer has determined that the APA applies to the agency and to the particular agency action under analysis. The question remains how the APA's provisions interact with other applicable (1) constitutional, (2) statutory, and (3) exec-utive-branch provisions, if any. We will take each of these three types of law one at a time, in discussing this third part of the analysis of APA applicability.

Constitutional provisions may influence the interpretation of an APA provision. For example, § 554(b) of the federal APA describes what information an agency must give to a person who is "**entitled to notice of an agency hearing**" in a formal adjudication. When a formal adjudication may deprive a person of liberty or property, the person is "**entitled** to notice" by the Due Process Clause of the Fifth Amendment. In such a formal adjudication, §554(b)'s notice requirement must be interpreted to satisfy the Due Process Clause's requirements for notice. In one case, for example, a court of appeals relied on due process to hold that an employer was entitled to notice under §554(b) before an agency ordered the employer to pay the attorney's fees of an employee who'd won a workers' compensation against the employer. *See, e.g., Todd Shipyards Corp. v. Director, Office of Workers' Compensation*, 545 F.2d 1176, 1180–1181 (9th Cir. 1976). This case shows how constitutional provisions may interact with APA provisions in the analysis of an agency action.

Statutory provisions may add to, modify, or render inapplicable otherwise applicable APA provisions. The federal APA and most state APAs just prescribe a set of default procedures that apply, according to their terms, unless a more specific statute says otherwise. As discussed earlier in this chapter, the federal APA has a a coordination provision, §559, reflecting that agency-specific legislation may add to, modify, or supersede the federal APA. A state APA may or may not have a coordinating provision. In the absence of one, the lawyer must resort to other means for determining how to resolve any inconsistencies between the APA and any other statute applicable to the problem at hand.

We mentioned earlier in this chapter one common situation in which statutes supplement APA requirements: hybrid rulemaking. Hybrid rulemaking occurs when the agency legislation governing an agency's rules adds procedural requirements over and above those required by §553 of the APA. Hybrid rulemaking illustrates Congress's broader power to customize the way in which the APA applies (or does not apply) to a particular agency action.

In addition to constitutional and statutory provisions, executive-branch material may supplement APA procedures. For example, several executive orders supplement the APA's rulemaking procedures. *See, e.g.,* Exec. Order No. 12,866, §6, 3 C.F.R. 638, 644 (1994) (requiring federal agencies to prepare economic impact analyses of proposed rules with annual impact of $100 million or more); Exec. Order No. 13,175, 3 C.F.R. 303 (2000) (prescribing principles and procedures for certain federal rules and other agency actions that "have tribal implications" for federally recognized Indian tribes). Besides executive orders, agency rules may supplement APA procedures. That is because an agency is usually free to add to the procedural requirements imposed by statute; statutory procedural requirements provide a procedural floor beneath which the agency may not go, rather than a ceiling.

Unlike constitutional and statutory provisions, however, agency rules and other material generated within the executive branch can only supplement—not modify or supersede—the APA and other statutorily required procedures. The President and all other entities within the federal executive branch must obey valid Acts of Congress, including the federal APA. Valid federal statutes come above executive-branch directives in the hierarchy of federal law. So, while an agency may be free to add to or elaborate upon statutorily required procedures, it cannot otherwise deviate from them.

The bottom line is that the APA and other legislation applicable to the agency problem at hand are to be read together and reconciled. Furthermore, an agency may promulgate rules that refine or supplement statutory procedures. Gaps in one source of law may be filled by provisions of another. Agency legislation or agency rules may augment the requirements that the APA otherwise permits the agency to follow. The better all of these sources of law fit together, the more coherent is the attorney's guide to the procedural law bearing on that particular administrative law problem.

Diagram 4-3. Outline for Analyzing APA Applicability

a. Does the APA apply to this *agency*? To answer that question, identify and analyze:

   1. the APA definition of "agency" (and, if necessary, case law interpreting the APA definition) and

   2. provisions (if any) in the agency legislation addressing APA's applicability to this agency (and, if necessary, case law interpreting the provisions in the agency legislation)

b. Does the APA apply to the particular agency *action* involved in the problem? To answer that question, consult:

   1. provisions in the APA addressing and defining various agency activities, including the APA provision defining "agency action" (and, if necessary, case law interpreting those provisions)

   2. provisions (if any) in the agency legislation or agency rules addressing APA's applicability to the agency action under analysis (and, if necessary, case law interpreting those provisions)

c. If the APA applies, how does it interact with *other laws* applicable to the problem at hand?

   1. Constitutional provisions take precedence over APA provisions and may affect their validity or interpretation.

   2. The agency legislation can add to APA requirements. Also, the agency legislation can modify or supersede APA requirements. But federal agency legislation enacted after the federal APA (in 1946) can effectively modify or supersede APA requirements only if it does so expressly. 5 U.S.C. § 559.

   3. Agency rules and other executive-branch material (e.g., executive orders) may add to or elaborate upon APA procedures, and may make APA requirements applicable to agency action that are otherwise exempt from the APA by its terms. Agency rules and other executive-branch material cannot, however, trump either the APA or the agency legislation — e.g., by exempting agency action that, according to the APA or the agency statute, is subject to the APA.

   If you prefer flow charts to outlines, the next diagram reflects our attempt to "flow chart" the above information. We offer this as an example to encourage you to try your hand at improving or modifying our example, and, in the future, composing your own, if that helps you grasp future material.

Diagram 4-4. Flow Chart for Analyzing APA Applicability

(1) Does the APA apply to this agency?

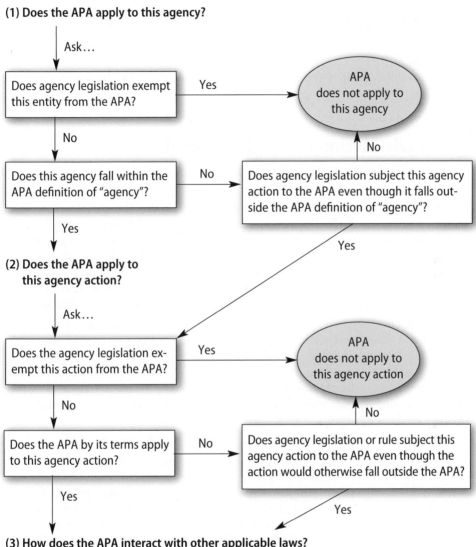

(2) Does the APA apply to this agency action?

(3) How does the APA interact with other applicable laws?
(In making this determination, consult any coordinating
provision such as federal APA § 559.)

D. The Fundamental Distinction between Rulemaking and Adjudication

Administrative law recognizes a fundamental distinction between rulemaking (or, more generally, legislative-type activity) and adjudication. This section explores the distinction.

1. The Distinction under the Federal APA

The general analysis of APA applicability described in the last section requires you, at the second step, to determine whether an agency's action is subject to the APA. To make that determination, you usually must first determine whether the agency action under analysis is rulemaking, adjudication, or something else. The determination will control which provisions of the APA, if any, apply to that agency action. For example, when a federal agency makes a rule, the agency may have to follow the rulemaking procedures in § 553 of the APA. When a federal agency adjudicates a case, the agency may have to follow the formal adjudication procedures in § 554. Like the federal APA, state APAs have separate procedural requirements for agency rulemaking and agency adjudication.

The distinction between agency rulemaking and agency adjudication is fundamental to the federal APA. The Attorney General's Manual on the APA says, "[T]he entire [Administrative Procedure] Act is based upon a dichotomy between rule making and adjudication." AGM 14. Thus, learning to distinguish between rulemaking and adjudication is fundamental to understanding the federal APA. This is also true of state APAs, which likewise prescribe separate procedures for agency rulemaking and agency adjudications. (Many state APAs call agency adjudications "contested cases.")

The Attorney General's Manual describes rulemaking as follows:

> Rule making is ... essentially legislative in nature, not only because it operates in the future but also because it is primarily concerned with policy considerations. The object of the rule making proceeding is the implementation or prescription of law or policy for the future, rather than the evaluation of a respondent's past conduct. Typically, the issues relate not to evidentiary facts, as to which the veracity and demeanor of witnesses would often be important, but rather to the policy making conclusions to be drawn from the facts.

AGM 14. Thus, the Manual characterizes rulemaking as legislative in nature because it is (1) future-oriented; (2) designed to implement law or policy; and (3) more concerned with policy considerations than evidentiary (historical) facts.

The Manual continues:

> Conversely, adjudication is concerned with the determination of past and present rights and liabilities. Normally, there is involved a decision as to whether past conduct was unlawful, so that the proceeding is characterized by an accusatory flavor and may result in disciplinary action. Or, it may involve the determination of a person's right to benefits under existing law so that the issues relate to whether he is within the established category of persons entitled to such benefits. In such proceedings, the issues of fact are often sharply controverted.

AGM 15. Thus, the Manual says adjudication (1) is about a person's present or past rights and liabilities; (2) is designed to determine rights and liabilities under existing law; and (3) often requires the resolution of disputed facts.

The Manual concludes, "Not only were the draftsmen and proponents of the bill [that became the APA] aware of this realistic distinction between rule making and adjudication, but they shaped the entire Act around it." AGM 15.

The APA creates the distinction between rulemaking and adjudication beginning in its definitional section, § 551. Section 551 defines the terms "**rule making**" and "**adjudication**" to mean agency processes relating to rules and orders, respectively.

---

5 U.S.C. § 551. Definitions ...

(5) "**rule making**" means agency process for formulating, amending, or repealing a rule ...

(7) "**adjudication**" means agency process for the formulation of an order ...

Thus, to understand the distinction between rulemaking and adjudication in the federal APA, you must understand the definitions of "**rule**" and "**order**."

---

5 U.S.C. § 551. Definitions ...

(4) "**rule**" means the whole or a part of an agency statement of general or particular applicability and future effect designed to implement, interpret, or prescribe law or policy or describing the organization, procedure, or practice requirements of an agency and includes the approval or prescription for the future of rates, wages, corporate or financial structures or reorganizations thereof, prices, facilities, appliances, services or allowances therefor or of valuations, costs, or accounting, or practices bearing on any of the foregoing ...

(6) "**order**" means the whole or a part of a final disposition, whether affirmative, negative, injunctive, or declaratory in form, of an agency in a matter other than rule making but including licensing ...

The APA definition of "**rule**" is dense but penetrable. It covers several different types of rules that you will learn more about later in this book. For now, notice that, consistently with the description in the Attorney General's Manual, the definition defines rules as having a future effect and as including the implementation of law or policy. Also notice, while we are in the neighborhood, that "**rule making**" includes a proceeding to amend or repeal a rule. Thus, an agency must follow the applicable APA rulemaking procedures not only when it promulgates a new rule but also when it modifies or repeals an existing rule.

You may wonder why the APA defines "**rule**" to include agency statements of "**general or particular** applicability." 5 U.S.C. § 551(4) (emphasis added). The Attorney General's Manual confirms that under this definition a rule may regulate the conduct of "a single person." AGM 14. The drafters of the definition probably had in mind a situation that was more common in 1946 than today: The term "**rulemaking**" includes agency action setting rates, and in 1946 many industries subject to federal agency ratemaking were monopolies. For example, there was only one phone company, American Telephone and Telegraph (AT&T, affectionately known as "Ma Bell"), for which the Federal

Communications Commission set rates. By defining **"rule"** to include agency statements of **"particular applicability,"** § 551(4) treated the FCC's process of setting rates for AT&T as rulemaking, even though it directly affected only one company.

Today, federal courts continue to hold that an agency action may be a rule under § 551(4) even if it applies only to one entity. Below we describe an example:

- *Hercules, Inc. v. Environmental Protection Agency*, 598 F.2d 91 (D.C. Cir. 1978)

In *Hercules*, the EPA exercised its power under the Clean Water Act to issue rules limiting companies from discharging certain toxic chemicals into the water, including toxaphene and endrin. At the time the EPA issued the rules, it just so happened that only one company in the country discharged toxaphene, and only one company discharged endrin.

The court of appeals held that the EPA's rules for those two chemicals were **"rules"** under § 551(4) even though each rule applied to only one company. The court observed that the EPA's rules were designed to implement policy and were of future effect (applicable only to discharges occurring after the rules were issued). The rules were based on consideration of statutorily specified factors such as toxicity, degradability, persistence, and effects on affected organisms, "rather than issues of fact concerning any particular entity's discharges." *Hercules*, 598 F.2d at 118. These statutory factors underlying the rules "are the same whether the substance is discharged by one manufacturer or one thousand." *Id*. Other courts reaching similar conclusions have reasoned that as long as the wording of a rule is generalized, and may therefore apply to future entities that engage in the regulated conduct, it does not matter that there just so happens to be only one entity affected by the rule at the time the rule is first issued.

Turning to the APA definition of **"order"**: The APA defines the term **"order"** in a residual way: An **"order"** is an agency final disposition in a matter **"other than"** rulemaking. Thus, all final dispositions by agencies that are not rules, are orders. Because **"order"** is defined in contradistinction to **"rule,"** classification of an agency's final disposition should begin by determining whether the final disposition is a rule. If not, it is an order.

The federal APA defines **"order"** to include the outcome of licensing. Thus, a license is a type of **"order,"** and licensing is a type of **"adjudication."** The federal APA defines the terms **"license"** and **"licensing"** as follows:

---

5 U.S.C. § 551. Definitions ...

(8) "license" includes the whole or a part of an agency permit, certificate, approval, registration, charter, membership, statutory exemption or other form of permission ...

(9) "licensing" includes agency process respecting the grant, renewal, denial, revocation, suspension, annulment, withdrawal, limitation, amendment, modification, or conditioning of a license ...

Significantly, "licensing" refers to agency action affecting a specific license; "licensing" does not include the process by which an agency establishes *criteria* for getting, keeping, or losing a license. That is because the process by which an agency establishes licensing criteria is a rulemaking process, and the resulting agency statement of licensing criteria is a rule. In contrast, when the agency applies those criteria to an applicant for, or the holder of, a license, the agency engages in adjudication and its final disposition of the matter is an order.

Diagram 4-5 reflects that, under the federal APA, the universe of "final dispositions" comprises rules and orders. One type of rule establishes criteria for getting and keeping a license. One type of order is entered in "licensing" cases, and may grant, deny, suspend, modify, or terminate a license.

Diagram 4-5. "Rules" and "Orders" under the Federal APA

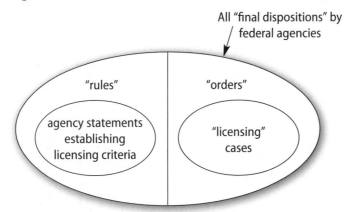

Once you have classified the action of a federal agency as a rule or an order under § 551 of the APA, you will know whether the next step of your analysis will take you to § 553 (entitled "**Rule making**") or instead to § 554 (entitled "**Adjudications**").

Agencies can complicate the lawyer's effort to classify agency action as a rule or an order. For one thing, agencies do not always call their rules "rules." Agencies may call them "standards," "directives," "general requirements," "guidelines," and many other things. Perhaps most annoyingly, some federal agencies call their rules "orders," which is the term that the federal APA uses for the outcome of adjudications! *See, e.g., MCI Telecomm. Corp. v. American Tel. & Tel. Co.*, 512 U.S. 218, 223 (1994) ("[T]he Commission released a Report and Order from the rulemaking proceeding."). Similarly, agencies do not always label their orders "orders." What an agency calls a "report" or "decision" may be an order. The bottom line is that not all agencies follow the APA terminology. It's annoying, but you can't take it personally.

Exercise: Distinguishing Rules from Orders under the Federal APA

Please identify whether each of the following agency actions is a "rule" or an "order," as the federal APA defines those terms, or neither:

1. The EPA establishes limits on the amount of greenhouse gases that new cars in the United States can emit.

2. The federal Commodity Futures Trading Commission concludes that a particular broker violated the Commodity Exchange Act when she conducted certain transactions involving commodity futures for a specific customer.

3. The federal Nuclear Regulatory Commission grants a license to Vermont Yankee Nuclear Power Corporation to operate a nuclear power plant in Vernon, Vermont.

4. The U.S. Civil Rights Commission holds hearings to investigate citizen complaints that voting officials in three counties of a particular State have harassed black people seeking to register to vote. The hearings culminate in a report

to Congress and the President making findings and recommendations. The recommendations are purely advisory; they have no legal effect.

5. After a formal hearing, the National Labor Relations Board concludes that the Hearst Publishing Company has committed an "unfair labor practice," in violation of a federal statute, by failing to negotiate with the union representing "newsboys" who sell its papers on the streets of Los Angeles.

6. Without holding a hearing, the U.S. Secretary of Transportation decides that a federally funded interstate highway should be located so as to cut through a municipal park in Memphis, Tennessee.

7. The U.S. Fish and Wildlife Service decides that the Lost River Sucker should be added to the Endangered Species List. This has the effect of generally prohibiting people (including federal agencies) from taking actions that threaten this species of fish or its "critical habitat."

8. The Federal Energy Regulatory Commission establishes rates that a company can charge for transmitting electric power in interstate commerce.

2. The Distinction under State APAs

If you determine that a governmental entity is a state "agency" under the state APA, you must next determine whether the agency's action is rulemaking or adjudication or something else under the state APA's definitions. Then you can decide whether to consult the state APA's rulemaking procedures, its adjudication procedures, or neither.

Here are the definitions of "order" and "rule" in the 1981 Model State APA that closely resemble or are identical to those in several States' APAs:

1981 Model State APA § 1-102. Definitions ...

(5) "Order" means an agency action of particular applicability that determines the legal rights, duties, privileges, immunities, or other legal interests of one or more specific persons ...

(10) "Rule" means the whole or a part of an agency statement of general applicability that implements, interprets, or prescribes (i) law or policy, or (ii) the organization, procedure, or practice requirements of an agency. The term includes the amendment, repeal, or suspension of an existing rule....

Compare these definitions with those of the federal APA. You will find they mesh pretty well. As a result, in most cases a state agency action that qualifies as a "rule" under the 1981 Model State APA's definition would, if taken by a federal agency, also qualify as a "rule" under the federal APA. Likewise for agency orders. But because the Model State APA's definitions differ from the federal APA's definitions, the correspondence is not perfect: An agency action that, if taken by a federal agency, would fall within the definition of **"rule"** under the federal APA could, if taken by a state agency, fall within the definition of **"order"** under that State's APA.

The most important example of this divergence is rate making. Under the 1981 Model State APA, when a state agency fixes the rates that a single (monopolistic) utility company will be allowed to charge in the future, the agency's decision is an "order," and is the result of an agency process that the Model State APA classifies as an adjudication. See 1981 Model State APA § 1-102, Official Comment. In contrast, the 1981 Model State APA treats an agency proceeding to fix rates for *multiple* utility companies as a rulemaking proceeding. *Id.* In contrast, the federal APA treats all ratemaking proceedings by federal agencies as rulemaking, regardless whether they set rates for a single entity or multiple entities. *See* 5 U.S.C. § 551(4); AGM 13. The different treatment of ratemaking in the 1981 Model APA and the federal APA reflects that an agency proceeding to fix future rates for, e.g., a public utility partakes of both rulemaking and adjudication.

Despite the gray area, the distinction between agency rulemaking and agency adjudication is universal throughout the field of administrative law. You might wonder why. It is because the distinction predates APAs, as discussed next.

3. The Distinction in U.S. Supreme Court Case Law

a. Introduction to the *Londoner/Bi-Metallic* Distinction

The U.S. Supreme Court has said, "The basic distinction between rulemaking and adjudication is illustrated by the Court's treatment of two related cases under the Due Process Clause of the Fourteenth Amendment." *United States v. Fla. E. Coast Ry.*, 410 U.S. 224 (1973). The two related cases to which the Court was referring are *Londoner v. City and County of Denver*, 210 U.S. 373 (1908), and *Bi-Metallic Investment Co. v. State Board of Equalization*, 239 U.S. 441 (1915), portions of which you will read shortly.

The Court's opinions in *Londoner* and *Bi-Metallic* are famous in administrative-law circles—so famous that the distinction between rulemaking and adjudication is often called the "*Londoner/Bi-Metallic* distinction." The term "*Londoner/Bi-Metallic* distinction" definitely belongs in your growing glossary of administrative law terms. Roughly speaking for the moment, the *Londoner/Bi-Metallic* distinction refers to the difference between, on the one hand, (1) government action that is *adjudicative* in nature, in the sense that it affects a small number of people on individualized grounds and, on the other hand, (2) government action that is *legislative* in nature, in the sense that it affects a large number of people, based on general principles.

The *Londoner/Bi-Metallic* distinction is used to determine whether the doctrine of procedural due process requires the government, before taking an action that affects one or more people's property or liberty, to give each affected individual (a) notice that the government intends to take the action; and (b) an opportunity to be heard (so that, for example, the affected individual can try to persuade the government *not* to take the proposed action). Procedural due process does generally impose those requirements on adjudicative governmental actions, but not on legislative-type governmental actions.

We introduce the *Londoner/Bi-Metallic* distinction now, while deferring our comprehensive exploration of procedural due process until later in the book, because the *Londoner/Bi-Metallic* distinction underlies the distinction between two types of agency activity—rulemaking and adjudication—that is necessary to understanding APAs.

b. The *Londoner* and *Bi-Metallic* Opinions

Please read the *Londoner* and *Bi-Metallic* opinions below with these questions in mind:

1.　What government *action* is being challenged in each case?

2. What government *entity* is taking the challenged action in each case?

3. Why does the Court invalidate the challenged government action in *Londoner* but uphold the challenged government action in *Bi-Metallic*?

Londoner v. City and County of Denver
210 U.S. 373 (1908)

Mr. Justice Moody delivered the opinion of the Court.

[The plaintiff Londoner and other land owners] began this proceeding in a state court of Colorado to relieve lands owned by them from an assessment of a tax for the cost of paving a street upon which the lands abutted. The relief sought was granted by the trial court, but its action was reversed by the Supreme Court of the State, which ordered judgment for the defendants [which include the City and County of Denver]. 33 Colorado, 104. The case is here on writ of error. The [Colorado] Supreme Court held that the tax was assessed in conformity with the constitution and laws of the State, and its decision on that question is conclusive....

The tax complained of was assessed under the provisions of the charter of the city of Denver, which confers upon the city the power to make local improvements and to assess the cost upon property specially benefited. It does not seem necessary to set forth fully the elaborate provisions of the charter regulating the exercise of this power, except where they call for special examination. The board of public works, upon the petition of a majority of the owners of the frontage to be assessed, may order the paving of a street. The board must, however, first adopt specifications, mark out a district of assessment, cause a map to be made and an estimate of the cost, with the approximate amount to be assessed upon each lot of land....

The board may then order the improvement, but must recommend to the city council a form of ordinance authorizing it, and establishing an assessment district, which is not amendable by the council. The council may then, in its discretion, pass or refuse to pass the ordinance. If the ordinance is passed, the contract for the work is made by the mayor.... The charter then provides for the assessment of the cost.... [Once the assessment is made, a lien upon property abutting the newly paved street automatically arises as a matter of state law. The plaintiffs in error sought judicial relief to remove the liens on their properties.]

The fifth assignment [of error], though general, vague and obscure, fairly raises, we think, the question whether the assessment was made without notice and opportunity for hearing to those affected by it, thereby denying to them due process of law. The trial court found as a fact that no opportunity for hearing was afforded, and the [Colorado] Supreme Court did not disturb this finding. The record discloses what was actually done, and there seems to be no dispute about it....

Upon these facts was there a denial by the State of the due process of law guaranteed by the Fourteenth Amendment to the Constitution of the United States?

In the assessment, apportionment and collection of taxes upon property within their jurisdiction the Constitution of the United States imposes few restrictions upon the States. In the enforcement of such restrictions as the Constitution does impose this court has regarded substance and not form. But where the legislature of a State, instead of fixing the tax itself, commits to some subordinate body the duty of determining whether, in what amount, and upon whom it shall be levied, and of making its assessment and apportionment, due process of law requires that at some stage of the proceedings before the tax becomes irrevocably fixed, the taxpayer shall have an opportunity to be heard, of which he must have notice, either personal, by publication, or by a law fixing the time and place of the hearing.... It must be remembered that the law of Colorado denies the landowner the right to object in the courts to the assessment, upon the ground that the objections are cognizable only by the [City Council, sitting as a] board of equalization.

If it is enough that, under such circumstances, an opportunity is given to submit in writing all objections to and complaints of the tax to the board, then there was a hearing afforded in the case at bar. But we think that something more than that, even in proceedings for taxation, is required by due process of law. Many requirements essential in strictly judicial proceedings may be dispensed with in proceedings of this nature. But even here a hearing in its very essence demands that he who is entitled to it shall have the right to support his allegations by [oral] argument however brief, and, if need be, by proof, however informal.... It is apparent that such a hearing was denied to the plaintiffs in error.... The assessment was therefore void, and the plaintiffs in error were entitled to a decree discharging their lands from a lien on account of it.... Judgment reversed.

THE CHIEF JUSTICE and MR. JUSTICE HOLMES dissent [without writing any dissenting opinions].

Bi-Metallic Investment Company v.
State Board of Equalization of Colorado
239 U.S. 441 (1915)

MR. JUSTICE HOLMES delivered the opinion of the Court.

This is a suit to enjoin the State Board of Equalization and the Colorado Tax Commission from putting in force, and the defendant Pitcher as assessor of Denver from obeying, an order of the boards increasing the valuation of all taxable property in Denver forty per cent. The order was sustained and the suit directed to be dismissed by the Supreme Court of the State. 56 Colorado, 512. See 56 Colorado, 343. The plaintiff is the owner of real estate in Denver and brings the case here on the ground that it was given no opportunity to be heard and that therefore its property will be taken without due process of law, contrary to the Fourteenth Amendment of the Constitution of the United States. That is the only question with which we have to deal....

For the purposes of decision we assume that the constitutional question is presented in the baldest way—that neither the plaintiff nor the assessor of Denver, who presents a brief on the plaintiff's side, nor any representative of the city and county, was given an opportunity to be heard, other than such as they may have had by reason of the fact that the time of meeting of the boards is fixed by law. On this assumption it is obvious that injustice may be suffered if some property in the county already has been valued at its full worth. But if certain property has been valued at a rate different from that generally prevailing in the county the owner has had his opportunity to protest and appeal as usual in our system of taxation, *Hagar v. Reclamation District*, 111 U.S. 701, 709, 710, so that it must be assumed that the property owners in the county all stand alike. The question then is whether all individuals have a constitutional right to be heard before a matter can be decided in which all are equally concerned—here, for instance, before a superior board decides that the local taxing officers have adopted a system of undervaluation throughout a county, as notoriously often has been the case. The answer of this court in the *State Railroad Tax Cases*, 92 U.S. 575, at least as to any further notice, was that it was hard to believe that the proposition was seriously made.

Where a rule of conduct applies to more than a few people it is impracticable that every one should have a direct voice in its adoption. The Constitution does not require all public acts to be done in town meeting or an assembly of the whole. General statutes within the state power are passed that affect the person or property of individuals, sometimes to the point of ruin, without giving them a chance to be heard. Their rights are protected in the only way that they can be in a complex society, by their power, immediate or remote, over those who make the rule. If the result in this case had been reached as it might have been by the State's doubling the rate of taxation, no one would suggest that the Fourteenth Amendment was violated unless every person affected had been allowed an opportunity to raise his voice against it before the body entrusted by the state constitution with the power. In considering this case in this court we must assume that the proper state machinery has been used, and the question is whether, if the state constitution had declared that Denver had been undervalued as compared with the rest of the State and had decreed that for the current year the valuation should be forty per cent higher, the objection now urged could prevail. It appears to us that to put the question is to answer it. There must be a limit to individual argument in such matters if government is to go on. In *Londoner v. Denver*, 210 U.S. 373, 385, a local board had to determine 'whether, in what amount, and upon whom' a tax for paving a street should be levied for special benefits. A relatively small number of persons was concerned, who were exceptionally affected, in each case upon individual grounds, and it was held that they had a right to a hearing. But that decision is far from reaching a general determination dealing only with the principle upon which all the assessments in a county had been laid.

Judgment affirmed.

c. Exploring the *Londoner/Bi-Metallic* Distinction

The Court in *Bi-Metallic* identifies three factors for distinguishing legislative-type action from adjudicative action for purposes of procedural due process:

(1) the number of people affected by the action: *Londoner* involved "a relatively small number of people." *Bi-Metallic* involved "all the assessments in a county."

(2) the way in which the government action affects these people: In *Londoner*, a small number of people were "exceptionally affected" because the assessment of benefits to their property gave rise to a lien on their properties. In *Bi-Metallic* the rule increasing property valuation was only a "general determination"; it did not have "bite" until the tax officials issued tax bills to individual property owners based on the new valuation rule.

(3) the basis on which the government action is taken: In *Londoner*, the assessment of "special benefits" was based on "individual grounds" — namely, the extent to which a particular property parcel benefited from the street paving. In *Bi-Metallic*, the valuation rule was based on "the principle" that, overall, the existing valuation rule undervalued property by 40%. As a result, the property owners affected by the 40% increase "all stand alike" and "are equally concerned."

The *Bi-Metallic* Court also justifies not requiring "individual argument" before legislative-type action takes effect:

> Where a rule of conduct applies to more than a few people, it is impracticable
> that everyone should have a direct voice in its adoption.... There must be a limit
> to individual argument in such matters if government is to go on.

239 U.S. at 445. This rationale (consistently with Justice Holmes' philosophy) is pragmatic.
The rationale has obvious implications for agency rulemaking. since the vast majority of
rules are agency statements "of general ... applicability." 5 U.S.C. § 551(4); *see also*, *e.g.*,
1981 Model State APA § 1-102(10) (defining "rule" to include agency statements "of general
applicability").

The Court does not indicate how to weigh the three factors listed above, and none of
them calls for a simple binary determination. For example, it is possible for a City Council
to adopt an ordinance that applies to a small number of identifiable businesses, such as
tattoo parlors. That does not mean the adoption of ordinance is an adjudicative action,
rather than a legislative one, especially if the ordinance imposes requirements applicable
to all tattoo parlors—both those now in operation and those which open in the future—
and is based on general principles (of health and hygiene, for example).

The second factor listed above needs explanation. One difference between legislative
and adjudicative action is that legislative action often does not have an immediate, direct
impact on individuals, whereas adjudicative action usually does.

Take, for example, the official actions in *Bi-Metallic* "increasing the valuation of all
taxable property in Denver forty per cent." Denver property owners didn't feel the bite of
this governmental action until they got their individual tax bills. Each tax bill was based
on applying the applicable tax rate to the individual property owner's property, as valued
under the newly increased valuation rule. The computation of each property owner's tax
bill is an adjudicative action. Due process entitled each tax payer to notice and an
opportunity to be heard on the computation of that taxpayer's tax bill. Due process did
not, however, entitle any taxpayer to individualized notice and an opportunity to be heard
at the earlier stage at which governmental entities decided to increase the valuation of all
property. This reflects that legislative-type actions often have no direct impact at the
individual level until they are applied to individuals through later, adjudicative actions.

Although legislative-type action does not always directly deprive people of their property,
sometimes it can. For example, someone who is found entitled to government benefits—
such as payments under a governmental program providing benefits for disabled people—has a "property" interest, within the meaning of the Due Process Clauses, in continued
receipt of the benefits. Even so, the government can abolish the entire program—and
so stop paying any further disability benefits to anyone—without having to give every
individual receiving benefits notice and an opportunity to be heard before losing his or
her benefits. *See Atkins v. Parker*, 472 U.S. 115, 129 (1985) ("The procedural component
of the Due Process Clause does not 'impose a constitutional limitation on the power of
Congress to make substantive changes in the law of entitlement to public benefits.'... The
participants in the food-stamp program [who brought this lawsuit] had no greater right
to advance notice of the legislative change [reducing benefits] ... than did any other
voters.") (quoting *Richardson v. Belcher*, 404 U.S. 78, 81 (1971)). Legislative abolition of
a benefits program has a direct effect on the recipients of benefits, but that does not entitle
them to individualized notice and a right to be heard before such legislation is enacted.
Why not, according to Justice Holmes?

Londoner and *Bi-Metallic* give us a set of non-exclusive factors for distinguishing predominantly legislative action from predominantly adjudicative action. We say
"predominantly" because, as Diagram 4-6 reflects, the difference between adjudicative-

type action and legislative-type action is a spectrum, not a hard-and-fast distinction. In addition, *Bi-Metallic* gives a pragmatic rationale for the distinction that should be considered when applying those factors. These factors, and the Court's rationale, create a framework for determining whether agency action that deprives or threatens to deprive someone of property or liberty must comply with the Due Process Clauses' demand for individualized notice and an opportunity to be heard.

Diagram 4-6: The *Londoner/Bi-Metallic* Distinction

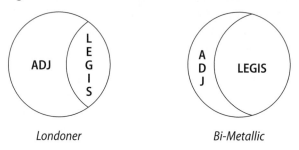

Londoner   Bi-Metallic

Exercise: Revisiting *Londoner* and *Bi-Metallic*

The Court in *Bi-Metallic* said that legislative-type action increasing the valuation of property for property tax purposes raised no due process concerns because the taxpayers' "rights are protected in the only way that they can be in a complex society, by their power, immediate or remote, over those who make the rule." *Bi-Metallic*, 239 U.S. at 445. The Court in a later case added this gloss: "The citizens who are taxed are given notice and a hearing through their representatives, whose power is a direct manifestation of the citizens' consent." *Missouri v. Jenkins*, 495 U.S. 33, 66 (1990).

This rationale makes sense when a legislative-type decision—e.g., a decision to raise the tax rate, or to raise the overall valuation of all property within a large geographic location by an across-the-board percentage, or to abolish a benefits program—is made by a legislative body of elected representatives, such as members of a state legislature or city council.

1. Articulate an argument that this rationale does not apply when a legislative rule is made by unelected officials in an agency (also known as "faceless bureaucrats").

2. Now articulate an argument that even unelected agency officials are "representatives" of the people.

Because unelected agency officials may not be as responsive to the public as elected officials, the federal and state legislatures have enacted APAs providing for public participation in the rulemaking process. Ordinarily, for example, APAs give members of the public the chance to file written comments on proposed rules. An open question is whether such statutorily required public participation is also required as a matter of constitutional due process. *Bi-Metallic* suggests not, but *Londoner* suggests maybe, because of its emphasis on the difference between a task done by the legislative body itself, versus a task delegated by the legislative body to "some subordinate body." *Londoner*, 210 U.S. at 385.

Exercise: Distinguishing Legislative from Adjudicative Activity for Due Process Purposes

L C & S, Inc., obtained a state liquor license from the State of Indiana and leased a building in the small town of Williamsport, Indiana, (population 1800) to operate a restaurant where liquor would be served. At the time L C & S leased the building and began renovating it, it was in a part of the town zoned for commercial use, including the operation of "taverns." Under this zoning, L C & S did not need permission of the zoning board to open and operate their restaurant and serve liquor there.

Before the restaurant opened, however, rumors spread that the restaurant would include a topless bar or would be operated as a gay bar. Apparently because of those rumors, the Town Council amended the zoning ordinance to classify all taverns as "special exceptions." This classification required L C & S to apply to the town's board of zoning appeals for permission to operate their restaurant. At the time the Town Council enacted this amendment, there was one other tavern in Williamsport. The Town Council "grandfathered" this existing tavern into the ordinance so that its owners did not have to get permission to keep operating.

The Town Council amended the zoning ordinance to make taverns "special exceptions" without giving L C & S notice or any opportunity to argue against the amendment (or to argue in favor of being "grandfathered in" like the existing tavern). L C & S sued the Town Council in federal court, claiming that the Town Council's amendment of the zoning ordinance violated procedural due process. In its defense, the Town Council argued that its amendment of the ordinance was legislative, not adjudicative, in nature under the *Londoner/Bi-Metallic* distinction and that L C & S was therefore not entitled to individualized notice and a right to be heard.

1. If you represent L C & S, what circumstances do you emphasize in support of your argument that the Town Council's action was adjudicatory under the *Londoner/Bi-Metallic* distinction?

2. If you represent the Town Council, what circumstances do you emphasize in support of your argument that the Town Council's action was legislative in nature under the *Londoner/Bi-Metallic* distinction?

See L C & S, Inc. v. Warren County Area Plan Commission, 244 F.3d 601 (7th Cir. 2001).

4. Differences between the APA Distinction between Rulemaking and Adjudication and the Procedural Due Process Distinction between Rulemaking and Adjudication

Londoner and *Bi-Metallic* addressed whether procedural due process required individualized notice and an opportunity to be heard before government action took effect. In addressing that issue, the U.S. Supreme Court distinguished between legislative-type activity and adjudicative activity. The distinction between legislative-type activity and adjudicative activity that the Court drew in *Londoner* and *Bi-Metallic* for procedural due process purposes is a forerunner of—but it is not identical to—the distinction between rulemaking and adjudication made in the federal APA. Nor is the *Londoner/Bi-Metallic* distinction made for procedural due process purposes necessarily identical to the distinction between rulemaking and adjudication made in state APAs.

In short, the *Londoner/Bi-Metallic* distinction is a procedural due process concept, not an APA concept. To determine whether an agency proceeding is rulemaking or adjudication under an APA, you consult that APA's definition of those terms. Because the *Londoner/Bi-Metallic* distinction is a procedural due process concept and not an APA concept, it is possible that an agency proceeding could be properly classified as "rulemaking" under the applicable APA while also being properly classified as adjudicative in nature for procedural due process purposes under the *Londoner/Bi-Metallic* distinction. This will be a rare situation. We raise it here, nevertheless, because the U.S. Supreme Court and the lower federal courts have recognized its existence.

The U.S. Supreme Court recognized in the following passage that an agency rulemaking may implicate the procedural due process requirements for adjudications:

> In prior opinions we have intimated that even in a rule making proceeding when an agency is making a "'quasi judicial'" determination by which a very small number of persons are "'exceptionally affected, in each case upon individual grounds,'" in some circumstances additional procedures may be required in order to afford the aggrieved individuals due process. *United States v. Florida East Coast R. Co.*, 410 U.S., at 242, 245, quoting from *Bi Metallic Investment Co. v. State Board of Equalization*, 239 U.S. 441, 446 (1915).

Vermont Yankee Nuclear Power Corp. v. Natural Resources Defense Council, 435 U.S. 519, 542 (1978). The *Vermont Yankee* Court held that the agency rulemaking proceeding before it did not implicate due process because it was "clearly a rulemaking proceeding in its purest form." *Id.* at 542 n.16. The dicta, however, suggested that due process could be required in rulemakings that affect a small number of people on individual grounds.

Besides this dicta, a lower federal court seemed to rely on due process to hold that ex parte communications invalidated a federal agency rulemaking. The court was the United States Court of Appeals for the District of Columbia, a court that decides many administrative-law cases and is highly influential for that reason. The case is old but well known to administrative lawyers: *Sangamon Valley Television Corp. v. United States*, 269 F.2d 221 (D.C. Cir. 1959).

Sangamon Valley involved an informal (notice-and-comment) rulemaking proceeding under the federal APA. In that proceeding, the Federal Communications Commission (FCC) had to decide whether to transfer VHF Channel 2 from Springfield, Illinois, to St. Louis, Missouri. While the rulemaking proceeding was underway, a person who supported the transfer—and who hoped to own the newly transferred station—had private meetings with the Commissioners of the FCC to plead his case. He also sent each of them a follow-up letter. The people opposing the transfer (which included the owners of the existing station in Springfield) never found out about these private, "ex parte" meetings or correspondence. *See* 269 F.2d at 223–224; *see also* 5 U.S.C. § 551(14) (defining "ex parte communication").

Because of the *Londoner/Bi-Metallic* distinction, ex parte contacts are forbidden as a matter of procedural due process only in proceedings that are adjudicative, rather than legislative, in nature. Ex parte contacts therefore ordinarily do not violate due process when they occur in rulemaking. Even so, the United States Court of Appeals for the D.C. Circuit invalidated the FCC's decision because of the ex parte contacts. The court explained:

> Ordinarily allocation of TV channels among communities is a matter of rule-making, governed by § 4 of the Administrative Procedure Act [5 U.S.C. § 553], … rather than adjudication governed by § 5 [5 U.S.C. § 554] … The Commission and the intervenor [the company whose president made the ex parte contacts] contend that because the proceeding now on review was "rule-making," ex parte attempts to influence the Commissioners did not invalidate it. The Department of Justice disagrees. On behalf of the United States, the Department urges that whatever the proceeding may be called it involved not only allocation of TV channels among communities but also resolution of conflicting private claims to a valuable privilege, and that basic fairness requires such a proceeding to be carried on in the open. We agree with the Department of Justice.

269 F.2d at 224. The *Sangamon Valley* court's reference to "basic fairness" suggests that it was relying on procedural due process. *See Sierra Club v. Costle*, 657 F.2d 298, 400 (D.C. Cir. 1981) (interpreting *Sangamon Valley* as based on due process). If so, *Sangamon Valley* holds that due process bars ex parte contacts in rulemakings that involve "resolution of conflicting private claims to a valuable privilege." 269 F.2d at 224. This holding emphasized that in reality the proceeding involved identified parties, not just the general public, locked in an adversary dispute over entitlement to a valuable government benefit that only one party would win.

The *Sangamon Valley* situation will be rare. The court that decided *Sangamon Valley*, the United States Court of Appeals for the D.C. Circuit, has construed its decision in *Sangamon Valley* narrowly to apply only to rulemaking proceedings that are really predominantly adjudicatory in nature. *See Action for Children's Television v. FCC*, 564 F.2d 458, 475 (D.C. Cir. 1976). Other lower federal courts have consistently applied the *Londoner/Bi-Metallic* distinction to hold that procedural due process requirements for adjudicative action do *not* apply in agency rulemaking proceedings. Here are examples:

- *Love v. U.S. Department of Housing & Urban Development*, 704 F.2d 100 (3rd Cir. 1983)

A federal statute required the U.S. Department of Housing and Urban Development (HUD) to issue rules for HUD-subsidized housing. The HUD rules had to identify types of lease provisions that were unreasonable and that therefore could not be included in leases of HUD-subsidized housing. The district court ordered HUD, when promulgating these rules, to ensure that individual tenants of HUD-subsidized housing had a chance to submit comments on provisions in their individual leases that the tenants considered unreasonable. The court of appeals reversed this order. The court of appeals rejected the tenants' argument that the Due Process Clause entitled the tenants to an individualized opportunity to comment on the rules. The court of appeals held that the Due Process Clause did not apply because the HUD rulemaking was legislative, not adjudicative, in nature.

- *Pickney Bros. v. Robinson*, 194 F.3d 1313, 1999 WL 801514 (6th Cir. 1999) (Table)

The Whitman County (Tennessee) Health Board issued rules imposing new, stricter licensing requirements on companies that installed sewage systems. A company subject to the rules complained that the Board did not give the company individual notice of the public meeting at which the Board considered the proposed rules. The court rejected this argument, holding that the Board's adoption of rules was a legislative act that did not trigger the procedural due process protections applicable to adjudicative action.

- *Anaconda Co. v. Ruckelshaus*, 482 F.2d 1301 (10th Cir. 1973)

The United States EPA proposed a rule under the Clean Air Act controlling sulfur oxide emissions in Deer Lodge County, Montana. Anaconda was the only company in that area that emitted sulfur oxide. Anaconda argued that due process entitled it to an evidentiary hearing before the EPA issued the rule. The court rejected Anaconda's argument. The rule was a legislative-type action, under the *Londoner/Bi-Metallic* distinction, even though, at the time of the rule's promulgation, the rule applied only to Anaconda. *Id.* at 1306–1307; *see also Hercules, Inc. v. EPA*, 598 F.2d 91, 118 (D.C. Cir. 1978); *S. Terminal Corp. v. EPA*, 504 F.2d 646, 660–661 (1st Cir. 1974).

In sum, the *Londoner/Bi-Metallic* distinction was used by the Supreme Court to determine when procedural due process applied to government actions affecting people's property interests. The distinction influenced drafters of the federal APA and state APAs.

The result of that influence is that APAs distinguish between rulemaking and adjudication. As you will see in later chapters, in rulemaking proceedings APAs typically require agencies to consider public input on proposed agency rules but do not entitle every single person who will be affected by a proposed rule to receive notice and a right to be heard. In contrast, in agency adjudications that deprive or threaten to deprive someone of property or liberty, APAs typically do require individualized notice and a right to be heard. There is thus a close correspondence, but not perfect overlap, between the *Londoner/Bi-Metallic* distinction and the rulemaking/adjudication distinction.

E. Chapter 4 Wrap Up and Look Ahead

From this chapter, you have learned that the federal and state APAs were enacted partly to bring more uniformity to the procedures that agencies followed, especially when making rules and adjudicating cases. Because of their broad applicability, APAs get much attention in the study as well as the practice of administrative law.

You have also learned about the purposes and structure of the federal APA. The purposes include not only providing uniform procedures for certain agency activities but also providing for public information about agency activities and for judicial review of agency action. The federal APA's procedural provisions address all three kinds of agency power: rulemaking, adjudication, and some executive (specifically, some investigative) powers. In learning about the federal APA's procedural provisions for rulemaking and adjudication, you were introduced to several important administrative law terms: formal rulemaking, informal (or notice-and-comment) rulemaking; formal adjudication; informal adjudication; ALJs; and hybrid rulemaking.

Having been introduced to APAs and impressed with their broad applicability, you next learned a framework for determining an APA's applicability to a particular administrative law problem. The framework entails analysis of (1) whether the APA applies to the agency involved in the problem; (2) if so, whether the APA applies to the particular agency action under analysis; and (3) if the APA does apply to the agency action under analysis, how it interacts with other applicable laws. You can use this framework, as part of the broader framework introduced in Chapter 2, to determine whether the APA is an external source of procedural requirements for the agency action under analysis.

Finally, you learned that the distinction between rulemaking and adjudication is not only central to the federal APA and most state APAs but, in fact, predates those statutes, being rooted in U.S. Supreme Court case law on procedural due process. The distinction, as it exists in procedural due process, is called the *Londoner/Bi-Metallic* distinction. The *Londoner/Bi-Metallic* distinction underlies, but is not identical to, the rulemaking/adjudication distinction made in APAs.

In later chapters, you will separately study the APA provisions for rulemaking and adjudication. The next chapter, however, addresses a subject that is as fundamental to administrative law in the United States as is the role of APAs. The next chapter addresses the relationship between federal and state law as they apply to administrative agencies.

Chapter Problem Revisited

1. The first two questions posed by the chapter problem require you to create an analytic framework and a research plan, respectively, for determining the applicability of the APA to your clients' problem. This chapter aims to provide such a framework.

2. The issue of the APA's applicability to a problem is purely a question of statutory interpretation. The issue turns upon interpreting relevant terms in the APA and the agency legislation. But disputes about APA applicability may end up in court, and produce a court opinion that has precedential value. Thus, the administrative lawyer often consults case law when analyzing the APA's applicability to a particular agency, a particular agency action, or particular agency legislation.

3. It is constitutional for an agency to adopt a rule that drives companies out of business because they can't afford to comply with the rule. The agency does not have to give each such company a right to be heard before adopting the rule. The Court said as much in *Bi-Metallic* when it said: "General statutes within the state power are passed that affect the person or property of individuals, sometimes to the point of ruin, without giving them a chance to be heard." 239 U.S. at 445. The same result may occur from promulgation of agency rules, and is likewise constitutional.

Professional Development Reflection Question

The chapter problem concerns a client who may go out of business if you cannot successfully challenge a new regulation. Suppose you conclude that the chances of a successful judicial challenge are nil. Does your responsibility to that client end, or does the client's imminent business failure give you any additional responsibilities?

Chapter 5

Administrative Law, Federal Supremacy, and Cooperative Federalism

Overview

A complete analysis of an agency's action requires you to analyze (1) laws that may give the agency power to take the action and (2) laws that may limit that power. Chapter 2 offers a framework for analyzing agency powers and limits on those powers. This chapter addresses how that analysis is influenced by our federal system.

Under our federal system, we have a national ("federal") government with nationwide power plus fifty state governments exercising power within state borders. The executive branch of the federal government includes hundreds of federal agencies, and the executive branch of each state government includes dozens of state agencies. It might be neat and tidy if federal agencies only had to worry about federal law, while state agencies only had to worry about state law. But that is not how things work.

Instead, here is the more complicated bottom line: (1) Federal agencies and federal officials must sometimes obey state-law limits on their power; (2) state agencies and state officials must constantly obey federal-law limits on their power. The adverbs "sometimes" and "constantly" in the last sentence are meant to emphasize that the situation is asymmetrical. Federal agencies and officials operate largely without regard to state-law restrictions, whereas state agencies and officials not only must obey federal law but often voluntarily become involved in administering federal law. The situation is asymmetrical, but it's not completely one sided, as you will learn.

The asymmetry exists for two mains reasons. The first reason is the Supremacy Clause of the U.S. Constitution. *See* U.S. Const. art. VI, § 1, cl. 2. The Supremacy Clause invalidates state law that either conflicts with federal law or meaningfully interferes with the execution of federal law. The second reason is "cooperative federalism." Cooperative federalism refers to situations in which States agree to help administer regulatory programs and benefits programs created by federal law. When a State agrees to help execute a federal program, it obligates itself to obey federal laws governing the program.

Interactions between federal and state law, and between federal and state agencies and officials, pervade administrative law in the United States. That is why we include the subject of this chapter here in Part One's foundational material on administrative law.

Here are the chapter sections' titles:

A. When Must Federal Agencies and Officials Obey State and Local Law?

B. When Must State and Local Agencies and Officials Obey Federal Law?

C. Chapter 5 Wrap Up and Look Ahead

Chapter Problem 1

You are legal advisor to the City Council. A member of the City Council contacts you about a vacant house that has become an eyesore and breeding ground for rats. Your investigation reveals that the house is owned by the U.S. Department of Housing and Urban Development (HUD). HUD came to own the house after the prior owners defaulted on a mortgage insured by the Federal Housing Administration. Federal statutes and regulations require HUD to sell houses like this as soon as possible, generally at the highest price possible. Conditions on the property violate several provisions of the City Health and Safety Code. The Council Member asks you whether the City Housing Inspector can get HUD to bring the house into compliance with the City Code.

1. What is the framework for analyzing whether HUD must obey the City Code? What sources of law must you analyze under that framework?

2. If the matter is doubtful as a legal matter, is there anything you can do as a practical matter to get HUD to take care of the problem?

Chapter Problem 2

Your client has applied to the State Department of Health and Welfare in her State for food stamps. That state agency denied your client's application, citing one of its rules for calculating food stamp eligibility. You know that the food stamp program is actually created by federal law, and that state agencies administer the food stamp program in their respective States under federal regulations issued by the U.S. Department of Agriculture (USDA). Your research reveals a USDA regulation on food stamp eligibility that clearly conflicts with the state agency rule cited to support denying your client's application for food stamps. Given this situation—where the state agency rule says one thing, but the federal agency rule says something different—which rule prevails?

A. When Must Federal Agencies and Officials Obey State and Local Law?

Federal agencies and federal officials must obey valid state and local laws in two situations: (1) when the state or local law does not meaningfully interfere with the execution of federal law and is not preempted by federal law; or (2) when a federal law requires federal agencies or officials to obey state and local law. This section addresses each situation.

1. Federal Agencies and Officials Must Obey a State or Local Law If that Law Does Not Meaningfully Interfere with the Execution of Federal Law and Is Not Preempted by Federal Law

a. Under the Doctrine of "Intergovernmental Immunity," a State or Local Law Is Invalid If It Meaningfully Interferes with the Execution of Federal Law

The doctrine of intergovernmental immunity holds that federal agencies and federal officials are "immune"—meaning they don't have to obey—state or local laws that meaningfully interfere with the execution of federal law. The doctrine is rooted in the Supremacy Clause of the Constitution. The doctrine carries an important negative implication: Federal agencies and federal officials *do* have to obey state and local laws that do *not* meaningfully interfere with the execution of federal law (and are not preempted). Courts sometimes express this negative implication by saying that federal agencies and officials must obey state and local laws that have only an "incidental" effect on the execution of federal law.

You may have encountered (or will encounter) the most famous case on intergovernmental immunity in a law school course on constitutional law. The case is *McCulloch v. Maryland*, 17 U.S. 316 (1819). The Court in *McCulloch* held that the Bank of the United States, which was an institution created by federal law, did not have to obey a tax law enacted by the State of Maryland. The Court grounded the national bank's immunity from the state tax law in the Supremacy Clause of the U.S. Constitution, article VI, section 1, clause 2, which says in relevant part:

U.S. Const. art. VI, § 1, clause 2

This Constitution, and the Laws of the United States which shall be made in Pursuance thereof; and all Treaties made, or which shall be made, under the Authority of the United States, shall be the supreme Law of the Land....

The *McCulloch* Court explained that federal instrumentalities operate for the benefit of everyone in the United States. Because state governments represent, and are accountable to, only a part of the nation, they cannot interfere with activities authorized by the national government for the benefit of the whole nation. The Court concluded:

> [T]he states have no power, by taxation or otherwise, to retard, impede, burden, or in any manner control, the operations of the constitutional laws enacted by Congress to carry into execution the powers vested in the general government. This is, we think, the unavoidable consequence of that supremacy which the constitution has declared.

McCulloch, 17 U.S. at 436.

McCulloch gave birth to what is today called the doctrine of "intergovernmental immunity." The doctrine's name misleads to the extent it implies the immunity is a two-way street. In truth, while the doctrine gives federal activities great protection from interference by state and local laws, the activities of state and local governments have almost no protection from federal regulation. True, state and local governments and officials do enjoy immunity from federal laws that try to "commandeer" state and local governments and their officials by compelling them to enforce federal laws. *See, e.g., Printz v. United States*, 521 U.S. 898 (1997) (striking down as unconstitutional a federal law that compelled local enforcement officials to enforce federal handgun laws). A federal law is invalid if it violates this anti-commandeering principle. That is a narrow principle, however. Most importantly, the anti-commandeering principle does not invalidate federal laws that regulate States and local governments comparably to the private sector. Suffice it to say that, for all practical purposes, intergovernmental immunity is an immunity that federal agencies and officials have from state law; the immunity seldom operates to immunize state agencies or officials from federal law.

An administrative law case illustrating intergovernmental immunity is *Mayo v. United States*, 319 U.S. 441 (1943). *Mayo* concerned a federal program under which the U.S. Secretary of Agriculture bought fertilizer for distribution to farmers throughout the country, including Florida. Florida law required all fertilizer distributed in Florida to be inspected and to have a label signifying the payment of a state inspection fee. The U.S. Secretary of Agriculture (through his minions) distributed the federally purchased fertilizer in Florida without having it inspected, without paying the fee, and without affixing any labels signifying payment of the fee. Florida officials threatened to seize the federal fertilizer, prompting the United States to sue Florida officials in federal court. The case eventually went to the U.S. Supreme Court.

The Court held that the Florida fertilizer law did not apply to fertilizer distributed by the federal government. Relying on *McCulloch*, the Court held that the Florida law's application to the federal government was "prohibited by the supremacy clause." 319 U.S. at 447; *see also Arizona v. California*, 283 U.S. 423, 451–459 (1931) (State of Arizona could not enjoin U.S. Secretary of Interior from constructing dam authorized by federal statute, even though Secretary did not get approval of state engineer, as required by state law). The Court broadly stated: "[T]he activities of the Federal Government are free from regulation by any state." 319 U.S. at 445.

Despite that broad statement, intergovernmental immunity does not shield federal agencies and federal officials from state and local laws that do not meaningfully interfere with the execution of federal law. An administrative law case illustrating this point is *Penn Dairies v. Milk Control Commission of Pennsylvania*, 318 U.S. 261 (1943). In *Penn Dairies*, a Pennsylvania state agency promulgated rules setting minimum prices for milk. The U.S. Supreme Court held that the state agency's minimum price rules could apply to milk sold to a U.S. Army facility in Pennsylvania. The Court recognized that the State's minimum price rules for milk increased the Army's cost of operating the facility, but the Court held that this effect was too indirect to bar the rules' application to the Army base. The state rules did not regulate the *Army*'s activities; they regulated milk dealers. The immunity doctrine does not invalidate a state or local law merely because the law increases the federal government's cost of operations by regulating private actors dealing with the federal government. *See North Dakota v. United States*, 495 U.S. 423, 434–435 (1990) (upholding North Dakota laws regulating companies that sold liquor to U.S. military bases in the State).

The applicability of intergovernmental immunity to federal officials is illustrated by *Johnson v. Maryland*, 254 U.S. 51, 55–58 (1920). In *Johnson*, a federal employee delivering the U.S. mail was arrested in Maryland for driving without a Maryland driver's license. The U.S. Supreme Court held that Maryland could not require federal employees to have a driver's license when carrying out official duties. The Court added that Maryland could, however, require federal employees to obey "general rules that might affect incidentally the mode of carrying out employment—as, for instance, a statute or ordinance regulating the mode of turning at the corners of streets." *Id.* at 56; *see also Howard v. Lyons*, 360 U.S. 593, 597–598 (1959) (federal official immune from state libel law when carrying out official duties). Thus, the immunity of federal officials carrying out official duties, like the immunity of federal agencies, protects only against state and local laws that meaningfully impede the execution of federal law, and not against state and local laws that have only an incidental effect on federal activities.

McCulloch probably captured the rationale of intergovernmental immunity best when it said, "[T]he power to tax involves the power to destroy." 17 U.S. at 431. In other words, if States could tax federal government operations, States could effectively prevent the national government from carrying out the will of the nation's people, as expressed through the elected representatives in Congress who enact laws that create and empower the federal agencies that carry out the federal government's operations. The Court has applied the same rationale to bar state *regulation* of the federal government's activities. *See Mayo*, 319 U.S. at 445.

b. Preemption of State and Local Law by Federal Statutes and Regulations

The doctrine of preemption holds that in certain situations a valid federal statute or federal agency's legislative rule may invalidate state or local law. The invalidation, known as *preemption*, arises from a clash between the federal law, on the one hand, and the state or local law, on the other hand. When this kind of clash occurs, federal law wins. Even state and local laws that do not meaningfully interfere with the execution of federal law cannot operate if they are preempted.

An administrative law case illustrating preemption is *GWN Petroleum Corp. v. Federal Deposit Insurance Corp.*, 998 F.2d 853 (10th Cir. 1993). A federal agency, the Federal Deposit Insurance Corporation (FDIC), took over a bank and became its receiver. As receiver, the FDIC collected money from an oil and gas company that owed money to the bank. The oil and gas company also owed money to the Four-O-One Corporation. Four-O-One filed an action against the FDIC to garnish the money that the oil company had paid the FDIC. Four-O-One based its garnishment action on state law. The court of appeals, however, held that the state law was preempted by a federal statute that protected money in the FDIC's possession from garnishment under state law. *Id.* at 856–857.

GWN Petroleum illustrates the preemptive force of a federal statute. State law can be preempted not only by a federal statute but also by a federal agency's legislative rule. That is called regulatory preemption. We discuss federal regulatory preemption in Chapter 16.C, as part of our examination of the legal effects of a valid, federal agency's legislative rule.

The thing to understand now is that the preemption doctrine differs from intergovernmental immunity. Preemption gives invalidating force to a federal *statute* or federal agency *rule*. In contrast, intergovernmental immunity gives certain federal *activities* protection from state and local law, whether or not the state or local law clashes with any particular federal statute or legislative rule. Thus, for example, in the *Mayo* case discussed above, the federal government was immune from Florida inspection laws even though those state laws did not conflict with any federal law or federal rule; the state laws could not operate because of their effect on federal government activities.

c. Preemption of State or Local Law by Federal Common Law

The preemption doctrine addresses the invalidating force of federal statutes and regulations, which are the respective products of the federal legislative and executive branches. The federal courts, too, have power to make federal law that displaces state and local law. *See generally Banco Nacional de Cuba v. Sabbatino*, 376 U.S. 398, 426 (1964). The federal-judge-made law is called "federal common law." Federal courts can make federal common law in certain situations that are not governed by any federal statute or rule but that involve "uniquely federal interest[s]." *E.g., Boyle v. United Technologies Corp.*, 487 U.S. 500, 507 (1988). Federal common law, like federal statutes and regulations, can preempt state and local law. *See, e.g., id.; Int'l Paper Co. v. Ouellette*, 479 U.S. 481, 488 (1987).

Two administrative law cases involving federal common law were addressed in *United States v. Kimbell Foods, Inc.*, 440 U.S. 715 (1979). In each case, a federal agency loaned money to a private entity under a lending program established by a federal statute. In one case, the Small Business Administration loaned money to a grocery company; in the other case, the Farmers Home Administration (FmHA) loaned money to a farmer. In each case, the agency got a security interest in the debtor's property. In each case, a dispute arose between the agency and another creditor about which lender's security interest had priority. This dispute over priority, in turn, raised another question: Was the issue of priority governed by state law or by federal law? No federal statute or regulation addressed the priority issue. The issue was whether a federal court should devise federal common law to fill the gap.

The Court in *Kimbell Foods* divided that issue into two questions. One was whether federal courts had power to make federal common law to govern the priority issue. The second was, if so, whether federal common law should take the form of a uniform priority rule, applicable throughout the country, or should, instead, simply incorporate the law of the States in which the loans were made.

On the first question, the Court held that federal courts could and should apply federal common law to govern the priority issue. The Court held that "the priority of liens stemming from federal lending programs must be determined by reference to federal law." *Id.* at 726. Of relevance to administrative lawyers, the Court explained, "When Government activities arise from and bear heavily upon a federal ... program, ... federal interests are sufficiently implicated to warrant the protection of federal law." *Id.* at 726–727 (internal quotation marks and brackets omitted). The Court relied on a case in which it had held that federal common law governed third party mineral rights in land that the United States acquired under the Migratory Bird Conservation Act. *United States v. Little Lake Misere Land Co.*, 412 U.S. 580, 592–594 (1973).

On the second question, the Court in *Kimbell Foods* decided that federal common law should incorporate state law. The Court considered: whether the nature of the federal programs required a uniform rule; "whether application of state law would frustrate specific objectives of the federal programs"; and whether "application of a federal rule would disrupt commercial relationships predicated on state law." *Id.* at 728–729. The Court did not see any strong federal interests in uniformity in administration of the loan programs, and the Court worried that a uniform federal rule would frustrate reliance of private creditors on state commercial law. Thus, Texas law (as incorporated into federal common law) governed the priority of the SBA loan to the Texas grocery company, and Georgia law (as incorporated into federal common law) governed the priority of the FmHA loan to the Georgia farmer.

d. Preemption Summary

Each branch of the federal government can make federal law, and when any of the branches validly does so, that federal law can preempt state and local law. Even in the absence of preemptive federal law, state and local law cannot significantly interfere with federal activities, including the activities of federal agencies. The combination of preemption and intergovernmental immunity largely frees federal agencies and officials from having to worry about state and local interference with the administration of federal law.

2. Federal Agencies and Officials Must Obey State and Local Laws When Required to Do So By Federal Law

The Court has held that Congress can subject federal instrumentalities and officials to state and local laws. *Mayo*, 319 U.S. at 446. Congress has done so, for example, in several federal environmental statutes. In addition, a federal agency may have authority under its legislation to adopt agency rules and policies subjecting the agency's activities to state and local laws.

The federal Clean Water Act subjects federal government activities to state and local water pollution laws in this provision:

---

33 U.S.C. § 1323. Federal facilities pollution control

(a) Each department, agency, or instrumentality of the executive, legislative, and judicial branches of the Federal Government (1) having jurisdiction over any property or facility, or (2) engaged in any activity resulting, or which may result, in the discharge or runoff of pollutants, and each officer, agent, or employee thereof in the performance of his official duties, shall be subject to, and comply with, all Federal, State, interstate, and local requirements, administrative authority, and process and sanctions respecting the control and abatement of water pollution in the same manner, and to the same extent as any nongovernmental entity including the payment of reasonable service charges. The preceding sentence shall apply (A) to any requirement whether substantive or procedural (including any recordkeeping or reporting requirement, any requirement respecting permits and any other requirement, whatsoever), (B) to the exercise of any Federal, State, or local administrative authority, and (C) to any process and sanction, whether enforced in Federal, State, or local courts or in any other manner. This subsection shall apply notwithstanding any immunity of such agencies, officers, agents, or employees under any law or rule of law....

See also 42 U.S.C. § 6961 (2012) (provision in federal Resource Conservation and Recovery Act subjecting federal entities to state and local laws "respecting control and abatement of solid waste or hazardous waste disposal and management"); 42 U.S.C. § 7418 (2012) (provision in federal Clean Air Act subjecting federal entities to state and local air pollution laws). The result of these federal statutory provisions is that state and local environmental laws can be enforced—by state and local environmental agencies, for example—against federal entities, such as military bases, that would otherwise have intergovernmental immunity from state and local regulation. *See, e.g., United States v. Tennessee Air Pollution Control Bd.*, 185 F.3d 529 (6th Cir. 1999) (upholding civil penalties assessed by Tennessee agency against U.S. Army for violations of state air pollution laws).

The method for enforcing state and local laws against federal entities depends on what enforcement methods Congress has authorized. Just because a federal statute subjects federal agencies or officials to certain state and local laws, that does not mean that these federal entities can be treated just like everyone else. To the contrary, Congress often restricts the means of enforcement. In one case, for example, the Court held that, although federal installations must obey state water pollution laws, they do not have to get the state permits required of non-federal entities. *EPA v. Cal. ex rel. State Water Resources Control Bd.*, 426 U.S. 200, 211–227 (1976). In another case, the State of Ohio sued the U.S. Department of Energy (DOE) alleging that a DOE uranium-processing plant was violating state pollution laws. The Court held that, even if DOE could be sued for judicial remedies to ensure future compliance with those laws, DOE could not be held liable for civil fines for its past violations. The Court interpreted the relevant federal statutes as preserving the federal government's sovereign immunity from liability for past violations. *See Dep't of Energy v. Ohio*, 503 U.S. 607 (1992).

Thus, Congress gets to decide, by statute, (1) whether to subject federal agencies and their officials to state and local laws; and (2) what means can be used to enforce those state and local laws against the federal government. All hail Congress!

Besides congressional authorization, a federal agency may have discretion to subject itself to state and local law. As you will learn, many federal agencies have broad power to make legislative rules to carry out their statutory missions. As mentioned above, that power can include the power to adopt legislative rules that preempt conflicting state and local law. By the same token, a federal agency's rulemaking power may include the power to adopt rules allowing state or local law to govern the agency's activities. A federal agency could decide to adopt such a rule when, for example, its activities are limited to a particular locality; when there is no strong need for a uniform federal rule; or when following state and local laws is wise policy because it shows respect for state and local regulation of activities that have state and local effect. *See, e.g., United States v. Palmer*, 956 F.2d 189 (9th Cir. 1992) (discussing National Park Service regulations that partially incorporated state drunk driving laws). Using the first chapter problem for this chapter as an example: It is entirely possible that the U.S. Department of Housing and Urban Development (HUD) would issue a regulation requiring HUD officials and their agents to obey local housing laws in the maintenance and upkeep of residential houses that HUD has come to own through foreclosures.

3. Summary

Let us relate the material in this section to the problem solving framework introduced in Chapter 2. The material in this section relates to the second of the three questions of the framework, which asks whether, in taking the action under analysis, the agency has obeyed limits on, and requirements for, exercising its power.

The material in this section enables you to determine when a federal agency or official is subject to limits or requirements created by state or local law. This section identifies two such situations: (1) when the state or local law doesn't meaningfully interfere with the execution of federal law (and isn't preempted); and (2) when Congress by statute, or an agency by rule, subjects federal activities to the state or local law.

Exercise: Analyzing Federal Immunity from State and Local Laws

The objective of this exercise is to help you construct for yourself a framework for analyzing whether a state or local law applies to a federal agency or official. We list the questions that you must ask. Your job is to construct a flow chart or other graphic organizer that maps an analysis to answer the question: Does this state or local law apply to federal agency action *X*? The questions, which you may reformulate for your flow chart, are:

1. Does the state or local law meaningfully interfere with federal agency action *X*?

2. Is the state or local law preempted by a federal statute, federal legislative rule, or federal common law?

3. Does a federal law require the federal agency to obey this state or local law when taking action *X*?

B. When Must State and Local Agencies and Officials Obey Federal Law?

State and local agencies and officials must obey federal law all the time. Not only must they obey the U.S. Constitution and valid federal statutes, federal regulations, and federal common law. In addition, in many situations state and local agencies and officials choose to administer programs created by federal law. When doing so, they must obey all applicable federal law.

1. State and Local Agencies and Officials Must Obey All Valid Federal Laws

State and local agencies and officials must obey the U.S. Constitution and all valid federal laws because of the Supremacy Clause. For example, state and local agencies and officials must obey the Fourteenth Amendment's Due Process and Equal Protection Clauses:

U.S. Const. amend. XIV, § 1

No State ... shall ... deprive any person of life, liberty, or property, without due process of law; nor deny to any person within its jurisdiction the equal protection of the laws.

We mention these Clauses because they come up later in the book.

State and local agencies and officials must also obey valid Acts of Congress. Indeed, state and local agencies and officials are subject to many federal statutes that also apply to the private sector. These include, for example, federal statutes that (1) require employees to be paid a federally prescribed minimum wage; (2) forbid employers from discriminating against employees or applicants for employment based on race, religion, disability, or national origin; and (3) regulate activities that produce air and water pollution. *See Chao v. Virginia Dep't of Transp.*, 291 F.3d 276 (4th Cir. 2002) (suit by federal government to enforce federal minimum wage laws against state agency); *Fitzpatrick v. Bitzer*, 427 U.S. 445 (1976) (suit by private plaintiffs against state officials for violation of federal statute barring gender discrimination in employment); *South Carolina Wildlife Fed'n v. Limehouse*, 549 F.3d 324 (4th Cir. 2008) (suit against state officials for violation of federal environmental statute). Although some federal statutes treat state and local governments differently from (often more leniently than) the private sector, that is because Congress has decided that special treatment is appropriate—not because the Constitution compels it.

While federal law can and does impose many substantive obligations on state and local governments, enforcement of those obligations can be tricky because of two immunity doctrines. The doctrine of state *sovereign* immunity makes it hard for private plaintiffs to sue States or state agencies for money out of the state treasury. The doctrine of *official* immunity makes it hard for private plaintiffs to sue state and local officials for money damages out of their own pockets. Even so, there are ways to get around both immunities. Most importantly, people can sue state officials in federal court for prospective relief against ongoing violations of federal law. *E.g., Virginia Office for Protection & Advocacy v. Stewart*, 131 S.Ct. 1632, 1639 (2011) (discussing doctrine of *Ex parte Young*, 209 U.S. 123 (1908)). The upshot is that, when Congress puts obligations on state and local agencies and officials, there are usually adequate ways to enforce those obligations.

In addition to obeying the U.S. Constitution and valid Acts of Congress, state and local agencies and officials must obey valid legislative rules issued by federal agencies. As we will discuss in Chapters 7 and 16, valid federal legislative rules have the same force and effect as do Acts of Congress. And as discussed above, federal common law can displace state and local law, and in the process impose federal-law obligations on state and local governments.

The upshot is that, when you are analyzing the action of a state or local agency or official, and in the process of that analysis you are searching for laws limiting that agency's or official's power, your search must include a search for any applicable *federal* laws. Applicable federal-law limits can come from the U.S. Constitution, federal statutes, federal agency rules, and the federal courts.

2. Cooperative Federalism

Federal law does impose many restrictions (e.g., "Don't discriminate in employment based on race!") and affirmative commands (e.g., "Pay your employees the federal minimum wage!") on state and local agencies and officials. Separate and apart from these mandatory federal laws are federal laws that create programs of "cooperative federalism." In a cooperative federalism program, Congress enacts statutes that do not *compel* state and local officials to enforce the federal laws. Rather, the federal statutes *allow* state and local governments, if they wish to do so, to assist the federal government in executing federal laws.

State and local governments usually participate in these programs voluntarily from one of two motives (or both). They participate either to get money from the federal government or to avoid having the federal government administer the program itself, perhaps in ways that are not sensitive to local conditions and concerns. Cooperative programs are voluntary. State and local governments do not have to participate.

If a state or local government wants to participate in a cooperative federalism program, the federal statutes creating the program require the state or local government to meet certain conditions — prescribed by the federal statute itself and by federal regulations. State or local administration of the program is overseen by a federal agency, which ensures the state or local administration complies with the federal statute and regulations.

Here are programs of cooperative federalism that may be familiar to you:

- The federal Medicaid program helps poor people get medical care.

"The Medicaid program … is a cooperative one; the Federal Government pays between 50% and 83% of the costs the State incurs for patient care, and, in return, the State pays its portion of the costs and complies with certain [federal] statutory [and regulatory] requirements for making eligibility determinations, collecting and maintaining information, and administering the program." *Arkansas Dep't of Health & Human Servs. v. Ahlborn*, 547 U.S. 268, 275 (2006) (citation omitted).

Every State has a state agency that administers the Medicaid program in that State. A State's "Medicaid agency" is usually the same agency that administers certain State-created (and State-funded) assistance programs for the poor. The state agency often goes by the name "[State] Department of Health and Welfare." These state agencies often administer not only the federal Medicaid program but also another federal program that operates using cooperative federalism: the federal Supplemental Nutrition Assistance Program (SNAP), which used to be called the "food stamp program." Furthermore, the state agency that administers Medicaid and SNAP probably administers benefits programs created by state law and funded by state taxes. Thus, thanks to cooperative federalism, people in many States can go to a single state office to apply for several different types of government benefits. They may even be able to apply for several types of benefits using a single form.

Even so, not all federal programs providing assistance to the poor are administered through cooperative federalism, and even those federal programs that *are* so administered are not all administered by a single agency within the State. Instead, some federal assistance programs are administered by the federal government itself, a prime example of which are programs created by the Social Security Act to provide benefits to the disabled. Other federal assistance programs may be administered by different state agencies within a State. The result is that, to get all the government benefits to which a poor person may be entitled, the person often must shuttle back and forth between multiple local, state, and federal agencies, each with its own paperwork requirements. This is the uncooperative side of federalism.

- Many federal environmental statutes authorize cooperative federalism, including the Clean Air Act (CAA) and Clean Water Act (CWA).

States administer portions of the CAA by developing state implementation plans according to criteria established by the CAA and the U.S. EPA. 42 U.S.C. § 7410 (2012). Similarly, States may administer portions of the CWA by developing state permit programs that comply with federally prescribed criteria. 33 U.S.C. § 1342 (2012). The result of these state permitting programs is that people may apply to the state agency for certain permits required by federal law.

- Many States administer programs to implement the federal Occupational Safety and Health Act of 1970 (OSH Act).

The OSH Act authorizes the U.S. Secretary of Labor to develop occupational safety and health standards (by rulemaking) and allows States to submit plans to the Secretary for enforcing those standards within their borders. 29 U.S.C. § 667 (2012). About half the States have federally approved plans for administering the OSH Act. In these States, it is state government employees who, for example, inspect work sites for compliance with federal workplace safety standards and issue citations for violations of those standards.

- Several federal anti-discrimination laws employ cooperative federalism.

Specifically, the federal law prohibiting employment discrimination, which is known as Title VII, allows state agencies to do the initial investigation of violations of Title VII if the state agency has power to enforce a comparable state law. 42 U.S.C. § 2000e-5(c) and (d) (2012). State agencies may similarly participate in investigation of age-discrimination charges under the federal Age Discrimination in Employment Act, 29 U.S.C. § 633(b) (2012), and the federal Americans with Disabilities Act, 42 U.S.C. § 12117(a) (2012).

* * *

States typically participate in cooperative federalism programs by enacting state law, and by having their agencies promulgate state rules, necessary to comply with federal requirements for participation. A state agency can enforce federal laws (such as the federal Clean Air Act and Clean Water Act) only if it has authority to do so under state law. *See*, *e.g.*, 33 U.S.C. § 1342(b) (2012) (requiring State to show that it has adequate authority under state law to administer Clean Water Act permit program). State agencies therefore administer cooperative federalism programs under restrictions of both state and federal law. The state laws must comply with all applicable federal laws or else they are preempted. As a result, a state agency's action in administering a cooperative federalism program may require analysis under federal statutes, federal regulations, federal common law, state statutes, and state regulations—not to mention the federal and state Constitutions!

Even when a state or local agency helps administer a federal program, it remains a state or local agency. It does not become a federal agency. Thus, a state or local agency administering a federal program does not have to follow the federal APA. The state or local agency need not follow the federal APA because it does not fall within the federal APA's definition of "**agency**" in § 551(1). Though not subject to the federal APA, the state or local agency still must follow federal statutory and regulatory provisions governing the federal program it cooperates in administering.

C. Chapter 5 Wrap Up and Look Ahead

Usually we talk about federal administrative law and state administrative law as if they were separate bodies of law that are administered, separately and respectively, by federal and state agencies. This chapter introduces the more complex reality.

Federal agencies and officials *do* administer federal law of course. But in doing so they must obey state and local laws that do not meaningfully interfere with the execution of federal law and are not preempted. Federal agencies and officials also must obey state and local law when Congress or their own rules require them to.

State and local agencies and officials must obey the U.S. Constitution and valid federal statutes, federal rules, and federal common law. Beyond that, many States and local governments voluntarily undertake to have their agencies and officials participate in administering programs created by federal statutes. When participating in these programs of cooperative federalism, state and local agencies are regulated not only by state and local law but also by federal law, typically including federal rules and policies adopted by the federal agency that oversees the state and local administration of the federal program.

Chapter Problem 1 Revisited

1.   It is not clear whether HUD is subject to the City Code.

   a.   Intergovernmental Immunity

   HUD has intergovernmental immunity from the City Code if compliance with the Code significantly interferes with HUD's administration of its program. You must research HUD's program to determine the program's policies, objectives, and activities. That will help you analyze whether compliance with the City Code would interfere with HUD's program so significantly as to be inapplicable because of intergovernmental immunity. In your research, you will find case law suggesting that the application of local housing laws to HUD-owned property does significantly interfere with HUD's policy of selling foreclosed property "as is." *See United States v. City of St. Paul*, 285 F.3d 750 (8th Cir. 2001); *see also Burroughs v. Hills*, 741 F.2d 1525 (7th Cir. 1984). Thus, although there are reasonable arguments to the contrary, HUD has case law supporting a claim of intergovernmental immunity from the City Health and Safety Code.

   b.   Preemption

   A valid federal statute or federal agency's legislative rule can preempt conflicting state and local law. Thus, Congress could enact a statute that expressly or impliedly authorizes HUD to own houses without obeying any state or local laws. In addition, HUD might have authority under its legislation to issue a legislative rule that protected HUD from having to obey state and local laws applicable to privately owned homes. Again, you must do research for any preemptive federal statutes or rules. (Our research revealed no such statutes or rules.)

   If no federal statute or rule preempts local law, federal common law could govern HUD's ownership of residential housing. *Kimbell Foods* states, "When Government activities arise from and bear heavily upon a federal ... program, ... federal interests are sufficiently implicated to warrant the protection of federal law." 440 U.S. at 726–727 (internal quotation marks and brackets omitted). This statement supports application of federal common law to this problem, in which HUD owns a house through a government program supporting home ownership. In addition, *Little Lake Misere Land Co.* held that federal common law governed an issue arising from the federal government's acquisition of land. This holding also supports application of federal common law to HUD's ownership of a house. If federal common law does govern HUD's ownership of the home in the chapter problem, the question would remain whether federal common law would incorporate state and local laws such as the City Code. You can reasonably argue this issue of incorporation either way.

c.   Federal Law Subjecting HUD or Its Contractors to Local Laws

Even if HUD might otherwise have intergovernmental immunity from the City Code, Congress could eliminate that immunity by enacting a statute requiring HUD to obey local law. In addition, HUD itself might have discretion under its legislation to adopt a policy committing itself to follow local law. You must do research for any such laws and policies.

Our research indicates that, in its contracts with property management companies, HUD requires those companies to follow certain local laws, such as snow removal laws, when maintaining HUD-owned houses. *See* U.S. Department of Housing and Urban Development, Mortgagee Letter 2010–18 (May 13, 2010), Exhibit A, HUD/FHA Property and Preservation Guidelines, § 6.F, at 11, http://portal.hud.gov/hudportal/HUD?src=/program_offices/housing/sfh/nsc/mcm. Thus, even if HUD itself isn't subject to the City Code, the problem house in Chapter Problem 1 may be in the hands of a management company that is subject to the City Code.

2.   Your preliminary research would probably show it is unclear whether HUD is subject to the City Code. Rather than litigate the issue, the City's best bet is probably to resolve the matter informally.

Toward that end, a good first step may be to determine whether HUD has hired a property management company to manage the property, and, if so, to approach that company. If the company manages many properties in the City besides the troublesome HUD property, the company may be motivated to stay on good terms with the City by bringing the property up to Code. If the company balks, the next step might be to identify and contact the HUD official with immediate responsibility for the property. If this official doesn't cooperate, you might next contact that official's boss. While you are pursuing these steps, you might take others, such as notifying the Member of the U.S. House of Representatives or the U.S. Senator whose constituents live in the City. Perhaps you could get the local news media to cover the story. Legislative representatives and the media may, if need be, generate some pressure on HUD to clean up its house. Remember, courts are not the only source for control of agency action.

Chapter Problem 2 Revisited

As discussed in this chapter, the food stamp program is a cooperative federalism program. This means that state agencies administer federal law. State agencies often must issue their own regulations to implement the federal laws. If the state regulations conflict with federal law, those regulations are invalid; they are preempted. Your research indicates that the state agency misinterpreted federal law in a way that has affected your client adversely. You should seek administrative review of the denial of your client's application for food stamps, based on the conflict between the state agency rule and federal law.

Professional Development Reflection Questions

This chapter discusses difficult constitutional law doctrines that may assume background knowledge that a reader may not have. It thus raises a question relevant for upper-level law students as well as lawyers: How do you identify and handle situations that require self-initiated, self-planned learning? For example, what do you do when, as a law student or a lawyer, you encounter a doctrine of constitutional law that you've never encountered before, in material that plainly assumes you have knowledge that, in fact, you don't yet have? These situations seem to require three steps.

First, you have to know what you don't know. In other words, you must learn not to gloss over material that you do not understand. You cannot assume that, since you don't understand it, you don't *need* to understand it. Many lawyers get into trouble by taking on projects that require more background knowledge, or that require skills, that, realistically, the lawyer won't be able to acquire well enough to provide adequate representation. As obvious as it may seem, knowing your limitations is a key component of professionalism.

Second, you have to be able to determine whether something that you don't know is something that you *need* to know, in order to achieve your objective. In this book, we strive for transparency in setting out what you are supposed to get out of the material. The chapter problems, for example, are meant to help you gauge whether you've learned what the chapter material is meant to teach. Law students don't have time to learn every nuance of every subject they encounter in a law school course. So, too, lawyers don't have time (and their clients don't have the money) for the endless research necessary to investigate the law and facts governing every conceivable aspect of a legal problem. As a law student and a lawyer, you must distinguish between, on the one hand, what you "need" to know or must be able to do and, on the other hand, what it "would be nice" to know or be able to do.

Third, once you identify what you need to know or be able to do, you must determine the best way to learn the needed information or skills. "The best" way means the most efficient and accurate way. The best lawyers identify reliable resources to which they can resort for needed knowledge and skills. Those resources are often other lawyers. They can also include treatises, training institutes, professional organizations, etc.

With all that in mind, we pose these questions:

1. Do you think you have the background knowledge of constitutional law necessary for learning what the chapter material is meant to teach?

2. If not, or if you encounter other material in the book that assumes background knowledge of constitutional law that you lack, what it the best way to acquire that knowledge?

RULEMAKING

Chapter 6

Introduction to Agency Rulemaking

Overview

This is the first chapter on agency rulemaking, the subject of Part Two of this book. This chapter introduces the subject of rulemaking and gives you a roadmap for this part of the book. The chapter consists of five sections, entitled:

A. Rulemaking in a Legal-Practice Context

B. Rulemaking within the Problem Solving Framework

C. Rulemaking from the Agency Perspective

D. The Role of Lawyers in Rulemaking

E. Roadmap of Part Two

A. Rulemaking in a Legal-Practice Context

To appreciate why you will benefit from studying rulemaking, it helps to put the subject into a practical context. Picture two common scenarios.

In scenario one, the client wants to do something the client knows has legal repercussions. The client wants to build a shopping center, start a business, or begin selling goods overseas. The client comes to you for help obeying "the law."

In scenario two, the client has already done something that's gotten the client into legal trouble. The client comes to you for help getting out of trouble with "the law."

In the United States today, much "law," other than criminal law, comes not directly from the legislative branch or the judicial branch of government. It comes from the executive branch—specifically, from the executive-branch agencies that exist at the federal, state, tribal, and local levels of government. This executive-branch law is not-so-affectionately known as "red tape." Most red tape takes the form of agency rules (also known as regulations). Thus, to learn "the law," it is incumbent upon law students to learn about agency rulemaking.

To help you learn about agency rulemaking, this part of the book approaches the subject within the problem solving framework introduced in Chapter 2.

B. Rulemaking within the Problem Solving Framework

The problem solving framework in Chapter 2 reflected that many administrative law problems involve agency action and that, broadly speaking, three kinds of legal questions can arise about an agency action:

(1) Is there a valid source of power for the agency to take this action?

(2) If so, has the agency obeyed limits on, and requirements for exercising, that power?

(3) If the agency lacks power to take the action, or has not obeyed limits on, or requirements for exercising, that power, what can be done about it?

For now we defer the third question. We defer it because this book, consistently with most administrative law courses, addresses the question "What can be done about invalid agency action?" primarily by exploring the availability of judicial relief for such action; and we devote Part 4 of this book to that subject. That leaves for now the first two questions, relating to (1) agency power and (2) limits on, and requirements for exercising, agency power.

To analyze these two questions as they apply to agency rules, you must understand the difference between legislative rules and non-legislative rules. These two kinds of rules differ in terms of both the nature of an agency's power to make each kind of rule and the nature of limits on, and requirements for exercising, that power. Because the distinction between legislative and non-legislative rules is a fundamental distinction in administrative law, we devote the next chapter to it.

C. Rulemaking from the Agency Perspective

To understand agency rulemaking it is useful to understand why agencies make rules. In general, agencies make rules to carry out their responsibilities. And so there is much truth to the saying: "Fish gotta swim, birds gotta fly, and agencies gotta make rules."[1] More specifically, though, the impetus for a particular rule may come from any of five sources: the legislature, legislators, the agency, executive officials outside the agency, and the people.

First, the agency legislation may require the agency to issue rules. For example, one of the statutes that the EPA administers required the Administrator of EPA by a certain date to issue regulations to reduce exposure to lead-based paint during home renovation and remodeling projects. *See* 15 U.S.C. § 2682(c)(1) (2012) (providing that by a certain date "the Administrator *shall* ... promulgate guidelines for the conduct of such renovation and remodeling activities") (emphasis added). EPA issued updated standards as required by this statute in 2010. *See* 75 Fed. Reg. 24,802 (2010).

Second, individual legislators or legislative committees may pressure an agency to issue rules. An agency will pay attention to a legislator, especially if the legislator is, say, on the committee that reviews the agency's budget request. Besides budget oversight, every agency is subject to substantive oversight by legislative committees, and these committees may

---

1. Apologies to Oscar Hammerstein & Jerome Kern, Can't Help Lovin' That Man (1928).

make "suggestions" for things the agency should do, which may include making rules on matters of concern to the committee. Sometimes you will see these suggestions appear in the records of legislative debates or the reports of legislative committees. Suggestions from individual legislators or legislative committees do not have the legal effect of statutes, and they are not judicially enforceable, but agencies that ignore them may face "grave political consequences." *Lincoln v. Vigil,* 508 U.S. 182, 193 (1993).

Third, officials inside an agency may decide to address a problem by issuing a rule. For example, the Consumer Product Safety Commission has authority to issue consumer product safety standards. In 2011 the Commission decided to use that authority to issue safety standards for firepots (also known as personal fireplaces) and the gel fuels used in them. The Commission took this step because of reports of many injuries and two deaths caused by these products over a fifteen-month period. *See* Office of Communications, U.S. Consumer Product Safety Commission, *CPSC Announces ANPR for Gel Fuels, Firepots to Address Flash Fire, Burn Hazards,* Press Release # 12-059 (Dec. 19, 2011).

Fourth, agencies in the executive branch are subordinate to the chief executive, and sometimes to other agencies, which may impel an agency to issue rules addressing a subject. For example, the President appoints the heads of all cabinet-level agencies, and can generally remove them at will. You can be sure that when the President suggests the need for a rule to one of these appointees, the appointee will take the suggestion very, very seriously. At any one time, it is a good bet that some high-profile instance of regulatory failure will be capturing attention from the news media, in which case there will be contacts between the White House and the responsible agency that are aimed to result in regulatory reform.

Fifth, people are entitled under the federal APA to petition an agency to promulgate a rule. *See* 5 U.S.C. § 553(e) (2012). Many state APAs have similar provisions. *See, e.g.,* Nev. Rev. Stat. Ann. § 233B.100(1) (West, Westlaw through 2011 Reg. Sess.). Such a rulemaking petition, for example, ultimately prompted the U.S. EPA to begin issuing rules limiting new car emissions of carbon dioxide and other pollutants linked to global warming. *See* 75 Fed. Reg. 25,324, 25,327 (2010).

The volume of agency rules is probably increasing over time, and it seems that agency regulation is becoming increasingly pervasive. Whether or not that is a good thing, it is a development that heightens the importance of studying agency rulemaking.

Exercise: Sources of Pressure to Make Rules

Pick an agency, any agency. Then imagine a scenario in which pressure on the agency to make a rule may come from an individual legislator or from the chief executive. You may find inspiration for the scenario in current news media.

D. The Role of Lawyers in Rulemaking

Lawyers participate in many aspects of agency rulemaking. Lawyers may participate as:

- employees of the agency
- representatives of private individuals or private businesses with economic interests

- representatives of private individuals or organizations with non-economic interests, such as environmental protection, electoral reform, the combating of racism, etc.

Lawyers get involved even when a rule is only a twinkle in someone's eye. For example, a lawyer outside the agency may petition the agency, on behalf of a client, to adopt a new rule. A lawyer inside the agency may evaluate a rulemaking petition or advise the agency on its legal authority to adopt a rule. After an agency decides to promulgate a rule (whether in response to a rulemaking petition or another impetus), an agency lawyer usually participates in drafting the rule, often working with other agency officials with subject-matter expertise (e.g., scientific or technical) on the subject of the rule.

Lawyers outside the agencies may monitor certain agencies to learn whether they are considering rules that may affect the lawyers' clients. For example, lawyers working for trade associations, such as the American Petroleum Institute, may use lawyers to watch for and evaluate proposed agency rules that affect the oil and gas industry. Other interest groups, such as AARP, may use lawyers to watch for and evaluate proposed agency rules affecting senior citizens. The lawyers may learn informally of agency plans to promulgate a rule, or they may get that information through government publications, such as the Federal Register or the regulatory agenda that federal agencies must publish semiannually under the Regulatory Flexibility Act, 5 U.S.C. § 602 (2012). The lawyer outside the agency often can serve a client most effectively by consulting with the agency while the agency is merely considering the promulgation of a rule and has not yet started drafting it.

Once the agency has drafted a rule, and publishes it as a proposed rule for public input, lawyers may draft written comments or prepare public hearing testimony on the proposed rule for their clients. Well-supported comments and testimony can shape the content of the final rule in ways that benefit the client. The comments or testimony also may lay groundwork for an eventual, successful, judicial challenge to the rule.

Once the rule becomes final, lawyers may: advise their clients on how to comply with the rule; petition the agency to clarify, modify, or exempt their client from the rule; or bring a lawsuit to challenge the rule. Alternatively, a judicial challenge to the rule might arise when the agency goes to court to enforce its rule against someone and that person challenges the rule's validity as a defense against its enforcement. Lawyers will participate, of course, in any judicial proceeding brought by the agency to enforce its rule or any judicial proceeding brought by someone other than the agency to challenge the rule.

The importance of agency rulemaking and the importance of lawyers in that process make agency rulemaking a worthwhile subject for study in a law school course on administrative law.

E. Roadmap of Part Two

We generally organize the material on rulemaking in this part of the book to discuss (1) the need for an agency to have a valid grant of power to make rules; (2) the need for the agency to obey limits on, and requirements for exercising, its rulemaking power; and (3) the legal effects of a valid, published rule. The more specific breakdown and sequence of chapters is as follows:

Chapter 7 explores the fundamental distinction between legislative and non-legislative rules. You must understand that distinction at the outset because it affects analysis of an agency's rulemaking power and limits on that power.

Chapter 8 explores the subject of rulemaking power. It identifies agency legislation as the usual source of an agency's power. It helps you learn how to identify when the agency legislation grants rulemaking power. Finally, it examines an important constitutional restriction on statutes granting legislative rulemaking power. The restriction is called the delegation doctrine or (interchangeably) the nondelegation doctrine. If a statute violates the delegation doctrine, the statute is invalid and therefore incapable of effectively granting rulemaking power to the agency.

Chapter 9 gives an overview of the potential sources of limits on, or requirements for exercising, agency rulemaking power.

Chapter 10 homes in on the most important source of procedural limits on agency rulemaking power: the applicable (federal or state) APA. Chapter 10 helps you learn how to determine whether the APA applies to a particular agency rulemaking proceeding and, when so, how to analyze the interaction of the APA and the agency legislation. Depending on that interaction, rulemaking under the Federal APA is classified as one of three types (each involving different procedures): informal rulemaking, formal rulemaking, and hybrid rulemaking. Chapter 11 gives an overview of these three types of rulemaking. Chapter 11 also discusses rulemaking under state APAs.

Chapters 12 through 14 examine in more detail informal, formal, and hybrid rulemaking.

Chapter 15 identifies and briefly describes laws in addition to the APA and agency legislation that may impose procedural requirements on agency rulemaking.

Finally, Chapter 16 discusses the legal effects of a valid, published legislative rule.

Professional Development Reflection Questions

Rulemaking is a distinctive power of administrative agencies, and it is one in which government lawyers are intimately involved. By one estimate, 7.5% of lawyers work for government agencies. *See* Law School Admissions Council (LSAC), Thinking About Law School, http://www.lsac.org/jd/think/being-a-lawyer.asp (visited June 3, 2012). Thus, very roughly speaking, if your administrative law course has 50 students, at least three or four of those students on average could end up working for a government agency. You might be one of them.

You may have heard about some of the supposed benefits of working for a government agency, such as the generally more humane working condition compared to the private sector. You may not have heard, however, about some of the distinctive obligations of government attorneys. The purposes of this discussion are to introduce the topic and to encourage you to learn more, if you are considering the possibility of working for an agency.

The distinctive obligations of government attorneys come from several sources. Specifically, statutes may restrict the activities of all government employees, including government attorneys. For example, the federal Hatch Act restricts political activities of federal employees. *See* 5 U.S.C. §§ 7321–7326 (2012). Besides statutes, federal rules prescribe "standards of ethical conduct" for all executive-branch employees. *See* 5 C.F.R. Part 2635 (2012). Individual agencies can supplement these rules. *See, e.g.,* 5 C.F.R. Part 8101 (2012) (supplemental ethical rules for employees of Consumer Product Safety Commission). More to the point, government lawyers are thought by some to have a duty to serve the public interest that lawyers with private-sector clients do not.

The 9/11 terrorist attacks on the United States caused a well-known incident raising the issue of the existence and nature of a government lawyer's duty to the public. After 9/11, lawyers in the U.S. Department of Justice wrote what came to be called the "torture memos." They described legal limits on "enhanced interrogation techniques" that government officials could use on suspected terrorists. One question they raised was whether it is appropriate for a government lawyer to advise government officials what the officials could "get away with," even if that advice counseled immoral activity. One way to put this question is to ask whether the government lawyers had a duty to consider the public interest, and not just their immediate clients' interest.

We relate this incident of the "torture memos" now because it bears on rulemaking: The lawyers who wrote the torture memos provided a legal foundation for rules allowing certain enhanced interrogation techniques such as "waterboarding." Although few agency rules have such a drastic effect on people's lives, many agency rules do have broad effect on the quality of lives of many, many people. For this reason, lawyers for government agencies can have a huge impact on the public.

With this in mind, please consider these questions.

1. Suppose you are an attorney for an environmental agency and are asked to draft a legal justification for a rule that the agency intends to propose and that would relax existing rules designed to protect children from exposure to lead-based paint. Assuming the law would support such a relaxation, do you have an ethical duty to your client to draft the requested justification?

2. Would you do this assignment even if you believed that the relaxation of existing standards disserved the public interest but was supportable under all applicable laws?

Chapter 7

The Distinction between Legislative Rules and Non-Legislative Rules

Overview

This chapter's objectives are to (1) introduce you to the distinction between legislative rules and non-legislative rules; (2) help you understand why the distinction matters; and (3) help you develop a framework for distinguishing between legislative and non-legislative rules.

This exploration of legislative and non-legislative rules comes at this point in Part Two because much of the material in the rest of Part Two is about legislative rules. Specifically, Part Two explores where agencies get the power to make legislative rules, what procedures agencies must follow to make legislative rules, and what is the legal effect of valid legislative rules.

This chapter has seven sections:

A. Why It Matters Whether a Rule Is a Legislative or a Non-Legislative Rule

B. Types of Non-Legislative Rules

C. To Make Legislative Rules, an Agency Needs Statutory Power to Make Legislative Rules

D. How to Tell If a Rule Is a Legislative or a Non-Legislative Rule

E. The Distinction between "Legislative" Rules and "Substantive" Rules

F. Types of Rules Recognized in APAs

G. Chapter 7 Wrap Up and Look Ahead

Chapter Problem

Email

From: Your friend, who is just starting the third year of law school

To: You, a newly licensed lawyer

Friend, I need your advice. As you probably know, to cover law school expenses, I've been getting a Direct PLUS Loan through the U.S. Department of Education. I had credit problems before law school, so to get the loan I needed a co-signer. Fortunately, my mother qualified to be a co-signor and she did co-sign for my loan. That worked fine for the first two years of law school.

But now the Department of Education won't give me a loan to cover my third year of law school. They say my mother no longer qualifies to co-sign for me, because *her* credit history disqualifies her from being a co-signor. Her credit history hasn't changed. What's changed is the way the Department of Education interprets its regulations.

A Department of Education regulation says a person can't be a co-signor if that person has any debts that are more than ninety days delinquent. My mother had a couple of old debts that were turned over to collection agencies. The Department of Education calls these "collection accounts." Up until now, her having these collection accounts did not disqualify her from being a co-signor under the regulation, because she was keeping up with her payments on those collection accounts.

Two months ago, though, the Department of Education decided to change the way it interprets the regulation. It now interprets the regulation to treat all collection accounts as reflecting debts that are more than ninety days delinquent. This means it doesn't matter that my mom is making regular payments on the collection accounts. Until she's paid off all the collection accounts entirely, she won't qualify to co-sign for me under the new interpretation.

I found out about this new interpretation of the regulation through an email from somebody at the Department of Education. They gave me citations to the regulation that they have reinterpreted. Under the regulation, my mom has been considered a "Parent PLUS borrower." Here is the part of the regulation that defines the eligibility of a Parent PLUS borrower:

Code of Federal Regulations, volume 34, § 685.200 Borrower eligibility …

(c) Parent PLUS borrower.

(1) A parent is eligible to receive a Direct PLUS Loan if the parent meets the following requirements: …

(vii)(A) The parent —

(1) Does not have an adverse credit history;

(2) Has an adverse credit history but has obtained an endorser who does not have an adverse credit history; or

(3) Has an adverse credit history but documents to the satisfaction of the Secretary that extenuating circumstances exist.

(B) For purposes of paragraph (c)(1)(vii)(A) of this section, an adverse credit history means that as of the date of the credit report, the applicant —

(1) Is 90 or more days delinquent on any debt …

I don't have anyone except my mom who can co-sign for my third year Direct PLUS Loan, and she doesn't have anyone who can co-sign for her (so the option in (c)(1)(vii)(A)(2) is not available to her).

I guess at this point my main questions are: How can they do this? And, what can I do about it? I mean, I understand the logic behind their new interpretation of the regulation, but is this interpretation now written in stone? Is this interpretation now "the law"? Don't they understand that I was counting on being able to use my mom as a co-signor to get money for my last year of law school?

I know that you took the administrative law course in law school. (I was planning to take it this year, if I get a chance!) I'd greatly appreciate any advice you can give me!

A. Why It Matters Whether a Rule Is a Legislative or a Non-Legislative Rule

1. Legislative Rules Have the Force and Effect of Law

An administrative lawyer must be able to distinguish legislative rules from non-legislative rules primarily because legislative rules have "the force and effect of law." *Chrysler Corp. v. Brown*, 441 U.S. 281, 295 (1979) (internal quotation marks omitted). Non-legislative rules do not.

A legislative rule has the force and effect of law in the sense that it operates like a statute—i.e., like legislation. *See Az. Grocery Co. v. Atchison, Topeka & Santa Fe Ry.*, 284 U.S. 370, 386 (1932) (agency with rulemaking power "speaks as the legislature, and its pronouncement has the force of a statute"). Like a statute, a legislative rule can create legally enforceable rights and duties for members of the public and the agency itself.

a. A Legislative Rule Binds Members of the Public

For members of the public, legislative rules can create legal duties and rights. To violate a legislative rule that prohibits certain conduct is like violating a statute. It can subject the violator to legislatively prescribed penalties, including imprisonment. By the same token, satisfying a legislative rule that prescribes criteria for a license or federal benefit—such as payments under the federal Medicare or Medicaid programs—may create a valuable entitlement.

An example may help. Suppose Congress enacted this hypothetical statute:

---

51 U.S.C. § 101. Inattentive driving in national parks

(a) Inattentive driving in a national park is prohibited.

(b) The Director of the National Park Service shall promulgate such rules as are necessary or appropriate to enforce subsection (a).

(c) A violation of subsection (a) or any rules promulgated under subsection (b) is punishable by a civil fine of up to $5,000, which the Secretary may recover in an action in a federal district court.

Subsection (a) is a substantive command—a "thou shalt not"—directed to the public. Subsection (b) will be construed as a grant of power to the Secretary to make legislative rules to implement subsection (a). Subsection (c) reflects Congress's power, when it grants an agency the power to make legislative rules that regulate people's conduct, to fix penalties for violations of those rules. *See United States v. Grimaud*, 220 U.S. 506 (1911) (upholding criminal conviction of defendants for grazing sheep on federal land in violation of Secretary of Agriculture's legislative rule; Court holds that Congress may empower an agency to issue regulations the violation of which carry criminal penalties, as long as Congress prescribes the penalties itself).

Now suppose that the Director of the Park Service uses the authority granted in subsection (b) of the above statute to issue the following, hypothetical legislative rule, which is published in the Code of Federal Regulations (C.F.R.):

---

51 C.F.R. § 201.01. Cell phone use while driving in national parks

Using a cell phone while driving in a national park is prohibited.

By promulgating this rule, the Secretary has used legislative rulemaking power for a typical purpose: to create a new standard of conduct. The new standard specifically targets cell phone use while driving. A particularized standard of conduct like this is easier to enforce than the vaguer, statutory standard of "inattentive driving."

This is a perfectly proper way for an agency to use legislative rulemaking power to implement a statute. Indeed, Congress often gives agencies power to make legislative rules so that the agency can devise detailed standards of conduct to implement a broad substantive command (here, the ban on inattentive driving). This is why the rule barring cell phone use is not objectionable merely because the statute itself does not mention cell phone use. Legislative rules can do more than merely parrot the statutory provision that they are designed to implement.

Now assume that, with this legislative rule on the books, the Director of the Park Service files an action in federal court seeking a fine against Amber for violating this rule. In that proceeding, the only arguments that Amber can raise to avoid liability are (1) she did not violate the rule; or (2) the rule is invalid. Importantly, Amber cannot avoid liability by persuading the judge that, although she may have violated the *rule*, she did not violate the underlying *statute*, because she was paying attention to her driving. Even if she was driving attentively, that does not matter. She still violated a legislative rule. The judge must follow the rule if it is valid, just as must Amber. And the rule is not invalid merely because one can argue that people like Amber can pay attention to driving while using a cell phone. A valid legislative rule stands in for the statute, in the sense that the rule, rather than the statute, supplies the standard of conduct for determining liability. It creates a new, discrete legal duty.

More generally, if your client violates a legislative rule, you can avoid whatever penalties the legislature has fixed for that violation by arguing that (1) your client did not violate the rule; or (2) the rule is invalid. (You will learn much more in this Part of the book about analyzing the validity of a legislative rule.) You cannot avoid the penalty, however, by arguing that your client did not violate the underlying statute. This does not matter because the rule, if valid, has "the force and effect of law." *Chrysler Corp. v. Brown*, 441 U.S. at 295 (internal quotation marks omitted).

b. A Legislative Rule Binds the Agency

A legislative rule binds not only the public but also the agency that makes it. Thus, when an agency makes a rule that limits the agency's discretion, the agency must follow the rule as long as it is in effect, just as the agency must obey a statute. If the agency does not want to follow its rule anymore, the agency must first change or repeal the rule. The agency usually must follow certain procedures to change or repeal a legislative rule; these procedures include giving members of the public a chance to give input on the proposed change or repeal. The agency cannot change or repeal a rule simply by deciding, in a particular case, not to follow the rule.

Perhaps the most famous case illustrating the principle that an agency must obey its legislative rules involved President Richard Nixon. *United States v. Nixon*, 418 U.S. 683 (1974). The U.S. Attorney General adopted regulations (legislative rules) for appointing a special prosecutor. Under these regulations the Attorney General appointed a special prosecutor to investigate the Watergate break-in. (For background on the break-in, see History.com, *Watergate Scandal*, http://www.history.com/topics/ Watergate (last visited June 3, 2012).) The special prosecutor, using power granted by the regulations, arranged for the issuance of a subpoena requiring President Nixon to turn over certain tape recordings. The President refused to turn over those tapes, invoking "executive privilege." The special prosecutor, again using power granted by one of the regulations, took President Nixon to court, seeking enforcement of the subpoena. President Nixon argued that he alone had the power to decide whether to turn over the tapes; the special prosecutor could not contest the President's claim of executive privilege, and the court could not hear the special prosecutor's request to enforce the subpoena. *United States v. Nixon*, 418 U.S. 683, 686–695 (1974).

The U.S. Supreme Court rejected President Nixon's argument and upheld the subpoena. Of the regulation authorizing the special prosecutor to enforce the subpoena, the Court said:

> So long as this regulation is extant it has the force of law.... [I]t is theoretically possible for the Attorney General to amend or revoke the regulation defining the Special Prosecutor's authority. But he has not done so. So long as this regulation remains in force the Executive Branch is bound by it, and indeed the United States as the sovereign composed of the three branches is bound to respect and to enforce it.

Id. at 695–696. This statement not only affirms the obligation of executive-branch agencies and officials to follow valid legislative rules but also recognizes the power of the judicial branch to compel executive obedience to legislative rules.

Now you know why agency power to make legislative rules is such a big deal, and worth close attention in the study of administrative law.

Exercise: Challenging the Application and Validity of Legislative Rules

The purpose of this exercise is to get you thinking about ways to challenge a legislative rule.

Suppose your client Amanda was charged with violating the Park Service rule, 51 C.F.R. § 201.01, and that the Park Service Ranger who cited her testified that he (the ranger) saw Amanda holding a cell phone while driving and that she had just entered the park.

Recall that, in a court enforcement proceeding, a person can ordinarily avoid liability for violating a legislative rule only by showing that (1) the person did not, in fact, violate the rule; or (2) the rule is invalid.

1. First, imagine factual scenarios under which a creative, zealous lawyer might be able to argue that, even if Amanda were holding a cell phone when the ranger saw her, she did not violate the rule.

2. Second, why is it important to know the procedures used by the Park Service to adopt the rule?

---

2. Other Differences between Legislative and Non-Legislative Rules

In addition to having the force and effect of law, legislative rules generally differ from non-legislative rules in four ways:

a. Different Procedures for Making

To make a legislative rule, the agency usually must follow certain legally required procedures. Those procedures typically include publishing a proposed rule for public input, and considering that input when finalizing the proposed rule. Agencies usually need not follow these notice-and-comment procedures to make non-legislative rules. Because the procedural requirements for legislative rules usually differ from the procedural requirements for non-legislative rules, you must determine whether a particular rule is a legislative rule or a non-legislative rule before you can analyze whether the agency followed the required procedures when making it.

b. Different Codification Requirements

Because they "make law," agencies' legislative rules are permanently and officially codified. Agencies' non-legislative rules often need not be so codified. For example, the legislative rules of federal agencies are permanently codified in the Code of Federal Regulations (CFR), which is organized by subject matter, updated annually, and has a comprehensive index. In contrast, the non-legislative rules of federal agencies have to be published in the Federal Register, but they don't have to be codified in the CFR. Because non-legislative rules don't have to be codified permanently in the CFR, they can be hard to find. The Federal Register is a chronological record that can be hard to search for relevant non-legislative rules.

c. Different Constitutional Implications

The U.S. Constitution and many state constitutions restrict the ability of legislatures to authorize executive-branch agencies to make legislative rules. This constitutional restriction is called the "delegation" or "nondelegation" doctrine. The nondelegation doctrine does not apply when a legislature authorizes an agency to make non-legislative rules. That is because, when an agency makes a non-legislative rule, the agency is not exercising a legislative, or even a "quasi-legislative," power. Instead, when an agency makes a non-legislative rule, the agency is considered to be exercising an *executive* power.

d. Different Scope of Federal Judicial Review

When an agency issues a rule to implement a statute, the agency often must interpret the statute. This is true whether the rule is a legislative or a non-legislative rule. For example, the National Park Service in the hypothetical situation discussed above had to interpret the statutory term "inattentive driving." One way to challenge an agency rule successfully in court is to argue that the rule rests on a misinterpretation of the statute that the rule is supposed to implement.

When a federal court reviews a federal agency's rule to determine whether the rule rests on a proper interpretation of a statute that the agency is responsible for administering, the court usually gives weight to the agency's interpretation. But here's the important thing to know about this "weight" right now: The amount of weight usually depends on whether the rule is a legislative rule or a non-legislative rule. Agency interpretations embodied in legislative rules typically get greater weight — the term of art is "deference" — than do interpretations embodied in non-legislative rules. We explore the differing levels of deference when we discuss judicial review in Chapter 32. We raise the issue now to identify an important difference between legislative rules and non-legislative rules.

Exercise: Differences between Legislative and Non-Legislative Rules

This exercise is meant to help you check your understanding of, and to remember, the differences between legislative rules and non-legislative rules.

1. In your own words, what do we mean when we say that legislative rules have "the force and effect of law"?

2. List three other ways in which legislative rules generally differ from non-legislative rules.

(1) _____

(2) _____

(3) _____

B. Types of Non-Legislative Rules

Non-legislative rules do not have the force and effect of law, and an agency generally has the power to adopt them without an express grant of statutory authority. An agency's power to make non-legislative rules inheres in the agency's responsibility for administering certain laws. You might say that the power of an executive-branch agency to make non-legislative rules comes with the territory. Indeed, although non-legislative rules lack the force and effect of law, they are often indispensable to an agency accomplishing its legislative mission.

There are two main types of non-legislative rules. The federal APA identifies them as:

(1) "**interpretative rules**" and

(2) "**general statements of policy.**"

5 U.S.C. § 553(b)(A) (2012). Some state APAs use similar terminology. *See, e.g.,* Ga. Code Ann. § 50-13-4(a) (LexisNexis 2012) (prescribing procedures for "the adoption, amendment, or repeal of any rule, other than interpretive rules or general statements of policy"). These are formal names; an agency may or may not use them. Indeed, non-legislative rules may go by many different names and may take various forms, including press releases, circulars, brochures, manuals, guidance documents, handbooks, policy statements, agency letters to affected members of the public, and FAQs. The 2010 Model State APA uses the term "guidance document" as a collective term for these non-legislative agency pronouncements:

2010 Model State APA § 102. Definitions ...

(14) "Guidance document" means a record of general applicability developed by an agency which lacks the force of law but states the agency's current approach to, or interpretation of, law, or describes how and when the agency will exercise discretionary functions....

You will now get an introduction to each type of non-legislative rule (guidance document).

1. Interpretative (Also Known as "Interpretive") Rules

Sometimes an agency does not want to make rules with the force and effect of law—or, indeed, lacks the statutory power to do so—but nonetheless wants to advise the public or its own employees how it interprets a statute or legislative rule that it is charged with administering. In that situation, the agency may issue what the federal APA calls an "interpretative" rule, and what many people (impatient of the extra syllable) call an "interpretive" rule. 5 U.S.C. § 553(b)(A). An interpretative (or interpretive) rule is "issued by an agency to advise the public of the agency's construction of the statutes and rules which it administers." *Shalala v. Guernsey Mem'l Hosp.*, 514 U.S. 87, 99 (1995) (quoting AGM 30 n.3). Whereas a legislative rule may create new legal duties, an interpretative rule merely "reminds affected parties of existing duties." *General Motors Corp. v. Ruckelshaus*, 742 F.2d 1561, 1565 (D.C. Cir. 1984) (internal quotation marks omitted).

An agency can issue interpretative rules not only to show how it interprets its statutes but also to clarify the agency's own legislative rules. The latter use of interpretative rules is legitimate and useful. When an agency issues a legislative rule, the agency cannot foresee all of the questions that may arise about how the rule applies in particular settings. After experience applying its legislative rule, the agency may wish to publicize how it interprets the rule, both to benefit the public and to ensure that all agency personnel are on the same page. In this situation, the agency may issue an interpretative rule to give the agency's official gloss on its legislative rule.

We can use the hypothetical "inattentive driving" statute discussed above to illustrate what it means to say that interpretative rules lack the force and effect of law. Here is the hypothetical statute again:

---

51 U.S.C. § 101. Inattentive driving in national parks

(a) Inattentive driving in a national park is prohibited.

(b) The Director of the National Park Service shall promulgate such rules as are necessary or appropriate to enforce subsection (a).

(c) A violation of subsection (a) or any rules promulgated under subsection (b) is punishable by a civil fine of up to $5,000, which the Secretary may recover in an action in a federal district court.

Suppose that the Park Service concludes that a driver's use of a cell phone cannot help but cause the driver to drive inattentively. The Park Service may decide to announce this conclusion as an interpretative rule, rather than as a legislative rule. After all, an agency with the power to make legislative rules does not have to exercise that power; it can choose instead to proceed by interpretative rule. The Park Service's hypothetical interpretative rule could look much like the hypothetical legislative rule discussed above, and the Park Service can even choose to publish this rule in the CFR (even though it's not required to):

---

51 C.F.R. § 201.01. Cell phone use while driving in national parks

Using a cell phone while driving in a national park will be deemed to be inattentive driving, which is prohibited.

Now when the Park Service goes to court to recover a fine from Amber for using a cell phone while driving in a national park, her liability will depend on whether she is found to have violated the statute prohibiting inattentive driving. Thus, it will be open to her to argue that, even though she was using a cell phone while driving, she was being attentive to her driving and therefore should not be fined. If the judge decides that Amber was not "inattentive" within the meaning of the statute, the judge cannot fine her, despite her acting inconsistently with the interpretative rule.

It is not accurate to say that Amber "violated" the interpretative rule because that rule is not law. The only thing she can violate is the statute, and a violation of the statute is therefore what the Park Service must prove in court to establish her liability.

Unfortunately for Amber, the judge may give weight to the Park Service's interpretative rule when deciding whether her conduct violated the statute. After all, Congress made the Park Service responsible for administering this statute, and the Park Service has developed experience in how best to enforce it. As a result, the Park Service's interpretation of its statute will carry more weight than Amber's or her lawyer's interpretation.

More generally, although interpretative rules are not law, one takes several risks by "violating" them. First, the agency will usually follow its interpretative rule, which means it will treat the "violator" as a law breaker. For example, the agency may initiate enforcement action against those who transgress the agency's interpretive rule. Second, although a court reviewing the enforcement action will not equate an interpretative rule to "the law," it will usually give the rule respect when the court determines what the law (the underlying statute) really means. Third, judicially challenging an interpretative rule does not earn the agency's good will, and that good will may be important to a company or person who has an ongoing relationship with the agency. For these reasons, the lawyer counseling a company or client about an interpretative rule may decide that the wisest course is to treat the interpretative rule as if it were a legislative rule, by simply obeying it.

Nonetheless, because interpretative rules lack the force and effect of law, when promulgated by federal agencies they are exempt from the federal APA's procedures requiring public input on rules in their proposed form. See 5 U.S.C. § 553(b)(A). For the same reason, some state APAs exempt interpretative rules from the rulemaking procedures required for legislative rules. *See, e.g.*, Wash. Rev. Code Ann. § 34.05.010(16) (LexisNexis 2012) (defining "interpretive statements" separately from "rules," only latter of which are subject to state APA rulemaking procedures); N.C. Gen. Stat. Ann. § 150B-2(8a)(c)

(LexisNexis 2012) (APA defines "rule" to exclude "[n]onbinding interpretative statements"). Even APAs that exempt interpretive rules from their rulemaking procedures still require agencies to publish their interpretive rules for the guidance of the public. For example, federal agencies must publish their interpretative rules in the federal government's official, daily publication of regulatory activity, the Federal Register. *See, e.g.*, 5 U.S.C. § 552(a)(1)(D).

2. General Statements of Policy

In addition to including interpretative rules, the class of non-legislative rules includes what the federal APA calls **"general statements of policy,"** and what are more commonly called, simply, "agency policy statements." *See* 5 U.S.C. § 553(b)(A). The Attorney General's Manual on the APA defined agency policy statements as "statements issued by an agency to advise the public prospectively of the manner in which the agency proposes to exercise a discretionary power." AGM 30 n.3. Similarly, the 2010 Model State APA defines "guidance document" to include agency statements of "how and when the agency will exercise discretionary functions." 2010 Model State APA § 102(1). The federal APA definition usefully links the concept of agency *policy* making to agency exercise of *discretion*.

Whereas interpretative rules explain what the agency thinks a statute or legislative rule means, general statements of policy describe how the agency intends to enforce its statutes and rules, or how it intends to exercise its other statutorily granted powers or duties. Agencies often have much discretion about how and when to enforce the laws that they are responsible for administering, and how and when to exercise their other statutorily assigned powers and duties. Policy statements inform the public (and the agency officials) how the agency will exercise its discretion in these matters.

For example, let us return to the hypothetical federal statute described above banning "inattentive driving" in national parks. The Park Service may decide to devote more resources to enforcing that statute at times of the year when many people are using the national parks, such as Memorial Day and the Fourth of July. After all, the high traffic volume at these times of the year makes inattentive driving in national parks particularly dangerous at these times. Stepped-up enforcement efforts make sense given the invariably limited resources that the Park Service has to carry out its many statutory duties.

It also makes sense for the Park Service to notify the public, as well as its own employees, of the agency policy of enforcing the statute particularly aggressively during summer holidays. The mere announcement of that policy could encourage more attentive driving. Plus, it may diminish the feelings of surprise and unfairness that folks might otherwise experience when they are caught. Accordingly, the Park Service may try to get the word out broadly by issuing a press release, publishing it on the Park Service website, and announcing it in public service advertisements. This shows that non-legislative rules can take many forms and go by different names. In any event, the public benefits when an agency publicizes its enforcement policies, just as the public benefits from the agency's publication of interpretative rules.

The Park Service's enforcement policy is one example of a "general statement of policy." The policy does not focus on interpreting the inattentive-driving statute; rather, it alerts the public to how the agency plans to enforce the statute.

Like a federal agency's interpretative rules, a federal agency's policy statements are generally exempt from the federal APA's notice-and-comment requirements for rulemaking, *see* 5 U.S.C. § 553(b)(A), and usually a federal agency's statutes will impose no procedural requirements for their adoption. To put a policy statement into effect, a federal agency usually just has to publish it in the Federal Register. *See* 5 U.S.C. § 552(a)(1). Because a federal agency can issue policy statements without going through the notice-and-comment procedures, an agency may have an incentive to attach the label "general statement of policy" to an agency pronouncement that, a court will later decide, is really a legislative rule that should have gone through those procedures. We leave for Chapter 10.C an exploration of these situations, which involve agency actions that straddle the line between general statements of policy, on the one hand, and legislative rules, on the other hand.

C. To Make Legislative Rules, an Agency Needs Statutory Power to Make Legislative Rules

Agencies have no inherent powers. For an agency to make legislative rules, the agency must have the power to make legislative rules. Because agencies are creatures of statute, agencies with the power to make legislative rules usually get that power from a statute. Usually, the statute is specific to that agency; it is what we have been calling "the agency legislation." For simplicity's sake, from here on out we will assume that an agency's power to make legislative rules, if any such power exists, will come from the agency legislation.

A statute that grants an agency power to make legislative rules is a grant of legislative, or at least "quasi-legislative," power. Graphically, it can be depicted as shown in Diagram 7-1.

Diagram 7-1. Statutory Delegation of Quasi-Legislative Power

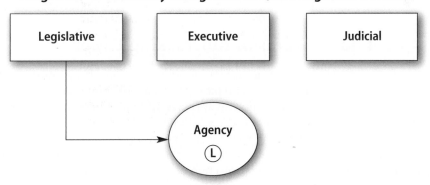

If the agency legislation does not grant the agency power to make legislative rules, the agency will almost always have other ways of carrying out its statutory responsibilities. For example, the agency can issue non-legislative rules to advise the public of how the agency interprets its legislation and how it intends to carry out its responsibilities under the agency legislation. An agency's power to issue non-legislative rules is considered an executive power. Graphically, the power can be depicted as shown in Diagram 7-2.

Diagram 7-2. Statutory Delegation of Executive Power

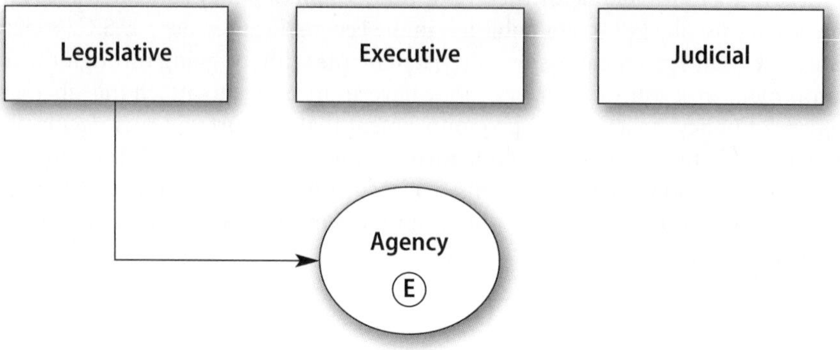

Legislative   Executive   Judicial

Agency
(E)

By now you may be wondering how to tell if the agency legislation grants power to make legislative rules. The answer is that any provision in the agency legislation authorizing an agency to make—or "issue" or "adopt" or "prescribe" or "promulgate"—"rules," "regulations," "criteria," "guidelines," or "standards" will probably be interpreted to authorize the agency to make legislative rules. To be so interpreted, the statutory provision need not use the term "legislative rule." Indeed, you will seldom if ever see the term "legislative rule" used in statutes that grant agencies the power to make legislative rules.

Even so, some statutory provisions are clearer than others in expressing the legislature's intention about whether to grant an agency the power to make legislative rules. We will first discuss how the federal courts have approached the vaguely worded, open-ended grants of rulemaking power found in so many federal statutes (and for that matter, in many state statutes). Then we will show you two kinds of statutory grants of rulemaking power that in administrative law circles are considered clearly to express the legislature's intent to authorize agencies to make legislative rules.

1. Open-Ended Grants of Rulemaking Power

Many federal agencies have agency legislation with provisions that grant rulemaking power in broad, open-ended terms. A typical provision will empower the agency "to promulgate all such rules and regulations as are necessary and appropriate" to administer the agency legislation. *See, e.g.,* 19 U.S.C. § 2612 (2012) (authorizing Secretary of the Treasury to "prescribe such rules and regulations as are necessary and appropriate to carry out the provisions of this chapter," with "this chapter" referring to federal statute implementing U.N. Convention on protection of cultural property); 30 U.S.C. § 189 (2012) (authorizing Secretary of Interior to "prescribe necessary and proper rules and regulations ... to carry out and accomplish the purposes" of the federal statute about mining on federally owned land); 47 U.S.C. § 201(b) (2012) (authorizing FCC to "prescribe such rules and regulations as may be necessary in the public interest to carry out the provisions of this chapter," with "this chapter" referring to the Communications Act of 1934). Federal courts consistently construe such open-ended grants of rulemaking power to give agencies the power to make legislative rules.

Consider the National Labor Relations Board's grant of rulemaking power, which is in the National Labor Relations Act:

29 U.S.C. § 156. Rules and regulations

The Board shall have authority from time to time to make, amend, and rescind, in the manner prescribed by subchapter II of chapter 5 of Title 5, such rules and regulations as may be necessary to carry out the provisions of this subchapter.

The U.S. Supreme Court construed this provision to authorize the Board to promulgate a legislative rule about collective bargaining by employees of acute care hospitals. *American Hosp. Ass'n v. NLRB*, 499 U.S. 606 (1991). The U.S. Supreme Court has interpreted similarly worded provisions in other federal agency legislation as grants of power to make legislative rules. *See Mourning v. Family Publ'ns Serv., Inc.*, 411 U.S. 356, 369 (1973); *see also AT&T Corp. v. Iowa Utils. Bd.*, 525 U.S. 366 (1999) (construing 47 U.S.C. § 201(b), which was quoted above, to authorize FCC to promulgate legislative rules).

Lower federal courts likewise interpret open-ended grants of rulemaking power like the NLRB's to authorize legislative rulemaking. A famous example is *National Petroleum Refiners Ass'n v. FTC*, 482 F.2d 672 (D.C. Cir. 1973). A provision in the Federal Trade Commission Act authorized the FTC to "make rules and regulations for the purpose of carrying out" specified provisions of the Act. One of the specified provisions outlawed "unfair or deceptive" trade practices. The FTC relied on these statutory provisions to promulgate what the court described as "substantive rules of business conduct." *Id.* at 673. One such rule required gas stations to display the octane ratings of gas on their gas pumps. As the court explained, this rule and ones like it had the force and effect of law:

> Once promulgated, the rules would be used by the agency in adjudicatory proceedings aimed at producing cease and desist orders against violations of the statutory standard [prohibiting "unfair or deceptive" trade practices]. The central question in such adjudicatory proceedings would be whether the particular defendant's conduct violated the rule in question.

Id. at 673. This explanation reflected the ability of the FTC's rules, as legislative rules, to supplant the underlying statute in an enforcement proceeding. Proof of a rule violation would establish a statutory violation.

The petroleum refiners argued that the octane rating rule exceeded the FTC's rulemaking authority. The refiners contended that the FTC's rulemaking power, which we quoted above, was limited to making non-substantive, non-legislative rules on procedural matters. The court rejected that argument in favor of a "libera[l]" interpretation of the FTC's statutory grant of rulemaking power. *Id.* at 678. Federal court cases since *National Petroleum Refiners* have taken a similar approach, by interpreting open-ended grants of rulemaking authority to confer the power to make substantive, legislative rules.

Two administrative law scholars have argued that *National Petroleum Refiners* was wrong to read the FTC's vaguely worded, open-ended statute to grant power to make legislative rules. These scholars argue that until recently Congress used a convention to express its intention to grant legislative rulemaking power, and that Congress did not use this convention in the statute at issue in *National Petroleum Refiners*. Under that supposed convention, "rulemaking grants coupled with a statutory provision imposing sanctions on those who violate the rules were understood to authorize rules with the force of law; rulemaking grants not coupled with any provision for sanctions were understood to authorize only interpretive and procedural rules." Thomas W. Merrill & Kathryn Tongue Watts, *Agency Rules with the Force of Law: The Original Convention*, 116 Harv. L. Rev. 467, 469 (2002). Professors Merrill and Watts recognize, however, that the Supreme Court and lower federal courts have ignored this convention in favor of one that generally treats vaguely worded, open-ended grants of rulemaking power as grants of power to make legislative rules. *See id.* at 472–473.

States do not have to take the same approach as the federal courts have taken to open-ended statutory grants of rulemaking power in agency legislation. Accordingly, the lawyer must be careful when analyzing a state statutory provision with an open-ended grant of rulemaking power. Specifically, the lawyer should do research to confirm that the provision under analysis has been construed to grant legislative rulemaking power. If the lawyer finds no case law directly on point, the lawyer must study state court case law interpreting other open-ended grants of rulemaking power. A State's courts may choose not to adopt the federal courts' liberal approach to interpreting such open-ended grants.

Exercise: The Stakes of Establishing the Legislative or Non-Legislative Status of a Rule

In *National Petroleum Refiners Ass'n v. FTC*, why did the petroleum refiners care whether the octane rating rule was legislative or non-legislative?

---

2. Statutory Grants of Power to Make Rules That, If Violated, Expose the Violator to Statutorily Authorized Sanctions

When the agency legislation grants the agency power to make rules and also makes violations of those rules unlawful, the grant of rulemaking power will always be construed to be a grant of power to make *legislative* rules. The "classic legislative rule" is a rule "the violation of which would, without more, establish violation of the [underlying] statute in a subsequent enforcement proceeding." *Alaska v. U.S. Dep't of Transp.*, 868 F.2d 441, 446 (D.C. Cir. 1989).

For example, the hypothetical federal statute reproduced earlier in this chapter grants rulemaking power and exposes those who violate those rules to specified sanctions:

---

51 U.S.C. § 101. Inattentive driving in national parks

(a) Inattentive driving in a national park is prohibited.

(b) The Director of the National Park Service shall promulgate such rules as are necessary or appropriate to enforce subsection (a).

(c) A violation of subsection (a) or any rules promulgated under subsection (b) is punishable by a civil fine of up to $5,000, which the Secretary may recover in an action in a federal district court.

This hypothetical agency statute shows a clear intention to grant legislative rulemaking power because it combines the grant of rulemaking power with penalties for violations of the resulting rules. Because a person cannot "violate" a non-legislative rule, a statute prescribing penalties for violations of rules necessarily implies that those rules are legislative rules.

An actual statute illustrating this combination comes from this provision in the Clean Water Act authorizing EPA to establish standards of performance for new sources of water pollution:

---

33 U.S.C. § 1316. National standards of performance ...

(b) (1) ...

(B) As soon as practicable ... the Administrator [of EPA] shall propose and publish regulations establishing Federal standards of performance for new sources ...

(e) ... After the effective date of standards of performance promulgated under this section, it shall be unlawful for any owner or operate of any new source to operate such source in violation of any standard of performance applicable to such source.

(Other provisions specify the penalties for violations of the performance standards. *See id.* § 1319.) Because this statute makes it unlawful to violate the rules establishing performance standards, it is clear that the rules will be legislative rules: Violations of the rules are tantamount to violations of the statute itself. Thus, the rules have the force and effect of law, which is the defining feature of legislative rules. Section 1316(b)(1)(B) is therefore a grant of legislative rulemaking power.

3. Statutory Grants of Power to Make Rules Necessary to Complete the Statutory Scheme

Sometimes agency legislation cannot fully operate until the agency exercises the rulemaking power granted by the legislation. This is another situation in which legislative intent to authorize legislative rules will be regarded as clear.

Here, for example, is a provision in the Securities Exchange Act of 1934 that grants rulemaking power to the Securities and Exchange Commission in connection with proxies:

---

15 U.S.C. § 78n. Proxies ...

(b) Giving or refraining from giving proxy in respect of any security carried for account of customer

(1) It shall be unlawful for any member of a national securities exchange, or any broker or dealer registered under this chapter, or any bank, association, or other entity that exercises fiduciary powers, in contravention of such rules and regulations as the Commission may prescribe as necessary or appropriate in the public interest or for the protection of investors, to give, or to refrain from giving a proxy ... in respect of any security registered pursuant to section 78*l* of this title, or any security issued by an investment company registered under the Investment Company Act of 1940 [15 U.S.C.A. § 80a-1 et seq.], and carried for the account of a customer....

You need not understand proxies to appreciate the significance of this statutory provision for administrative law purposes. The important thing to understand is that this provision forbids nothing *except* acts or omissions "in contravention of" the Commission's "rules and regulations." In effect, the statute issues a "thou shalt not _____" and lets the agency fill in the blank. This situation, in which a statutory provision cannot operate until the agency exercises the rulemaking power connected with the provision, is a sure sign of legislative intent to give the agency the power to make legislative rules. *See Am. Mining Cong. v. Mine Safety & Health Admin.*, 995 F.2d 1106, 1109 (D.C. Cir. 1993).

An analogous situation arises in agency legislation involving government loans, grants, and other types of benefits. Sometimes, Congress includes in the legislation provisions empowering the agency to make rules establishing eligibility for those benefits. An example is this federal statute administered by the Secretary of Health and Human Services:

---

42 U.S.C. § 5318. Urban development action grants ...

(b) Eligibility of cities and urban counties; criteria and standards; regulations

(1) Urban development action grants shall be made only to cities and urban counties which have ... demonstrated results in providing housing for low- and moderate-income persons and in providing equal opportunity in housing and employment for low- and moderate-income persons and members of minority groups. The Secretary shall issue regulations establishing criteria in accordance with the preceding sentence and setting forth minimum standards for determining the level of economic distress of cities and urban counties for eligibility for such grants. These standards shall take into account factors such as the age of housing; the extent of poverty; the extent of population lag; growth of per capita income; and the extent of unemployment, job lag, or surplus labor....

Grants under this statute cannot be made until the Secretary establishes "minimum standards" of "economic distress" for "eligibility for such grants." We say in administrative law circles that the rules establishing those standards are necessary to "fill a statutory gap" or, put another way, to "complete the statutory scheme." When the agency legislation authorizes rules to serve this purpose, the legislation is clearly authorizing legislative rules.

4. Summary

An agency can make legislative rules only if it has statutory power to do so. Federal statutory grants of rulemaking power that are vaguely but broadly worded—so as to give the agency, for example, power to make all rules "necessary for proper administration" of a statute—are consistently construed by the federal courts to authorize legislative rules. Besides that situation, a statute clearly authorizes legislative rules (1) when violation of the rules trigger statutorily authorized sanctions or (2) when the rules are necessary to complete a statutory scheme.

Exercise: Determining Whether Agency Legislation Grants Power to Make Legislative Rules

Determine whether these two statutes authorize an agency to make legislative rules.

33 U.S.C. § 499. Regulations for drawbridges

(a) Criminal penalties for violations; enforcement; rules and regulations
It shall be the duty of all persons owning, operating, and tending the drawbridges built prior to August 18, 1894, or which may thereafter be built across the navigable rivers and other waters of the United States, to open, or cause to be opened, the draws of such bridges under such rules and regulations as in the opinion of the Secretary of Transportation the public interests require to govern the opening of drawbridges for the passage of vessels and other water crafts. and such rules and regulations, when so made and published, shall have the force of law. Every such person who shall willfully fail or refuse to open, or cause to be opened, the draw of any such bridge for the passage of a boat or boats, as provided in such regulations, shall be deemed guilty of a misdemeanor, and on conviction thereof shall be punished by a fine of not more than $2,000 nor less than $1,000, or by imprisonment (in the case of a natural person) for not exceeding one year, or by both such fine and imprisonment, in the discretion of the court....

The next provision comes from the Hawaii Ocean and Submerged Lands Leasing Act. The Act authorizes the Board of Land and Natural Resources to lease state marine lands.

Hawai'i Revised Stat. Ann. § 190D-32. Rules

The board may adopt such rules as are necessary and appropriate to carry out the purposes and provisions of this chapter. The adoption of these rules shall be in accordance with [the Hawai'i Administrative Procedure Act].

No provision authorizes sanctions for rules adopted under this Hawai'i law.

D. How to Tell If a Rule Is a Legislative or a Non-Legislative Rule

In theory, the distinction between legislative rules and non-legislative rules is clear. In practice, too, it usually is easy to identify legislative rules: A rule will be a legislative rule if the agency has power to make legislative rules and has followed the required procedures for making them when it made the rule in question. If the agency lacks power to make legislative rules, or if it has the power but did not follow the required procedures for making legislative rules when it made the rule in question, the rule is valid, if at all, only as a non-legislative rule.

Sometimes, though, it is hard to determine whether a particular rule is a legislative or a non-legislative rule. Just because the agency has power to make legislative rules, that does not mean that every rule the agency issues is a legislative rule. The agency might decide in a particular situation to issue a non-legislative rule instead of a legislative rule. Furthermore, sometimes an agency intends (or later claims to have intended) to adopt a non-legislative rule, but someone adversely affected by the rule will challenge the rule in court on the ground that the rule is "really" a legislative rule, and, as such, is invalid because the agency did not follow the procedures required to make a legislative rule. Federal courts have often upheld such challenges, thereby refusing to accept the agency's characterization of its rule as non-legislative.

We will defer to Chapter 10.C.1.c our examination of this fairly rare, but tricky, situation in which someone judicially challenges a supposedly non-legislative rule on the ground that it is "really" a legislative rule. We raise the issue here simply to acknowledge what you probably already have recognized: the distinction between legislative rules and non-legislative rules is not always obvious.

E. The Distinction between "Legislative" Rules and "Substantive" Rules

This section introduces you to a semantic debate in administrative law. The debate involves the terms "*legislative* rule" and "*substantive* rule." The debate matters for lawyers who practice administrative law because those terms constantly crop up and can cause unnecessary confusion for those who do not know the background.

Often you will hear the term "substantive rule" used as a synonym for the term "legislative rule." The U.S. Supreme Court used the terms as synonyms, for example, in *Batterton v. Francis*. The Court said, "Legislative, or substantive, regulations are issued by an agency pursuant to statutory authority and ... implement the statute." 432 U.S. 416, 425 n.9 (1977) (internal quotation marks omitted). Likewise, the federal APA appears to use the term "substantive rule" to mean a legislative rule when it states that "a substantive rule" may not be issued "except within jurisdiction delegated to the agency and as authorized by law." 5 U.S.C. §558(b). Many courts and lawyers use the terms interchangeably.

Two administrative-law scholars believe that treating the terms as interchangeable "can be misleading." Michael Asimow & Ronald M. Levin, State and Federal Administrative Law 319 (3rd. ed. 2009). They explain that using the term "substantive rule" to mean rules that have the force and effect of law implies that the opposite of a substantive rule — namely a "procedural" rule — can never have the force and effect of law. In truth, procedural rules can have the force and effect of law, if the agency makes them under a grant of statutory authority to make legislative rules. These are procedural, legislative rules.

Indeed, several important Supreme Court cases have required federal agencies to follow their legislative rules, and among them are cases involving procedural, legislative rules. One famous case concerned an administrative proceeding to deport Joseph Accardi. *United States ex rel. Accardi v. Shaughnessy*, 347 U.S. 260 (1954). In the deportation proceeding, Mr. Accardi sought a form of relief called "suspension of deportation." Procedural regulations gave an agency called the Board of Immigration Appeals discretion to decide whether to grant this relief. Rather than exercising its own discretion, however, the Board apparently denied relief to Mr. Accardi because the Attorney General had put Mr. Accardi's name on a list of "unsavory characters" that, the Attorney General announced, he believed should be deported. *Id.* at 264. The Board received a copy of this list and apparently relied on it to deny Mr. Accardi relief from deportation.

The U.S. Supreme Court granted Mr. Accardi *habeas corpus* relief from immediate deportation because of the apparent violation of the procedural regulations that gave the Board, not the Attorney General, discretion to decide Mr. Accardi's request for relief. The Court observed that those regulations had "the force and effect of law." *Id.* at 265. The Attorney General therefore could not "sidestep" the Board by distributing the "unsavory characters" list. *Id.* at 267. The Court remanded the case so that the Board could follow the procedural regulations requiring it to exercise its own discretion in Mr. Accardi's case. The principle that an agency must follow its rules is now often called "the *Accardi* principle."

The *Accardi* principle illustrates that procedural rules can be legislative rules that, like all legislative rules, have the force of law. To make a procedural, legislative rule, an agency needs a statutory grant of authority, just as is required to make a substantive, legislative rule. Many federal statutes expressly grant agencies power to make procedural rules. An example is 42 U.S.C. §405 (2012), which relates to administration of a social security program:

---

42 U.S.C. § 405. Evidence, procedure, and certification for payments

(a) Rules and regulations; procedures

The Commissioner of Social Security shall have full power and authority to make rules and regulations and to establish procedures, not inconsistent with the provisions of this subchapter, which are necessary or appropriate to carry out such provisions, and shall adopt reasonable and proper rules and regulations to regulate and provide for the nature and extent of the proofs and evidence and the method of taking and furnishing the same in order to establish the right to benefits hereunder....

It is easy to forget that procedural rules can be legislative rules if you use the term "substantive rule" to mean all legislative rules. To avoid that danger, it is probably best, as Professors Asimow and Levin recommend, to use only the term "legislative rule" to refer to rules with the force and effect of law. Under this approach, some legislative rules are substantive rules; other legislative rules are procedural rules.

You may be wondering by now: What is the correct use of the term "substantive rule"? Generally, substantive rules do not concern agency procedures. Instead, they concern either the everyday conduct of people and companies (often called "primary conduct") or their entitlement to a government license or benefit. More refined definitions of the terms "procedural rule" and "substantive rule" have been devised by the Administrative Conference of the United States (ACUS), a group of scholars and practitioners who advise Congress on matters of administrative law. ACUS suggested that an agency procedural rule "relates solely to agency methods of internal operation or of interacting with regulated parties or the public." A substantive rule, in contrast, "affect[s] conduct, activity, or a substantive interest that is the subject of agency jurisdiction, or ... the standards for eligibility for a government program." ACUS Recommendation, 1 C.F.R. §305.92-1 (1993).

We can't improve on those definitions and, indeed, urge you to re-read them before moving on.

If you find all this terminology confusing, you are in great company. As mentioned above, courts and academic commentators have struggled with it. The terminology is challenging but worth learning. Learning it is an essential step in learning administrative law. Furthermore, because imprecision and confusion over terminology abound, mastering the terminology is a great way for you, as an attorney, to earn credibility with the administrative law experts who work as lawyers for agencies, or who serve as judges in courts that review agency action, or who may be your opposing counsel.

Diagram 7-3. Types of Rules

1. Legislative rules

    a. Substantive legislative rules

    b   Procedural legislative rules

2. Non-legislative rules

    a. Interpretative rules

    b. Agency policy statements

    c. Procedural non-legislative rules

F. Types of Rules Recognized in APAs

1. Federal APA

The distinction between legislative and non-legislative rules is reflected in the federal APA's definition of **"rule,"** and in other federal APA provisions. We examine the provisions here to help you relate the distinction between legislative rules and non-legislative rules to the text of the federal APA.

Let us begin with the federal APA's definition of **"rule"**:

---

5 U.S.C. § 551. Definitions ...

(4) **"rule" means the whole or a part of an agency statement of general or particular applicability and future effect designed to implement, interpret, or prescribe law or policy or describing the organization, procedure, or practice requirements of an agency and includes the approval or prescription for the future of rates, wages, corporate or financial structures or reorganizations thereof, prices, facilities, appliances, services or allowances therefor or of valuations, costs, or accounting, or practices bearing on any of the foregoing....**

We reproduced this definition in Chapter 4 to explore the distinction between rulemaking and adjudication under the federal APA. We return to the definition now with the aim of identifying the types of rules reflected in it.

The federal APA's definition of "**rule**" is dense, but worth unpacking, for it helps identify the type of rule that is subject to the APA's rulemaking requirements. The definition embraces four types of rules:

(1) The definition's reference to agency statements "**designed to *implement* ... or *prescribe* law or [statutory] policy**" encompasses substantive legislative rules.

(2) The definition's reference to agency statements "**designed to ... *interpret* ... law**" encompasses interpretative rules, which are one of the main types of non-legislative rules.

(3) The definition's reference to agency statements "**designed to implement, interpret or prescribe [*agency*] policy**" encompasses agency statements of policy, which are (along with interpretative rules) one of the main types of non-legislative rules.

(4) The definition's reference to agency statements "**describing the organization, procedure, or practice requirements of an agency**" are often called "agency procedural rules" for short. Agency procedural rules may be legislative or non-legislative, depending on whether or not they are promulgated under a statutory grant of power to make legislative rules.

The federal APA prescribes certain procedural requirements for federal agencies to follow when they make rules. As upcoming chapters detail, however, these procedural requirements generally apply only when agencies make the first type of rule listed above: **substantive legislative rules**. The second, third, and fourth types of rules are generally exempt from the federal APA's procedural requirements for agency rulemaking.

In Chapter 10.C we examine each type of rule more closely. For now keep in mind why it is important to understand which type of rule is subject to the APA's procedural requirements: Analysis of the validity of an agency rule must include consideration of not only whether the agency has the power to make the rule but also whether the agency has complied with all requirements, including procedural requirements, for exercising its rule-making power. Those requirements differ depending on the type of rule, which makes it important for administrative lawyers to be familiar with the different types of rules.

2. State APAs

Like the federal APA, some state APAs reflect the difference between legislative and non-legislative rules. The modern trend is reflected in the 2010 Model State APA. It uses the term "rule" to refer to legislative rules — meaning an agency statement that "has the force of law" — and uses the term "guidance document" to include non-legislative rules. Here are the definitions:

Section 102. Definitions.

In this [act]: ...

(14) "Guidance document" means a record of general applicability developed by an agency which lacks the force of law but states the agency's current approach to, or interpretation of, law, or describes how and when the agency will exercise discretionary functions....

(30) "Rule" means the whole or a part of an agency statement of general applicability that implements, interprets, or prescribes law or policy or the organization, procedure, or practice requirements of an agency and has the force of law. The term does not include: ...

(F) a guidance document....

The 2010 Model State APA prescribes rulemaking procedures only for rules, and not for "guidance documents." *See* 2010 Model State APA § 311(a).

In short, it is a fair generalization to say that many APAs prescribe rulemaking procedures for legislative rules, and not for non-legislative rules. The generalization does not avoid the need for careful study of the particular APA and case law construing it in the jurisdiction of the agency whose rule is under analysis. It is, however, a useful rule of thumb.

G. Chapter 7 Wrap Up and Look Ahead

Administrative law distinguishes legislative rules from non-legislative rules. The two types of rules differ in several ways, the most important of which is that legislative rules have the "force and effect of law"; non-legislative rules do not. For an agency to make legislative rules, it must have the power to do so, and that power usually comes from the agency legislation. This chapter introduced you to the knowledge and skills necessary to determine whether the agency legislation empowers the agency to make legislative rules.

Having introduced you to the distinction between legislative and non-legislative rules in this chapter, this book in upcoming chapters helps you learn how to analyze whether an agency rule falls within the agency's powers as well as the limits on, and requirements for, exercising that power.

Chapter Problem Revisited

Your friend's email makes it fairly clear that the Department of Education has adopted a new interpretation of an existing regulation and that your friend's problem stems from that interpretation. The interpretation is a rule, because it has general applicability and future effect. More specifically, it is an interpretative rule, a kind of non-legislative rule.

The interpretative rule is not "the law"; rather, it reflects the Department's view of what "the law" is. "The law," in this case, is the regulation quoted in the chapter problem. That regulation is a legislative rule; if valid, the regulation has the same force and effect as a statute. Thus, if the issue of your friend's eligibility for the PLUS loan ever came before a court, your friend's eligibility will be governed by the regulation (assuming it's valid), not the Department of Education's new interpretation of it. The court will independently determine what the regulation means, as its bears on your friend's situation. In making that determination, however, the court will likely give weight to the Department of Education. After all, it is the entity that Congress has authorized to administer the PLUS loan program.

Although the Department's interpretation is not "the law," the agency will view it as the law, and your friend will be hard-pressed to challenge that view as a practical matter. Your friend is probably in no position to go to court to challenge the interpretation. Even if he could, he might well lose, because the new interpretation appears reasonable. Nor is it likely that your friend (even with your help) can get the Department to change its mind and go back to the old interpretation. This situation illustrates that interpretative rules and other non-legislative rules can have great practical impact, even though they lack the force and effect of law.

Your friend's best bet is probably to try to take advantage of the portion of the regulation that allows his mother to "document to the satisfaction of the Secretary that extenuating circumstances exist." The Department might consider your friend to have extenuating circumstances if he can show that his mother is the only person whom he can get to be a co-signor, she has been diligently paying off her debts, and he has only one year of law school to complete.

If your friend decides to try this route, he may need your help figuring out the procedures for documenting extenuating circumstances. You must find the Department's procedural rules for this process. As you will learn, a federal agency must publish its procedural rules (and most other rules) in an official publication called the Federal Register. That will be your next stop. Besides that, your friend may try contacting his representatives in the U.S. Congress. They—or, more accurately, their staff—devote much time to helping constituents who have problems with federal agencies. Indeed, they may very well have designated staff people to deal with the Department of Education. Your friend's bid to get the Department to find that he has extenuating circumstances may well benefit from supportive phone calls to the relevant Department officials from staff members of your friend's congressional representatives.

Professional Development Reflection Question

The chapter problem illustrates a common situation in which one friend seeks legal advice from a friend who is a lawyer. If you are the lawyer in this situation, you owe it to your friend—and have a professional responsibility besides—to clarify the scope of the representation. We mention this because, when friends seek your legal advice, it's all too easy for you to conceive of giving the advice as merely an act of friendship. But it is more: It is providing legal services. You not only have to be licensed to practice in the relevant jurisdiction but also must obey the same rules of professional conduct that apply to a paying client whom you never met before being hired to provide representation.

When you begin practicing law (if not before), you will get requests for (free) legal advice from friends and family members. How will you deal with such requests? Specifically, which of these approaches do you tend to favor?

- Deny all requests for free legal advice, on the theory that this is the best way to avoid the problems that can arise when you undertake to provide such advice.

- Only give legal advice to family members, on the theory that this is a nice "bright line" that will avoid hard feelings on the part of your friends.

- Deal with these requests on a case-by-case basis, which gives you maximum flexibility and requires no forethought, but does, as a practical matter, mean you will have to explain (justify) turning down any requests for free advice from friends or family.

Chapter 8

Agency Rulemaking Power

Overview

Chapter 7 helped you learn to distinguish legislative rules from non-legislative rules. This chapter explores the question of rulemaking power. This chapter has four sections:

A. Sources of Power for Legislative and Non-Legislative Rules

B. The Nondelegation Doctrine as a Limit on Statutes Granting Federal Agencies Power to Make Legislative Rules

C. Other Limits on Statutes Granting Agencies Power to Make Legislative Rules

D. Chapter 8 Wrap Up and Look Ahead

Chapter Problem

Memo

From: Chief of Staff for Member of U.S. Congress

To: Staff Specialist on Federal Administrative Law

Our boss needs to decide how to vote on a bill and has concerns about the constitutionality of one of its current provisions. The bill is entitled the "Economic Stabilization Act of 2011" (Act). It appropriates $500 billion of stimulus money to spur hiring by the country's largest, private employers.

Our boss worries about a provision in the Act that would provide for a "Compensation Czar," to be appointed by the President with the advice and consent of the Senate. The Compensation Czar will have power to issue rules that limit the salaries of senior executives of all corporations that accept stimulus money under the Act. Violation of these rules will carry significant civil and criminal penalties under the bill.

The provision says that the rules issued by the Compensation Czar should "ensure that the salaries of individuals subject to this Act are not grossly excessive." Our boss thinks this "grossly excessive" standard for the Czar's rules is awfully vague but doubts that a majority could agree on any more precise standard. Our boss wonders whether it is constitutionally permissible for this legislation to give an executive-branch official such broad discretion over private-sector corporate salaries.

Would you please give me a one-pager on this issue? Thanks!

A. Sources of Power for Legislative and Non-Legislative Rules

The issue of rulemaking power divides into two further questions:

a)   Is there a grant of rulemaking power?

b)   Is the grant of rulemaking power valid?

As a practical matter, these questions of power usually arise in connection with legislative rules, and seldom if ever arise in connection with non-legislative rules. Questions of power do not arise for non-legislative rules because non-legislative rules lack the force and effect of law. Because non-legislative rules lack the force and effect of law, an agency does not need an express grant of power to make them. Rather, an agency's authority to make non-legislative rules inheres in the grant of responsibility for executing a body of laws (usually statutory laws).

Consider by way of analogy a police officer responsible for enforcing (executing) a law that makes "inattentive driving" illegal. To execute that law—in this case by issuing traffic tickets—the officer must interpret the law. Indeed, the officer interprets the law every time the officer decides to write a ticket for a violation of that law. The same is true of an agency's authority to interpret the statute that the agency is responsible for administering, and the agency's concomitant authority to announce that interpretation in non-legislative, interpretative rules. In addition to the inherent authority to interpret the inattentive driving law, our police officer also has inherent authority to decide how to execute the inattentive driving law most effectively. For example, the officer can decide to stake out intersections where many accidents have occurred because of inattentive driving. Similarly, an agency can devise policies to rationalize and prioritize the way its employees enforce the laws that the agency is responsible for administering. The agency does not need an express grant of power to interpret or make policies for enforcing the laws that it is responsible for administering. The power comes with the responsibility.

Thus, our examination of rulemaking power will focus on power to make legislative rules. And, as discussed in Chapter 7, to make legislative rules an agency needs a grant of power to make legislative rules. Chapter 7 also discussed how to identify those grants, which almost always take the form of statutory grants of power. In this chapter we will assume the lawyer has identified a source of power for the legislative rule under analysis.

The question then becomes: "Is the grant of rulemaking power *valid*?" We identified the reasons a statute could be invalid in Chapter 2.B. Recall that a federal statute is invalid if it violates the U.S. Constitution or has been expressly or impliedly repealed by a later federal statute; a state statute is invalid if it violates the U.S. or State constitutions; or has been expressly or repealed by a later state statute; or is preempted by or violates federal law.

We will focus in the next section on one particular constitutional limit. This limit specifically applies to statutes that give agencies power to make legislative rules. The limit is known interchangeably as the "delegation" or "nondelegation" doctrine. The U.S. Supreme Court has characterized the delegation doctrine as one facet of the broader separation of powers doctrine established by the U.S. Constitution. Many state supreme courts have similarly construed their state constitutions to contain a delegation doctrine limiting state statutes that give state agencies power to make legislative rules. In addition to the nondelegation doctrine found in federal and state law, the Due Process Clauses of the Fifth and Fourteenth Amendments limit delegations of governmental power to private entities; these situations involve "private delegations."

B. The Nondelegation Doctrine as a Limit on Statutes Granting Federal Agencies Power to Make Legislative Rules

The U.S. Constitution restricts federal statutes that delegate to federal agencies the "quasi-legislative" power to make legislative rules. The restriction, known as the nondelegation doctrine, can be depicted as shown in Diagram 8-1.

Diagram 8-1. U.S. Constitutional Restriction on Statutes Delegating Power to Make Legislative Rules to Executive-Branch Agencies

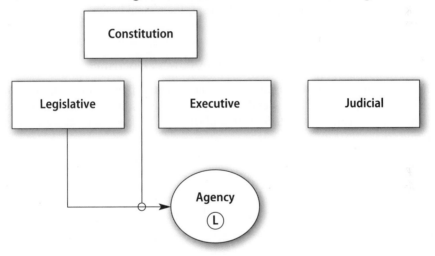

If a federal statute violates the U.S. Constitution's nondelegation doctrine, legislative rules issued under that statute will be invalid, too.

In practice, federal statutes are almost never invalidated under the nondelegation doctrine today. Nonetheless, administrative lawyers must know the federal nondelegation doctrine for three reasons. First, the federal nondelegation doctrine can cause federal courts to interpret narrowly statutes that grant unusually broad rulemaking power to federal agencies. Second, the federal nondelegation doctrine may continue to put a meaningful limit on federal agencies' power to define *criminal* conduct. Third, a nondelegation doctrine rooted — not in the separation of powers — but in the Due Process Clauses limits federal and state statutes delegating power to *private* entities.

Another reason to learn the federal nondelegation doctrine is that it resembles in concept the analogous nondelegation doctrine that many state courts have interpreted their state constitutions to contain as a matter of the separation of powers required under those constitutions. Furthermore, some States apply a version of the nondelegation doctrine that is more stringent than the federal version.

This section explores the nondelegation doctrine in four steps:

(1) Background on federal nondelegation doctrine

(2) Modern nondelegation doctrine—Federal

(3) Modern nondelegation doctrine—State

(4) Private delegations

The objectives of this section are to help you learn the source and substance of the nondelegation doctrines found in federal and state law, and to help you identify and analyze situations in which the nondelegation doctrine could arguably invalidate a statute.

1. Background on Federal Nondelegation Doctrine

a. Relevant Constitutional Text

The federal nondelegation doctrine is one facet of the broader separation of powers doctrine. Subsection (a) below discusses the textual basis for the separation of powers doctrine in general, and subsection (b) discusses the textual basis, in particular, for the nondelegation doctrine.

(i) Textual Basis for Federal Separation of Powers Doctrine

The U.S. Constitution vests legislative power, executive power, and judicial power in three separate branches of the federal government. The vesting occurs in three separate Articles of the Constitution: Articles I, II, and III. Here are the vesting clauses of Articles I, II, and III:

U.S. Const. art. I, § 1

All legislative Powers herein granted shall be vested in a Congress of the United States, which shall consist of a Senate and House of Representatives.

U.S. Const. art. II, § 1

The executive Power shall be vested in a President of the United States of America....

U.S. Const. art. III, § 1

The judicial Power of the United States, shall be vested in one supreme Court, and in such inferior Courts as the Congress may from time to time ordain and establish....

The U.S. Constitution's vesting of separate powers in separate branches, in separate articles of the Constitution, is a primary textual basis for construing the Constitution to require a separation of the three types of powers.

The separation of powers doctrine has several facets relevant to administrative law. The delegation doctrine is one facet of the separation of powers doctrine.

(ii) Textual Basis for Federal Nondelegation Doctrine

The textual basis for the nondelegation doctrine is in the vesting clause of Article I. Article I vests "all" legislative powers in Congress. In contrast, the adjective "all" does not appear in the vesting clauses of Articles II or III. Article I's vesting of "all" legislative power in a Congress has two related but distinct implications.

The clause implies, first, that Congress cannot give away (the term of art is "delegate") its legislative power to *anyone* else. Congress cannot delegate its legislative power to private persons, private entities, state or local governments, or entities within the executive or legislative branch created in Articles II and III. The clause seems to say to Congress not only "You get all the legislative power" but also "You must *keep* it all for yourself!". The clause seems to preclude delegation of federal legislative power to *any* agent.

The vesting clause of Article I further implies, when read together with the vesting clauses of Articles II and III, that Congress is specifically forbidden from delegating its legislative power to any agent in the executive or judicial branches of the federal government. This would not only constitute an abdication of the authority vested in Congress but would also upset the balance of powers by shifting some of the Article I power to a different branch. The shifting of legislative power to some other branch could increase the other branch's cumulative powers, causing what in constitutional circles is called "aggrandizement" of that other branch at the expense of Congress. Alternatively, the shifting of legislative power from Congress to another branch could undermine the other branch's ability to exercise the power properly belonging to it; this could occur, for example, if the judicial branch were given legislative power that impaired its ability impartially to exercise its judicial power. That result would be described as "encroachment" in constitutional law circles. Either aggrandizement or encroachment can upset the equilibrium of power among the three branches, weakening the system of checks and balances and possibly violating the separation of powers doctrine.

Despite textual evidence of limits on Congress's power to delegate legislative power, the U.S. Supreme Court has upheld federal statutes giving federal agencies broad power to make legislative rules. Generally, the Court concludes these statutes are permissible because they don't really delegate legislative power. Rather, they delegate only "quasi-legislative" power. This distinction has permitted the Court to uphold broad statutory grants of legislative rulemaking power while asserting that Congress cannot delegate its legislative power.

To bring in terminology from constitutional law scholars: The Court's approach to the delegation doctrine reflects "formalist" rhetoric that justifies a "functionalist" result. Interpreting the Constitution to create a watertight compartment of legislative power is often called a "formalist" approach to interpreting the separation of powers doctrine. The formalist approach contrasts with the so-called "functional" approach to interpreting the separation of powers doctrine. Whereas the formalist approach favors interpretations that create clear lines separating the three branches of the federal government, the functional approach reflects the "practical understanding that ... Congress simply cannot do its job absent an ability to delegate power under broad general directives." *Mistretta v. United States*, 488 U.S. 361, 372 (1989). Champions of the functional approach claim that their practical approach finds textual support in Congress's power "[t]o make all Laws which shall be necessary and proper for carrying into execution" powers granted by the Constitution. U.S. Const. art. I, § 8, cl. 18. They argue that it is both necessary and proper for Congress to give power to make legislative rules to other branches. *See, e.g., Mistretta v. United States*, 488 U.S. 361, 387–388 (1989).

The formalist and functional approaches to interpreting the separation of powers doctrine tend to lead to different results. A formalist approach will tend to invalidate laws that blur the lines between the three branches. A functional approach tends to tolerate this blurring of lines, if "necessary and proper."

Judging by results, the U.S. Supreme Court has generally taken a functional approach to the nondelegation doctrine. In modern times the Court has consistently upheld, against nondelegation challenges, broad statutory grants, by Congress, to federal agencies of the power to make legislative rules. Thus, the *results* of the Court's cases evince the functional approach, even though the *language* in some of its opinions sounds formalistic.

b. Historical U.S. Supreme Court Case Law

Early on, Congress began delegating legislative-type power to executive-branch officials. *See, e.g., Guiseppi v. Walling*, 144 F.2d 608, 618 n.23 (2nd Cir. 1944) (describing early examples), *aff'd sub nom. Gemsco, Inc. v. Walling*, 324 U.S. 244 (1945). Only twice in its history has the U.S. Supreme Court used the nondelegation doctrine to strike down federal statutory provisions. Both before and after these cases, the Court has consistently rejected nondelegation challenges. The two cases are worth knowing about, however, because the Court has never overruled them.

(i) Early Cases

An early case expressing the nondelegation doctrine is *Marshall Field & Co. v. Clark*, 143 U.S. 649 (1892). The Court in *Field v. Clark* said, "That Congress cannot delegate legislative power … is a principle universally recognized as vital to the integrity and maintenance of the system of government ordained by the Constitution." *Id.* at 692. Having said this, the Court held that the statute before it did not violate this principle, because it did not delegate legislative power.

The statute at issue in *Field v. Clark* had two relevant provisions. One provision exempted goods imported from certain foreign countries from import duties (taxes). Another provision authorized the President to "suspend" the exemption as to the goods from any of these countries that the President determined was discriminating against U.S. goods imported into that country. 143 U.S. at 680–681. The effect of the President's suspending the exemption was that the discriminating foreign country's goods became subject to import duties. The Court held that the President's suspension power did not violate the nondelegation doctrine because the suspension power was not a legislative power:

> Legislative power was exercised when congress declared that the suspension should take effect upon a named contingency. What the president was required to do was simply in execution of the act of congress. It was not the making of law. He was the mere agent of the law-making department to ascertain and declare the event upon which its expressed will was to take effect.

Id. at 693. *Field v. Clark* established Congress's ability to make the operation of statutory provisions depend on an executive official's determination of a "named contingency."

Field v. Clark is included in this historical section for three reasons. First, it contains an early, clear statement of the nondelegation doctrine. Second, *Field v. Clark* is one of several cases in which the Court has used "formalistic" verbiage (in stating the nondelegation principal) while reaching a "functionalist" result that recognizes Congress's need to leave details to the executive branch. Third, the case illustrates the frequent difficulty of classifying a power. Although the Court held that the President's suspension power was not legislative, surely Congress could appropriately have exercised the suspension power itself, by repealing the statute exempting goods from import duties if the President (or Congress) determined they came from countries that were discriminating against U.S. goods. Thus, the suspension power would have been "legislative" if Congress had exercised that power itself; yet it was not "legislative" when delegated to the President.

Indeed, many kinds of government power are hard to characterize. This led Justice John Paul Stevens to write in a later case that "governmental power cannot always be readily characterized" as legislative, executive, or judicial. Rather, a governmental power, "like a chameleon, will often take on the aspect of the office [meaning the branch of government] to which it is attached." *Bowsher v. Synar*, 478 U.S. 714, 749 (1986) (Stevens, J., concurring in the judgment). The idea that governmental powers may be hard to characterize is a justification cited to support a functional approach, rather than a formalistic approach, to separation of powers issues. (Do you see why?)

(ii) New Deal Cases

The Court during the New Deal era struck down provisions of New Deal legislation in two cases. These are the only cases in which the Court has found violations of the nondelegation doctrine.

The first case was *Panama Refining Co. v. Ryan*, 293 U.S. 388 (1935), known as the *Hot Oil Case*. A provision in the National Industrial Recovery Act (NIRA) authorized the President to ban interstate shipments of oil produced in violation of state law. The Court struck down the provision because it gave the President no guidance in determining when to ban a shipment of such "hot oil." The Court said:

> As to the transportation of oil production in excess of state permission, the Congress has declared no policy, has established no standard, has laid down no rule. There is no requirement, no definition of circumstances and conditions in which the transportation is to be allowed or prohibited.

Id. at 252–253. In failing to limit the President's discretion, this provision differed from the suspension provision upheld in *Field v. Clark*.

The second New Deal case was *A.L.A. Schechter Poultry Corp. v. United States*, 295 U.S. 495 (1935), known as the "*Sick Chicken Case*." *Schechter* involved another provision of the NIRA. This one authorized the President to approve "codes of fair competition" for the poultry industry and other industries. *Id.* at 521–522. The Court concluded that the provision was "an unconstitutional delegation of legislative power" because of its breadth and lack of constraints on executive discretion. *Id.* at 541–542.

The 1935 cases of *Panama Refining* and *Schechter Poultry* may have reflected the Court's skepticism toward statutes that attempted ambitious economic regulation. At around the same time, the Court struck down other statutes regulating economic activities on the grounds that they violated substantive due process or exceeded Congress's power under the Commerce Clause. Since 1935 the Court has upheld all of the many federal statutes that it has reviewed under the nondelegation doctrine. Many of those statutes delegated rulemaking authority to federal agencies under broad standards. Nonetheless, the Court has never overruled *Panama Refining* or *Schechter Poultry*. The nondelegation doctrine in federal law is therefore still alive, which is why lawyers must know it. As we will see in the next section, however, the doctrine does not have much bite in most contexts today, as it exists under federal law.

2. Modern Federal Nondelegation Doctrine

Subsection *a* below examines the most common situation in which the nondelegation doctrine arises, which is when the doctrine is used to challenge a federal statute that grants an agency broad power to make legislative rules. Subsection *b* below examines two other situations involving delegation issues: (i) when the nondelegation doctrine is used to interpret a statute; and (ii) when a statute delegates power to an agency to make legislative rules and prescribes criminal penalties for violations of those rules.

a. The Most Common Situation in Which the Nondelegation Doctrine Arises

The federal nondelegation doctrine limits the power of Congress. The doctrine therefore applies to federal *statutes*, not federal agency actions. Furthermore, not all federal statutes implicate the nondelegation doctrine. Instead, the delegation doctrine is implicated — and your nondelegation antennae should quiver — when a federal statute authorizes an agency to make *legislative* rules. In contrast, the doctrine is not implicated by statutes authorizing agencies to make *non-legislative* rules. Thus, to identify when a federal statute implicates the nondelegation doctrine, you must be able to determine when a federal statute authorizes an agency to make legislative rules. We presented material for making that determination in Chapter 7.C.

As the next case explains, a statute that empowers an agency to make legislative rules will violate the nondelegation doctrine if it does not give the agency an "intelligible principle" to follow when exercising that power. The case below also makes clear that the Court today applies the intelligible principle liberally, to allow Congress to give agencies broad rulemaking power.

Exercise: *Whitman v. American Trucking*

Please read *Whitman* with these questions in mind:

1. What agency action is being challenged in this case? How does the nondelegation challenge relate to the validity of the agency action?

2. How would you paraphrase the "intelligible principle" standard articulated by the Court, and its rationale?

3. What "intelligible principle" does the statute at issue here prescribe?

4. By what reasoning does the Court conclude that the statute at issue here satisfies the "intelligible principle" standard?

Whitman v. American Trucking Associations, Inc.

531 U.S. 457 (2001)

JUSTICE SCALIA delivered the opinion of the Court.

These cases present the following questions: (1) Whether § 109(b)(1) of the Clean Air Act (CAA) delegates legislative power to the Administrator of the Environmental Protection

Agency (EPA). (2) Whether the Administrator may consider the costs of implementation in setting national ambient air quality standards (NAAQS) under § 109(b)(1). (3) Whether the Court of Appeals had jurisdiction to review the EPA's interpretation of Part D of Title I of the CAA, 42 U.S.C. §§ 7501–7515, with respect to implementing the revised ozone NAAQS. (4) If so, whether the EPA's interpretation of that part was permissible.

[Editor's note: We excerpt only the part of the Court's opinion addressing the first question: the delegation of legislative power to the agency.]

I

Section 109(a) of the CAA, as added, 84 Stat. 1679, and amended, 42 U.S.C. § 7409(a), requires the Administrator of the EPA to promulgate NAAQS for each air pollutant for which "air quality criteria" have been issued under § 108, 42 U.S.C. § 7408. Once a NAAQS has been promulgated, the Administrator must review the standard (and the criteria on which it is based) "at five year intervals" and make "such revisions ... as may be appropriate." CAA § 109(d)(1), 42 U.S.C. § 7409(d)(1). These cases arose when, on July 18, 1997, the Administrator revised the NAAQS for particulate matter (PM) and ozone.... American Trucking Associations, Inc., and its co-respondents in No. 99-1257—which include, in addition to other private companies, the States of Michigan, Ohio, and West Virginia—challenged the new standards in the Court of Appeals for the District of Columbia Circuit, pursuant to 42 U.S.C. § 7607(b)(1)....

II ...

III

Section 109(b)(1) of the CAA instructs the EPA to set "ambient air quality standards the attainment and maintenance of which in the judgment of the Administrator, based on [the] criteria [documents of § 108] and allowing an adequate margin of safety, are requisite to protect the public health." 42 U.S.C. § 7409(b)(1). The Court of Appeals held that this section [violated the nondelegation doctrine.] We disagree.

In a delegation challenge, the constitutional question is whether the statute has delegated legislative power to the agency. Article I, § 1, of the Constitution vests "all legislative Powers herein granted ... in a Congress of the United States." This text permits no delegation of those powers, *Loving v. United States*, 517 U.S. 748, 771 (1996) ..., and so we repeatedly have said that when Congress confers decisionmaking authority upon agencies Congress must "lay down by legislative act an intelligible principle to which the person or body authorized to [act] is directed to conform." *J. W. Hampton, Jr., & Co. v. United States*, 276 U.S. 394, 409 (1928).

We agree with [the EPA] that the text of § 109(b)(1) of the CAA at a minimum requires that "for a discrete set of pollutants and based on published air quality criteria that reflect the latest scientific knowledge, [the] EPA must establish uniform national standards at a level that is requisite to protect public health from the adverse effects of the pollutant in the ambient air." Tr. of Oral Arg. in No. 99-1257, p. 5. Requisite, in turn, "means sufficient, but not more than necessary." *Id.* at 7. These limits on the EPA's discretion are strikingly similar to the ones we approved in *Touby v. United States*, 500 U.S. 160 (1991), which permitted the Attorney General to designate a drug as a controlled substance for purposes of criminal drug enforcement if doing so was " 'necessary to avoid an imminent hazard to the public safety.' " *Id.* at 163. They also resemble the Occupational Safety and Health Act provision requiring the agency to " 'set the standard which most adequately assures, to the extent feasible, on the basis of the best available evidence, that no employee will suffer any impairment of health'" — which the Court upheld in *Industrial Union Dept., AFL-CIO v. American Petroleum Institute*, 448 U.S. 607, 646 (1980)....

The scope of discretion § 109(b)(1) allows is in fact well within the outer limits of our nondelegation precedents. In the history of the Court we have found the requisite "intelligible principle" lacking in only two statutes ... *See Panama Refining Co. v. Ryan*, 293 U.S. 388 (1935); *A. L. A. Schechter Poultry Corp. v. United States*, 295 U.S. 495 (1935). We have, on the other hand, upheld the validity of § 11(b)(2) of the Public Utility Holding Company Act of 1935, 49 Stat. 821, which gave the Securities and Exchange Commission authority to modify the structure of holding company systems so as to ensure that they are not "unduly or unnecessarily complicated" and do not "unfairly or inequitably distribute voting power among security holders." *American Power & Light Co. v. SEC*, 329 U.S. 90, 104 (1946). We have approved the wartime conferral of agency power to fix the prices of commodities at a level that "'will be generally fair and equitable and will effectuate the [in some respects conflicting] purposes of the Act.'" *Yakus v. United States*, 321 U.S. 414, 420, 423–426 (1944). And we have found an "intelligible principle" in various statutes authorizing regulation in the "public interest." *See, e.g., National Broadcasting Co. v. United States*, 319 U.S. 190, 225–226 (1943) (FCC's power to regulate airwaves); *New York Central Securities Corp. v. United States*, 287 U.S. 12, 24–25 (1932) (ICC's power to approve railroad consolidations). In short, we have "almost never felt qualified to second guess Congress regarding the permissible degree of policy judgment that can be left to those executing or applying the law." *Mistretta v. United States*, 488 U.S. 361, 416 (1989) (Scalia, J., dissenting); *see id.* at 373 (majority opinion).

It is true enough that the degree of agency discretion that is acceptable varies according to the scope of the power congressionally conferred. *See Loving v. United States, supra*, at 772–773.... While Congress need not provide any direction to the EPA regarding the manner in which it is to define "country [grain] elevators," which are to be exempt from new stationary source regulations for grain elevators, *see* § 7411(i), it must provide substantial guidance on setting air standards that affect the entire national economy. But even in sweeping regulatory schemes we have never demanded, as the Court of Appeals did here, that statutes provide a "determinate criterion" for saying "how much [of the regulated harm] is too much." 175 F.3d at 1034. In *Touby*, for example, we did not require the statute to decree how "imminent" was too imminent, or how "necessary" was necessary enough, or even — most relevant here — how "hazardous" was too hazardous. 500 U.S. at 165–167. It is therefore not conclusive for delegation purposes that, as respondents argue, ozone and particulate matter are "nonthreshold" pollutants that inflict a continuum of adverse health effects at any airborne concentration greater than zero, and hence require the EPA to make judgments of degree. "[A] certain degree of discretion, and thus of law-making, inheres in most executive or judicial action." *Mistretta v. United States, supra*, at 417 (Scalia, J., dissenting) (emphasis deleted); *see* 488 U.S. at 378–379 (majority opinion). Section 109(b)(1) of the CAA, which to repeat we interpret as requiring the EPA to set air quality standards at the level that is "requisite" — that is, not lower or higher than is necessary — to protect the public health with an adequate margin of safety, fits comfortably within the scope of discretion permitted by our precedent.

We therefore reverse the judgment of the Court of Appeals remanding for reinterpretation that would avoid a supposed delegation of legislative power. It will remain for the Court of Appeals — on the remand that we direct for other reasons — to dispose of any other preserved challenge to the NAAQS under the judicial review provisions contained in 42 U.S.C. § 7607(d)(9)....

JUSTICE STEVENS, with whom JUSTICE SOUTER joins, concurring in part and concurring in the judgment.

Section 109(b)(1) delegates to the Administrator of the Environmental Protection Agency (EPA) the authority to promulgate national ambient air quality standards (NAAQS). In Part III of its opinion, ... the Court convincingly explains why the Court of Appeals erred when it concluded that § 109 effected "an unconstitutional delegation of legislative power." *American Trucking Assns., Inc. v. EPA*, 175 F.3d 1027, 1033 (C.A.D.C.1999) (per curiam). I wholeheartedly endorse the Court's result and endorse its explanation of its reasons, albeit with the following caveat.

The Court has two choices. We could choose to articulate our ultimate disposition of this issue by frankly acknowledging that the power delegated to the EPA is "legislative" but nevertheless conclude that the delegation is constitutional because adequately limited by the terms of the authorizing statute. Alternatively, we could pretend, as the Court does, that the authority delegated to the EPA is somehow not "legislative power." Despite the fact that there is language in our opinions that supports the Court's articulation of our holding, I am persuaded that it would be both wiser and more faithful to what we have actually done in delegation cases to admit that agency rule making authority is "legislative power." ...

Exercise: *Whitman* Revisited

1. Please look back at the EPA's formulation (at oral argument) of the intelligible principle in § 109(b)(1) of the Clean Air Act, which the Court approvingly quoted. What constraints does that formulation put on the EPA's discretion in promulgating NAAQSs?

2. The Court says, "[T]he degree of agency discretion that is acceptable varies according to the scope of the power congressionally conferred." *Whitman v. American Trucking Ass'ns*, 531 U.S. at 475. How would you characterize the scope of the power conferred by § 109(b)(1) to establish ambient air quality standards for the United States?

3. Why, do you suppose, we included in this excerpt a portion of Justice John Paul Stevens' separate opinion?

---

b. Other Situations Presenting Delegation Issues

(i) Interpreting Federal Statutes Narrowly to Avoid Delegation Problems

Although the U.S. Supreme Court has not used the nondelegation doctrine to invalidate a federal statute since 1935, the Court has used the doctrine to justify interpreting a federal statute narrowly.

The most important such case is *Industrial Union Department, AFL-CIO v. American Petroleum Institute*, 448 U.S. 607 (1980), known as the *Benzene Case*. In the *Benzene* case, a plurality of the Court narrowly construed statutes that authorized the Occupational Safety and Health Administration (OSHA) to regulate benzene and other toxic chemicals in the workplace. The plurality rejected OSHA's broad interpretation of OSHA's rulemaking power under the statutes because the plurality believed that, if OSHA's broad interpretation were accepted, the statutes "might" violate the nondelegation doctrine. *Id.* at 646. A fifth Justice concluded that it did not matter whether the statutes were construed narrowly or broadly; in either event they did indeed violate the nondelegation doctrine. *Id.* at 672 (Rehnquist, J., concurring in the judgment). *See also National Cable Television Ass'n v. United States*, 415 U.S. 336 (1974) (narrowly interpreting an FCC statute to avoid delegation problem).

The takeaway seems to be that if a broad reading of a federal statute would raise serious delegation problems, a federal court will adopt a narrower reading. Of course, the statute must be reasonably susceptible to broader and narrower readings and, to that extent, ambiguous.

Exercise: Interpreting Statutes to Avoid Delegation Problems

The objective of this exercise is to introduce you to a statute that would raise delegation concerns if interpreted broadly, according to a federal court of appeals.

The federal Age Discrimination in Employment Act (ADEA) generally makes it unlawful for an employer to discriminate against an employee in compensation or employment benefits because of the employee's age. *See* 29 U.S.C. § 623(a)(1) (2012). The ADEA is administered by the Equal Employment Opportunity Commission (EEOC). Section 9 of the ADEA authorizes the EEOC to issue rules creating exemptions from the ADEA. Specifically, the EEOC may under § 9 "establish such reasonable exemptions ... as [the EEOC] may find necessary and proper in the public interest." 29 U.S.C. § 628 (2012). Exercising its § 9 exemption authority, the EEOC issued a rule allowing employers to reduce retirees' health benefits to the extent those benefits were payable under Medicare or a comparable state health benefit plan. This reduction by employers is known as "coordinating" employer benefits with governmental health benefits.

The U.S. Court of Appeals for the Third Circuit held that, even if the coordination of benefits would otherwise violate the ADEA, the EEOC had authority under § 9 to create the exemption allowing the coordination. *American Ass'n of Retired Persons v. EEOC*, 489 F.3d 558, 562–567 (3d Cir. 2007). The court said, however, "We must narrowly interpret section 9 of the ADEA, if possible, to avoid any potential delegation problem." *Id.* at 564 n.6.

Please write down a short explanation of why § 9 could raise delegation concerns if construed broadly.

(ii) Statutes Granting an Agency the Power to Define Criminal Offenses

Some federal statutes not only grant agencies power to make legislative rules. They also make violations of those rules punishable as federal crimes. In this situation, agencies have the power to define criminal conduct.

Congress must satisfy two requirements to authorize a federal agency to define criminal conduct. First, Congress must expressly state in the statute that violations of the agency's rules are a crime. Second, Congress itself must prescribe the criminal penalties for violations. *Loving v. United States*, 517 U.S. 748, 768 (1996); *Grimaud*, 220 U.S. 506, 518 (1911); *see, e.g., United States v. O'Hagen*, 521 U.S. 642, 666–677 (1997) (upholding conviction for violating SEC Rule 14e-3(a)). Thus, if a federal statute grants an agency broad power to make legislative rules, but does not make violations of the rules a crime punishable by specific criminal sanctions, the agency acting alone cannot prescribe criminal penalties for violations of its rules. Congress must act expressly when it wishes to delegate to an agency the power to make legislative rules the violation of which carries criminal penalties, and Congress must prescribe the penalties.

It is possible that, when Congress does empower an agency to make rules identifying conduct that is subject to statutorily prescribed criminal punishment, Congress must restrict the agency's power more than is usually required by the "intelligible principle" standard. In a case before the U.S. Supreme Court, a criminal defendant argued that "something more than an 'intelligible principle' is required when Congress authorizes [the executive branch] to promulgate regulations that contemplate criminal sanctions." *Touby v. United States*, 500 U.S. 160, 165–166 (1991). In response to that argument, the Court admitted, "Our cases are not entirely clear as to whether more specific guidance is in fact required" in this situation. *Id.* at 166. The Court did not resolve the issue in that case, because the Court concluded that the challenged statute would be valid "even if greater congressional specificity is required in the criminal context." *Id.*; *see also United States v. Dhafir*, 461 F.3d 211, 216–217 (2nd Cir. 2006) (rejecting argument that the International Emergency Economic Powers Act was unconstitutional delegation of power to President to define criminal offenses, holding that Act satisfied even heightened specificity that might be required of such delegations of power). It is therefore an open question whether the nondelegation doctrine demands "greater congressional specificity" when an agency can make rules the violation of which carries criminal penalties.

Exercise: Agency Power to Make Rules Identifying Conduct Subject to Criminal Punishment

Why might the Court demand more specificity from Congress when it empowers a federal agency to make rules identifying conduct that is subject to statutorily prescribed criminal punishment?

Exercise: Making Sense of Federal Constitutional Limits on Delegations

The material in this section has addressed these situations:

1. use of the federal nondelegation doctrine to challenge the validity of federal statutes that delegate to executive-branch agencies the power to make legislative rules, including rules the violation of which carries criminal penalties.

2. use of the federal nondelegation doctrine as a basis for interpreting ambiguous federal statutes

Please explain in your own words the principles that apply in each situation.

3. Modern Nondelegation Doctrine in the States

This section emphasizes that States are not bound by U.S. Supreme Court and lower federal court precedent on the nondelegation doctrine that applies to federal statutes. It also briefly discusses the nondelegation doctrine in the States.

a. The Federal Nondelegation Doctrine Does Not Apply to the States

The federal nondelegation doctrine is a facet of the separation of powers doctrine established by the U.S. Constitution. The separation of powers doctrine concerns the relationship among the three branches of the national government. It does not apply to the relationship among branches of state government. Thus, "the concept of separation of powers embodied in the United States Constitution is not mandatory in state governments." *Sweezy v. New Hampshire*, 354 U.S. 234, 255 (1957); *see also Highland Farms Dairy, Inc. v. Agnew*, 300 U.S. 608, 612 (1937) ("How power shall be distributed by a state among its governmental organs is commonly, if not always, a question for the state itself.") In particular, the federal nondelegation doctrine does not restrict the ability of state legislatures to give state agencies power to make legislative rules.

b. The Sources and Prevalence of the Nondelegation Doctrine in the States

According to two administrative law scholars, about thirty-five States have state constitutions with provisions expressly requiring separation of powers. Michael Asimow & Ronald M. Levin, State and Federal Administrative Law 391 (3rd. ed. 2009). Here, for example, is the one in Kentucky's Constitution:

Kentucky Constitution, § 27

The powers of the government of the Commonwealth of Kentucky shall be divided into three distinct departments, and each of them be confined to a separate body of magistracy, to wit: Those which are legislative, to one; those which are executive, to another; and those which are judicial, to another.

Furthermore, even state constitutions that do not expressly require the separation of legislative, executive, and judicial powers may be interpreted—just as the U.S. Constitution is interpreted—to require a separation of powers and, more specifically, to limit the ability of state legislatures to delegate legislative rulemaking power to state agencies. In any event, the source of the nondelegation doctrine in a State will be that State's constitution. And because state constitutions differ, the nondelegation doctrine may differ in each State.

A State's nondelegation doctrine may of course also differ from the federal nondelegation doctrine. In particular, States are free to interpret their constitutions to put greater restrictions on their state legislatures than the federal nondelegation doctrine puts on Congress. Kentucky is one State that has done so. Illustrating Kentucky's more stringent approach is *Board of Trustees of Judicial Retirement System v. Attorney General of Commonwealth*, 132 S.W.2d 770 (Ky. 2003). There, the Kentucky Supreme Court held that a

Kentucky statute violated the State's nondelegation doctrine. The court reviewed the state statute under an "intelligible principle" standard. The court emphasized, however, that Kentucky does not agree with the "toothless" and "notoriously lax" version of that standard applied by the U.S. Supreme Court to federal statutes. "Kentucky holds to a higher standard," the state court said. *Id.* at 782.

The lesson to take from this discussion is that state courts may use similar standards (e.g., "intelligible principle") and express similar concerns (e.g., about unchecked agency discretion) in applying the state nondelegation doctrine. You cannot, however, assume that the state version of the doctrine is the same as the federal standard. You must identify the relevant state constitutional provisions and research the state case law.

4. Delegations of Power to Private Entities

Federal and state statutes that delegate governmental power to private entities are subject to restrictions under the Due Process Clauses of the Fifth and Fourteenth Amendments. The leading case on federal statutes delegating power to private entities is *Carter v. Carter Coal Co.*, 298 U.S. 238 (1936).

In *Carter Coal*, the Court struck down a statutory provision that allowed groups of private coal producers and private coal mine workers to establish minimum wages and maximum hours for the entire coal industry. In striking down the provision, the Court said:

> The power conferred upon the majority is, in effect, the power to regulate the affairs of an unwilling minority. This is legislative delegation in its most obnoxious form; for it is not even delegation to an official or an official body, presumptively disinterested, but to private persons whose interests may be and often are adverse to the interests of others in the same business.

Carter Coal, 298 U.S. at 311. In striking down the statute, the Court relied on the Due Process Clause of the Fifth Amendment. The Due Process Clause requires impartial decision makers, and delegation of governmental power to private entities raises concerns that the power will not be exercised impartially. *Id.*

The Due Process Clause does not prohibit *all* private participation in exercises of government power. To the contrary, the Court has made clear that a federal statute may constitutionally allow private entities, such as representatives of the regulated industry, to have input into governmental decision making, as long as the ultimate decision-making authority resides in the federal agency. *See, e.g., Sunshine Anthracite Coal Co. v. Adkins*, 310 U.S. 381, 399 (1940); *see also Nat'l Ass'n of Reg. Util. Comm'rs v. FCC*, 737 F.2d 1095, 1143–1144 (1984).

The due process limit on private delegations that the Court in *Carter Coal* found in the Due Process Clause of the Fifth Amendment also exists under the Due Process Clause of the Fourteenth Amendment. The latter limits state (including local) laws that delegate governmental authority to private entities. The U.S. Supreme Court cases addressing state laws have allowed private participation in regulatory decisions, when the private parties did not compete with the regulated parties and had a legitimate stake in the matter. *Cusack v. City of Chicago*, for example, upheld a Chicago ordinance that allowed billboards on residential streets only with the consent of the residents who owned the majority of frontage on the affected street. 242 U.S. 526, 529–531 (1917). The Court observed that it was common to let a neighborhood assess "the propriety of having carried on within it trades or occupations which are properly the subject of regulation in the exercise of the police power, ... such as the right to maintain saloons." *Id.* at 530. *See also Philly's v. Byrne,* 732 F.2d 87 (7th Cir. 1984) (rejecting due process challenge to state law that allowed voters in a precinct to ban all liquor stores in the precinct by majority vote, and noting that the law's "across-the-board" feature prevented voters from "ganging up" on any particular liquor store within a precinct).

Like the U.S. Supreme Court, state courts are particularly suspicious of statutes delegating legislative rulemaking power to private entities. An example is *Texas Boll Weevil Eradication Foundation, Inc. v. Lewellen,* 952 S.W.2d 454 (Tex. 1997). A Texas statute created an "Official Cotton Growers' Boll Weevil Eradication Foundation." *Id.* at 457 (quoting statute). The Foundation had statutory authority to impose fees on cotton growers to fund a boll weevil eradication program. The Foundation was a private, nonprofit organization, made up of growers. The Court held that the statute violated the special, stringent sets of standards required under Texas law for a private delegation. *Id.* at 472–475.

The takeaway from this discussion is that the Due Process Clauses of the Fifth and Fourteenth Amendments restrict delegations of governmental power to private entities. The restriction reflects concern that private entities will not use that power impartially. The restriction does not, however, prohibit all private participation in government decision making. State law, too, may restrict delegations of power to state agencies.

C. Other Limits on Statutes Granting Agencies Power to Make Legislative Rules

We have focused so far on the nondelegation doctrine because it is the only constitutional doctrine that uniquely applies to statutes that give agencies power to make legislative rules. Of course, federal and state statutes must obey all applicable provisions of the U.S. Constitution. No federal or state law, for instance, could validly authorize an agency to make rules violating people's freedom of speech under the First Amendment. But besides the nondelegation doctrine, we will not attempt to identify every provision or doctrine of constitutional law that might invalidate a statute that gives an agency the power to make legislative rules.

State statutes must not only comply with the U.S. Constitution. They also may not conflict with valid federal statutes or federal agency legislative rules, or else they are preempted. Under the preemption doctrine, a state statute that gave a state agency power to make legislative rules would be invalid if it conflicted with a valid federal statute or legislative rule. *See Rice v. Santa Fe Elevator Corp.,* 331 U.S. 218, 224–225, 236 (1947) (United States Warehouse Act preempted Illinois laws authorizing Illinois Commerce Commission to set rates for grain storage).

Exercise: Refining the Problem Solving Framework

First, devise an outline or flow chart or other graphic organizer depicting federal nondelegation analysis. Your outline should address the following questions:

a. When will a statute arguably implicate the nondelegation doctrine?

b. When a statute does so, does the statute involve the run-of-the-mill delegation doctrine situations such as involved in *Whitman* or one of the specialized situations discussed in this chapter (e.g., delegation to a private entity)?

c. How do you analyze each type of delegation situation?

d. What is the consequence of concluding that a statute violates the nondelegation doctrine?

Next, determine where in the problem solving framework below you should fit your nondelegation outline or flow chart or graphic organizer.

Problem Solving Framework for Problems Involving Agency Action

1. Is there a valid source of power for the agency to take this action?

   a. Is there a source of power? There are three possible sources of power for agency action:

      i. Constitutional

      ii. Statutory (most common)

      iii. Executive order or other executive-branch material

   b. Is the source of power valid?

2. If the agency has acted under a valid source of power, has the agency obeyed limits on, and requirements for exercising, that power? (For simplicity's sake, we use the term "limits" to include requirements.)

   a. Internal limits

      i. Internal substantive limits

      ii. Internal procedural limits

   b. External limits

      i. External substantive limits
      ii. External procedural limits

D. Chapter 8 Wrap Up and Look Ahead

To make a valid legislative rule, an agency must issue the rule under a valid statutory grant of power. For a statute granting such power to be valid, it must of course satisfy the Constitution. Of particular relevance, federal statutes that empower federal agencies to make legislative rules implicate the U.S. Constitution's nondelegation doctrine. The federal nondelegation doctrine generally requires a federal statute to supply an "intelligible principle" that limits the federal agency's discretion. Today, federal statutes will almost always meet this requirement. They may, however, warrant greater scrutiny if they give an agency power to define criminal conduct. They may also be interpreted narrowly to avoid significant delegation problems.

A state statute may delegate legislative rulemaking power to a state agency. The state constitution may be construed to limit such statutory delegations of rulemaking power, as a matter of the state constitution's separation-of-powers requirement.

Besides separation-of-powers limits on federal and state statutes delegating legislative rulemaking power, the Due Process Clauses limit statutes delegating governmental power to private entities.

If a statute violates one of these constitutional restrictions, legislative rules promulgated under the statute will also be invalid. Thus, one way to challenge a legislative rule is to argue that it has been promulgated under an invalid statute.

Even if a legislative rule rests on a valid statute, the rule still might be invalid. Indeed, the rule will be invalid if the agency has not obeyed limits on, and requirements for, exercising its rulemaking power. We begin examining those limits in the next chapter.

Chapter Problem Revisited

1. This book excerpts only one modern U.S. Supreme Court case on the non-delegation doctrine. If you encounter a nondelegation issue in practice, you would have to study dozens of cases from the relevant jurisdiction (state or federal), because, even just considering Supreme Court cases, every jurisdiction has abundant case law on the subject. Your research may extend to lower court case law as well. Even so, the material presented in this chapter should enable you to explain why the bill described in the chapter problem implicates the nondelegation doctrine.

2. What do you make of the possibility that the bill at issue in the chapter problem delegates power under a vague standard because Members of Congress could not agree on anything more specific? Is that a good reason or bad reason for delegation? As far as you can tell, does it matter under the case law?

3. The Court said in *Whitman v. American Trucking Associations*: "[E]ven in sweeping regulatory schemes we have never demanded, as the Court of Appeals did here, that statutes provide a 'determinate criterion' for saying 'how much [of the regulated harm] is too much.'" 531 U.S. at 475 (quoting court of appeals' opinion). How would analysis of the chapter problem change if the Court in *Whitman* had agreed with the court of appeals that a statute delegating power to make legislative rules must have a "determinate criterion"?

4. The bill in the chapter problem authorizes criminal penalties for violations of the Czar's rules. If, as the Court has suggested, greater congressional specificity is required in this context, how would you articulate a standard more specific than the "intelligible principle" standard?

Professional Development Reflection Question

In the chapter problem, the Chief of Staff asks the staff specialist for a "one pager." In other legal practice settings, too, junior lawyers are often expected to be extremely concise when writing up research results. We offer two bits of advice for this common situation. First, give the boss what he or she wants. If asked for a "one pager," don't produce a ten pager (heavily footnoted). Even if the ten pages are brilliant, that won't matter; the boss will remember only that you didn't follow instructions. Second, just because you are expected to produce an extremely short written product, that doesn't mean it won't take you much time. To the contrary, the opposite is usually true, as reflected in the statement that Blaise Pascal supposedly made in a letter: "I have written you a long letter because I did not have time to write a short one."

New lawyers often feel hard pressed to boil a complicated legal subject down to the short written products that senior lawyers expect. That feeling may indicate that the new lawyer hasn't grasped the subject well enough to express its essence. In any event, how do you plan to handle situations in which a client or supervising lawyer asks you to convey in one page a legal analysis that requires ten pages to do it justice?

Chapter 9

Limits on Agency Rulemaking Power

Overview

Chapter 8 discussed agency power to make rules. As this chapter discusses, even if an agency has power to make a rule, the rule may be invalid if the agency did not obey the limits on its rulemaking power. To identify those limits, we begin with the portion of the framework from Chapter 2 that classifies types of limits on agency power. The framework, modified for specific application to agency rulemaking, is as follows:

Has the agency obeyed limits on its rulemaking power? (For simplicity's sake, we use the term "limits" to include requirements for exercising.)

a. Internal limits

    i. Internal substantive limits

    ii. Internal procedural limits

b. External limits

    i. External substantive limits

    ii. External procedural limits

This chapter consists of three sections:

A. Internal Limits on Agency Rulemaking Power

B. External Limits on Agency Rulemaking Power

C. Chapter 9 Wrap Up and Look Ahead

The overall objective of this chapter is to give you a comprehensive "checklist" of potential limits on agency rulemaking power.

Chapter Problem

Email

To: Judge Able's Law Clerk

From: Judge Able

As a newly appointed judge, I need your help with important "homework." This homework is necessitated by my legal practice's focus on only one narrow area of administrative law that did not give me the big-picture understanding that I need now.

I have just been assigned by the Chief Judge to handle a lawsuit challenging a newly promulgated set of environmental regulations. It's a massive lawsuit.

Some parties—private companies who will be subject to the regulations—argue that the regulations are too stringent; other parties—people who live close to the regulated companies and non-profit environmental organizations—argue that the rules are too lax. Both sides are challenging the rules on all sorts of different theories.

I need you to construct a flow chart or other graphic way to depict a comprehensive framework for analyzing the validity of an agency rule. Only in this way can I hope to make sense of all of the arguments that all of the parties to this lawsuit are making about the various rules.

Thank you for your help with this!

Sincerely, Judge Able

A. Internal Limits on Agency Rulemaking Power

As discussed in Chapter 8, a legislative rule must rest on a valid grant of power to make legislative rules. That grant of power, if it exists, will ordinarily be found in the agency legislation. Agency legislation never gives an agency unfettered rulemaking power. Instead, the agency legislation invariably puts limits on, or prescribes requirements for, the agency's rulemaking power. We call these "internal" (or "intrinsic") limits. They may be substantive—addressing, for example, what topics the agency rules can address, or what considerations the rules must be based on—or procedural—addressing the process for making the rules.

Internal limits on the agency's rulemaking power may be hard to identify comprehensively. Agency legislation is often massive and complex. For example, the federal Clean Water Act alone has ninety-one separate sections. And it is only one of many statutes that the EPA administers. A particular EPA rule may be based on grants of rulemaking power in more than one of those statutes, in which event you must examine all of the applicable statutes for the relevant internal limits. The relatively small Consumer Product Safety Act has forty-six sections, and is only one of the statutes that make up the legislation that the Consumer Product Safety Commission administers.

With all its potential complexities and difficulties, however, the agency legislation is the place to start your search for limits on the agency's rulemaking power. Below we identify examples of the kinds of internal limits your research may reveal.

1. Internal Substantive Limits

a. Internal Substantive Limits on Agency Rulemaking Power— The "Ultra Vires" Concept

Some internal limits on agency power cause agency action that exceeds those limits to be labeled "ultra vires"—beyond the agency's authority. These are true limits on—not simply requirements for—valid agency action. Here are examples of cases in which the U.S. Supreme Court held that an agency's legislative rule was beyond its authority.

• *FDA v. Brown & Williamson Tobacco Corp.*, 529 U.S. 120 (2000)

The federal Food and Drug Administration (FDA) has power under one of its statutes to regulate "drugs" and medical "devices." The FDA relied on this power to issue rules for the marketing and sale of cigarettes. (The FDA essentially tried to characterize cigarettes as medical "devices" designed to deliver the "drug" nicotine). Tobacco companies challenged the rules.

The Supreme Court interpreted the FDA's statute as not authorizing the FDA to regulate cigarettes and accordingly found the FDA's rules ultra vires. An important P.S.: After the Supreme Court's decision, Congress enacted a new law authorizing the FDA to regulate cigarettes. Congress thus supplied the power that the Supreme Court had determined the FDA previously lacked. *See* Family Smoking Prevention and Tobacco Control Act, Pub. L. No. 111-31, 123 Stat. 1776 (2009), codified as 21 U.S.C. § 387a-1 (2012).

• *Addison v. Holly Hill Fruit Products*, 322 U.S. 607 (1944)

A federal statute, the Fair Labor Standards Act (FLSA), exempted from the federal minimum-wage laws certain people who worked in plants that processed things grown on farms. Specifically, these processing-plant workers were exempt from the minimum-wage law— meaning they could be paid less than the minimum wage—if they worked in a processing plant that was close to the farm where the goods being processed had been grown. This "local processing" exemption was part of a broader statutory exemption for agricultural workers.

The FLSA authorized a federal official—the Administrator of the Wage and Hour Division of the U.S. Department of Labor—to issue rules to define how close to the farms the processing plants had to be for its workers to fall within the local processing exemption. Specifically, the FLSA authorized the Administrator to define "the area of production," within which processing plants had to be located to take advantage of the local processing exemption. The Administrator relied on this statutory authority to promulgate a rule that supplied a geographical standard of proximity for a particular type of processing: canning. The rule said that, for a canning plant to fall within the local processing exemption, the canning plant had to be within the "immediate locality" of the farm where the goods being canned were grown. *Id.* at 609.

In addition to providing this geographic standard, the Administrator's rule said that large canning plants (plants with seven or more workers) had to pay the minimum wage, even if they were within the immediate locality of the farm. These large canning plants, in other words, could not take advantage of the local processing exemption, even though they met the geographical standard of being in the "immediate vicinity" of the farms from which the goods that they processed came. The Administrator created this large-plant exception to the local processing exemption to protect large, *urban* canning plants— which had to pay their workers at least the minimum wage—from unfair competition from large, *rural* canning plants.

The U.S. Supreme Court invalidated the part of the rule that required large, rural canning plants to pay the minimum wage. The Court interpreted the statute to "restric[t] the Administrator to the drawing of geographic lines." *Id.* at 619. The Court accordingly concluded: "[R]egulations which made discriminations within the [geographic] area defined by applying the exemption only to plants with less than seven employees are ultra vires." *Id.*

• *MCI Telecommunications Corp. v. American Telephone & Telegraph Co.*, 512 U.S. 218 (1994)

A federal statute required telephone companies to file tariffs with the Federal Communications Commission. A tariff lists the company's prices for various services. In addition to imposing this tariff filing requirement, the statute included a provision authorizing the Commission to makes rules to "modify" the statute's requirements.

The Commission issued a rule exempting a large class of phone companies from the tariff filing requirement. The Court held that this rule exceeded the Commission's authority, because it was too fundamental a change to be a mere "modification." The Court concluded:

> Certainly the Commission can modify the form, contents, and location of required filings, and can defer filing or perhaps even waive it altogether in limited circumstances. But what we have here goes well beyond that. It is effectively the introduction of a whole new regime of regulation (or of free-market competition), which may well be a better regime but is not the one that Congress established.

MCI v. AT&T, 512 U.S. at 234. The rule thus exceeded the Commission's statutory "modification" power.

* * *

The ultra vires concept can be easy to confuse with—but differs from—the nondelegation doctrine that was discussed in Chapter 8.B. The nondelegation doctrine limits the ability of the *legislature* to grant rulemaking power to an agency. Thus, the nondelegation doctrine is violated by *statutes*. We are now talking about situations in which *agency rules* exceed statutory authority.

b. Internal Substantive Requirements for Exercise of Agency Rulemaking Power

The ultra vires concept differs from other ways an agency's rule may violate the agency legislation. Suppose, for example, the agency legislation says that, when making a rule, the agency must consider factors *A*, *B*, and *C*. Further suppose that, contrary to that command, the agency considers only factors *A* and *B*—but not *C*—when making a particular rule. The agency's failure to consider factor *C* invalidates the rule. To use federal APA terminology, the rule is "**arbitrary, capricious, an abuse of discretion, or otherwise not in accordance with law.**" 5 U.S.C. § 706(2)(A) (2012). The rule is invalid, but not ultra vires.

The difference can be illustrated using the Consumer Product Safety Commission's rulemaking power under the Consumer Product Safety Act. The Act authorizes the Commission to promulgate safety standards for consumer products. 15 U.S.C. §§ 2056 & 2058. The Act has substantive limits on this rulemaking power that, if ignored, would cause a rule to be labeled ultra vires and other substantive limits that, if ignored, would simply cause a rule to be considered not "in accordance with law." 5 U.S.C. § 706(2)(A).

A substantive limit of the first kind is the Act's definition of "consumer product." 15 U.S.C. § 2052(5) (2012). The definition excludes tobacco products. *Id.* § 2052(5)(B). If the Commission issues a safety standard for tobacco products (e.g., cigarettes), that standard is ultra vires. The definition of "consumer product" puts a substantive limit establishing what might be called the Commission's regulatory "jurisdiction." *Cf.* 5 U.S.C. § 706(2)(C) (2012) (authorizing courts to invalidate agency action "in excess of statutory jurisdiction, authority, or limitations").

The Act requires consumer product safety standards to be "reasonably necessary to prevent or reduce an unreasonable risk of injury associated with such product." 15 U.S.C. § 2056(a). This is a substantive requirement because it sets a goal that safety standards must achieve. A safety standard fails to meet this requirement if the standard is more stringent or less stringent than "reasonably necessary." The standard is thus "not in accordance with law." 5 U.S.C. § 706(2)(A). But the standard wouldn't be labeled "ultra vires" merely because it wasn't stringent enough or was too stringent.

While the *ultra vires* concept can be useful, sometimes it does not matter. A case illustrating the point is *Ragsdale v. Wolverine World Wide, Inc.*, 535 U.S. 81, 84 (2002), in which the Court held that an agency rule was "contrary to the [statute that it was designed to implement] and beyond the Secretary of Labor's authority," without suggesting a difference between the concepts of a regulation being contrary to the statute and being ultra vires. *See also Miss. Power & Light Co. v. Miss. ex rel. Moore*, 487 U.S. 354, 381 (1988) (Scalia, J., concurring in judgment) ("[T]here is no discernible line between an agency's exceeding its authority and an agency's exceeding authorized application of its authority."). In short, the *ultra vires* concept is one that administrative lawyers must *be aware* of, given its prevalence, but it is also a concept to *beware* of, given its slipperiness and limited usefulness.

So far we have been discussing legislative rules. A non-legislative, interpretive rule is invalid if it substantively conflicts with the agency legislation that it is supposed to interpret. For example, the U.S. Equal Employment Opportunity Commission (EEOC) issued interpretive rules to give the public guidance on the federal statute known as Title VII. Title VII prohibits employment discrimination based on gender. An EEOC interpretive rule stated that employment discrimination based on a woman's being pregnant violated Title VII. The U.S. Supreme Court reviewed this rule in a lawsuit brought by an employee claiming that her employer discriminated against pregnant employees. The Court concluded that the EEOC interpretive rule was invalid because it misinterpreted Title VII. *General Elec. Co. v. Gilbert*, 419 U.S. 125, 140–146 (1976). One way to express this conclusion is to say that the EEOC's rule exceeded its interpretive authority under Title VII. An equally valid way to make the point is to say, simply, the EEOC's interpretation was wrong.[1]

The existence of internal substantive limits on agency rulemaking power is inevitable, given the nondelegation doctrine. The nondelegation doctrine says that, when Congress gives an agency power to make legislative rules, Congress must prescribe an "intelligible principle" for the agency to follow when exercising that power. To prescribe an intelligible principle, Congress must put substantive limits on the agency's rulemaking power. When a State's law includes a version of the nondelegation doctrine, state statutes granting legislative rulemaking power to state agencies likewise must put substantive limits on the agency's power.

2. Internal Procedural Limits

The agency legislation often gives the agency power to make rules but does not address what procedures the agency must use when exercising that power. In that situation, there are no internal procedural limits on the rulemaking power. Sometimes, however, the agency legislation does contain procedural requirements for the agency's exercise of rulemaking power.

The Consumer Product Safety Act provides an example. It prescribes detailed requirements—some of which are at least quasi-substantive—for the Consumer Product Safety Commission to follow when making consumer product safety rules. *See* 15 U.S.C. § 2058 (2012). The procedures and requirements include these steps:

---

1. In a sense, the EEOC got the last laugh. After the Court's decision, Congress amended Title VII expressly to ban discrimination based on pregnancy. *See* 42 U.S.C. § 2000e(k) (2012), added by Pub. L. No. 95-555, 92 Stat. 2076 (1978).

- The Commission must publish in the Federal Register an advance notice of public rulemaking. In this advance notice, the Commission must identify the product and the nature of the risk of injury that worries the Commission and invite people to identify existing standards — e.g., voluntary industry standards — that might adequately address the risk if adopted by the Commission as mandatory standards. The Commission must also offer to help any interested person develop a voluntary standard that might avoid the need for a mandatory standard.

- The Commission cannot propose a consumer product safety rule unless it concludes that a voluntary standard won't work and makes other determinations demonstrating the necessity of, and identifying regulatory alternatives to, a consumer product safety rule.

- The Commission must conduct a regulatory analysis identifying the potential benefits and costs of the proposed and final rule, and explaining why the Commission rejected regulatory alternatives to the rule.

- The Commission must follow the rulemaking procedures of § 553 of the federal APA, except that, in addition to allowing members of the public to submit written comments on a proposed consumer product safety rule, the Commission must also give interested people an opportunity "for the oral presentation of data, views, or arguments." 15 U.S.C. § 2058(d)(2).

- The Commission must consider "the special needs of elderly and handicapped persons to determine the extent to which such persons may be adversely affected by" a consumer product safety rules. *Id.* § 2058(e).

And these are not all. Congress did not make it easy for the Commission to adopt consumer product safety rules.

Most agency legislation does not have such detailed rulemaking requirements. Indeed, most agency legislation does not have *any* procedural requirements for agency rulemaking. As we will see, when the agency legislation says nothing about the procedural requirements for the agency's exercise of legislative rulemaking power, the applicable Administrative Procedure Act (state or federal) applies by default, and prescribes rulemaking procedures for all agencies subject to that APA.

Even so, your search for procedural requirements for agency rulemaking should begin with the agency legislation. That is because the agency legislation's procedural requirements, if any, will ordinarily control in the event of a conflict with the APA's rulemaking requirements. Requirements in the agency legislation will ordinarily control because of the principle of statutory construction that holds: If two statutory provisions conflict, the more specific provision controls, instead of the more general. *See, e.g., Gozlon-Peretz v. United States*, 498 U.S. 395, 407 (1991). In addition, conflicts between a federal agency's legislation and the federal APA are addressed by federal APA § 559, which says that other statutes can add to the APA's requirements, and statutes enacted after the APA (in 1946) can modify the APA's requirements if they do so expressly.

Exercise: Analyzing Internal Procedural Requirements for Agency Rulemaking

Please review the statutory provision reproduced above prescribing the procedures for making consumer product safety standards. As you do, keep these questions in mind and then answer them:

1. Why do you think the provision stresses Commission consideration of voluntary safety standards?

2. How do the procedural requirements for Commission consideration of voluntary safety standards affect the substance of the Commission's decisionmaking process?

No agency is an island. Accordingly, you must look outside the agency legislation to determine whether other laws limit (or impose requirements for exercising) the agency's rulemaking power.

B. External Limits on Agency Rulemaking Power

This section identifies and briefly describes four potential, external sources of limits on agency rulemaking power:

(1) constitutional law

(2) statutory law

(3) agency rules and other executive branch material

(4) limits imposed in connection with judicial review of agency action, including agency rulemaking

1. Constitutional Law

Because the U.S. Constitution limits government power and agencies are governmental entities, the Constitution limits agency power, including agency rulemaking power. In the everyday practice of administrative law, it is rare for agency rules to present even arguable violations of the U.S. Constitution. Some rules may do so, however, and so the administrative lawyer must be aware of that possibility. This section briefly discusses substantive and procedural constitutional limits.

a. Substantive Limits

A federal or state agency rule must obey substantive limits of the U.S. Constitution.

For example, the U.S. Supreme Court held that rules promulgated by the Federal Railroad Administration were subject to the Fourth Amendment's ban on unreasonable searches and seizures. The rules compelled railroads to do drug and alcohol testing of railroad employees involved in train accidents. (The Court held that the rules complied with the Fourth Amendment. *See Skinner v. Railway Labor Executives' Ass'n*, 489 U.S. 602 (1989).)

In another case, the U.S. Supreme Court reviewed rules promulgated by the U.S. Civil Service Commission. The rules excluded everyone except U.S. citizens and natives of Samoa from most federal jobs. The Court held that the Due Process Clause of the Fifth

Amendment includes a substantive, "equal protection"-like component that prohibits unjustified discrimination based on national origin. The Court held that the Civil Service Rules violated this equal protection component of substantive due process. *See Hampton v. Mow Sun Wong*, 426 U.S. 88 (1976).

b. Procedural Limits

The Due Process Clauses of the Fifth and Fourteenth Amendment are the primary constitutional sources of procedural requirements for government action other than criminal proceedings.

As discussed in Chapter 4.D.3, the doctrine of procedural due process will seldom impose any meaningful procedural limits on an agency's rulemaking process. Under the *Londoner/Bi-Metallic* distinction, the core procedural due process requirements of individualized notice and a right to be heard do not apply to legislative-type activity, which includes most agency rulemaking proceedings. Rather, procedural due process applies to adjudicative action by government that deprives or threatens to deprive someone of life, liberty, or property.

Although procedural due process will only rarely apply to an agency's rulemaking process, procedural due process can apply to an agency's procedural rules for an agency adjudicatory process. For example, in *Goldberg v. Kelly*, the U.S. Supreme Court reviewed New York City's rules for adjudicating individuals' eligibility for welfare benefits. The Court held that a person who's been found eligible for welfare benefits has a protected "property" interest in continuing to receive those benefits. An agency therefore must give the person notice and a right to be heard before terminating the person's welfare benefits on the ground that the person is no longer eligible for them. The Court held that New York City's rules for a proceeding to terminate an individual's welfare benefits did not satisfy procedural due process requirements because those rules did not give the individuals an adequate right to be heard. *Goldberg v. Kelly*, 397 U.S. 254 (1970).

We examine procedural due process limits on agency adjudication in Chapter 20. We mention the limits here because procedural due process limits do apply to an agency's procedural rules for agency adjudications that deprive or threaten to deprive people of property or liberty.

2. Statutory Law

In addition to obeying limits in the agency legislation, an agency rule must obey limits in all other valid statutes. Most such statutes will be what we have called "cross-cutting statutes," meaning statutes applicable to more than one agency.

a. Substantive Limits

An example of a cross-cutting federal statute that puts substantive limits on some federal agency rules is the Endangered Species Act (ESA). The ESA requires federal agencies to avoid actions that jeopardize endangered species or their critical habitats. Thus it prescribes a substantive limit in the form of a result (jeopardy to endangered species or their critical habitats) that an agency action, including an agency rule, cannot cause. *See* 16 U.S.C. § 1536(a)(2) (2012).

So far we have discussed cases involving federal agency rules. A state agency rule must comply with all valid state statutes. In addition, as discussed in Chapter 5.B, state agencies and officials must obey many different federal as well as state statutes. *See, e.g., Conroy v. N.Y. State Dep't of Correctional Servs.*, 333 F.3d 88, 100–101 (2d Cir. 2003) (holding that state agency's sick-leave policy would violate the federal Americans with Disabilities Act unless the policy was proven to serve a valid business necessity).

In addition, as discussed in Chapter 5.B.2, state agencies must follow federal law when they administer federal programs under a scheme of cooperative federalism. A case illustrating this requirement is *Van Lare v. Hurley*, 421 U.S. 338 (1975). *Van Lare* concerned New York regulations for calculating eligibility for benefits under a federal program called "Aid to Families with Dependent Children" (AFDC). The New York regulations reduced payments for shelter when an AFDC recipient had a "lodger." These "lodger regulations" assumed that lodgers contributed their own money toward the AFDC recipient's costs of shelter. The U.S. Supreme Court held that the New York lodger regulations violated the federal Social Security Act and were therefore invalid. *Id.* at 344–348.

b. Procedural Limits

The applicable (federal or state) Administrative Procedure Act is the most important cross-cutting statute, because it imposes procedural requirements on most agency proceedings to make legislative rules. The APA is so important that we discuss its applicability and the nature of its procedural requirements for rulemakings in the next several chapters.

But the APA is not the only cross-cutting statute that puts procedural limits on agency rulemaking power. To mention one example, the National Environmental Policy Act (NEPA) requires federal agencies to assess the environmental impact of actions, including agency rules, that significantly affect the environment. 42 U.S.C. § 4332(C) (2012). We discuss NEPA's requirements in more detail, and identify other federal statutes that impose procedural requirements on many agency rulemaking proceedings, in Chapter 15.

3. Agency Rules and Other Executive-Branch Material

It is helpful to discuss separately (a) the agency's own rules and (b) other valid executive-branch material. Agency rules and other executive-branch material can be sources of substantive and procedural requirements.

a. The Agency's Own Rules

(i) Substantive Limits

When an agency makes a legislative rule, the rule binds the agency as well as the public. The agency must follow that rule—including when it makes later rules—until the agency changes the prior rule.

It is rare for an agency to make a legislative rule in *Year 0* and then make a conflicting legislative rule in *Year +1*. This problem seldom arises because agencies know their own rules. If the agency wants to repeal or modify the legislative rule made in *Year 0*, the agency can do so in *Year +1* by following the same procedures used to promulgate the original rule.

A more common problem is this one: An agency makes a legislative rule in *Year 0*. Later, in *Year +1*, the agency issues a *non-legislative* rule that supposedly just *interprets* the prior rule but actually seeks to *change* the prior rule through the process of interpretation. A court may give weight to an agency's interpretation of its prior rule. But if the court concludes that the later "interpretative rule" conflicts with the earlier, legislative rule, the interpretative rule will be invalid. Agencies cannot change their legislative rules in the guise of interpreting them. *See, e.g., First Nat'l Bank v. Standard Bank & Trust*, 172 F.3d 472, 479 (7th Cir. 1999).

(ii) Procedural Limits

An agency must follow all rulemaking procedures required by statute. The applicable statutes, however, may not describe the required rulemaking procedures in much detail. Moreover, the applicable statutes ordinarily will not prevent the agency from imposing additional procedural requirements on itself. Accordingly, the agency may usually elaborate upon, or add to, the statutorily required rulemaking procedures by issuing procedural rules for its rulemaking proceedings. Here is the relevant principle:

> **An agency may usually *elaborate upon*, or *add to*, statutorily required procedures, but the agency may not *modify* the statutory procedures or provide *less* than the statutorily required minimum procedures.**

In general, statutes create a procedural "floor," but not a procedural "ceiling" for the agency's rulemaking process. An agency can raise the procedural ceiling by adopting rules committing the agency to following additional rulemaking procedures but cannot lower or otherwise modify the statutory floor.

For example, the federal APA's procedures for informal rulemaking allow an agency to restrict the public to filing written comments on a proposed rule. 5 U.S.C. § 553(c) (2012). The federal APA does not, however, prevent an agency from holding public hearings on a proposed rule, as well as inviting written comments. A federal agency, therefore, could adopt a policy providing for public hearings on many, or all, of its proposed rules. The agency might decide that this policy will enable the agency to get input that the agency will not get if it allows only written comments. If the agency adopts a policy of providing public hearings on some or all of its proposed rules, the agency will ordinarily establish that policy by adopting a procedural rule setting out the policy. *E.g.,* 24 C.F.R. § 10.1 (2012) (stating policy of Department of Housing and Urban Development "[f]or some rules" to use "additional methods of inviting public participation" such as "conducting public surveys, and convening public forums or panels").

When an agency does issue procedural rules providing for additional rulemaking procedures — over and above the statutorily required procedures — the agency ordinarily must obey them, for two reasons. For one thing, procedural rules have "the force and effect of law" if they rest on a statutory grant of power to make legislative rules. *See, e.g., United States ex rel. Accardi v. Shaughnessy*, 347 U.S. 260, 265 (1954). Such a power may exist in the agency legislation. *See, e.g.,* 42 U.S.C. § 405(a) (authorizing Commissioner of Social Security to make procedural rules for deciding social security claims). For another thing, even non-legislative procedural rules bind agencies in the sense that an agency's unjustified departure from its procedural rules may render its action "arbitrary and capricious" and thus subject to judicial invalidation. 5 U.S.C. § 706(2)(A); *see also* Thomas W. Merrill, *The Accardi Principle*, 74 Geo. Wash. L. Rev. 569, 598 (2006).

You can find a federal agency's procedural rules in the same place you will find its substantive rules: the Federal Register and the CFR. The federal APA requires agencies to publish their "rules of procedure" in the Federal Register, which is a daily publication. 5 U.S.C. § 552(a) (1) (C). Some procedural rules are then permanently codified, by subject matter, in the CFR. *See, e.g.,* 14 C.F.R. §§ 11.1–11.53 (2012) (FAA rules); 24 C.F.R. §§ 10.1–10.20 (2012) (HUD rules); 49 C.F.R. §§ 1110.1–1110.10 (2012) (Surface Transportation Board rules). These will not be the most exciting rules that you ever read, but you will find it useful to get a sense of what issues these rules address. Likewise, most state APAs require state agencies to publish their procedural as well as their substantive rules — usually in the State's administrative code. *See* 2010 Model State APA § 201(h).

b. Other Executive-Branch Material

Besides an agency's own rules, two other types of executive-branch material may limit agency rulemaking power: (i) rules of other agencies and (ii) executive orders. Here is an example of the first type of material: A federal agency called the Council on Environmental Quality has rules prescribing procedures that *other* federal agencies must follow to comply with the National Environmental Policy Act (NEPA). 40 C.F.R. §§ 1500–1508 (2012). Additional procedural requirements for many federal agency rulemaking proceedings can be found in executive orders, which are issued by the President at the federal level and by Governors at the state level. We discuss executive orders in more detail in Chapter 15.B.

4. Judicial Review

Agency rules and other agency actions are generally subject to judicial review. Judicial review usually occurs under statutes, such as the APA, that authorize courts to review the agency action for substantive and procedural validity. Two elements of substantive validity concern (1) the factual support for the agency action and (2) the rationality of the agency's decisionmaking process and of its ultimate decision. Procedural validity entails agency compliance with all valid procedural requirements.

Below we separately discuss these substantive and procedural limits imposed by judicial review of agency rules. In discussing judicial review of the procedural validity of agency rules, we distinguish (i) federal court review of federal agency action from (ii) state court review of state agency action.

a. Substantive Limits

(i) Factual Support

Agency rules often reflect the agency's factual determinations. The EPA, for example, may regulate arsenic in the drinking water based on a determination of how much arsenic people can consume safely. (We hope so!) The Federal Reserve Board may make factual determinations about economic conditions before it sets the "federal funds rate" for certain transactions between banks. The U.S. Department of Transportation may make factual determinations about the effect of a particular auto safety device when it makes rules on auto safety. Thus, although we usually associate fact finding with agency adjudication, factual determinations also occur in agency rulemaking.

Sometimes the agency legislation specifies the factual information on which an agency must base its rules. For example, the Endangered Species Act requires the Secretaries of Commerce and Interior to consider "the best scientific and commercial data available" when deciding whether or not to designate a species as endangered. 16 U.S.C. § 1533(b)(1)(A) (2012). The Safe Drinking Water Act requires the Administrator of EPA to regulate drinking water contaminants using "the best available, peer-reviewed science and supporting studies conducted in accordance with sound and objective scientific practices." 42 U.S.C. § 300g-1(b)(3)(A)(i) (2012). Agency rules that violate evidentiary requirements in the agency legislation are invalid as exceeding internal limits on agency action.

But an agency rule must have adequate factual support even if the agency legislation authorizing the rule does not expressly require it. Even when no statute or other law directly requires the agency to have adequate factual support for its rule, courts ordinarily require it when reviewing an agency rule. For example, when a federal court reviews a federal agency rule under the federal APA, the court can set aside (invalidate) the rule if the rule is "**arbitrary, capricious, an abuse of direction.**" 5 U.S.C. § 706(2)(A). The U.S. Supreme Court has construed this APA language to allow courts to review the factual basis for certain agency actions, including agency rules. *See, e.g., Motor Vehicle Mfrs. Ass'n v. State Farm Mut. Auto. Ins. Co.*, 463 U.S. 29, 43 (1983).

More generally, judicial review of most agency actions, including agency rules, usually includes judicial review of the factual support for the agency action. We can therefore appropriately say that, even if no statute expressly requires the agency itself to have adequate factual support for its rule, a rule will be invalid—in the sense that a reviewing court may invalidate the rule—if it lacks adequate factual support. For this reason, we list the requirement that a rule have adequate factual support separately from the requirement that a rule must comply with all applicable statutes.

Although requirements governing the factual support for an agency rule may be considered substantive, they have procedural aspects. The requirements are substantive in the sense they concern the substance of what the agency considers during the rulemaking process (e.g., by requiring the agency to consider the "best available peer-reviewed data"). They also will affect the substance of the resulting rule. On the other hand, requirements governing the factual support for an agency rule operate during the rulemaking process and affect the agency's gathering and evaluation of evidence on relevant factual matters. They thus affect the rulemaking process. However you classify them, requirements governing the factual support for an agency rule put important limits on agency rulemaking power.

(ii) Reasoned Decision Making

It is rare for the agency legislation expressly to require the agency to act rationally. Courts reviewing agency rules and other agency actions, however, have authority to invalidate the agency rule or other action if it is not the product of what courts call "reasoned decision making." Today, the requirement of reasoned decision making is captured by provisions in APAs and other statutes that authorize courts to set aside agency action that is "arbitrary and capricious" or an "abuse of discretion." *See FCC v. Fox Television Stations, Inc.*, 556 U.S. 502, 537 (2009) ("If an agency takes action not based on neutral and rational principles, the APA grants federal court power to set aside the agency's action as 'arbitrary' or 'capricious.'"); *Baltimore Gas & Elec. Co. v. Natural Res. Def. Council*, 462 U.S. 87, 104 (1983) (holding that agency rule was "within the bounds of reasoned decisionmaking required by the APA").

We will explore the meaning of the APA terms "arbitrary" and "capricious," and the requirement of reasoned decision making, in Chapter 34.B. The requirement of "reasoned decision making" entails five principles:

(1) The agency's reasoning process must be rational and comprehensible.

(2) The agency's decision should rest on consideration of all relevant factors.

(3) The agency's decision should not rest on consideration of irrelevant factors.

(4) There should be a clear, logical connection between the agency's factual determinations and its ultimate decision.

(5) The agency action should be consistent with prior agency action—and thus the agency must treat similar situations similarly—unless the agency adequately explains why it has changed course.

These requirements, like the requirement that an agency action have adequate factual support, stem from courts' authority to review agency action. As with the requirement for adequate evidentiary support, this requirement can reasonably be characterized as either procedural or substantive. It requires a rational decisionmaking process as well as a rational result.

b. Procedural Requirements

Courts usually can review an agency rule or other agency action for procedural validity. For example, the federal APA authorizes a court to set aside federal agency action "**found to be … without observance of procedure required by law.**" 5 U.S.C. § 706(2)(D). The 2010 Model State APA authorizes a state court to grant relief if the person challenging state agency action has been prejudiced because "the agency committed an error of procedure." 2010 Model State APA § 508(a)(3)(B).

The primary sources of procedural requirements for agency rulemaking are the APA and the agency legislation. Other statutes, however, can supply procedural requirements, as can executive-branch material such as agency procedural rules and executive orders.

(i) Federal Court Review of Federal Agency Action—
The *Vermont Yankee* Principle

An important question is whether federal courts, acting on their own, can devise procedural requirements for federal agencies to follow when making rules. The U.S. Supreme Court said "no," except perhaps in "extremely compelling circumstances," in *Vermont Yankee Nuclear Power Corp. v. Natural Resources Defense Council, Inc.*, 435 U.S. 519, 543 (1978). We excerpt the Court's *Vermont Yankee* opinion below.

Before setting out the Court's opinion, we want to explain the name of the case: *Vermont Yankee Nuclear Power Corp. v. Natural Resources Defense Council, Inc.* The case concerns an informal rulemaking proceeding of the U.S. Nuclear Regulatory Commission (Commission). The Vermont Yankee Nuclear Power Corporation (Vermont Yankee) supported the rule that resulted from that proceeding, whereas the Natural Resources Defense Council (NRDC) opposed that rule. The United States Court of Appeals for the District of Columbia invalidated the rule. After the court of appeals invalidated the rule, Vermont Yankee petitioned the U.S. Supreme Court for review of the court of appeals' decision. As the petitioner, Vermont Yankee is listed first in the official case name. In its written petition for U.S. Supreme Court review, Vermont Yankee listed the NRDC first among the opposing parties, which are called "respondents." As the first-listed respondent, NRDC's name becomes the second half of the case's official name in the U.S. Supreme Court. Hence: Vermont Yankee vs. NRDC. Even so, the federal agency at the heart of controversy—the Nuclear Regulatory Commission—was a party to the case and participated in the Supreme Court proceedings. The Commission naturally supported its rule and thus sided with Vermont Yankee.

This is a good place to make a broader point that newcomers to administrative law may find useful. The names of administrative law cases do not necessarily include the name of an agency. In some cases, like *Vermont Yankee*, this is because of the conventions for naming cases. In other cases, it's because an agency official, instead of the agency, is named as the party. In still other cases, a lawsuit is between private parties but an agency still plays an important role. The moral of the story is: In your administrative law research, do not overlook a case merely because its name does not include the name of an agency.

Exercise: *Vermont Yankee*

Please read *Vermont Yankee* with these questions in mind:

1. The Court's opinion describes two different sets of agency proceedings: One set of proceedings were adjudicatory; they concerned whether to grant Vermont Yankee the two permits or licenses necessary to construct, and then to operate, a nuclear power plant. The other proceeding was a rulemaking proceeding. How did the rulemaking proceeding relate to the permit (licensing) proceedings?

2. What procedures did the Commission follow in the rulemaking proceeding?

3. What additional procedures did the U.S. Court of Appeals for the D.C. Circuit hold the Commission *should have* provided in the rulemaking proceeding?

4. Why did the Supreme Court hold that the court of appeals erred in requiring these additional procedures?

Vermont Yankee Nuclear Power Corp. v. Natural Resources Defense Council, Inc.
435 U.S. 519 (1978)

MR. JUSTICE REHNQUIST delivered the opinion of the Court.

In 1946, Congress enacted the Administrative Procedure Act, which as we have noted elsewhere was not only "a new, basic and comprehensive regulation of procedures in many agencies," *Wong Yang Sung v. McGrath*, 339 U.S. 33 (1950), but was also a legislative enactment which settled "long continued and hard fought contentions, and enacts a formula upon which opposing social and political forces have come to rest." *Id.*, at 40. Section 4 of the Act, 5 U.S.C. § 553 (1976 ed.), dealing with rulemaking, requires in subsection (b) that "notice of proposed rule making shall be published in the Federal Register, ..." describes the contents of that notice, and goes on to require in subsection (c) that after the notice the agency "shall give interested persons an opportunity to participate in the rule making through submission of written data, views, or arguments with or without opportunity for oral presentation. After consideration of the relevant matter presented, the agency shall incorporate in the rules adopted a concise general statement of their basis and purpose." Interpreting this provision of the Act in *United States v. Allegheny-Ludlum Steel Corp.*, 406 U.S. 742 (1972), and *United States v. Florida East Coast R. Co.*, 410 U.S. 224 (1973), we held that generally speaking this section of the Act established the maximum procedural requirements which Congress was willing to have the courts impose upon agencies in conducting rulemaking procedures. Agencies are free to grant additional procedural rights in the exercise of their discretion, but reviewing courts are generally not free to impose them if the agencies have not chosen to grant them. This is not to say necessarily that there are no circumstances which would ever justify a court in overturning agency action because of a failure to employ procedures beyond those required by the statute. But such circumstances, if they exist, are extremely rare.

Even apart from the Administrative Procedure Act this Court has for more than four decades emphasized that the formulation of procedures was basically to be left within the discretion of the agencies to which Congress had confided the responsibility for substantive judgments. In *FCC v. Schreiber*, 381 U.S. 279, 290 (1965), the Court explicated this principle, describing it as "an outgrowth of the congressional determination that administrative agencies and administrators will be familiar with the industries which they regulate and will be in a better position than federal courts or Congress itself to design procedural rules adapted to the peculiarities of the industry and the tasks of the agency involved." The Court there relied on its earlier case of *FCC v. Pottsville Broadcasting Co.*, 309 U.S. 134, 138 (1940), where it had stated that a provision dealing with the conduct of business by the Federal Communications Commission delegated to the Commission the power to resolve "subordinate questions of procedure ... [such as] the scope of the inquiry, whether applications should be heard contemporaneously or successively, whether parties should be allowed to intervene in one another's proceedings, and similar questions."

It is in the light of this background of statutory and decisional law that we granted certiorari to review two judgments of the Court of Appeals for the District of Columbia Circuit because of our concern that they had seriously misread or misapplied this statutory and decisional law cautioning reviewing courts against engrafting their own notions of proper procedures upon agencies entrusted with substantive functions by Congress. We conclude that the Court of Appeals has done just that in these cases, and we therefore remand them to it for further proceedings....

I

Under the Atomic Energy Act of 1954, 68 Stat. 919, as amended, 42 U.S.C. § 2011 et seq., the Atomic Energy Commission[2] was given broad regulatory authority over the development of nuclear energy. Under the terms of the Act, a utility seeking to construct and operate a nuclear power plant must obtain a separate permit or license at both the construction and the operation stage of the project. In order to obtain the construction permit, the utility must [submit detailed safety information that is reviewed by the Commission staff and by a separate advisory group of experts. Each evaluates the information

---

2. The licensing and regulatory functions of the Atomic Energy Commission (AEC) were transferred to the Nuclear Regulatory Commission (NRC) by the Energy Reorganization Act of 1974, 42 U.S.C. § 5801 et seq. (1970 ed., Supp. V). Hereinafter both the AEC and NRC will be referred to as the Commission.

submitted and makes a report to the Commission.] Thereupon a three member Atomic Safety and Licensing Board conducts a public adjudicatory hearing, and reaches a decision[3] which can be appealed to the Atomic Safety and Licensing Appeal Board, and currently, in the Commission's discretion, to the Commission itself. The final agency decision may be appealed to the courts of appeals. The same sort of process occurs when the utility applies for a license to operate the plant, except that a hearing need only be held in contested cases and may be limited to the matters in controversy.[5] ...

In December 1967, after the mandatory adjudicatory hearing and necessary review, the Commission granted petitioner Vermont Yankee a permit to build a nuclear power plant in Vernon, Vt.... Thereafter, Vermont Yankee applied for an operating license. Respondent Natural Resources Defense Council (NRDC) objected to the granting of a license, however, and therefore a hearing on the application commenced on August 10, 1971. Excluded from consideration at the hearings, over NRDC's objection, was the issue of the environmental effects of operations to reprocess fuel or dispose of wastes resulting from the reprocessing operations. This ruling was affirmed by the Appeal Board in June 1972.

In November 1972, however, the Commission, making specific reference to the Appeal Board's decision with respect to the Vermont Yankee license, instituted rulemaking proceedings "that would specifically deal with the question of consideration of environmental effects associated with the uranium fuel cycle in the individual cost benefit analyses for light water cooled nuclear power reactors." The notice of proposed rulemaking offered two alternatives, both predicated on a report prepared by the Commission's staff entitled Environmental Survey of the Nuclear Fuel Cycle. The first would have required no quantitative evaluation of the environmental hazards of fuel reprocessing or disposal because the Environmental Survey had found them to be slight. The second would have specified numerical values for the environmental impact of this part of the fuel cycle, which values would then be incorporated into a table, along with the other relevant factors, to determine the overall cost-benefit balance for each operating license....

Much of the controversy in this case revolves around the procedures used in the rulemaking hearing which commenced in February 1973. In a supplemental notice of hearing the Commission indicated that while discovery or cross examination would not be utilized, the Environmental Survey would be available to the public before the hearing along with the extensive background documents cited therein. All participants would be given a reasonable opportunity to present their position and could be represented by counsel if they so desired. Written and, time permitting, oral statements would be received and incorporated into the record. All persons giving oral statements would be subject to questioning by the Commission. At the conclusion of the hearing, a transcript would be made available to the public and the record would remain open for 30 days to allow the filing of supplemental written statements. More than 40 individuals and organizations representing a wide variety of interests submitted written comments. On January 17, 1973, the Licensing Board held a planning session to schedule the appearance of witnesses and to discuss methods for compiling a record. The hearing was held on February 1 and 2, with participation by a number of groups, including the Commission's staff, the United

---

3. The Licensing Board issues a permit if it concludes that there is reasonable assurance that the proposed plant can be constructed and operated without undue risk, and that the environmental cost-benefit balance favors the issuance of a permit.

5. When a license application is contested, the Licensing Board must find reasonable assurance that the plant can be operated without undue risk and will not be inimical to the common defense and security or to the health and safety of the public. The Licensing Board's decision is subject to review similar to that afforded the Board's decision with respect to a construction permit.

States Environmental Protection Agency, a manufacturer of reactor equipment, a trade association from the nuclear industry, a group of electric utility companies, and a group called Consolidated National Intervenors which represented 79 groups and individuals including respondent NRDC.

After the hearing, the Commission's staff filed a supplemental document for the purpose of clarifying and revising the Environmental Survey. Then the Licensing Board forwarded its report to the Commission without rendering any decision. The Licensing Board identified as the principal procedural question the propriety of declining to use full formal adjudicatory procedures [in the rulemaking proceeding]. The major substantive issue was the technical adequacy of the Environmental Survey.

In April 1974, the Commission issued a rule which adopted the second of the two proposed alternatives described above. The Commission also approved the procedures used at the hearing, and indicated that the record, including the Environmental Survey, provided an "adequate data base for the regulation adopted." Finally, the Commission ruled that to the extent the rule differed from the Appeal Board decisions in *Vermont Yankee* "those decisions have no further precedential significance," but that since "the environmental effects of the uranium fuel cycle have been shown to be relatively insignificant … it is unnecessary to apply the amendment to applicant's environmental reports submitted prior to its effective date.…"

Respondents appealed from both the Commission's adoption of the rule and its decision to grant Vermont Yankee's license to the Court of Appeals for the District of Columbia Circuit.…

With respect to the challenge of Vermont Yankee's license, the court first ruled that in the absence of effective rulemaking proceedings, the Commission must deal with the environmental impact of fuel reprocessing and disposal in individual licensing proceedings. The court then examined the rulemaking proceedings and, despite the fact that it appeared that the agency employed all the procedures required by 5 U.S.C. § 553 (1976 ed.) and more, the court determined the proceedings to be inadequate and overturned the rule. Accordingly, the Commission's determination with respect to Vermont Yankee's license was also remanded for further proceedings.…

After a thorough examination of the opinion itself, we conclude that while the matter is not entirely free from doubt, the majority of the Court of Appeals struck down the rule because of the perceived inadequacies of the procedures employed in the rulemaking proceedings. The court first determined the intervenors' primary argument to be "that the decision to preclude 'discovery or cross examination' denied them a meaningful opportunity to participate in the proceedings as guaranteed by due process." 178 U.S.App.D.C., at 346, 547 F.2d, at 643. The court then went on to frame the issue for decision thus:

> Thus, we are called upon to decide whether the procedures provided by the agency were sufficient to ventilate the issues.…

In prior opinions we have intimated that even in a rule making proceeding when an agency is making a " 'quasi-judicial' " determination by which a very small number of persons are " 'exceptionally affected, in each case upon individual grounds,' " in some circumstances additional procedures may be required in order to afford the aggrieved individuals due process.[16] *United States v. Florida East Coast R. Co.*, 410 U.S., at 242, 245,

---

16. Respondent NRDC does not now argue that additional procedural devices were required under the Constitution. Since this was clearly a rulemaking proceeding in its purest form, we see nothing to support such a view. See *United States v. Florida East Coast R. Co*, 410 U.S. 224, 244–245 (1973);

quoting from *Bi Metallic Investment Co. v. State Board of Equalization*, 239 U.S. 441, 446 (1915). It might also be true, although we do not think the issue is presented in this case and accordingly do not decide it, that a totally unjustified departure from well settled agency procedures of long standing might require judicial correction.

But this much is absolutely clear. Absent constitutional constraints or extremely compelling circumstances the "administrative agencies 'should be free to fashion their own rules of procedure and to pursue methods of inquiry capable of permitting them to discharge their multitudinous duties.'" *FCC v. Schreiber*, 381 U.S., at 290, quoting from *FCC v. Pottsville Broadcasting Co.*, 309 U.S., at 143. Indeed, our cases could hardly be more explicit in this regard. The Court has, as we noted in *FCC v. Schreiber*, upheld this principle in a variety of applications ... [a]nd the basic reason ... was the ... very basic tenet of administrative law that agencies should be free to fashion their own rules of procedure.

We have continually repeated this theme through the years, most recently in *FPC v. Transcontinental Gas Pipe Line Corp.*, 423 U.S. 326 (1976), decided just two Terms ago. In that case, in determining the proper scope of judicial review of agency action under the Natural Gas Act, we held that while a court may have occasion to remand an agency decision because of the inadequacy of the record, the agency should normally be allowed to "exercise its administrative discretion in deciding how, in light of internal organization considerations, it may best proceed to develop the needed evidence and how its prior decision should be modified in light of such evidence as develops." *Id.*, at 333. We went on to emphasize:

> At least in the absence of substantial justification for doing otherwise, a reviewing court may not, after determining that additional evidence is requisite for adequate review, proceed by dictating to the agency the methods, procedures, and time dimension of the needed inquiry and ordering the results to be reported to the court without opportunity for further consideration on the basis of the new evidence by the agency. Such a procedure clearly runs the risk of "[propelling] the court into the domain which Congress has set aside exclusively for the administrative agency." *SEC v. Chenery Corp.*, 332 U.S. 194, 196 (1947). *Ibid.*

Respondent NRDC argues that § 4 of the Administrative Procedure Act, 5 U.S.C. § 553 (1976 ed.), merely establishes lower procedural bounds and that a court may routinely require more than the minimum when an agency's proposed rule addresses complex or technical factual issues or "Issues of Great Public Import." ... We have, however, previously shown that our decisions reject this view.... We also think the legislative history, even the part which it cites, does not bear out its contention.... And the Attorney General's Manual on the Administrative Procedure Act 31, 35 (1947), a contemporaneous interpretation previously given some deference by this Court because of the role played by the Department of Justice in drafting the legislation, further confirms that view. In short, all of this leaves little doubt that Congress intended that the discretion of the agencies and not that of the courts be exercised in determining when extra procedural devices should be employed.

There are compelling reasons for construing § 4 in this manner. In the first place, if courts continually review agency proceedings to determine whether the agency employed

---

Bowles v. Willingham, 321 U.S. 503 (1944); *Bi-Metallic Investment Co. v. State Board of Equalization*, 239 U.S. 441 (1915)....

procedures which were, in the court's opinion, perfectly tailored to reach what the court perceives to be the "best" or "correct" result, judicial review would be totally unpredictable. And the agencies, operating under this vague injunction to employ the "best" procedures and facing the threat of reversal if they did not, would undoubtedly adopt full adjudicatory procedures in every instance. Not only would this totally disrupt the statutory scheme [of the APA] ... but all the inherent advantages of informal rulemaking would be totally lost.

Secondly, it is obvious that the court in these cases reviewed the agency's choice of procedures on the basis of the record actually produced at the hearing, and not on the basis of the information available to the agency when it made the decision to structure the proceedings in a certain way. This sort of Monday morning quarterbacking not only encourages but almost compels the agency to conduct all rulemaking proceedings with the full panoply of procedural devices normally associated only with adjudicatory hearings.

Finally, and perhaps most importantly, this sort of review fundamentally misconceives the nature of the standard for judicial review of an agency rule. The court below uncritically assumed that additional procedures will automatically result in a more adequate record because it will give interested parties more of an opportunity to participate in and contribute to the proceedings. But informal rulemaking need not be based solely on the transcript of a hearing held before an agency. Indeed, the agency need not even hold a formal hearing. See 5 U.S.C. § 553(c) (1976 ed.). Thus, the adequacy of the "record" in this type of proceeding is not correlated directly to the type of procedural devices employed, but rather turns on whether the agency has followed the statutory mandate of the Administrative Procedure Act or other relevant statutes. If the agency is compelled to support the rule which it ultimately adopts with the type of record produced only after a full adjudicatory hearing, it simply will have no choice but to conduct a full adjudicatory hearing prior to promulgating every rule. In sum, this sort of unwarranted judicial examination of perceived procedural shortcomings of a rulemaking proceeding can do nothing but seriously interfere with that process prescribed by Congress.

In short, nothing in the APA, ... the circumstances of this case, the nature of the issues being considered, past agency practice, or the statutory mandate under which the Commission operates permitted the court to review and overturn the rulemaking proceeding on the basis of the procedural devices employed (or not employed) by the Commission so long as the Commission employed at least the statutory minima, a matter about which there is no doubt in this case.

There remains, of course, the question of whether the challenged rule finds sufficient justification in the administrative proceedings that it should be upheld by the reviewing court. Judge Tamm, concurring in the result reached by the majority of the Court of Appeals, thought that it did not. There are also intimations in the majority opinion which suggest that the judges who joined it likewise may have thought the administrative proceedings an insufficient basis upon which to predicate the rule in question. We accordingly remand so that the Court of Appeals may review the rule as the Administrative Procedure Act provides.... The court should engage in this kind of review and not stray beyond the judicial province to explore the procedural format or to impose upon the agency its own notion of which procedures are "best" or most likely to further some vague, undefined public good.[21] ... Reversed and remanded.

---

21. Of course, the court must determine whether the agency complied with the procedures mandated by the relevant statutes. *Citizens to Preserve Overton Park v. Volpe*, 401 U.S. 402, 417 (1971).

Mr. Justice Blackmun and Mr. Justice Powell took no part in the consideration or decision of these cases.

Exercise: *Vermont Yankee* Revisited

1. In administrative law circles you often hear references to the "*Vermont Yankee* principle." Please write a short description of that principle, based on your understanding of the Court's holding and rationale. In composing your version of the *Vermont Yankee* principle, make sure to address the legal foundation for the principle. For example, does the principle reflect that the APA restricts federal courts' power to make procedural rules for federal agencies? Or does the principle reflect that federal courts simply lack that power in the first place?

   In considering this question, you might find it helpful to know that, though *Vermont Yankee* concerned informal rulemaking, the Court in a later case relied on *Vermont Yankee* to hold that federal courts generally cannot devise procedural requirements for federal agencies to follow in informal adjudications. *See Pension Benefit Guaranty Corp. v. LTV Corp.*, 496 U.S. 633, 653–655 (1990). This means that the *Vermont Yankee* principle does not reflect simply an interpretation of the federal APA's rulemaking provision, § 553.

   Here is more food for thought when you consider the basis of the *Vermont Yankee* principle. Subject to certain restrictions, federal courts can use federal common law to devise procedural rules for their own proceedings. Maybe *Vermont Yankee* means that federal courts cannot rely on federal common law to devise procedural rules for federal agencies. If this is what *Vermont Yankee* means, what justifies this limit on federal common law?

2. Review the *Vermont Yankee* opinion to identify possible exceptions to the *Vermont Yankee* principle.

3. Although federal courts generally cannot devise procedural requirements for agency rulemaking, they can review whether the agency gave a sufficient justification for the fuel cycle rule in light of the data and other factual material before the agency. This type of review is justified by the federal APA provisions authorizing courts to set aside agency action that is "arbitrary and capricious." 5 U.S.C. § 706(2)(A) (2012). *See Vermont Yankee*, 435 U.S. at 549 ("There remains, of course, the question of whether the challenged rule finds sufficient justification in the administrative proceedings that it should be upheld by the reviewing court."). As mentioned earlier in this chapter, the "arbitrary and capricious" standard imposes on agencies an obligation to engage in reasoned decision making and have adequate factual support. The NRC's fuel cycle rule was eventually reviewed by the U.S. Supreme Court under this standard. The Court held that the rule was "within the bounds of reasoned decisionmaking required by the APA." *Baltimore Gas & Elec. Co. v. NRDC*, 462 U.S. 87, 104 (1983). Why didn't the Court decide this the first time the fuel cycle rule was before it?

But, as we indicated above, there is little doubt that the agency was in full compliance with all the applicable requirements of the Administrative Procedure Act.

Note Introducing "Open Record" vs. "Closed Record" Proceedings

You need background to appreciate fully the following part of the *Vermont Yankee* opinion:

> The court below uncritically assumed that additional procedures will automatically result in a more adequate record because it will give interested parties more of an opportunity to participate in and contribute to the proceedings. But informal rulemaking need not be based solely on the transcript of a hearing held before an agency.

435 U.S. at 547. Here the Court criticizes the lower court for ignoring that an informal rulemaking proceeding under the federal APA—such as the Nuclear Regulatory Commission proceeding on the fuel cycle rule—is not a "closed record" proceeding, to use administrative law terminology. Instead, informal rulemaking under the federal APA is an "open record" proceeding.

You will learn more throughout this book about the distinction between "closed record" and "open record" proceedings. The distinction is fundamental—comparable in importance to the distinction between rules and orders and the distinction between legislative and non-legislative rules. Now we will just introduce it.

In a nutshell, a closed record administrative proceeding has two essential characteristics:

1. The participants in a closed record proceeding—the parties and the court (or other decision maker)—know exactly what material will be the basis for the ultimate decision. They know this because a law governing the proceeding prescribes the material on which the agency must base its decision. This material constitutes "the record."

2. The decision maker must base the decision exclusively on the record.

A judicial proceeding has these same characteristics and is, indeed, the paradigm of a closed record proceeding.

In contrast, in an open record proceeding such as informal rulemaking under the federal APA, the decision maker is allowed to rely on material (e.g., material in agency files or within the expertise of agency employees) that may not be disclosed to everyone with an interest in the proceeding before the decision is made. Indeed, the agency may base its rule on not only material submitted by the public but also "materials in its files and the knowledge and experience of the agency." AGM 31–32. The rationale for allowing a federal agency in informal rulemaking proceedings to rely on material other than that presented by the public is that rulemaking is a legislative-type proceeding, and, just as legislators may rely on material other than that presented in, for example, committee hearings, agencies may rely on material other than that presented in public input.

So you may now be wondering: What does the distinction between open record proceedings and closed record proceedings have to do with *Vermont Yankee*? The answer is that Congress intended, in Section 4 of the federal APA (5 U.S.C. § 553), to make informal rulemaking an open record proceeding. The lower court in *Vermont Yankee* ignored Congress's intention by requiring a federal agency to follow procedures that were more appropriate for a closed record proceeding. So what is the problem with that? The problem is: If Congress enacts a statute telling agencies to bake bread, federal courts are not allowed to insist that an agency instead bake a soufflé.

(ii) State Court Review of State Agency Action

The *Vermont Yankee* principle concerns the relationship between federal courts and federal agencies, and Congress's intention in enacting the federal APA. *Vermont Yankee* does not concern the relationship between state courts and state agencies, or the proper interpretation of any state APA. Nothing in *Vermont Yankee*, or in any other U.S. Supreme Court precedent, prevents state law from authorizing state courts to craft rules of procedure for state agencies. Even so, a state court might interpret state law to deny state courts power to devise rulemaking requirements for executive-branch agencies. *See Int'l Council of Shopping Ctrs. v. Oregon Envt'l Quality Comm'n*, 597 P.2d 847, 849 (Or. App. 1979) (statute governing court's review of agency rules prevents courts from "apply[ing] any additional requirements of common law").

Occasionally state courts rely on state common law as a source of procedural requirements for agency proceedings. An example is *Shively v. Stewart*, 421 P.2d 475 (Cal. 1966). In *Shively*, the California Supreme Court relied on state common law to hold that a physician was entitled to prehearing discovery in a disciplinary proceeding before the state Board of Medical Examiners. *Id.* at 478–481. The Court observed that, at that time, the California APA did not expressly authorize prehearing discovery. The Court determined that the APA's silence "has left to the courts the question whether modern concepts of administrative adjudication call for common law rules to permit and regulate the use of the agencies' subpoena power to secure prehearing discovery." *Id.* at 479. California later amended its APA to include provisions for discovery in administrative adjudications. The California Supreme Court has not, however, repudiated *Shively*'s conclusion that common law can be a source of administrative procedure requirements. *See* 1 Witkin, California Evidence 4th (2000), Evid. § 77, p. 85, 1 WITEVID Ch. 1, § 78 (Westlaw).

The takeaway is that *Vermont Yankee* seems to rule out federal common law as a general source of procedural requirements for federal agencies. Common law also does not play a prominent role as a source of procedural requirements for state agencies. Still, you cannot count common law out entirely. Common law needs a place on the list of potential sources of procedural requirements.

C. Chapter 9 Wrap Up and Look Ahead

Limits on agency rulemaking power can come from within the agency legislation or outside it. In either event, some limits are substantive; other limits are procedural; and still others are hard to classify. This chapter has been comprehensive in its scope, with the aim of adapting the problem solving framework introduced in Chapter 2 for use in solving problems involving agency rules.

In the chapters immediately after this, our focus narrows to procedural requirements for agency rulemaking imposed by (1) the agency legislation, (2) the applicable (federal or state) APA, and, in the case of federal rulemaking, (3) other broadly applicable statutes and executive orders. This focus reflects the practical reality that most procedural requirements for agency rulemaking come from those three sources. As *Vermont Yankee* makes clear, the federal courts acting on their own are generally not a source of procedural requirements for federal agency rulemaking.

This book and courses on administrative law focus on procedural limits and requirements, rather than substantive ones, because the substantive law that agencies administer is way too broad to cover in one course and for that reason are the subject of separate books, and separate law school courses, on subjects such as environmental law, securities law, labor law, etc.

Chapter Problem Revisited

This chapter gives you a narrative description of the framework for analyzing an agency rule to determine whether the agency has obeyed limits on, and requirements for exercising, that power. The chapter problem asked you to convert that description into a graphic depiction. Doing so will help you remember the framework presented in this chapter and build on it as you work through future chapters on agency rulemaking, which flesh out certain limits and requirements. Your ability to develop user-friendly depictions of these frameworks will serve you particularly well in the practice of administrative law, because administrative law is such a sprawling topic and administrative law problems can be complex. It is easy to lose track of the big picture.

Professional Development Reflection Questions

One of the main things you must learn in law school is *how* to learn. That is because you can't learn everything you need to know to be a good lawyer. You have to do much learning on the job. A key to effective learning, as you've probably heard (perhaps ad nauseam) is "active learning." Active learning means you are doing more than passively absorbing information. Instead, you are using it in some way.

A good way to use the information you will learn in this book is to build on the framework that we introduced in Chapter 2 and will use throughout the book. By "building" on that framework, we mean creating your own outline, or mega-flow chart, or series of graphic organizers—anything that requires you to take the information and organize it in a personalized way.

Having emphasized the importance of "active learning" to your becoming a highly competent lawyer, we pose these questions (not to put you on the spot!):

1. At this point in your study of administrative law, what things do you regularly do, besides reading, to learn the material?

2. Realistically considering the demands on your time, how can you change your approach to learn the material more deeply, remember it better, and be more efficient in your approach to learning?

Chapter 10

The APA as a Source of Procedural Requirements for Agency Rulemaking

Overview

The major external source of procedural requirements for agency rulemaking is the applicable (federal or state) APA. The APA is the major such source because it is so broadly applicable. It is so broadly applicable because it was designed that way. As discussed in Chapter 4, both the Federal and state APAs were designed to create more uniformity in rulemaking procedures among agencies.

Because of the APA's broad applicability, when analyzing an administrative law problem, you must always determine whether the APA applies to the problem at hand and, if so, how it interacts with other applicable legal requirements. We introduced in Chapter 4.C a framework for analyzing the applicability of the APA to an administrative law problem. This chapter illustrates its use for analyzing the applicability of the APA to an agency rule.

The chapter's sections are entitled:

A. Framework for Analyzing APA's Applicability to An Agency Rule

B. Step 1 of Analysis: Does the APA Apply to This Agency?

C. Step 2 of Analysis: If the APA Does Apply to the Agency, Do the APA's Rule-making Requirements Apply to the Rule under Analysis? — Examining the APA Exemptions

D. Step 2 of Analysis, Continued: If the APA Does Apply to the Agency, Do the APA's Rulemaking Requirements Apply to the Rule under Analysis? — Examining the Agency Legislation and Agency Rules

E. Chapter 10 Wrap Up and Look Ahead

Chapter Problem

You are in-house counsel for a timber company. You specialize in employment and labor law. The company's Chief Legal Officer (CLO) asks for your advice on a letter the company has received from the U.S. Occupational Safety and Health Administration (OSHA). OSHA has power under the Occupational Safety and Health Act (OSH Act) to inspect workplaces for violations of safety rules and impose civil fines and other serious sanctions for those violations.

The letter from OSHA announces a new program for companies with particularly dangerous work places, which includes timber logging companies.

The program is called the Ensuring Safety Program (ESP). The OSHA letter describes the ESP as a "voluntary program."

Here is how the ESP works, according to the OSHA letter: Your company and about 13,000 other employers with particularly dangerous workplaces have been scheduled for a mandatory, comprehensive OSHA inspection within the next 15 months. Your company and these other companies can avoid the mandatory inspection, however, by adopting and implementing an OSHA-approved "Comprehensive Safety and Health Plan" (Plan). The Plan must require certain workplace safety procedures and must have certain substantive provisions. For example, the Plan must lay out steps for investigating both actual accidents and any "near-miss" incidents. The Plan must address substantive matters like ergonomic workplace tools and ergonomic work settings, and the proper handling of toxic substances and training for use of dangerous machinery.

The letter from OSHA stresses that an acceptable Plan will require employers to "go beyond mere compliance" with existing OSHA rules. The Plan must be designed "to address and prevent *all* workplace hazards," not just the specific hazards covered by OSHA rules. To achieve this purpose, Plans must obligate the employer to follow even otherwise "voluntary" standards developed, not by OSHA, but by the industries themselves. OSHA must approve each employer's Plan.

A company that implements an OSHA-approved Plan reduces its risk of a comprehensive OSHA inspection by 70–90%. That is significant because these comprehensive inspections can be disruptive and expensive for employers, whether or not the OSHA inspectors find any violations. And they invariably *do* find violations. Your company estimates that it spent $5 million accommodating the last OSHA inspection by activities like producing records for OSHA inspection and providing company officials to escort OSHA investigators around the worksite and answer their detailed follow-up questions. OSHA inspections distract workers from their jobs and can hurt workforce morale. They also can attract negative publicity when OSHA cites the company for safety violations found during the inspections.

A provision in the OSH Act grants OSHA broad power to make "such rules and regulations ... [as may be] necessary to carry out" the Act, "including rules and regulations dealing with the inspection of an employer's establishment." 29 U.S.C. § 657(g)(2) (2012). Neither the legislation governing the Department of Labor nor the Department of Labor's rules address the applicability of the APA to rules promulgated by the Department under the OSH Act.

The CLO notes that OSHA's grants of rulemaking power may authorize OSHA to promulgate a legislative rule establishing something like the ESP. But OSHA has not promulgated any legislative rule on the ESP. OSHA has simply sent out this form letter announcing the ESP without having followed the APA's rulemaking requirements. The CLO asks you to analyze the applicability of those requirements to the ESP. Can you even call the ESP a "rule"? It has the feel of one.

A. Framework for Analyzing APA's Applicability to an Agency Rule

We repeat here the framework from Chapter 4.C for analyzing the applicability of the APA to an agency action, modified to specify that the type of action under analysis will be a "rule," as defined in the applicable APA:

A. Does the APA apply to this agency? To answer that question, identify and analyze:

  1. the APA definition of "agency" (and, if necessary, case law interpreting the APA definition)

  2. provisions (if any) in the agency legislation addressing APA's applicability to this agency (and, if necessary, case law interpreting the provisions in the agency legislation)

B. If the APA does apply to this agency, do the APA's rulemaking requirements apply to this rule? To answer that question, consult:

  1. provisions in the APA (and, if necessary, case law interpreting those provisions)

  2. provisions (if any) in the agency legislation or agency rules addressing APA's applicability to the agency rule under analysis (and, if necessary, case law interpreting those provisions)

C. If the APA applies, how does it interact with other applicable legal requirements?

  1. Constitutional provisions take precedence over APA provisions and may affect their validity or interpretation.

  2. The agency legislation may add to APA requirements. Also, the agency legislation can modify or supersede APA requirements. But federal agency legislation enacted after the federal APA (in 1946) can effectively modify or supersede APA requirements only if it does so expressly. 5 U.S.C. § 559.

  3. Agency rules and other executive-branch material (e.g., executive orders) may add to or elaborate upon APA procedures, and may make APA requirements applicable to agency rules that are otherwise exempt from the APA by its terms. Agency rules and other executive-branch material cannot, however, trump either the APA or the agency legislation—e.g., by exempting an agency rule that, according to the APA or the agency statute, is subject to the APA.

The rest of this chapter fleshes out parts A and B of this framework.

The upshot of the framework, as applied to rulemaking under the federal APA, is that the APA is indeed widely applicable, but some rules are exempt from the APA. When the federal APA does apply, its interaction with the agency legislation may lead to one of three types of rulemaking proceedings: informal (i.e., notice-and-comment) rulemaking; formal rulemaking; and hybrid rulemaking.

State APAs differ from the federal APA and from each other in their applicability and rulemaking procedures. Generally, however, state APAs are broadly applicable to state agency rulemaking.

B. Step 1 of Analysis:
Does the APA Apply to This Agency?

As discussed in Chapter 4.C.2.a, to determine whether the relevant (federal or state) APA applies to the agency under analysis, you must interpret the APA and the agency legislation. Specifically, you look at the APA's definition of "agency" and case law construing that definition. *E.g.*, 5 U.S.C. § 551(1) (2012); 2010 Model State APA § 102(3). If the agency you are dealing with falls within that definition, or outside it, that usually concludes the matter of the APA's applicability. Even so, sometimes the agency legislation addresses the APA's applicability to the agency. If the agency legislation does address the issue, it ordinarily controls, under the maxim of statutory construction holding that, when a general statute and a specific statute conflict, the specific controls. *See* 2B Norman J. Singer & J.D. Shambie Singer, Sutherland Statutory Construction § 51:5, at 282–287 (2008).

Suppose you have examined both (1) the APA definition of "agency" and (2) the agency legislation; and you have determined that the APA applies to the agency under analysis. Then the APA *may* be a source of procedural requirements for the agency's rule. You must continue to step two.

C. Step 2 of Analysis:
If the APA Does Apply to the Agency,
Do the APA's Rulemaking Requirements
Apply to the Rule under Analysis? —
Examining the APA Exemptions

At step two you ask whether the APA's rulemaking requirements apply to the agency rule under analysis. To answer this question, you must look in: (1) the APA; and (2) the agency legislation and the agency's own rules. Your examination of those sources enables you to determine whether the APA's rulemaking requirements apply to the agency rule under analysis. If not, the APA drops out of the picture as a potential source of procedural requirements for the rule. If, on the other hand, the APA's rulemaking requirements do apply to the rule, then you must go to step three, which requires meshing the APA's rulemaking requirements with any other applicable procedural requirements for the rule.

In this section, we examine APA provisions that exempt certain rules from the APA's procedural requirements for rulemaking. In the next section, we examine agency legislation and agency rules exempting certain rules from the APA's procedural requirements for rulemaking.

1. Federal APA Rulemaking Exemptions

The federal APA provision on "**Rule making**," APA § 553, exempts certain rules from some or all of its requirements. To understand the exemptions, you must read all of § 553.

It is not long. If this is the first time you have read § 553 from start to finish, read it just to get a sense of its structure. To do so, ask yourself: What basic topic does each subsection address? Then read through it again paying particular attention to (a) and (b), where you will find the rulemaking exemptions, which are our present focus.

---

5 U.S.C. § 553. Rule making

(a) This section applies, according to the provisions thereof, except to the extent that there is involved —

   (1) a military or foreign affairs function of the United States; or

   (2) a matter relating to agency management or personnel or to public property, loans, grants, benefits, or contracts.

(b) General notice of proposed rule making shall be published in the Federal Register, unless persons subject thereto are named and either personally served or otherwise have actual notice thereof in accordance with law. The notice shall include —

   (1) a statement of the time, place, and nature of public rule making proceedings;

   (2) reference to the legal authority under which the rule is proposed; and

   (3) either the terms or substance of the proposed rule or a description of the subjects and issues involved.

Except when notice or hearing is required by statute, this subsection does not apply —

   (A) to interpretative rules, general statements of policy, or rules of agency organization, procedure, or practice; or

   (B) when the agency for good cause finds (and incorporates the finding and a brief statement of reasons therefor in the rules issued) that notice and public procedure thereon are impracticable, unnecessary, or contrary to the public interest.

(c) After notice required by this section, the agency shall give interested persons an opportunity to participate in the rule making through submission of written data, views, or arguments with or without opportunity for oral presentation. After consideration of the relevant matter presented, the agency shall incorporate in the rules adopted a concise general statement of their basis and purpose. When rules are required by statute to be made on the record after opportunity for an agency hearing, sections 556 and 557 of this title apply instead of this subsection.

(d) The required publication or service of a substantive rule shall be made not less than 30 days before its effective date, except —

   (1) a substantive rule which grants or recognizes an exemption or relieves a restriction;

   (2) interpretative rules and statements of policy; or

   (3) as otherwise provided by the agency for good cause found and published with the rule.

(e) Each agency shall give an interested person the right to petition for the issuance, amendment, or repeal of a rule.

Exercise: Outlining Federal APA § 553

Suppose you were drafting § 553 and, like modern statutory drafters, wished to give each subsection a short title (no more than six words). What title do you give to each subsection of § 553?

(a) _____

(b) _____

(c) _____

(d) _____

(e) _____

We encourage you to revisit your titles when you reach the end of this chapter and consider whether the titles need revision.

---

a. The Differences between the Exemptions in § 553(a) and Those in § 553(b)

Section 553 contains exemptions in subsection (a) and (b). It is hard to keep them straight. Therefore, let us start by identifying the differences between the exemptions in § 553(a) and those in § 553(b). The main difference concerns the scope of the exemptions. In addition, the § 553(a) exemptions differ in nature from the § 553(b) exemptions. The exemptions have several features in common, including the unfortunate tendency to provoke litigation.

(i) Scope of the Exemptions

The scope of the § 553(a) exemptions differs from the scope of the § 553(b) exemptions. Section 553(a) exempts certain rules from *all* of Section 553 (and in turn from §§ 556 and 557). In contrast, § 553(b) exempts certain rules only from § 553(b), § 553(c), § 556, and § 557. The practical effect is that rules falling within a § 553(b) exemption are exempt from all of § 553 except for § 553(e).

The scope of the § 553(a) exemptions is clear from § 553(a)'s opening words: "**This *section* applies ... except to the extent that there is involved ...**" Thus, a rule that falls within a § 553(a) exemption is exempt from all of § 553, which includes § 553(b), (c), (d), and (e).

Understanding the scope of the § 553(b) exemptions is trickier. Section 553(b) requires an agency to publish notice of proposed rulemaking. Section 553(c) then requires the agency to give the public a chance to participate in the making of those rules for which the agency has given notice under § 553(b). The whole point of giving the public notice under § 553(b) is to enable the public to give input under § 553(c). Thus, a rule that is exempt from § 553(b) is also exempt from § 553(c). That is because § 553(c) applies to all—but only—those rules as to which § 553(b) requires notice. In other words, if a rule falls within a § 553(b) exemption, it is exempt from § 553(c). Make sure you understand the connection between § 553(b) and § 553(c) before you move on.

A rule that is exempt from § 553(c) is ordinarily also exempt from §§ 556 and 557. That is because rules are subject to §§ 556 and 557 only when the condition in the last sentence of § 553(c) is satisfied. The last sentence requires a rule to be made in accordance with §§ 556 and 557 if a statute other than the APA—such as the agency legislation that authorizes the rule under analysis—requires the rule to be made **"on the record after opportunity for an agency hearing."** If a rule is not subject to § 553(c), it is not subject to that last sentence, which is the sentence that triggers the applicability of §§ 556 and 557 to some agency rules.

The upshot is that rules exempt from § 553(b)—most "interpretative rules," for example—are also exempt from § 553(c), § 556, and § 557. This means that, in general, a federal agency does not have to publish a notice of proposed rulemaking before issuing an interpretative rule, nor does the agency have to give the public a chance to give input on the agency's proposed interpretative rule. In general, all the agency has to do with an interpretative rule, under the federal APA, is to publish the interpretative rule, in its final form, in the Federal Register. 5 U.S.C. § 552(a)(1) (2012).

Section 553(b) does not exempt *all* interpretative rules. Under the sentence following § 553(b)(3), § 553(b)'s notice requirement *does* apply to an interpretative rule (and the other rules listed in § 553(b)(A) and (B)) **"when notice or hearing is required by statute."** For example, 12 U.S.C. § 43(a) (2012) requires federal banking agencies to publish in the Federal Register, for public comment, certain "interpretative rule[s]" that address the applicability of state laws to national banks. These interpretative rules are subject to § 553(b) because the statute requires **"notice"** of them. It is rare, however, for a statute to require notice or hearing for interpretative rules or for the other kinds of rules listed in § 553(b)(A) and (B) as exempt.

If you have worked your way through the text of § 553(b), and our explanation of it, up to this point, you understand (we hope) that agency rules that are exempt from § 553(b) are also exempt from §§ 553(c), 556, and 557. Now we take up § 553(**d**).

Section 553(**d**), in effect, exempts all rules that fall within a § 553(b) exemption. To begin with, § 553(d) applies only to **"substantive"** rules; thus, it does not apply to **"rules of agency organization, procedure, or practice,"** which are exempt from § 553(b) under § 553(b)(A). Moreover, § 553(d) itself exempts the other two types of exempt rules mentioned in § 553(b)(A)—namely, **"interpretative rules"** and **"statements of policy."** Finally, just as § 553(b)(B) allows an agency to find **"good cause"** to exempt a rule from the **"notice and public procedure"** requirements of § 553(b) and (c), § 553(d) allows an agency to find **"good cause"** to give less than 30 days for a newly published rule to take effect. Often (though not always), the same **"good cause"** that excuses a rule from the notice-and-comment requirements of § 553(b) and (c) will also justify excusing it from § 553(d)'s minimum-30-day-delay-for-taking-effect requirement.

In summary, rules that fall within a § 553(a) exemption are exempt from all of § 553. Rules that fall within a § 553(b) exemption are usually exempt from all of § 553 except for § 553(e), which requires an agency to give interested people a right to petition for the issuance, amendment or repeal of a rule. This right need not be given to people for rules that fall within a § 553(a) exemption. The reason seems to be that Congress considered the government to have great discretion in making, changing, and unmaking rules on the subjects (foreign affairs, etc.) that made them exempt under § 553(a).

(ii) Nature of the Exemptions

You will find three kinds of exemptions in §§ 553(a), 553(b)(A), and 553(b)(B).

(A) § 553(a)'s Subject Matter Exemptions

Section 553(a) exempts certain rules because of their subject matter. A rule on an exempt subject matter is exempt whether it is a legislative or non-legislative rule. This means that an agency can make a legislative rule on an exempt subject matter without following the APA's rulemaking procedures. The APA just requires the agency to publish its final rule in the Federal Register. 5 U.S.C. § 552(a)(1). If the rule falls within a statutory grant of power to make legislative rules, but concerns an exempt subject matter, it has the force and effect of law even if the public had no chance for input.

(B) § 553(b)(A)'s Exemptions for Certain Types of Rules

Section 553(b)(A) exempts certain *types* of rules — namely, rules other than substantive legislative rules. The types of rules exempted by § 553(b)(A) are known as interpretative rules, policy statements, and procedural rules.

(C) § 553(b)(B)'s Good Cause Exemption

Section 553(b)(B) creates an exemption that an agency can use on a rule-by-rule basis, when particular circumstances require a particular rule to be issued without the usual notice-and-comment procedures. This is an "ad hoc" exemption, in the sense that its applicability turns on the existence of particular circumstances that require a rule to be adopted without delay. In effect, for example, it allows emergency rules to be published without any prior opportunity for public input. In this way, it serves a function like provisions in many state APAs that expressly authorize state agencies to adopt emergency rules without following the usual procedures.

(iii) Common Elements of the Exemptions

The exemptions in § 553(a) and § 553(b) have three main things in common.

First and most importantly, all of these exemptions exempt rules from the notice-and-comment procedures in §§ 553(b) and (c), and from the formal rulemaking requirements of §§ 556 and 557. In short, rules falling into any of these exemptions aren't subject to *any* APA rulemaking procedures. The federal agency has only one procedural obligation under the federal APA when making one of these exempt rules: The agency generally must publish the rule in the Federal Register, as required by 5 U.S.C. § 552.

Second, all of the § 553 exemptions exempt rules from some or all of §§ 553, 556 and 557, *but not from other provisions of the APA.* As just mentioned, APA *§ 552* generally requires the agency to publish its rules in the Federal Register, whether or not they are exempt under § 553(a) or 553(b). In addition, rules that fall within a § 553 exemption are still subject to the provisions in APA *§§ 701–706*, which create a broad right to judicial review of **"agency action."** 5 U.S.C. § 704.

Third, most courts take the same approach to interpreting all the § 553 exemptions. The approach may have three components. First, of course, the court considers the statutory text of the exemption. It the court cannot tell from the text alone whether a particular falls within an exemption, the court considers the purposes of § 553's requirements and the purpose of the exemption. The court asks itself: Does it make sense, in light of these purposes, to conclude that this particular rule is exempt, or not exempt? Finally, if a court has done its best but still cannot tell whether a rule falls within a § 553 exemption, the court will ordinarily conclude that the exemption does *not* apply. This reflects the general principle of statutory interpretation requiring exemptions from statutory requirements to be interpreted narrowly.

Lawyers who practice federal administrative law must be familiar with both the exemptions and the courts' approach to interpreting them. Familiarity is valuable because the exemptions generate so much litigation. You can probably guess why. Agencies are only human; they tend to want to get by with minimal effort and therefore tend to interpret the exemptions broadly, to maximize the number of rules that can be made without following the APA's procedural requirements. On the flip side, members of the public affected by rules tend to interpret the exemptions narrowly, to maximize their opportunity to give input on proposed rule, as required by the APA's rulemaking requirements. When an agency, interpreting an exemption broadly, issues a rule without complying with the APA's rulemaking requirements, someone adversely affected by the rule may challenge it in court, arguing that the rule is procedurally defective because it is not, after all, exempt from the APA's requirements.

Exercise: The § 553 Exemptions

Please take a moment and jot down answers to these questions.

1. What are the differences between the § 553(a) and the § 553(b) exemptions?

2. What are the similarities between the § 553(a) and the § 553(b) exemptions?

Summary

Source of Exemptions	Nature of Exemptions	Scope of Exemptions	Federal Register Publication Required?
553(a)(1) & (2)	rules on certain subjects—e.g., military functions	exempt from all of §§ 553, 556 & 557	yes, except for rules related solely to internal personnel rules and practices. § 552(b)(2)
553(b)(A)	certain types of rules—e.g., interpretative rules	generally exempt from §§ 553(b) & (c) and 556 and 557	yes
553(b)(B)	certain rules for good cause	generally exempt from §§ 553(b) & (c) and 556 and 557	yes

---

(iv) Learning about Individual Exemptions

We will introduce you shortly to each APA rulemaking exemption, including each one's rationale. We first examine the § 553(a) exemptions and then the § 533(b) exemptions.

The objective of introducing you to them is to enable you to: (1) identify when an agency action arguably falls into one of these exemptions; and to (2) explain in your own words *why* the agency action arguably does so. Furthermore, (3) your explanation should include a context-specific analysis of the policies underlying the exemption and the policies underlying the APA procedures applicable to non-exempt rules.

The third objective requires you to know the policies underlying the APA rulemaking procedures for non-exempt rules. The key elements of those procedures are (1) public notice of proposed rulemaking and (2) an opportunity for public input on proposed rules.

Congress had three main purposes in requiring public notice and public input. The D.C. Circuit described those purposes as follows:

> First, notice improves the quality of agency rule making by ensuring that agency regulations will be "tested by exposure to diverse public comment." *BASF Wyandotte Corp. v. Costle*, 598 F.2d 637, 641 (1st Cir.1979). Second, notice and the opportunity to be heard are an essential component of "fairness to affected parties." *National Ass'n of Home Health Agencies v. Schweiker*, 690 F.2d 932, 949 (D.C.Cir.1982). Third, by giving affected parties an opportunity to develop evidence in the record to support their objections to a rule, notice enhances the quality of judicial review. *See Marathon Oil Co. v. EPA*, 564 F.2d 1253, 1272 n. 54 (9th Cir.1977) ("Such comment is often an invaluable source of information to a reviewing court attempting to evaluate complex statistical and technological decisions").

Small Refiner Lead Phase-Down Task Force v. U.S. EPA, 705 F.2d 506, 547 (D.C. Cir. 1983) (quoted in part in *Sprint Corp. v. FCC*, 315 F.3d 369, 373 (D.C. Cir. 2003)). In short, public notice and public input enhance the quality of agency decision making; insert a dose of democracy into the rulemaking process; and facilitate judicial review of agency rules.

Courts consider these purposes of the rulemaking procedures when deciding whether a particular agency rule is exempt from them. Specifically, courts consider whether the policies favoring public notice and input are outweighed by the policies underlying the exemptions that arguably apply to the rule under analysis. Of course, courts also consider judicial precedent construing the exemptions. Accordingly, our discussion below identifies the policies underlying the exemptions and describes some case law on them.

b. Subject-Matter Exemptions in Section 553(a)

Section 553(a) exempts rules on certain subjects from all of § 553, as well as from § 556 and 557.

(i) Military and Foreign Affairs Exemption

---

§ 553. Rule making

(a) **This section applies, according to the provisions thereof, except to the extent that there is involved—**

(1) **a military or foreign affairs function of the United States ...**

The exemption for rules relating to "a military ... function" presumably reflects the common understanding that the military is a world unto itself. The legislative history of the APA describes the purpose of the military function exemption as "self-explanatory." APA Legislative History at 15; *see also id.* at 358, 360.

The exemption for rules relating to a **"foreign affairs function"** was designed to apply to matters that, if encumbered by public rulemaking requirements, "would clearly provoke definitely undesirable international consequences." AGM 26 (internal quotation marks omitted).

A case illustrating the foreign affairs exemption is *Rajah v. Mukasey*, 544 F.3d 427 (2nd Cir. 2008). After terrorists attacked the United States on September 11, 2001, the Attorney General created a "Special Call-In Registration Program" for aliens who had come from certain countries and were then living in the U.S. The Attorney General created part of this call-in registration program without following the rulemaking requirements of the federal APA. The program was judicially challenged by aliens who could not show, when they registered under the program, that they were lawfully in the U.S., and were therefore deported.

The Second Circuit held that the program fell within the foreign affairs exemption, reasoning:

> There are at least three definitely undesirable international consequences that would follow from notice and comment rulemaking. First, sensitive foreign intelligence might be revealed in the course of explaining why some of a particular nation's citizens are regarded as a threat. Second, relations with other countries might be impaired if the government were to conduct and resolve a public debate over why some citizens of particular countries were a potential danger to our security. Third, the process would be slow and cumbersome, diminishing our ability to collect intelligence regarding, and enhance defenses in anticipation of, a potential attack by foreign terrorists.

Id. at 437.

(ii) Exemption for Agency Management or Personnel, Public Property, Etc.

---

§ 553. Rule making

(a) This section applies, according to the provisions thereof, except to the extent that there is involved — ...

  (2) a matter relating to agency management or personnel or to public property, loans, grants, benefits, or contracts....

Section 553(a)(2) actually contains two exemptions, one for rules on "**agency management or personnel**," the other for rules on "**public property, loans, grants, benefits, or contracts.**"

Rules on "**agency management or personnel**" concern the employment relationship between an agency and its employees. Examples include rules about agency employee "leaves of absence, vacation, [and] travel." AGM 18. Rules for disciplining and rewarding agency employees also fall within this exemption. Rules falling within this exemption are analogous to the sort of human resources policies and procedures that large, private companies have. As such, they are "solely the concern of the agency proper" and "d[o] not affect members of the public to any extent." AGM 18. Because they have no substantial effect on the public, they are exempt from the APA's notice-and-comment requirements.

Rules on **"public property, loans, grants, benefits, or contracts"** cover what the Attorney General's Manual on the APA called the "proprietary functions" of the government. AGM 27. Basically, the "proprietary functions" exemption reflects the government saying, "We, the Government, can give our property to; can give or lend our money to; and conduct our contractual business with, whomever we wish. The public has no right to meddle!" This attitude partly reflects due process principles of a bygone era, under which the receipt of government benefits was treated as a "privilege," not a "right." *See* Arthur Earl Bonfield, *Public Participation in Federal Rulemaking Relating to Public Property, Loans, Grants, Benefits, or Contracts*, 118 U. Pa. L. Rev. 540, 571 (1970). The right-privilege distinction has fallen into disfavor with the courts, but the proprietary functions exemption abides.

The proprietary functions exemption is broad. It covers rules for the sale or lease of public lands, as well as for the sale or lease of mineral, timber, or grazing rights in public lands. It covers the sale or lease of other types of public property, too, such as U.S. owned ships and buildings. AGM 27. The exemption covers loans and grants made by federal agencies, including loans and grants to state and local governments for airports, highways, etc. It covers government benefit programs and government contracts for procurement of goods and services.

The breadth of the proprietary functions exemption has been diminished in effect by agency-specific statutes, rules, and policy statements that subject rules otherwise covered by this exemption to the APA's rulemaking requirements. For example, 38 U.S.C. § 501 (2012) subjects to the APA's notice-and-comment procedures legislative rules promulgated by the Secretary of Veterans Affairs that "relat[e] to loans, grants, or benefits." Besides these statutes, several federal agencies have issued rules or policy statements that cause some of their rules to be subject to the APA's rulemaking requirements even though the rules would otherwise be exempt under § 553(a)(2)'s proprietary functions exemption. These agencies include the Department of the Interior, the Department of Housing and Urban Development, the Department of Agriculture, and the Department of Health and Human Services. *See* Jeffrey S. Lubbers, A Guide to Federal Agency Rulemaking 63 n.60 (4th ed. 2006).

c. Exemptions for Interpretative Rules, Policy Statements, and Procedural Rules

---

§ 553. Rule making . . .

(b) General notice of proposed rule making shall be published in the Federal Register . . . The notice shall include . . . [3 specific kinds of information.] —

Except when notice or hearing is required by statute, this subsection does not apply —

(A) to interpretative rules, general statements of policy, or rules of agency organization, procedure, or practice . . .

Section 553(b)(A) generally exempts three kinds of rules: (1) interpretative rules, (2) general statements of policy, and (3) rules of agency organization, procedure, or practice.

The exemption for these three types of rules does not apply, however, **"when notice or hearing is required by statute."** Thus, the agency legislation may override the exemptions by requiring the agency to use notice-and-comment procedures even if the APA, standing alone, does not. *E.g.*, *Alabama Power Co. v. FERC*, 160 F.3d 7, 11 (D.C. Cir. 1998).

As discussed earlier in this chapter, the three types of rules that are exempt under § 553(b)(A) are still subject to § 553(e), which gives **"an interested person the right to petition for the issuance, amendment, or repeal of a rule."** In contrast, they are exempt from § 553(d)'s delayed-effective-date requirement, by § 553(d) itself.

These three types of rules were introduced in Chapter 7.B and 7.E. Chapter 7 introduced them in exploring the distinctions (1) between legislative and non-legislative rules; and (2) between substantive and procedural rules. Thus, Chapter 7.B identified interpretative rules and agency policy statements as the main types of non-legislative rules. Chapter 7.E explained that "procedural rules" may be legislative or non-legislative, but in either event differ from "substantive rules." Now we return to these three types of rules with the objective of identifying the rules that fall within the § 553(b)(A) exemptions.

(i) "[R]ules of [A]gency [O]rganization, [P]rocedure, or [P]ractice"

Rules of agency organization, procedure, or practice are called "procedural rules" for short. The Administrative Conference of the United States (a group of administrative law scholars and practitioners) usefully defined a procedural rule as one that:

> (a) relates solely to agency methods of internal operations or of interacting with regulated parties or the public, and (b) does not (i) significantly affect conduct, activity, or a substantive interest that is the subject of agency jurisdiction, or (ii) affect the standards for eligibility for a government program.

1 C.F.R. 305.92-1, at 294 (1993). The exemption for procedural rules in § 553(b)(A) has provoked litigation because some arguably procedural rules affect people's legal rights and duties so strongly that they are challenged as really being substantive rules.

We summarize a case on the exemption for procedural rules.

- *JEM Broadcasting Co. v. Federal Communications Commission*, 22 F.3d 320 (D.C. Cir. 1994)

JEM Broadcasting concerned FCC rules under which companies could apply to the FCC for FM radio broadcast licenses. The rules were called the "hard look" rules. Under the hard look rules, the FCC rejected any application that had any mistake, even a minor typographical error. The FCC adopted the rules when it was receiving thousands of applications, many of which were sloppily prepared. The FCC adopted the hard look rules so that its processing would be more efficient and the public would more quickly get the benefit of new broadcasters. The FCC applied its hard look rules to reject an application from JEM Broadcasting Company. JEM judicially challenged the hard look rules, arguing that they were invalid because the FCC had not used the APA's notice-and-comment requirements when adopting them.

The court in *JEM Broadcasting* held that despite their impact the FCC's hard look rules were exempt from notice-and-comment requirements as procedural rules. The court observed, "Of course, procedure impacts on outcomes and thus can virtually always be described as affecting substance, but to pursue that line of analysis results in the obliteration of the distinction that Congress demanded" in enacting the exemption. *Id.* at 326 (internal quotation marks and citation omitted). The court explained, "[O]ur task is to identify which substantive effects are sufficiently grave so that notice and comment are needed to safeguard the policies underlying the APA." *Id.* at 327 (internal quotation marks and citation omitted). The court concluded:

> [A] license applicant's right to a free shot at amending its application is not so significant as to have required the FCC to conduct notice and comment rulemaking, particularly in light of the Commission's weighty efficiency interests. The APA's procedural exception embraces cases, such as this one, in which the interests promoted by public participation in rulemaking are outweighed by the countervailing considerations of effectiveness, efficiency, expedition and reduction in expense.

Id. (internal quotation marks and citation omitted). The court identified as the "critical fact" that "the 'hard look' rules did not change the substantive standards by which the FCC evaluates license applications, e.g., financial qualifications, proposed programming, and transmitter location." *Id.* Rather, the hard look rules affected a procedural right— the right to amend a defective application.

JEM Broadcasting provides a framework for analyzing the exemption for procedural rules: An agency rule may qualify as a procedural rule even if it affects substantive rights. The court must examine *how* the rule affects substantive rights. If the rule affects the way people assert their substantive rights, then the rule will ordinarily be procedural. On the other hand, if the rule affects the substantive legal standards being applied by the agency, it will not be a procedural rule. This can be a hard distinction to draw, and it reflects in part an effort to balance the "gravity" of a rule's impact against the agency's interests in avoiding the APA's procedural requirements for making non-exempt rules.

Exercise: Applying the Exemption for Procedural Rules

The federal Medicare program reimburses doctors and hospitals that treat Medicare patients (mostly folks age 65 and over). The program is administered by the U.S. Department of Health and Human Services (HHS). HHS hired private companies, which were called "Peer Review Organizations" (PROs), to review activities for which doctors and hospitals were claiming Medicare reimbursement. PROs reviewed whether reimbursement claims met the substantive standard prescribed in the Medicare statute for reimbursement: namely, whether the treatment was "reasonable and medically necessary." HHS sent "transmittals" to PROs that required them to give particularly close review in certain situations where, in HHS's experience, reimbursement was often sought for treatment that was *not* "reasonable and medically necessary." For example, one transmittal required PROs to review all hospital admissions of patients who had been discharged from a hospital within seven days of being readmitted. The American Hospital Association challenges these transmittals because HHS issued them without following the APA's notice-and-comment procedures. HHS argues that the transmittals are exempt as procedural rules. Please evaluate whether the transmittals are, indeed, procedural rules. *See American Hosp. Ass'n v. Bowen,* 834 F.2d 1037 (D.C. Cir. 1987).

(ii) "[G]eneral [S]tatements of [P]olicy"

The Attorney General's Manual on the federal APA defined "**general statements of policy**" as "statements issued by an agency to advise the public prospectively of the manner in which the agency proposes to exercise a discretionary power." AGM 30 n.3. This definition links policy statements to an agency's discretionary powers. The linkage reflects that, when an agency lacks discretion because its conduct is dictated by *law*, the agency has no room to make *policy*. An agency cannot make a policy that conflicts with legal requirements for agency conduct.

On the flip side, when an agency's conduct is not dictated by law—and the agency therefore possesses discretion—the agency may either exercise its discretion on an situation-by-situation basis (i.e., "ad hoc")—or it may adopt a policy that guides its exercise of discretion. By expressing that policy in a policy statement, the agency communicates that guidance to its employees. And by publishing the policy statement in the Federal Register, as required by § 552(a) (2012), the agency also informs the public of how it intends to exercise its discretion.

One big area where agencies exercise discretion concerns how to enforce their statutes and regulations. For example, regulatory agencies often can decide which possible violations of its statutes and regulations to investigate and which ones to punish. This enforcement discretion exists because, just as the police cannot ticket everyone who breaks a speed limit, agencies cannot punish all who violate agency rules or statutes. To be effective, agencies need enforcement priorities. These priorities focus agency attention on important matters and discourage idiosyncratic (or, worse, invidiously discriminatory) enforcement decisions by individual agency employees.

Congress probably exempted agency policy statements from the APA's notice-and-comment requirements to encourage agencies to adopt and publish policy statements. If agencies had to go through the APA's notice-and-comment requirements to issue policy statements, agencies might be reluctant to issue them. The result could be either fewer agency policies—and hence more ad hoc and idiosyncratic behavior—or more unwritten (or undisclosed) agency policies. Neither result is good. By avoiding these results, the exemption for agency policy statements serves a useful purpose.

The problem is that the exemption for policy statements, like other exemptions in § 553(b)(A), creates an opportunity for agencies to try to "pass off" non-exempt legislative rules as exempt rules. This way, the agency can "make law" (by issuing what are really legislative rules) without having to follow the notice-and-comment procedures normally required for legislative rules. Thus, the federal courts must often decide if an agency pronouncement is really a legislative rule or, instead, just a policy statement.

It can be hard to distinguish agency policy statements from legislative rules. One court said the distinction is "enshrouded in considerable smog." *Noel v. Chapman*, 508 F.2d 1023, 1030 (2nd Cir. 1975). To make the distinction, most courts consider how the agency pronouncement under analysis affects the agency's decision making. The more an agency pronouncement constrains agency discretion, the more likely it is to be found a legislative rule rather than a policy statement. The majority approach is illustrated by the following Ninth Circuit case.

• *Mada-Luna v. Fitzpatrick*, 813 F.2d 1006 (9th Cir. 1987)

Miguel Mada-Luna was a citizen of Mexico who committed a drug crime while living in the United States. Because of Mr. Mada's drug crime, federal immigration officials began a proceeding to deport him. Mr. Mada applied for discretionary relief from deportation called "deferred action," which, if granted, would put his deportation indefinitely on hold.

District Director Fitzpatrick, the local immigration official, denied Mr. Mada's application for deferred action. In denying relief, Fitzpatrick relied on an agency "Operating

Instruction" adopted in 1981. The 1981 Operating Instruction prescribed factors for im-migration officials to consider when ruling on applications for deferred action. The 1981 Operating Instruction made it harder for deportable aliens to get deferred action than the 1978 Operating Instruction that it replaced.

In seeking judicial review of the denial of relief, Mr. Mada argued that the 1981 Operating Instruction was invalid because it was a legislative rule adopted without no-tice-and-comment procedures. Mr. Mada wanted the 1981 Operating Instruction invalidated so that his application could be assessed under the more lenient 1978 Operating Instruction. The government, on behalf of District Director Fitzpatrick, argued that the 1981 Operating Instruction was a policy statement and therefore exempt from notice-and-comment requirements.

The Ninth Circuit agreed with the government (Fitzpatrick), holding that the 1981 Operating Instruction was a policy statement. The court stated this test for identifying policy statements:

> The critical factor to determine whether a directive announcing a new policy constitutes a rule or a general statement of policy is the extent to which the challenged [directive] leaves the agency, or its implementing official, free to exercise discretion to follow, or not to follow, the [announced] policy in an individual case.
>
> To the extent that the directive merely provides guidance to agency officials in exercising their discretionary powers while preserving their flexibility and their opportunity to make individualized determination[s], it constitutes a general statement of policy.... In contrast, to the extent that the directive narrowly limits administrative discretion or establishes a *binding norm* that so fills out the statutory scheme that upon application one need only determine whether a given case is within the rule's criterion, it effectively replaces agency discretion with a new binding rule of substantive law. In these cases, notice-and-comment rulemaking proceedings are required, as they would be for any other substantive rule.

813 F.2d at 1013–1014 (internal quotation marks and citation omitted; emphasis in original). The court's test resembles that of other courts and is called the "binding norm" test.

The Ninth Circuit determined that the 1981 Operating Instruction did not establish a binding norm. The court explained:

> [T]the wording and structure of the amended Instruction emphasizes the broad and unfettered discretion of the district director in making deferred action de-terminations. None of the factors listed in the 1981 Instruction establishes a binding norm: they require the district director to evaluate the sympathetic appeal of the deferred action applicant and to surmise the possible internal agency reaction and publicity that would result from his deportation and exclusion. The Instruction leaves the district director free to consider the individual facts in each case.

813 F.2d at 1017 (internal quotation marks omitted).

(iii) "[I]nterpretative [R]ules" (Also Known as "Interpretive" Rules)

An interpretative rule is "issued by an agency to advise the public of the agency's construction of the statutes and rules which it administers." *Shalala v. Guernsey Mem'l Hosp.*, 514 U.S. 87, 99 (1995) (quoting AGM 30 n.3). An agency may use interpretative rules to announce interpretations of the statutes that the agency is responsible for administering, as well as interpretations of the agency's own legislative rules. An interpretative rule is a type of non-legislative rule and, as such, it lacks the force and effect of law.

If a federal agency lacks statutory power to make rules having the force and effect of law, it cannot issue legislative rules. Thus, any rule that the agency issues that clarifies or explains the agency legislation must be merely interpretative. The agency generally need not follow the APA's notice-and-comment procedures to promulgate its interpretative rule. Because the rule lacks the force and effect of law, the agency may have to defend the validity of its interpretation if the interpretation is challenged, for example, in a court proceeding to enforce the statute or legislative rule that the interpretative rule interprets.

Many federal agencies do have the statutory power to make legislative rules. These agencies have a choice whether to promulgate a legislative rule or an interpretative rule. The agency may decide to issue an interpretative rule because the agency does not want to go through the notice-and-comment procedures generally required to promulgate a legislative rule. Although interpretative rules lack the force and effect of law, they still can have significant practical effect. Members of the public who are subject to the interpretative rule can expect the agency to act in accordance with that rule, and use it as a basis to impose penalties or grant benefits. Unless a member of the public can persuade the agency to change its interpretation, or can persuade a court that the rule is not a valid interpretation, the rule as a practical matter binds both the agency and the public.

Sometimes a federal agency intends (or claims to have intended) to issue an interpretative rule that is challenged as being "really" a legislative substantive rule. The federal courts have upheld those challenges in many cases. The courts, however, have taken many different approaches to distinguishing interpretative rules from legislative substantive rules. Among the factors that many courts consider are these:

- Does the rule actually interpret specific language in a particular statute or legislative rule?

If a rule does not merely state a gloss on statutory or regulatory language, but instead seems to make "new" law—such as by creating a new standard of conduct for regulated people and companies—this weighs against the rule's being interpretative. If, on the other hand, the rule seems designed to explain or clarify the actual text of a statute or legislative rule, the rule is more likely to be considered interpretative.

- Did the agency intend the rule to be an interpretative or, instead, a legislative rule?

If the agency calls its rule interpretative, then a court may be inclined to find the rule interpretative, and thus treat it only as an interpretation, and not give it the force and effect of law. Most courts do not treat the agency's label as conclusive in close cases, though, because agencies are fallible and, as discussed earlier in the chapter, agencies have an incentive to interpret the § 553 exemptions, including the exemption for interpretative rules, broadly.

- Was promulgation of the rule necessary to complete a legislative plan?

Sometimes the operation of a statute depends on an agency adopting rules, using a statutory grant of rulemaking authority. For example, a pollution statute that requires companies to comply "with such pollution standards as the Administrator shall promulgate" does not operate until the Administrator establishes those standards. *See, e.g.,* 33 U.S.C. § 1316(e) (2012) (making it illegal for the owner or operator of a "new source" of pollution to violate national performance standards promulgated by EPA). Rules that fill such statutory gaps are ordinarily found to be legislative rules, not interpretative rules.

- Does violation of the rule constitute a violation of a statute?

If the agency treats a violation of its rule as a violation of the underlying statute, this weighs in favor of treating the rule as a legislative rule, not an interpretative rule. In this situation, the agency seems to be giving its rule the force and effect of law.

- Does the agency consider itself bound by the rule?

If an agency considers itself to have no discretion to deviate from the rule, this suggests the rule is legislative, not interpretative. After all, to say that legislative rules have "the force and effect of law" means they are binding on both the public as well as the agency.

- Does the rule have mandatory language?

A rule that commands regulated people and companies to do things, or prohibits them from doing things, with no hint that the rule's command or prohibition reflects merely the agency's opinion, is often found to be legislative, not interpretative. In giving weight to the presence of mandatory language, courts sometimes observe that, as a practical matter, people who are subject to the rule will likely treat it as having the force and effect of law, and not merely as an interpretation.

- Should the rule under analysis be exempt from notice-and-comment procedures considering the purposes of those procedures and the purposes of the exemption for interpretative rules?

Many courts balance, on one side of the scale, the benefit of allowing the public to give input on the type of rule under analysis against, on the other side of the scale, the interest of the agency in being able to adopt the type of rule under analysis without the time and energy required to follow notice-and-comment procedures.

* * *

Having now discussed how to distinguish legislative rules from interpretative rules in close cases, we next turn to a related, but distinct, issue: Suppose an agency changes a longstanding interpretation of one of its legislative rules. Schematically, the situation is this:

- In 2000, the Agency adopts Interpretation 1, interpreting vague or ambiguous language in one of its own legislative rules.
- In 2010, Agency rejects Interpretation 1 in favor of Interpretation 2.
- Considered separately, each Interpretation is a genuine interpretative rule within the meaning of the APA exemption in § 553(b)(A).
- Accordingly, on neither occasion does the Agency use notice-and-comment procedures to adopt the interpretation.

May an agency change a longstanding interpretation of a legislative rule—i.e., in adopt Interpretation 2 in the hypothetical above—without notice-and-comment procedures, as long as the old interpretation and the new interpretation are, standing alone, genuine interpretations, and not covert attempts to amend the regulation?

The D.C. Circuit has said no, this is not permissible in certain situations. The leading case is *Alaska Professional Hunters Ass'n v. Federal Aviation Administration*, 177 F.3d 1030 (D.C. Cir. 1999). That case concerned whether people who worked as fishing and hunting guides in Alaska were "commercial operators" of airplanes, for purposes of the FAA's regulations, when they flew customers around the wilds of Alaska as part of one-price, package tours. For more than 30 years, the FAA told these Alaska guides that they were not "commercial operators" and therefore did not have to comply with regulations for commercial operators. The FAA's rationale was that these guides' piloting was "incidental" to their business. The FAA changed its mind in 1998 and issued a "Notice to Operators" announcing the change, under which the Alaska guides became subject to the regulations for commercial operators. The FAA issued the Notice to Operators without following the APA's notice-and-comment procedures. A professional group of fishing and hunting guides sued the FAA, contending that the Notice was procedurally invalid.

The D.C. Circuit agreed, holding that the FAA should have followed notice-and-comment procedures. The court made three points. First, it said, "Once an agency gives its regulation an interpretation, it can only change that interpretation as it would formally modify the regulation itself: through the process of notice and comment rulemaking." *Alaska Professional Hunters*, 177 F.3d at 1033–1034 (internal quotation marks omitted). For this point, the court relied on the APA's defining **"rule making"** to include the process for **"amending"** a rule, as well as for formulating it in the first place. *Id.* at 1034 (citing 5 U.S.C. § 551(4)). Second, the court observed that "Alaskan guide pilots and lodge operators relied on the advice FAA officials imparted to them—they opened lodges and built up businesses dependent on aircraft, believing their flights were [not subject to rules for commercial operators]." 177 F.3d at 1035. Third, the court reasoned that, "[h]ad guides and lodge operators been able to comment on [intervening changes in the underlying regulations for commercial operators], they could have suggested changes or exceptions that would have accommodated the unique circumstances of Alaskan air carriage." *Id.* at 1035–1036.

It is hard to know how broadly to read *Alaska Professional Hunters*. The court's first point suggests a broad principle that requires notice and comment for *any* change in an agency's interpretation of its regulations. But narrower readings of the court's opinion emphasize the longstanding nature of the regulation, the guides' reliance on the old interpretation, and the likelihood that giving the guides a chance to give input on the applicability of the underlying regulations would have altered the agency's new interpretation or the regulations themselves. In any event, one other federal court of appeals has adopted the *Alaska Professional Hunters* holding, and a second has cited it with approval. *See Shell Offshore, Inc. v. Babbitt*, 238 F.3d 622, 629 (5th Cir. 2001) (relying on *Alaska Professional Hunters* to hold that Department of Interior change in regulatory interpretation was subject to notice-and-comment requirements); *Dismas Charities, Inc. v. U.S. Dep't of Justice*, 401 F.3d 668, 682 (6th Cir. 2005) (citing *Alaska Professional Hunters* with approval but finding it inapplicable in that case). Whether *Alaska Professional Hunters* is read broadly or narrowly, it restricts an agency's ability to use interpretative rules to change the agency's prior interpretations of its legislative rules.

d. The Good Cause Exemption

---

5 U.S.C. § 553. Rule making ...

(b) General notice of proposed rule making shall be published in the Federal Register, unless persons subject thereto are named and either personally served or otherwise have actual notice thereof in accordance with law. The notice shall include ... —

Except when notice or hearing is required by statute, this subsection does not apply— ...

> **(B) when the agency for good cause finds (and incorporates the finding and a brief statement of reasons therefor in the rules issued) that notice and public procedure thereon are impracticable, unnecessary, or contrary to the public interest....**

Section 553(b)(B) creates a general "good cause" exemption that an agency can invoke on a rule-by-rule basis. The "good cause" exemption in § 553(b)(B) deserves attention because (1) agencies often invoke it; (2) "good cause" is a squishy term; and (3) consideration of when agencies use this broadly applicable exemption, and how courts interpret it, illuminates the purposes of the APA's procedural requirements for non-exempt rules.

To start with, do not confuse the "good cause" exemption in § 553(b)(B) with the good cause exemption in § 553(d)(3). The good cause exemption in § 553(b)(B) allows an agency to make a rule effective without following § 553's notice-and-comment procedures. In contrast, the good cause exemption in § 553(d)(3) allows an agency to publish a final rule that is not subject to the usual requirement of a 30-day delay before the rule takes effect. The two good cause exemptions exempt rules from different requirements.

Even so, the exemptions serve similar purposes: They allow the agency to skip the usual procedural requirements when there's good reason to do so. Indeed, when the agency has good cause to skip the notice-and-comment procedures, the agency often also has good cause to make the rule immediately effective, rather than delaying its effective date by 30 days.

The agency has good cause to skip notice-and-comment procedures when those procedures **"are impracticable, unnecessary, or contrary to the public interest."** The Attorney General's Manual on the federal APA described the following example of a situation in which delay would be **"impracticable"**: "[T]he CAB [now the Federal Aviation Administration] may learn from an accident investigation, that certain rules as to air safety should be issued or amended without delay; ... the Board [FAA] could find that notice and public rulemaking procedures would be impracticable." AGM 30–31. As a matter of fact, the FAA regularly invokes the good cause exemption today when issuing "airworthiness directives" requiring companies to make needed repairs on various models of airplanes. *See, e.g.,* Airworthiness Directives; Bombardier, Inc., Model CL-600-2819 (Regional Jet Series 100 & 440) Airplanes, 75 Fed. Reg. 10667 (2010); *see also Util. Solid Waste Activities Group,* 236 F.3d at 754–755 (quoting AGM's description of "impracticable").

Situations of genuine **"impracticability"** are not limited to those involving public safety. Sometimes an agency needs to get a regulation in place within a particular window of time. This is illustrated in *Oregon Trollers Ass'n v. Gutierrez,* 452 F.3d 1104 (9th Cir. 2006).

In early 2005, the National Marine Fisheries Service (NMFS) determined that a critically low number of Klamath Chinook would escape that season's harvest to survive and spawn in the wild. To increase the projected number of wild-spawning Klamath Chinook, NMFS issued "fishery management measures" (rules) limiting commercial and recreational fishing in the Klamath River Management Zone. In doing this, NMFS was exercising statutory authority; thus, these measures were legislative rules. NMFS nonetheless issued these measures without following notice-and-comment procedures. The Ninth Circuit held that NMFS had shown good cause under § 553(b)(B) to skip those procedures:

> Too long to reproduce in full here, the [NMFS's] good cause statement in this case fills nearly a page in the Federal Register, and it thoroughly explains why

the NMFS could not solicit public comment before the measures' effective date.... The NMFS justified its decision with specific fishery-related reasons, not generic complaints about time pressure and data collection difficulties. It observed that the data on which the management measures are based "are not available until January and February because spawning escapement continues through the fall[.]" The [Pacific Regional Fishery Management Council, a statutory entity that proposes fishery management rules to the NMFS,] does not finish its process until early April, and the season must begin on May 1. The NMFS thus has only a month to finalize the Council's proposals...."Delaying implementation of annual fishing regulations, which are based on the current stock abundance projections, for an additional sixty days would require that fishing regulations for May and June be set in the previous year without knowledge of current stock status." [Quoting NMFS's justification] ...

The NMFS also explained why season-specific measures, which cannot be ready until early May, must be in place by that time:

> [T]he 2005 forecast ocean abundance for Klamath River fall Chinook requires a reduction in the commercial season length from Humbug Mountain, OR, to the Oregon-California Border from being open from May–June 2004 to being closed in 2005. Without these, and similar restrictions in other areas in 2005, the projected Klamath River fall Chinook escapement floor [i.e., the minimum number of Chinook that had to escape the harvest in order to spawn] would not be met.

70 Fed. Reg. at 23063. Taken together, the NMFS's explanations set forth the "specific circumstances pertinent to the year at issue" we found missing in [a prior case rejecting an agency's good cause argument].

Oregon Trollers, 452 F.3d at 1124–1125. Thus, NMFS established good cause to act without notice and comment because of late-arriving information requiring action before the upcoming harvest. The agency had a narrow window of time in which to act.

Sometimes an agency is under a tight statutory deadline to issue rules and invokes the good cause exemption to meet the deadline. Sometimes federal agencies get away with this; other times they don't. The federal courts have said, "As a general matter, strict congressionally imposed deadlines, without more, by no means warrant invocation of the good cause exception." *United States v. Gould*, 568 F.3d 459, 480 (4th Cir. 2009) (quoting *Methodist Hosp. of Sacramento v. Shalala*, 38 F.3d 1225, 1236 (D.C. Cir. 1994)). "Nevertheless, deviation from APA requirements has been permitted where congressional deadlines are tight and where the statute is particularly complicated." *Methodist Hosp.*, 38 F.3d at 1236. Even in this situation, an agency must do its best to meet the deadline, and not wait until the last minute to begin the rulemaking process. Otherwise, the court will likely reject a "good cause" argument, finding that the agency itself created the urgency.

Federal agencies can invoke the good cause exemption when notice-and-comment procedures are **"unnecessary"** because of the uncontroversial nature of a proposed rule. The idea of dispensing with notice-and-comment procedures for uncontroversial rules has led to a practice among some federal agencies called "direct final rulemaking." Under this practice, a federal agency publishes a rule in the Federal Register as a final rule, without having first subjected it to notice-and-comment rulemaking. But, in publishing the final rule, the agency announces that it will withdraw the rule — and go through notice-and-comment procedures to promulgate it — if by a certain date the agency receives any adverse comments. If the agency receives no adverse comments by the deadline, the absence of adverse comment can be taken as proof that notice-and-comment procedures are "**unnecessary**" and that there is therefore "**good cause**" under § 553(b)(B) to dispense with them. *See* Ronald M. Levin, *Direct Final Rulemaking*, 64 Geo. Wash. L. Rev. 1, 11 (1995). If the agency gets any adverse comments, it withdraws the rule and republishes it as a proposed rule for normal notice-and-comment procedures.

A variation on direct final rulemaking is called "interim final rulemaking." In interim final rulemaking, a federal agency publishes in the Federal Register what it calls an "interim final rule" without having first gone through notice-and-comment procedures. The agency announces that the rule is final, but the agency will consider public comments, and may in light of those comments change the rule in the future. *See* Levin, 64 Geo. Wash. L. Rev. at 2–3. An "interim final rule," unlike a "direct final rule," remains effective even if the agency gets negative comments about it. Those negative comments may simply cause the agency to change the rule before making it a "final" final rule. The validity of interim final rulemaking, like that of direct final rulemaking, depends on the rule at issue falling within the "good cause" exemption or another exemption.

As for the situation at state law: Instead of providing a "good cause" exemption, many state APAs authorize state agencies to adopt "emergency rules" that take immediate effect and that can be adopted without following notice-and-comment procedures. The state APA itself ordinarily defines what constitutes an "emergency." Usually, too, the state APA will limit the life span of an emergency rule to (say) 180 days. The idea behind the limited life span is that, if the agency believes that the emergency rule should be made permanent, the agency can, during the life span of the emergency rule, use notice-and-comment procedures to adopt it as a permanent rule. *See, e.g.*, 2010 Model State APA §§ 309 & 317(d).

Exercise: Federal Agency Use of the "Good Cause" Exemption

Find a recent example of an agency's use of the "good cause" exemption. To do so, go to the GPO's Federal Digital System, and search on the phrase "good cause" in the most recent month of the Federal Register collection. Browse the results.

---

e. Researching the Exemptions

If you need to research federal case law interpreting an APA exemption, or simply want to learn more about the exemptions after reading the material on them in this book, three good research tactics help you tap into the case law:

1. You can search commercial database using the names or statutory citations for the exemptions, or both.

2. You can study annotations in U.S. Code Annotated (USCA). The USCA is produced by Thomson-West as a hard-copy resource and as a database on Westlaw. The organization follows that of the U.S. Code. For each provision of the U.S. Code, USCA gives short descriptions (annotations) of federal court opinions addressing the provision. Thus, the USCA entry for 5 U.S.C. § 553 includes an-

notations for all of the APA's rulemaking exemptions. LexisNexis has a similar annotated version of the U.S. Code; it is called the "U.S. Code Service" (USCS).

3. American Bar Association (ABA) Resources: The ABA's Section of Administrative Law and Regulatory Practice publishes two books useful for research on the APA's rulemaking exemptions:

   - JEFFREY S. LUBBERS, A GUIDE TO FEDERAL AGENCY RULEMAKING (4th ed. 2006). Professor Lubbers' Guide devotes much attention to the leading case law on the § 553 exemptions.

   - DEVELOPMENTS IN ADMINISTRATIVE LAW AND REGULATORY PRACTICE. This is the title of a book published each year by the Section. It discusses the year's most significant judicial opinions on the § 553 exemptions and other administrative law developments.

2. State APA Rulemaking Exemptions

State APAs, like the federal APAs, exempt some rules from their rulemaking procedures. Often you will find the exemptions in either, or both, of two places: (1) the APA's definition of "rule"; and (2) the APA provisions prescribing rulemaking procedures. For example, the Georgia APA contains them in both places.

Here is the Georgia APA's definition of "[r]ule":

Georgia Code Ann. § 50-13-2. Definitions

As used in this chapter, the term: ...

(6) "Rule" means each agency regulation, standard, or statement of general applicability that implements, interprets, or prescribes law or policy or describes the organization, procedure, or practice requirements of any agency. The term includes the amendment or repeal of a prior rule but does not include the following:

(A) Statements concerning only the internal management of an agency and not affecting private rights or procedures available to the public;

(B) Declaratory rulings issued pursuant to Code Section 50-13-11;

(C) Intra-agency memoranda;

(D) Statements of policy or interpretations that are made in the decision of a contested case;

(E) Rules concerning the use or creation of public roads or facilities, which rules are communicated to the public by use of signs or symbols;

(F) Rules which relate to the acquiring, sale, development, and management of the property, both real and personal, of the state or of an agency;

(G) Rules which relate to contracts for the purchases and sales of goods and services by the state or of an agency;

(H) Rules which relate to the employment, compensation, tenure, terms, retirement, or regulation of the employees of the state or of an agency;

(I) Rules relating to loans, grants, and benefits by the state or of an agency; or

(J) The approval or prescription for the future of rates or prices.

Next comes the Georgia APA provision prescribing rulemaking procedures; it exempts interpretive rules and general statements of policy from its requirements:

Georgia Code Ann. § 50-13-4. Procedure for adoption, amendment, or repeal of rules …

(a) Prior to the adoption, amendment, or repeal of any rule, other than interpretive rules or general statements of policy, the agency shall [follow certain procedures]….

You will find common rulemaking exemptions among APAs. For example, the Georgia APA and the federal APA both exempt interpretative rules and agency policy statements from their notice-and-comment procedures. In this area as in so many others, however, generalizations are dangerous. They are no substitute for the lawyer's careful identification and analysis of the particular APA applicable to the agency rule at hand.

D. Step 2 of Analysis, Continued: If the APA Does Apply to the Agency, Do the APA's Rulemaking Requirements Apply to the Rule under Analysis?—Examining the Agency Legislation and Agency Rules

The agency legislation governing an agency rule usually does not address the applicability of the APA's rulemaking requirements to that rule. Nor do the agency's own rules usually address the APA's applicability to that agency's rulemaking activities. Because the agency legislation and agency rules are usually silent on this subject, you can usually end your analysis of the APA's applicability to a particular rule by examining the APA: If you conclude that a particular rule does *not* fall within any of the APA's rulemaking exemptions, then ordinarily the agency must follow the APA's rulemaking requirements. By the same token, if you conclude that a particular rule *does* fall within one of the exemptions, then ordinarily the agency need not follow the APA's rulemaking requirements.

Sometimes, however, the agency legislation or the agency's own rules do address the applicability of the APA to the agency's rulemaking. Here are the possibilities:

(1) The agency legislation and agency rules are silent. As already stated, this is the most common situation.

(2) The agency legislation expressly *exempts* some or all of the agency's rules from the APA's rulemaking requirements.

(3) The agency legislation expressly *subjects* some or all of the agency's rules to the APA's rulemaking requirements.

(4)   The agency's own *rules* subject some or all of the agency's rules to the APA's rule-making requirements.

This section gives examples of each possibility.

1. The Agency Legislation and Agency Rules Are Silent

Many statutes give agencies the power to make legislative rules. Most of these statutes simply do not address the applicability of the APA. The agency's rules will also be silent on the matter. APAs are designed to supply a set of default rulemaking procedures to apply in just such situations.

The Internal Revenue Code includes a typically broad, typically silent grant of legislative rulemaking power to the Secretary of the Treasury:

---

26 U.S.C. § 7805. Rules and regulations

(a) Authorization. — Except where such authority is expressly given by this title to any person other than an officer or employee of the Treasury Department, the Secretary shall prescribe all needful rules and regulations for the enforcement of this title, including all rules and regulations as may be necessary by reason of any alteration of law in relation to internal revenue....

Because this statute is silent on the APA's applicability, the APA's rulemaking requirements apply to the Treasury's promulgation of rules under the statute, except for rules that fall within the APA's own rulemaking exemptions (e.g., for interpretative rules).

Not all statutory grants of rulemaking power are as broad as the Treasury Department's. Even much narrower grants, however, resemble the Treasury Department's grant in failing to address the applicability of the APA's rulemaking requirements to rules made under the grant.

2. The Agency Legislation Expressly Exempts Some or All of the Agency's Rules from the APA's Rulemaking Requirements

APAs establish default rulemaking procedures. They do not prevent the legislature from deciding that a particular agency's rules, or some of that agency's rules, should be exempt from the APA procedures. The federal APA has a provision, § 559, allowing later statutes expressly to modify or supersede the APA.

Here is an example of agency legislation exempting certain agency rules from the APA's rulemaking requirements. The statute authorizes oil from the North Slope of Alaska to be exported unless the President, with the assistance of the Secretaries of Commerce and Energy, decides to prohibit exports in the national interest:

30 U.S.C. § 185. Rights-of-way for pipelines through Federal lands ...

(s) Exports of Alaskan North Slope oil

(1) Subject to paragraphs (2) through (6) of this subsection and notwithstanding any other provision of this chapter or any other provision of law (including any regulation) applicable to the export of oil transported by pipeline over right-of-way granted pursuant to section 1652 of Title 43, such oil may be exported unless the President finds that exportation of this oil is not in the national interest....

(4) The Secretary of Commerce shall issue any rules necessary for implementation of the President's national interest determination, including any licensing requirements and conditions, within 30 days of the date of such determination by the President. The Secretary of Commerce shall consult with the Secretary of Energy in administering the provisions of this subsection....

(6) Administrative action under this subsection is not subject to sections 551 and 553 through 559 of Title 5....

This statute requires the Secretary of Commerce to issue rules to implement the President's national interest determination and, in subsection (s)(6), expressly exempts the Secretary's rules from provisions in Title 5 that codify the APA's rulemaking requirements.

Exemptions in agency legislation can be tricky to spot. One particularly tricky situation is this: The agency legislation includes one provision that generally requires the agency to follow the APA's rulemaking requirements and another provision that exempts certain agency rules from the APA. For example, the following provision generally requires the Secretary of Energy to follow the APA's rulemaking requirements (which are in "subchapter II of chapter 5 of Title 5 of the U.S. Code"):

42 U.S.C. § 7191. Procedures for issuance of rules, regulations, or orders

(a) Applicability of subchapter II of chapter 5 of Title 5

(1) Subject to the other requirements of this subchapter, the provisions of subchapter II of chapter 5 of Title 5 shall apply in accordance with its terms to any rule or regulation, or any order having the applicability and effect of a rule (as defined in section 551(4) of Title 5), issued pursuant to authority vested by law in, or transferred or delegated to, the Secretary, or required by this chapter or any other ct to be carried out by any other officer, employee, or component of the Department ... If any provision of any Act, the functions of which are transferred, vested, or delegated pursuant to this chapter, provides administrative procedure requirements in addition to the requirements provided in this subchapter, such additional requirements shall also apply to actions under that provision....

A separate provision, however, exempts certain rules of the Secretary's—namely, rules encouraging wind energy—from the APA's rulemaking requirements (and from the above provision):

---

42 U.S.C. § 9204. Research, development, and demonstration

(a) Areas of knowledge limiting system utilization

The Secretary shall initiate research and development or accelerate existing research and development in areas in which the lack of knowledge limits the widespread utilization of wind energy systems in order to achieve the purposes of this chapter.

(b) Development of system prototypes and improvements ...

The Secretary is authorized to enter into contracts, grants, and cooperative agreements with public and private entities for the purchase, fabrication, installation, and testing to obtain scientific, technological, and economic information from the demonstration of a variety of prototypes of advanced wind energy systems under a variety of circumstances and conditions ...

(d) Other provisions inapplicable

In carrying out the responsibilities under this section, the Secretary is not subject to the requirements of section 553 of Title 5 or section 7191 of this title.

This is a tricky situation because if you were aware of only the first provision reproduced above, you could reasonably, but incorrectly, conclude that the Secretary of Energy always must follow the APA's rulemaking requirements when making rules, as long as the APA itself does not exempt them.

Fortunately, neither Congress nor state legislatures routinely exempt rules from the applicable APA. Fortunately, too, although the exemptions may be hard to find, they are easy to recognize because they will ordinarily refer expressly to the APA's rulemaking requirements in stating that those requirements don't apply.

3. The Agency Legislation Expressly *Subjects* Agency Rules to the APA

Instead of expressly *exempting* an agency's rule from the APA's rulemaking requirements, the agency legislation may expressly *subject* the agency's rules to those requirements. Sometimes, the agency legislation expressly subjects the agency's rules to the APA simply to confirm the APA's applicability to those rules. Other times, however, the agency legislation expressly subjects the agency's rules to the APA because they would otherwise fall within one of the APA's rulemaking exemptions.

An example of the first situation comes from a statute—codified in Title 16, Chapter 52, of the U.S. Code—for conserving and enhancing salmon and steelhead fish:

---

16 U.S.C. § 3341. Regulations

The Secretary of Commerce and the Secretary of the Interior may each promulgate such regulations, in accordance with section 553 of Title 5, as may be necessary to carry out his functions under this chapter.

Even if this provision did not expressly require the Secretaries to follow the rulemaking procedures in § 553 of the federal APA, the APA procedures would still apply. Nothing about the regulations authorized under 16 U.S.C. § 3341 (2012) suggests that they are exempt from the APA's rulemaking requirements. The statute's express reference to § 553 therefore simply confirms the APA's applicability to regulations promulgated under 16 U.S.C. § 3341.

Sometimes agency legislation subjects to the APA's rulemaking requirements rules that would otherwise fall within one of the APA's rulemaking exemptions. An example comes from the statute granting rulemaking power to the Secretary of Veterans Affairs:

---

38 U.S.C. § 501. Rules and regulations

(a) The Secretary [of Veterans Affairs] has authority to prescribe all rules and regulations which are necessary or appropriate to carry out the laws administered by the Department and are consistent with those laws ...

(d) The provisions of section 553 of title 5 shall apply, without regard to subsection (a)(2) of that section, to matters relating to loans, grants, or benefits under a law administered by the Secretary.

This provision makes § 553 of the APA applicable "without regard to" § 553(a)(2). Section 553(a)(2) generally exempts from the APA's rulemaking requirements rules relating to "**public ... loans, grants, [or] benefits.**" 5 U.S.C. § 553(a)(2). This exemption would ordinarily apply to rules promulgated by the Secretary of Veterans Affairs "relating to loans, grants, or benefits." The exemption does not apply, however, because it is overridden by 38 U.S.C. § 501(d)'s statement that the rulemaking procedures of § 553 "shall apply, without regard to" the exemption. Consequently, the Secretary of Veterans Affairs must follow the rulemaking requirements of § 553 of the federal APA when making rules relating to loans, grants, or benefits for veterans, even though those rules are otherwise exempt from § 553.

In short, the agency legislation may confirm the applicability of the APA's rulemaking requirements or may subject, to those requirements, rules that are otherwise exempt from them.

Exercise: Analyzing Statutory References to APA Rulemaking Procedures

You may be familiar with a federal program that is commonly known as the "food stamp program" but that is now officially called the Supplemental Nutrition Assistance Program (SNAP). The SNAP program gives "vouchers" (commonly known as food stamps) to poor people to get food. The program is administered by the U.S. Department of Agriculture with the assistance of States. State agencies process applications for SNAP benefits and distribute those benefits under a co-operative federalism arrangement. *See generally* U.S. Dep't of Agriculture, Food and Nutrition Service, Supplemental Nutrition Assistance Program, http://www.fns.usda.gov/snap/ (modified May 31, 2012).

Here is the statute authorizing the SNAP:

7 U.S.C. § 2013. Establishment of supplemental nutrition assistance program

(a) In general

Subject to the availability of funds appropriated under section 2027 of this title, the Secretary is authorized to formulate and administer a supplemental nutrition assistance program under which, at the request of the State agency, eligible households within the State shall be provided an opportunity to obtain a more nutritious diet through the issuance to them of an allotment and, through an approved State plan, nutrition education, except that a State may not participate in the supplemental nutrition assistance program if the Secretary determines that State or local sales taxes are collected within that State on purchases of food made with benefits issued under this chapter. The benefits so received by such households shall be used only to purchase food from retail food stores which have been approved for participation in the supplemental nutrition assistance program. [B]enefits issued and used as provided in this chapter shall be redeemable at face value by the Secretary through the facilities of the Treasury of the United States.

(b) Food distribution program on Indian reservations ...[Editor's Note: This subsection allows tribal organizations to request a food distribution program that operates instead of, or in conjunction with, a standard SNAP program. It also has some specialized provisions applicable to food distribution program on Indian reservations.]

(c) Regulations; transmittal of copy of regulations to Congressional committees prior to issuance

The Secretary shall issue such regulations consistent with this chapter as the Secretary deems necessary or appropriate for the effective and efficient administration of the supplemental nutrition assistance program and shall promulgate all such regulations in accordance with the procedures set forth in section 553 of Title 5. In addition, prior to issuing any regulation, the Secretary shall provide the Committee on Agriculture of the House of Representatives and the Committee on Agriculture, Nutrition, and Forestry of the Senate a copy of the regulation with a detailed statement justifying it.

Please examine APA § 553(a)(1) and (a)(2), which exempt certain rules from § 553's rulemaking requirements, and then explain the reference to APA § 553 in 7 U.S.C. § 2013(c) (2012).

---

4. The Agency *Rules* Make the APA's Rulemaking Requirements Applicable

As discussed in Chapter 4.C.2.b(ii), an agency is usually free, by rule or policy statement, to subject its actions to the APA's requirements even though those actions are otherwise exempt from the APA. And an agency can by rule or policy usually add to the APA-required procedures, to give additional procedural protections to people dealing with the agency, as discussed in Chapter 4.C.2.c. Here is the relevant principle:

> **An agency may usually *elaborate upon*, or *add* to, statutorily required procedures, but it may not *modify* the statutory procedures or provide *less* than the statutorily required minimum procedures.**

This is an especially important principle for agency rulemaking. The principle has importance in rulemaking because several federal agencies have, by agency rule or agency policy statement, subjected their otherwise exempt rules to the APA's rulemaking requirements. They have thus exercised their power, consistently with the principle stated above, to impose procedural requirements upon themselves over and above those required by statute.

Here, for example, is the relevant rule expressing the policy of the Department of Housing and Urban Development (HUD):

---

24 C.F.R. § 10.1 Policy

It is the policy of the Department of Housing and Urban Development to provide for public participation in rulemaking with respect to all HUD programs and functions, including matters that relate to public property, loans, grants, benefits, or contracts even though such matters would not otherwise be subject to rulemaking by law or Executive policy. The Department therefore publishes notices of proposed rulemaking in the Federal Register and gives interested persons an opportunity to participate in the rulemaking through submission of written data, views, and arguments with or without opportunity for oral presentation.

This policy subjects to the APA's rulemaking requirements HUD rules that are otherwise exempt from the APA's rulemaking requirements as rules relating to **"public ... loans, grants, [or] benefits."** 5 U.S.C. § 553(a)(2).

Other agencies that likewise subject, to the APA's rulemaking requirements, rules that otherwise fall within the so-called "public benefits" exemption in § 553(a)(2) include the Department of Agriculture, the Department of Health and Human Services, the Department of Interior, the Department of Labor, the Department of Transportation, and the Small Business Administration. *See* Jeffrey S. Lubbers, A Guide to Federal Agency Rulemaking 63 n.60 (4th ed. 2006).

You may wonder: Why would an agency voluntarily undertake procedural obligations from which a statute otherwise exempts it? The answer is that several factors probably play a role. The agency may decide that public participation in rulemaking is justified by considerations of fairness and a desire to improve the quality of agency decision making. In addition, an agency might wish to avoid lawsuits by following the APA's rulemaking procedures. By following APA procedures, the agency creates a forum for public input that might otherwise be expressed by the filing of a legal challenge to the rules ultimately adopted. Moreover, the opportunity for input from people affected by the rule encourages buy-in: If they have a chance to be heard, they are more likely to comply with the resulting rule. Furthermore, public input may give the agency information and perspectives that the agency must consider to prevent its rule from later being found invalid by a reviewing court because of the agency's failure to consider that information and those perspectives.

Diagram 10-1. Flow Chart for Analyzing APA Applicability

(1) Does the APA apply to this agency?

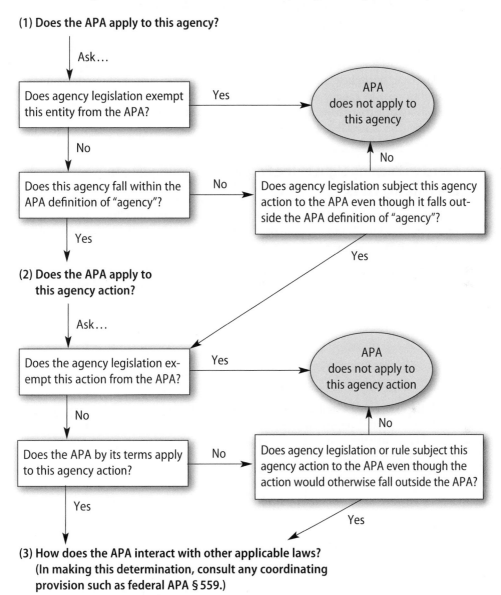

(3) How does the APA interact with other applicable laws? (In making this determination, consult any coordinating provision such as federal APA § 559.)

In sum, altruistic and practical reasons often lead an agency to subject its otherwise-exempt rules to the APA's rulemaking requirements.

Exercise: Learning the Framework for Analyzing the APA's Applicability to an Agency Rule

In Chapter 4, we presented a "Flow Chart for Analyzing APA Applicability." That flow chart was generic, applicable to any sort of agency action. We reproduce the flow chart again below. Please review the flow chart to ensure you understand its applicability to agency rules. You may wish to annotate it with specific APA provisions or other information from this chapter to help you review and remember the material in this chapter.

Exercise: Keeping Sight of the Forest while Continuing to Examine the Trees

Please review the problem solving framework presented in Chapter 2 — and reproduced below — and find the part of the framework to which the material in this chapter is relevant.

1. Is there a valid source of power for the agency to take this action?
    a. Is there a source of power? There are three possible sources of power for agency action:
        i.   constitutional
        ii. statutory
        iii. executive-branch material
    b. Is the source of power valid?
2. If the agency has acted under a valid source of power, has the agency obeyed limits on, and requirements for exercising, that power? (For simplicity's sake, we use the term "limits" to include requirements.)
    a. Internal limits
        i. Internal substantive limits
        ii. Internal procedural limits
    b. External limits
        i. External substantive limits
        ii. External procedural limits
3. If the agency lacks power to take the action, or has not obeyed limits on, or requirements for exercising, that power, what can be done about it? Five sources of control:
    a. agency
    b. judicial branch
    c. legislative branch
    d. executive branch
    e. the people

E. Chapter 10 Wrap Up and Look Ahead

The applicable (federal or state) APA may be an external source of procedural requirements for an agency's exercise of its rulemaking power. To determine whether the APA does indeed apply to a particular agency rule, you must use a three-step analysis. This chapter has examined the first two steps, which ask these questions:

(1) Does the APA apply to this agency?

(2) Does the APA apply to this rule?

To answer each question, you have to look both within and outside the APA. In looking outside the APA, you are looking, specifically, at the agency legislation and the agency rules. The agency legislation and agency rules usually say nothing about the APA's applicability. When they do address the APA's applicability, however, they ordinarily control rather than the more general provisions of the APA.

If your analysis of the first two questions leads you to conclude that the APA does apply to (1) the agency and (2) the rule at hand, a third question remains:

(3) How does the APA interact with other applicable legal requirements?

We turn to that question in the next chapter.

Chapter Problem Revisited

This problem is based on *Chamber of Commerce of the United States v. U.S. Dep't of Labor*, 174 F.3d 206 (D.C. Cir. 1999), and to a lesser extent on *U.S. Dep't of Labor v. Kast Metals Corp.*, 744 F.2d 1145 (5th Cir. 1984). The court in *Chamber of Commerce* held that a "voluntary" OSHA program much like the chapter problem's ESP was subject to the APA's rulemaking requirements.

1. The chapter problem tells you that neither the legislation governing the Department of Labor nor the Department's rules address the applicability of the federal APA's rulemaking requirements to rules promulgated under the OSH Act. This means the APA's applicability turns solely on analysis under the APA.

2. The Department of Labor is an executive department. Indeed, it is one of the cabinet-level departments. It easily fits within the federal APA's definition of **"agency."** If you had any doubt on this score, you could confirm the Department of Labor's status as an APA **"agency"** by searching for federal court decisions applying the APA to Department of Labor actions. You will find plenty of them.

3. In *Kast Metals*, the court held that an OSHA plan that determined when to inspect an employer was a **"rule,"** as defined in APA § 551(4), because it was designed to implement the agency's statutory power to make rules for workplace inspections. The court rejected the Secretary of Labor's argument that the OSHA plan was not a rule because it constituted only investigative activity. The court acknowledged that agency information gathering is often considered a separate activity from agency rulemaking. The court said, however, that the two are not mutually exclusive, and in this case the OSHA plan prescribed procedures for carrying out investigative activity. *See* 744 F.2d at 1149–1151.

4. In *Chamber of Commerce*, the court held that an ESP-like, "voluntary" OSHA program by which employers could avoid mandatory inspections did not fall within the APA exemption in § 553(b)(A) for procedural rules. The court emphasized that OSHA was pressuring employers to implement health and safety plans that required more than merely complying with existing OSHA rules. In this way OSHA's program changed the substantive legal standards for employers who adopted these plans. *Chamber of Commerce*, 174 F.3d at 212. In its analysis the court cited as precedent the case on the procedural-rule exemption discussed earlier in this chapter: *JEM Broadcasting Co. v. FCC*, 22 F.3d 320 (D.C. Cir. 1994).

5. The court in *Chamber of Commerce* also held that the OSHA program was not exempt from the APA's rulemaking requirements as a "**general statemen[t] of policy**" under § 553(b)(A). The court considered the same factors that a different court considered in *Mada-Luna v. Fitzpatrick*, 813 F.2d 1006 (9th Cir. 1987), a case discussed earlier in this chapter. Specifically, the *Chamber of Commerce* court noted that the OSHA program did not leave OSHA free to exercise discretion: OSHA had bound itself to inspecting comprehensively employers who did not adopt voluntary plans that went beyond existing legal requirements. In addition, employers who *did* adopt voluntary plans could not be removed from the program, and subjected to mandatory inspections, as long as they complied with their own plans. *Chamber of Commerce*, 174 F.3d at 212–213.

Professional Development Reflection Question

In law school, you take separate courses dealing with separate subjects. In practicing law, you will handle many matters that implicate multiple areas of law. Even the simplest case involving a lawsuit between people involved in a traffic accident requires you to know—and to integrate your knowledge of—torts, civil procedure, and evidence. Given the real-life overlap of subjects you study separately in law school, you benefit greatly from making connections among what you are learning and have learned in your law school courses.

Making the connection requires a deliberate effort on your part. That is because the material for a law school course is designed deliberately to focus on a particular subject. Thus, for example, the chapter problem involving a company facing OSHA citations could—but doesn't—explore the question whether a company's activities affect interstate commerce in a way that brings it within the scope of OSHA, which is an exercise of Congress's power to regulate interstate commerce. The interstate-commerce angle is covered in law school courses on constitutional law. Similarly, the chapter problem could have explored the issue whether OSHA's inspection of a work place implicated the Fourth Amendment's restrictions on unreasonable searches and seizures. But we refrained from exploring that issue because it is covered in law school courses on criminal procedure.

You will learn administrative law and other subjects better—i.e., in a way that makes your learning more useful in legal practice—if you look for connections between the material presented in your separate law school courses.

With that in mind, we pose a question to get you started: What are three specific topics or cases that we have presented in this book so far and that also have connections to other courses you have taken in law school or plan to take?

Chapter 11

Types of Rulemaking under the APA

Overview

Chapter 10 examined how to determine whether the APA applies to an agency rulemaking proceeding. Suppose you determine that the applicable APA does indeed apply to the proceeding. That brings you to the third question of the three-part framework for analyzing the APA's applicability:

(3) How does the APA interact with other legal requirements?

This chapter examines the specific question of how the APA may interact with the agency legislation governing the particular rule under analysis. The agency legislation for a federal agency may do one of three things, assuming that neither it nor the APA itself exempts the rule from the APA's rulemaking requirements (which is our working assumption for this chapter):

1. The agency legislation may, with respect to the particular agency rule under analysis, impose no procedural requirements for the agency's exercise of rulemaking power. In that event, the federal APA's informal rulemaking requirements apply by default. Informal (or notice-and-comment) rulemaking is probably the most common type of federal rulemaking proceeding.

2. The agency legislation may require the particular agency rule under analysis to be based on the record after an opportunity for an agency hearing. In that event, the agency legislation triggers the federal APA's formal rulemaking requirements. Formal rulemaking is the rarest type of federal rulemaking proceeding.

3. The agency legislation may, with respect to the particular agency rule under analysis, modify or add to the APA's informal rulemaking requirements. In that event, the rulemaking proceeding is called hybrid rulemaking because its procedures are a blend of the APA's rulemaking procedures and the agency legislation's rulemaking procedures. Hybrid rulemaking is a common type of federal rulemaking proceeding.

Unlike the federal APA, most state APAs do not have separate informal and formal rulemaking requirements. Instead, most state APAs have just one set of rulemaking procedures. Assuming that those procedures do apply to a particular state agency's rulemaking, the state agency's legislation may leave the APA's procedures alone or modify them.

This chapter's sections have the following titles:

A. The Three Types of Rulemaking under the Federal APA

B. Agency Legislation Requiring Informal Rulemaking under the Federal APA

A. The Three Types of Rulemaking under the Federal APA

It may help you understand the interaction between the federal APA and federal agency legislation if you think of the federal APA as an auto maker that makes only two kinds of rulemaking vehicles:

- **informal**—also known as **"notice-and-comment"**—**rulemaking** is governed by APA § 553(b) and 553(c). It is the basic, economy model of rulemaking vehicle. It provides a fairly efficient and reliable way to get an agency from point A (the decision to promulgate a rule) to point B (publication of the final rule). But it has no frills.

Less metaphorically, the APA's informal rulemaking provisions generally require the agency to publish a proposed version of the rule for public comment; consider written comments from the public on the proposed rule when drafting the final rule; and publish the final rule, along with an explanation of the basis and purpose of the rule, at least 30 days before it takes effect. In informal rulemaking, a federal agency is not limited to considering only the information submitted by the public but can also consider other material, including material from inside the agency. Informal rulemaking, which we examine in detail in Chapter 12, is probably the most common type of rulemaking proceeding.

- **formal rulemaking** is governed by APA §§ 553(b), 556, and 557. It is the top-of-the-line, heavy duty vehicle, loaded down with all available options. It is not terribly efficient or economical, and it usually gets from point A to point B more slowly than the informal rulemaking vehicle, but no one can complain about the lack of procedural bells and whistles when traveling by formal rulemaking. It's got everything the most luxury- (procedure-) conscious passenger could wish.

Less metaphorically, the APA's formal rulemaking provisions require the agency to hold an evidentiary hearing—rather than merely inviting written comments from the public—on a proposed version of the rule. The evidentiary hearing resembles a bench trial in its formality and is typically conducted by an "administrative law judge" (ALJ). The ALJ and all other officials involved in making the final rule must base the final rule exclusively on a formal record, which will include a transcript of the evidentiary hearing before the ALJ. Formal rule-making, which we examine in Chapter 13, is the rarest type of rulemaking proceeding.

When Congress enacts a statute authorizing an agency to make legislative rules, Congress can choose either the informal or the formal rulemaking vehicle for the agency to use when making rules under that statute. As a third alternative, Congress can customize the informal rulemaking vehicle by changing features or adding features so that the rulemaking vehicle provides more than basic, economical transportation without becoming as inefficient and cumbersome as formal rulemaking. When Congress chooses this third alternative, we say that Congress is providing for "**hybrid rulemaking**." The term "hybrid" indicates that the required procedures are a blend of APA procedures and procedures required by the agency legislation. Hybrid rulemaking, which is discussed in Chapter 14, is a common type of rulemaking proceeding.

The question becomes: Assuming the APA's rulemaking requirements apply to the rule under analysis, *where* does Congress express its choice of APA rulemaking vehicle? The answer is: Congress ordinarily expresses its choice in the agency legislation that authorizes the rule under analysis.

1. If Congress wants the agency to use the **informal rulemaking** vehicle, Congress usually need not say anything in the agency legislation. When the agency legislation is silent about the procedures to be followed when the agency exercises its power to make legislative rules, the APA's informal rulemaking procedures apply by default, as long as the agency fits the APA's definition of agency (in § 551(1)) and the rule is not exempt by the APA itself—for example, because it relates to a foreign affairs function. *See* 5 U.S.C. § 553(a)(1) (2012) (discussed in Chapter 10.C.1.b(i)). If the agency or rule is otherwise exempt from the APA's rulemaking provisions, Congress must expressly state in the agency legislation that the agency must follow the APA's rulemaking procedures, for the procedures to apply.

2. If Congress wants the agency to use the **formal rulemaking** vehicle, it must make clear in the agency legislation (or its legislative history) that the rule is "**required ... to be made on the record after opportunity for an agency hearing**." 5 U.S.C. § 553(c) (last sentence). Such a requirement triggers the formal procedures in APA §§ 556 and 557 instead of the informal, written-comment procedures of § 553(c).

3. If Congress wants the agency to use **hybrid rulemaking**, it must specify in the agency legislation how the APA's informal rulemaking procedures are to be customized for rules made under that agency legislation.

In the next sections you will see examples of statutes providing for each of the three APA rulemaking vehicles. Your objective in studying these examples should be to learn how to determine which type of rulemaking is required for a particular agency rule, once you have identified the agency legislation authorizing that rule.

Exercise: Learning the Three Types of Rulemaking under the Federal APA

The following chart helps you distinguish among the three types of rulemaking possible under the federal APA. At this point, please fill in the first column of the chart using the information given so far in this chapter.

	What APA procedural provisions apply?	What does agency legislation say, if anything?	What are the main procedural features?
informal			
formal			
hybrid			

B. Agency Legislation Requiring Informal Rulemaking under the Federal APA

As discussed in Section A, if the agency legislation is silent, ordinarily the APA's notice and comment rulemaking procedures apply by default. Even so, many federal statutes granting rulemaking power *expressly* subject rules made under them to the APA's informal rulemaking procedures. Below we examine each situation.

1. The Agency Statute Is Silent

Much, and perhaps most, federal agency legislation granting rulemaking power says nothing about the procedures that the agency should follow when exercising that power. In that situation, the agency usually must follow the informal rulemaking requirements of the federal APA.

For an example of an agency statute that says nothing about the procedures to be followed when the agency exercise its rulemaking power, look at the statutory grant of rulemaking power to the FCC in the Communications Act of 1934:

---

47 U.S.C. § 201. Service and charges ...

(b) ... The Commission may prescribe such rules and regulations as may be necessary in the public interest to carry out the provisions of this chapter....

Nothing in "this chapter" (meaning 47 U.S.C. §§ 151–621 (2012)) conditions this grant of rulemaking power on following any particular rulemaking procedures.

In this situation of an agency legislation's silence on procedural matters, the APA's informal rulemaking provisions will apply by default or, to put it somewhat more legalistically, will apply "by their own terms"—assuming (as we do throughout this chapter) that the APA applies to the agency and that neither the agency statute nor the APA itself exempts the rule from the APA's rulemaking requirements.

2. The Agency Statute Expressly Refers to the APA's Informal Rulemaking Requirements

Many federal statutes, when granting an agency power to make legislative rules, expressly refer to § 553, which is where the APA's informal rulemaking provisions are codified. Sometimes these express references cause the APA's rulemaking requirements to apply to a rule that would otherwise be exempt under the terms of the APA.

As discussed in Chapter 10, the statute granting rulemaking power to the Secretary of Veterans Affairs makes the APA's rulemaking requirements applicable to rules that are otherwise exempt from APA requirements because they concern government loans, grants, or benefits:

38 U.S.C. § 501. Rules and regulations

(a) The Secretary has authority to prescribe all rules and regulations which are necessary or appropriate to carry out the laws administered by the Department and are consistent with those laws....

(d) The provisions of section 553 of title 5 shall apply, without regard to subsection (a)(2) of that section, to matters relating to loans, grants, or benefits under a law administered by the Secretary.

We quoted this statute in Chapter 10.D.3 to illustrate Congress's ability to address in the agency legislation the applicability of the APA's rulemaking requirements. The statute's reference to "section 553" not only addresses *whether* the APA applies (and makes clear that the APA does indeed apply). It also makes clear *which kind* of APA rulemaking vehicle is to be used: the informal-rulemaking vehicle. That is why the statute is relevant here.

Exercise: Examining Federal Agency Legislation to Determine What Kind of Rulemaking Proceeding Is Required

The Nuclear Regulatory Commission has rulemaking power under this statutory provision:

42 U.S.C. § 2201. General Duties of Commission

In the performance of its functions the Commission is authorized to—

...

(p) Rules and regulations

make, promulgate, issue, rescind, and amend such rules and regulations as may be necessary to carry out the purposes of [the Atomic Energy Act]....

Nothing in the Atomic Energy Act addresses the procedures to be followed when exercising this power.

Assume that the Commission relies on this provision to issue rules requiring owners, operators, and employees of nuclear power plants to follow certain procedures when responding to various kinds of accidents at a nuclear power plant.

1. By way of review, are rules issued under this provision legislative or non-legislative rules?

2. Explain why the Commission must follow the notice-and-comment procedures of § 553(c) to promulgate these rules.

C. Agency Legislation Requiring Formal Rulemaking under the Federal APA

Whereas informal rulemaking is probably the most common rulemaking vehicle for making legislative rules under the federal APA, the rarest type is undoubtedly formal rulemaking. An agency must use formal rulemaking to make a rule when the agency legislation requires:

(1) the rule to be based exclusively on a formal record; and

(2) the agency to give an opportunity for a trial-like hearing.

Statutes that impose these two requirements are said to "trigger" formal rulemaking under the federal APA. This section gives background on formal rulemaking and gives examples of federal statutes that trigger formal rulemaking.

Informal rulemaking requirements are set out in APA § 553(b), which requires notice of proposed rulemaking, and in the first two sentences of § 553(c), which require that the agency invite and consider public comments on the proposed rule. Section 553(c) is set out below. Pay particular attention to § 553(c)'s third (and last) sentence:

---

5 U.S.C. § 553. Rule making . . .

(c) After notice required by this section, the agency shall give interested persons an opportunity to participate in the rule making through submission of written data, views, or arguments with or without opportunity for oral presentation. After consideration of the relevant matter presented, the agency shall incorporate in the rules adopted a concise general statement of their basis and purpose. When rules are required by statute to be made on the record after opportunity for an agency hearing, sections 556 and 557 of this title apply instead of this subsection. . . .

The last sentence of § 553(c) says that its first two sentences do not apply when a rule is **"required by statute to be made on the record after opportunity for an agency hearing."** In that event, § 553(c) directs us to §§ 556 and 557.

Sections 556 and 557 prescribe procedures for formal rulemaking (as well as formal adjudication). Specifically, § 556 requires a formal, evidentiary hearing before a presiding official who is usually an administrative law judge employed by the agency making the rule. This formal agency hearing may include testimony under oath and cross-examination of witnesses. *See* 5 U.S.C. § 556(c) & (d) (2012). Section 556 also requires the documents submitted in the proceeding and the material admitted into evidence at the hearing to be **"the exclusive record for decision in accordance with section 557."** *Id.* § 556(e). Section 557 generally requires the official who presided at the hearing to make an initial or recommended decision, which is subject to review by the head of the agency. *See id.* § 557(a) & (b) (2012). Section 557 generally forbids ex parte communications between people outside the agency and anyone inside the agency involved in the rulemaking proceeding. *See id.* § 557(d). In sum, rulemaking proceedings under §§ 556 and 557 are formal indeed, compared to the notice-and-comment procedures in APA § 553(c).

At this point, you will find it helpful to skim §§ 556 and 557, especially the subsections cited in the last paragraph. For now you just need a general sense of their contents. We explore them in detail in Chapters 22–24, in connection with formal adjudication.

Relatively few federal statutes trigger formal rulemaking. Formal rulemaking is rare for three reasons.

First, formal rulemaking is often elaborate and time-consuming. One notorious formal rulemaking proceeding lasted 9 years. The proceeding was conducted by the federal Food and Drug Administration to decide whether peanut butter should be required to contain a minimum of 90% peanuts or only 87%. *See* Robert W. Hamilton, *Rulemaking on a Record by the Food and Drug Administration*, 50 Tex. L. Rev. 1132, 1144 (1972); *see also Corn Prods. Co. v. FDA*, 427 F.2d 511 (3rd Cir. 1970) (rejecting challenge to the final rule), *cert. denied*, 400 U.S. 957 (1970). The cumbersomeness of formal rulemaking makes Congress hesitant to require it.

Second, formal rulemakings are "closed record" proceedings, which are generally considered inappropriate for the rulemaking process. A "closed record" proceeding is one in which the decision makers must base the decision exclusively on a formal record, the contents of which are clearly defined (usually by statute) and are generally created by the parties to the proceeding. In an "open record" proceeding, in contrast, the decision maker need not rely exclusively on input from people involved in the proceeding, and those people do not even necessarily know—at least before the proceeding ends—what material the decision maker will rely on in making a decision. Closed record proceedings are usually not considered appropriate for rulemaking because of rulemaking's quasi-legislative nature. Just as legislatures when drafting statutes do not rely solely on material gathered during legislative hearings—e.g., in hearings before legislative committees and subcommittees— agencies when drafting rules in informal rulemaking proceedings need not rely exclusively on input from the public on a proposed rule. For example, the agency may rely on information from inside the agency. It is generally thought that closed record proceedings are more suited to judicial and quasi-judicial proceedings than to legislative and quasi-legislative proceedings. The closed-record feature of formal rulemaking is another factor that leads Congress seldom to require it in agency legislation

Formal rulemaking was more common in the first half of the 20th century. In that era, federal agencies used formal rulemaking to fix the rates that large companies—such as the phone company (there used to be only one phone company), public utilities, railroads and other "common carriers"—could charge their customers. The federal APA classifies ratemaking proceedings as a type of rulemaking. *See* 5 U.S.C. § 551(4) (2012) (defining "rule" to include "the approval or prescription for the future of rates [and] ... prices"). Though classified as rulemakings, ratemaking proceedings have characteristics of adjudications. They usually involve a small number of identified entities—namely, the companies whose rates are being fixed—and affect those entities' property rights (the right to make money) based on individual circumstances (e.g., the companies' costs of doing business). Formal rulemaking, with its trial-like evidentiary hearing was thought suitable to ratemaking proceedings because they were as much "quasi-judicial" as "quasi-legislative." *See* AGM 33. As federal ratemaking became rarer (because of deregulation), so did formal rulemaking.

Third, the U.S. Supreme Court has signaled that lower federal courts, when in doubt, should avoid construing federal statutes to trigger formal rulemaking. The Court sent this signal in *United States v. Florida East Coast Railway*, 410 U.S. 224 (1973). There, the Court held that the APA's formal rulemaking requirements were not triggered by an agency statute that merely required a rule to be made "after hearing." *Id.* at 237–238. The Court explained this was not enough to trigger formal rulemaking because the statute did not express an intention that the rule be based exclusively on the record compiled at a formal, trial-like hearing. *See also United States v. Allegheny-Ludlum Steel Corp.*, 406 U.S. 742, 756–757 (1972) (reaching same conclusion about earlier version of the statute at issue in *Florida East Coast Railway*). After *Florida East Coast Railway*, a federal statute will not trigger formal rulemaking unless the statute both: (1) requires an opportunity for a formal agency hearing; *and* (2) requires the rule to be based "on the record." 5 U.S.C. § 553(c) (2012).

Here is an example of a federal statute that triggers formal rulemaking under the federal APA. This statute authorizes the U.S. Attorney General to make additions to, or subtractions from, the lists (called "schedules") of controlled substances regulated under the Controlled Substances Act:

---

21 U.S.C. § 811. Authority and criteria for classification of substances

(a) Rules and regulations of Attorney General; hearing

The Attorney General shall apply the provisions of this subchapter to the controlled substances listed in the schedules established by section 812 of this title and to any other drug or other substance added to such schedules under this subchapter. Except as provided in subsections (d) and (e) of this section, the Attorney General may by rule —

(1) add to such a schedule or transfer between such schedules any drug or other substance [if he or she makes specified findings]....

(2) remove any drug or other substance from the schedules [if he or she makes specified findings]....

Rules of the Attorney General under this subsection shall be made on the record after opportunity for a hearing pursuant to the rulemaking procedures prescribed by subchapter II of chapter 5 of Title 5....

The different schedules for controlled substances reflect the many different uses, dangers, and benefits associated with these substances. The Attorney General's classification of substances under this statute is likely to be highly fact-intensive. This may be why Congress chose to require formal rulemaking for the classification process.

Another example of a federal statute that has been interpreted to trigger formal rulemaking is the Agricultural Marketing Agreement Act. This Act authorizes the Secretary of Agriculture to issue "marketing orders" for certain fruits and vegetables. One marketing order, for example, governs the marketing of all California peaches. *See* 7 C.F.R. Part 917. That order regulates the grades and sizes of California peaches and prescribes procedures for inspecting, packaging, and labeling them. The main purpose of the Act is to ensure stable market conditions for agricultural goods.

Here are the provisions for the issuance of a marketing order:

---

7 U.S.C. § 608c. Orders ...

(3) Notice and hearing

Whenever the Secretary of Agriculture has reason to believe that the issuance of [a marketing] order will tend to effectuate the declared policy of this [Act] with respect to any commodity or product thereof specified in [this Act], he shall give due notice of and an opportunity for a hearing upon a proposed order.

(4) Finding and issuance of [a marketing] order

After such notice and opportunity for hearing, the Secretary of Agriculture shall issue an order if he finds, and sets forth in such order, upon the evidence introduced at such hearing ... that the issuance of such order ... will tend to effectuate the declared policy of this chapter with respect to such commodity....

Marketing orders are **"rules"** within the meaning of the APA. 5 U.S.C. § 551(4). The Secretary of Agriculture uses formal rulemaking under the federal APA to promulgate these rules. Section 608c(3) requires an opportunity for a hearing. Section 608c(4) requires the Secretary to base a marketing order "upon the evidence introduced at such hearing," which means that the Secretary must rely exclusively on the hearing record. These two provisions impose the two requirements necessary to trigger formal rulemaking. If you were a marketer of products subject to a marketing order, what arguments would you make in favor of the appropriateness of using formal rulemaking to promulgate marketing orders?

Although only a few federal statutes trigger formal rulemaking, this does not mean that APA §§ 556 and 557 are rarely used. Sections 556 and 557 supply procedures for both formal rulemaking *and* formal adjudications by federal agencies. The formal procedures of §§ 556 and 557 must be used for an agency adjudication when the statute authorizing the adjudication requires it **"to be determined on the record after opportunity for an agency hearing."** 5 U.S.C. § 554(a) (2012). Formal adjudication is more common than formal rulemaking.

Exercise: Identifying Statutes that Trigger Formal Rulemaking under the Federal APA

The following provision from the Marine Mammal Protection Act authorizes the Secretaries of Commerce and Interior (who both administer the Act) to issue regulations allowing the taking and importing of marine mammals:

16 U.S.C. § 1373. Regulations on taking of marine mammals

(a) Necessity and appropriateness

The Secretary, on the basis of the best scientific evidence available and in consultation with the Marine Mammal Commission, shall prescribe such regulations with respect to the taking and importing of animals from each species of marine mammal (including regulations on the taking and importing of individuals within population stocks) as he deems necessary and appropriate to insure that such taking will not be to the disadvantage of those species and population stocks and will be consistent with the purposes and policies set forth in section 1361 of this title.

(b) Factors considered in prescribing regulations ...

(c) Allowable restrictions ...

(d) Procedure

Regulations prescribed to carry out this section with respect to any species or stock of marine mammals must be made on the record after opportunity for an agency hearing....

1. Please explain in your own words why this statute triggers formal rulemaking. Include in your explanation a reference to the relevant federal APA provision that addresses when a statute should be interpreted to trigger formal rulemaking.

2. Please explain why Congress might have chosen to require formal rulemaking in this statute.

D. Agency Legislation Requiring Hybrid Rulemaking under the Federal APA

Congress requires hybrid rulemaking in what you might call the "Goldilocks situation." If Congress considers informal rulemaking to be too informal, and formal rulemaking too formal, it will require an agency, when making legislative rules under a particular statute, to follow procedures that are customized to be just right. Ordinarily, Congress achieves this by modifying the APA's informal rulemaking procedures. Section 559 of the federal APA allows such modifications of APA requirements. *See* 5 U.S.C. § 559 (2012).

Congress can modify the APA's informal rulemaking requirements in many different ways, ranging from minor tweaks to major changes. Because the range of hybrid rulemaking is broad, and because understanding it requires an understanding of the APA's informal rulemaking procedures, we defer until Chapter 14 an examination of hybrid rulemaking. Our present focus is identifying *when* a statute requires hybrid rulemaking, and not on the various forms that hybrid rulemaking can take.

Hybrid rulemaking statutes fall into three categories, according to the ease with which they can be identified as hybrid rulemaking statutes:

(1) statutes that expressly refer to the APA in the process of customizing the APA's informal rulemaking procedures;

(2) statutes that are plainly designed to modify the APA's informal rulemaking procedures but do not expressly mention the APA; and

(3) statutes that require rules to be made after a "hearing."

As discussed below, unlike statutes in the first two categories, statutes in the third category do not necessarily — or even usually — trigger hybrid rulemaking. Below you will see examples of statutes in each category.

1. Agency Legislation Expressly Modifying the APA

A well-known example of a hybrid rulemaking statute is the Magnuson-Moss Warranty-Federal Trade Commission Improvement Act of 1975. This 1975 Act modified the procedures that the Federal Trade Commission must follow to promulgate legislative rules defining unfair or deceptive trade practices. The modified procedures are a souped-up version of informal rulemaking:

---

15 U.S.C. § 57a. Unfair or deceptive acts or practices rulemaking proceedings

(a) Authority of Commission to prescribe rules and general statements of policy

(1) Except as provided in subsection (h) of this section, the Commission may prescribe —

(A) interpretive rules and general statements of policy with respect to unfair or deceptive acts or practices in or affecting commerce (within the meaning of section 45(a)(1) of this title), and

(B) rules which define with specificity acts or practices which are unfair or deceptive acts or practices in or affecting commerce (within the meaning of section 45(a)(1) of this title).... Rules under this subparagraph may include requirements prescribed for the purpose of preventing such acts or practices....

(b) Procedures applicable

(1) When prescribing a rule under subsection (a)(1)(B) of this section, the Commission shall proceed in accordance with section 553 of Title 5 (without regard to any reference in such section to sections 556 and 557 of such title), and shall also (A) publish a notice of proposed rulemaking stating with particularity the text of the rule, including any alternatives, which the Commission proposes to promulgate, and the reason for the proposed rule; (B) allow interested persons to submit written data, views, and arguments, and make all such submissions publicly available; (C) provide an opportunity for an informal hearing in accordance with subsection (c) of this section; and (D) promulgate, if appropriate, a final rule based on the matter in the rulemaking record (as defined in subsection (e)(1)(B) of this section), together with a statement of basis and purpose....

[Editor's note: Additional procedural requirement for rulemaking under this statute are omitted from this excerpt.]

This provision expressly adds to the informal rulemaking procedures prescribed in APA § 553. These customized rulemaking procedures are further tricked out in the FTC's procedural rules for its rulemakings. 16 C.F.R. §§ 1.7–1.20 (2012).

Not all hybrid rulemaking statutes make major modifications to the APA's informal rulemaking procedures. Some hybrid rulemaking statutes only tweak the informal rulemaking procedures—for example, by requiring the agency to allow people to make oral presentations on a proposed rule. Here, for example, is a provision authorizing the Secretary of Agriculture to make rules for handling poultry products:

---

21 U.S.C. § 463. Rules and regulations

(a) Storage and handling of poultry products; violation of regulations

The Secretary may by regulations prescribe conditions under which poultry products capable of use as human food, shall be stored or otherwise handled by any person engaged in the business of buying, selling, freezing, storing, or transporting, in or for commerce, or importing, such articles, whenever the Secretary deems such action necessary to assure that such articles will not be adulterated or misbranded when delivered to the consumer. Violation of any such regulation is prohibited.

(b) Other necessary rules and regulations

The Secretary shall promulgate such other rules and regulations as are necessary to carry out the provisions of this chapter.

(c) Oral presentation of views

In applying the provisions of section 553(c) of Title 5 to proposed rule making under this chapter, an opportunity for the oral presentation of views shall be accorded all interested persons.

This modifies the APA's informal rulemaking procedures, because the APA does not require an agency to allow oral presentation of views in informal rulemaking. Instead, APA § 553 allows public participation in the rulemaking proceeding "with *or without* opportunity for oral presentation." 5 U.S.C. § 553(c) (emphasis added). For examples of other hybrid rulemaking statutes requiring oral presentations, see, for example, 15 U.S.C. § 2309 (2012) (empowering Federal Trade Commission to make rules for consumer product warranties); 49 U.S.C. § 5103(b)(2) (2012) (empowering Secretary of Transportation to make rules for transportation of hazardous material); 49 U.S.C. § 32502(e) (2012) (empowering Secretary of Transportation to make rules for car bumpers).

Several federal environmental statutes require hybrid rulemaking by expressly modifying the APA's informal rulemaking requirements. They include provisions in the Toxic Substances Control Act, 15 U.S.C. § 2605(c) (2012); the Endangered Species Act, 16 U.S.C. § 1533(b)(4)-(6) (2012); the Safe Drinking Water Act, 42 U.S.C. §§ 300g-1 & 300h(a)(2) (2012); and the Clean Air Act, 42 U.S.C. § 7607(d) (2012).

2. Agency Statutes That Modify the APA's Informal Rulemaking Procedures without Mentioning the APA

Some hybrid rulemaking statutes modify the APA's informal rulemaking requirements without mentioning the APA. An example is a Clean Water Act provision authorizing the Administrator of the EPA to compile a list of toxic pollutants and establish effluent standards—which are "rule[s]" as defined in the APA, 5 U.S.C. § 551(4)—for each such pollutant. The excerpt of this provision includes not only procedural requirements but also substantive requirements for making effluent standards. See if you can tell them apart.

---

33 U.S.C. § 1317. Toxic and pretreatment effluent standards

(a) Toxic pollutant list; revision; hearing; promulgation of standards; effective date; consultation

(1) On and after December 27, 1977, the list of toxic pollutants or combination of pollutants subject to this chapter shall consist of those toxic pollutants listed in table 1 of Committee Print Numbered 95-30 of the Committee on Public Works and Transportation of the House of Representatives, and the Administrator shall publish, not later than the thirtieth day after December 27, 1977, that list. From time to time thereafter, the Administrator may revise such list and the Administrator is authorized to add to or remove from such list any pollutant....

(2) Each toxic pollutant listed in accordance with paragraph (1) of this subsection shall be subject to effluent limitations resulting from the application of the best available technology economically achievable.... The Administrator, in his discretion, may publish in the Federal Register a proposed effluent standard (which may include a prohibition) establishing requirements for a toxic pollutant.... Such published effluent standard (or prohibition) shall take into account the toxicity of the pollutant, its persistence, degradability, the usual or potential presence of the affected organisms in any waters, the importance of the affected organisms and the nature and extent of the effect of the toxic pollutant on such organisms, and the extent to which effective control is being or may be

achieved under other regulatory authority. The Administrator shall allow a period of not less than sixty days following publication of any such proposed effluent standard (or prohibition) for written comment by interested persons on such proposed standard. In addition, if within thirty days of publication of any such proposed effluent standard (or prohibition) any interested person so requests, the Administrator shall hold a public hearing in connection therewith. Such a public hearing shall provide an opportunity for oral and written presentations, such cross-examination as the Administrator determines is appropriate on disputed issues of material fact, and the transcription of a verbatim record which shall be available to the public....

This provision modifies the APA's informal rulemaking requirements by fixing the length of time for public comment at 60 days and by requiring a fairly formal "public hearing" if requested by an interested person.

For another example of a hybrid rulemaking statute that modifies the APA's informal rulemaking requirements without expressly referring to the APA, see the Occupational Safety and Health Act, 29 U.S.C. § 655(b) (2012).

3. Agency Statutes Requiring Rules to Be Made after a "Hearing"

A few federal statutes granting rulemaking authority require rules to be made after an opportunity, not for "oral presentations," but for a "hearing," and these statutes do not elaborate on what the required "hearing" should entail. Rulemaking statutes that require a "hearing"—but that do not require that "hearing" to be trial-like in its formality, or that the rule must be based exclusively on the record of the "hearing"—will often be interpreted to require only *informal* rulemaking—not formal rulemaking, and not even hybrid rulemaking. This is because of *United States v. Florida East Coast Railway*, 410 U.S. 224 (1973).

The statute in *Florida East Coast Railway* authorized the Interstate Commerce Commission (ICC) to make rules establishing how much money railroads had to pay for borrowing each other's freight cars. The statute required the ICC to make these rules "after hearing." *Id.* at 225 n.1. The statute did not say whether this "hearing" was supposed to be a trial-like hearing. Nor did the statute expressly require the ICC to base its rules exclusively on a defined "record" made at that hearing. The Court reached two important conclusions in *Florida East Coast Railway* about what the statute's reference to "hearing" meant.

One conclusion was discussed earlier in this chapter: The Court held that the statute's reference to a "hearing" did not trigger formal rulemaking. To trigger formal rulemaking, the Court held, the agency statute must require the rule to be based "on the record" after opportunity for a formal agency hearing. This holding relates to determining when a federal statute triggers formal rulemaking under the federal APA. *See Florida East Coast Railway*, 410 U.S. at 234–238.

A separate holding in *Florida East Coast Railway* relates to determining when a statute requires hybrid rulemaking: The Court held that the ICC could satisfy the statute's "hearing" requirement without allowing *any* oral presentations, formal or otherwise. The Court implied that the "hearing" could be purely a paper hearing, in which the ICC considered only written submissions from the public. The "hearing," in other words, could be the same opportunity for written public input given in informal rulemaking under § 553 of the federal APA. *Id.* at 238–246.

The result of *Florida East Coast Railway* was that an agency statute requiring a rule to be made "after hearing" not only did not trigger formal rulemaking—it did not even require hybrid rulemaking—when the statute contained nothing to indicate that the rule had to be based on the record of the hearing or that the hearing had to involve oral presentations. Good old informal rulemaking was good enough.

Few federal statutes resemble the one in *Florida East Coast Railway*, and so the question of what "hearing" means in this context does not come up often. We mention the issue— and *Florida East Coast Railway*'s determination of it—primarily because most law students and lawyers think that a "hearing" inevitably entails an oral presentation to a decision maker. But *Florida East Coast Railway* holds that oral presentations are usually not appropriate under statutes requiring "hearings" in agency rulemaking proceedings. "Hearings" in rulemaking proceedings may be no more than "paper hearings," in which interested persons are "heard" through written submissions.

In addition to knowing about this somewhat counterintuitive holding, you should also recall the reason for it. The reason is that rulemaking is a quasi-legislative activity, whereas formal evidentiary hearings with oral presentations are associated with judicial and quasi-judicial activities. Citing *Londoner v. City and County of Denver*, 210 U.S. 373 (1908), and *Bi-Metallic Investment Co. v. State Board of Equalization*, 239 U.S. 441 (1915), the Court in *Florida East Coast Railway* emphasized the "recognized distinction in administrative law between proceedings for the purpose of promulgating policy-type rules or standards, on the one hand, and proceedings designed to adjudicate disputed facts in particular cases on the other." 410 U.S. at 245. The Court described the ICC proceeding at issue there as involving "the formulation of a basically legislative-type judgment, for prospective application only, rather than ... adjudicating a particular set of disputed facts." *Id.* at 246. The clear implication was that oral presentations of the sort sometimes required as a matter of due process in adjudicatory proceedings are not ordinarily appropriate in quasi-legislative proceedings.

E. Types of Rulemaking under State APAs

A state agency's legislation, like that of a federal agency, often authorizes the agency to make legislative rules. Sometimes the state agency legislation addresses the procedures that the agency must follow when exercising their rulemaking power; other times the agency legislation is silent on this matter. Typically, when the state agency statute is silent, the state APA supplies the default set of rulemaking procedures for state agencies' legislative rules (and sometimes for other types of state agency rules).

Most state APAs, unlike the federal APA, do not prescribe two different sets of rulemaking procedures: formal and informal. Instead, most state APAs prescribe only *one* set of rule-making procedures. Of course, this generalization has exceptions. Every state APA is different. In this section we offer examples of approaches that state APAs take.

The 1961 Model APA has one set of rulemaking procedures. Those procedures, however, may have an oral component. The 1961 Model APA's rulemaking procedures at a minimum require the agency to publish a proposed rule and give the public a chance to submit written comments on a proposed rule. In addition, under the following circumstances, the agency must allow for the public to make oral presentations on a proposed rule:

1961 Model State APA § 3. [Procedure for Adoption of Rules] …

(a) Prior to the adoption, amendment, or repeal of any rule, the agency shall: …

(2) afford all interested persons reasonable opportunity to submit data, views, or arguments, orally or in writing. In case of substantive rules, opportunity for oral hearing must be granted if requested by 25 persons, by a governmental subdivision or agency, or by an association having not less than 25 members.…[1]

Under such a provision, any rulemaking proceeding on a substantive (i.e., non-procedural) rule may include an "oral hearing."

The term "oral hearing" is ambiguous, since it can mean anything from an informal conference to a trial-like, evidentiary hearing. To dispel the ambiguity, the 1981 Model APA provision addressing public participation in rulemaking, § 3-104, used the term "oral proceeding" instead of "the more ambiguous and troublemaking word 'hearing.'" 1981 Model State APA § 3-104 Official Comment. The drafters of the 1981 Model APA wanted to ensure, when the specified circumstances for an "oral proceeding" were satisfied, that the agency allowed more than just a "paper hearing," without having to hold "a trial-type hearing." *Id.* Thus, the drafters expected that public hearings on proposed rules will resemble the kinds of public hearings that legislatures hold on proposed legislation, or more informal "town hall" type meetings that a city council might hold on a proposed ordinance.

Unlike the 1961 Model APA and the many state APAs modeled upon it, the Massachusetts APA resembles the federal APA in providing two sets of rulemaking procedures. The Massachusetts APA has one set of procedures for "regulations requiring hearings," and a separate set of procedures for "regulations not requiring hearings." Mass. Gen. Laws ch. 30A, §§ 2 & 3 (West, Westlaw through Chap 65 of 2012 2nd Ann. Sess.). The provision for "regulations requiring hearings" explains when its procedures apply:

Mass Gen. Law ch. 30A, § 2. Regulations requiring hearings …

A public hearing is required prior to the adoption, amendment, or repeal of any regulation if: (a) violation of the regulation is punishable by fine or imprisonment; or, (b) a public hearing is required by the enabling legislation of the agency or by any other law; or, (c) a public hearing is required as a matter of constitutional right.…

The public hearing shall comply with any requirements imposed by law, but shall not be subject to the provisions of this chapter governing adjudicatory proceedings.

---

1. For state APAs with provisions similar to that of the 1961 Model APA quoted in the text, see, e.g., Ark. Code Ann. § 25-15-204(a)(2)(B) (West, Westlaw through end of 2011 Reg. Sess.); Ga. Code Ann. § 50-13-4(a)(2) (West, Westlaw through 2011 Reg. & Special Sess.); Idaho Code Ann. § 67-5222 (2) (Michie 2006); Okla. Stat. Ann. § 303(C) (West, Westlaw through emergency effective provisions through Chapter 27 of 2nd Reg. Sess. of 53rd Legislature (2012)); Vt. Stat. Ann. § 840(a) (West, Westlaw through laws No. 67, 69 to 72, 74 to 77 (except sections effective July 1, 2012), and 79 to 80 of the Adjourned Sess. of 2011–2012 Gen. Ass. (2012)).

This provision recognizes that the agency legislation ("the enabling legislation") or the state or federal constitution may require a "public hearing." The Massachusetts provision also reflects a judgment that rules punishable by fines or imprisonment are serious enough to warrant a "public hearing." Massachusetts case law makes clear, however, that the "public hearing" required under this provision need not be a trial-like hearing of the sort that is required for agency adjudicatory proceedings. *See Bd. of Health of Sturbridge v. Bd. of Health of Southbridge*, 962 N.E.2d 734, 741–743 (Mass. 2012). Thus, you see in the Massachusetts APA the same reluctance to require trial-type hearings in rulemakings that you find in the 1981 Model State APA and in the federal APA as construed in *Florida East Coast Railway*.

The takeaway is that at both the federal and state level you will seldom find statutorily required trial-type hearings for agency rulemaking proceedings. The default form of public participation in rulemaking will often be the opportunity to file written comments. This opportunity may sometimes be supplemented by the opportunity for "oral proceedings" in which members of the public have a chance to speak their piece.

F. Procedural Steps Common to All Types of Rulemaking under an APA

This chapter identified three types of rulemaking proceedings under the federal APA and explained that state APAs may provide one or more types of rulemaking proceeding. It is useful to keep in mind, however, that all types of rulemaking proceedings under the federal and state APAs generally require an agency to take at least five steps to make a legislative rule:

1. Notify the public of the proposed rulemaking.
2. Invite input on the proposed rule from people outside the agency.
3. Consider that input when deciding on the final rule.
4. Provide a written explanation for the final rule.
5. Publish the final rule before it takes effect.

The details of these steps vary, depending on the type of rulemaking (informal, formal, or hybrid). Even so, it's important to keep in mind the overall similarity of rulemaking under an APA.

G. Chapter 11 Wrap Up and Look Ahead

Once you determine that the applicable (federal or state) APA's rulemaking requirements apply to an agency rule, you must next determine how the APA's requirements interact with the rulemaking requirements of other laws. The most important category of "other laws" is the agency legislation authorizing the rule under analysis. The agency legislation is the source of the agency's rulemaking power, and in granting that power the legislature may impose procedural requirements as well as substantive requirements. This chapter explored the interaction between procedural requirements of an APA and procedural requirements (if any) in the agency legislation.

In discussing the way agency legislation may interact with an APA's rulemaking requirements, this chapter separately discussed (1) the interaction between federal agency statutes and the federal APA; and (2) the interaction between state agency statutes and a state APA. Rulemaking under the federal APA may take one of three forms, depending on what, if anything, the agency legislation requires in the way of rulemaking procedures: (1) informal rulemaking; (2) formal rulemaking; or (3) hybrid rulemaking. Rulemaking under most state APAs, in contrast, ordinarily will not include any proceeding analysis to formal rulemaking under the federal APA. Indeed, formal rulemaking is rare in the federal system today, partly because it requires a trial-type hearing that is thought inappropriate to the quasi-legislative activity of rulemaking.

Now you should be able to tell whether a federal agency statute requires informal rulemaking; formal rulemaking; or hybrid rulemaking. You should also have an introduction to how state APAs address rulemaking. The next step is to learn more about what each type of rulemaking proceeding (and its state analogue, if any) actually entails. Accordingly, the next three chapters deal with each type of rulemaking.

Professional Development Reflection Questions

The sprawling nature of administrative law makes it important to develop professional relationships to help you practice competently in this area of law. The need to develop these relationships is essential because you can only learn so much working alone, especially in the early years of your legal career. The question arises: How do you establish these relationships? The answer is: Practice, practice, practice. You can start practicing in law school.

Indeed, you can start practicing in your law school course on administrative law. Specifically, you can establish relationships with the professor who teaches the course and with classmates taking the course. These relationships can help you learn administrative law better and more enjoyably than you can learning it alone. For example, by developing a professional relationship with the teacher, you will feel more comfortable visiting the teacher during office hours to discuss questions that come up when you review the material. By developing a professional relationship with a classmate, you will have someone whom you can ask questions that you don't feel comfortable asking the professor (e.g., because you think they are "too obvious").

With this background on the value of professional relationships, please consider these questions:

1. What is one do-able step you can take to further your professional relationship with the teacher of your administrative law course?

2. What is one do-able step you can take to further your professional relationship with a classmate in your administrative law course?

Chapter 12

Informal Rulemaking

Overview

Chapter 11 identified three types of rulemaking under the federal APA, one of which is informal rulemaking. This chapter examines informal rulemaking under the federal APA and rulemaking under the 2010 Model State APA.

The chapter's sections are entitled:

A. The Federal Agency Publishes General Notice of Proposed Rulemaking.

B. The Federal Agency Gives the Public a Chance to File Written Comments on the Proposed Rule.

C. The Federal Agency Considers Public Input on the Proposed Rule and Other Relevant Matters When Deciding on the Final Rule.

D. The Federal Agency Publishes the Final Rule Along with a Concise General Statement of Its Basis and Purpose.

E. The Federal Agency Makes the Rule Effective No Sooner than 30 Days after Publication.

F. Rulemaking Requirements in State APAs

G. Chapter 12 Wrap Up and Look Ahead

The main objective of this chapter is to help you learn how to analyze whether a particular informal rulemaking proceeding complies with the federal APA and case law construing it. A secondary objective is to introduce enough information about rulemaking under state APAs that you become familiar with some similarities and differences among various APAs' rulemaking procedures.

Chapter Problem

Memo to: Legal Counsel

From: Executive Director, National Association of Residential Housing Contractors

Re: Proposed EPA Rule

I would like your help preparing written comments for our association opposing a rule that EPA has just proposed. The proposed rule amends an existing rule in a way that will be extremely burdensome for those of our members who are renovation firms.

As you know, the EPA issued a rule in April 2008 to reduce the dangers of lead-based paint in residential housing. The rule is known as the Lead Renovation, Repair, and Painting Program (RRP) rule. The RRP rule applies to firms that renovate houses constructed before 1978 (the year that lead-based paint was banned). The RRP rule requires these firms to go through an EPA-approved training program and get certified for handling lead paint safely in pre-1978 houses (so-called "target housing"). We estimate that compliance with the rule raises the cost of renovation projects by 15%, which is, of course, passed on to consumers.

EPA included an "opt out" provision in the 2008 RRP rule. The opt-out provision sometimes allows owners of pre-1978 residential housing to waive the requirements of the RRP rule. The opt-out provision is somewhat limited, because an owner of target housing can opt out only if the owner signs a written statement to the effect that no children under 6 years old or pregnant women live in the house. Even so, many of our members like the opt-out provision and use it to get a lot of work from people who want a price break on their renovation job.

Now EPA proposes to eliminate the opt-out provision in the 2008 RRP rule. Here is EPA's rationale, as set out in its notice of proposed rulemaking:

> **Environmental Protection Agency, Proposed Rule, Lead: Amendment to the Opt-out and Recordkeeping Provisions in the Renovation, Repair, and Painting Program, 74 Fed. Reg. 55506 (Oct. 28, 2009) [excerpt]**
>
> After further consideration of the opt-out provision, the Agency believes it is in the best interest of the public to remove the provision. EPA has decided it is important to require the RRP work practices and training and certification requirements in target housing even if there is no child under age 6 or pregnant woman residing there. While the RRP rule focused mainly on protecting young children and pregnant women from lead hazards, exposure can result in adverse health effects for older children and adults as well. By removing the opt-out provision the rule will go farther toward protecting older children and adults occupants of target housing where no child under age 6 or pregnant woman resides.
>
> In addition, the opt-out provision may not be sufficiently protective for children under age 6 and pregnant women, the vulnerable populations identified in the RRP rule, given that no known safe level of lead exposure has been identified.... As pointed out by a number of commenters on the RRP rule, the opt-out provision does not protect families with young children who may purchase recently renovated target housing. Removal of the opt-out will result in fewer homes being purchased with pre-existing lead hazards. Under the RRP rule, the opt-out provision was limited to owner-occupied target housing and did not extend to vacant rental housing because of the concern that future tenants could un-knowingly move into a rental unit where dust-lead hazards created by the renovation are present. In the same way, dust-lead hazards created during renovations in an owner-occupied residence conducted prior to a sale will be present for the next occupants. It is common for home owners to perform activities that disturb paint before selling a house, thus increasing the likelihood of lead hazards being present for someone buying a home, which may include a family with a child under age 6 or a pregnant woman.
>
> Renovations performed under the opt-out provision are also likely to result in exposures for vulnerable populations in other ways. Visiting

children who do not spend enough time in the housing to render it a child-occupied facility [subject to the RRP rule] may nevertheless be exposed to lead from playing in dust-lead hazards created by renovations. For example, children may spend time in the homes of grandparents, but those homes may be eligible for the opt-out provision of the RRP rule. A homeowner who signs an opt-out statement may not realize that she is pregnant. Eliminating the opt-out provision will also protect families with young children residing near or adjacent to homes undergoing renovations. Under the RRP rule, an owner occupant can take advantage of the opt-out provision even if a child under age 6 or a pregnant woman lives in an adjacent home. Renovations on the exterior of a residence can spread leaded dust and debris some distance from the renovation activity, which is why, for regulated renovations, EPA requires renovation firms to cover the ground with plastic sheeting or other impermeable material a distance of 10 feet from the renovation and take extra precautions when in certain situations to ensure that dust and debris does not contaminate other buildings or other areas of the property or migrate to adjacent properties. There are approximately 2 million owner-occupied, single-family attached homes built before 1978. Renovations on the exteriors of these homes are likely to contaminate neighboring yards and porches resulting in exposure outside the house as well as inside because dust can be tracked into the home. Many more owner-occupied, single-family detached homes are located in close proximity to each other, and renovations performed under the opt-out provision present a similar risk for these homes.

Moreover, EPA believes that implementing the regulations without the opt-out provision promotes, to a greater extent, the statutory directive to promulgate regulations covering renovation activities in target housing. Section 401(17) of TSCA [i.e., the Toxic Substances Control Act] defines target housing as "any housing constructed prior to 1978, except housing for the elderly or persons with disabilities (unless any child who is less than 6 years of age resides or is expected to reside in such housing for the elderly or persons with disabilities) or any 0-bedroom dwelling." Among other things, TSCA section 403(c)(3), in turn, directs EPA to promulgate regulations that apply to renovation activities in target housing....

EPA invoked, as the authority for the original RRP rule and this proposed amendment to it, provisions in the TSCA: 15 U.S.C. §§ 2682(c)(3), 2684, 2686, and 2687 (2012).

EPA recognized in the original RRP rule that it has discretion under TSCA's grant of rulemaking authority to include the opt-out provision. We must mount arguments, backed up with evidence, that EPA was right to include the opt-out provision in the first place, and should leave it in now.

I value your help as a newcomer to this project. My specific questions to you, as a newcomer, are: (1) what arguments might we make to oppose elimination of the opt-out provision; and (2) what evidence, if any, do we need to back up those arguments? Send me a memo when you've got your thoughts together.

A. The Federal Agency Publishes General Notice of Proposed Rulemaking

Section 553(b) of the APA requires a federal agency, as the first step of an informal rulemaking proceeding, to publish a notice of proposed rulemaking in the Federal Register. *See* 5 U.S.C. §553(b) (2012). The notice must have the information expressly required by §553(b)(1), (b)(2), and (b)(3). In addition to this information, many federal courts require agencies to disclose the technical basis of the proposed rule, such as the scientific data or reports on which the proposed rule rests. Yet another court-developed requirement prevents agencies from adopting final rules that are not a "logical outgrowth" of the previously published proposed rule.

This section discusses: (1) the purpose of §553(b) and its express requirements; (2) the court-developed requirement that an agency disclose the technical basis of a proposed rule; and (3) the court-developed "logical outgrowth" requirement.

1. The Purpose and Express Requirements of APA §553(b)

Let us start with the text of §553(b) (not including its exemptions, which we discussed in Chapter 10.C).

---

5 U.S.C. §553. Rule making ...

(b) General notice of proposed rule making shall be published in the Federal Register, unless persons subject thereto are named and either personally served or otherwise have actual notice thereof in accordance with law. The notice shall include—

(1) a statement of the time, place, and nature of public rule making proceedings;

(2) reference to the legal authority under which the rule is proposed; and

(3) either the terms or substance of the proposed rule or a description of the subjects and issues involved....

Federal agencies almost always publish a general notice of proposed rulemaking in the Federal Register, rather than personally serving notice on each person subject to a proposed rule. This discussion therefore focuses on the general notice of proposed rulemaking published in the Federal Register.

a. Purpose of Notice

The main purpose of requiring the agency to publish a general notice of proposed rulemaking is to alert the public, and supply the information necessary for the public to give meaningful input on the proposed rule. Public input, in turn, is supposed to serve three purposes: (1) It enhances the quality of agency decision making by exposing the agency's proposal to outside evaluation. (2) It inserts a dose of democracy into the rulemaking process by allowing the public to be heard on rules that determine legal rights and duties. Finally, (3) it enhances judicial review "by giving affected parties an opportunity to develop evidence in the record to support their objections to a rule." *Small Refiner Lead Phase-Down Task Force v. EPA*, 705 F.2d 506, 547 (D.C. Cir.1983) (internal quotation marks omitted).

The third purpose deserves particular attention because of its practical importance for lawyers. If your client opposes (or supports) a proposed agency rule and therefore wants you to develop evidence against it (or in favor of it), you must develop the evidence and present it to the agency during the period for public input on the proposed rule. Your evidence then becomes part of the "rulemaking record" that a court will review if the final rule is judicially challenged. You must "build your record" against (or in favor of) the agency rule during the rulemaking proceeding. That is because, when a court reviews an agency rule, the court usually considers only the evidence and other information that was presented to the agency. Thus, the quality of judicial review depends on the quality of the rulemaking record, which in turn depends on the quality of public input on the proposed rule.

b. The Federal Register

Section 553(b) requires federal agencies to publish the general notice of proposed rule-making in the Federal Register. The Federal Register has such an important place in federal administrative law that it deserves explanation.

The Federal Register owes its existence to the Federal Register Act of 1935, 44 U.S.C. §§ 1501–1511 (2012). This 1935 Act created an official daily publication of significant, executive-branch actions known as the Federal Register. The Federal Register has been published every business day since 1935. The Federal Register contains notices of proposed agency rulemaking. In addition, a federal agency must publish the final version of its rules in the Federal Register. Besides notices of proposed rulemaking and final rules, the Federal Register contains material about other agency activities, such as notices of agency meetings. The Federal Register also contains certain presidential documents.

The Federal Register Act established a second publication, the Code of Federal Regulations (CFR), which is where final legislative rules are permanently codified, and organized according to subject matter, after they are published in a daily edition of the Federal Register.

You can find the Federal Register and the CFR on the Government Printing Office's Federal Digital System website: http://www.gpo.gov/fdsys/. Every day's Federal Register has a section devoted exclusively to notices of proposed rulemaking. Many lawyers pay attention to the daily Federal Register to monitor proposed rules and other executive-branch actions that affect their clients. In addition, lawyers study the Federal Register to research the regulatory history of regulations. The Federal Register is useful for regulatory history research because, when the agency publishes a notice of proposed rulemaking in the Federal Register, and again when the agency publishes the final rule in the Federal Register, the agency also publishes an explanation that sheds light on the purposes and operation of the proposed and final rule.

c. Information Expressly Required by § 553(b)

The notice of proposed rulemaking—which is called the NOPR or NPRM in admin-istrative law circles—must have the three items of information specified in subsections 553(b)(1) through (b)(3).

As to § 553(b)(1): In most informal rulemaking proceedings, the agency allows the public to participate in the proceeding only by submitting written comments on the proposed rule. Accordingly, the NOPR satisfies § 553(b)(1) by describing how to submit written comments and identifying the deadline for submitting them. But sometimes the agency legislation or the agency's own rules require the agency to hold a public hearing on the proposed rule. In that event, the NOPR tells the public where and when the hearing will occur and how members of the public can participate in it.

Section 553(b)(2) requires the agency to identify the legal (usually statutory) source of authority for the proposed rule. This information matters because one question that may arise is whether a rule falls within the agency's rulemaking authority. If a court ultimately has to decide that question, the agency will usually have to stick with the purported sources of legal authority that it has cited in the notice of proposed rulemaking in accordance with § 553(b)(2). It will be hard for the agency to cite, for the first time on judicial review, some other statute as the source of authority for the rule.

Agencies usually satisfy § 553(b)(3) by reproducing the actual text — "the terms" — of the proposed rule, rather than simply "a description of the subjects and issues involved." Figure 12-A reproduces an NOPR from the Federal Register.

Exercise: Basic Analysis of a Notice of Proposed Rulemaking

Please review Figure 12-A with the objective of answering these questions:

1. How can you tell this is a Notice of Proposed Rulemaking?

2. What information does the caption contain?

3. Where in the notice you can find the information required by § 553(b) (1), (2), and (3)?

The caption of an NOPR has two elements that are sure to mystify. The "docket number" is assigned by the agency as a tracking number, so that the agency and others interested in the rulemaking can keep straight the events and filings associated with that rulemaking proceeding. The "RIN" is a "regulation identifier number." It is another number designed to help keep track of the regulation. Instead of being assigned by the agency (as is the docket number), the RIN is assigned by the Regulatory Information Service Center under Executive Order 12,866, § 4(b), 3 C.F.R. 638 (1994), for purposes of the "Unified Regulatory Agenda." The federal government publishes the Unified Regulatory Agenda twice a year, to enable people inside and outside the government to keep track of both the anticipated and the ongoing regulatory actions of all federal agencies. The idea of collecting all of this information in one unified agenda is to facilitate coordination of regulatory efforts among federal agencies, and to inform the public of what regulatory actions are "in the pipeline." Think of the Federal Register as serving the function of a daily newspaper of the federal government, and the Unified Regulatory Agenda as serving the function of a semi-annual almanac of federal regulatory activity.

Figure 12-A. Notice of Proposed Rulemaking (NPRM or NOPR) in Federal Register

12506

Proposed Rules

Federal Register

Vol. 77, No. 41

Thursday, March 1, 2012

This section of the FEDERAL REGISTER contains notices to the public of the proposed issuance of rules and regulations. The purpose of these notices is to give interested persons an opportunity to participate in the rule making prior to the adoption of the final rules.

DEPARTMENT OF TRANSPORTATION

Federal Aviation Administration

14 CFR Part 39

[Docket No. FAA–2012–0187; Directorate Identifier 2011–NM–094–AD]

RIN 2120–AA64

Airworthiness Directives; The Boeing Company Airplanes

AGENCY: Federal Aviation Administration (FAA), DOT.

ACTION: Notice of proposed rulemaking (NPRM).

SUMMARY: We propose to adopt a new airworthiness directive (AD) for certain The Boeing Company Model 757 airplanes. This proposed AD was prompted by fuel system reviews conducted by the manufacturer. This proposed AD would require modifying the fuel quantity indication system (FQIS) wiring or fuel tank systems to prevent development of an ignition source inside the center fuel tank. We are proposing this AD to prevent ignition sources inside the center fuel tank, which, in combination with flammable fuel vapors, could result in fuel tank explosions and consequent loss of the airplane.

DATES: We must receive comments on this proposed AD by April 30, 2012.

ADDRESSES: You may send comments, using the procedures found in 14 CFR 11.43 and 11.45, by any of the following methods:

• *Federal eRulemaking Portal:* Go to *http://www.regulations.gov.* Follow the instructions for submitting comments.

• *Fax:* 202–493–2251.

• *Mail:* U.S. Department of Transportation, Docket Operations, M–30, West Building Ground Floor, Room W12–140, 1200 New Jersey Avenue SE., Washington, DC 20590.

• *Hand Delivery:* Deliver to Mail address above between 9 a.m. and 5 p.m., Monday through Friday, except Federal holidays.

Examining the AD Docket

You may examine the AD docket on the Internet at *http://www.regulations. gov;* or in person at the Docket Management Facility between 9 a.m. and 5 p.m., Monday through Friday, except Federal holidays. The AD docket contains this proposed AD, the regulatory evaluation, any comments received, and other information. The street address for the Docket Office (phone: 800–647–5527) is in the **ADDRESSES** section. Comments will be available in the AD docket shortly after receipt.

FOR FURTHER INFORMATION CONTACT: Tak Kobayashi, Aerospace Engineer, Propulsion Branch, ANM–140S, FAA, Seattle Aircraft Certification Office (ACO), 1601 Lind Avenue SW., Renton, Washington 98057–3356; phone: 425–917–6499; fax: 425–917–6590; email: *takahisa.kobayashi@faa.gov.*

SUPPLEMENTARY INFORMATION:

Comments Invited

We invite you to send any written relevant data, views, or arguments about this proposal. Send your comments to an address listed under the **ADDRESSES** section. Include "Docket No. FAA–2012–0187; Directorate Identifier 2011–NM–094–AD" at the beginning of your comments. We specifically invite comments on the overall regulatory, economic, environmental, and energy aspects of this proposed AD. We will consider all comments received by the closing date and may amend this proposed AD because of those comments.

We will post all comments we receive, without change, to *http:// www.regulations.gov,* including any personal information you provide. We will also post a report summarizing each substantive verbal contact we receive about this proposed AD.

Discussion

The FAA has examined the underlying safety issues involved in fuel tank explosions on several large transport airplanes, including the adequacy of existing regulations, the service history of airplanes subject to those regulations, and existing maintenance practices for fuel tank systems. As a result of those findings, we issued a regulation titled "Transport Airplane Fuel Tank System Design Review, Flammability Reduction and

Maintenance and Inspection Requirements" (66 FR 23086, May 7, 2001). In addition to new airworthiness standards for transport airplanes and new maintenance requirements, this rule included Special Federal Aviation Regulation No. 88 ("SFAR 88," Amendment 21–78, and subsequent Amendments 21–82 and 21–83).

Among other actions, SFAR 88 requires certain type design (i.e., type certificate (TC) and supplemental type certificate (STC)) holders to substantiate that their fuel tank systems can prevent ignition sources in the fuel tanks. This requirement applies to type design holders for large turbine-powered transport airplanes and for subsequent modifications to those airplanes. It requires them to perform design reviews and to develop design changes and maintenance procedures if their designs do not meet the new fuel tank safety standards. As explained in the preamble to the rule, we intended to adopt airworthiness directives to mandate any changes found necessary to address unsafe conditions identified as a result of these reviews.

In evaluating these design reviews, we have established four criteria intended to define the unsafe conditions associated with fuel tank systems that require corrective actions. The percentage of operating time during which fuel tanks are exposed to flammable conditions is one of these criteria. The other three criteria address the failure types under evaluation: single failures, a combination of failures, and unacceptable service (failure) experience. For all four criteria, the evaluations included consideration of previous actions taken that may mitigate the need for further action.

We have determined that the actions identified in this proposed AD are necessary to reduce the potential of ignition sources inside the center fuel tank, which has been identified to have a high flammability exposure. Ignition sources inside the center fuel tank, in combination with flammable fuel vapors, could result in fuel tank explosions and consequent loss of the airplane.

The combination of a latent failure within the center fuel tank and a subsequent single failure of the fuel quantity indicating system (FQIS) wiring or components outside the fuel tank can cause development of an ignition source inside the center fuel tank. Latent in-tank failures, including corrosion/deposits at wire terminals, conductive debris on fuel system probes, wires or probes contacting the tank structure, and wire faults, could create a conductive path inside the center fuel tank. Out-tank single failures including hot shorts in airplane wiring and/or the FQIS processor could result in electrical energy being transmitted into the center fuel tank via the FQIS wiring. The electrical energy, if combined with a latent in-tank failure, could be sufficient to create an ignition source inside the center fuel tank, which, combined with flammable fuel vapors could result in a catastrophic fuel tank explosion.

SFAR 88 and Fuel Tank Flammability Reduction Rule

The National Transportation Safety Board (NTSB) determined that the combination of a latent failure inside the center fuel tank and a subsequent single failure of the FQIS wiring or components outside the fuel tank was the most likely ignition source inside the center fuel tank that resulted in the TWA Flight 800 explosion. After the TWA 800 accident, we issued AD 99–03–04, Amendment 39–11018 (64 FR 4959, February 2, 1999), and AD 98–20–40, Amendment 39–10808 (63 FR 52147, September 30, 1998), mandating separation of the FQIS wiring that penetrates the fuel tank from high power wires and circuits on the classic Boeing 737 and 747 airplanes. Those ADs resulted in installation of Transient Suppression Units (TSUs), Transient Suppression Devices (TSDs), or Isolated Fuel Quantity Transmitter (IFQT) as a method of compliance with the AD requirements.

After we issued those ADs, the findings from the SFAR 88 review showed that most transport category airplanes with high flammability fuel tanks needed TSUs, TSDs, or IFQTs to prevent electrical energy from entering the fuel tanks via the FQIS wiring in the event of a latent failure in combination with a single failure.

Installation of those FQIS protection devices, however, was determined unnecessary on those airplanes that are required to comply with the "Reduction of Fuel Tank Flammability in Transport Category Airplanes" rule (73 FR 42444, July 21, 2008), referred to as the Fuel Tank Flammability Reduction (FTFR) rule. The FTFR rule requires incorporation of a flammability reduction means (FRM) that converts high flammability fuel tanks into low flammability fuel tanks for certain airplane models. Therefore, the unsafe

condition identified by SFAR 88 is mitigated by incorporation of an FRM, as discussed in the FTFR rule.

This proposed AD is intended to address the unsafe condition associated with the FQIS wiring that penetrates the center fuel tank for all Boeing Model 757 airplanes that are not subject to the requirements of the FTFR rule. This proposed AD would apply to airplanes operated in all-cargo service and airplanes operated under Title 14 Code of Federal Regulations (CFR) part 91, since those airplanes are also not subject to the requirements of the FTFR rule. As explained in paragraph 2–5.a. of Advisory Circular 120–98, "Operator Requirements for Incorporation of Fuel Tank Flammability Reduction Requirements," dated May 7, 2009, to operate a pre-1992 airplane in passenger service after December 26, 2017, operators must incorporate an FRM that meets the requirements of § 26.33(c) before that date. For such airplanes on which an FRM is incorporated, further compliance with this proposed AD is not required.

The nitrogen generating system (NGS) being developed by Boeing to meet the FTFR rule addresses the unsafe condition of this AD, as well as providing other safety improvements. Paragraph (h) of this proposed AD provides that, for operators not required to comply with the FTFR rule, electing to comply with the FTFR rule would be an acceptable method of addressing the unsafe condition.

As discussed in the FTFR rule, the FAA recognized that separate airworthiness actions would be initiated to address the remaining fuel system safety issues for airplanes for which an FRM is not required. We have notified design approval holders that service instructions to support introduction of FQIS protection are now necessary for fuel tanks that are not required to be modified with an FRM by the FTFR rule. To date we have not received any service information from Boeing addressing this specific threat; therefore, we are proceeding with this proposal, which would require modifications using methods approved by the Manager of the Seattle Aircraft Certification Office.

We plan similar actions for those Boeing and Airbus airplanes with

similar FQIS vulnerabilities that are not affected by the FTFR rule.

FAA's Determination

We are proposing this AD because we evaluated all the relevant information and determined the unsafe condition described previously is likely to exist or develop in other products of the same type design.

Proposed AD Requirements

This proposed AD would require modifying the FQIS wiring or fuel tank systems to prevent development of an ignition source inside the center fuel tank.

Costs of Compliance

We estimate that this proposed AD affects 352 airplanes of U.S. registry. We have been advised that some of those airplanes are subject to the requirements of the FTFR rule and therefore are excluded from the requirements of this AD.

Because the manufacturer has not yet developed a modification commensurate with the actions specified by this proposed AD, we cannot provide specific information regarding the required number of work hours or the cost of parts to do the proposed modification. In addition, modification costs will likely vary depending on the operator and the airplane configuration. The proposed compliance time of 60 months should provide ample time for the development, approval, and installation of an appropriate modification.

Based on similar modifications, however, we can provide some estimated costs for the proposed modification in this NPRM. The modifications mandated by AD 99–03–04, Amendment 39–11018 (64 FR 4959, February 2, 1999), and Amendment 39–10808 (63 FR 52147, September 30, 1998), for the classic Boeing Model 737 and 747 airplanes (i.e., TSD, TSU, IFQT) are not available for Boeing Model 757 airplanes. But, based on the costs associated with those modifications, we estimate the cost of this new proposed modification to be no more than $100,000 per airplane. The Honeywell FQIS may need additional modifications, which may cost as much as $100,000 per airplane. The cost impact of the proposed AD therefore is estimated to be between $100,000 and $200,000 per airplane.

As indicated earlier in this preamble, we specifically invite the submission of comments and other data regarding the costs of this proposed AD.

Authority for This Rulemaking

Title 49 of the United States Code specifies the FAA's authority to issue rules on aviation safety. Subtitle I, section 106, describes the authority of the FAA Administrator. Subtitle VII: Aviation Programs, describes in more detail the scope of the Agency's authority.

We are issuing this rulemaking under the authority described in subtitle VII, part A, subpart III, section 44701: "General requirements." Under that section, Congress charges the FAA with promoting safe flight of civil aircraft in air commerce by prescribing regulations for practices, methods, and procedures the Administrator finds necessary for safety in air commerce. This regulation is within the scope of that authority because it addresses an unsafe condition that is likely to exist or develop on products identified in this rulemaking action.

Regulatory Findings

We determined that this proposed AD would not have federalism implications under Executive Order 13132. This proposed AD would not have a substantial direct effect on the States, on the relationship between the national Government and the States, or on the distribution of power and responsibilities among the various levels of government.

For the reasons discussed above, I certify this proposed regulation:

(1) Is not a "significant regulatory action" under Executive Order 12866,

(2) Is not a "significant rule" under the DOT Regulatory Policies and Procedures (44 FR 11034, February 26, 1979),

(3) Will not affect intrastate aviation in Alaska, and

(4) Will not have a significant economic impact, positive or negative, on a substantial number of small entities under the criteria of the Regulatory Flexibility Act.

List of Subjects in 14 CFR Part 39

Air transportation, Aircraft, Aviation safety, Incorporation by reference, Safety.

The Proposed Amendment

Accordingly, under the authority delegated to me by the Administrator, the FAA proposes to amend 14 CFR part 39 as follows:

PART 39—AIRWORTHINESS DIRECTIVES

1. The authority citation for part 39 continues to read as follows:

Authority: 49 U.S.C. 106(g), 40113, 44701.

§ 39.13   [Amended]

2. The FAA amends § 39.13 by adding the following new airworthiness directive (AD):

The Boeing Company: Docket No. FAA–2012–0187; Directorate Identifier 2011–NM–094–AD.

(a) Comments Due Date

We must receive comments by April 30, 2012.

(b) Affected ADs

None.

(c) Applicability

This AD applies to The Boeing Company Model 757–200, –200PF, –200CB, and –300 series airplanes; certificated in any category; for which compliance with 14 CFR 121.1117(d), 125.509(d), or 129.117(d) is not required; regardless of the date of issuance of the original certificate of airworthiness or export airworthiness approval.

(d) Subject

Joint Aircraft System Component (JASC)/Air Transport Association (ATA) of America Code 7397: Engine fuel system wiring.

(e) Unsafe Condition

This AD was prompted by fuel system reviews conducted by the manufacturer. We are issuing this AD to prevent development of an ignition source inside the center fuel tank caused by a latent in-tank failure combined with electrical energy transmitted into the center fuel tank via the fuel quantity indicating system (FQIS) wiring due to a single out-tank failure.

(f) Compliance

Comply with this AD within the compliance times specified, unless already done.

(g) Modification

Within 60 months after the effective date of this AD, modify the FQIS wiring or fuel tank systems to prevent development of an ignition source inside the center fuel tank, in accordance with a method approved by the Manager, Seattle Aircraft Certification Office (ACO), FAA.

Note 1 to paragraph (g) of this AD: After accomplishment of the actions required by paragraph (g) of this AD, maintenance and/or preventive maintenance under 14 CFR part 43 is permitted provided the maintenance does not result in changing the AD-mandated configuration (reference 14 CFR 39.7).

(h) Optional Installation of Flammability Reduction Means

As an alternative to the requirements of paragraph (g) of this AD, operators may elect to comply with the requirements of 14 CFR 121.1117 or 14 CFR 125.509 or 14 CFR 129.117 (not including the exclusion of cargo airplanes in Sections 121.1117(j), 129.117(j), and 125.509(j)). Following this election, failure to comply with Sections 121.1117, 129.117, and 125.509 is a violation of this AD.

(i) Alternative Methods of Compliance (AMOCs)

(1) The Manager, Seattle ACO, FAA, has the authority to approve AMOCs for this AD, if requested using the procedures found in 14 CFR 39.19. In accordance with 14 CFR 39.19, send your request to your principal inspector or local Flight Standards District Office, as appropriate. If sending information directly to the manager of the ACO, send it to the attention of the person identified in the Related Information section of this AD. Information may be emailed to: *9-ANM-Seattle-ACO-AMOC-Requests@faa.gov.*

(2) Before using any approved AMOC, notify your appropriate principal inspector, or lacking a principal inspector, the manager of the local flight standards district office/certificate holding district office.

(j) Related Information

For more information about this AD, contact Tak Kobayashi, Aerospace Engineer, Propulsion Branch, ANM–140S, FAA, Seattle Aircraft Certification Office (ACO), 1601 Lind Avenue SW., Renton, Washington 98057–3356; phone: 425–917–6499; fax: 425–917–6590; email: *takahisa.kobayashi@faa.gov.*

Issued in Renton, Washington, on February 21, 2012.

Ali Bahrami,

Manager, Transport Airplane Directorate, Aircraft Certification Service.

[FR Doc. 2012–4931 Filed 2–29–12; 8:45 am]

BILLING CODE 4910–13–P

DEPARTMENT OF JUSTICE

Drug Enforcement Administration

21 CFR Part 1308

[Docket No. DEA–345]

Schedules of Controlled Substances: Placement of Five Synthetic Cannabinoids Into Schedule I

AGENCY: Drug Enforcement Administration, Department of Justice.

ACTION: Notice of proposed rulemaking.

SUMMARY: The Drug Enforcement Administration (DEA) proposes placing five synthetic cannabinoids 1-pentyl-3-(1-naphthoyl)indole (JWH–018), 1-butyl-3-(1-naphthoyl)indole (JWH–073), 1-[2-(4-morpholinyl)ethyl]-3-(1-naphthoyl)indole (JWH–200), 5-(1,1-dimethylheptyl)-2-(3-hydroxycyclohexyl)-phenol (CP–47,497), and 5-(1,1-dimethyloctyl)-2-(3-hydroxycyclohexyl)-phenol (cannabicyclohexanol, CP–47,497 C8 homologue) including their salts, isomers, and salts of isomers whenever the existence of such salts, isomers, and salts of isomers is possible, into Schedule I of the Controlled Substances Act (CSA). This proposed action is pursuant to the CSA which requires that

2. The Requirement That an Agency Disclose the Technical Basis of a Proposed Rule

The text of § 553(b) requires the NOPR to include three items of information. One required item is "**either the terms or substance of the proposed rule or a description of the subjects and issues involved.**" 5 U.S.C. § 553(c)(3) (2012). Most agencies, as noted above, satisfy this requirement by reproducing the text — "**the terms**" — of the proposed rule. Some federal courts construe § 553(b) also to require agencies to disclose the technical basis, such as the scientific data or studies, for the proposed rule. The federal courts that impose this requirement justify it as necessary to give the public adequate notice and a meaningful chance to comment on the proposed rule.

The leading federal court case requiring a federal agency to disclose the technical basis of a proposed rule is *Portland Cement Ass'n v. Ruckelshaus*, 486 F.2d 375 (D.C. Cir. 1973). In that case, the Administrator of the U.S. EPA published proposed air pollution limits in the Federal Register without initially disclosing in full the scientific tests on which the air pollution limits were based. The D.C. Circuit said, "Obviously a prerequisite to the ability to make meaningful comment is to know the basis upon which the rule is proposed." *Id.* at 393 n.67. Because EPA did not disclose information necessary to allow the meaningful public comment that the court construed the APA to require, the D.C. Circuit held that EPA's final rule violated the APA's rulemaking requirements.

A more recent federal court case applying the *Portland Cement* principle is set out below. The case also illustrates the controversial nature of the requirement in federal law.

Exercise: *American Radio Relay League*

The case below concerns rules by the Federal Communication Commission designed to allow electric power lines to be used to give people access to the internet. The name for the technology is "Access BPL." Please read the case with these questions in mind:

1. What context does this case present for a judicial challenge to an agency rule? In other words, how does the case arise?

2. According to the majority, what is the purpose of requiring an agency to disclose the technical basis for a proposed rule? How does the purpose that the majority identifies relate to the three purposes previously identified earlier in this chapter for requiring agencies to publish general notice of proposed rulemaking for public input?

3. Why does Judge Tatel write a separate, concurring opinion?

4. Why does Judge Kavanaugh write separately?

American Radio Relay League, Inc. v. Federal Communications Commission

524 F.3d 227 (D.C. Cir. 2008)

Before: Rogers, Tatel, and Kavanaugh, Circuit Judges.

Opinion for the Court by Circuit Judge Rogers.

Concurring opinion by Circuit Judge Tatel.

Opinion concurring in part, concurring in the judgment in part, and dissenting in part by Circuit Judge Kavanaugh.

Rogers, Circuit Judge:

The American Radio Relay League, Inc., petitions on behalf of licensed amateur radio operators for review of two orders of the Federal Communications Commission promulgating a rule to regulate the use of the radio spectrum by Access Broadband over Power Line ("Access BPL") operators. The Commission concluded that existing safeguards combined with new protective measures required by the rule will prevent harmful interference to licensees from Access BPL radio emissions. The League challenges this conclusion.... We grant the petition in part and remand the rule to the Commission. The Commission failed to satisfy the notice and comment requirements of the Administrative Procedure Act ("APA") by redacting studies on which it relied in promulgating the rule....

I.

Section 302 of the [Communications] Act [of 1934] authorizes the Commission, "consistent with the public interest, convenience, and necessity," to promulgate regulations for manufacture and use governing "the interference potential of devices which in their operation are capable of emitting radio frequency energy ... in sufficient degree to cause harmful interference to radio communications." *Id.* § 302a(a). The Commission's rules, specifically Part 15, define "harmful interference" as "[a]ny emission, radiation or induction that endangers the functioning of a radio navigation service or of other safety services or seriously degrades, obstructs or repeatedly interrupts a radiocommunications service." 47 C.F.R. § 15.3(m). The rules governing unlicensed devices also include two provisions to protect licensed radio operators from unlicensed devices: an *ex ante* precondition of operation that a device not cause "harmful interference," *id.* § 15.5(b), and an *ex post* requirement that a device "cease" operation if "harmful interference" occurs, *id.* § 15.5(c).

The Commission, upon concluding that "the introduction of new high-speed [Access] BPL technologies warrants a systematic review of the Part 15 rules in order to facilitate the deployment of this new technology, promote consistency in the rules and ensure the ongoing protection of the licensed radio services," issued a notice of inquiry. Notice of Inquiry, Carrier Current Systems, Including Broadband Over Power Line Systems ("NOI"), 18 F.C.C.R. 8498, 8503 (April 28, 2003). Therein it stated that in the process of Access BPL transmission, devices installed along electric power lines transmit radio frequency energy over the 1.7-80 MHz spectrum, creating potential to interfere with the ability of nearby radio operators to send and receive signals on the same frequencies. *Id.* at 8499–500, 8505–06. Licensed radio operators on this part of the spectrum include public safety and federal government agencies, aeronautical navigation, maritime, radio-astronomy, citizen band radio, and amateur radio operators. *Id.* at 8506. Subsequently, in announcing a proposed rule, the Commission stated that its policy was to "promote and foster the development of [the] new technology [Access BPL] with its concomitant benefits while at the same time ensuring that existing licensed operations are protected from harmful interference." Notice of Proposed Rule Making, Carrier Current Systems, Including Broadband Over Power Line Systems ("NPRM"), 19 F.C.C.R. 3335, 3355 (Feb. 23, 2004).

In the final rule the Commission defined Access BPL and set technical and administrative requirements to protect licensed radio operators from harmful interference. See Amendment of Part 15 Regarding New Requirements and Measurement Guidelines for Access Broadband Over Power Line Systems, Carrier Current Systems ("Order "), 19 F.C.C.R. 21,265, 21,284–302 (Oct. 28, 2004)....

[T]he Commission stated that "[t]he record and our investigations indicate that [Access] BPL network systems can generally be configured and managed to minimize and/or eliminate ... harmful interference potential [to licensed radio services]." *Id.* at 21,266, 21,322. The Commission also relied on "information provided by our field tests," "our own field measurements of Access BPL installations," and "our own field testing." *Id.* at 21,275–76, 21,282, 21,296. Following issuance of the NOI, the League sought disclosure under the Freedom of Information Act ("FOIA") of the Commission's studies related to Access BPL systems. The Commission denied that request except as to one document that it placed in the record in the fall of 2003. When the League filed a second FOIA request citing the Order, the Commission released five studies in redacted form and made them part of the record in December 2004 after the rule was promulgated. The Commission stated that "[t]hese documents comprise internally-generated information upon which the Commission relied, in part, in reaching its determination." Submission by FCC Ofc. of Eng'g & Tech. to Sec'y (Dec. 22, 2004), filed in ET Docket Nos. 03-104 & 04-37.

The League sought reconsideration [by the FCC], and upon its denial ... the League petitioned for [judicial] review.

II.

The League seeks vacatur of the rule on four grounds. [Editor's note: This excerpt includes the court's discussion of only the second ground.] The League contends ... [s]econd, [that] because "[t]he lynchpin" of the rule "is a series of studies conducted by the [Commission's] engineers" that have never been made available in unredacted form, their non-disclosure violates the APA's notice and comment requirements. Pet.'s Br. at 18.

A. ...

B.

The APA requires an agency to publish "notice" of "either the terms or substance of the proposed rule or a description of the subjects and issues involved," in order to "give interested persons an opportunity to participate in the rule making through submission of written data, views, or arguments," and then, "[a]fter consideration of the relevant matter presented, the agency shall incorporate in the rules adopted a concise general statement of their basis and purpose." 5 U.S.C. §553(b)–(c). Longstanding precedent instructs that "[n]otice is sufficient 'if it affords interested parties a reasonable opportunity to participate in the rulemaking process,' and if the parties have not been 'deprived of the opportunity to present relevant information by lack of notice that the issue was there.'" *WJG Tel. Co., Inc. v. FCC*, 675 F.2d 386, 389 (D.C.Cir.1982) (citations omitted); *see Fla. Power & Light Co. v. Nuclear Regulatory Comm'n*, 846 F.2d 765, 771 (D.C.Cir.1988).

Under APA notice and comment requirements, "[a]mong the information that must be revealed for public evaluation are the 'technical studies and data' upon which the agency relies [in its rulemaking]." *Chamber of Commerce v. SEC (Chamber of Commerce II)*, 443 F.3d 890, 899 (D.C.Cir.2006) (citation omitted). Construing section 553 of the APA, the court explained long ago that "[i]n order to allow for useful criticism, it is especially important for the agency to identify and make available technical studies and data that it has employed in reaching the decisions to propose particular rules." *Conn. Light & Power Co. v. Nuclear Regulatory Comm'n*, 673 F.2d 525, 530 (D.C.Cir.1982) (emphasis added). More particularly, "[d]isclosure of staff reports allows the parties to focus on the information relied on by the agency and to point out where that information is erroneous or where the agency may be drawing improper conclusions from it." *Nat'l Ass'n of Regulatory Util. Comm'rs ("NARUC") v. FCC*, 737 F.2d 1095, 1121 (D.C.Cir.1984) (emphasis added); see *Portland Cement Ass'n v. Ruckelshaus*, 486 F.2d 375, 393 (D.C.Cir.1973)....

The failure to disclose for public comment is subject, however, to "the rule of prejudicial error," 5 U.S.C. §706, and the court will not set aside a rule absent a showing by the petitioners "that they suffered prejudice from the agency's failure to provide an opportunity for public comment," *Gerber v. Norton*, 294 F.3d 173, 182 (D.C.Cir.2002), in sufficient time so that the agency's "decisions ... [may be] framed with ... comment in full view," *NARUC*, 737 F.2d at 1121.

At issue are five scientific studies consisting of empirical data gathered from field tests performed by the [FCC's] Office of Engineering and Technology. Two studies measured specific Access BPL companies' emissions, and three others measured location-specific emissions in pilot Access BPL areas in New York, North Carolina, and Pennsylvania. In placing the studies in the rulemaking record, the Commission has redacted parts of individual pages, otherwise relying on those pages. In responding to the League's FOIA request, the Commission stated that "certain portions of [these] presentations have been redacted, as they represent preliminary or partial results or staff opinions that were part of the deliberative process, exempt from disclosure under Section 0.457(e) of the Commission's rules and Section 552(b)(5) of the FOIA." Letter from Edmond Thomas, Chief, FCC Ofc. of Eng'g & Tech., to Christopher Imlay, Gen. Counsel, Am. Radio Relay League (Jan. 4, 2005). Upon reconsideration, the Commission reaffirmed that "the redacted portions ... referred to internal communications that were not relied upon in the decision making process," while reiterating that Commission statements in the Order "point" to the partially redacted studies—including the Commission's "own field investigations of [Access] BPL experimental sites"—and "clarify[ing] that in this proceeding, the Commission relied ... on its own internally conducted studies." Reconsideration Order, 21 F.C.C.R. at 9324–25. The court, pursuant to the Commission's offer, Resp.'s Br. at 44 n. 35, has reviewed in camera the partially redacted pages in unredacted form; they show staff summaries of test data, scientific recommendations, and test analysis and conclusions regarding the methodology used in the studies. All pages in the studies are stamped "for internal use only."

It would appear to be a fairly obvious proposition that studies upon which an agency relies in promulgating a rule must be made available during the rulemaking in order to afford interested persons meaningful notice and an opportunity for comment. "It is not consonant with the purpose of a rule-making proceeding to promulgate rules on the basis of inadequate data, or on data that, [to a] critical degree, is known only to the agency." *Portland Cement Ass'n*, 486 F.2d at 393; *see NARUC*, 737 F.2d at 1121. Where, as here, an agency's determination "is based upon 'a complex mix of controversial and uncommented upon data and calculations,'" there is no APA precedent allowing an agency to cherry-pick a study on which it has chosen to rely in part....

The League has met its burden to demonstrate prejudice by showing that it "ha[s] something useful to say" regarding the unredacted studies, *Chamber of Commerce II*, 443 F.3d at 905, that may allow it to "mount a credible challenge" if given the opportunity to comment, *Gerber*, 294 F.3d at 184 (citation omitted); *see Owner-Operator Indep. Drivers Ass'n, Inc. v. Fed. Motor Carrier Safety Admin.*, 494 F.3d 188, 202–03 (D.C. Cir. 2007). As suggested by the League, the partially redacted pages indicate that a study's core scientific recommendations may reveal the limitations of its own data and that its conclusions may reveal methodology or illuminate strengths and weaknesses of certain data or the study as a whole. For example, the League points to the unredacted headings of otherwise redacted pages referring to "New Information Arguing for Caution on HF BPL" and "BPL Spectrum Tradeoffs," subjects on which it seeks the opportunity to comment. FCC Lab., BPL Summary After Briarcliff Manor, N.Y. Test, Sept. 8, 2004, at 17, filed in ET Docket Nos. 03-104 & 04-37. The unredacted pages thus appear to "contain information in tension with the [Commission's] conclusion" that "[Access] BPL's acknowledged interference risks are 'manageable.'" Pet.'s Br. at 18 (quoting Order, 19 F.C.C.R. at 21,276). Allowing such "omissions in data and methodology" may "ma[ke] it impossible to reproduce" an agency's results or assess its reliance upon them. *City of Brookings Mun. Tel. Co. v. FCC*, 822 F.2d 1153, 1168 (D.C.Cir.1987); *see also Sierra Club*, 657 F.2d at 334, 397–98; *United States v. Nova Scotia Food Prods. Corp.*, 568 F.2d 240, 252 (2d Cir.1977)....

The FOIA's deliberative process privilege, invoked by the Commission in responding to the League's FOIA request, "does not authorize an agency to throw a protective blanket over all information.... Purely factual reports and scientific studies cannot be cloaked in secrecy by an exemption designed to protect only those internal working papers in which opinions are expressed and policies formulated and recommended." *Bristol-Myers Co. v. Fed. Trade Comm'n*, 424 F.2d 935, 939 (D.C.Cir.1970) (footnote and internal quotation marks omitted). By choosing "to adopt or incorporate by reference" the redacted studies, *NLRB v. Sears, Roebuck & Co.*, 421 U.S. 132, 161, (1975), and thereby "us[ing] ... [them] in its dealings with the public," *Coastal States Gas Corp. v. Dep't of Energy*, 617 F.2d 854, 866 (D.C.Cir.1980), the Commission ceased treating them as internal working papers....

The narrowness of our holding under section 553 of the APA is manifest. The redacted studies consist of staff-prepared scientific data that the Commission's partial reliance made "critical factual material." *Owner-Operator Indep. Drivers Ass'n*, 494 F.3d at 201 (quoting *Air Transp. Ass'n of Am. v. FAA*, 169 F.3d 1, 7 (D.C.Cir.1999)). The Commission has chosen to rely on the data in those studies and to place the redacted studies in the rulemaking record. Individual pages relied upon by the Commission reveal that the unredacted portions are likely to contain evidence that could call into question the Commission's decision to promulgate the rule. Under the circumstances, the Commission can point to no authority allowing it to rely on the studies in a rulemaking but hide from the public parts of the studies that may contain contrary evidence, inconvenient qualifications, or relevant explanations of the methodology employed. The Commission has not suggested that any other confidentiality considerations would be implicated were the unredacted studies made public for notice and comment. The Commission also has not suggested that the redacted portions of the studies contain only "supplementary information" merely "clarify[ing], expand[ing], or amend[ing] other data that has been offered for comment." *See Chamber of Commerce II*, 443 F.3d at 903. Of course, it is within the Commission's prerogative to credit only certain parts of the studies. But what it did here was redact parts of those studies that are inextricably bound to the studies as a whole and thus to the data upon which the Commission has stated it relied, parts that explain the otherwise unidentified methodology underlying data cited by the Commission for its conclusions, and parts that signal caution about that data. This is a critical distinction and no precedent sanctions such a "hide and seek" application of the APA's notice and comment requirements. *See Gerber*, 294 F.3d at 181 (quoting *MCI Telecomms. Corp. v. FCC*, 57 F.3d 1136, 1142 (D.C.Cir.1995)).

As our colleague notes, see Concurring & Dissenting Op. by Judge Kavanaugh..., in *Vermont Yankee Nuclear Power Corp. v. Natural Resources Defense Council*, 435 U.S. 519 (1978), the Supreme Court has limited the extent that a court may order additional agency procedures, but the procedures invalidated in *Vermont Yankee* were not anchored to any statutory provision. *See id.* at 548; Richard J. Pierce, Jr., *Waiting for Vermont Yankee III, IV, and V? A Response to Beermann and Lawson*, 75 Geo. Wash. L.Rev. 902, 917 (2007). By contrast, the court does not impose any new procedures for the regulatory process, but merely applies settled law to the facts. The Commission made the choice to engage in notice-and-comment rulemaking and to rely on parts of its redacted studies as a basis for the rule. The court, consequently, is not imposing new procedures but enforcing the agency's procedural choice by ensuring that it conforms to APA requirements. It is one thing for the Commission to give notice and make available for comment the studies on which it relied in formulating the rule while explaining its non-reliance on certain parts. It is quite another thing to provide notice and an opportunity for comment on only those parts of the studies that the Commission likes best. Moreover, the court's precedent construing section 553 to require agencies to release for comment the "technical studies and data" or "staff reports" on which they rely during a rulemaking, *see, e.g., Conn. Light & Power Co.*, 673 F.2d at 530; *NARUC*, 737 F.2d at 1121, is not inconsistent with the view that "the Portland Cement doctrine should be limited to studies on which the agency actually relies to support its final rule." 1 Richard J. Pierce, Jr., Administrative Law Treatise 437 (4th ed.2002) (emphasis added).

On remand, the Commission shall make available for notice and comment the unredacted "technical studies and data that it has employed in reaching [its] decisions," *Conn. Light & Power Co.*, 673 F.2d at 530....

TATEL, Circuit Judge, concurring:

I write separately to emphasize that in my view, the disclosure ordered by the court in Part IIB is particularly important because the Commission's failure to turn over the unredacted studies undermines this court's ability to perform the review function APA section 706 demands. That provision requires us to set aside arbitrary and capricious agency action after reviewing "the whole record," 5 U.S.C. § 706, and the "whole record" in this case includes the complete content of the staff reports the Commission relied upon in promulgating the challenged rule....

KAVANAUGH, Circuit Judge, concurring in part, concurring in the judgment in part, and dissenting in part.

Applying the Administrative Procedure Act and our *Portland Cement* line of decisions, ... the majority opinion remands for the FCC to release redacted portions of certain FCC staff documents analyzing field tests of broadband over power lines. *See Portland Cement Ass'n v. Ruckelshaus*, 486 F.2d 375, 392–93 (D.C.Cir.1973). In light of our precedents, I concur in the judgment on this point; but I write separately because of concerns about our case law in this area....

I

[T]he Commission did not release certain redacted portions of the internal staff studies on which it relied. *Id.* Citing § 553 of the APA, petitioner says the FCC must release the redacted portions of the staff studies so that interested parties can comment on them and so the FCC, in turn, can consider those comments.

Petitioner's argument would be unavailing if analyzed solely under the text of APA § 553. The APA requires only that an agency provide public notice and a comment period before the agency issues a rule. *See* 5 U.S.C. § 553. The notice must include "the terms *or* substance of the proposed rule *or* a description of the subjects and issues involved." § 553(b)(3) (emphasis added). After issuing a notice and allowing time for interested persons to comment, the agency must issue a "concise general statement" of the rule's "basis and purpose" along with the final rule. § 553(c). One searches the text of APA § 553 in vain for a requirement that an agency disclose other agency information as part of the notice or later in the rulemaking process.

But beginning with the *Portland Cement* case in 1973—which was decided in an era when this Court created several procedural requirements not rooted in the text of the APA—our precedents have required agencies to disclose, in time to allow for meaningful comment, technical data or studies on which they relied in formulating proposed rules. *See Portland Cement Ass'n v. Ruckelshaus*, 486 F.2d 375, 392–93 (D.C.Cir.1973)....

The majority opinion concludes that the *Portland Cement* requirement does not allow the FCC to redact portions of studies when the studies otherwise must be disclosed under *Portland Cement.* I accept the majority opinion's conclusion as the best interpretation of our *Portland Cement* line of decisions.

I write separately to underscore that *Portland Cement* stands on a shaky legal foundation (even though it may make sense as a policy matter in some cases). Put bluntly, the *Portland Cement* doctrine cannot be squared with the text of § 553 of the APA. And *Portland Cement*'s lack of roots in the statutory text creates a serious jurisprudential problem because the Supreme Court later rejected this kind of freeform interpretation of the APA. In its landmark *Vermont Yankee* decision, which came a few years after *Portland Cement*, the Supreme Court forcefully stated that the text of the APA binds courts: Section 553 of the APA "established the *maximum procedural requirements* which Congress was willing to have the courts impose upon agencies in conducting rulemaking procedures." *Vermont Yankee Nuclear Power Corp. v. Natural Res. Def. Council, Inc.*, 435 U.S. 519, 524 (1978) (emphasis added)....

Because there is "nothing in the bare text of § 553 that could remotely give rise" to the *Portland Cement* requirement, some commentators argue that *Portland Cement* is "a violation of the basic principle of *Vermont Yankee* that Congress and the agencies, but not the courts, have the power to decide on proper agency procedures." Jack M. Beermann & Gary Lawson, *Reprocessing* Vermont Yankee, 75 Geo. Wash. L. Rev. 856, 894 (2007). At the very least, others say, the Supreme Court's decision in *Vermont Yankee* raises "a question concerning the continuing vitality of the *Portland Cement* requirement that an agency provide public notice of the data on which it proposes to rely in a rulemaking." 1 Richard J. Pierce, Administrative Law Treatise § 7.3, at 435 (4th ed.2002).

I do not believe *Portland Cement* is consistent with the text of the APA or *Vermont Yankee.* In the wake of *Vermont Yankee*, however, this Court has repeatedly continued to apply *Portland Cement* (albeit without analyzing the tension between *Vermont Yankee* and *Portland Cement*). In these circumstances, this three-judge panel must accept *Portland Cement* as binding precedent and must require the FCC to disclose the redacted portions of its staff studies. I therefore concur in the judgment as to Part IIB of the majority opinion.

Exercise: *American Radio Relay League* Revisited

You can find in Chapter 9 the Supreme Court's decision in *Vermont Yankee Nuclear Power Corp. v. Natural Resources Defense Council*, 435 U.S. 519 (1978) (reproduced in Chapter 9.B.4.b(i)). According to the majority in *American Radio Relay League*, the Court in *Vermont Yankee* invalidated court-imposed "[agency] procedures ... not anchored to any statutory provision." 524 F.3d at 239. Judge Kavanaugh in partial dissent similarly indicates that *Vermont Yankee* bars a court from imposing a procedural requirement upon an agency if there is "nothing in the bare text of § 553 that could remotely give rise" to the requirement. *Id.* at 246. On this reading of *Vermont Yankee*, consider these questions:

1. To what statutory language does the majority in *American Radio Relay League* anchor what Judge Kavanaugh calls "the *Portland Cement* requirement"? *Id.*

2. How would Judge Tatel justify the *Portland Cement* requirement?

3. Why would Judge Kavanaugh argue that the *Portland Cement Requirement* cannot be tied to § 553(b)'s reference to the "issues involved" in a rulemaking?

Note on Using the Freedom of Information Act to Learn the Technical Basis of a Proposed Rule

We have emphasized the need for opponents and supporters of a proposed rule to build the record against (or for) it during the rulemaking. The *Portland Cement* requirement reflects that, to challenge a proposed rule effectively, the opponent often needs to know the technical basis for it. The technical basis for a proposed rule may be contained in documents generated by and located within the agency. As *American Radio Relay League* illustrates, the Freedom of Information Act (FOIA) can help an opponent find out the technical basis for a proposed rule. The FOIA will become even more important for this purpose if the Supreme Court ever invalidates the *Portland Cement* requirement that lower courts have derived from APA § 553. Because of the FOIA's practical importance in rulemaking, this note gives some background.

Congress enacted the FOIA in 1966 as an amendment to Section 3 of the original APA. Congress enacted the FOIA in part to better protect "the citizens' right to be informed about what their government is up to." *U.S. Dep't of Justice v. Reporters Comm. for Freedom of the Press*, 489 U.S. 749, 773 (1989) (internal quotation marks omitted). The FOIA is codified in APA § 552 (not to be confused with § 553, which is the APA provision entitled "Rule making").

The FOIA imposes on federal agencies three types of disclosure requirements, codified in § 552(a)(1), (a)(2), and (a)(3). Section 552(a)(1) requires federal agencies to publish certain information in the Federal Register. Section 552(a)(2) requires federal agencies to make certain other information "available for public inspection and copying"; this information need not be published in the Federal Register, but it does have to be made available automatically, without anyone having to ask for it. Section 552(a)(3) is probably the best known part of the FOIA: It requires federal agencies to disclose, "upon any request," information that has not been made available under subsections (a)(1) or (a)(2). Section 552(a)(3) is what entitles people to file what are called "FOIA requests."

The American Radio Relay League made FOIA requests for the technical information underlying the FCC's proposed Access BPL rule. The League's second FOIA request brought to light the five studies that, the D.C. Circuit held, should have been disclosed when the FCC published the general notice of rulemaking. As the opinion in *American Radio Relay League* states, the League's FOIA requests produced the underlying studies only *after* the FCC had published the final version of the rule, at which point it was too late for the League to submit comments analyzing those studies. The League did use the FOIA disclosure successfully, however, in persuading the court to remand the rule to the FCC for consideration of the League's comments on the underlying studies.

As was true in *American Radio Relay League*, a FOIA request may not produce the requested information until after the rulemaking ends. Thus, the FOIA is no substitute for the *Portland Cement* requirement, which generally requires disclosure of the technical basis for a proposed rule when the proposed rule is published. Even so, a FOIA request serves the useful function, illustrated in *American Radio Relay League*, of helping ensure disclosure of the technical basis. Therefore, lawyers involved in rulemaking should consider making FOIA requests to help "flush out" all of the information underlying the agency rule.

Neither *Portland Cement* nor the FOIA requires an agency to disclose all information relevant to a proposed or final agency rule. As the *American Radio Relay League* case reflects, the FOIA has an exemption that allows an agency to refuse to disclose material covered by a "deliberative process privilege." 524 F.3d at 238–239. The court in *American Radio Relay League* held that the privilege did not cover the information that the FCC withheld. Agencies have used the privilege in other rulemaking cases, however, to withhold material that reflects the agency's internal deliberations, such as drafts of proposed rules. *E.g.*, *Pies v. IRS*, 668 F.2d 1350, 1354 (D.C. Cir. 1981) (draft regulations were covered by deliberative process privilege); *see also Lead Indus. Ass'n v. OSHA*, 610 F.2d 70, 85–86 (2nd Cir. 1979) (drafts of preamble to final regulations were covered by deliberative process privilege). The deliberative process privilege does not protect factual information that can be disclosed without revealing the deliberative portions of a document.

This book does not give sustained treatment to the FOIA. Especially good sources for research into the FOIA include:

- The U.S. Department of Justice Guide to the FOIA, http://www.justice.gov/oip/foia_guide09.htm

- Justin D. Franklin and Robert Bouchard, Guidebook to the Freedom of Information and Privacy Acts (C. Boardman, 2nd ed. 1986) (regularly updated).

3. Deviation between the Proposed Rule and the Final Rule

A recurring issue related to notice arises when the agency publishes a final rule that differs significantly from the proposed rule that was published in the NOPR. On the one hand, those adversely affected by the difference between the proposed and final rule may argue that they did not have adequate notice that the change was in the air and consequently lacked an adequate chance to comment on the change. On the other hand, the agency may argue that the whole purpose of soliciting public input is thwarted unless the agency can change a proposed rule in response to that public input.

Initially you might think that the agency can get out of this dilemma, whenever the agency decides to change a proposed rule, by publishing a revised version of the proposed rule and allowing public comment on the revised version. The problem with this approach is that it has the potential to prolong a rulemaking proceeding significantly, by requiring another round of public notice and comment every time the agency decides to change something in the proposed rule. That possibility, moreover, could discourage agencies from responding to public comments that demonstrate the need for changes to a proposed rule.

Many federal courts have adopted a test under which a final rule can differ from a proposed rule, without requiring another round of public notice and comment, as long as the change represents a "logical outgrowth" of the proposed rule. A well known federal court case applying the "logical outgrowth" test is *Chocolate Manufacturers Ass'n v. Block*, 755 F.2d 1098 (4th Cir.1985). In that case, the U.S. Department of Agriculture (USDA) proposed a rule that gave government subsidies to the poor for certain types of food, including flavored milk. The final rule, however, prohibited the use of the subsidies for flavored milk, because of its high sugar content. The Chocolate Manufacturers Association challenged the flavored milk prohibition on the ground that the Association had no notice that this change to the proposed rule might be made. The court agreed. The court found it significant that chocolate flavored milk had always been allowed in the USDA's subsidized food program and that the notice accompanying the proposed rule said nothing about changing this practice.

The teaching of *Chocolate Manufacturers* and other logical outgrowth case law is that, when an agency wants to change a proposed rule in a way that those adversely affected by the change could not reasonably have foreseen, the agency should publish the proposed change, and allow the public to comment on it, even if this prolongs the public comment period.

The "logical outgrowth" case law from the federal courts is subject to the same criticisms and defenses as the federal court case law requiring agencies to disclose the technical basis of a proposed rule. Both are tied to the purpose of giving adequate notice of what is at stake in a rulemaking proceeding, yet neither is clearly supported by the text of the APA provision on notice of proposed rulemaking: § 553(b). Perhaps the technical basis and logical outgrowth cases are better understood as resting on § 553*(c)*, rather than on § 553(b). After all, they are designed to ensure that the **"opportunity to participate in the rule making"** guaranteed to the public by § 553(c) is a meaningful opportunity.

Even with an alternative textual basis, however, the logical outgrowth and technical basis case law arguably involve federal courts "engrafting their own notions of proper procedures upon agencies entrusted with substantive functions by Congress," in violation of *Vermont Yankee*. 435 U.S. at 525; *see also American Radio Relay League Inc. v. FCC*, 524 F.3d 227, 246–247 (D.C. Cir. 2008) (Kavanaugh, J., concurring in part, concurring in the judgment in part, and dissenting in part) (reproduced above, criticizing technical data disclosure requirement as violating *Vermont Yankee* principle); *ConocoPhillips Co. v. U.S. EPA*, 612 F.3d 822, 834 & n.95 (5th Cir. 2010) (recognizing tension between logical outgrowth requirement and *Vermont Yankee* principle). The U.S. Supreme Court has not addressed the technical basis or logical outgrowth case law. The Court has recognized the existence of the logical outgrowth case law without directly addressing its validity. *Long Island Care at Home, Ltd. v. Coke*, 551 U.S. 158, 174 (2007).

The 2010 Model State APA codifies the logical outgrowth test by providing: "An agency may not adopt a rule that differs from the rule proposed in the notice of proposed rulemaking unless the final rule is a logical outgrowth of the rule proposed in the notice."

2010 Model State APA § 308. Some state APAs likewise codify a version of the logical outgrowth rule. *E.g.*, Idaho Code Ann. § 67-5227 (Westlaw, through 2012 Second Regular Session of 61st Legislature); Minn. Stat. Ann. § 14.05(2) (Westlaw, through 2012 Reg. Sess. through Ch. 131); Miss. Code Ann. § 25-43-3.107 (Westlaw, through end of 2011 Reg. Sess.). In other States, the state courts have endorsed the logical outgrowth rule as a gloss on their APA's notice provision. *See, e.g., In re Dep't of Pub. Serv. Respecting Application of Gen. Order 65*, 632 A.2d 1373, 1375 (Vt. 1993).

Exercise: The Logical Outgrowth Test

The court in *Chocolate Manufacturers* sent the case back to the USDA, instructing the agency "to reopen the comment period and thereby afford interested parties a fair opportunity to comment on the proposed changes in the rule." 755 F.2d at 1107. Please answer two questions about this disposition:

1. What kind of evidence do you think the Chocolate Manufacturers Association submitted to try to convince the USDA to keep subsidizing flavored milk?

2. Suppose the USDA did not change its mind after considering the Chocolate Manufacturers' evidence. Why might it still be worthwhile for the Chocolate Manufacturers to have forced USDA to reopen the comment period for the Chocolate Manufacturers to comment on the elimination of the subsidy for flavored milk?

B. The Federal Agency Gives the Public a Chance to File Written Comments on the Proposed Rule

The first sentence of § 553(c) requires public participation in informal rulemaking. We reproduce all of § 553(c) below, with the first sentence in bold face type, to present it in context with the rest of § 553(c).

---

5 U.S.C. § 553. Rule making ...

(c) After notice required by this section, the agency shall give interested persons an opportunity to participate in the rule making through submission of written data, views, or arguments with or without opportunity for oral presentation. After consideration of the relevant matter presented, the agency shall incorporate in the rules adopted a concise general statement of their basis and purpose. When rules are required by statute to be made on the record after opportunity for an agency hearing, sections 556 and 557 of this title apply instead of this subsection....

The first sentence requires an opportunity for public participation in informal rulemaking. The second sentence (which we will take up in Section C of this chapter) requires the agency to consider the public input and, when publishing the final rule, to provide a concise statement of the final rule's basis and purpose. The third sentence requires the agency to follow §§ 556 and 557 when the agency legislation authorizing the rule triggers what is called "formal rulemaking" (which we will discuss in Chapter 13).

The text of § 553(c)'s first sentence requires the agency to accept written data, written views, and written arguments of **"interested persons."** This does not mean that someone has to demonstrate an interest in a rulemaking to participate. Anyone who feels strongly enough to make a written submission on a proposed rule qualifies as an interested person. This is why the APA itself refers to § 553(c) as creating a *"public* procedure." 5 U.S.C. § 553(b)(B) (emphasis added). As a practical matter, though, it is unusual for broad segments of the public to comment on a proposed rule. Instead, many proposed rules draw comments from interest groups that represent only narrow segments of the public. For example, a proposed pollution regulation will draw comments from (1) entities that will be subject to the regulation, and who think it is too stringent; and (2) non-profit organizations dedicated to environmental protection, who think it is too lenient. Thus, § 553(c)'s reference to participation by **"interested persons"** is not restrictive, but is *descriptive* of those who typically participate in informal rulemaking. One could argue that rulemaking is not truly public given that interest groups dominate the public participation process, except in the same sense that a gladiatorial contest is "public."

Significantly, § 553(c) does not require the agency to allow members of the public to make an **"oral presentation"** to the agency. Section 553(c)'s first sentence lets the agency choose whether to allow a public hearing on a proposed rule. Most agencies elect not to hold public hearings in informal rulemakings if they are not required to by the agency legislation or the agency's own rules. Instead, they invite the public to make written submissions.

The written submissions on a proposed rule are generically called "comments," and informal rulemaking is often called "notice-and-comment" rulemaking. Effective written submissions, however, must do more than express the author's opinions about the proposed rule. The most effective comments offer relevant data, arguments on the relevant law, and relevant policy analysis. Indeed, comments on an agency rule may contain highly sophisticated economic, engineering, medical, or scientific data and analysis; and may challenge the validity and reliability of the data in opponents' comments.

Today people can usually submit comments either in hard copy by mail or as an electronic file uploaded to the internet. (See, for example, the Federal Register NOPR reproduced above in Figure 12-A, which invites submission of comments by mail or internet.) Indeed, the E-Government Act of 2002 states: "To the extent practicable, agencies shall accept submissions under section 553(c) of title 5, United States Code, by electronic means." Pub. L. No. 107-347, § 206(c), 116 Stat. 2916 (codified at 44 U.S.C. § 3501 Note (2012)). To carry out this requirement, the federal government has established a rulemaking portal where you can find proposed rules from about 300 federal agencies and can comment on them. The current link to the portal is as follows:

http://www.regulations.gov/#!home

This portal not only makes it easy for members of the public to submit comments in proposed federal agency rules. It also makes it easy to see all of the comments that other members of the public have submitted. This way, a commenter can readily tailor comments to ones that have previously been submitted.

This chance to "rebut" or buttress other public submissions is especially important if the rule is judicially challenged. If you oppose a proposed rule, for example, you do not want the court to be able to say that any evidence or comment supporting the rule "went unchallenged in the rulemaking proceeding." You want to challenge supporting evidence and comments during the public comment period, or else you will lose the chance to do so. Arguments and data not presented during the rulemaking ordinarily cannot be presented in a later judicial challenge to the rule. *Nuclear Energy Inst. v. EPA*, 373 F.3d 1251, 1290 (D.C. Cir. 2004).

In informal rulemakings, the notice of proposed rulemaking states the deadline for submission of comments. This is part of the information required by §553(b)(1). Section 553(c) itself does not require any minimum period for public comment. Executive Order 12,866, however, requires most federal agencies to allow at least sixty days for public comment on proposed rules. Exec. Order 12,866, §6(a)(1), 53 C.F.R. 638 (1994). For complicated proposed rules an agency may allow more than sixty days. Furthermore, if an agency receives more comments than it anticipated, it may extend the public comment period.

Exercise: Comments on Proposed Rules

Go to the federal government's rulemaking portal. Find public comments on rules for which the comment period is still open, and look at a sampling of the comments. Based on that sample, what are your initial impressions about what makes for an effective comment?

C. The Federal Agency Considers Public Input on the Proposed Rule and Other Relevant Matters When Deciding on the Final Rule

The second sentence of §553(c) addresses what happens in an informal rulemaking proceeding after the agency gives the public a chance to provide input on a proposed rule. The second sentence is reproduced in bold face type below:

---

5 U.S.C. §553. Rule making ...

(c) After notice required by this section, the agency shall give interested persons an opportunity to participate in the rule making through submission of written data, views, or arguments with or without opportunity for oral presentation. **After consideration of the relevant matter presented, the agency shall incorporate in the rules adopted a concise general statement of their basis and purpose.** When rules are required by statute to be made on the record after opportunity for an agency hearing, sections 556 and 557 of this title apply instead of this subsection....

The second sentence requires two things:

1. The agency must "**conside[r] … relevant matter presented.**"

2. The agency must incorporate in the final rule "**a concise general statement of [the rule's] basis and purpose.**"

This section of the chapter explores the agency's duty to consider relevant matter presented. The next section explores the agency's duty to accompany the final rule with a concise general statement of basis and purpose.

You can probably deduce the purpose of requiring the agency to consider the relevant matters presented. This "duty to consider" requires the agency to think about the significant input that it got from the public (and elsewhere). If the agency does not do this, the opportunity for public participation was a sham.

An agency's duty to "**conside[r] … relevant matter presented**" raises three questions:

(1) What is "**relevant**"?

(2) What does the "**matter presented**" include?

(3) How can you *tell* if a federal agency has "*consider[ed] … relevant matter presented*"?

Each question regularly arises in the practice of administrative law and therefore deserves our attention.

1. What Is "[R]elevant"?

What is relevant to a proposed rule depends mainly, but not only, upon the agency legislation governing the rule. The agency legislation may require the agency to consider certain things and prohibit the agency from considering other things. Other laws may also constrain the basis for the agency's decision making. These legal constraints, however, still usually leave the agency with much discretion to determine what's relevant when making a rule.

The agency statute often commands the agency to consider certain factors when making a rule. For example, the statute for determining whether a species is endangered or threatened under the Endangered Species Act requires the Secretaries of the Interior and Commerce to consider specific factors, such as loss of habitat. *See* 16 U.S.C. § 1533(a)(1) (2012). The Clean Water Act requires the EPA when setting certain water pollution standards to determine "the best available technology economically achievable." 33 U.S.C. § 1311(b)(2)(A)(i) (2012). These statutes specifically focus agency attention on certain matters, and in this way the statutes determine what is relevant to the agency rules implementing the statute. Even a statute broadly granting an agency power to make "such rules and regulations as may be necessary in the public interest to carry out this statute" determines relevance. *E.g.,* 47 U.S.C. § 201(b) (2012). It requires the agency to consider what may be necessary in the public interest to carry out the statute's provisions. If an agency fails to consider something that a court later finds relevant to the public interest, the court may invalidate the rule. Thus, even open-ended grants of power to legislative rules shape relevance.

Besides the agency legislation, other laws may affect relevance. For example, the National Environmental Policy Act requires federal agencies proposing rules that will significantly affect the environment to prepare an environmental impact statement that assesses "alternatives to the proposed action." 42 U.S.C. §4332(C) (2012). This requirement enables the agency, to the extent permitted by other laws, to consider the environmental impacts of its proposed action and ways to lessen those impacts. *See Massachusetts v. United States*, 522 F.2d 115, 119 (1st Cir. 2008). The Regulatory Flexibility Act requires federal agencies in most rulemakings to assess the effects of a proposed rule on small businesses and other small entities. 5 U.S.C. §§603(c) & 604(a)(5) (2012). These statutory duties impose procedural requirements with the objective of providing information that may be **"relevant"** for the agency to consider when making its rule.

Many court cases discuss what is relevant for an agency to consider when drafting a rule. Two cases show relevance can be hard to determine.

One case is *Whitman v. American Trucking Ass'ns, Inc.*, 531 U.S. 457 (2001). That case concerned an EPA rule establishing air quality standards under §109 of the Clean Air Act. The U.S. Supreme Court held that the EPA could not, when establishing air quality standards under §109, take into account how much it would cost industry to comply with the standards. The Court concluded that §109, "interpreted in its statutory and historical context ... unambiguously bars cost considerations" in setting air quality standards. 531 U.S. at 471. Thus, cost considerations were not **"relevant,"** within the meaning of APA §553(c), in proceedings to issue air quality standards under §109 of the Clean Air Act.

The Court reached a different conclusion, in a seemingly similar statutory setting, in *Entergy Corp. v. Riverkeeper, Inc.*, 556 U.S. 208 (2009). That case concerned EPA regulations issued under §316(b) of the Clean Water Act. The Court held that §316(b) permitted the EPA to consider costs (as well as benefits) when issuing regulations under that provision. 556 U.S. at 217–226. Thus, cost considerations were **"relevant,"** within the meaning of APA §553(c), in proceedings to issue rules under §316(b) of the Clean Water Act.

Whitman and *Entergy* reflect that every statute requires separate examination to determine what an agency may properly consider when making rules to implement the statute. *See also Catawba County, N.C. v. EPA*, 571 F.3d 20, 37 (D.C. Cir. 2009) (observing that statutory language requiring an agency rule to be "based on" specified information is "unquestionably ambiguous" about whether agency may also consider other information). *Whitman* and *Entergy Corp.* also show that, to determine what information on a proposed rule is **"relevant"** and therefore must be considered under §553(c), the agency itself often must interpret the agency legislation governing the rule. If the agency legislation precludes consideration of costs, for example, agency consideration of public comments presenting information about costs could render the resulting rule **"arbitrary, capricious, an abuse of discretion, or otherwise not in accordance with law,"** to use the terminology of the federal APA. 5 U.S.C. §706(2)(A) (2012). On the flip side, if a statute *requires* the agency to consider the costs of a proposed rule, failure to consider public comments providing cost information could also cause the rule to be **"arbitrary, capricious ... [etc.]."** In short, statutes—mainly including but not limited to the agency legislation—are a primary determinant of what is **"relevant"** under §553(c).

Many laws may require an agency to consider certain things, and prohibit it from considering other things, when drafting a rule. Even so, the agency is usually left with discretion to consider things that the agency, or the incumbent Administration, believes are relevant. The classic case making this point is *Chevron USA, Inc. v. Natural Resources Defense Council*, 467 U.S. 837 (1984). In *Chevron*, the EPA adopted an air pollution rule that reflected a business-friendly interpretation of an ambiguous provision in the Clean Air Act. The adoption of the rule coincided with the election of a new President who initiated a government wide reexamination of regulatory burdens on businesses. The Court upheld the EPA's business-friendly interpretation of the ambiguous statute, acknowledging that it reflected the political views of the new Administration:

> Judges are not experts in the field, and are not part of either political branch of the Government. Courts must, in some cases, reconcile competing political interests, but not on the basis of the judges' personal policy preferences. In contrast, an agency to which Congress has delegated policy-making responsibilities may, within the limits of that delegation, properly rely upon the incumbent administration's views of wise policy to inform its judgments. While agencies are not directly accountable to the people, the Chief Executive is, and it is entirely appropriate for this political branch of the Government to make such policy choices — resolving the competing interests which Congress itself either inadvertently did not resolve, or intentionally left to be resolved by the agency charged with the administration of the statute in light of everyday realities.

Id. at 865–866. The moral is that in informal rulemaking, a federal agency can, within legal constraints, treat as "relevant" the views of the Administration that controls the White House.

There are things an agency may not consider when making a rule, even though no law specifically bars their consideration. For example, an agency official could not ignore a comment on a proposed rule merely because it was submitted by a former law school classmate whom the agency official dislikes. Although no law specifically bars these agency practices, they will cause a court to invalidate the tainted rule on the ground that the agency did not use "reasoned decision making." *FCC v. Fox Television Stations, Inc.*, 556 U.S. 502, 520 (2009). The tainted rule is, in the words of the federal APA, "**arbitrary and capricious**" or an "**abuse of discretion**." 5 U.S.C. §706(2)(A) (2012).

An agency rule adopted through informal rulemaking is invalid if the agency bases the rule on factors that are not relevant, or if the agency adopts the rule without considering all relevant factors. As the Supreme Court has said, "Normally, an agency rule would be arbitrary and capricious if the agency has relied on factors which Congress has not intended it to consider [or] has entirely failed to consider an important aspect of the problem [to which the rule is addressed]." *Motor Vehicle Mfrs. Ass'n v. State Farm Mut. Auto Ins. Co.*, 463 U.S. 29, 43. (1983). This is true for all agency actions, not just rules adopted through informal rulemaking. *See Citizens to Preserve Overton Park, Inc. v. Volpe*, 401 U.S. 402, 416 (1971) (stating generally that, in reviewing agency action under the federal APA, "the court must consider whether the decision was based on a consideration of the relevant factors"). We discuss relevance now because of §553(c)'s express requirement that the agency consider "**relevant**" matters in informal rulemaking.

Exercise: Generally "Relevant" Considerations

The agency statute and other laws may leave an agency with varying degrees and types of discretion when making a rule. For example, the agency will often have discretion to consider factors relevant to what you might call "administrability":

- Comprehensibility: A rule should be easy for people who must follow it to understand.

- Enforceability: It should be as easy as possible for the agency to apply the rule. For regulatory rules, this means it must be easy for the agency to detect and correct violations. For rules related to getting government benefits or permits, it must be easy for agency decision makers (of whom there may be many non-lawyers) to determine whether the rule is satisfied.

- Efficiency: It shouldn't cost the agency too much to administer the rule, compared to the benefits of having the rule. Overly complicated rules, for example, may cost much agency personnel time to administer.

Other factors that the agency may have discretion to consider include:

- Burdens of compliance: If it is too hard (e.g., expensive) to comply with a rule, you might expect a lower compliance rate.

- Fairness: The rule should not single out certain people or businesses to bear an undue burden, or favor certain people or businesses over others without justification.

Please think of rules or policies that you have been subject to, or are aware of, that *violate* these principles. They can be, but need not be, government rules or policies. They can be rules or policies of your law school (e.g., rules on plagiarism) or a current or former employer (e.g., use of company computers), or a company with which you've done business (e.g., a retailer's return policy). This exercise attunes you to factors that agencies and other participants in agency rulemaking often consider when defending or opposing a rule.

---

2. What Does the "[M]atter [P]resented" Include?

The NOPR tells people how to submit written comments on a proposed rule or otherwise participate in the informal rulemaking proceeding. *See* Figure 12-A, *supra*. Public input submitted through the prescribed channels is plainly part of the **"matter presented"** that § 553(c) requires the agency to consider (if relevant). A recurring question is whether a federal agency may consider public input supplied through other channels, including back channels.

Suppose, for example, a politically powerful captain of industry phones the head of a federal agency and, during the conversation, persuades the agency head to change something in a proposed agency rule. Or perhaps the captain of industry meets the agency head for lunch and successfully makes the case for a change to the proposed rule. Oral communication like this can occur "off the record"; nothing in the federal APA expressly requires oral communications during informal rulemaking to be memorialized in any agency document, even if they influence the agency. Written communications may also occur off the record. Our captain of industry, for example, may send a personal note to her old law-school buddy, who is now the head of a federal agency, with authority to decide on the final form of a proposed rule that affects the industry captain's business. Nothing in the federal APA expressly requires the agency head to make a personal note part of a rulemaking record in an informal rulemaking proceeding. Informal rulemakings don't have formal records; that is why they are called "open record" proceedings. (As discussed below, however, the personal note in the example above might have to be included in the administrative record submitted to any court that reviews the final rule.)

Although the federal APA does not expressly require these back-channel communications to be included in any sort of formal rulemaking record, much less published for public comment, they are worrisome. If the back-channel communications are not made available for public comment, other members of the public ordinarily will never find out about them, much less have a chance to comment on them. These back-channel communications thus seem to short-circuit or circumvent the public participation process. Moreover, if a court ever reviews the agency's final rule, the court may never learn about the back-channel communications, even though they influenced the rule. These back-channel communications thus threaten the integrity and quality of judicial review.

Because the federal APA does not forbid these back-channel communications in informal rulemaking or require them to be exposed to public comment, they resemble ex parte communications in judicial proceedings, which are generally improper. Indeed, back-channel communications in informal rulemaking are often called "ex parte communications." This is technically inaccurate, though. The federal APA defines "**ex parte communication**" as one "**to which reasonable prior notice to all parties is not given.**" 5 U.S.C. § 551(14). Informal rulemaking, however, does not have "**parties**," unlike judicial proceedings and unlike two other kinds of administrative proceedings under the federal APA — namely, formal rulemaking and formal adjudication (as well as some hybrid rulemaking proceedings).

That is not to say that back-channel communications are perfectly all right. Here are the relevant principles for these back-channel (also called "off the record" or "ex parte") communications in federal agency rulemaking:

a. The federal APA generally does not forbid off-the-record communications in informal rulemaking. However:

b. If the off-the-record communication causes a federal agency to consider irrelevant factors, the agency's reliance on it could make the rule invalid.

c. A federal agency's own procedural rules or policies, or the agency legislation, may bar the agency from considering off-the-record communications in informal or hybrid rulemaking.

d. In formal rulemaking (as well as formal adjudication), the federal APA requires the agency to consider only evidence that has been made part of the record under provisions that restrict ex parte communications.

e. The President gets special treatment when it comes to communicating off-the-record with officials in executive-branch agencies during informal rulemaking.

f. In a judicial challenge to a rule made through informal rulemaking, the federal agency must submit to the reviewing court an "administrative record" containing all material on which the agency based the rule.

To elaborate briefly on each principle:

a. The Federal APA Generally Does Not Forbid Off-the-Record Communications in Informal Rulemaking

Informal rulemaking under the federal APA is not a "closed record" proceeding. This means that the agency may generally consider all relevant information without violating the federal APA. This is true whether the information comes from inside or outside the agency, and whether the information comes through normal channels or not. *See* AGM 31–32 (agency "is free to formulate rules on the basis of materials in its files, and the knowledge and experience of the agency"); *Town of Orangeburg v. Ruckelshaus*, 740 F.2d

185 (2nd Cir. 1984) ("[W]here an agency is not performing a judicial or quasi-judicial function, ex parte contacts between public officials and agency administrators are not necessarily proscribed.").

The idea behind the agency's freedom in informal rulemaking to consider information whatever its source and however it is supplied is that informal rulemaking is generally a legislative-type activity. A leading case on the subject explained:

> Where agency action resembles judicial action, where it involves formal rulemaking, adjudication, or quasi-adjudication among conflicting private claims to a valuable privilege, the insulation of the decision maker from ex parte contacts is justified by basic notions of due process to the parties involved. But where agency action involves informal rulemaking of a policymaking sort, the concept of ex parte contacts is of more questionable utility.
>
> Under our system of government, the very legitimacy of general policymaking performed by unelected administrators depends in no small part upon the openness, accessibility, and amenability of these officials to the needs and ideas of the public from whom their ultimate authority derives, and upon whom their commands must fall. As judges we are insulated from these pressures because of the nature of the judicial process in which we participate; but we must refrain from the easy temptation to look askance at all face-to-face lobbying efforts, regardless of the forum in which they occur, merely because we see them as inappropriate in the judicial context. Furthermore, the importance to effective regulation of continuing contact with a regulated industry, other affected groups, and the public cannot be underestimated. Informal contacts may enable the agency to win needed support for its program, reduce future enforcement requirements by helping those regulated to anticipate and shape their plans for the future, and spur the provision of information which the agency needs.

Sierra Club v. Costle, 657 F.2d 298, 400–401 (D.C. Cir. 1981) (internal quotation marks and citations omitted). As this excerpt notes and as discussed in Chapter 4.D.4, only the rare informal rulemaking proceeding—such as one that involves "conflicting claims to a valuable privilege"—may be sufficiently adjudicatory in character to trigger due process limits on ex parte contacts. *See also Sangamon Valley Television Corp. v. United States*, 269 F.2d 221, 224 (D.C. Cir. 1959).

Bottom line: The federal APA does not prohibit off the record (or "ex parte") communications in informal rulemaking (though due process occasionally may do so). Furthermore, ex parte communications are not necessarily a bad thing in this kind of proceeding.

b. If the Off-the-Record Communication Causes a Federal Agency to Consider Irrelevant Factors, the Agency's Reliance on It Could Make the Rule Invalid

As discussed above in the explanation of what is "relevant," a federal agency cannot base a rule on irrelevant information, regardless of its source. Thus, for example, an agency could not consider a Member of Congress's threat to cut off funding for an agency project unless the agency changed its mind about an unrelated matter. *See D.C. Federation of Civil Associations v. Volpe*, 459 F.2d 1231, 1247–1248 (D.C. Cir. 1972). That is because the Congress person's threat caused the agency in the unrelated matter to take into account "considerations that Congress could not have intended to make relevant." *Id.* at 1248. Similarly, an agency could not consider international political pressure in deciding whether a method of fishing for tuna caused depletion of dolphin stocks. *Earth Island Institute v. Hogarth*, 494 F.3d 757, 768 (9th Cir. 2007). That was improper because "Congress's clear intent [in the relevant statute] was to have the [agency] findings be based on science alone." *Id.* A rule is invalid if it rests on irrelevant factors, political or otherwise, whether supplied through normal or back channels. *See Sierra Club v. Costle*, 657 F.2d 298, 408–409 (D.C. Cir. 1981).

c. A Federal Agency's Own Rules or Policies, or the Agency Legislation, May Bar the Agency from Considering Off-the-Record Communications in Informal or Hybrid Rulemaking

Federal agencies may decide to insulate themselves from off-the-record communications in informal rulemaking or to have procedures for documenting them and exposing them to public input. This lets agency officials respond to off-the-record communications — which may come from a politically powerful person — by saying, "My hands are tied. I have to follow the rules!" An example of a federal agency rule regulating off-the-record contacts in informal rulemaking comes from the Federal Aviation Administration. *See* 14 C.F.R. Part 11, Appendix 1 (2012) (entitled "Oral Communications with the Public During Rulemaking").

Moreover, Congress can always decide to restrict off-the-record communications for particular rulemaking proceedings. Remember, APA § 559 allows for **"additional requirements imposed by statute"** to supplement the APA's requirements, including its rulemaking requirements. An example of a hybrid rulemaking statute limiting off-the-record communications is the Magnuson-Moss Warranty-Federal Trade Commission Improvement Act of 1975. 15 U.S.C. § 57a(i) (2012) ("Meetings with outside parties").

d. In Formal Rulemaking (as well as Formal Adjudication), the Federal APA Requires the Agency to Consider Only Evidence That Has Been Made Part of the Record under Provisions That Restrict Ex Parte Communications

This is a good time to introduce you to two important APA provisions that restrict ex parte contacts. The thing to remember for now is that neither applies to informal rulemaking proceedings.

Section 554(d)(1) generally forbids ex parte communications in formal adjudications under the APA. You can learn more about § 554(d)(1) in Chapter 24. For now, simply look at the title of § 554 and the text of § 554(a), to embed in your mind its inapplicability to informal rulemaking.

Section 557(d) generally forbids ex parte communications in both formal rulemaking and formal adjudications. You can learn more about § 557(d) in Chapter 24. For now, simply look at the following provisions, in the following order, that make clear § 557(d)'s inapplicability to informal rulemaking: §§ 557(a), 556(a), 553(c), and 554(a).

e. The President Gets Special Treatment When It Comes to Communicating Off-the-Record with Federal Officials in Executive-Branch Agencies during Informal Rulemaking

The President has a constitutional duty to take care that the laws are faithfully executed. The President also is entitled to ensure that agencies in the federal executive branch implement presidential policies and priorities, within the limits of the law. For these reasons, a well-known case recognized that the President and White House officials can generally communicate off-the-record with federal agency officials during informal rulemaking without having those communications disclosed to the public or to a reviewing court. *Sierra Club v. Costle*, 657 F.2d 298, 404–408 (D.C. Cir. 1981).

f. In a Judicial Challenge to a Rule Made through Informal Rulemaking, the Federal Agency Must Submit to the Reviewing Court an "Administrative Record" with All Material on Which the Agency Based the Rule

The federal APA does not require an agency to create a formal record or to base its decision exclusively on that record in informal rulemaking or informal adjudication. The federal APA's broadly applicable provision on judicial review, however, does require a reviewing court to **"review the whole record or those parts of its cited by a party."** 5 U.S.C. § 706. The U.S. Supreme Court has accordingly required federal agencies to submit to the reviewing court the "administrative record" to enable the court to review agency actions taken in informal proceedings. *See Fla. Power & Light Co. v. Lorion*, 470 U.S. 729, 744 (1985); *Camp v. Pitts*, 411 U.S. 138, 142–143 (1973). That record includes at least all documentary information on which the agency based its action, which could include documentary evidence (even if not oral communications) transmitted to the agency through back channels.

3. How Can You Tell If a Federal Agency Has "[C]onsider[ed] … [R]elevant [M]atter [P]resented"?

There are two times during informal rulemaking when a federal agency explains the rationale and basis for a rule. First, when the agency publishes the notice of proposed rulemaking in the Federal Register, the agency often explains the basis and purpose of the proposed rule. In addition, at the end of the rulemaking process, when the agency publishes the final rule in the Federal Register, the agency must include a **"concise general statement of [the rule's] basis and purpose."** 5 U.S.C. § 553(c). These two Federal Register entries are the main places that reviewing courts examine to determine if the agency considered all relevant matter, and only relevant matter, when making the rule.

The next section of this chapter, Section D, explores the **"concise general statement"** requirement of § 553(c). Right now it will help you to recognize that informal rulemaking proceedings can raise two issues, one connected with § 553(c)'s requirement to **"consider**

relevant matter presented," the other connected with § 553(c)'s requirement of a "**concise general statement**." The agency's duty to consider relevant matter is a "substantive" requirement; it relates to the substantive basis for the agency's decision. A separate issue is whether the agency has adequately *explained* (in the concise general statement or elsewhere) the considerations underlying the final rule. This latter "duty to explain," unlike the duty to consider, might be called a "procedural" requirement.

The duty to consider and the duty to explain are separate but connected. They are separate because an agency might, in fact, consider all relevant matters but fail adequately to explain what it considered. They are connected, however, because one might infer from an agency's failure to *say* that it considered Issue *X* that the agency in fact did not consider Issue *X*. (Otherwise, the argument goes, the agency would have mentioned in its explanation that it considered Issue *X*.) Indeed, courts will often conclude from an agency's failure to *discuss* an issue in the concise general statement (or elsewhere) that the agency failed to *consider* that issue when making the rule.

If a federal court concludes from a federal agency's failure to discuss an important issue that the agency indeed failed to consider that issue, the court will ordinarily set aside the rule as "arbitrary and capricious," which means the rule is substantively flawed. *See Arrington v. Davis*, 516 F.3d 1106, 1114 (9th Cir. 2008) ("The agency's lack of explanation for its choice renders its decision arbitrary and capricious.").

When a court reviews a rule, and finds the agency's explanation for the rule inadequate for its failure to address Issue *X*, the agency might persuade the court that the agency really did consider Issue *X*, even though the agency did not mention doing so in the concise general statement. This might prevent the court from finding the rule arbitrary and capricious. But the court could still find the rule procedurally invalid because the concise general statement was inadequate. *See Action on Smoking & Health v. Civil Aeronautics Bd.*, 713 F.2d 795, 799 (D.C. Cir. 1983) (stating that § 553(c) "contemplates that the [concise general statement] will *accompany* publication of a rule, not follow the rule long after it has been published") (citation omitted). If the court is uncertain whether an agency considered certain matters, or concludes that, regardless of what the agency considered, its explanation is inadequate, the court will ordinarily remand the matter to the agency.

Often it makes no difference whether a court invalidates an agency rule on substantive grounds or procedural grounds. Sometimes, however, the difference affects (a) whether the court, having found the agency rule invalid, not only remands the matter to the agency but also, pending remand, vacates (renders ineffective) the agency rule; and (b) what the agency must do on remand. On the first point, sometimes federal courts, having found an agency action invalid, nonetheless allow it to remain in effect — rather than vacating it — pending remand to the agency. A court is more likely to remand a rule without vacating it if the problem with the rule is an inadequate agency explanation rather than an agency failure to consider relevant matters. *See generally, e.g., Heartland Reg'l Med. Ctr. v. Sebelius*, 566 F.3d 193 (D.C. Cir. 2009). As to the second point, if a court finds the agency's explanation inadequate, then on remand the agency simply must supply a better explanation. If, instead, a court finds that the agency failed to consider relevant matters, the agency must consider those matters on remand and explain how those matters affect its decision. In short, the agency's conduct on remand depends on why the court is remanding the matter to the agency.

D. The Federal Agency Publishes the Final Rule along with a Concise General Statement of Its Basis and Purpose

The last step of informal rulemaking is publication of the final rule or set of rules, along with "**a concise general statement of their basis and purpose.**" 5 U.S.C. § 553(c).

1. Publication of the Final Rule

Publication of the final rule in the Federal Register is required by 5 U.S.C. § 552(a)(1). Final legislative rules published in the Federal Register are permanently codified by subject matter in the CFR, which is updated annually. When you encounter a federal agency's legislative rule, the citation for the rule will usually be to the CFR.

The CFR is not only the place to find current regulations but also a good source of information on a regulation's history. When the CFR reproduces a current rule, it also cites the places in the Federal Register where that rule, and earlier versions of the rule, were published. By locating the Federal Register pages cited, you can find not only the current rule and earlier versions of the rules, but also the agency's "concise general statement" of the basis and purpose of those rules. These statements give you insight into the rule, and its purpose and history. Also, the Federal Register entries publishing the final version of the rules will, in turn, cite to the earlier Federal Register entry in which the agency published the *proposed* version of the rule. When publishing the proposed rule, the agency will also have published an explanation for the proposed rule. That explanation will give you additional background information. All of this is to say that the CFR is the place to begin research on the regulatory history of a federal agency's legislative rule.

To illustrate how this works, Figure 12-B reproduces the last page of the CFR that reproduces 47 C.F.R. § 15.3, one of the rules discussed in the case excerpted earlier in this chapter: *American Radio Relay League, Inc. v. FCC*, 524 F.3d 227 (D.C. Cir. 2008). At the end of this rule, which contains definitions, you will see within bracketed text all of the Federal Register citations, dating back to 1989, where versions of this rule, in final form, were published.

Regulatory research is a staple of practicing administrative law. If you want to learn more about researching federal rules, we highly recommend an excellent lesson on the subject published by the Center for Computer-Assisted Legal Instruction (CALI), entitled "Researching Federal Administrative Regulations," by Sheri Lewis.

2. Concise General Statement

Federal agencies must accompany the final rule with a "**concise general statement**" of its basis and purpose, under 5 U.S.C. § 553(c):

---

5 U.S.C. § 553. Rule making ...

(c) After notice required by this section, the agency shall give interested persons an opportunity to participate in the rule making through submission of written

Figure 12-B. Page from Code of Federal Regulations
Reproducing Tail End of 47 C.F.R. § 15.3 (2011)

Federal Communications Commission   **§ 15.5**

are video cassette recorders and terminal devices attached to a cable system or used with a Master Antenna (including those used for central distribution video devices in apartment or office buildings).

(z) *Unintentional radiator.* A device that intentionally generates radio frequency energy for use within the device, or that sends radio frequency signals by conduction to associated equipment via connecting wiring, but which is not intended to emit RF energy by radiation or induction.

(aa) *Cable ready consumer electronics equipment.* Consumer electronics TV receiving devices, including TV receivers, videocassette recorders and similar devices, that incorporate a tuner capable of receiving television signals and an input terminal intended for receiving cable television service, and are marketed as "cable ready" or "cable compatible." Such equipment shall comply with the technical standards specified in § 15.118 and the provisions of § 15.19(d).

(bb) *CPU board.* A circuit board that contains a microprocessor, or frequency determining circuitry for the microprocessor, the primary function of which is to execute user-provided programming, but not including:

(1) A circuit board that contains only a microprocessor intended to operate under the primary control or instruction of a microprocessor external to such a circuit board; or

(2) A circuit board that is a dedicated controller for a storage or input/output device.

(cc) *External radio frequency power amplifier.* A device which is not an integral part of an intentional radiator as manufactured and which, when used in conjunction with an intentional radiator as a signal source, is capable of amplifying that signal.

(dd) *Test equipment* is defined as equipment that is intended primarily for purposes of performing measurements or scientific investigations. Such equipment includes, but is not limited to, field strength meters, spectrum analyzers, and modulation monitors.

(ee) *Radar detector.* A receiver designed to signal the presence of radio signals used for determining the speed of motor vehicles. This definition does not encompass the receiver incorporated within a radar transceiver certified under the Commission's rules.

(ff) *Access Broadband over Power Line (Access BPL).* A carrier current system installed and operated on an electric utility service as an unintentional radiator that sends radio frequency energy on frequencies between 1.705 MHz and 80 MHz over medium voltage lines or over low voltage lines to provide broadband communications and is located on the supply side of the utility service's points of interconnection with customer premises. Access BPL does not include power line carrier systems as defined in § 15.3(t) or In-House BPL as defined in § 15.3(gg).

(gg) *In-House Broadband over Power Line (In-House BPL).* A carrier current system, operating as an unintentional radiator, that sends radio frequency energy by conduction over electric power lines that are not owned, operated or controlled by an electric service provider. The electric power lines may be aerial (overhead), underground, or inside the walls, floors or ceilings of user premises. In-House BPL devices may establish closed networks within a user's premises or provide connections to Access BPL networks, or both.

[54 FR 17714, Apr. 25, 1989, as amended at 55 FR 18340, May 2, 1990; 57 FR 33448, July 29, 1992; 59 FR 25340, May 16, 1994; 61 FR 31048, June 19, 1996; 62 FR 26242, May 13, 1997; 64 FR 22561, Apr. 27, 1999; 65 FR 64391, Oct. 27, 2000; 66 FR 32582, June 15, 2001; 67 FR 48993, July 29, 2002; 70 FR 1373, Jan. 7, 2005]

data, views, or arguments with or without opportunity for oral presentation. After consideration of the relevant matter presented, **the agency shall incorporate in the rules adopted a concise general statement of their basis and purpose.** When rules are required by statute to be made on the record after opportunity for an agency hearing, sections 556 and 557 of this title apply instead of this subsection.

As a practical matter, one of the most important purposes of the concise general statement from the agency's point of view is to give a justification for the rule that will help the rule stand up to any later judicial challenge. To serve this purpose, the concise general statement often ends up being lengthy, rather than concise, and detailed, rather than general. (Agency lawyers are often involved in drafting it.) A leading case explained:

> [We] caution against an overly literal reading of the statutory terms "concise" and "general." These adjectives must be accommodated to the realities of judicial scrutiny.... We do not expect the agency to discuss every item of fact or opinion included in the submissions made to it in informal rule making. We do expect that, if the judicial review which Congress has thought it important to provide is to be meaningful, the "concise general statement of ... basis and purpose" mandated by Section 4 [5 U.S.C. § 553] will enable us to see what major issues of policy were ventilated by the informal proceedings and why the agency reacted to them as it did.

Auto. Parts & Accessories Ass'n v. Boyd, 407 F.2d 330, 338 (D.C. Cir. 1968).

To permit adequate judicial review of a rule, the agency often must do five things in its concise general statement (or in another document generated during the informal rulemaking). Whether you become an agency lawyer or a lawyer challenging agency rules, you can think of these as a checklist:

a.   The agency must respond to significant public comments.

b.   The agency must explain how the rule meets statutory requirements and purposes, unless this is obvious.

c.   The agency must explain the connection between its rule and the relevant data or other relevant evidence.

d.   The agency must consider significant alternatives to the approach taken in the final rule and explain why it rejected those alternatives.

e.   The agency must explain any "change in course."

If the agency fails to do these things, its concise general statement may violate § 553(c). A court may invalidate the agency's rule for that violation, either as procedurally flawed or as "arbitrary and capricious."

Because the five requirements for concise general statements come from case law, below we introduce case law applying these principles.

a. The Agency Must Respond to Significant Public Comments

Public comments are significant if they (a) are relevant to the proposed rule and (b) could, if accepted, affect the final rule. *Safari Aviation, Inc. v. Garvey*, 300 F.3d 1144, 1150 (9th Cir. 2002). Public comments do not require a response if they are vague or speculative. To ensure an agency response, lawyers preparing comments on proposed rules should be as specific as possible and support their comments with evidence and cogent analysis. For example, if a comment predicts that a proposed rule will have bad consequences, the comment should specify the consequences and support the prediction with logic and, if possible, evidence.

Here are two examples of cases in which a court held that the agency failed to respond to significant public comments, and one example of a case finding comments not significant:

- *Center for Biological Diversity v. National Highway Traffic Safety Administration*, 538 F.3d 1172 (9th Cir. 2008)

The National Highway Traffic Safety Administration (NHTSA) set fuel-efficiency standards for light trucks. The NHTSA used a cost-benefit analysis to determine the appropriate standards. Commenters argued the NHTSA should have included in its cost-benefit analysis the monetary benefits of reducing greenhouse gas emissions. The NHTSA did not consider these benefits. On judicial review, the court held that NHTSA did not adequately explain its failure to consider the monetary benefits of reducing greenhouse gases, and this made its fuel efficiency standards "arbitrary and capricious." *Id.* at 1198–1203.

- *United States v. Nova Scotia Food Products Corp.*, 568 F2d 240 (2nd Cir. 1977)

The Food and Drug Administration (FDA) adopted rules for processing smoked fish. When the FDA proposed the rules, members of the public asserted that the processing requirements were not commercially feasible for certain types of smoked fish, such as whitefish, because the processing would destroy the product. The court reviewing the rules held that the FDA should have responded to that assertion. The court explained:

> One may recognize that even commercial infeasibility cannot stand in the way of an overwhelming public interest. Yet the administrative process should disclose, at least, whether the proposed regulation is considered to be commercially feasible, or whether other considerations prevail even if commercial infeasibility is acknowledged.

Id. at 253.

- *City of Portland v. Environmental Protection Agency*, 507 F.3d 706 (D.C. Cir. 2007)

The EPA promulgated a rule requiring Portland, Oregon, and New York City to take steps to eliminate the parasite Cryptosporidium from their drinking water. The EPA issued this rule under the Safe Drinking Water Act (SDWA). The SDWA required the EPA to impose the most stringent feasible treatment technique for Cryptosporidium, regardless of the costs or benefits of that technique. For this reason, the court held, the EPA did not have to respond to comments on the proposed rule that criticized EPA data on the incidence and infectivity of Cryptosporidium. Since these data were not relevant to determining the most stringent feasible treatment technique, they could not have affected the final rule and they were therefore not significant comments to which the EPA had to respond. *Id.* at 714–715.

b. The Agency Must Explain How the Rule Meets Statutory Requirements or Purposes, Unless This Is Obvious

Since the agency legislation governing the agency rule is the primary determinant of what is relevant, the agency must explain, if it is not obvious, how the rule faithfully implements the agency legislation. Here are three examples of cases discussing this requirement:

- *Independent U.S. Tanker Owners Commission v. Dole*, 809 F.2d 847 (D.C. Cir. 1987)

The Secretary of Transportation issued a rule under the Merchant Marine Act of 1936, 46 U.S.C. §§ 1101–1295g (2012). The rule affected U.S. tanker vessels that had been authorized to operate in foreign commerce. These vessels had been built with large federal government subsidies so that the vessels could compete effectively with foreign vessels for foreign commerce. The Secretary's rule, for the first time, allowed a subsidized vessel to operate in *domestic* commerce—in competition with U.S. vessels that had not been built with subsidies from the federal government—if the subsidized vessel's owner repaid a portion of the subsidy to the federal government. The Secretary justified the rule as a means of increasing competition and economic efficiency in domestic commerce, and decreasing regulation. These objectives, however, were not among the five statutory objectives specified in the Merchant Marine Act.

The court held that "the Secretary's statement of basis and purpose fails to give an adequate account of how the ... rule serves these [statutory] objectives." 809 F.2d at 853. The court said, "[T]he Secretary is certainly free to consider factors that are not mentioned explicitly in the governing statute, yet she is not free to substitute new goals in place of the statutory objectives without explaining how these actions are consistent with her authority under the statute." *Id.* at 854.

- *Hazardous Waste Treatment Council v. U.S. Environmental Protection Agency*, 886 F.2d 355 (D.C. Cir. 1989)

The EPA proposed a rule establishing treatment standards for certain toxic wastes. The proposed standards were based on both the "best demonstrated available technology" and an analysis of health risks. The EPA explained that its consideration of both technology and health risks was the best way to carry out the agency legislation. Some members of Congress commented, however, that the agency legislation required purely technology-based treatment standards. In the final rule, the EPA adopted purely technology-based treatment standards. The EPA expressly rejected, however, the Congress members' argument that the agency legislation compelled a purely technology-based approach. Even so, the EPA stated that this approach was "best." *Id.* at 364 (quoting EPA's explanation). The reviewing court held that the EPA did not adequately explain how the approach that it ultimately chose better fulfilled statutory purposes, given the EPA's express disagreement with the Congress members' statutory argument. *Id.* at 364–366.

- *Alabama Association of Insurance Agents v. Board of Governors of Federal Reserve System*, 533 F.2d 224 (5th Cir. 1976), *vacated in part on other grounds*, 558 F.2d 729 (1977)

The Board of Governors of the Federal Reserve System issued regulations that allowed bank holding companies to sell certain kinds of insurance. The concise general statement accompanying the regulations merely paraphrased the relevant statutory language. Specifically, the Board's statement said that sales of the kinds of insurance that the regulations allowed bank holding companies to sell "have been determined by the Board to be so closely related to banking or managing or controlling banks as to be a proper incident thereto." *Id.* at 232 (quoting Board regulation which was, in turn, quoting agency legislation). The reviewing court held this statement satisfied the APA, even though the statement "does nothing to illuminate the process by which the Board arrived at the regulation." *Id.* at 236. The rule's purpose was "obviou[s]," and its basis could be discerned from several other sources: namely, the legislative history, Board decisions on individual applications by bank holding companies to sell insurance, and the detailed briefs of the parties before the court. *Id.* at 237.

c. The Agency Must Explain the Connection between Its Rule and the Relevant Data or Other Relevant Evidence

The U.S. Supreme Court has said that, for an agency's exercise of discretion to survive judicial review, the agency "must offer a rational connection between the facts found and the choice made." *Motor Vehicle Mfrs. Ass'n v. State Farm Mut. Auto. Ins. Co.*, 463 U.S. 29, 52 (1983) (internal quotation marks omitted). The Court has applied this principle — which governs any matter in which an agency has discretionary power — to an agency's adoption of a rule after informal rulemaking. *Bowen v. Am. Hosp. Ass'n*, 476 U.S. 610, 625 (1986) (plurality opinion); *Baltimore Gas & Elec. v. Natural Res. Def. Council*, 462 U.S. 87, 105 (1983). Courts rely primarily on the concise general statement required under § 553(c) to determine if the agency has rationally connected "the facts found" to the rule ultimately adopted in an informal rulemaking proceeding.

Here are three rulemaking cases about the need for the agency to "offer a rational connection between the facts found and the choice made." *State Farm*, 463 U.S. at 52.

- *American Farm Bureau Federation v. Environmental Protection Agency*, 559 F.3d 512 (D.C. Cir. 2009)

The EPA revised National Ambient Air Quality Standards for particulate matter under the Clean Air Act. Empirical data presented to the EPA indicated that the revised standards did not adequately protect children and other vulnerable populations, as required by the Act. The EPA did not adequately explain why, despite that data, the revised standards met statutory requirements. *Id.* at 524–526.

- *American Radio Relay League, Inc. v. Federal Communications Commission*, 524 F.3d 227 (D.C. Cir. 2008)

The FCC promulgated a rule designed to prevent a new type of internet technology, which uses electrical power lines, from interfering with licensed radio operators. The rule relied on a numerical "extrapolation factor" for estimating how quickly the radio frequency strength emitted from the power lines decays at various distances from the power lines. The FCC did not adequately explain why it chose the extrapolation factor that it did, despite empirical evidence and the agency's own analysis, which cast doubt on the accuracy of that factor. *Id.* at 240–241.

- *International Union, United Automobile Workers v. Pendergrass*, 878 F.2d 389 (D.C. Cir. 1989)

The Occupational Safety and Health Administration (OSHA) set maximum exposure levels for workplace formaldehyde. In determining that formaldehyde in the workplace can cause cancer, OSHA credited a particular analysis of workplace data by two scientists. OSHA implicitly rejected that same study, however, in determining the relationship between increasing levels of formaldehyde exposure and incidence of lung cancer. OSHA did not adequately explain why it relied on the study in finding carcinogenicity but rejected the study on the relationship between amount of exposure and incidence of lung cancer. *Id.* at 394–396.

d. The Agency Must Consider Significant Alternatives to the Approach Taken in the Final Rule and Explain Why It Rejected Those Alternatives

The rule that an agency ultimately adopts after informal rulemaking reflects the agency's judgment about how best to implement agency legislation. The agency legislation often constrains the agency's exercise of judgment by, for example, specifying factors for the agency to consider or objectives for the agency to achieve. Even so, the agency will ordinarily have discretion in designing the regulatory approach. When exercising that discretion through the adoption of a rule, the agency is not only making law but also making policy. "It is well settled that an agency has a duty to consider responsible alternatives to its chosen policy and to give a reasoned explanation for its rejection of such alternatives." *City of Brookings Mun. Tel. Co. v. FCC*, 822 F.2D 1153 (D.C. Cir. 1987); *see also American Radio Relay League*, 524 F.3d at 242 (duty extends only to "significant and viable alternatives"). As true of the agency's duty to respond to significant comments, the agency's duty to respond to significant alternatives is ordinarily satisfied (or not) in informal rulemaking by the contents of the concise general statement required under APA § 553(c).

The text of APA § 553 does not expressly require an agency in informal rulemaking either to consider significant alternatives to the approach that it ultimately chooses, or to explain why it rejected those alternatives. The courts have traced the first duty—the agency's duty to *consider* alternatives—to the need for the agency's rule to be "the product of reasoned thought and based upon a consideration of relevant factors." *Farmers Union Cent. Exch., Inc. v. FERC*, 734 F.2d 1486, 1511 (D.C. Cir. 1984) (internal quotation marks omitted). The second duty—the agency's duty to *explain* why it rejected alternatives— can, at least in informal rulemaking, be traced to § 553(c)'s requirement for a general statement of basis and purpose. *See Int'l Ladies' Garment Workers' Union v. Donovan*, 722 F.2d 795, 815 n.35 (D.C. Cir. 1983). More broadly, the U.S. Supreme Court has stated that an agency—whether promulgating a rule or taking other action—must "cogently explain why it has exercised its discretion in a given manner." *Motor Vehicle Mfrs. Ass'n v. State Farm Mut. Auto. Ins. Co.*, 463 U.S. 29, 48–49 (1983) (citing cases involving judicial review of agency actions other than informal rulemaking).

The most important case on a federal agency's duties to consider alternatives and explain why it rejected them is *Motor Vehicle Manufacturers Ass'n v. State Farm Mutual Automobile Insurance Co.*, 463 U.S. 29 (1983), known as the *State Farm* case. *State Farm* actually involved an agency's *rescission* of a previously adopted rule, but the Court reviewed the rescission under the same "arbitrary and capricious" standard as generally applies, under the federal APA, to an agency's adoption of a rule in the first place. *Id.* at 40–43. The Secretary of Transportation rescinded a rule that required auto makers to install either airbags or automatic seat belts in new cars. The Secretary determined that most auto makers would choose to install automatic seat belts that were detachable, and that these detachable belts would not make cars much safer. The Court held that the Secretary's rescission was "arbitrary and capricious" because he did not consider the alternative of requiring auto makers to install airbags (instead of detachable, automatic seatbelts). The airbag alternative was obvious because airbags were a device that the Secretary had already found made cars much safer. *Id.* at 48–51.

In the two rulemaking cases cited at the end of this paragraph, the courts held that the agency did not adequately explain why it chose one admittedly imperfect methodology over alternative methodologies. In both cases, alternative methodologies were urged upon the agency in public comments on the agency's proposed rule. These cases reflect the large overlap between the agency's duty to respond to significant comments and its duty to consider and explain the rejection of significant alternatives, *See City of Brookings*, 822 F.2d at 1168–1170; *Farmers Union*, 734 F.2d at 1511–1527. Thus, although we separately discussed above the agency's duty to respond to significant *comments*, that duty is not always separate from the agency's duty, now under discussion, to consider significant *alternatives* to the agency's chosen approach.

e. The Agency Must Explain Any "Change in Course"

Federal courts commonly review agency rules and other agency actions to ensure the agency engaged in "reasoned decision making." The "reasoned decision making" requirement obliges an agency to acknowledge and explain any way in which the agency action under review departs from or is inconsistent with a prior agency action, policy, or interpretation. For example, the U.S. Supreme Court said in the *State Farm* case that "an agency changing its course by rescinding a rule is obligated to supply a reasoned analysis for the change." *State Farm*, 463 U.S. at 42.

The Court in *State Farm* held that the Department of Transportation did not adequately explain why it was rescinding a rule that required cars to have passive restraints to protect people during accidents. Here are two other cases discussing an agency's duty to explain a "change in course" in a rulemaking proceeding.

- *Western Watershed Project v. Kraayenbrink*, 632 F.3d 472 (9th Cir. 2011)

The Bureau of Land Management regulates livestock grazing on 160 million acres of public land. In 2006, BLM proposed eighteen amendments to its grazing regulations. The BLM also prepared draft and final environmental impact statements (EISs) on the proposed amendments, as required by the National Environmental Policy Act (NEPA). Plaintiffs sued BLM and various officials under the federal APA, alleging that BLM violated NEPA by not adequately assessing the environmental effects of the amendments.

The court of appeals held that BLM did violate NEPA, partly because in the final EIS BLM did not adequately explain its change in course. The court observed that the regulatory amendments

> decreased [BLM's] regulatory authority over rangeland management, decreased the role of the public in overseeing that management, and granted [people with permits or leases to graze livestock] ... ownership rights. These changes are inconsistent with the 1995 Regulations and discordant with the lessons learned from the history of rangeland management in the west, which has been moving towards multiple use management and increased public participation. The BLM itself acknowledges in the Final EIS that public input helps identify environmental impacts.

Id. at 494. Although BLM said that public input is at times "inefficient" and "redundant," the court held that this rationale was not a "reasoned explanation" for BLM's change in course. *Id.* at 494–495.

- *National Cable & Telecommunications Association v. Federal Communications Commission*, 567 F.3d 659 (D.C. Cir. 2009)

Companies that offer television and other telecommunications services to consumers regularly have entered into "exclusivity contacts" with owners of apartment buildings. Under these contracts, the company agrees to wire the building for cable in exchange for the exclusive right to sell video (e.g., television) programming service to the building's residents. In 2003, the FCC considered whether to limit or ban these exclusivity contracts and decided not to. In 2007, however, the FCC changed its mind and banned them. The trade association for cable companies sought judicial review of the 2007 rule banning exclusivity contracts. The association argued that the FCC did not adequately explain its change in policy.

The court rejected the association's challenge and upheld the 2007 FCC rule. The court said that the association misconstrued the FCC's 2003 decision. The FCC's 2003 decision did not reflect a policy of allowing cable companies to use exclusivity contracts as long as they faced increasing competition from other telecommunications providers like satellite TV. Instead, the FCC's 2003 decision was based largely on the FCC's view that the evidence before it at that time did not justify banning the exclusivity contracts. In contrast, the 2007 rule was based on a record that the FCC found adequate to conclude that exclusivity contracts interfered with competition and raised prices for consumers. In short, the FCC met its obligation to explain its change in course.

E. The Federal Agency Makes the Rule Effective No Sooner Than 30 Days after Publication

Section 553(d) imposes what is often called a "delayed effective date" requirement on most substantive, legislative rules:

---

5 U.S.C. § 553. Rule making …

(d) The required publication or service of a substantive rule shall be made not less than 30 days before its effective date, except —

(1) a substantive rule which grants or recognizes an exemption or relieves a restriction;

(2) interpretative rules and statements of policy; or

(3) as otherwise provided by the agency for good cause found and published with the rule.…

As explained in Chapter 10, § 553(d) applies to most substantive, legislative rules. (See Chapter 10.C.1.a(i).) But § 553(d) does not apply to non-legislative rules — i.e., interpretative rules or agency policy statements. Nor does § 553(d) apply to rules that are exempt from all of § 553 under § 553(a) (exempting, e.g., rules on military affairs).

The purpose of the delayed-effective-date requirement is to give people a chance to learn about and, if necessary, bring themselves into compliance with a new rule. AGM 36. The requirement is that the rule take effect "*not less* than 30 days" after publication, which implies that the agency has discretion to delay a rule's effective date for *more* than 30 days after its publication. If you represent a client who will benefit from having more than 30 days to achieve compliance with a proposed rule, you should include in your comments on the proposed rule arguments for a longer delay in the effective date of the final rule.

The delayed-effective-date requirement does not apply to rules that grant exemptions or relieve restrictions, because these kinds of rules are liberalizing. People do not need time to comply with these kinds of rules. To the contrary, such rules grant benefits or relief that should be realized right away. AGM 37.

Section 553(d)(3) allows an agency to make a rule effective less than 30 days after publication for "**good cause found and published with the rule.**" As discussed in Chapter 10, this good cause requirement resembles, but differs from, the good cause exemption in § 553(b)(B). Section 553(b)(B) exempts a rule from the APA's notice-and-comment requirements "for good cause." In contrast, § 553(d)(3) exempts a rule from the 30-day-delayed-effective date requirement "for good cause." As a practical matter, of course, if a pressing need creates good cause for an agency to bypass the notice-and-comment requirements, that same pressing need may also create good cause for the agency to make the rule effective less than 30 days after publishing it.

The delayed-effective-date requirement of § 553(d) does not supersede provisions in other federal statutes that require a longer period between the publication of a rule and its effective date. The most important such statute is the Congressional Review Act, 5 U.S.C. §§ 801–808 (2012). The Congressional Review Act generally requires agencies to lay "major rules" before each House of Congress for *60* days before the rules can take effect. *Id.* § 801(a)(3); *see also id.* § 804(2) (defining "major rule" to include rules with annual effect on economy of $100 million or more). The 60-day delay gives Congress a chance, using a streamlined procedure, to enact a joint resolution disapproving the rule. A resolution of disapproval will invalidate the rule unless successfully vetoed by the President. If Congress does not disapprove the rule, it takes effect 60 days after it has been presented to Congress.

F. Rulemaking Requirements in State APAs

Most state APAs prescribe rulemaking requirements that, in broad outline, resemble those of the informal rulemaking procedures of the federal APA. As you know, however, the devil is in the details. Indeed, rulemaking procedures in state APAs invariably differ in many ways from the informal rulemaking procedures of the federal APA, and they differ among themselves. Even so, it may help you get a sense of rulemaking procedures under state APAs to discuss those of the 2010 Model State APA. This model Act may provide a template for revision of many existing state APAs. Even if it does not, it provides a useful comparison to the federal APA's informal rulemaking procedures.

The 2010 Model State APA has two provisions that are not found in the federal APA and that help the public and reviewing courts better understand a rulemaking proceeding. First, § 301 requires the state agency to establish a "rulemaking docket." The rulemaking docket serves a purpose like that of the docket in a judicial proceeding. The rulemaking docket must contain certain information about key events in the proceeding and include an index of documents related to the proceeding. 2010 Model State APA § 301(c). Second, § 302 requires the agency to maintain a "rulemaking record" for each proposed rule. *Id.* § 302. The rulemaking record must include almost every document generated by the agency, presented to the agency, or considered by the agency in formulating the proposed and final rules. From the rulemaking index and rulemaking record, the public and reviewing courts can understand the process leading to a rule and the information on which the rule was based.

Under the federal APA, the informal rulemaking process typically begins when the agency publishes a notice of proposed rulemaking, in which the agency presents the proposed rule. By contrast, the 2010 Model State APA expressly allows an agency to give public notice even before it begins drafting a proposed rule. Section 303 allows an agency to publish an "Advance Notice of Proposed Rulemaking." The purpose of the Advance Notice is to "gather information relevant to the subject matter of a potential rulemaking proceeding and [to] solicit comments and recommendations from the public." 2010 Model

State APA § 303(a). Section 303 also expressly allows negotiated rulemaking, which is a process that federal agencies may use, under the federal Negotiated Rulemaking Act, 5 U.S.C. §§ 561–570 (2012).

Similar to the federal APA, the 2010 Model State APA requires notice of proposed rulemaking (NOPR) and an opportunity for the public to file written comments on a proposed rule. 2010 Model State APA §§ 304–306. As discussed earlier in this chapter, the federal courts have held that a federal agency's NOPR must disclose the technical basis for the rule. The 2010 Model State APA expressly imposes a similar requirement. Specifically, § 304 requires a state agency to include in the notice of proposed rulemaking "a citation to and summary of each scientific or statistical study, report, or analysis that served as a basis for the proposed rule, together with an indication of how the full text of the study, report, or analysis may be obtained." 2010 Model State APA § 304(a)(6). The official comment on § 304 observes that it "codifies requirements used in federal administrative law." *Id.* Comment.

The 2010 Model State APA codifies another aspect of federal case law. Section 308 says, "An agency may not adopt a rule that differs from the rule proposed in the notice of proposed rulemaking unless the final rule is a logical outgrowth of the rule proposed in the notice." *Id.* § 308. As discussed earlier in this chapter, federal case law such as the *Chocolate Manufacturers* case construes the federal APA likewise to impose the logical outgrowth test to restrict agencies from publishing final rules with features that could not have been foreseen. *See Chocolate Manufacturers Ass'n v. Block*, 755 F.2d 1098 (4th Cir.1985).

Finally, like the federal APA's provisions for informal rulemaking, the 2010 Model State APA does not limit the agency to considering information presented by the public. The 2010 Model State APA says "An agency may consider any other information it receives concerning a proposed rule during the rulemaking." *Id.* § 306(b). The 2010 Model State APA requires the agency, however, to incorporate into the rulemaking record "[a]ny information considered by the agency." *Id.* The federal APA does not impose a similar requirement. But as discussed earlier in this chapter, federal courts reviewing federal agency actions generally require the agency to submit to the court an administrative record containing the material on which the agency based its action. *See Fla. Power & Light Co. v. Lorion*, 470 U.S. 729, 743 (1985).

The 2010 Model State APA exempts rules from its notice-and-comment procedures in three situations. First, it exempts non-legislative rules from those procedures by defining the term "rule" to exclude "guidance documents." 2010 Model State APA § 102(14) & (30). Second, it exempts "emergency rules" from the notice-and-comment procedures, while allowing emergency rules generally to be effective for no more than 180 days. *Id.* § 309. Third, the 2010 Model State APA allows a state agency to use a process called "direct final rulemaking." 2010 Model State APA § 310. In direct final rulemaking, the agency publishes a rule "with a statement … that it does not expect the adoption of the rule to be controversial and that the proposed rule takes effect 30 days after publication if no objection is received." *Id.* If no objection is received, the rule becomes final without going through notice-and-comment procedures. If an objection is received, the agency must go through notice-and-comment procedures. As discussed earlier in this chapter, some federal agencies use direct final rulemaking to adopt uncontroversial rules, though the federal APA does not expressly authorize it. *See* Jeffrey S. Lubbers, A Guide to Federal Agency Rulemaking 115–118 (4th ed. 2006).

The 2010 Model State APA, similar to the federal APA, requires agencies to publish their final rules, legislative or non-legislative, substantive or procedural. When publishing a final legislative rule, the 2010 Model State APA requires the agency to accompany it with a "concise explanatory statement." 2010 Model State APA § 313. The statement must include "the agency's reasons for not accepting substantial arguments made in testimony [in any public hearing] and comments." *Id.* This requirement to respond to significant comments is imposed on federal agencies by case law interpreting the federal APA's "concise statement of basis and purpose" requirement.

The purpose of this brief description of the 2010 Model State APA (many of the provisions of which are taken from actual state APAs) is to show you how state APAs may compare to the federal APA. This is no substitute, of course, for your careful study of the APA of the State in which you intend to practice.

G. Chapter 12 Wrap Up and Look Ahead

This chapter has explored the steps of informal rulemaking under the federal APA and introduced you to rulemaking procedures under state APAs. The next chapters explore two other kinds of rulemaking under the federal APA: formal rulemaking and hybrid rulemaking.

Chapter Problem Revisited

The main objective of this problem was to get you to think about a rulemaking proceeding as a type of legal proceeding in which lawyers exercise advocacy skills, which may include the skills of developing legal arguments and policy arguments, and developing evidence to support those arguments. A secondary objective was to have you apply the legal principle that in a rulemaking proceeding, parties opposing or supporting a proposed rule need to gather evidence that is "**relevant**" under § 553(c).

The client in this case presumably would like to argue that the proposed elimination of the opt-out provision (1) is too expensive for renovation firms and (2) counterproductive in that it could increase risks of lead-based paint.

The costs of eliminating the opt-out provision are obviously important to the client. Those costs may not be relevant, however, to EPA's consideration of the proposed rule. Initially, this is a question of statutory interpretation. The agency legislation might bar consideration of costs, as did the legislation in *Whitman v. American Trucking Ass'ns, Inc.*, 531 U.S. 457 (2001). On the other hand, the agency legislation might be construed to permit EPA to consider costs, as did the legislation in *Entergy Corp. v. Riverkeeper, Inc.*, 556 U.S. 208 (2009). A third possibility is that the agency legislation *requires* the agency to consider costs. Your comments might usefully address the proper interpretation of the applicable legislation.

If costs are at least arguably relevant, your next task will be gathering evidence to document the costs of eliminating the opt-out provision. One can only predict the likely costs, but even predictions can be supported with empirical evidence. That evidence should include the information underlying the client's estimate that compliance with the RRP rule raises the cost of renovation projects by an average of 15%. You will also need evidence about how much money business renovation firms would lose if the average price of projects increases 15%. As a lawyer, you may want to hire a social scientist to develop cogent evidence.

As to the argument that eliminating the opt-out provision will increase lead-based paint dangers, this argument seems relevant to EPA's consideration of the proposed rule (though your research needs to confirm this). The big challenge in making this argument is supporting it with evidence. You can imagine scenarios under which eliminating the opt-out provision will increase lead-paint dangers. For example, if renovations become too expensive for many people to afford, they may do the renovations themselves and, in the process, expose themselves to lead-based paint. Or perhaps people will delay renovation projects, thereby prolonging their exposure to dangers from, e.g., existing lead-based paint in their homes that is peeling. But without hard evidence this is just speculation that the agency is not bound to accept. Developing hard evidence may take ingenuity and the help of non-lawyer experts.

In developing possible arguments and evidence to support them, you will want to study the regulatory history of the 2008 RRP rule. Perhaps most importantly, your study should focus on why the EPA adopted the opt-out provision that it now proposes to eliminate. EPA's proposal to eliminate the provision requires it to explain its change in course. Perhaps something in the regulatory history provides material that EPA will now have a hard time explaining away.

The main things to take away from this chapter problem, related to drafting comments on a proposed agency rule, are the importance of (1) determining what is relevant; and (2) developing evidence to support arguments for or against a proposed rule.

Professional Development Reflection Questions

This chapter discussed the permissibility of "back-channel" communications in rulemaking. When you begin practicing law, you may very well be in a position to engage in such communications. If your law school class is typical, 7.5% of your class will work as lawyers for government agencies. Think of a law school classmate who might end up in that group. If that classmate ends up in a government agency that makes rules through informal rulemaking, do you think the classmate will be particularly susceptible to arguments about a proposed rule presented, face-to-face, by a close law school friend? If so, is there anything wrong with that?

In considering that question, please reflect on the material discussed in this chapter about back-channel communications. Also consider the possible bearing of the Model Rules of Professional Conduct., which have been adopted in most States. Specifically, Rule 3.9 is entitled "Advocate in Nonadjudicative Proceedings" and says:

> A lawyer representing a client before a legislative body or administrative agency in a nonadjudicative proceeding shall disclose that the appearance is in a representative capacity and shall conform to the provisions of Rules 3.3(a) through (c), 3.4(a) through (c), and 3.5.

Among the rules to which Rule 3.9 refers, the most relevant for the present discussion is Rule 3.5, entitled "Impartiality and Decorum of the Tribunal." The first two subsections of 3.5 state:

> A lawyer shall not:
>
> (a) seek to influence a judge, juror, prospective juror or other official by means prohibited by law;
>
> (b) communicate ex parte with such a person during the proceeding unless authorized to do so by law or court order ...

Elsewhere in the Rules, the term "tribunal" is defined as follows:

> "Tribunal" denotes a court, an arbitrator in a binding arbitration proceeding or a legislative body, administrative agency or other body acting in an adjudicative capacity. A legislative body, administrative agency or other body acts in an adjudicative capacity when a neutral official, after the presentation of evidence or legal argument by a party or parties, will render a binding legal judgment directly affecting a party's interests in a particular matter.

Rule 1.1(m). Do these rules address the permissibility of back-channel communications in informal rulemaking?

Chapter 13

Formal Rulemaking

Overview

Chapter 12 discussed informal rulemaking under the federal APA. This chapter discusses *formal* rulemaking under the federal APA. A federal agency must use formal rulemaking to make a legislative rule when the agency legislation requires the rule **"to be made on the record after opportunity for an agency hearing."** 5 U.S.C. § 553(c) (2012).

This chapter is short for three reasons. First, formal rulemaking is the rarest of the three types of federal rulemaking. Second, several of the steps of formal rulemaking are the same as those for informal rulemaking and were therefore discussed in the last chapter. Third, the main difference between formal rulemaking and informal rulemaking is that the public input and decisionmaking requirements for formal rulemaking are governed by §§ 556 and 557 of the federal APA, rather than by § 553(c). Sections 556 and 557 also govern the public input and decisionmaking requirements for formal *adjudication*. Because formal adjudication is much more common than formal rulemaking, this book explores the requirements of §§ 556 and 557 later, in our exploration of formal adjudication.

The sections of this chapter are entitled:

A.   Review: The Five Steps of Rulemaking under the Federal APA

B.   Similarities between Formal and Informal Rulemaking

C.   Differences between Formal and Informal Rulemaking

D.   Chapter 13 Wrap Up and Look Ahead

Chapter Problem

Please create a matrix or other graphic organizer to help you compare the procedural elements of informal, formal, and hybrid rulemaking proceedings under the federal APA. If you choose to make a matrix, the left hand side of the matrix should list the five common elements of rulemaking under the federal APA that were introduced in Chapter 11.F and are reproduced below in Section A.

The top of the matrix will horizontally list, next to this list of common elements, columns for informal, formal, and hybrid rulemakings. If you have already studied informal rulemaking, you can at this point fill in the column for informal rulemaking. At the end of this chapter, you should be able to fill out the column for formal rulemaking.

A. Review: The Five Steps of Rulemaking under the Federal APA

As stated in Chapter 11, proceedings to make legislative rules under the federal APA ordinarily involve five steps:

(1) Notify the public of the proposed rulemaking.

(2) Invite public input on the proposed rule.

(3) Consider that input when deciding on the final rule.

(4) Explain the final rule.

(5) Publish the final rule before it takes effect.

Both formal rulemaking and informal rulemaking involve all five steps. As Section B discusses, these steps are essentially identical, for both informal and formal rulemaking, at steps (1) and (5). As Section C discusses, they differ at steps (2), (3), and (4).

B. Similarities between Formal and Informal Rulemaking

Formal rulemaking begins (at step (1)) and ends (at step (5)) the same way as informal rulemaking.

Both types of rulemaking begin when the agency publishes a general notice of proposed rulemaking ("NOPR" or "NPRM") in the Federal Register, in accordance with federal APA § 553(b). APA § 553(b) requires the NOPR to include certain information, including **"the time, place, and nature of public rule making proceedings."**

The contents of the NOPR will differ depending on the type of rulemaking proceeding. In informal rulemaking, the NOPR will typically announce: how long the public has to submit written comments on the proposed rule (usually 30–60 days); and how to submit written comments. In formal rulemaking, the NOPR will typically announce: the date and location of the formal hearing; who may participate in that hearing; and how someone who wishes to participate in the hearing may do seek to do so. The NOPR in a formal rulemaking will also provide other details about the formal hearing.

Exercise: Recognizing an NOPR for Formal Rulemaking

Browse the NOPR for a formal rulemaking proceeding at 73 Fed. Reg. 69,588 (2008). You can find this Federal Register entry at GPO's Federal Digital System: http://www.gpo.gov/fdsys/search/home.action. The System allows you to retrieve a Federal Register entry by citation. Once you find the notice, browse it to get a sense of the contents of an NOPR for a formal rulemaking under the federal APA.

Both formal and informal rulemaking usually end with the publication of the final rule in the Federal Register, at least 30 days before the rule takes effect. Federal Register publication is required by APA § 552(a)(1)(D) (2012). The 30-day-delayed-effective-date requirement is imposed by § 553(d). Both § 552(a)(1)(D) and § 553(d) apply regardless of whether a rule was promulgated using informal or formal rulemaking.

C. Differences between Formal and Informal Rulemaking

Formal rulemaking differs from informal rulemaking in the way the public participates (step 2); the way the agency considers the public input in deciding on the final rule (step 3); and the way the agency explains the final rule (step 4).

1. Public Participation

People participate in informal rulemaking by submitting written comments on a proposed rule. People participate in formal rulemaking by becoming **"parties"** who participate at an oral, evidentiary **"hearing."** Anyone can participate in informal rulemaking. In contrast, not just anyone can become a party to a formal rulemaking proceeding. The federal APA does not itself identify who may participate as a party in a formal rulemaking proceeding. Eligibility for party status is addressed, instead, mainly by the agency legislation and the agency's procedural rules. Although agency legislation and agency rules vary in defining eligibility for party status, generally they restrict party status so that it is not available to everyone.

The hearing in a formal rulemaking proceeding is usually presided over by an administrative law judge (ALJ). *See* 5 U.S.C. § 556(b) (2012). The ALJ has several powers comparable to those of a trial judge. *See id.* § 556(c). Parties participate in the hearing in roughly the same way that parties do in a trial before a judge. Section 556(d) states, in general, **"A party is entitled to present his [or her] case or defense by oral or documentary evidence, to submit rebuttal evidence, and to conduct such cross-examination as may be required for a full and true disclosure of the facts."** *Id.* § 556(d).

A party's right to present oral evidence in formal rulemaking is subject to a limitation: **"In [formal] rule making ... an agency may, when a party will not be prejudiced thereby, adopt procedures for the submission of all or part of the evidence in written form."** *Id.* Thus, the "hearing" in a formal rulemaking may, in whole or in part, be a paper hearing. Even such a paper hearing will be more formal than informal rulemaking. For example, the ALJ in a formal rulemaking can exclude **"irrelevant, immaterial, or unduly repetitious evidence"**; no such evidence filtering occurs in informal rulemaking. Furthermore, the parties to the formal rulemaking have the right to rebut opposing evidence, even if all the evidence takes documentary form; no right of rebuttal exists in informal rulemaking.

2. Agency Consideration of Public Input

Section 553(c) of the federal APA requires the agency in an informal rulemaking simply to **"conside[r] ... the relevant matter presented."** Section 553(c) does not limit the agency to considering only relevant input supplied by the public. The agency can also consider "materials in its files and the knowledge and experience of the agency." AGM 31–32. In addition, the agency can consider off-the-record communications by people outside the agency, subject to the restrictions discussed in Chapter 12.C.2. In short, informal rulemaking is an open record proceeding.

In contrast, formal rulemakings are closed-record proceedings. **"The transcript of testimony and exhibits, together with all papers and requests filed in the proceeding, constitutes the *exclusive record* for decision."** 5 U.S.C. §556(d) (emphasis added). The federal APA prohibits ex parte communications in a formal rulemaking proceeding. *See id.* §557(d) (discussed in Chapter 24.D.2).

The federal APA does not prescribe any procedures for the agency to follow when it considers the relevant matter presented in an informal rulemaking. In contrast, §557 specifies a two-step decisionmaking process in formal rulemaking. First, the official who presided at the hearing makes a decision. *See* 5 U.S.C. §557(b) (2012). The parties to the proceeding can file objections to that decision. The decision is then subject to review by the head of the agency (or someone to whom the agency head has delegated reviewing authority). *See id.*

3. Agency Explanation of the Final Rule

In informal rulemaking, §553(c) of the federal APA requires the agency to accompany the final rule with a **"concise general statement of ... basis and purpose."**

In formal rulemaking, the federal APA requires both the presiding official's decision and the agency head's decision to contain **"findings and conclusions, and the reasons or basis therefore, on all the material issues of fact, law or discretion presented on the record."** 5 U.S.C. §557(c). This requirement of findings and conclusions resembles the requirement imposed on a federal judge, at the end of a bench trial, to issue a written decision with findings of fact and conclusions of law. *See* Fed. R. Civ. P. 52(a)(1).

D. Chapter 13 Wrap Up and Look Ahead

This chapter compared formal and informal rulemaking. It has aimed to give you enough information about formal rulemaking that you can understand at what stages it differs from informal rulemaking. The chapter also briefly introduced the formal hearing and formal decisionmaking requirements of APA §§556 and 557. The next chapter examines the third type of rulemaking under the federal APA: hybrid rulemaking.

Chapter Problem Revisited

This chapter should enable you to complete the graphic organizer to compare informal rulemaking to formal rulemaking under the federal APA. Do not worry—on the contrary, rejoice!—if you have many questions about formal rulemaking. Formal rulemaking differs from informal rulemaking primarily in having elaborate requirements for public (party) participation and for agency decisionmaking, under §§556 and 557, respectively. We examine those provisions in more detail when we discuss formal adjudication under the APA, which is the more common context in which lawyers encounter them.

Chapter 14

Hybrid Rulemaking

Overview

A federal agency must use hybrid rulemaking requirements to make a legislative rule when the agency legislation governing that rule modifies or adds to the informal rulemaking requirements of the federal APA. This chapter explores some ways in which agency statutes can modify the APA's informal rulemaking requirements.

It is hard to generalize about hybrid rulemaking because Congress can modify the APA's informal rulemaking requirements in infinite ways. This chapter introduces you only to some examples of modifications. The objectives of this chapter are to help you:

- learn that hybrid rulemaking exists, so you don't labor under the misimpression that the only kinds of rulemaking proceedings are the informal and formal rulemaking procedures prescribed in APAs;

- develop same familiarity with some common ways in which agency statutes modify the APA's informal rulemaking requirements, so they do not take you by surprise in your practice;

- gain a better understanding of informal and formal rulemaking, by learning about rulemaking proceedings that often lie somewhere between those two types of rulemaking in terms of their formality.

This chapter has four sections:

A. Context for Studying Hybrid Rulemaking

B. One Example of a Hybrid Rulemaking Statute

C. Advance Notice of Proposed Rulemaking

D. Chapter 14 Wrap Up and Look Ahead

Chapter Problem

Memo

To: New Associate

From: Senior Associate

Re: New Client Matter

We have been retained by a major pesticide manufacturer to represent it in a pending rulemaking proceeding. Specifically, the EPA has proposed a new rule regulating one of the client's pesticides under the Toxic Substances Control Act (TSCA). I have the citation for the place in the U.S. Code where TSCA starts: 15 U.S.C. § 2601 (2012). I seem to recall that TSCA modifies the usual notice-and-comment procedures, but I don't remember the details. Would you please take a look at TSCA and email me back with a summary of the modifications? I am particularly interested to know whether there is an opportunity for oral presentations.

Over time, I want you to become an expert in the rulemaking procedures for rules promulgated under TSCA. You must therefore locate and analyze any EPA procedural rules that elaborate on the statutory rulemaking procedures. For now, though, I just need you to get, and give me, the lay of the statutory landscape. Thank you.

A. Context for Studying Hybrid Rulemaking

Congress enacted the APA in 1946 to prescribe (1) informal rulemaking procedures for most proceedings by federal agencies to make substantive, legislative rules; and (2) formal rulemaking procedures for those now-relatively rare rules that are **"required by statute to be made on the record after opportunity for an agency hearing."** 5 U.S.C. § 553(c) (2012). In creating these two rulemaking vehicles, Congress recognized that they would not be suitable in all situations. Thus, Congress provided in § 559 of the federal APA that other laws can impose requirements in addition to those of the APA, and that laws enacted after the APA could displace the APA altogether if they did so expressly. By allowing in § 559 for the APA's rulemaking procedures to be added to, and modified, Congress understood that "two sizes would not fit all."

"Hybrid rulemaking" is the term used for situations in which the agency legislation governing a particular rule adds to or modifies the APA's informal rulemaking requirements for that rule. Besides the agency legislation, other laws may add to or modify the APA's procedures, including cross-cutting statutes such as the National Environmental Policy Act and the agency's own procedural rules. For now, we ignore these other sources of procedural requirements for agency rulemaking. As a matter of terminology, "hybrid rulemaking" usually refers to rulemaking in which the agency legislation, in particular, modifies or adds to APA requirements.

State legislatures began enacting APAs soon after Congress enacted the APA in 1946. Like the federal APA, the state APAs create a default set of rulemaking procedures, which the state legislature may modify for making particular rules. State legislatures can also enact cross-cutting statutes, besides an APA, that require additional rulemaking procedures in many instances. Finally state agencies — sometimes in conjunction with the State Attorney General — can adopt procedural rules for rulemaking that elaborate on or add to statutorily required rulemaking procedures.

B. One Example of a Hybrid Rulemaking Statute

There is no such thing as a typical hybrid rulemaking statute. In this section we introduce you to a hybrid rulemaking statute that we have chosen not because it is typical, but because it modifies the APA's informal rulemaking procedures significantly and thus shows you the range of ways Congress can customize the basic informal rulemaking vehicle.

When Congress drafts a hybrid rulemaking statute, it assumes the reader's familiarity with the APA's informal rulemaking procedures. When lawyers analyze a hybrid rulemaking statute, they determine how the statute modifies the APA's informal rulemaking procedures. Accordingly, this section gives you practice reading a hybrid rulemaking statute the way administrative lawyers do.

The statutory provision reproduced below modifies the APA's informal rulemaking requirements for many of the rules that EPA issues under the Clean Air Act. As modified, EPA rulemaking proceedings still follow the basic notice-and-comment procedure, but with lots of extra procedural bells and whistles. As you read the provision, pay attention to how it alters the informal rulemaking requirements of federal APA § 553.

---

42 U.S.C. § 7607. Administrative proceedings and judicial review ...

(d) Rulemaking

(1) This subsection applies to — [specified rules issued under various provisions of the Clean Air Act, including, just to give you some examples of the covered rules:]

(A) the promulgation or revision of any national ambient air quality standard under section 7409 of this title, ... (D) the promulgation of any requirement for solid waste combustion under section 7429 of this title, ... (G) the promulgation or revision of any regulation under subchapter IV-A of this chapter (relating to control of acid [rain]), ...

(I) promulgation or revision of regulations under subchapter VI of this chapter (relating to stratosphere and ozone protection), [and]

(J) promulgation or revision of regulations under part C of subchapter I of this chapter (relating to prevention of significant deterioration of air quality and protection of visibility)....

The provisions of section 553 through 557 and section 706 of Title 5 shall not, except as expressly provided in this subsection, apply to actions to which this subsection applies. This subsection shall not apply in the case of any rule or circumstance referred to in subparagraphs (A) or (B) of subsection 553(b) of Title 5.

(2) Not later than the date of proposal of any action to which this subsection applies, the Administrator shall establish a rulemaking docket for such action (hereinafter in this subsection referred to as a "rule"). Whenever a rule applies only within a particular State, a second (identical) docket shall be simultaneously established in the appropriate regional office of the Environmental Protection Agency.

(3) In the case of any rule to which this subsection applies, notice of proposed rulemaking shall be published in the Federal Register, as provided under section 553(b) of Title 5, shall be accompanied by a statement of its basis and purpose and shall specify the period available for public comment (hereinafter referred to as the "comment period"). The notice of proposed rulemaking shall also state the docket number, the location or locations of the docket, and the times it will

be open to public inspection. The statement of basis and purpose shall include a summary of—

(A) the factual data on which the proposed rule is based;

(B) the methodology used in obtaining the data and in analyzing the data; and

(C) the major legal interpretations and policy considerations underlying the proposed rule.

The statement shall also set forth or summarize and provide a reference to any pertinent findings, recommendations, and comments by the Scientific Review Committee established under section 7409(d) of this title and the National Academy of Sciences, and, if the proposal differs in any important respect from any of these recommendations, an explanation of the reasons for such differences. All data, information, and documents referred to in this paragraph on which the proposed rule relies shall be included in the docket on the date of publication of the proposed rule.

(4)(A) The rulemaking docket required under paragraph (2) shall be open for inspection by the public at reasonable times specified in the notice of proposed rulemaking. Any person may copy documents contained in the docket. The Administrator shall provide copying facilities which may be used at the expense of the person seeking copies, but the Administrator may waive or reduce such expenses in such instances as the public interest requires. Any person may request copies by mail if the person pays the expenses, including personnel costs to do the copying.

(B)(i) Promptly upon receipt by the agency, all written comments and documentary information on the proposed rule received from any person for inclusion in the docket during the comment period shall be placed in the docket. The transcript of public hearings, if any, on the proposed rule shall also be included in the docket promptly upon receipt from the person who transcribed such hearings. All documents which become available after the proposed rule has been published and which the Administrator determines are of central relevance to the rulemaking shall be placed in the docket as soon as possible after their availability.

(ii) The drafts of proposed rules submitted by the Administrator to the Office of Management and Budget for any interagency review process prior to proposal of any such rule, all documents accompanying such drafts, and all written comments thereon by other agencies and all written responses to such written comments by the Administrator shall be placed in the docket no later than the date of proposal of the rule. The drafts of the final rule submitted for such review process prior to promulgation and all such written comments thereon, all documents accompanying such drafts, and written responses thereto shall be placed in the docket no later than the date of promulgation.

(5) In promulgating a rule to which this subsection applies (i) the Administrator shall allow any person to submit written comments, data, or documentary information; (ii) the Administrator shall give interested persons an opportunity for the oral presentation of data, views, or arguments, in addition to an opportunity to make written submissions; (iii) a transcript shall be kept of any oral presentation; and (iv) the Administrator shall keep the record of such proceeding open for thirty days after completion of the proceeding to provide an opportunity for submission of rebuttal and supplementary information.

(6)(A) The promulgated rule shall be accompanied by (i) a statement of basis and purpose like that referred to in paragraph (3) with respect to a proposed rule and (ii) an explanation of the reasons for any major changes in the promulgated rule from the proposed rule.

(B) The promulgated rule shall also be accompanied by a response to each of the significant comments, criticisms, and new data submitted in written or oral presentations during the comment period.

(C) The promulgated rule may not be based (in part or whole) on any information or data which has not been placed in the docket as of the date of such promulgation....

After reading about the fairly elaborate procedures in § 7607(d), you might wonder whether it requires formal rulemaking. The answer is no. Section 7607(d) doesn't require formal rulemaking because it doesn't require an opportunity for a "hearing"; rather, it requires an opportunity for "oral presentations." Thus, § 7607(d) lacks one of the statutory elements necessary to trigger formal rulemaking. Instead, § 7607(d) just adds to the informal rulemaking procedures of federal APA § 553; it thus requires hybrid rulemaking.

In a moment we will compare rulemaking under § 7607(d) to informal rulemaking. Before that, you need an explanation of two references in § 7607(d). Knowing the background of these references not only helps you understand § 7607(d) itself but also introduces issues relevant to hybrid rulemaking proceedings under other statutes.

First, § 7607(d)(3)'s fourth sentence refers to "comments by the Scientific Review Committee established under section 7409(d) of this title." The provision referred to, 42 U.S.C. § 7409(d) (2012), applies specifically to EPA rules establishing National Ambient Air Quality Standards (NAAQSs). Section 7409(d) requires the Administrator of the EPA to appoint an independent scientific review committee. The committee's job is to review NAAQSs every five years and suggest changes or new NAAQSs to the EPA Administrator. This ensures EPA gets regular feedback on the NAAQSs from independent, scientific experts. Congress has also required EPA to consider reports and recommendations of the National Academy of Science on various aspects of environmental regulation.

Section 7409(d) has counterparts in other agency legislation. The central importance of accurate scientific data to many rulemaking proceedings has prompted Congress in § 7409(d) and other statutes to create procedures to ensure agency rules rest on sound science.

Second, § 7607(d)(4)(B)(ii) refers to "drafts of proposed rules submitted by the Administrator to the Office of Management and Budget for any interagency review process." This refers to a requirement imposed by various executive orders, the most important of which is Executive Order 12,866, 3 C.F.R. 638 (1994), on many federal agency rules. These executive orders require federal agencies, other than the independent federal agencies, to submit significant proposed rules to another federal agency, the Office of Management and Budget (OMB), for review. Executive Order 12,866 is discussed in Chapter 15.B.

As mentioned above, lawyers analyze hybrid rulemaking statutes in part by comparing the procedures they require to the APA's informal rulemaking procedures. Let us do the same.

1. Notify the Public of the Proposed Rulemaking

Section 7607(d)(3) requires EPA to publish the notice of proposed rulemaking (NOPR) required by § 553(b). Section 553(b) specifies three items of information that an NOPR must have. Section 7607(d)(3) requires additional information in NOPRs published under it.

Interestingly, some information that §7607(d)(3) expressly requires—namely, "the factual data on which the proposed rule is based" and the "methodology used in obtaining the data and in analyzing the data"—resembles what the federal courts, in cases such as *Portland Cement Ass'n v. Ruckelshaus*, 486 F.2d 375 (D.C. Cir. 1973), have construed §553(b) implicitly to require. *See* Chapter 12.A.2.

2. Invite Public Input on the Proposed Rule

Section 7607(d)(5) entitles "any person" to file written comments on the proposed rule. To this extent, it tracks APA §553(c)'s provision for **"interested persons"** to **"participate ... through submission of written data, views, or arguments."** Section 7607(d)(5) goes farther than APA §553(c), however, by allowing "interested persons" to make oral presentations as well. In addition, §7607(d)(5) requires EPA to make a transcript of the oral presentations and keep the record open so that people can rebut and supplement information in the oral presentations. This opportunity for rebuttal or supplementation of oral presentations does not create the same level of formality as characterizes evidentiary hearings in formal rulemaking. For example, §7607(d)(5) does not authorize cross-examination of witnesses or exclusion of immaterial evidence. Even so, §7607(d)(5) definitely creates a more formal process for public participation than occurs in informal rulemaking.

3. Consider That Input When Deciding on the Final Rule

Section 7607(d) essentially provides for a "closed record" proceeding, unlike APA §553, which allows informal rulemaking to be an "open record" proceeding. Section 7607(d) requires the agency to create a rulemaking docket and to base the rule solely on information in that docket. (Although §7607(d) implies a docket of physical documents, other federal legislation requires agencies to make these dockets digitally available on the internet "to the extent practicable." Pub. L. No. 107-347, §206(d)(2), codified at 44 U.S.C. §3501 Note (2012).)

The rulemaking docket created under §7607(d) differs from the record in a traditional formal rulemaking or formal adjudication, however, in one important way: The agency may add items to the rulemaking docket, which the agency may then rely on, apparently without any participants being able to challenge their addition or their contents. In a formal proceeding, the parties usually have an opportunity to challenge the admission of evidence and rebut unfavorable evidence. In addition, most of the evidence in a formal proceeding comes into the record on the initiative of one of the parties, except for information of which the decision maker takes official notice. In contrast, the agency in a proceeding under §7607(d) may take a more active role in determining the contents of the rulemaking docket, and non-agency participants have less control over the contents.

4. Explain the Final Rule

APA §553(c) requires a **"concise general statement of [a rule's] basis and purpose"** at the end of the rulemaking process. By comparison, §7607(d) is much more elaborate in describing the required contents of EPA's explanation of final rules adopted under that provision. *See* 42 U.S.C. §7607(d)(6). True, case law interpretations of §553(c)'s "concise general statement" requirement have caused it to resemble the requirements of §7607(d)(6) more than the differing texts of the two statutes might suggest. Even so, §7607(d) on its face imposes a more elaborate duty to explain the final rule than does APA §553(c) on its face.

5. Publish the Final Rule before It Takes Effect

Although §7607(d) largely displaces the informal and formal rulemaking provisions of the APA, it does not displace APA §552(a)(1) (2012), which generally requires federal agencies to publish their final rules in the Federal Register. Thus, the last required step of rulemaking—publication in the Federal Register—is the same in hybrid rulemaking under §7607(d) as in informal and formal rulemaking. Likewise, legislative rules made under §7607(d), like legislative rules made through informal and formal rulemaking, will be permanently codified in the CFR.

Section 553(d) of the federal APA generally requires an agency to publish a substantive, legislative rule at least 30 days before it takes effect. Section 553(d), however, apparently does not apply to rules made under §7607(d), because §7607(d)(1) makes §553 inapplicable "except as expressly provided in this subsection," and the subsection does not expressly provide for compliance with §553(d). Nor does §7607(d) itself require rules to be published before their effective date. This may be a legislative oversight. In any event, the Congressional Review Act requires "major rules" made under §7607(d) to take effect no sooner than sixty days after their publication in the Federal Register. 5 U.S.C. §801(a)(3) (2012); *see also id.* §804(2) (defining "major rule" to include rules with annual effect on economy of $100 million or more).

Exercise: Hybrid Rulemaking

Why do you think Congress required hybrid rulemaking for NAAQSs and the other rules covered by 42 U.S.C. §7607(d)?

C. Advance Notice of Proposed Rulemaking

Some federal agency statutes require the agency to publish an "advance notice of proposed rulemaking," known as an ANPRM. We introduce this feature of some hybrid rulemaking proceedings for two reasons. First, it is fairly common in federal agency rulemaking—either because an ANPRM is required by agency legislation or voluntarily provided by federal agencies. (Though fairly common, ANPRMs are not always required by statutes requiring hybrid rulemaking, as 42 U.S.C. §7607(d), the hybrid rulemaking statute examined above in Section B, shows.) Second, we introduce the ANPRM because it has counterparts in state APAs.

A federal agency publishes an ANPRM in the Federal Register to notify the public that the agency is thinking about initiating a rulemaking proceeding. Thus, the agency publishes the ANPRM *before* it publishes the NOPR. Typically, an agency uses the ANPRM to gather information from the public that will be helpful for the agency to have even before it begins drafting a proposed rule. The ANPRM may seek public information and opinions about the appropriate scope of the rulemaking; what issues are particularly important; and what perspectives the agency should consider when it sits down to compose its proposed rule.

Several federal statutes require federal agencies to publish ANPRMs. Here, for example, is the provision for the Consumer Product Safety Commission's promulgation of rules under the Consumer Product Safety Act:

---

15 U.S.C. § 2058. Procedure for consumer product safety rules

(a) Commencement of proceeding; publication of prescribed notice of proposed rulemaking; transmittal of notice

A proceeding for the development of a consumer product safety rule may be commenced by the publication in the Federal Register of an advance notice of proposed rulemaking which shall—

(1) identify the product and the nature of the risk of injury associated with the product;

(2) include a summary of each of the regulatory alternatives under consideration by the Commission (including voluntary consumer product safety standards);

(3) include information with respect to any existing standard known to the Commission which may be relevant to the proceedings, together with a summary of the reasons why the Commission believes preliminarily that such standard does not eliminate or adequately reduce the risk of injury identified in paragraph (1);

(4) invite interested persons to submit to the Commission, within such period as the Commission shall specify in the notice (which period shall not be less than 30 days or more than 60 days after the date of publication of the notice), comments with respect to the risk of injury identified by the Commission, the regulatory alternatives being considered, and other possible alternatives for addressing the risk;

(5) invite any person (other than the Commission) to submit to the Commission, within such period as the Commission shall specify in the notice (which period shall not be less than 30 days after the date of publication of the notice), an existing standard or a portion of a standard as a proposed consumer product safety standard; and

(6) invite any person (other than the Commission) to submit to the Commission, within such period as the Commission shall specify in the notice (which period shall not be less than 30 days after the date of publication of the notice), a statement of intention to modify or develop a voluntary consumer product safety standard to address the risk of injury identified in paragraph (1) together with a description of a plan to modify or develop the standard.
The Commission shall transmit such notice within 10 calendar days to the appropriate Congressional committees....

We encourage you, when re-reading this provision, to identify what specific issues members of the public must be invited to address.

A federal agency can always publish an ANPRM even if no statute requires it, and some federal agencies regularly do so. The agency usually does so on a situation-by-situation basis, as reflected in this procedural rule from the Coast Guard:

---

33 C.F.R. § 1.05-30. Advance notice of proposed rulemaking (ANPRM)

An advance notice of proposed rulemaking may be used to alert the affected public about a new regulatory project, or when the Coast Guard needs more information about what form proposed regulations should take, the actual need for a regulation, the cost of a proposal, or any other information. The ANPRM may solicit general information or ask the public to respond to specific questions.

ANPRMs generally benefit the agency and the public. The ANPRM benefits the agency by flushing out important issues and information before the agency devotes time and effort to drafting a rule. The ANPRM benefits the public by creating an opportunity for input before the agency has invested time and effort into — and accordingly begins to get entrenched in favor of — a particular regulatory approach. In addition to gathering public input for rules that the agency has decided to draft on its own initiative, or as a result of a statutory requirement, federal agencies may use ANPRMs when someone outside the agency petitions the agency to adopt, amend, or repeal a rule, and the agency wants input on that rulemaking petition. *See, e.g.*, 76 Fed. Reg. 10553 (Feb. 25, 2011) (notice published by U.S. Coast Guard seeking public comments on petition for rulemaking); *see also* 5 U.S.C. § 553(e) (2012) ("Each agency shall give an interested person the right to petition for the issuance, amendment, or repeal of a rule.").

State agencies also use ANPRMs. In some States, their use is addressed in the state APA. The Minnesota APA, for example, generally requires an ANPRM in all rulemakings:

Minn. Stat. Ann. § 14.101. Advice on possible rules

Subdivision 1. Required notice. In addition to seeking information by other methods designed to reach persons or classes of persons who might be affected by the proposal, an agency, at least 60 days before publication of a notice of intent to adopt or a notice of hearing, shall solicit comments from the public on the subject matter of a possible rulemaking proposal under active consideration within the agency by causing notice to be published in the State Register. The notice must include a description of the subject matter of the proposal and the types of groups and individuals likely to be affected, and must indicate where, when, and how persons may comment on the proposal and whether and how drafts of any proposal may be obtained from the agency.

This notice must be published within 60 days of the effective date of any new or amendatory law requiring rules to be adopted, amended, or repealed....

As true at the federal level, state agencies with rulemaking power will probably be considered to have the power to publish ANPRMs or something similar even if no statute expressly requires or authorizes them to do so, as a way to collect information to inform their exercise of rulemaking power.

In sum, ANPRMs are a required part of hybrid rulemaking proceedings under some federal agency legislation. Federal agencies sometimes use ANPRMs voluntarily. A state APA may require an ANPRM; may allow it; or may say nothing about the matter. Even if not required, state agencies generally will be considered to have authority to use the ANPRM device voluntarily. ANPRMs are great opportunities for administrative lawyers to shape the future of a rule when it is only a twinkle in an agency's eye.

Exercise: Comparing Hybrid Rulemaking to Other Types of Federal Rulemaking

Below is a chart to help you organize information about the three types of rulemaking under the federal APA that we have examined in Chapters 12 through 14. Please complete the chart using statutory provisions from the federal APA and sample hybrid rulemaking statute examined in this chapter, 42 U.S.C. § 7607(d).

	Informal Rulemaking	Formal Rulemaking	Hybrid Rulemaking under 42 U.S.C. § 7607(d)
1. Notice			
2. Input from Public or Parties			
3. Agency Considers Input (Closed Record or Open Record?)			
4. Agency Explains Final Rule			
5. Agency Publishes Final Rule			

D. Chapter 14 Wrap Up and Look Ahead

This chapter has examined one hybrid rulemaking statute that shows some ways Congress can (and does) modify the APA's informal rulemaking requirements. The chapter also introduced the ANPRM — a common element of hybrid rulemaking and other rulemaking proceedings at both the federal and state levels.

In addition to the APA modifications found in some federal agency legislation, Congress has enacted what we have been calling "cross-cutting statutes," besides the federal APA, that require additional procedures in many federal rulemaking proceedings. Presidents have done the same through executive orders. The next chapter turns to these other laws that are potential, external sources of procedural requirements for many federal rules. It also mentions the variety of state laws that may impose procedural requirements on state agency rulemaking.

Chapter Problem Revisited

The TSCA is codified in 15 U.S.C. §§ 2601–2629 (2012), as subchapter I ("Control of Toxic Substances") of Chapter 53 ("Toxic Substances Control") of Title 15 ("Commerce and Trade") of the U.S. Code. You can find out where TSCA is codified from the EPA's website, http://www.epa.gov/lawsregs/laws/tsca.html, or (for those who prefer good old books), the U.S. Code's "Popular Name Index," which gives citations for statutes, which are listed alphabetically by their popular names. If your boss did not know the name of the federal statute that regulates pesticides, then to find the statute's name you might consult the Washington Information Directory (CQ Press 2011–2012), which has an entry for "pesticides" in its index.

The provision of TSCA authorizing regulation of hazardous chemicals is 15 U.S.C. § 2605 ("Regulation of hazardous chemical substances and mixtures"). Subsection 2605(c) requires EPA to "provide an opportunity for an informal hearing" on rules proposed under TSCA, and spells out procedures for the hearing. *See id.* § 2605(c)(3). When you look at this provision, you will see that it requires a fairly formal "informal" hearing. For example, the EPA must allow cross-examination. Compare this with the hybrid procedures prescribed in the provision examined in this chapter, 42 U.S.C. § 7607(d)(5), which requires an opportunity for oral presentations without expressly allowing cross-examination. Hybrid rulemaking can encompass a range of procedures for public input.

If you really want to impress your boss, you will also want to find the EPA's procedural rules for informal hearings under § 2605(c). Here again, you have several options. A good option is the Index to the Code of Federal Regulations (CFR). The Index includes a particularly handy item called "Parallel Table of Authorities and Rules." That Table lists, in order, provisions in the U.S. Code and directs you the parts of the CFR where you will find regulations implementing those provisions. Thus, you would look for the Table's entry for 15 U.S.C. § 2605, which would direct you to the part of the CFR with procedural rules for informal hearings on rules proposed under 15 U.S.C. § 2605. *See* 40 C.F.R. Pt. 750 (2012) ("Procedures for rulemaking under section 6 of the Toxic Substances Control Act").

Professional Development Reflection Questions

One big difference between law school and legal practice is that in law school you are usually evaluated based solely on your own performance, while in legal practice you are often evaluated based on work product requiring collaboration with others. For example, the party in a complex agency rulemaking proceeding may be represented by a law firm that has several attorneys working together, each bringing his or her expertise to bear on facets of the case. In this kind of setting, a lawyer is judged not only by the quality of the collaborative work product but also on the lawyer's ability to work effectively as part of a team.

This distinction between the solo nature of law school, on the one hand, and the collaborative nature of legal practice, on the other hand, matters in at least two ways for a law student. First, the law student must affirmatively seek out opportunities to gain experience collaborating with others on legal projects. This is necessary not only for the value of learning collaboration skills but also because many prospective legal employers like to hire new lawyers who've gained that experience. Second, the law student must learn his or her strengths, weaknesses, and preferences when it comes to collaboration. This self-knowledge helps the student (a) address weaknesses when identifying skills that need development and (b) take the preferences into account when searching for a legal job.

With this background on collaboration in mind, please consider these questions:

1. If you were interviewing for a legal job today and the interviewer asked you to describe significant experiences that you've had since graduating from college in which you worked collaboratively, what would you say?

2. Considering your existing comfort level with collaborating on legal projects, what can you do in the next year to become involved in a collaborative legal project—e.g., moot court, pro bono projects, clinical experiences, law review—that would (a) be a "stretch" for you in terms of taking you out of your comfort zone but that would also (b) be something you could realistically commit to?

Chapter 15

Other Laws Creating Procedural Requirements for Rulemaking

Overview

The source of power for most agency rules is the agency legislation. The most important sources of limits on, or requirements for exercising, agency rulemaking power are the agency legislation and the applicable APA. In exploring these limits and requirements, we have tried to help you keep in mind that agency rules, too, may be a source of procedural requirements for agency rulemaking.

But there's more! This chapter introduces you to cross-cutting statutes other than the APA and to executive orders that apply in many proceedings by federal agencies to make substantive legislative rules. It also discusses comparable state laws. We have two objectives in introducing you to these provisions:

1. To introduce you to laws that you must learn about if your practice involves federal rulemaking.

2. To show the importance of taking a broad view when identifying potential, external sources of procedural requirements for rulemaking.

This chapter contains five sections:

A. Federal Statutes

B. Presidential Executive Orders

C. Dealing with the Complexity of Federal Rulemaking

D. State Laws

E. Chapter 15 Wrap Up and Look Ahead

A. Federal Statutes

This section introduces you to seven cross-cutting federal statutes that create procedural requirements for many federal rulemaking proceedings. You will learn each statute's purpose; its applicability to rulemaking; and its main requirements. The description below also touches upon the availability of judicial review of an agency's compliance with the statute.

1. National Environmental Policy Act

At the heart of the National Environmental Policy Act (NEPA) is a requirement that all federal agencies prepare environmental impact statements (EISs) on proposed actions that significantly affect the environment. 42 U.S.C. § 4332(C) (2012). Thus, NEPA requires an EIS for a proposed federal agency *rule* if that rule will significantly affect the environment. For example, NEPA required an EIS when the Bureau of Land Management amended rules for private livestock grazing on 160 million acres of public land. *See Western Watershed Project v. Kraayenbrink*, 632 F.3d 472 (9th Cir. 2011).

NEPA's EIS requirement serves two purposes. First, the EIS requirement ensures that, before the agency acts, the agency has identified and given written consideration to the environmental impacts of the proposed action. Second, the EIS requirement ensures that information on the environmental impacts of a proposed action will be available to "the larger audience that may also play a role in both the [agency's] decisionmaking process and the implementation of that decision." *Robertson v. Methow Valley Citizens Council*, 490 U.S. 332, 349 (1989).

An agency determines whether a proposed rule significantly affects the environment by preparing an Environmental Assessment (EA). If the agency concludes in its EA that the rule will not significantly affect the environment, the agency makes a "finding of no significant impact" (FONSI) and need not prepare an EIS. Otherwise the agency must prepare an EIS. To prepare the EIS, the agency must identify reasonable alternatives to its proposed rule and evaluate their environmental impacts. Further requirements for an EIS are spelled out in regulations promulgated by the Council on Environmental Quality (CEQ), an agency created by NEPA to further the purposes of the Act. *See* 40 C.F.R. §§ 1500.1–1508.28 (2012); *see also* 42 U.S.C. §§ 4342 & 4344 (2012).

Preparation of the EIS usually runs concurrently with the rulemaking process. Typically, the agency publishes a draft EIS when it publishes the proposed rule in the Federal Register. The agency must invite public comments on the draft EIS, just as in informal rulemaking the agency invites comments on the proposed rule itself. The agency publishes the final EIS when it publishes the final rule in the Federal Register. The agency must respond to significant comments on the draft EIS, just as the agency must respond to significant comments on the proposed rule.

By running in tandem with the rulemaking process, the NEPA process can affect the federal rulemaking process in three ways.

First, NEPA can influence the rulemaking record. When NEPA requires an EIS for a proposed rule, the EIS becomes part of the rulemaking record. The agency's final rule must have adequate support in the rulemaking record. For example, if the EIS shows that the rule ultimately adopted will have terrible environmental impacts, this prevents the agency from justifying it as environmentally friendly.

Second, and relatedly, NEPA may influence the agency's decision making. An EIS provides information that may constitute **"relevant matter presented,"** to quote the federal APA, which the agency must consider in order for the agency's rule not to be arbitrary and capricious. *See* 5 U.S.C. § 553(c) (2012). It is true that in theory, other laws governing a federal agency's rule could prohibit the agency from considering environmental impacts in devising its rule. Agency legislation, for example, could prescribe an exclusive list of factors that the agency should consider, and that list could exclude environmental impacts. Such legislation is rare, however, and for that reason NEPA procedures "are almost certain to affect the agency's substantive decision." *Robertson v. Methow Valley Citizens Council*, 490 U.S. 332, 350 (1989).

Third, NEPA can affect the agency's duty to explain why it rejected significant alternatives to the rule ultimately adopted. As noted above, the EIS must evaluate alternatives to the proposed agency action. True, NEPA does not require the agency to adopt the most environmentally friendly alternative. As the U.S. Supreme Court has said, "NEPA itself does not mandate particular results." *Methow Valley*, 490 U.S. at 350. Nevertheless, the agency must explain why the rule ultimately chosen is better, overall, than the alternatives, and the agency may have a harder time explaining that when the rule ultimately chosen causes greater harm to the environment than the alternatives. In that situation, the agency will have to show "that other values outweigh the environmental costs." *Id.*

A federal agency's compliance with NEPA is subject to judicial review under the federal APA. *E.g., Friends of Tims Ford v. Tenn. Valley Auth.*, 585 F.3d 955, 964 (6th Cir. 2009). If the court concludes the agency violated NEPA in connection with adopting a rule, the court may set aside the rule.

2. Regulatory Flexibility Act

The Regulatory Flexibility Act (RFA) is codified in 5 U.S.C. §§ 601–612 (2012). The purpose of the RFA is to require federal agencies to assess the impact of proposed rules on small businesses, small nonprofit organizations, and small government jurisdictions (like rural county governments). The idea behind the RFA is to get agencies to consider ways they can minimize the impact of their rules on small entities whose concerns might otherwise be ignored.

The RFA has procedural requirements resembling NEPA's. Whenever a federal agency is required by APA § 553 or any other law to publish a general notice of proposed rulemaking, the agency must assess whether the proposed rule will have a "significant economic impact on a substantial number of small entities." 5 U.S.C. § 605(b). If so, the agency must prepare an "initial regulatory flexibility analysis" (IRFA) on the proposed rule. *Id.* § 603. The IRFA must assess the impact of the proposed rule on small entities by estimating how many will be affected and describing the proposed rule's paperwork burden and other burdens of compliance. The agency also has to identify alternatives to its proposed rule that would have less of an adverse economic effect on small entities. 5 U.S.C. § 603(c) & (d).

The agency invites public comment on the IRFA and prepares a final regulatory flexibility analysis (FRFA). *See* 5 U.S.C. § 603(a). In the FRFA the agency responds to significant issues raised by the public comments on the IRFA. *Id.* § 604(a)(2). The agency also explains why it chose the action it did instead of the alternatives. *Id.* § 604(a)(6).

The RFA, like NEPA, is a procedural statute. The RFA does not require an agency to adopt a final rule that has the least adverse impact on small entities. The RFA does, however, require the agency to identify and assess these impacts. Moreover, the RFA entitles adversely affected small entities to seek judicial review of federal agencies' compliance with many of the RFA's procedural requirements. 5 U.S.C. § 611. The RFA therefore gives small entities leverage in rulemaking that they otherwise would lack.

3. Paperwork Reduction Act

The Paperwork Reduction Act (Paperwork Act) has the noble purpose of reducing the paperwork burdens imposed by the federal government. 44 U.S.C. § 3501(1) (2012). The Paperwork Act also aims to increase the efficiency of the federal government's collection of information. *Id.* § 3501(2). Federal agency rules often put paperwork burdens on the public. Many rules not only require people to do things—e.g., to maintain a safe workplace—but also to keep records—e.g., records of workplace accidents. Federal rules that impose recordkeeping and other paperwork burdens are subject to the Paperwork Act.

To be precise, the Paperwork Act applies to any agency rule that puts reporting or recordkeeping requirements on ten or more people. 44 U.S.C. § 3502(3)(A)(I). Such a rule constitutes the "collection of information" that triggers the Act's requirements. The Act requires an agency to give the public at least sixty days to comment on a proposed collection of information. An agency meets that requirement by including, in the general notice of proposed rulemaking, an invitation to the public to comment on the proposed rule's compliance with the Act.

In addition to inviting public comment on a proposed collection of information, the agency must have the proposed collection of information approved by a federal agency called the Office of Information and Regulatory Affairs (OIRA), which is a component of the Office of Management and Budget (OMB), which in turn is a unit within the Office of the White House. The public can submit comments directly to OIRA on the proposed collection of information. OIRA can disapprove the collection if it is not "necessary for proper performance" of the agency's functions. 44 U.S.C. § 3508.

Courts can review some claims that an agency has violated the Paperwork Act. Most cases have involved claims that federal forms requiring people to provide information (such as tax forms) lack the "control number" that signifies OMB approval of the form under the Act. *See, e.g., United States v. Partridge*, 507 F.3d 1092, 1095 (7th Cir. 2007) (holding that IRS Form 1040 complied with Paperwork Act).

4. Information Quality Act (Also Known as the Data Quality Act)

The Information Quality Act of 2001 required OMB to issue guidelines to ensure "the quality, objectivity, utility, and integrity of information (including statistical information) disseminated by Federal agencies." 44 U.S.C. § 3516 Note ("Policy and Procedural Guidelines"). The Information Quality Act is sometimes known as the "Data Quality Act." The Act required federal agencies to issue their own guidelines to achieve the Act's data quality goals, and to create procedures that people can use to correct information that the agency has disseminated and that violates OMB guidelines.

OMB's guidelines define "dissemination" broadly enough to include information published by an agency in rulemaking proceedings. *See* 67 Fed. Reg. 8452, 8459 (2002); *cf. Prime Time Int'l Co. v. Vilsack*, 599 F.3d 678 (D.C. Cir. 2010) (upholding OMB's view that the Act does not apply to information disclosed in agency adjudication). For example, an agency may disseminate, in a notice of proposed rulemaking, the technical basis for a proposed rule. The technical information underlying the proposed rule must meet the data quality standards of OMB's guidelines. If the information does not, people adversely affected by the information can ask the agency to correct it.

The Information Quality Act is controversial. Some commentators claim the Act was inspired by private industry to bog down the regulatory process. Defenders of the Act claim it prevents federal agencies from relying on, and spreading information based on, "junk science."

The Information Quality Act does not address whether courts can review claims that an agency has violated the Act. One federal court of appeals has held that the Act does not create legal rights enforceable in a federal court. *See Salt Inst. v. Leavitt*, 440 F.3d 156 (4th Cir. 2006).

5. Unfunded Mandate Reform Act

An "unfunded mandate" is a federal law that imposes costly requirements without any federal funding to cover the costs. Congress enacted the Unfunded Mandate Reform Act to control unfunded mandates, including those imposed by federal agencies' legislative rules. *See* 2 U.S.C. §§ 1501–1571 (2012). The Act creates procedures for any proposed federal rule that may impose more than $100 million per year in costs on the private sector or on state, local, or tribal governments. *Id.* § 1532(a).

For those proposed rules, the agency must prepare a regulatory analysis. The analysis must include "a qualitative and quantitative assessment of the anticipated costs and benefits of the Federal mandate ... as well as the effect of the Federal mandate on health, safety, and the natural environment." *Id.* § 1532(a)(2). The agency must summarize the results of this analysis in the notice of proposed rulemaking. *Id.* § 1532(b). If an agency does not do the required analysis for a rule covered by the Act, a court can require the agency to do it. *Id.* § 1571(a)(2)(B). The court may not, however, prevent the final rule from taking effect in the meantime. *Id.* § 1571(a)(3). That is a pretty toothless remedy.

The Unfunded Mandate Reform Act requires agencies to identify "a reasonable number of regulatory alternatives" to the proposed rule. 2 U.S.C. § 1535(a). In addition, the Act requires the agency to select the alternative that will achieve the agency's objective and is the least burdensome for state, tribal, or local governments. *Id.* There is one exception to the latter requirement, and it is a big exception: The agency does not have to select the least burdensome alternative if the agency publishes, with the final rule, an explanation of why it did not choose that alternative. *Id.* § 1535(b). The Act says to the agency, in other words, "You must do this unless you explain why you did not do this." What is more, even if the agency's explanation is lame, it probably is not subject to judicial review. *See id.* § 1571(b)(1).

6. Congressional Review Act

The Congressional Review Act requires federal agencies to submit all rules to Congress and the Comptroller General, who heads a congressional agency known as the General Accountability Office (GAO). 5 U.S.C. § 801(a)(1)(A) (2012). Along with a copy of the rule the agency must give Congress and the GAO information about the agency's compliance with the Regulatory Flexibility Act and the Unfunded Mandate Reform Act. *Id.* § 801(a)(1)(B).

A "major rule" cannot take effect until at least 60 days after it has been submitted to Congress for review. *Id.* § 801(a)(3); *see also id.* § 804(2) (defining "major rule" to include rules with annual effect on economy of $100 million or more). Thus, the Act modifies the 30-day-delayed-effective-date requirement of federal APA § 553(d) for major rules. The 60-day delay in a major rule's effective date gives Congress a chance to enact a joint resolution disapproving the rule. A joint resolution of disapproval, unless successfully vetoed by the President, nullifies the rule.

The Congressional Review Act does not seem to have had much real world effect. A GAO study in late 2008 reported that only one rule had been disapproved under the Act. This is one of more than 50,000 rules that had been submitted to Congress under the Act. *See* Curtis W. Copeland, *Congressional Review Act: Disapproval of Rules in a Subsequent Session of Congress* 1 (Sept. 3, 2008) (Congressional Research Service Report, Order Code RL34633). This 1-in-50,000 statistic, however, may be misleading. Perhaps the Act facilitates behind-the-scenes efforts by Members of Congress to influence agency rules. That is hard to gauge precisely because those efforts go on behind the scenes.

7. Negotiated Rulemaking Act

The federal APA requires an agency to publish notice of proposed rulemaking, but the federal APA does not prescribe procedures for devising a proposed rule. In 1990, Congress enacted the Negotiated Rulemaking Act to encourage federal agencies to use a negotiation process to devise proposed rules. The idea behind the legislation was to allow the interest groups that would be affected by a proposed rule to give input and seek consensus on a proposed rule before it was published for public comment. Congress hoped this negotiation process would "enhance the informal rulemaking process." 5 U.S.C. § 561 (2012); *see* Jeffrey S. Lubbers, *Agency Policymaking Consensus: The (Unfortunate) Waning of Negotiated Rulemaking*, 49 S. Texas L. Rev. 98 (2008).

The Negotiated Rulemaking Act mainly addresses two steps. One step is the establishment of a Negotiated Rulemaking Committee, which is the entity that will try to reach consensus on a proposed rule. The second step is the operation of that Committee.

The Act authorizes the head of a federal agency to establish a Negotiated Rulemaking Committee if the agency head determines that (1) there is a need for a rule; (2) the rule will significantly affect a limited number of identifiable interests; and (3) it is reasonably likely that a balanced committee can be convened to devise a proposed rule by consensus. 5 U.S.C. § 563(a) (2012). The second determination reflects that negotiation will not be practicable except when a rule will affect only a limited number of groups. The third reflects the reality that some rules will be so contentious that consensus is unlikely to occur, even if everyone acts in good faith. When an agency makes these three determinations just discussed, as well as others specified in the Act, the agency *may*, but is not required to, establish a Negotiated Rulemaking Committee.

If the agency head decides in favor of creating a Negotiated Rulemaking Committee, the agency publishes notice of that decision in the Federal Register. The notice includes information about the subject matter to be addressed by the rule, the interests that the agency believes will be significantly affected by the rule, and the proposed membership of the Committee. The public then has a chance to comment. People can also ask to serve on the Committee or nominate other people for membership. Based on the public input, the agency makes a final decision about whether to create the Committee and who should be on it. *See* 5 U.S.C. §§ 564 & 565 (2012).

The Act allows the Committee to pick a facilitator to help it reach consensus. 5 U.S.C. § 566(c) (2012). The Act defines "consensus" to mean "unanimous concurrence among the interests represented on a negotiated rulemaking committee," unless the committee itself agrees to change that definition. *Id.* § 562(2). (Unfortunately, the Act does not say whether, to change the Act's definition of "consensus," the committee must agree unanimously!)

If the Committee reaches consensus on a proposed rule, it reports the proposed rule to the agency. *Id.* § 566(f). The Act does not require the agency to adopt the Committee's proposed rule. But because the agency will have been represented on the Committee by someone authorized to act for the agency, the proposed rule as it comes from the Committee should already have the agency's blessing. At that point, the procedures for adoption of the proposed rule will be governed by the APA and other statutes, because, as mentioned above, the Negotiated Rulemaking Act addresses only the procedure for devising a proposed rule.

Even if the Committee does not reach a consensus on a proposed rule, it may reach a consensus on some issues, which should also be reported to the agency. This can help the agency when it drafts the proposed rule.

The Negotiated Rulemaking Act bars judicial review of "[a]ny action relating to es-tablishing, assisting, or terminating a negotiated rulemaking committee" under the Act. *Id.* § 570. This and other provisions in the Act give agencies almost complete discretion about whether and when to use negotiated rulemaking. The Act does direct the President to designate an agency or interagency committee to encourage the use of this process. *Id.* § 569(a). Despite this encouragement, Professor Lubbers found that its use at the federal level had declined to the point that most negotiated rulemaking proceedings as of 2008 were ones required by agency legislation for specific rules. Lubbers, 49 S. Tex. L. Rev. at 988.

B. Presidential Executive Orders

U.S. Presidents and state Governors issue "executive orders" and similar directives to control the operations of executive-branch agencies. Presidents must control executive-branch agencies because the President is the Chief Executive and required to take care that the laws are faithfully executed. *See* U.S. Const. art. II, § 3. State Governors typically have a similar constitutional obligation faithfully to execute state laws.

An executive order, like an agency rule, may be expressly authorized by statute, in which case the order, like an agency rule, has the force and effect of law; it can define the legal rights and duties of members of the public. *See, e.g., Ass'n for Women in Science v. Califano,* 566 F.2d 339, 344 (D.C. Cir. 1977); *Indep. Meat Packers Ass'n v. Butz,* 526 F.2d 228, 234 (8th Cir. 1975). Even executive directives that lack the force of law, and that therefore cannot define legal rights and duties of the public, still provide marching orders for the executive agencies and officials to which they apply.

Several executive orders create procedural requirements for many federal agency rulemaking proceedings. Before we summarize those orders, we give you background on presidential executive orders.

1. Background on Executive Orders

a. An Executive Order Cannot Conflict with a Valid Statute

Just as a federal agency's rules cannot violate a valid federal statute, other executive-branch directives, including executive orders, cannot violate a valid federal statute. *E.g.*, *Chamber of Commerce v. Reich*, 74 F.3d 1322, 1332–1339 (D.C. Cir. 1996); *Marks v. CIA*, 590 F.2d 997, 1003 (D.C. Cir. 1978). That is because executive orders and other executive-branch law, including agency rules, come below statutes in the pecking order of federal law (and both executive-branch law and statutes are of course subordinate to the Constitution). Reflecting their subordination to valid statutes, executive orders commonly command agencies to do things only "to the extent permitted by law." An agency cannot follow the executive order if doing so conflicts with valid statutory requirements.

For example, Executive Order 12,866 requires federal agencies to adhere to certain "[p]rinciples of [r]egulation," but only "to the extent permitted by law." Exec. Order 12,866, § 1(b), 3 C.F.R. 638 (1994). One principle of regulation directs agencies to consider the costs and benefits of its proposed rules. *Id.* § 1(b) (6). An agency could not, however, consider the costs of a proposed regulation if the statute authorizing that regulation precluded cost considerations. *See, e.g.*, *Whitman v. American Trucking Ass'ns, Inc.*, 531 U.S. 457, 471 (2001) (Clean Air Act provision "unambiguously bars cost considerations" in setting air quality standards). An executive order can add to, but cannot reduce or otherwise modify, statutory requirements.

The upshot is that the executive orders and similar directives can put substantive and procedural requirements on agency rulemaking, as long as the requirements don't conflict with statutory or constitutional requirements.

b. Violations of Executive Orders Are Usually Not Judicially Reviewable

Many executive orders state that they are not judicially enforceable. Here is the provision in Executive Order 12,866, 3 C.F.R. 638 (1994), that says so:

Exec. Order 12866. Regulatory Planning and Review . . .

Sec. 10. Judicial Review. Nothing in this Executive order shall affect any otherwise available judicial review of agency action. This Executive order is intended only to improve the internal management of the Federal Government and does not create any right or benefit, substantive or procedural, enforceable at law or equity by a party against the United States, its agencies or instrumentalities, its officers or employees, or any other person. . . .

Even executive orders that are issued in the exercise of statutory authority and that therefore have the force and effect of law may not be judicially enforceable when they have disclaimers like this. *Compare Indep. Meat Packers Ass'n*, 526 F.2d at 236 (judicial review of agency's violation of executive order was not available unless those challenging the agency's action could "demonstrate that it was intended to create a private right of action"), *with In re Surface Mining Regulation Litigation*, 627 F.2d 1346, 1357 (D.C. Cir. 1980) (implying that judicial review is available for agency violations of executive orders that are based on statutory authority). Indeed, although the case law is somewhat unsettled, the bulk of it indicates that you cannot get judicial enforcement of executive orders.

Because executive orders are generally not judicially enforceable, they too often get treated by many lawyers as the Rodney Dangerfields of administrative law — they get no respect.[1] Sophisticated administrative lawyers, however, recognize that there are ways besides judicial review to ensure agencies obey executive orders, and lawyers use these ways when necessary for good advocacy. For example, Executive Order 12,866 is enforced by an entity in the White House known as the Office of Information and Regulatory Affairs (OIRA). Lawyers who believe an agency is not obeying Executive Order 12,866 can meet with OIRA to point out the agency's deficiencies. In short, although executive orders are not judicially enforceable, they are important means of controlling agency action. *See, e.g.*, Curtis W. Copeland, Congressional Research Service, *Federal Rulemaking: The Role of the Office of Information and Regulatory Affairs* (RL32397, June 2009).

c. Many Executive Orders Do Not Apply at All, or Do Not Apply Fully, to Independent Agencies

Many executive orders are written to exclude independent agencies from some or all of their requirements. The limited applicability of executive orders to independent agency matters, because it contributes to independent agencies' independence from the President. Moreover, when you, as a lawyer, deal with rules made by an independent agency, you should not assume that the executive orders applicable to most agencies will apply to your independent agency. Instead, you must carefully check the executive order's definition of "agency" and other provisions of the executive order to see whether (as is often true) it excludes or applies only in part to independent agencies.

You may wonder why executive orders often do not apply, or do not apply fully, to independent agencies. The answer is unclear. Perhaps Presidents worry that applying executive orders to independent agencies would, in many instances, violate the statutes that establish them as independent agencies. As discussed above, an executive order cannot violate a valid statute.

d. Finding Executive Orders

Finding pertinent executive orders and other executive directives can be tricky. When the President first issues an executive order, it is published in the Federal Register. The President's executive orders are also codified, in chronological order, in Title 3 of the CFR. To locate executive orders on particular subjects, you can search on the commercial databases Westlaw ("Presidential Documents") and LexisNexis ("CIS Index Documents"). For executive orders from 1993 on, you can also search the "Compilation of Presidential Documents" collection on the GPO's publicly available Federal Digital System website: http://www.gpo.gov/fdsys/search/home.action. To find executive orders of state governors, your best bet is probably to begin at the governor's website, because it may publish recent

---

1. Rodney Dangerfield was a great comedian from the second half of the twentieth century. He was famous for self-deprecating jokes that typically began, "I don't get no respect." Example: "With my dog I don't get no respect. He keeps barking at the front door. He don't want to go out. He wants me to leave."

executive orders. For older executive orders of the governor, you may have to contact a bricks-and-mortar law library in the State.

2. Executive Orders on Federal Rulemaking

Among the executive-branch activities that the President seeks to control through executive orders is agency rulemaking. Below we summarize five executive orders on rulemaking. Notice as you read the summaries that the executive orders have substantive objectives they seek to achieve through procedural means. In other words, they require agencies to follow certain procedures to ensure the agencies consider certain substantive matters when rulemaking (to the extent permitted by law).

- Executive Order 12,866, 3 C.F.R. 638 (1993), is entitled "Regulatory Planning and Review." As mentioned above, Executive Order 12,866 sets out "principles" of regulation for all executive-branch federal agencies to follow. For example, one principle is that federal agencies should adopt regulations "only upon a reasoned determination that the benefits of the intended regulation justify its costs." *Id.* §1(b)(6). Also, Executive Order 12,866 requires federal agencies, other than independent agencies, to do a cost-benefit analysis of every economically significant proposed rule and to submit that analysis, along with the proposed rule, for review by an entity mentioned earlier in this section, the Office of Information and Regulatory Affairs (OIRA). *Id.* §§3(f)(1) & 6(a)(3)(B) & (C). (The cost-benefit analysis that Executive Order 12,866 requires is similar to the regulatory analysis required by the Unfunded Mandate Reform Act, which was discussed above.) OIRA reviews proposed rules "so that each agency's regulatory actions are consistent with applicable law, the President's priorities, and the principles [of regulation], and do not conflict with the policies or actions of another agency." *Id.* §6(b). OIRA cannot veto a proposed rule, but it can return the proposed rule to the agency "for further consideration." *Id.* §6(b)(3). In addition, OIRA objections can lead an agency to withdraw a proposed rule. "[D]isagreements or conflicts" that arise between the agency and OIRA and that cannot be resolved by the Administrator of OIRA "shall be resolved by the President with the assistance" of other officials. *Id.* §7(a).
- Executive Order 13,045, 3 C.F.R. 198 (1998), is entitled "Protection of Children From Environmental Health Risks and Safety Risks." It applies to major rules that "concern an environmental health risk or safety risk that an agency has reason to believe may disproportionately affect children." *Id.* §2-202(b). It requires an agency to gather information on the risk and give it to the OIRA to consider when reviewing a rule under Executive Order 12,866. *See* Executive Order 13,045, §5-501.
- Executive Order 13,132, 3 C.F.R. 206 (2000), is entitled "Federalism." It applies to rules that "have substantial direct effects on the States, on the relationship between the national government and the States, or on the distribution of power and responsibilities among the various levels of government." *Id.* §1(a). This order requires agencies to be sensitive to state concerns and to consult with state and local officials. *Id.* §§3 & 6; *see also* Presidential Memorandum on Preemption for the Heads of Executive Departments and Agencies, 74 Fed. Reg. 24,693 (May 20, 2009) (announcing policy for agency rulemaking and other agency actions that preempt state law).
- Executive Order 13,175, 3 C.F.R. 304 (2001), is entitled "Consultation and Coordination With Indian Tribal Governments." It applies to rules that "have substantial

direct effects on one or more Indian tribes, on the relationship between the Federal Government and Indian tribes, or on the distribution of power and responsibilities between the Federal Government and Indian tribes." Id. § 1(a). This order requires agencies to consult with Indian tribes about covered rules. *Id.* § 5(a). In addition, it directs agencies to prepare "tribal impact statements" for covered rules that impose "unfunded mandates" on Indian tribes, unless such mandates are required by federal statute. *Id.* § 5(b).

• Executive Order 12,630, 3 C.F.R. 554 (1989), is entitled "Governmental Actions and Interference With Constitutionally Protected Property Rights." It applies to "rules ... [or] regulations that propose or implement licensing, permitting, or other condition requirements or limitations on private property use." *Id.* § 2(a). It aims to minimize the impact of federal rules on people's use of private property.

Believe it or not, these are only some of the executive orders that may apply to a federal agency rulemaking. As discussed above, executive orders tend to get little respect outside of the agencies, because they are generally not judicially enforceable. They do, however, absorb agencies' time and attention, for they are commands of the President.

Exercise: Using Secondary Material to Identify Required Rulemaking Procedures

The objective of this exercise is to identify two useful secondary sources of information on legally required procedures for federal rulemaking. More generally, this exercise illustrates the usefulness of secondary material for administrative law research projects.

Professor Mark Seidenfeld published *A Table of Requirements for Federal Administrative Rulemaking* in 27 Fla. St. U. L. Rev. 533 (2000). Although the table is now more than 10 years old, it is a useful starting point.

The federal government has published a useful flowchart of federal rulemaking at www.reginfo.gov/public/reginfo/Regmap/regmap.pdf. It refers to many of the executive orders and other laws that govern federal agency rulemaking.

Find these two sources and look them over in enough detail to appreciate how the information they provide compares to the information this book provides. In addition, if you're interested specifically in the role of the OIRA in reviewing federal agency rules, you can find a useful flow chart in Curtis W. Copeland, Congressional Research Service, *Federal Rulemaking: The Role of the Office of Information and Regulatory Affairs* 16 (RL32397, June 2009), http://www.fas.org/sgp/crs/misc/RL32397.pdf.

C. Dealing with the Complexity of Federal Rulemaking

We hope it is clear by now that there are many potential, external sources of procedural requirements for federal rulemaking. This book has introduced you only to the major federal statutes and executive orders potentially applicable to federal rulemaking. The multiplicity of potentially applicable laws raises an issue for the legal system and an issue for lawyers.

The issue for the legal system is whether federal rulemaking procedures are too complicated. For example, do federal rulemaking procedures take so much agency time and effort that they prevent agencies from adopting needed rules when they are needed? Are they so complicated that ordinary members of the public cannot meaningfully participate, so "public input" is limited to wealthy, sophisticated interest groups? The increasing complexity of rulemaking procedures is called "ossification" by some people, to indicate that, as procedural requirements increase, rulemaking becomes more rigid. *See, e.g.,* Thomas O. McGarity, *Some Thoughts on "Deossifying" the Rulemaking Process,* 41 Duke L.J. 1385 (1992).

The issue for lawyers is how to learn and keep up with all legally required rulemaking procedures. This challenge arises throughout administrative law because of its sprawling and dynamic nature. Many lawyers respond to the challenge by specializing in certain substantive areas of administrative law, such as food and drug law, banking regulation, telecommunications, etc. In addition, lawyers use these sources to keep abreast of rulemaking developments:

- Government Websites

The OIRA, which conducts centralized review of federal agency rules under E.O. 12,866, has many resources on federal rulemaking, and regular visits to its website help lawyers keep abreast of changes in legally required procedures.

   http://www.reginfo.gov/public/ (see, in particular, the "FAQs/Resources" tab)

State-government websites ordinarily include information about the executive branch, which may give you access to the governor's executive orders and other information relevant to state agency rulemaking.

- Bar Association Publications

The American Bar Association has a Section of Administrative Law and Regulatory Practice that produces several valuable publications on federal administrative law, including:

1. Jeffrey S. Lubbers, *A Guide to Federal Agency Rulemaking* (4th ed. 2006). This guide tells you everything you need to know about the federal rulemaking process in general.

2. *Developments in Administrative Law and Regulatory Practice,* an annual publication that includes discussion of statutes, regulations, and court decisions on federal agency rulemaking.

3. *A Guide to Judicial and Political Review of Federal Agencies* (John F. Duffy & Michael eds. 2005), which discusses many issues relevant to judicial review of federal agency rules.

Many state bars include sections on administrative law, which can be a useful resource for keeping up-to-date on that State's administrative law.

- Commercial Sources

Many companies publish information to update lawyers on developments in various areas of administrative law. One useful general periodical is Pike & Fischer's *AdLaw Bulletin,* a monthly publication that covers developments in federal rulemaking and other administrative law topics.

In addition, commercial legal databases such as Westlaw and LexisNexis offer "clipping" services that can be customized to keep you abreast of developments in any area of law, including your favorite area of administrative law.

D. State Laws

A State's law, like federal law, usually includes cross-cutting statutes besides the APA that apply to multiple agencies' rulemaking proceedings. Further, the State's governor, like the President, can issue executive orders that impose additional procedural requirements on state agency rulemaking. This section mentions three kinds of state laws that many States have and that resemble federal laws discussed earlier in this chapter.

First, many States have "little NEPAs" requiring state agencies to assess the environmental impact of major state government actions, which can include state agency rulemaking. *See* Daniel R. Mandelker, NEPA Law and Litigation § 12:2, at 12-6–12-9 (2d ed. 2011).

Second, many States require state agencies to do cost-benefit analyses of proposed rule, as Executive Order 12,866 and the Unfunded Mandate Reform Act require for many proposed federal rules. *See* Robert W. Hahn, *Cost-Benefit Analysis: Legal, Economic, and Philosophical Perspectives*, 29 J. Legal Stud. 873 (2000). The requirement to do a cost-benefit analysis is built into the 2010 Model State APA (§ 305, entitled "Regulatory Analysis").

Third, many States require some or all agency rules to be reviewed by the state legislature, or a subpart of it, before they take effect. 3 Charles H. Koch, Jr., Administrative Law and Practice § 7.51, at 58–59 (2010). The idea behind this requirement, like the analogous requirement for "major" federal rules under the Congressional Review Act, is to give the legislature a chance to disapprove newly adopted regulations.

The moral of the story is that lawyers whose practice includes state agency rulemaking must be aware that multiple laws besides the state APA and state agency statute may be a source of procedural requirements.

E. Chapter 15 Wrap Up and Look Ahead

This chapter has introduced you to federal statutes and executive orders that are a source of procedural requirements for many federal rulemaking proceedings. It has made clear that States also have cross-cutting statutes and executive directives that apply to stage agency rulemaking. We hope that, from your study of the material in this chapter, you will recognize these provisions if you encounter them in practice and recall roughly what they concern. We also hope this chapter sensitizes you to the importance of identifying all potential sources of procedural requirements when analyzing the procedural validity of an agency rule.

The next chapter assumes that a legislative rule is procedurally and substantively valid and explores the question: What is the effect of a valid legislative rule?

Professional Development Reflection Questions

In most law school courses, you don't need to locate the material you need to learn. It's presented to you on a silver platter—well, in a casebook or course supplement, anyway. In contrast, practicing lawyers are presented with a problems (e.g., a client has a dispute with a government agency) or a project (e.g., the client needs a government permit), and the lawyer must find the material for addressing the problem or carrying out the project. Most of what the lawyer learns is learned for specific legal projects, but that project-specific type of learning is not enough, which is why most jurisdictions require lawyers to do continuing legal education (CLE).

In reality, the best lawyers do not rely on CLE programs to stay up to date in their fields. Instead, they develop habits and resources tailored to their needs and those of their clients. You might call these "do it yourself" (DIY) CLE methods. Several types of DIY CLE methods for administrative lawyers are described in this chapter. You will find it easier to use these methods as a lawyer if you start doing some DIY CLE as a law student.

With that in mind, we pose this question/challenge:

What is one, new method you could develop and stick to for learning about legal developments? Some new methods could include the following:

- Subscribing to a blog on an area of law in which you are likely to practice, and regularly reading its postings.

- Reading the "advance sheets" of opinions from the Supreme Court of the State in which you intend to practice.

- Meeting for lunch every two weeks with a lawyer practicing in an area in which you are interested.

Chapter 16

Legal Effect of a Valid Legislative Rule When Published

Overview

Chapter 7 introduced the principle that valid legislative rules have "the force and effect of law." *Chrysler Corp. v. Brown*, 441 U.S. 281, 295 (1979) (internal quotation marks omitted). At its heart, the principle means that valid legislative rules operate much like statutes. For example, violation of a legislative rule, like violation of a statute, can carry civil and criminal penalties.

This Chapter discusses three more ways that valid legislative rules operate like statutes:

- Like statutes, legislative rules sometimes operate retroactively.

- Like statutes, legislative rules, when properly published, put the public on notice of their contents.

- Like federal statutes, a federal agency's legislative rules can preempt state law.

We take up these features of legislative rules now, as we end our study of the legislative rulemaking process, because they concern the end products of that process. We could have discussed these features of legislative rules at the beginning of our study of rulemaking, because they reflect the earlier-discussed principle that a valid legislative rule operates like a statute. We deferred the discussion until now, however, because our earlier discussion of the principle focused primarily on distinguishing legislative rules from non-legislative rules, rather than on detailing similarities between legislative rules and statutes.

The titles of this chapter's sections are as follows:

A. Retroactive (Also Known as "Retrospective") Rules

B. Effect of Publication of Legislative Rules

C. Federal Regulatory Preemption

D. Chapter 16 Wrap Up and Look Ahead

Chapter Problem 1

Email

From: Judge

To: Judicial Clerk

Re: Homeland Security Case

I need your take on a new case. Mr. B is the plaintiff in the case; he challenges a decision of the defendant Transportation Security Administration (TSA), a federal agency within the Department of Homeland Security. Mr. B argues that TSA has applied a TSA rule to him retroactively, and that TSA lacks the authority to make retroactive rules. Here's the background.

A federal statute prohibits a State from licensing someone to transport hazardous waste unless TSA has checked the person's background and certified that the person poses no security risk. 49 U.S.C. § 5103a(a)(1) (2012). TSA implemented this federal statute by issuing a "threat assessment regulation" in 2003. TSA's 2003 threat assessment regulation creates a presumption that people convicted of certain crimes pose a security risk. The regulation allows someone to overcome that presumption only by submitting evidence satisfying TSA that the person is not actually a security risk.

Mr. B applied to California for a driver's license to transport hazardous waste commercially. California denied the license because TSA refused to certify that Mr. B posed no security risk. TSA determined that, under the 2003 regulation, Mr. B. is presumptively a security risk because he was convicted of possessing a bomb in 1975. TSA also determined that Mr. B did not overcome that presumption. Mr. B now sues TSA challenging its denial of certification.

Mr. B argues that TSA is applying its 2003 threat assessment regulation retroactively by considering a 1975 conviction. He further argues that TSA lacks authority to issue retroactive rules.

I would like your analysis of the first argument: Did TSA apply its rules retroactively by considering the 1975 conviction? Thanks!

Chapter Problem 2

Intake Interview Memo

From: Legal Aid Intern

To: Legal Aid Attorney

Re: Cynthia Harrison

Cynthia Harrison began receiving benefits from the Social Security Administration (SSA) in January. She would have applied for them 10 years ago — and it appears that she would have been eligible to begin receiving them 10 years ago — except that an employee at the local SSA office told her at the time — incorrectly, it appears — that she was not eligible.

An SSA legislative rule states that, to get SSA benefits, a person must file a written application and that no benefits can be awarded for any period prior to the filing of a written application. Ms. Harrison did not file a written application until last November, because until then she relied on the official who told her

10 years ago that she was not eligible. Now Ms. Harrison wants to recover the 10 years' worth of benefits for which it appears she would have been eligible if she had not relied on the bad advice from the local SSA office.

I told Ms. Harrison one of our attorneys would get back to her. Her contact info is below.

Thanks!

Chapter Problem 3

Interoffice Memo

From: Petra Partner

To: Alexia Associate

Re: Cortés case

Farmer Luis Cortés lost last fall's soybean crop because he used a new pesticide called Roust on it that killed the crop (as well as the bugs). My preliminary research suggests that Mr. Cortés may have several plausible claims against the manufacturer of Roust: negligent design; negligent manufacture; negligent testing; fraudulent labeling; negligent labeling; and breach of express warranty. All those claims would be based on our State's common law of torts and contracts.

I am worried, though, that some or all of these state common-law claims might be preempted by the Federal Insecticide, Fungicide, and Rodenticide Act (FIFRA). FIFRA says that a State "shall not impose or continue in effect any requirements for labeling or packaging in addition to or different from those required under [the Act.]" 7 U.S.C. § 136v(b) (2012). I have confirmed that FIFRA comprehensively regulates the labeling and packaging of Roust. Under FIFRA, EPA has promulgated legislative rules that require pesticide labeling and packaging to be accurate and complete. Moreover, as required by FIFRA, EPA specifically approved the proposed packaging and labeling for Roust.

Please give me a background memo describing how courts will analyze the preemption issue. Thanks.

A. Retroactive (Also Known as "Retrospective") Rules

Most legislative rules, like most statutes, operate only prospectively. A rule or statute, for example, prohibiting cellphone use while driving will punish people for that conduct only if it occurs after the rule is promulgated or the statute is enacted. Indeed, the federal APA defines **"rule"** to mean an agency statement **"of future effect."** 5 U.S.C. §551(4) (2012). Some legislative rules, however—like some statutes—operate based on past events. Not all such rules are "retroactive," and not all retroactive rules are invalid. A rule that operates based on past events raises two issues:

(1) Is the rule retroactive?

(2) If so, may the agency make retroactive rules?

As discussed below, it can be hard to tell if a particular rule is retroactive as applied to a particular situation. Beyond that, if you determine that a rule is being retroactively applied, you then face the challenge of determining whether the retroactive application is authorized by statute and is constitutional.

1. Determining Whether a Rule Is Retroactive

Two statements of the U.S. Supreme Court illustrate the difficulty of identifying retroactivity. On the one hand, the Court has described a retroactive law as one that "attaches new legal consequences to events completed before" the law's adoption. *Landgraf v. USI Film Prods.*, 511 U.S. 244, 269 (1994). On the other hand, the Court has said that a law "is not made retroactive merely because it draws upon antecedent facts [i.e., facts predating its adoption] for its operation." *Id.* at 269 n.24. How can a law "draw upon antecedent facts for its operation" without "attaching new legal consequences" to those facts? The Court has given guidance for answering that question when posed by federal agency legislative rules, and some state courts have followed that guidance to determine whether state statutes and state agency rules are retroactive.

a. Rules That Are Clearly Retroactive

Here is a clearly retroactive rule. Suppose the EPA publishes a final rule on January 1, 2013, that prohibits the manufacture of bullets containing lead. Also suppose that a violation of the rule exposes the violator to a large civil fine. Finally, suppose that the rule says it applies to all bullets manufactured after 1970. This rule is retroactive as applied to bullets manufactured before January 1, 2013. The rule is retroactive as to these bullets because it creates civil liability for conduct that occurred before the rule's adoption. *See Landgraf*, 511 U.S. at 280.

Our hypothetical bullet rule is retroactive even if, when the EPA publishes it as a final rule in the Federal Register on January 1, 2013, the EPA states that the rule's effective date is thirty days later, as required by federal APA § 553(d). All that means is that EPA will not begin *enforcing* the bullet rule until February 2013. The delayed effective date for enforcement may satisfy the federal APA's definition of **"rule"** as a statement of **"future effect."** 5 U.S.C. § 551(4) (2012). But the bullet rule will still be retroactive if EPA enforces it against companies for manufacturing bullets before January 1, 2013.

Exercise: Identifying Clearly Retroactive Rules

Using the bullet rule example, come up with your own hypothetical rule that is clearly retroactive. It may help to use a familiar context, such as a law school rule about class attendance.

---

b. Rules That Are Not Retroactive

Two recurring situations arise that do not involve retroactive rules but that are often thought to do so. In the first situation, an agency changes a rule after someone has applied for a government benefit or permit, and the agency applies the changed rule to deny the benefit or permit. In the second situation, an agency clarifies or interprets an existing rule or statute to someone's detriment.

The first situation arose in *Pine Tree Medical Associates v. Secretary of Health & Human Services*, 127 F.3d 118 (1st Cir. 1997). A medical clinic applied to the U.S. Department of Health and Human Services (HHS), asking HHS to designate the community served by the clinic a "medically underserved population" (MUP). If HHS granted that application, the clinic would get a higher rate of federal reimbursement for serving Medicare and Medicaid patients in that community. After the clinic filed the application, HHS changed the rules for designating a community an MUP; the change made it harder for the clinic to get the MUP designation. Indeed, HHS denied the clinic's application under the new rules, and the clinic sought judicial review of the denial.

The clinic argued in court that HHS should judge the clinic's application under the rules in effect when the clinic filed the application, because use of the changed rules to judge its application would make them "retroactive." The court disagreed. The court explained, "[T]he mere filing of an application is not the kind of completed transaction in which a party could fairly expect stability of the relevant laws as of the transaction date." *Pine Tree*, 127 F.3d at 121. *Pine Tree* shows that the mere filing of an application does not freeze the status quo, such that any change in applicable law thereafter will be considered "retroactive" if applied to that application.

The second situation involves agency clarifications or interpretations of existing rules. This situation arose in *Levy v. Sterling Holding Co., Inc.*, 544 F.3d 493 (3rd Cir. 2008). Mark Levy sued two companies for violating the Securities Exchange Act of 1934. The companies claimed that existing SEC rules exempted them from liability under the 1934 Act. The federal district court agreed and dismissed Mr. Levy's complaint. The United States Court of Appeals for the Third Circuit reversed, holding that the SEC's rules did not exempt the companies from liability. The Third Circuit remanded the case to the district court for further proceedings.

While the case was on remand, the SEC amended its rules to "clarify" the scope of the exemption. The amended SEC rules plainly *did* exempt from statutory liability the two companies that Mr. Levy had sued. Mr. Levy argued that the amended SEC rules could not be applied retroactively to defeat his lawsuit. The federal district court rejected that argument and entered summary judgment for the companies, finding them within the SEC's exemption rules.

On appeal, the Third Circuit affirmed, holding that application of the SEC's amended rules to Mr. Levy's case was not retroactive. The court relied on the principle that "where a new rule constitutes a clarification—rather than a substantive change—of the law as it existed beforehand, the application of that new rule to pre-promulgation conduct necessarily does not have an impermissible retroactive effect." *Levy*, 544 F.3d at 506. The court analogized an agency's clarification of an existing rule to a court's decision interpreting an unclear statute: "A rule simply clarifying an unsettled or confusing area of law ... is no more retroactive in its operation than is a judicial determination construing and applying a statute to a case at hand." *Id.* at 506 (internal quotation marks and some citations omitted) (quoting in part *Manhattan Gen. Equip. Co. v. Comm'r*, 297 U.S. 129, 135 (1936)).

No doubt people feel unfairly treated when, after applying for an agency permit or benefit, the agency changes the rules to make the permit or benefit harder to get; or when an agency clarifies or interprets an existing rule to someone's detriment. But neither situation involves retroactivity. In neither situation, therefore, does the agency need authority to make retroactive rules or need to defend its application against constitutional restrictions on retroactive rules.

c. Hard Cases and the Principles for Analyzing Them

An example of a hard retroactivity case is *Combs v. Commissioner of Social Security*, 459 F.3d 640 (6th Cir. 2006) (en banc). *Combs* also introduces a third, recurring situation that courts often treat as not involving retroactivity despite arguments to the contrary: Changes in procedural rules for adjudication are often not considered retroactive as applied to cases pending when the changes occurred.

Barbara Combs applied to the Social Security Administration (SSA) for disability insurance benefits under the Social Security Act. Ms. Combs claimed that her obesity made her eligible for those benefits. At the time of her application, SSA rules automatically treated obesity as a qualifying disability if it caused certain symptoms, such as high blood pressure. By the time SSA ruled on Ms. Comb's application, however, SSA had changed its rules to make it harder for people with obesity to show that they met the statutory standard for eligibility. Under the new rules, obesity with the symptoms identified in the old rule no longer led automatically to a conclusion of eligibility. SSA denied Ms. Combs' application under the new rules. She sought judicial review of SSA's denial of benefits.

The case was ultimately decided by the United States Court of Appeals for the Sixth Circuit sitting en banc. Fifteen judges participated in the Sixth Circuit's en banc decision. *Combs v. Comm'r of Soc. Security*, 459 F.3d 640 (6th Cir. 2006). The Sixth Circuit held that SSA's application of its new rules to Ms. Combs did not make the rules "retroactive." The fifteen judges deciding the case collectively produced four opinions, none of which had a support of the majority. The "lead" opinion, supported by seven of the fifteen judges, emphasized that the change in rules changed the *procedure* that SSA used for determining disability, rather than changing the substantive requirements for eligibility. The lead opinion relied on the principle that "changes to procedural rules generally do not have retroactive effects." *Id.* at 647 (Rogers, J.). This principle reflects a third recurring situation — namely, changes in procedural rules for adjudications — that courts ordinarily treat as not involving retroactivity.

An eighth judge concurred in the conclusion that SSA was not applying its rules retroactively. This judge, however, did not join the lead opinion's reliance on the supposedly procedural nature of the change in the rules. Instead, he reasoned that Ms. Combs did not, merely by applying for benefits, acquire any "vested right" to have her application judged by the rules in effect on the date of her application. This judge saw the case as analogous to *Pine Tree*, which was discussed above. *Id.* at 654–655 (Gilman, J., concurring in the judgment).

The judges in *Combs* agreed, as have many courts, that a major precedent for determining the retroactivity of an agency's legislative rule is *Landgraf*, 511 U.S. 244. *Landgraf* addressed whether a *statute* was retroactive, but lower federal courts and state courts have relied on *Landgraf* to analyze the retroactivity of legislative rules. *Landgraf* gives us the following guidance:

- The *Landgraf* Court approvingly quoted Justice Story's description of a retroactive law as one that "takes away or impairs vested rights acquired under existing laws, or creates a new obligation, imposes a new duty, or attaches a new disability, in respect to transactions or considerations already past." *Landgraf*, 511 U.S. at 269 (quoting *Soc'y for Propagation of the Gospel v. Wheeler*, 22 F. Cas. 756 (C.C.N.H. 1814)). The *Landgraf* Court used similar wording in its own description of the test for a retroactive law: "whether [the law] would impair rights a party possessed when he acted, increase a party's liability for past conduct, or impose new duties with respect to transactions already completed." 511 U.S. at 280; *cf. id.* at 269 (to determine retroactivity, "the court must ask whether the new provision attaches new legal consequences to events completed before its enactment").

- The *Landgraf* Court said, "A statute does not operate 'retrospectively' merely because [1] it is applied in a case arising from conduct antedating the statute's enactment ... or [2] upsets expectations based in prior law." *Id.* at 269 (bracketed numerals added). The *Landgraf* Court cited as an example of situation [1] *Cox v. Hart*, 260 U.S. 427 (1922). *Cox* involved a dispute between two people claiming ownership of public land. The Court in *Cox* resolved the dispute in favor of the person who had entered the land first and begun developing it. In resolving the dispute this way, the Court relied on a statute that was enacted *after* both disputants had entered onto the disputed land and begun developing it. The *Cox* Court held that the statute was not retroactive merely because it was applied to pre-enactment conduct (namely, entry onto, and development of land, by the earlier entrant). *Cox*, 260 U.S. at 435. The *Landgraf* Court cited as an example of situation [2] a new law prohibiting gambling in a jurisdiction where someone has bought land and started building a casino on it. 511 U.S. at 269 n.24.

- The *Landgraf* Court said, "The conclusion that a particular rule operates 'retroactively' [requires consideration of] the nature and extent of the change in the law and the degree of connection between the operation of the new rule and a relevant past event." *Id.* at 271. The Court added: "[F]amiliar considerations of fair notice, reasonable reliance, and settled expectations offer sound guidance." *Id.*

- The *Landgraf* Court said, "Changes in procedural rules may often be applied in suits arising before their enactment without raising concerns about retroactivity.... Because rules of procedure regulate secondary rather than primary conduct, the fact that a new procedural rule was instituted after the conduct giving rise to the suit does not make application of the rule at trial retroactive." *Id.* at 275.

Although the Court's statement in the last bullet point concerned changes in rules of *court* procedure that occur after a *lawsuit* is filed, the principle also applies to changes in rules of *agency* procedure that occur after an *administrative* case—such as an application for government benefits or a permit—has been filed. As mentioned above, one judge in the *Combs* case relied on this principle to reject a retroactivity challenge to changes in SSA rules for adjudicating disability claims based on obesity.

Now that you have read the criteria for retroactivity, you can appreciate why arguments that an agency rule is retroactive arise regularly. Agencies often adopt rules in response to a pre-existing problem. Such responsive rules often operate based on events pre-dating their adoption. That is simply to say, they are intended to address the problem that prompted their adoption.

Here is an example: A State's Department of Public Health (DPH) has statutory authority to license nurse aides and to issue legislative rules establishing requirements for getting and keeping a nurse aide's license. DPH finds, after a formal adjudication, that nurse aide Patricia Miller has committed patient abuse. After that adjudication, DPH promulgates a legislative rule prohibiting someone who has been found guilty of patient abuse from holding a nurse aide's license. Is this rule retroactive as applied to take away Ms. Miller's license? The state appellate court answered "yes"; that application of the rule was retroactive. *Miller v. DeBuono*, 652 N.Y.S.2d 313, 314 (N.Y. App. Div. 1997). To test your understanding of retroactivity, figure out how that conclusion is supported by the *Landgraf* principles summarized above. Also consider how those principles might be used to argue against the court's conclusion.

Landgraf and other U.S. Supreme Court precedent do not yield a clear framework for identifying retroactivity. The precedent, does, however, establish relevant considerations that both lower federal courts and some state courts have used to determine whether a particular application of a law is retroactive. *See, e.g., Thomas v. Color Country Mg'mt*, 84 P.3d 1201, 1210 (Utah 2004) ("While we have not, in the past, expressly aligned Utah law with federal court pronouncements on retroactive application of statutory amendments, the federal rule is entirely sound."); *see also Citizens for Equity v. N.J. Dep't of Env'tl Protection*, 599 A.2d 516, 524–525 (N.J. Super. Ct. App. Div. 1990) (relying on federal and state precedent to determine whether a state agency rule was retroactive). States can adopt their own distinctive ways of determining retroactivity, except when addressing federal constitutional challenges, and one State has done so. *See, e.g., Porter v. Galarneau*, 911 P.2d 1143, 1148–1150 (Mont. 1996) (discussing U.S. Supreme Court precedent on determining retroactivity and departing from it in one way).

Exercise: Devising an Analytic Approach for Identifying Retroactive Rules

The case law on retroactivity does not give us a precise formula for analyzing retroactivity. We can identify, however, three features of the law that, taken together, imply a loose framework.

1. The Court in *Landgraf* gave three descriptions of a retroactive law. Most broadly, the Court described a retroactive law as one that "attaches new legal consequences" to events occurring before the law's adoption. 511 U.S. at 269. That description seems too broad, however, to identify retroactive laws. Elsewhere in its opinion, the Court described retroactive laws more restrictively, as occurring only when *certain* new legal consequences attach to prior events. Specifically, the Court said a retroactive law "impair[s] rights a party possessed when he acted, increase[s] a party's liability for past conduct, or impose[s] new duties with respect to transactions already completed." *Id.* at 280. A third description, similar to the second, said a retroactive law "takes away or impairs vested rights acquired under existing laws, or creates a new obligation, imposes a new duty, or attaches a new disability, in respect to transactions or considerations already past." *Id.* at 269 (quoting *Soc'y for Propagation of the Gospel v. Wheeler*, 22 F. Cas. 756 (C.C.N.H. 1814)). The latter two descriptions overlap but are not entirely consistent, and they both contain ambiguous terms. Yet they are used by courts to analyze retroactivity, and so administrative lawyers must use them, too. It's fair to say that if a rule has one of the characteristics identified in these latter two descriptions, it is probably retroactive.

2. The Court in *Landgraf* and lower courts have identified certain situations when rules are usually *not* treated as retroactive—i.e., changes in rules occurring after an application for benefits or a permit; clarifications of existing laws; and changes in procedural rules.

3. The Court in *Landgraf* identified relevant factors for determining retroactivity—which will be especially useful in hard cases—such as "fair notice, reasonable reliance, and settled expectations." 511 U.S. at 270.

Please use these three features of the case law to create an ordered checklist of questions, flow chart, or other graphic organizer for retroactivity analysis.

2. Determining Whether an Agency May Adopt Retroactive Legislative Rules

If you determine that an agency's legislative rule is retroactive, then you must determine if the agency may properly make retroactive rules. This further determination actually involves two sub-issues: First, does the agency have statutory authority to make retroactive rules? Second, is the exercise of that power constitutional? You have to answer both questions "yes" for the retroactive application of a rule to be valid. We will discuss these issues in reverse order.

a. Federal Constitutional Restrictions on Retroactive Laws

The constitutionality of retroactive laws is often studied in courses on constitutional law. We will touch only briefly on the constitutional issue here.

The Due Process Clauses restrict, but do not completely bar, retroactive statutes and legislative rules. Instead, the Court has said that a retroactive law, when challenged on due process grounds, bears a greater burden of justification than a prospective law:

> The Due Process Clause ... protects the interests in fair notice and repose that may be compromised by retroactive legislation; a justification sufficient to validate a statute's prospective application under the Clause may not suffice to warrant its retroactive application.

Landgraf, 511 U.S. at 266. Even so, the Court has often rejected due process challenges to retroactive statutes. *See, e.g., Usery v. Turner Elkhorn Mining Co.*, 428 U.S. 1, 15–20 (1976) (rejecting due process challenge to federal statute that made coal companies retroactively liable for compensation to former employees who got black lung disease). Likewise, the lower federal courts have rejected due process challenges to federal statutes such as the Superfund Law, which imposes retroactive liability on land owners for the costs of cleaning up toxic waste sites created before Congress enacted the Superfund Law. *See United States v. Alcan Aluminum Corp.*, 315 F.3d 179, 188 (2d Cir. 2003).

The U.S. Constitution's Ex Post Facto Clauses also restrict retroactive federal and state laws. *See* U.S. Const. art. I, § 9, cl. 3; *id.* art. I, § 10, cl. 1. The Ex Post Facto Clauses apply, however, only to criminal laws and laws that, though labeled "civil" by the legislature or agency that made them, are "so punitive either in purpose or effect as to negate" the "civil" label. *Smith v. Doe*, 538 U.S. 84, 92 (2003) (sex offender notification and registration law did not violate Ex Post Facto Clause). An example of a legislative rule that violates the Ex Post Facto Clause is a rule governing the pardon and parole process that increased the time spent in prison by someone sentenced before the rule was adopted. *See Garner v. Jones.* 529 U.S. 244 (2000). Aside from rules affecting prison sentences or other criminal punishments, it will be rare for a legislative rule to implicate the Ex Post Facto Clauses.

The takeaway is that the Due Process Clause and Ex post Facto Clauses do restrict retroactive legislative rules but will seldom invalidate those rules.

b. Federal Agency Authority to Make Retroactive Rules

Retroactive legislative rules must not only satisfy constitutional restrictions on retroactive laws. They must also fall within the agency's statutory grant of rulemaking authority. In this respect, retroactive legislative rules are no different from any other legislative rule.

The U.S. Supreme Court has adopted a presumption against interpreting federal statutes to authorize retroactive legislative rules. The basis for the presumption is that retroactive legislative rules, like retroactive statutes, are disfavored. The Court adopted the presumption against interpreting federal statutes to authorize retroactive legislative rules in *Bowen v. Georgetown University Hospital*, 488 U.S. 204 (1988), summarized next.

- *Bowen v. Georgetown University Hospital*, 488 U.S. 204 (1988)

In *Georgetown Hospital*, the U.S. Department of Health and Human Services (HHS) changed the rules under which hospitals received Medicare reimbursement for caring for Medicare patients. The changes decreased Medicare reimbursement. The changes applied not only to care provided by hospitals after the rule was adopted but also to care provided (and costs incurred) before the rule was adopted. The Court invalidated the retroactive feature of the new rules, holding that HHS lacked authority to adopt retroactive rules.

The *Georgetown Hospital* Court began with the principle that "an administrative agency's power to promulgate legislative regulations is limited to the authority delegated by Congress." *Georgetown Hospital*, 488 U.S. at 208. Then it explained how to analyze a statutory grant of rulemaking authority to determine if it grants power to make retroactive legislative rules:

> Retroactivity is not favored in the law. Thus, congressional enactments and ad-ministrative rules will not be construed to have retroactive effect unless their language requires this result. By the same principle, a statutory grant of legislative rulemaking authority will not, as a general matter, be understood to encompass the power to promulgate retroactive rules unless that power is conveyed by Congress in express terms. *See Brimstone R. Co. v. United States*, 276 U.S. 104, 122 (1928) ("The power to require readjustments for the past is drastic. It … ought not to be extended so as to permit unreasonably harsh action without very plain words"). Even where some substantial justification for retroactive rulemaking is presented, courts should be reluctant to find such authority absent an express statutory grant.

Id. at 208–209. *Georgetown Hospital* adopts a principle of statutory interpretation, amounting to a presumption, under which federal statutes generally will not be interpreted to grant retroactive rulemaking power unless they do so expressly. *See Henry Ford Health Sys. v. Dep't of Health & Human Servs.*, 654 F.3d 660, 667 (6th Cir. 2011).

Some federal statutes do expressly authorize retroactive rulemaking. Indeed, after *Georgetown Hospital*, Congress amended the Medicare statute at issue in that case expressly to authorize HHS to make retroactive rules. As amended, the statute authorizes HHS to make retroactive rules if "such retroactive application is necessary to comply with statutory requirements … or … failure to apply the change retroactively would be contrary to the public interest." 42 U.S.C. § 1395hh(e)(1)(A) (2012). Another statute expressly authorizing retroactive rules is in the federal Internal Revenue Code. The Code gives the Secretary of the Treasury broad power to make "all needful rules and regulations for the enforcement" of the Code. 26 U.S.C. § 7805(a) (2012). This grant of power includes the power to make retroactive rules "to prevent abuse" of the tax system. *Id.* § 7805(b)(3).

Congress rarely gives federal agencies express authority to make retroactive legislative rules. Federal agencies often apply their legislative rules, however, in ways that "dra[w] upon antecedent facts" and that accordingly provoke retroactivity objections. *Landgraf*, 511 U.S. at 269 n.24. This discussion of retroactivity equips you, we hope, to analyze those instances.

Exercise: Identifying Retroactive Laws

1. Explain why the Medicare rule addressed in *Georgetown Hospital* was retroactive using the *Landgraf* definitions.

2. Explain why the Medicare rule addressed in *Georgetown Hospital* did not fall into one of the three recurring situations that, courts have found, do not involve retroactivity.

---

3. State Law on Retroactive Rulemaking by State Agencies

State courts do not have to apply the *Georgetown Hospital* presumption when they interpret state statutes to determine whether those state statutes grant retroactive rulemaking power. Even so, some state courts do take a similar approach. *See Kaho'ohanohano v. Dep't of Human Servs.*, 178 P.3d 538, 586–587 (Hawai'i 2008); *City of Cordova v. Medicaid Rate Comm'n*, 789 P.2d 346, 350 (Alaska 1990). In these States, a state statute may be interpreted to grant retroactive rulemaking power if it does so expressly. *See Alford v. City and County of Honolulu*, 109 P.3d 809, 823 (Hawaii 2005).

As noted above, the Due Process Clause of the 14th Amendment restricts retroactive state statutes and legislative rules. Further limits on retroactive state statutes and state agency rules may come from state constitutions and state statutes. For example, the Texas Constitution expressly prohibits any "retroactive law."[1] An Idaho statute states: "No part of these compiled laws is retroactive, unless expressly so declared." Idaho Code § 73-101 (Michie 2006). These State-specific laws may be interpreted to define retroactivity differently from the way it is defined under the federal case law we've discussed in this section.

---

1. Tex. Const. art. I. § 16 (West, Westlaw through end of 2011 Reg. Sess. & First Called Sess. of 82d Legis.); *Satterfield v. Crown Cork & Seal Co.*, 268 S.W.3d 190 (Tex. App. 2008) (interpreting this provision.); *see also* Ga. Const. art. I, § 1, para. X (West, Westlaw through 2011 Reg. & Special Sess.); Ohio Const. art. II, § 28 (West, Westlaw through all 2011 laws and statewide issues and 2012 Files 80, 82 through 88, 91, 92, 96, and 97 of the 129th Gen. Ass. (2011–2012)) (provisions similar to Texas's).

B. Effect of Publication of Legislative Rules

The federal APA requires federal agencies to publish their final legislative rules in the Federal Register. 5 U.S.C. § 552(a)(1)(C) & (D) (2012). Most state APAs impose similar requirements for state agencies' final rules. This section discusses the effect of an agency's *failure* to meet that requirement and one important effect of an agency's *compliance* with that requirement.

1. Effect of Agency's Failure to Publish a Rule

If a federal agency fails to publish a rule in the Federal Register as required by APA § 552(a)(1), the agency generally cannot rely on that rule to someone's disadvantage, unless the person has actual notice of the rule:

---

5 U.S.C. § 552. Public information; agency rules ...

(a) Each agency shall make available to the public information as follows:

(1) Each agency shall separately state and currently publish in the Federal Register for the guidance of the public — ...

(C) rules of procedure, descriptions of forms available or the places at which forms may be obtained, and instructions as to the scope and contents of all papers, reports, or examinations;

(D) substantive rules of general applicability adopted as authorized by law, and statements of general policy or interpretations of general applicability formulated and adopted by the agency; and

(E) each amendment, revision, or repeal of the foregoing.

Except to the extent that a person has actual and timely notice of the terms thereof, a person may not in any manner be required to resort to, or be adversely affected by, a matter required to be published in the Federal Register and not so published....

This restriction prevents the agency from relying on "secret law."

The federal APA restriction applied in *NI Industries, Inc. v. United States*, 841 F.2d 1104 (Fed. Cir. 1988). NI Industries had a contract with the federal government to manufacture ammunition. NI came up with an idea to change one of the contract specifications in a way that would reduce the cost of making the ammunition. The government had a program under which the first contractor to propose such a cost-saving idea could share the cost savings with the government. NI orally advised the federal government of its cost-saving idea, but did not submit the idea in writing until after a second company, with a contract to manufacture the same type of ammunition, had already submitted the same idea in writing. The government denied NI a share in the cost savings because of an unpublished rule stating that, to share the cost savings, a contractor had to be the first to submit the cost-saving idea *in writing*.

The United States Court of Appeals for the Federal Circuit reversed the government's denial of cost savings to NI. The court held that the government could not rely on the unpublished rule to NI's detriment. *NI Industries*, 841 F.2d at 1107–1108.

2. Effect of Publishing a Legislative Rule

The effect of properly publishing a legislative rule is that, like a properly published statute, the public is deemed to be on notice of the rule's requirements. This effect has great practical importance. It means that, if a government official gives someone advice that conflicts with a properly published legislative rule, that rule controls. The official's bad advice does not "estop" the government from applying the published rule. We summarize the classic case:

- *Federal Crop Insurance Corp. v. Merrill*, 332 U.S. 380 (1947)

Federal officials advised two Idaho farmers, A.A. Merrill and N.D. Merrill, that their spring wheat crop was insurable under a federal crop insurance program. The Merrills relied on that advice and applied for crop insurance under the program. The officials accepted the Merrills' insurance application. The officials turned out to be wrong: A published federal regulation prevented the crop insurance program from covering the portion of the Merrills' spring wheat crop that was reseeded on winter wheat acreage. A drought destroyed the entire crop. Relying on its regulation, the government refused to pay out on the portion of the destroyed crop that had been planted on reseeded winter acreage.

The Merrills sued the federal agency that administered the program, claiming that it had breached an insurance contract insuring their entire spring wheat crop. At trial, the Merrills put on evidence that they were not aware of the regulation and that they relied on the officials' advice that the Merrills' entire spring wheat crop was insurable. The Merrills won their case in the state court system but lost in the U.S. Supreme Court.

In ruling against the Merrills, the Court made two points relevant for administrative lawyers. First, the Court rejected the argument that the government could be held liable, like a private entity, for acts by its agents taken with "apparent authority." The *Merrill* Court held that the doctrine of apparent authority doesn't apply to the federal government. Instead,

> anyone entering into an arrangement with the Government takes the risk of having accurately ascertained that he who purports to act for the Government stays within the bounds of his authority. The scope of this authority may be explicitly defined by Congress or be limited by delegated legislation, properly exercised through the rule-making power. And this is so even though, as here, the agent himself may have been unaware of the limitations upon his authority.

Id. at 384. Second, the Court reasoned that, if the restriction on insuring reseeded winter wheat acreage were in a federal statute, the restriction would prevent the Merrills from relying on bad official advice; the result was the same even though the restriction was in a properly published legislative rule:

> Congress has legislated in this instance, as in modern regulatory enactments it so often does, by conferring the rule-making power upon the agency created for carrying out its policy.... Just as everyone is charged with knowledge of the United States Statutes at Large, Congress has provided that the appearance of rules and regulations in the Federal Register gives legal notice of their contents. 44 U.S.C. § 307.
>
> Accordingly, the Wheat Crop Insurance Regulations were binding on all who sought to come within the Federal Crop Insurance Act, regardless of actual knowledge of what is in the Regulations or of the hardship resulting from innocent ignorance.

Merrill, 332 U.S. at 384–385. The statute cited by the Court as "44 U.S.C. § 307" is codified today as 44 U.S.C. § 1507 (2012). It says that publication of a rule in the Federal Register "is sufficient to give notice of the contents of the [rule] to a person subject to or affected by it." *Id.* Thus, the Merrills were out of luck.

Merrill is one of several cases in which the U.S. Supreme Court has refused to find the federal government "estopped" because of bad official advice that someone relied upon to his or her detriment. We discuss more case law on estoppel in Chapter 26. The moral of the case law should be clear enough from *Merrill*, though: Although federal officials can be useful sources of information about the law, they are no substitute for examining the law itself.

Exercise: Relying on Government Advice

The objectives of this exercise are to help you remember the holding of *Federal Crop Insurance Corp. v. Merrill* and to reflect on its significance for the practice of administrative law.

1. What practical reasons support the Court's conclusion in *Merrill* that an official's bad advice cannot estop the government from applying a published legislative rule?

2. Assume that the Merrills had been represented by a lawyer, and that the lawyer, rather than the Merrills, had relied on the officials' advice without having read, or without understanding, the relevant regulation that barred insurance of reseeded wheat acreage. With the benefit of hindsight, evaluate the following ways a lawyer might minimize the risk of relying on bad official advice:

    a) Identify and analyze the applicable laws *before* seeking government advice on a matter, or, failing that, always check government advice against applicable laws after the fact. Do not rely on advice that conflicts with any applicable law. And be wary of advice that is not expressly supported by applicable law.

    b) Get the advice in writing, if possible. This prevents misunderstandings and may provide leverage if an official can lawfully honor the advice despite a later disinclination to do so.

    c) Get the advice from as high up in the agency as possible. All other things being equal, the higher you go in the agency, the more likely you are to get advice that is correct, or at least authoritative. Agencies usually establish law from the top down. Often, a rule or policy established by high-level officials gets distorted in the process of being interpreted and implemented by people lower in the agency hierarchy.

    d) Some agencies have procedures for issuing official, written interpretations of law in response to requests. *See, e.g., United States v. Mead Corp.*, 533 U.S. 218, 221–223 (2001) (describing procedure under which the federal government issues "tariff rulings" determining customs due on various imported goods). Consider requesting such an interpretation.

    e) Consider invoking the agency's authority to issue declaratory rulings. The federal APA authorizes a federal agency to **"issue a declaratory**

order to terminate a controversy or remove uncertainty." 5 U.S.C. § 554(e) (2012). A declaratory order resembles a court's declaratory judgment. The U.S. Supreme Court has spoken approvingly of the declaratory order device. *See Weinberger v. Hynson, Westcott & Dunning, Inc.*, 412 U.S. 609, 625–626 (1973). Even so, federal agencies don't use it much. That is probably partly because the federal APA does not clarify whether federal agencies can issue declaratory orders (1) only on matters as to which they have the power to hold formal adjudications; and (2) only after following the federal APA's procedures for formal adjudications. *See* Jeffrey S. Lubbers & Blake D. Morant, *A Reexamination of Federal Agency Use of Declaratory Orders*, 56 Admin. L. Rev. 1097 (2004). Many state APAs include provisions authorizing state agencies to issue declaratory orders. *See, e.g.*, 2010 Model State APA § 204(a) ("A person may petition an agency for a declaratory order that interprets or applies a statute administered by the agency or states whether or in what manner a rule, guidance document, or order issued by the agency applies to the petitioner.").

See generally William F. Fox, Understanding Administrative Law 208–210 (6th ed. 2012).

---

3. Publication of State Agency Rules

Many States have laws that, like the federal APA, (1) require agencies to publish their final rules and (2) prevent agencies from using unpublished rules to the detriment of someone without actual knowledge of the rules. The Alabama APA provides an example:

Alabama Code § 41-22-4. Adoption by agencies of rules governing organization, practice, etc.; public access to rules, orders, etc.; effect of rules, orders, etc., not made available to public

(a) In addition to the other rulemaking requirements imposed by law, each agency shall:

(1) Adopt as a rule a description of its organization, stating the general course and method of its operations and the methods whereby the public may obtain information or make submissions or requests;

(2) Adopt rules of practice setting forth the nature and requirements of all formal and informal procedures available, including a description of all forms and instructions used by the agency;

(3) Make available for public inspection and copying, at cost, all rules and all other written statements of policy or interpretations formulated, adopted or used by the agency in the discharge of its functions;

(4) Make available for public inspection and copying, at cost, and index by name and subject all final orders, decisions, and opinions which are issued after October 1, 1982, except those expressly made confidential or privileged by statute or order of court.

(b) No agency rule, order, or decision shall be valid or effective against any person or party nor may it be invoked by the agency for any purpose until it has been made available for public inspection and indexed as required by this section and the agency has given all notices required by Section 41-22-5. This provision is not applicable in favor of any person or party who has actual knowledge thereof, and the burden of proving such knowledge shall be on the agency.

Other States have similar provisions, many of which are based on the 1961 or 1981 Model State APAs. 1981 Model State APA § 2-101; 1961 Model State APA § 2.

State courts have addressed whether bad official advice can estop state or local governments from relying on published laws or legislative rules. If you have an administrative law problem involving this issue, you must carefully examine the State's case law. Some state courts suggest that bad official advice can never estop the government. Other States seem to take a more lenient approach. *See generally* P.H. Vartanian, Comment Note, *Applicability of Doctrine of Estoppel Against Government and Its Governmental Agencies*, 1 A.L.R.2d 338 (1948) (updated regularly).

The dangers of relying on official advice may remind you of the distinction with which we began our study of rulemaking—namely, the distinction between "the law" and an agency's or official's interpretation of the law. Neither lawyers nor their clients can afford to mistake official advice for "the law."

C. Federal Regulatory Preemption

Like a valid federal statute, a valid federal agency's legislative rule can invalidate—to use the technical term, it can "preempt"—state law. *See Hillsborough County v. Automated Med. Labs., Inc.*, 471 U.S. 707, 713 (1985) ("State laws can be pre-empted by federal regulations as well as by federal statutes."). The invalidation of state law by a federal rule is known as "regulatory preemption." This section introduces regulatory preemption and shows how it works.

You may study (or have already studied) the preemption doctrine in a law school course on constitutional law. The preemption doctrine stems from the Supremacy Clause of the Constitution:

U.S. Const. art. VI. . . .

This Constitution, and the Laws of the United States which shall be made in Pursuance thereof; and all Treaties made, or which shall be made, under the Authority of the United States, shall be the supreme Law of the Land; and the Judges in every State shall be bound thereby, any Thing in the Constitution or Laws of any State to the Contrary notwithstanding. . . .

The "Laws of the United States" include not only federal statutes but also federal agencies' legislative rules. Both forms of federal law, if valid, are the "supreme Law of the land … any Thing in the Constitution or Law of any State to the Contrary notwithstanding." No state constitution, state statute, state agency rule, or state common law can stand in the way of valid federal law. *See, e.g., Maryland v. Louisiana*, 451 U.S. 725, 746 (1981).

For a federal agency's legislative rule to be valid, and hence to have preemptive force, the rule must rest on a statute authorizing the agency to make legislative rules. The agency legislation may expressly authorize the agency's rules to preempt state law. This situation is known as "express preemption." Agency legislation, however, may also *impliedly* authorize an agency to make rules that have preemptive effect.

"A pre-emptive regulation's force does not depend on express congressional authorization to displace state law." *Fidelity Fed. Sav. & Loan Ass'n v. de la Cuesta*, 458 U.S. 141, 154 (1982). Even when the agency statute is silent, the agency's rules have preemptive force if they fall within the agency statute and are otherwise valid. *See, e.g., United States v. Shimer*, 367 U.S. 374, 377–385 (1961). Regulatory preemption in that situation is known as "implied preemption." We will examine express regulatory preemption and implied regulatory preemption separately.

1. Express Preemption

Express regulatory preemption can occur, for example, under the Federal Railroad Safety Act. 49 U.S.C. §§ 20101–20120 (2012). The Act authorizes the Secretary of Transportation to "prescribe regulations and issue orders for every area of railroad safety." *Id.* § 20103(a). The Act also includes an express preemption provision, which states in part:

---

49 U.S.C. § 20106. Preemption

(a) National uniformity of regulation....

(2) A State may adopt or continue in force a law, regulation, or order related to railroad safety or security until the Secretary of Transportation (with respect to railroad safety matters), or the Secretary of Homeland Security (with respect to railroad security matters), prescribes a regulation or issues an order covering the subject matter of the State requirement....

This provision causes a railroad safety regulation issued by the Secretary of Transportation to preempt state laws that "cove[r] the subject matter" of the regulation.

The Court interpreted this provision in the following case:

• *Norfolk Southern Railway Co. v. Shanklin*, 529 U.S. 344 (2000)

Shanklin arose from an accident at a railroad crossing. Eddie Shanklin was struck and killed by a train when he drove across railroad tracks that intersected a road in Tennessee. Mr. Shanklin's widow sued Norfolk Southern, which operated the train, asserting tort claims under state law. She claimed that Norfolk Southern was negligent, among other ways, in failing to have adequate warning devices at the railroad crossing.

The railroad crossing where Mr. Shanklin was killed did not have one of those familiar, red-and-white striped gates that come down, to the sound of clanging bells and flashing lights, before the train comes. The crossing, instead, just had advance warning signs and, at the fatal intersection, "reflectorized crossbucks, ... the familiar black-and-white X-shaped signs that read "RAILROAD CROSSING." *Norfolk Southern*, 529 U.S. at 350;

see also http://safety.fhwa.dot.gov/xings/com_roaduser/07010/sec04a.htm (Figure 12). Those passive warning devices were installed using federal funds and complied with federal regulations issued by the Secretary of Transportation under the Federal Railroad Safety Act.

The U.S. Supreme Court held that the Secretary's regulations preempted Ms. Shanklin's state-law tort claim challenging the adequacy of the warning devices. The Court emphasized that the federal regulations were "*mandatory* for all warning devices installed with federal funds." *Norfolk Southern*, 529 U.S. at 353. The regulations required the specific warning device actually installed at the fatal intersection — no more and no less. Once the devices were installed, the regulations "displaced Tennessee statutory and common law addressing the same subject, thereby pre-empting [plaintiff's] claim." *Id* at 359.

Several things about *Norfolk Southern* deserve highlighting:

- A state tort claim was held to be "a *law* ... related to railroad safety" within the meaning of an express preemption provision. Thus, state "laws" subject to preemption are not limited to state constitutional provisions, state statutes, and state agency rules; they can come from state common law. In another case, the Court held that state common-law claims could fall within an express preemption provision that preempted certain state "requirements." *See Medtronic v. Lohr*, 518 U.S. 470, 502–503 (1996) (plurality opinion); *id.* at 503–505 (Breyer, J., concurring in part and concurring in judgment); *id.* at 509–512 (O'Connor, J., concurring in part and dissenting in part). In contrast, the Court held that state tort claims did not fall within an express preemption provision that preempted certain state "safety standard[s]." *Geier v. American Honda Motor Co.*, 529 U.S. 861, 868 (2000). The point is that state tort claims may fall within an express preemption provision, but to determine whether they do you must always examine the language of the specific preemption provision, the statutory context in which the provision occurs, and any case law interpreting the provision.

- Ms. Shanklin apparently had state-law tort claims that were not preempted. Specifically, in the lower courts, she claimed that the train didn't blow its horn or hit its brakes when it should have. Norfolk Southern did not argue on appeal that those claims were preempted. *See Shanklin v. Norfolk S. Ry.*, 173 F.3d 386, 388–389 (6th Cir. 1999), *rev'd*, 529 U.S. 344 (2000). In *Shanklin*, as in other regulatory preemption cases, preemption may not bar all state tort claims arising from the plaintiff's injury. *See, e.g., Cipollone v. Liggett Group, Inc.*, 505 U.S. 504 (1992) (holding that federal statute regulating cigarette warnings preempted some of plaintiff's state tort claims, but not others).

- Unless Ms. Shanklin could prevail on her unpreempted state tort claims, she would be unable to recover any damages in a private lawsuit. She could not sue under the Federal Railroad Safety Act because it did not authorize private causes of action. The Act is not exceptional in this respect. Federal regulatory statutes often preempt state-law claims without supplying any private cause of action under federal law to replace the preempted state-law claims. *See, e.g., PLIVA, Inc. v. Mensing*, 131 S.Ct. 2567, 2592 (2011) (Sotomayor, J., dissenting) (decision of majority, which held that plaintiffs' state tort claims were preempted, "strips generic-drug consumers of compensation when they are injured by inadequate warnings").

- Justice Breyer said in a concurring opinion in *Shanklin* that the Secretary of Transportation could allow future tort suits like Ms. Shanklin's by amending the federal regulations that preempted her claim. The amended regulations could, for example, "specif[y] that federal money is sometimes used for 'minimum,' not 'adequate' [warning device installation programs], which minimum programs lack preemptive force." *Shanklin*, 529 U.S. at 360 (Breyer, J., concurring). The majority did not dispute this point, and it illustrates that federal agencies may have discretion about the preemptive effect of their legislative rules. Their power and discretion depend on the text of any express statutory preemption provision and the specifics of the agency's rulemaking authority.

When a federal statute expressly authorizes an agency's rules to have preemptive force, you must analyze the particular statute and the particular rule, and any available case law, to determine exactly what state laws are preempted.

Exercise: Express Preemption

Massachusetts enacted a law prohibiting billboards from advertising cigarettes within 1,000 feet of a playground or school. A cigarette company that wants to advertise on such a billboard challenges the Massachusetts law as preempted by federal law. The company relies on the federal statute that regulates the labeling and advertising of cigarettes and other tobacco products. The federal statute has a provision that prohibits any "requirement or prohibition based on smoking and health ... imposed under State law with respect to the advertising or promotion of cigarettes." 15 U.S.C. § 1334 (2012). Think up a reasonable argument that Massachusetts might make that the Massachusetts law is not preempted under this express preemption provision. *See Lorillard Tobacco Co. v. Reilly*, 533 U.S. 525, 547–550 (2001).

---

2. Implied Preemption

As the Court has said, "[a] pre-emptive regulation's force does not depend on *express* congressional authorization to displace state law." *Fidelity Fed. Sav. & Loan Ass'n v. de la Cuesta*, 458 U.S. 141, 154 (1982) (emphasis added). A federal agency's legislative rule may preempt state law through "implied preemption." "Implied preemption" means situations in which federal law invalidates conflicting state law even though nothing in a federal statute expressly says that the federal law can have this invalidating effect. Although the implied preemption doctrine has developed mostly in cases involving the question of whether a federal *statute* preempts state law, the same principles determine whether a federal agency's legislative rule preempts state law.

The U.S. Supreme Court has divided implied preemption into two types: "field" preemption and "conflict" preemption.

Field preemption occurs either (1) when "[t]he scheme of federal regulation [is] so pervasive as to make reasonable the inference that Congress left no room for the States to supplement it"; or (2) when federal law "touch[es] a field in which the federal interest is so dominant that the federal system will be assumed to preclude enforcement of state laws on the same subject." *Rice v. Santa Fe Elevator Corp.*, 331 U.S. 218, 230 (1947). Field preemption reflects that some matters require comprehensive, uniform regulation at the national level. Federal law on such matters acts like an 800-pound gorilla, which, when it sits down, squashes all state law beneath it, whether the state law is consistent or inconsistent with the federal law. For example, the Court has held that in the Atomic Energy Act Congress intended to occupy the field of the "radiological safety aspects involved in the construction and operation of a nuclear plant." *Pac. Gas & Elec. Co. v. State Energy Res. Conservation & Dev. Corp.*, 461 U.S. 190, 205 (1983). That holding meant that state law could not regulate the same subject, even if the state law was consistent with, and supportive of, federal law. In field preemption situations, the mere existence of state law conflicts with Congress's intent.

Unlike field preemption, "conflict" preemption occurs only when a state law contradicts or interferes with federal law. The Court has recognized two types of conflict preemption. One is where "compliance with both federal and state regulations is a physical impossibility." *Gade v. Nat'l Solid Waste Mg'mt*, 505 U.S. 88, 98 (1992). This type of preemption is known alternately as "actual" conflict preemption or "physical impossibility" preemption. "Physical impossibility" preemption occurs, for example, if state law requires a product sold in that State to be labeled in a way that federal law forbids. *See PLIVA, Inc. v. Mensing*, 131 S.Ct. 2567, 2577–2578 (2011). The second, more common type of conflict preemption is known as "obstacle" conflict preemption. It occurs when state law "stands as an obstacle to the accomplishment and execution of the full purposes and objectives of Congress." *Fidelity Fed. Sav. & Loan Ass'n v. de la Cuesta*, 458 U.S. 141, 153 (1982) (internal quotation marks omitted).

"Obstacle conflict preemption" occurred in the following regulatory preemption case:

- *Fidelity Federal Savings & Loan Association v. de la Cuesta*, 458 U.S. 141 (1982)

The Federal Home Loan Bank Board had statutory authority to regulate federal savings and loan associations (federal S&L's) "under such rules and regulations as it may prescribe." *Id.* at 145 (quoting agency legislation). The Board used this power to issue a legislative rule allowing federal S&Ls to use "due-on-sale" clauses in their mortgage contracts. Due-on-sale clauses stated that, if a homeowner sold the mortgaged home without the federal S&L's permission, the entire outstanding amount of the mortgage was immediately due. The Board allowed federal S&Ls to use these clauses so that the federal S&Ls could negotiate with the buyers of mortgaged homes for a higher interest rate upon assuming the mortgage. This in turn helped the federal S&Ls stay solvent.

When a federal S&L called Fidelity Federal Savings and Loan Association tried to enforce a due-on-sale clause against some home buyers, the home buyers sued Fidelity in California state court. The home buyers argued that the due-on-sale clause violated California state law. California state law allowed enforcement of due-on-sale clauses in only limited situations. Fidelity countered that the Federal Home Loan Bank Board's rule preempted California law.

The U.S. Supreme Court agreed that the Board's rule preempted California law. The Court recognized that it was "physically possible" for federal S&Ls to comply with both federal law and California law. The Board's regulation merely permitted, but did not require, federal S&Ls to use due-on-sale clauses; federal S&Ls would therefore not be violating the Board's regulation if they restricted their use of due-on-sale clauses to those situations permitted under California law. *Fidelity Federal*, 458 U.S. at 155. California law nonetheless conflicted with the Board's regulation by interfering with the purpose of the Board's regulation, which was to give federal S&Ls the "flexibility" to use these clauses as they saw fit. *Id.* Indeed, the Board considered that flexibility "essential to the economic soundness" of the S&L industry. *Id.* at 156. Under those circumstances, the Court held that "the State has created 'an obstacle to the accomplishment and execution of the full purposes and objectives' of the due-on-sale regulation." *Id.* (quoting *Hines v. Davidowitz*, 312 U.S. 52, 67 (1941)). That holding prevented California law from restricting the use of due-on-sale clauses by federal S&Ls in that State.

Fidelity Federal resembles *Shanklin* in two notable ways. First, both involved situations seemingly far removed from federal administrative law: a dispute connected with a home sale and a state-law tort suit over a car-train collision. The two cases show how federal regulatory preemption can "intrude" into traditional areas of state law. Second, in both situations the federal agency's intent in promulgating the preemptive regulations was an important consideration in the Court's decision finding preemption. *See Shanklin*, 458 U.S. at 154 ("[T]he Court of Appeal's narrow focus on Congress' intent to supersede state law was misdirected. Rather, the questions upon which resolution of this case rests are whether the Board meant to pre-empt California's due-on-sale law, and, if so, whether that action is within the scope of the Board's delegated authority."); *Norfolk Southern*, 529 U.S. at 355 (relying on agency's longstanding "understanding" of its regulations). Many people, including many lawyers, would be surprised not only that federal regulatory preemption arose in these factual settings but also that federal agencies have power and discretion to preempt state law. Now that you have studied this chapter, you will not be among the surprised.

Exercise: Mapping Regulatory Preemption

Please draw a graphic organizer of the types of preemption. Here they are:

- express preemption
- implied preemption
- field preemption
- conflict preemption
- physical impossibility (or "actual conflict") preemption
- obstacle preemption

Make sure your graphic organizer reflects that federal legislative rules, as well as federal statutes, can preempt state law.

D. Chapter 16 Wrap Up and Look Ahead

From this chapter you have learned three ways in which legislative rules operate like statutes. Specifically, you have learned that legislative rules, like statutes, sometimes operate retroactively (and are sometimes validly retroactive). You have also learned that a legislative rule, like a statute, when published puts the public on notice of its content. Finally, you have learned that a federal legislative rule, like a federal statute, can preempt state law. We hope that, from this and other things you have learned in this part of the book, you understand the awesomeness of an agency's power to make legislative rules.

This chapter ends our examination of rulemaking. This does not mean you have seen the last of agency rules in this book. Later chapters on judicial review of "agency action" include judicial review of agency rules. Thus, die-hard fans of rulemaking, fear not!

Chapter Problem 1 Revisited

TSA denied Mr. B a national security certification because, under TSA's 2003 threat assessment regulation, Mr. B's 1975 conviction created a presumption that he was a national security risk, and Mr. B did not overcome that presumption. The 2003 regulation operated based on past events in Mr. B's case, and so might be retroactive. We must analyze it more closely.

The regulation seems retroactive according to one of the Court's general descriptions of retroactive laws, but not others. Specifically, the regulation "attaches new legal consequences to events completed before" its adoption. *Landgraf v. USI Film Prods.*, 511 U.S. 244, 269 (1994). The new legal consequence of Mr. B's 1975 conviction is a presumption that he poses a national security risk. Unless he overcomes that presumption, TSA will not certify him to transport hazardous material.

In the case on which this chapter problem was based, the court concluded that TSA's threat assessment regulation was *not* retroactive. The Court used a different general description of retroactive laws than the one quoted in the last paragraph. Here is the court's reasoning:

> [I]n evaluating whether a statute or regulation has a retroactive effect we consider "whether it would impair rights a party possessed when he acted, increase a party's liability for past conduct, or impose new duties with respect to transactions already completed." [*Landgraf*, 511 U.S. at 280.] ... The Government argues the threat assessment regulation does not have any of the effects deemed retroactive in *Landgraf* because it does not bar an applicant with a disqualifying conviction from obtaining [a license to transport hazardous material] ... but rather creates "an evidentiary presumption" that an applicant with a disqualifying conviction in his past poses a security threat in the present; the applicant may rebut that presumption through the waiver process. Again, we agree. Although the presumption does, as the Amicus notes, "put[ ] the burden [of rebuttal] on an already-disqualified trucker," the presumption is nonetheless rebuttable and the disqualification hence merely provisional. The scheme therefore does not "impair rights [Boniface] possessed when he acted, increase [his] liability for past conduct, or impose new duties with respect to transactions already completed." *Landgraf*, 511 U.S. at 280.

Boniface v. U.S. Dep't of Homeland Sec., 613 F.3d 282, 288 (D.C. Cir. 2010). The court in *Boniface* relied on the general description of retroactivity in *Landgraf* that requires more than the attachment of a new "legal consequence" to past activity; the description favored in *Boniface* requires impairment of prior rights, increased liability, or new duties. This shows that retroactivity analysis may vary, depending on which general description of retroactivity one uses.

In addition, TSA's regulation might be considered non-retroactive under the exception for "procedural" rules. The regulation only creates an evidentiary burden that operates in a TSA adjudication on someone's application for a certification. Arguably, the presumption affects *how* someone like Mr. Boniface shows entitlement to certification, but it does not change the underlying substantive standard for certification. That standard remains tied to the question of whether a person poses a security risk.

Under the *Boniface* court's analysis, the critical issue is that the presumption in TSA regulation was rebuttable. Maybe the court would have found the regulation retroactive if it had absolutely disqualified Mr. Boniface from getting a certification because of his 1975 conviction. In that event, the regulation would be analogous to the rule discussed in this chapter that prohibited someone from working as a nurse aide because she committed patient abuse before the adoption of a rule disqualifying her from being a nurse aide because of that prior offense. Under *Boniface*, a state public health agency could adopt a rule denying nurse aide licenses to people who posed a risk of abusing patients, and creating a rebuttable presumption that people found guilty of such abuse pose such a risk.

Chapter Problem 2 Revisited

This problem is based on *Schweiker v. Hansen*, 450 U.S. 785 (1981) (per curiam). In that case, as in the chapter problem, an SSA regulation prevented the payment of benefits for periods of time that preceded the filing of a written application for benefits. The issue was whether, despite this regulation, a person could get benefits for the period prior to the filing of her written application, if the person relied on bad advice from an SSA official, who had advised the person not to file an application.

The Court held that SSA properly relied on its regulation to deny benefits for the period preceding a claimant's filing of a written application. Thus, the bad advice given by an SSA official did not "estop" the SSA from denying retroactive benefits. The Court acknowledged that some kinds of "affirmative misconduct" by a government official might support an estoppel claim, but negligently erroneous official advice was not enough. *Id.* at 790 ("In sum, [the official] Connelly's errors 'fal[l] far short' of conduct which would raise a serious question whether petitioner [agency] is estopped from insisting upon compliance with the valid regulation [requiring a written application for benefits].") (quoting *Montana v. Kennedy*, 366 U.S. 308, 314 (1961)).

Chapter Problem 3 Revisited

This is an express preemption case. Analysis focuses on which of the state-law claims, if any, fall within FIFRA's preemption provision. The preemption provision applies to "any requirements for labeling or packaging in addition to or different from those required under [the Act.]" 7 U.S.C. § 136v(b) (2012). To fall within the preemption provision, a state-law claim must have three features. It must be: (1) a requirement; (2) for labeling or packaging; (3) in addition to or different from requirements imposed under FIFRA.

As mentioned earlier in this chapter, the Court has held that a state common-law claim could be a "requirement" within the meaning of an express preemption provision. Even so, you must examine the specific preemption provision in the FIFRA, the FIFRA as a whole, and the case law on the FIFRA's preemptive effect, to determine whether FIFRA's preemption provision applied to state common-law claims.

Assuming that a state tort claim is a "requirement[t]" within the meaning of FIFRA's preemption provision, the tort claims for fraudulent and negligent labeling appear to be preempted. They seek to impose tort-law requirements "for labeling," and they are necessarily "in addition to or different" from FIFRA's requirements, considering that EPA found that Roust's labeling complied with FIFRA's labeling requirements.

The other state-law claims do not appear to be requirements for labeling or packaging, with the possible exception of the express warranty claim. If the alleged warranty was on Roust's label or in its packaging, the warranty claim arguably relates to the labeling or packaging. In the case on which this problem was based, however, the U.S. Supreme Court held that FIFRA's preemption provision did not preempt an express warranty claim based on state law. *See Bates v. Dow Agrisciences LLC.*, 544 U.S. 431, 444–445 (2005). The Court reasoned:

> [A] cause of action on an express warranty asks only that a manufacturer make good on the contractual commitment that it voluntarily undertook by placing that warranty on its product. Because this common-law rule does not require the manufacturer to make an express warranty, or in the event that the manufacturer elects to do so, to say anything in particular in that warranty, the rule does not impose a requirement "for labeling or packaging."

Id.

Professional Development Reflection Questions

Administrative lawyers often have clients that have regular dealings with a particular agency. For example, a mining company may have regular dealings with the federal Mine Safety and Health Administration (MHSA). The lawyer for the company may have regular contacts with the lawyers for the MHSA. The lawyer for the company may best serve the client by establishing a good working relationship with the MHSA lawyers. By establishing a good working relationship, the lawyer may be more effective, say, in resolving potential disputes informally.

Of course, problems can arise if a lawyer for a regulated entity gets too "buddy buddy" with a lawyer for the regulatory agency. This creates a risk that friendship between the lawyers will prevent one or the other lawyer (or both) from zealously representing the respective clients. The challenge for the lawyers on both sides is to develop a professional relationship that remains professional.

Think of someone—a law school classmate, professor, professional acquaintance, etc.—whom you believe could strike the balance of developing a cordial relationship with an attorney on the "other side" of the regulatory agency/regulated entity divide without having that relationship impair zealous representation of the client. What qualities does he or she possess? What lessons does this person have to teach you?

PART THREE

AGENCY ADJUDICATION

Chapter 17

Introduction to Agency Adjudication

Overview

This chapter introduces Part 3 of the book and the subject of Part 3: agency adjudication. The chapter also provides a roadmap for Part 3.

This chapter's sections are entitled:

A. How and Why Agencies Get Adjudicatory Power

B. What Lawyers Do in Agency Adjudications

C. How Agency Adjudication Compares to Court Adjudication

D. How Agency Adjudication Compares to Agency Rulemaking

E. Common Subjects of Agency Adjudication

F. The Distinction between the Agency as Adjudicator and the Agency as Litigant

G. Chapter 17 Wrap Up and Roadmap of Part 3

Chapter Problem

Email

From: State Senator Nguyen

To: Long-Time Friend and, Now, Lawyer Lovasco

Lovasco: You know I am just a citizen legislator, and that I count on you when I need a lawyer's perspective. I need that now.

I am struggling to develop a position on the current push in the State Legislature to do something about day care providers. You probably know better than I do that we are the only State that doesn't regulate day care providers, and I am honestly having a hard time figuring out why they should be regulated.

As I understand it, the sponsors of the push to regulate day care providers want them to get licenses. But who would they get licenses from? And why should we require someone to get a license in the first place? I am worried that the people handing out licenses will be faceless bureaucrats who impose all kinds of unrealistic requirements for getting a license, and who then take away providers' licenses for the smallest of infractions.

As it is now, if a problem arises because a day care provider does something wrong, we've got a court system where parents can sue, and a prosecutor can prosecute if something really bad happens. What's wrong with using the court system to keep day care providers in line?

Maybe I am missing something. I hope you can enlighten me. You usually do. Let me know what you think. Thanks!

A. How and Why Agencies Get Adjudicatory Power

When you first learned about "adjudication," you probably heard the term used for the process by which *courts* resolve disputes. Courts, however, are not the only governmental entities that have adjudicatory power. Many administrative agencies also have adjudicatory power. Thus, although we commonly associate the adjudicatory power with the judicial branch, in reality adjudicatory power is also exercised by many of the executive-branch entities that you have come to know and love as administrative agencies.

An executive-branch agency with adjudicatory power typically gets that power from a statute specifically concerning that agency (which we will continue to call "the agency legislation"). The legislature may give the agency adjudicatory power when enacting the statute that creates the agency or when enacting a later statute that alters the agency's powers (and duties). This produces what might seem like an odd arrangement, when you first encounter it: *Executive*-branch agencies exercise *judicial*-type power granted by the *legislative* branch. The following graphic illustrates the situation:

Diagram 17-1. Statutory Delegation of Quasi-Judicial Power

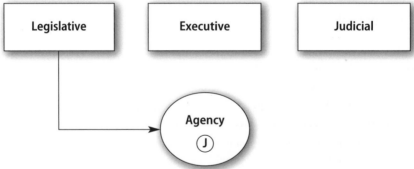

This is quite a stew! You might well wonder: How can the legislative branch give judicial-type power to the executive branch? And why would the legislature do such a thing?

As to how: Article III of the U.S. Constitution vests the judicial power of the federal government in the federal courts. And yet the first Congress gave executive-branch agencies powers that were at least "quasi-judicial." Specifically, the first Congress created the Treasury Department and gave the Comptroller of the Treasury power to decide individual monetary claims against the government—for example, claims for money by people who had supplied goods or services to the government. In debating the legislation creating the Treasury Department, James Madison observed that the Comptroller's power to decide monetary claims against the government "partakes strongly of the judicial character." 1 Annals of Cong. 635–636 (Joseph Gales ed. 1834). No one in Congress at the time seemed to think this was a problem. Congress has been authorizing executive agencies to exercise adjudicatory powers ever since. State legislatures have done the same, despite state constitutions that, like the U.S. Constitution, typically contemplate adjudicatory power being exercised by a judicial branch. In short, although the U.S. and state constitutions may vest *judicial* power exclusively in the judicial branch, the constitutions have generally been construed to allow some *adjudicatory* (admittedly quasi-judicial) power to be exercised by the executive branch.

As to why: Legislatures have many reasons to allow an agency, rather than a court, to adjudicate a matter initially. (We say "initially" because most agency adjudicatory decisions are subject to judicial review.) Some matters may be too routine to spend judicial resources on, such as the issuance of fishing licenses. Some matters may require specialized knowledge that judges lack, such as the decision whether to license a nuclear power plant. The sheer number of some matters may be too large for a court system to handle, such as claims for government welfare benefits. Other matters may involve so many interested persons with such varying interests and relationships that they do not fit the mold of the typical plaintiff vs. defendant controversy that courts are accustomed to deciding. An example of such a multiparty matter with varying sets of interests is a governmental decision whether to authorize the building of a natural gas pipeline that would extend over many States and kinds of land, including public land, private property, and tribal lands.

Because so many matters have been found by legislatures to be appropriately adjudicated by agencies instead of courts, today agencies adjudicate a much larger number of matters than do courts. This makes agency adjudication important to learn about. As you do, remember that an agency's decision in an agency adjudication is classified as an "order" under the federal APA and under many state APAs. *See, e.g.,* 5 U.S.C. § 551(6) (2012); 2010 Model State APA § 102(23). But we must warn you: Just as agencies don't always call their rules "rules," agencies don't always call their orders "orders." Don't be fooled by camouflage!

Exercise: Allocating Adjudicatory Authority between Agencies and Courts

Consider these matters that are ordinarily adjudicated initially by agencies rather than courts:

- the issuance of a license to practice medicine
- the approval of a new drug as safe and effective
- the determination of whether a company is the source of an illegal discharge of water pollution into a nearby river and, if so, what is an appropriate civil fine in light of the environmental damage caused by the discharge
- the determination of whether someone is too disabled to work and is therefore eligible for government-funded disability benefits
- the decision to approve a new pesticide

What factors identified in the discussion above could lead a legislature to confide each matter to an agency, instead of a court, for initial adjudication?

B. What Lawyers Do in Agency Adjudications

In many agency adjudications a party has a right to be represented by a lawyer. That right comes from the federal APA, for adjudications before federal agencies. The federal APA says, **"A party is entitled to appear … by or with counsel … in an agency proceeding,"** 5 U.S.C. § 555(b) (2012), and defines **"agency proceeding"** to include agency adjudications, *id.* § 551(7) & (12). Similarly, a state APA may create a entitlement to legal representation in state agency adjudications.[1] Besides the federal or state APA, the Due Process Clauses may entitle people to be represented by a lawyer in certain agency adjudications. *See Goldberg v. Kelly*, 397 U.S. 254, 270–271 (1970). To be clear, APAs do not entitle people to *free* lawyers, nor has the U.S. Constitution been construed to create such an entitlement. Even so, many lawyers devote some or all of their practice to representing clients in agency adjudications.

To represent clients effectively in agency adjudications, you need the same skills as required of lawyers in court adjudications. In particular, just as lawyers who practice in courts must master the intricacies of court procedure, lawyers who practice before an agency must master the intricacies of that agency's adjudicatory procedures. In both venues, the merits of a client's case don't count for much if they are not presented in compliance with the required procedures.

This is not to say that court adjudications are like agency adjudications, or that all agency adjudications are alike. To the contrary, lawyers who are new to agency adjudications often make one or more of these three, serious errors based on misconceptions about the relationship between agency and court adjudication:

1. The lawyer erroneously assumes that agency adjudications are just like court adjudications. That is a serious error because it can hurt the client's interests. For example, the client may lose the right to assert a claim or defense because the lawyer did not follow the proper agency procedures for asserting that claim or defense.

2. The lawyer erroneously assumes that all agency adjudications are alike. That is a serious error for the same reasons as the first error.

3. The lawyer erroneously assumes that the agency adjudication is merely a prelude to the "main event" — the "main event" being adjudication of the matter in a court.

The third mistake is so serious that it needs special attention. If you remember only one thing about agency adjudication, please remember this:

In 9 out of 10 cases, you will win or lose your case at the agency level. You must therefore make your best case before the agency.

There are three reasons why almost all adjudicatory matters are won or lost, for once and for all, at the agency level.

First, in many cases if you get a favorable decision for your client from the agency, you are done. For example, if your client applies to an agency for benefits and the first agency official responsible for reviewing the application grants it, you are done; you have won.

---

1. *See, e.g.*, Okla. Stat. Ann. tit. 75, § 310 (West, Westlaw through Chapter 3 of the Second Reg. Sess. of 53rd Legislature (2012)).

Normally, the agency has no reason or authority to review the initial grant of benefits further or seek judicial review, nor will anyone else have standing or authority to take the matter any further.

The same is often true when you persuade the "front-line" agency official to grant a license to your client or not to put a sanction on your client. The front-line official's action usually ends the matter. True, sometimes an application for a license or a decision whether to impose a sanction has such broad public importance that the matter will not end with a front-line official's decision favorable to the license applicant or potential target of the sanction. For example, an agency's initial decision to license a nuclear power plant may well be opposed by people who live near the plant, and those opponents may have legal rights to contest the granting of the license within the agency and, if not successful in the agency, in the courts. Similarly, people who live downstream from a company that has initially avoided a penalty for polluting a river may be able to challenge an agency's initial decision not to impose a sanction. But most licensing and penalty matters are not so momentous that anyone besides the license applicant or the potential sanctionee will care or have legal authority to complain. That is why the license applicant's or potential sanctionee's initial success usually equates to final victory.

A second reason for the need to make your best case at the agency level concerns the evidentiary basis for judicial review. A court will seldom take new evidence—much less hold a trial—when reviewing an agency's adjudicatory decision. *See* Chapter 31.D. Thus, if you did not present enough evidence to the agency to get a favorable decision for your client, you will not get a second chance in court. You must make your best case to the agency, which means you must present all favorable evidence, and challenge all unfavorable evidence, in the agency adjudication, in accordance with procedural requirements. To express the principle as commonly expressed in administrative law circles: "Judicial review is ordinarily based solely on the record before the agency."

The third reason you need to make your best case to the agency concerns the deferential standards of review that courts typically apply to the agency's factual and legal determinations in an adjudication. As discussed in Part 4, roughly speaking a court will uphold an agency's factual and legal determinations if they are reasonable, even if the court would have determined the matters differently. Not only do the standards of judicial review favor the agency: As a practical matter, many judges lack familiarity—and, though it pains us to add, they even lack interest—in administrative law cases. Legal and practical factors make it hard for lawyers to challenge agency adjudicatory decisions successfully in court.

There is much work—and much good work—that lawyers can do representing people in agency adjudications. But it is not an area in which to dabble. Competent representation of a client in an agency adjudication requires mastery of both the substantive law and procedural law governing the matter. This part of the book gives you a framework for analyzing substantive and procedural aspects of an agency adjudication. In keeping with the focus of administrative law courses, this part of the book pays particular attention to procedural requirements for agency adjudication.

Exercise: Introduction to Agency Adjudications

As you will learn, an agency adjudication may include an oral, evidentiary hearing. The formality of these hearings varies widely. To begin getting a sense of how these hearings operate, search YouTube for "administrative hearings" or "agency hearings." Here are two good presentations we found at the time of this writing:

- Guide to Social Services Agency Hearings in California, http://www.youtube.com/watch?v=W8RvrAJIKJE&feature=related (law-student-made video on benefits hearings in California) (last visited June 3, 2012)

- Michael P. Sullivan, SSDI Hearing Video, http://www.youtube.com/watch?v=LwFe3qk-KrQ&feature=related (simulation of hearing on claim for disability benefits under Social Security Act) (last visited June 3, 2012).

C. How Agency Adjudication Compares to Court Adjudication

As we emphasized above, agency adjudications differ from judicial proceedings. It helps to appreciate the differences from the start.

Agency adjudications differ from judicial proceedings in that most agency adjudications are less formal than judicial proceedings. Whereas most judicial proceedings could culminate in a trial, relatively few agency adjudications provide an opportunity for trial-type hearings. Instead, many agency adjudications involve a low-level agency employee making a decision based on paperwork. For agency adjudications in which trial-type hearings do occur, the rules of evidence are usually more relaxed than the rules of evidence for trials. Thus, for example, the administrative law judge or other officer presiding at the agency hearing may be able to admit hearsay. The agency hearing seldom will occur in a courtroom. The agency official presiding at the hearing may be called an "administrative judge" or "administrative law judge," but the official might not wear a judge's robes.

Agency adjudications vary much more widely in their procedures than do judicial proceedings. Most judicial proceedings, regardless of the court system in which they occur, have common elements: notice to parties; pleadings; discovery; pretrial motions; a trial before an impartial decision maker; and a decision based exclusively on a record, the contents of which are generally created exclusively by, and known in their entirety to, the parties. An agency adjudication may have none, some, or all of those procedural elements. Furthermore, an agency adjudication may even have procedural elements that we associate with rulemaking. For example, the EPA gives notice to the public, and an opportunity for public comment, before the EPA makes a final determination on whether to fine someone for violating certain water pollution laws. 33 U.S.C. § 1319(g)(4) (2012). In short, there is no such thing as a typical agency adjudication.

Chapter 19 identifies and introduces the potential sources of procedural requirements for agency adjudications. At this point we want to introduce the categories that administrative lawyers use to classify agency adjudications in terms of their procedural formality. We separately discuss federal agency adjudications and state agency adjudications.

1. Federal Agency Adjudications

Folks in administrative law circles divide federal agency adjudications into two types: formal adjudication and informal adjudication. Some administrative law folks further subdivide informal adjudications into those in which there is an opportunity for an oral, evidentiary hearing and those in which there is no such opportunity. We introduce these types of adjudication below.

a. Formal Adjudications

"Formal adjudications" are adjudications subject to the formal adjudication requirements of the federal APA. The formal adjudication requirements are in federal APA §§ 554, 556, and 557. Roughly speaking, an adjudication is subject to §§ 554, 556, and 557 when the agency legislation requires the adjudication to be decided (1) after an opportunity for a trial-type hearing and (2) exclusively on the basis of evidence admitted into the record at that hearing. To quote the federal APA, the formal adjudication requirements of §§ 554, 556, and 557 are required, with some exceptions, **"in every case of adjudication required by statute to be determined on the record after opportunity for an agency hearing."** 5 U.S.C. § 554(a) (2012).

Chapters 22–24 examine the federal APA's formal adjudication requirements. As those chapters discuss, formal adjudications resemble court proceedings in broad outline. In particular, formal adjudications include oral, evidentiary hearings in which parties put up live witnesses, seek admission of documentary evidence, and cross-examine opposing witnesses. These and other features make for proceedings that are relatively formal indeed. The formality reflects that formal adjudications typically involve important interests. Examples include adjudications involving certain government benefits or licenses, and adjudications involving sanctions for violations of regulatory statutes.

b. Informal Adjudications

The term "informal adjudication" is usually used to mean a federal agency adjudication that is not subject to the formal adjudication requirements in §§ 554, 556, and 557 of the federal APA. Used in this way, the term includes both truly informal adjudications as well as adjudications that—though not subject to §§ 554, 556, and 557—can be as formal as adjudications that *are* subject to those provisions.

For informal adjudications by federal agencies, procedural requirements will ordinarily come from one or more of four potential sources:

(1) §§ 555 and 558 of the federal APA;

(2) the agency legislation;

(3) the Due Process Clause; and

(4) the agency's procedural rules.

These same potential sources of procedural requirements may also apply to formal adjudications. But formal adjudications are *also* subject to §§ 554, 556, and 557, which do not apply to informal adjudications.

Sometimes one or more of the four sources listed above require procedures that make for an informal adjudication that actually has fairly formal procedures. An example is a proceeding to remove an alien from the United States under the federal immigration laws.

Removal proceedings, which used to be called deportation or exclusion proceedings, are not subject to federal APA §§ 554, 556, and 557. Those provisions do not apply because Congress has established an alternate set of procedures that, by statute, are exclusive. *See* 8 U.S.C. § 1229a (2012). The alternate procedural requirements for removal are elaborated upon and supplemented by agency rules. 8 C.F.R. pt. 1240 (2012). Together, the statutes and rules provide for a trial-type hearing and other procedural safeguards comparable in formality to those required by APA §§ 554, 556, and 557.

One procedural safeguard that is missing from removal proceedings — but that is a typical feature of formal adjudications under the federal APA — is the use of ALJs to preside over the hearings. Removal proceedings are presided over, not by ALJs, but instead by Immigration Judges (IJs) employed by the U.S. Department of Justice. IJs lack the job protections that ALJs have under the APA and that are designed to ensure impartiality. That lack of protection, coupled with a serious shortage of IJs and other systemic failings, have led many to believe that, despite the procedural trappings, the administrative system for adjudicating removal is often unfair. *See* Michele Benedetto, *Crisis on the Immigration Bench: An Ethical Perspective*, 28 J. Nat'l Ass'n Admin. L. Judiciary 471, 472–474 (2008); *see also, e.g.*, *Elias v. Gonzales*, 490 F.3d 444, 451 (6th Cir. 2007) ("During the course of the hearing, the IJ repeatedly addressed petitioner in an argumentative, sarcastic, and sometimes arguably insulting manner.").

Removal proceedings are only one example of federal agency adjudications that are not subject to federal APA §§ 554, 556, and 557, but that still require an opportunity for oral, evidentiary hearings and other features of formal adjudications. Two other examples are some nuclear licensing matters and some adjudications to remedy violations of environmental laws. *See* *City of West Chicago v. U.S. Nuclear Regulatory Comm'n*, 701 F.2d 632, 643–645 (7th Cir. 1983) (holding that NRC did not have to follow formal adjudication requirements in proceeding to amend license of facility that processed nuclear material and stored nuclear waste); *Chemical Waste Management, Inc. v. EPA*, 873 F.2d 1477, 1481–1483 (D.C. Cir. 1989) (upholding EPA regulations that did not require formal adjudication in agency adjudications relating to issuance of corrective orders under Resource Conservation and Recovery Act). These two types of adjudications occur under statutes that require the agency to hold a "hearing" but do not expressly require the agency to make a determination "on the record." *See* 42 U.S.C. § 2239(a)(1)(A) (2012); 42 U.S.C. § 6928(b) (2012). The statutes do not trigger the formal adjudication requirements of the federal APA, and so adjudications under these statutes are informal adjudications, even though they include an opportunity for oral, evidentiary hearings.

Though some informal adjudications are pretty formal, most are truly informal. They typically are authorized by statutes that prescribe little or no procedural requirements. The most famous example of informal adjudication is *Citizens to Preserve Overton Park v. Volpe*, 401 U.S. 402 (1971). In that case, the Secretary of Transportation had to decide whether to build an interstate highway through a municipal park in Memphis, or instead attempt to have the highway go around or under the park. The statutes governing the Secretary's decision said nothing about the procedures that the Secretary should follow when making the decision. Thus, they did not require the decision **"to be determined on the record after opportunity for an agency hearing."** 5 U.S.C. § 554(a). Because no statute triggered the federal APA's formal adjudication requirements, the Secretary's decision was an informal adjudication.

Every day, federal officials make countless decisions that are adjudicatory in the sense that they concern the application of law to individualized circumstances. The vast majority of these decisions are based only on paperwork, perhaps supplemented by informal conversations with those affected by the decision. These matters include, for example, many decisions on applications for government grants; many decisions affecting individual federal employees, federal prisoners, or federally owned land and other federally owned property; and many decisions about small-value government purchases of goods and services. The procedures for these decisions are necessarily minimal. Government would grind to a halt otherwise. (Of course, some folks would not consider that a bad thing!)

Summary: Distinguishing Formal from Informal Adjudication

	APA provisions actually or potentially imposing procedural requirements	May other laws impose procedural requirements?
formal adjudication	554, 555, 556, 557 & 558	Yes, including agency legislation, agency rules, and due process requirements
informal adjudication	555 and 558	Yes, including agency legislation, agency rules, and due process requirements

---

2. State Agency Adjudications

State agencies, like federal agencies, may get adjudicatory power from their legislative creator. As true for federal agencies, state agencies are sometimes required by legislation to provide an opportunity for a trial-type hearing and to base their decisions exclusively on an official record of the hearing. And so, like federal administrative law, state administrative law distinguishes (1) agency adjudications that are required to include those procedures from (2) agency adjudications that are not subject to those requirements. In many States, the first type of adjudications are called "contested cases." The second kind may be called "informal adjudication" or go by some other name.

All state APAs of which we are aware prescribe procedures for contested cases. A state APA may, or may not, prescribe procedures for informal adjudications. In any event, the lawyer involved with a state agency adjudication must always consider the applicability of the state APA.

More generally, the primary potential sources of procedural requirements for a state agency's adjudication are:

(1) the state APA

(2) the agency legislation

(3) the Due Process Clause of the Fourteenth Amendment

(4) the agency's procedural rules

When multiple sources of law put procedural requirements on a particular state agency adjudication, the lawyer must synthesize the requirements and reconcile any conflicts.

Exercise: Determining Agency Adjudication Procedures

1. Do the Federal Rules of Civil Procedure apply, of their own force, to federal agency adjudications? (Please identify the provision that answers this question.)

2. Do the Federal Rules of Evidence apply, of their own force, to federal agency adjudications? (Please identify the provision that answers this question.)

3. Would you expect a state court system's civil procedure rules or its rules of evidence to apply, of their own force, to adjudications by state agencies?

D. How Agency Adjudication Compares to Agency Rulemaking

As discussed in Chapter 4, administrative law recognizes a fundamental distinction between agency rulemaking and agency adjudication. True, some agency rulemakings procedurally resemble some agency adjudications. The prime example of this are formal rulemakings and formal adjudications under the federal APA, which are both subject to §§ 556 and 557 of the federal APA. *Generally*, however, agency adjudication differs from agency rulemakings in several ways that we introduce now because they provide context for our examination of agency adjudication. The differences concern (1) the procedures; (2) the nature of agency determinations; (3) and the legal effect of agency determinations. We make generalizations about these differences now, with the aim of returning to them, and refining them, in this part of the book.

1. Procedural Differences

Agency adjudication procedures differ from agency rulemaking procedures in terms of (a) notice of the initiation of the proceeding; (b) opportunity for participation; and (c) notice of the agency's final decision.

a. Notice of the Initiation of the Proceeding

Notice of the initiation of an agency adjudication typically differs from notice of the initiation of agency rulemaking in terms of (i) who gets notice; and (ii) what information the notice contains.

(i) In most agency adjudications, notice of the initiation of the adjudication goes only to the parties. In contrast, in most proceedings to make legislative rules, the entire public is notified of the initiation of the rulemaking by publication of a general notice of proposed rulemaking in the Federal Register or analogous state publication.

(ii) The notice of an agency adjudication ordinarily does not indicate whether the agency plans to use that adjudication to announce a new principle of law (e.g., a new interpretation of a statute that the agency is responsible for administering) or a new agency policy, or to overrule agency precedent. *See* Michael S. Gilmore & Dale D. Goble, *The*

Idaho Administrative Procedure Act: A Primer for the Practitioner, 30 Idaho L. Rev. 273, 308 (1993–1994). And yet agencies are generally free to use adjudication to announce such changes. (Exceptions to this general rule are discussed in Chapter 25.C.) In contrast, the general notice of proposed rulemaking ordinarily contains the text of the proposed rule and an explanation of how the proposed rule, if adopted, will change the law or agency policy.

b. Participation

Participation in agency adjudications differs from participation in agency rulemaking in terms of (i) who can participate; and (ii) what form participation takes.

(i) In most agency adjudications, only parties can participate. Someone wishing to participate in the adjudication who is not initially named as a party must seek to intervene. Some agencies authorize non-parties to participate in a more limited role, like that of an *amicus curiae* in a court case. Even so, participation in agency adjudication is restricted, in contrast to most agency rulemakings, in which anyone may participate.

(ii) An agency adjudication may include an opportunity for a trial-type hearing. This opportunity is rare in an agency rulemaking proceeding. If a rulemaking proceeding does include a live hearing at all, the hearing usually is like a hearing before a city council on a proposed ordinance, or a hearing before a legislative committee on a proposed statute, at which people get an opportunity to "speak their piece."

c. Notice of the Outcome of the Proceeding

The federal APA and most (if not all) state APAs require agencies to make their adjudicatory decisions publicly available. *See, e.g.*, 5 U.S.C. § 552(a)(2) (2012); 1961 Model State APA § 2(a)(4). The federal APA further requires, as do some state APAs, that agencies publish a general index of their adjudicatory decisions, which facilitates research into agency precedent.[2] Despite those requirements, it can be hard to research agency adjudicatory decisions.

In contrast, final rules must be published in the Federal Register or analogous state publication, and final legislative rules are then permanently codified by subject matter in the Code of Federal Regulations or analogous state administrative code. These codifications make it easier to identify the law relevant to your administrative law problem when that law is in agency rules than when it is in agency adjudicatory decisions.

2. Nature of Agency Determinations

Agency adjudications typically differ from agency rulemakings in terms of (a) the nature of the facts on which the agency bases a decision; and (b) the nature of the agency decision.

a. "Adjudicative Facts" vs. "Legislative Facts"

Most agency adjudications primarily concern particularized facts: The facts concern, for example, whether under applicable law a particular party is entitled to benefits or a

---

2. *See, e.g.*, 5 U.S.C. § 552(a)(2)(E); Fla. Stat. Ann. § 120.53(1)(a) (West, Westlaw through Apr. 13, 2012); Idaho Code § 67-5250(1) (Michie 2006); Ind. Code Ann. § 4-21.5-3-32(a) (West, Westlaw through Mar. 20, 2012).

permit—or should be sanctioned—because of that party's circumstances and conduct. Particularized facts of this sort are often called "adjudicative facts." They differ from the generalized facts on which agencies often base rules, which concern, for example, the conditions in the industry to be regulated or the risks to public health posed by a pollutant. These are called "legislative facts." The distinction between adjudicative facts and legislative facts, and its relevance for administrate law, were most famously explored by the administrative law scholar Kenneth Culp Davis. *See, e.g.*, Kenneth C. Davis, *Judicial Notice*, 55 Colum. L. Rev. 945, 952 (1955). The distinction is useful for distinguishing the differing kinds of fact that often dominate adjudication and rulemaking.

b. Applying Law vs. Making Law; Making Policy

Agency adjudication and agency rulemaking involve not only different kinds of fact but different kinds of determinations. The immediate aim of an agency in an adjudication is to determine how existing law applies to the facts of the case before it. Whereas agency adjudication primarily focuses on *applying* the law to a *present* situation, agency legislative rulemaking focuses on *making* law to govern *future* situations. In either setting, however, the agency often has discretion to base its determinations on consideration of policy.

3. Legal Effect

We explore the legal effect of an agency's adjudicatory decision in Chapter 26. In many ways, such a decision has legal effects like those of a court's decision. In contrast, as discussed in Chapter 16, an agency's legislative rule has legal effects like those of a statute.

4. Summary

Exceptions exist to every generalization made above. For example, although agencies do *apply* law in adjudications, they also "make law" to the extent their decision rests on principles that will guide that agency's decision making in future adjudications. The purpose of stating these generalizations is to help you learn about agency adjudication by relating it to an agency process—namely, rulemaking—with which you are already familiar, if you have studied Part Two of the book

E. Common Subjects of
Agency Adjudication

Collectively, agencies adjudicate many different matters. Many agency adjudications, however, fall into one of three categories. Those three categories correspond to three common types of agency activity. It will help you to keep these three categories of agency adjudication in mind. That is because adjudications in each of the three categories share certain features, and differ in some ways from adjudications in the other two categories. We discuss the three types of adjudication below. We also make the point that usually these agency adjudications involve a matter between the government and a private person, but sometimes they involve a matter between private persons.

1. Enforcement Proceedings

First, as discussed in Chapter 1, one common agency activity is telling people what to do. Agencies that spend most of their time telling people what to do are called regulatory agencies. Examples of federal regulatory agencies include the U.S. Environmental Protection Agency, the Occupational Safety and Health Administration, and the Federal Trade Commission. State agencies also exist to enforce state laws controlling environmental pollution, work place safety, and consumer transactions. Most local government have local agencies that tell people what they can and cannot do with their land; they are called land use agencies and are a type of regulatory agency.

Many regulatory agencies have the power to conduct adjudications to enforce the rules and statutes that they are responsible for administering. Those adjudications are often called "enforcement proceedings." An enforcement proceeding within an agency often begins when the agency issues a complaint or citation against a person (an individual or a company) that the agency believes has violated an agency rule or statute. The person charged with the violation can respond to the complaint. If the agency and the person charged cannot settle the matter and if the relevant facts are disputed, the matter might proceed to a trial-type hearing. An agency official presides over the hearing. The presiding official determines whether the charged violation has been proven by *another* agency official who acts as the prosecutor. The presiding official makes an initial decision or a recommended decision based on the evidence at the hearing, and that initial or recommended decision is then subject to review by someone higher up in the agency. If the agency makes a final decision finding a violation, the losing party can usually seek judicial review. Or, the agency itself may have to go to court to enforce whatever sanction or remedy it has ordered at the end of the adjudication.

2. Benefits Proceedings

In addition to or instead of regulating, many agencies distribute government benefits. Agencies that spend most or all of their time doing that are sometimes called "benefits agencies." Examples of federal benefits agencies include the Social Security Administration, the Department of Education, the Department of Agriculture, and the Department of Veterans Affairs, which, respectively, distribute benefits that include Medicare and Medicaid; student grants and loans; grants loans and subsidies to farmers; and veterans benefits. State agencies help administer certain federally created benefits programs, including Medicaid and what used to be called the Food Stamps Program. State and local agencies also administer benefit programs created by state law, such as programs that help poor people pay utility bills.

A benefits agency engages in an adjudication when someone applies to the agency for benefits. In that situation, unlike in an enforcement proceeding, someone outside the agency—namely, the applicant, rather than the agency itself—initiates the adjudication (by filing the application). The benefits agency may initiate an adjudication, however, to modify or terminate someone's continued receipt of ongoing benefit like payments under the federal disability insurance program. The legally required procedures for these benefits adjudications vary. Some adjudications, such as the processing of a college student's request for federal financial aid, are exclusively paperwork processes. Other benefits adjudications may include the opportunity for a trial-type hearing.

3. Licensing Proceedings

A third adjudicatory activity of many agencies is licensing. Examples of licensing agencies include the Nuclear Regulatory Commission and state boards of law examiners and medical examiners. Many commercial activities require multiple permits from multiple agencies. For example, creation of a large housing development may require permits from the local land use agency, as well as from state and federal environmental agencies—to mention just a few.

When an agency *establishes* criteria for getting and keeping a license, the agency is engaged in a type of rulemaking. In contrast, when an agency *applies* those criteria to decide whether a particular license applicant is entitled to a license, the agency is adjudicating. One type of licensing adjudication begins when someone applies for a license. Another type of licensing proceeding begins when the licensing agency seeks to terminate or modify a previously granted license. The granting of some licenses, such as driver's licenses and licenses to practice law and medicine, depend primarily on the applicant's passing a standardized test. The determination whether someone has passed a standardized test ordinarily will not require a trial-type hearing. Other licensing proceedings may involve analysis of highly technical data. As with benefits proceedings, licensing proceedings do not follow a typical path.

4. Parties to Agency Adjudication

Most matters adjudicated by agencies involve rights and duties between a private person and the government. That is true when someone seeks benefits or a license from the government, and when the government seeks to terminate someone's benefits or license. Likewise, in many enforcement proceedings, the agency's enforcement officials are pitted against a private person whom, the enforcement officials believe, has violated a law the agency is responsible for enforcing.

While most agency adjudications involve a private person with a matter before the government, some agency adjudications involve legal rights or duties that one private person owes another private person. Below we introduce three examples of "private person vs. private person" disputes that agencies adjudicate:

a. Workers' Compensation Schemes

All States and the federal government have enacted statutes creating workers' compensation schemes. In the typical workers' compensation scheme, a worker alleging an on-the-job injury files a claim for benefits with a workers' compensation agency. In the States, these are usually called the Workers' Compensation (or Industrial) Commission. The worker seeks compensation for the injury from either the employer or a state workers' compensation fund. A workers' compensation proceeding between the employee and employer is a dispute between private parties, in which the agency plays a judicial role by deciding whether the worker is entitled to benefits from the employer. In making that decision, the agency does not apply tort principles. Instead, the employer can be liable for an employee's on-the-job injury whether or not the employer is to blame. Workers' compensation schemes create no-fault liability determined according to substantive criteria established by statutes and regulations.

b. Reparations Claims

Some regulatory statutes allow people injured by regulatory violations to seek reparations from the violator through an administrative adjudication. The parties to reparation proceedings are the injured person and the violator. The agency plays a judicial role.

An example of a reparations scheme is established by the federal Commodity Exchange Act. 7 U.S.C. §§ 1–27f (2012). The Act regulates trading in commodity futures. (The classic example of a commodity for which futures used to be traded is pork bellies.) The Act also establishes a reparation scheme for disputes between commodity futures brokers and their customers. If a commodity futures broker violates the Act or rules issued under it and that violation causes financial injury to a customer, the customer can file a reparations claim against the broker with a federal agency called the Commodity Futures Trading Commission. *Id.* § 18; *see also Commodity Futures Trading Comm'n v. Schor*, 478 U.S. 833 (1986).

Other federal statutes creating reparation schemes are the Perishable Agricultural Commodities Act, 7 U.S.C. §§ 499a–499s (2012), and the Packers and Stockyards Act, 7 U.S.C. §§ 181–229c (2012). The reparation schemes established by those statutes give people a choice to seek reparations for regulatory violations in a federal court or before a federal agency. 7 U.S.C. §§ 209(b) & 499(b). What factors do you think influence the choice between those forums?

c. Patent Interference Proceedings

In general, the first person to invent something can patent the invention. A patent is issued by the federal government. The patent gives the person the exclusive right (for a time) to make and sell the invention. *See* 35 U.S.C. § 102(g) (2012).

Sometimes disputes arise about who was the first person to invent something. These disputes can be adjudicated by the Board of Patent Appeals and Interferences, an agency within the U.S. Patent and Trademark Office, which is itself an agency within the U.S. Department of Commerce. In such an adjudication, known as an "interference proceeding," the Board decides who, as between multiple inventors, was actually first. *See id.* § 135. Although an interference proceeding involves a government issued benefit—a patent— it resolves competing claims to that benefit by private persons.

5. Cautions

This discussion of types of agency adjudication ends with three cautions.

First, we emphasize that the three types of adjudication discussed above—enforcement proceedings, benefits proceedings, and licensing proceedings—do not account for all agency adjudications. Some agency adjudications do not fall into any of these categories. For example, when a government agency selects one company, among several bidders, to build a new aircraft carrier, the agency is adjudicating. Indeed, government procurement decisions like that are an important type of adjudication, even though they don't really fall into any of the three categories. Another kind of agency adjudication—reparation proceedings, which were mentioned earlier in this chapter—does not really fit into the three categories described in this section. The three categories are useful but not exhaustive.

Second, some agencies do more than one type of adjudication. Many agencies, for example, issue licenses and initiate enforcement proceedings against licensees who have violated the rules for licensees. Other agencies may administer benefits programs and regulatory programs. The larger the agency, the more likely it is to engage in many different types of adjudication.

Finally, you cannot assume that all enforcement proceedings are alike; or that all benefits proceedings are alike; or that all licensing proceedings are alike. The careful lawyer always identifies and analyzes all laws applicable to the agency adjudication under analysis.

Exercise: Common Types of Agency Adjudication

You learn better when you relate knowledge to be learned with knowledge you already have. With that in mind:

1. Identify *regulatory* laws (federal, state, or local) with which you or someone you know must comply.

2. Identify government *benefits* (federal, state, or local) that you or someone you know has gotten or is getting.

3. Identify government *licenses* (other than a driver's license) that you or someone you know has received.

F. The Distinction between the Agency as Adjudicator and the Agency as Litigant

So far in this chapter we have been discussing agency adjudications, in which an agency decides the legal rights and duties of identified parties. Now we distinguish situations in which an agency adjudicates a matter from situations in which the agency is a party to— i.e., a litigant in—a judicial proceeding. The two situations can be tricky to keep straight unless you know about them going into your study of agency adjudication. They are tricky partly because sometimes an *agency* adjudication leads to a *court* adjudication. We first address situations in which an agency adjudication is followed by a court action to which the agency is a party. We then address situations in which *no* agency adjudication precedes the court adjudication to which an agency is a party.

The first situation is graphically depicted in Diagram 17-2.

Diagram 17-2. Agency Adjudication Followed by Court Adjudication

Agency
Ⓙ

Time 1: Agency adjudication begins

Time 2: Agency issues Final Order in agency adjudication

Court

Time 3: Agency sues to enforce Agency's Final Order; or dissatisfied Person sues Agency to challenge Agency's Final Order

Time 4: Court enters final judgment in the case

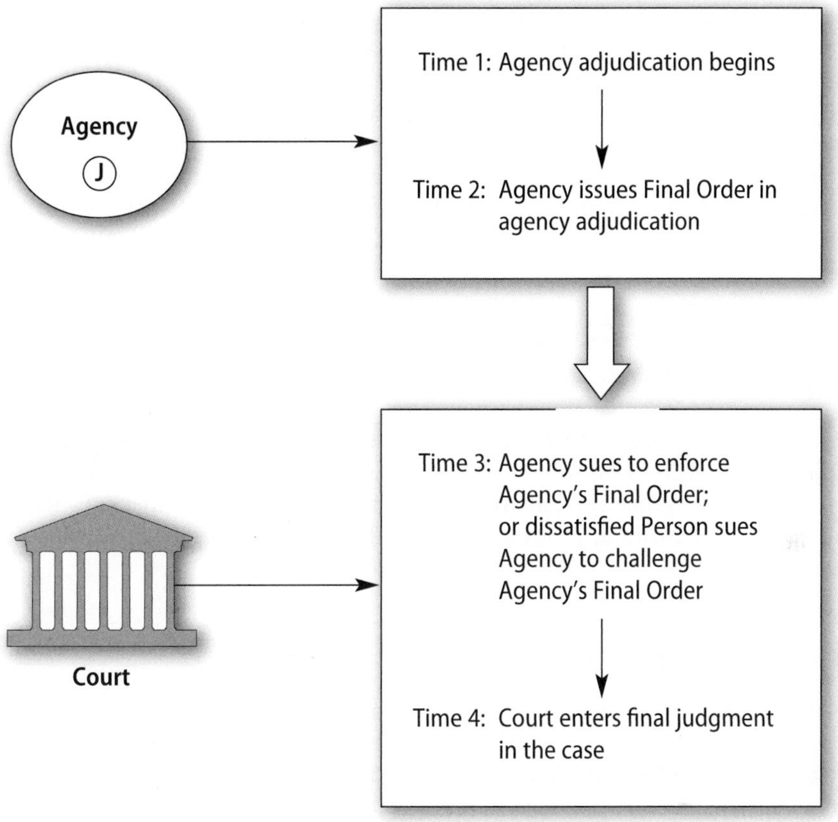

1. Agency Adjudication Followed by Court Adjudication

Sometimes a matter begins as an agency adjudication and later becomes the subject of a court proceeding. This sequence can occur in two situations. The sequence can occur (a) when an agency adjudicates a matter and someone dissatisfied with the agency's adjudicatory decision challenges that decision in court. The sequence can also occur (b) when an agency adjudicates a matter but must go to court to enforce its adjudicatory decision. We will explain each situation.

a. Judicial Review of Agency Orders

After an agency conducts an adjudication and enters a final order in that adjudication, someone adversely affected by that order usually can seek judicial review. For example, judicial review is normally available for agency decisions imposing sanctions, denying benefits, and denying licenses. In this situation, the agency is on the defensive in the court proceeding. Indeed, the agency may be named as the defendant.

b. Judicial Enforcement of Agency Orders

Sometimes, the agency goes to court as a plaintiff to enforce its adjudicatory decision. For example, the Federal Trade Commission may end a formal adjudication by entering a cease-and-desist order against a company that has violated the Federal Trade Commission Act. If the company does not obey the cease-and-desist order, the FTC can go to court for a court order requiring the company to obey. In that proceeding, the company can challenge the order on procedural or substantive grounds. If the court upholds the order, the court may enter an injunction compelling obedience. 15 U.S.C. § 45(l) (2012).

2. Court Adjudications Not Preceded by an Agency Adjudication

As described in subsection 1 above, an agency may go to court to defend or enforce its adjudicatory decision. But this is not the only scenario in which agencies go — or are taken — to court. Agencies end up in court in many other situations that are *not* preceded by an agency adjudication. In these other situations, the agency may be a plaintiff or a defendant.

a. The Agency as Plaintiff

Not all agencies have adjudicatory power. Suppose an agency lacks adjudicatory power and sees someone violating a law that the agency is responsible for enforcing. How does the agency enforce that law? The answer is: The agency often has the power to go to court and get a judicial remedy against the violator by proving the violation to the court's satisfaction.

An example of an agency that lacks broad adjudicatory power and that therefore must often go directly to court to enforce the law is the Equal Employment Opportunity Commission (EEOC). For example, the EEOC has authority under the federal law called "Title VII" to investigate complaints of employment discrimination by private employers. In addition to investigating those complaints, the EEOC can try to resolve the complaints by "informal methods of conference, conciliation, and persuasion." 42 U.S.C. § 2000e-5(b) (2012). The EEOC cannot, however, adjudicate an employment complaint to determine whether a private employer has violated Title VII and, if so, to impose a sanction. Instead, if the EEOC determines that a private employer has violated Title VII and deserves to be sanctioned, the EEOC must file a civil action in federal court. *See id.* § 2000e-5(f). By filing and litigating the lawsuit, EEOC is exercising an executive-type power. The situation is depicted in Diagram 17-3.

An agency also may have to go initially to court — even if it has some adjudicatory power — if it wants a remedy that the agency cannot itself order in an agency adjudication. For example, the SEC has power to adjudicate many different kinds of violations of the securities laws and, in its adjudications, impose sanctions such as cease-and-desist orders and large civil fines. The SEC must go to court, however, if the SEC wants to bar someone who has violated the securities laws from serving as an officer of a public company. *See* 15 U.S.C. § 78u(d)(2) (2012); *SEC v. Patell*, 61 F.3d 137 (2nd Cir. 1995). By statute, that particular remedy is available only from a court.

Diagram 17-3. Example of Agency as Litigant (Plaintiff)

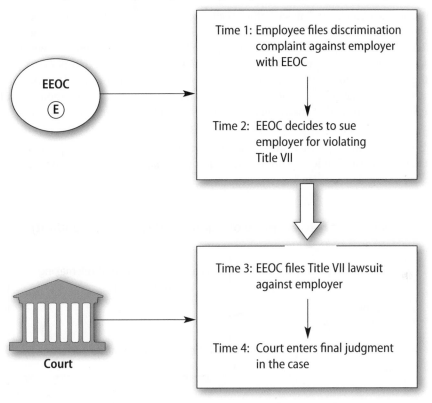

When an agency goes directly to court to enforce the law that it is responsible for administering, it is much like any other plaintiff. The agency will bear the burden of proving through admissible evidence the violation that it alleges in its court complaint. The defendant charged with the violation may take the case to trial. In fact, the defendant may even have a right to a jury trial. *See, e.g., EEOC v. W&O, Inc.,* 213 F.3d 600 (11th Cir. 2000) (discussing which issues could be decided by a judge and which had to be decided by a jury in a discrimination suit by EEOC). In any event, this situation does not involve judicial *review* of an agency adjudication, because there has been no agency adjudication. The court adjudicates the matter "de novo." In particular, any factual disputes will be resolved in the court proceeding (by the judge in bench trial or the jury in a jury trial), based on evidence presented in court.

There is one kind of remedy that can only come from a court and that an agency can never order: criminal punishment. An agency cannot impose a criminal penalty such as a prison term or criminal fines in an agency adjudication. Beyond that, most agencies cannot themselves even bring criminal prosecutions in court; they must refer the matter to a law enforcement agency. Federal agencies ordinarily refer potential criminal matters to the U.S. Department of Justice. State and local agencies refer potential criminal matters to state and local prosecutors. These law enforcement agencies have prosecutors who work with agency officials to build and present criminal charges in court against people who have allegedly committed regulatory crimes.

b. The Agency as Defendant

People sue agencies and agency officials all the time—and not just to get judicial review of agency adjudicatory decisions. For example, a person may sue an agency to get judicial review of a new legislative rule that the agency has promulgated and that will hurt the person. Alternatively, a person may sue an agency that has denied that person's petition asking the agency to commence rulemaking. To cite yet another example, a person may sue an agency because the agency has failed to take action—e.g., on an application for a permit. The point is that many agency actions—besides an agency's adjudicatory decision—can lead to judicial proceedings in which the agency defends itself as a litigant.

In these situations, unlike situations in which the agency is a plaintiff, the agency is on the defensive and indeed is often named as a defendant. These situations are depicted in Diagram 17-4.

Diagram 17-4. Example of Agency as Litigant (Defendant)

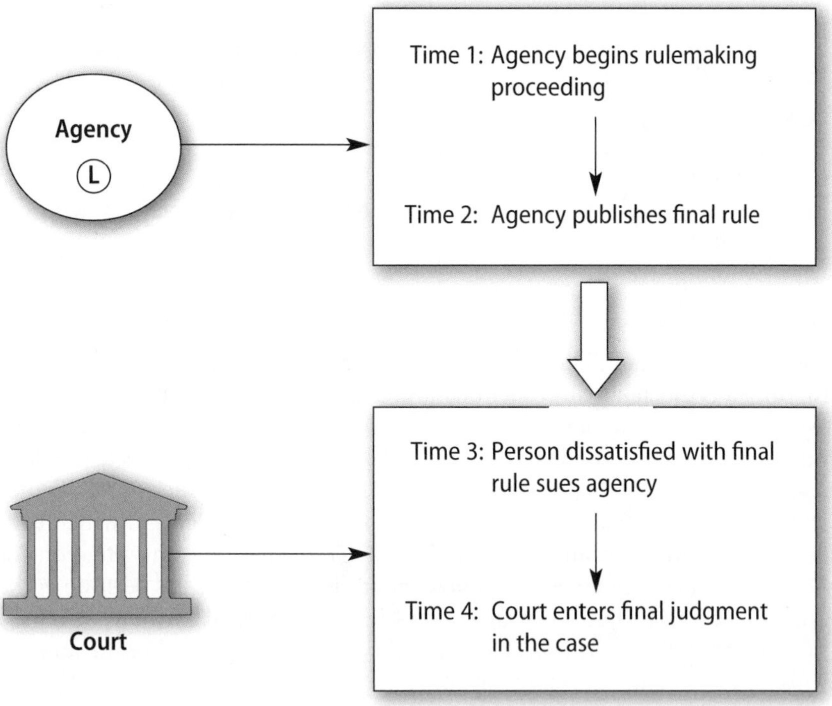

Exercise: Agency as Adjudicator and Litigant

The National Labor Relations Board has powers under 29 U.S.C. § 160 (2012) to prevent unfair labor practices. You don't have to know what an unfair labor practice is to identify the Board's powers to adjudicate and litigate cases involving alleged unfair labor practices. Please examine § 160 and answer these questions:

1. What subsection of § 160 authorizes the Board to adjudicate unfair labor practice charges?

2.   What subsection of § 160 authorizes the Board, as a litigant, to go to court to enforce a Board decision finding an unfair labor practice and ordering a remedy for that practice?

3.   What subsection of § 160 authorizes a person to make the Board a litigant (specifically a defendant) by seeking judicial review of a Board decision finding the person guilty of an unfair labor practice charge?

G. Agency Adjudication within the Problem Solving Framework

This part's exploration of agency adjudication, like Part Two's exploration of agency rulemaking, is organized to reflect the problem solving framework for agency action presented in Chapter 2. Recall that the framework incorporates three questions that commonly arise about an agency action:

(1) Is there a valid source of power for the agency to take this action?

(2) If so, has the agency obeyed limits on, and requirements for exercising, that power?

(3) If the agency lacks power to take the action, or has not obeyed limits on, or requirements for exercising, that power, what can be done about it?

As we did in Part Two for agency rulemaking, for now we defer the third question with respect to agency adjudication. We defer it because this book, consistently with most administrative law courses, addresses the question of "what can be done about invalid agency action"—including an invalid agency rule or adjudication decision—primarily by exploring the availability and scope of judicial relief for such action; and we devote Part Four of this book to that subject. That leaves for this part of the book the first two questions, relating to (1) agency power and (2) limits on, and requirements for exercising, agency power.

H. Chapter 17 Wrap Up and Roadmap of Part 3

We hope that this chapter gives you a foundation for exploring agency adjudication. From this chapter, you have learned that an agency can adjudicate only when it has the power to do so, and that an agency's adjudicatory power ordinarily comes from a statute. You have also learned how agency adjudication compares to court adjudication and agency rulemaking. You have learned what lawyers do, and should not do, in agency adjudications. You have gotten an introduction to the terms "informal adjudication," "formal adjudication," and "contested cases." You have also been introduced to the three common subjects of agency adjudication, and to the differing roles of an agency as an adjudicator and litigant.

Upcoming chapters explore agency adjudication using an approach similar to the one we used to explore agency rulemaking.

First, we take an overview of (1) the source of power for agency adjudication; and (2) the sources of *limits* on that power. This overview occurs in Chapters 18 and 19.

Then we home in on limits imposed by the constitutional doctrine of procedural due process and by the Administrative Procedure Act. We explore due process limits in Chapter 20, and we survey APA limits in Chapter 21.

The federal APA, in particular, prescribes procedural requirements for formal adjudications. We examine requirements for formal adjudications in Chapters 22 through 24. In the process, we touch upon state APA requirements for contested cases.

Having explored procedures for agency adjudication, in Chapter 25 we examine the discretion that many modern agencies have to choose either rulemaking or adjudication to carry out their missions.

Finally, we examine the legal effects of an agency's adjudicatory decision in Chapter 26.

Chapter Problem Revisited

This chapter problem concerns the reasons for licensing day care providers. Licensing is one form of adjudication. The objective of the chapter problem is to give you a concrete example for considering the reasons this particular type of administrative adjudication is used. In particular, we highlight three things about licensing.

First, licensing is a form of administrative adjudication that typically *supplements*, rather than supplanting, the court adjudication process. For example, a licensed day care provider can still be sued for negligence by, say, a parent whose child suffers an injury because of a provider's negligence. A licensed day care provider can still be criminally prosecuted for, say, reckless endangerment or criminal child abuse. In short, licensing typically overlays the traditional set of judicial remedies.

Second, unlike court adjudication, licensing seeks to prevent problems, rather than remedying them after they occur. By requiring someone to get a license before they provide day care, the government can screen prospective providers to make sure they have the appropriate background and training. For example, licenses can be denied to people who have a chronic history of physical violence. In this sense, licenses serve as barriers to entering a profession. Consider: What problems arise from creating such a barrier? What grounds justify creating the barrier?

Third, licensing systems cannot work without licensing *criteria*. The formulation of criteria for getting a license is a legislative or rulemaking activity. The legislature can make the criteria itself; leave the matter to the licensing agency; or adopt a middle ground by formulating some general criteria that the agency must elaborate upon. To the extent Senator Nguyen worries about unrealistic standards for getting and keeping a license, these worries might be addressed by a combination of (1) the legislature's restricting the ability of the agency to devise unduly onerous licensing requirements; (2) authorizing judicial review of licensing decisions to ensure compliance with legislatively prescribed licensing criteria; and (3) legislative oversight.

Professional Development Reflection Question

This chapter compares agency adjudication to judicial proceedings, and there are indeed similarities. In particular, lawyers in each type of proceeding act as advocates for clients. Moreover, many agency adjudications, like most judicial proceedings, are adversarial. Thus, the lawyer's client has an opponent, and the lawyer representing that client must deal with opposing counsel. Law students who are conflict-averse reasonably should consider whether a legal practice dominated by agency adjudication or court litigation is "for them." That is the question we pose for you to consider during your exploration of agency adjudication: Is it for you?

In considering that question, some background information may help. First, not all agency adjudication is, in fact, adversarial. For example, the Social Security Administration's processing of claims for benefits under the Social Security Act is nonadversarial; no government official or lawyer has the job of opposing the claim for benefits, though, of course, SSA officials do have the responsibility of determining eligibility. Furthermore, many agency adjudications do not require lawyers for the parties to duke it out, face to face, in front of a judge. Instead, they are adjudications based on written submissions. Finally, even agency adjudications that do revolve around trial-like, evidentiary proceedings don't feature the courtroom drama of the sort you see on television. That is because juries are never used in agency adjudications; the trier of fact is an agency official who will be most impressed—not by lawyers who are loud, flamboyant, and aggressive—but by lawyers who are well-prepared, well-organized, polite, efficient, and, perhaps most importantly, who know the rules for that particular agency adjudication.

In addition to considering whether agency adjudication may be something you'd be interested in doing as a lawyer, we ask that you take a moment and write down what you would guess are five qualities or habits of lawyers who meet with the least success, and earn the least credibility, in agency adjudications.

1. _____

2. _____

3. _____

4. _____

5. _____

Chapter 18

Agency Adjudicatory Power

Overview

Many administrative law problems involving agency adjudication pose these two questions:

(1) Is there a valid source of power for the agency adjudication?

(2) If so, has the agency obeyed limits on, and requirements for exercising, its adjudicatory power?

This chapter addresses the question of adjudicatory power. Chapter 19 and later chapters address limits on, and requirements for exercising, adjudicatory power. This chapter's sections are entitled:

A. Analyzing Agency Adjudicatory Power

B. Identifying and Analyzing Grants of Adjudicatory Power to Agencies

C. Federal Constitutional Restrictions on Statutory Grants of Adjudicatory Power to Federal Agencies

D. Modern State Law on Adjudicative Delegations to State Agencies

E. Chapter 18 Wrap Up and Look Ahead

Chapter Problem

You are an advisor to the President of the United States. The President has asked for your advice on how to respond to a massive oil spill off the coast of California. The President wants to ask Congress to set up an administrative system for compensating people who have suffered economic harm from the spill. The President believes an administrative system of adjudicating compensation claims will be faster and cheaper than forcing victims of the spill to file lawsuits.

The President wants your advice on minimizing the risk of a successful constitutional challenge to an administrative adjudicative system. Specifically, the President asks whether either of these two features could affect its constitutionality.

1. The money to compensate victims could come from two sources.

One source is the federal government itself. Under this approach, Congress would appropriate, say, $30 billion and put it in a compensation fund. The federal government would hope eventually to recover this much or more in separate proceedings the government itself would bring against the companies responsible for the spill. In the meantime, though, victims would file claims for compensation from the fund, not from the private companies apparently responsible for the spill.

The other possibility is for the money to come directly from the companies responsible for the spill. Under this approach, the government would administratively adjudicate claims by victims of the spill against the responsible companies, for money out of the companies' coffers.

Would one approach present less risk of unconstitutionality than the other?

2.   Assume the President goes with the second approach, under which victims file administrative claims directly against the apparently responsible private companies. Should the claims be administratively adjudicated simply under state tort law, or should the federal legislation creating this compensation scheme create federal substantive law—perhaps largely through federal agency rulemaking—establishing federal standards of liability as part of a larger federal regulatory scheme to prevent and remedy this and future environmental catastrophes?

In short, from a constitutional perspective, is it better for the administrative compensation scheme to rely on state tort law or on federal regulatory law?

A. Analyzing Agency Adjudicatory Power

We can subdivide into two parts the question of whether there is a valid source of power for a particular agency adjudication:

a)   Is there a grant of adjudicatory power?

b)   Is the grant of adjudicatory power valid?

The first question arises because agencies have no inherent power. An agency's power to adjudicate a matter must come from somewhere. Agencies with adjudicatory power usually get that power from the agency legislation. We will therefore generally refer to "the agency legislation" as the source of adjudicatory power. Even so, grants of adjudicatory power can come from other sources, such as executive orders and, for some state agencies, from state constitutions. For example, the U.S. Department of Labor depends partly on authority from an executive order to adjudicate some equal employment opportunity matters involving government contractors. *See* Exec. Order 11,246, pt. 2, 42 U.S.C. § 2000e Note (2012).

Whatever the source of an agency's adjudicatory power, administrative lawyers must know how to recognize those grants. In section B of this chapter, you will learn how to do that.

The second question arises because, for an agency adjudication to be valid, the statute granting the agency adjudicatory power must be valid. A federal statute is invalid if it violates the U.S. Constitution or has been expressly or impliedly repealed by a later federal statute; a state statute is invalid if it violates the State constitutions or federal law; or has been expressly or repealed by a later state statute; or is preempted by federal law.

Rather than canvass all possible grounds of invalidity, we will focus in section C of this chapter on constitutional restrictions on Congress's authority to delegate adjudicatory power to federal agencies. Those restrictions stem from Article III and the Seventh Amendment of the U.S. Constitution. We also touch in section D of this chapter on state constitutional restrictions on state statutes delegating adjudicatory power to state agencies.

Before moving on, we note that for agency adjudications, there is no distinction analogous to the distinction between legislative and non-legislative rules. True, sometimes an agency makes a non-binding, individualized determination about how the law applies to a particular set of facts. For example, an agency may give someone a non-binding opinion of how the law applies to that person's circumstances, while emphasizing that the agency cannot be held to that opinion and that the opinion does not have the force of law. Such an opinion, if rendered by a federal agency, probably falls outside the federal APA's definition of **"adjudication"** as the agency process for making an **"order,"** which the APA defines as a **"final disposition."** *See* 5 U.S.C. §551(6) & (7) (2012). An agency opinion that does not really "dispose" of a matter but merely reflects the agency's non-binding view on the matter may not be an **"adjudication"** at all.

B. Identifying and Analyzing Grants of Adjudicatory Power to Agencies

When you have an administrative law problem involving a potential or ongoing agency adjudication, you must identify and analyze the possible sources of statutory authority for the adjudication.

1. Identifying the Source of Adjudicatory Authority

Often the agency itself identifies its (supposed) source(s) of adjudicatory authority, but sometimes you must figure this out for yourself. You can use the following research strategies:

- Find out from the agency, by searching its website or contacting agency personnel directly (subject to legal constraints, discussed in Chapter 3.D, on contacting represented parties in litigation).
- Consult secondary sources (e.g., treatises and law review articles) discussing the particular kind of agency adjudication under analysis.
- Research court opinions on the particular kind of agency adjudication under analysis.
- Identify the statutes that the agency is responsible for administering, using strategies discussed in Chapter 3.C, and examine the ones that are most applicable to the adjudication under analysis.

This process may yield several possible sources of authority, or may reveal no evident sources of authority. Indeed, the agency's authority may become a disputed issue. In any event, you may have to study statutory provisions to determine whether they, in fact, authorize the adjudication under analysis.

2. Analyzing Potential Sources of Agency Adjudicatory Authority

Statutory grants of agency *rulemaking* power are usually easy to identify. They typically use verbs like "make," "adopt," "issue," "prescribe" or "promulgate"; and use direct objects such as "rules," "regulations," "criteria," "guidelines," or "standards." Statutory grants of *adjudicatory* power can be harder to identify. They usually authorize the agency to make individualized determinations that have legal effect, but they do not use terminology that is as standardized as that found in statutory grants of rulemaking power.

Because it can be hard to tell if a statute grants adjudicatory authority, we present below examples of statutes that do so. We select statutes granting adjudicatory power to agencies in each of the three common situations we identified in Chapter 17.E: enforcement proceedings, benefits proceedings, and licensing. We also give an example of a statute that an agency mistakenly believed gave it adjudicatory power.

As you study these examples, keep in mind that the specific statutory provisions granting adjudicatory power are part of larger pieces of agency legislation. Although we reproduce the specific statutory language granting adjudicatory authority, lawyers analyzing specific exercises of that statutory authority must study the entire statute in which the grant of adjudicatory power occurs. That is necessary to identify all intrinsic limits on that power. The lawyer must also identify all agency rules applicable to the exercise of a specific statutory grant of adjudicatory power.

Even in the isolated portions of statutes we reproduce below, you will find not only language granting adjudicatory power but also language limiting the exercise of that power. As you study these statutory provisions, pay attention to both the language that grants power and the language limiting it.

a. Statutes Granting Agencies Power to Conduct Enforcement Proceedings

The Securities and Exchange Commission (SEC) and the U.S. Department of Agriculture have power to use adjudication to enforce the laws they are responsible for administering. We will give examples of statutes granting that power.

The SEC has authority under the Securities Act of 1933 to conduct cease-and-desist proceedings to stop violations of the Act and of rules promulgated under the Act:

---

15 U.S.C. § 77h-1. Cease-and-desist proceedings

(a) Authority of Commission

If the Commission finds, after notice and opportunity for hearing, that any person is violating, has violated, or is about to violate any provision of this subchapter, or any rule or regulation thereunder, the Commission may publish its findings and enter an order requiring such person, and any other person that is, was, or would be a cause of the violation, due to an act or omission the person knew or should have known would contribute to such violation, to cease and desist from committing or causing such violation and any future violation of the same provision, rule, or regulation. Such order may, in addition to requiring a person to cease and desist from committing or causing a violation, require such person to comply, or to take steps to effect compliance, with such provision, rule or regulation, upon such terms and conditions and within such time as the Commission may specify in such order. Any such order may, as the Commission deems appropriate, require future compliance or steps to effect future compliance, either permanently or for such period of time as the Commission may specify, with such provision, rule, or regulation with respect to any security, any issuer, or any other person....

This provision grants the SEC adjudicatory power by authorizing it to "fin[d]" a violation and to "enter an order" requiring the person responsible for the violation to cease and desist. The newcomer to agency adjudications might not recognize this wording as a grant of adjudicatory power.

The Secretary of Agriculture has authority under the legislation creating the food stamp program to conduct adjudications to disqualify and impose civil penalties on grocery stores that violate the program. For example, a grocery store violates the program if it lets someone use food stamps to buy liquor or cigarettes. The statutes authorizing the Secretary to punish grocery stores for such violations say in relevant part:

---

7 U.S.C. § 2021. Civil penalties and disqualification of retail food stores and wholesale food concerns

(a) Disqualification

(1) In general

An approved retail food store or wholesale food concern that violates a provision of this chapter or a regulation under this chapter may be—

(A) disqualified for a specified period of time from further participation in the supplemental nutrition assistance program;

(B) assessed a civil penalty of up to $100,000 for each violation; or

(C) both.

(2) Regulations

Regulations promulgated under this chapter shall provide criteria for the finding of a violation of, the suspension or disqualification of and the assessment of a civil penalty against a retail food store or wholesale food concern on the basis of evidence that may include facts established through on-site investigations, inconsistent redemption data, or evidence obtained through a transaction report under an electronic benefit transfer system. . . .

(c) Civil penalty and review of disqualification and penalty determinations

(1) Civil penalty

In addition to a disqualification under this section, the Secretary may assess a civil penalty in an amount not to exceed $100,000 for each violation.

(2) Review

The action of disqualification or the imposition of a civil penalty shall be subject to review as provided in section 2023 of this title.

---

7 U.S.C. § 2023. Administrative and judicial review; restoration of rights

(a)(1) Whenever . . . a retail food store . . . is disqualified or subjected to a civil money penalty under the provisions of section 2021 of this title, . . . notice of such administrative action shall be issued to the retail food store . . .

(3) If such store . . . is aggrieved by such action, it may, in accordance with regulations promulgated under this chapter, within ten days of the date of delivery of such notice, file a written request for an opportunity to submit information in support of its position to such person or persons as the regulations may designate.

(4) If such a request is not made or if such store ... fails to submit information in support of its position after filing a request, the administrative determination shall be final.

(5) If such request is made by such store ... such information as may be submitted by the store..., as well as such other information as may be available, shall be reviewed by the person or persons designated by the Secretary, who shall, subject to the right of judicial review hereinafter provided, make a determination which shall be final and which shall take effect thirty days after the date of the delivery or service of such final notice of determination....

In these statutory provisions, adjudicatory powers are packed into language authorizing USDA to "disqualif[y]" food stores and to "asses[s] a civil penalty." The powers are limited, however, by substantive and procedural requirements in these provisions and elsewhere in the statutes.

b. Statutes Granting Agencies Power to Distribute Benefits

The largest benefits programs are administered by the Commissioner of Social Security. Here is the statutory provision authorizing the Commissioner to adjudicate claims for benefits under the program that pays monthly benefits to retirees:

42 U.S.C. § 405. Evidence, procedure, and certification for payments ...

(b) Administrative determination of entitlement to benefits; findings of fact; hearings; investigations; evidentiary hearings in reconsiderations of disability benefit terminations; subsequent applications

(1) The Commissioner of Social Security is directed to make findings of.fact, and decisions as to the rights of any individual applying for a payment under this subchapter....

The power to "make ... decisions as to the rights" of individual applicants is the power to adjudicate claims for benefits.

Many government benefits do not take the form of cash payments. The U.S. Department of Veterans Affairs administers many types of benefits programs. This provision, for example, authorizes services for mentally ill and homeless veterans:

38 U.S.C. § 2031. General treatment

(a) In providing care and services ... to veterans suffering from serious mental illness, including veterans who are homeless, the Secretary may provide ... —

(1) outreach services;

(2) care, treatment, and rehabilitative services (directly or by contract in community-based treatment facilities, including halfway houses); and

(3) therapeutic transitional housing assistance ...

The statutory authority to provide these services implies the authority to determine whether a particular veteran is eligible as one who is "suffering from serious mental illness." This statute therefore grants adjudicatory power, though it does so less obviously than the statute above authorizing the Commissioner of Social Security to "make ... decisions" on applications for benefits.

c. Statutes Granting Agencies Licensing Authority

The Secretary of Interior has authority under the Taylor Grazing Act to issue permits allowing people to use public land to graze cattle and other livestock. Here is the specific provision in the Act granting that authority:

---

43 U.S.C. § 315b. Grazing permits ...

The Secretary of the Interior is authorized to issue or cause to be issued permits to graze livestock on such grazing districts to such bona fide settlers, residents, and other stock owners as under his rules and regulations are entitled to participate in the use of the range, upon the payment annually of reasonable fees in each case to be fixed or determined from time to time in accordance with governing law....

The Secretary engages in adjudication when he or she "issue[s] or cause[s] to be issued [a] permi[t]." Thus, the verb "issue" can refer to adjudicatory conduct when applied to a permit, even while it refers to rulemaking activity when used in the phrase "issue such rules and regulations ...".

The U.S. EPA grants many types of permits. For example, the EPA grants permits under the National Pollutant Discharge Elimination System established by the Clean Water Act. These permits allow people to discharge pollutants into the water, subject to all kinds of restrictions. 33 U.S.C. § 1342 (2012). The statutory language authorizing the EPA Administrator to issue these permits is as follows:

---

33 U.S.C. § 1342. National pollutant discharge elimination system

(a) Permits for discharge of pollutants

(1) Except as provided in sections 1328 and 1344 of this title, the Administrator may, after opportunity for public hearing, issue a permit for the discharge of any pollutant, or combination of pollutants, notwithstanding section 1311(a) of this title, upon condition that such discharge will meet either (A) all applicable requirements under sections 1311, 1312, 1316, 1317, 1318, and 1343 of this title, or (B) prior to the taking of necessary implementing actions relating to all such requirements, such conditions as the Administrator determines are necessary to carry out the provisions of this chapter....

What verbs besides "issue" might a statute use when authorizing an agency to license an activity?

d. Statutes Not Granting Adjudicatory Power

Now we summarize a case in which the Consumer Product Safety Commission mistakenly believed that a statute granted it adjudicatory power.

- *Athlone Industries, Inc. v. Consumer Product Safety Commission*, 707 F.2d 1485 (D.C. Cir. 1983)

The Consumer Product Safety Act requires a company to notify the Consumer Product Safety Commission when the company thinks one of its products has a defect that makes the product dangerous. A violation of the notification requirement is a "prohibited act," as defined in 15 U.S.C. § 2068.

The Commission believed that Athlone Industries violated § 2068 by failing to notify the Commission about defects in the company's automatic baseball pitching machines. The Commission began an agency adjudication to assess civil penalties against Athlone. The Commission claimed authority to adjudicate the matter under 15 U.S.C. § 2069 (Supp. V 1981). Section 2069 stated in relevant part:

---

15 U.S.C. § 2069. Civil Penalties

(a) Amount of penalty

… Any person who knowingly violates section 2068 of this title shall be subject to a civil penalty not to exceed $2,000 for each such violation.…

(b) Relevant factors in determining amount of penalty

In determining the amount of any penalty to be sought upon commencing an action seeking to assess a penalty for a violation of section 2068(a) of this title, the Commission shall consider the nature of the product defect, the severity of the risk of injury, the occurrence or absence of injury, the number of defective products distributed, and the appropriateness of such penalty in relation to the size of the business of the person charged.

(c) Compromise of penalty …

Any civil penalty under this section may be compromised by the Commission. In determining the amount of such penalty or whether it should be remitted or mitigated and in what amount, the Commission shall consider [the same factors as are listed in § 2069(b)] …

The Commission relied on the language in this provision authorizing it to "commenc[e] an action seeking to assess a penalty." In the administrative adjudication, Athlone moved to dismiss the proceeding on the ground that this statutory language did not authorize the Commission to conduct adjudications. After the Commission denied Athlone's motion to dismiss, Athlone filed a federal court suit against the Commission seeking a permanent injunction against the Commission proceeding. Although a federal district denied Athlone relief, the United States Court of Appeals reversed, and held that Athlone was right: the Commission lacked statutory authority to adjudicate civil penalties.

The court of appeals cited three reasons to interpret § 2069 as not granting adjudicatory power to the Commission. First, the court determined that, when Congress uses the term "action," rather than the term "proceeding," Congress usually means a court action. Second, the court found evidence in the legislative history that Congress intended to require the Commission to bring a lawsuit when the Commission wanted to recover a penalty. Finally, the court believed that § 2069 resembled another statute that had been interpreted to require a federal agency to go to court when the agency wanted to recover a civil penalty. *Athlone*, 707 F.2d at 1490–1492.

In short, the Commission interpreted a statute as giving it adjudicatory power to assess penalties, but the statute actually required the Commission to act as a litigant, rather than an adjudicator, to enforce the statutory provision authorizing civil penalties for statutory violations. This meant that the Commission could recover a penalty only if proved a violation to the court's satisfaction, through evidence presented to the court in accordance with the rules of evidence, and sufficient to satisfy the burden of proof. The moral of the *Athlone* case is that statutory grants of adjudicatory power can be hard to identify. For a U.S. Supreme Court case illustrating the same moral, see *Coit Independence Joint Venture v. Fed. Sav. & Loan Ins. Corp.*, 489 U.S. 561, 572–579 (1989) (Federal Savings and Loan Insurance Corporation did not have power to adjudicate creditor's claims against insolvent banks).

Exercise: Identifying Statutory Grants of Adjudicatory Power to an Agency

The Indian Gaming Regulatory Act (IGRA) establishes a federal agency called the National Indian Gaming Commission, which has a Chairman. 25 U.S.C. § 2704 (2012). This provision requires the Chairman under certain conditions to approve tribal ordinances and resolutions authorizing "Class II gaming activity" (which includes bingo and certain card games).

25 U.S.C. § 2710. Tribal gaming ordinances ...

(b) Regulation of class II gaming activity ...

(2) The Chairman shall approve any tribal ordinance or resolution concerning the conduct, or regulation of class II gaming on the Indian lands within the tribe's jurisdiction if such ordinance or resolution provides that —

(A) except as provided in paragraph (4), the Indian tribe will have the sole proprietary interest and responsibility for the conduct of any gaming activity;

(B) net revenues from any tribal gaming are not to be used for purposes other than —

(i) to fund tribal government operations or programs;

(ii) to provide for the general welfare of the Indian tribe and its members;

(iii) to promote tribal economic development;

(iv) to donate to charitable organizations; or

(v) to help fund operations of local government agencies;

[and other conditions] ...

Please explain why this provision gives the Chairman adjudicatory power and how it limits that power.

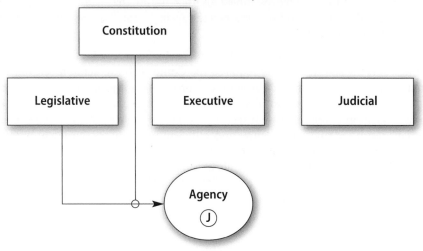

Diagram 18-1. Constitutional Limits on Statutory
Grants of Adjudicatory Power

C. Federal Constitutional Restrictions on Statutory Grants of Adjudicatory Power to Federal Agencies

The U.S. Constitution limits Congress's ability to delegate adjudicatory power to federal agencies. The limits are depicted in Diagram 18-1.

The objectives of this section are to help you learn the source and substance of the constitutional limits on legislative delegation of adjudicatory power, and to help you identify and analyze situations in which a statute arguably violates those limits. To achieve those objectives, we discuss (1) the relevant constitutional text; (2) historical case law interpreting that text; and (3) modern case law.

1. Relevant Constitutional Text

First we remind you of the textual bases in the U.S. Constitution for the separation of powers doctrine. Then we focus on the textual basis for the specific facet of the separation of powers doctrine that limits statutes delegating adjudicatory power to federal agencies. We also identify the Seventh Amendment as a limit on such statutes.

a. Textual Basis for Separation of Powers Doctrine

The textual bases for the separation of powers doctrine are the vesting clauses of Articles I, II, and III of the U.S. Constitution:

U.S. Const. art. I, § 1

All legislative Powers herein granted shall be vested in a Congress of the United States, which shall consist of a Senate and House of Representatives.

U.S. Const. art. II, § 1

The executive Power shall be vested in a President of the United States of America....

U.S. Const. art. III, § 1

The judicial Power of the United States, shall be vested in one supreme Court, and in such inferior Courts as the Congress may from time to time ordain and establish....

The separation of powers doctrine has several facets relevant to administrative law.

One facet is called the "delegation" or "non-delegation" doctrine. We examined the non-delegation doctrine in Chapter 8. The non-delegation doctrine limits Congress's ability to delegate to federal agencies the quasi-legislative power to make legislative rules. As construed by the U.S. Supreme Court, the non-delegation doctrine requires federal statutes to prescribe an "intelligible principle" for the agency to follow when making legislative rules.

The terms "delegation doctrine" and "non-delegation doctrine" refer only to constitutional limits on statutes granting agencies the quasi-legislative power to make legislative rules. The terms do not refer to constitutional limits on statutes granting agencies the quasi-judicial power to adjudicate cases administratively.

Nonetheless, there *are* constitutional limits on statutes delegating quasi-judicial power to agencies. We will refer to these statutes as "adjudicative delegations." As you will learn in this chapter, the constitutional limits on adjudicative delegations cannot be encapsulated in any shorthand phrase analogous to the "intelligible principle" standard used for federal statutes delegating quasi-legislative power.

b. Textual Basis for Separation of Powers Limits and Seventh Amendment Limits on Federal Adjudicative Delegations

Article III and the Seventh Amendment have been interpreted to limit adjudicative delegations by Congress to federal agencies.

Article III says that federal judicial power "shall be vested" in the U.S. Supreme Court and the lower federal courts. Article III's vesting language does not appear as strict as the language in Article I that vests "all" legislative power in Congress. Article III does not say that "all" judicial power must be vested in the specified federal courts. Despite that difference, Article III does appear to limit the judicial power to "courts" whose judges hold potentially lifetime appointments and irreducible salaries. *See* U.S. Const. art. III, § 1 ("The Judges, both of the supreme and inferior Courts, shall hold their Offices during good Behavior, and shall ... receive ... a compensation, which shall not be diminished...."). There is little doubt that at the time the Constitution was drafted, the word "court" referred to traditional courts of law. Thus, you could reasonably argue that in the federal system the judicial power may be exercised only by an Article III "court" presided over by an Article III "judge."

Neither Congress nor the Court, however, has interpreted Article III to prevent Congress from granting adjudicatory power to non-Article III entities. To the contrary, Congress has often granted adjudicatory power to entities other than Article III courts staffed by Article III judges. The Court has generally upheld these statutes against challenges based on Article III. Its grounds for doing so are discussed below.

Besides Article III limits, the Seventh Amendment may limit adjudicative delegations. The Seventh Amendment preserves the right to a jury trial in certain civil actions:

U.S. Const. amend. VII

In Suits at common law, where the value in controversy shall exceed twenty dollars, the right of trial by jury shall be preserved ...

The question has arisen: Can Congress authorize a federal *agency* to adjudicate a matter that, if adjudicated in federal court, the parties would have a Seventh Amendment right to have tried by a jury?

The next section summarizes the cases in which the Court has addressed Article III and Seventh Amendment limits on adjudicative delegations.

2. Historical U.S. Supreme Court Case Law

In early cases, the Court approved federal laws that delegated the power to adjudicate matters to non-Article III entities in three main situations. Non-Article III entities could serve as military courts, as territorial courts, and as tribunals for adjudicating "public rights." *Northern Pipeline Construction Co. v. Marathon Pipe Line Co.*, 458 U.S. 50, 65–68 (1982). In addition, non-Article III entities could serve as "adjuncts" to Article III courts. *Id.* at 78. The "public rights" and the "adjunct" situations are the most important for modern administrative law.

a. Public Rights

The Court defined "public rights" in early cases basically to mean non-constitutional rights asserted by people in disputes with the government. *See Crowell v. Benson*, 285 U.S. 22, 50 (1932). The Court gave as examples of disputes involving public rights: tax disputes; disputes over the reasonableness of rates charged to customers by a regulated entity such as a railroad or public utility; a dispute over whether a company has violated a federal statute by engaging in an unfair practice affecting interstate commerce; customs disputes; immigration disputes; and cases involving public lands, public money, and veterans benefits. *Id.* at 51 & n.13. The Court made clear that "administrative agencies" could be "created for the determination of such matters." *Id.* at 51. "Public rights" matters did not extend, however, to criminal prosecutions, even though the government is, of course, always a party to those prosecutions. *Northern Pipeline*, 458 U.S. 50, 70 n.24 (1982). Thus, public rights disputes were ordinary civil disputes between someone and the government.

The justification for allowing public rights to be adjudicated outside of Article III courts was essentially twofold. First, sovereign immunity generally bars people from suing the federal government without its consent. Since Congress did not have to allow people to sue the federal government over public rights matters at all (because of sovereign immunity), Congress could authorize suits involving public rights to be adjudicated by non-Article III entities. The idea is that the greater power to bar suits altogether includes the lesser power to restrict the suits to being adjudicated initially by non-Article III entities. Second, the public rights doctrine reflected that claims regarding public rights had historically been decided by legislatures or executive officials. For example, the first Congress assigned to Treasury Department officials adjudication of monetary claims against the government. Richard Fallon, *Of Legislative Courts, Administrative Agencies, and Article III*, 101 Harv. L. Rev. 915, 919 & n.17 (1988).

The public rights doctrine continues to justify the adjudicatory power of many modern federal agencies, as well as that of what are called "Article I" courts (or "legislative courts"). Current Article I courts include the Bankruptcy Courts, the U.S. Tax Court, the Court of Federal Claims, the Court of Appeals for the Armed Forces, and the Court of Appeals for Veterans Claims. Article I courts are created by federal statutes and staffed by "Article I judges," who, unlike Article III judges, serve fixed terms and lack constitutional protection against salary reductions. Article I courts are usually studied primarily in law school courses on the federal courts. We mention them here only to explain why we frame the current issue as involving the constitutional limits on adjudication of matters by "non-Article III entities," which include Article I courts as well as federal agencies.

Exercise: Identifying Public Rights

Please explain whether the following agency adjudications involve "public rights" as that term was historically defined.

1. The Federal Trade Commission determines in an enforcement proceeding that a company involved in interstate commerce has engaged in an unfair and deceptive trade practice.

2. At the end of an agency adjudication, the Department of the Interior issues a lease allowing a company to explore for oil and gas in an area of the Outer Continental Shelf, which is owned by the federal government.

3. The Social Security Administration determines in an adjudication that someone is not eligible for disability insurance payments from the government under the Social Security Act.

4. The U.S. Department of Labor determines in an adjudication that a private shipping company should pay benefits to one of its employees who was injured on the job and is therefore entitled to benefits under the federal Longshore and Harbor Workers' Compensation Act.

5. The federal Civil Board of Contract Appeals resolves through adjudication a contract dispute between a government contractor and a federal agency.

---

b. Agencies as Adjuncts to Courts

In addition to allowing non-Article III entities to adjudicate public rights, the Court made clear in early cases that non-Article III entities can serve as "adjuncts" to Article III judges. The Court grounded the "adjunct" theory on history. Courts of equity, for example, traditionally could farm out certain chores — especially ones related to gathering evidence and proposing findings of fact — to special masters who were not Article III judges. The special masters worked for judges; they had no independent decisionmaking power. They were adjuncts to the courts.

The adjunct theory permitted non-Article III entities, including administrative agencies, to gather evidence and do fact finding even in matters involving "private rights" — which were defined in early case law as rights that are asserted in disputes between private parties. Non-Article III entities could generally make findings of fact as long as an Article III court could (1) finally determine the legal significance of those factual determinations; and (2) freely review determinations of facts relevant to the agency's jurisdiction or to constitutional claims.

Under the adjunct theory, for example, the Court in *Crowell v. Benson*, 285 U.S. 22 (1932), upheld the administrative adjudication of claims under the federal Longshore and Harbor Workers' Compensation Act. The Act authorized an administrative official to award benefits to maritime employees injured on the job. The benefits were payable by employers. Because adjudications under the Act concerned rights as between the employee and employer, they concerned private rights, not public rights. The Court observed that, in disputes involving private rights, "there is no requirement that ... all determinations of fact ... shall be made by judges." *Id.* at 51. The adjunct theory upon which the Court relied in *Crowell v. Benson* has been cited in modern cases to uphold statutes granting agencies the power to adjudicate matters, as long as an Article III court has "plenary review" of "questions of law." *Gibas v. Saginaw Min. Co.*, 748 F.2d 1112, 1119–1120 (6th Cir. 1984).

c. Continuing Relevance of Historical Case Law

Historical case law allows federal agencies today to adjudicate "public rights" and to act as "adjuncts" to federal courts. As discussed below, under the Court's modern case law Congress can also authorize federal agencies to adjudicate in certain, additional situations that do not fall within the traditional definition of "public rights" or within the adjunct theory.

3. Modern Federal Law on Adjudicative Delegations

The Court in modern cases continues to refer to the distinction between public rights and private rights, and to the adjunct theory. The Court's modern decisions, however, have de-emphasized the public rights/private rights distinction when analyzing statutes delegating adjudicative power to federal agencies. The Court has also addressed Seventh Amendment limits on adjudicative delegations. We discuss Article III limits and Seventh Amendment limits separately.

a. Article III Limits

Below we describe the leading, modern cases on Congress's ability to delegate adjudicatory power to federal agencies consistently with Article III. As you read the descriptions, focus on this question: Under what circumstances can a federal agency initially adjudicate a matter *in addition to* (1) matters involving public rights; and (2) situations in which the agency acts only as an "adjunct" to an Article III court?

- *Thomas v. Union Carbide Agricultural Products Co.*, 473 U.S. 568 (1985)

In *Thomas*, the Court rejected an Article III challenge to provisions in the Federal Insecticide, Fungicide, and Rodenticide Act (FIFRA).

FIFRA requires pesticide manufacturers to register their pesticides with the EPA. To register a pesticide, the manufacturer must give EPA data about the pesticide's safety and its effect on health and the environment. FIFRA had special provisions for manufacturers who wanted to register pesticides similar to ones that were previously registered. These "follow-on" manufacturers could have EPA consider data submitted in connection with the previously registered, similar pesticide. For EPA to do this, however, the follow-on manufacturer had to agree to compensate the manufacturer of the previously registered pesticide. If the two manufacturers could not agree on the compensation, FIFRA required them to work it out in binding arbitration. The arbitrator's award was subject to only limited judicial review; a court could set aside the arbitration award only for "fraud, misrepresentation, or other misconduct." *Thomas*, 473 U.S. at 573–574 (quoting statute as it then existed).

FIFRA's compensation scheme was challenged by a manufacturer that was dissatisfied with an arbitrator's compensation award and with the limited scope of judicial review of that award. The manufacturer argued that the scheme delegated too much adjudicative authority to the non-Article III arbitrator. The manufacturer pointed out that the arbitrator adjudicated "private rights," involving how much money one private company owed another private company for use of privately owned data.

The Court rejected the Article III challenge. The Court said Article III analysis should turn on "practical attention to substance" instead of a formalistic distinction between public rights and private rights. *Id.* at 587. Having said this, the Court still found significant that the compensation right created by FIFRA "bears many of the characteristics of a 'public right.'" *Id.* at 589. In particular, the right to compensation was created by FIFRA; it was not a common law right of the sort that courts traditionally have adjudicated. In addition, the right was created, not just to benefit the owners of the data, but also to "serve a public purpose" of facilitating review of pesticide safety. *Id.* The right to compensation was, furthermore, closely intertwined with FIFRA's regulatory scheme. It was "an integral part of a program safeguarding the public health." *Id.* at 590. All these factors meant that, although the right to compensation was a private right, it was "so closely integrated into a public regulatory scheme as to be a matter appropriate for agency resolution with limited involvement by the Article III judiciary." *Id.* at 594.

The Court cited two other considerations. First, the arbitration scheme was a "pragmatic" response to a "near disaster" caused by an earlier version of FIFRA. *Id.* at 590. The earlier FIFRA had produced a "logjam of litigation" over EPA's use of one company's data to consider registration of other companies' pesticides. *Id.* at 573. Second, the arbitration scheme did not significantly depend for its effectiveness on judicial enforcement of arbitration awards. Instead, if a follow-on manufacturer failed to pay the arbitration award, EPA canceled the registration of the follow-on manufacturer's pesticide. If the manufacturer of a previously registered pesticide whose data was to be used in registering a follow-on pesticide refused to participate in the arbitration scheme, EPA would consider its data without compensation. Thus, EPA could—without the assistance of the courts—effectively require manufacturers to obey arbitration procedures and arbitral awards. This scheme largely avoided involving courts in enforcing administrative arbitral decisions the merits of which the courts had little power to review. *Id.* at 591.

Both the outcome and reasoning of *Thomas* are significant. The *outcome* was that the Court upheld adjudication of private rights by a non-Article III entity, subject to extremely limited judicial review. This result expanded Congress's power to delegate adjudicative authority beyond what the Court's precedent on public rights and the adjunct theory could reasonably have been read to allow. The Court's *reasoning* in *Thomas* was important because the Court avoided a formalistic reliance on the public rights/private rights distinction in favor of a pragmatic approach.

• *Commodity Futures Trading Commission v. Schor*, 478 U.S. 833 (1986)

In *Schor* the Court again upheld an administrative adjudication scheme against an Article III challenge.

A federal statute regulates trading in commodity futures. The statute is called the Commodity Exchange Act (CEA or Act). The Act creates the Commodity Futures Trading Commission to administer the Act.

The Act authorizes the Commission to adjudicate claims against commodity brokers by their customers. A customer can file an administrative claim against a broker for violating the substantive provisions of the Act or legislative rules promulgated under the Act. In the ensuing administrative adjudication before the Commission, the customer can seek damages, called "reparations," for the broker's violations.

A customer named Schor started a reparation proceeding before the Commission against his broker, a man named Conti. Customer Schor contended that broker Conti had violated the Act in ways that damaged Schor. In the reparation proceeding brought by customer Schor, broker Conti counterclaimed for the debit amount in Schor's brokerage account. Whereas customer Schor's reparation claim was based on federal law — namely, violations of the CEA — broker Conti's counterclaim for the account debit was a breach-of-contract claim based on state law.

An administrative law judge ruled in favor of broker Conti on both customer Schor's reparation claim and Conti's counterclaim. This meant that customer Schor did not recover reparations and was, in fact, ordered to pay the balance due on his account with broker Conti. The Commission allowed the ALJ's decision to become the agency's final decision.

As the case reached the U.S. Supreme Court, no one disputed that Congress could allow the Commission to adjudicate customer Schor's claim for reparations under the Act. *Id.* at 856 ("This reparations scheme itself is of unquestioned constitutional validity.") Although customer Schor's reparation claim involved a private right (a right to compensation from another private party), agency adjudication of it was constitutional under *Thomas*. Like the data compensation disputes in *Thomas*, a reparation claim under the CEA was "so closely integrated into a public regulatory scheme as to be a matter appropriate for agency resolution with limited involvement by the Article III judiciary." *Thomas*, 473 U.S. at 594. The issue in *Schor* was whether the Commission could *also* adjudicate broker Conti's state-law counterclaim to recover the debit amount in Schor's account. This state-law counterclaim not only involved a private right; as a claim based on state common law, it was "of the kind assumed to be at the 'core' of matters normally reserved to Article III courts." *Id.* at 852.

Even so, the Court held that the Commission's adjudication of the compulsory counterclaim did not violate Article III.

The Court said that Article III serves two functions. It "serves both to protect the role of the independent judiciary within the constitutional scheme of tripartite government … and to safeguard litigants' right to have claims decided before judges who are free from potential domination by other branches of government." *Id.* at 848. The first was a "structural" function; the second a "personal" function. *Id.*

Customer Schor had waived the personal protections of Article III; Schor waived them by submitting his reparations claim to the Commission for adjudication. By submitting his reparations claim to a federal agency for adjudication, Schor, in effect, consented to having the Commission adjudicate not only his reparation claim but also Conti's compulsory counterclaim.

To determine whether allowing the Commission to adjudicate the compulsory counterclaim violated Article III's structural function, the Court took a "pragmatic" rather than a "formalistic" approach. *Id.* at 851, 853. Under a pragmatic approach, the counterclaim's being a private right, rather than a public right, did not compel a conclusion that an agency's adjudication of it violated Article III. Instead, the Court had to consider, among other factors,

> the extent to which the essential attributes of judicial power are reserved to Article III courts, and, conversely, the extent to which the non-Article III forum exercises the range of jurisdiction and powers normally vested only in Article III courts, the origins and importance of the right to be adjudicated, and the concerns that drove Congress to depart from the requirements of Article III.

Id. at 851 (internal quotation marks omitted).

Considering these factors, the Court upheld the statutory scheme allowing the Commission to adjudicate state-law compulsory counterclaims like Conti's. The Court admitted that an agency's adjudication of "private common law rights," when challenged on Article III grounds, requires a "searching" examination. *Id.* at 854. The "origi[n]" of the right made it strongly suited for judicial rather than administrative adjudication. *Id.* at 851. The Court nonetheless upheld the agency's authority to adjudicate such rights based on four considerations:

1. The Commission's adjudicatory powers "depart from the traditional agency model in just one respect: [its] jurisdiction over common law counterclaims." *Id.* at 852.

2. Like the workers' compensation agency in *Crowell v. Benson*, the Commission deals only with a "particularized area of law." *Id.*

3. The Act did not require brokers and customers to submit their claims to an agency for adjudication; they could go to court instead. This choice of forums mitigated Article III concerns. The Court reasoned: "[I]t seems self-evident that just as Congress may encourage parties to settle a dispute out of court or resort to arbitration without impermissible incursions on the separation of powers, Congress may make available a quasi-judicial mechanism through which willing parties may, at their option, elect to resolve their differences." *Id.* at 855.

4. Congress had good reasons for allowing the Commission to adjudicate state common law counterclaims. The arrangement allowed for a single, inexpensive forum to resolve all disputes between a customer and broker arising from a particular transaction or series of transactions regulated by federal law. *See id.* at 855–856.

Schor's result and reasoning are important. The result was important in going farther than any previous case in allowing adjudicative delegations to federal agencies. Specifically, the Court in *Schor* for the first time allowed a federal agency to adjudicate a purely private right arising from state common law. *Schor*'s reasoning is important because it continues the "pragmatic" approach taken in *Thomas*.

- *Stern v. Marshall*, 131 S.Ct. 2594 (2011)

In *Stern*, the Court held that Congress violated Article III by giving Article I Bankruptcy Courts power to adjudicate a state tort claim asserted in a bankruptcy proceeding.

Although *Stern* involved adjudication by a bankruptcy court, not a federal agency, the Court's decision may bear on statutes granting adjudicatory power to federal agencies. That is because bankruptcy courts, like federal agencies, are not created under Article III of the Constitution. Bankruptcy judges lack the lifetime tenure and irreducible salaries that Article III guarantees to the judges of Article III courts. Statutes granting adjudicatory power to bankruptcy judges implicate Article III concerns, like statutes granting adjudicatory power to federal agencies, because they threaten to take away business that traditionally has belonged to the Article III courts.

Stern involved a counterclaim made by the bankruptcy trustee against a person who had first filed a claim against the bankruptcy estate. Specifically, in response to Pierce Marshall's claim against the bankruptcy estate, bankruptcy trustee Vickie Marshall counterclaimed that Pierce had tortiously interfered with a gift that Vickie's husband intended to give her at his death. Ms. Marshall's tortious-interference counterclaim rested on state tort law. The counterclaim did not have anything to do with bankruptcy law. It was an ordinary state tort claim of the sort that state courts routinely adjudicate and federal courts do, too, when exercising diversity or supplemental jurisdiction. In other words, there was nothing about the counterclaim that required the expertise of a bankruptcy judge. Furthermore, if bankruptcy judges were allowed to adjudicate state tort claims like Ms. Marshall's, they would apparently be allowed to adjudicate a broad range of claims that traditionally have been adjudicated by Article III courts.

In holding that Congress could not authorize a bankruptcy court to adjudicate the counterclaim, the Court determined that the counterclaim did not involve a public right and that the bankruptcy court was not acting merely as an adjunct to an Article III court. The counterclaim did not involve a public right even under the broadest conception that the Court's precedent had suggested, because the claim did not "derive[e] from a federal regulatory scheme," nor was its "resolution ... by an expert government agency ... essential to a limited regulatory objective within the agency's authority." 131 S.Ct. at 2613. In plain English, the counterclaim was nothing like the claims adjudicated by agencies in *Thomas* and *Schor*. Furthermore, the bankruptcy court was not acting merely as an adjunct because it did not "ma[k] only specialized, narrowly confined factual determinations regarding a particularized area of law or engage in statutorily channeled factfinding functions." *Id.* at 2618. Rather, the bankruptcy court was acting like an Article III court.

It is possible that *Stern* will not greatly affect analysis of statutes granting adjudicatory power to federal agencies. The Court emphasized in *Stern*: "We deal here not with any agency but with a court." *Id.* at 2615. The Court described the case before it as "markedly distinct from the agency cases" such as *Thomas* and *Schor*. *Id.* Because of this description, the opinion in *Stern* might not cut back on *Thomas* and *Schor*.

b. Seventh Amendment Limits

Suppose a private company has a dispute with the federal government over whether the company violated a federal regulation. Also suppose that, if a federal *court* adjudicates the dispute, the company will have a right to a jury trial under the Seventh Amendment. Can Congress eliminate the jury trial right by authorizing a federal agency, instead of a federal court, to adjudicate the dispute?

The answer is "yes," *if*, as is true in our hypothetical private company's case, the federal agency adjudicates public rights. The Court gave this answer in the following case:

- *Atlas Roofing Co. v. Occupational Safety & Health Review Commission*, 430 U.S. 442 (1977)

In *Atlas Roofing*, officials from the U.S. Department of Labor charged two companies with violating federal workplace safety rules. To contest the charges, the companies had to go through an administrative adjudication before an agency called the Occupational Safety and Health Review Commission. The Commission concluded that the companies had violated the rules, and it imposed civil penalties on the companies. The companies sought judicial review of the Commission's action, arguing that the administrative adjudication scheme violated the Seventh Amendment because the adjudication before the Commission offered no jury trial.

The U.S. Supreme Court rejected the companies' Seventh Amendment challenge. The Court held that Congress can authorize a federal agency to adjudicate a matter involving public rights even if—were a federal court to adjudicate the same matter—the Seventh Amendment would confer a right to a jury trial.

* * *

In *Atlas Roofing* and a later case, the Court suggested that the Seventh Amendment bars a federal agency from adjudicating "private rights" as to which a right to a jury trial exists, except when the agency is acting merely as an adjunct to a federal court. *See Atlas Roofing*, 430 U.S. at 4 ("In cases which do involve only 'private rights,' this Court has accepted factfinding by an administrative agency, without intervention by a jury, only as an adjunct to an Art. III court."); *Granfinanciera v. Nordberg*, 492 U.S. 33, 51–52 (1989) (Congress "lacks the power to strip parties contesting matters of private right of their constitutional right to a trial by jury."). If this suggestion ever hardens into a holding, the Seventh Amendment could prevent federal agencies from adjudicating certain private rights that Article III would not prevent them from adjudicating. It is possible, for example, that the Seventh Amendment would forbid federal agencies from adjudicating state common-law claims that the Court in *Schor* held could be adjudicated by the Commodity Futures Trading Commission without violating Article III. This is just speculation, though; the Court has left unclear Seventh Amendment restrictions on federal agency adjudications.

It is clear, however, that, just as the Seventh Amendment might bar agency adjudications that would not be barred by Article III, the converse is possible: Article III could bar agency adjudications that would not be barred by the Seventh Amendment. That is because the Seventh Amendment right to a jury trial does not attach to all private rights. Instead, the Seventh Amendment only applies to claims of private right that are the same or similar to claims as to which a jury trial right attached in 1789. *See, e.g.*, *Curtis v. Loether*, 415 U.S. 189, 192–195 (1974). Seventh Amendment concerns thus arise only when a federal agency adjudicates private rights to which a jury trial right attaches. Some private rights, such as those created by federal regulatory schemes, may not carry a Seventh Amendment jury trial right, even if asserted in a federal court.

Fortunately, administrative lawyers seldom encounter Seventh Amendment issues in agency adjudications for two reasons. First, the Seventh Amendment applies only to adjudications by the *federal* government. The Seventh Amendment does not apply to adjudications by state or local government courts or agencies. *See McDonald v. City of Chicago*, 130 S.Ct. 3020, 3035 n.13 (2010). Second, most federal agencies adjudicate matters involving either "public rights" or private rights that do not carry a right to a jury trial.

c. Federal Agency Adjudication of Fines and Other Penalties

As mentioned above, "public rights" matters do not include criminal actions. Criminal actions are special. The Constitution's Sixth Amendment gives criminal defendants a right to trial by jury, and related trial rights, that would be violated if an agency adjudicated a criminal matter. *See, e.g., Wong Wing v. United States*, 163 U.S. 228, 237–238 (1896). Congress can authorize federal agencies to impose civil fines and other civil sanctions, such as cease-and-desist orders or orders suspending, restricting, or revoking required licenses. *See, e.g., Oceanic Steam Navigation Co. v. Stranahan*, 214 U.S. 320, 337–338 (1909). But the Constitution bars federal agencies from imposing criminal punishments.

In theory, a civil sanction could be so extreme as to constitute a criminal punishment, and thus be beyond the power of a federal agency to impose. Just because Congress authorizes a federal agency to impose a sanction that Congress labels a civil sanction, that does not prevent a court from concluding, in an exceptional case, that the sanction really constitutes criminal punishment. But only a truly extreme civil sanction might be invalidated as a criminal punishment. *See Helvering v. Mitchell*, 303 U.S. 391, 398–405 (1938) (IRS assessed taxpayer a penalty representing 50% of tax underpayment; Court held that this penalty was a civil, not a criminal, sanction); *Atlas Roofing Co. v. Occupational Safety & Health Review Comm'n*, 518 F.2d 990 (5th Cir. 1995) (rejecting a company's argument that an OSHA fine was so large that it was really a criminal penalty, not a civil fine).

Exercise: Framework for Analyzing Adjudicative Delegations

Construct an outline or graphic organizer (e.g. flow chart) for analyzing federal adjudicative delegations. To get you started, here are key questions your framework must address:

1. Does the federal statute under analysis involve adjudication of only public rights?

2. Does the federal statute under analysis authorize the agency to act merely as an adjunct to a federal court?

3. If the federal statute under analysis does allow for a federal agency to adjudicate private rights, is agency adjudication of those rights justified under the "pragmatic" approach of *Thomas* and *Schor*?

4. If the federal statute under analysis does allow for a federal agency to adjudicate private rights, are the rights ones that, if litigated in a federal court, carry a right to a jury trial?

D. Modern State Law on Adjudicative Delegations to State Agencies

Most state constitutions, like Article III of the U.S. Constitution, assign judicial power to a judicial branch that is separate from the legislative and executive branches. By assigning judicial power to a separate branch, the state constitutions imply limits on the exercise of judicial power by executive-branch agencies. Many state constitutions also guarantee the right to a jury trial in certain civil actions. Thus, state courts have had to decide whether the state legislature can delegate adjudicatory power to state agencies consistently with their constitution's separation of powers and jury trial guarantees, just as the federal courts have done.

Different States have taken different approaches, though many recognize the distinction between public rights and private rights. Generally, state courts express most concern about state statutes delegating to state agencies the power to adjudicate private rights. Most state courts generally uphold these delegations, but put limits on the ability of state agencies to adjudicate private rights.

One of the oldest and most common situations in which agencies adjudicate private rights is under workers' compensation statutes. The typical workers' compensation statute allows an employee injured on the job to get compensation from the employer (or a state fund) whether or not the employer's fault caused the injury. The adjudication of a workers' compensation claim against a private employer involve private rights. Even so, administrative adjudication of workers' compensation claims is universally upheld against separation of powers challenges, often in part because workers' compensation schemes do not operate on the fault-based system of liability that characterizes the tort law administered by courts.

A well-known state court decision addressing agency adjudication of private rights is *McHugh v. Santa Monica Rent Control Bd.*, 777 P.2d 91 (Cal. 1989). The California Supreme Court in *McHugh* reviewed a local law empowering a local rent control board to adjudicate tenants' claims against landlords for excessive rents. The law was challenged on the ground that it violated the clause in the California Constitution that vests judicial power in the state courts. The court in *McHugh* discussed many court decisions from other States and discerned two principles that it adopted as California law:

> The better analyzed and more thoughtful decisions, as we read them, set out the following guidelines: An administrative agency may constitutionally hold hearings, determine facts, apply the law to those facts, and order relief—including certain types of monetary relief—so long as (i) such activities are authorized by statute or legislation and are reasonably necessary to effectuate the administrative agency's primary, legitimate regulatory purposes, and (ii) the "essential" judicial power (i.e., the power to make enforceable, binding judgments) remains ultimately in the courts, through review of agency determinations.

Id. at 106. Applying these principles, the court held that the rent control board could adjudicate excessive rent claims and award restitution. *Id.* at 108–109. The board could not, however, allow tenants to recover restitution by withholding future rent payments. Empowering the board to authorize tenants to withhold future rent would give the board's orders a "self-enforceable" character that would hinder effective judicial review of them. *Id.* at 109. Also, the board could not award treble damages. That power "pose[d] a risk of producing arbitrary, disproportionate results that magnify, beyond acceptable risks, the possibility of arbitrariness inherent in any scheme of administrative adjudication." *Id.* at 111.

The *McHugh* court observed that modern courts have not "rigidly construed" constitutional provisions vesting judicial power in a judicial branch. *Id.* 102. Rather, "a more tolerant approach to the delegation of judicial powers has emerged out of a perceived necessity to accommodate administrative adjudication of certain disputes and thereby to cope with increasing demands on our traditional judicial system." *Id.* The tolerant approach generally balances the need to have an agency exercise adjudicatory power against the degree to which the agency's exercise of this power infringes on the courts' traditional turf. *See, e.g., Gelb v. Dep't of Fire, Bldg. & Life Safety*, 241 P.3d 512 (Ariz. Ct. App. 2010) (holding that a state statute violated state constitution's separation of powers doctrine by allowing an agency to adjudicate disputes between homeowners and homeowners associations in planned communities). Of course, delegations also cannot violate constitutional provisions protecting individual rights, such as those of criminal defendants.

If you encounter a state statute that delegates adjudicative power to an agency in a way that causes your separation of powers antennae to quiver, you will want to do three things. First, identify and analyze the state constitutional provisions that have been construed to limit adjudicative delegations. Then identify and analyze the state court case law construing these constitutional provisions. Third, consider whether—in addition to or instead of arguing that the state statute under analysis exceeds constitutional limits—you should argue that the statute should be interpreted to avoid exceeding constitutional limits. A state court may be more open to interpreting a statute narrowly to avoid constitutional problems than to holding that the statute violates the state constitution. The narrow-construction approach finds support in a presumption that federal courts and many state courts make—namely, that the legislature acts within constitutional limits.

State constitutional provisions bearing on adjudicative delegations are not limited to provisions requiring separation of powers, vesting judicial power in the judicial branch, and guaranteeing a right to a jury trial. For example, many States have constitutional provisions guaranteeing open access to the courts.[1] State courts sometimes construe these "open courts" provisions to bar statutes that require people to adjudicate before an agency matters that are traditionally handled by courts. *See, e.g., State ex rel. Cardinal Glennon Mem. Hosp. v. Gaertner*, 583 S.W.2d 107 (Mo. 1979) (statute requiring medical malpractice claimants to assert the claim before an agency before going to court violated Missouri Constitution's open-courts provision). The upshot is that lawyers who practice administrative law before state agencies should be familiar with the relevant state constitutional limits.

E. Chapter 18 Wrap Up and Look Ahead

This chapter has focused on the requirement that an agency adjudication rest on a valid grant of adjudicatory power. From this chapter you have learned how to determine when a statute grants adjudicatory power. You have also learned about constitutional limits on statutes that grant adjudicatory power to agencies. Specifically, you have learned that, under U.S. Supreme Court precedent, federal agencies can generally adjudicate "public rights" and serve as adjuncts to Article III courts. Federal agencies also can adjudicate some private rights intertwined with their regulatory responsibilities. Many state agencies can be granted similar adjudicatory power without offending state constitutions. The competent lawyer will be able to tell when an adjudicative delegation approaches the constitutional limits and will require close study and research.

Having examined adjudicatory power in this chapter, in the next chapter we turn to limits on agency adjudicatory power.

---

1. *See* Colo. Const. art. II, §6 (West, Westlaw through Nov. 2, 2010 Gen. Election); Mo. Const. art. I, §14 (West, Westlaw through Nov. 2, 2010 Gen. Election); Utah Const. art. I, §11 (West, Westlaw through 2011 3d Spec. Sess.).

Chapter Problem Revisited

1. The administrative adjudication scheme will better withstand constitutional challenge if it uses government money to compensate victims. In that event, the compensation claims will involve "public rights," which federal agencies have long been allowed to adjudicate without violating Article III or the Seventh Amendment.

2. The administrative adjudication scheme will better withstand constitutional challenge if it relies on newly created federal regulatory law, instead of state tort law, to determine compensation claims. Under cases such as *Schor* and *Stern v. Marshall*, federal agency adjudication of state tort claims could violate Article III because they are the type of claim that Article III courts have traditionally adjudicated, they would not require agency expertise, and they would not be an integral part of a federal regulatory scheme.

Professional Development Reflection Questions

Many law students take judicial clerkships after law school. Clerkships have great benefits. Specifically, clerkships can be highly educational; they give you the chance to meet many lawyers and other people in the legal field; they may lead to a wonderful mentoring relationship with a judge; and they are a highly regarded credential. Although clerkships are not for everyone, they are a post-law-school option that every law student should consider.

You may be happy to know that clerkship opportunities exist for law students interested in administrative law. Specifically, at the federal level you can get great administrative experience clerking for the following courts, among which are "Article I" courts of the sort we discussed in this chapter:

- United States Court of Appeals for the D.C. Circuit
- United States Court of International Trade
- United States Court of Federal Claims
- United States Court of Appeals for the Armed Forces
- United States Tax Court
- United States Court of Appeals for Veterans Claims

In addition, many federal agencies use administrative law judges or other types of hearing officers to conduct administrative hearings in agency adjudications. Some of these ALJs and other hearing officers may hire new law school graduates as law clerks. A particularly large volume of cases is adjudicated by the Executive Office for Immigration Review (EOIR), which is in the U.S. Department of Justice. The EIOR has post-law-school job opportunities that will steep new graduates in administrative law.

At the state level, perhaps the most abundant opportunities for administrative-law-focused clerkships exist in States that have what are called "central panels." A central panel is typically a stand-alone state agency made up of administrative law judges who hold hearings for other state agencies. You can find links to many of the State's central panels at this website:

> Oregon Office of Administrative Hearings, *Other Central Panels*, http://www.oregon.gov/OAH/Other_Central_Panels.shtml (updated July 28, 2011).

Have you considered taking a judicial clerkship after graduation? If you have not made a firm decision *against* taking a clerkship, what "next step" can you commit to taking within the next month to advance your decision-making process on that question?

Chapter 19

Limits on Agency Adjudicatory Power

Overview

Even if an agency has power under a valid statute to adjudicate, its order in a particular adjudication may be invalid if the agency did not obey the limits on, or requirements for exercising, that power. To identify those limits and requirements, we use the problem-solving framework from Chapter 2. The framework, as applied to agency adjudication, is as follows:

Has the agency obeyed limits on its adjudicatory power? (For simplicity's sake, we use the term "limits" to include requirements for exercising.)

a. Internal limits

    i. Internal substantive limits

    ii. Internal procedural limits

b. External limits

    i. External substantive limits

    ii. External procedural limits

This chapter consists of three sections:

A. Internal Limits on Agency Adjudicatory Power

B. External Limits on Agency Adjudicatory Power

C. Chapter 19 Wrap Up and Look Ahead

While this chapter is comprehensive in identifying limits on agency adjudicatory power, later chapters will focus on procedural requirements put on that power by the agency legislation and the applicable (federal or state) APA. That focus reflects the standard focus of administrative law courses.

This chapter will remind you of Chapter 9, if you studied that chapter. Chapter 9 identified and gave examples of limits on agency *rulemaking* power. Those limits are generally similar to limits on agency adjudicatory power. Moreover, here, as in Chapter 9, we present those limits using the problem solving framework of Chapter 2. So do not worry if you get a sense of *déjà vu*. So do not worry if you get a sense of *déjà vu*.

Chapter Problem

Email

To: Law Clerk to Judge Able

From: Judge Able

I really appreciated the great work you did for me some weeks back, when you made me a flow chart for comprehensively analyzing the validity of an agency rule. I have consulted it repeatedly as we have worked our way through that big lawsuit challenging the environmental regulations.

May I get your help making something similar for analyzing agency adjudication? As you know, we have just been assigned a new lawsuit challenging an agency's imposition of enormous fines on a company for regulatory violations. In my legal practice before joining the bench, I dealt with agency adjudications only enough to learn that they differ from judicial adjudications.

Thank you for your help with this latest project!

Sincerely, Judge Able

A. Internal Limits on Agency Adjudicatory Power

When an agency adjudicates a matter, the agency must obey limits on its adjudicatory power imposed by the agency legislation. The limits may be substantive, procedural, or hard to classify as one or the other. The important thing is to identify all applicable internal limits as a prelude to determining whether the agency has obeyed them.

1. Internal Substantive Limits

When an agency order exceeds substantive limits in the agency legislation, sometimes the order will be considered "ultra vires." Other times, the agency order will be considered simply wrong. In this section we give examples of each.

a. Ultra Vires Agency Adjudications

In the following cases, federal courts held that agency orders were ultra vires.

• *Federal Maritime Commission v. Seatrain Lines, Inc.*, 411 U.S. 726 (1973)

The federal Shipping Act authorized the Federal Maritime Commission to review certain agreements between shippers. *Id.* at 726–727 & n.1 (discussing Shipping Act as it then existed). If the Commission approved an agreement, the agreement was exempt from antitrust laws. In this case, the Commission approved an agreement between two particular shippers under which one sold all of its assets to the other. The U.S. Supreme Court held that this agreement did not fall within the statutory definition of "agreement[s]" that the Commission could review and approve. In approving the agreement, the Commission therefore "overstepped the limits which Congress placed on its jurisdiction." *Id.* at 746.

- *Securities & Exchange Commission v. Sloan*, 436 U.S. 103 (1978)

The SEC had authority "summarily to suspend trading in any security" for up to ten days "[i]f in its opinion the public interest and the protection of investors so require." *Id.* at 105 & n.1 (quoting and discussing statute as it then existed). The SEC relied on that authority to issue a series of ten-day suspension orders that, cumulatively, suspended trading in a company's stock for more than one year. The SEC based the orders on a single set of shady events within the company. The U.S. Supreme Court held that the SEC lacked authority to enter a prolonged series of suspension orders all based on a single set of events. To suspend trading in a stock for more than 10 days based on a single set of events, the SEC had to go to court. The agency lacked authority to impose such a lengthy trading suspension through administrative adjudication.

- *Kyocera Wireless Corp. v. International Trade Commission*, 545 F.3d 1340 (Fed. Cir. 2008)

Broadcom filed a complaint with the International Trade Commission. Broadcom complained that its patent was being infringed by products that Qualcom was importing. After an adjudication, the Commission held that Qualcom was indeed infringing the patent. The Commission issued a "limited exclusion order" (LEO) excluding infringing products from being imported into the country. The LEO applied not only to Qualcom, which was a party to the Commission adjudication, but also to Qualcom's customers, who were not parties. The court held that the Commission lacked authority under its statute to issue an LEO extending beyond the party to the Commission's adjudication. To that extent, its LEO was "ultra vires." *Id.* at 1358.

* * *

The principle that agencies must act within the scope of their adjudicatory power is reflected in statutes authorizing judicial review of agency orders. For example, § 706(2)(C) of the federal APA authorizes a federal court to set aside agency action that is "**in excess of statutory jurisdiction, authority, or limitations.**" 5 U.S.C. § 706(2)(C) (2012). Many state APAs have similar judicial review provisions, which empower state courts to set aside ultra vires state agency action. The Maryland APA, for example, authorizes courts to reverse or modify an agency's decision in a contested case (formal adjudication) if the decision "exceeds the statutory authority or jurisdiction of the final decision maker." Md. Code Ann. State Gov't § 10-222(h)(3)(ii) (West, Westlaw through 2011 Reg. Sess.).

Exercise: Ultra Vires Adjudicatory Orders

A federal immigration statute allows an "order of deportation" (more commonly called an "order of removal" today) to be issued only by an immigration judge or other "administrative officer to whom the Attorney General has delegated the responsibility for determining whether an alien is deportable." 8 U.S.C. § 1101(a)(47)(A) (2012). In deportation proceedings, the immigration judge (IJ) initially determines whether other immigration officials, acting in a prosecutorial role, have proven that an alien is deportable. If so, the IJ may issue an order of deportation. If not, the IJ issues a decision holding that the case for deportation has not been proven.

Either the alien or the prosecutorial immigration officials can appeal the IJ's decision to the Board of Immigration Appeals (BIA). The BIA has statutory authority to "affirm [a deportation] order" entered by an IJ or to reverse it, but no statute expressly authorizes the BIA itself to enter a deportation order.

Thanks to your excellent advocacy, an IJ decided that your client has not been proven to be deportable. The government, however, appealed that decision to the BIA, which has not only reversed the IJ's decision but also entered a deportation order. By entering the deportation order itself rather than remanding the case to the IJ, the BIA has prevented you from requesting statutorily authorized discretionary relief from deportation, such as the withholding of removal. *See* 8 U.S.C. § 1231(b)(3) (2012).

You can seek judicial review of the BIA's decision in the federal court of appeals. Assuming that you do so, succinctly explain why the BIA acted ultra vires. *See, e.g., Salazar v. U.S. Attorney General*, 385 Fed. Appx. 948, 950 (11th Cir. 2010).

b. Other Violations of Substantive Internal Limits

Even if an agency acts within the scope of its adjudicatory power under the agency legislation, its order is invalid if it violates substantive provisions in the legislation. Here are examples of cases in which the U.S. Supreme Court held that a federal agency's order violated the agency legislation. The agency order was not labeled ultra vires; it was just wrong.

- *National Credit Union Administration v. First National Bank & Trust Co.*, 522 U.S. 479 (1998)

The National Credit Union Administration (NCUA) regulates federal credit unions under the Federal Credit Union Act. *See* 12 U.S.C. §§ 1752–1775 (2012) (current statute). A federal credit union that wants to expand its membership must get the NCUA's approval. The NCUA approved several requests by AT&T Family Federal Credit Union to expand its membership to include employees of employers other than the AT&T family of companies. The Court held that the NCUA erred in approving these requests, because, at the time NCUA granted these requests, the Act forbade a credit union from having members composed of multiple, unrelated employer groups.

Although the NCUA violated the Act by approving the requests, the NCUA acted within its statutory authority, for the statute authorized it to approve requests by credit unions to expand their membership. The NCUA simply misinterpreted its legislation, as the Court interpreted it. (An interesting postscript: In response to the Court's holding in this case, Congress amended the Act to authorize credit unions to include unrelated employer groups; the amendment statutorily "overruled" the Court's interpretation.)

- *Immigration & Naturalization Service v. Cardoza-Fonseca*, 480 U.S. 421 (1987)

The Board of Immigration Appeals (BIA) has authority under a federal statute to grant asylum to refugees who fear persecution in another country. The BIA denied Luz Marina Cardoza-Fonseca's asylum application because she did not establish a "clear probability of persecution." *Id.* at 425 (quoting Immigration Judge's opinion, which was affirmed by BIA). The Court concluded that, in holding Ms. Cardoza-Fonseca to such a high standard of proof, the BIA misinterpreted the asylum statute. The BIA acted within its authority to grant (or deny) asylum requests. In Ms. Cardoza-Fonseca's case, however, the BIA misinterpreted the asylum statute by imposing too high a standard for proving entitlement to asylum.

- *National Labor Relations Board v. Kentucky River Community Care, Inc.*, 532 U.S. 706 (2001)

The National Labor Relations Board ordered a mental health care facility to bargain with a union representing the facility's registered nurses. In entering this order, the Board exercised authority under the National Labor Relations Act. The Court held that the Board's order violated the provision in the Act excluding "supervisors" from the Act's protection. The Court determined that nurses were "supervisors" within the meaning of the Act, and that the Board's contrary conclusion therefore reflected a misinterpretation of the Act.

* * *

In the cases summarized above the Court concluded that the agency misinterpreted the agency legislation. When federal courts review a federal agency's interpretation of its legislation, the courts often give weight to the agency's interpretation. This weight is often called "deference." We examine the doctrine of deference in Part Four of this book, when we study judicial review of agency action.

2. Internal Procedural Limits and Quasi-Procedural/Quasi-Substantive Limits

The agency legislation may require the agency to follow certain procedures or consider certain factors when exercising adjudicatory power. Later chapters will discuss in more detail the sorts of procedural requirements that the agency legislation may put on the agency's adjudications. Now we simply introduce the concept that the agency legislation is an important source of procedural and quasi-procedural/quasi-substantive requirements for agency adjudication.

For example, the Administrator of the EPA can impose civil penalties for violations of the Clean Water Act. The provision in the Act giving the Administrator this power contains procedural requirements and also requires the Administrator to consider certain factors in determining the penalties. As you read the provision, notice that the procedures for imposing a "Class I" penalty include a hearing that is not subject to the formal adjudication requirements of the federal APA (found in §§ 554 and 556 of Title 5). The procedures also include opportunity for input by "interested persons" other than the target of the penalty proceeding. The latter procedures reflect that violations of the Clean Water Act may affect many members of the public.

---

33 U.S.C. § 1319. Enforcement ...

(g) Administrative penalties

(1) Violations

Whenever on the basis of any information available—

(A) the Administrator finds that any person has violated section 1311, 1312, 1316, 1317, 1318, 1328, or 1345 of this title, or has violated any permit condition or limitation implementing any of such sections in a permit issued under section 1342 of this title by the Administrator or by a State, or in a permit issued under section 1344 of this title by a State, ...

the Administrator ... may, after consultation with the State in which the violation occurs, assess a class I civil penalty or a class II civil penalty under this subsection.

(2) Classes of penalties

(A) Class I

The amount of a class I civil penalty under paragraph (1) may not exceed $10,000 per violation, except that the maximum amount of any class I civil penalty under this subparagraph shall not exceed $25,000. Before issuing an order assessing a civil penalty under this subparagraph, the Administrator ... shall give to the person to be assessed such penalty written notice of the Administrator's ... proposal to issue such order and the opportunity to request, within 30 days of the date the notice is received by such person, a hearing on the proposed order. Such hearing shall not be subject to section 554 or 556 of Title 5, but shall provide a reasonable opportunity to be heard and to present evidence.

(B) Class II ...

(3) Determining amount

In determining the amount of any penalty assessed under this subsection, the Administrator ... shall take into account the nature, circumstances, extent and gravity of the violation, or violations, and, with respect to the violator, ability to pay, any prior history of such violations, the degree of culpability, economic benefit or savings (if any) resulting from the violation, and such other matters as justice may require. For purposes of this subsection, a single operational upset which leads to simultaneous violations of more than one pollutant parameter shall be treated as a single violation.

(4) Rights of interested persons

(A) Public notice

Before issuing an order assessing a civil penalty under this subsection the Administrator ... shall provide public notice of and reasonable opportunity to comment on the proposed issuance of such order.

(B) Presentation of evidence

Any person who comments on a proposed assessment of a penalty under this subsection shall be given notice of any hearing held under this subsection and of the order assessing such penalty. In any hearing held under this subsection, such person shall have a reasonable opportunity to be heard and to present evidence.

(C) Rights of interested persons to a hearing

If no hearing is held under paragraph (2) before issuance of an order assessing a penalty under this subsection, any person who commented on the proposed assessment may petition, within 30 days after the issuance of such order, the Administrator ... to set aside such order and to provide a hearing on the penalty. If the evidence presented by the petitioner in support of the petition is material and was not considered in the issuance of the order, the Administrator ... shall immediately set aside such order and provide a hearing in accordance with paragraph (2)(A) in the case of a class I civil penalty and paragraph (2)(B) in the case of a class II civil penalty. If the Administrator ... denies a hearing under this subparagraph, the Administrator ... shall provide to the petitioner, and publish in the Federal Register, notice of and the reasons for such denial.

These procedures are fairly elaborate, though they provide for a hearing that need not be as elaborate as the hearing required by the federal APA's formal adjudication requirements.

B. External Limits on Agency Adjudicatory Power

This section introduces and briefly describes four, potential external sources of limits on agency rulemaking power:

(1) constitutional law

(2) statutory law

(3) agency rules and other executive-branch material

(4) limits imposed in connection with judicial review

Later chapters in this part of the book will explore certain of these sources in detail.

1. Constitutional Law

Of course, a federal agency order is invalid if it violates the U.S. Constitution. *See, e.g., BE & K Constr. Co. v. NLRB*, 536 U.S. 516 (2002) (holding that order entered by federal agency in a formal adjudication violated the First Amendment of the U.S. Constitution). A state agency adjudication must comply not only with the U.S. Constitution—which contains many provisions applicable to the States—but also with the applicable state constitution. *See, e.g., Pennsylvania v. Bd. of Directors*, 353 U.S. 230 (1957) (holding that local agency's refusal to admit black applicants to school administered by the agency violated the Equal Protection Clause of the Fourteenth Amendment of the U.S. Constitution).

a. Substantive Limits

The U.S. Constitution and state constitutions put substantive constraints on government power, including power exercised by administrative agencies. Agencies cannot, for example, violate the freedom of speech, the free exercise of religion, and the right to the equal protection of the laws. These substantive constitutional limits on government power are studied in law school courses on substantive areas of law, including constitutional law, civil rights law, and criminal procedure. We do not give them further attention in this book, as interesting as they are.

b. Procedural Limits

The U.S. Constitution puts important *procedural* limits on government power. The most important constitutional sources of procedural limits upon agency adjudications are the Due Process Clauses of the Fifth and Fourteenth Amendment. In fact, many agency adjudications are subject to due process limits. We accordingly explore those limits in detail, in Chapter 20.

2. Statutory Law

In addition to the agency legislation, other statutes may impose substantive and procedural limits — as well as limits that are hard to characterize as one or the other — upon an agency's adjudicatory power. We will give examples.

a. Substantive Limits

In Chapter 9.B.2.a, we identified the Endangered Species Act as a cross-cutting statute that substantively limits federal agency *rulemaking* power when it threatens an endangered species or its habitat. The ESA likewise applies to federal agency adjudications that pose such a threat. *See, e.g., Sierra Club v. Van Antwerp*, 661 F.3d 1147 (D.C. Cir. 2011) (reviewing Army Corps of Engineer's issuance of a permit for a Florida mall development for compliance with ESA).

Other statutes likewise can substantively limit agency adjudicatory power. An example arose in *NLRB v. Bildisco & Bildisco*, 465 U.S. 513 (1984). A building-supply company filed for bankruptcy. The Bankruptcy Court authorized the company to continue to operate the business as a "debtor-in-possession." After becoming debtor-in-possession, the company stopped honoring its collective bargaining agreement with a union that represented some of the company's employees. The union filed an unfair labor practice charge against the company with the National Labor Relations Board. The Board concluded after a formal adjudication that the company's rejection of the collective bargaining agreement was an unfair labor practice. The company, however, claimed the right to reject the agreement under the federal Bankruptcy Code. The Court agreed with the company, holding that the Board's unfair labor practice determination violated the Bankruptcy Code. *Id.* at 527–534.

b. Procedural Limits

The most important potential statutory source of procedural limits on agency adjudication is the applicable (federal or state) APA. It is so important that we examine it in detail in Chapters 21–24.

The APA is not the only statute, however, that may put procedural requirements on agency adjudication. In Chapter 9.B.2.b, we identified the National Environmental Policy Act (NEPA) as a cross-cutting statute that puts procedural requirements on many federal agency *rulemakings*. The NEPA can also apply to a federal agency *adjudication*, if the adjudication "significantly affect[s] the quality of the human environment." 42 U.S.C. §4332(2)(C) (2012). *See, e.g., Pit River Tribe v. U.S. Forest Serv.*, 469 F.3d 768, 782–784 (9th Cir. 2006) (holding that Bureau of Land Management and other agencies violated the NEPA in extending the terms of leases on federal land to permit development of geothermal energy plant). Although procedural in nature, the NEPA has the substantive objective of limiting environmental harm of federal agency actions.

Another example of cross-cutting statute that puts procedural requirements on federal agency adjudications is the National Historic Preservation Act (NHPA). It has the substantive objective of preserving sites and structures that have been listed or are eligible for listing on the National Register of Historic Places:

---

16 U.S.C. § 470f. Effect of Federal undertakings upon property listed in National Register; comment by Advisory Council on Historic Preservation

The head of any Federal agency having direct or indirect jurisdiction over a proposed Federal or federally assisted undertaking in any State and the head of any Federal department or independent agency having authority to license any undertaking shall, prior to the approval of the expenditure of any Federal funds on the undertaking or prior to the issuance of any license, as the case may be, take into account the effect of the undertaking on any district, site, building, structure, or object that is included in or eligible for inclusion in the National Register. The head of any such Federal agency shall afford the Advisory Council on Historic Preservation established under part B of this subchapter a reasonable opportunity to comment with regard to such undertaking.

This Act applied, for example, when the Federal Aviation Administration was asked to approve the demolition of a historic airplane hangar to make room for a real estate development. *Safeguarding the Historic Hanscom Area's Irreplaceable Resources, Inc. v. FAA*, 651 F.3d 202, 214–217 (1st Cir. 2011).

As mentioned in Chapter 15.D, in discussion of rulemaking, many States have "little NEPAs." Like the federal NEPA, these state mini-NEPAs can apply to both state agency rulemaking and state agency adjudication. *See* Daniel R. Mandelker, NEPA Law and Litigation § 12:2, at 12-6–12-9 (2d ed. 2011).

c. Mixed Substantive and Procedural Limits

The following case shows that statutes often combine procedural and substantive limits on agency adjudication.

• *Andrus v. Glover Construction Co.*, 446 U.S. 608 (1980)

Andrus involved the Bureau of Indian Affairs (BIA), a federal agency in the Department of Interior. The BIA awarded a contract to an Indian-owned company to repair and improve the Honobia Road in Pushmataha County, Oklahoma. (By way of review, why is the award of a government contract an adjudication?) The BIA awarded the contract under a BIA procurement policy implementing the Buy Indian Act. A non-Indian construction company challenged the award of the contract on the ground that it violated a separate federal statute, the Federal Property and Administrative Services Act. That Act, the construction company argued, required the BIA to advertise for bids before awarding the contract. The Court agreed and upheld the lower court judgment finding the contract "null and void." *Id.* at 611.

The Federal Property and Administrative Services Act, like many federal statutes, had both procedural and substantive provisions. The Act required "advertising" for bids, a seemingly procedural requirement. The provision of the Act that prescribed "Advertising requirements" included a substantive command: When an agency opened the bids received in response to advertising, the agency had to award the contract "to that responsible bidder whose bid ... will be most advantageous to the Government, price and other factors considered." 41 U.S.C. § 253(b) (1976). That was substantive because it provided a criterion for BIA's selection of the winning bidder.

* * *

The takeaway is that, when you analyze an agency adjudication for compliance with applicable statutes, you often devote much effort to determining the agency's compliance with the agency legislation. This is appropriate. External statutes, however, may also come into the picture.

3. Agency Rules and Other Executive-Branch Material

a. Compliance with the Agency's Own Rules

It is useful to distinguish three ways that an agency order may conflict with the agency's own rules. Different principles govern the three types of conflict.

(i)   The order conflicts with the agency's substantive legislative rule.

(ii)   The order conflicts with the agency's substantive non-legislative rule.

(iii) The order conflicts with the agency's procedural rule.

We discuss each separately.

(i) The Agency Order Conflicts with the Agency's Substantive Legislative Rule

In Chapter 7, we discussed the effect of a valid legislative rule. One effect is that the rule binds the agency until the agency changes or repeals it. Ordinarily, to change or repeal a legislative rule, the agency must follow the same procedures it used to promulgate the rule in the first place. For most legislative rules, these procedures involve notifying the public of the proposed rule and giving the public a chance to comment on the proposed rule. Without following these procedures, an agency cannot change or repeal a legislative rule in an adjudication. *See Marseilles Land & Water Co. v. FERC*, 345 F.3d 916 (D.C. Cir. 2003) ("[A]n administrative agency may not slip by the notice and comment rule-making requirements needed to amend a rule by merely adopting a de facto amendment to its regulation through adjudication.").

The practical consequence is that you can challenge an agency *order* on the ground that it conflicts that same agency's substantive legislative *rule*.

(ii) The Agency Order Conflicts with the Agency's Substantive Non-Legislative Rule

Agencies often issue interpretive rules and other guidance material to advise the public or its own employees, or both, of how the agency interprets and intends to enforce the statutes and legislative rules that the agency administers. Because agency guidance material does not have the "force and effect of law," the agency usually does not have to follow any particular procedures to change its mind about guidance that it has previously given. Once the agency changes its mind, it may issue new guidance material announcing the change or adopt the change in adjudicating a case.

Even so, an agency may have to *explain* why it has changed its mind. Suppose, for example, the agency has issued an interpretive rule that explains the agency's interpretation of an ambiguous statute. Later, the agency relies on a different interpretation to decide an adjudicatory matter. If an agency departs from its prior interpretation without explanation, a reviewing court may conclude that the agency's order is "arbitrary and capricious" to use standard administrative law terminology. Thus, to withstand judicial review, the agency changing course has to explain the change adequately. *See, e.g., FCC v. Fox Television Stations, Inc.*, 556 U.S. 502, 514–516 (2009).

(iii) The Agency Order Conflicts with the Agency's Procedural Rules

Do not let the small Roman numeral heading for this discussion fool you. Agencies with adjudicatory power often have procedural rules for their adjudications, and those rules are important for administrative lawyers to find and analyze. Agencies adopt these rules because, even if the agency legislation and the APA prescribe procedural requirements, those statutes will not address all of the procedural issues that will arise. Agencies issue procedural rules to address the procedural details that are too mundane to be addressed by the statutes but that are vital for the lawyer with a matter before the agency to master.

The agency's procedural rules may supplement, as well as elaborate upon, procedural requirements imposed by the agency legislation and other sources of law. This is true whether the agency's procedural rules pertain to agency adjudication or agency rulemaking. As we earlier stated the principle (in connection with agency rulemaking):

> Generally, an agency may *add* to statutorily required procedures, but it may not *modify* the statutory procedures or provide *less* than the statutorily required minimum procedures.

Indeed, on a day-to-day basis, agencies and people with adjudicatory matters before the agency will pay more attention to the agency's procedural rules than to the procedural provisions of the agency legislation. The devil is in the details, and the details are in the agency's procedural rules.

Federal agencies must publish the procedural rules for their adjudications. *See, e.g.*, 5 U.S.C. §552(a)(1)(B) & (C) (2012). Most state APAs require the same of their agencies. *See, e.g.*, 2010 Model State APA §202(a)(2). A federal agency's procedural rules will ordinarily be codified along with the agency's other rules in the Code of Federal Regulations. State agencies often publish their procedural rules in an analogous state administrative code. Agencies often call their procedural rules for adjudication something like "rules of practice and procedure." For example, the Federal Trade Commission calls them "rules of practice for adjudicative proceedings." As shown in Figure 19-A, you can find where those rules are codified in the C.F.R. by looking in the one-volume CFR Index and Finding Aids published each year.

Some agencies supplement their procedural rules for adjudication with internal manuals and other material designed primarily for instructing the agency's own employees. For example, the Social Security Administration has a "Program Operations Manual System" (POMS) that is "a primary source of information used by Social Security employees to process claims for Social Security benefits." https://secure.ssa.gov/apps10/. SSA publishes a "public version" of the POMS on its website. *Id.* The federal APA requires agencies to make material like the POMs **"available for public inspection and copying."** 5 U.S.C. §552(a)(2)(C) (2012). The APA describes material like the POMS as **"administrative staff manuals and instructions to staff that affect a member of the public."** *Id.* A state APA may also require such material to be publicly available. *See, e.g.*, Iowa Code Ann. §17A.3.1(d) (West, Westlaw through Mar. 28, 2012).

Figure 19-A. Page from 2011 Index to Code of Federal Regulations Showing Part of Entry for "Federal Trade Commission"; See First Subentry

Federal Retirement Thrift Investment Board   **CFR Index**

Series I bonds, definitive, regulations governing, 31 CFR 360

Series I bonds, offering, 31 CFR 359

Unfair or deceptive banking acts or practices (Regulation AA), 12 CFR 227

Federal Retirement Thrift Investment Board

Supplemental standards of ethical conduct for agency employees, 5 CFR 8601

Thrift savings plan, 5 CFR 1690

Administrative errors correction, 5 CFR 1605

Claims collection, 5 CFR 1639

Conduct standards, 5 CFR 1633

Court orders and legal processes affecting accounts, 5 CFR 1653

Death benefits, 5 CFR 1651

Employee elections to contribute to thrift savings plan, 5 CFR 1600

Expanded and continuing eligibility, 5 CFR 1620

Loan program, 5 CFR 1655

Methods of withdrawing funds, 5 CFR 1650

Nondiscrimination on basis of disability in federally conducted programs or activities, 5 CFR 1636

Participants' choices of funds, 5 CFR 1601

Periodic participant statements, 5 CFR 1640

Privacy Act regulations, 5 CFR 1630

Public observation of meetings, 5 CFR 1632

Records availability, 5 CFR 1631

Share prices calculation, 5 CFR 1645

Uniformed services accounts, 5 CFR 1604

Vesting, 5 CFR 1603

Federal Savings and Loan Insurance Corporation

See Federal Deposit Insurance Corporation; Thrift Supervision Office

Federal Service Impasses Panel

Employee responsibilities and conduct, 5 CFR 2415

Flexible or compressed work schedules, impasses arising pursuant to Agency determinations not to establish or to terminate, 5 CFR 2472

Legal proceedings, testimony by employees relating to official information and

production of official records, 5 CFR 2417

Official information availability, 5 CFR 2411

Privacy, 5 CFR 2412

Procedures of Panel, 5 CFR 2471

Purpose of regulations, definitions, 5 CFR 2470

Subpoenas, 5 CFR 2473

Federal-State relations

See Intergovernmental relations

Federal Trade Commission

Adjudicative proceedings practice rules, 16 CFR 3

Administrative interpretations, general policy statements, and enforcement policy statements, 16 CFR 14

Advertising allowances and other merchandising payments and services, 16 CFR 240

Advisory committee management, 16 CFR 16

Alternative fuels and alternative fueled vehicles, labeling requirements, 16 CFR 309

Amplifiers utilized in home entertainment products, power output claims, 16 CFR 432

Antitrust

Coverage rules, 16 CFR 801

Exemption rules, 16 CFR 802

Transmittal rules, 16 CFR 803

Automobile parts, rebuilt, reconditioned and used, industry guides, 16 CFR 20

Automotive fuel ratings, certification and posting, 16 CFR 306

Bait advertising, 16 CFR 238

Business opportunities, disclosure requirements and prohibitions, 16 CFR 437

CAN-SPAM Rule, 16 CFR 316

Children's online privacy protection rule, 16 CFR 312

Cigarettes in relation to health hazards of smoking, unfair or deceptive advertising and labeling of, 16 CFR 408

Consumer financial information, privacy, 16 CFR 313

Consumers' claims and defenses, preservation, 16 CFR 433

Contact lens rule, 16 CFR 315

Credit practices, 16 CFR 444

Not all agencies make their staff manuals and similar material publicly available, even if the law requires it. If you represent a client in an agency adjudication and you suspect that this material exists but cannot find it, you should ask the agency whether it exists and, if so, to make it available to you. If the agency refuses, you may wish to request the material under the federal Freedom of Information Act or comparable state law. Such a request may at least reveal whether the unpublished material exists. If the material does exist but the agency will not make it available, you must consider whether it is worth pursuing the material by seeking administrative or judicial review of the agency's refusal to disclose the information.

When you get involved as a lawyer in an agency adjudication, you will want to identify and analyze the agency's procedural rules for the adjudication, as well as other agency-generated material, and analyze this material together with all statutorily required procedures. Then you must synthesize them to determine how they interact. You will hope that the integration will be smooth, and not produce inconsistencies that require resolution.

Your efforts to identify the agency's procedural rules for agency adjudications is worth your time because agencies all too often depart from those rules. Indeed, such departures have generated a trio of famous U.S. Supreme Court cases. In *Accardi v. Shaughnessy*, 347 U.S. 260 (1954), a federal agency violated its procedural rules when rejecting Joseph Accardi's application for a suspension of deportation proceedings against him. In *Service v. Dulles*, 354 U.S. 363 (1957), a federal agency violated its procedural rules when firing John Service from his job in the Foreign Service. In *Vitarelli v. Seaton*, 359 U.S. 535 (1959), a federal agency again departed from its procedural rules when firing William Vitarelli. This trio of cases, all of which involve agencies departing from procedural rules for adjudication, underlie the fundamental principle that an agency must follow its own rules.

Although an agency must follow its procedural rules, not every violation of those rules will invalidate the agency's adjudication. Minor violations may be considered "harmless error." *See, e.g., Rabbers v. Comm'r of Soc. Sec. Admin.*, 582 F.3d 647 (6th Cir. 2009) (holding that agency decision maker violated agency regulations by failing to make findings on the severity of Mr. Rabbers' mental impairment, but this was harmless error because his impairment was not severe enough to make him eligible for disability benefits). Generally courts will not set aside agency action for errors that cause no prejudice to the person challenging the agency action. *See, e.g.,* 5 U.S.C. § 706 (requiring courts reviewing agency action to take "due account" of "the rule of prejudicial error"); 1961 Model State APA § 15(g) (authorizing courts reviewing agency orders to set aside an order "if substantial rights of the appellant have been prejudiced" because of specified flaws). Thus, the lawyer seeking to invalidate an agency order for a violation of the agency's procedural rule must be prepared to show that the violation did real damage to the client's interests.

b. Compliance with Other, Valid Executive-Branch Material

In Chapter 15, we discussed the power of U.S. Presidents and state Governors to issue executive orders and use other means to control executive-branch agencies. We also identified in Chapter 15 the major executive orders governing many federal rulemaking proceedings. Executive orders and other executive-branch actions also may apply to agency adjudications. There are no presidential executive orders, however, that apply broadly to federal agency adjudications.

Some executive orders, however, do affect some federal agency adjudications. For example, Executive Order 13,467 has requirements for most federal agency adjudications of whether an individual should be allowed access to classified information. 3 C.F.R. 196 (2009). To cite another example, Executive Order 11,246 authorizes the Secretary of Labor to conduct adjudications to determine a government contractor's compliance with federal laws requiring equal employment opportunities. 42 U.S.C. § 2000e Note (2012). The point is that an agency adjudication may be subject to executive orders, which may impose authority to adjudicate as well as substantive and procedural requirements for exercise of that authority.

Other executive-branch actions besides executive orders may also affect an agency's adjudication, because most agencies are within the executive branch and subject to control not only by the Chief Executive but also by other executive-branch entities that have a higher perch in the pecking order. For example, the Office of Management and Budget (OMB), which is part of the Executive Office of the President, regulates federal agency procurement and personnel matters. Many procurement and personnel decisions are adjudicative, and subject to procedures prescribed in OMB "Circulars" and other issuances.

State governors issue executive orders and have an inner circle of officials whose job is to help the governor steer the ship of state. The Governor and the Governor's Office may accordingly be a source of procedural directives for certain state agency adjudications. *See Cutler v. State Civil Serv. Comm'n*, 924 A.2d 706, 711–717 (Pa. Commw. Ct. 2007) (holding that executive-branch "management directive" relating to veterans preference for state employees violated state statute).

We know of no sure-fire way to identify executive-branch material that may supply procedural requirements for a particular agency adjudication. Here, as in many other settings, however, it may be useful and appropriate to ask an agency what laws govern the procedures in which your client is involved.

4. Judicial Review

Agency orders are generally subject to judicial review to ensure the agency has acted within substantive and procedural limits on its authority. We have already surveyed most of those substantive and procedural limits. Besides those limits, courts can generally review the factual basis and rationality of agency orders, as part of the court's authority to conduct judicial review. But the federal courts, at least, cannot devise their own procedural requirements for federal agency adjudication.

a. Substantive Limits

(i) Factual Support

An agency order almost always rests on certain factual determinations. But even before making those determinations, the agency has to decide what facts are relevant to the decision at hand. Relevance in agency adjudications, as in agency rulemaking, is determined primarily by law. In particular, the agency legislation will be the main law that determines relevance. For example, the agency legislation will determine whether a license applicant must meet a minimum age requirement. The agency legislation will prescribe criteria for the granting of benefits or the imposition of a sanction. In addition to addressing these substantive matters, the agency legislation or other laws will govern procedural matters such as what types of evidence the agency can consider and how someone involved in the adjudication can present the evidence. Finally, the law governs the issue of "burden of proof," an issue that is in the borderland between substance and procedure. Ordinarily, for example, the applicant for a license bears the burden of proving, by a preponderance of the evidence, that the applicant meets legal requirements for getting the license.

Often a lawyer's most important job in an agency adjudication is to gather as much relevant, favorable evidence as possible and to present it to the agency using the proper procedures. (The tasks of gathering and presenting relevant, favorable evidence includes evidence that successfully impeaches or rebuts unfavorable evidence.) These evidentiary tasks have such importance because in the vast majority of agency adjudications the *law* will be clear and undisputed, and the outcome will depend on the *facts*—or more precisely, on the evidence bearing on the facts.

If your client is adversely affected by an agency's decision in an adjudication—e.g., if the agency denies your client a license or benefit or assesses a penalty against your client—you ordinarily can seek judicial review of the agency's decision. Ordinarily, too, on judicial review a court can set aside an agency decision that lacks adequate factual support. But as we discuss in Part 4 of this book, a courts reviewing the factual basis for an agency order will not hear new evidence; instead, the court will only review the evidence before the agency. Nor will the reviewing court usually decide factual disputes de novo; instead, the court will, roughly speaking, only determine whether the agency's determination was reasonable. Even so, judicial review of the factual basis of an agency order puts an important substantive constraint on agency adjudicatory power.

(ii) Reasoned Decision Making

Another important substantive constraint on agency adjudicatory power lies in the authority of courts to review agency orders for rationality. This judicial authority is often described as the power to ensure the agency order is the product of "reasoned decision making." Today, the requirement of reasoned decision making is captured by provisions in APAs and other statutes that authorize courts to set aside agency action that is "arbitrary and capricious" or an "abuse of discretion." *See Allentown Mack Sales & Serv., Inc. v. NLRB*, 522 U.S. 359, 374 (1998) (stating that agency "adjudication is subject to the requirement of reasoned decisionmaking"). Because agencies have so much discretion in so many situations, courts' power to review agency action for an "abuse of discretion" and other forms of irrationality plays a key role in modern administrative law.

Judicial review of rationality entails, of course, review of the substance of the agency's order. We will explore the components of rationality ("reasoned decision making") when we examine the "arbitrary and capricious" standard of review in Chapter 34. Basically, the requirement entails five principles:

(1) The agency's reasoning process must be rational and comprehensible.

(2) The agency's decision should rest on consideration of all relevant factors,.

(3) The agency's decision should not rest on considerations of irrelevant factors.

(4) There should be a clear, logical connection between the agency's factual determinations and its ultimate decision

(5) The agency action should be consistent with prior agency action—and thus the agency must treat similar situations similarly—unless the agency adequately explains why it has changed course.

These requirements, like the requirement that an agency action have adequate factual support, stem from courts' authority to review agency action. As with the requirement for adequate evidentiary support, the reasoned-decisionmaking requirement, though predominantly substantive, has some procedural aspects: Courts require a rational decisionmaking process as well as a rational result.

b. Procedural Requirements

Courts usually can review an agency order or other agency action for procedural validity. For example, the federal APA authorizes a court to set aside federal agency action **"found to be ... without observance of procedure required by law."** 5 U.S.C. §706(2)(D). The 2010 Model State APA authorizes a court to grant relief if the person challenging state agency action has been prejudiced because "the agency committed an error of procedure." 2010 Model State APA §508(a)(3)(B).

The primary sources of procedural requirements for agency adjudication are the APA and the agency legislation. Other statutes, however, can supply procedural requirements, as can executive-branch material such as agency procedural rules and executive orders. Finally, procedural due process plays an important role in many agency adjudications — often by influencing the interpretation of the other laws (e.g., the APA, the agency legislation, and the agency rules) applicable to the particular adjudication.

For federal agencies, however, procedural requirements generally cannot be devised by federal courts acting on their own notions of appropriate procedure. As discussed in Chapter 9, the Court in *Vermont Yankee* held that federal court generally cannot devise procedural requirements for federal agency rulemaking. Instead, the federal courts generally can only enforce procedural requirements imposed by non-judicial sources. *See Vermont Yankee Nuclear Power Corp. v. Natural Resources Defense Council*, 435 U.S. 519 (1978) (discussed in Chapter 9.B.4.b(i)). In a later case, the Court relied on *Vermont Yankee* to hold that federal courts likewise generally cannot devise procedural requirements for federal agency *adjudications*. *See Pension Benefit Guar. Corp. v. LTV Corp.*, 496 U.S. 633, 655 (1990).

The *Vermont Yankee* principle governs the relationship between federal courts and federal agencies. *Vermont Yankee* does not govern the relationship between state courts and state agencies. Nothing in *Vermont Yankee*— or any other U.S. Supreme Court precedent— prevents state law from authorizing state courts to create rules of procedure for state agencies. Even so, a state court might construe the separation of powers provision of the state constitution, or other state laws, to deny it power to make rules for executive-branch agencies. *Cf. Ship Creek Hydraulic Syndicate v. Alaska Dep't of Transp. & Pub. Facilities*, 685 P.2d 715, 717–719 (Alaska 1984) (holding that state agency had to issue written decisions to explain their decisions even though statute did not require it; rejecting argument to the contrary based on *Vermont Yankee*).

C. Chapter 19 Wrap Up and Look Ahead

This chapter gives you a big-picture "inventory" of potential sources of legal limits on agency adjudication. By working your way through this chapter, you have (we hope) begun to internalize that inventory. The inventory will be useful in practice, for it can serve as an all-encompassing checklist. The inventory is also designed to help you put into context the rest of our examination of agency adjudication in this part of the book.

The next chapter examines in detail one potential source of external, procedural limits on agency adjudication: the doctrine of procedural due process.

Chapter Problem Revisited

This chapter gives you a narrative description of the framework for analyzing in a particular case whether an agency has obeyed limits on, and requirements for, exercising its adjudicatory power. Your challenge is to convert that narrative description into a graphic description that delineates the skeleton or the architecture of that framework. Doing so will help you remember the framework and enlarge on it as future chapters flesh out certain parts of that framework.

Professional Development Reflection Questions

A common conception about government lawyers is that they get paid less, but don't have to work as many hours, as lawyers in the private sector. Your casebook author's experience agrees with that conception. Though data on hours worked is hard to find, salary data is available. Specifically, the Association for Legal Career Professionals reported these salaries for law students graduating in 2010:

	National Median	National Mean
All types of legal jobs	$63,000	$84,111
Government legal jobs	$52,000	$55,014

NALP, *Starting Salaries — What New Law Graduates Earn — Class of 2010*, http://www.nalp.org/starting_salaries_-_what_new_law_graduates_earn_-_class_of_2010 (from NALP Bulletin, Nov. 2011).

Research suggests that money does not buy happiness, at least above the minimum needed for a decent level of comfort and security. Rather than depending on how much a job pays you, job happiness for most people depends more on (no surprises here): enjoying what you do (or at least finding it meaningful), enjoying most of the people with whom you work closely, believing your work is worthwhile, and feeling that you are good at it.

With that in mind, what would you say is a starting salary in your first post-law-school job that you would feel comfortable with?

Now, recognizing that your first job after law school may not be your ideal job, what will be the attributes of the job that would closely approximate your ideal?

If you have trouble answering that question, you may find helpful guidance from your law school's career development office and lawyers who seem to enjoy their jobs. Another excellent resource is a booklet by Lawrence S. Krieger entitled *A Deeper Understanding of Your Career Choices: Scientific Guidance for a Fulfilling Life and Career* (2007).

Chapter 20

The Due Process Clauses as Sources of Procedural Requirements for Agency Adjudications

Overview

In Chapter 19, we identified the Due Process Clauses of the Fifth and Fourteenth Amendments as sources of procedural requirements for agency adjudications. Now we examine (1) when the Clauses apply to an agency adjudication, and (2) what procedures the Clauses require, when they do apply.

In short, the Due Process Clauses apply to agency adjudications that deprive or threaten to deprive someone of life, liberty, or property. The U.S. Supreme Court has interpreted the Clauses to apply not only to traditional forms of property but also to "new" property such as government welfare benefits. Although most agencies lack the power to deprive people of liberty, some agencies do have that power, including, for example, the federal agencies responsible for deporting undocumented aliens. Fortunately, agencies lack the power to deprive people of life, except to execute court-entered death sentences. We therefore focus on deprivations of property and liberty.

When due process applies, its usual core requirements are that the person facing a potential deprivation of property or liberty gets notice and a right to be heard before any significant deprivation occurs. Because the notice and right to be heard usually must precede a significant deprivation, judicial review of agency actions that have already caused a significant deprivation usually is not enough to satisfy due process. Thus, the agency's own procedures must provide the required notice and opportunity to be heard.

This chapter has five sections:

A. Context

B. Text, Framework for Due Process Analysis, and Overview of Due Process Principles

C. Question One: Does Due Process Apply?

D. Question Two: If Due Process Applies, What Process is Due?

E. Chapter 20 Wrap Up and Look Ahead

Chapter Problem

Memo

From: General Counsel, University of West Dakota

To: Associate General Counsel

Re: Law student lawsuit

Linus Stafford was a law student at the University of West Dakota Law School until he was disqualified after his second year of law school for cheating on an exam. Mr. Stafford is now suing the dean of the law school and other law school officials in the state district court here in Capital City, West Dakota, claiming that the disqualification violated his rights under the Due Process Clause.

The associate dean of the law school says that the law school followed all procedures required in the law school's law student handbook and other relevant sources before it disqualified Mr. Stafford. You will have to conduct interviews and review documents to figure out if the law school followed its procedures in this case. In the meantime, assume for this research assignment that the law school did follow its procedures. I would like you to write a short memo for me to review and send to the President, to respond to questions the President has raised about this lawsuit. I will now paraphrase the President's questions as faithfully as I can.

First, how can Mr. Stafford claim a due process violation when he has the undoubted right—which he has exercised—to sue in state court, where he will be entitled to discovery and a trial with live testimony, cross-examination, etc.? He'll get his due process in this lawsuit, won't he?

Second, the Due Process Clause says people cannot be deprived of life, liberty, or property without due process. What "property" or "liberty" can Mr. Stafford claim we have deprived him of? I could understand him having a property interest in a license to practice law, but he's just a law student.

Third, even assuming Mr. Stafford had a due process "right" to stay in law school, that right was conditioned on his obeying the rules. He forfeited that right by breaking the rule against cheating on his exams! Whatever right he may have had is gone, right?

These are the President's immediate questions. Eventually, we will have to pin down how Mr. Stafford believes the procedures that we followed in his case fell short of due process. At this point, in addition to drafting answers to these questions I'd like you simply to review the procedures for disqualifying a student for cheating on an exam and identify any procedures (or any absence of procedures) you think may be objectionable on due process grounds.

I look forward to your draft.

A. Context

This section gives you context for our exploration of due process. In this section you will learn why we explore due process in a law school course on administrative law. You will also learn what branch of due process doctrine we explore in a course on administrative law. Finally, you will learn other important contextual information related to the role of due process in administrative law.

1. Why Study Due Process in an Administrative Law Course

The term "due process" conjures up lofty thoughts of the Magna Carta to many lawyers and judges, and seems far removed from the bureaucratic world of administrative law. Nonetheless, due process lies just beneath the surface of much administrative law, and it bobs up to the surface more often than you might expect. To understand the role that due process plays in administrative law, it helps to know some history.

When agencies began to dominate business life and personal life in the early twentieth century, concerns arose about their fairness. The fairness concerns centered on the procedures agencies used to carry out their statutory missions. In particular, the procedures that agencies used to adjudicate matters (e.g., grant and deny licenses) were challenged, sometimes successfully, on due process grounds.

You may wonder how due process could ever invalidate an agency action that is eventually subject to judicial review. After all, doesn't judicial review itself provide all the process that is constitutionally due? The answer is: not necessarily. That is because many agencies have power to deprive a person of property or liberty *before* the person can get judicial review. For example, the government can fire an employee who may have a property interest in his job. The firing causes an immediate deprivation, which it may take years to challenge through the court process. Judicial review alone may not be enough because, as you will see, due process generally requires the government to give you notice and "some kind of hearing" *before* it causes a significant deprivation of your liberty or property. Thus, while judicial review of agency action can provide a remedy for a wrongful agency deprivation after the fact, due process usually requires the agency itself to have procedures to prevent wrongful deprivations in the first place.

Because *judicial* process alone does not necessarily provide *due* process, legislatures enacted APAs and agency-specific legislation requiring administrative procedures to ensure fairness during agency adjudications. This legislation was designed to meet or exceed due process requirements. Today, legislatures continue to craft statutory procedural requirements for agency adjudications to meet or exceed due process requirements. In addition, sophisticated agencies (meaning agencies with good lawyers!) often elaborate upon and refine these statutory procedures by drafting their own procedural rules for their adjudications. Thus, procedural requirements imposed by statutes and agency rules are informed by due process concepts. In this way, due process lies below their surface.

Given this history, you can appreciate why understanding due process helps you understand procedural requirements that statutes and agency rules put on agency adjudications. When statutes and rules have been *drafted* to ensure due process, agencies and courts are likely to *interpret* those statutes and rules to ensure due process. Thus, lawyers who understand due process will be able to *predict*—and, by effective advocacy, to *influence*—how agencies and courts interpret those statutes and rules.

Indeed, due process arguments are used by administrative lawyers most effectively to influence the interpretation of procedural statutes and rules. In contrast, administrative lawyers will find it hard to argue successfully that a procedural statute, agency rule, or other agency action *violates* the applicable Due Process Clause. Such claims of out-and-out due process violations rarely succeed for three reasons. First, as we have said, procedural statutes, agency rules, and other agency actions usually meet or exceed due process requirements because they are consciously designed to do so. Second, courts and other decision makers are uncomfortable finding out-and-out due process violations because due process analysis can be highly imprecise and indeterminate. Courts and other decision makers feel on more solid ground interpreting statutes and agency actions to avoid finding due process violations and, indeed, courts are obligated to do so. Third, due process rulings can have broad implications, compared to rulings based on the interpretation of a particular statute, rule, or other agency action. Judges and other governmental decision makers tend to be conservative, and thus to avoid broad grounds for decision when narrower ones exist.

In sum, due process lies behind many statutes and rules imposing procedural requirements in agency adjudication, and that is why the lawyer working with these statutes and rules needs to understand due process.

2. What Due Process Doctrine We Study in Administrative Law

The Due Process Clauses of the Fifth and Fourteenth Amendments have been interpreted to have both a "substantive" and a "procedural" component. This book focuses on the procedural component, consistently with most law school courses on administrative law. To understand that focus, you must understand the difference between the substantive and procedural components of due process.

Roughly speaking, the doctrine of substantive due process addresses *what* actions the government can take, whereas the doctrine of procedural due process addresses *how* the government must take certain actions. More specifically, substantive due process prohibits government actions that interfere with fundamental liberties or are utterly arbitrary and malicious. Procedural due process requires the government to use fair procedures when it deprives someone of life, liberty, or property.

To cite an example relevant to administrative law, substantive due process might bar a government official from revoking a person's business license solely because that person reminded the official of a childhood bully who beat up the official on the playground. Such a substantive ground for an adjudicatory decision arguably violates substantive due process because of its utter arbitrariness. By comparison, procedural due process simply requires the government to use fair procedures before revoking the person's business license. Everyone realizes that the distinction between substantive and procedural due process is somewhat artificial and often blurry, but fortunately administrative lawyers encounter due process almost exclusively in its purely procedural form.

Exercise: Due Process in Context

Assume you represent the person described in the text above whose business license is revoked because the person resembles the childhood nemesis of the official who has revoked the license.

1. Assume your client contacts you as soon as the client has gotten notice that the government intends to revoke your client's business license. What legal research will you undertake, if this is your first case involving the revocation of a business license?

2. Assuming for the moment that you can prove the improper basis for the revocation, besides substantive due process, what other substantive grounds may exist for challenging the revocation?

3. In some agency adjudications, procedural due process requires a decision maker to give a written statement of reasons for the decision. Even when due process does not require a written explanation, it is often required by the agency legislation or agency rules. Please explain in your own words how the procedural requirement of a written explanation reinforces the requirement that the decision be substantively valid.

3. Other Contextual Considerations

Before we delve into due process analysis, you will benefit from three final pieces of contextual information.

The first point is that the primary remedy for an agency's due process violation is a requirement that the agency provide due process. This remedy often gives the agency the ability to reach the same result as before, after a procedural "re-do."

Suppose, for example, that you convince a court that a government agency fired your client from an agency job without following the procedures that were constitutionally due. In proving a violation of procedural due process, you have impugned the process but not necessarily the substantive correctness of the agency's decision. Assume for now that the agency correctly determined (say) that your client was drunk on the job. In that event, the agency probably had a valid substantive ground for firing your client. If so, all your client may get from a successful procedural-due-process challenge is some backpay and some extra time on the payroll while the agency again fires your client for being drunk on the job, this time using proper procedures. The broader point is that the primary judicial remedy for a violation of procedural due process is a court order requiring the government to provide due process. This may be cold comfort for a client.

The second point is that an agency's due process violation may be found "harmless" on judicial review, in which case the lawyer establishing the violation gets nothing at all for the client, not even extra process. The burden is on the person alleging a due process error to show how the error tainted the outcome. For example, if you argue to a court that the agency violated due process by refusing to allow you to cross-examine an adverse witness at the hearing before the agency, you'd better be prepared to explain precisely how your cross-examination would have hurt the witness's credibility and might have changed the outcome. (Furthermore, you'd better be able to demonstrate to the court that you made a timely objection at the agency hearing to the denial of cross-examination and made a proper proffer to the hearing officer of the basis for your proposed cross-examination.) The bottom line is that procedural due process arguments fail if they seem to be seeking more procedure just for procedure's sake.

The third and last point is that procedural due process analysis differs depending on whether you are analyzing adjudicative-type government action or legislative-type government action. Procedural due process puts significant procedural requirements on certain adjudicative actions by the government. In contrast, procedural due process puts few, if any, procedural requirements on legislative-type governmental action. The distinction between those two types of government action is called the "*Londoner/Bi-Metallic* distinction," after the two U.S. Supreme Court cases associated with the distinction: *Bi-Metallic Investment Co. v. State Board of Equalization*, 239 U.S. 441 (1915), and *Londoner v. City and County of Denver*, 210 U.S. 373 (1908). We examined those cases earlier, in Chapter 4.D.3. In the rest of this chapter we focus on procedural due process requirements for agency adjudications.

B. Text, Framework for Due Process Analysis, and Overview of Due Process Principles

The U.S. Constitution has two Due Process Clauses. The Due Process Clause of the Fifth Amendment forbids the federal government from depriving any person of life, liberty, or property without due process of law. The Due Process Clause of the Fourteenth Amendment forbids state and local governments from doing so. The two Clauses have been interpreted generally to mean the same thing. Thus, when it comes to procedural due process requirements, what's good for the federal goose is good for state and local ganders, and vice versa.

The Due Process Clauses can be understood as "If…, then" statements:

(1) *If*

- the government
- deprives
- a person
- of life, liberty, or property,

(2) *then* the government must provide due process.

This "If … then" formulation reflects the two overarching questions of procedural due process analysis:

(1) Does due process apply to the particular action under analysis?

(2) If so, what process is due?

The text of the Due Process Clauses gives guidance on the first question but not the second. As to the first question, due process applies when all conditions of the "if" clause are present. As to the second, the Clauses are silent.

We examine the case law relevant to the two questions in sections C and D below. Now we summarize the principles that the case law establishes and that matter to administrative lawyers:

(1) Due process may apply to situations in which a federal, state, or local government entity or official:

- reduces or terminates ongoing government benefits for which a person has previously been found eligible, such as payments under a government welfare program
- reduces or terminates a government service that a person has been receiving, such as residential electricity
- restricts or terminates a government license or permit for which a person has previously been found eligible, such as a license to operate a restaurant or practice medicine
- puts a tax on someone—e.g., a property tax assessment—or a civil sanction such as a fine or a cease-and-desist order—e.g., for a violation of pollution laws
- terminates a person's government job or otherwise takes adverse action against (e.g., demotes) a government employee
- terminates or breaches a contract with a person who has contracted with the government—e.g., to supply the government with goods or services
- punishes or takes other adverse action against (e.g., suspends) a public school student

The key to understanding why due process may apply to these situations is that the term "property" for due process purposes includes not only traditional forms of property such as land, personal property, and money, but also a person's interest in certain types of government benefits, such as welfare benefits, government-issued permits and licenses, and government employment. These nontraditional forms of "property" are known as "the new property" and account for many administrative law cases about procedural due process.

2. If you determine that due process applies to the situation, the question becomes what process is due in that situation—and, in particular, did the government provide it?

When due process does apply to a particular situation, questions may arise about (a) when the process must be provided; and (b) what the process must entail. The Court has held that timing and elaborateness of the required procedures depend on three factors:

   i.   the private interest at stake;

   ii.   the accuracy of existing procedures and the probable value, if any, of additional procedures; and

   iii.   the governmental and public interests at stake.

In practice, these considerations lead to a couple of important rules of thumb.

The rule of thumb about timing generally requires the government to give a person notice and a right to be heard *before* a significant deprivation occurs.

As for the rule of thumb about what due process entails: The person's pre-deprivation "right to be heard" usually must include a chance to present evidence supporting the person's version of any disputed facts and to confront adverse evidence. The pre-deprivation right to be heard does not, however, usually have to be as elaborate as a trial and indeed may consist only of a "paper hearing," with no opportunity for the person to come face-to-face with the decision maker. Due process does generally require the decision maker to be impartial.

Lawyers establish due process violations by showing that (1) the procedures actually used were actually unfair under the particular circumstances; and (2) the government readily could have cured the unfairness by using additional or different procedures. Theory and intricate analysis aside, due process comes down to fairness in the individual case.

Exercise: Due Process Framework

The objective of this exercise is to have you construct a framework into which you can integrate the material presented in the rest of this chapter.

Please create a flow chart or other graphic organizer that depicts the due process framework described above. Design your graphic organizer to leave room for elaboration and refinement in light of the material in the rest of this chapter. If you need inspiration, look over the headings and subheadings for the rest of this chapter.

C. Question One: Does Due Process Apply?

1. There Must Be Conduct Attributable to the Government

The Due Process Clauses generally apply only to governmental conduct, not private conduct. Yet sometimes private conduct *will* be attributable to the government. The "state action" doctrine identifies when private conduct will be attributable to the government. We will not explore the state action doctrine in detail because it is usually addressed in law school courses on constitutional law. We will, however, summarize two administrative-law cases from the U.S. Supreme Court addressing the state action doctrine, to show how the doctrine arises in this setting.

- *Blum v. Yaretsky*, 457 U.S. 991 (1982)

This was a lawsuit by residents of private nursing homes in New York. The nursing homes had either discharged these residents or transferred them to facilities that offered a lower level of care. The residents asserted that they did not get adequate notice or opportunity to be heard before the discharge or transfer decisions were made. They claimed that this violated their due process rights.

Each of the residents was eligible for government-funded health care under the Medicaid program. Consequently, their nursing homes got reimbursement from the Medicaid program for caring for them. Medicaid regulations required nursing homes periodically to assess all Medicaid-eligible residents to ensure that they continued to need the high level of care provided in a nursing home. If a resident was found not to require such a high level of care, Medicaid regulations did *not* require the nursing home to discharge or transfer the resident. Medicaid regulations did, however, reduce or terminate reimbursement to the nursing home for that resident.

The Court applied the state action doctrine to conclude that the private nursing homes' decisions to discharge or transfer residents were *not* attributable to the government, and so the nursing homes' decisions were not subject to due process restrictions. The Court made three points:

(1) Medicaid regulations did not exert such "coercive power or such significant encouragement" that a nursing home's decision to discharge or transfer a resident

should be treated under the state action doctrine as a decision attributable to the government. *Id.* at 1004. Medicaid regulations did decrease or terminate reimbursement for any resident who was found not to need the level of care provided in the current facility. The Medicaid regulations did not, however, affirmatively require a nursing home to discharge or transfer the resident.

(2) The extensive regulation of nursing homes that receive Medicaid reimbursement also was not enough to attribute the nursing homes' actions to the government under the state action doctrine. *Id.* at 1010–1011.

(3) Nursing homes do not "perform a function that has been traditionally the exclusive prerogative" of the government. *Id.* at 1011. Thus, the "traditional public function" principle did not justify finding state action in this case under the state action doctrine.

• *Jackson v. Metropolitan Edison Co.*, 419 U.S. 345 (1974)

Metropolitan was a private utility company. It held a certificate of public convenience from the Pennsylvania Utilities Commission that authorized Metropolitan to sell electricity to customers in Pennsylvania. Metropolitan cut off electricity to Catherine Jackson's home for nonpayment. Ms. Jackson sued Metropolitan claiming that the company had violated procedural due process by cutting off her electricity without first giving her adequate notice, a hearing, and a chance to pay the amounts past due.

The Court rejected Ms. Jackson's procedural due process claim, holding that Metropolitan's termination of her electric service was not attributable to the State and therefore was not subject to procedural due process requirements. The Court framed the question as "whether there is a sufficiently close nexus between the State and the challenged action of the regulated entity so that the action of the latter may be fairly treated as that of the State itself." *Id.* at 351.

The Court answered that question "no," after rejecting all of Ms. Jackson's arguments for treating the termination of her electricity as state action. The Court held it insufficient that Metropolitan might have a governmentally protected monopoly in providing electricity; and that the provision of electricity was "affected with a public interest." *Id.* at 354. On the second point, the Court explained that providing electricity was not a power "traditionally exclusively reserved to the State," and thus the case was distinguishable from cases finding "state action" when private actors were involved in holding elections for public office or running an entire town. *Id.* at 352–353. The Court also rejected the argument that, by approving the tariff (detailed filing) that Metropolitan filed with the Utilities Commission, the State had "specifically authorized and approved" Metropolitan's procedures for cutting off someone's electricity for nonpayment. *Id.* at 354–355. The Court concluded:

> All of petitioner's arguments taken together show no more than that Metropolitan was a heavily regulated, privately owned utility, enjoying at least a partial monopoly in the providing of electrical service within its territory, and that it elected to terminate service to petitioner in a manner which the Pennsylvania Public Utility Commission found permissible under state law. Under our decision this is not sufficient to connect the State of Pennsylvania with [Metropolitan's] ... action so as to make the latter's conduct attributable to the State for purposes of the Fourteenth Amendment.

Id. at 358.

Because the Court found no state action, the Court did not have to address whether Ms. Jackson had a "property" interest in continuing to receive electricity. *Id.* at 348 n.2.

In a later case, the Court held that state law can indeed give a customer a property interest in continued receipt of governmentally supplied electricity. *See Memphis Light, Gas & Water Division v. Craft*, 436 U.S. 1, 9–11 (1978).

* * *

Private action was not attributed to the government in either case just described. Indeed, private conduct will seldom be attributable to the government under the state action doctrine. For that reason, due process generally restricts only the actions of government authorities.

Exercise: The "State Action" Doctrine

Your client lives in a city that owns and operates the gas and electric company. This municipal gas and electric company operates just like a private company. It bills city residents for residential gas and electric service, and it cuts off a customer's gas and electric service if the customer does not pay. Assume that a customer has a "property" interest in the continued receipt of residential gas and electric service. Must the company comply with procedural due process when it cuts off a customer's gas and electric service?

---

2. The Conduct Must Cause a Deprivation

Usually you will have no trouble identifying a "deprivation" triggering procedural due process. Here we just highlight four important aspects of the term "deprivation."

- Procedural due process may apply even when the government just *threatens* a deprivation.

As a rule of thumb, procedural due process requires the government to give a person notice and an opportunity to be heard *before* it deprives that person of life, liberty, or property. If, for example, the government intends to terminate someone's welfare benefits, the government must notify the welfare recipient of its intention before cutting off those benefits. At the time the welfare recipient gets notice, the deprivation has not happened yet. Even so, the *threat* of the deprivation triggers procedural due process. To make that point in this book, we say that procedural due process applies when the government "deprives or threatens to deprive" someone of life, liberty, or property. We also refer to "deprivations or threatened deprivations." The point is, procedural due process usually comes into play even before the deprivation has occurred.

- Procedural due process may apply even to *temporary* deprivations.

If the government takes away your liberty or property, you have suffered a deprivation, even if the government gives it back later. Thus, for example, procedural due process applied when the government suspended a person's disability benefits but gave the person the right to get an award of back benefits by showing the suspension was not justified. *Mathews v. Eldridge*, 424 U.S. 319, 340 (1976). *See generally Fuentes v. Shevin*, 407 U.S. 67, 84–85 (1972) ("[I]t is now well settled that a temporary, nonfinal deprivation of property is nonetheless a 'deprivation.'").

- Procedural due process applies only to deprivations that are a direct result of government action.

Government action can have ripple effects. If a government action only indirectly causes someone to lose property or liberty, the government action may not constitute a "deprivation" for purposes of procedural due process.

The leading case is *O'Bannon v. Town Court Nursing Center*, 447 U.S. 773 (1980). In *O'Bannon* the government terminated a nursing home's eligibility to receive reimbursement under the Medicare and Medicaid programs for caring for patients. Because of the termination, some residents of that nursing home had to be discharged or transferred to a different nursing home. The residents argued that procedural due process entitled them to a hearing before the government finally terminated the nursing home's Medicare and Medicaid eligibility. The Court rejected that argument on the ground that the government's action affected them too indirectly to be a deprivation as to them. The Court determined that the discharge or transfer of the Medicare and Medicaid residents was only "an indirect and incidental result of the Government's enforcement action." *Id.* at 787. It therefore did not constitute a deprivation as to the residents.

Because government action can have broad ripple effects, the Court in *O'Bannon* worried about extending procedural due process rights to people other than direct victims of government action.

- Merely negligent government action cannot constitute a deprivation.

In *Daniels v. Williams*, 474 U.S. 327 (1986), a prisoner slipped and fell on a pillow that a deputy sheriff left on the jailhouse stairs. The prisoner sued the officer claiming a violation of procedural due process. The Court rejected the claim, holding that merely negligent conduct cannot constitute a deprivation of life, liberty, or property for due process purposes. The Court relied on the connotations of the word "deprive" and the history showing that due process applied to *deliberate* decisions by the government to deprive someone of life, liberty, or property.

Exercise: Deprivations

Please explain whether these government actions are deprivations:

1. A state Department of Motor Vehicles suspends a person's driver's license for thirty days because the person refused to take a breathalyzer test after a police officer stopped the person for suspected drunk driving.

2. The U.S. Department of Defense shuts down a military base in a rural area. This causes a restaurant located right outside the base to close down for loss of business.

3. A police car negligently collides with a motorcycle and kills its rider while pursuing a fleeing bank robber.

---

3. The Deprivation Must Affect a Person

The Due Process Clauses protect "person[s]." For administrative law purposes, there are two important things to understand about the term "person" as used in those Clauses.

First, a corporation or other artificial entity can be a "person" within the meaning of the Due Process Clauses. *Grosjean v. Am. Press Co.*, 297 U.S. 233, 244 (1936). Second, the term "person" includes every human being in United States, including undocumented aliens. A person's immigration status may affect what process is "due" in proceedings about that status. *See, e.g., Reno v. Flores*, 507 U.S. 292, 306–307 (1993). Immigration status, however, generally does not affect what process is "due" in other proceedings. *See generally Mathews v. Diaz*, 426 U.S. 67, 77–78 (1976) (discussing due process rights of aliens).

4. The Deprivation Must Be a Deprivation of Life, Liberty, or Property

Due process applies only to actual or threatened deprivations of life, liberty, or property. Governmentally authorized deprivations of *life* are generally the province of courts in criminal cases.

Administrative law cases can involve actual or threatened deprivations of *liberty*. As we will see, however, the Court has defined the term "liberty" for procedural due process purposes so narrowly that an administrative agency's adjudication will only rarely deprive someone of liberty.

Most administrative law cases implicating due process involve actual or threatened deprivations of *property*. We therefore start by examining how to identify "property" for due process purposes.

a. Property

As mentioned above, "property" includes not only traditional forms of property — such as land, personal property, and money — but also interests in certain kinds of government benefits — such as welfare benefits, government-issued permits and licenses, and government employment. This section focuses on modern U.S. Supreme Court case law recognizing the latter forms of "new property."

To understand current case law, it helps to know some history. Early case law distinguished "rights," on the one hand, from "privileges" (or "gratuities" or "bounties"), on the other hand. Certain interests that the law had traditionally protected were treated as "rights" that the government could not take away without due process. They included, for example, the right to own property, the right to make contracts, the right to be free from bodily restraint, and the right to practice certain professions or trades. Other interests were considered as mere privileges, gratuities, or bounties made available by the grace, and not the obligation, of the government. These privileges, being created by government benevolence, did not arise to the dignity of interests protected by due process. Examples of mere privileges included government employment and licenses to operate pool halls or sell liquor.

You will find references to the right/privilege distinction in older court cases. The distinction no longer controls the identification of interests protected by due process, however, because it has been discredited as intellectually bankrupt. The U.S. Supreme Court expressly rejected the relevance of the right/privilege distinction to due process analysis in *Goldberg v. Kelly*, 397 U.S. 254 (1970). *Goldberg* is a landmark case partly because it rejected the right/privilege distinction. *Goldberg* also replaced the earliest approach with a second, transitional approach to identifying interests protected by due process. We summarize *Goldberg* below:

- *Goldberg v. Kelly*, 397 U.S. 254 (1970)

John Kelly and other plaintiffs (collectively referred to here as "Mr. Kelly") had been receiving welfare benefits from New York City (referred to here as "the State"). The State terminated Mr. Kelly's welfare benefits on the ground that he was no longer eligible for them. Mr. Kelly sued a state official, Jack Goldberg, claiming a violation of procedural due process. Specifically, Mr. Kelly argued that due process entitled him, before his welfare benefits were terminated, to a live hearing at which he could present evidence showing his continued eligibility.

The U.S. Supreme Court ruled in favor of Mr. Kelly. The Court treated his interest in the continued receipt of welfare payments as tantamount to a "property" interest protected by due process. In addition, the Court held that due process required an evidentiary hearing before the State terminated his welfare benefits. Our present concern is with the Court's decision in *Goldberg* to treat Mr. Kelly's interest in his welfare benefits as tantamount to a "property" interest.

Curiously, the Court did not clarify whether it was actually holding that Mr. Kelly had a "property" interest at stake. The State did not dispute that procedural due process applied to the termination of welfare benefits. Thus, the Court did not have an adversary presentation by the parties on the issue whether welfare benefits are property. Perhaps for that reason, the Court equivocated. The Court addressed the issue mainly in a footnote, where the Court said: "It may be realistic today to regard welfare entitlements as more like 'property' than a 'gratuity.'" *Goldberg*, 397 U.S. at 262 n.8.

Despite *Goldberg*'s lack of an adversary presentation and lack of an unequivocal holding, the Court in a later case treated *Goldberg* as holding that Mr. Kelly's interest in welfare benefits was indeed "property" within the meaning of the Due Process Clause. *Board of Regents v. Roth*, 408 U.S. 564, 576–577 (1972). In extending procedural due process to government benefits, though tentatively, *Goldberg* is known as the first major case in which the Court recognized what is called "the new property."

The *Goldberg* Court gave two reasons for this extension of the concept of "property." One was that welfare benefits "are a matter of statutory entitlement for persons qualified to receive them." *Id.* at 262. The other was that a person's interest in continuing to receive welfare payments is "important"; their termination could cause "grievous loss." *Id.* at 262–263.

Goldberg led some lower courts and commentators to think that the right/privilege distinction had been replaced by a second approach, under which the applicability of due process to the deprivation of a government-created interest depended on the *weight* of the interest. Due process thus applied to interests that were sufficiently "important" that governmental deprivation of those interests would cause "grievous loss." This interest-weighing approach was short-lived, however, for the Court squarely rejected it two years after *Goldberg*, in two important cases: *Board of Regents v. Roth*, 408 U.S. 564 (1972), and *Perry v. Sindermann*, 408 U.S. 593 (1972).

Excerpts of *Board of Regents v. Roth* and *Perry v. Sindermann* are reproduced below. They establish the modern approach to determining whether government benefits of various types, including governmentally issued licenses and permits, are "property" for due process purposes. Instead of pursuing the interest-weighing rationale of *Goldberg*, the Court in *Board of Regents v. Roth* and *Perry v. Sindermann* pursued *Goldberg*'s "entitlement" rationale for identifying protected property interests. These two post-*Goldberg* cases reflected and fostered what has been called the "due process revolution." *See, e.g.,* Erwin N. Griswold, *The Due Process Revolution and Confrontation,* 119 U. Pa. L. Rev. 711 (1971).

Exercise: *Board of Regents v. Roth* and *Perry v. Sindermann*

Please read the excerpts below with these questions in mind:

1. Why does the Court in *Roth* reject an "interest weighing" approach to determining whether an interest constitutes "liberty" or "property" for procedural due process purposes? What role does interest weighing continue to serve in due process analysis?

2. How does the Court in *Roth* justify treating the interest in continued receipt of welfare payments as "property" for procedural due process purposes?

3. What is the significance of having a "legitimate claim of entitlement" to a government benefit? What makes a claim "legitimate"?

4. In *Roth* the Court found no property interest. In *Perry v. Sindermann,* the Court held that the plaintiff might have a property interest. How do you reconcile these results, considering that both cases involved untenured professors at public institutions?

Board of Regents v. Roth

408 U.S. 564 (1972)

Mr. Justice Stewart delivered the opinion of the Court.

In 1968 the respondent, David Roth, was hired for his first teaching job as assistant professor of political science at Wisconsin State University-Oshkosh. He was hired for a fixed term of one academic year. The notice of his faculty appointment specified that his employment would begin on September 1, 1968, and would end on June 30, 1969. The respondent completed that term. But he was informed that he would not be rehired for the next academic year.

The respondent had no tenure rights to continued employment. Under Wisconsin statutory law a state university teacher can acquire tenure as a "permanent" employee only after four years of year-to-year employment. Having acquired tenure, a teacher is entitled to continued employment "during efficiency and good behavior." A relatively new teacher without tenure, however, is under Wisconsin law entitled to nothing beyond his one-year appointment. There are no statutory or administrative standards defining eligibility for re-employment. State law thus clearly leaves the decision whether to rehire a nontenured teacher for another year to the unfettered discretion of university officials.

The procedural protection afforded a Wisconsin State University teacher before he is separated from the University corresponds to his job security. As a matter of statutory law, a tenured teacher cannot be "discharged except for cause upon written charges" and pursuant to certain procedures. A nontenured teacher, similarly, is protected to some extent *during* his one-year term. Rules promulgated by the Board of Regents provide that a nontenured teacher "dismissed" before the end of the year may have some opportunity for review of the "dismissal." But the Rules provide no real protection for a nontenured teacher who simply is not re-employed for the next year. He must be informed by February 1 "concerning retention or non-retention for the ensuing year." But "no reason for non-retention need be given. No review or appeal is provided in such case."

In conformance with these Rules, the President of Wisconsin State University-Oshkosh informed the respondent before February 1, 1969, that he would not be rehired for the 1969–1970 academic year. He gave the respondent no reason for the decision and no opportunity to challenge it at any sort of hearing.

[Mr. Roth sued, claiming the nonrenewal of his contract violated procedural due process.]

I

The requirements of procedural due process apply only to the deprivation of interests encompassed by the Fourteenth Amendment's protection of liberty and property.... [T]he range of interests protected by procedural due process is not infinite.

The District Court decided that procedural due process guarantees apply in this case by assessing and balancing the weights of the particular interests involved. It concluded that the respondent's interest in re-employment at Wisconsin State University-Oshkosh outweighed the University's interest in denying him re-employment summarily. 310 F.Supp., at 977–979. Undeniably, the respondent's re-employment prospects were of major concern to him — concern that we surely cannot say was insignificant. And a weighing process has long been a part of any determination of the form of hearing required in particular situations by procedural due process. But, to determine whether due process requirements apply in the first place, we must look not to the "weight" but to the nature of the interest at stake.... We must look to see if the interest is within the Fourteenth Amendment's protection of liberty and property.

"Liberty" and "property" are broad and majestic terms. They are among the "[g]reat [constitutional] concepts ... purposely left to gather meaning from experience.... [T]hey relate to the whole domain of social and economic fact, and the statesmen who founded this Nation knew too well that only a stagnant society remains unchanged." *National Mutual Ins. Co. v. Tidewater Transfer Co.*, 337 U.S. 582, 646 (Frankfurter, J., dissenting). For that reason, the Court has fully and finally rejected the wooden distinction between "rights" and "privileges" that once seemed to govern the applicability of procedural due process rights. The Court has also made clear that the property interests protected by procedural due process extend well beyond actual ownership of real estate, chattels, or money. By the same token, the Court has required due process protection for deprivations of liberty beyond the sort of formal constraints imposed by the criminal process.

Yet, while the Court has eschewed rigid or formalistic limitations on the protection of procedural due process, it has at the same time observed certain boundaries. For the words "liberty" and "property" in the Due Process Clause of the Fourteenth Amendment must be given some meaning.

II

[Editor's note: In part II of the Court's opinion, the Court held that the nonrenewal of Mr. Roth's contract did not deprive him of "liberty" for due process purposes. The Court's discussion is not relevant to our current examination of what constitutes "property" and, in any event, has been largely superseded by later Court precedent. That is why we omit it from this excerpt.]

III

The Fourteenth Amendment's procedural protection of property is a safeguard of the security of interests that a person has already acquired in specific benefits. These interests—property interests—may take many forms.

Thus, the Court has held that a person receiving welfare benefits under statutory and administrative standards defining eligibility for them has an interest in continued receipt of those benefits that is safeguarded by procedural due process. *Goldberg v. Kelly*, 397 U.S. 254 [(1970)]. See *Flemming v. Nestor*, 363 U.S. 603, 611 [(1960)]. Similarly, in the area of public employment, the Court has held that a public college professor dismissed from an office held under tenure provisions, *Slochower v. Board of Education*, 350 U.S. 551 [(1956)], and college professors and staff members dismissed during the terms of their contracts, *Wieman v. Updegraff*, 344 U.S. 183 [(1952)], have interests in continued employment that are safeguarded by due process. Only last year, the Court held that this principle "proscribing summary dismissal from public employment without hearing or inquiry required by due process" also applied to a teacher recently hired without tenure or a formal contract, but nonetheless with a clearly implied promise of continued employment. *Connell v. Higginbotham*, 403 U.S. 207, 208 [(1971)].

Certain attributes of "property" interests protected by procedural due process emerge from these decisions. To have a property interest in a benefit, a person clearly must have more than an abstract need or desire for it. He must have more than a unilateral expectation of it. He must, instead, have a legitimate claim of entitlement to it. It is a purpose of the ancient institution of property to protect those claims upon which people rely in their daily lives, reliance that must not be arbitrarily undermined. It is a purpose of the constitutional right to a hearing to provide an opportunity for a person to vindicate those claims.

Property interests, of course, are not created by the Constitution. Rather they are created and their dimensions are defined by existing rules or understandings that stem from an independent source such as state law—rules or understandings that secure certain benefits and that support claims of entitlement to those benefits. Thus, the welfare recipients in *Goldberg v. Kelly, supra*, had a claim of entitlement to welfare payments that was grounded in the statute defining eligibility for them. The recipients had not yet shown that they were, in fact, within the statutory terms of eligibility. But we held that they had a right to a hearing at which they might attempt to do so.

Just as the welfare recipients' "property" interest in welfare payments was created and defined by statutory terms, so the respondent's "property" interest in employment at Wisconsin State University-Oshkosh was created and defined by the terms of his appointment. Those terms secured his interest in employment up to June 30, 1969. But the important fact in this case is that they specifically provided that the respondent's employment was to terminate on June 30. They did not provide for contract renewal absent "sufficient cause." Indeed, they made no provision for renewal whatsoever.

Thus, the terms of the respondent's appointment secured absolutely no interest in re-employment for the next year.... Nor, significantly, was there any state statute or University rule or policy that secured his interest in re-employment or that created any legitimate claim to it.[16] In these circumstances, the respondent surely had an abstract concern in

---

16. To be sure, the respondent does suggest that most teachers hired on a year-to-year basis by Wisconsin State University-Oshkosh are, in fact, rehired. But the District Court has not found that there is anything approaching a "common law" of re-employment, see *Perry v. Sindermann*, 408 U.S. 593, [602 (1972)], so strong as to require University officials to give the respondent a statement of reasons and a hearing on their decision not to rehire him.

being rehired, but he did not have a property interest sufficient to require the University authorities to give him a hearing when they declined to renew his contract of employment....

We must conclude that ... respondent has not shown that he was deprived of liberty or property protected by the Fourteenth Amendment. The judgment of the Court of appeals, accordingly is reversed ...

[Editor's note: Justice Powell did not participate in the case. Justices Douglas and Marshall wrote separate dissenting opinions, which we omit from this excerpt.]

Perry v. Sindermann

408 U.S. 593 (1972)

[Editor's summary: Robert Sindermann taught at a state junior college in Texas for four successive years under a series of one-year contracts. After the fourth one-year contract expired, the college did not renew it. The college did not give Mr. Sindermann a chance to contest the nonrenewal, nor did it give him an official explanation of the nonrenewal. Mr. Sindermann sued, claiming that the nonrenewal of his contract violated procedural due process. A federal district court granted summary judgment against Mr. Sindermann on his procedural due process claim. The district court held that, because Mr. Sindermann did not have formal tenure, he could not establish a property interest in renewal of his contract. The federal court of appeals reversed the grant of summary judgment, and the U.S. Supreme Court affirmed that reversal. In the excerpt below, the Court held that even though Mr. Sindermann lacked formal tenure, he could establish a property interest if he could show that the state college had created a "de facto" tenure system.]

MR. JUSTICE STEWART delivered the opinion of the Court....

II

The respondent's lack of formal contractual or tenure security in continued employment at Odessa Junior College ... is highly relevant to his procedural due process claim. But it may not be entirely dispositive.

We have held today in *Board of Regents v. Roth*, 408 U.S. 564, that the Constitution does not require opportunity for a hearing before the nonrenewal of a nontenured teacher's contract, unless he can show that the decision not to rehire him somehow deprived him of an interest in "liberty" or that he had a "property" interest in continued employment, despite the lack of tenure or a formal contract. In *Roth* the teacher had not made a showing on either point to justify summary judgment in his favor.

Similarly, the respondent here has yet to show that he has been deprived of an interest that could invoke procedural due process protection....

But the respondent's allegations—which we must construe most favorably to the respondent at this stage of the litigation—do raise a genuine issue as to his interest in continued employment at Odessa Junior College. He alleged that this interest, though not secured by a formal contractual tenure provision, was secured by a no less binding understanding fostered by the college administration. In particular, the respondent alleged that the college had a de facto tenure program, and that he had tenure under that program. He claimed that he and others legitimately relied upon an unusual provision that had been in the college's official Faculty Guide for many years:

"Teacher Tenure: Odessa College has no tenure system. The Administration of the College wishes the faculty member to feel that he has permanent tenure as long as his teaching services are satisfactory and as long as he displays a cooperative attitude toward his co-workers and his superiors, and as long as he is happy in his work."

Moreover, the respondent claimed legitimate reliance upon guidelines promulgated by the Coordinating Board of the Texas College and University System that provided that a person, like himself, who had been employed as a teacher in the state college and university system for seven years or more has some form of job tenure.[6] Thus, the respondent offered to prove that a teacher with his long period of service at this particular State College had no less a "property" interest in continued employment than a formally tenured teacher at other colleges, and had no less a procedural due process right to a statement of reasons and a hearing before college officials upon their decision not to retain him.

We have made clear in *Roth, supra,* [408 U.S.] at 577, that "property" interests subject to procedural due process protection are not limited by a few rigid, technical forms. Rather, "property" denotes a broad range of interests that are secured by "existing rules or understandings." *Id.*, at 577. A person's interest in a benefit is a "property" interest for due process purposes if there are such rules or mutually explicit understandings that support his claim of entitlement to the benefit and that he may invoke at a hearing. *Ibid.*

A written contract with an explicit tenure provision clearly is evidence of a formal understanding that supports a teacher's claim of entitlement to continued employment unless sufficient "cause" is shown. Yet absence of such an explicit contractual provision may not always foreclose the possibility that a teacher has a "property" interest in reemployment. For example, the law of contracts in most, if not all, jurisdictions long has employed a process by which agreements, though not formalized in writing, may be "implied." 3 A. Corbin on Contracts §§ 561–572A (1960). Explicit contractual provisions may be supplemented by other agreements implied from "the promisor's words and conduct in

---

6. The relevant portion of the guidelines, adopted as "Policy Paper 1" by the Coordinating Board on October 16, 1967, reads:

"A. Tenure

"Tenure means assurance to an experienced faculty member that he may expect to continue in his academic position unless adequate cause for dismissal is demonstrated in a fair hearing, following established procedures of due process.

"A specific system of faculty tenure undergirds the integrity of each academic institution. In the Texas public colleges and universities, this tenure system should have these components:

"(1) Beginning with appointment to the rank of full-time instructor or a higher rank, the probationary period for a faculty member shall not exceed seven years, including within this period appropriate full-time service in all institutions of higher education. This is subject to the provision that when, after a term of probationary service of more than three years in one or more institutions, a faculty member is employed by another institution, it may be agreed in writing that his new appointment is for a probationary period of not more than four years (even though thereby the person's total probationary period in the academic profession is extended beyond the normal maximum of seven years)....

"(3) Adequate cause for dismissal for a faculty member with tenure may be established by demonstrating professional incompetence, moral turpitude, or gross neglect of professional responsibilities."

The respondent alleges that, because he has been employed as a "full-time instructor" or professor within the Texas College and University System for 10 years, he should have "tenure" under these provisions.

the light of the surrounding circumstances." *Id.*, at § 562. And, "[t]he meaning of [the promisor's] words and acts is found by relating them to the usage of the past." *Ibid.*

A teacher, like the respondent, who has held his position for a number of years, might be able to show from the circumstances of this service — and from other relevant facts — that he has a legitimate claim of entitlement to job tenure ...[7]

In this case, the respondent has alleged the existence of rules and understandings, promulgated and fostered by state officials, that may justify his legitimate claim of entitlement to continued employment absent "sufficient cause." We disagree with the Court of Appeals insofar as it held that a mere subjective "expectancy" is protected by procedural due process, but we agree that the respondent must be given an opportunity to prove the legitimacy of his claim of such entitlement in light of "the policies and practices of the institution." 430 F.2d, at 943. Proof of such a property interest would not, of course, entitle him to reinstatement. But such proof would obligate college officials to grant a hearing at his request, where he could be informed of the grounds for his nonretention and challenge their sufficiency. [The Court affirmed the court of appeals' judgment remanding the case to the district court for further proceedings.]

[Editor's note: Justice Powell did not participate in the case. Justices Brennan and Marshall each wrote separate opinions dissenting in part. Chief Justice Burger wrote a concurring opinion. We omit these separate opinions.]

Exercise: *Board of Regents v. Roth* and *Perry v. Sindermann* Revisited

1. Administrative lawyers must consider what they can win for their client in a lawsuit if they successfully establish a procedural due process violation. This exercise is meant to help you think about remedies in *Perry v. Sindermann*.

    The Court in *Perry v. Sindermann* says that even if Mr. Sindermann proves entitlement to procedural due process, he will not be automatically entitled to reinstatement but, instead, will only be entitled to a hearing at which he can challenge the sufficiency of the reasons for his nonrenewal. To prove entitlement to procedural due process, he will have to show that he enjoys "de facto tenure," meaning that he can't be fired without "sufficient cause."

    This raises three practical questions: (1) How might Mr. Sindermann establish that he has a right to be retained in the absence of "sufficient cause" for his firing? (2) What are examples of reasons that might be "sufficient cause" for firing a college teacher? (3) What remedy, do you suppose, Mr. Sindermann will get if he shows there was not "sufficient cause" for his nonrenewal?

2. Footnote 7 of *Perry v. Sindermann* mentions an important potential obstacle to Mr. Sindermann's ability to prove he is entitled to procedural due process because he enjoys de facto tenure. Footnote 7 says he cannot prove entitlement

---

7. We do not now hold that the respondent has any such legitimate claim of entitlement to job tenure. For "[p]roperty interests ... are not created by the Constitution. Rather, they are created and their dimensions are defined by existing rules or understandings that stem from an independent source such as state law...." *Board of Regents v. Roth, supra,* 408 U.S., at 577. If it is the law of Texas that a teacher in the respondent's position has no contractual or other claim to job tenure, the respondent's claim would be defeated.

"[i]f it is the law of Texas that a teacher in the respondent's position has no contractual or other claim to job tenure." 408 U.S. at 602 n.7.

This means that Texas could defeat future claims like Mr. Sindermann's by enacting a statute expressly disclaiming tenure rights in circumstances like those of Mr. Sindermann. The statute might say, for example, that state college teachers without formal tenure "have no legitimate expectation of continued employment after the term of their contract ends and in particular no legitimate expectation of contract renewal." That statute invalidates any state college rules or policies that purport to grant de facto tenure. That is because state law is the source of any property interest that Mr. Sindermann might claim, and, in the hierarchy of law, valid state statutes are superior to state agency legislative and non-legislative rules. *See, e.g., Cheveras Pacheco v. Rivera Gonzalez,* 809 F.2d 125, 127 (1st Cir. 1987) (rejecting procedural due process claim of government employee who was classified as a "transitory employee" who, under a Puerto Rico statute, could be "removed from service at any time"); *Freeman v. Poling,* 338 S.E.2d 415, 417 (1985) (employees did not qualify for job security under civil service statutes and therefore had no property interest despite assurances from the official who hired them).

Footnote 7 thus allows federal, state, and local governments to enact statutes defeating "de facto tenure" claims resting on agency rules or other legal material subordinate to statutes. We pose this question, then, to help you internalize the footnote's significance: If your client is a fired government employee who claims that her former agency employer had policies creating "de facto tenure," what should your research on that claim include?

3. The objective of this exercise is to introduce you to the relationship between, on the one hand, a "legitimate claim of entitlement" to a government benefit—which is necessary to establishing a protected property interest in that benefit—and, on the other hand, laws limiting the discretion of the government authority that has the power to grant or take away that benefit.

Mr. Sindermann claimed that Texas state law—including the Coordinating Board's Policy Paper 1—gave him de facto tenure preventing him from being fired unless the decision makers had "sufficient cause." In contrast, the Wisconsin law governing Mr. Roth's situation did not constrain the decision maker's discretion; the Court said in Roth's case, "State law ... clearly leaves the decision whether to rehire a nontenured teacher for another year to the *unfettered discretion* of university officials." 408 U.S. at 567 (emphasis added).

Suppose the state governor appoints Joe to a government job under a state statute that gives the governor not only the power to appoint a person to that job but also says, "the Governor may remove the person who holds this position at will." Further suppose the state governor appoints Jane to a different government job under a statute that authorizes the Governor to make the appointment but also says: "The governor may remove the person who holds this position only for malfeasance, misfeasance, or neglect of office." (Don't you love those legalese siblings Malfeasance and Misfeasance?)

Please explain in your own words why, under *Board of Regents v. Roth* and *Perry v. Sindermann,* Joe does not have a "legitimate claim of entitlement" to his government job, whereas Jane *does* have a "legitimate claim of entitlement" to her government job.

Another question: Suppose the governor fires Jane on the ground that she took bribes. Does Jane have a legitimate claim of entitlement to her job even if she has taken bribes?

Board of Regents v. Roth and *Perry v. Sindermann* establish the modern approach to identifying "property" for procedural due process purposes. Under that approach, "property interests protected by procedural due process extend well beyond actual ownership of real estate, chattels, or money." *Roth*, 408 U.S. at 571–572. Property includes interests in government benefits, including government employment, supported by legal "rules or mutually explicit understandings" (*Perry v. Sindermann*, 408 U.S. at 601) establishing a "legitimate claim of entitlement" to the benefit (*Roth*, 408 U.S. at 577).

The modern approach makes it important to determine whether applicable rules or understandings give the government "unfettered discretion" to take away the benefit, for valid laws explicitly granting unfettered discretion to deprive a person of a benefit will defeat claims of entitlement. *Roth*, 408 U.S. at 567.

Many hard questions remain about the modern approach. We will briefly mention two important questions for administrative lawyers. One is: How much discretion does it take to defeat a claim of legitimate entitlement to a government benefit? Does it really have to be totally unfettered? The second is: Can a person have a legitimate claim of entitlement to a benefit for which the government has not yet found the person eligible? The first question, about discretion, was discussed in a case we summarize next.

- *Town of Castle Rock v. Gonzales*, 545 U.S. 748 (2005)

This case arose from horrible events: Jessica Gonzales's estranged husband murdered their three children after Ms. Gonzales failed to get the police in Castle Rock, Colorado, to enforce the restraining order against the estranged husband. Ms. Gonzales sued the town for violating her procedural due process rights by refusing adequately to consider her pleas for enforcement of the restraining order.

The Court rejected Ms. Gonzales's procedural due process claim. The Court held that Ms. Gonzales did not have a protected "property" interest in police enforcement of the restraining order. She had no property interest because she had no legitimate claim of entitlement to enforcement of the order. The Court said, "Our cases recognize that a benefit is not a protected entitlement if government officials may grant it or deny it in their discretion." *Id.* at 756. The Court interpreted Colorado law to give police discretion in enforcing restraining orders. The Court recognized that a Colorado statute on restraining orders entered in domestic violence cases contained mandatory language, which stated, for example: "A peace officer shall use every reasonable means to enforce a restraining order." *Id.* at 758 (quoting Colorado statute). The Court believed that this mandatory language did not actually alter the "well established tradition of police discretion." *Id.* at 760.

The Court in *Castle Rock* found no legitimate claim of entitlement because Colorado law did not make police enforcement of restraining orders "mandatory." That does not mean, however, that the police had totally unfettered discretion. More generally, many agencies and officials have some discretion about implementing the laws that they are responsible for administering, including laws granting individual benefits. Hard questions, requiring careful thought and research, often arise about how much governmental discretion it takes to defeat a legitimate claim of entitlement to the benefit.

* * *

The second question posed above was whether applicants for benefits have a property interest. The question arises from this common scenario: A statute entitles people who meet specific criteria *A*, *B*, and *C* to a specific benefit (including a license). Someone applies for the benefit, claiming to meet the statutorily specified criteria. Does such an *applicant* for a government benefit have a "property" interest — does the applicant, in other words, have a "legitimate claim of entitlement" to the benefit — if the applicant *claims* to meet the criteria but has not yet been *found* by the government to meet those criteria? You can appreciate the importance of this question when you consider the tens of millions of applications that people file each year for government benefits. The Social Security Administration alone processed more than 10 million claims for benefits under its most popular benefits programs in fiscal year 2010. *See* Social Security Administration, Annual Statistical Supplement 2011, Tables 2.F.4 through 2.F.6, http://www.ssa.gov/policy/docs/statcomps/supplement/ (released Feb. 2012).

The U.S. Supreme Court has not settled whether applicants for government benefits have property interests protected by due process before the government has found them eligible for the benefits. The Court's cases recognizing property interests in government benefits have involved people already found eligible for, and receiving, those benefits. In cases involving applications for government benefits, the Court has suggested that applicants often may lack a property interest in the benefit itself, but can sometimes establish a property interest in the *claim* for the benefit. *See American Mfrs. Mut. Ins. Co. v. Sullivan*, 526 U.S. 40, 58–61 & 61 n.13 (1999); *id.* at 61–62 (Ginsburg, J., concurring in part and concurring in the judgment); *id.* at 62–63 (Breyer, J., joined by Souter, J., concurring in part and concurring in the judgment); *id.* at 63–64 (Stevens, J., concurring in part and dissenting in part) (all discussing whether a protected property interest existed in workers' compensation benefits or a claim for such benefits); *see also Lujan v. G&G Fire Sprinklers, Inc.*, 532 U.S. 189, 195 (2001) ("assum[ing], without deciding," that a subcontractor on a government contract had a property interest in its claim for payments under the subcontract).

If an applicant for government benefits does have a property interest in the claim for benefits, procedural due process requires the government to use fair procedures in adjudicating that claim. The procedures for adjudicating the claim, however, might not have to be as elaborate as the procedures required if the government sought to terminate benefits that a person was already receiving. After all, people tend to distinguish between not getting something they want, and losing something desirable that they already have. In short, procedural due process may distinguish between the bird in the bush and the bird in the hand, or, if you prefer a gentler image, between the cat on the windowsill and the cat in the lap.

Exercise: Identifying Protected Property Interests

Ann and Thomas Harrington have sued Suffolk County, New York, contending that the police violated procedural due process by failing adequately to investigate the traffic accident in which their son died. They allege that an adequate investigation would have revealed their son was killed by a drunk driver. They claim entitlement to an adequate investigation under a provision in the Suffolk County Code stating: "It shall be the duty of the Police Department to preserve the public peace, prevent crime, detect and arrest offenders, protect the rights of persons and property, and enforce all laws and ordinances applicable to the county." Please analyze whether they have a property interest protected by procedural due process in the investigation of their son's death. *See Harrington v. County of Suffolk*, 607 F.3d 31 (2nd Cir. 2010).

b. Liberty

Administrative agencies rarely have adjudicative authority to deprive someone of liberty. Sometimes, though, they do have that authority. We focus on four situations in which agencies can deprive people of liberty.

(i) Removal of Aliens from the United States by Immigration Agencies

More than 396,000 people were deported or excluded—or "removed," to use the current omnibus term—from the United States in fiscal year 2011. *See* Immigration and Customs Enforcement, U.S. Department of Homeland Security, Removal Statistics, http://www.ice.gov/removal-statistics/ (visited June 3, 2012). The removal of a person because of the person's immigration status deprives the person of liberty and accordingly must satisfy procedural due process. *See, e.g., Reno v. Flores*, 507 U.S. 292, 306–307 (1993). The procedures by which someone can challenge their detention and deportation are elaborate. The volume of these cases is huge.

Immigration procedures are so specialized and elaborate that we cannot attempt to discuss them in detail. Moreover, the procedural due process analysis governing those procedures are distinctive. It is worth knowing, however, that two federal agencies are involved. The first is the Department of Homeland Security, which enforces the immigration laws by bringing removal proceedings. People can challenge their removal through an immigration "court" system administered by a second agency, the Executive Office for Immigration Review, which is a component of the U.S. Department of Justice.

Here is a good, succinct description of the process and the volume of cases:

> [T]he Executive Office for Immigration Review (EOIR) administers the immigration court system, composed of both trial and appellate tribunals. The trial level consists of the immigration courts, which a Chief Immigration Judge oversees. Removal proceedings begin when the Department of Homeland Security (DHS) files with the immigration court a formal charging document, called a Notice to Appear (NTA), against an alien. EOIR's immigration judges must first decide whether the alien is removable from the United States based on the DHS charges and then whether the alien is eligible for and merits any relief or protection from removal. The immigration courts are high-volume tribunals that received more than 2.1 million matters, which include proceedings, bonds and motions, throughout the past six years. In Fiscal Year (FY) 2010, the courts received more than 325,326 proceedings, which are spread out among 268 immigration judges in 59 immigration courts....
>
> The appellate level of EOIR is the Board of Immigration Appeals (BIA).... The BIA has nationwide jurisdiction and hears appeals of the decisions of immigration judges. The BIA is composed of 15 Board Members, supported by a staff of attorney advisers, and headed by a Chairman. Like the immigration courts, the BIA is a high-volume operation; in FY 2010, the BIA issued more than 33,000 decisions. In addition, the BIA issues binding precedent decisions

interpreting complex areas of immigration law and procedure. Either the alien or DHS may file an appeal with the BIA. An alien who loses his or her appeal before the BIA may seek review of that decision in the federal courts, [usually a federal court of appeals]. DHS, however, may not seek review of a BIA decision in federal court.

Statement of Juan P. Osuna, Director, EOIR, before the Judiciary Committee of the U.S. Senate (May 18, 2011), *available at* United States Senate, Judiciary Committee, http://www.judiciary.senate.gov/pdf/5-18-11%20Osuna%20Testimony.pdf (last visited June 3, 2012).

(ii) Treatment of Prisoners and Other Institutionalized Persons

In 2010, federal and state governments held a total of about 1.5 million people in prison. Lauren E. Glaze, *Correctional Populations in the United States, 2010,* U.S. Dep't of Justice, Bureau of Justice Statistics Bulletin NCJ 236319, at p. 3 Table 1 (December 2011), http://bjs.ojp.usdoj.gov/content/pub/pdf/cpus10.pdf (last visited June 3, 2012). As true of immigration proceedings, the procedural due process case law governing prisoners is distinctive—something of a world unto itself. *See Sandin v. Conner,* 515 U.S. 472, 483–485 (1995) (discussing when actions by prison officials implicate a prisoner's liberty interest).

Even so, a well-educated lawyer should know that a criminal conviction does not totally wipe out a person's liberty interests. Some official actions taken by prison officials against prisoners cause additional deprivations of liberty and therefore must comply with procedural due process. *See, e.g., Wilkinson v. Austin,* 545 U.S. 209 (2005) (state prisoners had a liberty interest in avoiding transfer to "supermax" facility; procedures governing transfer satisfied procedural due process).

(iii) Corporal Punishment of Public School Children

In *Ingraham v. Wright,* 430 U.S. 651 (1977), public school students challenged Florida laws allowing corporal punishment of students for misconduct. The Court held that the Eighth Amendment's Cruel and Unusual Punishment Clause does not apply to corporal punishment of public school students, but the Due Process Clause does apply. The Court said: "[W]here school authorities, acting under color of state law, deliberately decide to punish a child for misconduct by restraining the child and inflicting appreciable physical pain, we hold that Fourteenth Amendment liberty interests are implicated." *Id.* at 674.

(Having found that due process applied, the Court in *Ingraham* addressed what process is due. The Court's answer was: very little. Due process was satisfied by a student's entitlement, under the common law of Florida, to sue the teacher in state court for excessive corporal punishment. *Id.* at 674–682.)

(iv) Harm to Reputation

In the following case, the Court addressed when government action hurting someone's reputation will constitute a deprivation of liberty. Its answer: Almost never.

- *Paul v. Davis,* 424 U.S. 693 (1976)

Local police put Edward Charles Davis's name and photo on a flyer that was entitled "Active Shoplifters" and was distributed to local merchants. Mr. Davis had been arrested for shoplifting, but the charges had been dropped. Mr. Davis sued the police claiming that they deprived him of his liberty interest in his reputation without due process. The Court rejected Mr. Davis's due process claim, holding that he failed to assert a liberty interest.

The Court considered Mr. Davis's claim really to be a claim for defamation, not a due process claim. The Court worried that allowing people to bring tort claims masquerading as due process claims would make the Due Process Clause of the Fourteenth Amendment "a font of tort law to be superimposed upon whatever systems may already be administered by the States." *Id.* at 701. The Court held that defamatory conduct by the government does not constitute a deprivation of liberty protected by due process unless the conduct adversely alters or extinguishes a right or status previously protected by law. Basically, to constitute a deprivation of liberty the defamatory conduct must impose a legal disability. This requirement is often called the "stigma-plus" test or requirement.

Here is an example of a situation that may satisfy the stigma-plus test for defamatory conduct that implicates a liberty interest under *Paul v. Davis*: A public school fires a teacher and announces that it has done so because the teacher accepted bribes from students in exchange for good grades. The announcement may deprive the teacher of a liberty interest if the charge of bribery, once disclosed, barred the teacher under the jurisdiction's laws from getting another public school teaching job. *Cf. Brandt v. Bd. of Co-Op. Educ. Servs.*, 820 F.2d 41, 44–45 (2nd Cir. 1987) (plaintiff could prove that being fired from his teaching job for sexual misconduct deprived him of liberty if plaintiff proved that prospective employers were likely to see his personnel record and refuse to hire him because of the sexual misconduct charge). *See generally* Application of Stigma-Plus Due Process Claims to Education Context, 41 A.L.R.6th 391 (2009). To satisfy additional requirements imposed by the Court in other cases of defamatory government conduct, the teacher would also have to show that the bribery charge was false and was publicly disclosed without the teacher's consent. *See Bishop v. Wood*, 426 U.S. 341, 348–349 (1976); *Codd v. Velger*, 429 U.S. 624, 627 (1977).

D. Question Two: If Due Process Applies, What Process Is Due?

If due process does not apply to the situation under analysis, then due process drops out of the analysis; it is not an external source of procedural requirements. In contrast, if due process *does* apply to the situation under analysis, the question becomes: What process is due in that situation?

The question of what process is due in agency adjudications is answered today by applying *Mathews v. Eldridge*, 424 U.S. 319 (1976).[1] Although *Mathews v. Eldridge* concerned the government's termination of disability benefits, the Court has used the *Mathews v. Eldridge* framework is other settings. Every administrative lawyer knows *Mathews v. Eldridge*, and so it is the star of this section.

This section begins with the *Mathews v. Eldridge* opinion. After that, we identify two important due process principles recognized in *Mathews v. Eldridge*. Finally, we explore an almost invariable element of due process: the requirement of an unbiased decision maker.

---

1. Notice that *Mathews* is spelled unusually: with only one "t."

1. *Mathews v. Eldridge*

a. Context for Studying *Mathews*

When lawyers think about due process, they tend to think about court proceedings, not agency adjudications. In court proceedings, the procedures include:

- notice to the parties of the proceeding (e.g., by service of process)

- right of parties to be represented by a lawyer

- a live, evidentiary hearing—i.e., a trial before an impartial decision maker that includes:

  - a chance for each party to present documentary and live witnesses supporting the party's position

  - a chance for each party to confront and cross-examine adverse witnesses

  - a chance for each party to rebut each opposing party's case

- a decision by the decision maker based on the whole record, and only the record, of the proceeding

- a written explanation of the decision, if the decision maker is not a jury, that includes findings of fact, conclusions of law, and an explanation of how discretion was exercised

One way to decide what process is due in an agency adjudication would be to determine which of these elements of judicial proceedings must be included to ensure fairness. This approach could be called the judicial model; it treats a court proceeding as a template for due process.

At the beginning of the due process revolution, the U.S. Supreme Court used the judicial model. The prime example of this is *Goldberg*. The Court in *Goldberg* held that, before terminating welfare benefits, the agency adjudication had to include many elements of a court proceeding, including the right to be represented by a lawyer and to confront and cross-examine adverse witnesses. The Court broke from the judicial model in *Mathews v. Eldridge* and established the modern framework for determining what process is due in administrative adjudications.

b. The *Mathews v. Eldridge* Opinion

Please read *Mathews v. Eldridge* with these points in mind:

1. *Mathews* concerns disability benefits under the Social Security Act. The federal government administers the disability benefits program through the Social Security Administration (SSA).

SSA administers the disability benefits program with the help of States. Specifically, state agencies examine applicants to determine whether they have a disability. State agencies also monitor the continued eligibility of people who have been found eligible for disability benefits. As you read the opinion, please pay attention to what role state officials played and what role federal officials played in the adjudication of Mr. Eldridge's continued eligibility.

2. Under *Mathews v. Eldridge*, analysis of what process is due requires analysis of what process is currently being given. Therefore, please pay close attention to

the description of the existing procedures for termination of disability benefits that Mr. Eldridge challenged. In particular, be on the lookout for the answer to this question: At what point in the administrative process did Mr. Eldridge stop getting his disability benefits? Specifically, did he stop getting his benefits before he had a right to an evidentiary hearing?

Mathews v. Eldridge
424 U.S. 319 (1976)

MR. JUSTICE POWELL delivered the opinion of the Court.

The issue in this case is whether the Due Process Clause of the Fifth Amendment requires that prior to the termination of Social Security disability benefit payments the recipient be afforded an opportunity for an evidentiary hearing.

I

Cash benefits are provided to workers during periods in which they are completely disabled under the disability insurance benefits program created by the 1956 amendments to Title II of the Social Security Act. Respondent Eldridge was first awarded benefits in June 1968. In March 1972, he received a questionnaire from the state agency charged with monitoring his medical condition. Eldridge completed the questionnaire, indicating that his condition had not improved and identifying the medical sources, including physicians, from whom he had received treatment recently. The state agency then obtained reports from his physician and a psychiatric consultant. After considering these reports and other information in his file the agency informed Eldridge by letter that it had made a tentative determination that his disability had ceased in May 1972. The letter included a statement of reasons for the proposed termination of benefits, and advised Eldridge that he might request reasonable time in which to obtain and submit additional information pertaining to his condition.

In his written response, Eldridge disputed one characterization of his medical condition and indicated that the agency already had enough evidence to establish his disability.[2] The state agency then made its final determination that he had ceased to be disabled in May 1972. This determination was accepted by the Social Security Administration, which notified Eldridge in July that his benefits would terminate after that month....

... Eldridge commenced this action challenging the constitutional validity of the administrative procedures established by the Secretary of Health, Education, and Welfare for assessing whether there exists a continuing disability....

[The federal district court] held that prior to termination of benefits Eldridge had to be afforded an evidentiary hearing of the type required for welfare beneficiaries [under *Goldberg v. Kelly*]. [The federal court of appeals affirmed, and the U.S. Supreme Court granted certiorari.] ... We reverse.

---

2. Eldridge originally was disabled due to chronic anxiety and back strain. He subsequently was found to have diabetes. The tentative determination letter indicated that aid would be terminated because available medical evidence indicated that his diabetes was under control, that there existed no limitations on his back movements which would impose severe functional restrictions, and that he no longer suffered emotional problems that would preclude him from all work for which he was qualified. App. 12–13. In his reply letter he claimed to have arthritis of the spine rather than a strained back.

II

[Editor's note: In part II of the opinion, which we omit, the Court held that the federal courts had jurisdiction over Mr. Eldridge's constitutional claim.]

III

A

... The Secretary does not contend that procedural due process is inapplicable to terminations of Social Security disability benefits. He recognizes, as has been implicit in our prior decisions, that the interest of an individual in continued receipt of these benefits is a statutorily created "property" interest protected by the Fifth Amendment.... Rather, the Secretary contends that the existing administrative procedures, detailed below, provide all the process that is constitutionally due before a recipient can be deprived of that interest.

This Court consistently has held that some form of hearing is required before an individual is finally deprived of a property interest. *Wolff v. McDonnell*, 418 U.S. 539, 557–558 (1974).... Eldridge agrees that the review procedures available to a claimant before the initial determination of ineligibility becomes final would be adequate if disability benefits were not terminated until after the evidentiary hearing stage of the administrative process. The dispute centers upon what process is due prior to the initial termination of benefits, pending review.

In recent years this Court increasingly has had occasion to consider the extent to which due process requires an evidentiary hearing prior to the deprivation of some type of property interest even if such a hearing is provided thereafter. In only one case, *Goldberg v. Kelly*, 397 U.S., at 266–271, has the Court held that a hearing closely approximating a judicial trial is necessary. In other cases requiring some type of pretermination hearing as a matter of constitutional right the Court has spoken sparingly about the requisite procedures....

... [O]ur prior decisions indicate that identification of the specific dictates of due process generally requires consideration of three distinct factors: First, the private interest that will be affected by the official action; second, the risk of an erroneous deprivation of such interest through the procedures used, and the probable value, if any, of additional or substitute procedural safeguards; and finally, the Government's interest, including the function involved and the fiscal and administrative burdens that the additional or substitute procedural requirement would entail. See, *e. g., Goldberg v. Kelly, supra*, 397 U.S., at 263–271.

We turn first to a description of the procedures for the termination of Social Security disability benefits and thereafter consider the factors bearing upon the constitutional adequacy of these procedures.

B

The disability insurance program is administered jointly by state and federal agencies. State agencies make the initial determination whether a disability exists, when it began, and when it ceased. 42 U.S.C. § 421(a). The standards applied and the procedures followed are prescribed by the Secretary, see § 421(b), who has delegated his responsibilities and powers under the Act to the SSA....

In order to establish initial and continued entitlement to disability benefits a worker must demonstrate that he is unable

> "to engage in any substantial gainful activity by reason of any medically determinable physical or mental impairment which can be expected to result in

death or which has lasted or can be expected to last for a continuous period of not less than 12 months...." 42 U.S.C. § 423(d)(1)(A).

To satisfy this test the worker bears a continuing burden of showing, by means of "medically acceptable clinical and laboratory diagnostic techniques," § 423(d)(3), that he has a physical or mental impairment of such severity that

> "he is not only unable to do his previous work but cannot, considering his age, education, and work experience, engage in any other kind of substantial gainful work which exists in the national economy, regardless of whether such work exists in the immediate area in which he lives, or whether a specific job vacancy exists for him, or whether he would be hired if he applied for work." § 423(d)(2)(A).

The principal reasons for benefits terminations are that the worker is no longer disabled or has returned to work. As Eldridge's benefits were terminated because he was determined to be no longer disabled, we consider only the sufficiency of the procedures involved in such cases.

The continuing-eligibility investigation is made by a state agency acting through a "team" consisting of a physician and a nonmedical person trained in disability evaluation. The agency periodically communicates with the disabled worker, usually by mail in which case he is sent a detailed questionnaire or by telephone, and requests information concerning his present condition, including current medical restrictions and sources of treatment, and any additional information that he considers relevant to his continued entitlement to benefits....

Information regarding the recipient's current condition is also obtained from his sources of medical treatment. If there is a conflict between the information provided by the beneficiary and that obtained from medical sources such as his physician, or between two sources of treatment, the agency may arrange for an examination by an independent consulting physician. Whenever the agency's tentative assessment of the beneficiary's condition differs from his own assessment, the beneficiary is informed that benefits may be terminated, provided a summary of the evidence upon which the proposed determination to terminate is based, and afforded an opportunity to review the medical reports and other evidence in his case file. He also may respond in writing and submit additional evidence.

The state agency then makes its final determination, which is reviewed by an examiner in the SSA Bureau of Disability Insurance.... If, as is usually the case, the SSA accepts the agency determination it notifies the recipient in writing, informing him of the reasons for the decision, and of his right to seek de novo reconsideration by the state agency.... Upon acceptance by the SSA, benefits are terminated effective two months after the month in which medical recovery is found to have occurred....

If the recipient seeks reconsideration by the state agency and the determination is adverse, the SSA reviews the reconsideration determination and notifies the recipient of the decision. He then has a right to an evidentiary hearing before an SSA administrative law judge. The hearing is nonadversary, and the SSA is not represented by counsel. As at all prior and subsequent stages of the administrative process, however, the claimant may be represented by counsel or other spokesmen.... If this hearing results in an adverse decision, the claimant is entitled to request discretionary review by the SSA Appeals Council, § 404.945, and finally may obtain judicial review. 42 U.S.C. § 405(g); 20 CFR § 404.951 (1975).

Should it be determined at any point after termination of benefits, that the claimant's disability extended beyond the date of cessation initially established, the worker is entitled to retroactive payments....

C

Despite the elaborate character of the administrative procedures provided by the Secretary, the courts below held them to be constitutionally inadequate, concluding that due process requires an evidentiary hearing prior to termination. In light of the private and governmental interests at stake here and the nature of the existing procedures, we think this was error.

Since a recipient whose benefits are terminated is awarded full retroactive relief if he ultimately prevails, his sole interest is in the uninterrupted receipt of this source of income pending final administrative decision on his claim. His potential injury is thus similar in nature to that of the welfare recipient in *Goldberg*, see 397 U.S., at 263–264....

Only in *Goldberg* has the Court held that due process requires an evidentiary hearing prior to a temporary deprivation. It was emphasized there that welfare assistance is given to persons on the very margin of subsistence:

> "The crucial factor in this context—a factor not present in the case of ... virtually anyone else whose governmental entitlements are ended—is that termination of aid pending resolution of a controversy over eligibility may deprive an eligible recipient of the very means by which to live while he waits." 397 U.S., at 264.

Eligibility for disability benefits, in contrast, is not based upon financial need.... Indeed, it is wholly unrelated to the worker's income or support from many other sources ...

As *Goldberg* illustrates, the degree of potential deprivation that may be created by a particular decision is a factor to be considered in assessing the validity of any administrative decisionmaking process.... The potential deprivation here is generally likely to be less than in *Goldberg*, although the degree of difference can be overstated. As the District Court emphasized, to remain eligible for benefits a recipient must be "unable to engage in substantial gainful activity." ... 361 F.Supp., at 523....

As we recognized last Term in *Fusari v. Steinberg*, 419 U.S. 379, 389 (1975), "the possible length of wrongful deprivation of ... benefits (also) is an important factor in assessing the impact of official action on the private interests." The Secretary concedes that the delay between a request for a hearing before an administrative law judge and a decision on the claim is currently between 10 and 11 months. Since a terminated recipient must first obtain a reconsideration decision as a prerequisite to invoking his right to an evidentiary hearing, the delay between the actual cutoff of benefits and final decision after a hearing exceeds one year.

In view of the torpidity of this administrative review process, ... and the typically modest resources of the family unit of the physically disabled worker, ... the hardship imposed upon the erroneously terminated disability recipient may be significant. Still, the disabled worker's need is likely to be less than that of a welfare recipient.... In view of ... potential sources of temporary income, there is less reason here than in *Goldberg* to depart from the ordinary principle, established by our decisions, that something less than an evidentiary hearing is sufficient prior to adverse administrative action.

D

An additional factor ... is the fairness and reliability of the existing pretermination procedures, and the probable value, if any, of additional procedural safeguards. Central to the evaluation of any administrative process is the nature of the relevant inquiry. In order to remain eligible for benefits the disabled worker must demonstrate by means of "medically acceptable clinical and laboratory diagnostic techniques," 42 U.S.C. § 423(d)(3), that he is unable "to engage in any substantial gainful activity by reason of *any medically determinable* physical or mental impairment...." § 423(d)(1)(A) (emphasis supplied). In short, a medical assessment of the worker's physical or mental condition is required. This is a more sharply focused and easily documented decision than the typical determination of welfare entitlement. In the latter case, a wide variety of information may be deemed relevant, and issues of witness credibility and veracity often are critical to the decisionmaking process. *Goldberg* noted that in such circumstances "written submissions are a wholly unsatisfactory basis for decision." 397 U.S., at 269.

By contrast, the decision whether to discontinue disability benefits will turn, in most cases, upon "routine, standard, and unbiased medical reports by physician specialists," *Richardson v. Perales*, 402 U.S., at 404, concerning a subject whom they have personally examined.[28] ... To be sure, credibility and veracity may be a factor in the ultimate disability assessment in some cases. But procedural due process rules are shaped by the risk of error inherent in the truthfinding process as applied to the generality of cases, not the rare exceptions. The potential value of an evidentiary hearing, or even oral presentation to the decisionmaker, is substantially less in this context than in *Goldberg*.

The decision in *Goldberg* also was based on the Court's conclusion that written submissions were an inadequate substitute for oral presentation because they did not provide an effective means for the recipient to communicate his case to the decisionmaker. Written submissions were viewed as an unrealistic option, for most recipients lacked the "educational attainment necessary to write effectively" and could not afford professional assistance. In addition, such submissions would not provide the "flexibility of oral presentations" or "permit the recipient to mold his argument to the issues the decision maker appears to regard as important." 397 U.S., at 269. In the context of the disability-benefits-entitlement assessment the administrative procedures under review here fully answer these objections.

The detailed questionnaire which the state agency periodically sends the recipient identifies with particularity the information relevant to the entitlement decision, and the recipient is invited to obtain assistance from the local SSA office in completing the questionnaire. More important, the information critical to the entitlement decision usually is derived from medical sources, such as the treating physician. Such sources are likely to be able to communicate more effectively through written documents than are welfare recipients or the lay witnesses supporting their cause. The conclusions of physicians often are supported by X-rays and the results of clinical or laboratory tests, information typically more amenable to written than to oral presentation....

A further safeguard against mistake is the policy of allowing the disability recipient's representative full access to all information relied upon by the state agency. In addition, prior to the cutoff of benefits the agency informs the recipient of its tentative assessment, the reasons therefor, and provides a summary of the evidence that it considers most relevant. Opportunity is then afforded the recipient to submit additional evidence or arguments, enabling him to challenge directly the accuracy of information in his file as well as the correctness of the agency's tentative conclusions. These procedures, again as

---

28. The decision is not purely a question of the accuracy of a medical diagnosis since the ultimate issue which the state agency must resolve is whether in light of the particular worker's "age, education, and work experience" he cannot "engage in any ... substantial gainful work which exists in the national economy...." 42 U.S.C. § 423(d)(2)(A). Yet information concerning each of these worker characteristics is amenable to effective written presentation.... Similarly, resolution of the inquiry as to the types of employment opportunities that exist in the national economy for a physically impaired worker with a particular set of skills would not necessarily be advanced by an evidentiary hearing. The statistical information relevant to this judgment is more amenable to written than to oral presentation.

contrasted with those before the Court in *Goldberg*, enable the recipient to "mold" his argument to respond to the precise issues which the decisionmaker regards as crucial.

Despite these carefully structured procedures, *amici* point to the significant reversal rate for appealed cases as clear evidence that the current process is inadequate. Depending upon the base selected and the line of analysis followed, the relevant reversal rates urged by the contending parties vary from a high of 58.6% for appealed reconsideration decisions to an overall reversal rate of only 3.3% ... Bare statistics rarely provide a satisfactory measure of the fairness of a decisionmaking process. Their adequacy is especially suspect here since the administrative review system is operated on an open-file basis. A recipient may always submit new evidence, and such submissions may result in additional medical examinations. Such fresh examinations were held in approximately 30% to 40% of the appealed cases, in fiscal 1973, either at the reconsideration or evidentiary hearing stage of the administrative process.... In this context, the value of reversal rate statistics as one means of evaluating the adequacy of the pretermination process is diminished. Thus, although we view such information as relevant, it is certainly not controlling in this case.

E

In striking the appropriate due process balance the final factor to be assessed is the public interest. This includes the administrative burden and other societal costs that would be associated with requiring, as a matter of constitutional right, an evidentiary hearing upon demand in all cases prior to the termination of disability benefits. The most visible burden would be the incremental cost resulting from the increased number of hearings and the expense of providing benefits to ineligible recipients pending decision. No one can predict the extent of the increase, but the fact that full benefits would continue until after such hearings would assure the exhaustion in most cases of this attractive option. Nor would the theoretical right of the Secretary to recover undeserved benefits result, as a practical matter, in any substantial offset to the added outlay of public funds. The parties submit widely varying estimates of the probable additional financial cost. We only need say that experience with the constitutionalizing of government procedures suggests that the ultimate additional cost in terms of money and administrative burden would not be insubstantial.

Financial cost alone is not a controlling weight in determining whether due process requires a particular procedural safeguard prior to some administrative decision. But the Government's interest, and hence that of the public, in conserving scarce fiscal and administrative resources is a factor that must be weighed. At some point the benefit of an additional safeguard to the individual affected by the administrative action and to society in terms of increased assurance that the action is just, may be outweighed by the cost. Significantly, the cost of protecting those whom the preliminary administrative process has identified as likely to be found undeserving may in the end come out of the pockets of the deserving since resources available for any particular program of social welfare are not unlimited....

But more is implicated in cases of this type than ad hoc weighing of fiscal and administrative burdens against the interests of a particular category of claimants. The ultimate balance involves a determination as to when, under our constitutional system, judicial-type procedures must be imposed upon administrative action to assure fairness. We reiterate the wise admonishment of Mr. Justice Frankfurter that differences in the origin and function of administrative agencies "preclude wholesale transplantation of the rules of procedure, trial and review which have evolved from the history and experience of courts." *FCC v. Pottsville Broadcasting Co.*, 309 U.S. 134, 143 (1940). The judicial model of an evidentiary hearing is neither a required, nor even the most effective, method of decisionmaking in all circumstances. The essence of due process is the requirement that "a person in jeopardy of serious loss (be given) notice of the case against him and opportunity to meet it." *Joint Anti-Fascist Comm. v. McGrath*, ... [341 U.S. 123, 171–172 (1951)] (Frankfurter, J., concurring).... In assessing what process is due in this case, substantial weight must be given to the good-faith judgments of the individuals charged by Congress with the administration of social welfare programs that the procedures they have provided assure fair consideration of the entitlement claims of individuals....

We conclude that an evidentiary hearing is not required prior to the termination of disability benefits and that the present administrative procedures fully comport with due process.

The judgment of the Court of Appeals is

Reversed.

[Editor's note: Justice Stevens did not participate in the case. Justice Brennan, joined by Justice Marshall, dissented in an opinion that we omit.]

c. Significance of *Mathews v. Eldridge*

Mathews v. Eldridge is a leading modern case on procedural due process because it establishes a three-part framework for analyzing what process is due. Indeed, the case's fame makes it all too easy to lose sight of the individual, George Eldridge, whose case led to the Court's framework. Mr. Eldridge's situation is described in Cynthia R. Farina, *Due Process at Rashomon Gate: The Stories of* Mathews v. Eldridge, in Administrative Law Stories 231–233 (Peter L. Strauss ed. 2009). Here, we examine and pose questions about each part of that framework.

(i) Private Interest

The first element of the *Mathews v. Eldridge* framework is the nature of the private interest implicated by the government action. Courts must consider (A) the nature of the interest and (B) whether the erroneous deprivation of the private interest would be permanent or temporary under the challenged procedures, and, if temporary, how long it may last.

In considering the nature of the private interest and the duration of an erroneous deprivation, the Court in *Mathews v. Eldridge* compared the private interest in the case before it to the private interest in *Goldberg v. Kelly.* The Court said that in considering the private interest and the other two elements of the framework, we consider the "generality of cases," not just the situation of the party before the court. *E.g.*, *Walters v. Nat'l Ass'n of Radiation Survivors*, 473 U.S. 305, 330 (1985).

Using this guidance, please determine whether each private interest at stake in the following situations has more weight, less weight, or is about the same as the private interest in *Mathews v. Eldridge*. Then decide which private interest below is *most* weighty and which one is *least* weighty. (Each situation involves an interest that the Court has found to be protected by procedural due process.) In each case, it may help you to consider the matter from the perspective of a typical victim of the deprivation (the "generality of cases") and to assume that the deprivation is erroneous:

- A public school student suffers corporal punishment when school officials whack the student on the butt with a wooden paddle for school-related misconduct. *Ingraham v. Wright*, 430 U.S. 651 (1977).

- A public school student is suspended from school for ten days for school-related misconduct. *Goss v. Lopez*, 419 U.S. 565 (1975).

- A government employee who can be fired only for cause is fired for lying about his criminal record on his employment application. *Cleveland Bd. of Educ. v. Loudermill*, 470 U.S. 532 (1985).

- A government security officer who can be fired only for cause is suspended without pay from his job pending disposition of criminal charges for possessing illegal drugs with intent to distribute them. *Gilbert v. Homar*, 520 U.S. 924 (1997).

- A U.S. citizen is detained by U.S. military forces in an active combat zone on suspicion of bearing arms against the United States and is confined in the United States as a suspected enemy combatant. *Hamdi v. Rumsfeld*, 542 U.S. 507, 529–535 (2004) (plurality opinion); *see also id.* at 553–554 (Souter, J., concurring in part, dissenting in part, and concurring in the judgment). *But see id.* at 575 (Scalia, J., dissenting); *id.* at 594 (Thomas, J., dissenting).

- A person whom the police have stopped on suspicion of drunk driving has his driver's license suspended for thirty days for refusing to take a breathalyzer test. *Mackey v. Montrym*, 443 U.S. 1 (1979).

The point of this exercise is that it can be hard to weigh deprivations, yet most people can agree at the extremes about what types of deprivation are the most and the least weighty.

(ii) Risk of Error

The second *Mathews v. Eldridge* factor analyzes the risk of error. In applying the second factor, a court must assess (A) the risk that existing procedures will produce erroneous deprivations and (B) the marginal value of additional or different procedures.

In applying the second factor, the Court in *Mathews v. Eldridge* examined existing procedures to identify potential sources of error and means for correcting those errors. In this examination, the Court was wary of "bare statistics" on reversal rates. The main additional or different procedure that the Court analyzed was an evidentiary hearing with live witnesses, and an opportunity for cross-examination. The Court determined that, because of the nature of the determinations, a live hearing would not improve the quality of decision making much, if any, compared to determinations based on documentary material.

First, please review the Court's analysis of the second factor to identify when, in the Court's view, live testimony will have significant value.

Second, please explain in your own words what it would mean for a deprivation to be "erroneous" in *Mathews v. Eldridge*.

In general, the term "erroneous" is trickier than it might at first seem when you consider the various matters that agencies adjudicate. The criteria for disability benefits are fairly objective and give the decision makers little, if any, discretion. But agencies decide other matters under criteria that leave room for discretion. For example, an environmental agency may have discretion under a statute to impose a fine of "up to $50,000" for a violation of a pollution rule. If a company admits that it violated that rule, does it have a right to "some kind of hearing" on the appropriate amount of the fine? This pollution scenario concerns whether due process aims to not only prevent bald errors by agencies but also to ensure well-informed exercises of agency discretion.

A separate question is whether due process entitles a person to argue that a decision maker should show leniency by departing from legal criteria restricting the decision maker's discretion. The answer implied by Supreme Court cases is "no." *See Cleveland Bd. of Educ. v. Loudermill*, 470 U.S. 532, 543 & n.8 (1985).

(iii) Government and Public Interest

The third *Mathews v. Eldridge* factor is "the Government's interest, including the function involved and the fiscal and administrative burdens that the additional or substitute procedural requirement would entail." 424 U.S. at 335.

The Court in *Mathews v. Eldridge* describes the third factor alternatively as the "public interest" and "the Government's interest," and says it includes consideration of "societal costs" in the form of public costs of additional procedures. *Id.* at 335, 347. The cost of additional procedures varies according to whether a situation involves a high-volume type of adjudication, such as adjudicating continued eligibility for welfare benefits, or a low-volume litigation, such as licensing nuclear power plants.

In later cases applying the third *Mathews v. Eldridge* factor, the Court has considered the government's interest in acting promptly when it thinks a deprivation is justified—for example, when it believes a dangerous driver should immediately lose driving privileges.

With these considerations in mind, review the situations listed above in the discussion of the private interest factor. Identify in a generic way the government function involved in each and whether the situation involves high-volume adjudication or low volume adjudication. Also identify which situation involves the weightiest government interest and which situation involves the least weighty government interest.

2. Due Process Principles

The Court in *Mathews v. Eldridge* did more than establish a three-factor framework. It also cited two principles of procedural due process that serve as rules of thumb. The Court stated those principles as follows:

(1) "This Court consistently has held that some form of hearing is required before an individual is finally deprived of a property interest." *Mathews v. Eldridge*, 424 U.S. at 333.

(2) "[T]he ordinary principle, established by our decisions, [is] that something less than an evidentiary hearing is sufficient prior to adverse administrative action." *Id.* at 343. By "evidentiary hearing," the Court meant a proceeding including an opportunity for a person "to defend by confronting any adverse witnesses and by presenting his own arguments and evidence orally." *Id.* at 325 n.4.

The first principle concerns *timing*; it ordinarily requires what is often called a "pre-deprivation" hearing.

The second principle concerns the *elaborateness* of the pre-deprivation procedures. Under this principle, the pre-deprivation "right to be heard" can involve "something less" than a trial-like evidentiary hearing.

a. The Timing Principle: Generally Requiring a Pre-Deprivation Notice and Right to Be Heard

Procedural due process generally aims to prevent erroneous deprivations before they happen. To that end, procedural due process generally requires the government to give a person notice and a chance to be heard *before* any significant deprivation occurs. *See, e.g., Fuentes v. Shevin*, 407 U.S. 67, 82 (1972).

We will discuss the notice requirement in more detail when we discuss formal adjudications under the APA in Chapter 22. For now, you should understand the connection between pre-deprivation *notice* and a pre-deprivation *right to be heard*. You are entitled to notice of the government's intention to deprive you of liberty or property so you can prepare a defense against the deprivation. Because notice is meant to help you prepare a defense, the notice must do more than give you a vague "heads up" of the impending deprivation. The notice must explain the *grounds* for the proposed deprivation in enough detail that you can defend against it when given the right to be heard.

The notice and right to be heard ordinarily must precede any significant deprivation. The Court has said, for example, that this rule of thumb generally "requires 'some kind of hearing' prior to the discharge of an employee who has a constitutionally protected property interest in his [government] employment." *Cleveland Bd. of Educ. v. Loudermill*, 470 U.S. 532, 542 (1985) (quoting *Board of Regents v. Roth*, 408 U.S. at 569–570). Deprivation of one's job, even temporarily — as occurs when one is suspended from a job pending an investigation — is a significant deprivation for most people, which is why ordinarily due process requires some kind of pre-deprivation hearing.

The principle requiring some kind of pre-deprivation hearing has exceptions. For example, after stating the principle in *Loudermill*, a case involving a government employee, the Court qualified the principle by saying that a government agency can immediately suspend a government employee, before any hearing, "in those situations where the employer perceives a significant hazard in keeping the employee on the job." *Loudermill*, 470 U.S. at 544–545. The Court added in a later case that, when the immediate suspension of a government employee is justified, pending an investigation, the suspension can be a suspension without pay. *Gilbert v. Homar*, 520 U.S. 924 (1997). The Court found immediate suspension justified in *Gilbert v. Homar* because the employee, a state college campus police officer, was arrested on suspicion of drug offenses. *Id.* at 926–927; *see also Fed. Deposit Ins. Corp. v. Mallen*, 486 U.S. 230 (1988) (upholding immediate suspension of bank official by federal banking agency that took over a troubled bank). The exception to the requirement of a pre-deprivation right to be heard is often called the emergency exception.

Next we summarize the most famous case on the emergency exception.

- *North American Cold Storage Co. v. City of Chicago*, 211 U.S. 306 (1908)

City of Chicago health officials visited the North American Cold Storage Company one day in 1906 and demanded that the company turn over forty-seven barrels of poultry that allegedly had become "putrid, decayed, poisonous or infected in such a manner as to render it unsafe or unwholesome for human food." *Id.* at 308. The City Code authorized the officials to seize and immediately destroy the poultry if it was unsafe or unwholesome as alleged. North American refused to hand over the allegedly putrid poultry, prompting the City officials to shut down the company's entire operation. North American sued City officials for an injunction preventing them from interfering with its business. North American argued that due process entitled it to a judicial determination of whether the poultry was putrid *before* the poultry was seized and destroyed.

The Court rejected the due process argument. The Court held that because the public safety was at stake, the City had the discretion to seize and destroy the allegedly unsafe food before any hearing. The Court rejected North American's argument that the officials could have seized the poultry but refrained from destroying it until after a hearing on whether it was putrid. This option presented practical problems (e.g., what to do with the poultry in the meantime) that the City officials had the discretion to decide required immediate destruction. Due process was satisfied by the right of the poultry's owner to sue City officials for damages after they destroyed the poultry. "[I]n that action those who destroyed it can only successfully defend if the jury shall find the fact of unwholesomeness as claimed by them." *Id.* at 316.

In addition to the government employment cases and the putrid poultry case, cases about drivers licenses illustrate the rule of thumb generally requiring hearings before significant deprivations, including the limits of that rule.

The earliest case was *Bell v. Burson*, 402 U.S. 535 (1971). *Bell* addressed a state law that suspended the driver's license of any uninsured driver who was in a car accident, unless the driver posted a bond for the damages claimed by others involved in the accident. The Court held that the state law violated due process because it could cause the suspension of a person's license before a hearing on whether that person was to blame for the accident. The Court broadly stated: "[I]t is fundamental that except in emergency situations (and this is not one) due process requires that when a State seeks to terminate an interest such as that here involved, it must afford notice and opportunity for hearing appropriate to the nature of the case *before* the termination becomes effective." *Id.* at 542 (footnote and internal quotation marks omitted; emphasis in original).

The Court cut back on that statement in later cases, in which it upheld state laws suspending driver's licenses without prior hearings. *See Mackey v. Montrym*, 443 U.S. 1 (1979); *Dixon v. Love*, 431 U.S. 105 (1977). One such statute automatically revoked the driver's license of any driver whose license had been suspended for moving violations three times within the last ten years. *Dixon v. Love*, 431 U.S. at 109. A driver whose license was automatically revoked could have a hearing before the revocation became final—and so in that sense automatic revocations were provisional—but pending the successful outcome of the hearing the driver lost driving privileges. The Court upheld the statute against a due process challenge, after evaluating the statute under the general framework established in *Mathews v. Eldridge*, 424 U.S. 319 (1976).

Perhaps the best way to summarize the timing rule is to say that the government cannot deprive a person of liberty or property, without first giving the person notice and a right to be heard, unless the government has a very good reason for immediate action.

Exercise: The General Rule Requiring Pre-Deprivation Notice and Some Kind of Hearing

A state statute authorizes the State Board of Medicine to temporarily suspend the license of a physician if the Board develops probable cause to believe that temporary suspension is immediately necessary to prevent serious harm to the public or particular people. The Board may exercise this suspension authority after notice to the physician, but before the physician has a chance to be heard. In all suspension cases, however, the Board must immediately file an action in court to get a court order supporting the suspension. The administrative suspension cannot last more than seven days unless, after a hearing before a court at which the physician is entitled to appear and make a defense, a court extends the suspension. Please evaluate whether this violates due process.

---

b. The Elaborateness Principle: The Pre-Deprivation Hearing Need Not Be as Elaborate as a Trial

The timing principle discussed above requires "*some* kind of hearing" before a significant deprivation of property or liberty. *E.g., Goss v. Lopez*, 419 U.S. 565, 579 (1975) (emphasis in original); *Wolff v. McDonnell*, 418 U.S. 539, 557–558 (1974). The hearing need not be as elaborate as a trial. It need not even be a face-to-face encounter between the decision maker and the person threatened with the deprivation. The Court in *Mathews* upheld a pre-deprivation process in which the government relied almost exclusively on paperwork to make its decision. *See* 424 U.S. at 325 n.4 & 343. The term "some kind of hearing" should be understood to require "some kind of right to be *heard from*," if only through a written submission

The most barebones type of pre-deprivation hearing that the Court has allowed is in *Goss v. Lopez*, 419 U.S. 565 (1975). The Court held that public school students were deprived of property and liberty interests when they were suspended from public school for up to ten days. The students facing suspension, however, were not entitled to much pre-suspension process. In most instances, a student was entitled to "first be told what he [or she] is accused of doing and what the basis of the accusation is." *Id.* at 582. The student would then have "an opportunity to explain his [or her] version of the facts." *Id.* After being advised of what the student was accused of doing wrong, the student was not entitled to have any time to prepare a defense. The student had to respond immediately. Furthermore, the student had no right to present evidence other than the student's own account of the relevant events. In sum, the Court concluded that due process required only the briefest delay, and the most "rudimentary" process, between the occurrence of the alleged misconduct and the suspension. *Id.* at 581.

In terms of the elaborateness of pre-deprivation hearings, *Goss* is at one end of the spectrum; *Goldberg* is at the other end. *Goldberg* required a trial-like pre-deprivation hearing. In cases after *Goldberg*, the Court made clear that due process rarely requires such elaborate pre-deprivation procedures in civil cases involving property interests. To analyze cases between these extremes, a lower court would apply the *Mathews v. Eldridge* framework we examined above.

The *Mathews v. Eldridge* framework is not mathematical. The framework does not yield precise answers about how much process is due in various settings. Smart agencies ensure that their statutes and agency rules provide more than enough to provide the process that is constitutionally due. That puts the agency in a good position to argue that, in assessing what process is constitutionally due, the reviewing court should give "substantial weight" to the judgment of the agency officials who devised the procedures. *Mathews v. Eldridge*, 424 U.S. at 349.

Exercise: "Some Kind of Hearing"

The state medical board has authority to conduct administrative adjudications to discipline physicians for professional misconduct. An administrative adjudication can result in revocation of a physician's license (though the physician can seek judicial review of an administrative revocation order). One such adjudication arises when a patient accuses a physician of offering to sell the patient a prescription for amphetamines without first examining the patient to determine whether the patient actually needed them for a legitimate medical purpose. The physician disputes the patient's account; the physician claims that the patient pressured the physician to prescribe amphetamines, and that the physician refused. Would due process require an oral evidentiary hearing in this situation before the Board makes a decision about whether to discipline the physician?

3. An Unbiased Decision Maker

a. The Opinion in *Withrow v. Larkin*

Due process requires an unbiased decision maker. This requirement is even more unbending than the principles about the timing and elaborateness of the right to be heard discussed above. That is why we devote a separate subsection to this requirement. In the next case, *Withrow v. Larkin*, the Court explained how the impartial-decision-maker requirement applies to a common situation in administrative agencies: Officials who head the agency participate in investigative and prosecutorial roles as well as in quasi-judicial roles. The Court held that this common situation does not pose such a risk of bias that it categorically violates due process.

Exercise: *Withrow v. Larkin*

As you read the excerpt below, please keep these questions in mind:

1. At what points in the opinion does the Court compare administrative adjudicators to judges?

2. At what points in the opinion does the Court expressly seek to limit its holding?

Withrow v. Larkin

421 U.S. 35 (1975)

[Editor's summary: This case concerned the Wisconsin Medical Examining Board. The Board was made up of practicing physicians. The Board had power under Wisconsin law to issue licenses to practice medicine in Wisconsin and to regulate license holders. The Board's powers included the power to investigate whether a licensee was violating any of the Wisconsin statutes defining and forbidding various acts of professional misconduct. The Board also had power to issue a reprimand or temporarily suspend a license for misconduct. Finally, the Board had power to bring a criminal action or a civil action to revoke a license, if it found probable cause to believe that there were grounds for either such action.

Dr. Duane Larkin held a license to practice medicine in Wisconsin. He used the license to perform abortions. The Board notified Dr. Larkin that it would hold an investigative hearing on whether he had committed professional misconduct. At the hearing, witnesses testified and Dr. Larkin was represented by a lawyer. The Board offered Dr. Larkin a chance to appear before the Board to explain any of the evidence presented against him. The Board decided based on the investigative hearing that it would hold a "contested hearing" (meaning an adjudicative hearing) to decide whether to suspend his license. Dr. Larkin, however, got a federal district court to grant a temporary restraining order, and later a preliminary injunction, preventing the Board from holding the contested hearing.

Instead of holding a contested hearing, the Board held a "final investigative session" and issued a decision finding "probable cause" for criminal sanctions and a revocation of Dr. Larkin's license. The Board apparently found probable cause that Dr. Larkin had practiced medicine in Wisconsin under an alias; had allowed an unlicensed physician in his office to perform abortions; and violated the statute outlawing "fee splitting." *See* Brief for Appellants at 8, *Withrow v. Larkin*, 421 U.S. 35 (1975) (No. 73-1573); Brief for Appellee at 14, *Withrow v. Larkin*.

The federal district court based the preliminary injunction on its view that the Wisconsin statute violated procedural due process by allowing members of the Board to both investigate charges against Dr. Larkin and then act as judges of those charges by determining whether they justified temporarily suspending his license.]

MR. JUSTICE WHITE delivered the opinion of the Court....

III

... On the present record, it is quite unlikely that appellee would ultimately prevail on the merits of the due process issue presented to the District Court, and it was an abuse of discretion to issue the preliminary injunction.

Concededly, a "fair trial in a fair tribunal is a basic requirement of due process." *In re Murchison*, 349 U.S. 133, 136 (1955). This applies to administrative agencies which adjudicate as well as to courts. *Gibson v. Berryhill*, 411 U.S. 564, 579 (1973). Not only is a biased decisionmaker constitutionally unacceptable but "our system of law has always endeavored to prevent even the probability of unfairness." *In re Murchison, supra*, 349 U.S., at 136.... In pursuit of this end, various situations have been identified in which experience teaches that the probability of actual bias on the part of the judge or decisionmaker is too high to be constitutionally tolerable. Among these cases are those in which the adjudicator has a pecuniary interest in the outcome ... and in which he has been the target of personal abuse or criticism from the party before him....

The contention that the combination of investigative and adjudicative functions necessarily creates an unconstitutional risk of bias in administrative adjudication has a much more difficult burden of persuasion to carry. It must overcome a presumption of honesty and integrity in those serving as adjudicators; and it must convince that, under a realistic appraisal of psychological tendencies and human weakness, conferring investigative and adjudicative powers on the same individuals poses such a risk of actual bias or pre-judgment that the practice must be forbidden if the guarantee of due process is to be adequately implemented.

Very similar claims have been squarely rejected in prior decisions of this Court. In *FTC v. Cement Institute*, 333 U.S. 683 (1948), the Federal Trade Commission had instituted proceedings concerning the respondents' multiple basing-point delivered-price system. It was demanded that the Commission members disqualify themselves because long before the Commission had filed its complaint it had investigated the parties and reported to Congress and to the President, and its members had testified before congressional committees concerning the legality of such a pricing system. At least some of the members had disclosed their opinion that the system was illegal. The issue of bias was brought here and confronted "on the assumption that such an opinion had been formed by the entire membership of the Commission as a result of its prior official investigations." *Id.*, at 700.

The Court rejected the claim saying:

"[T]he fact that the Commission had entertained such views as the result of its prior ex parte investigations did not necessarily mean that the minds of its members were irrevocably closed on the subject of the respondents' basing point practices. Here, in contrast to the Commission's investigations, members of the cement industry were legally authorized participants in the hearings. They produced evidence—volumes of it. They were free to point out to the Commission by testimony, by cross-examination of witnesses, and by arguments, conditions of the trade practices under attack which they thought kept these practices within the range of legally permissible business activities." *Id.*, at 701.

In specific response to a due process argument, the Court asserted:

"No decision of this Court would require us to hold that it would be a violation of procedural due process for a judge to sit in a case after he had expressed an opinion as to whether certain types of conduct were prohibited by law. In fact, judges frequently try the same case more than once and decide identical issues each time, although these issues involve questions both of law and fact. Certainly, the Federal Trade Commission cannot possibly be under stronger constitutional compulsions in this respect than a court." *Id.*, at 702–703....

That is not to say that there is nothing to the argument that those who have investigated should not then adjudicate. The issue is substantial, it is not new, and legislators and others concerned with the operations of administrative agencies have given much attention to whether and to what extent distinctive administrative functions should be performed by the same persons. No single answer has been reached. Indeed, the growth, variety, and complexity of the administrative processes have made any one solution highly unlikely. Within the Federal Government itself, Congress has addressed the issue in several different ways, providing for varying degrees of separation from complete separation of functions to virtually none at all. For the generality of agencies, Congress has been content with § 5 of the Administrative Procedure Act, 5 U.S.C. § 554(d), which provides that no employee engaged in investigating or prosecuting may also participate or advise in the adjudicating function, but which also expressly exempts from this prohibition "the agency or a member or members of the body comprising the agency."

... When the Board instituted its investigative procedures, it stated only that it would investigate whether proscribed conduct had occurred. Later in noticing the adversary hearing, it asserted only that it would determine if violations had been committed which would warrant suspension of appellee's license.... [T]here was no more evidence of bias or the risk of bias or prejudgment than inhered in the very fact that the Board had investigated and would now adjudicate.... The processes utilized by the Board ... do not in themselves contain an unacceptable risk of bias.... [A]ppellee and his counsel were permitted to be present throughout; counsel actually attended the hearings and knew the facts presented to the Board.... No specific foundation has been presented for suspecting that the Board had been prejudiced by its investigation or would be disabled from hearing and deciding on the basis of the evidence to be presented at the contested hearing. The mere exposure to evidence presented in nonadversary investigative procedures is insufficient in itself to impugn the fairness of the board members at a later adversary hearing. Without a showing to the contrary, state administrators "are assumed to be men of conscience and intellectual discipline, capable of judging a particular controversy fairly on the basis of its own circumstances." *United States v. Morgan*, 313 U.S. 409, 421 (1941)....

IV

Nor do we think the situation substantially different because the Board, when it was prevented from going forward with the contested hearing, proceeded to make and issue formal findings of fact and conclusions of law asserting that there was probable cause to believe that appellee had engaged in various acts prohibited by the Wisconsin statutes....

Judges repeatedly issue arrest warrants on the basis that there is probable cause to believe that a crime has been committed and that the person named in the warrant has committed it. Judges also preside at preliminary hearings where they must decide whether the evidence is sufficient to hold a defendant for trial. Neither of these pretrial involvements has been thought to raise any constitutional barrier against the judge's presiding over the criminal trial and, if the trial is without a jury, against making the necessary determination of guilt or innocence.... It is also very typical for the members of administrative agencies to receive the results of investigations, to approve the filing of charges or formal complaints instituting enforcement proceedings, and then to participate in the ensuing hearings. This mode of procedure does not violate the Administrative Procedure Act, and it does not violate due process of law....

That the combination of investigative and adjudicative functions does not, without more, constitute a due process violation, does not, of course, preclude a court from determining from the special facts and circumstances present in the case before it that the risk of unfairness is intolerably high....

The judgment of the District Court is reversed and the case is remanded....

b. Significance of *Withrow v. Larkin*

Withrow held that the due process requirement of an unbiased decisionmaker applies to administrative adjudications. *Withrow* also established a broad "presumption of honesty and integrity in those serving as [administrative] adjudicators." 421 U.S. at 35. *Withrow* identified two situations in which that presumption is overcome: cases "in which the adjudicator has a pecuniary interest in the outcome ... and in which he has been the target of personal abuse or criticism from the party before him." Finally, and most importantly for the structure of many modern agencies, *Withrow* held that an agency official's involvement in both investigative and prosecutorial functions, on the one hand, and adjudicative functions, on the other hand, is *not* one of those situations that categorically overcomes the presumption of honesty and integrity and establishes a violation of due process.

In the next subsections we briefly discuss later decisions that involve the scope of the due process rule requiring unbiased agency adjudicators; and the two categorical situations that the Court identified as involving unconstitutional bias (pecuniary interests and personal animosity).

c. Scope of the Due Process Rule Requiring Unbiased Agency Adjudicators

Withrow discussed the due process rule generally requiring agency adjudicators to be unbiased. This subsection discusses (i) the scope of that rule; and (ii) an often recognized exception to the rule.

(i) Who Is an Administrative "Adjudicator" for Purposes of the *Withrow* Rule?

The due process requirement of an unbiased decision maker applies to agency officials serving as adjudicators. The requirement does not apply with equal force to agency officials serving investigative or prosecutorial functions.

The Court distinguished agency investigators and prosecutors, on the one hand, from agency adjudicators, on the other hand, in *Marshall v. Jerrico, Inc.*, 446 U.S. 238 (1980). *Jerrico* concerned enforcement of federal statutes limiting child labor. The statutes authorized civil penalties for violations. The statutes were enforced by an entity within the U.S. Department of Labor called the Employment Standards Administration (ESA). Under the enforcement scheme, an ESA assistant regional administrator would initially determine whether an employer had violated the child labor laws and assess an appropriate fine. If the employer disputed the fine, the employer could get an evidentiary hearing before a federal administrative law judge (ALJ), who reviewed the matter de novo. An employer, Jerrico, argued that the statutory scheme violated procedural due process because the money collected in fines could flow back to assistant regional administrators to reimburse their regional offices for enforcement costs.

The Court rejected Jerrico's procedural due process argument. The Court determined that assistant regional administrators should not be treated like the judges and agency adjudicatory officials that the Court had held in prior due process cases called *Tumey* and *Ward* must be unbiased:

> The assistant regional administrator simply cannot be equated with the kind of decisionmakers to which the principles of *Tumey* and *Ward* have been held applicable. He is not a judge. He performs no judicial or quasi-judicial functions. He hears no witnesses and rules on no disputed factual or legal questions. The function of assessing a violation is akin to that of a prosecutor or civil plaintiff. If the employer excepts to a penalty—as he has a statutory right to do—he is entitled to a de novo hearing before an administrative law judge. In that hearing the assistant regional administrator acts as the complaining party and bears the burden of proof on contested issues.... It is the administrative law judge, not the assistant regional administrator, who performs the function of adjudicating child labor violations. As the District Court found, the reimbursement provision of § 16(e) is inapplicable to the Office of Administrative Law Judges.

Id. at 247–248. The Court concluded that "the strict requirements of neutrality cannot be the same for administrative prosecutors as for judges." *Id.* at 248; *see also Ward v. Village of Monroeville*, 409 U.S. 57, 59–62 (1972) (Village finances were funded by fines, forfeitures, and costs collected from defendants by Mayor's Court of Village for various infractions; Court found due process violation in this arrangement because it biased the Mayor's Court against defendants); *Tumey v. Ohio*, 273 U.S. 510, 522 (1927) (mayor was paid for trying minor offenses only when he found defendants guilty; Court found due process violation under principles applicable to officials acting "in a judicial or quasi judicial capacity").

Lawyers unfamiliar with *Jerrico* could easily consider the front line officials who enforce regulatory programs to be adjudicators. Indeed, when a police officer writes a traffic ticket, the officer is engaging in adjudication in the sense that the officer applies the law to the facts of a particular situation (a "case"?) and, if the person who is cited for the traffic violation does not contest it, that ticket becomes the final decision, having legal effect. *Jerrico* shows us, however, that a narrower concept of "adjudicator" operates when it comes to the due process requirement for an unbiased administrative adjudicator.

(ii) An Exception to the Rule Requiring Unbiased Adjudicators: "The Rule of Necessity"

Due process generally requires an unbiased adjudicator, which generally precludes a decision maker from judging a case in which the adjudicator has a personal (e.g., pecuniary) interest. What happens, then, if the only official in an agency with authority to decide a case has a personal interest in that case, or some other conflict of interest? The answer is that a "rule of necessity" allows the official to decide the case as long as the parties know of the personal interest. The rule of necessity for federal agencies comes from federal court case law. In other systems, it may be codified in a statute or agency rule. *See* 2010 Model State APA § 403(g) (codifying rule of necessity based on California Government Code § 11512(c) (West, Westlaw through urgency legislation through Ch. 8 of 2012 Reg. Sess.). The rules comes into play most often when the law requires a specific official to make a decision and does not permit that official to delegate decisionmaking authority to anyone else. The rule allows the official to decide matters in which a conflict of interest would otherwise be disqualifying.

d. Improper Pecuniary Interests

An example of a case involving improper pecuniary interests is *Gibson v. Berryhill*, 411 U.S. 564 (1973). The Court's decision in *Gibson* turned upon unusual facts, but we summarize the case because it involves a generically common situation in administrative law: An agency headed by members of the same profession that the agency is responsible for licensing and regulating.

- *Gibson v. Berryhill*, 411 U.S. 564 (1973)

The Alabama Board of Optometry was the state agency that licensed and regulated optometrists. Membership on the multi-person *Board* that headed this *state* agency was limited by law to members of the Alabama Optometric *Association*, which was a *private* entity. The Association restricted its membership to self-employed ("independent") optometrists; the Association excluded from membership optometrists employed by other persons or entities. Because membership on the *Board* was restricted to members of the *Association*, the Board was made up exclusively of self-employed optometrists.

At the urging of the Association, the Board began an administrative proceeding against the optometrists who worked for Lee Optical Company. The Board alleged that Alabama law prohibited optometrists from working as employees for business corporations like Lee Optical. (The Alabama Supreme Court ultimately rejected this understanding of state law in a later, separate proceeding.) The Lee-Optical optometrists sued the Board in federal court, alleging that the Board's administrative proceeding against them violated due process because the members of the Board were biased.

The federal district court held that the Board's conduct violated procedural due process, essentially sustaining the plaintiffs' allegation of bias. The district court found that the Board's aim was to revoke the licenses of all optometrists in Alabama who worked for business corporations. The district court also found that almost half of the optometrists in Alabama worked for business corporations. The district court found that revoking all these corporate optometrists' licenses could financially benefit the Board's members, all of whom were independent optometrists. This possible financial benefit to Board members was particularly disturbing because all of the Board's members had to be selected from a private organization that excluded corporate optometrists. Thus, the optometrists who worked for Lee Optical and other companies "were denied participation in the governance of their own profession." *Id.* at 571.

The U.S. Supreme Court affirmed the district court's decision that the Board members' "personal interest" in the proceeding against the Lee-Optical optometrists was "sufficient to disqualify them" as a matter of due process. *Id.* at 578. The Court said that "those with substantial pecuniary interest in legal proceedings should not adjudicate these disputes." *Id.* at 579. The Court emphasized that the district court was in a superior position to determine whether the arrangement created a substantial pecuniary interest, and the Court saw no reason to disturb the district court's determination on that score.

It is not unusual for members of a profession to head the state agency that regulates the profession. *Gibson* was unusual because of the restricted membership of the Board and the high risk that its members would benefit financially by revoking the licenses of a large segment of the State's profession who were apparently treated as outsiders and "others" by the segment of the profession to which the Board members belonged.

e. Personal Animosity

Withrow identified as one situation in which the risk of bias is constitutionally unacceptable the situation in which the adjudicator "has been the target of personal abuse or criticism from the party before him." 421 U.S. at 47. More generally, if it seems highly likely that the adjudicator has personal animosity against a party, the risk of bias disqualifies the adjudicator as a matter of due process. The evidence has to be strong, however. The "presumption of honor and integrity" established in *Withrow* amounts to a presumption that adjudicators have extremely thick skin when applied to allegations that an adjudicator bears personal animosity to a party. *See, e.g., Hortonville Joint Sch. Dist. No. 1 v. Hortonville Educ. Ass'n*, 426 U.S. 482 (1976) (rejecting due process argument attributing undue bias to members of local school board who fired public school teachers in that district for going on strike after contract dispute with that same board).

f. Ex parte Contacts

Closely related to the need for an impartial decision maker is the need for the decision maker not to be exposed to ex parte contacts with interested parties. We discuss due process restrictions on ex parte contacts in Chapter 24.D.3, when we discuss APA restrictions on ex parte contacts.

E. Chapter 20 Wrap Up and Look Ahead

If you were trying to pitch the subject of this chapter to a movie producer, you might describe it as "Magna Carta meets the Motor Vehicle Code." Indeed, the lofty principles of procedural due process strongly influence procedures for agency adjudications that threaten to deprive people of property or liberty.

Many agency adjudications today do implicate "property," as that term has been understood to encompass government entitlements, as well as people's money and their traditional forms of property such as land and chattels. Agency adjudications may implicate liberty interests as well, especially among those whose liberty can within some limits be restrained by the government, such as public school students, undocumented aliens, and prisoners.

This chapter has introduced you to principles and analytic frameworks for analyzing which agency adjudications implicate procedural due process and for determining whether the procedures used in those adjudications afford the process that is constitutionally due. Having examined the Due Process Clauses as a potential, external source of procedural requirements for agency adjudications in this chapter, in the next chapter we turn to APAs as another potential, external source of procedural requirements for agency adjudications.

Chapter Problem Revisited

The material in this chapter aims to give you principles and frameworks for determining whether a person such as a student at a public law school is entitled to due process before the law school kicks the student out and, if so, whether the school provided due process.

1. Due process ordinarily is not satisfied by judicial review of agency action that has caused a deprivation, because due process ordinarily requires notice and a right to be heard *before* a significant deprivation has occurred. For that reason, if Mr. Stafford has a protected liberty or property interest in staying in law school, the law school itself or another administrative entity must provide the required notice and right to be heard, unless this presents one of those fairly rare cases in which due process does not require pre-deprivation notice and a right to be heard. You would want to consider cases illustrating what is sometimes called the "emergency exception" such as *North American Cold Storage Co. v. City of Chicago*, 211 U.S. 306 (1908).

2. Mr. Stafford probably has a subjective expectation that he is entitled to stay in law school until he completes graduation requirements, as long as he obeys the rules for staying in good standing. He must show, however, more than a unilateral expectation. He must show that the expectation was mutual. He must be able to point to law school rules or something else official to support a legitimate claim of entitlement. He would seek, similar to the professor in *Perry v. Sindermann*, 408 U.S. 593 (1972), to show at least a "de facto" system that gave law students a legitimate expectation that they could stay at the law school until they completed the program. Consider what evidence he might use to prove the existence of such a system.

3. The law school *cannot* defeat Mr. Stafford's due process claim by showing that his entitlement, if any, was conditioned on his obeying the rules, and that his entitlement accordingly vanished when he broke them by cheating on an exam. This argument assumes he was guilty of breaking the rules. That is not an assumption that due process analysis makes. If due process applies here, it entitles him to notice and a right to be heard (either before or after disqualification) precisely so he can show that the deprivation is erroneous. Of course, if he admits his guilt, then there may be nothing to have a hearing about. Therefore, to make a procedural due process argument, he will have to assert that he did not deserve to be disqualified for cheating under the relevant law school rules. He may have legal or factual arguments. The point is, he cannot be deprived of the right to make those arguments by assuming that the deprivation he is challenging was correct.

4. If Mr. Stafford had a property or liberty interest in staying in law school, the question becomes whether he received due process. That question is governed by *Mathews v. Eldridge*, 424 U.S. 319 (1976), and the timing and elaborateness principles discussed in this chapter. In addition to studying that case and those principles, you would want to identify lower federal court and state court cases applying *Mathews* to determine what process is due public law students disqualified for academic misconduct. *See, e.g.*, *Gagne v. Trustees of Indiana Univ.*, 692 N.E.2d 489 (Ind. Ct. App. 1998).

Professional Development Reflection Question

This question is based on the facts of the chapter problem. Assume the following additional facts. You have agreed to represent Mr. Stafford. Mr. Stafford has admitted to you that he cheated on a law school exam. The law school's rules do not, however, require that students who cheat on law school exams be expelled. As an alternative to expulsion, a student who cheats on an exam can be suspended from studies for one or two semesters, if there were extenuating circumstances. Mr. Stafford has a dubious claim of extenuating circumstances: He says he was sick the week before exams and therefore didn't have enough time to study; also, he broke up with his boyfriend. A much more favorable circumstance is revealed, however, by your preliminary research: The law school made several procedural mistakes in disqualifying Mr. Stafford, and you've discovered an email from an associate dean who clearly disliked Mr. Stafford and was glad to see him expelled regardless of his guilt for cheating. These facts probably didn't affect the result, but they provide respectable grounds for getting a preliminary injunction that will keep Mr. Stafford in school long enough to get the credits required to graduate.

Here is the question: Is it ethical for you to seek a preliminary injunction to keep Mr. Stafford in law school long enough to graduate, in effect using a lawsuit to gain delay that will advantage Mr. Stafford, even though you think that he got what he deserved and eventually a court is highly likely to uphold his expulsion if the case doesn't "moot out"? In considering this question, you may find relevant Model Rule of Professional Conduct 3.2, which says, "A lawyer shall make reasonable efforts to expedite litigation consistent with the interests of the client." Other Rules might also be relevant.

Chapter 21

The APA as a Source of Procedural Requirements for Agency Adjudications

Overview

Chapter 19 identified the applicable APA as one of the important potential sources of procedural requirements for agency adjudication. APAs are important because they have broad applicability. The idea behind their broad applicability is to establish uniform procedures for certain agency activities, including adjudication.

Although APAs are broadly applicable, they do not apply to every agency action. Part One of the book introduced a general framework for determining the APA's applicability to an administrative law problem. This chapter shows how you can use that framework to determine the APA's applicability to an agency adjudication.

This chapter's sections are entitled:

A. Identifying an "Adjudication" or "Order" for Purposes of the Federal APA

B. Framework for Determining the Federal APA's Applicability to a Federal Agency Adjudication

C. First Step: Does the Federal APA Apply to the Agency under Analysis?

D. Second Step, Part (a): If the Federal APA Does Apply to the Agency under Analysis, and the Agency Action under Analysis Is an Adjudication, Do the APA's Formal Adjudication Requirements Apply to This Adjudication?

E. Second Step, Part (b): If the Federal APA Does Apply to the Agency under Analysis, and the Agency Action under Analysis Is an Adjudication, Does Federal APA §§ 555 or 558 Apply to This Adjudication?

F. Third Step: If the Federal APA Does Apply to the Agency Adjudication under Analysis, How Does the APA Interact with Other Laws Applicable to the Adjudication?

G. Determining the Applicability of a State APA to a State Agency Adjudication

H. Chapter 21 Wrap Up and Look Ahead

Chapter Problem

Your clients own a small farm. After a flood destroyed their crops, they applied to the U.S. Department of Agriculture (USDA) for disaster relief aid. The local

USDA officials responsible for processing their application denied it. You have done enough research to believe your clients have good grounds for challenging the local officials' denial of their application for disaster relief.

Your research has revealed that your clients can appeal the local officials' decision to the National Appeals Division (Division), an entity within USDA. An appeal to the Division can involve two steps. First, a hearing officer employed by the Division will hold a hearing and make a decision on your clients' application for relief. Second, if the hearing officer rules against your clients, they can appeal to the head of the Division, who is known as the "Director." The relevant statute says:

---

7 U.S.C. § 6997. Division hearings

(a) General powers of Director and hearing officers

(1) Access to case record

The Director and hearing officer shall have access to the case record of any adverse decision appealed to the Division for a hearing.

(2) Administrative procedures

The Director and hearing officer shall have the authority to require the attendance of witnesses, and the production of evidence, by subpoena and to administer oaths and affirmations....

(b) Time for hearing

Upon a timely request for a hearing under section 6996(b) of this title, an appellant shall have the right to have a hearing by the Division on the adverse decision within 45 days after the date of the receipt of the request for the hearing.

(c) Location and elements of hearing

(1) Location

A hearing on an adverse decision shall be held in the State of residence of the appellant or at a location that is otherwise convenient to the appellant and the Division.

(2) Evidentiary hearing

The evidentiary hearing before a hearing officer shall be in person, unless the appellant agrees to a hearing by telephone or by a review of the case record. The hearing officer shall not be bound by previous findings of fact by the agency in making a determination.

(3) Information at hearing

The hearing officer shall consider information presented at the hearing without regard to whether the evidence was known to the agency officer, employee, or committee making the adverse decision at the time the adverse decision was made. The hearing officer shall leave the record open after the hearing for a reasonable period of time to allow the submission of information by the appellant or the agency after the hearing to the extent necessary to respond to new facts, information, arguments, or evidence presented or raised by the agency or appellant.

(4) Burden of proof

The appellant shall bear the burden of proving that the adverse decision of the agency was erroneous.

(d) Determination notice

The hearing officer shall issue a notice of the determination on the appeal not later than 30 days after a hearing or after receipt of the request of the appellant to waive a hearing, except that the Director may establish an earlier or later deadline. If the determination is not appealed to the Director for review under section 6998 of this title, the notice provided by the hearing officer shall be considered to be a notice of an administratively final determination....

Now you must determine whether this statute triggers the formal adjudication procedures of § 554 of the federal APA. You must make that determination for two reasons. One is to gain a general sense of the procedures for hearings before the Division. The other is that, if hearings before the Division *are* subject to the formal adjudication provisions of § 554, your clients may be able to recover attorney's fees.

The possibility of recovering attorney's fees arises from the Equal Access to Justice Act (EAJA). The EAJA requires a federal agency "that conducts an adversary adjudication" to award to a "prevailing party" in the adjudication that party's attorney's fees and certain other expenses. 5 U.S.C. § 504(a)(1) (2012). The EAJA defines "an adversary adjudication" generally to mean "an adjudication under section 554 of this title in which the position of the United States is represented by counsel or otherwise." *Id.* § 504(b)(1)(C)(i). You have already determined that the position of the United States will be represented if your clients appeal to the Division: the USDA will have lawyers opposing their appeal. Thus, the applicability of the EAJA depends on whether the appeal is "an adjudication under section 554" of the federal APA. If the EAJA does indeed apply to your client's appeal and creates the possibility of recovering the costs of their appeal to the Division, the appeal may be more financially feasible for your clients. (As discussed in Chapter 35.B.5, the EAJA also authorizes people involved in *court* proceedings against the government to recover the attorney's fees and costs of the court proceedings in certain situations. *See* 5 U.S.C. § 2412(d) (2012).)

Sketch out notes on how to analyze whether the appeal to the Division is subject to the formal adjudication requirements of § 554 of the federal APA.

A. Identifying an "Adjudication" or "Order" for Purposes of the Federal APA

As discussed in Chapter 4, in analyzing the applicability of the APA to an agency action, you must classify the agency action. That is because different APA provisions apply to different agency actions. Determining the applicability of the APA's provisions for adjudications depends initially on classifying the agency activity under analysis as "**adjudication**" as that term is defined for purposes of the federal APA.

The federal APA defines **"adjudication"** as the **"agency process for the formulation of an order."** 5 U.S.C. § 551(7) (2012). The federal APA defines an **"order,"** in turn, as **"the whole or a part of a final disposition … of an agency in a matter other than rule making."** *Id.* § 551(6). Thus, the federal APA divides final dispositions into two categories: orders and rules. An agency's final disposition of a matter must be an order if it is not a rule. And if it is indeed an order, then the process leading to it must be an adjudication.

As defined in the federal APA, **"adjudication"** encompasses agency final dispositions from the mundane to the momentous. For example, suppose that, when leaving a national park, you put in the park's suggestion box a note suggesting the park install snack vending machines along the park's hiking trails. When the official who reads your suggestion crumples it up and throws it into the paper recycling bin instead of passing it along to someone higher up in the agency, that official has engaged in adjudication by finally disposing of your request, which concerns a matter other than rulemaking. When the International Trade Commission enters an order blocking the importation of a product that infringes a U.S. patent, the agency is issuing an **"order"** after an **"adjudication."** The latter adjudication will involve much more elaborate procedures than the adjudication of your suggestion about vending machines along a park's hiking trails. And a good thing, too! *See* 19 U.S.C. § 1337(c) (2012).

Although the federal APA defines **"order"** broadly, the term does not encompass all individualized determinations by a federal agency. The most important category of individualized determinations that federal agencies make and that are not **"orders"** occur in agency *investigations*. Agency investigations do not finally dispose of anyone's legal rights or liabilities, and for this reason they are not **"adjudications"** as defined in the federal APA and thus not subject to the federal APA's requirements for adjudications.

The distinction between agency adjudication and agency investigation is broadly recognized in administrative law circles. The federal APA simply reflects the distinction. Three cases illustrate the distinction. They show that even when an agency investigation leads to a preliminary determination, that outcome will not be an agency **"order"** as defined in the federal APA:

  · *Hannah v. Larche*, 363 U.S. 420 (1960)

The U.S. Civil Rights Commission exercised statutory authority to investigate reports that Louisiana voting officials were violating black people's voting rights. The investigation could culminate in a report to Congress and the President making findings and recommendations. During the investigation, the Commission subpoenaed the voting officials to testify at an investigative hearing held by the Commission. The Commission's rules did not allow the voting officials to find out who had accused them of voting rights violations or to cross-examine their accusers. The officials argued that the Commission's investigative procedures violated the Due Process Clause and the federal APA.

The U.S. Supreme Court rejected both arguments. Of particular importance to our present focus, the Court held that the Commission's investigative hearing was not subject to the formal adjudication requirements of the federal APA. The Court explained that those requirements do not apply to "nonadjudicative, fact-finding investigations." *Id.* at 446; *see also id.* at 452–453. The Court thus drew a distinction between an agency investigation and an agency adjudication.

  · *National Transportation Safety Board v. Gibson*, 118 F.3d 1312 (9th Cir. 1997)

An airplane carrying about ninety people and flying at about 39,000 feet altitude suddenly veered to the right and plunged in a spiral dive six miles towards the earth before the pilot regained control of the plane. The National Transportation Safety Board investigated the incident and issued a report finding that the pilot was partly to blame. The pilot sought judicial review of the Board's report under a statute authorizing judicial review of the Board's "orders."

The Ninth Circuit denied review, holding that the report was not an "order." The court relied partly on the federal APA's definition of **"order"** as a **"final disposition."** The court cited U.S. Supreme Court precedent interpreting **"final disposition"** to require "some determinate consequences for the party to the proceeding." 118 F.3d at 1314 (quoting *Int'l Tel, & Tel. Corp v. Int'l Bhd. of Elec. Workers*, 419 U.S. 428, 443 (1975)). The Ninth Circuit determined that the Board's report did not determine any legal rights or liabilities.

- *Georator Corp. v. Equal Employment Opportunity Commission*, 592 F.2d 765 (4th Cir. 1979)

An employee filed a charge with the Equal Employment Opportunity Commission that accused her employer of violating the federal anti-discrimination statute known as Title VII. The Commission investigated the employee's charge by seeking documents from the employer. The Commission ultimately determined that there was "reasonable cause" to believe the charge was true. The employer sought judicial review of the Commission's reasonable cause determination. The employer claimed a right to judicial review under the provision in the federal APA authorizing judicial review of final **"agency action."** 5 U.S.C. §704 (2012). The federal APA defines **"agency action"** to include an **"order."** 5 U.S.C. §551(13).

The Fourth Circuit held that the Commission's reasonable cause determination was not an **"order"** because it was not a **"final disposition."** The reasonable cause determination was not a final disposition because it did not have "determinate consequences for" the employer. *Id.* at 768 (quoting *Int'l Tel, & Tel. Corp v. Int'l Bhd. of Elec. Workers*, 419 U.S. 428, 443 (1975)). The Fourth Circuit explained that the reasonable cause determination, "[s]tanding alone ... is lifeless, and can fix no obligation nor impose any liability upon [the] employer." 592 F.2d at 768.

* * *

Although an agency investigation differs from an agency adjudication, an agency investigation may lead to an agency adjudication. The same is true of other agency information gathering activities, such as agency requests for information and agency inspections of business premises. Many agencies have powers (1) to investigate suspected violations of the laws and rules that they are responsible for administering and, if that investigation reveals an apparent violation, (2) to conduct an agency adjudication to determine whether a violation has indeed occurred and, if so, what sanction is appropriate. Often the adjudication phase begins with the agency issuing a formal complaint. Because the complaint commences the adjudication, the Court has held that the complaint qualifies as an **"order"** under the federal APA. The complaint is **"a part of a final disposition ... in a matter other than rulemaking."** *FTC v. Standard Oil of California*, 449 U.S. 232, 238 n.7 (1980). The complaint is only **"a part of"** a final disposition, however, because it signifies only the beginning, not the end, of the adjudication. And because it marks only the beginning of the adjudication, the complaint is not a **"*final* agency action"** of which APA §704 authorizes immediate judicial review. *See FTC v. Standard Oil*, 449 U.S. at 239–245. The broader point is that, although an agency order is the whole or part of a **"final *disposition*,"** it may not qualify as a **"final *agency action*"** for purposes of judicial review.

We explore § 704's **"final agency action"** requirement for judicial review in Chapter 29.B.2.b. We introduce § 704's **final agency action** concept here only to distinguish it from the **final disposition** concept found in § 551's definition of "**order**."

Exercise: Identifying Agency Adjudication

Please explain whether or not the following agency actions are adjudications.

1. The EPA issues a compliance order against the owners of property, in which the EPA determines that the property owners have violated the Clean Water Act by discharging a pollutant into a "water of the United States" without getting the required permit.

2. The Federal Emergency Management Agency denies a home owner's application for disaster relief to pay for housing after a tornado has destroyed her home.

3. The U.S. Department of Justice decides to begin an investigation of a shooting in Florida to determine whether there are grounds to prosecute the shooter for violating the victim's federal civil rights.

B. Framework for Determining the Federal APA's Applicability to a Federal Agency Adjudication

Once you have classified a federal agency action as an **"order,"** you must determine whether, in entering that order, the agency must follow APA procedures for agency adjudication. You can make that determination by using the basic framework for analyzing APA applicability that we introduced in Chapter 4. For adjudications by federal agencies, however, you must apply the framework with an understanding of the different ways that the federal APA treats rulemaking and adjudication.

Chapter 4 introduced a general framework for analyzing the APA's applicability to an administrative law problem. The framework, as formulated for agency adjudications, is as follows:

(1) Does the APA (federal or state) apply to this *agency*?

(2) If so, does the APA apply to the agency *adjudication* under analysis?

(3) If the APA does apply to the agency adjudication under analysis, how does the APA interact with *other laws* applicable to adjudication?

The second step is tricky, as applied to federal agency adjudications, especially if you have studied the material in Chapter 11 about the APA's applicability to agency rulemaking. The trickiness arises from the federal APA's differing treatment of rulemaking and adjudication.

As Chapter 11 explained, the federal APA prescribes two types of proceedings for making legislative rules. One type is informal rulemaking. The informal rulemaking procedures apply, with some exceptions, when the agency legislation says nothing about the procedures the agency should follow. The second type of rulemaking is formal rulemaking. The formal rulemaking requirements apply only if the agency legislation requires the rule **"to be made on the record after opportunity for an agency hearing."** 5 U.S.C. § 553(c) (2012). (A third type of rulemaking, known as "hybrid rulemaking," is required when the agency legislation modifies the federal APA's informal rulemaking requirements but does not trigger the formal rulemaking procedures.)

For adjudications, the federal APA prescribes—not two—but only *one* set of procedures. That set of adjudication procedures is called "formal adjudication" procedures or requirements. The formal adjudication requirements are in federal APA §§ 554, 556, and 557. They include procedures for a trial-type hearing. They apply only if the agency legislation requires the adjudication is **"to be determined on the record after opportunity for an agency hearing."** 5 U.S.C. § 554(a) (2012). The federal APA does not prescribe a comprehensive set of procedures for agency adjudications that are *not* **"required by statute to be determined on the record after opportunity for an agency hearing."** *Id.* Instead, for such "informal adjudications," the federal APA has only two provisions—§§ 555 and 558—that prescribe procedural requirements in some situations.

Because the federal APA treats rulemaking and adjudication differently, the framework for analyzing the federal APA's applicability to agency adjudications differs from the framework for analyzing the federal APA's applicability to agency rulemaking. The difference concerns the second part of the framework:

(2) If the APA does apply to the agency under analysis, does the APA apply to the adjudication under analysis?

That question can be subdivided for analysis of adjudications:

(2) If the APA does apply to the agency under analysis, and the agency's action involves adjudication,

(a) Do the APA's formal adjudication requirements (in §§ 554, 556, and 557) apply to this adjudication?

(b) Does APA §§ 555 or 558 apply to this adjudication?

Now that we have introduced this refinement to the framework for analyzing the federal APA's applicability to a federal agency adjudication, we look at each step of the framework.

C. First Step: Does the Federal APA Apply to the Agency under Analysis?

The federal APA defines the term **"agency"** broadly to include most government authorities with adjudicatory power, other than the federal courts. 5 U.S.C. § 551(1). As broad as an APA's definition of "agency" may be, the definition will invariably exclude some governmental entities. Therefore, when you encounter an unfamiliar government entity in your legal practice, you must always consult the APA definition of "agency" to see whether the entity falls within that definition. You may also have to examine case law interpreting the APA definition of "agency" to see how courts have interpreted the definition as applied to the entity with which you are dealing, or similar entities.

In addition to consulting the APA definition of "agency" and case law interpreting that definition, you must examine the agency legislation (and, if necessary, case law interpreting it). The agency legislation may *exempt* the entity from the APA, even though the entity otherwise falls within the APA's definition of "agency." Alternatively, the agency legislation may *subject* an entity to the APA even though the agency does not otherwise fall within the APA's definition of "agency." In either event, the agency legislation ordinarily controls as the more specific statute.

Let us suppose that you have determined, at the first step of the analysis, that the agency under analysis is subject to the APA. Let us also suppose that the agency activity under analysis is an agency adjudication. The next step is to determine the APA's application to the particular adjudication.

D. Second Step, Part (a): If the Federal APA Does Apply to the Agency under Analysis, and the Agency Action under Analysis Is an Adjudication, Do the APA's Formal Adjudication Requirements Apply to This Adjudication?

If the federal APA applies to the agency under analysis, an adjudication by that agency will ordinarily be subject to the federal APA's formal adjudication requirements only on three conditions:

(1) The agency legislation must not exempt the adjudication from the APA's formal adjudication requirements.

(2) The agency legislation must require the adjudication "**to be determined on the record after opportunity for an agency hearing.**" 5 U.S.C. § 554(a).

(3) The adjudication must not fall within one of the exemptions prescribed in federal APA §§ 554(a)(1) through (a)(6).

Below we examine each condition separately.

1. The Agency Legislation Must Not Exempt the Adjudication from the APA's Formal Adjudication Requirements

Federal APA § 559 states that a statute enacted after the APA was enacted in 1946 can "**supersede or modify**" any provision of the APA "**to the extent that it does so expressly.**" We mentioned in Chapter 17 that the largest and most important type of federal agency adjudications that Congress has expressly exempted from the federal APA's formal adjudication requirements are proceedings under the immigration laws to remove (i.e., deport or exclude) an alien. 8 U.S.C. § 1229a (2012) (prescribing procedures for removal proceedings and stating, in subsection (a)(3), that "a proceeding under this section shall be the sole and exclusive procedure for determining whether an alien may be ... removed from the United States"); *see also Marcello v. Bonds*, 349 U.S. 302, 310 (1955); Chapter 17.C.1.b.

Aside from the statutory exemption for removal proceedings, few if any federal statutes expressly exempt agency adjudications from the federal APA's formal adjudication requirements. The express exemption in the removal statute was necessary to "overrule" a decision in which the U.S. Supreme Court held that formal adjudication was required in deportation proceedings. *See Marcello*, 349 U.S. at 306–310. More frequently, federal statutes simply fail to include the language necessary to trigger the federal APA's formal adjudication requirements, which is the next condition that we discuss.

2. The Agency Legislation Must Require the Adjudication "[T]o [B]e [D]etermined on the [R]ecord after [O]pportunity for an [A]gency [H]earing"

Section 554, entitled "**Adjudications,**" addresses its applicability in subsection (a):

---

5 U.S.C. § 554. Adjudications

(a) This section applies, according to the provisions thereof, in every case of adjudication required by statute to be determined on the record after opportunity for an agency hearing, [with six exemptions]....

Adjudications subject to § 554 are also subject to §§ 556 and 557, because of § 554(c)(2):

---

5 U.S.C. § 554. Adjudications ...

(c) The agency shall give all interested parties opportunity for—

(1) the submission and consideration of facts, arguments, offers of settlement, or proposals of adjustment when time, the nature of the proceeding, and the public interest permit; and

(2) to the extent that the parties are unable so to determine a controversy by consent, hearing and decision on notice and in accordance with sections 556 and 557 of this title....

Thus, §§ 554, 556, and 557 apply to agency adjudications only if the adjudication is "**required by statute to be determined on the record after opportunity for an agency hearing.**"

Newcomers to administrative law may be mystified by § 554(a)'s phrase "**required by statute to be determined on the record after opportunity for an agency hearing.**" The phrase generally means this: Sections 554, 556, and 557 apply when the agency legislation governing the adjudication requires the agency (1) to provide an opportunity for a trial-like hearing; and (2) to base its decision exclusively on the official record of the proceeding, which will include a transcript of the hearing, plus hearing exhibits and all other evidence admitted into the record. Thus, the **"statute"** to which § 554 refers usually means the agency legislation authorizing the adjudication. The **"agency hearing"** is an oral, evidentiary hearing in which the parties or their representatives appear in person before an agency official — usually an Administrative Law Judge — to present testimony of live witnesses, as well as other evidence, such as documentary exhibits. The requirement that the adjudication be **"determined on the record"** means the agency decision must be based *exclusively* on the evidence admitted into the record.

Determining whether the agency legislation triggers § 554 (and §§ 556 and 557) can be tricky. It helps to distinguish three situations:

a)   The agency legislation requires both an opportunity for a hearing and a determination on the record.

b)   The agency legislation requires the agency to provide an opportunity for a "hearing," but does not expressly require an on-the-record determination.

c)   The agency legislation is unclear, but the Due Process Clause applies to the adjudication.

a. The Agency Legislation Requires Both an Opportunity for a Hearing and a Determination on the Record

Many federal statutes authorizing agency adjudication clearly trigger the formal adjudication requirements of the APA. These statutes operate in one of two ways. Either they expressly require both an opportunity for a hearing and a decision based on the record, or they expressly refer to § 554 (and, sometimes, to §§ 556 and 557 as well).

In the first category are statutes that track the language of § 554(a) closely. An example is the United States Warehouse Act, which regulates warehouses for agricultural commodities. The Act authorizes the Secretary of Agriculture to license warehouses and make legislative rules for their operation. The following provision in the Act authorizes the Secretary to impose civil penalties on people who violate the Act or its regulations:

---

7 U.S.C. § 254. Penalties for noncompliance

If a person fails to comply with any requirement of this chapter (including regulations promulgated under this chapter), the Secretary may assess, on the record after an opportunity for a hearing, a civil penalty —

(1) of not more than $25,000 per violation, if an agricultural product is not involved in the violation; or

(2) of not more than 100 percent of the value of the agricultural product, if an agricultural product is involved in the violation.

The phrase "on the record after opportunity for a hearing" closely tracks the trigger language required by federal APA § 554(a).

Some statutes trigger the formal adjudication requirements using less clear trigger language. An example is the Federal Trade Commission Act. As you read the following provision from the Act, look for the language that requires an opportunity for a hearing and the language that requires the Commission's determination to be made on the basis of the evidence admitted into the hearing record.

---

15 U.S.C. § 45. Unfair methods of competition unlawful; prevention by Commission …

(b) Proceeding by Commission; modifying and setting aside orders

Whenever the Commission shall have reason to believe that any such person, partnership, or corporation has been or is using any unfair method of competition or unfair or deceptive act or practice in or affecting commerce, and if it shall appear to the Commission that a proceeding by it in respect thereof would be to the interest of the public, it shall issue and serve upon such person, partnership, or corporation a complaint stating its charges in that respect and containing a notice of a hearing upon a day and at a place therein fixed at least thirty days after the service of said complaint. The person, partnership, or corporation so complained of shall have the right to appear at the place and time so fixed and show cause why an order should not be entered by the Commission requiring such person, partnership, or corporation to cease and desist from the violation of the law so charged in said complaint.… If upon such hearing the Commission shall be of the opinion that the method of competition or the act or practice in question is prohibited by this subchapter, it shall make a report in writing in which it shall state its findings as to the facts and shall issue and cause to be served on such person, partnership, or corporation an order requiring such person, partnership, or corporation to cease and desist from using such method of competition or such act or practice.…

Section 45(b) is confusing partly because the language requiring an opportunity for a hearing is separate from the language requiring an on-the-record determination. Moreover, both sets of language are obscure. Section 45(b) provides an opportunity for a hearing by requiring the Commission to issue a "notice of a hearing" at which a person has "the right to appear." Section 45(b) requires an on-the-record determination by requiring the Commission to base its opinion "upon such hearing." The phrase "upon such hearing" means the Commission must base its determination exclusively on the hearing record.

Now we show you two statutes that trigger formal adjudication requirements by expressly referring, in one case, to §§ 554, 556, and 557, and in the other case only to § 554. In either case, the result is the same. Both statutes trigger the formal adjudication requirements of the federal APA.

The first provision comes from the federal Grain Standards Act, which regulates the handling and weighing of grain:

---

7 U.S.C. § 86. Refusal of inspection and weight services; civil penalties …

(d) Opportunity for hearing; temporary refusal without hearing pending final determination

Before official inspection or services related to weighing is refused to any person or a civil penalty is assessed against any person under this section, such person shall be afforded opportunity for a hearing in accordance with sections 554, 556, and 557 of Title 5....

This provision deserves our appreciation for the clarity with which it triggers the formal adjudication requirements. Compare it to the murky Federal Trade Commission Act provision (15 U.S.C. § 45(b) (2012)) reproduced above!

The next provision comes from the Endangered Species Act:

---

16 U.S.C. § 1540. Penalties and enforcement

(a) Civil penalties

(1) Any person who knowingly violates, and any person engaged in business as an importer or exporter of fish, wildlife, or plants who violates, any provision of this chapter, or any provision of any permit or certificate issued hereunder, or of any regulation issued in order to implement subsection (a)(1)(A), (B), (C), (D), (E), or (F), (a)(2)(A), (B), (C), or (D), (c), (d) (other than regulation relating to recordkeeping or filing of reports), (f) or (g) of section 1538 of this title, may be assessed a civil penalty by the Secretary of not more than $25,000 for each violation. Any person who knowingly violates, and any person engaged in business as an importer or exporter of fish, wildlife, or plants who violates, any provision of any other regulation issued under this chapter may be assessed a civil penalty by the Secretary of not more than $12,000 for each such violation. Any person who otherwise violates any provision of this chapter, or any regulation, permit, or certificate issued hereunder, may be assessed a civil penalty by the Secretary of not more than $500 for each such violation. No penalty may be assessed under this subsection unless such person is given notice and opportunity for a hearing with respect to such violation. Each violation shall be a separate offense. Any such civil penalty may be remitted or mitigated by the Secretary. Upon any failure to pay a penalty assessed under this subsection, the Secretary may request the Attorney General to institute a civil action in a district court of the United States for any district in which such person is found, resides, or transacts business to collect the penalty and such court shall have jurisdiction to hear and decide any such action. The court shall hear such action on the record made before the Secretary and shall sustain his action if it is supported by substantial evidence on the record considered as a whole....

(2) Hearings held during proceedings for the assessment of civil penalties authorized by paragraph (1) of this subsection shall be conducted in accordance with section 554 of Title 5....

This provision requires proceedings "in accordance with section 554." Section 554 applies only when an adjudication is **"required by statute to be determined on the record after opportunity for an agency hearing."** 5 U.S.C. § 554(a). Thus, the statutory reference to § 554 clearly triggers the formal adjudication requirements of §§ 554, 556, and 557.

In short, an agency generally must follow formal adjudication requirements if it adjudicates under either (1) a statute that expressly requires an opportunity for a hearing and a determination on the record; or (2) a statute that expressly requires compliance with federal APA § 554.

Exercise: Federal Statutes Triggering Formal Adjudication under the Federal APA

You may have noticed a common feature of all the statutes reproduced above as examples of statutes triggering formal adjudication under the federal APA. All of them involve agency adjudications to impose a civil sanction. This is no coincidence. Many of the federal statutes that trigger formal adjudication are statutes that authorize agencies to impose civil sanctions. Why, do you suppose, Congress often requires formal adjudication for imposition of civil sanctions?

b. The Agency Legislation Requires the Agency to Provide an Opportunity for a "Hearing," but Does Not Expressly Require an On-the-Record Determination

Some federal statutes require an agency adjudicating a matter to provide an opportunity for a "hearing" but do not expressly require the agency to base its decision on the record. Here are three examples:

- A provision in the Clean Water Act exempts the owner or operator of a source of pollution from certain requirements if the owner or operator demonstrates, "after opportunity for public hearing," that the requirements should be relaxed in a particular situation. 33 U.S.C. § 1326(a) (2012). The provision does not expressly require the EPA to rely on the hearing record when deciding whether to grant an exemption.

- The Atomic Energy Act says that in any proceeding under the Act for the granting, suspending, revoking, or amending of any license or construction permit, the Nuclear Regulatory Commission "shall grant a hearing upon the request of any person whose interest may be affected by the proceeding." 42 U.S.C. § 2239(a)(1)(A) (2012). The Act does not expressly require the Commission to base its decision in such a proceeding on the record of that proceeding.

- The Resource Conservation Recovery Act (RCRA) authorizes EPA to order corrective actions for certain RCRA violations. The RCRA says that a corrective order becomes final unless, within 30 days after EPA issues it, "the person or persons named therein request a public hearing." 42 U.S.C. § 6928(b) (2012). The RCRA does not expressly require EPA's decision after such a hearing to be based on the record of the hearing.

Do statutes like these — which require an opportunity for a "hearing" in an agency adjudication but do not expressly require the agency's decision in the adjudication to be based on the record — trigger the federal APA's formal adjudication requirements? The question is important but unresolved.

The question matters for both agencies and parties with cases before the agencies.

All other things being equal, most agencies prefer not to have to follow the federal APA's formal adjudication requirements. That is not necessarily because the agencies want to avoid hearings altogether, or because the agencies want to rely on matters outside the record to make their decisions. To the contrary, agency regulations implementing statutes like those cited above often require both evidentiary hearings and on-the-record determinations. Those hearings, however, may not be as elaborate as required by federal APA §§ 554 and 556. Moreover, the agency's decisionmaking process may not comply with the elaborate decisionmaking requirements of APA § 557. The elaborate hearing and decisionmaking requirements of formal adjudication take much agency time and effort to meet.

By the same token, parties with matters before an agency tend to want the formal adjudication requirements to apply. Those requirements give parties the maximum opportunity to present their case, to rebut evidence adverse to their case, and generally to influence the decisionmaking process. Moreover, the formal adjudication procedures require the agency to be rigorous in its decision making—for example, by requiring the agency to make written findings **"on all the material issues of fact, law, or discretion presented on the record."** 5 U.S.C. § 557(c)(3)(A) (2012).

Despite the importance of the issue, the U.S. Supreme Court has not decided whether the federal APA's formal adjudication requirements are triggered by federal statutes that require the agency to provide an opportunity for a "hearing" in an adjudication, but do not expressly require an on-the-record determination.

The Court addressed a similar issue in *Florida East Coast Railroad v. United States*, 410 U.S. 224 (1973), a case discussed in Chapter 11.D.3. There, the Court held that a federal statute requiring an agency to hold a hearing in a *rulemaking* proceeding did not trigger the formal *rulemaking* requirements of the federal APA. *Id.* at 237–238. The Court relied partly on the view that rulemaking involves legislative-type determinations that are not suited to the quasi-judicial procedures that the federal APA requires for formal rulemaking. *See id.* at 244–246. That view does not apply to the interpretation of statutes authorizing the quasi-judicial activity of agency adjudication, rather than agency rulemaking, and therefore *Florida East Coast* does not seem relevant to the question whether a statute requiring a "hearing" in an agency adjudication triggers the federal APA's formal adjudication requirements.

In the absence of Supreme Court guidance, the lower federal courts disagree. Some lower courts hold that statutes requiring a hearing in an agency adjudication trigger the formal adjudication requirements only if the statute's text or legislative history clearly expresses congressional intent to require formal, on-the-record proceedings. *See, e.g., Five Points Road Joint Venture v. Johanns*, 542 F.3d 1121, 1126 (7th Cir. 2008). Other courts, in older cases, took the nearly opposite approach, presuming that statutes requiring a hearing in an agency adjudication ordinarily trigger the formal adjudication requirements. *Marathon Oil Co. v. Envt'l Protection Agency*, 564 F.2d 1253, 1262 (9th Cir. 1977). A third group of courts treats these statutes as ambiguous and defers to the interpretation that they are given by the agencies responsible for administering them. The agencies invariably interpret these statutes *not* to trigger formal adjudication requirements. *See, e.g., Dominion Energy Brayton Point, LLC v. Johnson*, 443 F.3d 12, 16–19 (1st Cir. 2006).

The U.S. Supreme Court may eventually have to resolve the conflicting approaches to interpreting federal statutes that require "hearings" in federal agency adjudications, but that do not expressly require on-the-record determinations. In the meantime, you may be wondering: What does a lawyer do if involved in an agency adjudication under such a statute? Here is a suggested approach:

- First determine what adjudication procedures the agency actually provides. You can usually determine that by examining the agency's procedural rules for the adjudication.

- Next, determine how those procedures differ from the procedures that the agency would be required to provide under the federal APA's formal adjudication requirements.

- Determine whether the procedures that the agency actually provides are inadequate, compared to formal adjudication procedures, in terms of their usefulness for advocating your client's case.

- If the existing procedures are inadequate, consider asking the agency voluntarily to adopt additional procedures to remedy the inadequacies that you have identified. After all, the agency usually has discretion to adopt additional procedural protections — even beyond those required by its regulations and legislation — as long as doing so will not prejudice other parties or the public interest. If you do request additional procedures, be sure to document your request, and support it with a specific explanation of how the existing procedures are inadequate, in terms of your client's ability to present its case.

- If the agency ultimately uses adjudication procedures that you have determined are inadequate, be sure, in the agency adjudication, to preserve your objection to their adequacy and to build a record showing specifically how they are inadequate. For example, if the agency does not allow you to cross-examine adverse witnesses, you may ask to make a proffer of evidence showing the grounds on which you would have conducted cross-examination, if permitted.

- If the agency adjudication leads to an adverse decision, after exhausting all administrative remedies, seek judicial review, if possible, in a court that has the most favorable case law upon which to argue that the agency statute requires formal adjudication. (You will hope to be able to seek review in a court that is in the second group of courts described above). Be prepared to argue to the reviewing court that, even if the agency statute did not require the agency to use formal adjudication, the agency still did not provide procedures sufficient to satisfy the opportunity for a hearing required by its statute. (This argument, of course, depends on what the term "hearing" means in the particular statute governing the adjudication.)

c. The Agency Legislation Does Not Plainly Trigger Formal Adjudication, but the Due Process Clause Applies to the Adjudication

Section 554(a) makes the APA's formal adjudication procedures applicable, with some exceptions, **"in every case of adjudication required *by statute* to be determined on the record after opportunity for an agency hearing."** 5 U.S.C. § 554(a) (emphasis added). This wording has raised an important and unsettled issue of interpretation. The issue arises in this situation: A federal statute authorizes an agency adjudication, but the statute itself does not expressly require the adjudication to be determined on the record after opportunity for an agency hearing. (Perhaps the statute only requires a hearing, without expressly requiring an on-the-record determination.) But here is the kicker: The Due Process Clause applies to the adjudication because the adjudication threatens someone with a deprivation of liberty or property. If the Due Process Clause applies, but the statute is unclear on the matter, does the statute trigger the federal APA's formal adjudication requirements? The U.S. Supreme Court answered that question: "Yes; when procedural due process applies to a federal agency's adjudication, the agency must follow the federal APA's formal adjudication requirements." The Court gave this answer in old cases, however, that some people think are no longer good law.

The leading case is *Wong Yang Sung v. McGrath*, 339 U.S. 33 (1950). Wong Yang Sung, a citizen of China, was subjected to a deportation proceeding before immigration officials. The deportation proceeding did not comply with the federal APA's formal adjudication requirements. The proceeding resulted in an order requiring that Wong Yang Sung be deported. On judicial review of the deportation order, the government argued that deportation proceedings did not have to comply with the formal adjudication requirements of the federal APA because they occurred under a statute that did not expressly require the determinations to be made on the record after an opportunity for a hearing.

The Court rejected the government's argument and held that the federal APA's formal adjudication requirements applied to deportation proceedings. The Court reasoned that deportation proceedings are subject to the Due Process Clause because they threaten to deprive people of their liberty. The Clause therefore requires fair procedures in deportation proceedings. The federal APA's formal adjudication requirements reflect Congress's judgment of what is required for fairness in adjudications involving serious interests like those at stake in deportation proceedings. The deportation statute must be construed to incorporate that standard of fairness, and thereby to trigger the formal adjudication requirements, to ensure the statute's constitutionality. *See Wong Yang Sung*, 339 U.S. at 48–51.

The Court followed *Wong Yang Sung* in several later cases. *See* William Funk, *The Rise and Purported Demise of* Wong Yang Sung, 58 Admin. L. Rev. 881, 886–887 (2006). Even so, some people believe that *Wong Yang Sung* is no longer good law, for three main reasons.

First, the Court has changed its mind since *Wong Yang Sung* about what procedural due process requires. At the time the Court decided *Wong Yang Sung* (1950), the Court used a judicial model for analyzing due process requirements. (See Chapter 20.D.1 for a description of the judicial model.) Under the judicial model, procedural due process generally required agency adjudications to resemble judicial proceedings. Today, the Court doesn't use the judicial model anymore. Instead, the Court uses the framework of *Mathews v. Eldridge*, 424 U.S. 319 (1976). Under that framework, procedural due process ordinarily does *not* require agency proceedings to be as formal as judicial proceedings. Indeed, the modern Court has construed procedural due process to impose only rudimentary procedural requirements in some agency adjudications. On the Court's modern view, the federal APA's formal adjudication requirements go far beyond what procedural due process typically requires. One can therefore argue that the Court today would not interpret statutory "hearing" requirements to incorporate the federal APA's formal adjudication requirements in adjudications to which the Due Process Clause applies.

Second, Congress responded to *Wong Yang Sung* by amending the deportation statute to exempt deportation proceedings from the formal adjudication requirements. The Court held in *Marcello v. Bonds*, 349 U.S. 302 (1955), that the amendment was effective and constitutional. It remains true today that deportation proceedings—which are now called "removal proceedings"—are exempt from the federal APA's formal adjudication requirements. 8 U.S.C. § 1229a (2012). The procedures required under the removal statutes are still fairly elaborate, though, reflecting the requirements of procedural due process. Even so, one can argue that, by legislatively "overruling" *Wong Yang Sung*, Congress rejected the Court's reasoning in that case.

The third reason that some people doubt the continuing validity of *Wong Yang Sung* is that, since *Wong Yang Sung*, the Court has developed a doctrine of "deference" that may supersede the approach that the Court took in *Wong Yang Sung*. Today, the Court generally requires federal courts to defer to a federal agency's reasonable interpretation of a statute that the agency is responsible for administering. *See Chevron, U.S.A. Inc. v. Natural Resources Def. Council*, 467 U.S. 837 (1984). Some lower federal courts have relied on *Chevron* to defer to agencies that have interpreted statutory provisions requiring "hearings" in agency adjudications as not triggering the formal adjudication requirements. *See, e.g., Dominion Energy Brayton Point, LLC v. Johnson*, 443 F.3d 12, 16–19 (1st Cir. 2006).

Despite doubt about the continuing validity of *Wong Yang Sung*, some lower courts still follow it. An example is *Collord v. U.S. Dep't of the Interior*, 154 F.3d 933 (9th Cir. 1998). *Collord* involved a federal agency adjudication to determine the validity of Marjorie and James Collord's mining claims. The federal statute authorizing the adjudication did not expressly require an opportunity for an agency hearing or a determination on the record. The Ninth Circuit nonetheless held that the adjudication was subject to the federal APA's formal adjudication requirements under *Wong Yang Sung* because the Collords' mining claims "are property interests and the Constitution requires a hearing before the agency can cancel these claims." *Id.* at 936. The *Collord* court's adherence to *Wong Yang Sung* reflects that the Court alone has the "prerogative of overruling its own decisions." *Rodriguez de Quijas v. Shearson/American Express, Inc.*, 490 U.S. 477, 484 (1989).

What does it mean for the administrative lawyer if, as the court in *Collord* held, *Wong Yang Sung* is still good law? It means that the lawyer must give special attention to federal statutes that require the agency in an adjudication to provide an opportunity for a "hearing," but that do not expressly require an on-the-record determination. The lawyer must determine whether adjudications under the statute must comply with procedural due process requirements. If so, *Wong Yang Sung* indicates that the adjudication must also comply with the federal APA's formal adjudication requirements. The lawyer may find, however, that lower court case law in the relevant jurisdiction treats *Wong Yang Sung* as no longer good law. As a practical matter, such lower court case law may be controlling until the Court decides to address *Wong Yang Sung*'s continuing vitality.

3. The Adjudication Must Not Fall within One of the Exemptions Prescribed in Federal APA §§ 554(a)(1) through (a)(6)

Even if the agency legislation requires an adjudication "**to be determined on the record after opportunity for an agency hearing**," the adjudication is not subject to the formal adjudication requirements if it falls within an exemption. Section 554 creates six exemptions:

---

5 U.S.C. § 554. Adjudications

(a) This section applies, according to the provisions thereof, in every case of adjudication required by statute to be determined on the record after opportunity for an agency hearing, except to the extent that there is involved—

(1) a matter subject to a subsequent trial of the law and the facts de novo in a court;

(2) the selection or tenure of an employee, except a administrative law judge appointed under section 3105 of this title;

(3) proceedings in which decisions rest solely on inspections, tests, or elections;

(4) the conduct of military or foreign affairs functions;

(5) cases in which an agency is acting as an agent for a court; or

(6) the certification of worker representatives....

An adjudicatory matter that falls within one of these exemptions is generally exempt from § 554, as well as from §§ 556 and 557. Exempt adjudications, like other informal adjudications, will be governed by the procedural requirements, if any, of four main sources:

(1) the federal APA §§ 555 and 558;

(2) the agency legislation;

(3) the Due Process Clause; and

(4) the agency's procedural rules.

Below we briefly discuss each of the exemptions. The main objective of this discussion is to give you general familiarity with the scope and purpose of each.

a. "[A] [M]atter [S]ubject to a [S]ubsequent [T]rial of the [L]aw and the [F]acts de [N]ovo in a [C]ourt"

This exemption arises only when a statute authorizes someone dissatisfied with an agency's adjudication of a matter to have a court adjudicate the matter all over again. In that event, the court will hear evidence and make up its own mind about how to resolve any factual and legal disputes. The court will, at most, give some consideration to the agency's view of the facts, the legal issues, and the proper outcome, depending on the quality of the agency's handling of the matter. *See* AGM 43. Since the court will otherwise essentially start from scratch, however, it would not make sense to require the agency to follow the formal adjudication requirements. It would be a waste of time and effort.

This exemption is rare. An agency's decision in an adjudication is usually subject to judicial review, which is not the same as a judicial "re-do." Ordinarily, when the court reviews the agency's decision, the court reviews only the evidentiary material that the agency considered. The court does not hear new evidence. Indeed, an important principle of administrative law is that courts ordinarily review agency action based solely on the record before the agency. Moreover, on judicial review a court usually gives deference to the agency's factual determinations. The reviewing court doesn't make its own factual determinations.

Although it is rare for a statute to authorize de novo trial of facts that have already been determined by an agency, some important types of agency adjudications are subject to such de novo review and therefore fall within this first exemption. For instance, applicants for patents can get a trial de novo on their entitlement to a patent in federal district court, if they are dissatisfied with the decision of the Board of Patent Appeals and Interferences. *See* 35 U.S.C. § 145 (2012); *In re Gartside*, 203 F.3d 1305, 1313 (Fed. Cir. 2000). In addition, some adjudicatory decisions by the Internal Revenue Service are subject to de novo review in the U.S. Tax Court. *See Comm'r of Internal Revenue v. Neal*, 557 F.3d 1262 (11th Cir. 2009).

b. "[T]he [S]election or [T]enure of an [E]mployee, [E]xcept an [A]dministrative [L]aw [J]udge [A]ppointed under [S]ection 3105 of [T]his [T]itle"

This exemption frees federal agencies from following formal adjudication requirements when deciding on the selection and retention of agency employees. The legislative history of the APA indicates that the exemption reflects the broad discretion that the government has as an employer. AGM 44.

The exemption contains an exception for administrative law judges (ALJs). We explore the role of ALJs and their special job protections in Chapter 22.

c. "[P]roceedings in [W]hich [D]ecisions [R]est [S]olely on [I]nspections, [T]ests, or [E]lections"

As the Attorney General's Manual on the APA explained, decisions based on inspections, tests, or elections do not lend themselves to the trial-type hearing and decisionmaking process required by §§ 554, 556, and 557. AGM 44 (quoting legislative history).

d. "[T]he [C]onduct of [M]ilitary or [F]oreign [A]ffairs [F]unctions"

The government traditionally has broad discretion in military and foreign affairs. Thus, adjudications on those matters are exempt from the federal APA's formal adjudication requirements, just as rules on those matters are exempt from § 553's rulemaking requirements. AGM 45; *see also* 5 U.S.C. § 553(a)(1).

e. "[C]ases in [W]hich an [A]gency [I]s [A]cting as an [A]gent for a [C]ourt"

We do not know of any modern situations in which federal agencies act as agents for federal courts, and the legislative history of the APA leaves the scope and purpose of the exemption unclear.

f. "[T]he [C]ertification of [W]orker [R]epresentatives"

Certain federal statutes, including the National Labor Relations Act, provide for individuals or organizations (such as unions) to be selected by workers to represent those same workers. An agency gives effect to the worker's selection by certifying the result of the selection process. *See, e.g.*, 29 U.S.C. § 159(e) (2012). The selection is typically based on an election or other process that is not suited for formal adjudication procedures.

* * *

Section 554(a)'s exemptions can be overridden by a specific agency statute, so as to subject an otherwise-exempt agency adjudication to the formal adjudication requirements of §§ 554, 556, and 557. An example is a federal statute authorizing a federal agency to impose civil penalties and other sanctions for violations of federal mining laws. Many violations of the mining laws are detected through inspections of the mines. The owner or operator of a mine who contests a proposed sanction is entitled under the statute to "an opportunity for a hearing (in accordance with section 554 of Title, but *without regard to subsection (a)(3) of such section)*." 30 U.S.C. § 815(d) (2012) (emphasis added). The "without regard to" phrase subjects an agency adjudication on a proposed sanction to the formal adjudication requirements, even though the proposed sanction is based on an inspection and the process for imposing that sanction would therefore otherwise be exempt from § 554.

Exercise: Determining Whether an Agency Statute Triggers Formal Adjudication under the Federal APA

The Consumer Product Safety Commission has authority under its organic statute to determine whether a consumer product presents a "substantial product hazard." 15 U.S.C. § 2064 (2012). Please examine § 2064 and explain whether proceedings before the Commission under this provision must follow the federal APA's formal adjudication requirements.

E. Second Step, Part (b):
If the Federal APA Does Apply to the Agency under Analysis, and the Agency Action under Analysis Is an Adjudication, Does Federal APA §§ 555 or 558 Apply to This Adjudication?

A federal agency adjudication may be subject to the federal APA, even if it is not subject to the federal APA's formal adjudication provisions. Specifically, informal adjudications may be subject to two other sets of APA provisions. First, as discussed in Chapter 29 on judicial review, most federal agency actions, including agency decisions in informal adjudications, are subject to the APA's provision on judicial review, which are in §§ 701–706. Second, and relevant to our current focus, some informal adjudications are subject to some of the procedures in APA §§ 555 and 558.

Although applicable to informal adjudications, Sections 555 and 558 are not specifically aimed at agency adjudications. Section 555, entitled **"Ancillary matters,"** prescribes procedural rights that attach in various agency proceedings, including but not limited to formal and informal adjudications. Section 558 is entitled **"Imposition of sanctions; determination of application for licenses; suspension, revocation, and expiration of licenses."** As this title implies, § 558 primarily (but not exclusively) addresses licensing, which is a type of adjudication. *See* 5 U.S.C. § 551(6).

We will examine §§ 555 and 558 separately, in each case focusing on their application to informal adjudications.

1. § 555

a. Introduction

The U.S. Supreme Court has identified § 555 as a source of "minimal requirements" for "informal adjudication." *Pension Benefit Guar. Corp. v. LTV Corp.*, 496 U.S. 633, 655 (1990). Although § 555 imposes only "minimal requirements," administrative lawyers should know about § 555 because informal adjudication accounts for so much federal agency activity that affects people's legal rights.

Now is a good time to skim § 555. Before you do, though, you may find it helpful to keep two things in mind as you get acquainted with this quirky provision.

First, § 555 does not modify any other procedural requirements imposed elsewhere in §§ 551–559. This is made clear by § 555(a):

---

5 U.S.C. § 555. Ancillary matters

(a) This section applies, according to the provisions thereof, except as otherwise provided by this subchapter....

For example, § 555(e) requires an agency to give a **"brief statement"** of the grounds for denying any written application, petition, or other request in an agency proceeding. This "brief statement" requirement does not supersede the detailed requirements of § 557 for written decisions in formal rulemaking and formal adjudications. *See* 5 U.S.C. § 557(c). For many informal adjudications, however — which are not subject to § 557 — § 555(e) imposes an important, albeit minimal, written-explanation requirement.

Second, § 555 contains some easily confused, but distinct, terms for (1) who enjoys various rights, and (2) in what settings those rights exist. Some rights granted in § 555 extend to **"persons"**; others extend only to **"interested persons"**; still others extend only to **"parties."** Some rights granted in § 555 apply only in **"agency proceedings"**; other rights extend to other **"agency functions."** We mention this array of terms to help you begin to appreciate the array of agency activities to which § 555 applies, and the array of groups to which various aspects of § 555 applies.

You need not gain a complete grasp of all these terms at this point. The most important things to understand are that the terms do differ; they were selected with care for use in § 555; and three of them are defined in APA § 551: **"person,"** **"party,"** and **"agency proceeding."** 5 U.S.C. § 551(2), (3) & (12).

Skim § 555 with the idea of getting a general sense of the subjects it addresses. Below we lift out the parts of § 555 particularly relevant to informal adjudications.

b. § 555 Provisions Most Relevant to Informal Adjudications

Three parts of § 555 impose procedural requirements on informal adjudications, and one part provides a right to counsel, to help ensure agency compliance with the procedural requirements. In studying these aspects of § 555, your objective should be to understand both the nature and the scope of these requirements, meaning: What do the requirements involve? Do they apply not only in informal adjudications but also in other agency proceedings or in connection with other agency activities?

(i) Right to Appear with Counsel

Section 555(b) creates a right to counsel in its first two sentences:

---

5 U.S.C. § 555. Ancillary matters ...

(b) A person compelled to appear in person before an agency or representative thereof is entitled to be accompanied, represented, and advised by counsel or, if permitted by the agency, by other qualified representative. A party is entitled to appear in person or by or with counsel or other duly qualified representative in an agency proceeding....

The first sentence creates a right to appear with counsel when an agency uses a subpoena or similar compulsory order to compel someone to appear before the agency, usually to give evidence in an agency investigation or at an adjudicatory hearing. The second sentence creates a right to appear with counsel in an **"agency proceeding."** 5 U.S.C. § 551(12). The term **"agency proceeding"** includes formal and informal adjudications (as well as rulemakings), but not agency investigations. Thus, a person's right to appear with counsel in an agency investigation arises only when the agency compels the person to appear in that investigation. In contrast, in an adjudication a person has a right to appear with counsel (if the person is a "party") even if the person's appearance is not compelled.

A person's right to have a lawyer in an informal adjudication is important because the lawyer can help the person use the three procedural rights discussed next.

(ii) Right of Informal Appearance

First, Section 555(b) gives **"an interested person"** a qualified right to **"appear"** informally before the agency or its officials in an agency proceeding or in connection with an agency function. This gives someone a chance to meet with the agency informally. This right to appear before the agency informally is granted by § 555(b)'s third sentence:

---

5 U.S.C. § 555. Ancillary matters ...

(b) ... So far as the orderly conduct of public business permits, an interested person may appear before an agency or its responsible employees for the presentation, adjustment, or determination of an issue, request, or controversy in a proceeding, whether interlocutory, summary, or otherwise, or in connection with an agency function....

The Attorney General's Manual on the APA explains this provision:

> It means, for example, that upon request any person should be allowed, where this is feasible, to present his reasons as to why a particular loan or benefit should be made or granted to [her or] him. It would also seem to mean that [she or] he can present [her or] his reasons as to why a particular controversy should be settled informally rather than in formal proceedings with attendant publicity.

AGM 64. Roughly speaking, § 555(b)'s third sentence entitles someone with a matter before an agency, including an informal adjudication, to communicate about that matter with a live human being in the agency who is in a position to influence the matter. That entitlement, however, has restrictions.

First, the entitlement exists only "[s]o far as **the orderly conduct of public business permits.**" The quoted language gives agencies so much discretion that their decisions about how to honor this entitlement are probably not subject to judicial review. Instead, they are likely to be regarded as decisions that are "**committed to agency discretion by law,**" of which the federal APA precludes judicial review. 5 U.S.C. §701(a)(2) (2012); *see also infra* Chapter 29.D.2.a(ii) (discussing this preclusion provision).

Furthermore, §555(b) entitles a person to appear "**before an agency or its responsible employees.**" This means that the person is not necessarily entitled to meet with the head of the agency. Instead, the person is entitled only to "confer with an official of such status that [she or] he knows the agency's policy, and is able to bring unusual or meritorious cases to the attention of the officials who shape the policy or make final decisions." AGM 63.

Finally, the right to "**appear before**" an agency official does not necessarily entail a face-to-face meeting. The "**orderly conduct of public business**" may permit only a phone call or an email exchange between the person and an agency official.

Though the right to appear informally is a weak right, if exercised properly it can make a big difference. It can enable a person with a matter before an agency to make a personal connection with someone in the agency who is in a position to influence the outcome. The personal connection can make the difference between victory and defeat.

(iii) Agency Duty to Conclude Matters within a Reasonable Time

Section 555(b) requires an agency to conclude a matter reasonably promptly. Here is the relevant statutory text:

---

5 U.S.C. § 555. Ancillary matters ...

(b) ... With due regard for the convenience and necessity of the parties or their representatives and within a reasonable time, each agency shall proceed to conclude a matter presented to it....

This agency duty to conclude a matter within a reasonable time applies to informal adjudications, as well as other agency matters such as rulemaking and formal adjudication.

The agency duty to act reasonably promptly is sometimes judicially enforceable under APA §706(1). Section 706(1) of the federal APA authorizes "**a reviewing court**" to "**compel agency action unlawfully withheld or unreasonably delayed.**" 5 U.S.C. §706(1). As discussed in Chapter 35, however, for various reasons it is hard to get a court to compel agency action even in cases of long agency delay. Section 555(b) does give lawyers a legal basis for objecting to agency foot dragging in informal adjudications and other proceedings.

(iv) Prompt Notice of, and Brief Statement Explaining, Agency Denial of a Written Request

Section 555(e) requires a federal agency to give prompt notice of, and to explain, its denial of "**a written application, petition, or other request of an interested person made in connection with any agency proceeding.**" The complete text of §555(e) follows:

5 U.S.C. § 555. Ancillary matters ...

(e) Prompt notice shall be given of the denial in whole or in part of a written application, petition, or other request of an interested person made in connection with any agency proceeding. Except in affirming a prior denial or when the denial is self-explanatory, the notice shall be accompanied by a brief statement of the grounds for denial.

The requirements in § 555(e) apply only to agency denials of written requests. Thus, for example, when a federal agency denies a request for a loan or government license or benefit, the agency has to explain the denial. Likewise, § 555(e) requires an agency to explain its denial of a petition for rulemaking. *E.g.*, *Massachusetts v. EPA*, 549 U.S. 497, 527 (2007).

An explanation serves two purposes. It ensures the agency considered the request. In addition, it provides a basis for seeking judicial review of the agency's denial. The explanation may reveal substantive or procedural flaws in the agency's decision.

(v) Summary

In sum, § 555 creates a right to counsel and three procedural rights in some informal adjudications. The person who will be affected by the informal adjudication can informally appear before the agency to plead his or her case. The agency must conclude the matter within a reasonable time. If the agency denies a person's request (e.g., for a government loan, license, or benefit), the agency has to notify the person of the denial and explain it. These are indeed, as the Court described them, "minimal" requirements for informal adjudications. *Pension Benefit Guar. Corp. v. LTV Corp.*, 496 U.S. 633, 655 (1990). But they are better than nothing, and lawyers representing clients in informal adjudications should know about them.

Exercise: Exercising Rights under § 555 of the Federal APA in Informal Adjudications

This exercise challenges you to think about how, as a practical matter, people involved in informal adjudications with federal agencies exercise rights under § 555.

Consider an informal adjudication with which you may be familiar. Many students in college and graduate schools apply for loans and other types of financial aid from the federal government. They do so by completing a "Free Application for Federal Student Aid" (FAFSA), by which they apply for funding under several federal education funding programs. The FAFSAs are processed by the Federal Student Aid Office (FSA) in the U.S. Department of Education. In fiscal year 2010, FSA processed more than 21 million FAFSAs, according to its annual report. The financial aid award to an individual student is administered by the school that the student attends. The schools ensure their students' continued eligibility for financial aid.

1. First, make sure you understand why FSA's decision on an individual FAFSA is an informal adjudication.

2. Then consider when a student who has applied for financial aid might need the four rights granted under § 555.

3. Finally, what factors affect the way in which the FSA honors those rights?

2. § 558

a. Introduction

Here is the complete text of § 558 of the federal APA:

---

5 U.S.C. § 558. Imposition of sanctions; determination of applications for licenses; suspension, revocation, and expiration of licenses

(a) This section applies, according to the provisions thereof, to the exercise of a power or authority.

(b) A sanction may not be imposed or a substantive rule or order issued except within jurisdiction delegated to the agency and as authorized by law.

(c) When application is made for a license required by law, the agency, with due regard for the rights and privileges of all the interested parties or adversely affected persons and within a reasonable time, shall set and complete proceedings required to be conducted in accordance with sections 556 and 557 of this title or other proceedings required by law and shall make its decision. Except in cases of willfulness or those in which public health, interest, or safety requires otherwise, the withdrawal, suspension, revocation, or annulment of a license is lawful only if, before the institution of agency proceedings therefor, the licensee has been given —

(1) notice by the agency in writing of the facts or conduct which may warrant the action; and

(2) opportunity to demonstrate or achieve compliance with all lawful requirements.

When the licensee has made timely and sufficient application for a renewal or a new license in accordance with agency rules, a license with reference to an activity of a continuing nature does not expire until the application has been finally determined by the agency.

You can think of § 558 as having two parts. The first part consists of subsections (a) and (b). Together, they express a fundamental principle: An agency must act within the scope of its authority. This principle applies not only to "**order[s]**" and "**substantive rule[s]**" but also to "**sanction[s]**," a term that § 551(10) defines to include many different adverse agency actions—not just the imposition of penalties or fines. The second part of § 558 is subsection (c), which specifically addresses licensing. Because licensing is a kind of adjudication, we focus on subsection (c) in the next section.

b. § 558's Requirements for Licensing

Federal laws require licenses for many activities, and so many federal agencies engage in "**licensing**," as defined in the federal APA. (Be sure to review that definition, found in 5 U.S.C. § 551(9), as well as the definition of "**license**" in § 551(8).) For example, the Bureau of Land Management issues grazing permits under the Taylor Grazing Act that allow people to graze livestock on federal land. The Environmental Protection Agency issues permits under the Clean Water Act allowing companies to discharge limited amounts of pollutants into the water. The Federal Communications Commission issues licenses for telecommunications activities involving radio, television, the internet, and telephones. The Food and Drug Administration licenses drugs and medical devices. The Federal Energy Regulation Commission licenses hydroelectric power projects. Licensing is one of the main types of adjudication in which federal agencies—as well as state and local agencies, for that matter—engage. Many administrative lawyers represent agencies or private clients in licensing proceedings.

Section 558(c) has three sentences, each of which addresses a separate aspect of licensing by federal agencies:

- The first sentence addresses applications for licenses.
- The second sentence addresses suspension or revocation of existing licenses.
- The third sentence addresses renewals of existing licenses.

The first sentence addresses the timeframe for agency action on a license application. The sentence's main purpose is to require an agency to act with reasonable speed. The agency cannot act so hastily, however, that it fails to give "**due regard for the rights and privileges of all the interested parties or adversely affected persons.**" 5 U.S.C. § 558(c).

The first sentence does not prescribe procedures for ruling on license applications. It just tells the agency to complete all proceedings "**required to be conducted**" by the laws applicable to a particular license application. The first sentence recognizes that, for some license applications, the agency may be required by applicable law to follow the formal adjudication requirements in §§ 556 and 557. The first sentence itself, however, does not require the agency to follow those requirements. *See, e.g., City of West Chicago v. U.S. Nuclear Regulatory Comm'n*, 701 F.2d 632, 644 (7th Cir. 1983). A license-application proceeding requires formal adjudication procedures only if a statute external to § 558 requires it. To clarify this important limitation, it would have been better if § 558(c) had been written to say that, when someone applies for a license, the agency "**shall set and complete proceedings,** *if any*, **required to be conducted in accordance with sections 556 and 557 …**"

The second sentence of § 558(c) gives existing licensees an important right: Before the agency can begin a proceeding to suspend or revoke the license, the agency must give the licensee written notice of the "**facts or conduct**" that may warrant suspension or revocation, followed by an "**opportunity to demonstrate or achieve compliance with all lawful requirements.**" This opportunity offers two alternatives. First, if the licensee believes it is in compliance, the licensee has a chance to prove compliance. Alternatively, if the licensee believes it is out of compliance, it has a chance to achieve compliance. The latter opportunity to "**achieve compliance**" gives the licensee a "second chance" to comply with all requirements for keeping the license.

The "second chance" opportunity has limits. It does not apply "**in cases of willfulness.**" "Willfulness" seems to encompass situations in which a licensee deliberately violates the law. The second-chance opportunity also does not apply in cases "**in which public health, interest, or safety requires otherwise.**" These cases probably include those in which a licensee, after getting an opportunity to achieve compliance, thereafter repeatedly falls out of compliance. As one court put it, "The purpose of § 558(c) is to give permittees a 'second chance,' not a third, fourth, and fifth chance." *Buckingham v. Secretary of U.S. Dep't of Agric.*, 603 F.3d 1073, 1086 (9th Cir. 2010).

The third sentence of § 558(c) protects a person who holds a license for "**an activity of an ongoing nature.**" That person is protected from having the license expire because of agency delay in acting on the person's "**timely and sufficient application for**" renewal or for a new license to replace the existing one. The agency may "**finally determin[e]**" that the application should be granted or should be denied. But either way, the existing license does not expire until the agency makes that final determination. This protection has particular importance for people whose livelihood depends on having a valid license in effect at all times.

Because licensing plays such an important role in state administrative law, this is a good place to mention (while the federal APA provision is fresh in your mind) that many state APAs, like the federal APA, include provisions specifically addressing licenses. License provisions in many state APAs, like § 558, address the issues of (1) agency proceedings to suspend or revoke licenses; and (2) agency delay in acting upon applications for licenses for activities of a continuing nature.

The 2010 Model State APA addresses both issues in the following provisions. After you read them, go back and compare them with § 558. You will find important differences, which illustrate the need to study the particular APA provision that governs any licensing problems that you encounter in your practice.

2010 Model State APA, § 419. Licenses . . .

(a) If a licensee has made timely and sufficient application for the renewal of a license or a new license for any activity of a continuing nature, the existing license does not expire until the agency takes final action on the application and, if the application is denied or the terms of the new license are limited, until the last day for seeking review of the agency order or a later date fixed by the reviewing court.

(b) A revocation, suspension, annulment, or withdrawal of a license is not lawful unless, before the institution of agency proceedings, the agency notifies the licensee of facts or conduct that warrants the intended action, and the licensee is given an opportunity to show compliance with all lawful requirements for the retention of the license. If the agency finds that imminent peril to public health, safety, or welfare requires emergency action and incorporates a finding to that effect in its order, summary suspension of a license may be ordered pending proceedings for revocation or other action. These proceedings must be promptly instituted and concluded.

The takeaway from this discussion is that adjudications involving licenses, including informal adjudications, often are subject to APA provisions specifically governing licenses.

Exercise: License Provisions

1. What, do you suppose, is the purpose of the provision in § 419(a) of the 2010 Model State APA stating that—if an agency finally denies a renewal or new license for any activity of an ongoing nature, or restricts the terms of the new or renewed license—the existing license does not expire "until the last day for seeking review of the agency order or a later date fixed by order of the reviewing court"? The aim of this question is to get you to start thinking about what it means for an agency to "finally" determine an application for renewal or a new license. Does "final" really mean final?

2. Suppose you represent a roofing contractor who has a license from the State to engage in roof replacement and repair. Also suppose the state agency that

licenses roofing contractors has given your client notice of on-the-job conduct by your clients' employees because of which the agency intends to revoke your client's license. Which provision is more favorable to your client: § 558(c)'s second sentence, or 2010 Model State APA § 419(e)? Why? (We realize that § 558(c) is a provision of federal law, but for purposes of this question suppose that you might find an identical provision in some state APAs.)

F. Third Step:
If the Federal APA Does Apply to the Agency Adjudication under Analysis, How Does the APA Interact with Other Laws Applicable to the Adjudication?

You must identify the agency legislation that governs an agency adjudication to determine if the APA applies to that adjudication. So far we have discussed three possibilities:

(1) The agency legislation exempts the adjudication from the APA.

(2) The agency legislation triggers the federal APA's formal adjudication requirements.

(3) The agency legislation does not exempt the adjudication from the APA but also does not trigger the federal APA's formal adjudication requirements.

In any of these situations, the agency legislation itself may prescribe procedural requirements for the agency adjudication. In the first situation, however, you do not have to synthesize the procedural requirements in the agency legislation with those of the APA, because the latter are inapplicable. In the second and third situations, however, you may have to do such a synthesis of—and, perhaps, to reconcile inconsistencies or outright conflicts between—the agency statute and the APA.

When reconciling procedural requirements of the agency legislation and the federal APA, the key provision is federal APA § 559. Section 559 has two relevant sentences:

5 U.S.C. § 559. Effect on other laws; effect of subsequent statute

[The provisions of the APA] do not limit or repeal additional requirements imposed by statute or otherwise recognized by law.... Subsequent statute may not be held to supersede or modify [the APA], except to the extent that it does so expressly.

Under § 559's first sentence, the agency legislation may *add* to the procedural requirements of the APA. Under § 559's second sentence, the agency legislation may *modify* or *displace* the APA's procedural requirements, but statutes enacted after the APA (in 1946) may do so only to the extent that they do so expressly.

An example of a statute that adds to the federal APA's procedural requirements for agency adjudications is 33 U.S.C. § 1319 (2012). Section 1319 authorizes the EPA and the

Secretary of the Army to assess civil penalties for certain violations of the Clean Water Act. Section 1319 divides the penalties into two classes, depending on their severity:

---

33 U.S.C. § 1319. Enforcement …

(g) Administrative penalties

(1) Violations

Whenever on the basis of any information available—

(A) the Administrator finds that any person has violated section 1311, 1312, 1316, 1317, 1318, 1328, or 1345 of this title, or has violated any permit condition or limitation implementing any of such sections in a permit issued under section 1342 of this title by the Administrator or by a State, or in a permit issued under section 1344 of this title by a State, or

(B) the Secretary of the Army (hereinafter in this subsection referred to as the "Secretary") finds that any person has violated any permit condition or limitation in a permit issued under section 1344 of this title by the Secretary,

the Administrator or Secretary, as the case may be, may, after consultation with the State in which the violation occurs, assess a class I civil penalty or a class II civil penalty under this subsection.

(2) Classes of penalties

(A) Class I

The amount of a class I civil penalty under paragraph (1) may not exceed $10,000 per violation, except that the maximum amount of any class I civil penalty under this subparagraph shall not exceed $25,000. Before issuing an order assessing a civil penalty under this subparagraph, the Administrator or the Secretary, as the case may be, shall give to the person to be assessed such penalty written notice of the Administrator's or Secretary's proposal to issue such order and the opportunity to request, within 30 days of the date the notice is received by such person, a hearing on the proposed order. Such hearing shall not be subject to section 554 or 556 of Title 5, but shall provide a reasonable opportunity to be heard and to present evidence.

(B) Class II

The amount of a class II civil penalty under paragraph (1) may not exceed $10,000 per day for each day during which the violation continues; except that the maximum amount of any class II civil penalty under this subparagraph shall not exceed $125,000. Except as otherwise provided in this subsection, a class II civil penalty shall be assessed and collected in the same manner, and subject to the same provisions, as in the case of civil penalties assessed and collected after notice and opportunity for a hearing on the record in accordance with section 554 of Title 5. The Administrator and the Secretary may issue rules for discovery procedures for hearings under this subparagraph….

Assume (as is true) that the EPA and the Secretary of the Army are agencies subject to the APA. From prior material in this chapter and this book, you should be able to answer these questions:

(1) Why is a proceeding to impose a Class I or Class II civil penalty an **"adjudication,"** as defined in the APA?

(2) Why is a proceeding to impose a Class I civil penalty an informal adjudication?

(3) Why is a proceeding to impose a Class II civil penalty a formal adjudication?

As an informal adjudication, a proceeding to impose a Class I civil penalty is subject to the requirements of APA § 555. Section 1319(g)(2)(A) adds to § 555's requirements by requiring the agency to "provide a reasonable opportunity to be heard and to present evidence."

As a formal adjudication, a proceeding to impose a Class II civil penalty is subject to the requirements of APA §§ 554, 556, and 557. Section 555 also applies, to the extent it is consistent with §§ 554, 556, and 557. In addition, both proceedings to impose Class II penalties and proceedings to impose Class I penalties are subject to the following public notice-and-comment procedures in § 1319(g)(4):

---

33 U.S.C. § 1319. Enforcement . . .

(g) Administrative penalties . . .

(4) Rights of interested persons

(A) Public notice

Before issuing an order assessing a civil penalty under this subsection the Administrator or Secretary, as the case may be, shall provide public notice of and reasonable opportunity to comment on the proposed issuance of such order.

(B) Presentation of evidence

Any person who comments on a proposed assessment of a penalty under this subsection shall be given notice of any hearing held under this subsection and of the order assessing such penalty. In any hearing held under this subsection, such person shall have a reasonable opportunity to be heard and to present evidence.

(C) Rights of interested persons to a hearing

If no hearing is held under paragraph (2) before issuance of an order assessing a penalty under this subsection, any person who commented on the proposed assessment may petition, within 30 days after the issuance of such order, the Administrator or Secretary, as the case may be, to set aside such order and to provide a hearing on the penalty. If the evidence presented by the petitioner in support of the petition is material and was not considered in the issuance of the order, the Administrator or Secretary shall immediately set aside such order and provide a hearing in accordance with paragraph (2)(A) in the case of a class I civil penalty and paragraph (2)(B) in the case of a class II civil penalty. If the Administrator or Secretary denies a hearing under this subparagraph, the Administrator or Secretary shall provide to the petitioner, and publish in the Federal Register, notice of and the reasons for such denial. . . .

This provision adds procedural requirements resembling those of informal rulemaking under APA § 553. A member of the public, by commenting on a proposed civil penalty order, becomes entitled to participate in the hearing provided for in § 1319(g)(2), which was reproduced in relevant part above. These procedural additions to the APA's adjudication requirements are authorized under APA § 559, which states that the APA does not **"limit** or repeal *additional* requirements imposed by statute." 5 U.S.C. § 559 (2012) (emphasis added).

Section 559 of the federal APA also says that a subsequent statute — i.e., a statute enacted after the APA was enacted in 1946 — may **"supersede or modify"** the APA's requirements, if it **"does so expressly."** 5 U.S.C. § 559. For example, in a series of appropriation acts Congress authorized federal hearing officers who were not Administrative Law Judges to preside at hearings on claims for benefits under the Black Lung Benefits Act. The lower federal courts relied on APA § 559 to upheld these appropriation acts against challenges based on the APA, which generally requires ALJs to preside at hearings in formal adjudications. See, *e.g.*, *Director, Office of Workmen's Compensation Program v. Alabama*, 560 F.2d 710, 720 (5th Cir. 1977) ("Because the language of … the appropriation acts expressly modifies the administrative law judge requirement of [the APA], the acts do not contravene 5 U.S.C. § 559."). Congress ultimately enacted permanent legislation requiring ALJs to conduct these hearings, thus eliminating the modification expressly effected by the prior appropriation acts. 33 U.S.C. § 919(d) (2012).

In sum, a federal agency adjudication will be either exempt from the federal APA or subject to it. If the adjudication is subject to the federal APA, the adjudication will be either subject to the APA's formal adjudication requirements or not subject to those requirements. Whether or not the agency adjudication is subject to the APA's formal adjudication requirements, the adjudication may be subject to the minimal requirements of APA § 555 and, if it concerns licensing, to § 558. Besides considering the APA's procedural requirements for the adjudication under analysis, the lawyer must also determine whether the agency legislation adds to or modifies APA requirements. The lawyer also should identify all agency rules applicable to the adjudication.

G. Determining the Applicability of a State APA to a State Agency Adjudication

The same basic framework used to determine the applicability of the federal APA to a federal agency adjudication can be used to determine the applicability of a state APA to a state agency adjudication:

(1) Does the APA apply to this agency?

(2) If so, does the APA apply to the agency adjudication under analysis?

(3) If the APA does apply to the agency adjudication under analysis, how does the APA interact with other laws applicable to the agency adjudication under analysis?

As is true when applied to a federal agency adjudication, when applied to a state agency adjudication, the tricky step in this three-part framework is the second. It helps at the outset to know why this second step is tricky.

Most state APAs have procedures for agency adjudications that are required by law to include an opportunity for a trial-like hearing. States differ, however, in their approach to determining *when* "the law" requires an opportunity for a hearing in an agency adjudication. Roughly speaking, States take one of three approaches:

- Some States take the same approach as federal law. Under that approach, the state APA itself does not identify when an opportunity for a trial-like hearing is required.

Instead, you must look outside the state APA—ordinarily to the agency legislation—to see if a trial-like hearing is required. This approach is sometimes called the "external law" approach.

- In a second group of States, the state APA itself identifies when an opportunity for a trial-like hearing is required.

- A third group of States takes a hybrid approach, under which either the state APA or external laws may require an opportunity for a trial-like hearing in a particular agency adjudication.

The first ("external law") approach is illustrated in the 1961 Model State APA. The 1961 Model State APA uses the term "contested case" to mean roughly what is meant by the term "formal adjudication" in federal law. The 1961 Model State APA defines "contested case" as follows:

1961 Model State APA § 1. [Definitions]

As used in this Act: …

(2) "contested case" means a proceeding, including but not restricted to ratemaking, [price fixing], and licensing, in which the legal rights, duties, or privileges of a party are required by law to be determined by an agency after an opportunity for hearing.…

This definition requires examination of "law" outside the APA to determine whether it requires "an opportunity for hearing." The "law" may include a constitutional or statutory provision. If the external "law" does require an opportunity for a hearing, the 1961 Model State APA prescribes a set of procedural requirements, including requirements for a trial-like hearing and a decision based exclusively on the record.

The second approach is taken by, for example, North Carolina and Florida. Under the second approach, the APA itself determines when an opportunity for a trial-like hearing is required in a particular agency adjudication. For example, the North Carolina APA generally requires an opportunity for a trial-like hearing in any agency adjudication that cannot be settled informally. *See* N.C. Gen Stat. §§ 150B-22, 150B-23 & 150B-25 (West, Westlaw through S.L. 2012-1 of 2011 Reg. Sess.). The Florida APA creates an opportunity to be heard in "all proceedings in which the substantial interests of a party are determined by an agency." Fla. Stat. § 120.569(1) (West, Westlaw through Mar. 29, 2012). The nature of the opportunity to be heard under Florida law depends on whether or not a proceeding involves disputed issues of material fact. If so, the Florida APA requires an elaborate, oral, evidentiary hearing. *Id.* § 120.57(1)(b). If there are no disputed issues of material fact, the Florida APA gives parties an opportunity to submit oral or written evidence. *Id.* § 120.57(2). What North Carolina and Florida have in common is that their APAs themselves, rather than external laws, determine the availability of an adjudicatory hearing.

Some States take neither of the approaches described above. For example, Oregon takes a hybrid approach. The Oregon APA itself requires an opportunity for a hearing in some categories of adjudications and prescribes the procedures, including the hearing procedures, for those adjudications. Those same procedural requirements also govern adjudications in which a law external to the Oregon APA requires an opportunity for a hearing. Oregon's hybrid approach is created by the Oregon APA's definition of "contested case":

Or. Rev. Stat. § 183.310. Definitions . . .

(2) (a) "Contested case" means a proceeding before an agency:

(A) In which the individual legal rights, duties or privileges of specific parties are required by statute or Constitution to be determined only after an agency hearing at which such specific parties are entitled to appear and be heard;

(B) Where the agency has discretion to suspend or revoke a right or privilege of a person;

(C) For the suspension, revocation or refusal to renew or issue a license where the licensee or applicant for a license demands such hearing; or

(D) Where the agency by rule or order provides for hearings substantially of the character required by ORS 183.415, 183.417, 183.425, 183.450, 183.460 and 183.470. . . .

This provision in the Oregon APA requires, in (2)(A) and (2)(D), examination of external laws to determine whether they require a hearing. The provision itself, in (2)(B) and (2)(C), prescribes situations in which a hearing is required. In any event, hearings required under an external law or the provision itself must comply with hearing procedures prescribed elsewhere in the Oregon APA.

Having sampled the different state approaches, keep in mind that, regardless of a State's approach, the lawyer analyzing a state agency adjudication must always specifically analyze the applicability of the state APA, because state APAs invariably prescribe procedures for certain agency adjudications (contested cases) and are invariably designed to be broadly applicable.

H. Chapter 21 Wrap Up and Look Ahead

From this chapter, you should be able to determine the applicability of the APA to an agency adjudication.

To make that determination for a federal agency adjudication, you must examine the agency legislation and (if *Wong Yang Sung* is still good law) the doctrine of procedural due process. The agency legislation or procedural due process may trigger the federal APA's formal adjudication requirements. Even if those requirements do not apply, a federal agency adjudication may be subject to procedural requirements in federal APA §§ 555 or 558.

Determining the applicability of a state APA to a state agency adjudication requires an analysis like that required under the federal APA. Many state APAs, however, take different approaches. Under any approach, you will have to examine the agency legislation as well as the APA.

The federal APA and most state APAs have procedures for trial-type hearings in certain agency adjudications. The federal APA refers to adjudications in which these procedures are required as "formal adjudications." Under many state APAs, they are known as "contested cases."

Moving forward, we will assume that the APA's formal adjudication (contested case) procedures apply to an agency adjudication and, in the next three chapters, explore those requirements.

Exercise: Keeping Sight of the Forest While Continuing Your Scrutiny of the Trees

Please review the problem solving framework that was introduced in Chapter 2 and that is reproduced below, and identify where in the framework the material in this chapter should go.

1. In taking the action under analysis, has the agency acted under a valid source of power?

   a. Is there a source of power? There are three possible sources of power for agency action:

      i.   constitutional

      ii. statutory

      iii. executive-branch material

   b. Is the source of power valid?

2. If the agency has acted under a valid source of power, has the agency obeyed limits on, and requirements for exercising, that power? (For simplicity's sake, we use the term "limits" to include requirements.)

   a. Internal limits

      i. Internal substantive limits

      ii. Internal procedural limits

   b. External limits

      i. External substantive limits

      ii. External procedural limits

3. If the agency lacks power to take the action, or has not obeyed limits on, or requirements for exercising, that power, what can be done about it? There are five sources of control:

   a. agency

   b. judicial branch

   c. legislative branch

   d. executive branch

   e. the people

Chapter Problem Revisited

This problem is based on *Aageson Grain & Cattle v. U.S. Department of Agriculture*, 500 F.3d 1038 (9th Cir. 2007). Before reading that case, determine how many of these questions and issues you identified as relevant to the applicability of the Federal APA's formal adjudication requirements:

1. There doesn't seem much question that the Division falls within the APA's definition of "**agency**." 5 U.S.C. §551(1) (2012). You would still have to examine the entire agency legislation of the Division and the USDA to

determine whether the Division in particular or the USDA as a whole is exempted the Division from the APA. *See* 7 U.S.C. §§ 6991–7002 (2012) (Division's organic statute); 7 U.S.C. §§ 2201–2279h (2012) (USDA's organic statute).

2.   The proceeding on your client's application for disaster relief fits the APA's definition of "**adjudication.**" 5 U.S.C. § 551(7). Again, you would have to consult the agency legislation to determine whether it exempted hearings before the Division from the APA.

3.   Assuming the federal APA applies to this adjudication, the question becomes whether this is an "**adjudication required by statute to be determined on the record after opportunity for an agency hearing.**" *Id.* § 554(a). (This case does not fall within any of the exemptions from § 554 listed in § 554(a)(1) through (6).)

4.   The agency legislation, in § 6997(b), requires an opportunity for a hearing. But § 6997 does not in so many words require the hearing officer to base the decision solely on the hearing record. Even so, such a requirement can fairly be inferred from § 6997(c)(3), which requires the hearing record to remain open for post-hearing information relevant to the decision. This provision would seem unnecessary unless the hearing officer were bound to base his or her decision on that record. You would want to research case law at this stage of the analysis to see if it addresses whether the agency legislation triggers formal adjudication procedures.

5.   You might wonder in light of this chapter's discussion of *Wong Yang Sung v. McGrath*, 339 U.S. 33 (1950), whether the statute in this chapter problem should be interpreted to trigger formal adjudication in order to ensure due process. If you have studied the due process material in Chapter 20, you might have remembered that it is unsettled whether an applicant for government benefits has a property interest in benefits or the claim for benefits before the government has found the applicant eligible for those benefits. If not, then your clients have no due process rights.

6.   You can probably appreciate the importance of determining whether attorney's fees are available for a successful appeal. Since your clients are seeking disaster relief, they may not be able to afford an appeal. Furthermore, an appeal might not make economic sense, depending on how much disaster relief they might receive.

Professional Development Reflection Questions

Surveys of law students suggest that, when choosing a law school, many future law students consider the school's location. Location may also influence the choice of lawyers deciding what legal job they will take. This makes sense. A person's surroundings inevitably affect the person's mood and can affect other issues related to qualify of life, such as access to friends and family and to cultural and recreational opportunities.

As a law student you must consider location at least to the extent of choosing the State in which you will initially seek admission to practice. That is the State whose bar exam you will take. Once you are licensed to practice in a State, you can seek to be admitted to practice before various federal courts and agencies, usually without having to take a separate bar exam. (The best-known exception is the patent bar exam, required to represent people applying for patents or prosecuting them before the U.S. Patent and Trademark Office.) To cite a typical example, the Consumer Product Safety Commission authorizes people in adjudications before it to be represented by "[a]ny attorney at law who is admitted to practice before any United States court or before the highest court of any State, the District of Columbia, or any territory or commonwealth of the United States." 16 C.F.R. § 1025.64 (2012). Of course, the Commission also has authority to disqualify from appearing before it attorneys who misbehave. *Id.* § 1025.66.

With that background, please consider these questions:

1. In what State or States are you considering initially seeking admission to practice law? What's your rationale for that choice (or those choices)?

2. Reflecting on the agencies you've encountered so far, in this book or your other experiences, what agencies, if any, appeal to you as possible ones before which you would like to practice, or which you would like to represent? It may help you answer this question to identify areas of law that interest you and that are administered by agencies.

3. Are any of the agencies you identified in Question 2 located in the State or States where you are considering seeking admission to practice? Remember that many federal agencies have regional offices outside of Washington, D.C., and of course you will find state, tribal, and local agencies throughout the country. You don't have to live in Washington, D.C., or a state capital to work for, or appear before, an agency.

Chapter 22

Formal Adjudications under an APA — Initiation and Prehearing Procedures

Overview

Chapter 21 showed you how to tell if a federal statute triggers formal adjudication under the federal APA. Chapter 21 also discussed how to determine whether a state APA's "contested case" provisions apply to a state agency adjudication. This chapter begins an examination of the procedural requirements for formal adjudications under the federal APA and contested cases under state APAs. Specifically, this chapter examines the procedures leading up to the formal hearing. Chapter 23 examines procedural requirements for the hearing itself. Finally, Chapter 24 examines decisionmaking requirements after the hearing.

This chapter's sections are entitled:

A. Context for Examining the Federal APA's Formal Adjudication Requirements

B. Stages of a Formal Adjudication under the APA

C. Initiation of a Formal Adjudication under the Federal APA

D. Prehearing Procedures in Formal Adjudications under the Federal APA

E. Initiation and Prehearing Procedures in Contested Cases under a State APA

F. Chapter 22 Wrap Up and Look Ahead

Chapter Problem

One morning you come into your office to find the following recorded phone message from a client. This client owns a specialty metal fabrication plant.

> Good morning, Counselor. Could you please call me back at your earliest convenience? I had one of my periodic visits from the OSHA [Occupational Safety and Health Administration] inspectors yesterday, and this time the inspectors found problems that they said they were probably going to cite me for. I've never been in trouble with OSHA before, so I have no idea what kind of trouble I'm in for. So call me back as soon as you can. Thanks!

You promptly call the client back and learn that the OSHA inspectors were concerned that some employees were not wearing adequate protective gear and that the lighting in one area of the plant was inadequate. The client is highly motivated to address any safety problems, for the sake of the employees and the company's reputation. The client wants your help avoiding any penalties from OSHA.

You know two things going in. First, your client is subject to OSHA regulation because the client does fabrication work for customers outside the State, including international customers. *See* 29 U.S.C. §§ 652(5) & 654 (2012). Second, although the Occupational Safety and Health Act (OSH Act) allows States voluntarily to adopt programs to enforce the federal OSHA standards (under a cooperative federalism arrangement), your client is in a State that does not administer the OSH Act, leaving it instead to the federal agency, OSHA.

Now you must work out a research plan, sensitive to your client's budget and the seemingly modest nature of the suspected violations. What questions do you have to answer, and where do you look for those answers?

A. Context for Examining the Federal APA's Formal Adjudication Requirements

Though we will focus on the federal APA's procedural requirements for formal adjudication, it is rare for a federal agency's formal adjudication to be governed solely by those requirements. Instead, additional procedural requirements for a federal agency's formal adjudication can come from: (1) the agency legislation; (2) the agency's procedural rules for formal adjudications; and (3) the doctrine of procedural due process. Thus, in formal adjudications as in most other agency proceedings, there may be a web of relevant law for the lawyer to master.

Accordingly, while we will focus on federal APA requirements for formal adjudications in this and the next two chapters, we will point out the aspects of formal adjudications that are often also shaped by agency legislation or agency rules. We will also flag aspects of formal adjudications in which procedural due process has influenced the drafting or interpretation of APA provisions.

B. Stages of a Formal Adjudication under the APA

We divide the formal adjudication process into five stages, to help you organize your understanding of it. The five stages are:

(1) initiation of the adjudication

(2) prehearing procedures

(3) the hearing

(4) the decision of the official who presided at the hearing

(5) administrative review of the presiding official's decision

These five stages occur in both formal adjudications under the federal APA and contested cases under most state APAs.

Let us illustrate the five stages with a typical formal adjudication by a federal agency. The Federal Trade Commission can initiate a formal adjudication to order a company to cease and desist an unfair trade practice. The adjudication typically comes after an agency investigation. The investigation is not considered to be part of the adjudication. The investigation may be prompted by a consumer complaint. In response to that complaint or other impetus, the initiation of an FTC investigation may be authorized by the multi-person body that heads the FTC, a body that we will hereafter refer to as the "Commission," to distinguish it from the agency as a whole, which we will call the "FTC." Instead of the Commission authorizing the initiation of an investigation, a lower-level official to whom the Commission has delegated its authority may authorize the initiation of an investigation. *See* 16 C.F.R. § 2.1 (2012). Let us suppose that the FTC has investigated a company that sells breakfast cereal and that advertises its cereal as good for heart health. Also suppose the results of the investigation are presented to the Commission, and show patently fraudulent health claims. What comes next?

(1) The initiation of an adjudication against the company would occur when, based on the results of the investigation, the Commission by majority vote approves the issuance of a complaint against the company. 16 C.F.R. § 3.11(a) (2012). Let us suppose the complaint charges that the company's health claims are false and misleading, in violation of the Federal Trade Commission Act and FTC rules. The FTC will serve the complaint on the company.

(2) In the prehearing stage, the breakfast cereal company will have a chance to file a document answering the complaint. Lawyers for the company will ordinarily meet with FTC lawyers to exchange information about facts and legal arguments and to discuss a possible settlement. If the parties cannot reach a settlement, the company may request a formal hearing before an Administrative Law Judge (ALJ) employed by the FTC.

(3) At the hearing, FTC lawyers acting as prosecutors will present evidence to the ALJ, perhaps including live witnesses as well as documentary evidence, to prove the violations alleged in the complaint. The breakfast cereal company's lawyers will present evidence in defense to the ALJ. The parties will also present legal arguments through written briefs and orally argued motions.

(4) After the hearing, the ALJ will make an initial or recommended decision on whether the company has committed the charged violations.

(5) The ALJ's decision may be reviewed by the Commission, which will be advised by the FTC's Office of General Counsel. If the Commission reviews the ALJ's decision, the Commission will make the final decision for the agency.

From this brief illustration you can see that different parts of an agency play different roles in a formal adjudication. Specifically, four components of the FTC could be involved in our hypothetical breakfast cereal case. The investigation and prosecuting functions would probably be handled by the FTC's Bureau of Consumer Protection. The evidentiary hearing would be held by an ALJ from the FTC's Office of Administrative Law Judges. The five-member Commission, in consultation with the Office of the General Counsel, could be involved in the decision to initiate the investigation, the decision to issue the complaint, and the review of the ALJ's decision. Now find these components on the FTC's organizational chart in Figure 22-A.

We have deliberately included a chart with the names of the people who headed the FTC's components at the time of this writing. As a practical matter, a lawyer often needs to know the names of the human beings in the bureaucracy with whom the lawyer must deal. For that reason, administrative lawyers often like to get their hands on not only the organizational chart showing the heads of various components but also the agency's staff directory, which will identify their minions. The organizational chart and staff directories are ordinarily public records that can be found on the internet or requested under the Freedom of Information Act.

Not every formal adjudication goes through all five stages listed above. Like court adjudications, agency adjudications may end before they go to a hearing. For instance, agency adjudications may get dismissed or settled. In addition, many agencies have rules for deciding cases without a hearing if no dispute of material fact exists. Furthermore, if an agency case *does* go to a hearing and the presiding official makes a decision, the losing party may accept that decision and not seek administrative review.

The next sections of this chapter go into detail about the first two stages — (1) initiation and (2) prehearing procedures — in formal adjudications under the federal APA.

C. Initiation of a Formal Adjudication under the Federal APA

This section examines three aspects of the initiation of a formal adjudication under the federal APA: (1) who may initiate a formal adjudication; (2) how and to whom notice of the adjudication is given; and (3) who participates as parties to the adjudication.

1. Who Initiates the Adjudication

Sometimes the agency initiates the formal adjudication; other times, it doesn't. The identity of the initiator depends on the nature of the adjudication.

The issue of who initiates the formal adjudication matters for several reasons. One reason is that the initiator of the adjudication bears certain procedural burdens like those of the plaintiff in a court adjudication. For example, the initiator usually bears the burden of production and the burden of proof. We will explore in later sections these burdens and other aspects of being the initiator of an agency adjudication. For now you just have to understand that being the initiator is a distinctive role.

Let us examine who initiates formal adjudications in the three most common types of adjudications: enforcement proceedings, licensing proceedings, and benefits proceedings.

a. Enforcement Proceedings

Many regulatory agencies have power under their statutes to initiate agency adjudications to enforce the laws they are responsible for administering. These enforcement proceedings

Figure 22-A. Federal Trade Commission Organizational Chart

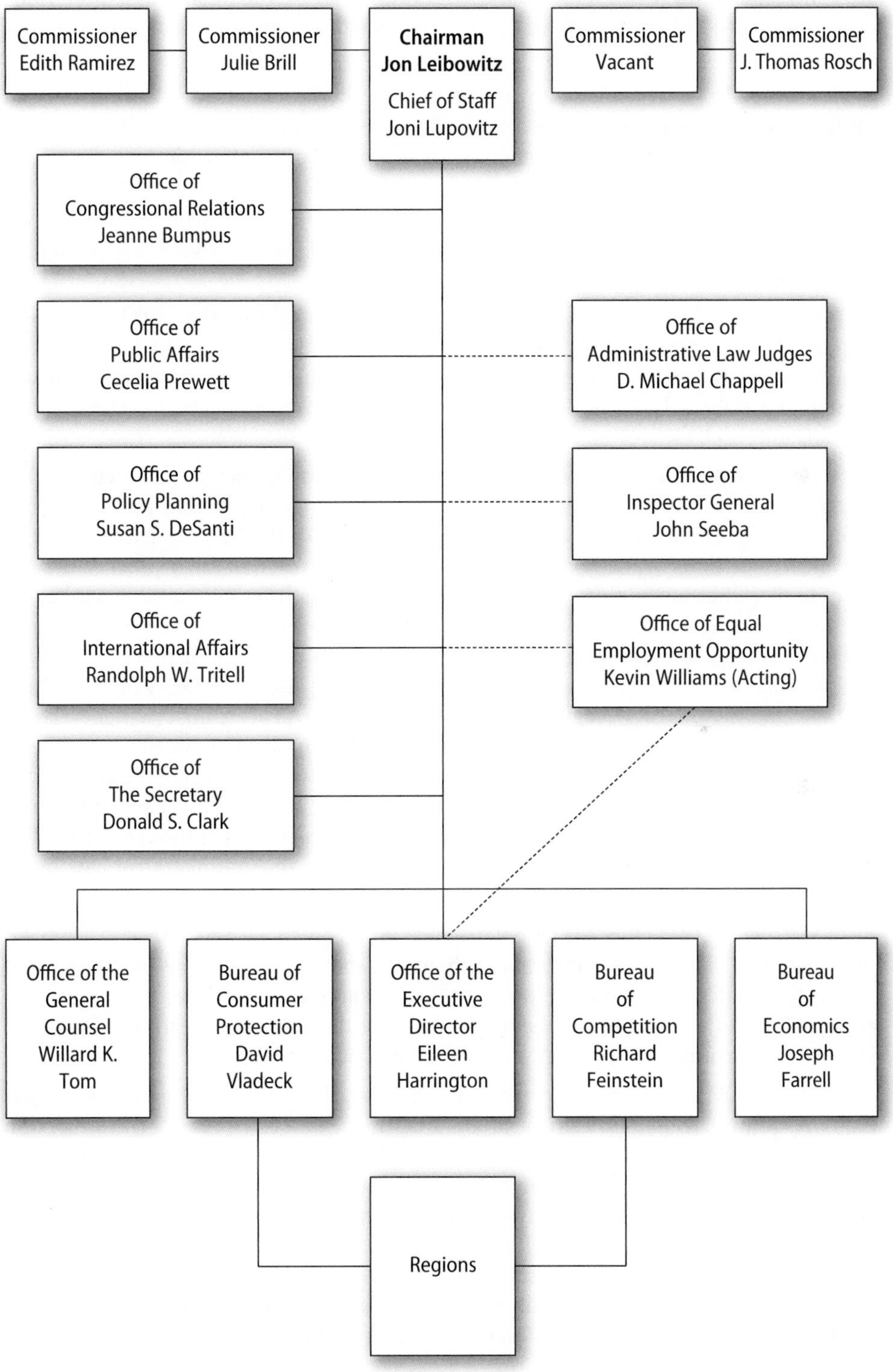

| Commissioner Edith Ramirez | Commissioner Julie Brill | **Chairman Jon Leibowitz** Chief of Staff Joni Lupovitz | Commissioner Vacant | Commissioner J. Thomas Rosch |

Office of Congressional Relations Jeanne Bumpus

Office of Public Affairs Cecelia Prewett

Office of Administrative Law Judges D. Michael Chappell

Office of Policy Planning Susan S. DeSanti

Office of Inspector General John Seeba

Office of International Affairs Randolph W. Tritell

Office of Equal Employment Opportunity Kevin Williams (Acting)

Office of The Secretary Donald S. Clark

| Office of the General Counsel Willard K. Tom | Bureau of Consumer Protection David Vladeck | Office of the Executive Director Eileen Harrington | Bureau of Competition Richard Feinstein | Bureau of Economics Joseph Farrell |

Regions

are initiated by the head of the agency or by someone else in the agency who has "prosecutorial" power. (Despite the term "prosecutorial," administrative enforcement proceedings are *not* criminal proceedings; they can result only in a civil remedy, such as a money fine or a cease-and-desist order.) We will give two concrete examples of agency initiation of enforcement proceedings.

First example: As described above in Section B, the Federal Trade Commission can initiate an enforcement proceeding against someone who, the Commission has reason to believe, has committed an "unfair method of competition or unfair or deceptive act or practice in or affecting commerce." 15 U.S.C. § 45 (2012). The decision to initiate the proceeding is made by the five-member body that heads the Commission. *See* 16 C.F.R. § 3.11(a) (2012). That body, which we have been calling "the Commission," initiates the enforcement proceeding by issuing a complaint.

You can find copies of Commission complaints on the FTC's website, http://www.ftc.gov/os/adjpro/. There, you can find complaints alleging violations of 15 U.S.C. § 45 as well as other laws that the FTC is responsible for administering. Your understanding of formal adjudication will benefit from examining litigation documents like these. (Hint, hint!)

Second example: The National Labor Relations Board can initiate an enforcement proceeding against someone who, it believes, has committed an unfair labor practice. *See* 29 U.S.C. § 160(b) (2012). Unfair labor practices are defined by the National Labor Relations Act and by decisions of the Board interpreting the Act. An unfair labor practice occurs, for example, when an employer fires an employee because the employee supports having a union represent the workers in dealings with the employer. Unfair labor practice cases often begin with someone (e.g., an employee) filing an unfair labor practice "charge" against someone else (e.g., an employer) with the Board. *See* 29 U.S.C. § 160(b) (2012) (authorizing the Board to begin an unfair labor practice proceeding "[w]henever it is charged that any person has engaged in or is engaging in any such unfair labor practice"). A Board employee in one of the Board's regional offices will investigate the charge. *See* 29 C.F.R. § 101.4 (2012). If the matter is not settled, the "Regional Director" will issue a complaint. *See id.* § 101.8. A Board attorney will thereafter prosecute the complaint. The charges in the complaint may ultimately be tried before an Administrative Law Judge employed by the Board.

In FTC, NLRB, and other agency enforcement proceedings, we say "the agency" initiates the proceeding. The two examples above, however, show that the details of exactly who, within the agency, is responsible for initiating the adjudication differ from agency to agency. The initiator is not necessarily the head of the agency. Instead, the initiator's identity is determined by the agency legislation and agency rules.

A lawyer may need to find out what specific official or entity within an agency has authority to initiate an enforcement proceeding. If the lawyer represents the target of a potential enforcement proceeding, the lawyer might persuade that official or body not to initiate a proceeding at all. Indeed, both the FTC and the NLRB have procedures for settling enforcement matters before formal enforcement proceedings begin. *See* 16 C.F.R. §§ 2.31– 2.34 (2012) ("Consent Order Procedure"); 29 C.F.R. § 101.7 (2012) ("Settlement"). Yet a second lawyer, however, may represent someone who has been harmed by a violation, or believes the violation should be punished. This second lawyer may seek to persuade the responsible official to initiate an enforcement proceeding rather than settle the matter.

Both lawyers' clients have a qualified right under federal APA § 555(b) to appear informally before the agency or a **"responsible [agency] employe[e]"** to argue their points of view. *See* Chapter 21.E.1.b(ii) (discussing the right of informal appearance under § 555). The procedures for exercising that right are likely to be spelled out in the agency's procedural rules or other agency guidance material.

Once "the agency" decides to initiate an enforcement proceeding, the proceeding generally does not end until the agency reaches a final decision. Thus, if your client is the defendant in an enforcement proceeding, you must initially work within the agency to get a favorable result. This is ordinarily true even if you think the entire proceeding is improper—for example, because the agency lacks authority over your client. In general, courts require people to exhaust all remedies within the agency and obtain the final decision of the agency before challenging the agency's "jurisdiction" over the target of an agency enforcement proceeding. *Myers v. Bethlehem Shipbuilding Corp.*, 303 U.S. 41, 49–50 (1938). There are exceptions to these "exhaustion" and "finality" requirements, but you cannot assume an exception exists merely because you believe an agency is acting improperly. *See, e.g., FTC v. Standard Oil of Cal.*, 449 U.S. 232 (1980) (federal court could not review FTC's issuance of an administrative complaint against oil companies); *see also infra* Chapter 30 (discussing finality and exhaustion requirements).

Exercise: Advocacy at the Initiation Stage

The objective of this exercise is to help you think in practical terms about an agency's discretion to initiate an enforcement proceeding.

Sometimes, but only rarely, a statute will constrain an agency's discretion about whether to initiate an enforcement proceeding. Such a rare statute might say, for example, if the agency finds "reasonable cause" to believe a violation has occurred, it "shall" take a specified enforcement action. Usually, though, no such statute exists and, as a result, the agency has broad discretion about whether to initiate enforcement action against a particular, possible violator.

Suppose, for a moment, your client is being investigated by an agency for a suspected violation of a law that the agency is responsible for enforcing. Thinking generically, what *kinds* of arguments might you make to convince the agency not to take enforcement action against your client?

---

b. Licensing Proceedings

These days you cannot do much without getting a license from some government agency. For many activities, such as developing a shopping center, you probably need multiple licenses and permits. When you apply to an agency for a license, you are initiating an adjudication. In contrast, the agency may initiate an adjudication to revoke, suspend, or restrict an existing license.

Considering first the application process: Your license application may initially be processed by a "front-line" agency official. The initial application process may be informal, with the front-line official simply reviewing your paperwork and perhaps informally contacting you for more information. If the front-line official grants the license, the process has usually ended; "the agency" has made a "final" decision on your application. If, on the other hand, the front-line official denies your application, ordinarily you can seek administrative review—often by a higher-level official. Indeed, the applicable agency legislation may entitle you, at some stage, to initiate a formal adjudication by requesting a trial-like hearing before an ALJ or other hearing officer. As the "moving party," you will ordinarily bear the burden of proving at the hearing that you are entitled to the license. You may have, as your opponent in this formal adjudication, an agency official who defends the agency's initial decision to deny you a license. The ALJ will make an initial or recommended decision, which the losing party will be entitled to appeal to a higher authority in the agency. The agency's final decision on the application will ordinarily be subject to judicial review.

Now contrast a proceeding on an application for a license with a proceeding against an existing licensee: The licensing agency may initiate an adjudication against an existing license holder who, for example, has violated a condition of the license, a statutory provision, or an agency rule governing licensees. Again, the relevant agency legislation may entitle the licensee to a formal adjudication on the agency's proposed adverse action against the licensee. As the initiating party, the agency will ordinarily bear the burden of proof at the hearing before an ALJ. Once again, the ALJ will make a decision that the losing party can appeal to a higher authority within the agency. The agency's final decision will ordinarily be subject to judicial review.

c. Benefits Proceedings

Benefits proceedings typically resemble licensing proceedings in terms of who initiates them. A person who seeks benefits initiates an adjudication by applying for them. If the front-line agency official denies the application, the applicable agency legislation may entitle the applicant to a formal adjudication before an ALJ, followed by an appeal to someone higher up in the agency, if the ALJ denies the benefits.

Once benefits are granted, if they are ongoing benefits, the agency may later initiate an adjudication to terminate or reduce the benefits if the agency comes to believe that termination or reduction is justified by a change in circumstances or a change in the law. The applicable agency legislation may require a formal adjudication on the agency's effort to terminate or reduce the benefits.

The burden of proof in benefits proceedings ordinarily corresponds to the identity of the initiator. Thus, the applicant for benefits ordinarily bears the burden of proving entitlement. When the agency seeks to terminate or limit benefits, however, the agency bears the burden of proof.

2. Notice

Notice in a formal adjudication under the federal APA is addressed by § 554(b):

---

5 U.S.C. § 554. Adjudications ...

(b) Persons entitled to notice of an agency hearing shall be timely informed of—

(1) the time, place, and nature of the hearing;

(2) the legal authority and jurisdiction under which the hearing is to be held; and

(3) the matters of fact and law asserted.

When private persons are the moving parties, other parties to the proceeding shall give prompt notice of issues controverted in fact or law; and in other instances agencies may by rule require responsive pleading. In fixing the time and place for hearings, due regard shall be had for the convenience and necessity of the parties or their representatives....

Section 554(b) addresses three issues: (a) who is entitled to timely notice; (b) what information the notice must contain; and (c) how other parties may be required to respond to the "**moving part[y]**."

a. Who Is Entitled to Notice

Section 554(b) requires timely notice of the agency hearing to "[p]**ersons entitled to notice**." This requirement involves *individualized* notice to particular people. Thus, it differs from the "[g]*eneral* **notice of proposed rulemaking**" that § 553(b) requires to be published in the Federal Register at the beginning of a rulemaking proceeding.

The notice requirement of § 554(b) fulfills a purpose like the requirement in a civil action that the plaintiff serve a summons and complaint on the defendant. Both requirements reflect that agency adjudications and civil actions often implicate property or liberty interests protected by due process. Due process generally requires "notice reasonably calculated, under all the circumstances, to apprise interested parties of the pendency of the action and afford them an opportunity to present their objections." *Mullane v. Cent. Hanover Bank & Trust Co.*, 339 U.S. 306, 314 (1950). Accordingly, courts construe § 554(b) to ensure it meets due process requirements in formal adjudications that implicate due process. *See, e.g., Pub. Serv. Comm'n v. FERC*, 397 F.3d 1004, 1012 (D.C. Cir. 2005); *Todd Shipyards Corp. v. Director, Office of Workers' Compensation*, 545 F.2d 1176, 1180–1181 (9th Cir. 1976).

Section 554(b) does not specify who is entitled to timely notice, or when notice will be considered timely. These matters may be addressed by the agency legislation or agency rules, as well as by judicial or agency precedent interpreting the legislation and rules. Sometimes the issues of who is entitled to notice and when the notice must be given are determined or influenced by due process analysis.

For example, the Federal Trade Commission Act addresses the issues of who gets notice of a hearing in formal adjudications under that Act and when the notice must be served:

---

15 U.S.C. § 45. Unfair methods of competition unlawful; prevention by Commission ...

(b) Proceeding by Commission; modifying and setting aside orders

Whenever the Commission shall have reason to believe that any such person, partnership, or corporation has been or is using any unfair method of competition or unfair or deceptive act or practice in or affecting commerce, and if it shall appear to the Commission that a proceeding by it in respect thereof would be to the interest of the public, it shall issue and serve upon such person, partnership, or corporation a complaint stating its charges in that respect and containing a notice of a hearing upon a day and at a place therein fixed at least thirty days after the service of said complaint....

Thus, §45 identifies those named in a complaint as the **"persons entitled to notice"** under §554(b), and specifies that the notice is **"timely"** under §554(b) if served at least thirty days before the hearing on the charges. The Act does not address the method for serving a complaint. The FTC's procedural rules do so, however:

---

16 C.F.R. §4.4 Service

(a) By the Commission.

(1) Service of complaints, initial decisions, final orders and other processes of the Commission under 15 U.S.C. 45 may be effected as follows:

(i) By registered or certified mail. A copy of the document shall be addressed to the person, partnership, corporation or unincorporated association to be served at his, her or its residence or principal office or place of business, registered or certified, and mailed; service under this provision is complete upon delivery of the document by the Post Office; or

(ii) By delivery to an individual. A copy thereof may be delivered to the person to be served, or to a member of the partnership to be served, or to the president, secretary, or other executive officer or a director of the corporation or unincorporated association to be served; service under this provision is complete upon delivery as specified herein; or

(iii) By delivery to an address. A copy thereof may be left at the principal office or place of business of the person, partnership, corporation, or unincorporated association, or it may be left at the residence of the person or of a member of the partnership or of an executive officer or director of the corporation, or un-incorporated association to be served; service under this provision is complete upon delivery as specified herein....

Another example of a statutory provision addressing the timing of notice and identity of those entitled to notice comes from the Longshore and Harbor Workers' Compensation Act, which authorizes formal adjudication of claims by injured longshore and harbor workers against their employers:

---

33 U.S.C. §919. Procedure in respect of claims ...

(b) Notice of claim

Within ten days after such claim is filed the deputy commissioner, in accordance with regulations prescribed by the Secretary, shall notify the employer and any other person (other than the claimant), whom the deputy commissioner considers an interested party, that a claim has been filed. Such notice may be served personally upon the employer or other person, or sent to such employer or person by registered mail.

(c) Investigations; order for hearing; notice; rejection or award

The deputy commissioner shall make or cause to be made such investigations as he considers necessary in respect of the claim, and upon application of any interested party shall order a hearing thereon. If a hearing on such claim is ordered the deputy commissioner shall give the claimant and other interested parties at least ten days' notice of such hearing, served personally upon the claimant and other interested parties or sent to such claimant and other interested parties by registered mail or by certified mail ...

This provision requires the agency official to give notice of the claim and a separate notice of the hearing. Again, agency rules elaborate on procedural details of formal adjudication under this statute. *See* 20 C.F.R. §§ 702.301–702.394 (2012) ("Adjudication Procedures").

The question of who is entitled to notice of a formal adjudication is thus ordinarily answered by an amalgam of the agency legislation and agency rules. The statutes and regulations may, especially if ambiguous or unclear, have been interpreted in judicial or agency precedent. Your statutory and regulatory research should therefore include a search for judicial and agency precedent.

b. Contents of Notice

Section 554(b) requires the notice to include three items of information. The most important are the legal authority for the adjudication and the **"matters of fact and law asserted."** Information on the claimed legal authority enables the parties to determine the scope of the agency's authority and, if appropriate, to challenge the agency's exercise of it in the particular adjudication. *See* AGM 47. Information on the **"matters of fact and law asserted"** refers to matters of fact and law asserted by the moving party, meaning the party who initiated the adjudication.

As to what the moving party will assert: Like the plaintiff in a court adjudication, the party initiating the adjudication will ordinarily have to assert (allege) certain matters of fact and law to support the desired result. In an adjudication under the federal APA, the desired result will be the issuance of an **"order."** 5 U.S.C. § 551(7) (2012). The order may, for example, grant a license or a benefit, or impose a sanction. The party seeking the order—whom the APA calls the **"proponent of ... [the] order"** (5 U.S.C. § 556(d))— will try to make the factual and legal assertions required under applicable substantive law to justify the order. In short, the moving party faces a burden resembling a civil plaintiff's burden to plead the elements of a cause of action.

It will help you understand this part of § 554(b) if you consider it in a specific context, the most frequently litigated of which concerns formal adjudications to impose agency sanctions. The agency is the moving party in a proceeding to impose sanctions. The agency must give notice to the proposed target of the sanctions. The notice must allege facts and law justifying the sanction. For example, the agency must allege specific conduct by the target that violated specific statutes or regulations. This enables the target to prepare a defense.

An agency violates § 554(b)(3) if it alleges conduct X as the basis for the proposed sanction and ends up imposing a sanction based on conduct Y. If the sanction deprives the target of property or liberty, this lack of adequate notice also violates due process. Lack of adequate notice happens more often than you might think. Here are two examples that reached federal courts of appeals:

- *Wyoming v. Alexander*, 971 F.2d 531 (10th Cir. 1992)

Wyoming received a grant from the U.S. Department of Education (DOE) under a federal statute. Wyoming was supposed to use the grant for vocational education of people with disabilities. The DOE audited Wyoming's use of the grant. Based on the audit, a DOE official wrote Wyoming a letter demanding that Wyoming pay back the grant money.

The letter said that Wyoming had improperly used the money for students who were not disabled. Wyoming administratively appealed the official's decision to the DOE's Education Appeal Board, which held a formal adjudication on the matter.

The Board determined, contrary to the DOE official, that Wyoming had used the grant for students with disabilities. But the Board on its own initiative raised a different problem. The Board believed that Wyoming had not used the proper accounting method in allocating the grant. On this new ground, the Board ordered Wyoming to repay the money. The Secretary of Education did not disturb the Board's decision within thirty days, as a result of which the Board's decision became the final decision of DOE. Wyoming sought judicial review in the federal court of appeals.

The court of appeals held that the DOE acted unfairly and violated § 554(b)(3). The court reasoned that the party to a formal adjudication must be "reasonably apprised of the issues in controversy." 971 F.2d at 542 (internal quotation marks and citation omitted). Wyoming did not get reasonable notice that the DOE thought Wyoming had used the wrong accounting method. The court vacated the DOE decision ordering Wyoming to refund the grant money. The court also remanded the case to the DOE "in order that Wyoming be afforded an opportunity to present evidence on the question now raised about its cost approach for this grant." *Id.* at 543. Thus, Wyoming might not get to keep the money that it supposedly had accounted for improperly, but it did live to fight another day.

- *Yellow Freight System, Inc. v. Martin*, 954 F.2d 353 (6th Cir. 1992)

Yellow Freight, a transportation company, fired one of its truck drivers, Thomas Moyer. Mr. Moyer filed a complaint against Yellow Freight with the Occupational Safety and Health Administration (OSHA), an agency in the U.S. Department of Labor. Mr. Moyer claimed that Yellow Freight violated a federal statute by firing him. Specifically, Mr. Moyer argued that Yellow Freight fired him for refusing to drive a truck one day in February 1988 when he was too sick to drive. OSHA notified Yellow Freight of the claim and asked Yellow Freight to respond to Mr. Moyer's charge that he was fired "in reprisal for not operating his commercial vehicle because of illness." *Id.* at 355. After Yellow Freight responded, OSHA's regional administrator determined that Yellow Freight had not violated federal law.

Mr. Moyer requested and obtained a formal evidentiary hearing before an ALJ. At the hearing, Mr. Moyer testified about a new theory for his firing: Mr. Moyer alleged that Yellow Freight also fired him for testifying at an administrative hearing in support of *another* Yellow Freight driver whom Yellow Freight had supposedly fired for refusing to drive while sick. The ALJ held that Yellow Freight had not violated federal law under either theory.

On review of the ALJ's decision, however, the Secretary of Labor adopted the new theory that Mr. Moyer introduced at the hearing. The Secretary found that Yellow Freight fired Mr. Moyer for testifying in favor of a fellow driver. The Secretary refused to reopen the administrative record to allow Yellow Freight to present evidence rebutting this new theory. The Secretary ordered Yellow Freight to rehire Mr. Moyer. Yellow Freight sought judicial review of the Secretary's decision in the federal court of appeals.

The court of appeals held that the Secretary violated Yellow Freight's due process rights. The court summarized the relevant principles:

> The fundamental elements of procedural due process are notice and an opportunity to be heard. *Mullane v. Central Hanover Bank & Trust Co.*, 339 U.S. 306, 313

(1950). Congress incorporated these notions of due process in the Administrative Procedure Act. Under the Act, "[p]ersons entitled to notice of an agency hearing shall be timely informed of … the matters of fact and law asserted." 5 U.S.C. § 554(b). To satisfy the requirements of due process, an administrative agency must give the party charged a clear statement of the theory on which the agency will proceed with the case. *Bendix Corp. v. FTC*, 450 F.2d 534, 542 (6th Cir.1971). Additionally, "an agency may not change theories in midstream without giving respondents reasonable notice of the change." *Id.* (quoting *Rodale Press, Inc. v. FTC*, 407 F.2d 1252, 1256 (D.C.Cir.1968)).

954 F.2d at 357. The court concluded that the Secretary violated those principles.

The court first determined that Yellow Freight did not get adequate notice of the new theory before the ALJ hearing. This was not fatal in and of itself to the agency's decision, however, the court said: "Notwithstanding the possible lack of notice prior to the administrative hearing, due process is not offended if an agency decides an issue the parties fairly and fully litigated at a hearing." *Id.* at 358. In addition, the court determined that evidence of the new theory came up at the ALJ hearing, and Yellow Freight did not object to the evidence.

Ultimately, the court determined that the evidence of the new theory presented at the hearing was not obvious enough to conclude that Yellow Freight "impliedly consented" to litigate the new theory. *Id.* at 359. Yellow Freight therefore did not have an opportunity to "fairly and fully litigate" the new theory. *Id.* at 358. Because Yellow Freight lacked adequate notice, the court remanded the case to the Secretary, to give the Secretary a chance to "re-examine" the new theory of a statutory violation "after giving Yellow Freight proper notice and a full and fair opportunity to respond." *Id.*

* * *

Wyoming v. Alexander and *Yellow Freight* show how notice problems can arise. They often arise because the adjudication involves multiple decision makers. The first agency decision maker may base a decision on different grounds from that of a later agency decision maker. The lawyer opposing the agency must guard against such "drift" in the agency's rationale. Initially, the lawyer may request that the agency make the **"matters of fact and law asserted"** (5 U.S.C. § 554(b)(3) (2012)) in the notice as specific as possible. Vague or ambiguous allegations can lead to drift. Second, the lawyer must ensure the agency uses only evidence relevant to its original allegations; the lawyer must object to evidence on new issues. In these efforts, the lawyer behaves like the lawyer for a party in a civil action, who must object to the admission of evidence that varies from the opposing party's pleadings.

c. Responses to the Matters Asserted by the Moving Party

Section 554(b) says:

---

5 U.S.C. § 554. Adjudications …

(b) …

When private persons are the moving parties, other parties to the proceeding shall give prompt notice of issues controverted in fact or law; and in other instances agencies may by rule require responsive pleading.

This statement takes a bit of unpacking. In plain English, it requires all parties to a formal adjudication to state their factual and legal positions at the beginning of the adjudication, to put other parties on notice of where each party stands.

The first clause addresses formal adjudications in which a private person is the moving party. This includes, for example, most formal adjudications involving applications for licenses or benefits.

An example of a formal adjudication to which the first clause applies is an adjudication on a claim under the Longshore and Harbor Workers' Compensation Act. As mentioned above, that Act authorizes adjudication of claims by injured longshore and harbor workers against their employers. The **"other part[y]"** in such an adjudication will be the employer or the employer's insurance carrier, as the agency rules tell us. 20 C.F.R. § 702.333 (2012). Section 554(b) requires the employer or insurance carrier to **"give prompt notice of issues controverted in fact or law."**

If, for example, the employer disputes that an injury is connected to the claimant's job (as required for the injury to be compensable), the employer must give **"prompt notice"** of this controverted issue. The employer is in a position analogous to that of a defendant, who must file a motion or responsive pleading to give notice of defenses and objections. An agency rule spells out how the employer does so in an adjudication under the Longshore and Harbor Workers' Compensation Act:

---

20 C.F.R. § 702.251 Employer's controversion of the right to compensation

Where the employer controverts the right to compensation after notice or knowledge of the injury or death, or after receipt of a written claim, he shall give notice thereof, stating the reasons for controverting the right to compensation, using the form prescribed by the Director. Such notice, or answer to the claim, shall be filed with the district director within 14 days from the date the employer receives notice or has knowledge of the injury or death. The original notice shall be sent to the district director having jurisdiction, and a copy thereof shall be given or mailed to the claimant.

The employer's statement of reasons for controverting a claim serves a purpose like that of an answer or other responsive pleading in a court adjudication. It helps identify the disputed issues that may have to be tried at an oral, evidentiary hearing.

In addition to addressing formal adjudications in which a private party is a moving party, § 554(b) addresses **"other instances,"** which refers to formal adjudications in which the agency, rather than a **"private perso[n],"** is the moving party. Agencies are typically the moving party, for example, in enforcement proceedings and proceedings to suspend, terminate, or restrict a previously granted license or benefits. In these formal adjudications, § 554(b) says, **"agencies may by rule require responsive pleading."** Thus, the agency will initiate the proceeding by issuing a complaint or other document that gives notice of the reasons for its proposed action. The agency **"may by rule"** require the person against whom the proceeding is brought, whom we might call the administrative defendant, to file a document that responds to the allegations in the agency's complaint. In this way the agency can identify what issues, if any, are in dispute.

You know what can happen to the defendant in a civil action who fails to respond to a complaint. What do you suppose can happen to an administrative defendant who fails to file the **"responsive pleading"** that the agency may, under § 554(b), require by rule? In both settings the defendant may lose by default. After entry of an administrative default judgment, the administrative defendant may, or may not, be able to ask the agency to vacate the default judgment. That depends on whether the agency rules authorize this relief. If not, or if the agency denies that relief, the administrative defendant must pin hope on a reviewing court, which may or may not grant relief. *Compare Lion Raisins, Inc. v. U.S. Dep't of Agriculture*, 2005 WL 6406066 (E.D. Cal. May 12, 2005) (setting aside administrative default judgment) *with Kirk v. U.S. Immigration & Naturalization Serv.*, 927 F.2d 1106 (9th Cir. 1991) (upholding administrative default judgment).

The case of *Lion Raisins v. U.S. Department of Agriculture* involved an administrative default judgment and shows the danger of assuming that agency adjudications are just like court adjudications. That case involved an agency within USDA called the Agricultural Marketing Service (AMS). The AMS initiated a formal adjudication charging that Lion Raisins had forged a Department of Agriculture document and then sent it to a client. The AMS served the forgery complaint on Lion Raisins, together with a copy of the agency's Rules of Practice. The Rules of Practice required Lion Raisins to file an answer to the complaint within twenty days and said that the failure to file a timely answer constituted an admission to the charge and a waiver of the right to a hearing. Instead of filing an *answer* to the complaint, Lion Raisins' lawyer filed a *motion to dismiss* the complaint. That would have been perfectly OK under the Federal Rules of Civil Procedure, but the agency's Rules of Practice required an *answer* and did not permit a response in the form of a motion to dismiss. The AMS moved for a default judgment, which the Judicial Officer of the Department of Agriculture ultimately upheld, which in turn became the Department of Agriculture's final decision. Lion Raisins did successfully challenge the default judgment in a federal district court. The district court held that a default judgment was disproportionately harsh considering the quasi-criminal nature of the sanctions involved. But don't let Lion Raisins' ultimate victory obscure that it took Lion Raisins two-and-a-half years to un-do its lawyer's apparent, erroneous belief that the rules for responding to the complaint in this agency adjudication were the same as the rules for responding to a complaint in a civil action. *See* 2005 WL 6406066, at *1–*9.

3. Who Participates as Parties to the Adjudication

Every formal adjudication will include, as parties, people who have an obvious and direct stake in the outcome, such as the applicant for a license or government benefit, or the target of an agency enforcement proceeding. The agency itself will be a party to adjudications that the agency itself has initiated to, for example, impose a sanction or revoke a license. In some formal adjudications, a person whose interest is not direct or obvious may seek to participate as a party. If the agency does not automatically give that person party status, the person may seek to become a party by asking to intervene.

The question of who is entitled to participate as a party to a formal adjudication has importance for three reasons. The first reason becomes clear when you ask yourself: Why would someone want to become a party to an adjudication? The usual answer is: to influence the outcome. Parties have procedural rights of participation that give them a chance to influence the outcome. Second, the number and identity of the parties may influence the complexity and duration (not just the outcome) of the adjudication. Neither the agency nor most parties want an overly long, complicated proceeding. Third, sometimes judicial review of the agency's decision in a formal adjudication will be restricted, by statute, to those who were parties to the litigation. *See, e.g.,* 16 U.S.C. § 825*l*(b) (2012)

("Any *party* to a proceeding [before the Federal Energy and Regulatory Commission] aggrieved by an order issued by the Commission in such proceeding may obtain [judicial] review of the order. . . .") (emphasis added). If such a statute exists, someone who wants eventually to get judicial review of the agency's decision must seek to intervene in the adjudication. In short, the question of who may participate in a formal adjudication can affect the proceeding's nature and outcome, and who may seek judicial review of the agency decision.

Sometimes the question of who can be a party to an agency adjudication is called a question of "standing." We mention the term so you will understand it when you see it used in this context. But beware: "Standing" ordinarily refers to the question of who is entitled to sue in *court*, not who is entitled to intervene in an *agency adjudication*. The rules for standing in court are not necessarily identical to the rules for becoming a party to an agency adjudication. (A federal agency may, however, adopt the federal-court standing rules as its own standards for determining who can be parties to the agency's adjudications.) Turning to the state level, you cannot assume that the rules for standing in a State's courts govern who can be a party in a state agency's contested case. In short, do not be misled by the use of the term "standing" in the two different contexts of court proceedings and agency proceedings.

Rather than being addressed by the rules of judicial standing, the question of who may be a party to a formal adjudication before a federal agency is governed by a hodgepodge of laws. The federal APA does not squarely address the matter. The agency legislation sometimes addresses the matter, but often only in vague terms. This leaves the agency — and, initially, the ALJ or other official assigned to preside over the case — with much discretion. Though generalizations are difficult, it seems that agencies often have much discretion both in (1) how to interpret vague standards in statutes or agency rules on party participation; and (2) how to apply those standards in particular cases. If an agency's decision on whether a particular person may participate does not violate any legal restrictions, courts generally review the agency decision under the lenient, "abuse of discretion" standard. *See, e.g., Nichols v. Board of Trustees of Asbestos Workers Local 24, Pension Plan*, 835 F.2d 881, 897–898 (D.C. Cir. 1987).

Below we briefly explore the extent to which intervention may be addressed by the APA, the agency legislation, and agency rules

a. The APA

The federal APA addresses obliquely, at best, the issue of who is entitled to be a party to a formal adjudication. Section 554(b) describes the contents of the notice of a hearing that is supposed to be given to **"persons entitled to notice"** in a formal adjudication. 5 U.S.C. §554(b) (2012). Those **"persons"** are presumably the parties to the formal adjudication. In any event, §554(b) does not explain how you identify who those **"persons"** are, in a particular agency adjudication.

Section 555 of the federal APA may address the issue of who is entitled to participate in a formal adjudication. Section 555(b) gives **"an interested person"** a qualified right to **"appear . . . in a proceeding."** 5 U.S.C. §555(b) (2012) (discussed in Chapter 21.E.1.b(ii)). This language in §555(b) might provide a legal basis for someone to claim entitlement to intervene in a formal adjudication, since that is an agency **"proceeding."** 5 U.S.C. §551(12). But the right to appear conferred by §555(b) is qualified: it exists only **"[s]o far as the orderly conduct of public business permits."** *Id.* Because that phrase gives the agency great discretion to refuse to allow people to appear before the agency, § 555(b) does not give much help to would-be intervenors. And because the phrase is vague, it does not give much guidance to agencies faced with requests to intervene.

b. The Agency Legislation

The agency legislation may address the right of people to intervene in formal adjudication under that legislation. Unfortunately, even if the agency legislation does address the issue, it may not do so clearly.

For example, here is language from the statutory provision for unfair labor practice proceedings before the National Labor Relations Board:

---

29 U.S.C. § 160. Prevention of unfair labor practices ...

(b) Complaint and notice of hearing; answer; court rules of evidence inapplicable

Whenever it is charged that any person has engaged in or is engaging in any such unfair labor practice, the Board, or any agent or agency designated by the Board for such purposes, shall have power to issue and cause to be served upon such person a complaint stating the charges in that respect, and containing a notice of hearing before the Board or a member thereof, or before a designated agent or agency, at a place therein fixed, not less than five days after the serving of said complaint.... The person so complained of shall have the right to file an answer to the original or amended complaint and to appear in person or otherwise and give testimony at the place and time fixed in the complaint. In the discretion of the member, agent, or agency conducting the hearing or the Board, any other person may be allowed to intervene in the said proceeding and to present testimony....

This provision gives party status to the person charged with an unfair labor practice. Otherwise, it leaves to the discretion of agency officials whether "any other person may be allowed to intervene."

Not all statutes are so vague. For example, a provision in the Consumer Product Safety Act allows "interested parties, including consumer organizations, an opportunity for a hearing" to determine whether a product poses a substantial hazard and, if so, how to address it. 15 U.S.C. § 2064(d)(1) (2012). This provision gives affected consumer organizations a statutory right to intervene in the Commission's formal adjudications. To cite another example of a specific intervention provision, the Federal Power Act says that the Federal Energy Regulation Commission (FERC),

> in accordance with such rules and regulations as it may prescribe, may admit as a party any interested State, State commission, municipality, or any representative of interested consumers or security holders, or any competitor of a party to such proceeding, or any other person whose participation in the proceeding may be in the public interest.

16 U.S.C. § 825g(a) (2012). This provision allows the FERC to issue procedural rules addressing the standards and logistics of intervention, which FERC has done. 18 C.F.R. § 385.214 (2012).

We have shown you provisions in agency legislation that address who may participate in a formal adjudication. Often, however, the agency legislation will be silent on this matter.

c. Agency Rules

Agency rules may address the question of who may participate as a party to a formal adjudication. An example of an agency rule that does so in detail is in the SEC's "Rules of Practice." 17 C.F.R. §201.210 (2012) ("Parties, limited participants, and amicus curiae"). The SEC rule addresses three levels of participation: party status, "limited participants," and amici curiae. Each level has different rights of participation. The SEC rule is rare in the detail with which it addresses intervention. *Cf.*, *e.g.*, 14 C.F.R. §385.11 (2012) (Department of Transportation rule authorizing ALJs, without elaboration, to "[g]rant or deny intervention in formal proceedings"). It is not unusual, however, for federal agencies that hold formal adjudications to address the issue of intervention in their procedural rules for those adjudications. When an agency does have a rule addressing intervention, its interpretation of that rule as applied to a particular person seeking intervention will receive "great deference" from a reviewing court. *Koniag, Inc., Village of Uyak v. Andrus*, 580 F.2d 601, 607 (D.C. Cir. 1978).

d. Case Law

Federal courts have addressed people's entitlement to intervene in federal agencies' formal adjudications. An early, famous case seemed to require agencies to grant intervention on the same liberal grounds that the federal courts were developing to govern the "standing" of plaintiffs suing in federal courts. A more recent case takes a different approach by deferring to the agency's judgment on intervention standards. Because both cases are well known in administrative law, we describe them next:

- *Office of Communication of the United Church of Christ v. Federal Communications Commission*, 359 F.2d 994 (D.C. Cir. 1966)

This case is famous because: (1) it involved a racially charged situation during the Civil Rights Era of the 1960s; (2) the opinion was written by then-judge, later-Chief Justice of the U.S. Supreme Court Warren Burger; and (3) although then-Judge (later Justice) Burger was considered to be conservative, the court reached a "liberal" result, in the sense that the court's decision forced a well-respected federal agency (the FCC) to be more open and participatory (and, it seemed, open-minded) than the agency was inclined to be, left to its own devices. Many later court decisions have taken this same "liberal" approach to the issue of who is entitled to participate as parties in federal agency adjudications.

In 1964, a television station in Jackson, Mississippi — WLBT — applied to the FCC for a renewal of its broadcast license. Over the years, the FCC had received several complaints that the station was hostile to black people. As the court described the complaints:

> [T]he first complaints go back to 1955 when it was claimed that WLBT had deliberately cut off a network program about race relations problems on which the General Counsel of the NAACP [National Association for the Advancement of Colored People] was appearing and had flashed on the viewers' screens a "Sorry, Cable Trouble" sign. In 1957 another complaint was made to the Commission that WLBT had presented a program urging the maintenance of racial segregation and had refused requests for time to present the opposing viewpoint. Since then numerous other complaints have been made.

359 F.2d at 998.

When WLBT applied for license renewal in 1964, a church organization, its local congregation, and two members of the congregation filed a petition with the FCC opposing renewal and seeking to intervene in the relicensing proceeding. The two individuals seeking intervention were local civil rights leaders and viewers of the station's broadcasts. One was president of the Mississippi NAACP. "Each has had a number of controversies with WLBT over allotment of time to present views in opposition to those expressed by WLBT editorials and programs." *Id.* They claimed an interest in the proceeding on three grounds: (1) on a personal level, they had been denied an equal opportunity to appear on the station to answer their critics, whose views the station aired; (2) they represented "the nearly one half of WLBT's potential listening audience who were denied an opportunity to have their side of controversial issues presented ... and who were more generally ignored and discriminated against in WLBT's programs"; and (3) they asserted the right of the entire viewing audience "that the station be operated in the public interest." *Id.* at 998–999.

The relevant statute at the time authorized "[a]ny party in interest" to petition the FCC to deny a license renewal. Further, the statute required the Commission to hold a formal hearing on the license renewal if the petition and other material raised "a substantial and material question of fact" or if the Commission determined that it was unable to find that renewing the license would be in the public interest. 47 U.S.C. §309(d) (1964). At that hearing, the petitioners opposing renewal could participate as parties.

The Commission denied the petition opposing WLBT's license renewal and seeking intervention in a formal hearing on the matter. On the intervention issue, the Commission applied what it considered to be the standard that a federal court at the time would have used to determine if someone had standing in federal court to seek judicial review of a decision by the Commission. Specifically, the Commission held that standing to participate in an adjudication before the Commission, like standing to challenge the Commission's decision in a federal court, "is predicated upon the invasion of a legally protected interest or an injury which is direct and substantial." *Office of Communication*, 359 F.2d at 999 (quoting Commission's written decision). The Commission did not think the petitioners met this standard because "petitioners ... can assert no greater interest or claim of injury than members of the general public." *Id.* (quoting Commission's written decision).

The court of appeals reversed the Commission's denial of the petition for intervention. The court followed the lead of the parties before it in assuming that "the same standards are applicable to determining standing before the Commission and standing to appeal a Commission order to this court." *Id.* at 1000 n.8. On that assumption, the court held that the Commission took too restrictive a view of standing. The court noted that people in the petitioners' position sought to act as representatives of the licensee's audience, and that this audience had a clear-cut interest in the renewal of the license:

> [T]he listeners ... are most directly concerned with and intimately affected by the performance of a licensee. Since the concept of standing is a practical and functional one designed to insure that only those with a genuine and legitimate interest can participate in a proceeding, we can see no reason to exclude those with such an obvious and acute concern as the listening audience. This much seems essential to insure that the holders of broadcasting licenses be responsive to the needs of the audience, without which the broadcaster could not exist.

Id. at 1002. The Commission argued that it did not need the public's help in ensuring that licensees operated in the public interest; that was the Commission's job. Doubting that argument, the court observed that, but for petitioners' persistence, the Commission would have renewed the license of a station that the Commission itself recognized had provoked a long history of apparently legitimate complaints, and that the Commission itself could not find was currently operating in the public interest. *Id.* at 1003–1004.

The court upheld what has come to be called "viewer standing" to participate in an FCC adjudication partly because of concern about a problem known as "agency capture," though the court did not use that term. "Agency capture" occurs when an agency that is supposed to regulate a certain group becomes too sympathetic to the group's concerns to regulate it effectively. Concern about agency capture does not apply only to the Federal Communication Commission. This and other aspects of the court's reasoning justified recognizing a broad right of participation in other agency proceedings. Accordingly, many other federal courts relied on *Office of Communication of the United Church of Christ* in addressing administrative standing by people seeking to represent the public interest in other agency adjudications.

- *Envirocare of Utah, Inc. v. Nuclear Regulatory Commission*, 194 F.3d 72 (D.C. Cir. 1999)

Two companies applied for licenses from the Nuclear Regulatory Commission that would permit the companies to accept and store radioactive waste from other generators. Envirocare sought to intervene in the formal adjudications on the license applications, and to oppose them. If the licenses were granted, they would enable the licensees to compete with Envirocare, which itself was in the business of storing radioactive waste. The Commission denied intervention in both proceedings, and Envirocare sought judicial review of the Commission's rulings on its intervention requests.

Envirocare's requests to intervene were governed by a provision of the Atomic Energy Act (AEA):

---

42 U.S.C. § 2239. Hearings and judicial review

(a) (1)(A) In any proceeding under this chapter, for the granting, suspending, revoking, or amending of any license or construction permit, ... the Commission shall grant a hearing upon the request of any person whose interest may be affected by the proceeding, and shall admit any such person as a party to such proceeding....

The Commission determined that Envirocare's economic interest in opposing the issuance of licenses to would-be competitors did not qualify as an "interest" within the meaning of this provision. *See Envirocare*, 194 F.3d at 76. The Commission concluded, "Our understanding of the AEA requires us to insist that a competitor's pecuniary aim of imposing additional regulatory restrictions or burdens on fellow market participants does not fall within those 'interests' that trigger a right to hearing and intervention under [§ 2239(a)(1)(A)]." *Id.* at 75 (quoting Commission's written decision).

The Commission's conclusion led to a counterintuitive result: Envirocare lacked administrative "standing" to intervene in the licensing proceedings even though Envirocare could meet the "standing" requirements to bring a federal-court challenge to the Commission's licensing decisions in those proceedings. The reviewing court framed the issue posed by Commission's decision this way: "May an agency refuse to grant a hearing to persons who would satisfy the criteria for judicial standing and refuse to allow them to intervene in administrative proceedings?" *Id.* at 74.

The court of appeals held that this particular agency could do so, under the particular statute governing intervention in its proceedings. The court reviewed the Commission's interpretation of the AEA intervention provision under the doctrine of *Chevron U.S.A. Inc. v. Natural Resources Defense Council, Inc.*, 467 U.S. 837 (1984). The *Chevron* doctrine generally requires federal courts to accept a federal agency's reasonable interpretation of a statute that the agency is charged with administering. The court of appeals determined that the term "interest" in 42 U.S.C. § 2239 is ambiguous, and that the Commission's interpretation of the term was reasonable. *See Envirocare*, 194 F.3d at 75–79.

The *Envirocare* court gave no weight to *Office of Communication of United Church of Christ*, for three reasons: *Office of Communication* (1) involved a different statute and (2) was decided before *Chevron*. (3) "Furthermore, despite some broad language in *Office of Communication* about administrative standing, the agency there equated standing to appear before it with standing to obtain judicial review and so the court had no occasion to examine whether the two concepts might be distinct." *Envirocare*, 194 F.3d at 78.

Envirocare stands for three propositions, two of which are indubitable and the third of which would probably be followed by other federal courts. First, in analyzing intervention a court must closely examine the particular agency legislation addressing the subject. Second, the rules for judicial standing need not be the same as the standards for intervention in an agency adjudication. A third principle that some other federal courts are likely to follow is that the *Chevron* doctrine governs review of the agency's interpretation of its legislation's intervention provision.

These three propositions—especially the third—rob *Office of Communication of United Church of Christ* of most of its force as precedent. Even so, the earlier case remains one that every student of administrative law should learn about, not only for its historical value but also its discussion of the stake that a broad segment of the public may have in an agency adjudication, and of the potential problems that arise when an agency is the sole judge of the public interest.

D. Prehearing Procedures in Formal Adjudications under the Federal APA

Prehearing procedures in formal agency adjudications, as in judicial litigation, may include: (1) assignment of the case to the official who will preside at the evidentiary hearing (if it occurs); (2) discovery; (3) settlement negotiations; (4) prehearing conferences; and (5) summary judgment. We will take up each of these potential elements of prehearing procedures.

1. Administrative Law Judges

a. Officials Who May Preside at the Formal Hearing

Section 556(b) of the federal APA addresses who "shall preside at the taking of evidence" in a formal adjudication (or, for that matter, in a formal rulemaking). It provides three main options:

---

5 U.S.C. § 556. Hearings; presiding employees; ...

(b) There shall preside at the taking of evidence—

(1) the agency;

(2) one or more members of the body which comprises the agency; or

(3) one or more administrative law judges appointed under section 3105 of this title.

This subchapter does not supersede the conduct of specified classes of proceedings, in whole or in part, by or before boards or other employees specially provided for by or designated under statute....

Section §556(b)(1) uses the term **"agency"** to mean the head of the agency. This can be an individual, such as the Secretary of the Interior, or a multi-member body, such as the Federal Trade Commission (FTC). Under §556(b)(2), a hearing for an agency headed by a multi-member body can be presided over by one or more of the members of that body.

In practice, §§556(b)(1) and (b)(2) seldom apply, because the heads of agencies don't have time to hold oral, evidentiary hearings. In most formal adjudications, the job of presiding goes to an ALJ, as provided in §556(b)(3).

Federal ALJs work for the agency for which they hold the hearings. Every federal agency that conducts formal rulemakings or formal adjudications employs ALJs to conduct the formal hearings in those proceedings. Currently there are more than 1,300 federal ALJs, who work for 31 different federal agencies. The largest employer of federal ALJs is the Social Security Administration, for which ALJs hold hearing on claims for benefits under the Social Security Act.

Although most evidentiary hearings in formal adjudications are held by ALJs, §556(b) allows **"specified classes of proceedings"** to be conducted **"by or before boards or other employees specially provided for by or designated under statute."** Examples of statutes that provide for non-ALJ hearing officers in formal adjudications are the Railroad Retirement Act, 45 U.S.C. §355(c) (2012), which provides for hearings by the Railroad Retirement Board; and the statute establishing the Board of Veterans' Appeals, which authorizes the Board to conduct hearings on claims for veterans benefits, 38 U.S.C. §§7101–7112 (2012).

But because ALJs preside over the hearings in most formal adjudications, from now on we generally refer to ALJs alone as the presiding officials. The agency will typically assign an ALJ to a case before it goes to hearing, which means that the ALJ will not only preside at the hearing but may also be involved in a case at the prehearing stage. That is why we discuss ALJs as part of the examination of the prehearing stage.

b. ALJ Independence

Section 556(b) requires the ALJ and all other agency employees involved in deciding a formal adjudication to act **"in an impartial manner."** That requirement reflects the APA's goal of addressing complaints that, before the APA, the agency officials who conducted evidentiary hearings "were mere tools of the agency ... and subservient to the agency heads." *Ramspeck v. Federal Trial Examiners Conf.*, 345 U.S. 128, 131 (1953). The requirement of decisionmaker impartiality also reflects the demands of the Due Process Clause, which applies to many formal adjudications and under which "a biased decision maker is constitutionally unacceptable." *Withrow v. Larkin*, 421 U.S. 35, 47 (1975).

Three main provisions in the federal APA ensure ALJ impartiality. As explained below, however, ALJs are not totally independent of the agencies for which they work.

First, § 554(d)(2) says an ALJ **"may not ... be responsible to or subject to the supervision or direction of an employee or agency engaged in the performance of investigative or prosecuting functions for an agency."** This provision requires the agency's ALJs to be located in a separate part of the agency's organizational structure, and to be independent, from the agency's investigators and prosecutors. This provision is called a "separation of functions" provision because it separates ALJs, who carry out a quasi-judicial function, from officials who carry out investigative or prosecutorial functions. The result of the separation of function provision is that ALJs work for the agency, but not for the agency's investigators or prosecutors.

Second, ALJs are hired through a nonpolitical process, and can be suspended, demoted, or fired only for "**good cause.**" 5 U.S.C. § 7521(a) (2012). Moreover, the agency employing the ALJ must establish the good cause to the satisfaction of a separate federal agency, the Merit System Protection Board, in a formal adjudication. The "good cause" standard, plus the requirement that this standard be judged by a different agency from the one that employs the ALJ, ensures that the ALJ cannot be fired merely for making decisions that are adverse to the employing agency. *See Long v. Soc. Sec. Admin.*, 635 F.3d 526, 534 (Fed. Cir. 2011) ("good cause" does not exist if it is "based on reasons which constitute an improper interference with the ALJ's performance of ... quasi-judicial functions") (internal quotation marks omitted). We should all have such job protection!

Third, § 556(b) authorizes disqualification of the ALJ assigned to hear a case (as well as any other agency employee who participates in deciding the case) in cases of bias:

---

§ 556. Hearings; presiding employees ...

(b) ... A presiding or participating employee may at any time disqualify himself. On the filing in good faith of a timely and sufficient affidavit of personal bias or other disqualification of a presiding or participating employee, the agency shall determine the matter as a part of the record and decision in the case....

Under federal law, ALJs "are presumed to be unbiased." *Valentine v. Comm'r of Soc. Sec. Admin.*, 574 F.3d 685, (9th Cir. 2009). But that presumption "can be rebutted by a showing of conflict of interest or some other specific reason for disqualification." *Id.*

Although ALJs must be impartial and they have job protections, they are not totally independent of the agency. ALJs are agency employees, and as such they must follow the agency's policies and its interpretations of its legislation and rules. This is necessary to ensure that an agency's ALJs decide similar cases similarly. *See Nash v. Bowen*, 869 F.2d 675, 678–681 (2nd Cir. 1989) (rejecting ALJ's challenge to agency procedures for ensuring quality and efficiency of ALJ decisions); *D'Amico v. Schweiker*, 698 F.2d 903, 906 (7th Cir. 1983) (instead of suing agency to contest agency policy, ALJs were required to obey the policy and let those directly affected by it bring the judicial challenge). Thus, ALJs lack the independence of, say, federal district court judges.

Exercise: ALJ Independence

Please look back at Figure 22-A, the FTC's organizational chart, to determine how the organizational structure satisfies the "separation of functions" required by federal APA § 556(d)(2).

---

2. Discovery

The federal APA does not directly address discovery in formal adjudications. *See Citizens Awareness Network v. United States*, 391 F.3d 338, 350 (1st Cir. 2004). Instead, four APA provisions address discovery obliquely or in part, or address other ways to get information for use in an agency adjudication. Besides the federal APA, sometimes agency legislation addresses discovery. More often, discovery in formal adjudications under the federal APA is governed primarily by agency rules. Although federal agency rules on discovery vary, they ordinarily satisfy due process.

a. APA Provisions

Two of the four APA provisions that bear on discovery are in provisions that govern formal adjudications—namely, §§ 554 and 556. The other two are in §§ 555 and 552. We discuss these provisions in the order in which we just mentioned them.

Section 554(c) requires agencies to give the parties an opportunity for **"the submission and consideration of facts"** before the hearing. In isolation, this opportunity might be interpreted to require the parties to exchange relevant factual information. In context, however, the opportunity is probably just meant to facilitate settlement:

---

5 U.S.C. § 554. Adjudications ...

(c) The agency shall give all interested parties opportunity for—

(1) the submission and consideration of facts, arguments, offers of settlement, or proposals of adjustment when time, the nature of the proceeding, and the public interest permit; and

(2) to the extent that the parties are unable so to determine a controversy by consent, hearing and decision on notice and in accordance with sections 556 and 557 of this title....

The Attorney General's Manual on the APA states that Congress intended this provision "to provide, so far as practicable, for the informal settlement or adjustment of controversies in lieu of formal adjudicatory proceedings." AGM 48. That intention can be served without requiring formal discovery among the parties. For that reason, § 554(c)(1)'s reference to **"the submission and consideration of facts"** probably just means that parties may informally exchange information in their effort to settle the dispute.

Section 556 allows the ALJ to issue subpoenas and arrange for depositions, but only when a law outside the APA authorizes the agency to do so:

---

5 U.S.C. § 556. Hearings; presiding employees; powers and duties ...

(c) Subject to published rules of the agency and *within its powers*, employees presiding at hearings may— ...

(2) issue subpenas authorized by law; ...

(4) take depositions or have depositions taken when the ends of justice would be served....

(Emphasis added.) The Attorney General's Manual on the APA explained that §556(c) "vests in hearing officers only such of the enumerated powers as the agency itself possesses." AGM 74. Thus, the availability of subpoenas and depositions in a formal adjudication depends on whether the agency legislation or other law external to the APA authorizes the agency to use those discovery devices. If so, §556(c) devolves that authority on ALJs in the agency's formal adjudications. If not, the ALJ cannot issue subpoenas or order depositions.

The third APA provision bearing on discovery comes from §555. Specifically, §555(d) ensures that private parties to adjudications have the same access to the agency's subpoena power as does the agency itself:

---

5 U.S.C. §555. Ancillary Matters ...

(d) Agency subpenas authorized by law shall be issued to a party on request and, when required by rules of procedure, on a statement or showing of general relevance and reasonable scope of the evidence sought....

Like §556(c), §555(d) comes into play only when a law outside the APA authorizes the agency to issue subpoenas in an adjudication.

Some federal agencies do have that authority. For example, the Commissioner of Social Security can issue subpoenas in agency adjudications and other proceedings under Title II of the Social Security Act:

---

42 U.S.C. §405. Evidence; procedure ...

(d) Issuance of subpenas in administrative proceedings

For the purpose of any hearing, investigation, or other proceeding authorized or directed under this subchapter, or relative to any other matter within the Commissioner's jurisdiction hereunder, the Commissioner of Social Security shall have power to issue subpenas requiring the attendance and testimony of witnesses and the production of any evidence that relates to any matter under investigation or in question before the Commissioner of Social Security....

When an agency has adjudicatory subpoena authority, §555(d) requires the agency to make this power available to any party on request. At the same time, §555(d) allows the agency to adopt rules requiring a person to show a need for the subpoenaed evidence. A person usually makes that showing in a formal adjudication by submitting a subpoena request to the ALJ assigned to hear the case. The ALJ, then, is authorized by §556(c)(2) to exercise the agency's subpoena power.

The way adjudicatory subpoenas ordinarily work is that they order a person to show up, or produce documentary evidence, or both, at the evidentiary hearing before the ALJ. Thus, subpoenas ordinarily do not produce information during the prehearing stage, and are therefore not useful as a discovery tool. They do, however, provide a compulsory process for a party to get the evidence needed to support that party's position.

The fourth APA provision bearing on discovery is §552, the Freedom of Information Act (FOIA). FOIA entitles **"any person"** — not just parties to an agency adjudication — to request agency records from any federal agency — including, but not limited to, the agency before which the requester has an adjudicatory matter. 5 U.S.C. §552(a)(3)(A) (2012). The agency must make the records **"promptly available."** *Id.* A party to an agency adjudication can use FOIA to get records from federal agencies except to the extent the record contains information that FOIA exempts from disclosure. *Id.* §553(b). Although FOIA has its limits, the party to an agency adjudication should always consider using FOIA for discovery. *See* Edward Tomlinson, *Use of the Freedom of Information Act for Discovery Purposes*, 43 Md. L. Rev. 119 (1984).

In sum, the APA does not address discovery in agency adjudications comprehensively, nor does it grant agencies any discovery authority. The APA does, however, have provisions of which the lawyer must be aware when preparing a case for the hearing.

b. The Agency Legislation

Sometimes the agency legislation addresses discovery in formal adjudications. For example, here is a portion of a provision from the Comprehensive Environmental Response, Compensation, and Liability Act (CERCLA), commonly known as the "Superfund Law." The provision authorizes civil penalties for certain CERCLA violations:

---

42 U.S.C. §9609. Civil Penalties and awards …

(b) Class II administrative penalty

A civil penalty of not more than $25,000 per day for each day during which the violation continues may be assessed by the President in the case of any of the following [violations].… In any proceeding for the assessment of a civil penalty under this subsection the President may issue subpoenas for the attendance and testimony of witnesses and the production of relevant papers, books, and documents and may promulgate rules for discovery procedures.…

The President has delegated power under this provision to the EPA and the Coast Guard. *See* Exec. Order No. 12,580, §4(b)(2), (c)(2) & (d)(2), 3 C.F.R. 193 (1988).

c. Agency Rules

Most of the time, discovery powers and procedures are addressed in detail, if at all, only by the agency's own rules. The agency may have express or implied authority to adopt such rules under the same agency legislation that authorizes the agency to conduct formal adjudications. *See, e.g.*, 35 U.S.C. §316(a)(5)–(7) (2012) (requiring Director of U.S. Patent and Trademark Office to issue regulations governing discovery in certain proceedings). In addition, the agency's own executive authority may justify its adoption of procedural rules for carrying out its statutory responsibilities. Armed with such authority, the agency may pattern its discovery rules on the Federal Rules of Civil Procedure. Alternatively, the agency may adopt or modify the discovery rules of other agencies.

Some federal agencies have detailed rules for discovery. For example, the Securities and Exchange Commission has "Rules of Practice" that include rules for subpoenas, depositions upon oral examination, and depositions upon written questions. *See* 17 C.F.R. §§201.232–201.234 (2012). The Federal Trade Commission's Rules of Practice likewise address discovery tools in detail. 16 C.F.R. §§3.31–3.40 (2012).

d. Due Process

Due process applies to a formal adjudication that deprives or threatens to deprive someone of liberty or property. Due process does not, however, create an across-the-board right to prehearing discovery in those formal adjudications. *See, e.g., NLRB v. Interboro Contractors, Inc.*, 432 F.2d 854, 857–858 (2d Cir. 1970), *cert. denied*, 402 U.S. 915 (1971). Instead, due process may require an agency to grant discovery to a party if the agency has the power to do so and if the discovery is necessary for fairness in that particular agency adjudication. *See McClelland v. Andrus*, 606 F.2d 1278, 1285–1286 (D.C. Cir. 1979).

Here are two situations in which due process might require discovery in an agency adjudication:

- The State Board of Medical Examiners issues a complaint charging a physician with making unwanted sexual advances to several patients. Before the administrative hearing on that complaint, the physician requests copies of any written statements that the complaining patients made to Medical Board personnel.

- The EPA has issued an order assessing large civil fines against a company for contaminating a nearby stream. The company asks for a hearing on that order before an ALJ. Before the hearing, the company asks the EPA prosecutors to disclose the identity of any agency official who will testify at the hearing about the basis for the agency's determination that the company was the source of the contamination. The company also requests any written reports prepared by any such official.

The most important thing to understand is that, in situations like the two above, the agency legislation or the agency rules almost always allow discovery. That is because due process requirements will have been considered, and provided for, by the legislature, when authorizing the adjudications, or by the agency, when making rules for the adjudications. For that reason, it is rare for courts to hold that an agency's denial of discovery violated due process. More often, the court will find that an agency has violated its own discovery rules, or the agency legislation authorizing discovery. The lawyer seeking discovery from the agency may wish to argue that the agency rules and legislation must be interpreted in light of due process concerns.

3. Settlement

Many agency adjudications end by settlement. Indeed, an adjudicatory matter may settle even before the adjudication formally begins.

Section 556(c) of the federal APA contemplates that the ALJ or other official assigned to preside at the hearing may hold a settlement conference and encourage other means of resolving the matter without a hearing:

---

5 U.S.C. § 556. Hearings; presiding employees; powers and duties ...

(c) Subject to published rules of the agency and within its powers, employees presiding at hearings may— ...

(6) hold conferences for the settlement or simplification of the issues by consent of the parties or by the use of alternative means of dispute resolution as provided in subchapter IV of this chapter;

(7) inform the parties as to the availability of one or more alternative means of dispute resolution, and encourage use of such methods; [and]

(8) require the attendance at any conference held pursuant to paragraph (6) of at least one representative of each party who has authority to negotiate concerning resolution of issues in controversy....

Settlement has huge importance because it is so commonly used to resolve agency adjudications. Generalizations about it, however, are difficult and dangerous, as true of other subjects of administrative law. We introduce three questions that attorneys must ask themselves about settlement:

a.   Must someone in the agency approve the settlement, and, if so, who?

b.   What is the procedure for settlement?

c.   Can someone dissatisfied with the settlement seek judicial review?

Below we briefly examine each question.

a. Agency Approval of Settlements

In most *court* cases, the parties alone decide whether to settle. They do not need the court's approval. *See, e.g.,* Fed. R. Civ. P. 41(a)(1) (authorizing voluntary dismissal without court approval except in certain cases, such as certified class actions and derivative actions). The court usually must approve the settlement only if the parties want to enter into a judicially enforceable consent decree.

Turning to the administrative context: It can be complicated, and yet essential, to determine who needs to approve settlement of an agency adjudication. It is essential, for example, because, if the wrong agency official approves a settlement, the settlement will probably be invalid. *See, e.g.,* In re *Buckley v. Town of Wappinger*, 785 N.Y.S. 2nd 98 (App. Div. 2004) (town Board resolution authorizing town supervisor and town attorney to execute a stipulation settling a zoning enforcement action was unenforceable because it usurped the authority of Zoning Administrator, Zoning Board of Appeals, and Planning Board); *see also Federal Crop Insurance Corp. v. Merrill*, 332 U.S. 380, 384 (1947) ("[A]nyone entering into an arrangement with the Government takes the risk of having accurately ascertained that he who purports to act for the Government stays within the bounds of his authority."). It can be complicated to determine who within an agency, if anyone, must approve a settlement partly because agencies may have multiple roles in adjudicatory matters.

In some agency adjudications, the parties to the adjudication are private individuals or entities, and the agency acts only in a quasi-judicial role. An example of this is a workers' compensation agency, which adjudicates workers' compensation claims by employees against their employers. *See, e.g., Oceanic Butler, Inc. v. Nordahl*, 842 F.2d 773 (5th Cir. 1988) (discussing settlement of workers' compensation claim adjudicated before the U.S. Department of Labor under the federal Longshore and Harbor Workers' Compensation Act); *see also Melton v. Pasqua*, 339 F.3d 222 (4th Cir. 2003) (discussing settlement of administrative claims asserted by a customer against a commodity futures trading company and its employees, asserting violations of the federal Commodity Exchange Act). If the agency plays only a quasi-judicial role in the adjudication, its role in the settlement may be limited to accepting the parties' stipulation to a voluntary dismissal of a private party's claims against another private party. On the other hand, the agency may have to approve the settlement, just as judges sometimes must.

In other agency adjudications, part of the agency is a party to the litigation and another part of the agency acts in a quasi-judicial role. This scenario most commonly arises when an agency initiates an agency adjudication against someone who has supposedly violated an agency statute or rule. Part of the agency will prosecute the case by proving the violation to the satisfaction of another part of the agency that acts as the judge. *See, e.g., Action on Safety & Health v. Federal Trade Comm'n*, 498 F.2d 757 (D.C. Cir. 1974) (discussing procedure by which Federal Trade Commission issued consent order settling claims that Volvo, Inc., violated Federal Trade Commission Act by false and deceptive advertising). Settlement of these cases may involve the agency's investigative or prosecutorial officials, its quasi-judicial officials, or both. *See id.* at 759.

Lawyers whose clients have adjudicatory matters before agencies must keep settlement in mind as a possible way of resolving the matter favorably to the client, and must determine who in the agency, if anyone, must approve the settlement.

b. Agency Settlement Procedures

Agency settlement procedures are ordinarily governed by the agency legislation and the agency's own rules. The federal APA requires an agency to provide an opportunity for settlement in formal adjudications but qualifies that opportunity and says nothing about the procedures for settlement:

---

5 U.S.C. § 554. Adjudications ...

(c) The agency shall give all interested parties opportunity for—

(1) the submission and consideration of facts, arguments, offers of settlement, or proposals of adjustment when time, the nature of the proceeding, and the public interest permit ...

The agency legislation may or may not address settlement. If not, then the agency rules are the exclusive source of procedural requirements. Rather than explore the range of possibilities, we will examine settlement of matters before the Consumer Product Safety Commission (CPSC).

The CPSC has authority under the Consumer Product Safety Act (CPSA) to initiate a formal adjudication under the federal APA to remedy "substantial product hazards." 15 U.S.C. § 2064(c) & (d) (2012). The CPSA contemplates that parties to the adjudication may include not only the agency and the company that makes or distributes the hazardous product, but also "consumers and consumer organizations." *Id.* § 2064(c)(1) & (d)(1). The CPSA further indicates that at the formal hearing in the adjudication the parties may submit a settlement proposal to the ALJ:

---

15 U.S.C. § 2064. Substantial product hazards ...

(f) Hearing

(1) Except as provided in paragraph (2), an order under subsection (c) or (d) of this section may be issued only after an opportunity for a hearing in accordance with section 554 of Title 5.... Any settlement offer which is submitted to the

presiding officer at a hearing under this subsection shall be transmitted by the officer to the Commission for its consideration unless the settlement offer is clearly frivolous or duplicative of offers previously made....

A CPSC regulation prescribes procedures for submitting settlement offers to the ALJ who presides at the hearing, and for the ALJ's transmitting those offers to the Commission. 16 C.F.R. § 1025.26 (2012).

Interestingly, a *separate* CPSC regulation authorizes settlements to occur even before the Commission initiates an adjudication. This regulation authorizes settlements between a manufacturer and the Commission staff. In particular, the regulation authorizes the Commission staff to settle a matter by entering into a "consent order agreement," subject to Commission approval. Set out next is the portion of the regulation detailing the process for entry of a consent order agreement. You will see that the process includes a chance for the public to comment on a proposed consent order agreement:

---

16 C.F.R. 1115.20. Voluntary remedial actions ...

(b) Consent order agreements under section 15 of CPSA. The consent order agreement (agreement) is a document executed by a subject firm (Consenting Party) and a Commission staff representative which incorporates both a proposed complaint setting forth the staff's charges and a proposed order by which such charges are resolved.

(1) Consent order agreements shall include, as appropriate [specified terms] ...

(2) At any time in the course of an investigation, the staff may propose to a subject firm which is being investigated that some or all of the allegations be resolved by a consent order agreement. Additionally, such a proposal may be made to the staff by a subject firm.

(3) Upon receiving an executed agreement, the Commission may:

(i) Provisionally accept it;

(ii) Reject it and issue a complaint (in which case an administrative and/or judicial proceeding will be commenced); or

(iii) Take such other action as it may deem appropriate.

(4) If the consent order agreement is provisionally accepted, the Commission shall place the agreement on the public record and shall announce provisional acceptance of the agreement in the Commission's public calendar and in the Federal Register. Any interested person may request the Commission not to accept the agreement by filing a written request in the Office of the Secretary. Such written request must be received in the Office of the Secretary no later than the close of business of the fifteenth (15th) calendar day following the date of announcement in the Federal Register.

(5) If the Commission does not receive any requests not to accept the agreement within the time period specified above, the consent order agreement shall be deemed finally accepted by the Commission on the twentieth (20th) calendar day after the date of announcement in the Federal Register, unless the Commission determines otherwise. However, if the Commission does receive a request not to accept the consent order agreement, then it will consider such request and

vote on the acceptability of such agreement or the desirability of further action. After the consent order agreement is finally accepted, the Commission may then issue its complaint and order in such form as the circumstances may require. The order is a final order in disposition of the proceeding and is effective immediately upon its service upon the Consenting Party pursuant to the Commission's Rules of Practice for Adjudicative Proceedings (16 CFR part 1025). The Consenting Party shall thereafter be bound by and take immediate action in accordance with such final order.

(6) If the Commission does not accept the consent order agreement on a final basis, it shall so notify the Consenting Party. Such notification constitutes withdrawal of the Commission's provisional acceptance unless the Commission orders otherwise. The Commission then may:

(i) Issue a complaint, in which case an administrative and/or judicial proceeding will be commenced;

(ii) Order further investigation; or

(iii) Take such other action as it may deem appropriate....

This regulation reflects that many manufacturers and distributors of consumer products will want to settle matters before the Commission initiates a proceeding formally charging the existence of a "substantial product hazard." Without studying the Commission's rules, the lawyer with such a client won't even know this pre-complaint settlement process exists because, as noted above, the statute refers only to settlement offers made at the hearing.

The chances are good that an agency that conducts formal adjudications will have rules governing settlement. The lawyer representing private clients with adjudicatory matters before the agency should aim to master those rules as completely as the agency's lawyers are likely to have done.

c. Judicial Review of Settlements

The CPSC settlement procedure discussed above gives the public a chance to object to the Commission's acceptance of a proposed consent order agreement. The opportunity for public objections reflects that agency adjudications may affect the public as well as the parties. Members of the public may not like a settlement that the parties have reached. If the non-parties feel strongly enough (and have the resources), they may want judicial review of the settlement.

Sometimes judicial review will be available; other times it will not. It depends on the statutes governing the settlement and judicial review. Three cases illustrate the statute-specific nature of the availability of judicial review of settlements of adjudicatory matters before agencies.

- *National Labor Relations Board v. United Food & Commercial Workers Union, Local 23 (NLRB v. Food Workers)*, 484 U.S. 112 (1987)

In this case, the U.S. Supreme Court held that judicial review of the settlement of an administrative case was not available.

The United Food Workers union filed a document with the Pittsburgh, Pennsylvania, regional office of the National Labor Relations Board (NLRB). In that document, the Food Workers charged another union, the United Steelworkers, plus a grocery store chain,

Charley Brothers, with an unfair labor practice. Specifically, the Food Workers charged that the Steelworkers had entered into a collective bargaining agreement with Charley Brothers to represent the employees at a particular Charley Brothers store, but the employees at that store had not actually validly chosen the Steelworkers to represent them. Under these circumstances, the collective bargaining agreement violated those workers' rights under the National Labor Relations Act to decide which union, if any, would represent them in bargaining with their employer about terms and conditions of employment. (As you might guess, the Food Workers wanted to be the union for that Charley Brothers store.)

The Regional Director of the Pittsburgh office of the NLRB investigated the charges and began settlement negotiations with Charley Brothers and the Steelworkers. No settlement was reached. The Regional Director then filed a formal complaint that initiated an unfair labor practice proceeding—a type of formal adjudication—against Charley Brothers and the Steelworkers (the "charged parties"). The case was scheduled for an oral, evidentiary hearing before an ALJ employed by the Board. Before the hearing, however, the Regional Director reached a tentative, informal settlement with the two charged parties. The Regional Director invited the Food Workers, as the "charging party," to join the agreement, but the Food Workers refused. The Regional Director nonetheless went ahead by settling the unfair labor practice charges against the Steelworkers and Charley Brothers.

The Food Workers administratively appealed the Regional Director's decision to settle the matter to the General Counsel of the NLRB. The General Counsel upheld the Regional Director's decision, after which the Food Workers sought judicial review of the General Counsel's decision.

The U.S. Supreme Court held that the General Counsel's decision approving the settlement was not subject to judicial review under either of the two statutes upon which the Food Workers relied in seeking judicial review.

The Court held, first, that the General Counsel's decision was not subject to review under the National Labor Relations Act because the Act authorizes review only of decisions of the Board—i.e., the five-member body that heads the agency—and the General Counsel's decision was not a decision of the Board. The Court explained that Congress differentiated between decisions of the General Counsel, who plays investigative and prosecutorial roles under the Act, from decisions of the Board, which plays an adjudicative role under the Act. The General Counsel's decision to settle, rather than to *prosecute*, an unfair labor practice charge could not be equated to an *adjudicative* decision by the Board, which had not yet held an evidentiary hearing on the charge. *See* 484 U.S. at 117–130.

The Court further held that the General Counsel's decision upholding the settlement was not subject to review under the federal APA. The federal APA does not authorize judicial review if another statute "preclude[s] judicial review." 5 U.S.C. § 701(a)(1) (2012). The Court concluded that the National Labor Relations Act does preclude judicial review of a "prosecutorial" action such as the General Counsel's decision to sustain a post-complaint, prehearing informal settlement without the charging party's consent. The Court based its decision on a close study of the National Labor Relations Act and the consequences of allowing judicial review of settlement agreements. *See* 484 U.S. at 130–134.

In sum, judicial review of the settlement was unavailable in *NLRB v. Food Workers* because the agency legislation not only failed to authorize judicial review; it precluded judicial review under the federal APA.

- *Baltimore Gas & Electric Co. v. Federal Energy Regulatory Commission (BG&E v. FERC)*, 252 F.3d 456 (D.C. Cir. 2001)

In *Baltimore Gas & Electric*, a court of appeals held that the settlement of an administrative case was not subject to judicial review.

The Federal Energy Regulatory Commission (FERC) administers the Natural Gas Act, which regulates companies that produce natural gas and sell it in interstate commerce. FERC licenses natural gas companies to provide services at specified levels. FERC learned that one company, called "Columbia," was providing natural gas through one of its pipelines at a lower capacity than FERC had approved. The multi-person Commission that heads FERC (the Commission) directed FERC's General Counsel to investigate whether Columbia's failure to provide natural gas at the FERC-approved levels violated the Natural Gas Act.

After a four-year investigation, the Commission approved a settlement between Columbia and the FERC General Counsel. One of Columbia's natural gas customers, Baltimore Gas & Electric (BG&E), objected to this settlement. Specifically, BG&E objected that the settlement did not require Columbia to pay money damages to its customers. The Commission rejected that objection and issued an order approving the settlement. BG&E sought judicial review of the Commission's order in the United States Court of Appeals for the District of Columbia Circuit.

The D.C. Circuit held that the federal APA precluded judicial review of the Commission's order. The APA precludes judicial review **"to the extent that ... agency action is committed to agency discretion by law."** 5 U.S.C. § 701(a)(2). The D.C. Circuit held that Commission's approval of the settlement was committed to the Commission's discretion by law. The D.C. Circuit relied on the U.S. Supreme Court's decision in *Heckler v. Chaney*, 470 U.S. 821 (1985). The U.S. Supreme Court in *Heckler v. Chaney* held that a federal agency's decision not to undertake enforcement action against a supposed violator is presumptively **"committed to agency discretion by law"** within the meaning of § 701(a)(2) of the APA. *Id.* at 831. That was because an agency's decisions about how to enforce its statute and regulations ordinarily rests on considerations that courts are not well equipped to second guess. In a case decided before the *BG&E* case arose, the D.C. Circuit had held that "the [*Heckler v.*] *Chaney* presumption of nonreviewability extends not just to a decision whether to bring an enforcement action, but to a decision to settle." *BG&E v. FERC*, 252 F.3d at 459. In *BG&E v. FERC*, the D.C. Circuit relied on that prior holding to refuse review of the Commission's order approving settlement of the Columbia matter.

In *Heckler v. Chaney*, the U.S. Supreme Court said that the presumption of nonreviewability is overcome when a statute restricts an agency's enforcement discretion. The D.C. Circuit in *BG&E v. FERC* held that the Natural Gas Act did not restrict FERC's enforcement discretion. "Nowhere does the [Natural Gas Act] place an affirmative obligation on FERC to initiate an enforcement action, nor does it impose limitations on FERC's discretion to settle such an action." 252 F.3d at 460.

The Court in *Heckler v. Chaney* suggested other situations in which the presumption of nonreviewability might be overcome. The D.C. Circuit held in *BG&E v. FERC* that the case before it did not present any of those situations. Specifically, FERC's action did not rest on FERC's erroneous view of its authority, nor did FERC's action reflect a "general policy that is so extreme as to amount to an abdication of its statutory responsibility." *Id.* at 460 (quoting *Heckler v. Chaney*, 470 U.S. at 833 n.4).

Thus, judicial review of the settlement was unavailable in *BG&E v. FERC* because of the provision in § 701(a)(2) of the federal APA, as construed in *Heckler v. Chaney*, precluding judicial review when the law commits a matter to the agency's discretion.

- *Oceanic Butler, Inc. v. Nordahl*, 842 F.2d 773 (5th Cir. 1988)

In *Oceanic Butler*, a court reviewed an agency order approving a settlement between private parties. The agency legislation authorized judicial review of the agency's decisions and constrained the agency's authority to approve settlements.

Stig Nordahl, a longshoreman, filed a workers' compensation claim against his employer, Oceanic Butler, for an on-the-job injury. Mr. Nordahl claimed a right to compensation under the federal Longshore and Harbor Workers' Compensation Act (Longshore Act). Mr. Nordahl filed his workers' compensation claim with the agency that administers the Longshore Act, the U.S. Department of Labor.

While Mr. Nordahl's claim was pending before the Department of Labor, Mr. Nordahl reached a settlement with Oceanic Butler and its insurance company. A provision in the Longshore Act required the Department of Labor to approve this settlement. Specifically, the relevant statutory provision required the Department of Labor to approve the settlement "unless [the settlement] is found to be inadequate or procured by duress." *Id.* at 776 & n.2 (quoting statute, 33 U.S.C. § 908(i)(1), as it then existed; emphasis omitted). The settlement of Mr. Nordahl's claim was submitted to the Department of Labor for approval.

Before the Department of Labor could approve it, Mr. Nordahl died. At that point, Oceanic Butler and its insurer sought to withdraw from the settlement. The Department of Labor held that they could not withdraw. That holding mattered because the settlement, if approved, would still benefit Mr. Nordahl's estate. The Department of Labor's final order approving the settlement was made by an entity within the Department called the Benefits Review Board.

Oceanic Butler and its insurer sought judicial review of the Benefits Review Board's order approving the settlement under this statute:

---

33 U.S.C. § 921. Review of compensation orders ...

(c) Court of appeals ...

Any person adversely affected or aggrieved by a final order of the [Benefits Review] Board may obtain a review of that order in the United States court of appeals for the circuit in which the injury occurred, by filing in such court within sixty days following the issuance of such Board order a written petition praying that the order be modified or set aside. A copy of such petition shall be forthwith transmitted by the clerk of the court, to the Board, and to the other parties, and thereupon the Board shall file in the court the record in the proceedings as provided in section 2112 of Title 28. Upon such filing, the court shall have jurisdiction of the proceeding and shall have the power to give a decree affirming, modifying, or setting aside, in whole or in part, the order of the Board and enforcing same to the extent that such order is affirmed or modified....

Oceanic Butler and its insurer argued that they had a right to withdraw from the settlement while it was pending for Board approval. They also argued that the Board violated the Longshore Act by approving a settlement that was "inadequate" within the meaning of 33 U.S.C. § 908(i)(1) (quoted in relevant part above).

The court of appeals rejected both arguments and affirmed the Board's decision. More importantly for our purposes, the court *did* review the Board's order approving the settlement. Thus, the court implicitly held that judicial review of the agency's approval of the settlement was available.

You may be wondering: Why was judicial review of the settlement available in this case, while it was not available in *NLRB v. Food Workers* or *BG&E v. FERC*? The *Nordahl* case differs from each of those cases in relevant ways. In *NLRB v. Food Workers*, the Court held that a statute (the National Labor Relations Act) precluded judicial review. In *Nordahl*, in contrast, a statute authorized judicial review. In *BG&E v. FERC*, the court held that FERC's approval of the settlement was **"committed to agency discretion by law,"** because the Natural Gas Act did not restrict FERC's discretion to settle the case before it. 252 F.3d at 462 (quoting APA § 701(a)(2)). In *Nordahl*, in contrast, a statute did restrict the agency's discretion to settle a case: The statute required the agency to approve the settlement unless the settlement was "found to be inadequate or procured by duress." *Nordahl*, 842 F.2d at 776 & n.2 (quoting statute, 33 U.S.C. § 908(i)(1), as it then existed; emphasis omitted). That statutory restriction on agency discretion overcame the presumption of nonreviewability applied in *BG&E v. FERC*.

Your takeaway from this discussion of judicial review of settlements of adjudicatory matters should be that the availability of judicial review is highly statute-specific, like so many other matters of administrative law. The competent lawyer must understand the availability of judicial review before settling an adjudicatory matter with an agency.

4. Prehearing Conferences

Section 556 of the federal APA authorizes the ALJ or other presiding official to hold prehearing conferences:

---

5 U.S.C. § 556. Hearings; presiding employees; powers and duties ...

(c) Subject to published rules of the agency and within its powers, employees presiding at hearings may— ...

(6) hold conferences for the settlement or simplification of the issues by consent of the parties or by the use of alternative means of dispute resolution as provided in subchapter IV of this chapter ...

This power, like the ten other powers of presiding officials listed in § 556(c), is subject to the agency's published rules and may be exercised only **"within [the agency's] powers."** *Id*. Section 556(c) thus vests in the ALJ or other presiding official the eleven enumerated powers only if a statute outside the APA has given those powers to the agency. *See* AGM 74. Of course, some of those powers—including the power to hold a prehearing conference—would ordinarily be implied by the agency's power to hold the hearing.

Although § 556(c) mentions only two purposes for prehearing conferences—to explore settlement or simplify issues—prehearing conferences may explore other issues. Typically, the ALJ assigned to a formal adjudication will issue an order scheduling the prehearing conference and identifying the issues that the parties' lawyers must address at the conference. For example, Figure 22-B reproduces an order from an ALJ in an FTC adjudication scheduling a prehearing conference.

The Commission rule cited in the order in Figure 22-B states:

Figure 22-B. Sample Agency Order Scheduling Prehearing Conference

UNITED STATES OF AMERICA
FEDERAL TRADE COMMISSION
OFFICE OF ADMINISTRATIVE LAW JUDGES

In the Matter of	)
	)
GRACO INC.,	)
a corporation, and	)
	) DOCKET NO. 9350
ILLINOIS TOOL WORKS INC.,	)
a corporation, and	)
	)
ITW FINISHING LLC,	)
a limited liability company,	)
Respondents.	)

ORDER SETTING SCHEDULING CONFERENCE

Pursuant to Commission Rule 3.21(b), which requires a scheduling conference within ten days after the Answer is filed, the initial scheduling conference will be held on January 12, 2012, at 1:00 p.m. in Room 532, Federal Trade Commission Building, 600 Pennsylvania Avenue NW, Washington, DC.

The parties are directed to meet before the scheduling conference and to comply with Commission Rule 3.21(a) and (b). The expected scheduling order will be provided to the parties in advance of the scheduling conference.

ORDERED: _DM Chappell_____
                              D. Michael Chappell
                              Chief Administrative Law Judge

Date: January 4, 2012

16 C.F.R. § 3.21 Prehearing procedures.

(a) Meeting of the parties before scheduling conference. As early as practicable before the prehearing scheduling conference described in paragraph (b) of this section, but in any event no later than 5 days after the answer is filed by the last answering respondent, counsel for the parties shall meet to discuss the nature and basis of their claims and defenses and the possibilities for a prompt settlement or resolution of the case. The parties shall also agree, if possible, on (1) a proposed discovery plan specifically addressing a schedule for depositions of fact witnesses, the production of documents and electronically stored information, and the timing of expert discovery pursuant to § 3.31A. The parties' agreement regarding electronically stored information should include the scope of and a specified time period for the exchange of such information that is subject to §§ 3.31(b)(2), 3.31(c), and 3.37(a), and the format for the disclosure of such information, consistent with § 3.31(c)(3) and § 3.37(c); (2) a preliminary estimate of the time required for the evidentiary hearing; and (3) any other matters to be determined at the scheduling conference.

(b) Scheduling conference. Not later than 10 days after the answer is filed by the last answering respondent, the Administrative Law Judge shall hold a scheduling conference. At the scheduling conference, counsel for the parties shall be prepared to address: (1) their factual and legal theories; (2) the current status of any pending motions; (3) a schedule of proceedings that is consistent with the date of the evidentiary hearing set by the Commission; (4) steps taken to preserve evidence relevant to the issues raised by the claims and defenses; (5) the scope of anticipated discovery, any limitations on discovery, and a proposed discovery plan, including the disclosure of electronically stored information; (6) issues that can be narrowed by agreement or by motion, suggestions to expedite the presentation of evidence at trial, and any request to bifurcate issues, claims or defenses; and (7) other possible agreements or steps that may aid in the just and expeditious disposition of the proceeding and to avoid unnecessary cost....

If the prehearing conference makes clear that the parties probably won't settle, the conference results in an order scheduling deadlines for events, such as the completion of discovery, that must occur before the hearing. For example, Figure 22-C reproduces a portion of the scheduling order that resulted from the prehearing scheduling conference in the FTC matter that was the subject of the order reproduced above in Figure 22-B.

5. Administrative Summary Judgment

Formal adjudications under the federal APA are, by definition, adjudications in which a statute requires an opportunity for a hearing. 5 U.S.C. § 554(a). In some formal adjudications, however, there will be no need for a hearing, because there will be no genuine dispute of material fact. The U.S. Supreme Court has made clear that in such situations, federal agencies can use an administrative version of summary judgment to make decisions:

- *Weinberger v. Hynson, Westcott & Dunning, Inc.*, 412 U.S. 609 (1973)

This case arose under the Federal Food, Drug, and Cosmetic Act of 1938. As amended in 1962, the Act required the Food and Drug Administration (FDA) to review the efficacy of drugs that the FDA had previously approved. The Act also required the FDA, after

Figure 22-C. Excerpt of Scheduling Order in FTC Adjudication

UNITED STATES OF AMERICA
FEDERAL TRADE COMMISSION
OFFICE OF ADMINISTRATIVE LAW JUDGES

In the Matter of)
 	
GRACO INC.,)
   a corporation, and)
 	
ILLINOIS TOOL WORKS INC.,)
   a corporation, and)
 	
ITW FINISHING LLC,)
   a limited liability company,)
      Respondents.)
	DOCKET NO. 9350

SCHEDULING ORDER

January 26, 2012   -   Complaint Counsel provides preliminary witness list (not including experts) with a brief summary of the proposed testimony.

February 9, 2012   -   Deadline for issuing document requests, requests for admission, interrogatories and subpoenas *duces tecum*, except for discovery for purposes of authenticity and admissibility of exhibits.

February 9, 2012   -   Respondents' Counsel provides preliminary witness lists (not including experts) with a brief summary of the proposed testimony.

February 14, 2012   -   Complaint Counsel provides expert witness list.

February 21, 2012   -   Respondents' Counsel provides expert witness list.

March 16, 2012   -   Close of discovery, other than discovery permitted under Rule 3.24(a)(4), depositions of experts, and discovery for purposes of authenticity and admissibility of exhibits.

March 23, 2012   -   Deadline for Complaint Counsel to provide expert witness reports.

"notice and opportunity for hearing" to withdraw a drug's approval if the FDA determined, on the record, "that there [was] a lack of substantial evidence" of the drug's efficacy. *Hynson*, 412 U.S. at 617 n.9 (quoting statute). The Act defined "substantial evidence" to mean:

> evidence consisting of adequate and well-controlled investigations, including clinical investigations, by experts qualified by scientific training and experience to evaluate the effectiveness of the drug involved, on the basis of which it could fairly and responsibly be concluded by such experts that the drug will have the effect it purports or is represented to have.

Id. at 613 n.3 (quoting statute).

The FDA issued legislative rules providing "detailed guidelines" (*id.* at 617) on what constituted "substantial evidence" as defined in the Act. The Court observed that the rules' "strict and demanding standards, barring anecdotal evidence indicating that doctors 'believe' in the efficacy of a drug, are amply justified by the legislative history [showing] a marked concern that impressions or beliefs of physicians, no matter how fervently held, are treacherous." *Id.* at 619. The FDA's rules also included a rule providing for "administrative summary judgment." *Id.* at 617. As the Court described it:

> FDA ... by regulation, requires any applicant who desires a hearing to submit reasons "why the application ... should not be withdrawn, together with a well-organized and full-factual analysis of the clinical and other investigational data he [or she] is prepared to prove in support of his [or her] opposition to the notice of opportunity for a hearing.... When it clearly appears from the data in the application and from the reasons and factual analysis in the request for the hearing that there is no genuine and substantial issue of fact..., e.g., no adequate and well-controlled clinical investigations to support the claims of effectiveness," the [FDA] Commissioner may deny a hearing and enter an order withdrawing the application based solely on these data. [Citation to the FDA's summary judgment rule is omitted.] What the agency has said, then, is that it will not provide a formal hearing where it is apparent at the threshold that the applicant has not tendered any evidence which on its face meets the statutory standards as particularized by the regulations.

Id. at 620. The Court held that the FDA's summary judgment procedure was "appropriate," and consistent with both the statutory provision requiring an "opportunity for a hearing" and due process. The Court said, "We cannot impute to Congress the design of requiring, nor does due process demand, a hearing when it appears conclusively from the applicant's 'pleadings' that the application cannot succeed." *Id.* at 621.

In light of the Court's decision in *Hynson*, "[a]dministrative summary judgment is ... widely accepted" by the lower federal courts, even in adjudications under statutes or agency rules requiring an opportunity for a hearing. *Puerto Rico Aqueduct & Sewer Auth. v. EPA*, 35 F.3d 600 (1st Cir. 1994). *But cf. Kirkendall v. Dep't of the Army*, 479 F.3d 830, 844–845 (Fed. Cir. 2007) (en banc) (interpreting statutes to give an absolute right to a hearing to a veteran claiming discrimination by the Army). You can generally expect to find agency rules for administrative summary judgment when the agency uses that process to decide some adjudicatory matters. Sometimes, though, the process goes by a different name. *See, e.g.,* 16 C.F.R. § 1025.25 (2012) (Consumer Product Safety Commission rule providing for "[s]ummary decisions and orders"); *cf. Crestview Parke Care Ctr. v. Thompson*, 373 F.3d 743, 749–750 (6th Cir. 2004) (HHS rule providing for administrative summary judgment was in unpublished, "interpretive" rule). Many lower federal courts review a federal agency's decision on administrative summary judgment using the same standard of review they use for a decision made after an evidentiary hearing. *See Cedar Lake Nursing Home v. U.S. Dep't of Health & Human Servs.*, 619 F.3d 453, 457 (5th Cir. 2010).

An agency with both rulemaking power and adjudicatory power may use its rulemaking power to facilitate summary disposition of adjudications. The most famous case illustrating this use of the rulemaking power is *United States v. Storer Broadcasting Co.*, 351 U.S. 192 (1956), a case cited in *Hynson*, 412 U.S. at 620, 625. *Storer* involved an FCC rule that generally limited the number of broadcasting stations a company could own. The FCC could rely on this rule to deny a license for a new station to a company that already had the maximum number of stations permitted under the rule and that did not justify a waiver of the rule. A broadcast company challenged the rule, arguing that it violated a statute requiring the FCC to hold a "full hearing" on license applications. *Storer Broadcasting*, 351 U.S. at 202 (quoting statute). The Court rejected the company's argument. The Court held that an agency may use its rulemaking power to make rules that, as applied, dispense in certain cases with the need for adjudicatory hearings otherwise required by statute. *See id.* at 202–205. Together, *Hynson* and *Storer Broadcasting* allow an agency to adopt across-the-board rules to address recurrent issues, and thereby summarily decide adjudications that would otherwise require evidentiary hearings. *See* Richard E. Levy & Sidney A. Shapiro, *Administrative Procedure and the Decline of the Trial*, 51 U. Kan. L. Rev. 473, 481 (2003).

You should know about administrative summary judgment for two reasons. For one thing, you might otherwise wonder whether an agency can decide an adjudicatory matter without a hearing when a statute requires an opportunity for a hearing. For another thing, understanding administrative summary judgment helps you appreciate the synergy that can exist between an agency's rulemaking power — when used to make across-the-board rules like the one at issue in *Storer Broadcasting* — and its adjudicatory power.

E. Initiation and Prehearing Procedures in Contested Cases under a State APA

The 2010 Model State APA does not use the term "formal adjudication." Instead, the 2010 Model State APA, like most state APAs, uses the term "contested case" to mean agency adjudication in which the law requires an opportunity for an evidentiary hearing. The 2010 Model State APA defines a "contested case" as "an adjudication in which an opportunity for an evidentiary hearing is required by the federal constitution, a federal statute, or the constitution or a statute of this state." 2010 Model State APA § 102 (7); *see also* 1961 Model State APA § 1(2) (defining "contested case" as one "in which the legal rights, duties, or privileges of a party are required by law to be determined by an agency after an opportunity for hearing"). The 2010 Model State APA also prescribes procedures for contested cases.

This section discusses procedures relating to the initiation and prehearing procedures in a contested case. This discussion of procedures under the 2010 Model State APA includes some comparisons to formal adjudications under the federal APA and to contested cases under particular state APAs.

1. Initiation of Contested Cases

Many contested cases begin when an agency takes an action adverse to a person. An agency many deny benefits, deny a license, or decide a person should be fined or suffer another sanction for a statutory or regulatory violation. These agency actions, often taken by a "front line" agency official, can spark a contested case if the person adversely affected has a right to an evidentiary hearing before the agency to contest that action.

The 2010 Model State APA requires the agency to notify the person of the adverse action. The notification "must be in writing, set forth the agency action, inform the person of the right, procedure, and time limit to file a contested case petition, and provide a copy of the agency procedures governing the contested case." 2010 Model State APA § 403(b). This notice requirement, which has no counterpart in the federal APA, is separate from the requirement that comes into play once a contested case begins and that requires parties receive notice of the evidentiary hearing.

Once a contested case begins, the agency must give notice of its commencement. The 2010 Model State APA makes the agency responsible for giving notice regardless whether the contested case has been initiated by the agency itself—as is true, for example, in enforcement proceedings—or the contested case has been initiated instead by someone other than the agency—such as a person who has been denied a license or benefits. *See* 2010 Model State APA § 405(a). The required contents of the notice, however, differ depending on whether the agency initiated the case or someone else did. If the agency commenced the case, the notice must contain "a short and plain statement of the matters asserted, including the issues involved" and "a statement of the legal authority under which the hearing will be held citing the statutes and any rules involved." *Id.* § 405(c)(2) & (3).

Like the federal APA, the 2010 Model State APA does not identify who will be parties to a contested case. This omission probably reflects the impossibility of general rules for determining party status, considering the wide variety of agency adjudications that may occur under the APA. The 2010 Model State APA does include a provision addressing intervention; it is modeled on Federal Rule of Civil Procedure 24, which governs intervention in cases in the federal district courts. *See* 2010 Model State APA § 409.

2. Prehearing Procedures

The 2010 Model APA addresses who may preside at an evidentiary hearing. The 2010 Model State APA allows the presiding official to be (1) the individual who heads the agency (if the agency is headed by one person); (2) one or more member of the multi-person body that heads the agency (if the agency is headed by a multi-member body); or (3) an administrative law judge. 2010 Model State APA § 402(a). The 2010 Model State APA also authorizes a fourth option: The presiding official may be "an individual designated by the agency head" as long as that is not "prohibited by" state law. *Id.* Administrative law judges are probably the most common presiding officials in contested cases under state APAs, as is true in formal adjudications under the federal APA.

Federal ALJs are employed by the agency for which they hold hearings. About half the States likewise make an ALJ an employee of the state agency for which that ALJ holds hearings. The other half of the States take a different approach. They put their ALJs into an agency all its own. This is called the "central panel" approach. In States that take the central panel approach, the ALJs do not work for the agencies for which they hold hearings. They work for a separate agency with a name like "Office of Administrative Hearings." An ALJ in a central panel State may hold hearings for many different state agencies. The central panel approach is thought to make ALJs more independent of the agencies for which they hold hearings. The central panel approach also can give ALJs a broader perspective, by allowing them to preside over hearings in a wide variety of kinds of cases. The central panel approach has never been used in the federal government, though some scholars and practitioners have advocated it.

Although federal ALJs work for the agencies for which they hold hearings, the federal APA requires them to be impartial and has three provisions to assure impartiality. Those provisions, discussed earlier in this chapter, (1) require federal ALJs to be independent of the agency's investigative and prosecutorial officials (the "separation of functions" provision; (2) regulate the hiring and firing of ALJs to insulate them from agency pressure and bias; and (3) authorize disqualification of ALJs for bias.

The 2010 Model State APA has provisions comparable to the first and third. The 2010 Model State APA says that a person may not serve as an ALJ in a case if that person is "subject to the authority, direction, or discretion of an individual who has served as investigator, prosecutor, or advocate at any stage" of the same case. 2010 Model State APA § 402(b). The 2010 Model State APA also authorizes disqualification of ALJs "for bias, prejudice, financial interest, ex parte communications…, or any other factor that would cause a reasonable person to question the impartiality of" the ALJ. *Id.* § 402(c). The 2010 Model State APA does not address the hiring and firing of ALJs, except for a set of provisions designed for States with central panels. *See id.* §§ 601–605.

As discussed earlier in this chapter, the federal APA addresses prehearing discovery at most obliquely. In contrast, the 2010 Model State APA addresses discovery in detail in § 411. Section 411 reflects that "[c]ontested case proceedings can vary widely in the length and complexity of the issues to be decided." 2010 Model State APA, Official Comment to § 411. Section 411 accordingly offers "a range of options for discovery procedures." *Id.* Subsection 411(b) mandates disclosure of certain information by the parties, with protective orders provided for in subsection 411(d) and orders compelling discovery provided for in subsection 411(e). Subsection 411(f) allows an ALJ to bypass some or all of the other provisions in Section 411 by authorizing "discovery in accordance with the rules of civil procedure." Finally, subsection 411(g) allows an agency to exempt some or all of its contested cases from some or all of § 411 if the agency makes certain findings to the effect that the § 411 procedures are not appropriate.

As true of formal adjudications under the federal APA, contested cases under a state APA will often settle. Settlement can occur before, during, or after an evidentiary hearing. The 2010 Model State APA authorizes an ALJ to "refer the parties in a contested case to mediation or other dispute resolution procedure." The federal APA has a similar provision. *See* 5 U.S.C. § 556(c)(7) (2012). The 2010 Model State APA also authorizes "an agency" to "dispose of a contested case without a hearing by stipulation, agreed settlement, [or] consent order." 2010 Model State APA § 403(l). This authority to dispose of the case without a hearing by settlement or other means resides in the "agency," which means that the ALJ presiding over a contested case may or may not have final settlement authority, depending on the agency legislation and agency rules.

F. Chapter 22 Wrap Up and Look Ahead

This chapter has examined how formal adjudications begin and what happens before the hearing in a formal adjudication. The applicable federal or state APA will provide the framework for the initiation and prehearing stages, but inevitably many details remain to be filled in by the agency legislation, agency rules, and judicial and agency precedent interpreting the legislation and rules. This is a good place to mention that most agencies have unwritten rules governing how they do things, including how they do formal adjudications. The resourceful lawyer finds ways to discover these unwritten agency practices.

The next chapter discusses the hearing itself.

Chapter Problem Revisited

This chapter problem reflects the reality that many clients who may be subject to an agency adjudication in the form of an enforcement proceeding want to avoid the proceeding entirely or if that's not possible, end it as soon as possible.

Roughly speaking, the questions you must answer correspond to the three questions that form the problem solving framework presented in Chapter 2, relating to:

1. agency power: What can OSHA do to your client?

2. limits on agency power: Specifically, for example, what substantive rules for workplace safety exist that your client may have violated? What is the process that OSHA must use if it wants to penalize your client for violations of those rules?

3. remedies: If OSHA exceeds its powers or limits on that power, what can you do?

Two of the main sources for answering questions about these three issues are the agency legislation and the agency rules. You can expect the agency rules to include not only substantive rules about matters like worker safety gear but also procedural rules about the process for citing employers for violating the safety rules. There are likely to be both legislative rules, published in the CFR, and non-legislative rules, such as OSHA inspection manuals, that you must find and analyze. The agency rules are also likely to address the all-important issue of procedures for settling a matter informally.

We hope this chapter has alerted you to the need also to get an organization chart for the agency. This, together with the agency's procedural rules, will help you identify what components of the agency have various powers and responsibilities. If you can get your hands on an agency staff directory, you can even find out the names of the people who staff these components. For example, it would be good for you to know exactly who in the OSHA can settle any regulatory problems that arise for your client.

The OSH Act is 29 U.S.C. §§ 651–677 (2012). If you are interested in looking at the specific OSHA regulations relevant to this chapter problem, the regulations governing workplace inspections and citations are at 29 C.F.R. §§ 1903.1–1903.22 (2012). We found the citation for these regulations by first finding the statutory authority for OSHA inspections in the Westlaw database. The information accompanying that statutory authority (29 U.S.C. § 657) included citations to the regulations implementing the statute. Title 29 of the CFR has other OSHA rules. The regulations address settlement and other issues. *See* 29 C.F.R. § 1903.20 (2012).

Professional Development Reflection Question

This question concerns a case described in this chapter: *Lion Raisins, Inc. v. U.S. Dep't of Agriculture*, 2005 WL 6406066 (E.D. Cal. May 12, 2005). Lion Raisins suffered an administrative default judgment because its lawyer filed a motion to dismiss the complaint, instead of an answer, the latter of which was required by the agency's rules. Imagine you are Lion Raisins' attorney and that, through sheer oversight, you failed to understand that AMS rules required you in the formal adjudication to file an answer for Lion Raisins, not a motion to dismiss. What ethical obligations, if any, do you owe to (1) admit your mistake to your client; and (2) take other steps to make up for it?

Formal Adjudications under an APA — Hearings

Overview

Chapter 22 explored the pre-hearing stages of formal adjudications. This chapter examines the hearing stage of formal adjudications. As in Chapter 22, this chapter discusses formal adjudications under the federal APA separately from contested cases under a state APA and uses the 2010 Model State APA as the focus for discussing contested cases.

This chapter includes 4 sections:

A. Powers of a Presiding Official in a Formal Adjudication under the Federal APA

B. The Course of the Hearing in a Formal Adjudication under the Federal APA

C. The Course of the Hearing in a Formal Adjudication (Contested Case) under a State APA

D. Chapter 23 Wrap Up and Look Ahead

Chapter Problem

Memo

To: New Associate

From: Partner

Re: Help preparing for a hearing on OSHA citations

We have a client who owns a metal fabrication plant. Last week officials from the Occupational Safety and Health Administration (OSHA) inspected the plant, and the inspectors informally advised the client that OSHA was likely to issue citations for violations of several OSHA workplace safety standards.

I hope we can settle this without going to a hearing, but I want to prepare for all contingencies. The statute authorizing employers to challenge OSHA citations and get a hearing is 29 U.S.C. §659(c) (2012). According to this statute, citations are administratively reviewed and hearings held by an entity that is separate from OSHA; it's called the Occupational Safety and Health Review Commission.

I gather that hearings before the Commission are formal adjudications, though I would like you to confirm this. I'd also like you to find and examine the Commission's rules for these adjudications and brief me on what they add to the federal APA provisions on formal adjudication. If you can get back to me tomorrow, that would be great. Thanks!

A. Powers of a Presiding Official in a Formal Adjudication under the Federal APA

As discussed in Chapter 22, an ALJ usually presides at the hearing in a formal adjudication under the federal APA. The ALJ's main jobs at the hearing are to ensure that (1) the parties have a fair chance to present their case and (2) the hearing produces a record adequate for a good decision by the ALJ and by the agency head or other official or entity with authority to review the ALJ's decision.

Hearing procedures are governed primarily by § 556 of the federal APA. Section 556(c) gives the ALJ specific powers. We discussed some of those powers in Chapter 22, because they are ordinarily exercised *before* the hearing. As you review § 556(c) below, underline or put a check mark beside each power that would ordinarily be used *at* the hearing:

---

5 U.S.C. § 556. Hearings; presiding employees; powers and duties ...

(c) Subject to published rules of the agency and within its powers, employees presiding at hearings may—

(1) administer oaths and affirmations;

(2) issue subpenas authorized by law;

(3) rule on offers of proof and receive relevant evidence;

(4) take depositions or have depositions taken when the ends of justice would be served;

(5) regulate the course of the hearing;

(6) hold conferences for the settlement or simplification of the issues by consent of the parties or by the use of alternative means of dispute resolution as provided in subchapter IV of this chapter;

(7) inform the parties as to the availability of one or more alternative means of dispute resolution, and encourage use of such methods;

(8) require the attendance at any conference held pursuant to paragraph (6) of at least one representative of each party who has authority to negotiate concerning resolution of issues in controversy;

(9) dispose of procedural requests or similar matters;

(10) make or recommend decisions in accordance with section 557 of this title; and

(11) take other action authorized by agency rule consistent with this subchapter....

Section 556(c) makes all these powers **"subject to the published rules of the agency,"** which means the agency may make procedural rules for the ALJ's use of the powers.

Section 556(c) reminds us that it does not, itself, *grant* any of the listed powers. Instead, § 556(c) provides that, if a statute outside the APA includes these **"within [the agency's] powers,"** they devolve upon the ALJ in a formal adjudication. Even so, not all of these powers must be specifically granted in the agency legislation for them to exist. For example, agency legislation authorizing formal adjudications would ordinarily be understood implicitly to include powers incidental to conducting an evidentiary hearing, such as administering oaths and affirmations.

We explore the actual course of the hearing in the next section.

B. The Course of the Hearing in a Formal Adjudication under the Federal APA

A lawyer preparing for a hearing before an ALJ in a formal adjudication needs answers to the following questions:

(1) Who bears the burden of proof?

(2) What is the standard of proof?

(3) What evidence is admissible?

(4) May the parties cross-examine other parties' witnesses?

(5) Can facts be established by means other than adducing evidence?

We answer each question below. Before we do, please read § 556(d) of the federal APA with these questions in mind, and jot down the answers that it suggests:

---

5 U.S.C. § 556. Hearings; presiding employees; powers and duties; burden of proof; evidence; record as a basis for decision ...

(d) Except as otherwise provided by statute, the proponent of a rule or order has the burden of proof. Any oral or documentary evidence may be received, but the agency as a matter of policy shall provide for the exclusion of irrelevant, immaterial, or unduly repetitious evidence. A sanction may not be imposed or rule or order issued except on consideration of the whole record or those parts thereof cited by a party and supported by and in accordance with the reliable, probative, and substantial evidence. The agency may, to the extent consistent with the interests of justice and the policy of the underlying statutes administered by the agency, consider a violation of section 557(d) of this title sufficient grounds for a decision adverse to a party who has knowingly committed such violation or knowingly caused such violation to occur. A party is entitled to present his case or defense by oral or documentary evidence, to submit rebuttal evidence, and to conduct such cross-examination as may be required for a full and true disclosure of the facts. In rule making or determining claims for money or benefits or applications for initial licenses an agency may, when a party will not be prejudiced thereby, adopt procedures for the submission of all or part of the evidence in written form....

---

1. Burden of Proof

The first sentence of § 556(d) puts the **"burden of proof"** on the **"proponent of a rule or order,"** unless a statute provides otherwise. As discussed in Chapter 22, the proponent of a rule or order typically is the party who initiates the proceeding. For example, an applicant for a license is the proponent of an order granting the license. Similarly, an applicant for government benefits is the proponent of an order awarding the benefits. On the other hand, an agency seeking to revoke an existing license or to terminate benefits is the proponent of an order revoking the license or an order terminating the benefits. An agency seeking to promulgate a rule is the proponent of that rule. Whoever (or whatever) the proponent is, that person or entity bears the burden of proof.

Below we excerpt the leading U.S. Supreme Court case on the term **"burden of proof"** in § 556(d). It is a useful case to read for several reasons. First, in addressing the meaning of **"burden of proof,"** the Court distinguishes between two related concepts that all lawyers must learn: namely, the "burden [of production]" and the "burden of persuasion." Second, the opinion addresses the complex interaction of the federal APA and agency legislation in a specific setting. Third, the opinion introduces a feature of some agency adjudication schemes for granting government benefits, which is that they are tilted in favor of benefits claimants.

Exercise: *Director, Office of Workers' Compensation Programs, Department of Labor v. Greenwich Collieries*

As you read the next case, please keep in mind these questions:

1. What is the "true doubt rule"? Where does the rule come from? What, do you suppose, is its purpose?

2. Who is challenging the true doubt rule, and on what ground?

3. What does the Court address in part II of its opinion? In part III?

4. How would you summarize the Court's interpretation of § 556(d) of the APA in one sentence?

Director, Office of Workers' Compensation Programs, Department of Labor v. Greenwich Collieries
512 U.S. 267 (1994)

Justice O'Connor delivered the opinion of the Court.

In adjudicating benefits claims under the Black Lung Benefits Act (BLBA), 83 Stat. 792, as amended, 30 U.S.C. § 901 et seq. (1988 ed. and Supp. IV), and the Longshore and Harbor Workers' Compensation Act (LHWCA), 44 Stat. 1424, as amended, 33 U.S.C. § 901 *et seq.*, the Department of Labor applies what it calls the "true doubt" rule. This rule essentially shifts the burden of persuasion to the party opposing the benefits claim— when the evidence is evenly balanced, the benefits claimant wins. This litigation presents the question whether the rule is consistent with § 7(c) of the Administrative Procedure Act (APA), which states that "[e]xcept as otherwise provided by statute, the proponent of a rule or order has the burden of proof." 5 U.S.C. § 556(d). [Editor's note: In the rest of this excerpt, we replace the Court's references to "§ 7(c)" of the APA with "§ 556(d)," which is the provision in Title 5 of the U.S. Code where § 7(c) is currently codified.]

I

We review two separate decisions of the Court of Appeals for the Third Circuit. In one, Andrew Ondecko applied for disability benefits under the BLBA after working as a coal miner for 31 years. The Administrative Law Judge (ALJ) determined that Ondecko had pneumoconiosis (or black lung disease), that he was totally disabled by the disease, and that the disease resulted from coal mine employment. In resolving the first two issues, the ALJ relied on the true doubt rule. In resolving the third, she relied on the rebuttable presumption that a miner with pneumoconiosis who worked in the mines for at least 10 years developed the disease because of his employment. 20 CFR § 718.203(b) (1993). The Department's Benefits Review Board affirmed, concluding that the [ALJ] had considered all the evidence, had found each side's evidence to be equally probative, and had properly resolved the dispute in Ondecko's favor under the true doubt rule. The Court of Appeals vacated the Board's decision, holding that the true doubt rule is [invalid]....

In the other case, Michael Santoro suffered a work-related back and neck injury while employed by respondent Maher Terminals. Within a few months Santoro was diagnosed with nerve cancer, and he died shortly thereafter. His widow filed a claim under the LHWCA alleging that the work injury had rendered her husband disabled and caused his death. After reviewing the evidence for both sides, the ALJ found it equally probative and, relying on the true doubt rule, awarded benefits to the claimant. The Board affirmed, finding no error in the ALJ's analysis or his application of the true doubt rule. The Court of Appeals reversed, holding that the true doubt rule is inconsistent with § 556(d) of the APA. 992 F.2d 1277 (1993). In so holding, the court expressly disagreed with *Freeman United Coal Mining Co. v. Office of Workers' Compensation Programs*, 988 F.2d 706 (CA7 1993). We granted certiorari to resolve the conflict....

II

As a threshold matter, we must decide whether § 556(d)'s burden of proof provision applies to adjudications under the LHWCA and the BLBA. Section 556(d) of the APA applies "[e]xcept as otherwise provided by statute," and the Department argues that the statutes at issue here make clear that § 556(d) does not apply. We disagree.

The Department points out that in conducting investigations or hearings pursuant to the LHWCA, the "Board shall not be bound by common law or statutory rules of evidence or by technical or formal rules of procedure, except as provided by this chapter." 33 U.S.C. § 923(a). But the assignment of the burden of proof is a rule of substantive law, *American Dredging Co. v. Miller*, 510 U.S. 443, 454 (1994), so it is unclear whether this exception even applies. More importantly, § 923 by its terms applies "except as provided by this chapter," and the chapter provides that § 556(d) does indeed apply to the LHWCA. 33 U.S.C. § 919(d) ("[N]otwithstanding any other provisions of this chapter, any hearing held under this chapter shall be conducted in accordance with [the APA]"); 5 U.S.C. § 554(c)(2). We do not lightly presume exemptions to the APA, *Brownell v. Tom We Shung*, 352 U.S. 180, 185, (1956), and we do not think § 923 by its terms exempts the LHWCA from § 556(d).

The Department's argument under the BLBA fares no better. The BLBA also incorporates the APA (by incorporating parts of the LHWCA), but it does so "except as otherwise provided ... by regulations of the Secretary." 30 U.S.C. § 932(a). The Department argues that the following BLBA regulation so provides: "In enacting [the BLBA], Congress intended that claimants be given the benefit of all reasonable doubt as to the existence of total or partial disability or death due to pneumoconiosis." 20 CFR § 718.3(c) (1993). But we do not think this regulation can fairly be read as authorizing the true doubt rule and rejecting the APA's burden of proof provision. Not only does the regulation fail to mention the true doubt rule or § 556(d), it does not even mention the concept of burden shifting or burdens of proof. Accordingly—and assuming, *arguendo*, that the Department has the authority to displace § 556(d) through regulation—this ambiguous regulation does not overcome the presumption that these adjudications under the BLBA are subject to § 556(d)'s burden of proof provision.

III

We turn now to the meaning of "burden of proof" as used in § 556(d). Respondents contend that the Court of Appeals was correct in reading "burden of proof" to include the burden of persuasion. The Department disagrees, contending that "burden of proof" imposes only the burden of production (i.e., the burden of going forward with evidence). The cases turn on this dispute, for if respondents are correct, the true doubt rule must fall: because the true doubt rule places the burden of persuasion on the party opposing the benefits award, it would violate § 556(d)'s requirement that the burden of persuasion rest with the party seeking the award.

A

Because the term "burden of proof" is nowhere defined in the APA, our task is to construe it in accord with its ordinary or natural meaning. *Smith v. United States*, 508 U.S. 223, 228 (1993). It is easier to state this task than to accomplish it, for the meaning of words may change over time, and many words have several meanings even at a fixed point in time.... Here we must seek to ascertain the ordinary meaning of "burden of proof" in 1946, the year the APA was enacted.

For many years the term "burden of proof" was ambiguous because the term was used to describe two distinct concepts. Burden of proof was frequently used to refer to what we now call the burden of persuasion—the notion that if the evidence is evenly balanced, the party that bears the burden of persuasion must lose. But it was also used to refer to what we now call the burden of production—a party's obligation to come forward with evidence to support its claim. See J. Thayer, Evidence at the Common Law 355–384 (1898) (detailing various uses of the term "burden of proof" among 19th-century English and American courts)....

... [T]he dual use of the term continued throughout the late 19th and early 20th centuries.... To remedy this problem, writers suggested that the term "burden of proof" be limited to the concept of burden of persuasion, while some other term—such as "burden of proceeding" or "burden of evidence"—be used to refer to the concept of burden of production....

This Court tried to eliminate the ambiguity.... *Hill v. Smith*, 260 U.S. 592 (1923)....

In the two decades after *Hill*, our opinions consistently distinguished between burden of proof, which we defined as burden of persuasion, and an alternative concept, which we increasingly referred to as the burden of production or the burden of going forward with the evidence ...

The emerging consensus on a definition of burden of proof was reflected in the evidence treatises of the 1930's and 1940's. "The burden of proof is the obligation which rests on one of the parties to an action to persuade the trier of the facts, generally the jury, of the truth of a proposition which he has affirmatively asserted by the pleadings." W. Richardson, Evidence 143 (6th ed. 1944); see also 1 B. Jones, Law of Evidence in Civil Cases 310 (4th ed. 1938) ("The modern authorities are substantially agreed that, in its strict primary sense, 'burden of proof' signifies the duty or obligation of establishing, in the mind of the trier of facts, conviction on the ultimate issue"); J. McKelvey, Evidence 64 (4th ed. 1932) ("[T]he proper meaning of [burden of proof]" is "the duty of the person alleging the case to prove it," rather than "the duty of the one party or the other to introduce evidence").

We interpret Congress' use of the term "burden of proof" in light of this history, and presume Congress intended the phrase to have the meaning generally accepted in the legal community at the time of enactment.... These principles lead us to conclude that the drafters of the APA used the term "burden of proof" to mean the burden of persuasion.... Accordingly, we conclude that as of 1946 the ordinary meaning of burden of proof was burden of persuasion, and we understand the APA's unadorned reference to "burden of proof" to refer to the burden of persuasion.

B

We recognize that we have previously asserted the contrary conclusion as to the meaning of burden of proof in § 556(d) of the APA. In *NLRB v. Transportation Management Corp.*, 462 U.S. 393 (1983), we reviewed the National Labor Relations Board's (NLRB's) conclusion that the employer had discharged the employee because of the employee's protected union activity. In such cases the NLRB employed a burden shifting formula typical in dual motive cases: The employee had the burden of persuading the NLRB that antiunion animus contributed to the employer's firing decision; the burden then shifted to the employer to establish as an affirmative defense that it would have fired the employee for permissible reasons even if the employee had not been involved in union activity. *Id.*, at 401–402. The employer claimed that the NLRB's burden shifting formula was inconsistent with the National Labor Relations Act (NLRA), but we upheld it as a reasonable construction of the NLRA. *Id.*, at 402–403.

The employer in *Transportation Management* argued that the NLRB's approach violated § 556(d)'s burden of proof provision, which the employer read as imposing the burden of persuasion on the employee. In a footnote, we summarily rejected this argument, concluding that "[§ 556(d)] … determines only the burden of going forward, not the burden of persuasion. *Environmental Defense Fund, Inc. v. EPA*, [548 F.2d 998, 1004, 1013–1015 (CADC 1976)]." *Id.*, at 404, n. 7. In light of our discussion in Part II-A above, we do not think our cursory conclusion in the *Transportation Management* footnote withstands scrutiny....

Moreover, *Transportation Management* reached its conclusion without referring to *Steadman v. SEC*, 450 U.S. 91 (1981), our principal decision interpreting the meaning of § 556(d). In *Steadman* we considered what *standard* of proof § 556(d) required, and we held that the proponent of a rule or order under § 556(d) had to meet its burden by a preponderance of the evidence, not by clear and convincing evidence. Though we did not explicitly state that § 556(d) imposes the burden of persuasion on the party seeking the rule or order, our reasoning strongly implied that this must be so. We assumed that burden of proof meant burden of persuasion when we said that we had to decide "the degree of proof which must be adduced by the proponent of a rule or order *to carry its burden of persuasion* in an administrative proceeding." *Id.*, at 95 (emphasis added). More important, our holding that the party with the burden of proof must prove its case by a preponderance only makes sense if the burden of proof means the burden of persuasion. A standard of proof, such as preponderance of the evidence, can apply only to a burden of persuasion, not to a burden of production....

C

In addition to the *Transportation Management* footnote, the Department relies on the Senate and House Judiciary Committee Reports on the APA to support its claim that burden of proof means only burden of production.... We find this legislative history unavailing....

D

In part due to Congress' recognition that claims such as those involved here would be difficult to prove, claimants in adjudications under these statutes benefit from certain statutory presumptions easing their burden. See 33 U.S.C. § 920; 30 U.S.C. § 921(c); *Del Vecchio v. Bowers*, 296 U.S. 280, 286 (1935). Similarly, the Department's solicitude for benefits claimants is reflected in the regulations adopting additional presumptions. See 20 CFR §§ 718.301–718.306 (1993); *Mullins Coal*, 484 U.S., at 158. But with the true doubt rule the Department attempts to go one step further. In so doing, it runs afoul of the APA, a statute designed "to introduce greater uniformity of procedure and standardization of administrative practice among the diverse agencies whose customs had departed widely from each other." *Wong Yang Sung v. McGrath*, 339 U.S. 33, 41 (1950). That concern is directly implicated here, for under the Department's reading each agency would be free to decide who shall bear the burden of persuasion. Accordingly, the Department cannot allocate the burden of persuasion in a manner that conflicts with the APA.

IV

Under the Department's true doubt rule, when the evidence is evenly balanced the claimant wins. Under § 556(d), however, when the evidence is evenly balanced, the benefits claimant must lose. Accordingly, we hold that the true doubt rule violates § 556(d) of the APA....

JUSTICE SOUTER, with whom JUSTICE BLACKMUN and JUSTICE STEVENS join, dissenting....

Exercise: *Greenwich Collieries* Revisited

Please answer these questions about the Court's decision:

1. The Court says, "We do not lightly presume exemptions to the APA." *Greenwich Collieries*, 512 U.S. at 271. Why does that matter for purposes of the Court's reasoning in this case? Also, explain how the Court's presumption against APA exemptions accords, in this case, with the portion of § 556(d) that states, "**Except as otherwise provided by statute**," and with § 559 of the federal APA.

2. The Court says, "[C]laimants in adjudications under [the LHWCA and BLBA] benefit from certain statutory presumptions easing their burden." *Greenwich Collieries*, 512 U.S. at 280. As examples of statutory presumptions "easing" the burden of claimants, the Court cites 33 U.S.C. § 920, which is in the LHWCA, and 30 U.S.C. § 921(c), which is in the BLBA. Examine the current versions of these statutes and explain in your own words how these provisions, unlike the true doubt rule, are consistent with the burden of proof required under § 556(d).

The Court in *Greenwich Collieries* observed that the LHWCA and BLBA create presumptions that make it easier for claimants to establish eligibility. In other benefits programs, too, Congress or the agency responsible for administering the programs creates ways to help claimants. The most important example of such benefits programs are those established by the Social Security Act. A regulation on benefits claims under the Act says that the Social Security Administration (SSA) conducts "the administrative review process in an informal, nonadversary manner." 20 C.F.R. § 404.900(b) (2012). In addition, in a hearing before an ALJ on a benefits claim, the SSA has no representative before the ALJ to oppose the claim for benefits. The ALJ's approach to the hearing is "inquisitorial rather than adversarial. It is the ALJ's duty to investigate the facts and develop the arguments both for and against granting benefits." *Sims v. Apfel*, 530 U.S. 103, 111 (2000). If the ALJ's decision is adverse to the claimant, the ALJ may appeal to the SSA's Appeals Council, which likewise reviews the claim for benefits in a nonadversary way, without any SSA representative responsible for opposing the claim. *See id.*

The broader point is that not all formal adjudications are adversary proceedings. When someone applies to an agency for a license, for example, the applicant and the agency are not necessarily opponents. Indeed, sometimes, the agency's initial decision is to grant the license, but that decision becomes the subject of a request for a hearing because another private party opposes the license. Sometimes, as in SSA hearings, hearings are not adversarial because the statute or the agency regulations create an inquisitorial model — or what Judge Friendly in a famous article called an "investigatory" model — of agency adjudication. Henry Friendly, *Some Kind of Hearing*, 123 U. Pa. L. Rev. 1267, 1290 (1975). The practitioner preparing for a formal adjudication with which the practitioner has no past experience cannot assume that the atmosphere and tenor of that adjudication will be just like a court proceeding.

2. Standard of Proof

Section 556(d) states, "A sanction may not be imposed or rule or order issued except on consideration of the whole record or those parts thereof cited by a party and supported by and in accordance with the reliable, probative, and substantial evidence." The U.S. Supreme Court has interpreted the phrase "substantial evidence" in § 556(d) to impose a preponderance-of-the-evidence standard of proof in formal adjudications. The case adopting that interpretation was discussed in the *Greenwich Collieries* case above and is summarized next:

• *Steadman v. Securities & Exchange Commission*, 450 U.S. 91 (1981)

Steadman involved a formal adjudication in which the Securities and Exchange Commission sanctioned Charles Steadman for securities fraud. Mr. Steadman argued that § 556(d) does not address the standard of proof in formal adjudications. He further argued that, because of the inferential nature of the evidence against him, and the seriousness of the charges and of the sanctions sought, the SEC should have to prove the charges by clear and convincing proof. *See Steadman*, 450 U.S. at 92–95.

The Court rejected those arguments. The Court held that the term "substantial evidence" in § 556(d) refers to the standard of proof required to support a sanction. The Court determined that the legislative history of § 556(d) showed that the amount Congress intended to require was a preponderance of the evidence.

Although *Steadman* concerned a "sanction," its holding applies to all proceedings under § 556(d), including formal adjudications leading to other kinds of orders. The holding in *Steadman* does not, on the other hand, apply to informal adjudications, even ones that include formal evidentiary hearings before hearing officers. Indeed, the Court in *Steadman* noted that, in removal proceedings under the immigration laws, the government must prove the grounds for removal by "clear, unequivocal, and convincing evidence." *Steadman*, 450 U.S. at 102 n.22 (citing *Woodby v. Immigration & Naturalization Serv.*, 385 U.S. 276, 286 (1966)); *see also* 8 U.S.C. § 1229a(c)(3)(A) (2012). Finally, even in formal adjudications under the APA, § 556(d) applies "[e]xcept as otherwise provided by statute," which means that the agency legislation governing a particular formal adjudication can impose a different standard of proof if it does so expressly. *See* 5 U.S.C. § 559 (2012). No statute or rule in *Steadman* altered the standard of proof in § 556(d).

Exercise: Standard of Proof

Please read the following provision and explain (1) why it triggers formal adjudications under the APA and (2) how it modifies the standard of proof ordinarily applicable in formal adjudications.

---

25 U.S.C. § 458aaa-6. Provisions relating to the Secretary [of Health and Human Services

(a) Mandatory provisions ...

(2) Reassumption

(A) In general

Compacts or funding agreements negotiated between the Secretary and an Indian tribe shall include a provision authorizing the Secretary to reassume operation of a program, service, function, or activity (or portions thereof) and associated funding if there is a specific finding relative to that program, service, function, or activity (or portion thereof) of—

(i) imminent endangerment of the public health caused by an act or omission of the Indian tribe, and the imminent endangerment arises out of a failure to carry out the compact or funding agreement; or

(ii) gross mismanagement with respect to funds transferred to a tribe by a compact or funding agreement, as determined by the Secretary in consultation with the Inspector General, as appropriate.

(B) Prohibition

The Secretary shall not reassume operation of a program, service, function, or activity (or portions thereof) unless—

(i) the Secretary has first provided written notice and a hearing on the record to the Indian tribe; and

(ii) the Indian tribe has not taken corrective action to remedy the imminent endangerment to public health or gross mismanagement.

(C) Exception ...

(D) Hearings

In any hearing or appeal involving a decision to reassume operation of a program, service, function, or activity (or portion thereof), the

> Secretary shall have the burden of proof of demonstrating by clear and convincing evidence the validity of the grounds for the reassumption....

---

3. Admissibility of Evidence

Section 556(d) says that "[a]ny oral or documentary evidence may be received," subject to agency policy excluding "irrelevant, immaterial, or unduly repetitious evidence." The most important thing to understand about this part of § 556(d) is that it does not require agencies to follow the Federal Rules of Evidence in formal adjudications. *See* AGM 76. This inapplicability of court rules of evidence makes sense because many of those rules aim to prevent juries from considering unreliable evidence; agency hearings, of course, do not use juries.

Section 556(d) allows an agency to have a policy that excludes irrelevant, immaterial, or unduly repetitious evidence. Many agencies have such policies, which they express in their procedural rules. What is more, a few federal agencies have policies that are more stringent in that they apply the Federal Rules of Evidence to agency hearings. *See, e.g.*, 10 C.F.R. § 820.29 (2012) (Department of Energy). More often, if an agency policy refers to the Federal Rules of Evidence at all, it simply gives the ALJ (presiding official) discretion or encouragement to follow those Rules, to the extent appropriate. *See, e.g.*, 4 C.F.R. § 22.16(h) (2012) (General Accountability Office Contract Appeals Board). Although generalizations are always dangerous, most agencies seem to give the ALJ much discretion about admissibility of evidence at the hearing.

Unlike the Federal Rules of Evidence, § 556(d) does not restrict the admission of hearsay. In some early cases, however, federal courts held that an agency could not base a decision solely on hearsay that would be inadmissible in a court proceeding; the decision had to rest at least partly on "legally competent" evidence. This was known as the "legal residuum rule." The U.S. Supreme Court impliedly rejected the "legal residuum rule" for federal court review of federal agency decisions in the famous decision summarized next.

- *Richardson v. Perales*, 402 U.S. 389 (1971)

Pedro Perales applied for disability insurance benefits under the federal Social Security Act. Under the Act, state agencies initially determine whether a claimant is disabled. In Mr. Perales's case, a Texas agency determined that Mr. Perales was not disabled. Mr. Perales then exercised his right to a formal, evidentiary hearing before a federal ALJ employed by the Social Security Administration (SSA).

The case went to the U.S. Supreme Court because of the evidence at the hearing before the ALJ. At the hearing, Mr. Perales introduced his testimony and the testimony of his doctor. The ALJ rejected Mr. Perales's claim based on written reports from doctors who had been hired by the state agency to examine Mr. Perales and who found no medical evidence to support his claim of a severe impairment. These adverse, written reports were hearsay. The SSA's Appeals Council affirmed the ALJ's denial of benefits, and Mr. Perales sought judicial review under a provision in the Social Security Act that required the agency's decision to be upheld "if supported by substantial evidence." *Richardson v. Perales*, 402 U.S. at 390 (quoting statute); *see also* 42 U.S.C. § 405(g) (2012) (current statute, which still prescribes "substantial evidence" standard of judicial review). On judicial review, Mr. Perales argued that the adverse, written reports of the doctors were not "substantial evidence."

The Court rejected that argument. The Court assumed, without deciding, that Mr. Perales was entitled to procedural due process in the administrative proceeding. Thus, the question was whether, consistently with due process,

> physicians' written reports of medical examinations they have made of a disability claimant may constitute "substantial evidence" supportive of a finding of nondisability, within the [statutory] standard [for judicial review], when the claimant objects to the admissibility of those reports and when the only live testimony is presented by his side and is contrary to the reports.

Richardson v. Perales, 402 U.S. at 390. The Court answered this question "yes." The Court's conclusion rested partly on Mr. Perales's failure to follow the agency's rules for issuing subpoenas requiring the attendance at the hearing of the physicians who wrote the adverse reports:

> We conclude that a written report by a licensed physician who has examined the claimant and who sets forth in his report his medical findings in his area of competence may be received as evidence in a disability hearing and, despite its hearsay character and an absence of cross-examination, and despite the presence of opposing direct medical testimony and testimony by the claimant himself, may constitute substantial evidence supportive of a finding by the hearing examiner adverse to the claimant, when the claimant has not exercised his right to subpoena the reporting physician and thereby provide himself with the opportunity for cross-examination of the physician.

Id. at 402. The Court cited several factors that ensured the "reliability and probative value" of the reports, including:

- The reports were prepared by "independent physicians" who examined Mr. Perales and had no stake in the outcome. *Id.* at 403.

- The disability benefit program, including the use of State-hired physicians, cast the agency in the role of "an adjudicator and not as an advocate or adversary," ensuring its impartiality. *Id.*

- The reports were highly detailed and had information of obvious value in determining disability.

- The examinations were done by a range of specialists, reflecting "a patient and careful endeavor by the state agency and the examiner to ascertain the truth." *Id.* at 404.

- There was "no inconsistency whatsoever" in the specialists' reports. *Id.*

- Mr. Perales did not take advantage of agency rules that entitled him to request subpoenas compelling the attendance at the hearing of the physicians who wrote the adverse reports. The agency rules required Mr. Perales to request the subpoenas five days before the hearing, but this five-day requirement "afforded no real obstacle," because the agency notified him that he could examine the documentary evidence on file; thus he had the opportunity to learn that the adverse reports were in the file and to subpoena the authors so that he could cross-examine them at the hearing. *Id.* at 405.

- Given the huge number of disability claims hearings, "the cost of providing live medical testimony at those hearings, where need has not been demonstrated by a request for a subpoena, over and above the cost of the examinations requested by hearing examiners, would be a substantial drain" on the money available to support the program "and on the energy of physicians already in short supply." *Id.* at 406.

In short, the Court allowed the SSA to base its decision against Mr. Perales exclusively on hearsay, and in doing so the Court implicitly rejected the residuum rule. *Johnson v. United States.* 628 F.2d 187, 190–191 (D.C. Cir. 1980). The Court upheld the SSA's reliance on hearsay because of: the hearsay's apparent reliability; the opposing party's failure to follow the rules that would have enabled him to cross-examine the authors of the hearsay; and the nature of the adjudication. The Court did not take an "anything goes" approach to agency reliance on hearsay in formal adjudications. Indeed, the Court in *Richardson v. Perales* explained that its decision was consistent with its statement in a prior opinion that "[m]ere uncorroborated hearsay or rumor does not constitute substantial evidence." *Id.* at 407 (quoting *Consolidated Edison Corp. v. NLRB*, 305 U.S. 197, 230 (1938)). The prior statement simply required an agency order to be based on "evidence having rational probative force." 389 U.S. at 407. The written reports adverse to Mr. Perales had such force.

Exercise: Reliance on Hearsay in Formal Adjudications

John Doe works for a federal agency. Mr. Doe's teenage daughter, Jane Doe, accuses Mr. Doe of sexually molesting her. Jane Doe makes this accusation to a social worker while Jane Doe is in a psychiatric hospital after a failed suicide attempt. The social worker includes the accusation in a report that the social worker sends to a state agency. The federal agency for which Mr. Doe works discovers the social worker's report and relies on it to fire Mr. Doe after a formal adjudication. Mr. Doe testifies at the hearing before the ALJ and denies the accusation. He also introduces into evidence documents supporting his claim that his daughter was emotionally disturbed when she made the accusation. Mr. Doe seeks judicial review of the agency's decision to fire him.

1. By way of review, please identify who has the burden of proof in this formal adjudication and what is the standard of proof. Assume that both issues are governed exclusively by the federal APA.

2. Please explain whether the federal APA permits the agency to rely on the social worker's report in the formal adjudication relating to Mr. Doe's firing.

3. Please explain whether the court should uphold the agency's decision under a "substantial evidence" standard of judicial review.

See Doe v. United States, 132 F.3d 1430 (Fed. Cir. 1997).

The law in some States, like federal case law before *Richardson v. Perales*, limits agency reliance on hearsay through the "residuum rule." As codified in the New Jersey APA, for example, the rule says that, although hearsay is admissible in contested cases, "some legally competent evidence must exist to support each ultimate finding of fact to an extent sufficient to provide assurances of reliability and to avoid the fact or appearance of arbitrariness." N.J. Admin. Code § 1:1-15.5 (West, Westlaw through Feb. 6, 2012). In other words, hearsay alone cannot support an "ultimate finding of fact"; the hearsay must be buttressed by "legally competent evidence"—meaning evidence admissible under standard rules of evidence applicable in a court proceeding.

In jurisdictions where the residuum rule applies, the lawyer should introduce non-hearsay supportive evidence into the administrative record, even if it duplicates hearsay evidence. If that is not possible, the lawyer should seek to show that some of the hearsay upon which the lawyer relies falls within one of the exceptions to the rule barring admission of hearsay and therefore is "legally competent" evidence.

4. Cross-Examination

Section 556(d) entitles a party in a formal adjudication to "**conduct such cross-examination as may be required for a full and true disclosure of the facts.**" On its face, this right of cross-examination is not absolute. One federal court interpreted this provision to allow an agency to give the officials who preside at the hearing discretion to decide whether the person seeking cross-examination has demonstrated the need for it. *See Citizens Awareness Network, Inc. v. United States*, 391 F.3d 338, 351, 354 (1st Cir. 2004).

The right of cross-examination relates to the discussion above about agency reliance on hearsay. The benefits claimant in *Richardson v. Perales* objected to the agency's reliance on hearsay (written reports by physicians) partly because it prevented him from cross-examining the authors of the hearsay documents. 402 U.S. at 404–405. In rejecting that objection, the Court emphasized that the claimant failed to follow agency rules for requesting a subpoena for the document's author. The Court thus implied that a person can lose the right of cross-examination by failing to follow reasonable agency rules for requesting subpoenas. *Id.* at 405.

A restriction on cross-examination can raise due process concerns in an agency adjudication that involves a deprivation or threatened deprivation of liberty or property, as the Court in *Richardson v. Perales* assumed was true there. *See id.* at 401–402. In later cases involving social security benefits, most federal courts have interpreted *Richardson v. Perales* as not recognizing an absolute due process right of cross-examination. *See Passmore v. Astrue*, 533 F.3d 658 (8th Cir. 2008).

The federal APA and due process are not the only potential sources of a right of cross-examination in agency hearings. For example, a federal statute gives a person in removal proceedings "a reasonable opportunity ... to cross-examine witnesses presented by the Government." 8 U.S.C. § 1229a(b)(4)(B) (2012). A federal court found a violation of this statute in *Malave v. Holder*, 610 F.3d 483 (7th Cir. 2010). The government ordered Manuela Malave removed on the ground that she had entered into a sham marriage with a U.S. citizen to become a permanent resident alien. At the hearing before an Immigration Judge (IJ), the government had admitted into evidence a written statement by the man she had married as part of the alleged sham. The IJ refused Ms. Malave's request to issue a subpoena compelling this man to attend the hearing, so that she could cross-examine him. On review of the order removing Ms. Malave, the court of appeals held that the IJ's denial of her request for a subpoena violated her statutory right to a reasonable opportunity to cross-examine an adverse witness. *Id.* at 487–488.

Exercise: The Right of Cross-Examination

Suppose the IJ in *Malave* had issued a subpoena for the man with whom Ms. Malave had allegedly entered into a sham marriage, and that, despite best efforts to serve the subpoena, the man could not be found. Would this prevent the government from relying on the man's written statement at Ms. Malave's removal proceeding?

---

5. Proof by Methods Other Than Ordinary, Record Evidence

a. Inferences, Presumptions, Methods of Proof

In a court case, the judge or jury infers or presumes things based on logic and experience. The ALJs in formal adjudications do, too. Beyond the inferences and presumptions made by the individual decision makers, in administrative adjudications the legislature and the agency can prescribe presumptions and other rules for evaluating evidence. We will give examples of evidential inferences used in agency adjudications.

Federal courts have recognized that ALJs in formal adjudications, like the trier of fact in civil actions, can draw inferences based on logic and experience. To cite two examples:

- Suppose that the circumstances indicate that a party certainly would have called a particular person as a witness if that person could testify favorably to that party. When those circumstances exist, the party's failure to call the person as a witness can support an inference that the witness would, in fact, have testified unfavorably to the party. *Underwriters Labs., Inc. v. NLRB*, 147 F.3d 1048, 1054 (9th Cir. 1988).

- Suppose that a party fails to testify in his or her own defense. Although that failure cannot be held against the defendant in a criminal trial, it can support an adverse inference against the party in an agency adjudication. *See Brenner v. Commodity Futures Trading Comm'n*, 338 F.3d 713, 720 (7th Cir. 2003); *Pagel, Inc. v. SEC*, 803 F.2d 942, 946–947 (8th Cir. 1986).

An agency may develop presumptions that not only reflect experience and common sense but that are also driven by policy considerations—including, but not limited to, policies established by statute. The agency generally has discretion to develop presumptions by rulemaking or adjudication. Here are examples of each:

- The Social Security Administration and the U.S. Department of Labor have promulgated regulations establishing presumptions designed to help miners establish eligibility under the Black Lung Benefits Act, of which the following is one example:

  > 20 C.F.R. §718.203. Establishing relationship of pneumoconiosis to coal mine employment
  >
  > (a) In order for a claimant to be found eligible for benefits under the Act, it must be determined that the miner's pneumoconiosis arose at least in part out of coal mine employment. The provisions in this section set forth the criteria to be applied in making such a determination.
  >
  > (b) If a miner who is suffering or suffered from pneumoconiosis was employed for ten years or more in one or more coal mines, there shall be a rebuttable presumption that the pneumoconiosis arose out of such employment.
  >
  > (c) If a miner who is suffering or suffered from pneumoconiosis was employed less than ten years in the nation's coal mines, it shall be determined that such pneumoconiosis arose out of that employment only if competent evidence establishes such a relationship.

- After the National Labor Relations Board has certified a union as the representative of a defined group of employees (a "bargaining unit"), the union "usually is entitled to a conclusive presumption of majority status for one year following the certification." *Fall River Dyeing & Finishing Corp. v. NLRB*, 482 U.S. 27, 37 (1987). That presumption prevents the employer, during that year, from refusing to bargain with the union on the ground that it has lost the support of a majority of the employees in the bargaining unit. The Board has developed this presumption in a series of adjudicatory decisions. The presumption is based "not so much" on actual experience as on the National Labor Relations Act's "overriding policy" favoring "industrial peace." *Fall River Dyeing*, 482 U.S. at 38.

Statutes, as well as regulations, can create presumptions applicable in formal adjudications. In our earlier discussion of *Greenwich Collieries*, we cited examples from the Longshore and Harbor Workers' Compensation Act and the Black Lung Benefits Act. Another example comes from a statute providing compensation for members of the armed services whose service has caused certain illnesses. 38 U.S.C. § 1112 (2012) (entitled "Presumptions relating to certain diseases and disabilities").

The takeaway from this discussion is that agencies adjudicate specialized matters, which often call for specialized rules of adjudication. Those rules can be found in agency adjudicatory decisions, agency rules, or the agency legislation. They overlay the more familiar "rules of thumb" used by triers of fact in court adjudications.

b. Rules Establishing Generalized Facts

Lawyers familiar with court adjudications are accustomed to thinking that litigation facts must be established specifically and be individually tailored to each case. In addition, when an adjudication is subject to the demands of procedural due process, the individualized "right to be heard" implies the right to a decision based on the individual facts of the case.

But some agency adjudications involve generalized facts that are not specific to an individual litigant and that arise in case after case. An agency may use its rulemaking power to establish such generalized facts. The leading U.S. Supreme Court case addressing this use of rulemaking power by a federal agency is *Heckler v. Campbell*, 461 U.S. 458 (1983):

* *Heckler v. Campbell*, 461 U.S. 458 (1983)

Heckler v. Campbell concerns legislative rules issued by the Secretary of Health and Human Services to implement the disability benefits program created by the Social Security Act. To get disability benefits, a claimant must, because of a disability,

> "not only [be] unable to do his [or her] previous work but [must be unable], considering his [or her] age, education, and work experience, [to] engage in any other kind of substantial gainful work which exists in the national economy, regardless of whether such work exists in the immediate area in which he [or she] lives, or whether a specific job vacancy exists for him [or her], or whether he [or she] would be hired if he [or she] applied for work."

Id. at 460 (quoting Social Security Act). Once a claimant is found unable to return to the previous job, the Secretary (through the Social Security Administration (SSA)) must make two assessments. First, the SSA must assess the claimant's physical ability, age, education, and work experience. Second, the SSA must assess "whether jobs exist in the national economy that a person having the claimant's qualifications could perform." *Id.* at 461.

In *Heckler v. Campbell*, the SSA made an individualized assessment of Carmen Campbell's physical ability, age, education, and work experience. But to determine whether there were jobs in the national economy that she could perform, the SSA relied on legislative rules called the "medical-vocational guidelines." One of the rules, for example, stated that "a significant number of jobs exist for a person who can perform light work, is closely approaching advanced age, has a limited education but who is literate and can communicate in English, and whose previous work has been unskilled." *Id.* at 462 n.4. The SSA had promulgated the medical-vocational guidelines to improve "the uniformity and efficiency" of the determination whether alternative work was available to claimants who could not do their former jobs. *Id.* at 461. The guidelines avoided the need for a vocational expert to testify in each case about the availability of jobs in the national economy for a person with the claimant's characteristics.

The Court upheld the medical-vocational guidelines against the objection that they violated the Social Security Act. Although the Act "contemplates that disability hearings will be individualized determinations," that did not "bar the Secretary from relying on rulemaking to resolve certain classes of issues." *Id.* at 467. The Court had in past cases "recognized that even where an agency's enabling statute expressly requires it to hold a hearing, the agency may rely on its rulemaking authority to determine issues that do not require case-by-case consideration." *Id.* (citing *United States v. Storer Broadcasting Co.*, 351 U.S. 192, 205 (1956), and other cases). The Court observed: "A contrary holding would require the agency continually to relitigate issues that may be established fairly and efficiently in a single rulemaking proceeding." *Heckler v. Campbell*, 461 U.S. at 467.

As the Court described *Heckler v. Campbell* in a later case, *Heckler v. Campbell* establishes that, "even if a statutory scheme requires individualized determinations, the decisionmaker has the authority to rely on rulemaking to resolve certain issues of general applicability unless Congress clearly expresses an intent to withhold that authority." *American Hosp. Ass'n v. NLRB*, 499 U.S. 606, 612 (1991).

c. Official Notice

A court may take "judicial notice" of facts that are matters of common knowledge. Judicial notice means: "[a] court's acceptance, for purposes of convenience and without requiring a party's proof, of a well-known and indisputable fact." Black's Law Dictionary 923 (Bryan A. Garner ed. 9th ed. 2009). For example, a judge can take judicial notice that water freezes at 32 degrees Fahrenheit. *Id.* By taking judicial notice of this fact, the court finds a fact without relying on evidence in the record.

A similar doctrine allows an agency in an adjudication to take "official" or "administrative" notice of certain facts known to the agency. Thus, the doctrine of official (administrative) notice allows agencies to treat, as proven, facts that are not proven through evidence admitted into the record under the usual evidentiary rules.

Though official notice serves a function similar to that of judicial notice, official notice differs from judicial notice. Most importantly, official notice can include not only facts of which a court can take judicial notice but also facts within the agency's expertise. As the Attorney General's Manual on the APA argued:

> [T]he process of official notice should not be limited to the traditional matters of judicial notice but extends properly to all matters as to which the agency by reason of its functions is presumed to be expert, such as technical or scientific facts within its specialized knowledge.

AGM 80. This view of official notice is accepted in the federal system and some state systems. It is reflected in the 2010 Model State APA:

2010 Model State APA § 404. Evidence in Contested Case ...

(7) The presiding officer may take official notice of all facts of which judicial notice may be taken and of scientific, technical, or other facts within the specialized knowledge of the agency. A party must be notified at the earliest practicable time of the facts proposed to be noticed and their source, including any staff memoranda or data. The party must be afforded an opportunity to contest any officially noticed fact before the decision becomes final....

The idea is that, because agencies have specialized statutory missions, they develop specialized bodies of knowledge and experience. That justifies allowing them to take notice not only of facts that are well-known to the general public but also facts that are well-known to the agency as a result of its specialized mission. This can include not only facts known personally to agency officials but also facts in the agency's files. *See, e.g., Banks v. Schweiker*, 654 F.2d 637, 639–641 (9th Cir. 1981) (ALJ in social security case could take official notice based on his knowledge of customs and practices in offices that processed social security claims); *Bonnafons v. U.S. Dep't of Energy*, 646 F.2d 548, 555 (Temp. Emer. Ct. App. 1981) (agency could take official notice of past proceedings to make a finding in a later proceeding about "the precarious nature of the [oil] refining industry in Puerto Rico").

An agency generally must give parties the chance to rebut a fact of which the agency has taken or proposes to take official notice, if the fact is reasonably disputable. The right to rebut is required, for example by the provision in the 2010 Model State APA reproduced above. *See* 2010 Model State APA § 404(7). The federal APA also requires it, in § 556(e):

---

5 U.S.C. § 556. Hearings; ... record as basis of decision ...

(e) The transcript of testimony and exhibits, together with all papers and requests filed in the proceeding, constitutes the exclusive record for decision in accordance with section 557 of this title and, on payment of lawfully prescribed costs, shall be made available to the parties. When an agency decision rests on official notice of a material fact not appearing in the evidence in the record, a party is entitled, on timely request, to an opportunity to show the contrary.

Even if no statute creates an opportunity to rebut an officially noticed fact, in some cases a person will have a due process right to an opportunity to rebut. *See, e.g., Ohio Bell Tel. Co. v. Pub. Utils. Comm'n of Ohio*, 301 U.S. 292, 301–302 (1937). After all, even seemingly indisputable facts — such as that water freezes at 32 degrees Fahrenheit — can sometimes be disputed (and even disproven) — such as when the water in question is impure or under pressure.

In sum, there are three main things to keep in mind about official notice. First, it is analogous to judicial notice and thus may operate in an agency adjudication. Second, it is addressed in many APA provisions on formal adjudications (or contested cases). Third, and perhaps most importantly, official notice tends to be used only to establish facts that are not reasonably subject to dispute. If an agency official seeks to take official notice of controvertible facts, the official must give notice to the parties and a chance to controvert the facts of which the official proposes to take official notice.

6. Hearings Based Solely on Documentary Evidence

The federal APA allows a federal agency in some formal adjudications and in formal rulemakings to have some or all evidence submitted in written form:

---

5 U.S.C. § 556. Hearings; presiding employees; powers and duties; burden of proof; evidence; record as basis of decision ...

(d) ... In rulemaking or determining claims for money or benefits or applications for initial licenses an agency may, when a party will not be prejudiced thereby, adopt procedures for the submission of all or part of the evidence in written form....

This last sentence of § 556(d) authorizes agencies to adopt procedures for "paper hearings."

The main thing to notice about the sentence for now is that it applies only to formal adjudications on three subjects—claims for money, claims for benefits, and applications for initial licenses—and even then only when no party will be prejudiced. The Attorney General's Manual on the APA explained that an agency can require evidence supporting claims for money or benefits to be in writing only when "the veracity and demeanor of witnesses are not important," and thus there is no need for live testimony subject to cross-examination. AGM 78. Applications for initial licenses "frequently involve extensive technical or statistical data" that an agency could require "be submitted in orderly exhibit form rather than be read into the record by witnesses." *Id.* Here too, however, "[t]o the extent that cross-examination is necessary to bring out the truth, the party should have it." *Id.* (quoting legislative history of APA). When the agency allows all or part of the evidence to be submitted in written form, the party claiming prejudice from that procedure will have to show the agency (and later, if need be, the reviewing court) specifically how the procedure prevented the party from effectively challenging the adverse evidence. *See, e.g., Chauffeur's Training Sch. v. Spellings*, 478 F.3d 117, 131 (2d Cir. 2007).

In sum, § 556(d)'s last sentence identifies when the evidentiary "**hearing**" held under § 556 can be wholly or partly a paper hearing. Even paper hearings may be unnecessary if there is no genuine issue of material fact, because in that event agencies often have power to use administrative summary judgment to decide formal adjudications. We discussed administrative summary judgment in Chapter 22.D.5.

C. The Course of the Hearing in a Formal Adjudication (Contested Case) under a State APA

The same questions naturally arise for a lawyer facing a contested case hearing under a state APA as arise for a lawyer facing a formal adjudication under the federal APA:

(1) Who bears the burden of proof?

(2) What is the standard of proof?

(3) What evidence is admissible?

(4) May the parties cross-examine other parties' witnesses?

(5) Can facts be established by means other than adducing evidence?

A state APA may answer some or all of these questions. As always, however, the lawyer must examine other potential sources of procedural requirements for the hearing, including the agency legislation, the agency rules, and judicial and agency precedent interpreting the APA, the agency legislation, and the agency rules. Sometimes, too, due process will shape the interpretation of the state APA, the agency legislation, and the agency rules.

In this section we identify portions of the 2010 Model APA, if any, addressing these questions.

1. Burden of Proof

Unlike the federal APA, the 2010 Model State APA does not address the burden of proof in formal adjudications (contested cases). Some state APAs do, however.[1]

2. Standard of Proof

The 2010 Model APA does not expressly address the standard of proof in contested cases, but some state APAs do so.[2]

3. Admissibility of Evidence

The 2010 Model APA addresses the admissibility of evidence in the following provision:

2010 Model State APA § 404. Evidence in Contested Case

The following rules apply in a contested case:

(1) Except as otherwise provided in paragraph (2), all relevant evidence is admissible, including hearsay evidence, if it is of a type commonly relied on by a reasonably prudent individual in the conduct of the affairs of the individual.

(2) The presiding officer may exclude evidence in the absence of an objection if the evidence is irrelevant, immaterial, unduly repetitious, or excludable on constitutional or statutory grounds or on the basis of an evidentiary privilege

---

1. *E.g.*, Ariz. Rev. Stat. § 41-1065 (West, Westlaw through Mar. 29, 2012) (in hearings on agency's denial of license or permit, applicant has burden of proof); Ark. Code Ann. § 25-15-213(4) (West, Westlaw through end of 2011 Reg. Sess.) (providing in adjudications and on-the-record rulemakings: "Except as otherwise provided by law, the proponent of a rule or order shall have the burden of proof."); Del. Code Ann. tit. 29 § 10125(c) (West, Westlaw through 78 Laws 2011) (stating that in agency adjudications "[t]he burden of proof shall always be upon the applicant or proponent").

2. *E.g.*, Md. Code Ann., State Gov't § 10-217 (West, Westlaw through Chaps 1 & 2 of 2012 Reg. Sess.) ("The standard of proof in a contested case shall be the preponderance of the evidence unless the standard of clear and convincing proof is imposed on the agency by regulation, statute, or constitution."); N.C. Gen. Stat. Ann. § 150B-29(a) (West, Westlaw through S.L. 2012-1 of 2011 Reg. Sess.) ("The party with the burden of proof in a contested case must establish the facts required by [another APA provision] by a preponderance of the evidence.").

recognized in the courts of this state. The presiding officer shall exclude the evidence if objection is made at the time the evidence is offered.

(3) If the presiding officer excludes evidence with or without objection, the offering party may make an offer of proof before further evidence is presented or at a later time determined by the presiding officer.

(4) Evidence may be received in a record if doing so will expedite the hearing without substantial prejudice to a party. Documentary evidence may be received in the form of a copy if the original is not readily available or by incorporation by reference. On request, parties must be given an opportunity to compare the copy with the original....

---

4. Cross-Examination

The 2010 Model APA says: "In a contested case, to the extent necessary for full disclosure of all relevant facts and issues, the presiding officer shall give all parties the opportunity to respond, present evidence and argument, conduct cross-examination, and submit rebuttal evidence." 2010 Model State APA § 403(d). It is useful to compare this with the federal APA's provision on cross-examination in formal adjudications. *See* 5 U.S.C. § 556(d).

5. Proof by Methods Other Than Ordinary, Record Evidence

As discussed earlier in this chapter, both the 2010 Model APA and the federal APA address one way that evidence may be established other than by ordinary evidence: "official notice." *Compare* 2010 Model State APA § 404(7) *with* 5 U.S.C. § 556(e).

D. Chapter 23 Wrap Up and Look Ahead

From this chapter you have learned that the hearing in a formal adjudication under the federal APA or in a contested case under a state APA raises many of the same questions that arise in trials before courts. The APAs do not always answer those questions in the same way as does the law governing trial court procedures. Indeed, the biggest mistake a lawyer can make is assuming equivalency.

As in other areas of administrative law, procedural requirements for hearings come from different sources. The APAs establish some uniformity among agency hearings, but the lawyer who participates in formal adjudications before different agencies will still find much variety.

The next chapter discusses what happens after the hearing. It describes what is essentially a two-stage decisionmaking process. First, the ALJ or other hearing officer makes an initial or recommended decision. Second, that decision is subject to review by the head of the agency or another entity within the agency to which the agency head has delegated its review power.

Chapter Problem Revisited

This chapter problem has two main objectives: (1) to introduce you to a scheme of administrative review called a "split enforcement scheme"; and (2) to introduce you to the relationship between, on the one hand, the federal APA's requirements for hearings in formal adjudications and, on the other hand, the agency's procedural rules for those hearings.

(1) Bear with us as we trot out the herd of acronyms: The Occupational Safety and Health Act (OSH Act) is enforced by the Occupational Safety and Health Administration (OSHA), an agency within the U.S. Department of Labor. OSHA enforces the OSH Act by inspecting workplaces and issuing citations for violations of safety standards issued under the Act.

Administrative review of OSHA citations is conducted by an independent entity called the Occupational Safety and Health Review Commission (OSHRC).

The OSHRC's independence is established by the statute providing for the three people who head the Commission to be appointed by the President, with the advice and consent of the Senate, for six-year terms. *See* 29 U.S.C. §661 (2012). The President can remove a commissioner only for cause. *Id.* This makes the Commission accountable to the President, rather than the Secretary of Labor or OSHA.

This arrangement is known as a "split enforcement scheme." As the Court has described this scheme:

> Under most regulatory schemes, rulemaking, enforcement, and adjudicative powers are combined in a single administrative authority. See, *e.g.*, 15 U.S.C. §41 *et seq.* (Federal Trade Commission); 15 U.S.C. §§77s–77u (Securities and Exchange Commission); 47 U.S.C. §151 *et seq.* (Federal Communications Commission). Under the OSH Act, however, Congress separated enforcement and rulemaking powers from adjudicative powers, assigning these respective functions to two different administrative authorities. The purpose of this "split enforcement" structure was to achieve a greater separation of functions than exists within the traditional "unitary" agency, which under the Administrative Procedure Act (APA) generally must divide enforcement and adjudication between separate personnel, see 5 U.S.C. §554(d). See generally Johnson, The Split-Enforcement Model: Some Conclusions from the OSHA and MSHA Experiences, 39 Admin. L. Rev. 315, 317–319 (1987).

Martin v. Occupational Safety & Health Review Comm'n, 499 U.S. 144, 151 (1991). The Court in *Martin* had to decide which entity was entitled to deference from the federal courts when the courts reviewed the two entities' competing interpretations of regulations issued under the OSH Act. The Court inferred from the structure and history of the Act that OSHA got the deference. *Id.* at 152.

(2) The procedural rules of the Occupational Safety and Health Review Commission are at 29 C.F.R. §§2200.1–2200.211 (2012). You can find these rules in at least two ways. One is to look up the statute governing the Commission, 29

U.S.C. §661 (2012), in the "Parallel Table of Authorities and Rules" in the CFR Index. The Table identifies rules in the CFR implementing that statute. Another way is to find those statutes in a commercial database such as Westlaw and LexisNexis, which likewise link the statute to its implementing regulations.

The Commission's procedural rules create two sets of procedures: regular and simplified. You may want to alert your partner to several differences between regular and simplified procedures:

- Under the regular procedures, issues to be tried at the hearing are determined through pleadings, motions, and pre-hearing conferences; under simplified procedures, pleadings are not required, and so the issues to be tried are determined more informally through discussion.

- Under the regular procedures, the Federal Rules of Evidence apply at the hearing; they do not apply under the simplified procedures.

- Under the regular procedures the parties file post-hearing briefs; under the simplified procedures the parties present oral arguments at the end of the hearing,

For each set of procedures, you will want to determine how the rules add to or elaborate upon the federal APA provisions. You will also want to identify any inconsistencies between the rules and the federal APA. Last but not least, you must determine which set of procedures—the regular or simplified ones—will apply to your case.

Professional Development Reflection Questions

If your legal practice includes adjudication before agencies or courts, you may end up having to prepare a client or other witness to testify whose truthfulness you seriously doubt. Suppose, for example, you represent a client in an administrative proceeding on the client's claim for workers' compensation, under a scheme similar to that in *Director, Office of Workers' Compensation Programs, Department of Labor v. Greenwich Collieries*, 512 U.S. 267 (1994). And suppose your client proposes to testify that her workplace injury has restricted her daily activities much more severely than you believe is true, based on your observation of the client and your review of her medical records.

1. What steps, if any, do you take to limit the risk that she will lie when she testifies?

2. What steps, if any, do you take if she ends up giving testimony that you strongly suspect contains lies?

In pondering these questions, please check the Model Rules of Professional Responsibility for guidance.

Chapter 24

Formal Adjudications under an APA — Decisions

Overview

Chapter 23 explored what happens at the hearings in formal adjudications under the federal APA and touched upon provisions in the 2010 Model State APA governing hearings in contested cases. This chapter discusses what happens after the hearing.

The post-hearing decision-making process in formal adjudications under the federal APA is governed primarily by § 557 of the APA. This chapter will examine its provisions as well as other sources of procedural requirements for the decision-making process in formal adjudications. This chapter will also examine state APA provisions on agency decisions in formal adjudications (contested cases).

The sections of this chapter are entitled:

A.   Context and Essential History: Agency Decisions in Formal Adjudications as Institutional Decisions

B.   Decision Requirements in Agency Legislation and Agency Rules

C.   Decision Requirements in the Federal APA

D.   Restrictions on Ex Parte Communications under Federal Law

E.   Decision Requirements under a State APA

F.   Chapter 24 Wrap Up and Look Ahead

Chapter Problem

Email

To: New Associate

From: Senior Associate

Re: Your new assignment

The senior partner (SP) just told me you've been assigned to the Northern Power Company case. As SP probably told you, this case involves a long-running proceeding before the Federal Energy Regulatory Commission (FERC). Specifically, the case concerns a formal adjudication before FERC on the lawfulness of proposed rates for the transmission of electricity in interstate commerce by Northern Power. The rates are subject to regulation by FERC under the Federal Power Act, 16 U.S.C. §§ 824–824w (2012). Our client is a customer of Northern Power, and our client objects to Northern Power's proposed rates. At this point, an ALJ has held a hearing and we are expecting an initial decision from the ALJ anytime now. We think the ALJ may uphold the proposed rates, in which event we will advise our client to seek further review.

I suggest you get up to speed on the statutes and regulations governing the next step. The statute governing the proceeding is 16 U.S.C. § 824d. You'll find the FERC rules for these proceedings beginning at 18 C.F.R. § 385.101 (2012). These FERC rules implement the formal adjudication requirements of the federal APA, with which the SP tells me you already have some familiarity.

Please review this statute and these rules well enough so that, in your own mind, you understand the sequence of procedural events that will follow the ALJ's initial decision. You may want to make a sort of mini-timeline for yourself. I'll stop by tomorrow and make sure you have a handle on those events. Then I will help you start familiarizing yourself with the filings in this proceeding.

I look forward to having your assistance on this case. Thank you.

A. Context and Essential History: Agency Decisions in Formal Adjudications as Institutional Decisions

A formal adjudication resembles a judicial proceeding in many ways but differs in important ways, too. One important difference concerns the nature of the decision-making enterprise: In a judicial proceeding, an individual judge is personally responsible for making a decision that is correct in the individual case. In an agency adjudication, many individuals work together to produce a decision for "the agency." The result is an institutional decision, not the decision of any one individual, and it is designed not only to decide a particular case correctly but also to further the agency's statutorily assigned mission.

We mention this difference as background to essential history. In the early years of the administrative state, the contrast between court adjudications and agency adjudications appeared to present irreconcilable conflicts. Somehow an accommodation would have to be reached if the agency model for decision making was to survive. The struggle for that accommodation led to a group of U.S. Supreme Court cases known as "the *Morgan* cases," decided between 1938 and 1941. We summarize the *Morgan* cases in the next subsection, because they are essential history that every well-educated administrative lawyer knows. They were firmly in the minds of the drafters of the federal APA, research for which began in 1939, and the drafters of early state APAs.

1. Description of the *Morgan* Cases

In a series of four opinions in the *Morgan* cases, the U.S. Supreme Court addressed a statutory issue that, in the Court's view, had to be resolved with an eye toward due process requirements. The statutory issue was whether companies regulated by the U.S. Secretary of Agriculture received the "full hearing" to which the agency legislation entitled them. *Morgan v. United States*, 298 U.S. 468 (1936) (quoting statute). In arguing that they did not receive a "full hearing," the companies made two main points: (1) After the evidentiary hearing, the companies had almost no further input into the agency's decision-making process. (2) The ultimate decision maker — namely, the Secretary of Agriculture — had little or no direct knowledge of the hearing record. Instead, in making his decision, the Secretary relied primarily on information from other officials in the Department of Agriculture.

The U.S. Supreme Court ruled in favor of the companies the first two times the case came before it. In its final *Morgan* opinion, however, the Court reemphasized that courts should not "probe the mental processes" of the agency decision makers. *Morgan v. United States*, 304 U.S. 1, 18 (1938). This restriction on "probing mental processes" makes it difficult for people challenging agency actions to show that the officials ultimately responsible for exercising adjudicative power have adequately discharged that responsibility. Indeed, today the *Morgan* cases' chief significance is the "anti-probing" principle.

As a foundation for a fuller exploration of the *Morgan* cases' significance, we summarize the statutory background for the cases. They arose under the authority of the Packers and Stockyards Act of 1921. Exercising authority under that Act, the Secretary of Agriculture investigated the rates charged by "market agencies" (middlemen) for buying and selling livestock at the Kansas City stock yards. The Act authorized the Secretary to determine whether those rates were reasonable, and, if not, to set new rates. The Act also entitled the market agencies to a "full hearing" in such a ratemaking proceeding. The market agencies got a hearing before a Department of Agriculture employee called an "examiner." (Today such a hearing is usually held by an ALJ.) The hearing generated about 10,000 pages of transcripts of live testimony and about 1,000 pages of statistical exhibits. After the hearing, the market agencies presented oral argument before the Acting Secretary of Agriculture. Eventually, the Secretary of Agriculture issued an order fixing the future rates that the market agencies could charge. The Secretary's rate order was accompanied by findings of fact, conclusions, and a recital of "careful consideration of the entire record in this proceeding." *Morgan v. United States*, 298 U.S. 468, 476–477 (1936) (*"Morgan I"*). The market agencies brought a federal-court challenge to the rate order.

The first time the challenge went to the Supreme Court, the Court held that, if the market agencies' assertions were true, the Secretary of Agriculture deprived them of the "full hearing" to which the Act entitled them. The market agencies asserted:

> [T]he Secretary at the time he signed the order in question had not personally heard or read any of the evidence presented at any hearing in connection with the proceeding, and had not heard or considered oral arguments relating thereto or briefs submitted on behalf of the plaintiffs, but ... the sole information of the Secretary with respect to the proceeding was derived from consultation with employees in the Department of Agriculture out of the presence of the plaintiffs or any of their representatives.

Morgan I, 298 U.S. at 476 (summarizing the market agencies' allegations). In concluding that the Secretary's asserted approach to decision making did not provide a "full hearing," the Court in *Morgan I* analogized a ratemaking proceeding to a judicial proceeding and analogized the Secretary's obligation to a judge's:

> ... The requirement of a "full hearing" has obvious reference to the tradition of judicial proceedings in which evidence is received and weighed by the trier of the facts.... The "hearing" is the hearing of evidence and argument. If the one

who determines the facts which underlie the order has not considered evidence or argument, it is manifest that the hearing has not been given....

There is thus no basis for the contention that the authority conferred by section 310 of the Packers and Stockyards Act is given to the Department of Agriculture, as a department in the administrative sense, so that one official may examine evidence, and another official who has not considered the evidence may make the findings and order.... For the weight ascribed by the law to the findings— their conclusiveness when made within the sphere of the authority conferred— rests upon the assumption that the officer who makes the findings has addressed himself to the evidence, and upon that evidence has conscientiously reached the conclusions which he deems it to justify. That duty cannot be performed by one who has not considered evidence or argument. It is not an impersonal obligation. It is a duty akin to that of a judge. The one who decides must hear.

298 U.S. at 480–481. The Court qualified this duty—that "[t]he one who decides must hear." The Court said the Secretary could have a hearing examiner take evidence, and the evidence could "be sifted and analyzed by subordinates." *Id.* at 481. But still, the officer who made the final determinations "must consider and appraise the evidence which justifies them." *Id.* at 482.

On remand from the Court's decision in *Morgan I*, the district court held a trial on the decision-making process used by the Secretary. At that trial, the Secretary testified about his role in the process. The Court in *Morgan II* summarized the Secretary's trial testimony as follows:

The part taken by the Secretary himself in the departmental proceedings is shown by his full and candid testimony. The evidence had been received before he took office. He did not hear the oral argument. The bulky record was placed upon his desk and he dipped into it from time to time to get its drift. He decided that probably the essence of the evidence was contained in appellants' briefs. These, together with the transcript of the oral argument, he took home with him and read. He had several conferences with the Solicitor of the Department and with the officials in the Bureau of Animal Industry[, the office within the Department of Agriculture that was responsible for representing the Department in the hearing], and discussed the proposed findings[, which were prepared by officials in that same Bureau]. He testified that he considered the evidence before signing the order. The substance of his action is stated in his answer to the question whether the order represented his independent conclusion, as follows: "My answer to the question would be that that very definitely was my independent conclusion as based on the findings of the men in the Bureau of Animal Industry. I would say, I will try to put it as accurately as possible, that it represented my own independent reactions to the findings of the men in the Bureau of Animal Industry."

Save for certain rate alterations, he "accepted the findings." ...

Morgan v. United States, 304 U.S. 1, 17–18 (1938) (*Morgan II*).

The Court in *Morgan II* held that this was not good enough to provide the statutorily required "full hearing." The Court explained: "Congress, in requiring a 'full hearing,' had regard to judicial standards—not in any technical sense but with respect to those fundamental requirements of fairness which are of the essence of due process in a proceeding of a judicial nature." *Morgan II*, 204 U.S. at 19. The Secretary did not adhere to judicial standards because he relied largely on conversations with agency officials that went on behind the scenes after the hearing. Although the market agencies made a post-hearing oral argument and written submissions, they did so in a vacuum. The hearing examiner made no report. The government never proposed findings of fact to which the market agencies could respond. The Court said something more was necessary after the hearing than the ex parte process described at the trial on remand: "The requirements of fairness are not exhausted in the taking or consideration of evidence, but extend to the concluding parts of the procedure as well as to the beginning and intermediate steps." *Id.* at 20. The Court invalidated the Secretary's rate order.

The *Morgan* case went to the Court a third time on a question that arose in the wake of the Court's invalidation of the Secretary's rate order: What rates could the market agencies lawfully charge pending litigation challenging that same order? The Court addressed this issue in *Morgan III*. *United States v. Morgan*, 307 U.S. 183 (1939). After *Morgan III*, the Secretary of Agriculture issued a new rate order addressing lawful rates during the period consumed by litigation of the Secretary's prior rate order. The market agencies challenged the new rate order. A federal district court invalidated the new rate order. The case went to the U.S. Supreme Court for the fourth time. *United States v. Morgan*, 313 U.S. 409 (1941) (*Morgan IV*).

In *Morgan IV*, the Court rejected the market agencies' challenge and ruled in favor of the Secretary. In the most often quoted passage, the Court in *Morgan IV* disapproved the close scrutiny that the federal district court had allowed the market agencies to conduct into the Secretary's and other officials' thought processes:

> Over the Government's objection the district court authorized the market agencies to take the deposition of the Secretary.... He was questioned at length regarding the process by which he reached the conclusions of his order, including the manner and extent of his study of the record and his consultation with subordinates. His testimony shows that he dealt with the enormous record in a manner not unlike the practice of judges in similar situations, and that he held various conferences with the examiner who heard the evidence.... [T]he short of the business is that the Secretary should never have been subjected to this examination. The proceeding before the Secretary "has a quality resembling that of a judicial proceeding." *Morgan v. United States*, 298 U.S. 468, 480. Such an examination of a judge would be destructive of judicial responsibility. We have explicitly held in this very litigation that "it was not the function of the court to probe the mental processes of the Secretary." 304 U.S. 1, 18. Just as a judge cannot be subjected to such a scrutiny, so the integrity of the administrative process must be equally respected. It will bear repeating that although the administrative process has had a different development and pursues somewhat different ways from those of courts, they are to be deemed collaborative instrumentalities of justice and the appropriate independence of each should be respected by the other.

Morgan IV, 313 U.S. 409 at 421–422. This reflected a change in heart from *Morgan I* and *II*, and the upshot was ironic: The Court in *Morgan I* and *II* had analogized the ratemaking proceeding to a judicial proceeding to justify requiring the Secretary to examine the evidence personally rather than relying on subordinates. The Court in *Morgan IV* relied on the same judicial analogy to hold that courts could not inquire into whether the Secretary had actually given adequate personal attention to the matter.

2. Significance of the *Morgan* Cases

The *Morgan* cases have influenced federal administrative law in three ways. They relate to delegation within agencies; judicial inquiry into the administrative decision-making process; and the decision-making requirements of the federal APA. We discuss the first two issues below, and the third in Section C of this chapter.

a. Delegation within Agencies

In *Morgan I* and *II*, the Court held that the agency official with authority to make the final decision for the agency had to give personal attention to the relevant evidence and legal issues. But the Court left open the possibility that this requirement could be satisfied (within statutory constraints) if the head of the agency delegated final decision-making authority to the subordinate who was personally familiar with the evidence and issues. Thus, the Court suggested, perhaps the Secretary of Agriculture could delegate final authority for making the rate order to the Assistant Secretary, who, in the actual proceeding, had received the hearing record compiled by the hearing examiner and heard oral arguments from the parties. *See Morgan I*, 298 U.S. at 478–479.

Following up on this suggestion, some federal agencies after the *Morgan* cases made delegations within the agency so that lower-level officials had authority to make final decisions for the agency in formal adjudications. These are sometimes called "subdelegations," because they arise from statutes that "delegate" power to an official, who in turn "subdelegates" it to a subordinate. To cite a pertinent example of delegation (or subdelegation, if you prefer), soon after the *Morgan* litigation ended, Congress enacted legislation authorizing the Secretary of Agriculture to delegate the Secretary's statutory responsibilities to others within the Department. Act of Apr. 4, 1940, ch. 75, § 2, 54 Stat. 81. Under this legislation, the Secretary has delegated authority to make final decisions in formal adjudications to an official in the Department called the Judicial Officer (JO). 7 C.F.R. § 2.35(a)(2) (2012) (current version of regulation, authorizing JO to "[a]ct as final deciding officer in adjudicatory proceedings subject to 5 U.S.C. 556 and 557"). Thus, the Judicial Officer makes the final decision for the Secretary of Agriculture in formal adjudications; the Secretary cannot overrule the JO.

Other agencies have created multi-person, internal entities to make final agency decisions in formal adjudications. For example, the Social Security Administration (SSA) has created an Appeals Council that has power to review ALJ decisions and make final decisions for the Commissioner of SSA in many adjudications under the Social Security Act. *See* 20 C.F.R. § 422.210(a) (2012). To cite another example, the EPA contains the Environmental Appeals Board, which reviews ALJ decisions and makes final decisions for the EPA Administrator in many adjudications under the federal environmental laws. *See* 40 C.F.R. § 1.25(e) (2012). These delegates are better able than the head of the agency to become personally familiar with the evidence and issues in each adjudication and can therefore supply the personal attention that *Morgan I* and *II* held was required.

Of course, delegations within the agency must comply with the agency legislation. Sometimes, the agency legislation expressly addresses the permissibility of delegations of statutory powers and duties within the agency. *E.g.*, 15 U.S.C. § 2076(b)(9) & (10) (2012) (authorizing five-member body heading the Consumer Product Safety Commission to delegate powers, other than the subpoena power, to "any officer or employee of the Commission"). If the agency legislation does not expressly address delegation, some courts presume delegation is permitted in the absence of evidence of contrary congressional intent. *See, e.g., Frankl v. HTH Corp.*, 650 F.3d 1334, 1350 (9th Cir. 2011). Even so, the validity of a particular delegation may pose a difficult issue of statutory interpretation. Some statutes are interpreted to give an official nondelegable powers or duties. *See, e.g., Cudahy Packing Co. of La. v. Holland*, 315 U.S. 357 (1942) (interpreting federal statute to bar delegation of power to issue subpoenas).

As an alternative to complete delegation of final decision-making authority to a subordinate, an agency may (if the agency legislation permits) authorize the head of the agency to conduct discretionary, case-by-case review of the subordinate's decisions. The Federal Communications Commission has delegated some of its statutory authority to decision makers subordinate to the five-person Commission that heads the agency. The five-person Commission retains, however, authority to review the decisions made by subordinates exercising delegated authority. The Commission may review a decision upon request or on its own motion. *See* 47 C.F.R. §§ 1.115 & 1.117 (2012).

The takeaway from this discussion is that statutes often grant authority to a specific official or entity, but the authority may end up being delegated to a subordinate official or entity. The delegations may occur in agency rules, as illustrated above, or other agency directives. *See, e.g.*, 16 C.F.R. § 1000.11 (2012) (Consumer Product Safety Commission's delegations of authority under its organic act "are documented in the Commission's Directives System"); 40 C.F.R. § 1.5(b) (2012) ("EPA's Directives System contains definitive statements of ... delegations of authority."). *Morgan I* and *II* prompted many such delegations of adjudicatory authority through their insistence that the final decision maker give personal attention to the relevant evidence and legal issues.

b. Judicial Probing of Administrators' Thought Processes

As noted above, *Morgan* stands today for severely restricting courts' "probing the mental processes" of agency officials. *Morgan*, 304 U.S. at 18. A famous illustration of the restriction is *National Nutritional Foods Association v. FDA*, 491 F.2d 1141 (2d Cir. 1974). Plaintiffs in that case sought review of rules made by the Food and Drug Administration (FDA) through formal rulemaking. Those rules were the result of a two-year-long agency hearing producing more than 32,000 pages of testimony and thousands of pages of documents. The FDA Commissioner approved these rules, along with fourteen others, within two weeks of taking office. The plaintiffs argued that the Commissioner could not possibly have given adequate personal attention to the rules before approving them, and sought leave to depose the Commissioner to explore the approval process.

The Second Circuit upheld the denial of the plaintiffs' request for a deposition, concluding:

> With the enormous increase in delegation of lawmaking power which Congress has been obliged to make to agencies ... and in the complexity of life, government would become impossible if courts were to insist on anything of the sort [that plaintiffs claim was required]. It would suffice under the circumstances that Commissioner Schmidt considered the summaries of the objections and of the answers contained in the elaborate preambles and conferred with his staff about them. There is no reason why he could not have done this even in the limited time available.... In any event, absent the most powerful preliminary showing to the contrary, effective government requires us to presume that he did.

Id. at 1145–1146 (footnotes and internal citations omitted). Although the court did say that Commissioner Schmidt had to give personal attention to the matters, the court also said that the court had to assume that he fulfilled that requirement in the absence of "the most power preliminary showing to the contrary."

That is where federal law stands today.

Exercise: Applying the *Morgan* Cases

On July 1, 2010, a federal court of appeals vacated and remanded a decision of the National Labor Relations Board because the decision had been made by a two-member panel of the Board, instead of the minimum three-member panel required by the agency legislation. On July 14, 2010, a three-member panel was assigned to reconsider the case. On August 1, 2010, the three-member panel adopted the decision of the original two-member panel. The case was a relatively complex one. For this reason, the losing party sought judicial review of the three-member panel's decision, arguing that the panel could not possibly have given adequate personal attention to the record and legal arguments in the case. Please analyze this argument. *See NLRB v. County Waste of Ulster, LLC*, 455 Fed. Appx. 32 (Jan. 6, 2012).

B. Decision Requirements in Agency Legislation and Agency Rules

The agency legislation always should be analyzed to determine to what extent it controls the agency's decision methods in formal proceedings. Does it permit delegation or must the agency head decide? The agency legislation may require or permit creation of an intermediate review board. The agency legislation may define the scope of the agency's authority on review of a decision reached by subordinates. It is the agency that has ultimate responsibility for the decision, although it may be aided in that process by its subordinates. Thus, the legislature may have shaped the relationship between the agency and its staff in terms of decision-making authority and responsibility.

When the agency legislation does allow delegation of decision-making authority in formal proceedings, those delegations are often reflected in the agency's own published rules or other publicly available material. The public availability of this information reflects the federal APA's requirement that each agency publish in the Federal Register **"statements of the general course and method by which its functions are channeled and determined."** 5 U.S.C. § 552(a)(1)(B) (2012). For an example of material providing this information for the EPA, see 40 C.F.R. §§ 1.1–1.61 (2012).

C. Decision Requirements in the Federal APA

1. APA Decisional Requirements in a Nutshell

The drafters of the Administrative Procedure Act considered the *Morgan* cases when drafting the decision-making requirements for formal adjudications in § 557. Here in a nutshell is how § 557 ordinarily works. Section 557 prescribes a two-step decision-making process. At step one, the ALJ who presides at the hearing makes a decision. At step two, the ALJ's decision may be reviewed by "the agency," meaning the head of the agency or the subordinate to whom the head of the agency has delegated decision-making authority. On review of the ALJ's decision, the agency is not bound by the ALJ's decision but may instead make findings of fact and conclusions of law de novo. Throughout this decision-making process, both the ALJ and the agency base their decisions exclusively on the record and cannot engage in ex parte contacts.

2. Original Decisions by the ALJ (or Other Hearing Officer)

Section 557(b) addresses what happens after the formal hearing at which evidence is received. Take a deep breath before you dive in. This part of the APA is as intricate as a Russian novel:

---

5 U.S.C. § 557. Initial decisions; conclusiveness; review by agency; submissions by parties; contents of decisions; record ...

(b) When the agency did not preside at the reception of the evidence, the presiding employee or, in cases not subject to section 554(d) of this title, an employee qualified to preside at hearings pursuant to section 556 of this title, shall initially decide the case unless the agency requires, either in specific cases or by general rule, the entire record to be certified to it for decision. When the presiding employee makes an initial decision, that decision then becomes the decision of the agency without further proceedings unless there is an appeal to, or review on motion of, the agency within time provided by rule. On appeal from or review of the initial decision, the agency has all the powers which it would have in making the initial decision except as it may limit the issues on notice or by rule. When the agency makes the decision without having presided at the reception of the evidence, the presiding employee or an employee qualified to preside at hearings pursuant to section 556 of this title shall first recommend a decision, except that in rule making or determining applications for initial licenses—

(1) instead thereof the agency may issue a tentative decision or one of its responsible employees may recommend a decision; or

(2) this procedure may be omitted in a case in which the agency finds on the record that due and timely execution of its functions imperatively and unavoidably so requires....

In most cases, the head of the agency does **"not preside at the reception of the evidence."** That task is left instead to a **"presiding employee,"** most often an ALJ. After the ALJ has presided at the hearing, taken evidence, and compiled the record for decision, one of three things may happen.

1. First, and most often, the ALJ **"shall initially decide the case."** The ALJ's initial decision can then be reviewed by the agency, either on an appeal by the dissatisfied party, or on the agency's own motion. If not reviewed, the ALJ's initial decision becomes the final decision of the agency.

2. Instead of letting the ALJ make an initial decision, the agency may **"requir[e] ... the entire record to be certified to it for decision."** In that event, the ALJ will normally **"first recommend a decision."** The agency will consider the recommended decision and then make the initial and final decisions. AGM 81.

3. Instead of making an initial decision or recommended decision, the ALJ may make no decision at all **"in [formal] rule making or determining applications for initial licenses."** In those two types of proceedings, the ALJ compiles the record but the agency itself may make a tentative decision or have a subordinate agency official make a recommended decision. The agency can even dispense with a tentative decision or a recommended decision, however, when **"the agency finds on the record that due and timely execution of its functions imperatively and unavoidably so requires."**

3. Review of Original Decisions

a. Initial Decisions

Section 557(b) says that, if there is no appeal from, or review of, an ALJ's initial decision by the agency, the initial decision will become the final decision of the agency without further proceedings. That does not mean, however, that a person dissatisfied with the now-final decision of the ALJ can seek judicial review, having foregone the opportunity for review within the agency. To the contrary, as we will discuss in Chapter 30, the dissatisfied person often will be unable to get judicial review because of the failure to "exhaust administrative remedies." The moral of this story is that the person dissatisfied with the ALJ's initial decision should seek review of that decision within the agency, following the agency's rules for doing so. The initial decision may be reviewed by the head of the agency or by an official or entity to whom the agency head has delegated reviewing authority. For simplicity's sake, however, we will usually refer to the reviewing entity as "the agency" or "the agency head."

When the agency reviews the ALJ's initial decision, the agency is not bound by the initial decision of the ALJ. AGM 83. Instead, § 557 (b) states, **"On appeal from or review of the initial decision, the agency has all the powers which it would have in making the initial decision except as it may limit the issues on notice or by rule."** In plain English, the agency head can make its own findings of fact, conclusions of law, and discretionary judgments. But the ALJ's initial decision will be part of the record and will be taken into account if a court ultimately reviews the matter, especially where demeanor and credibility of witnesses are material factors related to the fact findings. AGM 84. An agency thus can make findings of fact de novo, but when it does so based on the "cold record," the agency will have to explain why any of its findings differ from those of the ALJ, especially on matters of demeanor and credibility. Otherwise, the agency's decision may become vulnerable to a successful judicial challenge.

b. Recommended Decisions

A recommended decision is purely advisory and does not bind the agency. AGM 83. But it will carry weight where demeanor and credibility of witnesses are material factors. AGM 84. The agency must consider and determine all issues that are properly presented for review, but it may require precise exceptions supported by specific citations to the record. AGM 84. If it desires, the agency may adopt the ALJ's recommended findings and conclusions or make them anew, or remand to the ALJ for further proceedings, subject to few limitations. AGM 84–85.

c. Tentative Decisions and Recommended Decisions of Responsible Employees

As discussed above, tentative decisions by an agency may occur when rulemaking or initial licensing is involved. Since rulemaking is legislative in nature and because initial licensing was considered to be non-accusatory when the APA was enacted, its drafters made provision in § 557(b) for agencies to issue a tentative decision or have a "**responsible employee**" recommend a decision. AGM 82.

4. Right to Submit Proposed Findings and Conclusions, Exceptions, and Supporting Reasons

The Court in *Morgan II* invalidated a decision-making process that largely excluded parties from participating after the hearing ended. To avoid that problem, § 557(c) gives the parties to a formal proceeding the right to give input during the post-hearing decision-making process. Section 557(c) also ensures that the agency decision makers respond to that input.

---

5 U.S.C. § 557. Initial decisions; conclusiveness; review by agency; submissions by parties; contents of decisions; record ...

(c) Before a recommended, initial, or tentative decision, or a decision on agency review of the decision of subordinate employees, the parties are entitled to a reasonable opportunity to submit for the consideration of the employees participating in the decisions—

(1) proposed findings and conclusions; or

(2) exceptions to the decisions or recommended decisions of subordinate employees or to tentative agency decisions; and

(3) supporting reasons for the exceptions or proposed findings or conclusions.

The record shall show the ruling on each finding, conclusion, or exception presented....

Section 557(c) prevents, for example, an ALJ's initial or recommended decision from being reviewed by the agency head without the parties first having an opportunity to poke holes in the ALJ's decision. *Cf. Koniag, Inc. v. Andrus*, 580 F.2d 601, 608–610 (D.C. Cir. 1978) (holding that due process was violated by administrative scheme that did not allow parties to see ALJ's recommended decision before it was reviewed by higher authority in the agency).

The Attorney General's Manual on the APA observed that, ordinarily, the parties submit proposed findings of fact and conclusions of law to the ALJ before the ALJ makes an initial or recommended decision; then, after the ALJ makes the initial or recommended decision, the parties file exceptions to that decision, for consideration by the agency head when reviewing the ALJ's decision. AGM 85. Agencies may by rule require proposed findings, conclusions, and exceptions to be supported by a precise citation to the record or to legal authorities. AGM 85. Section 557(c)(3) entitles the parties to file briefs or memos with arguments supporting the parties' proposed findings and conclusions and exceptions. AGM 85.

The purpose of the requirement that the record show the ruling on each finding, conclusion, or exception presented is "to preclude later controversy as to what the agency has done." AGM 86. The ALJ may reject proposed findings and conclusions or, to the contrary, may adopt them. However, a reviewing court will scrutinize closely an ALJ's action adopting virtually all findings submitted by one party while rejecting all findings proposed by another party. *Gimbel v. Commodity Futures Trading Comm'n*, 872 F.2d 196 (7th Cir. 1989). This follows for the reason that administrative law judges are responsible for developing the case fully and for preparing an adequate record for consideration by others within the agency. Furthermore, § 556(b) requires those participating in decision making to conduct their functions **"in an impartial manner."** Thus, the ALJ's responsibilities should not be confused with those of trial judges, who commonly accept the findings and conclusions drafted by the winning party at the close of a lawsuit.

5. Required Contents of Decisions

a. APA Requirements

Section 557(c) requires all decisions to have written explanations addressing the facts, the law, and the exercise of discretion:

---

5 U.S.C. § 557. Initial decisions; conclusiveness; review by agency; submissions by parties; contents of decisions; record …

(c) … All decisions, including initial, recommended, and tentative decisions, are a part of the record and shall include a statement of—

(A) findings and conclusions, and the reasons or basis therefor, on all the material issues of fact, law, or discretion presented on the record; and

(B) the appropriate rule, order, sanction, relief, or denial thereof. …

This provision on its face might suggest that, when the agency head reviews the ALJ's decision, the agency head must revisit every issue that the ALJ addressed. This is not true, however, as the Attorney General's Manual explained. Instead, the agency head can limit the issues it will review when it reviews initial decisions. The agency head, for example, could adopt a rule restricting it to reviewing questions of law posed by the ALJ's initial decision, but not questions of fact. Similarly, when the agency head reviews an ALJ's recommended decision, the agency head can limit its review to issues and objections specifically raised by the parties. AGM 84–85.

b. The Distinction between "Basic" Facts and "Ultimate" Facts

The outcome of many adjudications depends on the resolution of factual disputes. Like court adjudications, many agency adjudications are "He said—She said" affairs. For that reason, parties to the agency adjudication push the ALJ to make favorable findings of fact. By the same token, the party who loses before the ALJ must impugn those findings to prevail on review. Administrative lawyers thus spend much time analyzing officials' findings of fact and the evidence underlying them.

The law has long recognized a distinction between "basic" and "ultimate" facts. "Basic" facts are also known as "elemental," "primary," "historical" or "pure" facts. "Ultimate" facts are also known as "mixed questions of law and fact" or "law-application determinations." The following case, though old, is still well known for its articulate discussion of the distinction. The distinction continues to matter for reasons discussed after the case.

Saginaw Broadcasting Co. v. Federal Communications Commission (Gross et al., Intervenors)
96 F.2d 554 (D.C. Cir. 1938), cert. denied, 305 U.S. 613 (1938)

Before GRONER, Chief Justice, and STEPHENS and MILLER, Associate Justices. [Editor's note: At this time, federal court of appeals judges were called "Justices." They aren't called that today, probably to their regret.]

STEPHENS, ASSOCIATE JUSTICE

This is an appeal taken under Section 402(b)(1) of the Communications Act of 1934, 47 U.S.C.A. 402(b)(1), from an order of the Broadcast Division of the Federal Communications Commission denying the application of the appellant for a radio station construction permit, and granting the application of the intervenors for such a permit.

On September 30, 1935, the Saginaw Broadcasting Company, the applicant (hereinafter referred to as such), filed an application for a permit to construct a radio station in Saginaw, Michigan, to operate on the frequency of 1200 kilocycles with a power of 250 watts until local sunset and 100 watts at night. The hours of operation were to be those portions of the broadcast day not occupied by WMPC, a station already in operation on the same frequency in Lapeer, Michigan, a city 40 miles from Saginaw. On February 21, 1936, Harold F. Gross and Edmund C. Shields, the intervenors (hereinafter referred to as such), filed an application for a permit to construct a station in Saginaw to operate on the frequency of 950 kilocycles with a power of 500 watts. Continuous operation was proposed during the day until local sunset; no broadcasts were to be made at night. . . .

... [T]he Broadcast Division designated these applications for hearing and later a joint hearing was held thereon before a trial examiner. The examiner recommended that the appellant's application be granted, and that that of the intervenors be denied. Oral argument was had before the Broadcast Division on exceptions to the examiner's report. The Division refused to adopt the recommendation of the examiner and entered an order on February 9, 1937, granting the application of the intervenors and denying that of the appellant.... The Commission's statement of facts and grounds for decision was filed on March 16, 1937 [and the Commission later denied rehearing]....

The appellant assigns as reasons for its appeal numerous alleged errors of the Commission in making, and in failing to make, specific findings of fact from the evidence adduced at the hearing. These assignments require an inquiry into the purpose and necessary content of findings of fact under the Communications Act.

The Act in Section 319(a), 47 U.S.C.A. 319(a), provides that the Commission may grant a construction permit for a radio station, if public convenience, interest, or necessity will be served. Section 402(b) of the Act provides that an appeal may be taken to this court from a denial of an application for a construction permit. Section 402(c) provides that ... the Commission shall ... thereafter file "a full statement in writing of the facts and grounds for its decision as found and given by it." Section 402(e) provides that the review by the court shall be limited to questions of law, and that findings of fact by the Commission, if supported by substantial evidence, shall be conclusive unless they shall clearly appear to be arbitrary or capricious. Thereby the Act has set out a criterion to govern the Commission in granting or refusing to grant a construction permit, has required a full statement in writing of the facts and grounds for its decision, and has provided the standards for judicial review.

The requirement that courts, and commissions acting in a quasi judicial capacity, shall make findings of fact, is a means provided by Congress for guaranteeing that cases shall be decided according to the evidence and the law, rather than arbitrarily or from extralegal considerations; and findings of fact serve the additional purpose, where provisions for review are made, of apprising the parties and the reviewing tribunal of the factual basis of the action of the court or commission, so that the parties and the reviewing tribunal may determine whether the case has been decided upon the evidence and the law or, on the contrary, upon arbitrary or extralegal considerations. When a decision is accompanied by findings of fact, the reviewing court can decide whether the decision reached by the court or commission follows as a matter of law from the facts stated as its basis, and also whether the facts so stated have any substantial support in the evidence. In the absence of findings of fact the reviewing tribunal can determine neither of these things. The requirement of findings is thus far from a technicality. On the contrary, it is to insure against Star Chamber methods, to make certain that justice shall be administered according to facts and law. This is fully as important in respect of commissions as it is in respect of courts.

In discussing the necessary content of findings of fact, it will be helpful to spell out the process which a commission properly follows in reaching a decision. The process necessarily includes at least four parts: (1) evidence must be taken and weighed, both as to its accuracy and credibility; (2) from attentive consideration of this evidence a determination of facts of a basic or underlying nature must be reached; (3) from these basic facts the ultimate facts, usually in the language of the statute, are to be inferred, or not, as the case may be; (4) from this finding the decision will follow by the application of the statutory criterion. For example, before the Communications Commission may grant a construction permit it must, under the statute, be convinced that the public interest, convenience, or necessity will be served. An affirmative or negative finding on this topic would be a finding of ultimate fact. This ultimate fact, however, will be reached by inference from basic facts, such as, for example, the probable existence or non-existence of electrical interference, in view of the number of other stations operating in the area, their power, wave length, and the like. These basic facts will themselves appear or fail to appear, as the case may be, from the evidence introduced when attentively considered. Thus, upon the issue of electrical interference evidence may be introduced concerning power and wave length of a proposed station and of existing stations, and expert opinion based upon this evidence may be offered as to the likelihood of interference; and expert opinion based on evidence of field measurements of signal strength of existing stations may also be offered. This testimony may conflict. It is the Commission's duty to find from such evidence the basic facts as to the operation of the proposed and present stations in respect of power, wave length, and the like, and whether or not electrical interference will result from the operation of the proposed station, and then to find as an ultimate fact whether public interest, convenience, or necessity will be served by granting or not granting the application.

We ruled in [a prior case] ... that findings of fact ... must include what have been above described as the basic facts, from which the facts in the terms of the statutory criterion are inferred. It is not necessary for the Commission to recite the evidence, and it is not necessary that it set out its findings in the formal style and manner customary in trial courts. It is enough if the findings be unambiguously stated, whether in narrative or numbered form, so that it appears definitely upon what basic facts the Commission reached the ultimate facts and came to its decision.

... [A] reviewing court cannot properly exercise its function upon findings of ultimate fact alone, but must require also findings of the basic facts which represent the determination of the administrative body as to the meaning of the evidence, and from which the ultimate facts flow.... [The court determined that the Commission's findings of fact were sketchy, highly inferential, and inaccurate in places. Accordingly, they did not demonstrate that the Commission had based its decision on careful consideration of the evidence in the record.]

The language of Mr. Justice Butler in *Atchison, T. & S.F. Ry. Co. v. United States*, 295 U.S. 193 (1935), that:

> "This court will not search the record to ascertain whether, by use of what there may be found, general and ambiguous statements in the report intended to serve as findings may by construction be given a meaning sufficiently definite and certain to constitute a valid basis for the order. In the absence of a finding of essential basic facts, the order cannot be sustained." 295 U.S. 193, at pages 201, 202,

seems pertinent. It is not the duty of the court to make findings for the Commission and when the Commission has failed in its duty to make such findings, it is impossible for the court to review its conclusion....

Reversed and remanded.

* * *

The basic facts/ultimate facts distinction remains valid more than seventy-five years after *Saginaw* was decided. The distinction should be kept in mind for several reasons.

First, as discussed above, the federal APA requires all decisions—initial, recommended, tentative, and final—to include findings of basic facts and conclusions of law. 5 U.S.C. § 557(c)(3)(A). State APAs likewise will typically be construed to require ALJs in contested cases to make findings of basic facts. *See* 1961 Model State APA § 12 Official Comment (citing *Saginaw* as expressing "the degree of explicitness" required in agency findings). Careful study of an ALJ's proposed fact findings, or those of the agency, should indicate whether they are flawed. If the attorney can show that proper basic fact findings, based on the record evidence and supporting the proposed decision, have not been made, the ALJ's decision cannot be valid. However, if allowed to go unchallenged, it could survive.

Second, as also discussed above, the federal APA generally permits parties to submit proposed findings of fact. 5 U.S.C. §557(c)(1). Understanding the basic fact/ultimate fact distinction is essential to the proper drafting of proposed findings so that, if they are accepted, the decision will not later be vulnerable to being set aside as it was in *Saginaw* and in the cases discussed in *Saginaw*.

Third, as *Saginaw* illustrates, on judicial review courts will respond to the basic fact/ultimate fact distinction and will set aside decisions based on improper fact findings. Courts are familiar with the distinction between "basic" and "ultimate" facts because the distinction is not limited to administrative law. *E.g.*, *County Court v. Allen*, 442 U.S. 140, 156–157 (1979) (discussing distinction in criminal case). The ability to recognize their impropriety gives the astute attorney another potential ground on which to seek reversal of an unfavorable decision.

c. Rehearing and Reopening

Agencies often have authority to rehear, reconsider, or reopen their decisions and correct erroneous ones. (We will use the term "rehear" generically to refer to all three forms of revisiting a prior decision.) If consistent with applicable statutes, the agency rules may permit rehearing for errors of law as well as for factual errors. For example, regulations of the Social Security Administration authorize the Social Security Appeals Council to reopen cases under certain circumstances. 20 CFR §§404.987–404.996 and 416.1487–416.1494 (2012); *Cole v. Barnhart*, 288 F.3d 149, 152 n.9 (5th Cir. 2002).

Special principles govern federal court review of a federal agency's decision denying a party's request to reopen or rehear a decision. We discuss those principles in Chapter 35.A.3.

D. Restrictions on Ex Parte Communications under Federal Law

As you know, court proceedings are adversarial in nature, which means that each side has a chance to put on an affirmative case and to rebut or impeach the opposing party's case. Central to the integrity of the adversary process is a ban on ex parte communications, in which one party "gets the judge's ear" when other parties are not around to hear what is said (or otherwise communicated).

Similarly, ex parte communications are restricted in formal adjudications. The federal APA defines **"ex parte communications"** in 5 U.S.C. §551(14) (2012). In addition, two provisions of the federal APA restrict ex parte communications in formal adjudications: §§554(d) and 557(d). This section examines those provisions and mentions the Due Process Clauses as additional, potential sources of restrictions on ex parte communications.

1. § 554(d)

---

5 U.S.C. § 554. Adjudications ...

(d) The employee who presides at the reception of evidence pursuant to section 556 of this title shall make the recommended decision or initial decision required by section 557 of this title, unless he becomes unavailable to the agency. Except to the extent required for the disposition of ex parte matters as authorized by law, such an employee may not—

(1) consult a person or party on a fact in issue, unless on notice and opportunity for all parties to participate; or
(2) be responsible to or subject to the supervision or direction of an employee or agent engaged in the performance of investigative or prosecuting functions for an agency.

An employee or agent engaged in the performance of investigative or prosecuting functions for an agency in a case may not, in that or a factually related case, participate or advise in the decision, recommended decision, or agency review pursuant to section 557 of this title, except as witness or counsel in public proceedings. This subsection does not apply—

(A) in determining applications for initial licenses;

(B) to proceedings involving the validity or application of rates, facilities, or practices of public utilities or carriers; or

(C) to the agency or a member or members of the body comprising the agency....

Section 554(d) limits ex parte communications and other undue influence in three ways: (1) It limits what officials presiding at the hearing (ALJs) can do; (2) it separates the ALJs from the agency prosecutors and investigators; and (3) it limits what investigating and prosecuting officials can do.

First, § 554(d)(1) prohibits the ALJ from communicating ex parte with any person or party on a fact in issue. The ALJ thus may not consult, ex parte, with people inside or outside the agency about facts in issue. The ALJ may, however, consult with someone else inside the agency on pure issues of *law*, as long as that other agency official is not involved in investigating or prosecuting the case. In short, ALJs can consult other neutral agency officials about issues of law. ALJs may not consult people outside the agency even about issues of law because of § 557(d), which is discussed below.

Second, § 554(d)(2) makes ALJs independent of agency investigators and prosecutors. This "separation of functions" provision was discussed in Chapter 22's discussion of ALJs' job protections. Specifically, it ensures that ALJs don't feel pressured to rule in favor of those officials in proceedings that pit those officials against a private individual or company.

Third, Section 554(d) prohibits any agency official involved in investigating or prosecuting a case from participating in the decision in that case or a factually related case. Agency investigators and prosecutors can't have ex parte input into the ALJ's decision or that of any agency superior who reviews the ALJ's decision. The only way an agency investigator or prosecutor can give input is as a witness or lawyer. But neither of those roles permits ex parte contacts with the decision makers.

Section 554(d) creates three exceptions to these restrictions. The most confusing exception is the exception for agency heads. Let us try to minimize the confusion by starting with the one thing that the agency head exception was clearly meant to allow, and the one thing that the exception clearly does not allow. The agency head exception was clearly meant to allow the head of the agency to be involved in investigating, prosecuting, and adjudicating the same case. Thus, for example, the five-member commission that heads the Federal Trade Commission can be involved in (1) authorizing investigations of suspected unfair trade practices; (2) authorizing enforcement proceedings against companies and people who, the Commission has reason to believe, have committed unfair trade practices; and (3) making the final decision in those proceedings about whether unfair trade practices have indeed occurred. There is one main thing that the agency head exception clearly does *not* allow: It does not allow an agency head to discuss a case ex parte with agency investigators or prosecutors. Thus, for example, once an FTC enforcement proceeding has begun, the FTC Commissioners cannot discuss the case ex parte with the FTC lawyer who is prosecuting the case.

There is one main question that the agency head exception doesn't answer: Can the agency head discuss the facts of a case with the ALJ who presided over the hearing in that case? The answer may lie in § 554(d)(1), which prohibits the ALJ from discussing a fact in issue ex parte with any **"person."** The key question is whether the agency head is a **"person."** That is unclear. Section 551(2) defines **"person"** to **"include[e] an individual, partnership, corporation, association, or public or private organization other than an agency."** The agency head is an individual, but might be exempted by the phrase **"other than an agency,"** unless that phrase only refers to the agency as a whole, as distinguished from the agency head. Besides the ambiguity about the meaning of **"person"** in § 554(d)(1), it is unclear whether the agency head exception makes § 554(d)(1) inapplicable to discussions between an ALJ and an agency head. On the one hand, you can argue that the exception doesn't lift § 554(d)(1)'s restriction on the *ALJ*. On the other hand, you can argue that any ex parte discussion to which the agency head is a party, even a discussion with an ALJ, falls within the agency head exception. If your head is spinning by this point, you get the point.

Besides questions arising from the ambiguous statutory text, it is a hard question of policy whether the agency head should be able to discuss a case with the ALJ. This depends on whether you conceive of the relationship between the ALJ and the agency head as more like the relationship between a subordinate employee to a superior employee—in which case ex parte contacts between the agency head and the ALJ should be allowed—or more like the relationship between a trial court and an appellate court—in which case ex parte contacts should be forbidden. The reality is that the ALJ is both subordinate to the agency head but also has some decision-making independence like that of a trial judge.

The importance of this issue—whether the ALJ and agency head can discuss a case ex parte—is somewhat diminished by two facts. First, the ALJ and the agency head must base their decision in a formal adjudication exclusively on the record. They may not rely on factual information from any other source, including an ex parte contact. 5 U.S.C. § 556(e). This does not prevent them, however, from discussing the significance of evidence in the record. Second, the agency legislation or an agency rule may prohibit ex parte contacts, including contacts between the ALJ and the agency head, even if the federal APA does not do so.

2. § 557(d)

The provision discussed above, § 554(d), applies only to formal adjudications. The provision we now examine, § 557(d), applies to both formal adjudications and formal rulemakings.

---

5 U.S.C. § 557. Initial decisions; conclusiveness; review by agency; submissions by parties; contents of decisions; record

(a) This section applies, according to the provisions thereof, when a hearing is required to be conducted in accordance with section 556 of this title....

(d)(1) In any agency proceeding which is subject to subsection (a) of this section, except to the extent required for the disposition of ex parte matters as authorized by law—

(A) no interested person outside the agency shall make or knowingly cause to be made to any member of the body comprising the agency, administrative law judge, or other employee who is or may reasonably be expected to be involved in the decisional process of the proceeding, an ex parte communication relevant to the merits of the proceeding;

(B) no member of the body comprising the agency, administrative law judge, or other employee who is or may reasonably be expected to be involved in the decisional process of the proceeding, shall make or knowingly cause to be made to any interested person outside the agency an ex parte communication relevant to the merits of the proceeding;

(C) a member of the body comprising the agency, administrative law judge, or other employee who is or may reasonably be expected to be involved in the decisional process of such proceeding who receives, or who makes or knowingly causes to be made, a communication prohibited by this subsection shall place on the public record of the proceeding:

(i) all such written communications;

(ii) memoranda stating the substance of all such oral communications; and

(iii) all written responses, and memoranda stating the substance of all oral responses, to the materials described in clauses (i) and (ii) of this subparagraph;

(D) upon receipt of a communication knowingly made or knowingly caused to be made by a party in violation of this subsection, the agency, administrative law judge, or other employee presiding at the hearing may, to the extent consistent with the interests of justice and the policy of the underlying statutes, require the party to show cause why his claim or interest in the proceeding should not be dismissed, denied, disregarded, or otherwise adversely affected on account of such violation; and

(E) the prohibitions of this subsection shall apply beginning at such time as the agency may designate, but in no case shall they begin to apply later than the time at which a proceeding is noticed for hearing unless the person responsible for the communication has knowledge that it will be noticed, in which case the prohibitions shall apply beginning at the time of his acquisition of such knowledge....

Section 557(d) limits ex parte communications in two ways. First, §557(d)(1)(A) prohibits interested people outside the agency from communicating ex parte about the merits of the case with people inside the agency who are involved in deciding the case. Second, §557(d)(1)(B) prohibits people inside the agency who are involved in deciding the case from communicating ex parte with interested people outside the agency about the merits of the case. The two prohibitions are mirror images.

In addition to §557(d)'s bars on ex parte contacts, §557(d)(1)(C) prescribes procedures for handling ex parte contacts; §557(d)(1)(D) authorizes penalties for ex parte contacts caused by parties; and §557(d)(1)(E) identifies when the restrictions begin.

To illustrate the operation of §557(d), we will describe a leading case on it. The case illustrates the operation of §557(d)'s substantive restrictions and the scope of §557(d)'s term **"interested person outside the agency."** As you read the description, please make sure that you understand how the incidents discussed in the cases should be analyzed under §557(d) and why some points of the analysis don't yield clear answers.

- *Professional Air Traffic Controllers Organization (PATCO) v. Federal Labor Relations Authority*, 685 F.2d 547 (D.C. Cir. 1982)

The Professional Air Traffic Controllers Organization (PATCO) was a union designated by federal law as the exclusive bargaining representative for air traffic controllers employed by the Federal Aviation Administration (FAA). In 1981, more than 70% of the air traffic controllers went out on strike, significantly disrupting private and commercial air travel. The strike violated federal law prohibiting government employees from striking. *Id.* at 550 (discussing statutes). In addition, PATCO arguably violated federal law, and committed an unfair labor practice, by failing to disavow the strike.

The government set a deadline for the striking workers to return to work. Eleven thousand air traffic controllers did not obey the deadline; they were fired. In addition, the FAA filed an unfair labor practice charge against PATCO, alleging that PATCO committed an unfair labor practice by failing to disavow the strike. The FAA filed this charge with the federal agency responsible for federal labor relations, the Federal Labor Relations Authority (FLRA or Authority).

An FLRA Regional Director issued a complaint on the charge, and a hearing was scheduled. FLRA unfair labor practice hearings are formal adjudications under the APA, so §557(d) applied to the proceeding. In that proceeding, the General Counsel's Office of the FLRA prosecuted the unfair labor practice complaint against PATCO. After the hearing, the presiding ALJ recommended revocation of PATCO's status as the bargaining representative for FAA air traffic controllers. PATCO appealed the ALJ's recommended decision to the three-member body that heads the FLRA. The FLRA affirmed the ALJ's decision. PATCO then petitioned for judicial review.

On judicial review, allegations arose of ex parte communications during the FLRA proceeding. The court remanded for an evidentiary proceeding before an ALJ on the issue. The ALJ found three ex parte contacts to be significant, but determined that none

---

1. 685 F.2d at 567. The FLRA General Counsel was held to be **"outside the agency"** even though in fact he worked for the same agency, the FLRA, whose three-member body was considering the case. Although it seems odd that a person employed by the agency can be **"outside the agency"** under §557(d), the court's conclusion may have been influenced by the FLRA rule barring ex parte contacts, which classifies the FLRA General Counsel as a person outside the agency for purposes of any case in which the FLRA General Counsel's office is prosecuting an unfair labor practice. The court cited that

of them sufficiently affected the decision to require remand. The court of appeals referred to the "three troubling incidents" and assessed each of them. 685 F.2d at 566.

The first incident occurred while the General Counsel of the FLRA was in the office of one of the three members who then headed the FLRA, Member Applewhaite. The FLRA General Counsel was there to discuss with Member Applewhaite budgetary and administrative matters relating to the general operations of the FLRA, of which they were both employees. During their discussion, a staff attorney came in to give Member Applewhaite a memorandum addressing whether the Civil Service Reform Act mandates revocation of a striking union's exclusive bargaining agent status. That was the precise issue before Member Applewhaite in the PATCO case. The FLRA General Counsel and Member Applewhaite asked the staff attorney questions about her memorandum.

The court did not decide whether this incident violated § 557(d) but did find the ex parte contact, "such as it was," both "inadvertent" and "innocuous" and therefore not serious enough to "void" the FLRA's decision. *Id.* at 567. The court nonetheless found many of the elements of a § 557(d) violation. Specifically, the court held that the FLRA General Counsel was a **"person outside the agency"** under § 557(d).[1] The General Counsel, as a person outside the agency, made a communication to someone inside the agency, namely Member Applewhaite. The court recognized that the communication involved an issue relevant to the merits of the PATCO case, but still found the communication "innocuous" because "[n]either the General Counsel nor Member Applewhaite expressed any view on the correct statutory interpretation, the General Counsel made no arguments to Member Applewhaite, and the facts of the PATCO case were not mentioned." *PATCO*, 685 F.2d at 567. The court seemed to conclude that, if this first incident violated § 557(d), it was a harmless error.

The second incident happened when the Secretary of Transportation telephoned an FLRA member while the case was pending before the FLRA. The Secretary said he was not calling about the substance of the PATCO case, but wanted the member to know that, contrary to news reports, no meaningful efforts to settle the strike were underway. The Secretary also said that the Department of Transportation would appreciate expeditious handling of the case. To avoid discussing the PATCO case, the member replied, "I understand your position perfectly, Mr. Secretary." *PATCO*, 685 F.2d at 558. The member offered to convey the Secretary's message to another member, but the Secretary said that he would call the other member personally.

The court found that the Secretary of Transportation was an **"interested person outside the agency"** under § 557(d) and that his communications would have violated § 557(d) if he had sought to discuss the merits of the PATCO case. *See PATCO*, 685 F.2d at 568. Furthermore, the court said, "even a procedural inquiry may be a subtle effort to influence an agency decision." *PATCO*, 685 F.2d at 568. Nevertheless, the court concluded that, even if the Secretary of Transportation's phone call violated § 557(d), this communication, like the first incident, did not taint the proceedings or prejudice PATCO.

The third incident involved a person who was President of the American Federation of Teachers, and was a member of the Executive Council of the AFL-CIO. This labor leader had become a professional and social friend of an FLRA member. While in Washington, D.C., on business, the labor leader made arrangements to have dinner with the

---

[1] rule in support of its conclusion. 685 F.2d at 567; *see also* 5 C.F.R. § 2413.3(a) (2012) (current version of rule). And indeed, when prosecuting the unfair labor practice complaint in the PATCO case, the FLRA General Counsel was in effect representing the interests of the FAA, which filed the unfair labor practice charge against PATCO.

member. The labor leader candidly admitted he wanted to have dinner with the member because he felt strongly about the PATCO case and wanted to communicate directly his sentiments, expressed in public statements, that PATCO should not be severely punished for the strike.

The court said this was the most troubling incident. The labor leader was an **"interested person"** within the meaning of §557(d) (and was obviously **"outside the agency"**). The labor leader had a special and well known interest in the union movement. In addition, he felt that the hard line taken against PATCO might have an adverse effect on other government employee unions, at both federal and state levels. He had urged in public statements that PATCO should not be severely punished. The court said: "We in no way condone ... [the labor leader's] behavior in this case." 685 F.2d at 573.

However, the court found that the dinner meeting had not "irrevocably tainted the Authority's decision process or resulted in a decision either unfair to the parties or to the public interest." 685 F.2d at 574. In light of that finding, the Court concluded: "There is no reason to vacate the FLRA decision or to remand the case to the FLRA for any further proceedings." 685 F.2d at 575.

PATCO shows that judicial relief for violations of §557(d) may depend on proof that the violations "tainted" the proceeding. Perhaps the need for such proof reflects some courts' view that in the "small world" of Washington, D.C., ex parte contacts are inevitable. Certainly it is hard to create a complete barrier when people like the General Counsel of the FLRA and a Member of the FLRA have an undisputed need to discuss matters of common concern to the agency that employs them. Likewise, friendships, marriages, etc., can exist between a person who is outside the agency (such as the labor leader in the PATCO case) and someone who is inside the agency (the FLRA member in the PATCO case). Section 557(d) prevents them from communicating about the merits of a proceeding before the agency, but this restriction is hard to enforce, and perhaps it is even unrealistic to expect complete compliance. On the other hand, one can argue that, by refusing to void agency action for violations of §557(d), courts encourage future violations.

3. Due Process

As discussed in Chapter 20, the Due Process Clauses apply to any state or federal adjudicatory proceeding that deprives or threatens to deprive a person of life, liberty, or property. In such a proceeding, the procedural component of the Due Process Clause requires fair procedures. Fairness ordinarily forbids harmful ex parte contacts. "Harmful" in this context means contacts that lead a decision maker to have information that is not subject to adversarial testing—evidence that the person facing the deprivation had not had a chance to rebut or otherwise address. Due process restrictions on ex parte contacts are important for the administrative lawyer to keep in mind, because they may influence a court's interpretation of the APA's restrictions on ex parte contacts and they may apply in adjudications to which the APA restrictions don't apply, including informal adjudications that deprive or threaten to deprive someone of liberty or property.

Exercise: Ex Parte Contacts

1. In a formal adjudication to revoke a pilot's FAA license, an ALJ employed by the National Transportation Safety Board made an initial decision in favor

of revoking the license. The pilot appealed the ALJ's decision to the five-member body that heads the Board. While the case was pending before the Board, a Board employee who investigated the case wants to meet with the chair of the Board to explain the real significance of a procedure that the pilot regularly neglected to perform. The Board investigator testified about this at the hearing before the ALJ, but is convinced that the ALJ did not understand the investigator's testimony. Is a one-on-one meeting between the Board investigator and the chair of the Board OK?

2. The federal agency head hearing an appeal in a formal adjudication to assess civil fines against an industrial polluter wants to consult her personal scientific advisor—who is employed by the agency and works "at the elbow" of the agency head—on some technical matter that has arisen in the proceeding. May the agency head do so?

3. Assume the same facts as presented in Question 2, plus: The personal scientific advisor later becomes a lawyer employed in the office of the agency that prosecutes proceedings to impose fines. May personal-advisor-turned-agency-prosecutor be involved in a proceeding against the same polluter for a later supposed instance of pollution?

4. In a formal adjudication, the ALJ employed by a federal agency is preparing a recommended decision and wants to discuss some statistical information submitted during that adjudication with an economist in the agency's bureau of statistics. Is that all right? Alternatively, may the ALJ discuss the statistical information with an economist friend outside the agency?

5. Ordinarily, when goods are imported into the United States, they are held in the custody of U.S. customs officials until the importer pays a fee and files certain paperwork to "release" the goods into the United States. But this process can be expedited for people whose business is importing goods, who are known as "customs brokers." A customs broker can get a "term special permit" to import goods into the United States without first paying an "entry fee." The "term special permit" entitles the broker to "immediate release" of imported goods into the United States, without the delay that would occur in the absence of the permit. But a customs broker who holds a permit must file certain paperwork and pay certain fees within ten days after release of the goods, or else the broker will receive a nasty warning letter about the "late entry" from the relevant agency, which is today the U.S. Customs and Border Protection (formerly the U.S. Customs Service).

More than that, a customs broker can have his or her term special permit suspended or revoked if the broker repeatedly has late entries despite repeated official warnings. A federal official, the District Director of the Customs and Border Protection, has the authority to suspend a term special permit. Before the District Director can do so, however, regulations give the customs broker (1) a chance to review the records documenting the late entries, to ensure they are accurate; and (2) a chance to meet informally with the District Director, to correct any inaccurate information in the record and to plead mitigating circumstances. The statute authorizing the District Director to suspend or revoke a term special permit does not trigger the federal APA's formal adjudication requirements nor, indeed, expressly provide for any hearing.

It is the practice of the District Director, before an informal meeting with a customs broker whose term special permits is proposed to be suspended or revoked, to meet with a lower-level official who has reviewed all agency records on the broker's late entries. The lower-level official will brief the District Director on the content of the records. This "pre-meeting meeting" between the District Director and the subordinate is ex parte. Is this ex parte meeting permissible?

Some of these questions are based on an excellent lesson created by the Center for Computer-Assisted Legal Instruction (CALI) entitled "Ex parte Communications in Administrative Law," by Professor William Andersen. We highly recommend it if you want further instruction on this important topic.

E. Decision Requirements under a State APA

Many state APAs have procedures for formal adjudications (contested cases) that roughly resemble those of the federal APA. The state procedures generally create a two-step decision-making process. At the first step, the official who presided at the hearing, often called an ALJ, makes an initial or recommended decision that is subject to review by either the agency head or a subordinate to whom the agency head has delegated reviewing authority. *E.g.*, 2010 Model State APA §§ 413–415; 1981 Model State APA §§ 4-215 & 4-216.

The main difference between state and federal procedures is that about half of the States organize their ALJs into a separate agency, which deploys the ALJs to hold hearings for various agencies. These are called "central panel" States, reflecting that ALJs all come from a central location, an agency separate from the agencies for which they hold hearings. The central panel approach gives ALJs a greater sense of independence, and creates a stronger public perception of independence, than the alternative approach, under which the ALJ works for the agency for which he or she holds hearings. ALJs on central panels are not subject to supervision or direction by the prosecutors or investigators of the agencies for whom they hold hearings. The central panel system thus "builds in" a separation of those functions that, in States that do not use central panels, must be created within the agency.

Like the federal APA, state APAs commonly have provisions to ensure the impartiality and freedom from ex parte contacts of both the official who presides at the evidentiary hearing and all other officials who serve the quasi-judicial function. For example, the 2010 Model APA prohibits the presiding official for a particular case from having served as an "investigator, prosecutor, or advocate" at any stage of that case. 2010 Model State APA § 402(b). The 2010 Model State APA also authorizes parties to move for disqualification of the presiding officer or the official with final decision-making authority "for bias, prejudice, financial interest, ex parte communications as provided in Section 408, or any other factor that would cause a reasonable person to question the impartiality" of the official. In Section 408, the 2010 Model State APA generally bars the presiding official and the final decision maker from making or receiving any ex parte communications, with certain exceptions. *See* 2010 Model State APA § 408(b).

The most significant exception concerns the agency head. Like the drafters of the federal APA, the drafters of the 2010 Model APA struggled with the permissibility of ex parte communications between the agency head and agency "employee[s] or representative[s]" other than the agency prosecutors or investigators. *See* 2010 Model APA § 408 Official Comment. They settled on a compromise that, roughly speaking, allows the agency head to discuss a contested case with an agency employee or agency representative if the discussion doesn't modify the evidence in the record and seeks to clarify a technical point raised by the evidence or to shed light on agency precedent, policies or procedures. *See id.* § 408(e).

F. Chapter 24 Wrap Up and Look Ahead

This chapter has introduced you to the two-stage decision-making process that ordinarily occurs in formal adjudications under the federal APA, with ALJs making decisions that may be reviewed by the agency head or a reviewing entity or official to whom the agency head has delegated reviewing authority. The chapter has introduced model state APA procedures providing for similar two-stage decision making in contested cases by state agencies.

This chapter ends our exploration of formal adjudications under an APA. The next chapter discusses an issue that arises when an agency has the power to use both rulemaking and adjudication to carry out its statutory mission. The issue is: What are the legal constraints on the agency's choice between using its rulemaking power and its adjudication power?

Chapter Problem Revisited

This chapter problem presents you with a formal adjudication for which you are given the authorizing statute and the procedural rules. The general challenge is how to familiarize yourself with this material. Like many administrative law problems, the challenge involves weaving together agency legislation, agency rules, and the APA.

You would probably want to begin with the agency legislation, 16 U.S.C. § 824d, for its provisions control in the event of any conflict between it and the agency rules, and in the event of any conflict between it and the federal APA. You might also want to identify useful case law annotations to § 824d and secondary material to help you learn more about ratemaking proceedings under the Act.

As you begin examining the procedural rules, you will find they elaborate upon the formal adjudication procedures prescribed in the federal APA for procedures after the hearing. Section 824d(e) has little to say about such procedural matters. Thus, you will see regulations governing the hearing before the ALJ, 18 C.F.R. §§ 385.501–385.510; the ALJ's initial decision, *id.* § 385.708; and the right to file exceptions to the ALJ's initial decision, which will be considered by the

Commission on review of the initial decision, *id.* §385.711. The rules also implement the APA's restrictions on ex parte communications. *Id.* §385.2201.

Your study of the agency statute and rules together with the APA will begin to give you a structure to which you can add as you begin to immerse yourself in the specifics of the case you've been assigned. The chances are good that you will have many questions about the procedural details of the case. For this reason, you cannot rely solely on solitary review of the relevant law. You will have to develop a relationship with the Senior Associate so you can develop a solid understanding of the proceeding as quickly, efficiently, and accurately as possible. Such professional relationships can be personally and professionally enriching.

Professional Development Reflection Questions

In the discussion above revisiting the chapter problem, we mentioned the importance of forming a relationship with experienced lawyers to learn what you need as quickly and efficiently as possible. More broadly, lawyers beginning their practice often benefit from having mentors. You can find much advice in your career development office and on the internet about how to get mentors.

We would emphasize two things on this subject. First, lawyers expect to become mentors as they gain more experience and increasingly find themselves in a position to work with and advise less experienced lawyers. Thus, no senior lawyer will be surprised or offended to learn that a less experienced lawyer wants to have the senior lawyer as a mentor. Our point is that getting a mentor is not like calling someone out of the blue at supper time to convince them to refinance their mortgage with a company they've never heard of. Second, mentoring is a two-way street. True, less experienced lawyers have a strong need for good mentors. But mentors derive satisfaction from serving as mentors, for the same reasons a coach enjoys the success of the coach's "coachees."

We hope these points encourage you to seek out mentors. You can start while in law school. These questions may help get you started.

1. Please think back to someone outside your family who has served as a role model and personal advisor to you. What impact did she or he have on you? What made you choose that person?

2. Considering the qualities that you valued in past role models, do you know anyone now who might serve as a professional mentor for you in your law school and early legal career? If not, what "next step" can you realistically commit to take that would help you find such a person?

Chapter 25

Agency Choice between Rulemaking and Adjudication

Overview

Past chapters have examined agency rulemaking and agency adjudication. This chapter addresses how agencies choose between these two ways of doing their job when they have rulemaking and adjudicatory powers. This issue is sometimes called the "choice of means" issue.

The general principle for federal agencies is clear: Federal agencies generally have broad discretion to choose whether to proceed by rulemaking or adjudication. This general principle for federal agencies was established in *Securities & Exchange Commission v. Chenery*, 332 U.S. 194 (1947). States may choose to adopt the *Chenery* choice of means principle, but they don't have to.

The *Chenery* principle has exceptions. This chapter explores the principle and its exceptions.

The chapter is organized into these sections:

A.   Context

B.   The General Rule for Federal Agencies

C.   Exceptions to the Choice of Means Principle

D.   Court-Ordered Adjudication

E.   Chapter 25 Wrap Up and Look Ahead

Chapter Problem

A state statute addresses the safety of people seasonally employed on farms to pick crops. The statute refers to them as "field workers." The statute authorizes the State Department of Agriculture (Department) to inspect farms to ensure that field workers "are not exposed to unreasonably dangerous conditions."

If the Department finds unreasonably dangerous conditions on a farm during an inspection, the state statute authorizes the Department to assess fines against the farm owner. The fines may be imposed only after a contested case with an opportunity for a hearing before a hearing officer. The hearing officer's decision is subject to review by the state Secretary of Agriculture. Under the state APA, both the Secretary and the hearing officer must produce written decisions with findings of fact, conclusions of law, and explanations of the basis for any discretionary decisions such as why the particular amount of the fine was chosen. The state APA also authorizes judicial review of the Secretary's final decision.

One ground for a court to set aside the Secretary's decision is for an abuse of discretion.

In addition to authorizing agency adjudication, the state statute authorizes the Department to promulgate rules to ensure the safety of field workers. The statute does not, however, expressly require the Department to promulgate these rules, and, indeed, the Department has not done so.

One summer day a field worker collapses from heat stroke and almost dies before receiving the necessary medical attention. The Department conducts an adjudication leading to a severe fine against the owner of the farm where the field worker collapsed. In the written decision explaining the fine, the Department concludes that the farm owner exposed the field workers to "unreasonably dangerous" conditions on the day the field worker collapsed. Also in its written decision, the Department lays out eight specific requirements farm owners must take to protect field workers from heat stroke and heat exhaustion when the "heat index" reaches specified levels.

The farm owner seeks judicial review of the Department's decision to impose a fine. The farm owner argues that the Department should have used rulemaking instead of adjudication to adopt guidelines for protecting field workers from heat-related illness. The farm owner points out that the Department has regularly inspected the farm, including in torrid heat, and has never cited the farm owner for failure to provide adequate protection or even suggested that the farm owner should take any protective measures. The farm owner also points out that she provides the same measures of protection (e.g., shaded areas, opportunities for voluntary breaks) as every other farmer in the area. She feels unfairly singled out for these standards that, from her perspective, hit her like a bolt from the blue.

You are a State Supreme Court Justice reviewing the case. Your Court has no clear precedent on when, if ever, an agency is required to proceed by rulemaking instead of adjudication to carry out its statutory mission. Write an opinion responding to the farm owner's arguments and providing a principle or principles to guide future cases in your state court system involving an agency's use of adjudication to announce new standards of primary conduct. Your opinion will also have to ground the principle or principles in a source of law: e.g., the statute, the federal or state constitution, or common law or equitable principles.

A. Context

Before we get into the legal principles governing an agency's choice between rulemaking and adjudication, let us explain how this issue of choice typically arises. Typically, it arises in one of two ways, which present flip sides of the coin: Sometimes a person argues that an agency erred when it proceeded by adjudication instead of rulemaking. Other times, a person argues that an agency erred when it proceeded by rulemaking instead of adjudication.

Take an agency like the Federal Trade Commission. The FTC has statutory power to issue legislative rules defining unfair trade practices. The FTC also has statutory power to hold an administrative adjudication to determine whether a company has violated the statutory prohibition on unfair trade practices. Suppose the FTC begins investigating internet-based companies that sell gold to consumers as an investment. And suppose the FTC finds much activity that the FTC believes is unfair and deceptive. If certain unfair practices by gold selling companies are common, the FTC may adopt rules prohibiting those practices. The FTC could then conduct administrative adjudications to enforce those rules. Alternatively, the FTC may decide against adopting rules to govern the industry, at least initially, and instead conduct adjudications charging certain companies with violations of the *statutory* prohibition on unfair and deceptive practices. Under this approach, the FTC will act like a common law court, using its own case decisions to develop and announce principles for identifying what's unfair and deceptive within the meaning of the statute.

If the FTC chooses to adopt rules for the retail gold sales industry, and initiates a proceeding to enforce one of those rules against a particular company, the company might complain that the FTC rule is not nuanced enough. The company may argue that, although the company engaged in conduct that violated the rule, the conduct was not misleading under the particular circumstances. Suppose, for example, an FTC rule requires a company that sells gold to abide by the price advertised on its website (a rule designed to prohibit hidden fees and charges). Also suppose the company violates this rule inadvertently, because its website had a typographical error in the advertised price that the company didn't detect until after it charged several hundred customers the true price. The company has a respectable argument that the rule is overbroad if applied to punish its conduct. Indeed, many arguments challenging an agency's choice of rulemaking focus on the inability of rules to take into account unforeseen circumstances.

If, on the other hand, the FTC does not adopt rules for the retail gold sales industry before initiating adjudications to curb unfair and deceptive practices, the companies targeted may complain that they did not have adequate notice that the FTC would find their conduct unfair and deceptive. The companies will point out that the statutory standard is vague, and the FTC should have fleshed out that standard by making rules for their industry before seeking to penalize individual members of the industry. Arguments challenging an agency's use of adjudication often focus on the perceived unfairness or retroactive impact of adjudication.

The broader points of this discussion are twofold. First, agencies often have a choice whether to use rulemaking or adjudication to carry out their mission. Second, people adversely affected by agency action may have cause to complain whichever choice the agency makes. We turn to how the courts deal with those complaints.

Exercise: Factors Influencing the Choice between Rulemaking and Adjudication

A state law requires "day care centers" to have licenses and subjects licensees to regulation by the State Department of Health, Education, and Welfare (State HEW). The state law authorizes State HEW to assess fines of up to $1,000 per day for licensees who fail to provide "adequate supervision and stimulation" for children in their care. The law also authorizes State HEW to "promulgate regulations defining adequate supervision and stimulation."

From the perspective of a day care center licensee, what are the benefits and disadvantages of State HEW's promulgating rules on this subject? How might the disadvantages be minimized by the way the rules are drafted?

B. The General Rule for Federal Agencies

The general rule is that federal agencies have broad choice in deciding whether to accomplish their statutory mission by rulemaking or by adjudication. Sometimes this general rule is known as the "choice of means" principle. The principle is most famously associated with *Securities & Exchange Commission v. Chenery Corp.*, 332 U.S. 194 (1947). *SEC v. Chenery* addresses other important principles of administrative law, too, which are included in the excerpt below. After that excerpt we introduce you to the major exceptions to the *Chenery* choice of means principle.

Exercise: *SEC v. Chenery*

As you read *SEC v. Chenery*, please pay particular attention to the procedural history of the case (which made two trips to the U.S. Supreme Court, the second of which produces the opinion below). Also read the opinion with these questions in mind:

1. What was the legal basis for the SEC's first order, which approved a reorganization plan only with amendments to which the management objected?

2. Why did the U.S. Supreme Court decide the SEC's first order was incorrect?

3. What was the legal basis for the SEC's decision on remand to reject an application to amend the reorganization plan?

4. On the case's second trip to the U.S. Supreme Court, upon what grounds did the plaintiffs challenge the SEC's order on remand?

5. How does the "choice of means" principle come into play?

6. What is the legal basis for the "choice of means" principle?

If you want to learn about the background of this case, an excellent essay is: Roy Schotland, *A Sporting Proposition — SEC v. Chenery*, in Administrative Law Stories 168 (Peter Strauss ed. 2006).

Securities and Exchange Commission v. Chenery Corporation
332 U.S. 194 (1947)

Mr. Justice Murphy delivered the opinion of the Court.

This case is here for the second time. In *S.E.C. v. Chenery Corp.*, 318 U.S. 80, we held that an order of the Securities and Exchange Commission could not be sustained on the grounds upon which that agency acted. We therefore directed that the case be remanded to the Commission for such further proceedings as might be appropriate. On remand, the Commission reexamined the problem, recast its rationale and reached the same result. The issue now is whether the Commission's action is proper in light of the principles established in our prior decision.

When the case was first here, we emphasized a simple but fundamental rule of administrative law. That rule is to the effect that a reviewing court, in dealing with a determination or judgment which an administrative agency alone is authorized to make, must judge the propriety of such action solely by the grounds invoked by the agency. If those grounds are inadequate or improper, the court is powerless to affirm the administrative action by substituting what it considers to be a more adequate or proper basis. To do so would propel the court into the domain which Congress has set aside exclusively for the administrative agency.

We also emphasized in our prior decision an important corollary of the foregoing rule. If the administrative action is to be tested by the basis upon which it purports to rest, that basis must be set forth with such clarity as to be understandable. It will not do for a court to be compelled to guess at the theory underlying the agency's action; nor can a court be expected to chisel that which must be precise from what the agency has left vague and indecisive. In other words, "We must know what a decision means before the duty becomes ours to say whether it is right or wrong." *United States v. Chicago, M., St. P. & P. R. Co.*, 294 U.S. 499, 511.

Applying this rule and its corollary, the Court was unable to sustain the Commission's original action. The Commission had been dealing with the reorganization of the Federal Water Service Corporation (Federal), a holding company registered under the Public Utility Holding Company Act of 1935, 49 Stat. 803. During the period when successive reorganization plans proposed by the management were before the Commission, the officers, directors and controlling stockholders of Federal purchased a substantial amount of Federal's preferred stock on the over-the-counter market. Under the fourth reorganization plan, this preferred stock was to be converted into common stock of a new corporation; on the basis of the purchases of preferred stock, the management would have received more than 10% of this new common stock. It was frankly admitted that the management's purpose in buying the preferred stock was to protect its interest in the new company. It was also plain that there was no fraud or lack of disclosure in making these purchases.

But the Commission would not approve the fourth plan so long as the preferred stock purchased by the management was to be treated on a parity with the other preferred stock. It felt that the officers and directors of a holding company in process of reorganization under the Act were fiduciaries and were under a duty not to trade in the securities of that company during the reorganization period. And so the plan was amended to provide that the preferred stock acquired by the management, unlike that held by others, was not to be converted into the new common stock; instead, it was to be surrendered at cost plus dividends accumulated since the purchase dates. As amended, the plan was approved by the Commission over the management's objections.

The Court interpreted the Commission's order approving this amended plan as grounded solely upon judicial authority. The Commission appeared to have treated the preferred stock acquired by the management in accordance with what it thought were standards theretofore recognized by courts. If it intended to create new standards growing out of its experience in effectuating the legislative policy, it failed to express itself with sufficient clarity and precision to be so understood. Hence the order was judged by the only standards clearly invoked by the Commission. On that basis, the order could not stand. The opinion pointed out that courts do not impose upon officers and directors of a corporation any fiduciary duty to its stockholders which precludes them, merely because they are officers and directors, from buying and selling the corporation's stock.... The opinion further noted that neither Congress nor the Commission had promulgated any general rule proscribing such action as the purchase of preferred stock by Federal's management....

After the case was remanded to the Commission, Federal Water and Gas Corp. (Federal Water), the surviving corporation under the reorganization plan, made an application for approval of an amendment to the plan to provide for the issuance of new common stock of the reorganized company. This stock was to be distributed to the members of Federal's management on the basis of the shares of the old preferred stock which they had acquired during the period of reorganization, thereby placing them in the same position as the public holders of the old preferred stock. The intervening members of Federal's management joined in this request. The Commission denied the application....

The latest order of the Commission definitely avoids the fatal error of relying on judicial precedents which do not sustain it. This time, after a thorough reexamination of the problem in light of the purposes and standards of the Holding Company Act, the Commission has concluded that the proposed transaction is inconsistent with the standards of §§ 7 and 11 of the Act. It has drawn heavily upon its accumulated experience in dealing with utility reorganizations. And it has expressed its reasons with a clarity and thoroughness that admit of no doubt as to the underlying basis of its order.

The argument is pressed upon us, however, that the Commission was foreclosed from taking such a step following our prior decision. It is said that, in the absence of findings of conscious wrongdoing on the part of Federal's management, the Commission could not determine by an order in this particular case that it was inconsistent with the statutory standards to permit Federal's management to realize a profit through the reorganization purchases. All that it could do was to enter an order allowing an amendment to the plan so that the proposed transaction could be consummated. Under this view, the Commission would be free only to promulgate a general rule outlawing such profits in future utility reorganizations; but such a rule would have to be prospective in nature and have no retroactive effect upon the instant situation.

We reject this contention, for it grows out of a misapprehension of our prior decision and of the Commission's statutory duties. We held no more and no less than that the Commission's first order was unsupportable for the reasons supplied by that agency. But when the case left this Court, the problem whether Federal's management should be treated equally with other preferred stockholders still lacked a final and complete answer. It was clear that the Commission could not give a negative answer by resort to prior judicial declarations. And it was also clear that the Commission was not bound by settled judicial precedents in a situation of this nature. 318 U.S. at 89. Still unsettled, however, was the answer the Commission might give were it to bring to bear on the facts the proper administrative and statutory considerations, a function which belongs exclusively to the Commission in the first instance. The administrative process had taken an erroneous rather than a final turn. Hence we carefully refrained from expressing any views as to the propriety of an order rooted in the proper and relevant considerations.

When the case was directed to be remanded to the Commission for such further proceedings as might be appropriate, it was with the thought that the Commission would give full effect to its duties in harmony with the views we had expressed.... This obviously meant something more than the entry of a perfunctory order giving parity treatment to the management holdings of preferred stock. The fact that the Commission had committed a legal error in its first disposition of the case certainly gave Federal's management no vested right to receive the benefits of such an order.... After the remand was made, therefore, the Commission was bound to deal with the problem afresh, performing the function delegated to it by Congress. It was again charged with the duty of measuring the proposed treatment of the management's preferred stock holdings by relevant and proper standards. Only in that way could the legislative policies embodied in the Act be effectuated.... The absence of a general rule or regulation governing management trading during reorganization did not affect the Commission's duties in relation to the particular proposal before it. The Commission was asked to grant or deny effectiveness to a proposed amendment to Federal's reorganization plan whereby the management would be accorded parity treatment on its holdings. It could do that only in the form of an order, entered after a due consideration of the particular facts in light of the relevant and proper standards. That was true regardless of whether those standards previously had been spelled out in a general rule or regulation. Indeed, if the Commission rightly felt that the proposed amendment was inconsistent with those standards, an order giving effect to the amendment merely because there was no general rule or regulation covering the matter would be unjustified.

It is true that our prior decision explicitly recognized the possibility that the Commission might have promulgated a general rule dealing with this problem under its statutory rule-making powers, in which case the issue for our consideration would have been entirely different from that which did confront us. 318 U.S. 92–93. But we did not mean to imply thereby that the failure of the Commission to anticipate this problem and to promulgate a general rule withdrew all power from that agency to perform its statutory duty in this case. To hold that the Commission had no alternative in this proceeding but to approve the proposed transaction, while formulating any general rules it might desire for use in future cases of this nature, would be to stultify the administrative process. That we refuse to do.

Since the Commission, unlike a court, does have the ability to make new law prospectively through the exercise of its rule-making powers, it has less reason to rely upon ad hoc adjudication to formulate new standards of conduct within the framework of the Holding Company Act. The function of filling in the interstices of the Act should be performed, as much as possible, through this quasi-legislative promulgation of rules to be applied in the future. But any rigid requirement to that effect would make the administrative process inflexible and incapable of dealing with many of the specialized problems which arise. Not every principle essential to the effective administration of a statute can or should be cast immediately into the mold of a general rule. Some principles must await their own development, while others must be adjusted to meet particular, unforeseeable situations. In performing its important functions in these respects, therefore, an administrative agency must be equipped to act either by general rule or by individual order. To insist upon one form of action to the exclusion of the other is to exalt form over necessity.

In other words, problems may arise in a case which the administrative agency could not reasonably foresee, problems which must be solved despite the absence of a relevant general rule. Or the agency may not have had sufficient experience with a particular problem to warrant rigidifying its tentative judgment into a hard and fast rule. Or the problem may be so specialized and varying in nature as to be impossible of capture within the boundaries of a general rule. In those situations, the agency must retain power to deal with the problems on a case-to-case basis if the administrative process is to be effective. There is thus a very definite place for the case-by-case evolution of statutory standards. And the choice made between proceeding by general rule or by individual, ad hoc litigation is one that lies primarily in the informed discretion of the administrative agency.

Hence we refuse to say that the Commission, which had not previously been confronted with the problem of management trading during reorganization, was forbidden from utilizing this particular proceeding for announcing and applying a new standard of conduct. That such action might have a retroactive effect was not necessarily fatal to its validity. Every case of first impression has a retroactive effect, whether the new principle is announced by a court or by an administrative agency. But such retroactivity must be balanced against the mischief of producing a result which is contrary to a statutory design or to legal and equitable principles. If that mischief is greater than the ill effect of the retroactive application of a new standard, it is not the type of retroactivity which is condemned by law.

And so in this case, the fact that the Commission's order might retroactively prevent Federal's management from securing the profits and control which were the objects of the preferred stock purchases may well be outweighed by the dangers inherent in such purchases from the statutory standpoint. If that is true, the argument of retroactivity becomes nothing more than a claim that the Commission lacks power to enforce the standards of the Act in this proceeding. Such a claim deserves rejection.

... As we have noted, the Commission avoided placing its sole reliance on inapplicable judicial precedents. Rather it has derived its conclusions from the particular facts in the case, its general experience in reorganization matters and its informed view of statutory requirements. It is those matters which are the guide for our review. The Commission concluded that it could not find that the reorganization plan, if amended as proposed, would be "fair and equitable to the persons affected thereby" within the meaning of § 11(e) of the Act, under which the reorganization was taking place. Its view was that the amended plan would involve the issuance of securities on terms "detrimental to the public interest or the interest of investors" contrary to §§ 7(d)(6) and 7(e), and would result in an "unfair or inequitable distribution of voting power" among the Federal security holders within the meaning of § 7(e). It was led to this result "not by proof that the interveners [Federal's management] committed acts of conscious wrongdoing but by the character of the conflicting interests created by the interveners' program of stock purchases carried out while plans for reorganization were under consideration." ...

Drawing upon its experience, the Commission indicated that all these normal and special powers of the holding company management during the course of a ... reorganization placed in the management's command "a formidable battery of devices that would enable it, if it should choose to use them selfishly, to affect in material degree the ultimate allocation of new securities among the various existing classes, to influence the market for its own gain, and to manipulate or obstruct the reorganization required by the mandate of the statute." In that setting, the Commission felt that a management program of stock purchase would give rise to the temptation and the opportunity to shape the reorganization proceeding so as to encourage public selling on the market at low prices....

Turning to the facts in this case ... the Commission admitted that the good faith and personal integrity of this management were not in question.... The scope of our review of an administrative order wherein a new principle is announced and applied is no different from that which pertains to ordinary administrative action. The wisdom of the principle adopted is none of our concern. Our duty is at an end when it becomes evident that the Commission's action is based upon substantial evidence and is consistent with the authority granted by Congress.

We are unable to say in this case that the Commission erred in reaching the result it did. The facts being undisputed, we are free to disturb the Commission's conclusion only if it lacks any rational and statutory foundation. In that connection, the Commission has made a thorough examination of the problem, utilizing statutory standards and its own accumulated experience with reorganization matters. In essence, it has made what we indicated in our prior opinion would be an informed, expert judgment on the problem.

It has taken into account "those more subtle factors in the marketing of utility company securities that gave rise to the very grave evils which the Public Utility Holding [Company] Act of 1935 was designed to correct."

Such factors may properly be considered by the Commission in determining whether to approve a plan of reorganization of a utility holding company, or an amendment to such a plan.... The very breadth of the statutory language precludes a reversal of the Commission's judgment save where it has plainly abused its discretion in these matters ... Such an abuse is not present in this case....

There is thus a reasonable basis for a judgment that the benefits and profits accruing to the management from the stock purchases should be prohibited, regardless of the good faith involved. And it is a judgment that can justifiably be reached in terms of fairness and equity, to the end that the interests of the public, the investors and the consumers might be protected. But it is a judgment based upon public policy, a judgment which Congress has indicated is of the type for the Commission to make.

The Commission's conclusion here rests squarely in that area where administrative judgments are entitled to the greatest amount of weight by appellate courts. It is the product of administrative experience, appreciation of the complexities of the problem, realization of the statutory policies, and responsible treatment of the uncontested facts. It is the type of judgment which administrative agencies are best equipped to make and which justifies the use of the administrative process. Whether we agree or disagree with the result reached, it is an allowable judgment which we cannot disturb.

Reversed.

[Editor's note: Justice Burton concurred in the result without writing a separate opinion. Chief Justice Vinson and Justice Douglas took no part in the consideration of decision of the case. Justice Jackson wrote a dissenting opinion in which Justice Frankfurter joined. We omit the dissenting opinion.]

* * *

The Court in *Chenery* allowed an agency to use adjudication to address an issue of first impression. In a later case, the Court allowed an agency to use adjudication to *change* its position on an issue that the agency had addressed in a prior adjudication: *NLRB v. Bell Aerospace Co.*, 416 U.S. 267 (1974). The Court in *Bell Aerospace* held that the National Labor Relations Board could use an adjudication to decide, contrary to the Board's precedent, that a certain category of employees were entitled to the protections of the National Labor Relations Act and did not fall within the Act's exemption for "managerial employees." As a result of this change in the Board's treatment of this category of employees, the Board found the Bell Aerospace Company guilty of an unfair labor practice for failing to bargain with a union representing these newly protected employees. The Court recognized that the company had reasonably relied on the Board's precedent to the contrary but explained:

> It has not been shown that the adverse consequences ensuing from such reliance are so substantial that the Board should be precluded from reconsidering the issue in an adjudicative proceeding. Furthermore, this is not a case in which some new liability is sought to be imposed on individuals for past actions which were taken in good-faith reliance on Board pronouncements. Nor are fines or damages involved here.

Id. at 295. This quotation makes clear that an agency change in policy that imposes fines or damages on the party to an adjudication might require a stronger justification than simply: "We've changed our minds." But the reality is that agencies, just like courts, can abandon precedent and, in the process, cause a party to lose who would have won under old law. That's the way the "common law" process of developing the law works.

Chenery and *Bell Aerospace* establish the general rule for federal agencies. Some States have adopted this choice of means principle for their agencies as a matter of state law. *E.g., In re Water Use Permit Applications,* 9 P.3d 409, 481 (Haw. 2000); *Town of Brookline v. Comm'r of Dep't of Envt'l Quality Eng.,* 439 N.E.2d 792, 799 (Mass. 1982); *Bunge Corp. v. Comm'r of Revenue,* 305 N.W.2d 779, 785 (Minn. 1981). Indeed, "[m]ost States follow *Chenery,*" according to an official comment in the 2010 Model State APA. 2010 Model State APA § 418 Comment (citing Michael Douglas Jacobs, *Illuminating a Bureaucratic Shadow World: Precedent Decisions under California's Revised Administrative Procedure Act,* 21 J. Nat'l Ass'n Admin. L. Judges 247, 261 n.68 (2001)). The *Chenery* choice of means principle is not, however, universal.

Nor, as discussed in the next section, is the *Chenery* principle absolute at the federal level. To the contrary, it has several important exceptions

---

Exercise: *Chenery* Revisited

1. Please look back at *Chenery* to find the "simple but fundamental rule of administrative law" the Court announced on the case's first trip to the Court. How was that rule illustrated in the case itself? Does this rule benefit agencies or, instead, people who challenge agency action?

2. Please look back at *Chenery* to find the "important corollary" to the rule referenced in Question 1. What is the rationale for this important corollary?

3. The SEC lost the first time this case went to the Court. Why did the SEC get a "re-do"?

C. Exceptions to the Choice of Means Principle

The *Chenery* choice of means principle has four main exceptions:

(1) A federal agency's decision to proceed by adjudication rather than by rulemaking may constitute an abuse of discretion and therefore be subject to judicial invalidation—for example, because of retroactivity or because of the nature of the problem to be addressed.

(2) A statute may require an agency to promulgate rules before it adjudicates. If the agency fails to promulgate the required rules, adjudications in the absence of the required rules may be judicially invalidated.

(3) Constitutional principles of due process or equal protection may require an agency to proceed by rulemaking or adjudication.

(4) A state agency may be required by a state court, relying on common law or equitable considerations, to proceed by rulemaking rather than adjudication.

We discuss these exceptions below. Most of the time, cases involving the "choice of means" principle involve someone arguing that an agency should have used rulemaking instead of adjudication. Some cases, however, present the converse situation: someone argues that an agency should have used adjudication instead of rulemaking. We discuss the converse situation in Section D of this chapter.

1. Abuse of Discretion

Courts reviewing an agency action often can set aside the agency action for an "abuse of discretion." *E.g.*, 5 U.S.C. § 706(2)(A) (2012). The Court in *SEC v. Chenery* suggested that an agency's use of adjudication instead of rulemaking could be an abuse of discretion because of the adjudication's retroactive effect. Besides retroactive impact, other reasons can cause an agency's choice of adjudication to be an abuse of discretion. Beware, though: It is *rare* for a court to find that an agency's use of adjudication was an abuse of discretion.

It is rare for the retroactive impact of an adjudication to invalidate an agency's choice of adjudication because a retroactive impact is almost inevitable anytime an agency adopts a new standard of conduct in an adjudication. In this situation, the Court said,

> such retroactivity must be balanced against the mischief of producing a result which is contrary to a statutory design or to legal and equitable principles. If that mischief is greater than the ill effect of the retroactive application of a new standard, it is not the type of retroactivity which is condemned by law.

SEC v. Chenery, 332 U.S. at 203. In other words, the retroactive impact of a newly announced principle of conduct may be justified by the need for the agency to avoid making a decision contrary to statutory design (or nonstatutory law). An agency doesn't have to approve wrongful conduct merely because it's never encountered that conduct before. Nor does conduct of a type that the agency has previously approved get a perpetual pass, if the agency comes to view the conduct as wrongful. Agencies, like people, live and learn from experience.

What is more, courts put a thumb on the scale in favor of the public interest when they balance retroactivity against the public interest served by an agency's adoption of a new standard of conduct. The facts of *Chenery* make clear that the retroactive impact of a newly announced principle will cause an agency's use of adjudication to be an "abuse of discretion" only when the retroactive impact is both (1) severe; and (2) unjustified. After all, the retroactive impact in *Chenery* was severe: The family owners of a business could not maintain control of the business that they had built up. And the justification for denying them continued control had nothing to do with anything *they* did wrong. There was no showing that the family members were attempting to take advantage of others, that they were attempting to avoid the law, or that they were anything other than honorable people. Nevertheless, the Court permitted the agency to affect them significantly and retroactively in a case decision because of the agency's view that as a general matter their proposed course of conduct disserved the public interest sought to be protected by the agency legislation. The public interest (as judged by the agency under statutory standard) justified the private impact.

Considering the Court's leniency toward federal agencies' use of adjudication to announce new principles, we should not be surprised that it is hard to find any recent lower court precedent relying on an adjudication's retroactive impact to find an abuse of discretion. For old cases finding an abuse of discretion based on retroactivity, see *NLRB v. E & B*

Brewing Co., 276 F.2d 594 (6th Cir. 1960), and *NLRB v. Guy F. Atkinson Co.*, 195 F.2d 141 (9th Cir. 1952). For a fairly old case finding an abuse of discretion on other grounds, see *Curry v. Block*, 738 F.2d 1556 (11th Cir. 1984), in which the court held that adjudication was too slow a process for the agency to use to develop criteria for a loan program designed to meet the urgent need of farmers. For a more recent case suggesting in dicta that an agency abused its discretion by using adjudication to adopt broadly applicable timetables, see *City of Arlington, Texas v. FCC*, 668 F.3d 229, 241–243 (5th Cir. 2012).

2. Mandatory Language in Agency Legislation

An agency doesn't have the choice of using adjudication when the agency legislation requires the agency to use rulemaking. For instance, the agency legislation may state that the agency "shall promulgate rules ..." addressing a certain subject, but for whatever reason the agency has not done so. In this situation courts intervene to enforce the legislation's choice of means. When an agency disobeys a legislative directive to use a particular means of addressing a problem, courts will more readily intervene than when the agency's choice of means is simply challenged as an abuse of discretion.

A case from the state courts illustrates the point. In *Captain's Quarters Motor Inn v. S.C. Coastal Council*, 413 S.E.2d 13 (S.C. 1991), a seaside hotel applied to an agency for a permit to rebuild a seawall that had been damaged by Hurricane Hugo. The agency legislation authorized the rebuilding of such a structure only if it was "less than fifty percent damaged." *Id.* at 13 (quoting statute). The agency denied the permit, finding that, under the agency's test for assessing what percent of the seawall was damaged, the applicant's seawall was more than fifty percent damaged. The agency's damage-assessment test had never been promulgated as a regulation. The agency legislation, however, said that, by a date that had already passed, the agency "shall publish and make available the ... rules and regulations it will follow in evaluating permit applications." *Id.* at 14 (quoting statute). The court set aside the agency's denial of the permit because it was based on a test that should have been promulgated as a regulation but was not.

Questions may arise about whether the legislature actually has commanded the agency to promulgate rules if the legislative language drifts away from a direct statement mandating promulgation of rules. It is even possible that a statutory provision stating the agency "shall" promulgate regulations will be interpreted as expressing a legislative expectation, but not a requirement. In that event, you will face the additional problem of convincing the court that the legislative language does, indeed, constitute an obligation that the agency must honor. Of course, the agency also must be given a reasonable time to fulfill its obligation. Thus, you should be prepared to demonstrate to the court that the agency delay is not justifiable.

3. Constitutional Considerations — Due Process and Equal Protection

a. Equal Protection

The fundamental command of the Equal Protection Clause is that government treat similarly situated people alike. *Cleburne v. Cleburne Living Center, Inc.*, 473 U.S. 432, 439

(1985). This command can be hard for an agency to satisfy if it has multiple decision makers adjudicating cases under a vague statutory standard that has not been particularized by the promulgation of legislative rules. For example, suppose a state statute authorizes any of the dozen hearing officers in a State Department of Motor Vehicles to issue probationary licenses to drivers whose licenses have been suspended. And suppose that statute does no more than indicate probationary licenses should be issued if consistent with public safety and if justified by the individual driver's circumstances. This statutory scheme leaves plenty of room for disparate treatment of different drivers by the multiple hearing officers with power to grant probationary licenses. By contrast, as the U.S. Supreme Court noted in upholding a rules-based, "point" system for taking away people's drivers' licenses, clear, objective rules can "promot[e] equality of treatment among similarly situated [people]." *Dixon v. Love*, 431 U.S. 105, 115 (1977).

Nonetheless, equal protection challenges to agency choice of adjudication have not fared well. You must go years back to find support for the equal protection argument in federal appellate law. *See Hornsby v. Allen*, 326 F.2d 605 (5th Cir. 1964).

The equal protection argument has several problems. For one thing, in most settings, an equal protection argument triggers a "rational basis" standard of review. *E.g., Enquist v. Oregon Dep't of Agric.*, 553 U.S. 591, 602 (2008). As long as the agency has a rational basis for treating two cases differently, the differential treatment does not violate the equal protection guarantee. For another thing, when you can show that an agency *has* treated similar cases differently, you are better off arguing that the disparity renders the agency's decision "arbitrary and capricious" under the federal APA or similar judicial review provision, than to make the argument as a constitutional one. Courts may feel they are "going out on a limb" when they strike down agency action as unconstitutional. They feel more comfortable invalidating agency action under a judicial review statute in which the legislature has authorized the courts to set aside agency action that is "arbitrary and capricious." In the latter situation, courts are simply doing the job that the legislature has assigned them and that is a well accepted part of administrative law. Thus, an "arbitrary and capricious" argument can encompass an equal-protection-type argument while giving courts a familiar, statutory "hook" for invalidating agency action.

b. Due Process

A state supreme court used due process to invalidate an agency's choice of adjudication in a case that we excerpt below because it is well known in administrative law circles and provides a blue print for due process challenges to an agency's failure to promulgate rules particularizing a vague statutory standard.

Elizondo v. Department of Revenue

570 P.2d 518 (Colorado 1977)

[Editor's summary: Maria Elizondo accumulated thirteen points on her driver's record over about eight months. Her drivers' license was suspended for three-and-a-half months after a hearing conducted by a hearing officer in the Motor Vehicles Division of the Colorado Department of Revenue. Ms. Elizondo requested a probationary license for the period of the suspension, asserting that her business and personal circumstances required that she drive. The hearing officer denied the request. The statute authorizing the issuance of probationary licenses indicated only that they should be issued if consistent with public safety and if justified by the individual driver's circumstances. Ms. Elizondo appealed the denial of a probationary license to the district court.

The district court held that the statute on probationary licenses unconstitutionally delegated legislative power to the Department of Revenue. On review, the Colorado Supreme Court held that the statute did not unconstitutionally delegate legislative power but was unconstitutional for a different reason: It violated procedural due process. The Court's procedural due process discussion is below.]

Opinion by: CARRIGAN

The [probationary license] statute as applied ... fails to adequately protect the right of a driver to procedural due process in determining whether or not a probationary license shall be granted. A major concern in reviewing administrative actions is to protect against arbitrary decisions by agency personnel. Standards supplied by the legislature, no matter how detailed, can only provide partial protection. Here, however, the General Assembly went beyond merely indicating the broad policies to be forwarded. The statute also provided for adoption, by the agency, of more specific rules and regulations to limit the exercise of the admittedly broad discretionary power. Section 42-1-204, C.R.S. 1973. By failing to follow that statutory suggestion, the Department has left the granting or denial of probationary drivers' licenses solely to the unfettered discretion of individual hearing officers. As a result, neither the public nor the courts have any means of knowing in advance what evidence might be considered material to any particular decision. Nor is there any assurance that each hearing officer will not, consciously or subconsciously, follow standards quite different from those applied by his or her colleagues.

In the instant case, for example, the record fails to indicate why the hearing officer denied Ms. Elizondo's request for a probationary license. Although the hearing officer's integrity is not questioned, in this case as in every other, there is no way for a reviewing court to determine whether a hearing officer has or has not abused his discretion. Without some stated guidelines, and specific findings of fact, judicial review is a hollow gesture. "[J]udicial review can correct only the most egregious abuses. Judicial review must operate to ensure that the administrative process itself will confine and control the exercise of discretion. Courts should require the administrative officers to articulate the standards and principles that govern their discretionary decisions in as much detail as possible. Rules and regulations should be freely formulated by administrators, and revised when necessary. Discretionary decisions should more often be supported with findings of fact and reasoned decisions. When administrators provide a framework for principled deci-sion-making, the result will be to diminish the importance of judicial review by enhancing the integrity of the administrative process, and to improve the quality of judicial review in those cases where judicial review is sought." *Environmental Defense Fund, Inc. v. Ruckelshaus*, 142 U.S.App.D.C. 74, 439 F.2d 584, 598 (1971).

In the instant case, even though legislative prescription of more specific standards would serve little practical purpose, the breadth of the power delegated assumes that the agency, through rules and regulations, will provide its own guidelines and limitations. Absent such guidelines, an applicant who meets all stated requirements for a probationary license has no idea what further factors might influence a hearing officer's decision. Moreover, if his request is denied, he has no right to a statement of reasons and no basis upon which to attack the decision on appeal.

The use of motor vehicles on the public highways of this state is an adjunct of the con-stitutional right to acquire, possess, and use property which cannot be taken away without due process of law. *Love v. Bell*, 465 P.2d 118 (1970) ... Therefore, we hold that due process requires that the Department of Revenue promulgate rules or regulations to guide hearing officers in their decisions regarding requests for probationary licenses. See *Holmes v. New York City Housing Authority*, 398 F.2d 262 (2d Cir.1968); *Barnes v. Merritt*, 376 F.2d 8 (5th Cir.1967); *Hornsby v. Allen*, 326 F.2d 605 (5th Cir.1964); ... *Baker-Chaput v. Cammett*, 406 F.Supp. 1134 (D.N.H.1976); ... These rules or regulations must be sufficiently specific to inform the public what factors will be considered relevant by Department hearing officers, so that requests for probationary licenses may be supported by relevant evidence and arguments. Furthermore, to make judicial review a meaningful process, the rules or regulations must require that hearing officers specifically state, in each case where a probationary license is denied, the reasons for the denial ...

Although these requirements cannot guarantee a fair hearing, they will reduce significantly the possibility that the decision process will be arbitrary. "[A] requirement of procedural regularity at least renders arbitrary action more difficult. Moreover, proper procedures will surely eliminate some of the arbitrariness that results, not from malice, but from innocent error." *Board of Regents v. Roth*, 408 U.S. 564, 591 (1972) (Marshall J., dissenting)....

The suspension of drivers' licenses, being based on a point system, involves no discretion on the part of an administrator, and therefore is not subject to abuse of discretion.... Thus, we hold that it was error to invalidate the suspension of Ms. Elizondo's license. Rather, because a hearing meeting due process standards was never held, the action must be remanded for a new hearing on the merits of Ms. Elizondo's request for a probationary license. The suspension of her license was valid, however, and must be reinstated.

We further order that the Department of Revenue, Division of Motor Vehicles, shall not deny any requests for probationary drivers' licenses until adequate rules or regulations setting out standards to govern probationary licensing hearings have been promulgated. It may be argued that this order raises the possibility that incompetent or unsafe drivers may be granted probationary licenses, but the Department can eliminate that danger by prompt action under the emergency rules provision of subsection 24-4-103(6), C.R.S. 1973 [Colorado APA]. Under this provision, temporary or emergency rules may be adopted without notice, are effective upon adoption and may remain in effect up to three months. If the Department complies with this subsection, it can insure protection of the public safety immediately and during the time required to fulfill formal rule-making requirements and promulgate permanent rules....

Exercise: *Elizondo* Revisited

1. The statutory scheme in *Elizondo* allowed hearing officers to make final decisions for the agency on whether to grant probationary drivers' licenses. The hearing officers' decisions apparently were not subject to review by a higher authority within the agency. If a higher agency authority did exist, and had issued written, published opinions explaining specific decisions granting and denying probationary licenses, those opinions might serve as agency case precedent to provide decision-making criteria to guide the public and the hearing officers. In the absence of such an internal reviewing authority, there was indeed a great risk that individual hearing officers would apply disparate criteria in deciding whether to issue probationary licenses. What specific requirements does the court in *Elizondo* adopt to reduce that risk?

2. The procedural due process problem identified in *Elizondo* differs from the due process problem underlying unconstitutionally vague statutes. The U.S. Supreme Court has held that a statute is unconstitutionally vague, and therefore violates the Due Process Clause, when people of common intelligence "must necessarily guess at its meaning and differ as to its application." *Keyishian v. Bd. of Regents*, 385 U.S. 589, 604 (1967) (internal quotation marks omitted). Overly vague statutes violate due process because they don't give people fair notice of what the law is. The *Elizondo* court, however, did not find the probationary license statute unconstitutionally vague. Instead, the *Elizondo* court adopted a due process rationale that has no direct support (nor is there any directly contrary case law) in the U.S. Supreme Court's precedent. According to the *Elizondo* court, why exactly did the case before it involve a violation of the Due Process Clause?

3. To what extent did the *Elizondo* court rely on the agency legislation as a basis for requiring the Department to promulgate rules establishing criteria for probationary licenses? In considering this question, look back at the portion of the opinion referring to the "statutory suggestion" implied by the statutory grant of rulemaking power, and the court's statement that "the breadth of the power delegated assumes that the agency, through rules and regulations, will provide its own guidelines and limitations."

c. Common Law or Equitable Principles

In some state court cases, state courts have required agencies to use rulemaking to ensure that members of the public know the "rules of the game." These courts reason that persons regulated by an agency are entitled to something more specific than a general declaration of legislative purpose to guide their conduct. This is based on the theory that one is entitled to know what the law is, if one is to be obligated to comply with it. In some cases applying this theory, one may suspect that constitutional due process of law principles also lurk in the background as an unarticulated basis for the court action (e.g. no prior notice by statute, regulation or previous case decisions that specified conduct is a violation). For the reason that the court opinions do not expressly apply nor expressly refer to due process of law, they are, in theory, based on something else. Professor Kenneth Culp Davis suggested these cases are based on common law or equitable considerations. 2 Kenneth Culp Davis, Administrative Law Treatise § 7:26, at 131 (2nd ed. 1979)

We summarize next a well-known case that apparently relies on common law or equitable considerations to require an agency to use rulemaking rather than adjudication.

- *Sun Ray Drive-In Dairy v. Oregon Liquor Control Commission*, 517 P.2d 289 (Or. Ct. App. 1973)

The Oregon Liquor Control Commission denied a liquor license to the Sun Ray Drive-In Dairy, a convenience store. The denial occurred under a statute that allowed the Commission to deny a license if there were already "sufficient licensed premises in the locality" or if the granting of the license was "not demanded by public interest or convenience." *Id.* at 290 (quoting statute).

In the administrative adjudication on Sun Ray's license application, each official in the decision-making process gave different reasons for denying the license. The lowest-level official recommended denial of the license because of the neighbors' objections and the number of other licensed premises in the area. That recommendation went to a second official, who claimed to have "no yardstick" for his decision but relied on his "past experience and judgment." *Id.* at 291. The final decision maker, the Commission's Director of Licensing, relied primarily on his view that Sun Ray was not "a legitimate grocery store," a factor not mentioned in any statute or regulation but apparently relevant under unpublished agency policy. *Id.* He determined that Sun Ray was not a "legitimate grocery store" because, among other facts, "the store's inventory listed only three packages of Birdseye creamed peas." *Id.*

The Oregon Court of Appeals vacated the Commission's denial of Sun Ray's license application. The court ordered the Commission not to act on the application until it had promulgated rules under the Oregon APA establishing standards for deciding license applications. The court said that, for example, if the Commission wanted to limit licenses to "grocery stores," it should promulgate a rule expressing that requirement and defining "grocery store." *Id.* at 294. The Commission should also by rule identify other criteria that the Commission considered relevant and indicate the comparative importance of the criteria.

The court did not identify the legal theory for its decision, which has led commentators to speculate that the court relied on common law or equitable considerations. The court did, however, justify its decision on these grounds:

- "A legislative delegation of power in broad statutory language such as the phrase 'demanded by public interest or convenience' places upon the administrative agency a responsibility to establish standards by which that law is to be applied." *Id.* at 292.

- "The policies of an agency in a democratic society must be subject to public scrutiny. Published standards are essential to inform the public. Further, they help assure public confidence that the agency acts by rules and not from whim or corrupt motivation. In addition, interested parties and the general public are entitled to be heard in the process of rule adoption under the Administrative Procedures Act." *Id.* at 293.

- "An applicant for a license should be able to know the standards by which his application will be judged before going to the expense in time, investment and legal fees necessary to make application. Thereafter, he is entitled to even treatment by rule of law and reasonable confidence that he has received such treatment. This cannot be achieved without published rules." *Id.*

- "The parties to a hearing of a contested case must know what is to be heard in the hearing. The agency and the applicant are entitled to know what they are required to prove and disprove in order to gather and present their evidence. The hearings officer must have standards so that he can determine questions of materiality and relevance and propose appropriate findings and conclusions to the commission." *Id.*

- "Written standards enable the decision-making body, in this case the commission, to make its decisions by rule of law rather than for subjective or ad hominem reasons." *Id.*

- "The legislature is entitled to know whether or not the policies and practices of the agency are consistent with the legislative policies upon which the delegation of legislative power to the agency is based. In the absence of published rules, members of the legislature must form their judgments instead upon rumor, individual cases, isolated news reports and other fragmentary, impressionistic and often unreliable sources of information. Published standards are necessary to the proper performance of the duty of legislative oversight of executive agencies operating under legislative delegations of power." *Id.* at 294.

- "Finally, and most directly applicable to this case, the parties to a contested case are entitled to judicial review under ORS 183.480. Judicial review is among the safeguards which serve to legitimatize broad legislative delegations of power to administrative agencies.... In the absence of standards, however, the courts are unable to perform that task of judicial review. We cannot determine whether substantial evidence supported the findings because we cannot know what as in issue at the hearing. For example, we do not have a definition of 'grocery store'... and, if we did, we are unable to ascertain the legal significance of a finding under that definition. It is not for the court, but for the administrative agency with its statutory mandate and its expertise to develop standards." *Id.* at 294.

Although the court did not directly rely on the Equal Protection or Due Process Clauses, the court did cite considerations of equal treatment of similarly situated applicants and procedural fairness.

Exercise: *Sun Ray Drive-In Dairy*

We included many quotations from the *Sun Ray* opinion because it comprehensively discusses reasons why agencies should use rulemaking to particularize vague statutory standards. Please review the quotations above and summarize in your own words five reasons given by the court:

1. _____

2. _____

3. _____

4. _____

5. _____

You will not find any federal court case law comparable to the Oregon court's decision in *Sun Ray*. Indeed, if the *Sun Ray* decision is understood as merely "engrafting ... [judicial] notions of proper procedures upon agencies entrusted with substantive functions" by the legislation, the *Vermont Yankee* principle would bar federal courts from following *Sun Ray*. *Vermont Yankee Nuclear Power Corp. v. Natural Resources Defense Counsel, Inc.*, 435 U.S. 519, 525 (1978). But *Sun Ray* need not be read to conflict with *Vermont Yankee*. The *Sun Ray* Court relied in part on the rationale that it could not intelligently conduct judicial review without administrative standards by which to judge individual agency decisions. This rationale does not derive from common law or equitable principles; rather, it reflects the need for courts to carry out statutes requiring judicial review of agency action. Because the rationale is not grounded in principles of common law or equity, a federal court might rely on this rationale without violating the *Vermont Yankee* principle.

Indeed, the U.S. Supreme Court has endorsed a similar rationale for the requirement that a federal agency adequately explain its adjudicatory decisions. This adequate-explanation requirement, the Court has noted, does not conflict with the *Vermont Yankee* principle because it reflects the federal APA provision directing courts to set aside agency action that is "arbitrary and capricious" or otherwise not in accordance with law. That direction, the Court has explained, "imposes a general 'procedural' requirement of sorts by mandating that an agency take whatever steps it needs to provide an explanation that will enable the court to evaluate the agency's rationale at the time of [the agency's] decision." *Pension Benefit Gty. Corp. v LTV Corp.*, 496 U.S. 633, 654 (1990).

In any event, *Sun Ray* is a useful case for its articulate discussion of the benefits of agencies using rulemaking to particularize vague statutory standards, especially when those standards must be applied by multiple decision makers processing a large volume of cases.

D. Court-Ordered Adjudication

In most cases where courts are asked to review an agency's choice of means, the person challenges an agency's decision to use adjudication instead of rulemaking. Some cases, however, present the converse situation: A person judicially challenges agency action on the ground that the agency should have used adjudication instead of rulemaking. The U.S. Supreme Court has addressed such challenges in several cases, three of which we describe below. The Court's decisions reflect that the *Chenery* principle applies in this converse situation: These decisions give federal agencies broad discretion to choose rulemaking instead of adjudication to carry out their statutory mission. Courts almost never order an agency to proceed by adjudication instead of rulemaking.

- *United States v. Storer Broadcasting*, 351 U.S. 192 (1956)

The Federal Communications Commission issued "multiple ownership" rules capping the number of broadcast stations that a single company could own. One rule, for example, said a company could not own more than five televisions stations serving the same broadcast area. Storer Broadcasting owned five television stations in Miami and wanted more, so Storer judicially challenged the multiple ownership rules.

In its challenge, Storer relied on § 309 of the Communications Act, which entitled a license applicant to a "full hearing" on whether the requested license would serve "the public interest, convenience, and necessity." 351 U.S. at 195 n.5 (quoting statute). Storer argued that the rules deprived it of a "full hearing" because the FCC would deny Storer's application for an additional license *without a hearing* unless Storer could make the showing that the FCC required for a waiver of those rules.

The Court rejected Storer's challenge. The Court said:

> We do not read the hearing requirement … as withdrawing from the power of the Commission the rulemaking authority necessary for the orderly conduct of its business. As conceded by Storer, Section 309(b) does not require the Commission to hold a hearing before denying a license to operate a station in ways contrary to those that the Congress has determined are in the public interest. The challenged Rules contain limitations against licensing not specifically authorized by statute. But that is not the limit of the Commission's rulemaking authority. [Provisions in the Communications Act] grant general rulemaking power not inconsistent with the Act or law.

Id. at 202–203. In other words, the Commission could use its legislative rulemaking power to determine, as a categorical matter, that it would not be in the public interest for a single company to own more than five television stations in the same area.

The Court emphasized that an agency's rules must allow "flexibility" for waiving the rules or exempting people from them in appropriate situations. *Id.* at 204. The Court found the needed flexibility in the Commission's rule allowing a waiver of the multiple ownership rules:

> We read the Act and Regulations as providing a "full hearing" for applicants who have reached the existing limit of stations, upon their presentation of applications conforming to [the waiver rules], that set out adequate reasons why the Rules should be waived or amended. The Act, considered as a whole, requires no more.... We do not think Congress intended the Commission to waste time on applications that do not state a valid basis for a hearing.

Id. at 205. Thus, the Court suggests that agencies generally should have procedures for waiving their rules at least in exceptional circumstances demanding consideration of individualized circumstances. The waiver procedures can require those requesting a waiver to "set out adequate reasons" for a waiver. *Storer Broadcasting*, 351 U.S. at 205; *see also American Airlines, Inc. v. Civil Aeronautics Bd.*, 359 F.2d 624, 633 (D.C. Cir. 1966) (en banc) ("Nowhere in the record is there any specific proffer by petitioners as to the subjects they believed required oral hearings, what kind of facts they proposed to adduce, and by what witnesses, etc. Nor was there any specific proffer as to particular lines of cross-examination which required exploration at an oral hearing.").

More broadly, *Storer Broadcasting* stands for this principle: Just because a statute entitles someone to a "hearing," that does not mean the person is entitled to a hearing if there's nothing to have a hearing about. An agency can use rulemaking power to make objective rules that avoid the need to hold hearings in cases where there is no dispute about how the rules apply. We previously discussed *Storer* in Chapter 22's discussions of administrative summary judgment. *Storer* illustrates an agency's use of rulemaking power to facilitate summary disposition of adjudicatory matters, which is a facet of an agency's discretion about how to use its rulemaking and adjudicatory powers.

The Court has followed *Storer Broadcasting* in several later cases. A brief description of two of them will give you additional examples of statutory schemes that the Court has interpreted not to foreclose the use of rulemaking to establish general principles for agencies to decide cases without individualized determinations.

- *American Hospital Association v. National Labor Relations Board*, 499 U.S. 606 (1991)

The Court held that the statutory obligation of the National Labor Relations Board to determine the appropriate bargaining unit "in each case" did not preclude the Board from adopting a rule prescribing the number and composition of appropriate bargaining units in all acute care hospitals. In short, the statute did not constrain the agency's choice of means. The Court relied on the *Storer Broadcasting* and later cases following it for the proposition: "[E]ven if a statutory scheme requires individualized determinations, the decisionmaker has the authority to rely on rulemaking to resolve certain issues of general applicability unless Congress clearly expresses an intent to withhold that authority." *Id.* at 612.

- *Lopez v. Davis*, 531 U.S. 230 (2001)

Lopez involved a regulation of the Bureau of Prisons (BOP) that categorically denied early release to federal prisoners who had been convicted of a felony attended by the carrying, possession, or use of a firearm. The Court rejected a prisoner's argument that BOP had to make case-by-case determinations of the appropriateness of releasing a prisoner early. The Court observed that the statute did not require case-by-case determinations and that, considering the high volume of those determinations, BOP's use of a case-by-case approach "could invite favoritism, disunity, and inconsistency." *Id.* at 244.

Exercise: The *Storer Broadcasting* Line of Cases

This exercise is for students who have studied the due process material in Chapter 20. The exercise helps you to connect that material with the current material.

A drivers' license is a form of property protected by due process. This means that a license holder generally cannot be deprived, even temporarily, of the license without notice and a right to be heard. Suppose a state agency uses rulemaking power to make rules under which a person's license will be automatically suspended if multiple offenses within a specified period of time have earned the person a specified number of "points."

1. Please explain how the *Storer Broadcasting* principle supports such a rule (assuming the principle existed as a matter of state administrative law).

2. Please explain how these rules can be made consistent with the due process entitlement to notice and an opportunity to be heard.

E. Chapter 25 Wrap Up and Look Ahead

Agencies generally have broad discretion to choose between rulemaking and adjudication. The discretion springs from the legislature's choice to give an agency both powers to carry out its statutory duties. The discretion can be eliminated by a statutory requirement that an agency promulgate rules addressing a subject. In addition, in rare instances a court may find that an agency has abused its discretion by choosing adjudication instead of rulemaking. Alternatively, in the rare case, a court might rely on principles of common law, equity, or even constitutional principles of due process or equal protection to find that an agency erroneously used adjudication instead of rulemaking.

Cases also present the converse situation, in which the agency uses rulemaking to establish general principles or general facts, and then relies on those rules to decide entire cases, or certain issues in cases, summarily. Ordinarily, this is a permissible use of an agency's rulemaking power, even when it avoids the need for a statutorily required opportunity for a hearing.

Agencies that have broad discretion to proceed by adjudication instead of rulemaking can use adjudication to announce new principles or interpretations of law, and even to change principles or interpretations announced in prior agency adjudications. Thus, one potential effect of an agency adjudication is a binding determination of legal rights and duties that has retroactive impact. The next chapter explores other effects of an agency's adjudicatory decision.

Chapter Problem Revisited

This chapter problem confronts you with the problem courts face when deciding whether to constrain agency choice between rulemaking and adjudication. The problem actually raises two questions:

1.   Does any source of law constrain agency choice?

2.   If so, how?

1.   The possible legal sources of a duty to proceed by rulemaking are (a) the court's power to set aside the agency decision for an "abuse of discretion"; (b) the agency legislation; (c) due process or equal protection principles in the federal or state constitutions; or (d) common law or equitable principles. You should consider each of these bases as discussed in this chapter.

2.   Depending on what source of law the state court chooses, the state court will have varying degrees of latitude to structure a choice of means principle for state agencies. For example, a state court can define an "abuse of discretion" in the choice-of-means context differently from the way the Court in *SEC v. Chenery* defined it. A state court could interpret the agency legislation, like the *Elizondo* court did, to require the agency to proceed by rulemaking because of the legislation's vague substantive standard coupled with the "statutory suggestion" implied by a grant of power to make rules transforming the vague statutory standard into specific regulatory criteria. State courts must obey U.S. Supreme Court precedent when interpreting the federal due process and equal protection guarantees, of course, but that did not prevent the *Elizondo* court from formulating a due process rationale for which there was no directly applicable U.S. Supreme Court precedent. State courts have even more interpretive freedom when construing their own State's constitution, and they may also have much latitude when drawing upon common law or equitable considerations. In other words, a State Supreme Court Justice has much room to make the "best" choice. What choice would you make?

Professional Development Reflection Questions

Drivers' license suspension cases are a high-volume type of administrative adjudication in every State. As illustrated in *Elizondo v. Department of Revenue*, 570 P.2d 518 (Colorado 1977), these adjudications typically occur before the state department of motor vehicles and include the right to an oral, evidentiary hearing. Many lawyers handle drivers' license suspension cases, along with the criminal proceedings with which they are often connected. For example, a person arrested for drunk driving may face an administrative adjudication on the suspension of his or her drivers' license and a prosecution for drunk driving. Lawyers who specialize in administrative or judicial adjudications about driving offenses are sometimes called "drivers license lawyers" or "DUI/DWI" lawyers, in the case of those who specialize in driving offenses involving alleged driver impairment. The administrative adjudications on drivers' licenses represent a big slice of administrative law practice.

We introduce this specialized field of administrative law practice because it raises two questions of general importance for law students and lawyers.

1.   Many drivers are threatened with a loss of their license after they fail a roadside sobriety test in which a police officer uses an electronic testing device such as a "breathalyzer" to detect alcohol. As you may know, a driver often can avoid having his or license suspended by showing that the testing device was improperly calibrated or used. Is it ethical for a lawyer to rely on

such "technicalities" if all other evidence, including a client's driving history, makes it highly likely that the client was driving while impaired in the particular case in which the technicality arises? (Of course, the law is full of such technicalities that can be used to resolve matters without getting to the "merits." Thus, the question has general applicability.)

2. Many lawyers have perceptions of how prestigious particular legal positions are. Thus, the lawyer who works in a "white shoe" law firm representing large corporations in complicated business transactions may be perceived as having a more prestigious job than the lawyer who works in a small firm or is a solo practitioner representing ordinary folks in cases involving, say, charges of drunk driving. Preoccupation with these perceived differences in prestige level is a major source of unhappiness (and not just in the legal profession). More to the point, how important is it to you to have a post-law-school job that is perceived among lawyers as prestigious?

Chapter 26

Effect of Valid Agency Adjudicatory Decisions

Overview

Past chapters explored agency adjudications. This chapter examines the effects of an agency adjudication. As you'll see, the effects resemble those of a court decision in some ways. But because agency adjudicatory power is only "quasi-judicial" and because some agency adjudications differ dramatically from judicial proceedings, there are also differences between the effects of agency adjudications and court adjudications.

The chapter's sections are entitled:

A.   Direct Effect of the Agency Decision on the Agency and the Parties

B.   Administrative Stare Decisis

C.   Administrative Res Judicata

D.   Special Rules That Differ From, But Are Easy to Confuse With, Administrative Res Judicata; Agency Non-Acquiescence

E.   Chapter 26 Wrap Up and Look Ahead

Chapter Problem 1

You work in the general counsel's office of Splendor, Inc., a company that sells an herbal weight-loss product called "Splendor." You have just found out that the Federal Trade Commission has made a final decision in a formal adjudication you've been following. In that formal adjudication, the Commission has concluded that one of your company's competitors, ThinAgain, Inc., has violated the Federal Trade Commission Act in advertising its weight-loss product, ThinAgain. Specifically, the Commission has found that certain claims in ads for ThinAgain are "deceptive" within the meaning of the Act. *See* 15 U.S.C. §45(a)(1) (2012).

ThinAgain contains the same active ingredient as your company's product, Splendor. Moreover, your company's advertising for Splendor makes claims strongly resembling the ones in the ThinAgain ads that the Commission found misleading.

You must write a memo for your general counsel about the Commission's ThinAgain decision. In addition to summarizing the decision, you want to address the following questions that you anticipate the general counsel will have about the decision's relevance for your company:

1. Assuming the Commission's ThinAgain decision is not set aside on judicial review, is the Commission's ThinAgain decision binding on your company, Splendor, even though Splendor was not a party to the adjudication?

2. You have spoken with the attorney for ThinAgain. The attorney says ThinAgain will appeal the Commission's ThinAgain decision to the U.S. Court of Appeals for the Ninth Circuit. If the Ninth Circuit sets aside the Commission's decision and the U.S. Supreme Court does not grant further review, will the Ninth Circuit's decision prevent the Commission from taking enforcement action against Splendor?

Chapter Problem 2

For this problem, assume that the Federal Trade Commission has issued a decision about the weight-loss product ThinAgain like the one described in Chapter Problem 1. Now, though, instead of representing another company that makes a competing product, you represent a class of consumers who bought and used ThinAgain and have filed a civil action against ThinAgain for state-law fraud in a federal district court in New Jersey.

Write a memo to the file addressing what legal effect, if any, the Commission's ThinAgain decision might have in your pending class action against ThinAgain in New Jersey federal court. In that memo, consider three possible scenarios: (1) the Commission's ThinAgain decision is not reviewed by any court; (2) the Commission's ThinAgain decision is reviewed by the U.S. Court of Appeals for the Ninth Circuit and set aside; and (3) the Commission's ThinAgain decision is reviewed by the Ninth Circuit and upheld.

A. Direct Effect of the Agency Decision on the Agency and the Parties

The direct effect of an agency decision in an adjudication may strongly resemble the direct effect of a court decision. Like a court, an agency with adjudicatory power can make a legally binding determination of the parties' legal rights and duties. But some agencies — unlike the federal courts, at least — may issue advisory opinions that have little or no binding effect.

An agency adjudication ordinarily binds both the agency and the parties with respect to the case at hand. For example, an agency's decision to issue a license or grant benefits may create a property interest protected by due process. If so, the agency must honor that property interest; the agency cannot take it away without according due process. To take another example, an agency's decision to impose a civil fine on a party creates a legal duty to pay the fine, though sometimes the agency must go to court to enforce that duty. An agency may order a party to cease and desist activity found to violate an agency rule or the agency legislation, and violation of that cease-and-desist order may subject the party to civil and criminal sanctions prescribed by the agency legislation.

An agency's decision need not have the same binding effect as a court decision. Unlike the federal courts and many state courts, which cannot render advisory opinions, many agencies can issue advisory opinions. An agency may issue an advisory opinion at the request of individuals or companies that want to obey the law but need guidance on what the law means. When an agency issues an advisory opinion, the opinion may have only limited legal effect on the agency and others. For example, an important U.S. Supreme Court case concerned a "tariff ruling" by the U.S. Customs Service. Tariff rulings addressed how particular imported goods would be classified for purposes of paying tariffs. These tariff rulings were, by regulation, "binding on all Customs Service personnel ... until modified or revoked." *United States v. Mead Corp.*, 533 U.S. 218, 222 (2001) (quoting agency regulation). The kicker is that they could be modified or revoked at any time. In effect, they were binding as long as the agency wanted to be bound by them! Although you might think this is the agency having its cake and eating it, too, tariff rulings and similar advisory rulings do not just benefit the agency. The public also benefits from an agency's flexibility in being able to offer its tentative views of a matter without being forever pinned down by those views. *See Nat'l Automatic Laundry & Cleaning Council v. Shultz*, 443 F.2d 689, 699 (D.C. Cir. 1971).

The point is that agency adjudications can, and often are, as binding as court decisions but, as is true in so many areas of administrative law, generalizations are dangerous and the wary administrative lawyer always identifies and analyzes the law governing the binding effect of the particular agency decision. An agency decision may look adjudicatory, in that the decision explains how the law applies to a set of facts, but not be as binding as a court's decision.

Exercise: Statutes and Agency Rules for Advisory Opinions

To get a concrete sense of how and why agencies issue advisory opinions, please either go to the website of the Federal Election Commission and search on the term "advisory opinions" or examine the relevant statute and rules for the Commission's issuance of advisory opinions: 2 U.S.C. § 437f(a)(1) (2012), and 11 C.F.R. §§ 112.1–112.6 (2012).

B. Administrative Stare Decisis

Beyond its immediate effect on the agency and the parties to the adjudication, an agency's decision in an adjudication may also serve as precedent for the agency in future cases. This effect is called "administrative stare decisis." Because many agencies do follow their own precedent, people with adjudications before the agency must identify and analyze the relevant agency precedent. The important things for you to understand about the stare decisis effect of an agency adjudicatory decision are: (1) the nature and extent of that effect; (2) an agency's power to depart from its precedent; and (3) how to find agency precedent.

In general, an agency's decision doesn't have as strong a stare decisis effect on the agency's later decision making as an appellate court's precedent has on that court's later decision making. Thus, the U.S. Supreme Court has referred to "the *qualified role* of stare decisis in the administrative process." *Atchison, Topeka & Santa Fe Ry. v. Wichita Bd. of Trade*, 412 U.S. 800, 807 (1973) (internal quotation marks omitted; emphasis added). By "qualified," the Court means that agencies have more freedom to depart from their precedent than courts have to depart from judicial precedent.

Agencies have greater freedom because they are supposed to use their adjudicatory and other powers to fulfill statutorily assigned missions, not simply to get the law "right" in individual cases. An agency's views on how best to carry out its mission may change because of: (1) changed conditions in the area for which the agency has responsibility (e.g., global warming may affect an environmental agency's approach); (2) changes in the agency's view of how best to further its mission in light of the agency's experience in administering a statute; and (3) electoral changes, as newly elected or appointed officials take over the leadership of the agency after an election. In short, an agency's administration of its legislation—including through the agency's exercise of adjudicatory powers—is recognized as dynamic and flexible, whereas courts are characterized more by stability and gradualism in their approach to developing the law. Stare decisis is a defining feature of courts. As for agencies, not so much.

When an agency establishes legal precedent through adjudication, the agency can use adjudication or rulemaking (if it has rulemaking power) to depart from that precedent. In either event, the agency has to acknowledge and explain the departure. The requirements to acknowledge and explain a departure from agency precedent stem from the principle of "reasoned decisionmaking" that courts enforce when reviewing agency decisions. *Motor Vehicles Mfrs. Ass'n of United States v. State Farm Mut. Auto. Ins. Co.*, 463 U.S. 29, 52 (1983). "But [the agency] need not demonstrate to a court's satisfaction that the reasons for the new policy are *better* than the reasons for the old one; it suffices that the new policy is permissible under the statute, that there are good reasons for it, and that the agency *believes* it to be better, which the conscious change of course adequately indicates." *FCC v. Fox Television Stations, Inc.*, 556 U.S. 502, 515 (2009).

If an agency intends to use its adjudicatory decisions as precedent, the agency must make the decisions publicly available. Unfortunately, although an agency's precedential decisions are publicly available, that does not mean it will be easy for you to find the specific agency decisions relevant to the case in which you are involved. On the one hand, the Federal APA requires agencies to make their decisions in adjudications publicly available along with an index of those decisions, or else the agency cannot rely on them to someone's detriment. 5 U.S.C. § 552(b)(2) (2012). Some state APAs similarly require state agencies to publish their precedential decisions along with an index, and they restrict the use of undisclosed agency precedent. *E.g.*, Wash. Rev. Code Ann. § 42.56.070 (5)(b) (West, Westlaw through May 1, 2012). Other state APAs, however, do not expressly require agencies to keep an index of their decisions, in the absence of which it can be quite hard to locate relevant agency precedent. Wyo. Stat. § 16-3-102 (West, Westlaw through 2011 Gen. Sess.). Besides that, even in the federal system and in States that do require indexing of state agency decisions, agency indices vary widely in their usefulness. State laws typically require the index to list agency decisions "by name and subject," which can make looking for relevant precedent a treasure hunt. *E.g.*, Miss. Code Ann. § 25-43-2.102(1) (West, Westlaw through end of 2011 Reg. Sess.). Moreover, there is no centralized reporting system for federal agency decisions, nor do States have such centralized systems.

The situation is improving. Some States, like Florida, have laws requiring state agency indices of agency decisions to have certain, useful features. *E.g.*, Fla. Stat. Ann. § 120.53 (West, Westlaw through Apr. 20, 2012). Florida has gone even further by allowing state agencies, as an alternative to indexing their agency precedent, to create a full-text database of agency precedent searchable by conventional computer-research methods. *Id.* § 120.53(1)(a)2.b. Besides the state-law developments, commercial services such as Westlaw and LexisNexis include more and more databases of state agency decisions in adjudications. Despite all these developments, however, it remains true that the law in agency adjudicatory decisions is harder to find than the law in agency rules.

Exercise: Agency Precedent

The objective of this exercise is to have you lay your eyes on agency precedent. You've got two options.

1. If you're particularly interested in federal administrative law, please visit the website of the Federal Trade Commission or the National Labor Relations Board and look at recent opinions in formal adjudications by the Commission or the Board. Consider how they compare to appellate court decisions you've read in your law school courses. Also assess the website's tools for searching agency decisions.

2. If you're particularly interested in state administrative law, find the websites in a State of your choice for the State's public utilities commission or workers' compensation commission. These two agencies often issue written decisions in formal adjudications (or formal rulemaking) and post them on their websites. Look at some agency decisions and assess the website's search tools.

C. Administrative Res Judicata

"Res judicata" is a doctrine you may have learned about in law school courses on civil procedure or the federal courts. Maybe you thought you were finished with this obscurely named but important doctrine. Not so! We now take up the doctrine known as "administrative res judicata."

1. Defining Administrative Res Judicata and Distinguishing It from Other, Similar Situations and Doctrines

a. The Situation in Which Administrative Res Judicata Operates

Administrative res judicata operates when an agency's decision in an adjudication precludes the litigation of an issue or claim in a later adjudicatory proceeding. Thus, administrative res judicata operates when there are two separate proceedings: (1) an agency adjudication followed by (2) a later, separate adjudicatory proceeding. The later proceeding may be an adjudicatory proceeding before the same agency, a different agency, or a court. Law school courses on administrative law, however, tend to focus on situations in which the later proceeding is a judicial proceeding, and we will do the same in this book.

We also adopt two other conventions in exploring administrative res judicata. First, we use the term "traditional" res judicata to mean situations in which an earlier *judicial* proceeding has preclusive effect in a later judicial proceeding. Thus, "traditional" res judicata is used in contradistinction to administrative res judicata, in which an *agency adjudication* has preclusive effect in a later judicial proceeding. Second, we use the term "res judicata" in both a broad and narrow sense. We sometimes use it broadly, to include collateral estoppel (today often called "issue preclusion"). Other times, we use "res judicata" more narrowly, to refer only to what today is called "claim preclusion." We recognize that the second convention contributes to confusion about the traditional doctrine. In an attempt to mitigate the confusion, we will often use the more modern terms claim preclusion and issue preclusion.

To describe those terms in a nutshell, and ignoring "privity": Traditional claim preclusion generally prevents a party in a lawsuit from asserting a claim that the party did assert or could have asserted in a prior lawsuit against the same opposing party, if the prior lawsuit ended in a valid, final, judgment on the merits. Traditional issue preclusion generally prevents a party in a lawsuit from relitigating an issue that the party litigated in prior lawsuit if: (1) the issue was actually litigated and determined in the prior lawsuit; (2) its determination was necessary to the judgment in the prior lawsuit; and (3) the prior lawsuit ended in a valid, final judgment.

Just replace the words "prior lawsuit" with "prior agency adjudication" and you have the gist of how administrative res judicata works. Here is an example:

- *Bowen v. United States*, 570 F.2d 1311 (7th Cir. 1978)

Thomas Bowen crashed his Bellanca Viking aircraft while trying to land in Marion, Indiana. The Federal Aviation Administration (FAA) suspended Mr. Bowen's pilot license. Mr. Bowen appealed the FAA's suspension decision to the National Transportation Safety Board, which held a hearing on the causes of the crash. The Board determined that Mr. Bowen violated federal aviation safety regulations by trying to land a plane that was not equipped with de-icing equipment under conditions that he knew or should have known would cause ice to accumulate on his airplane's wings. The Board affirmed the FAA's suspension of Mr. Bowen's license. Mr. Bowen did not seek judicial review of the Board's order, which accordingly became final.

Mr. Bowen then sued the United States in federal court under the Federal Tort Claims Act. The Act exposes the United States to money damages for conduct by a federal employee that injures the plaintiff and that is tortious under the law of the State where the conduct occurred. Mr. Bowen claimed that federal air traffic controllers in Indiana negligently failed to warn him of icy conditions at the Marion airport. The federal district court held that the Board's determination precluded Mr. Bowen from relitigating the issue of whether he violated federal safety regulations by flying his airplane into conditions that he knew or should have known would cause icing on his wings. The district court determined that Mr. Bowen's violation of the regulations constituted contributory negligence and absolutely barred recovery under Indiana tort law. His lawsuit thus did not get off the ground because of administrative res judicata.

Bowen illustrates an agency adjudication having issue preclusive effect against a private party. Agency adjudication can also have claim preclusive effect in a later adjudication. In *Bowen* the party precluded was a private party, and preclusion operated to the benefit of the government. An agency adjudication can also have preclusive effect *against* the government when the government tries to relitigate against a party an issue that it litigated against that same party and lost in a prior agency adjudication. *See, e.g., Al Mutarreb v. Holder*, 561 F.3d 1023, 1031 (9th Cir. 2009) (administrative res judicata would bar agency from seeking to remove alien on grounds that agency relied on, or could have relied on, in prior removal proceeding that led to a final judgment on the merits); *Drummond v. Comm'r of Social Sec.*, 126 F.3d 837, 840–843 (6th Cir. 1997) (administrative res judicata prevented an ALJ from finding a disability claimant was capable of performing medium-level work, because in prior proceeding an ALJ had found the claimant capable of performing only light work).

b. Distinguishing Administrative Res Judicata from Other Situations

We briefly explain how administrative res judicata differs from:

- administrative stare decisis; and
- judicial review of an agency's adjudicatory decision.

(i) Administrative Res Judicata Vs. Administrative Stare Decisis

Administrative res judicata differs from administrative stare decisis. As discussed above in Section B, administrative stare decisis refers to the precedential effect of an agency's adjudicatory decision in a later adjudication *by that same agency*. Administrative stare decisis thus means an agency will generally stand by its own prior decisions. In contrast, administrative res judicata may operate not only in a later adjudication by the same agency but also in a later adjudication by a different agency or a court. This feature of administrative res judicata's operation was illustrated in the case summarized above, *Bowen v. United States*, in which a National Transportation Safety Board decision had preclusive effect in a later court proceeding.

Perhaps another way of expressing the same difference is to say that administrative res judicata, like traditional res judicata, precludes *parties* from litigating certain claims or issues; administrative stare decisis, like judicial stare decisis, binds the adjudicative entity (agency or court). Thus. if an agency interprets its legislation in a particular way in an adjudication in 2011, the agency is at least mildly bound by administrative stare decisis to adhere to that interpretation in an adjudication in 2014 that raises the same issue of interpretation as the 2011 adjudication. This is true whether or not the 2014 adjudication involves the same parties or events as the 2011 adjudication.

Despite these differences, both administrative res judicata and administrative stare decisis seek to bring consistency and predictability to decision making in which agencies are involved.

(ii) Administrative Res Judicata Vs. Judicial Review

Administrative res judicata can operate when an agency proceeding is followed by a later, *separate* judicial proceeding involving the same issue or claim as the earlier, agency proceeding. Administrative res judicata does not operate when a court *reviews* an agency's decision in an adjudication. Judicial review of an agency's adjudicatory decision is really a continuation of the same case. When a court reviews the agency's adjudicatory decision, the court may decide some issues de novo while giving weight to the agency's determination of other issues. But in no event will the reviewing court say that administrative res judicata precludes judicial review. Put another way, administrative res judicata only operates once the agency's decision in the adjudication has become final, having either survived judicial review or not been challenged on judicial review. *Astoria*, 501 U.S. at 107; *see Sunshine Anthracite Coal Co. v. Adkins*, 310 U.S. 381, 390–391, 401–402 (1940) (according preclusive effect to agency determination in prior proceeding where agency's determination was upheld on judicial review).

We turn in the next section to the sources of law that establish requirements for administrative res judicata.

Exercise: Identifying Situations in Which Administrative Res Judicata Potentially May Operate

Please indicate whether administrative res judicata could operate (assuming the requirements for it were satisfied) in these settings:

1. The Federal Trade Commission concludes after a formal adjudication that a company has engaged in an unfair and deceptive trade practice, in violation of the Federal Trade Commission Act. The company does not seek judicial review. A consumer sues the company for damages caused by the unfair and deceptive practice found by the Commission.

2. The Federal Trade Commission concludes after a formal adjudication that a company has engaged in an unfair and deceptive trade practice, in violation of the Federal Trade Commission Act. The company seeks judicial review.

3. The Federal Trade Commission concludes after a formal adjudication that a company has engaged in an unfair and deceptive trade practice, in violation of the Federal Trade Commission Act. The company seeks judicial review. The reviewing court upholds the FTC's decision. A consumer sues the company for damages caused by the unfair and deceptive practice found by the Commission in the prior adjudication.

4. The Federal Trade Commission concludes after a formal adjudication that a company's method of advertising the price of its product violates the Federal Trade Commission Act. In a later proceeding involving a different company but a highly similar method of advertising, the Commission relies on its prior decision in holding that the second company's conduct violated the Act.

---

2. Requirements for Administrative Res Judicata

a. Sources of Requirements

Before you delve into the requirements for administrative res judicata, you must know where those requirements come from. The source of the requirements differs depending on whether the litigation under analysis is in federal or state court and whether the agency adjudication under analysis is that of a federal or state agency.

- *Federal courts dealing with prior adjudicatory decisions by federal agencies*

When a federal court must determine the administrative res judicata effect of the adjudicatory decision of a federal agency, the court usually relies on federal common law. The U.S. Supreme Court established the federal common law requirements for administrative res judicata in *United States v. Utah Construction & Mining Co.*, 384 U.S. 394 (1966), which is discussed below.

There is, however, at least one situation, and possibly two, in which a federal court would not use the federal common law principles of *Utah Construction & Mining* to analyze the administrative res judicata effect of a federal agency's adjudicatory decision. First, as discussed below, Congress can modify or eliminate the federal common law principles of administrative res judicata. *See Astoria Fed. Sav. & Loan Ass'n v. Solimino*, 501 U.S. 104, 107–108 (1991). Second, it is possible that when a federal court is deciding a state-law claim—in the exercise of its diversity or supplemental jurisdiction—the administrative res judicata effect of a federal agency's prior adjudicatory decision upon that state-law claim would be governed by *state* law, either under the *Erie* doctrine or on the theory that in this situation federal common law should incorporate state law. *See Murray v. Alaska Airlines, Inc.*, 522 F.3d 920, 922 (9th Cir. 2008); *see also Semtek Int'l Inc. v. Lockheed Martin Corp.*, 531 U.S. 497, 508 (2001); 18B Arthur R. Miller et al., Federal Practice and Procedure § 4475, at 133 (2011 Supp.).

- *Federal courts dealing with prior adjudicatory decisions by state agencies that have been upheld by state courts on judicial review ("reviewed" state agency decisions)*

When a state agency adjudicates a case and its decision is upheld by a state court, the state court judgment affirming the state agency's decision gets "full faith and credit" in federal courts under the Full Faith and Credit statute, 28 U.S.C. § 1738 (2012). The Full Faith and Credit statute requires a federal court to give the state court judgment the same preclusive effect as it would have in a court of the State that rendered the judgment. Thus, if a rendering State's state courts would give preclusive effect to the state agency decision upheld by the prior state court judgment, a federal court must give preclusive effect, too. *Kremer v. Chem. Constr. Corp*, 456 U.S. 461 (1982). In short, a federal court "pretends" to be a state court in the State whose court upheld a state agency decision, when analyzing the preclusive effect of that state agency decision.

- *Federal courts dealing with prior adjudicatory decisions by state agencies that were not reviewed by state courts ("unreviewed" state agency decisions)*

The U.S. Supreme Court has held that when a state agency adjudicates a case and the state agency's adjudicatory decision is not reviewed by a state court, the Full Faith and Credit statute doesn't apply. Nonetheless, an unreviewed state agency decision may still get preclusive effect in later litigation in federal court. Here's the rule: If the unreviewed state agency decision (1) satisfies the federal common law requirements for giving preclusive effect to a *federal* agency's adjudicative decision, then (2) the unreviewed state agency decision is entitled to the same preclusive effect the courts of that State would give it. So, federal common law requirements act as a filtering device. A state agency decision that isn't filtered out gets the same treatment from a federal court that it would get from a state court in the State whose agency made the decision.

This two-stage method for determining the preclusive effect, if any, of unreviewed state agency decisions rests on federal common law, and may be modified by federal statute. *Univ. of Tenn. v. Elliott*, 478 U.S. 788 (1986).

- *State courts* dealing with prior adjudicatory decisions by their own *state agencies*

Every State has its own law of preclusion, and many States' courts, like the federal courts, recognize the doctrine of administrative res judicata. The state courts do not, however, have to adopt the same requirements for the administrative res judicata effect of their state agencies that the U.S. Supreme Court has adopted for the federal courts.

* * *

You are not alone if you have trouble keeping straight the permutations discussed above. The main thing to remember is that, when it comes to administrative res judicata, no one body of law controls all situations. Instead, the applicable body of law varies depending on the court in which the issue of administrative res judicata arises and the agency in which the prior adjudication occurred.

Below we focus on the federal common-law requirements for administrative res judicata, which apply, unless modified by statute or deemed to incorporate state-law principles of administrative res judicata, to determine whether a federal agency adjudication can have preclusive effect in later litigation in a federal court.

b. Federal Common Law Requirements for Administrative Res Judicata

We first summarize below the leading modern case on the federal common law requirements for administrative res judicata. Then we elaborate briefly on those requirements. Finally we remind you that, if you decide the requirements for *administrative* res judicata are satisfied in a particular case, you must then analyze whether the *traditional* res judicata requirements are satisfied.

- *United States v. Utah Construction & Mining Co.*, 384 U.S. 394 (1966)

Utah Construction and Mining Company had a contract with the federal government for a building project at an atomic energy facility. The contract required disputes under the contract to be submitted to a government agency called the Advisory Board of Contract Appeals. The Company submitted two claims to the Board asking for more money under the contract and more time to complete the contract. The claims were based on problems that the Company encountered while performing the contract and that, the Company claimed, caused delays and increased costs and were not the Company's fault. The Board made findings about the causes of the delays. Under both the contract and the federal statute governing review of the Board's findings, those findings were "final and conclusive." *Id.* at 399 nn.2 & 3.

The Company sued the United States in the federal Claims Court, arguing that the government's unreasonable delay breached the contract. One issue in the suit was whether the Claims Court could determine the causes of the delay de novo or was, instead, bound by the Board's findings. The U.S. Supreme Court held that under both the contract, as modified by the federal statute governing judicial review, and principles of administrative res judicata (which the Court interchangeably calls "collateral estoppel"), the Board's findings had preclusive effect in the Claims Court suit:

> Although the decision here rests upon the agreement of the parties as modified by the Wunderlich Act, we note that the result we reach is harmonious with general principles of collateral estoppel. Occasionally courts have used language to the effect that res judicata principles do not apply to administrative proceedings, but such language is certainly too broad. When an administrative agency is acting

in a judicial capacity and resolved disputed issues of fact properly before it which the parties have had an adequate opportunity to litigate, the courts have not hesitated to apply res judicata to enforce repose.

Id. at 421–422. Thus, the Court conditioned administrative res judicata on an agency's (1) "acting in a judicial capacity"; and (2) resolving disputed issues of fact properly before it that the party to be precluded had "an adequate opportunity to litigate."

Lower federal court case law has elaborated on each requirement. In reading our brief description of that case law, your objective should be to gain an understanding of the central concern underlying each requirement. When you are an administrative lawyer and have to analyze the administrative res judicata effect, if any, of a particular determination by a particular agency, you should search first for case law on the preclusive effect of that particular determination by that particular agency. That is because case law addressing the preclusive effect of, say, Federal Trade Commission determinations may not control the preclusive effect of determinations by the Social Security Administration (SSA). Beyond that, not even all determinations by a single agency—say SSA—will necessarily have the same preclusive effect. Here, as in other areas of administrative law, a highly contextual analysis is required.

Utah Mining & Construction's "judicial capacity" requirement generally limits administrative res judicata to agency determinations made in adjudications in which the party to be precluded had an opportunity for an unbiased decision maker to make a decision based on an adversary presentation of evidence. This leaves out notice-and-comment rulemaking, of course, but it also leaves out many informal adjudications that involve no more than an official reviewing paper work before making a decision. For example, a court denied preclusive effect to a federal agency's adjustment of a person's immigration status. The adjustment-of-status determination was not "judicial" because it was not adversarial in nature and did not involve an Immigration Judge. *Andrade v. Gonzales*, 459 F.3d 538, 545 (5th Cir. 2006); *see also Reich v. Youghiogheny & Ohio Coal Co.*, 66 F.3d 111, 115 (6th Cir. 1995) (nondiscretionary "ministerial" calculation by agency official lacked preclusive effect). In contrast, preclusive effect may attach to determinations made in federal agency proceedings to remove aliens from the United States, because removal proceedings are adversarial and decided by an Immigration Judge.

Utah Mining & Construction's "adequate opportunity to litigate" requirement means that the more elements of a trial the agency adjudication offered, the better. An agency adjudication is most likely to qualify for preclusive effect when it provides an opportunity for an oral, evidentiary hearing before an impartial decision maker; an opportunity for cross-examination; a decision based exclusively on the record; and a written decision with particularized determinations of law and fact—a formal adjudication, in other words. As those features drop away or become bob-tailed, the chances a court will give it preclusive effect fade. *See, e.g., Nasem v. Brown*, 595 F.2d 801, 806–807 (D.C. Cir. 1979). The agency only has to provide the *opportunity* for trial-like procedures, however; if the party to be precluded does not take advantage of them, the agency's decision might still have preclusive effect. *See, e.g., McGowen v. Harris*, 666 F.2d 60, 65 (4th Cir. 1981).

An agency adjudication that satisfies the *Utah Construction & Mining* requirements for administrative res judicata does not automatically get preclusive effect. Instead, meeting those requirements means that the agency adjudication may get the same preclusive effect that a court adjudication would have. *See Int'l Union of Operating Engineers, Local No. 714 v. Sullivan Transfer, Inc.*, 650 F.2d 669, 673 (5th Cir. 1981). Thus, once you determine that an agency adjudication satisfies the *Utah Construction & Mining* requirements, you turn to whether the agency adjudication satisfies the traditional requirements for preclusion. As adapted for agency adjudications, issue preclusion, for example, will prevent a party in a lawsuit from relitigating an issue that the party previously and unsuccessfully litigated in an agency adjudication if: (1) the issue was actually litigated and determined in the agency adjudication lawsuit; (2) its determination was necessary to the judgment in the agency adjudication; and (3) the agency adjudication ended in a valid, final judgment.

Even beyond these traditional requirements, sometimes federal courts reserve the right to deny preclusive effect to an agency adjudication when giving it preclusive effect would be unfair. The U.S. Court of Appeals for the Ninth Circuit said so in an opinion written by then-Judge, now-Justice Anthony Kennedy:

> Administrative res judicata ... is not applied with rigidity. Its application must be tempered by fairness and equity. Both administrative res judicata and administrative collateral estoppel are qualified or rejected when their application would contravene an overriding public policy or result in manifest injustice. Fairness in the administrative decision-making process is our principal concern, outweighing the importance of administrative finality.

Martin v. Donovan, 731 F.2d 1415 (9th Cir. 1984) (citations and internal quotation marks omitted). On this ground the Ninth Circuit refused to give preclusive effect to a state agency's determination that Peter Martin was fired for being drunk on the job. The state agency determination not only lacked preclusive effect in the federal court. It also could not be given preclusive effect by a federal agency—namely the U.S. Department of Labor—when that agency considered Mr. Martin's claims for unemployment benefits under a federal statute.

The Ninth Circuit in *Martin* may have been influenced not only by fairness but also by the "pro-employee" policy of the federal statute under which Mr. Martin sought benefits. *See id.* at 1416. If so, *Martin* is consistent with case discussed next, which shows that a statute can modify the federal common law requirements for administrative res judicata.

c. Statutory Modification of Administrative Res Judicata

The administrative lawyer cannot assume an agency adjudication will have preclusive effect in later litigation. In federal court litigation, the administrative res judicata of federal and state agency adjudicatory decisions will often be governed by federal common law. Similarly, the administrative res judicata in many state court systems is a doctrine that the state courts have developed on their own using the common law method. As a creature of common law, administrative res judicata can be modified or eliminated by statute. To give you a sense of how courts determine whether a statute modifies or eliminates the doctrine, we briefly describe two cases in which the U.S. Supreme Court held that federal statutes prevented agency adjudications from having administrative res judicata effect.

The facts of the two U.S. Supreme Court cases were similar: A state agency investigated a charge of illegal employment discrimination and ruled against the employee who claimed discrimination. Rather than seeking review of the state agency's ruling in state court, the employee sued the employer in federal court, asserting a claim under a federal employment discrimination statute. In each case, the Court interpreted the federal statute as denying administrative res judicata effect to state agency determinations that had not been reviewed by a state court. *Astoria Federal Savings & Loan Ass'n v. Solimino*, 501 U.S. 104 (1991) (Age Discrimination in Employment Act); *University of Tennessee v. Elliott*, 478 U.S. 788 (1986) (Title VII of the Civil Rights Act of 1964). Because the federal statutes denied preclusive effect to state agency adjudications, it didn't matter whether the state agency adjudications would have satisfied the federal common law requirements for administrative res judicata articulated in *Utah Construction & Mining*. The federal statutes displaced federal common law.

The Court explained the proper analytic approach in *Astoria Federal Savings & Loan Association v. Solimino*: Federal courts should presume that Congress "has legislated with an expectation" that administrative res judicata will apply "except when a statutory purpose to the contrary is evident." 501 U.S. at 108. This presumption reflects that "Congress is understood to legislate against a background of common-law adjudicatory principles," which include the administrative res judicata principles of *Utah Construction & Mining*. *Id.* But to overcome that presumption, Congress need not make a "clear statement" of an intention to override the common law *Id.* Instead, the court must determine what Congress intended regardless whether that intent is clear. In *Astoria* and *Elliott*, the Court found evidence of Congress's intent in the fact that Congress required discrimination complainants to give state agencies a chance to investigate and resolve their complaints before the complainants could file federal court lawsuits. Ordinarily, a complainant would file a federal court lawsuit only if the state agency ruled against the complainant. But if the state agency's ruling against the complainant had preclusive effect in the complainant's later federal court lawsuit, that lawsuit would be pointless. Congress could not have intended that result, and therefore could not have intended state agency determinations to have preclusive effect in later, federal court lawsuits.

The broader point is that a statute can modify federal common law requirements for administrative res judicata. Administrative res judicata analysis is thus highly sensitive to the statutory setting in which the analysis occurs. When researching an administrative res judicata problem, the administrative lawyer must examine the relevant statutes and case law interpreting those statutes.

Exercise: Reflecting on Reasons for Statutory Modification or Elimination of Administrative Res Judicata

Many hard administrative res judicata issues arise from decisions by the Social Security Administration (SSA) on individuals' rights to disability benefits. Roughly speaking, a person is entitled to benefits if a disability prevents the person from doing his or her old job and, considering the person's disability and the person's age and education, there is no other work the person can do. According to SSA, as of December 2011, 8.6 million disabled workers were receiving $9.5 billion annually in disability benefits. (This does not count benefits due to dependents and survivors of disabled workers.) *See* Social Security Administration, Social Security Basic Facts, http://www.ssa.gov/pressoffice/basicfact.htm (May 15, 2012).

First, consider why the program sometimes permits a person to apply for disability benefits even if that person previously applied and was turned down. When should the law allow new applications? Next consider why, while permitting people to apply for disability benefits multiple times, there are good reasons to prevent people from filing duplicative claims. In light of these competing considerations, frame a rule that allows people to re-file for disability benefits when it is appropriate for them to do so without allowing them to file duplicative claims.

D. Special Rules That Differ From, but Are Easy to Confuse with, Administrative Res Judicata; and Agency Non-Acquiescence

We briefly discuss two sets of special rules that differ from, but are easily confused with, administrative res judicata:

(1) special rules governing the use of the doctrine of *equitable* estoppel—not to be confused with *collateral* estoppel—against the government; and

(2) special rules in traditional res judicata for cases in which the government is a party.

An administrative lawyer should be aware of these special rules—because they are important in their own right—and understand how they differ from administrative res judicata. Our objective is to help you attain that knowledge.

We also introduce you in this section to a practice of many government agencies— known as "non-acquiescence"—related to the government's frequent litigation of cases throughout the country raising the same legal question.

1. Special Rules for Invoking Equitable Estoppel against the Government

The doctrine of equitable estoppel is used by courts to prevent one person from taking unfair advantage of another person. Suppose, for example, Petra and Danielle get into an auto accident apparently caused by Danielle's negligence. Petra and Danielle begin negotiating a settlement to avoid a lawsuit but they haven't reached a settlement when the statute of limitations on filing a lawsuit is about to expire. Danielle assures Petra: "Don't worry: If we can't settle this and you sue me, I won't raise a statute of limitations defense." If they ultimately cannot settle the matter and Petra sues Danielle after the statute of limitations has expired, Danielle will be equitably estopped from asserting a statute of limitations defense, because it would be unfair to let her do so given her prior assurance.

The U.S. Supreme Court has said, "[I]t is well settled that the [Federal] Government may not be estopped on the same terms as any other litigant." *Heckler v. Community Health Servs. of Crawford County, Inc.*, 467 U.S. 51 (1984). We discussed a leading example of the government's special treatment in Chapter 16.B.2: In *Federal Crop Insurance Corp. v. Merrill*, 332 U.S. 380 (1947), the Court held that the government could not be estopped by bad advice that a federal official gave a pair of farmers about the insurability of the farmers' winter wheat crop. The advice was bad—and ineffective in binding the government to a contract to insure the crop—because it conflicted with a published legislative rule. This is one important effect of a legislative rule, when properly published. In another leading case on estoppel involving the government, the Court held that a federal official's bad advice could not authorize a court to order the federal government to make a payment that no statute authorized. Use of equitable estoppel to require an unauthorized payment of government funds would violate the Appropriations Clause. *Office of Personnel Mg'mt v. Richmond*, 496 U.S. 414, 424 (1990).

The Court has come close to saying that equitable estoppel can never operate against the federal government, but the Court has expressly refused to say that the federal government can never be equitably estopped. *Id.* at 434. Good reasons support the Court's "What, never? (Well, hardly ever!)" attitude toward equitably estopping the federal government.[1]

On the one hand, holding the government responsible for the misleading (but usually well intentioned) advice or conduct of its officials could have bad results. It could discourage officials from giving any advice, even though most advice is accurate, useful, and free. Furthermore, if courts started allowing people to rely on the bad advice of officials, the effect would sometimes be to allow these people to ignore laws that other people must follow (often at great effort and expense). Getting bad advice could be like hitting the lottery. Still further, if courts gave effect to bad official advice, officials might be able to nullify laws with which they did not agree by simply giving advice contradicting the law.

On the other hand, there are situations in which equitable estoppel against the government avoids unfairness without undermining the rule of law. Indeed, lower federal courts have sometimes applied equitable estoppel against the federal government. We summarize an example:

- *Molton, Allen & Williams, Inc. v. Harris*, 613 F.2d 1176 (D.C. Cir. 1980)

The firm Molton, Allen & Williams (Molton) successfully bid on federally insured mortgages and options that a federal agency was authorized to sell. The federal official responsible for the sale phoned Molton to say that: (1) the agency had accepted Molton's bids; (2) the agency had signed the bids to signify the agency's acceptance; and (3) in modern parlance, everything was "good to go." But before the official put the signed bid forms into the mail for return to Molton, the agency suspended the sales program and the official was instructed not to mail the signed forms to Molton. Molton sued government officials for breach of contract. The government argued that no contract existed because an agency manual said that acceptance of bids was not final until the signed forms reached the buyer (in this case Molton).

The court of appeals held that the agency was equitably estopped from relying on the agency manual, because of the assurances that the agency official gave Molton on the phone. The court emphasized that the official who spoke with Molton had the authority to both accept the bids on behalf of the federal government and to waive any provisions

---

1. The quoted phrase comes from a song in the 1878 play *H.M.S. Pinafore* by W.S. Gilbert and Arthur Sullivan, in which the Captain of the *Pinafore* makes two absolute assertions that, when questioned by the chorus of sailors, he is forced to qualify:

Captain: … I am never known to quail
At the fury of a gale,
And I'm never, never sick at sea!
Chorus: What, never?
Captain: No, never!
Chorus: What, never?
Captain: Well, hardly ever! …
Captain: Bad language or abuse,
I never, never use,
Whatever the emergency;
Though "bother it" I may
Occasionally say,
I never use a big, big D —
Chorus: What, never?
Captain: No, never!
Chorus: What, never?
Captain: Well, hardly ever! …

in the agency manual, including the provision making acceptance effective only upon the buyer's receipt of the signed bid forms. These circumstances distinguished the case from *Merrill*, in which federal officials purported to enter into a contract (with farmers) that the officials lacked authority to make and that violated a published, legislative rule. The court of appeals explained, "The rationale [of *Merrill*] is that a single official cannot override a statue or regulation, and that citizens dealing with the government are charged with knowledge of the law." *Id.* at 1178. That rationale did not apply in Molton's case.

Other lower court decisions on equitable estoppel against the government are collected in *Fredericks v. Comm'r of Internal Revenue*, 126 F.3d 433 (3rd Cir. 1997). They make it clear that it is possible, though rare, for equitable estoppel to operate against the federal government.

2. Special Rules of Traditional Res Judicata for Cases to Which the Government Is a Party

Government agencies not only adjudicate cases administratively but also participate as parties to judicial proceedings. We discussed the difference between the government as an adjudicator and as a litigant in Chapter 17.F. Our focus in this subsection is on the government as a litigant.

When the government (including one of its agencies) is a party to a lawsuit, the government must generally follow the same rules as other litigants. In some areas, though, the government gets special treatment. One such area concerns the rules of res judicata. For the federal government, you should be familiar with two key cases. Together, the cases establish that nonmutual issue preclusion cannot be used against the federal government in federal court.

- *United States v. Stauffer Chemical Co.*, 464 U.S. 165 (1984)

In 1980, EPA officials went to a plant in Wyoming owned by Stauffer Chemical Company and sought to inspect it under authority of the Clean Air Act. The EPA officials brought along private contractors to help with the inspection. Stauffer refused to allow the private contractors into the plant on the ground that they lacked authority under the Clean Air Act to participate in the inspection. After the EPA got an administrative warrant to inspect the Wyoming plant, Stauffer sued in Wyoming federal district court and got an injunction preventing the private contractors from participating in the EPA inspection. The U.S. Court of Appeals for the Tenth Circuit affirmed the injunction, holding that private contractors lacked statutory authority to participate in the inspection. So, Stauffer won and the EPA lost in the Tenth Circuit.

While the Wyoming litigation was going on, EPA officials tried to inspect another plant owned by Stauffer, this one in Tennessee. Again, Stauffer refused to allow the private contractors accompanying the EPA officials to participate in the inspection, contending the private contractors lacked statutory authority to do so. This time the EPA went to federal court first, seeking to hold Stauffer in civil contempt for refusing to obey an administrative warrant. The federal district court in this Tennessee lawsuit ruled in favor of the EPA. On appeal to the U.S. Court of Appeals for the Sixth Circuit, Stauffer not only made its lack-of-statutory-authority argument but also argued that, because of the intervening decision of the Tenth Circuit that ruled against the EPA, the EPA was collaterally estopped from relitigating the issue of the private contractors' authority under the Clean Air Act to participate in the search. In modern parlance, Stauffer sought to assert mutual, defensive issue preclusion. The question before the U.S. Supreme Court was whether mutual, defensive issue preclusion can be asserted against the federal government in federal court.

The U.S. Supreme Court held "yes." The Court determined that all of the elements for issue preclusion applied: the Tennessee litigation and the Wyoming litigation involved the same parties and same issue, and there were no changes of law to justify revisiting the issue. The Court also made three important points in rejecting the government's arguments for special treatment in the case before it:

1. The government argued that "the application of collateral estoppel in government litigation involving recurring issues of public importance will freeze the development of the law." *Id.* at 173. The Court responded that frozen law could be avoided by allowing only claims of *mutual* issue preclusion against the government. By requiring mutuality, for example, although the EPA could not relitigate the same issue against Stauffer that had previously been decided against the EPA, the EPA could still relitigate the issue with other companies. This reasoning strongly suggests that *nonmutual* issue preclusion cannot be used against the federal government in federal court. The Court largely confirmed that suggestion in the next case summarized, *United States v. Mendoza*, 464 U.S. 154 (1984).

2. The government also cited precedent in which the Court had "recognize[d] an exception to the applicability of the principles of collateral estoppel for 'unmixed questions of law' arising in 'successive actions involving unrelated subject matter.'" *Id.* at 171 (quoting *Montana v. United States*, 440 U.S. 147, 162 (1979)). The Court in *Stauffer* said the exception did not apply in the case before it, because the Wyoming and Tennessee lawsuits involved related subject matter. The Court also cast doubt on the validity of any exception to collateral estoppel for "unmixed questions of law."

3. The Court in *Stauffer* reserved the question whether collateral estoppel against the federal government should work differently when issues arise under the federal tax laws. *Id.* at 172 n. 5.

• *United States v. Mendoza*, 464 U.S. 154 (1984)

In *Mendoza* the Court held that the doctrine of nonmutual, offensive issue preclusion cannot be used against the federal government in federal court.

This issue arose from two lawsuits against the federal government. In the first, plaintiffs sued the United States claiming that its administration of an immigration statute denied Filipino nationals due process. This set of plaintiffs prevailed on their due process claim in a federal district court decision that the government did not appeal. Later, Sergio Mendoza, a Filipino national, asserted the very same due process claim against the United States as had the plaintiffs in the earlier litigation. Mr. Mendoza asserted his claim in seeking to become a naturalized U.S. citizen. Mr. Mendoza was not a party to the prior lawsuit.

The Court held that the federal government was not estopped in Mr. Mendoza's case from relitigating the due process issue that had been decided against it in the prior lawsuit. In so holding, the Court adopted a categorical rule barring the use of nonmutual, offensive issue preclusion against the federal government in federal court. Its reasoning (reinforced by the decision in *Stauffer Chemical*) seems likewise to preclude nonmutual, *defensive* issue preclusion from being used against the federal government. The Court relied on the broad range of issues of public importance that the federal government often litigates in cases involving different parties. The Court worried that, if the federal government had only one shot to litigate an issue and were thereafter precluded from relitigating it against anyone else, the law would become frozen with respect to many important issues that need to be revisited from time to time in light of changes in the law and the outside world.

* * *

As we leave this subject, we emphasize the special rules for the federal government relate specifically to nonmutual issue preclusion. Under those rules, the federal government simply is not subject to nonmutual issue preclusion, whereas it *is* subject to defensive, mutual issue preclusion. (The Court has not addressed whether offensive, mutual issue preclusion can be asserted against the federal government.) As distinguished from issue preclusion, claim preclusion can indeed be asserted against the federal government seemingly on the same terms as private parties. *See, e.g., Nevada v. United States*, 463 U.S. 110 (1983) (res judicata prevented United States from suing for water rights in addition to those awarded to the United States in prior lawsuit). Thus, the United States may not assert against another party a claim that the United States asserted or could have asserted in a prior lawsuit against the same party, if that prior suit ended in a valid, final judgment on the merits.

Lower federal courts have suggested that state governments might also get special treatment in federal court litigation where a party asserts nonmutual issue preclusion against them. *See, e.g., Chambers v. Ohio Dep't of Human Servs.*, 145 F.3d 793 (6th Cir. 1998). Some state courts have held as a matter of state common law that nonmutual issue preclusion is not available in their courts against their State. *See, e.g., Sikorsky Aircraft Corp. v. Comm'r of Revenue Servs.*, 1 A.3d 1033, 1037–1038 (Conn. 2010).

The takeaway from this discussion is that the preclusion doctrines must be handled with care when someone seeks to use them against a government entity. Preclusion may be available in some situations but not in others.

3. Agency Non-Acquiescence

Above we discussed U.S. Supreme Court cases holding that nonmutual issue preclusion is not available against the federal government. The idea behind these cases is that, to prevent the development of the law from freezing, the government should be able to relitigate against party *B* an issue that the government has previously litigated—unsuccessfully—against party *A*. Thus, in *Stauffer Chemical*, although EPA lost in a Wyoming lawsuit on the issue whether private contractors could participate in EPA inspections under the Clean Air Act, the EPA could relitigate that issue elsewhere in the country, as long as the EPA didn't try to relitigate the issue against the same party (Stauffer Chemical) that prevailed in the prior lawsuit.

When you play out this scenario, you will see that, while it allows development of the law, it also poses risks of disuniformity and unequal treatment under the law.

You may recall that the EPA's litigation with Stauffer Chemical in Wyoming went up to the Tenth Circuit, which held that private contractors lacked authority under the Clean Air Act to participate in inspections. The Court's decision in *Stauffer Chemical* suggests that the EPA could refuse to be bound by the Tenth Circuit's holding—at least for inspections EPA conducted outside the geographic boundaries of the Tenth Circuit. If the EPA took that suggestion and continued to try to include private contractors in inspections in other circuits, the EPA would be engaging in "inter-circuit non-acquiescence." In fact, several federal agencies do engage in inter-circuit non-acquiescence.

You might wonder: How does this encourage development of the law? The answer is: It heightens the possibility that either the U.S. Supreme Court will review an issue or a lower federal court will reconsider its decision. If the EPA thinks the Tenth Circuit's decision is wrong but nonetheless complies with that decision in inspections throughout the United States, the Tenth Circuit's decision will be the final word. In contrast, if the EPA continues to try to use private contractors for inspections outside the Tenth Circuit, other federal courts, including other federal courts of appeals, may eventually consider the issue. If they disagree with the Tenth Circuit, the U.S. Supreme Court may then grant review to resolve the conflict among the circuits on the issue of whether private contractors can participate in inspections under the Clean Air Act. Alternately, perhaps the Tenth Circuit will eventually reconsider its decision if enough other federal courts disagree with it. Given that possibility, the EPA may even be justified, at some point, in engaging in *intra-circuit* non-acquiescence, to give the Tenth Circuit a vehicle for revisiting its earlier decision. In short, agency non-acquiescence may be an appropriate way to keep an issue percolating through the legal system, with the objective of having multiple courts weigh in, heightening the opportunity for an ultimately correct, uniform result—which may differ from the result reached by the first court to address the issue.

It may take a while for an issue to be resolved by the U.S. Supreme Court or for the lower federal courts to reach agreement on its proper resolution. In the meantime, people in different parts of the country may be subject to different legal regimes. For example, companies in the Tenth Circuit would not be exposed to EPA inspections that included private contractors, but companies in the Sixth Circuit would be so exposed (if the Sixth Circuit disagrees with the Tenth Circuit's view that private contractors lack authority to participate in inspections). Allowing development of the law inevitably entails a period of disuniformity and unequal treatment.

For this reason, administrative law scholars who've studied agency non-acquiescence generally agree that, assuming it's appropriate, agencies should do what they can to facilitate U.S. Supreme Court review of the issue as to which the agency does not acquiesce—such as by petitioning for U.S. Supreme Court review or by not opposing U.S. Supreme Court review in an appropriate case. Agencies should also be willing to throw in the towel when they keep losing after repeatedly litigating the same issue in different parts of the country.

The non-acquiescence issue arises more often for issues arising in agency adjudications than for issues arising in agency rulemaking. If a federal court of appeals sets aside an agency *rule*, that invalidates the rule completely, according to one federal court of appeals; the rule can't operate anywhere. *See Nat'l Mining Ass'n v. U.S. Army Corp of Eng'rs*, 145 F.3d 1399, 1409 (D.C. Cir. 1998); *see also Monsanto Co. v. Geertson Seed Farms*, 130 S.Ct. 2743, 2761 (2010) (accepting government's representation that federal district court's vacatur of agency decision would have nationwide effect). If that's correct, the agency has no option to refuse to acquiesce in the court's decision by treating the rule as still valid outside the geographic boundaries of the court of appeals' jurisdiction. In contrast, a court decision setting aside an agency's adjudicatory decision does not bind the agency in adjudications involving other parties in courts in other jurisdictions.

Even so, a federal court could decide that an agency's decision in an adjudication— say, an adjudication of person *A*'s entitlement to benefits under the Social Security Act— rests on a legal error that infects adjudications throughout the United States. Could the court in that situation enter a nationwide injunction to prevent the agency from repeating the error in adjudications that arise outside the geographic boundaries of the court's jurisdiction and that involve parties *B*, *C*, etc.? Surprisingly, the U.S. Supreme Court has never directly addressed that issue. If a federal court could enter such a nationwide injunction, this would prevent agency non-acquiescence. That very result could weigh against its validity if the Court considers it important to allow an agency to litigate the same issue multiple times to permit development of the law.

Of course, once the U.S. Supreme Court decides an issue adversely to the agency, there is no question that the agency is bound by that decision. (That is why they call it Supreme!) Until then, the Court's decisions freeing the federal government from the restrictions of nonmutual issue preclusion allow it to litigate the same issue in cases throughout the country as long as each case involves a different party and the agency determines that non-acquiescence is warranted.

Before we leave this topic, make sure you understand its relationship to the government's freedom from nonmutual issue preclusion. This freedom, designed to prevent the law's development from freezing, allows the government to relitigate (with different parties) issues that have been resolved against it in prior litigation, at least when the relitigation takes place outside the jurisdiction of the court that decided the prior case. Although the term "non-acquiescence" implies improper intransigence, the propriety of the practice is not so simple.

E. Chapter 26 Wrap Up and Look Ahead

An agency decision in an adjudication, once final, generally (1) binds the parties and the agency with respect to the particular case decided; (2) may serve as precedent for the agency in future adjudications; and (3) may have claim- or issue-preclusive effect in later court proceedings. Exceptions or qualifications exist to all of these effects, however, including (1) an agency's issuance of non-binding advisory opinions; (2) an agency's relative freedom to depart from its precedent as long as it acknowledges and justifies the departure; and (3) situations in which a statute modifies or eliminates the preclusive effect of an agency's decision in a later, judicial proceeding. When you put these general principles and qualifications together, you can understand why we call agency adjudicatory power only a "quasi-judicial" power.

In exploring the effects of an agency adjudication, this chapter introduced you to three other areas of administrative law. They concern (1) the limited (hardly ever!) availability of equitable estoppel against the government; (2) the federal government's freedom from having nonmutual issue preclusion asserted against it in federal court; and (3) the government's selective practice of non-acquiescence in lower court decisions as a means of allowing for the development of the law.

This chapter completes our exploration of agency adjudication. The next chapter begins our examination of judicial review of "agency action," a term that is both colloquially used, and often statutorily defined, to include agency adjudication, agency rulemaking, and other agency action, including the failure to act.

Chapter Problem 1 Revisited

1. We hope that after studying this chapter you appreciate the complexity underlying the question whether the Commission's decision in an adjudication

involving ThinAgain, Inc. is "binding" on Splendor, Inc. The Commission's ThinAgain decision does not directly bind Splendor, because Splendor was not a party to the Commission proceeding. But the Commission's decision on the legality of conduct by ThinAgain has relevance for the legality of similar conduct by Splendor. Setting aside for the moment the issue of judicial review, if the Commission commences an adjudication against Splendor, the Commission presumably will follow its ThinAgain decision under the doctrine of administrative stare decisis. If you represent Splendor, you therefore must convince the Commission either that it should not follow its precedent or that the precedent is distinguishable in a way that causes it not to control your case.

2. If the Ninth Circuit invalidates the Commission's ThinAgain decision, Splendor cannot use defensive, nonmutual issue preclusion to prevent the Commission from seeking to re-litigate any issues that arose in the litigation against ThinAgain. But the Ninth Circuit's decision in the ThinAgain case will serve as precedent for the Ninth Circuit, and the Ninth Circuit will presumably follow that precedent with respect to its decision on issues of law, if those same issues arise on review of the Commission's decision in the Splendor case. Therefore, if Splendor loses in the adjudication before the Commission, it should seek judicial review in the Ninth Circuit if possible, to take advantage of the favorable precedent. Splendor's ability to seek review in the Ninth Circuit will depend on the law governing venue in cases seeking judicial review of the Commission's decisions.

Chapter Problem 2 Revisited

Chapter Problem 2 asks you to take the perspective of a lawyer representing plaintiffs in a class action against ThinAgain. The first question concerns what effect, if any, the Commission decision might have on the class action. The second question asks about the effect of a court of appeals' affirmance or invalidation of the Commission's ThinAgain decision.

1. The Commission's adjudicatory decision against ThinAgain, if not set aside on judicial review, may have administrative res judicata effect in a civil action in federal court against ThinAgain. Specifically, ThinAgain may have litigated and lost on some issues before the Commission that could also arise in the class action. For example, if the Commission found that ThinAgain's advertisements were deliberately false, that determination might have preclusive effect in the class action for fraud against ThinAgain.

Something similar happened in a traditional collateral estoppel setting in *Parklane Hosiery Co., Inc. v. Shore*, 439 U.S. 322 (1979). The Securities and Exchange Commission (SEC) sued Parklane Hosiery and other defendants in federal court for issuing a materially false and misleading proxy statement. The federal court ruled in favor of the SEC, holding that the proxy statement was materially false and misleading. In a separate federal court lawsuit, a stockholder sued Parklane and other defendants seeking to hold them civilly liable for issuing that very same proxy statement. The U.S. Supreme Court held that Parklane and the other defendants were collaterally estopped from relitigating in the stockholder suit the issue whether the proxy statement was materially false and misleading.

The chapter problem, unlike *Parklane Hosiery*, involves an initial adjudication before an agency, rather than a court. The question is whether the agency adjudication has administrative res judicata effect. To determine whether the decision has such effect, you will have to research and analyze these issues:

a. What source of law governs whether the Commission's decision may have administrative res judicata effect? As discussed in the chapter, the federal common law principles of *Utah Construction & Mining* presumptively apply, unless modified by a federal statute or by the federal court's determination, when adjudicating your client's state-law claims, that state law should govern under either the *Erie* doctrine or the theory that federal common law should incorporate state law in a diversity action involving the administrative res judicata effect of a federal agency's adjudicatory decision.

b. Whatever law governs, how does it apply here? For example, if the *Utah Construction & Mining* principles govern, you must analyze whether the Commission was acting in a judicial capacity and whether ThinAgain had an adequate opportunity to litigate in the Commission adjudication. In general, formal adjudications by federal agencies will satisfy the *Utah Construction & Mining* requirements for administrative res judicata. Still, a complete analysis must include examination of the agency legislation and agency rules for the Commission adjudication, the record of the proceeding against ThinAgain, and case law on the preclusive effect of Commission decisions.

c. Assuming the Commission's adjudication can have administrative res judicata effect in the class action, the question remains whether the traditional res judicata requirements are satisfied. For example, are any of the issues in the class action indeed the same as any issues actually litigated and decided in the Commission adjudication and necessary to the Commission's decision in that adjudication?

2. If the Ninth Circuit sets aside the Commission's ThinAgain decision, the decision can have no preclusive effect in the New Jersey class action. The Ninth Circuit's decision setting aside the Commission's decision, though favorable to ThinAgain, cannot have any preclusive effect against your clients, the plaintiffs in the New Jersey class action, because they were not parties (nor were they in privity with any parties) to the Ninth Circuit action. The Due Process Clause prevents the preclusion doctrine from operating against your clients. *See Richards v. Jefferson County*, 517 U.S. 793, 798 (1996).

If the Ninth Circuit upholds the Commission's ThinAgain decision, the Commission's decision has essentially the same preclusive effect, if any, as if it had gone unreviewed by any court. In other words, The Ninth Circuit's decision upholding the Commission's decision does not give the Commission's decision any "extra" preclusive effect, under the federal common law of administrative res judicata. Furthermore, the Ninth Circuit decision itself—as distinguished from the Commission decision upheld by the Ninth Circuit—is unlikely to have any preclusive effect in the New Jersey class action. That is because, under the statute authorizing judicial review of Commission decisions, the Ninth Circuit will only determine whether "substantial evidence" supports the Commission's factual determination. That determination won't be relevant in the New Jersey class action. For example, the plaintiffs in the New Jersey class action may have to prove by a preponderance of the evidence that ThinAgain made deliberately false claims about its product. Perhaps the Commission itself found such deliberate falsity by a preponderance of the evidence. The Commission's finding may have preclusive effect. But for reasons that will become apparent when we discuss the "substantial evidence" standard of judicial review in Chapter 33, the Ninth Circuit's determination that there was substantial evidence to support that finding doesn't really help the New Jersey plaintiffs in their effort to meet the preponderance-of-the-evidence standard. This is why the Ninth Circuit's decision doesn't add to the preclusive effect of the Commission's decision.

Professional Development Reflection Question

The chapter problem involves a lawyer who works as an in-house counsel to a corporation. Besides working for corporations, lawyers work in other institutional settings, such as government agencies and law firms. One of the challenges for a lawyer taking a job in some institutional setting is learning the institutional culture. This can pose a particular challenge for new law school graduates who have not had much experience working for an organization. And law schools do not teach students explicitly how to meet that challenge. Perhaps it can't be taught outside experiential settings such as internships.

Just the same, it may interest you to read an experienced lawyer's advice about the culture of law firms:

> ... After you start working at [a] firm, ... put a lot of effort into learning the culture of the firm.
>
> The "myths" and "legends" of the firm can help you out. If the managing partners of the firm shared a table in the library for their first few years in the firm, you'll want to hesitate before you demand new furniture. An oft-repeated tale of a female partner who called into the office within an hour of giving birth to a child can give you a clue as to what lawyers will think of your request for substantial paternity leave ...
>
> ... Talk to people and listen carefully to the stories ...

Dennis Kennedy, *Twenty Lessons for Lawyers Starting Their Careers* (Mar. 2005), available at American Bar Association, Law Practice Management Section, http://apps.americanbar.org/lpm/lpt/articles/mgt03053.html (May 2012). To this advice, we would only add that you are even better off learning as much as possible about a firm's culture *before* you start working at the firm. After all, given the choice, you may not want to work at a firm that will begrudge you furniture and paternity (or maternity) leave.

To help you internalize the importance of learning institutional culture, we pose this question: Suppose a student had just transferred to your law school and asked you to explain the law school's culture. What would you say?

PART FOUR

Judicial Review

Chapter 27

Introduction to Judicial
Review of Agency Action

Overview

This short chapter introduces Part Four of this book, which explores judicial review of agency action. The chapter's sections are entitled:

A. Importance of Judicial Review of Agency Action

B. Two Aspects of Judicial Review of Agency Action

C. Roadmap of Part 4

A. Context

Judicial review of agency action is an important subject in administrative law. It has importance for our system of government, for the people affected by agency action, for the agency itself, and for students and practitioners of administrative law.

Judicial review has importance for our system of government because it helps ensure executive-branch officials and agencies obey the law. A famous scholar said: "The availability of judicial review is the necessary condition, psychologically if not logically, for a system of administrative power which purports to be legitimate, or legally valid." Louis L. Jaffe, Judicial Control of Administrative Action 320 (1965). From this perspective, a landmark case of constitutional law is also a landmark case in administrative law. That case is *Marbury v. Madison*, which established the power of courts to review actions of the executive branch. 5 U.S. (1 Cranch) 137 (1803).

Judicial review has importance for the public interests and private interests affected by agency action. The public has an interest in agency regulation of the environment, food safety, regulation of the financial sector, and many other matters. Agency action also affects the ability of individuals to pursue livelihoods and even in many cases to keep roofs over their heads and to receive life-sustaining health care. Public health, individual livelihoods, and even individual lives depend on agencies obeying the law, which judicial review helps ensure.

Judicial review has importance for agencies because agency behavior is influenced by the operation and even the mere prospect of judicial review. Courts have the power to grant remedies from wrongful agency action; in this sense, agencies are ultimately subordinate to the courts. Moreover, agencies shape their behavior to avoid lawsuits and to ensure that, when they are sued, their action is defensible. The mere potential for judicial review helps keep agencies in line.

Finally, judicial review has importance for law students and lawyers even though only a small percentage of agency matters becomes the subject of a lawsuit for judicial review. The lawyer strives to resolve a matter favorably to the client when the matter is before the agency. Yet the lawyer also handles the matter at the agency level to maximize the chance of a successful judicial challenge if that becomes necessary. To achieve that aim, the student must learn and the lawyer must understand the law of judicial review of agency action.

B. Two Aspects of Judicial Review of Agency Action

In law school courses on administrative law, the topic of judicial review is customarily divided into two sub-topics named (1) the *availability* of judicial review; and (2) the *scope* of judicial review. Material on the availability of judicial review answers the broad question:

(1) How do you get judicial review of agency action?

Material on the scope of judicial review answers the broad question:

(2) When you get judicial review, what exactly do you get? In other words, what does judicial review of agency action involve?

It may be helpful for you to know the basic answers to these questions up front:

(1) Availability: Judicial review of agency action is usually available to someone adversely affected by the agency action.

(2) Scope: Courts often give agencies the benefit of the doubt when it comes to (a) the agencies' interpretation of the statutes that they administer and the rules they issue; and (b) the agencies' factual determinations relevant to the matter before the agency. If the court nonetheless decides that agency action is flawed, the court typically sets aside the agency action.

C. Roadmap of Part Four (Judicial Review)

As discussed above, the study of judicial review divides into learning the law, and learning how to analyze, (1) the availability of judicial review; and (2) the scope of judicial review. We will enumerate the elements of each subject.

Availability: To get judicial review of agency action, you must (a) find a court that has jurisdiction to review that particular agency action; (b) have a cause of action entitling you to review of that particular agency action; and (c) seek judicial review at the appropriate time. These requirements are examined in Chapters 28 through 30:

- Chapter 28. Jurisdiction and Venue
- Chapter 29. Cause of Action
- Chapter 30. Timing

Scope: Chapter 31 gives a big-picture view of the subject of scope of review. Chapters after that examine: specific *standards* of judicial review that courts apply when reviewing various aspects of various agency actions; and the judicial *remedies* available when agency action fails judicial review:

- Chapter 32. Questions of Law
- Chapter 33. Substantial Evidence
- Chapter 34. Arbitrary and Capricious
- Chapter 35. Specialized Review Situations; Remedies

Chapter 36 bids you farewell.

Chapter 28

Jurisdiction and Venue

Overview

To get judicial review of an administrative agency's action, you must identify a court with jurisdiction. Jurisdiction is a multi-faceted concept, but it boils down to a matter of power. In this book, within this chapter, we focus on three requirements for a court to have jurisdiction (power) to review agency action. The first requirement is that a statute must authorize the federal court to exercise subject matter jurisdiction over the case. The second requirement is that the lawsuit seeking judicial review cannot be barred by sovereign immunity. The third requirement is that the plaintiff must have "standing."

This chapter not only explores jurisdiction but also touches on venue, which lawyers often group with jurisdiction, though the concepts are distinct.

Here are the titles of this chapter's sections:

A. Jurisdiction: The Requirement for a Statute Granting Jurisdiction

B. Jurisdiction: Sovereign Immunity

C. Jurisdiction: Standing Requirements in Federal Court

D. Jurisdiction: Standing Requirements in State Courts

E. Venue

F. Chapter 28 Wrap Up and Look Ahead

Chapter Problem

You have offered your services pro bono to a local group of bird watchers, who prefer to call themselves "birders" and who call their group "Birders of Paradise" (BOP). BOP has asked you to assess the likelihood of a successful federal-court challenge to a shopping mall development. BOP opposes the development because it will destroy 150 acres of wetlands that members of BOP regularly visit to watch birds.

You are currently analyzing the "dredge and fill permit" issued for the project by the U.S. Army Corps of Engineers. The permit allows the mall developers to fill in the existing wetlands, if they create other wetlands in the area and take other mitigation measures. The Corps issued the permit under §404 of the Clean Water Act (CWA), 33 U.S.C. §1344 (2012), and implementing regulations.

You believe the Corps' issuance of the permit may have violated two federal statutes: §404 of the CWA, which, as implemented by regulations, puts stringent conditions on issuance of a permit; and the National Environmental Policy Act (NEPA), 42 U.S.C. §4332(2)(C) (2012), which requires an environmental impact statement (EIS) for proposed federal actions significantly affecting the environment. In this case, the Corps did not prepare an EIS because it believed that the development will not significantly affect the environment.

Now you must analyze whether BOP can get judicial review of the permit and challenge it as violating the CWA and the NEPA. You have so far determined that the CWA has a "citizen suit" provision in 33 U.S.C. § 1365 (2012); in contrast, the NEPA lacks a citizen suit provision.

As you see it, your next steps are to:

1. Analyze the CWA's citizen suit provision to determine whether it gives a court jurisdiction over BOP's CWA claim, its NEPA claim, or both.

2. If not, consider what other statute might confer jurisdiction on some court over those claims.

3. Consider whether sovereign immunity might bar a lawsuit by BOP against the Corps.

4. Analyze whether BOP has standing to assert its CWA and NEPA claims in federal court.

You will want to write out your thoughts as you work through each step.

A. Jurisdiction: The Requirement for a Statute Granting Jurisdiction

Because federal courts are courts of limited power, the plaintiff seeking relief from a federal court has the burden of establishing that the court has power to decide the plaintiff's suit. One thing the plaintiff must do to meet that burden is identify a statute granting subject matter jurisdiction over the suit. In most federal-court suits seeking review of federal agency action, one of two kinds of federal statutes will grant subject matter jurisdiction:

(1) specialized jurisdictional statutes; or

(2) general jurisdictional statutes.

This section explores these two types of jurisdictional statutes. It also explains that the federal APA is *not* a jurisdiction-granting statute. Then it discusses the jurisdiction of state courts to review state agency action.

1. Specialized Statutory Grants of Jurisdiction

The agency legislation or other federal statute may grant subject matter jurisdiction to specific courts to review specific agency actions. These are called "special review" statutes.

Although we now focus on how these special review statutes grant subject matter jurisdiction, special review statutes may also carry out other functions related to judicial review of agency action. First, in addition to granting subject matter jurisdiction, special review statutes also usually create a *cause of action* — i.e., an entitlement to judicial relief for improper agency action. We will examine the cause of action requirement in Chapter 29. In addition, special review statutes may govern venue; establish time limits within which judicial review must be sought; and impose other requirements for judicial review, such as the requirement that the plaintiff have first exhausted all administrative remedies. In short, many special review statutes work like Swiss army knives.

As a general rule, when a special review statute applies, it provides the exclusive way to get judicial review. Hard questions can arise about whether a special review statute applies to a particular lawsuit seeking review of a particular agency action and, if so, whether the special review statute should be interpreted, in accordance with the general rule, to be exclusive.

a. Examples of Special Review Statutes

We will show examples of (1) special review statutes granting subject matter jurisdiction to federal courts of appeals and (2) special review statutes granting subject matter jurisdiction to federal district courts.

Special review statutes may designate judicial review in a federal court of appeals. Under these statutes, the plaintiff (often called a "petitioner") skips the federal district court. For example, this special review statute authorizes court-of-appeals review of certain actions of the Administrator of the EPA under the Clean Air Act:

---

42 U.S.C. § 7607. Administrative proceedings and judicial review [from Clean Air Act] ...

(b) Judicial review

(1) A petition for review of action of the Administrator [of EPA] in promulgating any national primary or secondary ambient air quality standard, any emission standard or requirement under section 7412 of this title, any standard of performance or requirement under section 7411 of this title, any standard under section 7521 of this title (other than a standard required to be prescribed under section 7521(b)(1) of this title), any determination under section 7521(b)(5) of this title, any control or prohibition under section 7545 of this title, any standard under section 7571 of this title, any rule issued under section 7413, 7419, or under section 7420 of this title, or any other nationally applicable regulations promulgated, or final action taken, by the Administrator under this chapter may be filed only in the United States Court of Appeals for the District of Columbia....

This provision actually accomplishes several things in one fell swoop: It waives the federal government's sovereign immunity from private actions; it grants a cause of action; and, most relevant for our current discussion, it gives the U.S. Court of Appeals for the D.C. Circuit subject matter jurisdiction (and specifies that same court as the appropriate venue). In portions of the provision that we have omitted, the provision also addresses mechanics of judicial review such as deadlines for seeking it.

The special review statute above came from the agency legislation, the Clean Air Act being one of the many statutes that the EPA administers. Not all special review statutes are located in agency legislation. The Hobbs Act, also known as the Administrative Orders Review Act, is a well-known special review statute that is codified in the Judicial Code: Title 28 of the U.S. Code. The central provision in the Hobbs Act reads as follows:

---

28 U.S.C. § 2342. Jurisdiction of court of appeals

The court of appeals (other than the United States Court of Appeals for the Federal Circuit) has exclusive jurisdiction to enjoin, set aside, suspend (in whole or in part), or to determine the validity of—

(1) all final orders of the Federal Communications Commission made reviewable by section 402(a) of title 47;

(2) all final orders of the Secretary of Agriculture made under chapters 9 and 20A of title 7, except orders issued under sections 210(e), 217a, and 499g(a) of title 7;

(3) all rules, regulations, or final orders of—

(A) the Secretary of Transportation issued pursuant to section 50501, 50502, 56101–56104, or 57109 of title 46 or pursuant to part B or C of subtitle IV, subchapter III of chapter 311, chapter 313, or chapter 315 of title 49; and

(B) the Federal Maritime Commission issued pursuant to section 305, 41304, 41308, or 41309 or chapter 421 or 441 of title 46;

(4) all final orders of the Atomic Energy Commission made reviewable by section 2239 of title 42;

(5) all rules, regulations, or final orders of the Surface Transportation Board made reviewable by section 2321 of this title;

(6) all final orders under section 812 of the Fair Housing Act; and

(7) all final agency actions described in section 20114(c) of title 49.

Jurisdiction is invoked by filing a petition as provided by section 2344 of this title.

The Hobbs Act not only grants exclusive subject matter jurisdiction to the courts of appeals for review of the specified agency actions but also, in other provisions that we will not reproduce here, addresses venue and various mechanics of judicial review, such as deadlines for seeking judicial review.

Where agency decisions are voluminous, highly fact specific, and focused on individual characteristics, a special review statute may authorize review in a federal district court. For example, judicial review of adjudications by the Social Security Administration on claims for benefits are reviewed in the district courts under 42 U.S.C. § 405(g) (2012):

---

42 U.S.C. § 405. Evidence, procedure, and certification for payments ...

(g) Judicial review

Any individual, after any final decision of the Commissioner of Social Security made after a hearing to which he was a party, irrespective of the amount in controversy, may obtain a review of such decision by a civil action commenced within sixty days after the mailing to him of notice of such decision or within such further time as the Commissioner of Social Security may allow. Such action shall be brought in the district court of the United States for the judicial district in which the plaintiff resides, or has his principal place of business, or, if he does not reside or have his principal place of business within any such judicial district, in the United States District Court for the District of Columbia. As part of the Commissioner's answer the Commissioner of Social Security shall file a certified copy of the transcript of the record including the evidence upon which the findings and decision complained of are based. The court shall have power to enter, upon the pleadings and transcript of the record, a judgment affirming, modifying, or reversing the decision of the Commissioner of Social Security, with or without remanding the cause for a rehearing.…

Even when review occurs in the district court, rather than the court of appeals, judicial review is ordinarily limited to the record before the agency. The district court usually does not take additional evidence, much less hold a trial. We explore this feature of judicial review in more detail in Chapter 31.D.

b. Exclusivity of Special Review Statutes

Administrative lawyers often encounter questions about how to interpret a special review statute. Two such questions are:

- whether a particular special review statute authorizes review of a particular agency action; and,
- if so, whether a special review statute provides the *exclusive* way to get review of the agency action that the statute covers.

Because these two types of question arise often, it will help you to see an example of each.

The Court had to decide whether a special review statute covered a particular agency action in *Florida Power & Light Co. v. Lorion*, 470 U.S. 729 (1985). The Atomic Energy Act authorized federal courts of appeals to review, pursuant to the Hobbs Act, orders entered by the Nuclear Regulatory Commission in certain licensing "proceeding[s]." *Id.* at 733 (discussing and quoting statutes). The question was whether a licensing decision made by the Commission without a hearing was made in a "proceeding" within the meaning of the Atomic Energy Act. The Court held that the Commission's decision was made in a "proceeding," and that the Hobbs Act therefore gave the federal court of appeals exclusive jurisdiction over a judicial challenge to that decision. *Id.* at 734–746. The Court based its holding partly on legislative history indicating that Congress intended to avoid the duplication of judicial effort that would occur if Commission decisions were subject to review by a district court and then by a court of appeals. *Id.* at 741–745.

When a special review statute authorizes review of a particular agency action, the statute may expressly state that it provides the exclusive way to get judicial review of the agency actions it covers. For example, a provision in the Mine Safety and Health Act says that judicial review of mine safety and health standards issued under the Act occurs exclusively in the United States Court of Appeals for the District of Columbia Circuit. *See* 30 U.S.C. § 811(d) (2012). Therefore, if someone sues in a federal *district* court to challenge a mine safety and health standard, the district court must dismiss the suit for lack of subject matter jurisdiction or transfer it to the D.C. Circuit. *See, e.g., In re Howard*, 570 F.3d 752, 756 (6th Cir. 2009); *see also* 28 U.S.C. § 1631 (2012).

Sometimes a special review statute does not make clear whether it provides the exclusive way to get judicial review of an agency action it covers. Indeed, sometimes a special review statute is worded permissively. For example, a provision in the Occupational Safety and Health Act says a person adversely affected by a workplace safety and health standard promulgated under that Act "*may* … fil[e] a petition … for a judicial review of such standard" in the U.S. Court of Appeals where the person resides or has his or her principal place of business. 29 U.S.C. § 655(f)

(2012) (emphasis added). Despite the permissive wording of § 655(f), courts have construed it to provide the exclusive means for judicial review of OSHA workplace safety and health standards. *See, e.g., Public Citizen Health Research. Grp.*, 314 F.3d 143, 150–151 (3rd Cir. 2002). Thus, the permissive language "may ... file" just means you have the option of seeking judicial review or not. But it does not give you an option of either seeking judicial review as it prescribes or, instead, seeking judicial review under a different statute, such as the federal question statute. The moral is that you shouldn't take a special review statute at face value without having studied the case law interpreting it.

The case law interpreting 29 U.S.C. § 655(f) to prescribe the exclusive means for judicial review of covered agency OSHA actions reflects a more general principle: "If ... there exists a special statutory review procedure, it is ordinarily supposed that Congress intended that procedure to be the exclusive means of obtaining judicial review in those cases to which it applies." *City of Rochester v. Bond*, 603 F.2d 927, 931 (D.C. Cir. 1979). The rationale is that "coherence and economy are best served if all suits pertaining to designated agency decisions are segregated in particular courts." *Id.* at 936.

One special review statute, the Hobbs Act, is especially special. The D.C. Circuit has interpreted the Hobbs Act to authorize review of a type of agency action — namely, agency delay — not expressly covered by the Act. In the case adopting this interpretation, the plaintiffs — who are called "petitioners" under the Hobbs Act — claimed that the Federal Communications Commission (FCC) had unreasonably delayed taking final action in proceedings about supposed overcharges by the phone company AT&T. *Telecomm. Research & Action Ctr. v. FCC*, 750 F.2d 70 (D.C. Cir. 1984) (hereafter referred to as the *TRAC* case). The Hobbs Act gives the federal courts of appeals exclusive jurisdiction to review final orders of the FCC. *See* 28 U.S.C. § 2342(1) (2012). But the plaintiffs in *TRAC* weren't challenging any final order of the FCC; "indeed, the lack of a final order [was] the very gravamen of the petitioners' complaint." *TRAC*, 750 F.2d at 75. The D.C. Circuit nonetheless held that it, rather than a federal district court, had exclusive jurisdiction over the claim of unreasonable delay by the FCC.

The D.C. Circuit based its jurisdiction in *TRAC* on the Hobbs Act together with the All Writs Act. The All Writs Act authorizes the federal courts to issue "all writs necessary or appropriate in aid of their respective jurisdictions." 28 U.S.C. § 1651 (2012). The D.C. Circuit reasoned that it had to take jurisdiction over a claim about the FCC's unreasonable delay to protect its jurisdiction to review the ultimate outcome of the FCC proceeding. The court reasoned: "Because the statutory obligation of a Court of Appeals to review [the FCC's final order] on the merits may be defeated by an agency that fails to resolve disputes, a Circuit Court may resolve claims of unreasonable delay in order to protect its future jurisdiction." *TRAC*, 750 F.2d at 76. That reasoning extends to claims of delay by other federal agencies the actions of which are subject to review exclusively in the federal courts of appeals under the Hobbs Act.

The upshot of this discussion is that analysis of the availability of judicial review of a particular agency action begins with a search for any special review statute. If such a statute exists and applies to the agency action under analysis, it ordinarily provides the exclusive way to get judicial review of the agency action.

Exercise: Identifying Special Review Statutes

The Consumer Product Safety Act is codified at 15 U.S.C. §§ 2051–2089 (2012). Please review the Act to find its special review provision. Does it address whether it provides the exclusive way to get judicial review of the agency actions it covers?

---

2. General Jurisdiction Statutes

If no special statutory review provision confers subject matter jurisdiction, the plaintiff must identify another statute as the basis for jurisdiction in the court in which the plaintiff has sued. Several federal statutes grant subject matter jurisdiction in broad terms, earning them the name "general jurisdiction statutes."

The most important general jurisdiction statute, without question, is the federal question statute: 28 U.S.C. § 1331 (2012). It gives federal district courts "original jurisdiction of all civil actions arising under the Constitution, laws, or treaties of the United States." *Id.* The federal question statute is probably the most commonly used general jurisdiction statute for review of federal agency action. Virtually all lawsuits for review of federal agency action present a federal question and therefore fall within the federal district courts' federal question jurisdiction — unless a special review statute provides for exclusive review elsewhere for a particular agency action.

The federal question statute, unlike many special review statutes, only grants subject matter jurisdiction. It does not create a cause of action for review of federal agency action. Therefore, plaintiffs who rely on the federal question statute for subject matter jurisdiction must look elsewhere for a law creating a cause of action. The most common such law, by far, is the good old federal APA.

The federal question statute is not the only broad grant of subject matter jurisdiction that may provide a jurisdictional platform for challenging federal agency action. Other remedies available under broad statutory grants of subject matter jurisdiction include habeas corpus under 28 U.S.C. §§ 2241–2255 (2012); district court mandamus actions brought under 28 U.S.C. § 1361 (2012), to compel an officer of the government or an agency to perform a nondiscretionary duty owed to the plaintiff, *see United States ex rel. Schonbrun v. Commanding Officer*, 403 F.2d 371 (2d Cir. 1968); and actions for money damages under the Federal Tort Claims Act, 28 U.S.C. § 1346(b) (2012). If you find this growing list of jurisdictional possibilities daunting, you will be glad to know that a federal statute authorizes the transfer of a case "in the interest of justice" from one federal court to another when the first court lacks jurisdiction over the case. 28 U.S.C. § 1631 (2012).

Even so, careful research is necessary both to identify jurisdictional statutes that exist but are not yet known to the attorney as well as to confirm that statutes believed to be applicable do indeed supply the requisite grant of jurisdiction. For example, the Declaratory Judgment Act, 28 U.S.C. §§ 2201–2202 (2012), is a well-known statute that is often pleaded as a basis for subject matter jurisdiction but that has been held, in fact, not to confer any jurisdiction on the federal courts. *Franchise Tax Bd. v. Construction Laborers Vacation Trust*, 463 U.S. 1 (1983). As we discuss next, the APA is another statute that may appear to grant jurisdiction but that does not.

3. The Federal Administrative Procedure Act

The federal APA creates a broad right to judicial review. In particular, § 702's first sentence says: "**A person suffering legal wrong because of agency action, or adversely affected or aggrieved by agency action within the meaning of a relevant statute, is entitled to judicial review thereof.**" Section 704's first sentence says: "**Agency action made reviewable by statute and final agency action for which there is no other adequate remedy in a court are subject to judicial review.**"

You might think these two sentences give federal courts subject matter jurisdiction over actions for judicial review of agency actions. Some lower courts thought so, too, until the Supreme Court corrected them in *Califano v. Sanders*, 430 U.S. 99 (1977). The Court in *Califano* held that the APA does not grant subject matter jurisdiction. Some lower courts continue mistakenly to treat the APA as jurisdictional. *See, e.g., Trudeau v. Fed. Trade Comm'n*, 456 F.3d 178, 184 (D.C. Cir. 2006) (discussing the confusion). Aren't you glad you won't make that mistake!

Rather than granting jurisdiction, § 704's first sentence creates a cause of action for review of "**final agency action for which there is no other adequate remedy in a court.**" 5 U.S.C. § 704; *see Bennett v. Spear*, 520 U.S. 154, 175 (1997). And § 702's first sentence identifies the people who are entitled to assert the cause: namely, people "**suffering legal wrong because of agency action, or adversely affected or aggrieved by agency action within the meaning of a relevant statute.**" We discuss this cause of action in Chapter 29. For now, the important thing to understand is that §§ 702 and 704 do not grant subject matter jurisdiction. Consequently, the plaintiff asserting the cause of action created by §§ 702 and 704 must identify another statute granting subject matter jurisdiction to the court in which the plaintiff has sued. As stated above, the federal question statute ordinarily will provide such a grant of jurisdiction to the federal district courts, unless a special review statute grants exclusive jurisdiction to another court.

Exercise: Non-Jurisdictional Nature of the Federal APA

This sentence comes from a decision of the U.S. Court of Appeals for the Tenth Circuit: "Having jurisdiction to review the [Nuclear Regulatory Commission's] licensing decision under 28 U.S.C. § 2342(4) and 42 U.S.C. § 2239(b), as well as the Administrative Procedures Act ("APA"), 5 U.S.C. § 702, we DENY the petition for review and uphold the NRC's licensing decision in all respects." *Morris v. U.S. Nuclear Regulatory Comm'n*, 598 F.3d 677, 681 (10th Cir. 2010). Who do you think initially made the mistake: the lawyers for the parties, the judge's law clerk, or the judge who wrote the opinion?

---

4. Jurisdiction of State Courts to Review State Agency Action

In many States, you will find a situation similar to the federal system in two ways. First, the State will have a general jurisdictional statute authorizing one of the State's courts to review most agency actions, or most agency actions of a certain type (such as decisions in contested cases), plus specialized statutes authorizing judicial review of certain other agency actions.[1] Second, judicial review of state agency actions may occur in a trial level court or in an appellate court. In Idaho, for example, final orders of the State's workers' compensation agency are subject to judicial review in the Idaho Supreme Court. *See* Idaho Appellate Rule 11(d) (West, Westlaw through amendments received through May 15, 2011).

States vary when it comes to where they codify their jurisdictional grants. Some States put their general jurisdictional grant in their APA, following the 1961 Model APA's approach.[2] Other States codify their general jurisdictional grant, not in a statute, but in rules for the state courts.[3] A good place to begin your search for the applicable jurisdictional grants is the index to the State's code of laws. That index should have entries for "Administrative Agencies" and "Jurisdiction." For finding grants of jurisdiction, the index of the State's legal code is even better than Google.

B. Jurisdiction: Sovereign Immunity

You generally cannot sue the government without its consent, because of sovereign immunity. Thus, if you sue the federal government or one of its agencies in federal court without its consent, the court must dismiss the case for lack of subject matter jurisdiction. The same is often true of lawsuits filed in state court against the state government, for States have sovereign immunity, too. Fortunately for administrative lawyers, laws exist at both the federal and state level that consent to—and thereby waive the government's sovereign immunity from—lawsuits seeking review of most agency actions. We discuss the federal and state situations separately.

1. Suits against the Federal Government and Its Agencies and Officials for Review of Federal Agency Action

Section A of this chapter discussed the need for a plaintiff seeking judicial review of agency action to identify a statute granting subject matter jurisdiction to the court in

---

1. *See, e.g.*, Mont. Code Ann. § 2-4-702(2)(a) (West, Westlaw through 2011 laws) (general jurisdictional statute in Montana APA authorizing review of agency decisions in contested cases); *id.* § 69-3-402(1) (specialized jurisdictional statute for judicial review of decisions of Montana Public Service Commission).

2. *See* 1961 Model APA §§ 7 & 15; *see, e.g.*, Wis. Stat. Ann. § 227.40 (West, Westlaw through 2011 Act 119, published Mar. 16, 2012) (giving circuit courts jurisdiction over declaratory judgment proceedings on validity of agency rules); *id.* § 227.53 (giving circuit courts jurisdiction over proceedings for review of some agency adjudicatory decisions).

3. *See, e.g.*, Ky. Const. § 111(2) (West, Westlaw through end of 2011 legislation) (Kentucky Court of Appeals "may be authorized by rules of the Supreme Court to review directly decisions of administrative agencies of the Commonwealth"); Minn. R. Civ. App. P., Rule 103.03(g) (West, Westlaw through amendments received through Mar. 1, 2012) (generally authorizing court of appeals to review appeals from "a final order, decision or judgment affecting a substantial right made in an administrative or other special proceeding").

which the plaintiff seeks review. For example, the federal question statute grants federal district courts subject matter jurisdiction over many lawsuits seeking review of federal agency action. Statutes granting subject matter jurisdiction, however, do not waive the government's sovereign immunity. *United States v. Nordic Village, Inc.*, 503 U.S. 30, 37–38 (1992); *Blatchford v. Native Village of Noatak*, 501 U.S. 775, 786 (1991). Thus, in addition to identifying a statute granting subject matter jurisdiction, the plaintiff must identify a law waiving sovereign immunity. A grant of subject matter jurisdiction and a waiver of sovereign immunity are two separate requirements.

The federal APA waives federal sovereign immunity from most lawsuits challenging federal agency action. The waiver is in § 702. The waiver does not announce itself boldly. See if you can find it:

---

5 U.S.C. § 702. Right of review

A person suffering legal wrong because of agency action, or adversely affected or aggrieved by agency action within the meaning of a relevant statute, is entitled to judicial review thereof. An action in a court of the United States seeking relief other than money damages and stating a claim that an agency or an officer or employee thereof acted or failed to act in an official capacity or under color of legal authority shall not be dismissed nor relief therein be denied on the ground that it is against the United States or that the United States is an indispensable party. The United States may be named as a defendant in any such action, and a judgment or decree may be entered against the United States: Provided, That any mandatory or injunctive decree shall specify the Federal officer or officers (by name or by title), and their successors in office, personally responsible for compliance. Nothing herein (1) affects other limitations on judicial review or the power or duty of the court to dismiss any action or deny relief on any other appropriate legal or equitable ground; or (2) confers authority to grant relief if any other statute that grants consent to suit expressly or impliedly forbids the relief which is sought.

The waiver is in the second sentence. Review the sentence considering these questions:

- Does it waive federal sovereign immunity from suits for all kinds of judicial relief?
- Is the waiver limited to suits based on the cause of action created by the APA?
- Is the waiver limited to suits in federal court or does it encompass suits in state court?

Below we discuss these questions, and we mention federal statutes other than the federal APA that waive federal sovereign immunity from lawsuits challenging federal agency action.

The most important feature of § 702's waiver is that it allows only actions "**seeking relief other than money damages.**" 5 U.S.C. § 702 (2012). Thus, § 702 allows the plaintiff in most cases to get declaratory or injunctive relief invalidating an agency action or compelling agency action improperly withheld. But it almost never allows the plaintiff to get a money judgment. We say "*almost* never" because of one U.S. Supreme Court case: *Bowen v. Massachusetts*, 487 U.S. 879 (1988). There, the Court construed § 702's waiver to allow Massachusetts to sue the federal government to get reimbursed for certain Medicaid expenditures the State had made. The challenge, if successful, would require the federal government to pay money to Massachusetts, but the Court held that this would not be a payment of "**money *damages***" under § 702. *Bowen v. Massachusetts* was an unusual case, however, and the Court has read it narrowly. *See Dep't of Army v. Blue Fox, Inc.*, 525 U.S. 255, 261–264 (1999) (§ 702 does not waive sovereign immunity from creditors enforcing liens on government property); *see also Great-West Life & Annuity Ins. Co. v. Knudson*, 534 U.S. 204, 210 (2002) ("Almost invariably ... suits seeking ... to compel the defendant to pay a sum of money are suits for 'money damages,' as that phrase has traditionally been applied.").

Ordinarily you must find some waiver of sovereign immunity other than the one in § 702 if you want to sue the federal government for money payable out of the U.S. Treasury. Such waivers do exist. The big two are in the Tucker Act and the Federal Tort Claims Act. The Tucker Act waives federal sovereign immunity from claims against the federal government for breach of contract or for just compensation under the Fifth Amendment. *See* 28 U.S.C. §§ 1346(a)(2), 1491 (2012). The Federal Tort Claims Act waives federal sovereign immunity from certain tort claims based on the tortious conduct of federal employees. *See* 28 U.S.C. §§ 1346(b), 2671–2680 (2012). We will not explore these two statutes in this book so that we can focus on lawsuits challenging agency action under the APA and special review statutes that generally incorporate the grounds for judicial relief in the APA.

On that score, § 702's waiver of sovereign immunity is not limited to suits asserting the cause of action created by the APA itself. To the contrary, § 702's waiver applies to almost all federal-court suits against federal agencies or officials for relief other than money damages. For example, § 702's waiver has been construed to allow a suit against the U.S. Department of Agriculture asserting claims under the Patent Act. *See Delano Farms Co. v. Calif. Table Grape Comm'n*, 655 F.3d 1337, 1343–1350 (Fed. Cir. 2011). In addition, the waiver allows actions for what is called "nonstatutory review" of federal executive branch conduct. *See Trudeau v. Fed. Trade Comm'n*, 456 F.3d 178, 185–187 (D.C. Cir. 2006). (We discuss nonstatutory review in Chapter 29.B.3.) The waiver also applies in lawsuits seeking judicial review under most special review statutes. Just remember that the waiver in § 702 is, however, limited to suits in federal court; it doesn't authorize lawsuits in state court. *See, e.g., Fed. Nat'l Mortg. Ass'n v. Le Crone*, 868 F.2d 190, 193 (6th Cir. 1989).

As comprehensive as it is, the waiver in § 702 is not the only waiver provision that may apply in a federal court lawsuit seeking nonmonetary relief against federal agency action. Specifically, special review provisions may be interpreted to waive federal sovereign from the actions they authorize. *See, e.g., U.S. Dep't of Energy v. Ohio*, 503 U.S. 607 (1992) (interpreting waivers of federal sovereign immunity in Clean Water Act and Resource Conservation and Recovery Act). To cite another example, a federal statute called the McCarran Amendment waives federal sovereign immunity from certain state-court suits in which the United States claims water rights. 43 U.S.C. § 666(a) (2012); *e.g., United States ex rel. Director v. Idaho Dep't of Water Resources*, 508 U.S. 1 (1993). In short, many federal statutes waive sovereign immunity, and the plaintiff seeking judicial review of federal agency action needs to find one applicable to the plaintiff's suit. *See Loeffler v. Frank*, 486 U.S. 549, 562 (1988) (analyzing interaction of two statutory provisions waiving federal sovereign immunity).

2. Suits against States and Their Agencies and Officials

In many States, sovereign immunity still exists unless waived by statute. The State's constitution is the place to begin your research on whether the State has retained its sovereign immunity and, if so, to what extent.[4] In States that retain their sovereign immunity, people seeking review of state agency action will often find that state statutes authorizing review of agency action have been interpreted as waiving sovereign immunity.[5] Even so, the careful administrative lawyer includes sovereign immunity among the potential barriers to be overcome in seeking judicial review of state agency action.

Exercise: Sovereign Immunity Research

Please pick the State in which you expect to practice; then research whether the State's constitution addresses sovereign immunity.

C. Jurisdiction: Standing Requirements in Federal Court

The doctrine of standing restricts *who* can sue in federal court. The doctrine includes three sets of requirements: (1) constitutional requirements, which come from Article III and the separation of powers doctrine; (2) "prudential" requirements, which the U.S. Supreme Court has developed and which supplement the constitutional requirements; and (3) statutory restrictions on who can sue under a particular statute, which are often called statutory "standing" restrictions (though the adjective is a bit misleading in this context, as you will see). All three of these types of standing requirements must be considered in a complete analysis of each claim that a plaintiff asserts in a federal-court lawsuit.

You have probably encountered the standing doctrine before, if you've taken a law school course on constitutional law or the federal courts. If so, you may recall that the standing doctrine applies in all federal courts, including the U.S. Supreme Court, and that, if the federal court determines at any point in the case that the plaintiff lacks standing, the federal court must dismiss the case for lack of subject matter jurisdiction. That is why we examine standing as one of the requirements for a federal court to have jurisdiction to review agency action. Recognizing that you may have encountered the standing doctrine before, we will examine the standing doctrine from the administrative law perspective.

Administrative lawyers know that, when it comes to standing, the world is divided into easy standing cases and hard standing cases. The easy standing cases are the majority.

---

4. *See, e.g.,* Ala. Const. art. I, § 14 (West, Westlaw through amendments ratified through Nov. 23, 2010) (generally preserving State's sovereign immunity); *see also* Ga. Const. art. 1, § 2, Paragraph IX (West, Westlaw through 2011 Regular & Special Sessions) (waiving sovereign immunity to some extent). *But see* Pa. Const. art. I, § 11 (West, Westlaw through 2012 Reg. Sess. Act 20) (authorizing suits against the State "as the Legislature may by law direct"); Tenn. Const. art. I, § 17 (West, Westlaw through laws from 2012 Reg. Sess., eff. through Feb. 9, 2012) (authorizing suits against the State "as the Legislature may by law direct").

5. *See, e.g., Southern LNG, Inc. v. MacGinnitie,* 719 S.E.2d 473, 474 (Ga. 2011) (Georgia APA provision authorizing judicial review of agency rules waives sovereign immunity); *Tex. Dep't of Protective & Reg. Servs. v. Mega Child Care, Inc.,* 145 S.W.3d 170, 198 (Tex. 2004) (Texas APA provision authorizing review of decisions in contested cases waives sovereign immunity).

In these cases, the plaintiff's standing is so clear that it is a non-issue. In other cases, however, standing is not clear. Our examination of standing therefore begins by helping you distinguish the easy cases from the hard cases.

Once the administrative lawyer identifies his or her case as a hard standing case, the lawyer knows how to apply the frameworks for analyzing three types of standing restrictions to which we alluded above: namely, constitutional, prudential, and statutory standing requirements. We examine each set of standing requirements in this section, emphasizing their application to administrative law cases. Our objective is to help you learn to ask the right questions in these hard standing cases. These questions may not have clear answers, however, unless you are a federal judge. Thus your main objective should be to learn the right questions to ask, in the right sequence. The three sets of standing requirements are depicted in Diagram 28-1.

Diagram 28-1. Three Kinds of Standing Requirements

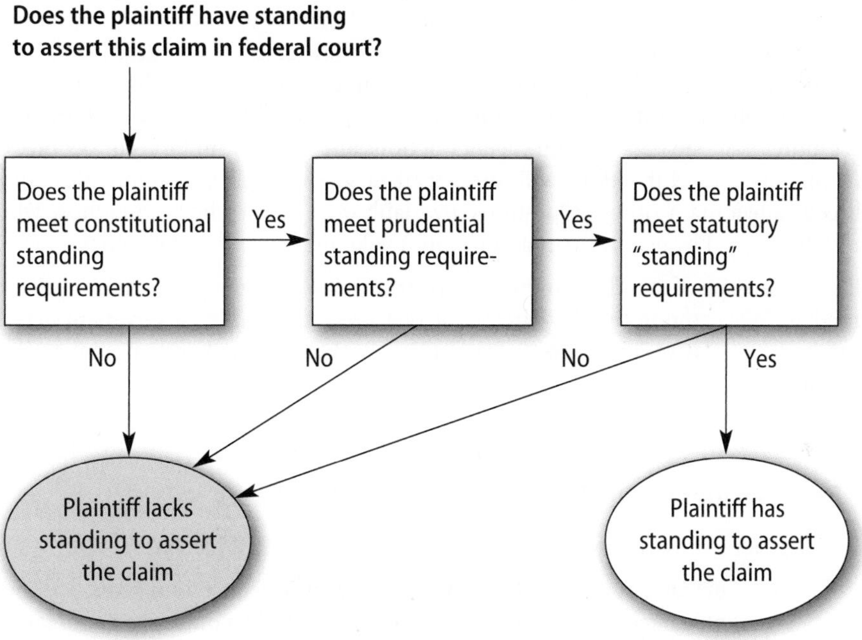

1. Standing in the Administrative Law Context

Not everyone who seeks judicial review of agency action has to worry about standing. A person who is directly affected by an agency action in a tangible, individualized way so clearly has standing that the issue of standing probably will not even arise. In contrast, when the person challenging agency action is not directly affected by the agency action or asserts an interest that is unclear, diffuse, or nontraditional, standing may be hard.

Easy standing cases involve (1) traditionally recognized injuries that (2) result directly from the challenged government action. Thus, standing is obvious when an agency ends an agency adjudication by denying, restricting, or terminating the plaintiff's governmentally required license or government benefits; or imposing a fine on, or issuing a cease-and-desist order against, the plaintiff. Standing is likewise obvious when an agency issues a rule increasing the costs or restricting the activities of the plaintiff. Many other kinds of agency action, such as agency demands for information, have direct targets and cause clearcut injury. In short, when an agency acts, it is usually easy to tell whose ox is gored, or, if you prefer, who will have an axe to grind with the agency. The plaintiffs with gored oxen and dull axes will have easy standing cases.

Hard standing cases arise when the person challenging agency action is not directly affected by the agency action or is claiming an interest that tends toward the abstract or diffuse. Many hard standing cases arise when the plaintiff claims that an agency has failed to enforce—or failed to enforce stringently enough—a law that targets someone other than the plaintiff. Thus, the U.S. Supreme Court has said that "when the plaintiff is not himself the object of the government action or inaction he challenges, standing is not precluded but it is ordinarily substantially more difficult to establish." *Lujan v. Defenders of Wildlife*, 504 U.S. 555, 561–62 (1992) (internal quotation marks omitted). The plaintiff may also have trouble showing standing when the plaintiff's real stake in the lawsuit seems to consist simply of ideological opposition to a government action or policy.

Even though most cases you encounter as an administrative lawyer will be easy standing cases, administrative lawyers still must understand the law of standing. That is because many of the hard standing cases are administrative law cases. If you think about it, this is not surprising. The actions (and inactions) of administrative agencies almost by definition affect the public interest and are designed to serve public purposes. Those actions often affect more than one person; some agency actions affect tens of millions of people. Government action (and inaction) will directly affect some people and companies but only indirectly affect many others. Questions invariably arise about who among those who are adversely affected by government action can invoke the powers of the courts.

Thus, the issue of standing in the administrative law context can be more realistically framed as: Who among those indirectly or obscurely affected by government action or inaction—the relative "outsiders"—can judicially challenge that government action (or inaction)?

Exercise: Identifying Easy and Hard Standing Cases

Please identify the following cases as easy or hard standing cases:

1. The Nuclear Regulatory Commission denies a license that would allow Vermont Yankee Nuclear Power Corporation to build a nuclear power plant. Vermont Yankee seeks judicial review.

2. The Nuclear Regulatory Commission grants a license that would allow Vermont Yankee Nuclear Power Corporation to build a nuclear power plant. Groups opposed to nuclear power seek judicial review.

3. The U.S. EPA establishes restrictions on emissions of carbon dioxide and other greenhouse gas from new cars made in the United States. The Ford Motor Company seeks judicial review of the restrictions.

4. The U.S. EPA relaxes existing restrictions on emissions of carbon dioxide and other greenhouse gases from new cars made in the United States. The American Lung Association seeks judicial review of the restrictions on behalf of members claiming EPA's action will make their respiratory illnesses worse.

5. The Department of Interior issues new safety rules for companies that hold leases from the federal government to explore for oil and gas on the Outer

Continental Shelf (OCS). The rules are designed to lower the risk of massive oil spills by requiring expensive new technology and safety procedures. Oil and gas companies that hold OCS leases seek judicial review.

6. The Department of Interior issues new safety rules for companies who hold leases from the federal government to explore for oil and gas on the Outer Continental Shelf (OCS). The rules are designed to lower the risk of massive oil spills. Scientists who study forms of marine life that may suffer from a massive oil spill seek judicial review of the rules on the grounds that they are not stringent enough.

2. Constitutional Standing Requirements

Article III of the U.S. Constitution limits the federal courts to deciding nine categories of "cases" or "controversies." The U.S. Supreme Court has held that the terms "cases" and "controversies" limit federal courts to resolving disputes "traditionally thought to be capable of resolution through the judicial process." *Flast v. Cohen*, 392 U.S. 83, 97 (1968) (emphasis added); *see also Arizona Christian Sch. Tuition Org. v. Winn*, 131 S. Ct. 1436, 1441 (2011) (the terms "cases" and "controversies" "restric[t] the federal judicial power to the traditional role of the Anglo-American courts") (internal quotation marks omitted). Disputes that fit this description are said to be "justiciable."

For a dispute to be justiciable in federal court, it has to meet certain requirements, one of which is that the plaintiff satisfies constitutional requirements for standing. The Court has summarized the constitutional standing requirements as follows:

> [T]he irreducible constitutional minimum of standing contains three elements. First, the plaintiff must have suffered an "injury in fact"—an invasion of a legally protected interest which is (a) concrete and particularized[1] and (b) actual or imminent, not conjectural or hypothetical. Second, there must be a causal connection between the injury and the conduct complained of—the injury has to be "fairly ... trace[able] to the challenged action of the defendant, and not ... th[e] result [of] the independent action of some third party not before the court." [Citation omitted.] Third, it must be likely, as opposed to merely speculative, that the injury will be redressed by a favorable decision.

Lujan v. Defenders of Wildlife, 504 U.S. 555, 560–561 (1992) (some internal quotation marks omitted). The three constitutional standing requirements are known as (1) "injury in fact"; (2) "traceability"; and (3) "redressability."

Before we examine these requirements, we mention three principles that administrative lawyers must know when analyzing and seeking to establish constitutional standing in federal court.

First, the person seeking federal court review of agency action bears the burden of proving that the person meets the three constitutional standing requirements. To meet that burden, the person may have to submit affidavits and other evidence to the federal court. A federal court will consider such evidence, even though it generally will not

---

1. [Court's footnote:] By particularized, we mean that the injury must affect the plaintiff in a personal and individual way.

consider additional evidence when reviewing the *merits* of the agency's decision. As discussed in Chapter 31.D, courts generally review the merits of agency action based solely on the evidence before the agency. But since standing implicates the federal court's jurisdiction, the court may decide that issue without limiting itself to the evidence before the agency. The moral of the story is that, if you think your client has a hard standing case, you'd better consider submitting material to the court proving your client's standing. *See, e.g., Ass'n of Flight Attendants-CWA, AFL-CIO v. U.S. Dep't of Transp.*, 564 F.3d 462, 464 (D.C. Cir. 2009).

Second, standing is "relief-specific." If the plaintiff seeks only backward looking ("retrospective") relief—such as money damages to compensate for a past injury or a court order setting aside an agency action—the plaintiff only needs to show a past injury. If, on the other hand, the plaintiff seeks future-oriented ("prospective") relief such as an injunction, the plaintiff must show a threat of imminent *future* injury. For example, a plaintiff lacked standing to seek an injunction against a police department's use of chokeholds on arrestees because, although the police had put a chokehold on him in the past, he could not show a "real and immediate threat" that the police would put a chokehold on him in the future. *Los Angeles v. Lyons*, 461 U.S. 95, 105 (1983). In other cases, the Court has emphasized that the threat of future injury must be "imminent" to constitute injury in fact. *E.g., Summers v. Earth Island Inst.*, 555 U.S. 488, 493 (2009). This requirement to prove an actual, imminent threat of future injury can be difficult to satisfy in administrative law cases where risk is hard to gauge, as discussed below.

Third, an organization can establish standing by showing the challenged agency action harms either the organization itself or its members. On its own behalf, for example, an organization could challenge a tax on organizational income. *See, e.g., Indep. Ins. Agents v. Comm'r of Internal Revenue*, 998 F.2d 989 (11th Cir. 1993). An organization can sue on behalf of its members if it shows that (1) at least one of its members meets the three constitutional standing requirements identified above (injury in fact, etc.); (2) the interests that the organization seeks to protect through its lawsuit are germane to the organization's purpose; and (3) neither the claim asserted nor the relief requested requires individual members to participate in the lawsuit. The second and third requirements are not usually hard to meet in administrative law cases. In particular, the third requirement is usually satisfied as long as the organization seeks only to invalidate agency action or get an injunction. Thus, the "hard standing cases" brought by organizations are usually hard because of doubt whether one of the organization's members can satisfy the constitutional standing requirements. *See Hunt v. Wash. State Apple Advertising Comm'n*, 432 U.S. 333, 343 (1977). Many important administrative law cases are brought by organizations.

Below we explore each of the three constitutional standing requirement as it applies to administrative law cases.

a. Injury in Fact

The hard standing cases in administrative law have often involved one of five types of asserted injury, which we take up separately below.

(i) Aesthetic or Recreational Injury

The Court held in *Sierra Club v. Morton*, 405 U.S. 727, 736 (1972), that the Sierra Club's "longstanding concern ... and expertise" in natural resources did not give it standing to challenge the government's plans to develop a Disney resort in the Sequoia National

Park. To have standing, the Court said, the organization had to show that one or more of its members had aesthetic or recreational interests that would be impaired by development of a specific piece of public land.

Taking this suggestion, plaintiffs in environmental cases today often rely on recreational or aesthetic injury to challenge government action. To seek prospective relief such as an injunction, the plaintiffs must show that they themselves regularly use (e.g., hike through or hunt in) the specific area that will be affected and thus confront an actual, imminent injury to their enjoyment of that area. *See, e.g., W. Watersheds Project v. Kraayenbrink,* 632 F.3d 472, 484 (9th Cir. 2011). Environmental organizations can sue on behalf of their members if they can show that one or more of their members regularly use the specific area that could be degraded by the challenged government action.

The Court has been a stickler in analyzing standing based on recreational and aesthetic interests. Three cases illustrate the Court's stickliness:

- *Lujan v. Defenders of Wildlife,* 504 U.S. 555 (1992)

The Court denied standing to an organization. The organization claimed that two federal-agency projects occurring overseas threatened endangered species. The organization's members alleged that they had visited these two overseas locations before and intended to return sometime in the future in an effort to see the endangered species that were threatened by the projects. The Court said that "[s]uch 'some day' intentions—without any description of concrete plans, or indeed any specification of *when* the some day will be—do not support a finding of the actual or imminent injury that our cases require." *Id.* at 564.

- *Lujan v. National Wildlife Federation,* 497 U.S. 871 (1990)

The Court denied standing to an organization whose members could only allege that they used land "in the vicinity of" the area that would be environmentally harmed by the challenged agency action. *Id.* at 886–887. Those allegations were not specific enough to defeat the government's summary judgment motion challenging the organization's standing. The Court said summary judgment could not be avoided by "averments which state only that one of respondent's members uses unspecified portions of an immense tract of territory, on some portions of which mining activity has occurred or probably will occur by virtue of the governmental action." *Id.* at 889. (The Court also addressed the "ripeness" of the organization's challenge in a portion of the opinion that we examine in Chapter 30.B.)

- *Summers v. Earth Island Institute,* 555 U.S. 488 (2009)

Organizations sued to challenge Forest Service rules that exempted small sales of timber on forest service land from statutory notice-and-comment procedures. The organizations could not show that any particular member used any particular forest service land that would be affected by one of these small timber sales. The organizations argued, instead, that there was a "statistical probability" that some members would visit areas of national forests where sales would occur. *Id.* at 497–498. The Court rejected this approach to standing because it conflicted with "prior cases, which have required plaintiff-organizations to make specific allegations "establishing that at least one identified member had suffered or would suffer harm." *Id.* at 498.

Exercise: Identifying Cognizable Aesthetic Injury

Phillip drives through a national park every day on his way to work. He particularly enjoys seeing a particular dogwood tree on the side of the road. One day he learns from a news article that the road through the park is going to be widened, and tree clearing will begin soon. Assume Phillip can prove that his cherished dogwood is one of the trees marked for removal. Does he have a cognizable interest to support a federal lawsuit challenging the tree's removal?

(ii) Risk

The Court in *Earth Island* denied standing to an organization that could not show "at least one identified member had suffered or would suffer harm." 555 U.S. at 498. In particular, the Court rejected a probability-based standing argument positing that unidentified members of the organization would probably suffer harm. Even so, a federal court plaintiff often must rely on probability-based arguments in a different way: The plaintiff must show that the plaintiff personally faces—or, if the plaintiff is an organization, a specific member personally faces—a threat (i.e., a risk or probability) of future injury. That is required to seek prospective relief. But establishing the required level of risk can be hard to do when the challenged agency action involves highly uncertain risks.

For example, the Natural Resources Defense Council (NDRC) sued to challenge an EPA rule regulating methyl bromide on the ground that the rule was not stringent enough. As its basis for standing, NRDC submitted expert evidence that "two to four of NRDC's nearly half a million members will develop cancer as a result of the rule." *NRDC v. EPA*, 464 F.3d 1, 7 (D.C. Cir. 2006). The court held that this risk constituted "injury in fact." *Id.* at 6–7. The court relied on prior cases in which it had required plaintiffs to show a "substantial probability" of injury. *Id.* at 6. The court noted that other federal courts had used a different standard, by requiring plaintiffs to show a "scientifically demonstrable increase in the threat of death or serious illness." *Id.* Whatever standard is used, the methyl bromide case shows that standing based on small risk can be hard to establish, at least unless you are a large organizational plaintiff. Even then, the *Earth Island* case discussed above forecloses some probability-based theories of injury in fact.

A 2010 opinion by the U.S. Supreme Court addresses whether the plaintiff established sufficient risk to establish standing, but the opinion does not give clear guidance on how much risk is required to establish injury in fact:

• *Monsanto v. Geertson Seed Farms, Inc.*, 130 S.Ct. 2743 (2010)

Growers of organic alfalfa sought judicial review of the U.S. Department of Agriculture's decision to stop regulating genetically modified (GM) alfalfa. The Department of Agriculture challenged the growers' standing. The Court upheld the growers' standing. In upholding standing, the Court relied at least partly on its determination that the growers had shown a "significant risk" that the GM alfalfa would contaminate the growers' non-GM alfalfa. *Id.* at 2755; *see also id.* at 2754–2755 (stating that plaintiffs showed a "substantial risk" of contamination); *id.* at 2754 (quoting district court's finding that plaintiffs established a "reasonable probability" of contamination).

But the Court's decision leaves unclear whether "significant risk" is necessary or sufficient to establish injury in fact. On the one hand, the Court doesn't say that "significant risk" is the minimum level of risk required, and so it is possible that a lower level of risk suffices to show injury in fact—such as a "scientifically demonstrable increase in the threat of death or serious injury" that some lower courts have found sufficient. *See NRDC v. EPA*, 464 F.3d at 6. On the other hand, it is also possible to read *Monsanto* as holding that significant risk alone is not sufficient to establish injury in fact. That reading is possible because the Court determined that the growers would suffer harms "even if their crops are not infected" with the GM alfalfa. *Id.* at 2755. Specifically, the growers had to spend money to test their crops regularly so they could assure their customers that their alfalfa was uncontaminated. They also had to spend money on measures to lower the risk of contamination. *Id.* Thus, quite apart from the "significant risk" of future contamination, the growers proved ongoing injury in the form of increased costs to abate the risk. This ongoing injury may have supported the Court's holding that plaintiffs showed injury in fact.

* * *

Monsanto, together with the methyl bromide case discussed above (*NRDC v. EPA*), shows that "injury in fact" is often hard to analyze when the plaintiff contends that an agency has not done enough to regulate risk. *See Public Citizen, Inc. v. Nat'l Highway Traffic Safety Admin.*, 489 F.3d 1279, 1289 (D.C. Cir. 2007) ("Claims that a safety regulation is good—but not good enough—can pose difficult issues of standing."). These hard standing cases are not for the fainthearted or underfunded plaintiff. In *NRDC v. EPA*, for example, NRDC convinced a court of appeals to uphold standing only after NRDC petitioned the court for rehearing and submitted additional information about the risk. Basing standing on risk can be risky.

Exercise: Risk as Injury in Fact

How do you distinguish the probability-based injury theory that the Court rejected in *Summers v. Earth Island Institute*, 555 U.S. at 497–498, from the probability-based injury theory that a lower court accepted in *NRDC v. EPA*, 464 F.3d at 6–7?

(iii) Fear

In two cases the Court has addressed whether fear of harm can constitute injury in fact. The Court's cases imply that *reasonable* fear can indeed constitute injury in fact. But to show that the fear is reasonable the plaintiff will often have to show a sufficient risk of harm. Thus, allegations of *fear* of harm will often be analyzed like allegations of *risk* of harm. We summarize the two cases below.

- *Los Angeles v. Lyons*, 461 U.S. 95 (1983)

Adolph Lyons alleged a fear that he would again be stopped by the Los Angeles police and put into a chokehold. Mr. Lyons sought injunctive relief limiting the L.A. Police Department's use of chokeholds. The Court said that, to have standing, Mr. Lyons' fear had to be reasonable, which required it to rest on actual risk:

> The reasonableness of Lyons' fear is dependent upon the likelihood of a recurrence of the allegedly unlawful conduct. It is the reality of the threat of repeated injury that is relevant to the standing inquiry, not the plaintiff's subjective apprehensions.

Id. at 107 n.8. The Court determined that Lyons did not have standing because he could not "credibly allege that he faced a realistic threat" of being put in a chokehold in the future, and for this reason he lacked standing. *Id.* at 106 n.7. The Court's demand for proof of a "realistic threat" may be consistent with its conclusion in the later case of *Geertson* that plaintiffs showing a "significant risk" demonstrated injury in fact. 130 S.Ct. at 2755. On this view, Mr. Lyons' assertion of subjective "fear" didn't really matter; injury in fact turned on objective risk, and that risk had to be "realistic" ("significant"?) to constitute injury in fact.

The case summarized next, however, suggests that a plaintiff might sometimes establish fear-based standing without proof of risk.

- *Friends of the Earth, Inc. v. Laidlaw Envt'l Servs. (TOC), Inc.*, 528 U.S. 167 (2000)

Environmental organizations sued a company that had repeatedly violated its EPA permit limiting the amount of pollutants the company could discharge into a river. In particular, the company repeatedly discharged more mercury into the water than its EPA permit allowed. Even so, the plaintiffs could not show that the violations caused any environmental harm and thus posed any risk. The plaintiffs alleged, however, that some of their members' concerns about the pollution in the river led those members to stop making recreational use of the river. Another member alleged that her home was near the river and she believed the river's reputation for being polluted depressed her property's value. The Court held that the organizations had standing because the members' "reasonable concerns about the effects of [the company's] ... discharges directly affected [their] recreational, aesthetic, and economic interests." *Id.* at 183–184. This holding seems to mean that reasonable fear affecting cognizable interests can establish injury in fact.

The Court in *Laidlaw* did not explain why the members' pollution concerns were "reasonable" despite lack of proof of environmental harm. Perhaps they were reasonable because the company's discharges did, after all, violate its EPA permit, which presumably was based on an expert agency's judgment about what levels of discharge were safe. Most reasonable people, knowing that a company was discharging illegal amounts of mercury into a river, probably would avoid recreating in and around the river. Perhaps significantly, the plaintiffs in *Laidlaw* sued under a "citizens suit" provision that broadly authorized "a person or persons having an interest which is or may be adversely affected" to sue companies that violated the Clean Water Act. *See id.* at 173 (quoting statute). This broad procedural right to sue may have influenced the Court's analysis, though the Court did not come out and say so. In other cases, the Court has said, "Congress has the power to define injuries and articulate chains of causation that will give rise to a case or controversy where none existed before." *Massachusetts v. EPA*, 549 U.S. 497, 516 (2007). Congress may have done just that in broadly authorizing suits by people who use rivers affected by illegal discharges of water pollution, even if they can't prove the discharges have caused harm.

* * *

Although *Geertson* and *Laidlaw* are not entirely clear, their gist is that reasonable fear can establish standing if that fear reflects a significant risk of cognizable harm or causes present injuries to cognizable interests.

Exercise: Fear as Injury in Fact

Congress amended the Foreign Intelligence Surveillance Act in 2008 to allow the government to conduct ongoing, widespread, electronic surveillance of "non-U.S. persons" (people other than U.S. citizens and permanent resident aliens) located in a foreign country. The plaintiffs sue federal officials challenging the 2008 amendments and asserting claims under the First and Fourth Amendments. The plaintiffs are lawyers, journalists, and organizations. The individual plaintiffs and the organizations' members regularly communicate with non-U.S. persons outside the United States whom the federal government, according to plaintiffs, is likely to target for surveillance under the 2008 amendments. Do the plaintiffs allege injury in fact? *See Amnesty Int'l USA v. Clapper*, 638 F.3d 118 (2d Cir. 2011), *cert granted*, 132 S.Ct. 2431 (2012).

(iv) Information

The Freedom of Information Act authorizes people to request documents from the federal government and to sue the government if the documents are not disclosed within a certain amount of time. *See* 5 U.S.C. §552(a)(3) (2012). The Act and the following Supreme Court case show that statutes like the FOIA can create a right to information, denial of which constitutes injury in fact.

• *Federal Election Commission v. Akins*, 524 U.S. 11 (1998)

The Federal Election Campaign Act requires that "political committee[s]" disclose to the public information about their donors and their expenditures. *Id.* at 14–15 (quoting and discussing Act). The Act is administered by the Federal Election Commission (FEC). A group of voters asked the FEC to enforce the Act against the American Israel Public Affairs Committee (AIPAC). The FEC refused the voters' request because the FEC determined that the AIPAC was not a "political committee" and therefore not subject to the Act. The voters then sued the FEC in federal court. *Id.* at 14–18. They claimed that the FEC's refusal to take enforcement action against AIPAC injured their right to information under the Act. The Court held that the plaintiffs had established injury in fact:

> The "injury in fact" that [plaintiffs] have suffered consists of their inability to obtain information—lists of AIPAC donors (who are, according to AIPAC, its members), and campaign-related contributions and expenditures—that, on [plaintiffs'] view of the law, the statute requires that AIPAC make public. There is no reason to doubt their claim that the information would help them (and others to whom they would communicate it) to evaluate candidates for public office, especially candidates who received assistance from AIPAC, and to evaluate the role that AIPAC's financial assistance might play in a specific election. Respondents' injury consequently seems concrete and particular. Indeed, this Court has previously held that a plaintiff suffers an "injury in fact" when the plaintiff fails to obtain information which must be publicly disclosed pursuant to a statute. *Public Citizen v. Department of Justice*, 491 U.S. 440, 449 (1989) (failure to obtain information subject to disclosure under Federal Advisory Committee Act "constitutes a sufficiently distinct injury to provide standing to sue"). See also *Havens Realty Corp. v. Coleman*, 455 U.S. 363, 373–374 (1982) (deprivation of information about housing availability constitutes "specific injury" permitting standing).

The Court's recognition of informational injury is important. Many statutes require agencies or private entities to make information available to the public. The Court's decision in *Akins* suggests that at least some of these statutes create informational rights enforceable in federal courts.

(v) Procedural Injury

You cannot sue a government agency merely because you object to the agency's failure to follow legally required *procedures*. Instead, to have standing, you must show the procedural defect occurred when the agency took an action that affected a concrete, personal interest of yours. When you have a concrete, personal interest at stake, however, you will find it easier to establish standing when the law gives you a "procedural right."

• *Lujan v. Defenders of Wildlife*, 504 U.S. 555 (1992)

In this case the Court rejected "procedural injury," standing alone, as cognizable injury in fact.

The Endangered Species Act (ESA) requires federal agencies to follow certain procedures before they take actions that could jeopardize endangered species or their critical habitat. The purpose of the procedures is to minimize the jeopardy. The Departments of Interior and Commerce issued a joint rule stating that federal agencies did not have to follow ESA procedures when they took actions in foreign countries. The plaintiff environmental organizations challenged the rule. One of the plaintiff's theories of why they had standing rested on the ESA's "citizen suit provision," which authorizes "any person" to sue government agencies for certain violations of the ESA. *Id.* at 571–572 (quoting statute). This theory was labeled a claim of "procedural injury," reflecting the plaintiffs' assertion of a right under the citizen suit provision to have the government follow ESA procedures.

The Court rejected the procedural injury theory. The Court held that the ESA cannot, consistently with Article III, be interpreted literally to allow anyone to sue the government for its failure to follow statutory procedures. That interpretation would violate Article III by giving standing to people based on their abstract interest in seeing that "the Government be administered according to law." *Id.* at 574 (internal quotation marks omitted). The Court said, "We have consistently held that a plaintiff raising only a generally available grievance about government—claiming only harm to his and every citizen's interest in proper application of the Constitution and laws, and seeking relief that no more directly and tangibly benefits him than it does the public at large—does not state an Article III case or controversy." *Id.* at 574–575.

The Court emphasized that some people do have standing to sue the government for failure to follow legally required procedures. A plaintiff can sue the government for procedural violations if the plaintiff shows that the procedural violation "could impair a separate concrete interest" of the plaintiff—for example, "the procedural requirement for a hearing prior to denial of [the plaintiff's] license application, or the procedural requirement for an environmental impact statement before a federal facility is constructed next door to [the plaintiff's home]." *Id.* at 572. The Court also explained that "procedural rights" are "special" in two senses:

> The person who has been accorded a procedural right to protect his concrete interests can assert that right without meeting all the normal standards for redressability and immediacy. Thus, under our case law, one living adjacent to the site for proposed construction of a federally licensed dam has standing to challenge the licensing agency's failure to prepare an environmental impact statement [a procedure required by the National Environmental Policy Act (NEPA)], even though he cannot establish with any certainty that the statement will cause the license to be withheld or altered, and even though the dam will not be completed for many years. (That is why we do not rely, in the present case, upon the Government's argument that, even if the other agencies were obliged [under the Endangered Species Act] to consult with the Secretary, they might not have followed his advice.)

Id. at 572 n.7. This means that if the law puts a procedural obligation on the government that the plaintiff has a statutory right to sue to enforce, the plaintiff will find it easier to prove standing in two ways:

(1) The plaintiff does not have to show as strong a likelihood as is usually required that the relief requested by the plaintiff—for example, an injunction requiring the government to follow the statutorily mandated procedure—will redress the plaintiff's injury.

(2) The plaintiff does not have to show as imminent ("immediate") a threat of future injury as is usually required to establish the injury in fact necessary for standing to seek prospective relief.

The plaintiff authorized to sue for procedural violations must still show that a concrete, personal interest of the plaintiff is threatened by the challenged government action.

Exercise: Analyzing Injury in Fact

Please complete Diagram 28-2, which is a flow chart for analyzing injury in fact.

Diagram 28-2. Analyzing Injury in Fact

Has the plaintiff suffered injury in fact to support this claim?

Does the plaintiff seek retrospective or prospective relief?

Has plaintiff shown **past** injury?

Has plaintiff shown an _____ threat of **future** injury?

Yes   No

No

Yes

Future threat is not imminent

Plaintiff lacks standing for this kind of relief

No

Is plaintiff asserting a _____ right?

Yes

Plaintiff has injury in fact for this kind of relief

Now analyze traceability and redressability

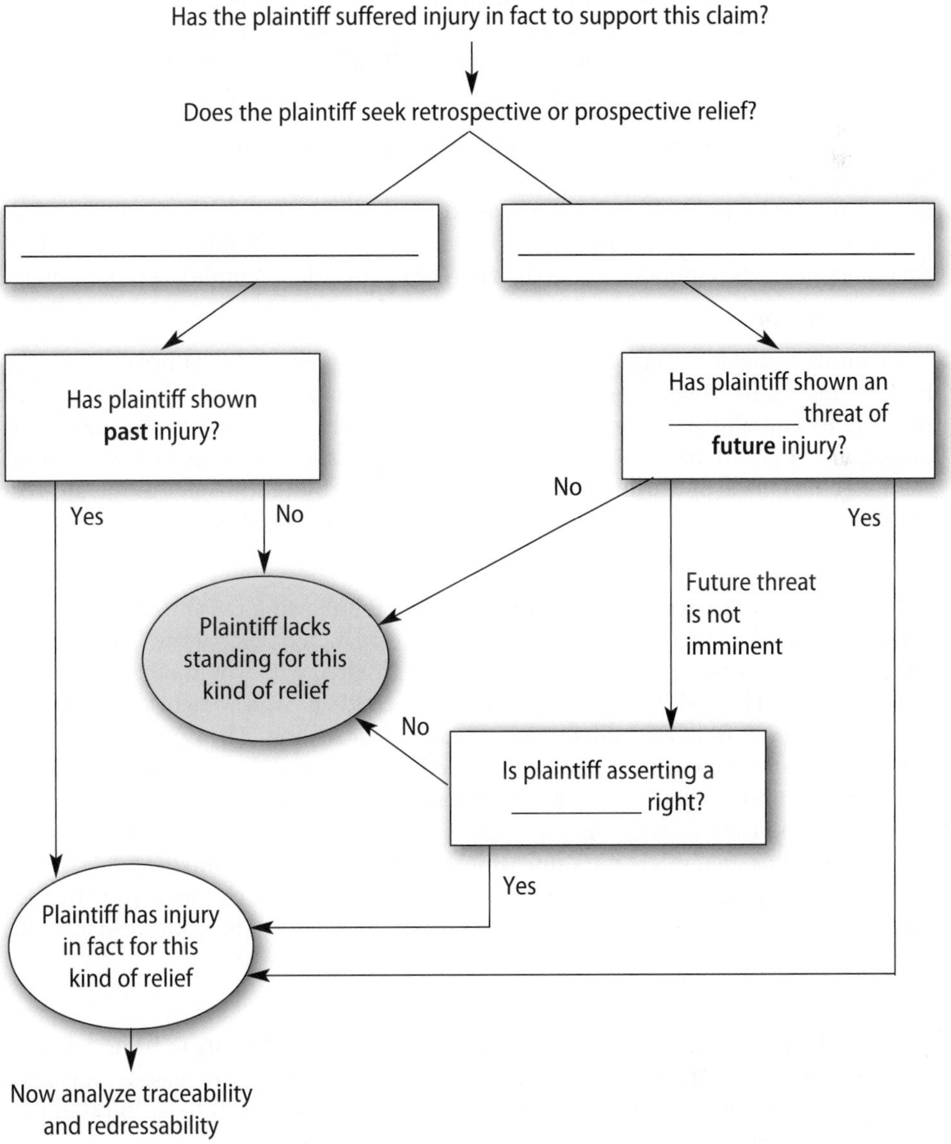

b. Traceability

Under Supreme Court precedent, in addition to injury in fact "there must be a causal connection between the injury and the conduct complained of—the injury has to be 'fairly … trace[able] to the challenged action of the defendant, and not … th[e] result [of] the independent action of some third party not before the court.'" *Defenders of Wildlife*, 504 U.S. at 560–561 (quoting *Simon v. Eastern Ky. Welfare Rights Organization*, 426 U.S. 26, 41–42 (1976)). *Accord Bond v. United States*, 131 S.Ct. 2355, 2366 (2011). Many hard traceability cases involve the "third party problem."

Three cases illustrate the problem. In all of them either the plaintiffs' injury or the relief they sought from the court, or both, depended significantly on the actions of someone other than the government agencies or officials named as defendants.

• *Simon v. Eastern Kentucky Welfare Rights Organization*, 426 U.S. 26 (1976)

Plaintiffs were poor people and their advocacy organizations. They complained that the Internal Revenue Service's change in tax policy would make free health care harder to get from charitable hospitals. The Court was not convinced that invalidating the IRS's change in tax policy would get plaintiffs the free health care they sought; this depended on how charitable hospitals responded to the change. The Court held plaintiffs lacked standing.

• *Warth v. Seldin*, 422 U.S. 490 (1975)

Plaintiffs complained that a town's restrictive zoning laws made affordable housing hard to find in that town. The Court held that the plaintiffs had not shown that their inability to find affordable housing was the result of the restrictive zoning laws. The availability of affordable housing seemed to depend less on decisions of town officials than on "the efforts and willingness of third parties to build low- and moderate-cost housing" in the town. *Id.* at 505. The Court held plaintiffs lacked standing.

• *Allen v. Wright*, 468 U.S. 737 (1984)

Plaintiffs sued Department of Treasury officials for allowing racially discriminatory private schools to retain their tax-exempt status, in violation of federal law. The plaintiffs alleged that these private schools soaked up white children who would otherwise attend public schools. This "white flight" prevented their children, who were black children in the public schools, from attending racially mixed public schools. The Court held that the plaintiffs did not show a close enough connection between their children's inability to attend racially mixed public schools and the tax-exempt status of the racially discriminatory private schools. The Court thought that, even if the IRS took away these private schools' tax-exempt status, that might not cause white children to flow back into the public school system. It depended on how the private schools and parents of children who attended those schools responded to the schools' loss of tax-exempt status. The Court held plaintiffs lacked standing.

* * *

These three cases show that when an administrative lawyer wants to bring a federal court lawsuit with the "third party problem," the lawyer must prepare to make a convincing showing of standing, because, in the Court's words, standing is likely to be "substantially more difficult" to get. *Warth*, 422 U.S. at 505.

c. Redressability

When the plaintiff seeks federal court review of a federal agency action, the traceability and redressability requirements for standing are often connected. The connection exists because the plaintiff alleges that the plaintiff's injury is fairly traceable to the agency action and seeks judicial relief invalidating that agency action. If the plaintiff's injury is indeed traceable to the agency action, judicial invalidation of the agency action is likely to redress the injury. By the same token, if the plaintiff's injury is more closely connected to the conduct of a third party not before the court than to the challenged agency action, redressability may be doubtful to the extent it rests on the third party's response to invalidation of the agency action. *See Warth*, 422 U.S. at 505. In short, the redressability and traceability analyses are usually flip sides of the same coin.

3. Prudential Standing Requirements

The plaintiff seeking federal court review of agency action not only must satisfy the three constitutional standing requirements. The plaintiff may also have to satisfy "prudential" standing requirements. The prudential standing requirements have been developed by the U.S. Supreme Court as "self-imposed limits on the exercise of federal jurisdiction." *Allen v. Wright*, 468 U.S. 737, 751 (1984). The prudential standing requirements include:

[1] the general prohibition on a litigant's raising another person's legal rights,
[2] the rule barring adjudication of generalized grievances more appropriately addressed in the representative branches, and [3] the requirement that a plaintiff's complaint fall within the zone of interests protected by the law invoked.

Id. (bracketed numerals added).

You might say the prudential standing requirements are "inspired" but not "required" by the Constitution. The prudential standing requirements identify situations that fall within federal judicial power but are thought by the Court to be better suited for resolution elsewhere, such as in the political branches or the States. *See Elk Grove Unified Sch. Dist. v. Newdow*, 542 U.S. 1, 12 (2004). Because the prudential standing requirements are not constitutional, Congress can modify or eliminate them in statutes authorizing federal court review of agency action. As we will see, Congress has indeed modified or eliminated prudential standing requirements in some special review statutes. But because the prudential standing requirements have been developed by the U.S. Supreme Court, the lower federal courts must apply those requirements unless Congress has modified them.

a. Third-Party Standing

As a general rule, the rights you assert in a federal court lawsuit must be your own. You generally cannot assert someone else's rights because it is up to them to decide whether to assert those rights, and, if so, where and how. The biggest exception to this rule against "third party" standing (also known, for you Latin fans, as *jus tertii*) was mentioned earlier in this section: An organization can sue on behalf of its members under certain conditions, and these conditions will often be satisfied in lawsuits for review of agency action. As a practical matter, therefore, administrative lawyers seldom have to deal with issues of third-party standing.

b. Generalized Grievances

The Court has said that as a prudential matter federal courts should not exercise jurisdiction over suits in which "the asserted harm is a generalized grievance shared in substantially equal measure by all or a large class of citizens." *Warth*, 422 U.S. at 499 (internal quotation marks omitted). The prudential restriction barring federal courts from hearing generalized grievances has importance for administrative lawyers because many agency actions broadly affect the public. Members of the public who challenge these agency actions in federal court lawsuits may confront government arguments that they present merely a generalized grievance. As discussed above, the Court relied on the "generalized grievance" principle to reject a bare claim of "procedural injury" in *Lujan v. Defenders of Wildlife*, 504 U.S. 555, 573–578 (1992).

In a later important case the Court distinguished widespread injury that is abstract from widespread injury that is concrete and personalized. The Court in *Federal Election Commission v. Akins*, 524 U.S. 11 (1998), held that the plaintiffs had standing based on their interest as voters in getting information that, they claimed, the Federal Election Campaign Act required an organization to make public. The Court rejected the government's argument that the plaintiffs asserted a non-cognizable, "generalized grievance" about the Federal Election Commission's failure to make the organization disclose the data. The Court explained:

> Often the fact that an interest is abstract and the fact that it is widely shared go hand in hand. But their association is not invariable, and where a harm is concrete, though widely shared, the Court has found "injury in fact." … Such an interest, where sufficiently concrete, may count as an "injury in fact." This conclusion seems particularly obvious where (to use a hypothetical example) large numbers of individuals suffer the same common-law injury (say, a widespread mass tort), or where large numbers of voters suffer interference with voting rights conferred by law. We conclude that, similarly, the informational injury at issue here, directly related to voting, the most basic of political rights, is sufficiently concrete and specific such that the fact that it is widely shared does not deprive Congress of constitutional power to authorize its vindication in the federal courts.…

Id. at 23–25.

c. Zone of Interests

The U.S. Supreme Court has included among the prudential standing rules "the requirement that a plaintiff's complaint fall within the zone of interests protected by the law invoked." *Allen v. Wright*, 468 U.S. 737, 751 (1984). Although this "zone of interests" requirement began life as a prudential standing requirement, it has been codified in a judicial review provision of the federal APA and in some special review statutes. As a result of this statutory codification, administrative lawyers today encounter the zone of interests requirement primarily as a restriction on statutory causes of action for judicial review of certain agency actions. We will discuss the zone of interests requirement (sometimes known as the zone of interests "test") in the next subsection, which addresses statutory "standing." Also, do not be surprised when you see the zone of interests test mentioned in the next chapter, which focuses on the cause of action requirement.

4. Statutory "Standing" Requirements

The federal APA and many special review statutes collectively create causes of action authorizing judicial review of most final agency actions. In creating this cause of action, the APA and special review statutes usually specify *who* is entitled to judicial review. As discussed above, the "zone of interests" test is an example of such a restriction. These statutory restrictions on who is entitled to judicial review are often called "statutory standing requirements." We discuss such requirements in this section.

Before we do, though, you should know that calling these "statutory *standing*" requirements is arguably inaccurate. "Standing" refers to restrictions on the federal courts' *jurisdiction*. But statutory restrictions on who can seek judicial review are generally not restrictions on standing; they are restrictions on the cause of action. (The "zone of interests" requirement may be an exception because of its dual nature as a judicially devised prudential standing requirement and a statutory restriction on who has a right to judicial review.) Ordinarily, if the plaintiff cannot satisfy the requirements for a statutory cause of action, the plaintiff's suit should be dismissed for failure to state a claim for which relief can be granted, *see* Fed. R. Civ. P. 12(b)(6), not for lack of subject matter jurisdiction, *see id.* Rule 12(b)(1). *See Steel Co. v. Citizens for a Better Env't*, 523 U.S. 83, 97 (1998). The difference between a standing requirement and a requirement for a cause of action matters to an administrative lawyer because the failure to meet a standing requirement is a defect that the parties cannot waive, and a court may raise on its own (*"sua sponte"*) at any stage of the proceeding. For that reason, we urge you to internalize the quotation marks we use when we talk about statutory "standing" requirements.

Below we discuss two types of statutory "standing" restrictions:

a)   the zone of interests requirement

b)   "party" restrictions

a. Zone of Interests Requirement

We separately discuss below (i) the origin of the zone of interests requirement (or "test"); (ii) what the requirement means; and (iii) how to recognize when the requirement applies.

In brief, the zone of interests requirement began life as a requirement for having standing in the federal courts. The Court later clarified that it is a prudential standing requirement. Despite its origins as a standing requirement, however, administrative lawyers encounter the requirement primarily because the Court has held that it is codified in the federal APA and special review statutes that create rights to judicial review of federal agency actions.

Roughly speaking, in administrative law cases the zone of interests requirement means that the plaintiff must show that the plaintiff's interests in bringing the lawsuit are not incongruent with the interests that are meant to be protected or regulated by the statutory provision that the plaintiff claims has been violated by the defendant. This showing is not too burdensome. In particular, the plaintiff doesn't have to show that, in enacting the statutory provision, Congress affirmatively intended to protect or regulate the interests that the plaintiff is asserting. Rather, the plaintiff can meet the zone of interests requirement unless it seems quite unlikely that Congress would have intended someone like the plaintiff to sue to enforce the provision.

The plaintiff must satisfy the zone of interests requirement when the plaintiff's cause of action rests on the federal APA or any special review provision that incorporates the requirement. The requirement is common in administrative law, because the Court has held that Congress is presumed to legislate with knowledge of the requirement and to intend the requirement to apply unless there's evidence of a contrary intent. The main situation in which the Court finds evidence of congressional intent to relax or negate the requirement is in citizen suit provisions, which typically authorize suits by "any person" who can satisfy constitutional standing requirements.

Below we go into detail about the zone of interests requirement. We warn you, though, that its unusual origins and elusive meaning cause some who study it to feel like they have entered the Twilight Zone.[6]

(i) Origin of Requirement

The zone of interests test is basically a vestige of a now-discarded test for standing known as the "legal interest" or "legal right" test.

At one time, to show standing the plaintiff in a federal court lawsuit had to show that defendant violated a "legal interest" or, synonymously, a "legal right" of the plaintiff. These terms referred to an individualized interest (or right) protected *by law*, such as by the law of property or contract. Under the legal interest test, it wasn't enough for the plaintiff to show actual injury; the plaintiff had to show injury to the plaintiff's legally protected interest (or right).

Under the legal interest test, for example, the Court held that a private power company, the Tennessee Electric Power Company (Tennessee Electric), lacked standing to challenge the Act of Congress creating the Tennessee Valley Authority (TVA). The TVA was a government power project that would supply power to the same customers that Tennessee Electric served. Everyone admitted, and the Court recognized, that the TVA would cause severe competitive injury to Tennessee Electric; today we would call it "injury in fact." The actual injury that the statute would cause Tennessee Electric did not matter because no *law* protected Tennessee Electric from competition. To quote the Court, Tennessee Electric lacked standing because it could not show invasion of "a legal right, ... one of property, one arising out of contract, one protected against tortious invasion, or one founded on a statute which confers a privilege." *Tennessee Elec. Power Co. v. TVA*, 306 U.S. 118, 137 (1939). Tennessee's competitive injury was real, but was not (to use the jargon) "legally cognizable" under the law as it then stood.

The Court abandoned the legal interest (i.e., legal right) requirement in *Association of Data Processing Service Organizations v. Camp*, 397 U.S. 150 (1970) (hereafter cited as *Data Processing*); *see also Barlow v. Collins*, 397 U.S. 159 (1970) (companion case to *Data Processing*). *Data Processing*, like *Tennessee Electric*, concerned competitive injury. An association of companies that sold data processing services sued the Comptroller of the Currency for deciding to allow banks to sell data processing services to certain customers. The Court upheld the association's standing. In analyzing standing, the Court said, "The first question is whether the plaintiff alleges that the challenged action has caused him *injury in fact*, economic or otherwise." *Id.* at 152 (emphasis added). The Court meant

---

6. The Twilight Zone was a fantasy/science fiction television show first aired in the early 1960s and famous for its eerie opening music and introduction, one version of which was: "You unlock this door with the key of imagination. Beyond it is another dimension: a dimension of sound, a dimension of sight, a dimension of mind. You're moving into a land of both shadow and substance, of things and ideas. You've just crossed over into ... the Twilight Zone." http://www.youtube.com/watch?v=NzlG28B-R8Y.

actual injury, as distinguished from injury to a legal interest or right. The Court determined that the association's members would suffer injury in fact from the Comptroller's decision because that decision allowed banks to compete with them. *Id.* This threatened injury in fact satisfied Article III's requirement that the plaintiff present a "case" or "controversy."

The conclusion that the association presented a case or controversy did not end the *Data Processing* Court's standing analysis. The Court explained there was another step:

> The question of standing ... concerns, apart from the "case" or "controversy" test, the question whether the interest sought to be protected by the complainant is arguably within the *zone of interests* to be protected or regulated by the statute or constitutional guarantee in question. Thus the Administrative Procedure Act grants standing to a person "aggrieved by agency action within the meaning of a relevant statute." 5 U.S.C. § 702 (1964 ed., Supp. IV). That interest, at times, may reflect aesthetic, conservational, and recreational as well as economic values.

Data Processing, 397 U.S. at 153–154 (emphasis added). Thus, the Court identified the zone of interests requirement as an additional standing requirement — existing over and above the "injury in fact" requirement — and the Court found this additional standing requirement codified in language in § 702 of the APA referring to **"aggrieve[ment] ... within the meaning of a relevant statute."** In later cases, the Court clarified that, unlike the "injury in fact" requirement, the zone of interests requirement is a prudential standing requirement, which means that Congress can alter it. *See, e.g., Bennett v. Spear*, 520 U.S. 154, 163–164 (1997).

The Court in *Data Processing* determined that the data processing companies were arguably within the zone of interests protected by the federal statutory restrictions on the activities of banks. *Data Processing*, 397 U.S. at 156. The Court cited legislative history of one banking statute showing Congress's intent to restrict banks to banking activities (apparently to keep them from getting into trouble by taking on activities that were too risky or that they weren't competent to perform). The Court found Congress's intent congruent with the purposes of companies that would suffer competitive injury from a decision allowing banks to perform nonbanking activities. The congruence was close enough that the relevant statute "arguably brings a competitor within the zone of interests protected by it." *Id.* at 155–156.

In sum, *Data Processing* abandoned the legal interest (legal right) requirement in favor of requiring "injury in fact" plus satisfaction of the zone of interests requirement. The legal basis for this change in standing law is not clear. Perhaps *Data Processing* reflected a compromise. Perhaps some Justices — but not a majority — wanted to require only "injury in fact," while others would not approve a purely fact-based approach to analyzing the harm requirement for standing. Thus, the Court adopted the "zone of interests" test to ensure that the actual injury asserted by the plaintiff had some loose, arguable connection with the law that the plaintiff claimed the defendant was violating. *See Data Processing*, 397 U.S. at 167 (Brennan, J., concurring and dissenting) (arguing that Court should only require showing of injury in fact; imposing the zone of interests requirement "comes very close to perpetuating the discredited requirement that conditioned standing on a showing by the plaintiff that the challenged governmental action invaded one of his legally protected interests").

In any event, plaintiffs no longer must show injury to a legal right or interest to have standing. They still, however, must satisfy the zone of interests requirement in many federal court lawsuits seeking review of federal agency action, and so administrative lawyers must know what the requirement means.

(ii) Meaning of Requirement

The zone of interests requirement demands some degree of congruence between, on the one hand, the plaintiff's interests in bringing a lawsuit to enforce a statutory or constitutional provision and, on the other hand, the purposes of the provision to be enforced. We will focus on lawsuits to enforce statutory provisions, because they predominate in administrative law. So focused, the Court has said that the zone of interests requirement

> denies a right of review if the plaintiff's interests are so marginally related to or inconsistent with the purposes implicit in the statute that it cannot reasonably be assumed that Congress intended to permit the suit. The test is not meant to be especially demanding; in particular, there need be no indication of congressional purpose to benefit the would-be plaintiff.

Clarke v. Sec. Indus. Ass'n, 479 U.S. 388, 399 (1987).

You take three steps to determine whether the plaintiff in a particular lawsuit satisfies the zone of interests test.

1. You identify the plaintiff's interest in bringing the lawsuit. You do this by examining the interests that the plaintiff claims have been harmed or are threatened with harm by the defendant's conduct. Thus, this first step studies the "injury in fact" asserted by the plaintiff. In *Data Processing*, for example, the plaintiff association's members' interest was to prevent banks from selling data processing services in competition with the members.

2. You identify the interests sought to be protected or regulated by the statutory provision that plaintiffs seek to enforce—i.e., the provision that plaintiffs claim has been violated. In *Data Processing*, for example, the Court examined banking statutes to find that Congress had an interest in limiting banks to banking activities.

3. You decide whether the interests identified at steps 1 and 2 have the degree of congruence required by the statute that creates the plaintiff's cause of action. The *Data Processing* Court held that the cause of action created by the federal APA is "generous," meaning that it requires only very rough congruence between the plaintiff's interests and those of the provision sought to be enforced. 397 U.S. at 156. In another case, the Court held that the special review provision in the Endangered Species Act required even less congruence than the APA and perhaps even "negated" the requirement entirely. *Bennett v. Spear*, 520 U.S. 154, 164 (1997). More generally, the Court has said, "The breadth of the zone of interests varies according to the provisions of law at issue, so that what comes within the zone of interests of a statute for purposes of obtaining judicial review of administrative action under the generous review provisions of the APA may not do so for other purposes." *Id.* at 163.

Thus, the test requires analysis of two different statutory provisions. At step two you examine the provision that the plaintiff seeks to enforce, which "generates" the interests that Congress sought to protect and with which with which plaintiff's must bear some degree of congruence. At step three you examine the provision that creates the plaintiff's cause of action, which may be the federal APA or a special review statute. That provision generates the zone—i.e., establishes the required degree of congruence that must exist between the plaintiff's interests and the interests regulated or protected by the statute that plaintiff seeks to enforce.

By this point you may wonder: Why does this zone of interests requirement exist? The Court's decisions suggest two answers. The Court's decisions characterizing the requirement as a prudential standing requirement imply that the Court imposes this requirement as a judicially "self-imposed limi[t] on … federal jurisdiction." *Allen v. Wright*, 468 U.S. 737, 751 (1984). In contrast, the Court's decisions construing the requirement as codified in the federal APA and special review statutes treat the requirement as a congressionally imposed restriction on the scope of the cause of action created in these statutes. Perhaps in administrative law cases the zone of interests requirement reflects both judicial policies and, at least presumptively, congressional intent.

We excerpt below a leading administrative law case on the operation of the zone of interests requirement, *Bennett v. Spear*, 520 U.S. 154 (1997). We include in the excerpt the Court's discussion of constitutional standing for two reasons. First, constitutional standing relates to the zone of interests test, as the zone test began life as a standing requirement and continues to exist as one outside the administrative-law context. Second, *Bennett* discusses an issue of constitutional standing we discussed above: the "third party problem," which can make it hard for a plaintiff to show traceability.

Exercise: *Bennett v. Spear*

Please read *Bennett* with these questions in mind:

1. What three claims of statutory violations did the plaintiffs make? Which of these claims did the Court find fell within the cause of action created by the ESA's citizen suit provision? Which of these claims did the Court find fell within the federal APA's cause of action? What difference does it make which statute supplied the cause of action for which claims?

2. According to the Court, how does the ESA's citizen suit provision affect the zone of interests requirement? What's the Court's rationale for its determination of how the ESA's citizen suit provision affects the zone of interests requirement?

3. According to the Court, why do the plaintiffs meet the federal APA's zone of interests requirement?

4. What would have happened if the plaintiffs had failed to meet the federal APA's zone of interests requirement?

Bennett v. Spear

520 U.S. 154 (1997)

JUSTICE SCALIA delivered the opinion of the Court.

This is a challenge to a biological opinion issued by the Fish and Wildlife Service in accordance with the Endangered Species Act of 1973 (ESA), concerning the operation of the Klamath Irrigation Project by the Bureau of Reclamation, and the project's impact on two varieties of endangered fish. The question for decision is whether the petitioners, who have competing economic and other interests in Klamath Project water, have standing to seek judicial review of the biological opinion under the citizen suit provision of the ESA, § 1540(g)(1), and the Administrative Procedure Act (APA), 5 U.S.C. § 701 *et seq.*

I

The ESA requires the Secretary of the Interior to promulgate regulations listing those species of animals that are "threatened" or "endangered" under specified criteria, and to designate their "critical habitat." 16 U.S.C. § 1533. The ESA further requires each federal agency to "insure that any action authorized, funded, or carried out by such agency ... is not likely to jeopardize the continued existence of any endangered species or threatened species or result in the destruction or adverse modification of habitat of such species which is determined by the Secretary ... to be critical." § 1536(a)(2). If an agency determines that action it proposes to take may adversely affect a listed species, it must engage in formal consultation with the Fish and Wildlife Service, as delegate of the Secretary, *ibid.*, after which the Service must provide the agency with a written statement (the Biological Opinion) explaining how the proposed action will affect the species or its habitat, 16 U.S.C. § 1536(b)(3)(A). If the Service concludes that the proposed action will "jeopardize the continued existence of any [listed] species or result in the destruction or adverse modification of [critical habitat]," § 1536(a)(2), the Biological Opinion must outline any "reasonable and prudent alternatives" that the Service believes will avoid that consequence, § 1536(b)(3)(A). Additionally, if the Biological Opinion concludes that the agency action will not result in jeopardy or adverse habitat modification, or if it offers reasonable and prudent alternatives to avoid that consequence, the Service must provide the agency with a written statement (known as the "Incidental Take Statement") specifying the "impact of such incidental taking on the species," any "reasonable and prudent measures that the [Service] considers necessary or appropriate to minimize such impact," and setting forth "the terms and conditions ... that must be complied with by the Federal agency ... to implement [those measures]." § 1536(b)(4).

The Klamath Project, one of the oldest federal reclamation schemes, is a series of lakes, rivers, dams and irrigation canals in northern California and southern Oregon. The project was undertaken by the Secretary of the Interior pursuant to the Reclamation Act of 1902, and the Act of Feb. 9, 1905, 33 Stat. 714, and is administered by the Bureau of Reclamation, which is under the Secretary's jurisdiction. In 1992, the Bureau notified the Service that operation of the project might affect the Lost River Sucker (*Deltistes luxatus*) and Shortnose Sucker (*Chasmistes brevirostris*), species of fish that were listed as endangered in 1988. After formal consultation with the Bureau ..., the Service issued a Biological Opinion which concluded that the "'long term operation of the Klamath Project was likely to jeopardize the continued existence of the Lost River and shortnose suckers.'" The Biological Opinion identified "reasonable and prudent alternatives" the Service believed would avoid jeopardy, which included the maintenance of minimum water levels on Clear Lake and Gerber reservoirs. The Bureau later notified the Service that it intended to operate the project in compliance with the Biological Opinion.

Petitioners, two Oregon irrigation districts that receive Klamath Project water and the operators of two ranches within those districts, filed the present action against the director and regional director of the Service and the Secretary of the Interior. Neither the Bureau nor any of its officials is named as defendant. The complaint asserts that the Bureau "has been following essentially the same procedures for storing and releasing water from Clear Lake and Gerber reservoirs throughout the twentieth century"; that "there is no scientifically or commercially available evidence indicating that the populations of endangered suckers in Clear Lake and Gerber reservoirs have declined, are declining, or will decline as a result" of the Bureau's operation of the Klamath Project; that "there is no commercially or scientifically available evidence indicating that the restrictions on lake levels imposed in the Biological Opinion will have any beneficial effect on the ... populations of suckers in

Clear Lake and Gerber reservoirs"; and that the Bureau nonetheless "will abide by the restrictions imposed by the Biological Opinion."

Petitioners' complaint included three claims for relief that are relevant here. The first
and second claims allege that the Service's jeopardy determination with respect to Clear
Lake and Gerber reservoirs, and the ensuing imposition of minimum water levels, violated
§ 7 of the ESA, 16 U.S.C. § 1536. The third claim is that the imposition of minimum
water elevations constituted an implicit determination of critical habitat for the suckers,
which violated § 4 of the ESA, 16 U.S.C. § 1533(b)(2), because it failed to take into consideration the designation's economic impact. Each of the claims also states that the
relevant action violated the APA's prohibition of agency action that is "arbitrary, capricious,
an abuse of discretion, or otherwise not in accordance with law." 5 U.S.C. § 706(2)(A).

The complaint asserts that petitioners' use of the reservoirs and related waterways for
"recreational, aesthetic and commercial purposes, as well as for their primary sources of
irrigation water" will be "irreparably damaged" by the actions complained of, and that
the restrictions on water delivery "recommended" by the Biological Opinion "adversely
affect plaintiffs by substantially reducing the quantity of available irrigation water." In
essence, petitioners claim a competing interest in the water the Biological Opinion declares
necessary for the preservation of the suckers.

The District Court dismissed the complaint for lack of jurisdiction.... The Court of
Appeals for the Ninth Circuit affirmed. It held that the "zone of interests" test limits the
class of persons who may obtain judicial review not only under the APA, but also under
the citizen suit provision of the ESA, 16 U.S.C. § 1540(g), and that "only plaintiffs who
allege an interest in the preservation of endangered species fall within the zone of interests
protected by the ESA."

In this Court, petitioners raise two questions: first, whether the prudential standing
rule known as the "zone of interests" test applies to claims brought under the citizen suit
provision of the ESA; and second, if so, whether petitioners have standing under that
test notwithstanding that the interests they seek to vindicate are economic rather than
environmental. In this Court, the Government has made no effort to defend the reasoning
of the Court of Appeals. Instead, it advances three alternative grounds for affirmance:
(1) that petitioners fail to meet the standing requirements imposed by Article III of the
Constitution; (2) that the ESA's citizen suit provision does not authorize judicial review
of the types of claims advanced by petitioners; and (3) that judicial review is unavailable
under the APA because the Biological Opinion does not constitute final agency action.

II

We first turn to the question the Court of Appeals found dispositive: whether petitioners
lack standing by virtue of the zone of interests test. Although petitioners contend that
their claims lie both under the ESA and the APA, we look first at the ESA because it may
permit petitioners to recover their litigation costs, see 16 U.S.C. § 1540(g)(4), and because
the APA by its terms independently authorizes review only when "there is no other adequate
remedy in a court," 5 U.S.C. § 704....

The "zone of interests" formulation was first employed in *Association of Data Processing
Service Organizations, Inc. v. Camp*, 397 U.S. 150 (1970).... *Data Processing*, and its companion
case, *Barlow v. Collins*, 397 U.S. 159 (1970), applied the zone of interests test to suits under
the APA, but later cases have applied it also in suits not involving review of federal administrative
action.... We have made clear, however, that the breadth of the zone of interests varies according
to the provisions of law at issue, so that what comes within the zone of interests of a statute

for purposes of obtaining judicial review of administrative action under the "'generous review provisions'" of the APA may not do so for other purposes, *Clarke v. Securities Industry Assn.*, 479 U.S. 388, 400, n. 16 (1987) (quoting *Data Processing, supra*, at 156).

Congress legislates against the background of our prudential standing doctrine, which applies unless it is expressly negated. The first question in the present case is whether the ESA's citizen suit provision, set forth in pertinent part in the margin,[2] negates the zone of interests test (or, perhaps more accurately, expands the zone of interests). We think it does. The first operative portion of the provision says that "any person may commence a civil suit"—an authorization of remarkable breadth when compared with the language Congress ordinarily uses. Even in some other environmental statutes, Congress has used more restrictive formulations, such as "[any person] having an interest which is or may be adversely affected," 33 U.S.C. § 1365(g) (Clean Water Act); see also 30 U.S.C. § 1270(a) (Surface Mining Control and Reclamation Act) (same); "any person suffering legal wrong," 15 U.S.C. § 797(b)(5) (Energy Supply and Environmental Coordination Act); or "any person having a valid legal interest which is or may be adversely affected ... whenever such action constitutes a case or controversy," 42 U.S.C. § 9124(a) (Ocean Thermal Energy Conversion Act). And in contexts other than the environment, Congress has often been even more restrictive. In statutes concerning unfair trade practices and other commercial matters, for example, it has authorized suit only by "any person injured in his business or property," 7 U.S.C. § 2305(c); see also 15 U.S.C. § 72 (same), or only by "competitors, customers, or subsequent purchasers," § 298(b).

Our readiness to take the term "any person" at face value is greatly augmented by two interrelated considerations: that the overall subject matter of this legislation is the environment (a matter in which it is common to think all persons have an interest) and that the obvious purpose of the particular provision in question is to encourage enforcement by so called "private attorneys general" ...

It is true that the plaintiffs here are seeking to prevent application of environmental restrictions rather than to implement them. But the "any person" formulation applies to

---

2. "(1) Except as provided in paragraph (2) of this subsection any person may commence a civil suit on his own behalf—

"(A) to enjoin any person, including the United States and any other governmental instrumentality or agency (to the extent permitted by the eleventh amendment to the Constitution), who is alleged to be in violation of any provision of this chapter or regulation issued under the authority thereof; or ...

"(C) against the Secretary where there is alleged a failure of the Secretary to perform any act or duty under section 1533 of this title which is not discretionary with the Secretary.

"The district courts shall have jurisdiction, without regard to the amount in controversy or the citizenship of the parties, to enforce any such provision or regulation, or to order the Secretary to perform such act or duty, as the case may be....

"(2)(A) No action may be commenced under subparagraph (1)(A) of this section—

"(i) prior to sixty days after written notice of the violation has been given to the Secretary, and to any alleged violator of any such provision or regulation;

"(ii) if the Secretary has commenced action to impose a penalty pursuant to subsection (a) of this section; or

"(iii) if the United States has commenced and is diligently prosecuting a criminal action ... to redress a violation of any such provision or regulation....

"(3)(B) In any such suit under this subsection in which the United States is not a party, the Attorney General, at the request of the Secretary, may intervene on behalf of the United States as a matter of right.

"(4) The court, in issuing any final order in any suit brought pursuant to paragraph (1) of this subsection, may award costs of litigation (including reasonable attorney and expert witness fees) to any party, whenever the court determines such award is appropriate." 16 U.S.C. § 1540(g).

all the causes of action authorized by § 1540(g) — not only to actions against private violators of environmental restrictions, and not only to actions against the Secretary asserting underenforcement under § 1533, but also to actions against the Secretary asserting overenforcement under § 1533.... The Court of Appeals therefore erred in concluding that petitioners lacked standing under the zone of interests test to bring their claims under the ESA's citizen suit provision.

III

The Government advances several alternative grounds upon which it contends we may affirm the dismissal of petitioners' suit....

A

The Government's first contention is that petitioners' complaint fails to satisfy the standing requirements imposed by the "case" or "controversy" provision of Article III....

Petitioners allege, among other things, that they currently receive irrigation water from Clear Lake, that the Bureau "will abide by the restrictions imposed by the Biological Opinion," and that "the restrictions on lake levels imposed in the Biological Opinion adversely affect [petitioners] by substantially reducing the quantity of available irrigation water." The Government contends, first, that these allegations fail to satisfy the "injury in fact" element of Article III standing because they demonstrate only a diminution in the aggregate amount of available water, and do not necessarily establish (absent information concerning the Bureau's water allocation practices) that the petitioners will receive less water. This contention overlooks, however, the proposition that each element of Article III standing "must be supported in the same way as any other matter on which the plaintiff bears the burden of proof, i.e., with the manner and degree of evidence required at the successive stages of the litigation." *Defenders of Wildlife, supra,* at 561. Thus, while a plaintiff must "set forth" by affidavit or other evidence "specific facts," to survive a motion for summary judgment, Fed. Rule Civ. Proc. 56(e), and must ultimately support any contested facts with evidence adduced at trial, "at the pleading stage, general factual allegations of injury resulting from the defendant's conduct may suffice, for on a motion to dismiss we 'presume that general allegations embrace those specific facts that are necessary to support the claim.'" *Defenders of Wildlife, supra,* at 561 (quoting *Lujan v. National Wildlife Federation,* 497 U.S. 871, 889 (1990)). Given petitioners' allegation that the amount of available water will be reduced and that they will be adversely affected thereby, it is easy to presume specific facts under which petitioners will be injured — for example, the Bureau's distribution of the reduction pro rata among its customers. The complaint alleges the requisite injury in fact.

The Government also contests compliance with the second and third Article III standing requirements, contending that any injury suffered by petitioners is neither "fairly traceable" to the Service's Biological Opinion, nor "redressable" by a favorable judicial ruling, because the "action agency" (the Bureau) retains ultimate responsibility for determining whether and how a proposed action shall go forward. See 50 CFR § 402.15(a) (1995) ("Following the issuance of a biological opinion, the Federal agency shall determine whether and in what manner to proceed with the action in light of its section 7 obligations and the Service's biological opinion"). "If the petitioners have suffered injury," the Government contends, "the proximate cause of their harm is an (as yet unidentified) decision by the Bureau regarding the volume of water allocated to petitioners, not the biological opinion itself." This wrongly equates injury "fairly traceable" to the defendant with injury as to which the defendant's actions are the very last step in the chain of causation. While, as we have said, it does not suffice if the injury complained of is "'the result [of] the independent action of some third party not before the court,'" *Defenders of Wildlife, supra,* 504 U.S. at 560–561 (emphasis added) (quoting *Simon v. Eastern Ky. Welfare Rights Organization,* 426 U.S. 26, 41–42 (1976)), that does not exclude injury produced by determinative or coercive effect upon the action of someone else.

By the Government's own account, while the Service's Biological Opinion theoretically serves an "advisory function," 51 Fed. Reg. 19928 (1986), in reality it has a powerful coercive effect on the action agency:

> "The statutory scheme ... presupposes that the biological opinion will play a central role in the action agency's decisionmaking process, and that it will typically be based on an administrative record that is fully adequate for the action agency's decision insofar as ESA issues are concerned.... [A] federal agency that chooses to deviate from the recommendations contained in a biological opinion bears the burden of 'articulating in its administrative record its reasons for disagreeing with the conclusions of a biological opinion,' 51 Fed. Reg. 19,956 (1986). In the government's experience, action agencies very rarely choose to engage in conduct that the Service has concluded is likely to jeopardize the continued existence of a listed species." Brief for Respondents 20–21.

What this concession omits to say, moreover, is that the action agency must not only articulate its reasons for disagreement (which ordinarily requires species and habitat investigations that are not within the action agency's expertise), but that it runs a substantial risk if its (inexpert) reasons turn out to be wrong. A Biological Opinion of the sort rendered here alters the legal regime to which the action agency is subject. When it "offers reasonable and prudent alternatives" to the proposed action, a Biological Opinion must include a so called "Incidental Take Statement"—a written statement specifying, among other things, those "measures that the [Service] considers necessary or appropriate to minimize [the action's impact on the affected species]" and the "terms and conditions ... that must be complied with by the Federal agency ... to implement [such] measures." 16 U.S.C. § 1536(b)(4). Any taking that is in compliance with these terms and conditions "shall not be considered to be a prohibited taking of the species concerned." § 1536(o)(2). Thus, the Biological Opinion's Incidental Take Statement constitutes a permit authorizing the action agency to "take" the endangered or threatened species so long as it respects the Service's "terms and conditions." The action agency is technically free to disregard the Biological Opinion and proceed with its proposed action, but it does so at its own peril (and that of its employees), for "any person" who knowingly "takes" an endangered or threatened species is subject to substantial civil and criminal penalties, including imprisonment. See §§ 1540(a) and (b) (authorizing civil fines of up to $25,000 per violation and criminal penalties of up to $50,000 and imprisonment for one year) ...

The Service itself is, to put it mildly, keenly aware of the virtually determinative effect of its biological opinions. The Incidental Take Statement at issue in the present case begins by instructing the reader that any taking of a listed species is prohibited unless "such taking is in compliance with this incidental take statement," and warning that "the measures described below are nondiscretionary, and must be taken by [the Bureau]." Given all of this, and given petitioners' allegation that the Bureau had, until issuance of the Biological Opinion, operated the Klamath Project in the same manner throughout the twentieth century, it is not difficult to conclude that petitioners have met their burden—which is relatively modest at this stage of the litigation—of alleging that their injury is "fairly traceable" to the Service's Biological Opinion and that it will "likely" be redressed—i.e., the Bureau will not impose such water level restrictions—if the Biological Opinion is set aside.

B

Next, the Government contends that the ESA's citizen suit provision does not authorize judicial review of petitioners' claims. The relevant portions of that provision provide that

"any person may commence a civil suit on his own behalf—

"(A) to enjoin any person, including the United States and any other governmental instrumentality or agency ... who is alleged to be in violation of any provision of this chapter or regulation issued under the authority thereof; or ..."(C) against the Secretary [of Commerce or the Interior] where there is alleged a failure of the Secretary to perform any act or duty under section 1533 of this title which is not discretionary with the Secretary." 16 U.S.C. § 1540(g)(1).

The Government argues that judicial review is not available under subsection (A) because the Secretary is not "in violation" of the ESA, and under subsection (C) because the Secretary has not failed to perform any nondiscretionary duty under § 1533.

1

Turning first to subsection (C): that it covers only violations of § 1533 is clear and unambiguous. Petitioners' first and second claims, which assert that the Secretary has violated § 1536, are obviously not reviewable under this provision. However, as described above, the third claim alleges that the Biological Opinion implicitly determines critical habitat without complying with the mandate of § 1533(b)(2) that the Secretary "take into consideration the economic impact, and any other relevant impact, of specifying any particular area as critical habitat." This claim does come within subsection (C)....

2

Having concluded that petitioners' § 1536 claims are not reviewable under subsection (C), we are left with the question whether they are reviewable under subsection (A), which authorizes injunctive actions against any person "who is alleged to be in violation" of the ESA or its implementing regulations. The Government contends that the Secretary's conduct in implementing or enforcing the ESA is not a "violation" of the ESA within the meaning of this provision. In its view, § 1540(g)(1)(A) is a means by which private parties may enforce the substantive provisions of the ESA against regulated parties—both private entities and Government agencies—but is not an alternative avenue for judicial review of the Secretary's implementation of the statute. We agree....

IV

The foregoing analysis establishes that the principal statute invoked by petitioners, the ESA, does authorize review of their § 1533 claim, but does not support their claims based upon the Secretary's alleged failure to comply with § 1536. To complete our task, we must therefore inquire whether these § 1536 claims may nonetheless be brought under the Administrative Procedure Act, which authorizes a court to "set aside agency action, findings, and conclusions found to be ... arbitrary, capricious, an abuse of discretion, or otherwise not in accordance with law," 5 U.S.C. § 706.

A

No one contends (and it would not be maintainable) that the causes of action against the Secretary set forth in the ESA's citizen suit provision are exclusive, supplanting those provided by the APA. The APA, by its terms, provides a right to judicial review of all "final agency action for which there is no other adequate remedy in a court," 5 U.S.C. § 704, and applies universally "except to the extent that—(1) statutes preclude judicial review; or (2) agency action is committed to agency discretion by law," § 701(a). Nothing in the ESA's citizen suit provision expressly precludes review under the APA, nor do we detect anything in the statutory scheme suggesting a purpose to do so. And any contention that the relevant provision of 16 U.S.C. § 1536(a)(2) is discretionary would fly in the face of its text, which uses the imperative "shall."

In determining whether the petitioners have standing under the zone of interests test to bring their APA claims, we look not to the terms of the ESA's citizen suit provision, but to the substantive provisions of the ESA, the alleged violations of which serve as the gravamen of the complaint. See *National Wildlife Federation*, 497 U.S. at 886. The classic formulation of the zone of interests test is set forth in *Data Processing*, 397 U.S. at 153: "whether the interest sought to be protected by the complainant is arguably within the zone of interests to be protected or regulated by the statute or constitutional guarantee in question." The Court of Appeals concluded that this test was not met here, since petitioners are neither directly regulated by the ESA nor seek to vindicate its overarching purpose of species preservation. That conclusion was error.

Whether a plaintiff's interest is "arguably ... protected ... by the statute" within the meaning of the zone of interests test is to be determined not by reference to the overall purpose of the Act in question (here, species preservation), but by reference to the particular provision of law upon which the plaintiff relies.... As we said with the utmost clarity in *National Wildlife Federation*, "the plaintiff must establish that the injury he complains of ... falls within the 'zone of interests' sought to be protected by the statutory provision whose violation forms the legal basis for his complaint." *National Wildlife Federation*, *supra*, at 883 (emphasis added).

In the claims that we have found not to be covered by the ESA's citizen suit provision, petitioners allege a violation of § 7 of the ESA, 16 U.S.C. § 1536, which requires, *inter alia*, that each agency "use the best scientific and commercial data available," § 1536(a)(2). Petitioners contend that the available scientific and commercial data show that the continued operation of the Klamath Project will not have a detrimental impact on the endangered suckers, that the imposition of minimum lake levels is not necessary to protect the fish, and that by issuing a Biological Opinion which makes unsubstantiated findings to the contrary the defendants have acted arbitrarily and in violation of § 1536(a)(2). The obvious purpose of the requirement that each agency "use the best scientific and commercial data available" is to ensure that the ESA not be implemented haphazardly, on the basis of speculation or surmise. While this no doubt serves to advance the ESA's overall goal of species preservation, we think it readily apparent that another objective (if not indeed the primary one) is to avoid needless economic dislocation produced by agency officials zealously but unintelligently pursuing their environmental objectives. That economic consequences are an explicit concern of the Act is evidenced by § 1536(h), which provides exemption from § 1536(a)(2)'s no jeopardy mandate where there are no reasonable and prudent alternatives to the agency action and the benefits of the agency action clearly outweigh the benefits of any alternatives. We believe the "best scientific and commercial data" provision is similarly intended, at least in part, to prevent uneconomic (because erroneous) jeopardy determinations. Petitioners' claim that they are victims of such a mistake is plainly within the zone of interests that the provision protects....

The Court of Appeals erred in affirming the District Court's dismissal of petitioners' claims for lack of jurisdiction. Petitioners' complaint alleges facts sufficient to meet the requirements of Article III standing, and none of their ESA claims is precluded by the zone of interests test. Petitioners' § 1533 claim is reviewable under the ESA's citizen suit provision, and petitioners' remaining claims are reviewable under the APA.

The judgment of the Court of Appeals is reversed, and the case is remanded for further proceedings consistent with this opinion.

Exercise: *Bennett v. Spear* Revisited

1. Notice that the plaintiffs did not name the Bureau of Reclamation or any of its officials, even though they are the ones most directly responsible for the loss of water with which plaintiffs are threatened. Why do you think plaintiffs chose not to name them as defendants?

2. Please describe in your own words (a) the relationship between the zone of interests test and the provision that supplies the cause of action for—i.e., right to judicial review of—a plaintiff's claim of a statutory violation; and (b) the relationship between the zone of interests test and the statute that the plaintiff claims has been violated.

3. *Bennett* reaches an arguably counterintuitive result: Plaintiffs whose interests were seemingly antithetical to endangered species were allowed to sue for a violation of the major federal statute designed to protect endangered species. How do you reconcile that result with the idea that, under the zone of interests test, the interests asserted by the plaintiffs must be at least roughly congruent with the interests regulated or protected by the statute they seek to enforce?

(iii) Determining When the Requirement Applies

In administrative law cases, the zone of interests requirement applies to any claim asserted under (A) the cause of action created by the federal APA; or (B) a special review provision incorporating the requirement.

The Court in *Data Processing* traced the federal APA's zone of interests requirement to the italicized portion of the first sentence of § 702:

---

§ 702. Right of review

A person suffering legal wrong because of agency action, *or adversely affected or aggrieved by agency action within the meaning of a relevant statute,* **is entitled to judicial review thereof....**

This sentence as a whole extends a cause of action to two categories of people: someone **"suffering legal wrong because of agency action"**; and (2) someone **"adversely affected or aggrieved by agency action within the meaning of a relevant statute."** The first category of people are ones who could have satisfied the old legal interest/legal right test for standing that the Court applied in cases like *Tennessee Electric Power Co. v. TVA*, 306 U.S. 118 (1939). This includes, for example, people whose business is regulated by the agency rule of which they seek judicial review, or who seek to challenge an agency fine, denial of a permit, or other adverse order. It is the second category of people who are subject to the zone of interests test. They must not only show injury in fact but also that their injury is not incongruent with the interests that Congress sought to protect in the **"relevant statute"** — meaning, the statute that they claim the defendant has violated.

The zone of interests test is not just a federal APA requirement. The Court said in *Bennett v. Spear*, "Congress legislates against the background of our prudential standing doctrine, which applies unless it is expressly negated." 520 U.S. at 163. Since the zone of interests test originated as a prudential standing requirement, the Court's statement means that a special review statute incorporates the test unless something in its text, legislative history, or other contextual information shows congressional intent to "negate" or modify the test. The Court found such an intent in the ESA's citizen suit provision. In contrast, the Court held in a more recent case that Congress intended to codify the traditional zone of interests test in a special review provision authorizing suits by a "person claiming to be aggrieved" by a statutory violation. *Thompson v. North American Stainless, LP.*, 131 S. Ct. 863, 869 (2011) (quoting the statute). This holding may broadly imply that a special review provision's use of the term "aggrieved" will be interpreted presumptively to incorporate the traditional zone of interests requirement.

In any event, as we leave the zone of interest, we express the hope that this discussion has held your interest and been illuminating enough that you don't feel too much like you have crossed over into … the Twilight Zone.

Exercise: Identifying When the Zone of Interests Requirement Applies

The objective of this exercise is to have you consider the possibility that Congress can not only expand the zone of interests, as the Court held Congress did in the ESA's citizen suit provision, but also contract it. The Court in *Bennett* quoted a special review provision authorizing a lawsuit by "[a]ny person suffering legal wrong." 520 U.S. at 165 (quoting statute). That provision comes from the Energy Supply and Environmental Coordination Act of 1974 (ESECA), which encourages power plants to burn coal as their primary energy source. The ESECA's special review provision authorizes suits for violations of (a) a provision that requires power plants, if possible, to burn coal as their primary energy source and (b) a provision that prohibits unauthorized disclosure of trade secrets and similar information that an energy company has been required to provide to the government. 15 U.S.C. § 797 (2012).

1. How do you think the special review provision in the ESECA affects the zone of interests requirement?

2. Describe a hypothetical lawsuit that could be brought under the ESECA's special review provision, including a description of the plaintiff and the claimed violation.

---

b. Party Restrictions

Some special review provisions authorizing judicial review of agency orders in adjudications limit the cause of action to people who were *parties* to the adjudication. *See, e.g.*, 16 U.S.C. § 825*l*(b) (2012) ("Any party to a proceeding under this chapter aggrieved by an order issued by the [Federal Energy Regulatory] Commission in such proceeding may obtain a [judicial] review of such order ..."); 2 U.S.C. §437g(a)(8)(A) (2012) (granting right of judicial review to "[a]ny party aggrieved by an order of the [Federal Election] Commission dismissing a complaint filed by such party" under §437g(a)(1)). This type of special review provision makes it important for the administrative lawyer planning eventual judicial review first to seek party status for the client in the agency adjudication—if party status is not accorded automatically—by following the statutory provisions and agency rules for timely intervention.

You might wonder what happens if the agency denies intervention: Can the would-be intervenor get judicial review of the agency's denial, or is judicial review precluded because the would-be intervenor never got "party" status? Courts construing one of the special review provisions limiting judicial review to parties, 16 U.S.C. §825*l*, have sensibly interpreted that provision to allow judicial review, reasoning:

> It would be grossly unfair to deny judicial review to a petitioner objecting to an agency's refusal to grant party status on the basis that the petitioner lacks party status. Such a petitioner must obviously be considered a party for the limited purpose of reviewing the agency's basis for denying party status.

Northern Colo. Water Conservancy Dist. v. FERC, 730 F.2d 1509, 1515 (D.C. Cir. 1984); *see Green Island Power Authority v. FERC*, 577 F.3d 148, 159 (2nd Cir. 2009). This means that, if you follow the agency statute and rules for seeking intervention but are denied, you can get judicial review of that denial, and, if successful, then hope to get invited to the party—we mean the agency proceeding in which you sought to intervene. *See Green Island Power*, 577 P.3d at 165 (after holding that FERC erroneously denied intervention, matter will be remanded to FERC to consider motion to intervene under proper standards).

Exercise: Synthesizing Standing Requirements

Here is a skeletal outline of the types of standing requirements and the subtopics that we discussed within each type:

1. Constitutional standing requirements
   a. injury in fact
   b. traceability
   c. redressability
2. Prudential standing requirements
   a. third-party standing
   b. generalized grievance
   c. zone of interests
3. Statutory standing requirements
   a. zone of interests
   b. citizen suit provisions
   c. party restrictions

Please use this outline as a basis for a more detailed outline or a graphic organizer that shows the relationship among the types of standing and, for each type of standing, the relationship among the subtopics listed above. In building your outline or graphic organizer, strive to identify the points most likely to have practical relevance for you as an administrative lawyer.

D. Jurisdiction: Standing Requirements in State Courts

"[T]he state courts are not bound to adhere to federal standing requirements." *ASARCO Inc. v. Kadish*, 490 U.S. 605, 617 (1989). Some state supreme courts, however, tend to follow federal precedent on standing, treating it as persuasive though not binding. Other state supreme courts do not follow federal-court standing principles, at least for some kinds of lawsuits.

The Oregon Supreme Court, for example, has held that a provision in the Oregon APA gives, quite literally, "any person" standing to challenge administrative rules in the State's courts. *See Kellas v. Dep't of Corrections*, 145 P.3d 139 (Ore. 2006) (discussing and quoting statute). Under that holding, anyone who cares enough to sue can do so. In contrast, the U.S. Supreme Court held in *Lujan v. Defenders of Wildlife* that a federal statute authorizing "any person" to sue in federal court for certain violations of the Endangered Species Act did not give standing to a plaintiff who lacked a concrete, personal interest in the suit. *Lujan v. Defenders of Wildlife*, 504 U.S. 555, 571–578 (1992). Leave it to Oregon to go its own way.

The broader point is that States can, and do, differ in their standing requirements for people challenging state agency action in their courts.

Exercise: State Court Standing

Suppose someone who would lack standing in federal court challenges an Oregon agency's rule in Oregon state court on the ground that the rule violates the U.S. Constitution. Also suppose that the Oregon state courts, including the Oregon Supreme Court, rejects the plaintiff's federal constitutional challenge to the Oregon rule. Can the U.S. Supreme Court review the Oregon Supreme Court's judgment if the plaintiff petitions for a writ of certiorari? *See Doremus v. Bd. of Educ.*, 342 U.S. 429, 434 (1952); *cf. ASARCO Inc. v. Kadish*, 490 U.S. 605, 617–624 (1989).

E. Venue

Whereas jurisdiction is all about the courts' power, venue is all about — to use the realtors' motto — location, location, location. Venue law identifies which court is located in the appropriate geographic location for a particular lawsuit. You will usually find the applicable venue law in statutes, and both the federal system and most States have two types of venue statutes: (1) special venue provisions for certain lawsuits and (2) general venue statutes for lawsuits that don't fall into a special provision. We will use federal statutes as examples.

Special federal venue provisions are usually found in the same special review provisions that grant *jurisdiction* to particular courts. For example, a venue provision can be found in the Clean Water Act's citizen suit provision. That provision grants jurisdiction to the district courts over suits alleging that a source of water pollution (known as a "discharge source") has violated a rule limiting water pollution (known as an "effluent standard or limitation"). The CWA's citizen suit provision includes this provision on venue:

---

33 U.S.C. § 1365. Citizen suits …

(c) Venue; intervention by Administrator …

(1) Any action respecting a violation by a discharge source of an effluent standard or limitation or an order respecting such standard or limitation may be brought under this section only in the judicial district in which such source is located.…

This CWA provision addresses venue for suits brought in federal district court. Special review provisions authorizing the federal courts of appeals to review certain agency actions may include venue provisions identifying which court of appeals can conduct the review. For example, venue for review of decisions of the National Labor Relations Board may be laid "in the circuit wherein the unfair labor practice in question was alleged to have been engaged in or wherein such person [seeking review] resides or transacts business, or in the United States Court of Appeals for the District of Columbia Circuit." 29 U.S.C. § 160(f) (2012). When a special venue provision like the ones cited in this paragraph applies, it governs.

In the federal system, the general venue statute for the federal district courts is 28 U.S.C. § 1391 (2012). In particular, § 1391(e) addresses venue in actions against federal agencies and officials. There is no comparable general venue provision for the federal courts of appeals, though the U.S. Court of Appeals for the Federal Circuit is the designated forum for review of certain actions by certain agencies, such as the Board of Patent Appeals and Interferences and the International Trade Commission. 28 U.S.C. §§ 1295 & 1296 (2012). The federal APA does not control venue, though it does includes a provision, § 703, entitled **"Form *and venue* of proceeding."** Contrary to what the italicized portion of that title might suggest, the Attorney General's Manual on the APA made clear that § 703 does not change existing venue provisions. AGM 98. Venue is governed by other statutes.

Lest the challenge of laying venue cause you to lay (or is it lie?) awake at night, you will be glad to know that federal law and most States authorize transfers of venue when a case is initially brought in the wrong venue, if the transfer is "in the interest of justice." *E.g.*, 28 U.S.C. § 1406(a) (2012).

F. Chapter 28 Wrap Up and Look Ahead

For a court to review agency action, the court must have jurisdiction. This chapter has focused on three jurisdictional requirements important for administrative lawyers to be able to analyze: (1) the requirement of a statute granting subject matter jurisdiction; (2) the requirement of a waiver of sovereign immunity, for lawsuits otherwise barred by sovereign immunity; and (3) the requirement that the plaintiff have standing. This chapter also touched upon the related subject of (4) venue.

Analysis of statutory subject matter jurisdiction begins by locating and analyzing the applicability of any special review provisions. If no special review provisions apply, analysis turns to general jurisdictional statutes.

Analysis of sovereign immunity involves finding the applicable statute waiving sovereign immunity. The federal APA serves that function for many federal-court lawsuits seeking review of federal agency actions. In addition to the federal APA, special federal review statutes may also waive sovereign immunity. Similarly, some state APAs waive state sovereign immunity, but other state laws may do so as well.

Standing analysis is multi-layered for hard standing cases, requiring consideration of constitutional, prudential, and statutory standing requirements.

With venue, though, we return to an analysis that is predominantly statutory, like so many other aspects of administrative law.

You have probably heard the expression "All dressed up with nowhere to go." If you have identified a court that is an appropriate venue and that has jurisdiction to hear your challenge to agency action, you have somewhere to go. But just as it is bad to go anywhere without the proper attire, you do not want to go to court without a cause of action — or, better yet, several causes of action. The next chapter examines the cause of action requirement.

Chapter Problem Revisited

1. When you research jurisdiction for a potential lawsuit challenging agency action, you begin by identifying and analyzing any special review statutes, because if a special review provision applies to your planned lawsuit, it will usually be exclusive. Here, you have identified one potentially applicable special review provision: 33 U.S.C. § 1365. The issue is whether it gives a court jurisdiction over either of the claims that you intend to assert.

   If you've examined § 1365, you know that it plainly does not include the NEPA claim; you may not readily be able to tell whether it covers the CWA claim. In fact, § 1365 does not cover the CWA claim, either. This should remind you, more generally, that a special review provision does not necessarily cover all claimed violations of the agency legislation in which the special review provision appears. The objective of having you read § 1365 is to illustrate the importance of the question whether a special review provision covers a particular lawsuit or a claim within that lawsuit. To answer the question, you must not only analyze the text of the statute but also may have to research case law to determine whether the special review provision has been construed to cover the kind of claims that you intend to assert.

2. The chapter problem notes that NEPA does not contain any special review provision. For this reason, NEPA suits are generally grounded on the federal-question grant of jurisdiction, which gives jurisdiction to the federal district courts. (The federal APA provides the cause of action for NEPA claims.)

3. Sovereign immunity is no bar to a suit that seeks simply to invalidate the Army's issuance of the permit. The APA supplies the waiver of sovereign immunity for both the NEPA and the CWA claim.

4. BOP can assert organizational standing if at least one of its members has standing. You must consider all three sets of standing requirements explored in this chapter. When you've done so, you should conclude that BOP satisfies all standing requirements.

Professional Development Reflection Question

The chapter problem involves a pro bono project. Pro bono projects are considered by many lawyers to be their most gratifying work. Their gratifying nature alone is a great reason for you to get into the habit of taking on pro bono work. This is not to mention the quasi-imperative to do pro bono work in the Model Rules of Professional Responsibility. *See* Model Rule of Professional Conduct 6.1.

There is a crying need for pro bono work in many areas of administrative law. Those areas include immigration matters, environmental matters, prisoners' rights, veterans' rights, elder rights, the rights of people with disabilities, and aid to the poor. For those of you who are interested in business law, many start-up businesses and nonprofit organizations would treasure pro bono help navigating administrative laws relating to the creation of business entities and obtaining tax-favored organizational status.

Of course, the gratifying nature of pro bono work depends on your finding pro bono projects that you care deeply about. What that in mind, what are three law-related issues you care about? What might you do as a law student to advance the ball on those issues through pro bono projects?

Chapter 29

Cause of Action

Overview

As discussed in Chapter 28, the person seeking judicial review of agency action must identify a court with jurisdiction to conduct the review. The person also must establish a cause of action, as discussed in this chapter. This chapter explains that statutes, and in particular APAs, are the most common source of a cause of action for review of agency actions. In addition to discussing the law creating causes of action, this chapter explores the rare situations in which, rather than creating a cause of action, the law precludes judicial review.

The sections' titles are:

A. The Requirement of a Cause of Action

B. Sources of a Cause of Action for Review of Federal Agency Action

C. Sources of a Cause of Action for Review of State Agency Action

D. Preclusion of Review

E. Chapter 29 Wrap Up and Look Ahead

Chapter Problem

Memo

To: Staffer

From: Representative White Eagle

Re: Funding Program

We are putting the finishing touches on a statute that will authorize the U.S. Department of Health and Human Services (HHS) to administer a new federal grant program. The program will award grants to people who design websites, posters, and public service advertisements to combat childhood obesity. The statute spells out criteria for HHS to consider in making awards, including factors like artistic merit, ingenuity, humor, informational value, and other factors.

Right now the draft legislation doesn't address whether someone who applies for a grant and is turned down can get judicial review. If the legislation remains silent on that matter, can someone who is turned down for a grant get judicial review of the denial? If so, should we consider putting something in the legislation to prevent judicial review? If we do decide to prohibit judicial review, can we prohibit even constitutional challenges to a denial of funding? (I ask that because I can imagine some poster artist claiming that the denial of an application for funding of a controversial poster violated the First Amendment. I'm not sure how I feel about allowing courts to review such claims. Still, I'd like to know whether such a lawsuit could be brought if we enact this program without mentioning any right of judicial review.) On the other hand, do we want to include special provisions authorizing judicial review under this program? What happens if the statute doesn't say anything about judicial review?

Thank you for your guidance on these questions.

A. The Requirement of a Cause of Action

It is not enough for a person seeking judicial review of agency action to show that he, she, or it has standing. The person must also plead and prove a cause of action (sometimes called a "right of review" in administrative law circles). The requirement that the plaintiff have a cause of action differs from the requirement that the plaintiff have standing. But the two are easy to confuse because each requires proof that the defendant has caused (or threatens) injury to the plaintiff. This section distinguishes the two requirements.

Recall that 50 years ago restaurants could refuse to serve black people. When a restaurant refused to serve a black person because that person was black, that person could have established *standing* to sue the restaurant under the modern law of constitutional standing: The refusal of service would constitute injury in fact; the injury would be traceable to the restaurant; and it would be redressable by a judicial award of damages or an injunction requiring the restaurant to serve the plaintiff. But the black person usually had no *cause of action* against the restaurant until Congress and the individual States enacted laws banning racial discrimination in restaurants (and other places of public accommodation) and authorizing lawsuits by the victims of such discrimination. It took time for the legal system to recognize the need for the victims of discrimination to be able to sue for remedies — i.e., to have causes of action — for the injuries actually caused by race discrimination.

If you have nonetheless found it hard to distinguish standing from a cause of action, you may be happy to know that, in fact, federal law did not always distinguish between them. As discussed in Chapter 28, until about the mid-twentieth century, to have standing in a federal court the plaintiff had to show that the defendant had deprived the plaintiff of a "legal right" or (synonymously) a "legal interest," terms which the Court defined to mean "one of property, one arising out of contract, one protected against tortious invasion, or one founded on a statute which confers a privilege." *Tennessee Elec. Power Co. v. Tennessee Valley Auth.*, 306 U.S. 118, 137 (1939). Under this old view of standing, proof of standing required proof that the defendant caused a "legal wrong" to the plaintiff by interfering with a "legal right" (or interest), which was tantamount to proving a cause of action. But the Court explicitly abandoned the legal right/legal interest concept in 1970. In two companion cases decided that year, the Court held that to have constitutional standing a plaintiff need not establish injury to some *legal* interest or right but instead needs only to show injury "*in fact*." *Ass'n of Data Processing Serv. Orgs. v. Camp*, 397 U.S. 150, 152 (1970); *Barlow v. Collins*, 397 U.S. 159, 163 (1970). The injury in fact concept separated the issue of whether the plaintiff had standing from the issue of whether plaintiff could establish a cause of action. *See* Cass R. Sunstein, *What's Standing After* Lujan? *Of Citizen Suits, "Injuries," and Article III*, 91 Mich. L. Rev. 163, 181–182 (1992).

That is why, when you devise a checklist of requirements for judicial relief against agency action, you must include standing and a cause of action as separate requirements.

B. Sources of a Cause of Action for Review of Federal Agency Action

The question naturally arises: Where do causes of action come from? The answer is that causes of action can come from any type of law: international law, constitutional law, common law, statutory law, and legislative rules. Statutes, however, are the main source of causes of action for judicial review of agency action. To be systematic about it, folks in administrative law circles recognize three general sources of a cause of action: (1) special statutory review; (2) general statutory review; and (3) "nonstatutory" review.

1. Special Statutory Review

We discussed in Chapter 28.A that special review statutes may grant jurisdiction to a particular court to review specified agency actions. These special review statutes also typically create a cause of action for review of the specified agency actions. Now we focus on their cause-of-action-creating function.

A common type of special review statute creating a cause of action is called a "citizen suit provision." Citizen suit provisions have that name because they create causes of action that are available to a broad range of plaintiffs. Many citizen suit provisions are in statutes designed to protect the environment or confer other benefits shared in common by broad segments of the population. Citizen plaintiffs help enforce these statutes by suing under the citizen suit provisions.

The citizen suit provision reproduced below comes from the Surface Mining Control and Reclamation Act of 1977 (SMCRA), 30 U.S.C. §§ 1251–1279 (2012). SMCRA is administered by the Secretary of the Interior and authorizes States to adopt programs to regulate surface mining within their borders. As you read SMCRA's citizen suit provision, please pay particular attention to:

- *who* may bring a citizen suit,
- *whom* the citizen may sue,
- *what* the citizen may sue about,
- *what requirements* the citizen must meet to sue, and
- *what judicial remedies* are available if the suit is successful.

Answering these questions will help you learn the scope and requirements for establishing a cause of action under this provision. As an added bonus, you will get practice analyzing a special review statute the way administrative lawyers do.

30 U.S.C. § 1270. Citizens suits

(a) Civil action to compel compliance with this chapter

Except as provided in subsection (b) of this section, any person having an interest which is or may be adversely affected may commence a civil action on his own behalf to compel compliance with this chapter—

(1) against the United States or any other governmental instrumentality or agency to the extent permitted by the eleventh amendment to the Constitution which is alleged to be in violation of the provisions of this chapter or of any rule, regulation, order or permit issued pursuant thereto, or against any other person who is alleged to be in violation of any rule, regulation, order or permit issued pursuant to this subchapter; or

(2) against the Secretary or the appropriate State regulatory authority to the extent permitted by the eleventh amendment to the Constitution where there is alleged a failure of the Secretary or the appropriate State regulatory authority to perform any act or duty under this chapter which is not discretionary with the Secretary or with the appropriate State regulatory authority.

The district courts shall have jurisdiction, without regard to the amount in controversy or the citizenship of the parties.

(b) Limitation on bringing of action

No action may be commenced—

(1) under subsection (a)(1) of this section—

(A) prior to sixty days after the plaintiff has given notice in writing of the violation (i) to the Secretary, (ii) to the State in which the violation occurs, and (iii) to any alleged violator; or

(B) if the Secretary or the State has commenced and is diligently prosecuting a civil action in a court of the United States or a State to require compliance with the provisions of this chapter, or any rule, regulation, order, or permit issued pursuant to this chapter, but in any such action in a court of the United States any person may intervene as a matter of right; or

(2) under subsection (a)(2) of this section prior to sixty days after the plaintiff has given notice in writing of such action to the Secretary, in such manner as the Secretary shall by regulation prescribe, or to the appropriate State regulatory authority, except that such action may be brought immediately after such notification in the case where the violation or order complained of constitutes an imminent threat to the health or safety of the plaintiff or would immediately affect a legal interest of the plaintiff.

(c) Venue; intervention

(1) Any action respecting a violation of this chapter or the regulations thereunder may be brought only in the judicial district in which the surface coal mining operation complained of is located.

(2) In such action under this section, the Secretary, or the State regulatory authority, if not a party, may intervene as a matter of right.

(d) Costs; filing of bonds

The court, in issuing any final order in any action brought pursuant to subsection (a) of this section, may award costs of litigation (including attorney and expert witness fees) to any party, whenever the court determines such award is appropriate. The court may, if a temporary restraining order or preliminary injunction is sought require the filing of a bond or equivalent security in accordance with the Federal Rules of Civil Procedure.

(e) Effect on other enforcement methods

Nothing in this section shall restrict any right which any person (or class of persons) may have under any statute or common law to seek enforcement of any of the provisions of this chapter and the regulations thereunder, or to seek any other relief (including relief against the Secretary or the appropriate State regulatory authority).

(f) Action for damages

Any person who is injured in his person or property through the violation by any operator of any rule, regulation, order, or permit issued pursuant to this chapter may bring an action for damages (including reasonable attorney and expert witness fees) only in the judicial district in which the surface coal mining operation complained of is located. Nothing in this subsection shall affect the rights established by or limits imposed under State Workmen's Compensation laws.

This provision is typical of citizen suit provisions in allowing two kinds of lawsuits by private plaintiffs:

(1) private actions against defendants who violate the agency legislation or agency rules. These defendants may include private entities as well as federal, state, and local governmental entities subject to the agency legislation; and

(2) private actions against the agencies or officials (in this case both federal and state agencies and officials) who are responsible for administering the legislation and who have failed to take a nondiscretionary action required under the legislation.

The idea behind citizen suit provisions is to use citizens as "private attorneys general" to help enforce the law (1) against people who violate it and (2) even against the government itself, if the government doesn't enforce the law properly. *See, e.g., Bennett v. Spear*, 520 U.S. 154 (1997); *Associated Indus. of N.Y. v. Ickes*, 134 F.2d 694, 704 (2nd Cir. 1943) (famous old case, with opinion by famous jurist Jerome Frank, using the phrase "private Attorney Generals" to describe role of plaintiffs under statutes granting broad right to private parties to seek judicial review of administrative action), *vacated as moot*, 320 U.S. 707 (1943). These provisions, by authorizing lawsuits against agencies and officials, permit judicial review of agency action.

As discussed in Chapter 28.A, some special review statutes grant jurisdiction to the federal courts of appeals, rather than to the federal district courts. Most of these statutes, too, not only grant jurisdiction but also create a cause of action for judicial review. For example, this provision authorizes the federal court of appeals to review final orders of the Securities and Exchange Commission:

---

15 U.S.C. § 78y. Court review of orders and rules

(a) Final Commission orders; persons aggrieved; petition; record; findings; affirmance, modification, enforcement, or setting aside of orders; remand to adduce additional evidence

(1) A person aggrieved by a final order of the Commission entered pursuant to this chapter may obtain review of the order in the United States Court of Appeals

for the circuit in which he resides or has his principal place of business, or for the District of Columbia Circuit, by filing in such court, within sixty days after the entry of the order, a written petition requesting that the order be modified or set aside in whole or in part.

(2) A copy of the petition shall be transmitted forthwith by the clerk of the court to a member of the Commission or an officer designated by the Commission for that purpose. Thereupon the Commission shall file in the court the record on which the order complained of is entered, as provided in section 2112 of Title 28 and the Federal Rules of Appellate Procedure.

(3) On the filing of the petition, the court has jurisdiction, which becomes exclusive on the filing of the record, to affirm or modify and enforce or to set aside the order in whole or in part.

(4) The findings of the Commission as to the facts, if supported by substantial evidence, are conclusive.

(5) If either party applies to the court for leave to adduce additional evidence and shows to the satisfaction of the court that the additional evidence is material and that there was reasonable ground for failure to adduce it before the Commission, the court may remand the case to the Commission for further proceedings, in whatever manner and on whatever conditions the court considers appropriate. If the case is remanded to the Commission, it shall file in the court a supplemental record containing any new evidence, any further or modified findings, and any new order....

(c) Objections not urged before Commission; stay of orders and rules; ...

(1) No objection to an order ... of the Commission, for which review is sought under this section, may be considered by the court unless it was urged before the Commission or there was reasonable ground for failure to do so.

(2) The filing of a petition under this section does not operate as a stay of the Commission's order ... Until the court's jurisdiction becomes exclusive, the Commission may stay its order ... pending judicial review if it finds that justice so requires. After the filing of a petition under this section, the court, on whatever conditions may be required and to the extent necessary to prevent irreparable injury, may issue all necessary and appropriate process to stay the order or rule or to preserve status or rights pending its review; but (notwithstanding section 705 of Title 5) no such process may be issued by the court before the filing of the record or the materials set forth in subsection (b)(2) of this section unless: (A) the Commission has denied a stay or failed to grant requested relief, (B) a reasonable period has expired since the filing of an application for a stay without a decision by the Commission, or (C) there was reasonable ground for failure to apply to the Commission....

Please compare this provision to the SMCRA citizen suit provision reproduced earlier in terms of how this provision describes: who may sue, whom a plaintiff can sue, what the plaintiff can sue about, what requirements the plaintiff must meet to sue, and what judicial remedies are available. This will help you internalize the important point that not all special review provisions are alike, and it will give you more practice reading a review provision the way administrative lawyers do.

As discussed in Chapter 28.A, when a special review statute covers an agency action, the special review statute ordinarily will be interpreted to provide the exclusive route for judicial review of that agency action, even if there is nothing in the statute expressly making it exclusive. Special review provisions say in effect, "It's my way or the highway." If you don't follow their requirements for bringing suit (such as their deadlines), you probably won't be able to take advantage of the "general statutory review" option discussed next.

2. General Statutory Review

Agency legislation often empowers the agency to take various actions but does not contain a special review provision authorizing judicial review of all actions that the agency is empowered to take. When no special review provision creates a cause of action authorizing judicial review of a particular agency action, the federal APA itself supplies a cause of action. When the plaintiff relies on this APA-created cause of action, the plaintiff is said to be seeking "general statutory review." We will first identify the portions of the APA that create this "fallback" or "default" cause of action. Then we will identify the limits on this APA-created cause of action.

a. APA's Creation of a Cause of Action

The main provision establishing the APA cause of action is the first sentence of § 704:

---

5 U.S.C. § 704. Actions reviewable

Agency action made reviewable by statute and final agency action for which there is no other adequate remedy in a court are subject to judicial review....

This sentence identifies two categories of agency action: (1) "[a]gency action made reviewable by" a special review statute; and (2) "final agency action for which there is no other adequate remedy in a court." For the first category, the special review statute provides the cause of action, and plaintiffs must follow the requirements in that special review statute to get judicial review. *See Bowen v. Massachusetts*, 487 U.S. 879, 903 (1988) ("§ 704 'does not provide additional judicial remedies in situations where the Congress has provided special and adequate review procedures.'") (quoting AGM 101). For the second category of agency action described in § 702's first sentence, the APA itself provides the cause of action.

Section 704 identifies the agency actions that are subject to judicial review under the APA-created cause of action. Section 702, in turn, identifies who can pursue the cause of action:

---

5 U.S.C. § 702. Right of review

A person suffering legal wrong because of agency action, or adversely affected or aggrieved by agency action within the meaning of a relevant statute, is entitled to judicial review thereof....

Section 702 makes the cause of action created in § 704 available to (1) someone who has suffered "legal wrong," which means an invasion of a "legal right" (or legal interest); and (2) someone within the "zone of interest" arguably protected by the statute that the defendant is alleged to have violated. We discussed the legal right/legal interest and zone of interests requirements in Chapter 28.C.4.a.

Section 703 confirms that the APA-created cause of action is available only when no special review statute applies or when the special review statute is "**inadequate[e]**." Section 703 also supplies useful information about whom to name as the defendant in suits relying on the APA-created cause of action:

---

5 U.S.C. § 703. Form and venue of proceeding

The form of proceeding for judicial review is the special statutory review proceeding relevant to the subject matter in a court specified by statute or, in the absence or inadequacy thereof, any applicable form of legal action, including actions for declaratory judgments or writs of prohibitory or mandatory injunction or habeas corpus, in a court of competent jurisdiction. If no special statutory review proceeding is applicable, the action for judicial review may be brought against the United States, the agency by its official title, or the appropriate officer....

Finally, § 706 establishes the grounds for getting judicial relief in a cause of action under the APA and the type of relief available:

---

5 U.S.C. § 706. Scope of review

To the extent necessary to decision and when presented, the reviewing court shall decide all relevant questions of law, interpret constitutional and statutory provisions, and determine the meaning or applicability of the terms of an agency action. The reviewing court shall—

(1) compel agency action unlawfully withheld or unreasonably delayed; and

(2) hold unlawful and set aside agency action, findings, and conclusions found to be—

(A) arbitrary, capricious, an abuse of discretion, or otherwise not in accordance with law;

(B) contrary to constitutional right, power, privilege, or immunity;

(C) in excess of statutory jurisdiction, authority, or limitations, or short of statutory right;

(D) without observance of procedure required by law;

(E) unsupported by substantial evidence in a case subject to sections 556 and 557 of this title or otherwise reviewed on the record of an agency hearing provided by statute; or

(F) unwarranted by the facts to the extent that the facts are subject to trial de novo by the reviewing court.

In making the foregoing determinations, the court shall review the whole record or those parts of it cited by a party, and due account shall be taken of the rule of prejudicial error.

The APA-created cause of action serves most often to authorize judicial review of agency action taken under, or subject to, agency statutes that do not themselves authorize judicial review of the agency action. In one famous case, for example, the organization

Citizens to Preserve Overton Park sued the Secretary of Transportation for deciding to build an interstate highway through a public park in Memphis, Tennessee. *See Citizens to Preserve Overton Park, Inc. v. Volpe*, 401 U.S. 402 (1971). The organization claimed that the Secretary's decision violated provisions in two statutes: the Department of Transportation Act of 1966 and the Federal-Aid Highway Act of 1968. *Id.* at 404–405. Those statutes did indeed restrict the Secretary's power to build highways through public parks, but they did not create a private cause of action to enforce their restrictions. The federal APA filled by gap by providing a cause of action through which the plaintiff organization could assert their statutory claims. *See also, e.g., Fanin v. U.S. Dep't of Veterans Affairs*, 572 F.3d 868, 875 (11th Cir. 2009) (plaintiff's complaint contained nine statutory-violation claims, all of which were "routed through the APA").

The APA-created cause of action supports claims of statutory violations as well as other types of claims. Statutory-violation claims like the ones in *Overton Park* are provided for in two places in §706: §706(2)(A)'s reference to agency action "**not in accordance with law**" and §706(2)(C)'s reference to agency action "**in excess of statutory ... limitations.**" Other grounds for relief are also available under §706, including the ever popular complaint that agency action is "**arbitrary, capricious, or an abuse of discretion.**" This ground for relief is so popular we devote a separate chapter to it: Chapter 34.

Exercise: Determining the Scope of the APA-Created Cause of Action

The purpose of this exercise is to help you identify and remember textual limits on the APA-created cause of action.

Please review the first sentence of §704. Then identify (1) *what* is subject to judicial review in the APA-created cause of action; and (2) what circumstance must exist for the APA-created cause of action to exist.

(1) _____

(2) _____

Now please review the first sentence of §702. Then paraphrase the two categories of people entitled to the cause of action created by the APA:

(3) _____ ;
   or
(4) _____

---

b. Limits on the Scope of the APA-Created Cause of Action

The exercise immediately above had you identify limits on the scope of the APA-created cause of action. Now we examine those limits.

(i) There Must be an "Agency Action"

The APA-created cause of action applies to final "**agency action,**" a term defined in §551(13):

---

5 U.S.C. § 551. Definitions ...

(13) "agency action" includes the whole or a part of an agency rule, order, license, sanction, relief, or the equivalent or denial thereof, or failure to act ...

Not everything an agency does is **"agency action"** as defined in § 551(13). By the same token, although § 551(13) defines **"agency action"** to include an agency's **"failure to act,"** not everything an agency *fails to do* constitutes a **"failure to act"** under § 551(13). The terms **"agency action"** and **"failure to act"** have been interpreted to have specialized meanings that may not be obvious on the face of § 551(13).

The U.S. Supreme Court has interpreted **"agency action"** to require the plaintiff to identify a *discrete* agency action of the type specified in § 551(13), or its equivalent. Thus, the Court held in one case that the term **"agency action"** did not include what the plaintiff called a "land withdrawal review program," under which the Bureau of Land Management (BLM) reviewed past decisions withdrawing public lands from availability for mining and other activities:

> The term "land withdrawal review program" (which as far as we know is not derived from any authoritative text) does not refer to a single BLM order or regulation, or even to a completed universe of particular BLM orders and regulations. It is simply the name by which [the government defendants] ... have occasionally referred to the continuing (and thus constantly changing) operations of the BLM in reviewing withdrawal revocation applications and the classifications of public lands and developing land use plans as required by [federal law]. It is no more an identifiable "agency action" — much less a "final agency action" — than a "weapons procurement program" of the Department of Defense or a "drug interdiction program" of the Drug Enforcement Administration.

Lujan v. Nat'l Wildlife Fed'n, 497 U.S. 871, 890 (1990). "Under the terms of the APA," the Court concluded, the plaintiff "must direct its attack against some particular 'agency action' that causes it harm." *Id.* at 891. In a later case, the Court emphasized that the plaintiff in an APA action must challenge a "*discrete* action" of the type listed in § 551(13) or its equivalent. *Norton v. Southern Utah Wilderness Alliance (SUWA)*, 542 U.S. 55, 63 (2004). The Court explained in *Norton v. SUWA* that the limitation to discrete agency action precludes "broad programmatic" challenges under the APA to the way an agency administers its statutes. *Id.* at 64.

The Court in *Norton v. SUWA* also interpreted the part of § 551(13) that defines **"agency action"** to include **"failure to act."** The Court said two important things about the meaning of **"failure to act."** First, the term is "properly understood as a failure to take an *agency action* — that is, a failure to take one of the agency actions (including their equivalents) earlier defined in § 551(13)." *Norton v. SUWA*, 542 U.S. at 62. This means that the plaintiff challenging an agency's failure to act must identify some "*discrete* action" of the sort specified in § 551(13) that the agency failed to take. *Id.* at 63. Plaintiffs can't meet this requirement with just general complaints of agency under-enforcement. Second, "[a] 'failure to act' is not the same thing as a 'denial.'" 542 U.S. at 63. A denial "is the agency's act of saying no to a request"; a failure to act "is simply the omission of an action without formally rejecting a request — for example, the failure to promulgate a rule or take some decision by a statutory deadline." *Id.* A denial is an affirmative type of agency action; a failure to act is inaction.

These glosses on **"failure to act"** set up the Court's further holding in *Norton v. SUWA* that "the only action that can be compelled under the APA is action legally *required*." 542 U.S. at 63 (emphasis in original). Thus, when a plaintiff asks a court under APA § 706(1) to **"compel *agency action* unlawfully withheld or unreasonably delayed"** (emphasis added), the plaintiff must:

1. identify a discrete action — i.e., a rule, order, or one of the other specific actions listed in § 551(13), or its equivalent;

2. show that the law required the agency to take that specific action; and

3. show that the agency failed to take that discrete, legally required action.

The plaintiffs in *Norton v. SUWA* did identify one discrete agency action that the agency failed to take. Specifically, the plaintiffs challenged the BLM's failure to exclude off-road vehicles (ORVs) from public lands in Utah that had been designated as "wilderness study areas." 542 U.S. at 65. The problem was that none of the laws identified by the plaintiffs specifically compelled BLM to exclude ORVs from these areas. Instead, the laws imposed on BLM only more general obligations to avoid impairing these areas' potential for being designated as wilderness. The legal obligations they imposed were not specific enough to satisfy the second required showing listed above. *Id.* at 66–67.

In sum, as the Court has interpreted § 551(13), not everything that an agency does constitutes **"agency action,"** and not everything that an agency fails to do constitutes a **"failure to act."** The Court's interpretation matters, because if you can't identify an agency action to challenge, you don't have an APA cause of action.

Exercise: Identifying "Agency Action" under the Federal APA

Plaintiffs sue the National Security Agency (NSA). They challenge what media accounts have called the NSA's "Terrorist Surveillance Program." The program reportedly intercepts telephone calls and emails between people in the United States and people outside the United States. According to media accounts, the program intercepts these communications if NSA suspects at least one of the parties to the intercepted communication is connected to the terrorist group Al Qaeda. In their lawsuit challenging the program, plaintiffs rely in part on the APA-created cause of action. Does the Terrorist Surveillance Program constitute **"agency action"** as defined in the APA? *See American Civil Liberties Union v. NSA*, 493 F.3d 644, 677–679 (6th Cir. 2007).

(ii) The Agency Action Must Be "[F]inal"

The APA and many special review statutes limit judicial review to agency actions that are final. Because the finality requirement is not unique to the APA-created cause of action, and because it is one of four doctrines that all can affect the timing of judicial review of agency action, we discuss it separately, along with other timing doctrines, in Chapter 30. Though we include finality among the timing doctrines, keep in mind it is an element of the APA-created cause of action.

(iii) There Must Be "[N]o [O]ther [A]dequate [R]emedy in a [C]ourt"

In keeping with its default role, the APA-created cause of action does not exist when there is some **"other adequate remedy"** in a court. 5 U.S.C. §704; *see also id.* §703. The other remedy can come from any of three sources: It may come (1) from a special review statute, as discussed above, or (2) from some form of "nonstatutory review," as discussed below. Finally, besides special review statutes and nonstatutory review, (3) other statutes may supply an adequate remedy. For example, the Tucker Act allows people to recover money from the federal government for breach of contract and for taking private property for public use without just compensation. *See* 28 U.S.C. §§ 1346(a)(2) & 1491 (2012). If a plaintiff has an adequate Tucker Act remedy, the plaintiff won't have a cause of action under the APA. *See, e.g., Christopher Village, L.P. v. United States*, 360 F.3d 1319 (Fed. Cir. 2004).

As you might guess, abundant case law addresses whether some remedy other than an APA cause of action is **"adequate."** *See, e.g., Bowen v. Massachusetts*, 487 U.S. 879, 901–908 (1988); *Garcia v. Vilsack*, 563 F.3d 519 (D.C. Cir. 2009). One thing is clear, though: The remedy provided under a special review statute is not inadequate merely because the plaintiff fails to meet its pre-conditions for filing a lawsuit under it. For example, many special review statutes severely limit the amount of time for seeking judicial review— e.g., requiring lawsuits to be commenced within thirty, sixty, or ninety days of the agency action. A person who fails to satisfy the special review provision's deadline cannot fall back on the APA-created cause of action—which is subject to a generous six-year statute of limitations, 28 U.S.C. §2401(a) (2012)—on the ground that the person's own failure to meet the special review provision's deadline renders its remedy inadequate. *See, e.g., Brem-Air Disposal v. Cohen*, 156 F.3d 1002, 1005 (9th Cir. 1998).

The moral of the story is that the administrative lawyer contemplating judicial review of agency action must identify—and quickly—rights of review that may displace the APA-based cause of action.

(iv) The Plaintiff Must Either Be "[S]uffering [L]egal [W]rong [B]ecause of [A]gency [A]ction, or [Be] [A]dversely [A]ffected or [A]ggrieved by [A]gency [A]ction within the [M]eaning of a [R]elevant [S]tatute"

Section 702's first sentence entitles two categories of people to judicial review. We discussed these two categories in Chapter 28.C.4, in discussing statutory "standing." A person must show they are within one of those categories to assert the cause of action created in §704's first sentence.

c. Warning! "Danger, Will Robinson!"[1]

From this discussion of the federal APA's role as the default source of a cause of action, please do not take away the misimpression that the federal APA does not do anything else. It does much more! Perhaps most importantly, the APA has judicial review provisions

---

1. The phrase "Danger, Will Robinson!" comes from the 1960s television show "Lost in Space." The phrase was often used by the robot who served as sidekick to and guardian of the young protagonist Will Robinson, who, along with his family, was indeed lost in space. Fans of the show remember the phrase partly because of the distinctive voice in which the robot intoned it. http://www.youtube.com/watch?v=REvmhBO99I4&feature=related. We figured allusions to "Lost in Space" may resonate for students of administrative law.

in §§ 701–706 that generally apply even when the plaintiff relies on the cause of action in a special review statute or seeks "nonstatutory" review (discussed below). In particular, § 706 prescribes grounds on which a court may compel agency action or set aside agency action, whether the judicial challenge to that agency action rests on the APA-created cause of action or some other law, unless the other law displaces § 706. *See* 5 U.S.C. § 706; *see also, e.g.*, *Green Island Power Auth. v. FERC*, 577 F.3d 148, 158 (2nd Cir. 2009) (because special review statute "does not set forth a separate standard of review for FERC's actions," court reviews those actions under § 706 of APA). The result is that, even when a plaintiff relies on a non-APA cause of action, the APA governs judicial review except to the extent that other law provides otherwise. *See* 5 U.S.C. § 559. Thus, for example, a plaintiff relying on a special review statute for the cause of action can still get relief by showing that the challenged agency action is **"arbitrary, capricious, [or] an abuse of discretion"** within the meaning of § 706(2)(A).

Exercise: Special Statutory Review

The Endangered Species Act (ESA) requires a federal agency to consult with the Director of the Fish and Wildlife Service (FWS) if the agency intends to take an action that would jeopardize an endangered species that FWS is responsible under the Act for protecting. If a federal agency violates this consultation requirement, the agency is subject to suit under the ESA's citizen suit provision, 16 U.S.C. § 1540(g). That provision requires a person, before suing under it, to give notice to the agency that is supposedly violating the consultation requirement. *Id.* § 1540(g)(2)(A)(i).

Plaintiffs sue the Bureau of Land Management (BLM) in federal court. Plaintiffs claim that the BLM violated the ESA by failing to consult with the FWS before issuing leases of public lands to cattle ranchers. Plaintiffs claimed that the ranching activity on these leased lands would jeopardize the endangered sage grouse.

Plaintiffs did not notify the BLM before bringing their lawsuit, as required by the ESA's citizen suit provision. When the BLM moves to dismiss the lawsuit because of plaintiff's failure to give notice, plaintiffs argue that, even if their claim cannot rest on the ESA's citizen suit provision, they can assert it, in the alternative, under the APA-created fallback cause of action. Please explain why plaintiffs have no cause of action under the APA.

---

3. "Nonstatutory" Review

"Nonstatutory" review refers today mainly to lawsuits in which the plaintiff asserts a cause of action that was originally developed by the courts, including ye olde English courts, rather than being created by statute. For example, nonstatutory review includes actions for writs of mandamus, prohibition, *quo warranto*, *habeas corpus*, and common law certiorari, as well as suits for injunctive and declaratory relief against executive-branch conduct that violates a statute or the Constitution. Today, these nonstatutory forms of relief are most often sought in suits for special statutory or general statutory review, such as APA suits in which the plaintiff seeks an injunction. In short, nonstatutory remedies serve as adjuncts to review under the APA or special review statutes. It is rare for a plaintiff challenging government action to rely exclusively on nonstatutory review. Because non-statutory review does not have great independent significance, we limit our discussion of nonstatutory review to the three things we believe administrative lawyers should know.

First, the term "nonstatutory" is misleading. For one thing, many of the remedies developed by courts are today codified in statutes or in rules that have the force and effect of statutes. For example, federal courts have power to issue writs of mandamus and other writs under 28 U.S.C. § 1361 (2012). Injunctive relief in the federal courts is governed by Federal Rule of Civil Procedure 65. For another thing, even if the plaintiff asserts a cause of action not codified in a federal statute or federal rule, if the plaintiff is in federal court the plaintiff will have to identify a statute validly granting subject matter jurisdiction. Plaintiff's lawsuit is "statutory" to that extent.

The second thing to know about nonstatutory review is that sometimes only nonstatutory review will do. Specifically, nonstatutory review is necessary when a plaintiff challenges government conduct that is not reviewable under either the APA's cause of action or any special review statute. Here are three examples:

- *Trudeau v. Federal Trade Commission*, 456 F.3d 178 (D.C. Cir. 2006)

Kevin Trudeau sued the Federal Trade Commission (FTC) over a press release the FTC issued about its settlement of a lawsuit against Mr. Trudeau. Mr. Trudeau asserted that the press release was false and misleading. He claimed the issuance of the press release exceeded the FTC's statutory authority and violated his First Amendment rights. The court held that the claims could not rest on the APA-created cause of action because an agency's issuance of a press release does not fall within the APA's definition of "**agency action.**" 5 U.S.C. § 551(13).

The court observed, however, that nonstatutory review is available for a claim that an agency has acted outside its authority. Moreover, the court had previously adjudicated First Amendment claims not resting on any statutory cause of action. The court accordingly reviewed Mr. Trudeau's claims on the merits (and rejected them). *See Trudeau*, 456 F.3d at 188–191. Mr. Trudeau thus got nonstatutory review of an agency activity that fell outside the federal APA's definition of "**agency action**" and that was not covered by any special review statute.

- *Rhode Island Dep't of Environmental Management v. United States*, 304 F.3d 31 (1st Cir. 2002)

Four employees of a Rhode Island agency filed whistleblower claims against that state agency with the U.S. Department of Labor (USDOL). The employees asserted that the agency had retaliated against them for reporting that the agency was not properly imple-menting the federal Solid Waste Disposal Act. They based their administrative claims on a provision in the Act authorizing USDOL to adjudicate retaliation complaints. Before USDOL completed these adjudications, the Rhode Island agency sued in federal court to enjoin the adjudications on the ground they were barred by state sovereign immunity.

The court held that Rhode Island did not have a cause of action under the federal APA, because USDOL had not yet taken "**final agency action.**" Instead, the court held that Rhode Island could get nonstatutory review of USDOL's conduct. The court discussed the traditional requirements for nonstatutory review and held that Rhode Island met them. *Id.* at 42–45. *Cf. Alaska v. EEOC*, 564 F.3d 1062, 1065 n.1 (9th Cir. 2009) (*en banc*) (relying on collateral order doctrine to review similar sovereign immunity claim under federal APA).

- *Chamber of Commerce v. Reich*, 74 F.3d 1322 (D.C. Cir. 1996)

The Chamber of Commerce and others sued the Secretary of Labor to enjoin him from implementing an Executive Order that, the plaintiffs claimed, violated the National Labor Relations Act. The court observed that the plaintiffs could not base their challenge to the Executive Order on the APA-created cause of action because the President (as issuer of the executive order) is not an **"agency"** within the meaning of the APA. *Id.* at 1326 (citing *Franklin v. Massachusetts*, 505 U.S. 788, 797 (1992)). Accordingly, the court conducted nonstatutory review of the executive order (and held that the Executive Order did indeed conflict with the National Labor Relations Act). 74 F.3d at 1326–1328, 1332–1339.

* * *

You should know a third thing about nonstatutory review: Sovereign immunity from nonstatutory review is generally waived by § 702 of the APA. This conclusion illustrates, as discussed earlier in this chapter, that § 702's waiver is not limited to claims resting on the APA-created cause of action.

C. Sources of a Cause of Action for Review of State Agency Action

State agencies must obey both state and federal law. Consequently, both state and federal law can supply causes of action for judicial review of state agencies' actions.

The law in many States resembles federal law in this way: Judicial review of state agency actions is widely available through one of three routes: (1) under special review provisions authorizing review of specified agency actions; (2) under a state APA that creates a broadly available, fallback right of review; or (3) under nonstatutory review obtained, for example, through requests for writs of mandamus or certiorari. The 2010 Model APA reflects this pattern. *See* 2010 Model State APA §§ 501–508; *see also, e.g., Ottman v. Town of Primrose*, 796 N.W.2d 411, 420 (Wis. 2011) ("Certiorari is a mechanism by which a court may test the validity of a decision rendered by ... an administrative agency.").

Certain federal regulatory statutes put legal restrictions and obligations on state and local agencies. These statutes may have provisions authorizing private actions to enforce them against state and local agencies. Earlier in this chapter, for example, we reproduced a special review provision from the Surface Mining Control and Reclamation Act that authorized suits for violations of the Act against "the United States or any other governmental instrumentality or agency to the extent permitted by the eleventh amendment." 30 U.S.C. § 1270(a)(1) (2012). The reference to the "eleventh amendment" is the tip-off that States and state agencies (as well as local and federal agencies) can be sued for violations of the Act. The Eleventh Amendment gives the States, including their agencies, sovereign immunity from many lawsuits brought by private plaintiffs. As you can learn in a law school course on the federal courts, however, state sovereign immunity has exceptions, one of which permits private suits against state officials for prospective relief against ongoing violations of federal law. These suits are allowed under the case of *Ex parte Young*, 209 U.S. 123 (1908), and may include suits to enforce regulatory laws like the Clean Water Act. *See, e.g., Cox v. City of Dallas*, 256 F.3d 281, 307–309 (5th Cir. 2001). The cause of actions for such suits may be provided by special review provisions in the Clean Water Act. SMCRA, and other regulatory statutes.

Though federal law may apply to many activities of many state agencies, the practical reality is that most suits seeking review of state agency action will rest on the state APA and simply challenge the factual basis for the agency action or dispute the state agency's understanding of state law. Even so, the resourceful administrative lawyer keeps federal law in mind when considering potential bases for judicially challenging a state agency action.

D. Preclusion of Review

The law today supplies a cause of action for review of most agency actions. As this section discusses, however, on rare occasions the law affirmatively *precludes* judicial review of certain agency actions.

Preclusion is rare today because the federal APA and most state APAs create a broad right to judicial review of agency action when no special review statute applies. Though rare, preclusion of judicial review does occur. Moreover, sometimes problems of preclusion arise— not when someone takes the initiative of filing a lawsuit challenging agency action—but instead when a person against whom an agency brings an enforcement proceeding challenges agency action as a *defense* to the enforcement proceeding. This section briefly examines preclusion in the context of the presumption of the availability of judicial review.

1. Presumption of Reviewability

a. Federal Law

The U.S. Supreme Court has consistently applied a "strong presumption" that judicial review of federal agency action is available. *Bowen v. Michigan Academy of Family Physicians*, 476 U.S. 667, 670 (1986). Two cases illustrate the presumption in federal law, and the later of the two cases links it to the federal APA.

• *American School of Magnetic Healing v. McAnnulty*, 187 U.S. 94 (1902)

The American School of Magnetic Healing and its general manager sought federal court review of an order of the Postmaster General. The Postmaster General's order forbade the local postmaster from delivering mail to the school, because the Postmaster General determined that the school was using the mail to defraud its customers, in violation of a federal statute. The Postmaster General's order required the local postmaster to return all mail addressed to the school back to the post offices from which it had been sent, after stamping the word "fraudulent" plainly on the front of each piece.

The Court concluded that the Postmaster General acted outside the scope of his statutory authority. The Court then concluded that judicial relief had to be available for this ultra vires action: "Otherwise, the individual is left to the absolutely uncontrolled and arbitrary action of a public and administrative officer, whose action is unauthorized by any law and is in violation of the rights of the individual." 187 U.S. at 110. This conclusion was significant because no statute gave the school a cause of action for review of the Postmaster's conduct. The Court thus used what we would today call "nonstatutory review" to keep alive the promise of magnetic healing.

- *Abbott Laboratories v. Gardner*, 387 U.S. 136 (1967)

Congress amended the federal Food, Drug, and Cosmetic Act (Food and Drug Act) to require drug manufacturers to print the generic name of a drug on labels and in print advertisements for the drug. This was so consumers would know, for example, that, whether they bought Excedrin or Bufferin, they were buying the same thing: acetylsalicylic acid (or aspirin). To implement the statutory amendment, the Food and Drug Administration (FDA) promulgated a legislative rule. The FDA rule required drug manufacturers to print the generic name of a drug alongside the commercial name *every time* the commercial name appeared on a label or in an advertisement. Drug manufacturers challenged the "every time regulation" in federal court on the ground it exceeded the FDA's statutory authority. *Id.* at 155.

The FDA argued that the Food and Drug Act precluded judicial review of the manufacturers' challenge. The FDA did not point to anything in the Act expressly precluding review. Instead, the FDA pointed out that the Act authorized judicial review of certain FDA regulations, but not the type of regulation of which the "every time regulation" was one. Thus, the FDA argued that by authorizing judicial review of certain regulations, the Act impliedly precluded review of others.

The Court rejected this argument. The Court said, "The mere fact that some acts are made reviewable should not suffice to support an implication of exclusion as to others...." *Id.* at 141 (quoting Louis Jaffe, Judicial Control of Administrative Action 357 (1965)). More generally, the Court emphasized that its case law established a presumption of judicial review, which had been "reinforced by" the federal APA. *Id.* at 140. The Court concluded that preclusion of review should occur "only upon a showing of clear and convincing evidence" of congressional intent to preclude review. *Id.* at 141 (internal quotation marks omitted).

Abbott Laboratories helps the APA serve its gap filling function. Agency legislation often has a special review provision that does not cover all actions that an agency may take under that legislation. *Abbott Laboratories* establishes that the mere existence of a special review provision covering some agency actions will not preclude judicial review of non-covered agency actions under the APA.

In a later case, the Court emphasized that the presumption of the availability of judicial review "is just that—a presumption." *Block v. Community Nutrition Inst.*, 467 U.S. 340, 349 (1984). Subsection 2 below explores situations in which, under federal law, the presumption is overcome.

b. State Law

States will vary in whether they have a presumption that judicial review of agency action is available or some stronger guarantee of judicial review, and, if so, where that presumption or guarantee comes from and whether it is absolute or subject to exceptions. For example, some state constitutions have provisions creating a right to judicial review of actions taken by administrative agencies in their "judicial" or "quasi-judicial" capacity.[2] In other States, too, state courts have relied on various state constitutional provisions as creating a broad right to review of agency action. New York's highest state court, for example, has held that the state constitution permits limited judicial review of agency

---

2. *See, e.g.*, Mich. Const. art. VI, §28 (West, Westlaw through amendments approved at Nov. 2010 general election); S.C. Const. art. I, §22 (West, Westlaw through end of 2011 Reg. Sess.).

action even when a statute purports to preclude it.[3] Courts in other States recognize non-statutory methods of judicial review of agency action that supplement statutory review at least when necessary to correct egregious agency action. *See, e.g., Barnes v. Bd. of County Comm'rs*, 259 P.3d 725, 730 (Kan. 2011). In short, every State has its own tradition and laws governing the availability of judicial review of agency action. Though it is safe to say that judicial review is broadly available, that generalization is no substitute for analysis of the particular agency action of which judicial review is sought, in light of the specific State's laws.

2. Preclusion of Judicial Challenges to Agency Action

a. Federal Law

The federal APA precludes judicial review of federal agency action in two situations, described in § 701(a)(1) and (a)(2):

---

5 U.S.C. § 701. Application; definitions

(a) This chapter applies, according to the provisions thereof, except to the extent that —

(1) statutes preclude judicial review; or

(2) agency action is committed to agency discretion by law. . . .

Section 701 does more than restrict the availability of the APA-created cause of action. It precludes review even when a person seeks review under a special review statute.

A case in which § 701 precluded review under a special review statute is *Interstate Commerce Commission v. Brotherhood of Locomotive Engineers*, 482 U.S. 270 (1987). In that case, Unions sought judicial review under the Hobbs Act of a decision of the Interstate Commerce Commission (ICC) refusing to reconsider an earlier ICC ruling. The unions had sought reconsideration on the ground that the ICC made a material error in its earlier ruling. The Court held that judicial review of the ICC's denial of reconsideration was precluded. The Court based this holding partly on the Hobbs Act and partly on § 701(a)(2) of the APA. The Court explained why it was appropriate to look to § 701 in an action for judicial review under the Hobbs Act:

> While the Hobbs Act specifies the form of proceeding for judicial review of ICC orders, see 5 U.S.C. § 703, it is the Administrative Procedure Act (APA) that codifies the nature and attributes of judicial review, including the traditional principle of its unavailability "to the extent that . . . agency action is committed to agency discretion by law." 5 U.S.C. § 701(a)(2).

---

3. *See N.Y.C. Dep't of Envt'l Protection v. N.Y.C. Civil Serv. Comm'n*, 579 N.E. 2d 1385 (N.Y. 1991); *see also Int'l Ass'n of Fire Fighters, Local 188 v. Public Employment Rel'ns Bd.*, 245 P.3d 845 (Cal. 2011) ("The California Constitution gives rise to a presumption in favor of at least limited judicial review of state administrative agency actions."); *Saldin Secs., Inc. v. Snohomish County*, 949 P.2d 370, 373 (Wash. 1998) ("The superior court has inherent power [under the state constitution] to review administrative decisions for illegal or manifestly arbitrary acts.").

Thus, § 701 states generally applicable limits on judicial review of federal agency action.

Section 701(a) bars judicial review in two situations. One is where a statute precludes judicial review. 5 U.S.C. § 701(a)(1) (2012). The other is where the law commits an agency action to agency discretion. *Id.* § 701(a)(2). The difference between the two may seem obscure until you consider examples of each.

(i) Statutes Precluding Review (§ 701(a)(1))

It is rare for a federal statute expressly to preclude judicial review altogether. Still, some statutes do so. For example, immigration statutes expressly preclude judicial review of certain orders removing aliens from the United States. *See, e.g.,* 8 U.S.C. § 1225(b)(1)(A)(i) (2012) (authorizing removal of certain aliens "without further hearing or review"); *id.* § 1252(a)(2) (identifying "[m]atters not subject to judicial review"). But even statutes that expressly preclude judicial review are usually interpreted to permit constitutional challenges to agency action. *See Webster v. Doe,* 486 U.S. 592, 603 (1988); *Johnson v. Robison,* 415 U.S. 361, 373–374 (1974). *See generally* Ron Levin, *Understanding Unreviewability in Administrative Law,* 74 Minn. L. Rev. 689 (1990) (synthesizing case law). Indeed, it is unclear whether Congress constitutionally could altogether bar federal-court review of constitutional challenges to executive-branch action.

While it's rare for a statute to preclude judicial review expressly, it is even rarer for a federal statute to be interpreted as *impliedly* precluding judicial review. The best-known case holding that a federal statute impliedly precluded review is *Block v. Community Nutrition Institute,* 467 U.S. 340 (1984). The challengers in that case were consumers of milk; they challenged orders by the Secretary of Agriculture setting minimum prices for the sale of milk by dairy farmers to milk processors. The Court held that the agency legislation impliedly precluded milk consumers from challenging the pricing orders. The Court emphasized the elaborate procedures in the legislation contemplating that milk processors, rather than consumers, would be the ones who judicially challenged pricing orders. In the final analysis, *Community Nutrition Institute* may be more a case about who had "statutory standing" to challenge milk orders than a case about outright preclusion of judicial review. *See* Peter Strauss et al., *Gellhorn and Byse's Administrative Law* 1317 (11th ed. 2011). In any event, the Court has made clear that federal courts should not readily find implied preclusion of significant legal challenges. *See Bowen v. Mich. Academy of Family Physicians,* 476 U.S. 667 (1986).

More often than precluding judicial review altogether, Congress channels judicial review by enacting restrictions that may postpone judicial review—or shunt it to a particular court—but don't preclude it altogether. In one well-known case, for example, the Thunder Basin Coal Company brought a federal-court lawsuit challenging a letter from a district manager of the federal Mine Safety and Health Administration (MSHA). The district manager's letter instructed Thunder Basin to designate two employees to serve as representatives of Thunder Basin's work force for purposes of the federal statute regulating surface mine safety. These employees would have the right under the statute to accompany MSHA officials during inspections of Thunder Basin's mines and to review safety information from the company. The U.S. Supreme Court held that the federal district court lacked subject-matter jurisdiction over Thunder Basin's lawsuit, because the statute precluded "pre-enforcement" suits like Thunder Basin's. Instead, Thunder Basin could get judicial review only by: (1) violating the instructions in the district manager's letter; (2) administratively challenging the citation that the MHSA would presumably issue to Thunder Basin because of its violation; and, after exhausting administrative remedies, (3) seeking judicial review in a federal court of appeals. In short, Congress didn't preclude judicial review, but did intend to "channe[l] and streamlin[e]" the enforcement process by barring pre-enforcement lawsuits. *Thunder Basin Coal Co. v. Reich*, 510 U.S. 200, 216 (1994).

Exercise: Statutory Preclusion

Under the Consumer Product Safety Act (CPSA), the Consumer Product Safety Commission has authority to determine, after a formal adjudication, whether a consumer product poses a "substantial product hazard." 15 U.S.C. § 2064 (2012). If the Commission determines that a consumer product does pose such a hazard, it can order the manufacturer, distributors, and retailers of the product to take corrective actions such as recalling the product and refunding consumers the purchase price. *Id.* The CPSA authorizes judicial review of the Commission's *rules*, but omits any provision authorizing judicial review of the Commission's *orders* in formal adjudications. Please explain (1) why this omission should not be interpreted to preclude judicial review of Commission orders; and (2) what law provides a cause of action for review of such orders.

(ii) Agency Action Committed to Agency Discretion by Law (§ 701(a)(2))

The U.S. Supreme Court has interpreted § 701(a)(2) in several cases. In the process, the Court has addressed several kinds of agency action. We summarize two leading cases on § 701(a)(2).

- *Heckler v. Chaney*, 470 U.S. 821 (1985)

The FDA got a petition from death row inmates in state prison. These state prisoners asked the FDA to take enforcement action against state prison officials. The prisoners claimed that the prison officials were violating federal law because they planned to execute the prisoners using drugs that had not been approved by the FDA for use in human executions.[4] The FDA denied the prisoners' petition on the grounds that (1) the FDA's jurisdiction over the matters alleged in the petition was unclear; and (2) even if the FDA did have jurisdiction, it chose to devote its limited enforcement resources to more serious matters of public health. The prisoners sought judicial review of the FDA's denial of their petition.

The Court held that judicial review was precluded under § 701(a)(2). More broadly, the Court concluded that an agency's decision not to undertake enforcement action is presumptively "**committed to agency discretion by law**" and therefore not subject to judicial review. The Court based this conclusion mainly on "the general unsuitability" of judicial review of this type of agency action. *Id.* at 831. The Court explained:

> First, an agency decision not to enforce often involves a complicated balancing of a number of factors which are peculiarly within its expertise. Thus, the agency must not only assess whether a violation has occurred, but whether agency

---

4. As grimly comic as this may sound, the Court later had to address whether certain methods of lethal injection to carry out death sentences violate the Constitution's ban on cruel and unusual punishment. *See Baze v. Rees*, 553 U.S. 35 (2008).

resources are best spent on this violation or another, whether the agency is likely to succeed if it acts, whether the particular enforcement action requested best fits the agency's overall policies, and, indeed, whether the agency has enough resources to undertake the action at all. An agency generally cannot act against each technical violation of the statute it is charged with enforcing. The agency is far better equipped than the courts to deal with the many variables involved in the proper ordering of its priorities....

In addition to these administrative concerns, we note that when an agency refuses to act it generally does not exercise its coercive power over an individual's liberty or property rights, and thus does not infringe upon areas that courts often are called upon to protect. Similarly, when an agency does act to enforce, that action itself provides a focus for judicial review, inasmuch as the agency must have exercised its power in some manner. The action at least can be reviewed to determine whether the agency exceeded its statutory powers. Finally, we recognize that an agency's refusal to institute proceedings shares to some extent the characteristics of the decision of a prosecutor in the Executive Branch not to indict—a decision which has long been regarded as the special province of the Executive Branch, inasmuch as it is the Executive who is charged by the Constitution to "take Care that the Laws be faithfully executed." U.S. Const., Art. II, §3.

The Court emphasized that the presumption of unreviewability may be overcome. The Court cited *Dunlop v. Bachowski*, 421 U.S. 560 (1975), as an example of a case in which the presumption was overcome. In that case a statute constrained an agency official's discretion about whether to take enforcement action. The statute said that if the Secretary of Labor investigated a union election and found "probable cause" that the election violated federal law, the Secretary "*shall* ... bring a civil action" to set aside the election. *Id.* at 833 (quoting statute; emphasis added). The statute's mandatory language made it clear that, once the Secretary found probable cause of a violation, the Secretary had no choice but to take enforcement action (by filing a civil action to set aside the tainted election). Thus, the statute "quite clearly withdrew discretion from the agency and provided guidelines for exercise of its enforcement power." *Heckler v. Chaney*, 470 U.S. at 834. The statute thus overcame the presumption of unreviewability. No similar statute restricted the FDA's discretion to deal with the prisoners' petition.

- *Lincoln v. Vigil*, 508 U.S. 182 (1993)

For several years, the Indian Health Service funded health clinics for disabled American Indian children in the southwestern part of the United States. The funds for these regional clinics came from yearly lump-sum appropriations from Congress. In 1985, the Service decided to close the regional program and use the funds instead for a nationwide health program for Indian children and teenagers. Children who were eligible for services from the regional program sued the Indian Health Service claiming that the termination of the program violated federal law.

The Court held the Service's termination of the program was generally not subject to judicial review. More broadly, the Court concluded that a federal agency's decision about how to spend its lump sum appropriation is **"committed to agency discretion by law"** within the meaning of APA §701(a)(2). The Court observed that "the very point of a lump-sum appropriation is to give an agency the capacity to adapt to changing circumstances and meet its statutory responsibilities in what it sees as the most effective or desirable way." 508 U.S. at 192. The agency's decisions about how to spend those funds typically rest on factors that agencies are better equipped than courts to weigh and consider.

Congress is always free to put statutory restrictions on an agency's use of funds, but in the absence of such restrictions, the agency's spending decisions are not reviewable, with one possible exception: The Court observed that the plaintiffs' constitutional challenge to the Service's termination of the program had not yet been fully developed in the lower courts, and remained to be addressed on remand. The Court's express preservation of the constitutional claim may reflect the principle mentioned earlier in this chapter that statutes generally won't be interpreted to preclude constitutional challenges to executive-branch conduct.

* * *

This summary introduced you to § 701(a)(2). The Court has addressed § 701(a)(2) in other cases, as have the lower federal courts. We discussed one important lower court case in Chapter 22: *Baltimore Gas & Electric Co. v. Federal Energy Regulatory Commission (BG&E v. FERC)*, 252 F.3d 456 (D.C. Cir. 2001) (discussed in Chapter 22.D.3.c). In *BG&E v. FERC*, the D.C. Circuit held that a federal agency's decision to settle an enforcement proceeding is presumptively committed to agency discretion by law under § 701(a)(2). Given the prevalence of settlement in administrative law, this holding has great importance.

The broader point to take away from this discussion is that sometimes a court finds an agency action unsuitable for judicial review of nonconstitutional challenges, and thus committed to agency discretion by law, partly because the court doubts its competence to conduct the review. Courts tend to have a high opinion of their competence, however, and they therefore seldom find review precluded under § 701(a)(2).

b. State Law

Under the federal APA, preclusion can occur when a statute precludes review or when the "law" — which may include judicially developed principles limiting judicial review — commits a matter to agency discretion. Similarly, preclusion of judicial review in the courts of a State may occur by virtue of statutes or other forms of law, such as judicially developed restrictions. *See, e.g., Laurels of Bon Air, LLC v. Med. Facilities of America LIV Ltd. Partnership*, 659 S.E.2d 561, 595 (Va. App. 2008) (citing *Heckler v. Chaney*, 470 U.S. 821 (1985), in holding that state law provided "no meaningful standard" for judicial review of agency decision). Sometimes these judicially developed restrictions are rooted in state constitutional provisions, such as those requiring a separation of powers among the three branches of state government. *See Shepard v. Attorney General*, 567 N.E.2d 187, 190 (Mass. 1991) (judicial review of executive branch's enforcement discretion would violate state constitution's separation of powers provision). The point is that judicial review can be precluded under state laws that may take different forms: statutory, judicial, constitutional.

3. Preclusion in Enforcement Proceedings

Sometimes a person is minding his or her own business when an agency begins a judicial enforcement proceeding against the person. For example, the agency may sue the person for violating an agency rule and seek civil fines for the violation. In that enforcement proceeding, can the person challenge the validity of the agency rule that the person has supposedly violated? The question, more generally, is as follows: In a civil or criminal proceeding to enforce an agency rule or other prior agency action, can the target of the enforcement challenge the agency rule or the other agency action that the agency seeks to enforce?

The answer in the federal courts is generally "yes," under the last sentence of § 703 of the federal APA:

---

§ 703. Form and venue of proceeding

… Except to the extent that prior, adequate, and exclusive opportunity for judicial review is provided by law, agency action is subject to judicial review in civil or criminal proceedings for judicial enforcement.

The last sentence recognizes that, to quote § 703's title, one "[f]orm" of judicial review proceeding is an agency enforcement proceeding. The target of the enforcement proceeding can seek review of the agency rule or other agency action to be enforced, "**except to the extent that prior, adequate, and exclusive opportunity for judicial review is provided by law.**" The 2010 Model State APA has a provision nearly identical to the last sentence of § 703, including its exception. *See* 2010 Model State APA § 502(b).

The exception is not merely academic. On the contrary, some federal statutes do expressly provide for exclusive, pre-enforcement judicial review of agency action. One such statute is the Clean Water Act. The Act has provision that not only authorizes pre-enforcement judicial review of certain actions taken by the EPA Administrator under the Act (in subsection (b)(1)) but also precludes challenges to those actions in enforcement proceedings (in subsection (b)(2)):

---

33 U.S.C. § 1369. Administrative procedure and judicial review …

(b) Review of Administrator's actions; selection of court; fees

(1) Review of the Administrator's action (A) in promulgating any standard of performance under section 1316 of this title, (B) in making any determination pursuant to section 1316(b)(1)(C) of this title, (C) in promulgating any effluent standard, prohibition, or pretreatment standard under section 1317 of this title, (D) in making any determination as to a State permit program submitted under section 1342(b) of this title, (E) in approving or promulgating any effluent limitation or other limitation under section 1311, 1312, 1316, or 1345 of this title, (F) in issuing or denying any permit under section 1342 of this title, and (G) in promulgating any individual control strategy under section 1314(l) of this title, may be had by any interested person in the Circuit Court of Appeals of the United States for the Federal judicial district in which such person resides or transacts business which is directly affected by such action upon application by such person. Any such application shall be made within 120 days from the date of such determination, approval, promulgation, issuance or denial, or after such date only if such application is based solely on grounds which arose after such 120th day.

(2) Action of the Administrator with respect to which review could have been obtained under paragraph (1) of this subsection shall not be subject to judicial review in any civil or criminal proceeding for enforcement.…

See also 42 U.S.C. § 4915(a) (2012) (similar provision in Noise Control Act); *id.* § 6976(a)(1) (similar provision in Resource Conservation and Recovery Act); *id.* § 7607(b)(2) (similar provision in Clean Air Act). Besides express preclusion provisions like the Clean Water

Act's § 1369(b)(2), even special review statutes that lack express preclusion provisions may be interpreted to prohibit challenges to agency action in enforcement proceedings. For example, if a special review statute puts a deadline on seeking judicial review of the agency action and the enforcement proceeding occurs after the deadline has expired, a challenge to the agency action raised in the enforcement proceeding might be rejected as untimely.

Three decisions by the U.S. Supreme Court confirm, as the exception in § 703's last sentence indicates, that if Congress provides an adequate method for pre-enforcement review of agency action and intends that method to be exclusive, the agency action cannot be challenged in an enforcement proceeding.

- *Yakus v. United States*, 321 U.S. 414 (1944)

Albert Yakus was convicted of selling beef at prices exceeding the wartime price set by a federal agency regulation. The Court held that Mr. Yakus could not challenge the regulation in the criminal proceeding against him because Congress had expressly established an alternative, pre-enforcement method for review of the price regulation's validity. The Court emphasized, however, that Mr. Yakus apparently could have brought a pre-enforcement challenge to the regulation but failed to do so. The Court also determined that the pre-enforcement method of review satisfied due process requirements. *Id.* at 431–437.

- *Adamo Wrecking Co. v. United States*, 434 U.S. 275 (1978)

The Adamo Wrecking Company was prosecuted for violating an EPA rule regulating the handling of asbestos. The rule was promulgated under agency legislation that authorized pre-enforcement judicial review of EPA "emission standards" and expressly precluded challenges to EPA "emission standards" in judicial enforcement proceedings. *Id.* at 277 (quoting statute current version of which is codified as 42 U.S.C. § 7607(b)(2) (2012)). The Court held that Adamo *could* argue in its prosecution that the EPA rule Adamo had supposedly violated was not really an "emission standard" and thus not subject to the express preclusion provision. Further, the Court agreed with Adamo that the EPA rule was not, in fact, an "emission standard" and therefore could be challenged in the prosecution. But in dicta, the Court said that if the rule had been an emission standard after all, Adamo could not have judicially challenged it in the prosecution. *Id.* at 279–286.

Adamo did not challenge the constitutionality of the exclusive, pre-enforcement method of judicial review that Congress prescribed for emission standards. Concurring in *Adamo Wrecking*, Justice Powell said if the constitutional issue had been raised, "it would have merited serious consideration." *Id.* at 289 (Powell, J., concurring). Justice Powell worried that many people subject to emission standards did not have enough notice or time to seek pre-enforcement judicial review under the method Congress had prescribed. For this reason, he thought foreclosing challenges to emission standards in enforcement proceedings might violate due process. In fact, the next case shows that the pre-enforcement opportunity for challenging agency action must satisfy due process for that opportunity to foreclose a challenge in an enforcement proceeding.

- *United States v. Mendoza-Lopez*, 481 U.S. 828 (1987)

Jose Mendoza-Lopez and Angel Landeros-Quinones were prosecuted for re-entering the United States after having been ordered deported. In their prosecution they wanted to challenge the deportation orders. The government argued that they could not challenge the deportation orders in their prosecution because they could have sought judicial review of the deportation orders at the time those orders were entered. The U.S. Supreme Court rejected this argument because the original deportation proceeding violated due process. That proceeding—which included a group deportation hearing for thirteen deportees at once—did not adequately inform the deportees of their right to judicial review and did not result in a valid waiver of that right.

* * *

The last sentence of federal APA § 703 reflects U.S. Supreme Court cases holding that judicial review of agency action in enforcement proceedings can be limited, but the limits must leave an adequate opportunity for pre-enforcement judicial review. This all sounds sensible enough, but the truth is that complications lie beneath the surface, as becomes clear when you explore lower federal court case law. If you are interested in exploring it further, a good place to start is with this article: Ronald M. Levin, *Statutory Time Limits on Judicial Review of Rules: Verkuil Revisited*, 32 Cardozo Law Rev. 2203 (2011). Our discussion is primarily meant to introduce the ideas that enforcement proceedings are one **"form"** of judicial review proceeding and that this form of judicial review can be limited by statute. 5 U.S.C. § 703.

E. Chapter 29 Wrap Up and Look Ahead

You need a cause of action to get judicial review of agency action. Causes of action can come from the APA, special review statutes, or a nonstatutory source. If a special review statute authorizes judicial review, it will ordinarily be interpreted to be exclusive, and will thus control matters like the forum for judicial review. Although agency action is presumptively reviewable, review can be precluded altogether, channeled to certain venues at certain times, or restricted to certain challengers.

The next chapter examines judicially developed timing doctrines that you must also consider when planning your judicial challenge.

Chapter Problem Revisited

This problem concerns the availability of judicial review of an agency's decision to deny a grant application. Federal law creates a presumption that judicial review of agency action is available, and that presumption is implemented by the broad right of judicial review that the federal APA creates.

Moving beyond the presumption, though, you must analyze whether the elements of an APA cause of action exist: Is HHS's denial of a grant application **"final agency action"**? Is the disappointed applicant for a grant a person **"adversely affected or aggrieved ... within the meaning of a relevant statute"**? To answer these questions definitively, you will have to draw upon upcoming material in Chapter 30 on finality and upon the prior material in Chapter 28 on the "zone of interests" test. You also must consider whether review is precluded under APA § 701(a). In considering preclusion, recall that preclusion of constitutional challenges is strongly disfavored and may not even be constitutional.

A complete analysis leads to the conclusion that a person whose grant application is finally denied by HHS *can* get judicial review of the denial. You might doubt this conclusion in light of *Lincoln v. Vigil*, 508 U.S. 182 (1992).

Lincoln v. Vigil, like the chapter problem, involves a challenge to the way an agency spends money. But *Lincoln v. Vigil* differs from the chapter problem, because the draft legislation in the chapter problem specifies factors that HHS is required to consider; the legislation is not a lump-sum appropriation.

Of course, it is one thing to say that a disappointed applicant can get judicial review of HHS's denial. It is quite another thing to say that a court will invalidate HHS's decision. The court will review HHS's decision under § 706, as interpreted by case law on the "scope of review." We explore the scope of review in upcoming chapters.

Representative White Eagle has asked you to consider whether, on the one hand, judicial review should be precluded or, on the other hand, whether the APA cause of action should be modified or displaced by a special review provision. The Representative's questions remind you that, under § 701(a)(1), a statute may affirmatively preclude judicial review. Do you think that's appropriate here? Alternatively, is there some reason Congress should modify or depart from the APA cause of action? You should advise Representative White Eagle that, although the legislation could expressly preclude judicial review, a preclusion provision probably would not be interpreted to bar First Amendment claims like the one he mentioned.

Professional Development Reflection Question

When you analyze a case to identify feasible causes of action, you are, in effect, trying to fit your case into one or more legal boxes, each labeled with the name of a cause of action (e.g., negligence, breach of contract, APA-type challenge). It can be easy during this analytical process to lose sight of the needs of your client. For example, although your client may have a very promising APA challenge to an agency action, the client may not have the time or money to sustain that challenge. And, even if the client has the resources for a successful challenge, success may not give the client what she, he, or it really wants. Filing a lawsuit is a big step, and before taking that step, you must be sure the step is the right one for the client to take.

You can only be sure that's the right step if you've done a good job communicating with your client. A major barrier to good communication is the preconceptions that the lawyer, as well as the client, brings to any conversation. It takes deliberate self-awareness to recognize and dispel those preconceptions. A parable illustrating the point comes from Stephen Covey's book, The 7 Habits of Highly Effective People 33 (1990), recounting a story told by Frank Koch at Naval Institute proceedings:

> Two battleships assigned to the training squadron had been at sea on maneuvers in heavy weather for several days. I was serving on the lead battleship and was on watch on the bridge as night fell. The visibility was poor with patchy fog, so the captain remained on the bridge keeping an eye on all activities.
>
> Shortly after dark, the lookout on the wing of the bridge reported, "Light, bearing on the starboard bow."
>
> "Is it steady or moving astern?" the captain called out.

Lookout replied, "Steady, captain," which meant we were on a dangerous collision course with that ship.

The captain then called to the signalman, "Signal that ship: We are on a collision course, advise you to change your course 20 degrees."

Back came the signal, "Advisable for you to change course 20 degrees."

The captain said, "Send, I'm a captain, change course 20 degrees."

"I'm a seaman second class," came the reply. "You had better change course 20 degrees."

By that time, the captain was furious. He spat out, "Send, I'm a battleship. Change course 20 degrees."

Back came the flashing light, "I'm a lighthouse."

We changed course.

The point is that what looks like a stunning judicial victory to you as a lawyer may look like a pig in a poke to your client.

To help you remember the importance of good communication, we challenge you to recall an actual situation in your life in which you played the pilot, or the light house keep, in the story above.

Chapter 30

Timing

Overview

Judicial review of agency action can be delayed or barred by three timing doctrines: the doctrines of finality, ripeness, and exhaustion of administrative remedies. In addition, a fourth doctrine—that of "primary jurisdiction"—can cause a court to decline jurisdiction over a lawsuit if the lawsuit raises an issue that should initially be decided by an agency. Primary jurisdiction can thus delay a court's consideration of an issue until after it's been determined by an agency. A final timing consideration is that, like any lawsuit, lawsuits challenging agency action may be barred as untimely if not commenced within the time prescribed in the applicable statute of limitations. This chapter explores these doctrines, all of which can affect the timing, and which therefore concern the availability, of judicial review of agency action.

The chapter's sections are as follows:

A. Finality

B. Ripeness

C. Exhaustion

D. Relationship among Finality, Ripeness, and Exhaustion

E. Primary Jurisdiction

F. Statutes of Limitations for Lawsuits Seeking Review of Agency Action

G. Chapter 30 Wrap Up and Look Ahead

Chapter Problem 1

Springer held a license from the Federal Aviation Administration as an aircraft mechanic. The FAA suspended Springer's license for one year, however, when Springer's mandatory urine test tested positive for the active ingredient in marijuana. Springer's lawyer contested the suspension and requested a hearing before an ALJ employed by the National Transportation Safety Board. At the hearing, Springer argued that the testing method was flawed. The ALJ issued an initial decision upholding the suspension. A Board regulation says, "A party may appeal from [an ALJ's] initial decision" by filing an appeal with the five-member body that heads the Board. 49 C.F.R. § 821.47(a) (2012). Another regulation says that, if no appeal is taken, the ALJ's initial decision "shall become final with respect to the parties." *Id.* § 821.43. The relevant statute mirrors the Board's regulations in permitting, but not requiring, a person dissatisfied with an FAA order to appeal the order to the Board. 49 U.S.C. § 44709(d)(1) (2012).

Springer's lawyer appealed the ALJ's decision to the Board but was late in filing the brief for Springer with the Board. The Board's rules say that the filing of a timely brief is necessary to perfect the appeal to the Board. The Board's rules also say that, if an appellant's brief is filed late, the Board may dismiss the appeal. 49 C.F.R. § 821.48 (2012). That is what happened. The Board dismissed Springer's appeal on the ground that Springer did not perfect the appeal by filing a timely brief.

Springer fired the lawyer who filed the late brief and has hired you to seek judicial review of the Board's decision. The relevant statute is 49 U.S.C. § 1153(a) (2012). The questions before you are:

1. How long do you have to seek judicial review?

2. Does Springer's failure properly to exhaust his administrative remedies bar judicial review of the Board's order?

3. If judicial review is not barred, may the court review Springer's challenge to the testing method?

Chapter Problem 2

You are a law clerk to a federal district judge to whom the case described below has been assigned. The EPA has moved to dismiss the case. Please evaluate the EPA's arguments in support of dismissal.

Chantell and Michael Sackett own land near a lake in Idaho. They began to build a home on the land. During the building project, their contractors filled in part of their land with rock and dirt. Later, the EPA determined that the Sacketts had filled in a wetland without getting the permit required by federal law. The EPA issued a compliance order directing the Sacketts to restore the land according to an EPA-created restoration plan.

The EPA issued the compliance order under the Clean Water Act, 33 U.S.C. § 1319(a)(3) (2012). The issuance of the compliance order had two effects. First, it doubled the daily amount of civil penalties to which the Sacketts were subject if EPA brought a civil action against them and proved an ongoing violation of the Act. Second, it lowered their chances of getting a permit to fill a wetland on their land in the event that they conceded, or a court eventually determined, that their land did indeed have a wetland the filling of which required a federal permit.

The Act does not authorize either administrative review or judicial review of a compliance order. Nonetheless, Mr. and Ms. Sackett have sued the EPA in federal court, seeking judicial review of the compliance order under the federal APA. Their primary argument is that their land never had any wetland on it that was subject to the EPA's jurisdiction.

The EPA has moved to dismiss the action, arguing that judicial review is not available. The EPA makes three arguments:

1. The compliance order is not final. For one thing, the EPA told the Sacketts in the cover letter for the compliance order that it encouraged them to have informal discussions with EPA officials about the terms of the restoration plan. The cover letter also encouraged them to let the EPA know if they

thought the compliance order rested on any inaccurate statements about conditions on their land or their construction activity on that land. For another thing, EPA must bring a civil action to collect any penalty for the violations of the Clean Water Act underlying the compliance order, and in that civil action, the EPA will bear the burden of proving—at a trial, if need be—that the Sacketts violated the Act. Thus, the Sacketts can't be fined merely for violating the compliance order, unless the court independently determines that they have violated the Act.

2. The Sacketts have not exhausted their administrative remedies. As stated above, the EPA has invited them to have informal discussions about the terms of the restoration plan or any factual inaccuracies underlying the compliance order. The Sacketts did not pursue this option before suing.

3. The Clean Water Act impliedly precludes judicial review under the APA. The Act expressly authorizes judicial review of certain EPA actions, but it does not authorize judicial review of a compliance order.

A. Finality

This section examines the origin and rationale of the finality requirement, and the test for determining whether an agency action is final.

1. What Is the Finality Requirement? What Is Its Rationale? Where Do You Find It?

A court usually will review only agency action that is final. The idea behind this finality requirement is that the agency decision-making process should be finished and have legal consequences before judicial review of any aspect of that process is sought.

The finality requirement in administrative law resembles the general rule in court systems that only the "final" decisions of a trial court are immediately appealable; nonfinal rulings, also known as "interlocutory" rulings, are not usually immediately appealable. The reasons for requiring finality are similar in both settings. Review of nonfinal decisions can delay the agency's or trial court's coming to a final decision, and such delay alone is a reason not to allow it. What is more, review of nonfinal decisions can waste the time of the reviewing court, because the nonfinal decision might get reconsidered by the agency or the trial court, or because the nonfinal decision may end up not mattering—for example, when a party complains about the exclusion of evidence from a hearing but that party ends up winning anyway.

But despite similarity between the concepts and rationales for requiring finality of agency action and of trial-court decisions before review, the two finality doctrines are different, because judicial review of agency action differs from an appellate court's review of a trial court's decision.

The finality requirement in administrative law is a judicially created doctrine that today has been codified in APAs and many special review statutes. Specifically, the federal APA creates a cause of action only for "*final* agency action." 5 U.S.C. § 704 (2012) (emphasis added). Similarly, the 2010 Model State APA authorizes review of "*final* agency action." 2010 Model State APA § 501 (emphasis added). The finality requirement is also codified, for example, in the special review statutes covering decisions of the Commissioner of Social Security; the statute authorizes judicial review only of certain "*final* decision[s]" of the Commissioner. 42 U.S.C. § 405(g) (2012) (emphasis added); *id.* § 1395ff(b)(1)(A). Even if a judicial review statute does not expressly require finality, the statute will ordinarily be interpreted to require it. *Bell v. New Jersey*, 461 U.S. 773, 778 (1983) ("The strong presumption is that judicial review will be available only when agency action becomes final."). Finality is thus commonly required for judicial review of agency action.

Because finality is commonly required, the question naturally arises: How do you tell if an agency action is final? We turn to that question next.

2. How Do You Tell If an Agency Action Is Final?

a. General Framework

The Court set out a two-part test for determining the finality of federal agency action in *Bennett v. Spear*, 520 U.S. 154 (1997):

> As a general matter, two conditions must be satisfied for agency action to be "final": First, the action must mark the "consummation" of the agency's decisionmaking process — it must not be of a merely tentative or interlocutory nature. And second, the action must be one by which "rights or obligations have been determined," or from which "legal consequences will flow" ...

Id. at 177–178 (internal citations omitted). The first part of the test focuses on whether the agency has finished its process; the second focuses on the effect of that process. Sometimes the Court has described the second part of the test as requiring consideration of whether the agency action's "impact 'is sufficiently direct and immediate' and has a 'direct effect on ... day-to-day business.'" *Franklin v. Massachusetts*, 505 U.S. 788, 796–797 (1992) (quoting *Abbott Labs. v. Gardner*, 387 U.S. 136, 152 (1967)). This alternative wording emphasizes the immediacy and directness of the effect — as distinguished from the legal effect, which is what the *Bennett* formulation emphasizes.

The Court applied this two-part test in *Bennett* to find that a Biological Opinion issued by the Fish and Wildlife Service (FWS) under the Endangered Species Act was "**final**" agency action within the meaning of federal APA § 704 and therefore subject to judicial review. The Opinion directed a federal agency, the Bureau of Reclamation, to take certain measures when operating the Klamath Irrigation Project to avoid jeopardizing two endangered species of fish. The measures included maintaining minimum water levels in two reservoirs that formed part of the Project. Ranchers and irrigation districts that used water from the Project challenged the Biological Opinion in federal court. The FWS argued that its Opinion was not final agency action. There was no dispute that the Opinion marked the consummation of FWS's decision-making process and thus satisfied the first part of the test for finality. The dispute was over whether the Opinion had the kind of practical or legal effect necessary to satisfy the second part of the test. The Court held that the Opinion did have the requisite effect because it "alter[ed] the legal regime" to which the Bureau of Reclamation was subject. 520 U.S. at 169. For example, if the Bureau did not adopt the protective measures outlined in the Opinion, Bureau officials could be held civilly or even criminally liable for violations of the Endangered Species Act. *See id.*

at 169–170. In sum, the Opinion was an agency action from which legal consequences flowed.

Bennett v. Spear illustrates the general operation of the Court's two-part test for finality. Below we explore how the test applies in four recurring situations in which finality concerns arise. They further illustrate the operation of *Bennett*'s two-part test.

Exercise: The Two-Part Test for Federal Agency Action to Be Final

To help the two-part test of *Bennett v. Spear* stick in your brain, jot down shorthand descriptions of each part of the test below:

1. _____ ;

   and

2. _____ .

Now notice the relationship between the two parts.

Tentative or interlocutory agency decisions often lack legal or practical effect precisely because they are tentative or interlocutory. But that isn't always true. Consider the impact, by way of comparison, of interlocutory trial court rulings like orders compelling disclosure of documents withheld in discovery as privileged by, say, the attorney-client privilege. The disclosure of privileged documents may have great impact on the person claiming the privilege, but the order of disclosure is still interlocutory and, as such, not immediately appealable as a final judgment. *Cf. Mohawk Indus. v. Carpenter*, 130 S.Ct. 599, 608 (2009) (trial court order compelling disclosure of documents allegedly covered by attorney-client privilege is not immediately appealable under collateral order doctrine, even though disclosure will sometimes be highly consequential).

By the same token, an agency decision that reflects the consummation of the agency decision-making process often has legal or practical consequences of some sort. Otherwise, the decision would be pointless. The question is whether the consequences are the types of consequences that "count" under the finality case law.

---

b. Finality When Decision Making Involves Multiple Governmental Entities

In one recurring situation raising finality concerns, one agency makes a decision that another agency or government entity must act upon, and the question is whether the first agency's decision is final. The answer is "no," if the first decision is in the nature of a recommendation.

For example, in *Franklin v. Massachusetts*, the U.S. Census Bureau produced a report of census results for the President. 505 U.S. 788 (1992). The Court held that the Census Bureau's report was not final. Although the Bureau had finished its decision-making process, the report had no legal effect until the President approved it. Thus, the Census Bureau report was not reviewable under the APA as **"final agency action"** because it was not **"final."** (And the action taken by the President on the Census Bureau report was not reviewable under the APA as **"final agency action"** because the President is not an **"agency"** for APA purposes.)

To cite another, similar example, in *Dalton v. Specter*, 511 U.S. 462 (1994), an agency made recommendations to the President about what military bases should be closed. The agency recommendations came at the end of that agency's decision-making process, but they had no legal effect until the President approved them and were therefore not final. As in *Franklin*, neither the agency's decision nor the President's was subject to review under the APA.

Franklin and *Dalton* show that, even if an agency action is "final" in the sense that the agency has finished its job, that does not mean the agency action will be "final" for purposes of judicial review.

c. Finality of Interlocutory Agency Decisions

An agency often makes interlocutory rulings in the course of a proceeding such as an agency adjudication or a rulemaking proceeding. People dissatisfied with these interlocutory rulings generally cannot challenge them until the agency finishes its proceeding because those rulings are not themselves considered final. They don't meet the first part of *Bennett*'s two-part test.

The nonfinality of agency interlocutory rulings is reflected, somewhat obliquely, in the second sentence of APA § 704:

---

5 U.S.C. § 704. Actions reviewable

... A preliminary, procedural, or intermediate agency action or ruling not directly reviewable is subject to review on the review of the final agency action....

The Attorney General's Manual on the APA explained that § 704's second sentence codified existing practice, under which courts generally reviewed the interlocutory rulings of an agency in an agency proceeding only when the courts reviewed the agency's final decision in that proceeding. AGM 103. Even so, § 704's second sentence implies that some **"preliminary, procedural, or intermediate agency action[s] or ruling[s]"** *are* **"directly [i.e., immediately] reviewable."**

The general unreviewability of interlocutory agency decisions is illustrated in the case summarized next:

- *Federal Trade Commission v. Standard Oil of California*, 449 U.S. 232 (1980)

This is known as the *SOCAL* case in administrative law circles. In *SOCAL*, the FTC issued an administrative complaint against Standard Oil of California and other oil companies averring that the FTC had "reason to believe" that the companies were violating the Federal Trade Commission Act by restraining trade. *Id.* at 234 (quoting FTC complaint). The administrative complaint was the first step in a formal adjudication to determine whether violations had indeed occurred. Rather than go through that agency adjudication, Standard Oil sued the FTC in federal court. In that lawsuit, Standard Oil challenged the administrative complaint on the ground that it did not rest on adequate evidence and was issued under political pressure from members of Congress.

The *SOCAL* Court held that the FTC complaint was not **"final agency action"** within the meaning of federal APA § 704 and therefore was reviewable, if at all, only on review of a final agency action against Standard Oil, such as a cease-and-desist order. 449 U.S. at 238. Relevant to the first part of the two-part test for finality, the FTC complaint reflected only a tentative determination of a violation of the law. It merely began, rather than consummating, the agency's decision-making process. Relevant to the second part of the test for finality, the FTC complaint had no immediate impact on Standard Oil's day-to-day operations or any other legal consequences "except to impose upon [Standard Oil] the burden of responding to the charges made against it." *Id.* at 240–243. The Court explained, "[A]lthough this burden certainly is substantial, it is different in kind and legal effect from the burdens attending what heretofore has been considered to be final agency action." *Id.* at 242.

The *SOCAL* Court rejected Standard Oil's argument that the FTC complaint was **"directly reviewable"** under the second sentence of § 704 by analogy to the "collateral order" doctrine. That doctrine, as you may know, allows federal courts of appeals to review some interlocutory rulings of federal district courts immediately. *See Standard Oil*, 449 U.S. at 246. The *SOCAL* Court held that the FTC complaint did not fit the criteria for a collateral order established in *Cohen v. Beneficial Loan Corp.*, 337 U.S. 541 (1949). *See SOCAL*, 449 U.S. at 246. The *SOCAL* Court did not, however, rule out the possibility that a doctrine analogous to the collateral order doctrine might render some interlocutory agency rulings **"directly reviewable"** under § 704 of the federal APA.

* * *

Indeed, some lower federal courts have applied an administrative-law analogue of the collateral order doctrine to review some interlocutory agency actions directly. For example, the U.S. Court of Appeals for the Ninth Circuit relied by analogy on the collateral order doctrine to review an interlocutory ruling of the Equal Employment Opportunity Commission (EEOC). *Alaska v. EEOC*, 564 F.3d 1062, 1065 n.1 (9th Cir. 2009) (*en banc*). In the Ninth Circuit case, two former employees in the Alaska Governor's office complained of sex discrimination, prompting the EEOC to commence a formal adjudication against Alaska. An ALJ denied Alaska's motion to dismiss the adjudication as barred by state sovereign immunity, and the Commission that heads the EEOC affirmed the ALJ's ruling. The EEOC's rejection of Alaska's sovereign immunity defense was interlocutory, because it did not end the adjudication; rather, it allowed the adjudication to go forward. Even so, the Ninth Circuit held that Alaska could seek immediate judicial review of the agency's ruling under the federal APA, because it fit the criteria for a collateral order. *Cf. Rhode Island Dep't of Environmental Management v. United States*, 304 F.3d 31, 42–45 (1st Cir. 2002) (relying on nonstatutory review to consider similar claim of sovereign immunity by Rhode Island agency).

The Ninth Circuit's use of the collateral order doctrine accords with text in § 704's second sentence implying that some interlocutory agency rulings are **"directly reviewable."** Moreover, it accords with practice of state courts under state APAs that allow review of some interlocutory agency rulings. *See, e.g.*, Kan. Stat. Ann. § 77-608 (West, Westlaw through end of 2011 Reg. Sess.) (authorizing "interlocutory review of nonfinal agency action" under specified conditions). Most courts, however, worry about piecemeal review of agency action and will therefore rarely treat interlocutory agency rulings as final.

Exercise: Finality of Interlocutory Agency Rulings

The Federal Energy Regulatory Commission (FERC) has found cause to believe that Sunshine Natural Gas Company has violated the Natural Gas Act. FERC has accordingly begun an adjudication to determine whether Sunshine has indeed violated the Act. During the adjudication, Sunshine files a discovery request for records of FERC's investigation of Sunshine. FERC prosecutors refuse to hand over the documents. The ALJ assigned to the case holds that the documents are not subject to discovery under FERC's procedural rules, and the Commission that heads FERC affirms that holding. Now Sunshine seeks judicial review of the Commission's decision that the documents are not disclosable in discovery. Sunshine argues that it will suffer irreparable injury unless it gets the documents, because they are critical to Sunshine's defense. In opposing judicial review, FERC argues that the Commission's decision is not final. Please evaluate the finality argument, on the assumption (which is true) that the special review statute authorizes review only of "final orders" of FERC. *See Energy Transfer Partners, L.P. v. FERC*, 567 F.3d 134 (5th Cir. 2009).

---

d. Finality of Agency Guidance Documents

Many agencies give informal advice to individual companies or people who request it, and give guidance to the public at large by issuing interpretative rules, policy statements, and other guidance documents. When someone seeks judicial review of agency guidance documents, finality concerns often arise. The finality of guidance documents is analyzed using the two-part test of *Bennett v. Spear*, under which some guidance documents will be found final and others won't. The finality of a guidance document depends on the content and function of the specific document, the authority of the specific official who issues it, and the specific statutory and regulatory scheme under which it is issued.

We summarize below an old but still leading authority on the finality of agency guidance documents.

- *National Automatic Laundry & Cleaning Council v. Schultz*, 443 F.2d 689 (D.C. Cir. 1971)

At issue was whether 1966 amendments to the Fair Labor Standards Act caused the Act's minimum-wage and overtime provisions to apply to coin-operated laundry businesses and dry cleaning businesses. A trade association of those businesses requested advice on the Act's applicability from the Administrator of the U.S. Department of Labor's Wage and Hour Division. The Administrator replied in a letter that the Act, as amended, did indeed apply to those businesses. The trade association sued in federal court, challenging the Administrator's letter. The government defendants argued that the lawsuit was not ripe. As we discuss in Section B of this chapter, one usual requirement for a lawsuit to be ripe is that it concern "final" agency action.

The court of appeals held that the Administrator's letter reflected final agency action. The court cited these considerations in finding finality:

- The letter was not based on hypothetical facts; it was based on facts about the actual operations of the association's members.

- The letter did not concern future conduct not yet undertaken; the association's members had been paying employees on a pay scale that did not comply with the Act, relying on a 1963 ruling from the Administrator stating that those business were not subject to the Act (as it then stood).

- The process leading to issuance of the letter was not formal like that of legislative rulemaking, a consideration that weighed against, but did not preclude, finality.

- The letter was from the head of the agency, not a subordinate, and nothing in the wording of the letter suggested that the Administrator's view was tentative.

- The letter addressed a broad legal issue affecting an entire industry group.

Although the court held that the agency letter in this case was final, the court emphasized that courts should hesitate to treat agency guidance documents as final, because the prospect of judicial review would discourage agencies from providing useful guidance to the public. *Id.* at 699. Agencies would shy away from providing guidance, figuring: why stick our neck out by venturing legal advice, and thereby offering a target for a lawsuit?

e. Finality of Agency Inaction

An almost metaphysical question is: When is an agency's *failure to act* final? The question arises because the federal APA defines **"agency action"** to include an agency's **"failure to act."** 5 U.S.C. §§ 551(13) & 701(b)(2) (2012). For an agency failure to act to be subject to judicial review under the APA, the failure to act, like any other agency action, must be **"final"** within the meaning of § 704. But as any procrastinator knows, the failure to act can last indefinitely.

The lower federal courts have held that an agency's failure to act may be final in either of two situations:

1. The agency fails to meet a specific statutory deadline for taking a specific action — e.g., the agency fails to meet a statutory deadline for promulgating regulations on a particular subject. In this situation, the federal APA allows a court to **"compel agency action *unlawfully* withheld."** 5 U.S.C. § 706(1) (italics added).

2. The law requires the agency to take a specific action without specifying a deadline, but the agency's delay becomes so egregious that a court believes the agency delay can be treated as final. Section 706(1) of the federal APA allows a court to compel not only agency action unlawfully withheld but also **"agency action ... *unreasonably delayed."** Id.* (italics added); *see also id.* § 555(b) (requiring an agency "to conclude a matter presented to it" with "due regard for the convenience and necessity of the parties or their representatives and within a reasonable time"). In one case, for example, a court held that the FCC's six-year delay in obeying the court's mandate justified judicial relief under § 706(1). *In re Core Communications, Inc.,* 531 F.3d 849, 856 (D.C. Cir. 2008).

These situations identify agency action that is final enough to be the subject of judicial review. The judicial relief available in these situations is discussed in Chapter 35.A.5.

f. Final Thoughts on Finality

We have focused on tricky finality situations, but finality will be obvious in most lawsuits seeking judicial review of agency action. It usually is not hard to tell whether an agency has finished its decision-making process. Furthermore, when someone cares enough about the outcome of that process to file a lawsuit, it's a good bet that the outcome of that process has sufficient practical or legal effect to satisfy the second part of the two-part test for finality.

Perhaps the clearest example of a final federal agency action occurs when the agency publishes in the Federal Register a legislative rule that the agency designates as its "final" rule. No doubt about finality can arise in that situation. A final legislative rule, however, may not be subject to an immediate judicial challenge. Instead, an immediate judicial challenge may be barred because the challenge will be deemed not "ripe." We explore the ripeness doctrine in the next section.

Exercise: Identifying Agency Actions That Raise Finality Concerns

Please say whether or not the following agency actions could raise finality issues, for purposes of seeking judicial review of each as a **"final agency action"** under §704 of the APA.

1. An agency publishes as a "final rule" in the Federal Register a rule that has not gone through notice-and-comment rulemaking because, in the agency's view, the rule is exempt from those procedures.

2. An agency official sends an email to a company responding to the company's request for advice on how to comply with an agency regulation.

3. Before the scheduled hearing in a formal agency adjudication, an ALJ denies a motion for administrative summary judgment filed by one of the parties, and the head of the agency affirms the ALJ's denial of administrative summary judgment. (Administrative summary judgment is discussed in Chapter 22.D.5.)

4. The Department of Labor issues a citation to a mining company for a violation of the Mine Safety Act. The citation is issued under 30 U.S.C. §814 (2012), and is subject to administrative review under 30 U.S.C. §815 (2012), which states in relevant part:

---

30 U.S.C. §815. Procedure for enforcement

(a) Notification of civil penalty; contest

If, after an inspection or investigation, the Secretary issues a citation or order under section 814 of this title, he shall, within a reasonable time after the termination of such inspection or investigation, notify the operator by certified mail of the civil penalty proposed to be assessed under section 820(a) of this title for the violation cited and that the operator has 30 days within which to notify the Secretary that he wishes to contest the citation or proposed assessment of penalty. A copy of such notification shall be sent by mail to the representative of miners in such mine. If, within 30 days from the receipt of the notification issued by the Secretary, the operator fails to notify the Secretary that he intends to contest the citation or the proposed assessment of penalty, and no notice is filed by any miner or representative of miners under subsection (d) of this section within such time, the citation and the proposed assessment of penalty shall be deemed a final order of the Commission and not subject to review by any court or agency. Refusal by the operator or his agent to accept certified mail containing a citation and proposed assessment of penalty under this subsection shall constitute receipt thereof within the meaning of this subsection....

B. Ripeness

Federal courts and many state courts cannot hear a case that is not "ripe." This ripeness requirement has relevance for administrative lawyers, as demonstrated by the fact that the leading U.S. Supreme Court cases on ripeness involve judicial review of the actions of administrative agencies. This section explores the ripeness doctrine. As you will see, most cases raising ripeness issues involve one of two situations: (1) A person seeks judicial review under the APA of an agency legislative rule that has not yet been enforced against that person. These are called "pre-enforcement challenges." (2) A person seeks judicial review of some informal agency action—often some sort of non-legislative rule or policy statement—that does not have any immediate, obvious legal effect (and for that reason may not even be "final").

1. What Is the Ripeness Requirement? What Is Its Rationale? Where Do You Find It?

The U.S. Supreme Court has traced the federal law of ripeness to Article III of the U.S. Constitution and prudential principles reflecting the proper role of the federal courts. *See, e.g., Nat'l Park Hospitality Ass'n v. Dep't of the Interior*, 538 U.S. 803, 808 (2003). The Court has said that the purpose of the ripeness doctrine is "to prevent the courts, through avoidance of premature adjudication, from entangling themselves in abstract disagreements over administrative policies, and also to protect the agencies from judicial interference until an administrative decision has been formalized and its effects felt in a concrete way by the challenging parties." *Id.* (internal quotation marks omitted). So the doctrine protects courts and agencies, and it may be used to prevent someone who wants immediate judicial review from getting it.

As a judicially developed doctrine, ripeness law is found almost exclusively in case law. Though not expressly codifying ripeness, the APA leaves room in § 702's last sentence for courts to apply the ripeness doctrine:

---

5 U.S.C. § 702. Right of review

… Nothing herein … affects other limitations on judicial review or the power or duty of the court to dismiss any action or deny relief on any other appropriate legal or equitable ground …

The **"other limitations"** include justiciability limits such as ripeness. *See* H.R. Rep. 94-1656, at 12 (1976), *reprinted in* 1976 U.S.C.C.A.N. 6121, 6132 (1978).

Because the federal APA supplies the cause of action for so many lawsuits seeking review of federal agency action, and (impliedly) codifies traditional ripeness doctrine, administrative lawyers must understand the traditional doctrine. After exploring it, we will discuss how special review statutes can modify (as well as codify) the traditional doctrine.

2. How Do You Tell If a Lawsuit Challenging Agency Action Is Ripe?

We explore the ripeness doctrine of federal law in three steps. First we examine the traditional doctrine, by examining the classic cases. Second, we discuss an important situation in which federal statutes modify the classic doctrine—namely, by authorizing so-called "pre-enforcement challenges" to agency rules. Third, we discuss ripeness analysis of informal agency actions.

a. The Traditional Ripeness Doctrine

The Court adopted a two-part test for assessing ripeness in a famous set of cases decided in 1967 known as the "*Abbott Labs* trilogy." That two-part test requires a court to consider "[1] the fitness of the issues for judicial decision and [2] the hardship to the parties of withholding court consideration." *Abbott Laboratories v. Gardner*, 387 U.S. 136, 149 (1967) (bracketed numerals added). In a later case, the Court reformulated the two-part into a three-part inquiry as described below. But the reformulation does not change the traditional analysis.

(i) The *Abbott Labs* Trilogy

Below we reproduce an excerpt of one of the three cases in the *Abbott Labs* trilogy and then summarize the other two.

Exercise: *Abbott Laboratories v. Gardner*

As you read *Abbott Laboratories*, please consider these questions:

1. Why do the plaintiffs want to challenge the FDA's regulation now, instead of waiting until the FDA seeks to enforce it against them?

2. What is the relationship between finality and the Court's two-part test for ripeness?

Abbott Laboratories v. Gardner

387 U.S. 136 (1967)[1]

[Editor's note: You will recognize the facts of this case if you studied Chapter 29.D.1's discussion of preclusion of judicial review, which included this case.

Editor's summary: Congress amended the federal Food, Drug, and Cosmetic Act (Food and Drug Act) to require drug manufacturers to print the generic name of a drug on labels and in print advertisements for the drug. This was so consumers would know, for example, that, whether they bought Excedrin or Bufferin, they were buying the same thing: acetylsalicylic acid (aspirin). The Food and Drug Administration exercised its

---

1. You will find a red flag and red stop sign attached to *Abbott Labs* in the Westlaw and LexisNexis databases, respectively. They signify that the Court in *Abbott Labs* made a statement about the federal APA that the Court later repudiated. The Court in *Abbott Labs* said in a part of the opinion not included in our excerpt that the APA grants subject matter jurisdiction. 387 U.S. at 141. The Court later held in *Califano v. Sanders*, 430 U.S. 99, 105 (1977), that the federal APA does not grant subject matter jurisdiction. *Abbott Labs* is still good law for the ripeness analysis we reproduce here. We note that the holding in *Califano v. Sanders* likewise repudiated language about the APA's granting subject matter jurisdiction in another famous, "red flagged" administrative law case, *Citizens to Preserve Overton Park, Inc. v. Volpe*, 401 U.S. 402 (1971), which we have excerpted in Chapter 34.

statutory authority to promulgate a legislative rule implementing the statute. The FDA rule required drug manufacturers to use the generic name of a drug *every time* the commercial name appeared on a label or in a print advertisement. Drug manufacturers brought a federal court lawsuit challenging the FDA's "every time regulation" on the ground that it exceeded the FDA's statutory authority. They sought declaratory and injunctive relief against enforcement of the regulation.

In part I of its opinion, the Court rejected the FDA's argument that the Food and Drug Act impliedly precluded judicial review by authorizing judicial review of *some* FDA regulations, but not the type of regulations of which the "every time regulation" was one. We summarized that part of the Court's opinion in Chapter 29.D.1. In Part II of the opinion, reproduced below, the Court addressed ripeness.]

MR. JUSTICE HARLAN delivered the opinion of the Court....

II

... The injunctive and declaratory judgment remedies are discretionary, and courts traditionally have been reluctant to apply them to administrative determinations unless these arise in the context of a controversy "ripe" for judicial resolution.... The problem is best seen in a twofold aspect, requiring us to evaluate both the fitness of the issues for judicial decision and the hardship to the parties of withholding court consideration.

As to the former factor, we believe the issues presented are appropriate for judicial resolution at this time. First, all parties agree that the issue tendered is a purely legal one: whether the statute was properly construed by the Commissioner to require the established name of the drug to be used every time the proprietary name is employed. Both sides moved for summary judgment in the District Court, and no claim is made here that further administrative proceedings are contemplated....

Second, the regulations in issue we find to be "final agency action" within the meaning of § 10 of the Administrative Procedure Act, 5 U.S.C. § 704, as construed in judicial decisions. An "agency action" includes any "rule," defined by the Act as "an agency statement of general or particular applicability and future effect designed to implement, interpret, or prescribe law or policy," §§ 2(c), 2(g), 5 U.S.C. §§ 551(4), 551(13). The cases dealing with judicial review of administrative actions have interpreted the "finality" element in a pragmatic way. Thus in *Columbia Broadcasting System v. United States*, 316 U.S. 407, ... this Court held reviewable a regulation of the Federal Communications Commission setting forth certain proscribed contractual arrangements between chain broadcasters and local stations. The FCC did not have direct authority to regulate these contracts, and its rule asserted only that it would not license stations which maintained such contracts with the networks. Although no license had in fact been denied or revoked, and the FCC regulation could properly be characterized as a statement only of its intentions, the Court held that "Such regulations have the force of law before their sanctions are invoked as well as after. When as here they are promulgated by order of the Commission and the expected conformity to them causes injury cognizable by a court of equity, they are appropriately the subject of attack ..." 316 U.S., at 418–419 ...

We find decision in the present case following *a fortiori* from [our] precedents. The regulation challenged here, promulgated in a formal manner after announcement in the Federal Register and consideration of comments by interested parties is quite clearly definitive. There is no hint that this regulation is informal, or only the ruling of a subordinate official, or tentative. It was made effective upon publication, and the Assistant General Counsel for Food and Drugs stated in the District Court that compliance was expected....

This is also a case in which the impact of the regulations upon the petitioners is sufficiently direct and immediate as to render the issue appropriate for judicial review at this stage. These regulations purport to give an authoritative interpretation of a statutory provision that has a direct effect on the day-to-day business of all prescription drug companies; its promulgation puts petitioners in a dilemma that it was the very purpose of the Declaratory Judgment Act to ameliorate. As the District Court found on the basis of uncontested allegations, "Either they must comply with the every time requirement and incur the costs of changing over their promotional material and labeling or they must follow their present course and risk prosecution." 228 F.Supp. 855, 861.... If petitioners wish to comply they must change all their labels, advertisements, and promotional materials; they must destroy stocks of printed matter; and they must invest heavily in new printing type and new supplies. The alternative to compliance—continued use of material which they believe in good faith meets the statutory requirements, but which clearly does not meet the regulation of the Commissioner—may be even more costly. That course would risk serious criminal and civil penalties for the unlawful distribution of "misbranded" drugs.[19]

... Where the legal issue presented is fit for judicial resolution, and where a regulation requires an immediate and significant change in the plaintiffs' conduct of their affairs with serious penalties attached to noncompliance, access to the courts under the Administrative Procedure Act and the Declaratory Judgment Act must be permitted, absent a statutory bar or some other unusual circumstance, neither of which appears here....

... [T]he Government urges that to permit resort to the courts in this type of case may delay or impede effective enforcement of the Act. We fully recognize the important public interest served by assuring prompt and unimpeded administration of the ... [Food and Drug Act], but we do not find the Government's argument convincing. First, in this particular case, a pre-enforcement challenge by nearly all prescription drug manufacturers is calculated to speed enforcement. If the Government prevails, a large part of the industry is bound by the decree; if the Government loses, it can more quickly revise its regulation....

In addition to all ... [of the procedural and equitable safeguards] against what the Government fears, it is important to note that the institution of this type of action does not by itself stay the effectiveness of the challenged regulation. There is nothing in the record to indicate that petitioners have sought to stay enforcement of the "every time" regulation pending judicial review. See 5 U.S.C. § 705. If the agency believes that a suit of this type will significantly impede enforcement or will harm the public interest, it need not postpone enforcement of the regulation and may oppose any motion for a judicial stay on the part of those challenging the regulation....

MR. JUSTICE BRENNAN took no part in the consideration or decision of this case.

[Justice Fortas, in an opinion joined by Chief Justice Warren and Justice Clark, dissented from the Court's opinion in this case and in the other case in the trilogy that found the challenge ripe: *Gardner v. Toilet Goods*, summarized next. These same three Justices concurred in the third case in the trilogy, which found the challenge in that case unripe: *Toilet Goods v. Gardner*. Justice Fortas's dissenting opinion is omitted.]

---

19. Section 502(e)(1)(B) declares a drug not complying with this labeling requirement to be "misbranded." Section 301, 21 U.S.C. § 331, designates as "prohibited acts" the misbranding of drugs in interstate commerce. Such prohibited acts are subject to injunction, § 302, 21 U.S.C. § 332, criminal penalties, § 303, 21 U.S.C. § 333, and seizure, § 304(a), 21 U.S.C. § 334(a).

• *Gardner v. Toilet Goods Association*, 387 U.S. 167 (1967)

Gardner, like the *Abbott Labs* case excerpted above, was a pre-enforcement challenge to FDA regulations that, the challengers argued, exceeded the FDA's statutory authority. The regulations challenged in *Gardner* regulated color additives in foods, drugs, and cosmetics. The Court held that the challenge was ripe, using the two-part test of *Abbott Labs*.

As to fitness, the color additive regulations were final. Moreover, the lawsuit posed a "straightforward legal" issue the resolution of which would not be facilitated if the issue was raised "in the context of a specific attempt to enforce the regulations." *Id.* at 171.

As to hardship, the color additive regulations were "self-executing, and ha[d] an immediate and substantial impact" on the challengers. *Id.* The Food and Drug Act prescribed penalties for violations of the color additive regulations and presented the challengers with a dilemma. They could either refuse to comply with the regulations and risk substantial penalties if the regulations were upheld, or they could pursue costly measures to comply with the regulations pending their legal challenge. This was the same hardship found sufficient in *Abbott Labs* to justify judicial review of a pre-enforcement challenge. *Id.* at 171–174.

• *Toilet Goods Association v. Gardner*, 387 U.S. 158 (1967)

Toilet Goods is the only case of the trio that held a pre-enforcement challenge to an agency rule unripe. Thus, *Toilet Goods* shows that a judicial challenge to an agency action that is *final* will not necessarily be *ripe*. Ripeness requires more than finality.

The FDA regulation in *Toilet Goods* required companies that made color additives to give FDA inspectors "free access" to the companies' facilities and certain records. *Id.* at 161 (quoting regulation). If a company refused access for an inspection, the FDA could "suspend certification service" to the company. *Id.* This was a serious sanction because, unless the FDA "certified" a color additive as suitable and safe, the additive was generally deemed "unsafe"—and cosmetics containing the additive were deemed "adulterated" and hence barred from interstate commerce. *Id.* at 161 n.1.

The manufacturers in *Toilet Goods* challenged the inspection regulation as exceeding the FDA's statutory authority. The Court applied the two-part test of *Abbott Labs* to conclude that the challenge to the inspection regulation was not ripe.

First, the legal issue was not fit for judicial review. This was true even though "this regulation—promulgated in a formal manner after notice and evaluation of submitted comments—is a 'final agency action' under § 10 [§ 704] of the [APA]." 387 U.S. at 162. It was also true that the challenge "presents a purely legal question: whether the regulation is totally beyond the agency's power under the statute." *Id.* at 163.

The purely legal question was nonetheless not fit for review. For one thing, the regulation gave the FDA discretion in determining when and how to apply the regulation. The regulation said only that the FDA *may* under certain circumstances order inspection of certain facilities and data. The FDA *may* refuse certification of additives to those who do not permit an inspection. For another thing, the FDA had statutory authority to promulgate regulations "for the efficient enforcement" of the Food and Drug Act. *Id.* at 163 (quoting statute). Whether the regulation was justified under that standard depended "not merely on an inquiry into statutory purpose, but concurrently on an understanding of what types of enforcement problems are encountered by the FDA, the need for various sorts of supervision in order to effectuate the goals of the Act, and the safeguards devised to protect legitimate trade secrets." *Id.* at 163–164. The Court believed that "judicial appraisal of these factors is likely to stand on a much surer footing in the context of a specific application of this regulation than could be the case in the framework of a generalized [pre-enforcement] challenge." *Id.* at 164. The Court, in short, wanted to see the rubber hit the road before judicial review occurred.

On the hardship factor, the inspection regulation did not cause immediate hardship, like the "every time" regulation did. The inspection regulation did not require any immediate change in the manufacturers' "day-to-day affairs." *Id.* at 165. The inspection regulation did not operate unless and until FDA asked a particular manufacturer to permit an inspection. The Court summarized: "This is not a situation in which primary conduct is affected." *Id.* at 164. Furthermore, refusal to submit to an inspection would lead only to suspension of certification service, a sanction that was subject to administrative and then judicial review. *Id.* at 166.

* * *

The *Abbott Labs* trilogy expanded the availability of pre-enforcement review of agency rules in federal courts through its articulation and application of a two-part test for ripeness, which is said to have a "fitness prong" and a "hardship prong."

Exercise: Revisiting the *Abbott Labs* Trilogy

1. A lower federal court understood the "fitness prong" to require consideration of at least three factors: "[1] whether the issue presented is a purely legal one, [2] whether consideration of that issue would benefit from a more concrete setting, and [3] whether the agency's action is sufficiently final." *Ciba-Geigy Corp. v. EPA*, 801 F.2d 430, 435 (D.C. Cir. 1986) (bracketed numerals added). Please look back at the *Abbott Labs* excerpt above to confirm the Court's consideration of those three factors. Do the first two factors reflect concern about avoiding interference with the agency's process, or about the court's ability adequately to review the agency action?

2. *Abbott Labs* says: "Where the legal issue presented is fit for judicial resolution, and where a regulation requires an immediate and significant change in the plaintiffs' conduct of their affairs with serious penalties attached to noncompliance, access to the courts under the Administrative Procedure Act and the Declaratory Judgment Act must be permitted, absent a statutory bar or some other unusual circumstance." 387 U.S. at 153. Notice how this statement suggests that the hardship prong of the ripeness test can usually be satisfied when the target of a rule shows that the rule requires the target to make immediate, significant changes to its day-to-day operations or else risk serious penalties. Explain how this generalization may make it easier for the targets of an agency rule to show ripeness than it will be for plaintiffs challenging an agency rule on the ground that it doesn't regulate its targets stringently enough.

(ii) A Recasting of *Abbott Labs*' Two-Part Test

We summarize the next case for two reasons. First, the Court recasts the *Abbott Labs* test from a two-part test into a three-part inquiry. Second, the Court addressed the ripeness of a challenge to agency regulatory action brought by a plaintiff who, unlike the plaintiffs in the *Abbott Labs* trilogy, was not the target of the regulatory action.

- *Ohio Forestry Association, Inc. v. Sierra Club*, 523 U.S. 726 (1998)

The Sierra Club challenged a land and resource management plan (Plan) that the U.S. Forest Service adopted for the Wayne National Forest in Ohio. The Forest Service adopted the Plan as required by the National Forest Management Act of 1976 (NFMA). The Sierra Club argued that the Plan allowed too much logging and too much use of a specific logging method, clearcutting. These flaws, the Sierra Club contended, caused the Plan to violate the NMFA and to be **"arbitrary, capricious, an abuse of discretion, and not in accordance with law,"** under §706(2)(A) of the federal APA. The Court unanimously held that the Sierra Club's suit was not ripe.

The Court described the framework for ripeness analysis as follows:

> In deciding whether an agency's decision is, or is not, ripe for judicial review, the Court has examined both the "fitness of the issues for judicial decision" and the "hardship to the parties of withholding court consideration." [Quoting *Abbott Labs*, 387 U.S. at 149.] To do so in this case, we must consider: (1) whether delayed review would cause hardship to the plaintiffs; (2) whether judicial intervention would inappropriately interfere with further administrative action; and (3) whether the courts would benefit from further factual development of the issues presented. These considerations, taken together, foreclose review in the present case.

Ohio Forestry, 523 U.S. at 733. The Court's three-part formulation specifies that, in analyzing ripeness, courts should consider whether immediate judicial review will impede the agency's ability to carry out its statutory mission. The Court in *Abbott Labs* had considered that factor. *See Abbott Labs*, 387 U.S. at 154–155. But the need to consider it was reflected only indirectly and perhaps incompletely in the two-part test's attention to whether the agency has finished its decision-making process. In short, *Ohio Forestry*'s reformulation of the two-part test as a three-part test may be best understood as a clarification.

Assessing hardship to the Sierra Club, the Court in *Ohio Forestry* concluded that delayed review would not cause "effects of a sort that traditionally would have qualified as harm." 523 U.S. at 733. The Court explained:

> [The provisions of the challenged Plan] do not command anyone to do anything or to refrain from doing anything; they do not grant, withhold, or modify any formal legal license, power, or authority; they do not subject anyone to any civil or criminal liability; they create no legal rights or obligations. Thus, for example, the Plan does not give anyone a legal right to cut trees, nor does it abolish anyone's legal authority to object to trees being cut.

Id. at 733. Nor did the Plan "inflict significant practical harms" on the Sierra Club. *Id.* The Sierra Club could seek judicial review when the Forest Service sought to implement the Plan by proposing to permit logging on particular sites. In the meantime, the Plan did not "force [the Sierra Club] to modify its behavior to avoid future adverse consequences, as, for example, agency regulations can sometimes force immediate compliance through fear of future sanctions." *Id.* at 733–734. Thus, the Sierra Club had trouble showing hardship partly because it was not the target of the regulatory action it challenged.

Addressing hardship to the Forest Service, the Court said that "immediate judicial review ... could hinder agency efforts to refine its policies" in the course of applying the Plan to specific sites in the forest. *Id.* at 735. The Court emphasized that the possibility of these refinements was "not theoretical, but real" given the Forest Service's past practice in implementing plans. *Id.* The Court concluded, "Hearing the Sierra Club's challenge now could thus interfere with the system that Congress specified for the agency to reach forest logging decisions." *Id.* at 736.

The final consideration—whether the court would benefit from further factual development—also weighed against judicial review of the Plan before its implementation. The Court explained:

> ... [R]eview of the Sierra Club's claims regarding logging and clearcutting now would require time-consuming judicial consideration of the details of an elaborate, technically based plan, which predicts consequences that may affect many different parcels of land in a variety of ways, and which effects themselves may change over time. That review would have to take place without benefit of the focus that a particular logging proposal could provide. Thus, for example, the court below in evaluating the Sierra Club's claims had to focus upon whether the Plan as a whole was "improperly skewed," rather than focus upon whether the decision to allow clearcutting on a particular site was improper, say, because the site was better suited to another use or logging there would cumulatively result in too many trees being cut....
>
> This type of review threatens the kind of "abstract disagreements over administrative policies," *Abbott Laboratories*, 387 U.S., at 148, that the ripeness doctrine seeks to avoid. In this case, for example, the Court of Appeals panel disagreed about whether or not the Forest Service suffered from a kind of general "bias" in favor of timber production and clearcutting. Review where the consequences had been "reduced to more manageable proportions," and where the "factual components [were] fleshed out, by some concrete action" might have led the panel majority either to demonstrate that bias and its consequences through record citation (which it did not do) or to abandon the claim. All this is to say that further factual development would significantly advance our ability to deal with the legal issues presented and would aid us in their resolution.

Id. at 736–737 (some internal quotation marks omitted). Thus, the Court didn't feel comfortable assessing the challenge at the broad programmatic level that Sierra Club sought, preferring instead to await more "bite-sized" challenges to the implementation of the Plan with respect to specific sites proposed for logging.

Several times the Court in *Ohio Forestry* cited its prior decision in *Lujan v. National Wildlife Federation*, 497 U.S. 871 (1990). *Lujan v. National Wildlife Federation*, like *Ohio Forestry*, involved a broad programmatic challenge to agency action. The National Wildlife Federation (NWF) challenged an agency's "land withdrawal review program." In a portion of the opinion discussed in Chapter 29, the Court held in *Lujan v. National Wildlife Federation* that this program was not "**agency action**" for purposes of APA § 704 and therefore was not subject to judicial review under the APA. The Court in *Lujan v. National Wildlife Federation* also addressed the ripeness of such a programmatic challenge:

> [NWF] alleges that violation of the law is rampant within this program ... Perhaps so. But [NWF] cannot seek wholesale improvement of this program by court decree, rather than in the offices of the Department or the halls of Congress, where programmatic improvements are normally made. Under the terms of the APA, respondent must direct its attack against some particular "agency action" that causes it harm. Some statutes permit broad regulations to serve as the "agency action," and thus to be the object of judicial review directly, even before the concrete effects normally required for APA review are felt. Absent such a provision, however, a regulation is not ordinarily considered the type of agency action "ripe"

for judicial review under the APA until the scope of the controversy has been reduced to more manageable proportions, and its factual components fleshed out, by some concrete action applying the regulation to the claimant's situation in a fashion that harms or threatens to harm him. (The major exception, of course, is a substantive rule which as a practical matter requires the plaintiff to adjust his conduct immediately. Such agency action is "ripe" for review at once, whether or not explicit statutory review apart from the APA is provided. See *Abbott Laboratories v. Gardner*, 387 U.S. 136, 152–154 (1967); *Gardner v. Toilet Goods Assn., Inc.*, 387 U.S. 167, 171–173 (1967). Cf. *Toilet Goods Assn., Inc. v. Gardner*, 387 U.S. 158, 164–166 (1967).)

Id. at 891–892. Thus, the Court seemed to lay down a rule generally barring pre-enforcement challenges to agency rules and other programmatic agency actions under the APA. Such pre-enforcement challenges are possible under the APA, the Court suggests, only when authorized by a special review statute or brought by someone whose conduct is immediately affected by the agency action — *i.e.*, a regulatory target.

Having examined cases applying traditional ripeness analysis, below we focus on the way special review statutes may modify traditional ripeness analysis.

Exercise: *Ohio Forestry Association v. Sierra Club*

Suppose the Plan had included a provision allowing motorcycles and all-terrain vehicles to use a specific area of the Wayne National Forest that had previously been off limits to motorized vehicles and reserved for bird watching. Would the Sierra Club have a ripe challenge to the Plan, or that particular provision in the Plan, if one of its members regularly used the affected area for bird watching and wished to continue doing so? How do you analyze ripeness in this situation?

---

b. Special Review Statutes Authorizing Pre-Enforcement Review of Agency Rules

The Court in *Ohio Forestry Association* remarked that Congress has enacted laws authorizing pre-enforcement review of some agency rules. 523 U.S. at 737. One such law is in the Clean Air Act. Specifically, 42 U.S.C. §7607(b) (2012) authorizes pre-enforcement judicial review of certain EPA rules.

The Court suggested in a case arising under 42 U.S.C. §7607(b) that §7607(b) and similar special review provisions modify the ripeness analysis of pre-enforcement challenges but do not make all pre-enforcement challenges brought under them ripe. The case was *Whitman v. American Trucking Associations, Inc.*, 531 U.S. 457, 479–480 (2001). In *Whitman*, the Court held that a pre-enforcement challenge under 42 U.S.C. §7607(b) to an EPA implementation plan was ripe. And the Court said that statutes such as §7607 "permit judicial review ... even before the concrete effects normally required for APA review are felt." 531 U.S. at 479–480. Thus, the *Whitman* Court treated the review statute's authorization of pre-enforcement challenges as relaxing the hardship prong, but not affecting the fitness prong. Furthermore, the Court in *Whitman* still analyzed ripeness using the *Abbott Labs* framework. 531 U.S. at 479–480. *Whitman* thus suggests that a special review statute authorizing pre-enforcement challenges spares a challenger from having to show that the challenged agency action will have an immediate impact on the challenger's day to day affairs, but doesn't otherwise modify *Abbott Labs*.

c. Informal Agency Action

The *Abbott Lab* trilogy involved an agency's legislative rules. As you know, agencies act in less formal ways than issuing legislative rules after notice-and-comment proceedings. Judicial review of informal agency action can pose particularly tricky ripeness issues. That is why we examine the situation separately. Even so, federal courts still use the two-pronged *Abbott Labs* analysis for informal agency actions. The next case illustrates the analysis.

- *Ciba-Geigy Corp. v. U.S. Environmental Protection Agency*, 801 F.2d 430 (D.C. Cir. 1986)

Ciba-Geigy got a letter from EPA's Director of Pesticide Programs. The letter said that unless Ciba-Geigy changed the label on one of its pesticide products immediately, the EPA would consider the product misbranded under the Federal Insecticide, Fungicide, and Rodenticide Act (FIFRA). A misbranded product subjects its manufacturer to enforcement actions for civil and criminal penalties. The EPA letter rejected Ciba-Geigy's view, expressed in earlier correspondence, that FIFRA required the EPA to go through a formal adjudication before the EPA could require Ciba-Geigy to change its product label. The EPA thought that no such preliminary procedural step was necessary before the EPA ordered and enforced a label change.

Ciba-Geigy sued the EPA in federal district court challenging the interpretation of FIFRA reflected in the EPA's letter. On appeal, the D.C. Circuit applied the two-pronged *Abbott Labs* approach, assessing fitness and hardship, and held that Ciba-Geigy's challenge to the EPA letter was ripe.

The court concluded that the lawsuit presented an issue that was fit for review. The court said the fitness inquiry requires consideration of at least three factors: "whether the issue presented is a purely legal one, whether consideration of that issue would benefit from a more concrete setting, and whether the agency's action is sufficiently final." *Id.* at 435. Only the third, finality factor was in dispute here. The court said that in gauging finality federal courts "look primarily to whether the agency's position is 'definitive' and whether it has a '"direct and immediate ... effect on the day-to-day business"' of the parties challenging the action." *Id.* at 436 (quoting *Federal Trade Comm'n v. SOCAL*, 449 U.S. 232, 239 (1980) (quoting *Abbott Labs*, 387 U.S. at 151–152)).

To determine the letter's definitiveness, the court examined the content of EPA's letter to Ciba-Geigy, other related EPA actions, and the authority of the EPA official who wrote the letter. The court found the letter definitive on the issue of statutory interpretation that Ciba-Geigy's lawsuit presented. Because the agency had spoken its "final word" on the subject and was "at rest," judicial review would not "disrupt the orderly process of administrative decisionmaking." *Id.* at 437.

The court further found that the letter had immediate practical and legal effect. As a practical matter, the letter confronted Ciba-Geigy with the choice of changing its label or facing civil and criminal penalties. As a legal matter, the interpretation of FIFRA in the EPA letter could "comman[d] deference" by a court reviewing the merits of that interpretation. *Id.* at 437.

Having found the lawsuit presented an issue fit for review, the court assessed hardship. The court believed that "the hardship here is indistinguishable from that deemed compelling by the Supreme Court" in *Abbott Labs*. *Ciba-Geigy*, 801 F.2d at 438. The challenged agency action in both cases confronted the challenger with a choice between "costly compliance" and the risk of serious civil and criminal penalties. *Id.* at 438–439.

* * *

Ciba-Geigy not only illustrates ripeness analysis of informal agency action but also highlights two points at which ripeness analysis and finality analysis overlap. First, finality analysis considers the "definitiveness" of agency action partly to ensure that judicial review will not "disrupt" the administrative process. 801 F.2d at 437. Similarly, ripeness analysis considers "whether judicial intervention would inappropriately interfere with further administrative action." *Ohio Forestry Ass'n, Inc. v. Sierra Club*, 523 U.S. 726, 733 (1998). Second, finality analysis considers whether the challenged agency action has a "direct and immediate ... effect on the day-to-day business" of the party challenging the agency action. *Ciba-Geigy*, 801 F.2d at 436. Likewise, the hardship prong of ripeness analysis considers whether agency action has a "sufficiently direct and immediate" impact on the challenger to justify immediate judicial review, such as through an "effect on the day-to-day business" of the challenger. *Abbott Labs*, 387 U.S. at 136. These areas of overlap simply reflect that finality is an element of ripeness and that both doctrines reflect a "pragmatic" and "flexible" balancing of the factors favoring immediate judicial review against the factors favoring postponement of judicial review. *See Ciba-Geigy*, 802 F.2d at 434, 435. We mention the overlap so that you are not surprised when your ripeness analysis of an agency action partly duplicates your finality analysis.

Exercise: Determining the Ripeness of Informal Agency Action

The Consumer Product Safety Commission investigated a company, Reliable Sprinklers, that made automatic sprinkler heads for inclusion in the automatic fire sprinkler systems installed in commercial buildings. The Commission's Office of Compliance sent a letter to Reliable. The letter stated that it was "the intention of the Compliance staff to make the preliminary determination that these sprinklers present a substantial product hazard, as defined by 15 U.S.C. § 2064(a)." That statement was significant because, if the Office made the preliminary determination, that could lead to a formal adjudication before the Commission to decide whether, indeed, the sprinkler heads posed a substantial product hazard. And if the Commission concluded that such a hazard did exist, it could order Reliable to take corrective actions such as recalling the product and giving refunds to purchasers.

The letter from the Office of Compliance told Reliable that, before the Office actually made a preliminary determination of a substantial product hazard, Reliable was invited to take "voluntary corrective action" under the Commission's regulations. Under those regulations, a company can avoid a formal adjudication by agreeing to voluntary corrective action, as reflected in a "corrective action plan." 16 C.F.R. § 1115.20(a) (2012). The Commission's regulations say that a corrective action plan "has no legally binding effect." *Id.* If a company doesn't agree to take voluntary corrective action, the Commission may then issue a formal complaint commencing a formal adjudication to make a final determination whether a consumer product presents a substantial product hazard. Such a final determination by the Commission is subject to judicial review under the APA.

Reliable wants to sue the Commission on the ground that its sprinklers are not "consumer products" as defined in the Commission's legislation and therefore are not within the Commission's authority. Please analyze whether such a suit, which would focus on the letter from the Office of Compliance, is ripe for review. *See Reliable Automatic Sprinkler Co., Inc. v. Consumer Product Safety Comm'n*, 324 F.3d 726 (D.C. Cir. 2003).

3. Ripeness in State Law

The ripeness doctrine developed by the U.S. Supreme Court and lower federal courts for review of federal agency action does not bind the States and thus does not govern state court review of state agency action. That is because the federal law of ripeness is derived from Article III, which governs the power of the *federal* courts, and from prudential concerns about the proper role of the federal courts. Even so, many States have developed ripeness rules to identify when lawsuits in their courts are premature. Like the federal law on ripeness, state law on ripeness is typically devised by the courts and is thus found primarily in case law.

Although the state law of ripeness will be found mostly in case law, one statute found in many States addresses the most common situation in which ripeness issues arise in federal courts: namely, pre-enforcement challenges to agency rules. The state statutes are based on the 1961 Model APA:

§ 7. [Declaratory Judgment on Validity or Applicability of Rules].

The validity or applicability of a rule may be determined in an action for declaratory judgment in the [District Court of ... County], if it is alleged that the rule, or its threatened application, interferes with or impairs, or threatens to interfere with or impair, the legal rights or privileges of the plaintiff. The agency shall be made a party to the action. A declaratory judgment may be rendered whether or not the plaintiff has requested the agency to pass upon the validity or applicability of the rule in question.[2]

This provision authorizes some pre-enforcement challenges to agency rules. Even so, a State's ripeness law could limit the kinds of claims that could be asserted in declaratory judgment actions under this provision. Reflecting the types of limits that ripeness principles developed in state-court case law might impose, an Oregon statute authorizes courts in a pre-enforcement declaratory judgment proceeding to determine only whether an agency rule violates constitutional provisions, exceeds the agency's statutory authority, or was adopted without compliance with applicable rulemaking procedures. Or. Rev. Stat. § 183.400(4) (West, Westlaw through emergency legislation through Ch. 39 of 2012 Reg.

---

2. For state statutes based on this model code provision, see, *e.g.*, Ark. Code Ann. § 25-15-207(a) (West, Westlaw through end of 2011 Reg. Sess.); Idaho Code Ann. § 67-5278(1) (2006); Kan. Stat. Ann. § 16a-6-408 (West, Westlaw through end of 2011 Reg. Sess.); Vernon's Tex. Stat. & Code Ann. Gov't Code § 2001.038(a) (West, Westlaw through end of 2011 Reg. Sess. & First Called Sess. of 82d Legislature).

Sess.). These limits, expressed on the face of the Oregon statute, might be imposed in other States through application of ripeness principles reflected in state court case law.

The upshot is that States have their own ripeness law, and a State's ripeness law may differ from federal ripeness law.

4. Ripeness Is Necessary but Not Sufficient for Judicial Review

If a court determines that a legal challenge to agency action is ripe, the court must also have determined that the agency action is final. But finality and ripeness alone are not enough. Ordinarily, the person challenging agency action must have exhausted available administrative remedies before seeking judicial review. The next section explores the exhaustion requirement.

C. Exhaustion

It may help for you to understand up front how exhaustion differs from finality and ripeness. To illustrate the difference, we will use formal adjudication as an example. In a typical formal adjudication under the federal APA, an ALJ can hold a hearing and issue an initial decision. 5 U.S.C. §557(a) (2012). The ALJ's initial decision becomes the final decision of the agency if not reviewed by the head of the agency or the entity or official to whom the agency head has delegated reviewing authority. *Id.* §557(b). Suppose the party who does not like the ALJ's initial decision goes immediately to court to challenge it, instead of seeking review of the ALJ's decision within the agency. This party has a final decision of the agency, and may be able to show that a judicial challenge is ripe, especially if the ALJ's decision, once final, has an immediate adverse effect on the challenger's day-to-day activities and the challenge involves a purely legal issue. But the party has not exhausted administrative remedies, because the party has not sought review within the agency, and that failure will ordinarily bar judicial review, under the traditional exhaustion doctrine, even if the agency action is final and ripe.

In this section we explore (1) the traditional exhaustion doctrine, including exceptions to the exhaustion requirement under the traditional doctrine; (2) statutory modification of the traditional doctrine; (3) the effect of a failure to exhaust; and (4) a subdoctrine known as issue preclusion. Far from exhausting, we hope our exploration is exhilarating.

1. The Traditional Doctrine

a. Sources and Rationales of, and Exceptions to, the Exhaustion Requirement

In *McCarthy v. Madigan*, 503 U.S. 140 (1992), the U.S. Supreme Court discussed:
- the traditional exhaustion doctrine, including its rationale and exceptions
- legislative power to alter the traditional doctrine

Because of the opinion's comprehensive treatment of exhaustion, we reproduce it below. As you read it, please consider these questions:

1. The Court describes the exhaustion doctrine in Part II of its opinion, which consists of II.A, II.B. and II.C. If you were to give a short, descriptive heading to each subpart, what would it be?

2. What is the relationship between subparts II.B and II.C?

3. The Court applies the exhaustion doctrine in Part III of its opinion. How would you summarize its reasons for holding that John McCarthy did not have to exhaust administrative remedies?

McCarthy v. Madigan

503 U.S. 140 (1992)

[Editor's summary: John McCarthy, while in federal prison, filed a federal-court lawsuit against four prison employees. Mr. McCarthy claimed that the defendants subjected him to cruel and unusual punishment, in violation of the Eighth Amendment, because they were deliberately indifferent to his medical needs. In his lawsuit, Mr. McCarthy sought only money damages. The federal district court dismissed the lawsuit because Mr. McCarthy did not exhaust the grievance procedures the federal Bureau of Prisons established for prisoners with complaints like his. The court of appeals affirmed the dismissal. In the following excerpt, the Court discussed the exhaustion requirement and held that Mr. McCarthy did not have to exhaust administrative remedies.]

Justice BLACKMUN delivered the opinion of the Court.

... Under 28 CFR pt. 542 (1991), setting forth the general "Administrative Remedy Procedure for Inmates" at federal correctional institutions, a prisoner may "seek formal review of a complaint which relates to any aspect of his imprisonment." § 542.10. When an inmate files a complaint or appeal, the responsible officials are directed to acknowledge the filing with a "signed receipt" which is returned to the inmate, to "[c]onduct an investigation," and to "[r]espond to and sign all complaints or appeals." §§ 542.11(a)(2) to (4). The general grievance regulations do not provide for any kind of hearing or for the granting of any particular type of relief.

To promote efficient dispute resolution, the procedure includes rapid filing and response timetables. An inmate first seeks informal resolution of his claim by consulting prison personnel. § 542.13(a). If this informal effort fails, the prisoner "may file a formal written complaint on the appropriate form, within fifteen (15) calendar days of the date on which the basis of the complaint occurred." § 542.13(b). Should the warden fail to respond to the inmate's satisfaction within 15 days, the inmate has 20 days to appeal to the Bureau's Regional Director, who has 30 days to respond. If the inmate still remains unsatisfied, he has 30 days to make a final appeal to the Bureau's general counsel, who has another 30 days to respond. §§ 542.14 and 542.15. If the inmate can demonstrate a "valid reason for delay," he "shall be allowed" an extension of any of these time periods for filing. § 542.13(b)....

II

... Of paramount importance to any exhaustion inquiry is congressional intent. Where Congress specifically mandates, exhaustion is required. But where Congress has not clearly required exhaustion, sound judicial discretion governs....

A

This Court long has acknowledged the general rule that parties exhaust prescribed administrative remedies before seeking relief from the federal courts. See, *e.g.*, *Myers v. Bethlehem Shipbuilding Corp.*, 303 U.S. 41, 50–51, and n. 9 (1938) (discussing cases as far back as 1898). Exhaustion is required because it serves the twin purposes of protecting administrative agency authority and promoting judicial efficiency.

As to the first of these purposes, the exhaustion doctrine recognizes the notion, grounded in deference to Congress' delegation of authority to coordinate branches of Government, that agencies, not the courts, ought to have primary responsibility for the programs that Congress has charged them to administer. Exhaustion concerns apply with particular force when the action under review involves exercise of the agency's discretionary power or when the agency proceedings in question allow the agency to apply its special expertise. The exhaustion doctrine also acknowledges the commonsense notion of dispute resolution that an agency ought to have an opportunity to correct its own mistakes with respect to the programs it administers before it is haled into federal court....

As to the second of the purposes, exhaustion promotes judicial efficiency in at least two ways. When an agency has the opportunity to correct its own errors, a judicial controversy may well be mooted, or at least piecemeal appeals may be avoided. And even where a controversy survives administrative review, exhaustion of the administrative procedure may produce a useful record for subsequent judicial consideration, especially in a complex or technical factual context.

B

... [T]his Court has declined to require exhaustion in some circumstances even where administrative and judicial interests would counsel otherwise. In determining whether exhaustion is required, federal courts must balance the interest of the individual in retaining prompt access to a federal judicial forum against countervailing institutional interests favoring exhaustion. [Administrative] remedies need not be pursued if the litigant's interests in immediate judicial review outweigh the government's interests in the efficiency or administrative autonomy that the exhaustion doctrine is designed to further. Application of this balancing principle is intensely practical, because attention is directed to both the nature of the claim presented and the characteristics of the particular administrative procedure provided.

C

[T]his Court's precedents have recognized at least three broad sets of circumstances in which the interests of the individual weigh heavily against requiring administrative exhaustion. First, requiring resort to the administrative remedy may occasion undue prejudice to subsequent assertion of a court action. Such prejudice may result, for example, from an unreasonable or indefinite timeframe for administrative action....

Second, an administrative remedy may be inadequate because of some doubt as to whether the agency was empowered to grant effective relief. For example, an agency, as a preliminary matter, may be unable to consider whether to grant relief because it lacks institutional competence to resolve the particular type of issue presented, such as the constitutionality of a statute. In a similar vein, exhaustion has not been required where the challenge is to the adequacy of the agency procedure itself, such that the question of the adequacy of the administrative remedy ... [is] for all practical purposes identical with the merits of [the plaintiff's] lawsuit. Alternatively, an agency may be competent to adjudicate the issue presented, but still lack authority to grant the type of relief requested.

Third, an administrative remedy may be inadequate where the administrative body is shown to be biased or has otherwise predetermined the issue before it.

III

In light of these general principles, we conclude that petitioner McCarthy need not have exhausted his constitutional claim for money damages. As a preliminary matter, we find that Congress has not meaningfully addressed the appropriateness of requiring exhaustion in this context. Although respondents' interests are significant, we are left with a firm conviction that, given the type of claim McCarthy raises and the particular characteristics of the Bureau's general grievance procedure, McCarthy's individual interests outweigh countervailing institutional interests favoring exhaustion.

A

Turning first to congressional intent, we note that the general grievance procedure was neither enacted nor mandated by Congress....

B

Because Congress has not required exhaustion of a federal prisoner's ... claim, we turn to an evaluation of the individual and institutional interests at stake in this case. The general grievance procedure heavily burdens the individual interests of the petitioning inmate in two ways. First, the procedure imposes short, successive filing deadlines that create a high risk of forfeiture of a claim for failure to comply. Second, the administrative "remedy" does not authorize an award of monetary damages—the only relief requested by McCarthy in this action. [Editor's note: The Court apparently inferred that money damages were not available through the administrative grievance procedure, an inference that seems well founded.] The combination of these features means that the prisoner seeking only money damages has everything to lose and nothing to gain from being required to exhaust his claim under the internal grievance procedure....

We do not find the interests of the Bureau of Prisons to weigh heavily in favor of exhaustion in view of the remedial scheme and particular claim presented here. To be sure, the Bureau has a substantial interest in encouraging internal resolution of grievances and in preventing the undermining of its authority by unnecessary resort by prisoners to the federal courts. But other institutional concerns relevant to exhaustion analysis appear to weigh in hardly at all. The Bureau's alleged failure to render medical care implicates only tangentially its authority to carry out the control and management of the federal prisons. Furthermore, the Bureau does not bring to bear any special expertise on the type of issue presented for resolution here.

The interests of judicial economy do not stand to be advanced substantially by the general grievance procedure. No formal factfindings are made. The paperwork generated by the grievance process might assist a court somewhat in ascertaining the facts underlying a prisoner's claim more quickly than if it has only a prisoner's complaint to review. But the grievance procedure does not create a formal factual record of the type that can be relied on conclusively by a court for disposition of a prisoner's claim on the pleadings or at summary judgment without the aid of affidavits.

C

... Congress, of course, is free to design or require an appropriate administrative procedure for a prisoner to exhaust his claim for money damages. Even without further action by Congress, we do not foreclose the possibility that the Bureau itself may adopt an appropriate administrative procedure consistent with congressional intent....

Chief Justice REHNQUIST, with whom Justice SCALIA and Justice THOMAS join, concurring in the judgment....

Exercise: *McCarthy* Revisited

1. Congress legislatively "overruled" *McCarthy* in the Prison Litigation Reform Act of 1995, which requires a prisoner to exhaust administrative remedies even if those remedies do not include the money damages that a prisoner wishes to seek. *See Booth v. Churner*, 532 U.S. 731, 740–741 (2001). Explain how the PLRA's requirement can be reconciled with the Court's statement in *McCarthy* that exhaustion is not required if it will not yield "effective" relief. 503 U.S. at 147.

2. The Court in *McCarthy* said that under the traditional doctrine, exhaustion is not required "where the administrative body is shown to be biased or has otherwise predetermined the issue before it." *Id.* at 148. As discussed in Chapter 20, an unbiased decision maker is required as a matter of due process in an adjudication involving the deprivation or risk of deprivation of life, liberty, or property. In decisions interpreting *McCarthy*, however, courts have said that it takes a strong showing of bias or closemindedness to excuse exhaustion. "A pessimistic prediction or a hunch that further administrative proceedings will prove unproductive is not enough to sidetrack the exhaustion rule." *Portela-Gonzalez v. Sec'y of the Navy*, 109 F.3d 74, 78 (1st Cir. 1997). What sort of evidence do you think you realistically might find to show that an administrative entity is biased or has predetermined a matter against your client, in a case like that of Mr. McCarthy?

3. Courts sometimes say that exhaustion is not required if it would be "futile." *See, e.g., Shalala v. Illinois Council on Long Term Care, Inc.*, 529 U.S. 1, 13 (2000). Review the exceptions discussed in *McCarthy* and explain how they are consistent with the "futility" exception.

---

b. The Traditional Requirement of "Proper" Exhaustion

To satisfy the exhaustion requirement, a person must exhaust administrative remedies *properly*. The Court discussed the proper exhaustion requirement in *Woodford v. Ngo*, 548 U.S. 81 (2006). Viet Ngo, a state prisoner, filed a grievance complaining about the way he was disciplined for "inappropriate activity" in the prison chapel. *Id.* at 86. The prison officials denied Mr. Ngo's grievance because he did not file it within the fifteen-day period prescribed by prison regulations. The Court upheld the dismissal of Mr. Ngo's lawsuit because of his failure to exhaust administrative remedies, as required by the Prison Litigation Reform Act. The Court held that the Act incorporated the traditional exhaustion doctrine's requirement that the person seeking judicial review *properly* exhaust administrative remedies. The Court said, "Proper exhaustion demands compliance with an agency's deadlines and other critical procedural rules because no adjudicative system can function effectively without imposing some orderly structure on the course of its proceedings." *Id.*

at 90. Thus, the court linked the requirement of "proper" exhaustion to the integrity of the administrative procedures that the exhaustion requirement is designed to protect.

2. Statutory Alteration of Traditional Exhaustion Doctrine

The Court in *McCarthy* said, "Of paramount importance to any exhaustion requirement is congressional intent." 503 U.S. at 144. This means that Congress can by statute codify, modify, or eliminate the traditional exhaustion requirement. (If Congress does not address exhaustion, "sound judicial discretion governs." *Id.*) In this section we separately discuss (a) the general subject of statutory alteration of the exhaustion requirement and (b) the specific alteration to the exhaustion doctrine made by the federal APA.

a. Statutory Alteration in General

Congress can alter the traditional exhaustion requirement. When a statute addresses exhaustion, questions can arise about the extent to which the statute codifies, modifies, or eliminates the traditional requirement. Thus, when analyzing the availability of judicial review, the lawyer must be alert to possible statutory alterations of the exhaustion doctrine.

An example of statute expressly requiring exhaustion concerns civil actions challenging actions of the U.S. Department of Agriculture:

---

7 U.S.C. § 6912. Authority of Secretary to delegate transferred functions ...

(e) Exhaustion of administrative appeals

Notwithstanding any other provision of law, a person shall exhaust all administrative appeal procedures established by the Secretary or required by law before the person may bring an action in a court of competent jurisdiction against —

(1) the Secretary;

(2) the Department; or

(3) an agency, office, officer, or employee of the Department.

This expressly requires exhaustion but has raised interpretive questions. One question is whether it codifies any of the traditional exceptions. *See Forest Guardians v. U.S. Forest Serv.*, 641 F.3d 423, 431–432 (10th Cir. 2011). You can probably appreciate the competing arguments on that question: On the one hand, the statute speaks in absolute terms: "shall exhaust." On the other hand, maybe we should presume Congress enacted the exhaustion requirement with knowledge of, and tacit approval of, traditional exceptions to the requirement.

Now we show a statute expressly dispensing with the exhaustion requirement. The statute authorizes the Federal Crop Insurance Corporation to insure crops. The statute requires the Corporation, however, to exclude coverage of losses due to a farmer's failure to follow good farming practices. The statute has an exhaustion provision related to determinations of whether a farmer used good farming practices, and authorizes judicial review of decisions by the Corporation to deny claims made by farmers under crop insurance policies.

---

7 U.S.C. § 1508. Crop insurance

(a) Authority to offer insurance

(1) In general

... [T]he Corporation may insure, or provide reinsurance for insurers of, producers of agricultural commodities grown in the United States ...

(3) Exclusion of losses due to certain actions of producer

(A) Exclusions

Insurance provided under this subsection shall not cover losses due to— ...

(iii) the failure of the producer to follow good farming practices ...

(B) Good farming practices

(i) Informal administrative process

A producer shall have the right to a review of a determination regarding good farming practices made under subparagraph (A)(iii) in accordance with an informal administrative process to be established by the Corporation....

(iii) Judicial review

(I) Right to review

A producer shall have the right to judicial review of the determination [that a farmer has failed to use good farming practices] without exhausting any right to a review under clause (i)....

The important point is that, although courts and commentators refer to "the" exhaustion doctrine, it is not a unitary doctrine. There *is* a traditional version in federal law, as discussed and applied in *McCarthy*, but as a judicial creation it is subject to legislative codification, modification, and elimination. The most important federal statute modifying the doctrine is the federal APA, as discussed next.

b. Federal APA Modification of Traditional Exhaustion Doctrine

To distinguish exhaustion from ripeness and finality, we described at the beginning of this section a formal adjudication in which the party dissatisfied by an ALJ's initial decision goes right to court to challenge that decision instead of seeking review within the agency. That happens to be the main situation in which the U.S. Supreme Court has held that the federal APA modifies the traditional exhaustion doctrine.

Traditional exhaustion doctrine requires the dissatisfied party in this situation to seek review within the agency, even if that review is nominally "optional" and even if, pending administrative review, the ALJ's initial decision takes immediate effect—e.g., by ordering the party to cease and desist from some activity on pain of incurring serious penalties. Under traditional doctrine, if there are administrative remedies to exhaust, they must be exhausted.

The U.S. Supreme Court, however, has interpreted the federal APA to modify the exhaustion requirement in that situation. As modified, a person dissatisfied with the ALJ's initial decision must seek administrative review of that decision only if either (1) a statute expressly requires exhaustion of administrative remedies; or (2) agency rules expressly require exhaustion and, pending exhaustion, the ALJ's initial decision is inoperative. The Court adopted that interpretation in *Darby v. Cisneros*, 509 U.S. 137 (1993). The *Darby* Court traced the APA's modification of the traditional exhaustion doctrine to the last sentence of federal APA § 704:

---

5 U.S.C. § 704. Actions reviewable

… Except as otherwise expressly required by statute, agency action otherwise final is final for the purposes of this section whether or not there has been presented or determined an application for a declaratory order, for any form of reconsideration, or, unless the agency otherwise requires by rule and provides that the action meanwhile is inoperative, for an appeal to superior agency authority.

The *Darby* Court explained that § 704 modifies the exhaustion doctrine to ensure that people must exhaust administrative remedies only when the law makes it clear that they must. 509 U.S. at 146–147.

Section § 704 allows agencies to adopt rules requiring appeals within the agency if, pending the administrative appeal, the agency action appealed from is "**inoperative.**" The idea is to spare the appellant from immediate compliance with an initial agency action that may later be invalidated by the agency. After *Darby,* many federal agencies issued rules expressly (1) requiring people dissatisfied with an ALJ decision or some other initial agency action to appeal the action administratively and (2) making the initial action inoperative — e.g., through an automatic "stay" of the initial action — pending administrative review. Although these rules limit the importance of *Darby,* the decision is still important for federal administrative lawyers to know about because so many lawsuits challenging agency action rest on the APA-created cause of action and because the text of § 704's last sentence does not mention exhaustion (which is why *Darby* surprised many experienced administrative lawyers and scholars!).

c. State Law on Exhaustion

Many States require people to exhaust administrative remedies before seeking judicial review of agency action, subject to exceptions for situations in which exhaustion would be futile or would cause irreparable injury. In some States, the state APA expressly includes the exhaustion requirement. *See, e.g.,* Ala. Code 1975 § 41-22-20(a) (West, Westlaw through Act 2012-78 of 2012 Reg. Sess.).

3. Effect of Failure to Exhaust Administrative Remedies

The exhaustion doctrine is often more than just a timing doctrine. Specifically, the *failure* to exhaust administrative remedies can bar judicial review altogether. This can happen when a statute or agency rule puts a deadline on seeking an administrative remedy.

If a person foregoes that remedy and instead seeks judicial review immediately, and the court ultimately holds that exhaustion is required, by the time the court makes that decision, the deadline for pursuing the administrative remedy may have expired. If so, the person will never be able to satisfy the exhaustion requirement and will therefore never be able to get judicial review. Nor can the person argue for an exception on the ground that the administrative remedy is no longer available and that therefore trying to pursue it would be "futile." In short, failure to exhaust can be fatal to judicial review.

Exhaustion is nonetheless called a "timing" doctrine in administrative law circles. That is because satisfying the exhaustion requirement takes time; it delays judicial review. The Court has repeatedly said that the prospective costs and delay of pursuing administrative remedies, even if substantial, do not excuse you from exhausting them. *See, e.g., SOCAL*, 449 U.S. at 244 ("Mere litigation expense, even substantial and unrecoupable cost, does not constitute irreparable injury.") (internal quotation marks omitted). Only if an administrative procedure is shown to be a "black hole" from which litigants seldom emerge — and then only after a long time with resulting legal prejudice — will the court excuse resort to that procedure. *Coit Independence Joint Venture v. Fed. Sav. & Loan Ins. Corp.*, 489 U.S. 561, 586 (1989) (exhaustion was not required when federal agency delay could cause claimants' state law claims to be time-barred and could be used to coerce claimants into unfair settlements with the agency). Victims of routine administrative sloth are not excused from the exhaustion requirement, though.

4. Issue Exhaustion

One purpose of exhaustion is to give agencies a chance to correct their mistakes and to apply their expertise to a matter. In line with that purpose, sometimes courts reviewing challenges to agency action refuse to consider issues that the challenger did not present to the agency first. This refusal reflects the doctrine of "issue exhaustion." Courts apply the issue exhaustion doctrine most often when they review agency adjudications, but courts also sometimes apply the doctrine when they review agency rulemaking. We separately discuss issue exhaustion in agency adjudication and in agency rulemaking.

a. Agency Adjudication

The leading modern case on issue exhaustion under federal law is *Sims v. Apfel*, 530 U.S. 103 (2000). The Court in *Sims* explained the nature, sources, and rationale of the doctrine.

* *Sims v. Apfel*, 530 U.S. 103 (2000)

Juatassa Sims applied to the Social Security Administration (SSA) for benefits under the Social Security Act, claiming she was disabled. After an ALJ denied her application for disability benefits, Ms. Sims appealed to the SSA's Appeals Council, which denied further review. Ms. Sims then sought federal court review of SSA's denial of benefits. In her judicial challenge, Ms. Sims made arguments about the ALJ's decision that she did not make to the Appeals Council. The federal court of appeals refused to consider those arguments because she had not presented them to the Appeals Council.

The U.S. Supreme Court reversed the court of appeals' decision. The Court held that "issue exhaustion" is a viable doctrine, but the doctrine didn't apply in Ms. Sims' case.

The Court said that "requirements of administrative issue exhaustion are largely creatures of statute." *Id.* at 107. The Court cited as examples 29 U.S.C. § 160(e) (2012), which bars courts, when reviewing decisions of the National Labor Relations Board, from considering any "objection that has not been urged before the Board"; and 16 U.S.C. § 825*l*(b) (2012), which generally prevents courts, when reviewing orders of the Federal Energy Regulatory Commission under the Federal Power Act, from considering any objection to a Commission order that has not been presented to the Commission in a petition for rehearing. But, the Court remarked, no statute required issue exhaustion in Ms. Sims' case.

The Court observed that, in addition to statutes requiring issue exhaustion, "it is common for an agency's regulations to require issue exhaustion in administrative appeals." 530 U.S. at 108. The Court cited as an example a regulation of the U.S. Department of Labor's Benefits Review Board, which reviews ALJ decisions on claims for benefits under certain federal statutes. *Id.* (citing regulation currently codified at 20 C.F.R. 802.211(b) (2012)). When agency regulations do require issue exhaustion, the Court said with apparent approval, "courts reviewing agency action regularly ensure against the bypassing of that requirement by refusing to consider unexhausted issues." 530 U.S. at 108. But, the Court observed, no SSA regulation required issue exhaustion in Ms. Sims' case.

The Court acknowledged, "[W]e have imposed an issue-exhaustion requirement even in the absence of a statute or regulation." *Id.* at 108. The Court had done so based on "an analogy to the rule that appellate courts will not consider arguments not raised before trial courts." *Id.* at 108–109. If no statute or regulation requires issue exhaustion, "the rationale for [courts to] requir[e] issue exhaustion is at its greatest" when "the parties are expected to develop the issues in an adversarial administrative proceeding." *Id.* at 110. Thus, the application of the judicially developed issue exhaustion rule depends on how analogous the administrative proceeding is to a trial-court proceeding.

A plurality of four Justices concluded that the analogy was too weak in Ms. Sims' case to require issue exhaustion in the absence of any statute or agency rule requiring it. Far from being adversarial, benefits proceedings under the Social Security Act are nonadversarial, investigatory proceedings:

> It is the ALJ's duty to investigate the facts and develop the arguments both for and against granting benefits, and the Council's review is similarly broad. The Commissioner has no representative before the ALJ to oppose the claim for benefits, and we have found no indication that he opposes claimants before the Council.

Id. at 111. Reinforcing the agency's affirmative duty to develop arguments and evidence favorable to the claimant, the official form that claimants like Ms. Sims could use to seek Appeals Council review had only three lines on which claimants could fill in their reasons for seeking appeal. The form also assured claimants that it would take them only about ten minutes to read the form, gather the information needed to complete it, and fill out the form. All this "strongly suggests that the Council does not depend much, if at all, on claimants to identify issues for review." *Id.* at 112. These circumstances, coupled with the large portion of claimants who have no lawyer to represent them before the Appeals Council, made the analogy to adversary judicial proceedings weak indeed, and correspondingly weak was the justification for judicially imposed issue exhaustion.

Justice O'Connor concurred in the plurality's conclusion that issue exhaustion didn't apply in Ms. Sims' case. Justice O'Connor observed that the Court was unanimous in recognizing, as a principle of administrative law, that "[i]n most cases, an issue not presented to an administrative decisionmaker cannot be argued for the first time in federal court." *Id.* at 112 (O'Connor, J., concurring in part and concurring in the judgment). Justice O'Connor did not, however, agree with the plurality's rationale for not requiring issue exhaustion in Ms. Sims' case. Justice O'Connor based her vote against requiring issue exhaustion on three circumstances:

> In this case, the SSA told [Ms. Sims] ... (1) that she could request review by sending a letter or filling out a 1-page form that should take 10 minutes to complete, (2) only that failing to request Appeals Council review would preclude judicial review, and (3) that the Appeals Council would review her entire case for issues. She did everything that the agency asked of her. I would not impose any additional requirements.

Id. at 114. Unlike the plurality's approach, Justice O'Connor's approach might have left SSA free to require issue exhaustion without changing the non-adversary character of its proceedings, as long as it changed its form to make the issue-exhaustion requirement plain to people like Ms. Sims.

In any event, the Court's decision in *Sims* indicates that issue exhaustion is the general rule for judicial review of agency decisions in agency adjudications—as a matter of statute, agency rule, or judicial practice. Yet *Sims* leaves open many questions about how to apply the doctrine when issue exhaustion is required. In addition, hard questions can arise about whether a particular statute or agency rule is properly interpreted to require issue exhaustion. For example, a court may have to decide whether a statute expressly requiring exhaustion of administrative *remedies* prior to judicial review requires initial presentation to the agency of all *issues* presented on judicial review. *See, e.g., Garcia-Carbajal,* 625 F.3d 1233, 1237 (10th Cir. 2010) (issue exhaustion has been required under statute requiring exhaustion of remedies in proceedings to remove aliens from the United States). Another interpretive issue can concern whether a statute or rule should be interpreted to allow for *exceptions* to the issue exhaustion requirement.

As if the exhaustion-of-remedies doctrine were not exhausting enough, issue exhaustion may really make you struggle for that second wind.

b. Agency Rulemaking

It is unsettled how issue exhaustion applies, if at all, when federal courts review federal agency rules, as distinguished from orders entered in adjudications. Of course, if the special review statute governing judicial review of the rule requires issue exhaustion, courts must obey the statute. An example of such a statute is 42 U.S.C. § 7607(d)(7)(B) (2012). It says of certain EPA rules issued under the Clean Air Act: "Only an objection to a rule or procedure which was raised with reasonable specificity during the period for public comment (including any public hearing) may be raised during judicial review." *Id.* Section 7607(d)(7)(B) is rare, however, in expressly requiring issue exhaustion in rulemaking, and in the absence of such a statutory requirement or any agency rule expressly requiring issue exhaustion in the rulemaking proceeding, courts must decide whether to apply a judicially created issue exhaustion requirement to a particular lawsuit seeking judicial review of an agency rule.

Sims v. Apfel may cast doubt on the legitimacy of applying judicially imposed issue exhaustion to agency rulemaking. The Court in *Sims* said, "[T]he rationale for requiring issue exhaustion is at its greatest" when "the parties are expected to develop the issues in an adversarial administrative proceeding." 530 U.S. at 110. Rulemaking proceedings don't have parties (except for formal rulemakings, which are rare), and they are not usually considered adversarial but are, instead, quasi-legislative. Even so, some lower federal courts apply a judicially imposed issue exhaustion requirement to rulemaking proceedings.

See BCCA Appeal Group v. EPA, 355 F.3d 817, 828–830 & 829 n.10 (5th Cir. 2003). This includes the D.C. Circuit, which handles so many cases involving judicial review of federal agency rules. *See, e.g., Nat'l Ass'n of Mfrs. v. U.S. Dep't of Interior*, 134 F.3d 1095, 1111 (D.C. Cir. 1998). The U.S. Supreme Court may have to address the issue eventually.

D. Relationship among Finality, Ripeness, and Exhaustion

If you find it hard to distinguish among the doctrines of finality, ripeness, and exhaustion, you are in good company with federal judges, among other folks. In one famous federal court of appeals case, all three judges on the panel agreed that judicial review of a challenge to an agency's enforcement authority was not available, but the judges could not agree on a rationale. One judge concluded the agency action was not final; a second judge held that the judicial challenge was not ripe; and the third judge held that the challenger had failed to exhaust administrative remedies. *See Ticor Title Ins. Co. v. FTC*, 814 F.2d 731 (D.C. Cir. 1987). The doctrines do overlap, largely because they share the purpose of preventing premature judicial interference with agency processes.

These three generalizations may help you understand how they differ.

1. Finality Is Usually Necessary, but Not Always Sufficient, to Produce a Ripe Challenge

Usually, an agency action must be final for a judicial challenge to the action to be ripe. Some nonfinal agency actions, however, will be ripe for immediate judicial review. Section 702 of the federal APA indeed implies that some **"preliminary ... [and] intermediate agency action[s] or ruling[s]"** will be **"directly reviewable."** Furthermore, courts have used an administrative collateral order doctrine to review some interlocutory agency rulings. An example is the Ninth Circuit decision reviewing the EEOC's refusal to dismiss on sovereign immunity grounds a formal adjudication against Alaska. *See Alaska v. EEOC*, 564 F.3d 1062, 1065 n.1 (9th Cir. 2009) (en banc). But usually only truly final agency action can be the subject of a ripe judicial challenge.

By the same token, the finality of an agency action does not guarantee that a judicial challenge will be ripe. The prime examples are certain pre-enforcement challenges to agency rules. *See Toilet Goods Ass'n v. Gardner*, 387 U.S. 158 (1967).

2. Exhaustion Is Neither Sufficient nor Always Necessary to Produce a Final Decision That Is Ripe for Any Judicial Challenge

You may exhaust administrative remedies but end up with agency action that is neither final nor ripe for review. Suppose, for example, you seek an advisory opinion from an agency about how to comply with a regulation, using all of the right procedures for making the request. The resulting advisory opinion may be too tentative, and lack sufficient effect, to be final. And, because it is not final, it cannot be the subject of a judicial challenge that would be considered ripe. Yet you may have no further remedies to exhaust. The same is true of your participation in notice-and-comment rulemaking. The notice-and-comment process ends with the publication of a final rule, and no one can say, if you participated in the rulemaking proceeding, that you didn't exhaust your administrative remedies. Yet your pre-enforcement challenge to the final rule may not be ripe. *See Toilet Goods Ass'n v. Gardner*, 387 U.S. 158, 161–166 (1967).

On the flip side, exhaustion is not always necessary to produce a final agency action that can be the subject of a ripe judicial challenge. Suppose you apply to an agency for some benefit and are turned down by a low-level official. Also suppose that, although you have a right to appeal that official's decision, you do not appeal. Typically, agency regulations will provide that, after the time for appeal has expired, the low-level official's decision becomes the "final" decision of the agency. *See, e.g.,* 13 C.F.R. § 124.704 (2012). A judicial challenge to that final decision could be ripe (depending on the particular nature of your legal challenge), but you have not exhausted your administrative remedy and your failure to do so will ordinarily bar your judicial challenge, even though finality and ripeness won't pose obstacles.

In short, exhaustion is neither sufficient nor always necessary to produce a final agency action that may be the subject of a ripe judicial challenge. Even so, exhaustion is usually required. It's just not the only requirement that you must satisfy.

3. Ripeness Alone among the Timing Doctrines Invariably Considers the Precise Nature of the Particular Legal Challenge

Exhaustion focuses on completing the agency *process*. Finality focuses on the *outcome* of that process. Ripeness focuses on the propriety of a *court's reviewing* the outcome of the agency process. As part of ripeness analysis, the court considers the fitness of the issues for judicial review. This means that ripeness analysis always considers the particular issues that the challenger presents for review. For this reason, it is possible for *some* issues presented in a lawsuit to be ripe, while other issues in the same lawsuit will be found *not* ripe, even though all the issues concern the same challenger and the same agency action. For example, "facial" challenges to an agency rule are more likely to be found ripe, all other things being equal, than are "as applied" challenges to an agency rule. *See Nat'l Treasury Employees Union v. Chertoff*, 452 F.3d 839, 855 (D.C. Cir. 2006).

Because some challenges to a particular agency action may not be ripe—even though a different challenge to that very same agency action could be ripe—it makes no sense to discuss whether or not an *agency action* is, or is not, "ripe." The question is whether a particular *judicial challenge* to the agency action is, or is not, ripe.

* * *

The finality, ripeness, and exhaustion doctrines concern the timing of judicial review of agency action. By contrast, the doctrine of primary jurisdiction, discussed next, typically operates when a person begins a lawsuit in court without having first participated in any agency proceeding.

E. Primary Jurisdiction

Our objectives in this section are to: (1) identify the source of the primary jurisdiction doctrine; (2) identify the situations in which the doctrine may operate; (3) distinguish those situations from those in which the exhaustion doctrine operates; (4) identify the rationales for the doctrine; and (5) describe the effects of the doctrine. We recommend that your overall objective be to gain a general familiarity of these aspects of the doctrine.

The doctrine of primary jurisdiction is a judicially developed doctrine found in both federal law and in the law of many States. The doctrine entered federal law in *Texas & Pacific Railway Co. v. Abilene Cotton Oil Co.*, 204 U.S. 426 (1907). The Abilene Cotton Oil Company brought a state court suit against the railroad that transported Abilene's cotton oil to buyers. Abilene asserted that the railroad's rates were unreasonable and claimed a right under the common law to recover the excess rates that it had paid. The Court held that, instead of initially going to a court with a common law claim, Abilene "must ... primarily invoke redress through the Interstate Commerce Commission." *Id.* at 448. The Interstate Commerce Act had given the Commission primary responsibility to determine the reasonableness of rates. Only if the Commission found the rates unreasonable might the company have a cause of action enforceable in a court. This conclusion requiring initial resort to the ICC reflected a doctrine that the Court later called the "primary jurisdiction" doctrine. *See ICC v. Chicago, Rhode Island & Pac. Ry.*, 218 U.S. 88, 110 (1910) (using the term and attributing the doctrine to *Abilene Cotton*).

In the typical situation where primary jurisdiction operates, a private plaintiff sues a private defendant in a court. The suit either (1) involves a claim by the plaintiff that can be presented to some agency, as well as to a court; or (2) presents some issue (arising from a claim or defense) that an agency has statutory authority to address. The common feature of cases in which primary jurisdiction operates is that *both* a court *and* an agency have the authority to decide a claim or issue initially. *See Reiter v. Cooper*, 507 U.S. 258, 268 (1993). Thus, for example, the Court in *Abilene Cotton Oil* acknowledged that state courts had long entertained common law actions by companies against railroads for charging unreasonable rates. The dilemma arose because the ICC, too, could now entertain claims of unreasonable rates. In other words, the court and the agency concurrently have initial jurisdiction in cases in which the doctrine of primary jurisdiction operates. And those cases pose the question whether the court should abstain from initially deciding the matter itself to give the agency a first whack at deciding it. Should the court say to the agency, "Please; you first"?

This situation differs from situations where the exhaustion doctrine operates. The exhaustion doctrine operates when an agency alone has authority to decide a matter initially. Exhaustion disputes concern whether the party seeking judicial review of the agency's decision has given the agency an adequate chance to reach a decision. Thus, the exhaustion doctrine concerns the proper timing of judicial *review* of an agency decision. By comparison, primary jurisdiction concerns which of two eligible entities—agency or court—should make the initial decision on a matter. *See United States v. Western Pac. R.R.*, 352 U.S. 59, 65 (1956) (explaining difference between exhaustion and primary jurisdiction). In deciding whether to require exhaustion, courts initially look for a statute or rule addressing the issue, in the absence of which they generally balance the value of allowing the agency to finish its decision-making process against the value of providing judicial review before the agency has finished. By contrast, in primary jurisdiction cases, a court will refer a matter to an agency when the court determines that doing so (1) serves interests in uniformity of law and (2) draws upon an agency's expertise and experience. In sum, primary jurisdiction and exhaustion are quite different. *See, e.g., Farmers Ins. Exchange v. Superior Court*, 826 P.2d 730, 738–739 (Cal. 1992) (distinguishing exhaustion from primary jurisdiction).

While the uniformity and experience rationales weigh in favor of requiring initial resort to the agency under the traditional doctrine of primary jurisdiction, the applicability of the doctrine ultimately turns on whether Congress intended initial resort to the agency in the particular situation before the court. The issue of congressional intent has come up in some citizen suits under the Resource Conservation and Recovery Act (RCRA), the federal law authorizing the U.S. EPA to regulate hazardous wastes through a program of cooperative federalism. Defendants in some RCRA citizen suits have argued that state agencies, which may help administer RCRA, have primary jurisdiction over certain claims or issues asserted in the citizen suits. The lower federal courts have generally rejected these arguments, based partly on the existence of a citizen suit provision in RCRA. The existence of the citizen suit provision arguably reflects Congress's determination that courts are as competent as state agencies to decide issues commonly presented in such suits. *Baykeeper v. NL Indus.*, 660 F.3d 686, 691 (3rd Cir. 2011). The broader point is that because the primary jurisdiction doctrine is judicially created, Congress can modify or override it.

When a court concludes that an agency has primary jurisdiction over an entire case or some issue in the case, the court may dismiss the lawsuit or stay it. In choosing between dismissal and a stay, courts consider at least two factors. One is whether the agency's determination is likely to resolve the entire controversy. If so, dismissal is more likely than it would be if the agency's determination probably *won't* resolve the entire controversy. Another relevant factor is whether, if the court dismisses the action, the party who sought judicial review will be able to get judicial review later, in the event that the agency's decision does not resolve the entire controversy. *See Carnation Co. v. Pac. Westbound Conf.*, 383 U.S. 213, 222–223 (1966); *Far East Conf. v. United States*, 342 U.S. 570, 576–577 (1952). Thus, application of the primary jurisdiction doctrine can delay a lawsuit or defeat it altogether.

The primary jurisdiction doctrine does not come up all that often, compared to issues of finality, ripeness, and mootness. Because primary jurisdiction is a rather rare bird, some familiarity with the doctrine is the mark of a well-educated administrative lawyer. For that reason and because it can be tricky to distinguish from the exhaustion doctrine, we thought it worthwhile to introduce you to it.

Exercise: Distinguishing Primary Jurisdiction from Exhaustion

Please try your hand at making a visual depiction to illustrate the differences between the primary jurisdiction doctrine and the exhaustion doctrine.

F. Statutes of Limitations for Lawsuits Seeking Review of Agency Action

Earlier sections of this chapter discussed doctrines that tell you when it's too soon to seek judicial review of agency action. This section introduces you to laws that tell you when it's too late. These laws almost always take the form of statutes, and in administrative law as in other areas of law, they are called statutes of limitations.

The key to determining the applicable statute of limitations is determining the source of your cause of action. As you know, the statute of limitations for a lawsuit claiming negligence often differs from the statute of limitations for a lawsuit claiming a breach of contract. So too, the statute of limitations for a claim based on an APA may differ from the statute of limitations for a claim based on a special review statute. This means that you must identify all possible causes of action as early as possible in planning for judicial review of agency action so you can file your lawsuit within the shortest statutory limitations period. It would be a shame (if not malpractice) if your best claim were time-barred!

The timing of lawsuits in federal court seeking review of federal agency action is odd. Lawsuits based on the APA-created cause of action are generally subject to a luxurious six-year statute of limitations. *See* 28 U.S.C. § 2401(a) (2012). In sharp contrast, many special review statute require lawsuits challenging covered agency actions to be filed within as little as thirty days. *See, e.g.*, 49 U.S.C. § 521(b)(9) (2012) (time limit for judicial review of orders of Secretary of Transportation imposing civil penalties). The more generous special review statutes give you sixty days. *See, e.g.*, 42 U.S.C. § 7607(b)(1) (2012) (time limit for seeking judicial review of wide range of actions by Administrator of EPA under Clean Air Act). Remember that, when a special review provision applies, it is generally exclusive, which means that if you miss its deadline for seeking judicial review, you cannot take advantage of the APA-created cause of action. If you miss the special review boat, you are sunk.

You can expect to find in the States a similar combination of statutes of limitations: Actions seeking review of state agency action under the state APA may be subject to a general statute of limitations. Actions under special review statutes may be subject to a separate statute of limitations. The time limits may be quite short. For example, the North Carolina APA requires petitions for review of agency decisions in contested cases to be filed within thirty days after service of the decision. N.C. Gen. Stat. Ann. § 150B-45(a) (West, Westlaw through S.L. 2012-1 of 2011 Reg. Sess.). The statute does, however, grant relief from that time limit "[f]or good cause shown." *Id.* § 150B-45(b). As a further example, many state APAs put a two-year time limit for judicial challenges asserting an agency promulgated a rule without following the required rulemaking procedures. *See, e.g.*, Ga. Code Ann. § 50-13-4(d) (West, Westlaw through 2011 Reg. & Special Sess.).

Once you identify the applicable statute of limitations, more questions may arise, such as: When does the statute of limitations begin to run and when does it stop? Here is one more hard, important question: If someone requests that an agency reconsider (or rehear or reopen) its decision, does the statutory limitations period begin running on the date of the agency's original decision, or only on the (later) date on which the agency rules upon the request? (Hereafter we use the term "rehear" generically to mean all three forms of revisiting a decision.) A statute may address the effect of a rehearing request on the statute of limitations for seeking review of the original decision. *See* 16 U.S.C. § 825*l*(b) (2012). If not, the rule from federal case law appears to be that, if a request for rehearing is required to exhaust administrative remedies in a particular situation, then the statute of limitations only begins running when the agency has ruled on the request. When the filing of a rehearing request is optional and rehearing is not requested, of course, then the statute of limitations begins running on the date of the original decision. Suppose, however, that the filing of a rehearing request is optional, but someone requests rehearing anyway. In that situation, does the statute of limitations run from the date of the original decision or from the date of the ruling on the rehearing request? The federal courts have not resolved that question, despite its importance. *See Green v. White*, 319 F.3d 560, 563–568 (3rd Cir. 2003); *see also Interstate Commerce Comm'n v. Brotherhood of Locomotive Eng'rs*, 482 U.S. 270, 284–285 (1986). All we can hope is that time will tell.

Administrative lawyers, like other lawyers, pay constant attention to court deadlines. As an administrative lawyer, your approach to these deadlines will be generally the same as it will be for other issues: Your first step is to identify the applicable law (which will usually take the form of a statute), and your second step will be to analyze how the law applies to the case at hand. Of course, deadlines require as a third step that you meet them.

Exercise: Statutes of Limitation for Judicial Review of Agency Action

The National Marine Fisheries Service (NMFS) issued regulations under the Magnuson-Stevens Fishery Conservation and Management Act of 1976 (Magnuson Act), 16 U.S.C. §§ 1801–1891d (2012). The regulations reopened a Hawaii-based fishery that fishes for swordfish. The fishery had been closed down by NMFS for five years because its prior operations had harmed sea turtles. NMFS issued regulations reopening the fishery because NMFS concluded the sea turtle population had recovered enough, and the fishery technology had improved enough, to allow the fishery to operate without threatening the sea turtle population too much.

Five months after NMFS issued the regulations, the Turtle Island Restoration Network filed a lawsuit challenging them in federal district court. Turtle Island's complaint did not claim a violation of the Magnuson Act. Instead, it asserted violations of NEPA, the Migratory Bird Treaty Act, the Endangered Species Act, and the federal APA. NMFS moved to dismiss the lawsuit as untimely based on 16 U.S.C. § 1855(f)(1) (2012), which says that "regulations issued under" the Magnuson Act "shall be subject to judicial review ... if a petition for such review is filed within thirty days after the date on which the regulations are promulgated." Turtle Island contends that this thirty-day time limit doesn't apply because it is not asserting a violation of the Magnuson Act. Please evaluate the timeliness of the lawsuit. *See Turtle Island Restoration Network v. U.S. Dep't of Commerce*, 438 F.3d 937 (9th Cir. 2006).

G. Chapter 30 Wrap Up and Look Ahead

To bake a good cake, you can't take it out of the oven too soon or too late. Likewise, timing matters when it comes to seeking judicial review of agency action. Judicial challenges brought too soon may be barred by the doctrines of finality, ripeness, or exhaustion. If someone goes right to court without going to the agency first, the doctrine of primary jurisdiction may send that person off to the agency. By the same token, you can't file your judicial challenge to agency action too late, or else you and your client are burned.

The timing of judicial review is one aspect of a more general topic: the availability of judicial review. This chapter ends our exploration of the availability of judicial review. The next begins our examination of the *scope* of judicial review. This next set of material answers the question: Once you get judicial review, what exactly do you get?

Chapter Problem 1 Revisited

1. The special review provision applicable here requires you to seek judicial review "no later than 60 days after the order of the Board is issued." 49 U.S.C. § 1153(a) (2012). That's not much time compared to the statute of limitations for ordinary civil actions. As discussed in this chapter, if you miss that deadline, you won't be able to seek judicial review under the APA-created cause of action, which is subject to a generous six-year statute of limitations, because review under the special review provision provides an "adequate remedy in a court" and thereby forecloses use of the APA-created cause of action. *See* 5 U.S.C. § 704.

    You might wonder whether the sixty days runs from the ALJ's initial decision or the Board's dismissal order, because the Board did not actually decide the case on the merits and arguably did not even take jurisdiction of the administrative appeal. Even so, the Board's order is the event that starts the sixty-day clock running, because the review statute authorizes judicial review of the *Board*'s order, not the ALJ's.

2. The second question asked if Springer's failure properly to exhaust his administrative remedies barred judicial review of the Board's order. The short answer is that the court can review the Board's determination that Springer did not properly exhaust his administrative remedies in this case. But that's all.

    You might think that logically the first question is whether Springer was required to exhaust administrative remedies. That turns out to be a hard question, and one that probably is not necessary to answer. Regardless whether Springer was required to exhaust, he did try to exhaust. He didn't just go to court after the ALJ rendered the initial decision. By appealing to the Board, Springer obtained a final decision of the Board, and it is the Board's decision, not the ALJ's, of which judicial review is statutorily authorized. Thus, the central question is the correctness of the Board's decision.

    An entity, like the Board, that reviews ALJ decisions can surely put a reasonable deadline on seeking review of those decisions and refuse a decision when the deadline is missed. At most, Springer can ask the court to review (1) the validity of the Board's rule imposing a deadline for perfecting an appeal and (2) the Board's determination that Springer did not meet that deadline. Conceivably, for example, Springer might argue that the time limit was unreasonably short or that in other cases, the Board regularly ignored the time limit and accepted belatedly filed briefs. But if the court concludes that the rule is valid and that the Board applied it correctly, the court should uphold the Board's order without reviewing Springer's challenge to the testing method.

3. As discussed above, if the court upholds the Board's determination that Springer did not properly perfect the appeal, the court should not reach Springer's argument about the testing method. In the case on which this chapter problem is based, the court of appeals held that the person seeking judicial review "forfeited" his right to challenge the testing method by failing to file a timely brief with the Board. *Cornish v. Federal Aviation Administration*,

429 F.3d 806, 809 (8th Cir. 2005). That is another way of saying that the Board can impose reasonable rules for seeking its review of ALJ decisions, and it is reasonable for those rules to include reasonable deadlines. For those deadlines to have meaning, courts must give them effect by refusing to review claims that weren't timely presented.

Chapter Problem 2 Revisited

This problem is based on *Sackett v. United States Environmental Protection Agency*, 132 S.Ct. 1367 (2012), a case decided as this book went to press.

1. The Court held that the compliance order is final under the two-part test of *Bennett v. Spear*, 520 U.S. 154 (1997). First, the order determined legal obligations by imposing on the Sacketts the legal obligation to restore their land according to the EPA's restoration plan. The order also had legal consequences: It doubled the potential civil penalty to which the Sacketts were subject, and it restricted their ability to get a permit to fill the wetland on their property. Second, the compliance order marked the consummation of the agency's decision-making process. It didn't matter that the EPA invited the Sacketts to discuss the matter informally. "The mere possibility that an agency might reconsider in light of 'informal discussion' and invited contentions of inaccuracy does not suffice to make an otherwise final agency action nonfinal." *Sackett*, 132 S.Ct. at 1372.

2. The Sacketts did not fail to exhaust any required administrative remedies. Because they relied on the APA-created cause of action, exhaustion analysis is governed by APA § 704 as interpreted in *Darby v. Cisneros*, 509 U.S. 137 (1993). If the informal discussions in which they were invited to participate are construed as an opportunity for **"reconsideration"** under Section 704, they were not required to pursue them because reconsideration was not **"expressly required by statute."** The analysis is similar if the invitation for informal discussions is construed instead as an opportunity for **"appeal to superior agency authority."** Section 704 would require the Sacketts to pursue the opportunity, in the absence of a statute expressly requiring it, only if the EPA had a rule that expressly required it and that, pending the informal discussions, stayed the operation of the compliance order.

    Even under traditional exhaustion analysis, the Sacketts probably would not be required to pursue informal discussions. Somewhat similar to John McCarthy in *McCarthy v. Madigan*, 503 U.S. 140 (1992), the Sacketts apparently could not get what they wanted through informal discussions. They wanted the EPA off their backs and off their land so they could build their house. In their view, the EPA lacked jurisdiction over the asserted "wetland" on their property. The informal discussions to which they were invited, however, seemed to permit only the opportunity to bargain about the terms of the restoration of the land, not the EPA's jurisdiction or the permissibility of building on the land. The Sacketts' case seems to fall within the traditional exception to the exhaustion requirement, under which the person seeking judicial review is not required first to exhaust remedies that are inadequate because they are incapable of granting effective relief. *Id.* at 147–148.

3. The Court in *Sackett* rejected the EPA's argument that the Clean Water Act precluded judicial review. The Court held that the Act's authorization of a civil action by EPA to enforce a compliance order should not be interpreted to prevent an action brought under the APA by the targets of a compliance order for review of the order. The Court likewise rejected the EPA's reliance on another special review provision in the Clean Water Act authorizing judicial review in a different situation. Ultimately, the Court held that the EPA had not overcome the presumption of the availability of judicial review codified in the APA. *See Sackett*, 132 S.Ct. at 1372–1374.

Professional Development Reflection Question

Chapter Problem 1 involves a lawyer who files a brief late and, in the process, deprives the client of the right to challenge agency action on the merits. This situation seems like malpractice per se. Do you, as the lawyer who inherits this mess, have a duty to tell your client or anyone else—e.g., bar officials—that your predecessor has apparently committed malpractice? *See* Model Rule of Professional Conduct 8.3.

Chapter 31

Introduction to the
Scope of Judicial Review

Overview

Chapters 28 through 30 examined the availability of judicial review. Beginning in this chapter, we assume judicial review is available, and introduce you to the question: What does judicial review involve? The answers to this question concern a topic customarily called the "scope" of judicial review.

This chapter contains 6 sections, entitled:

A. The Connection between the Cause of Action and the Scope of Judicial Review

B. Overview of the Scope of Review under the APA

C. Identifying Grounds for an APA-Type Challenge to Agency Action

D. The Appellate Model for Judicial Review of APA-Type Challenges to Agency Action

E. Standards of Judicial Review in APA-Type Challenges to Agency Action

F. Overview of Chapters on Scope of Judicial Review in APA-Type Challenges to Agency Action

A. The Connection between the Cause of Action and the Scope of Judicial Review

The short answer to the question "What does judicial review of agency action involve?" is: It depends on the cause of action asserted by the person challenging the agency action. The law creating the cause of action will determine what the challenger needs to prove to get judicial relief and what type of judicial relief the challenger can get.

In the upcoming chapters, we will focus on the proof needed, and the relief available, in most lawsuits seeking judicial review of agency actions. The majority rests on either the APA-created cause of action or a special review statute that authorizes judicial relief on the grounds and of the type authorized in the APA. With regard to the relationship between special review statutes and the APA, the typical special review statute does not exhaustively list the grounds or types of relief available; it leaves those matters to be filled in, by default, by the APA. At most, the special review statute will modify the APA only in certain ways. And, to the extent that the special review statute does not modify the

APA, the court will evaluate the challenged agency action under the APA. *See, e.g., Green Island Power Auth. v. FERC*, 577 F.3d 148, 158 (2nd Cir. 2009).

We will illustrate the point using the case just cited, *Green Island Power Authority v. FERC*. In that case, the Green Island Power Authority challenged an order of the Federal Energy Regulatory Commission. Green Island's cause of action rested on this special review provision:

---

16 U.S.C. § 825*l*. Review of orders ...

Any party to a proceeding under this chapter aggrieved by an order issued by the Commission in such proceeding may obtain a review of such order in the United States Court of Appeals for any circuit wherein the licensee or public utility to which the order relates is located or has its principal place of business, or in the United States Court of Appeals for the District of Columbia, by filing in such court, within sixty days after the order of the Commission upon the application for rehearing, a written petition praying that the order of the Commission be modified or set aside in whole or in part. A copy of such petition shall forthwith be transmitted by the clerk of the court to any member of the Commission and thereupon the Commission shall file with the court the record upon which the order complained of was entered, as provided in section 2112 of Title 28. Upon the filing of such petition such court shall have jurisdiction, which upon the filing of the record with it shall be exclusive, to affirm, modify, or set aside such order in whole or in part. No objection to the order of the Commission shall be considered by the court unless such objection shall have been urged before the Commission in the application for rehearing unless there is reasonable ground for failure so to do. The finding of the Commission as to the facts, if supported by substantial evidence, shall be conclusive. If any party shall apply to the court for leave to adduce additional evidence, and shall show to the satisfaction of the court that such additional evidence is material and that there were reasonable grounds for failure to adduce such evidence in the proceedings before the Commission, the court may order such additional evidence to be taken before the Commission and to be adduced upon the hearing in such manner and upon such terms and conditions as to the court may seem proper. The Commission may modify its findings as to the facts by reason of the additional evidence so taken, and it shall file with the court such modified or new findings which, if supported by substantial evidence, shall be conclusive, and its recommendation, if any, for the modification or setting aside of the original order. The judgment and decree of the court, affirming, modifying, or setting aside, in whole or in part, any such order of the Commission, shall be final, subject to review by the Supreme Court of the United States upon certiorari or certification as provided in section 1254 of Title 28.

The court relied on this statute to address some issues, such as whether certain factual determinations by the Commission were supported by "substantial evidence" and should therefore be upheld. The court relied on the APA, however, as authority to determine whether the Commission's refusal to allow Green Island to intervene in a Commission proceeding was **"arbitrary, capricious, an abuse of discretion, or otherwise not in accordance with law."** 5 U.S.C. § 706(2)(A) (2012); *see Green Island*, 577 F.3d at 158 & 162–165.

This is typical. Many special review statutes authorize judicial review of agency action without exhaustively addressing the grounds for judicial relief or the scope of review. Any aspects of judicial review that are not addressed in the special review statute will be governed, by default, by the good old APA—specifically, by its judicial review provisions: §§ 701–706. Of particular importance, § 706 authorizes courts reviewing agency action— whether review occurs under the federal APA's cause of action or a special review statute— to set aside agency action that exceeds the agency's authority, violates substantive or procedural law, lacks an adequate factual basis, or fails to reflect reasoned decision making. In this way, the APA brings some uniformity as well as comprehensiveness to judicial review of federal agency actions. From now on, we will refer to lawsuits resting on the APA or on a special review statute that by default generally authorizes review under the APA's judicial-review provisions as an "APA-type challenge." APA-type challenges are characterized by a private plaintiff seeking to invalidate agency action as contrary to law, lacking an adequate factual basis, or contrary to reasoned decision making.

To understand what we mean by an APA-type challenge, some counterexamples may help. APA-type challenges do not include lawsuits against the government asserting tort claims, breach-of-contract claims, claims for just compensation, and quiet title claims. For one thing, these lawsuits often seek monetary relief, which is not available in APA-type challenges, or some form of affirmative relief. More fundamentally, these lawsuits seek to establish a specific sort of wrong by the government or a specific entitlement on the part of the plaintiff. In contrast, APA-type challenges often present a wide variety of claims about why the challenged action is invalid.

Some administrative law course books and courses discuss these non-APA-type lawsuits. To achieve depth of coverage in a book of reasonable length, this book does not discuss them.

Exercise: APA-Type Challenges

Please read the special review statute authorizing judicial review of safety standards issued by the Consumer Product Safety Commission (CPSC): 15 U.S.C. § 2060 (2012). In a federal-court action under this provision to challenge a safety standard, may the court set aside the safety standard if it is **"arbitrary"** or **"capricious"** within the meaning of § 706(2)(A) of the federal APA? On what other grounds in § 706(2) may a court set aside a CPSC safety standard on review under § 2060?

B. Overview of the Scope of Review under the APA

Section 706 of the federal APA addresses the grounds for judicial relief and the type of relief generally available in APA-type challenges:

---

5 U.S.C. § 706. Scope of review

To the extent necessary to decision and when presented, the reviewing court shall decide all relevant questions of law, interpret constitutional and statutory

provisions, and determine the meaning or applicability of the terms of an agency action. The reviewing court shall—

(1) compel agency action unlawfully withheld or unreasonably delayed; and

(2) hold unlawful and set aside agency action, findings, and conclusions found to be—

(A) arbitrary, capricious, an abuse of discretion, or otherwise not in accordance with law;

(B) contrary to constitutional right, power, privilege, or immunity;

(C) in excess of statutory jurisdiction, authority, or limitations, or short of statutory right;

(D) without observance of procedure required by law;

(E) unsupported by substantial evidence in a case subject to sections 556 and 557 of this title or otherwise reviewed on the record of an agency hearing provided by statute; or

(F) unwarranted by the facts to the extent that the facts are subject to trial de novo by the reviewing court.

In making the foregoing determinations, the court shall review the whole record or those parts of it cited by a party, and due account shall be taken of the rule of prejudicial error.

The 2010 Model State APA and many state APAs have a provision that, like § 706, is entitled "Scope of Review." 2010 Model State APA § 508. Many of these state provisions prescribe standards of judicial review—notably including the "arbitrary and capricious" standard and the "substantial evidence" standard—that, in name at least, are the same as ones found in § 706. For now, we will focus on § 706 of the federal APA.

Section 706 prescribes the scope of judicial review of "**agency action.**" For purposes of § 706, "**'agency action' includes the whole or a part of an agency rule, order, license, sanction, relief, or the equivalent or denial thereof, or failure to act …**" 5 U.S.C. § 551(13) (2012); *see also* 5 U.S.C. § 701(b)(2) (making definition of "agency action" in § 551 applicable to §§ 701– 706). Agency action taking the form of a *failure to act* is addressed by § 706(1); § 706(2), in contrast, addresses the other, affirmative types of agency action listed in the definition.

We have previously discussed some aspects of getting relief under § 706(1) for an agency's failure to act and will discuss remaining aspects in a future chapter. In Chapter 29, we discussed how to determine whether an agency's failure to act constitutes an "**agency action**" of which judicial review is available under the APA-created cause of action. *See* Chapter 29.B.2.b(i). In Chapter 30, we discussed the additional requirement that an agency's failure to act be "**final,**" as required for review under the APA. *See* Chapter 30.A.2.e. We will defer until Chapter 35 our discussion of the standard for judicial review, and the remedies available, for this rather specialized situation of agency inaction. *See* Chapter 35.A.5.

Moving on to § 706(2), § 706(2) lists grounds for judicial relief that concern two types of issues:

- Various questions of law are addressed by the last phrase in § 706(2)(A) ("**otherwise not in accordance with law**") and by § 706(2)(B), (2)(C), and (2)(D).

- Questions of the factual basis for the agency action are addressed by § 706(2)(E) and (2)(F).

This leaves one phrase unaccounted for: § 706(2)(A)'s **"arbitrary, capricious, an abuse of discretion"** ground for invalidating agency action. This ground for relief is known as the "arbitrary and capricious" standard. As we will discuss in Chapter 34, it has been interpreted to serve two functions:

1. The "arbitrary and capricious" standard imposes a requirement of "reasoned decisionmaking" on all agency action subject to review under § 706.

2. The "arbitrary and capricious" standard provides the standard for judicial review of the factual basis for agency actions that are not subject to either the "substantial evidence" standard of review prescribed in § 706(2)(E) or the "de novo" standard of review prescribed in § 706(2)(F).

As a whole, § 706(2) enables federal courts to review federal agency action for compliance with applicable legal requirements, adequate evidentiary support, and overall rationality. It thus authorizes comprehensive review.

Even so, an examination of the text of § 706 alone does not fully expose the realities of (1) how administrative lawyers systematically identify grounds for an APA-type challenge to a particular agency action; or (2) how courts review these challenges. The remaining sections begin to expose those realities. You've heard of "L.A. Confidential"? Think of the upcoming sections as "APA Confidential."

C. Identifying Grounds for an APA-Type Challenge to Agency Action

In Chapter 2 we identified three questions raised by most administrative law problems:

(1) Has the agency acted under a valid source of power?

(2) If so, has the agency obeyed limits on, and requirements for exercising, that power?

(3) If the agency lacks power to take the action, or has not obeyed limits on that power, what can be done about it?

The first two questions not only undergird a broad framework for identifying grounds for a legal challenge to most agency actions. They also reflect two broad, potential arguments for an APA-type challenge to agency action, which, as elaborated consistently with the problem solving framework presented in Chapter 2, are as follows:

(1) The agency has *not* acted under a valid source of power, because:

    (a) the agency lacks a source of power; or

    (b) the source of power under which the agency has acted is invalid.

(2) The agency has *not* obeyed one or more of the following limits on, or requirements for exercising, its power:

    (a) internal (intrinsic) limits:

        (i) substantive limits

        (ii) procedural limits

    (b) external (extrinsic) limits:

    (i)   substantive limits

    (ii) procedural limits

When we first introduced this analytic architecture, you had little background knowledge to help you build it out. By now, however, you should be able to appreciate the following about this framework:

(1) *Sources of power:* The most common source of power under which agencies act is the agency legislation, which assigns the agency a job to do along with powers to do that job. If the agency legislation is invalid, agency action taken under that legislation will be invalid. Let us separately consider federal agency legislation and state agency legislation.

Federal agency legislation is invalid if the legislation has been validly repealed or violates the U.S. Constitution. Focusing on the latter ground of invalidity, this book has examined three sets of federal constitutional restrictions on agency legislation:

- the non-delegation doctrine, which restricts federal statutes that delegate to federal agencies the quasi-legislative power to make legislative rules (discussed in Chapter 8)

- the doctrines based on Article III and the Seventh Amendment that limit federal statutes delegating to federal agencies the quasi-judicial power to adjudicate cases (discussed in Chapter 18)

- the doctrine of procedural due process, which requires fair procedures when a federal statute authorizes the deprivation of life, liberty, or property (discussed in Chapter 20)

As for state agency legislation, it too must comply with the U.S. Constitution and all valid federal statutes and federal legislative rules, as well as with the state constitution. We explored in Chapter 5 the general subject of the extent to which federal law restrains state agencies. In addition, in Chapter 16 we addressed the power of a federal agency's legislative rule to preempt conflicting state law, which can include state agency legislation.

(2)(a) *Internal limits on agency power:* Many lawsuits include the argument that an agency has exceeded its authority under the agency legislation or violated the agency legislation in some other way. The agency legislation invariably imposes substantive limits on, or requirements for exercising, agency power. In addition, the agency legislation may contain procedural requirements for the exercise of agency powers, including the agency's rulemaking or adjudicatory powers.

(2)(b) *External limits on agency power:* External limits on agency power include limits imposed by the U.S. Constitution. Of particular relevance to administrative lawyers, the Due Process Clauses require agencies to use fair procedures when their adjudicatory conduct deprives or threatens to deprive someone of liberty or property, including "new property" in the form of certain government benefits or government employment. External limits also come from cross-cutting statutes such as the APA, the agency's own rules, and other executive-branch material such as executive orders. The external limits may be substantive or procedural.

Earlier chapters examined procedural requirements in the APA and agency legislation, focusing on procedures for rulemaking and adjudication. (See Chapters 9–15 and 19–24.)

In addition to an APA's procedural limits, an APA's judicial review provisions typically allow a court to review agency action for rationality and for an adequate factual basis, two forms of review that are predominantly substantive and that both enforce and augment limits imposed by the law directly controlling the agency's powers. We introduced these judicial-review limits that judicial review puts on agency action in Chapters 9.B.4 and 19.B.4. We explore them in upcoming chapters.

The next section turns to how courts review APA-type challenges to agency action.

D. The Appellate Model for Judicial Review of APA-Type Challenges to Agency Action

Today courts generally use what is called the "appellate model" for judicial review of APA-type challenges to agency action. *See generally* Thomas W. Merrill, *Article III, Agency Adjudication, and the Origins of the Appellate Model of Administrative Law*, 111 Colum. L. Rev. 939 (2011) (tracing evolution of appellate model). The term "appellate model" means that judicial review of agency action resembles appellate court review of a trial court's judgment. Specifically, the appellate model for judicial review of agency action has two features:

(1) The court ordinarily reviews the agency action based solely on the record before the agency, just as an appellate court ordinarily reviews a trial court's decision based solely on the trial court record. The record before the agency is called "the administrative record."

(2) The court generally does not review the factual basis for the agency action de novo, just as an appellate court ordinarily does not conduct de novo review of a trial court's findings or a jury's verdict. Instead, in each setting, the court reviews factual determinations deferentially.

The appellate model is generally used by both trial courts and appellate courts when they review APA-type challenges to agency action. Also, the appellate model is generally used both by federal courts to review APA-type challenges to federal agency action, and by state courts to review APA-type challenges to state agency actions. The appellate model analogy is depicted in Diagram 31-1.

Diagram 31-1. The "Appellate Model" for Judicial Review of APA-Type Challenges to Agency Action

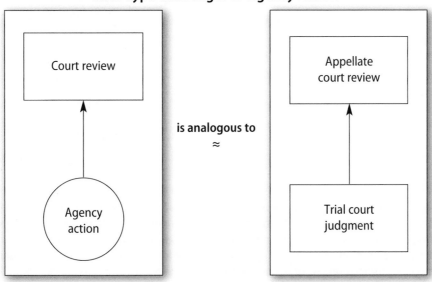

The term "appellate model" reflects only a rough analogy. The analogy is imperfect in two important ways.

For one thing, when an appellate court reviews a lower court decision, the appellate court is reviewing the action of another judicial-branch entity, an entity that occupies a subordinate position within that branch. In contrast, when a court reviews an agency action, the court is reviewing the decision of an entity that is in a different branch of government and that is therefore not formally subordinate to the court. Although a court may have authority to invalidate an agency decision, the court and agency are more like partners in a joint venture than like a superior and a subordinate. *See generally FCC v. Pottsville Broadcasting Co.*, 309 U.S. 134, 141–144 (1940) (discussing differences between appellate court review of lower court decisions and judicial review of agency action). Appellate review of lower court decisions is depicted in Diagram 31-2.

Diagram 31-2. Appellate Review of Lower Court Decisions

Legislative   Executive   Judicial

Supreme Court

Court of Appeals

Trial Court
Judgement

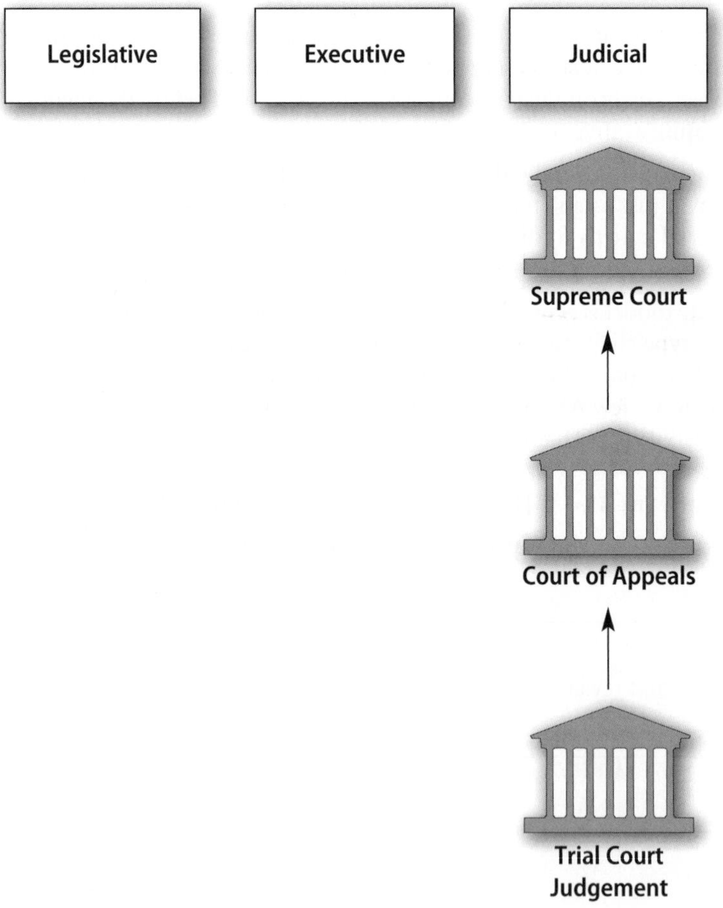

For another thing, when an appellate court reviews a lower court decision, the appellate court invariably reviews an adjudicatory action. In contrast, when a court reviews an agency action, the court may be reviewing an agency adjudication, an agency rule, or other agency action, such as an agency's exercise of executive power to conduct an inspection. Judicial review of agency decisions is depicted in Diagram 31-3.

Diagram 31-3. Judicial Review of Agency Action

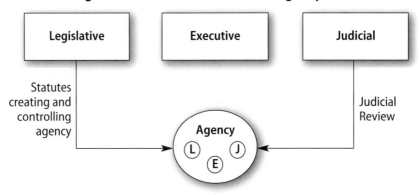

You would think these differences between appellate court review of lower court decisions, on the one hand, and court review of administrative agency action, on the other hand, would produce differences in the scope of review. And you would be right, as you will see.

In the next section we introduce the subject of the standard of judicial review that courts use under the appellate model.

E. Standards of Judicial Review in APA-Type Challenges to Agency Action

In the appellate model for judicial review of agency action, as is true when an appellate court reviews a trial court's decision, the *standard* for judicial review varies, depending on whether review concerns a question of law or a question of fact. Thus, to identify what standard of judicial review applies to a particular issue that arises on judicial review of agency action, you usually will have to determine whether the issue involves a question of law or a question of fact.

Even so, no sharp line separates questions of fact from questions of law. The absence of a sharp line explains why lawyers distinguish among "pure" questions of law, "pure" questions of fact, and "mixed questions of law and fact." An example of a pure question of law is: What does the term "cruel and unusual punishment" in the Constitution mean? An example of a pure question of fact is: What punishment did State *A* impose on Prisoner *X* for *X*'s conviction of crime *Y*? A mixed question of law and fact is: Was Prisoner *X*'s sentence "cruel and unusual" under the Constitution? Mixed questions of law and fact are also sometimes called questions of "ultimate" fact, to distinguish them from questions of "basic" fact (also known as elemental, primary, or historical fact). Many if not all mixed questions involve the application of law to a particular situation, and for that reason mixed questions are sometimes also classified as "law-application questions." The multitude of terms should alert you to the underlying complexity of the law/fact distinction.

Appellate court review of trial court decisions reflects the lack of a sharp line between law and fact. At one end of the spectrum, appellate courts use a de novo standard to review trial court determinations of pure questions of law. At the other end of the spectrum, appellate courts use a deferential standard to review trial court findings of basic facts—upholding those findings, for example, unless they are "clearly erroneous." As for mixed questions of law, the standard of appellate review varies. The variance reflects that the determination of the appropriate standard of review for mixed questions is often "as much a matter of allocation as it is of analysis." *Miller v. Fenton*, 474 U.S. 104, 113–114 (1985). In other words, policy concerns and practical concerns often drive the standard of review in this gray area.

The difficulty of drawing a sharp line between questions of law and questions of fact carries over into judicial review of agency action. Here, too, the distinction often depends on policy and pragmatic considerations. A well-known administrative law scholar put it this way:

> In truth, the distinction between "questions of law" and "questions of fact" really gives little help in determining how far the courts will review [agency action]; and for the good reason that there is no fixed distinction. They are not two mutually exclusive *kinds* of questions, based upon a difference of subject-matter. Matters of law grow downward into roots of fact, and matters of fact reach upward, without a break, into matters of law. The knife of policy alone effects an artificial cleavage at the point where the court chooses to draw the line between public interest and private right.

John Dickinson, Administrative Justice and the Supremacy of Law in the United States 55 (1927). The last sentence of the block quotation means that questions often get classified as questions of "law" when, because of their breadth, their resolution affects the public interest; and as questions of "fact" when, because of their narrowness, their resolution primarily affects the private rights of individuals. The law/fact distinction is depicted in Diagram 31-4.

Because the line between questions of law and questions of fact is not hard and fast, do not be surprised if you find the distinction abstract at this point. It will become more concrete as you learn about specific cases in which courts review agency action in the upcoming chapters. The next (and final) section of this chapter explains the organization of the upcoming chapters and puts them into context.

F. Overview of Chapters on Scope of Judicial Review in APA-Type Challenges to Agency Action

In the upcoming chapters, we examine the main standards of review that courts use to analyze issues that arise when the courts hear APA-type challenges to agency action. We start with the main standards governing review of questions of law. Then we take up the main standards governing review of questions of fact. Finally, we examine specialized standards of review developed for specialized situations. We also discuss judicial remedies available in APA-type challenges.

Specifically, our objective is to introduce you to the following standards of judicial review or analytic frameworks that courts use to review agency action:

Diagram 31-4. The Law/Fact Distinction

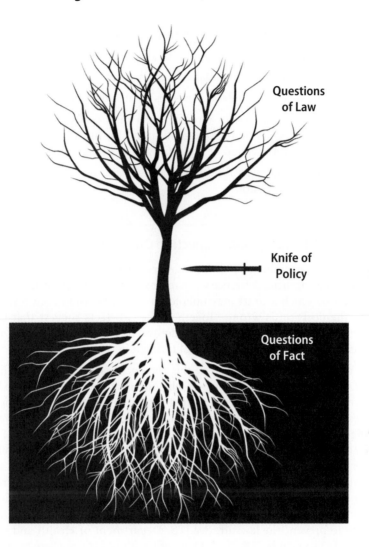

- de novo review
- the *Chevron/Mead* doctrine
- *Auer* deference
- the "arbitrary and capricious" standard
- the "substantial evidence" standard

For each of these standards and for the *Chevron/Mead* doctrine, the material in this part of the book is designed to enable you to answer three questions:

(1) When does this standard (or doctrine) apply?

(2) What does it mean?

(3) What is its rationale?

In addition, we briefly identify in Chapter 35 specialized standards federal courts use to review the following agency actions or types of legal challenges to agency action:

(1) claims of selective enforcement

(2) agency choice of sanction

(3) agency denial of request to rehear, reopen, or reconsider prior decision

(4) agency denial of rulemaking petitions

(5) claims of unreasonable or unlawful agency delay

Also in Chapter 35, we discuss judicial remedies in APA-type challenges.

If you find yourself hankering for more material on judicial review of agency action, do not worry; there is plenty more! One good source for further study comes from the American Bar Association's Section of Administrative Law and Regulatory Practice:

- *A Guide to Judicial and Political Review of Federal Agencies* (John E. Duffy and Michael Herz eds. 2005)

Professional Development Reflection Question

Agencies hate publicity. This fact matters when you couple it with the fact that courts give agencies deference when reviewing many aspects of agency action, as a result of which a court may uphold an agency decision even if the court thinks the decision is wrong. Together, the two facts suggest that lawyers challenging agency action should consider whether they can "try" their case in the media instead of, or in addition to, trying it in court.

An example of an effective use of this approach was taking place at the time of this writing. Specifically, a group of religious organizations is suing the federal government challenging agency rules that require employers to pay for their employees to receive birth control services. *See, e.g.*, Complaint, Diocese of Fort Wayne-South Bend Inc. v. Sebelius, No. 1:12-cv-00159-ECL-RBC (N.D. Ind. May 21, 2012); *see also* 76 Fed. Reg. 46,621 (2011) (amendments to challenged rules); 75 Fed. Reg. 41,276 (2010) (challenged rules). At the same time, the organizations began a media blitz even before the lawsuit, issuing press releases and holding press conferences denouncing the rules on the ground they infringe religious liberty. The media blitz caused some loosening of the rules, but not enough to prevent the lawsuit. *See* U.S. Department of Health and Human Services, A Statement by U.S. Department of Health and Human Services Secretary Kathleen Sebelius, *available at* http://www.hhs.gov/news/press/2012pres/01/2012 0120a.html (Jan. 20, 2012).

Is it ethical to use adverse media publicity to pressure an opposing party to resolve your lawsuit against that party on terms favorable to you? Does it matter whether the opposing party is the government or a private party? Does it matter whether the lawyer uses the media to pressure the opposing party as distinguished from the judge or jury? *See* Model Rule of Professional Responsibility 3.6 ("Trial Publicity").

Chapter 32

Questions of Law

Overview

This chapter discusses how courts decide questions of law that arise when the courts review agency action. We focus on federal court review of federal agency action, but also touch upon state court review of state agency action.

In a nutshell, the federal courts review most questions of law de novo, with two main exceptions. First, the federal courts use the *Chevron/Mead* doctrine to review a federal agency's interpretation of a statute that the agency administers. Second, the federal courts use what is called "*Auer* deference" to review a federal agency's interpretation of its own rules.

Most state courts use a de novo standard to decide most issues of law. Many state courts give special treatment, however, to a state agency's interpretation of a statute that the agency administers. Some state courts also give special treatment to a state agency's interpretation of its own rules.

This chapter consists of five sections:

A. Questions of Law in General

B. Federal Agencies' Interpretation of Statutes They Administer

C. Federal Agencies' Interpretation of Their Own Rules

D. State Agencies' Interpretations of Statutes They Administer and of Their Own Rules

E. Chapter 32 Wrap Up and Look Ahead

Chapter Problem

The Federal Insurance Contribution Act (FICA) requires employers and employees to pay taxes on all "wages," which FICA defines to mean "remuneration for employment." 26 U.S.C. §§ 3101(a), 3111(a) & 3121(a) (2012). FICA exempts from taxation, however, compensation for "service performed in the employ of ... a school, college, or university ... if such service is performed by a student who is enrolled and regularly attending classes [at the school]." *Id.* § 3121(b)(10). FICA is administered by the Department of Treasury and is part of the Internal Revenue Code. The Code has a provision authorizing Treasury to "prescribe all needful rules and regulations for the enforcement" of the Code. 26 U.S.C. § 7805(a) (2012).

Treasury used notice-and-comment rulemaking to promulgate a rule addressing FICA's application to medical residents and others who work full time for compensation but also are learning on the job. The rule categorically provides that employees who ordinarily work at least forty hours a week and their employers are subject to FICA taxes.

A hospital that employs medical residents brings a federal court action challenging the rule as an invalid interpretation of FICA. The hospital argues that medical residents fall within FICA's exemption for students regularly attending classes. The hospital notes that, while medical residents do work from fifty to eighty hours each week caring for patients, the residents also regularly attend lectures and other classes. The hospital also points out that, until 2005, Treasury used a case-by-case approach to determining whether medical residents fell within the FICA exemption for students, by asking whether their care of patients in a particular residency program was "incidental" to their course work.

Please analyze the Treasury rule under the relevant standard of judicial review.

A. Questions of Law in General

At least since *Marbury v. Madison,* federal courts have always considered it "emphatically the province and duty of the judicial department to say what the law is." 5 U.S. (1 Cranch) 137, 177 (1803). In practice, this has meant that federal courts independently determine most questions of law that arise when reviewing federal agency action. This includes the questions:

- Does the agency action comply with the U.S. Constitution?

- Does the agency legislation under which the agency acted comply with the U.S. Constitution?

- Does the agency action comply with all applicable cross-cutting statutes, including the APA?

When we say courts decide these questions "independently," we mean they make up their own mind about what is the right answer. In short, they use a "de novo" standard of review for these questions of law.

The federal courts use a de novo standard not only for most "pure" questions of law but also for most "mixed questions of law and fact." For example, a pure question of law determined de novo is: Does this FDA rule on its face violate the First Amendment? A mixed question of law determined de novo is: Does the FDA's application of its rule to this particular broadcaster, under the circumstances of this particular case, violate the First Amendment? The same de novo standard applies to the issues involving the interpretation of cross-cutting statutes such as the APA. For example, federal courts independently interpret the provisions in the APA exempting certain agency rules from the APA's notice-and-comment procedures, and they independently determine whether a particular agency rule falls within one of those exemptions.

Now that you know that federal courts review "most" questions of law de novo, you may be wondering: What are the exceptions? There are two main types of issues of law that federal courts treat exceptionally, using the doctrine or standard listed next to each:

Question:	Standard or doctrine used to answer this question:
1. Has a federal agency properly interpreted a statute that it administers, i.e., the agency legislation?	*Chevron/Mead* doctrine

2. Has a federal agency properly interpreted the agency's
own rule?   *Auer* deference

3. Other questions of law, such as the three questions
bulleted at the beginning of this section: *De novo*

You can appreciate the importance of the first two questions (and the resulting importance of how courts decide them) when you consider *how* they arise and how *often* they arise.

When an agency adjudicates a case, the agency decides how the law applies to the facts of that case. "The law" applied by the agency is often the agency legislation. For example, the agency may decide whether to penalize someone for violating the agency legislation, or the agency may decide whether someone satisfies requirements in the agency legislation for getting government benefits or a license. Thus, many agency adjudications involve the agency interpreting (in the course of applying) the agency legislation. And any APA-type challenge to the agency's adjudicatory decision can argue that the decision rests on a flawed interpretation of the agency legislation. In assessing that argument, a federal court does not ask whether the agency's statutory interpretation was correct. Rather, the court analyzes the agency's interpretation using the *Chevron/Mead* doctrine.

When an agency, instead of adjudicating, makes a rule, the agency must ensure the rule is consistent with the agency legislation. Indeed, the agency rule may have the specific purpose of explaining how the agency interprets some provision in the agency legislation. Alternatively, the agency rule may be designed to implement agency legislation by creating substantive legislative rules that establish legal rights and obligations that do not exist in the agency legislation. In either event, the agency must ensure its rule accords with the agency legislation under which the rule is issued. This requires the agency to interpret its legislation. Thus, almost all agency rules involve the interpretation of agency legislation. And any APA-type challenge to the agency's rule can raise the question whether the agency has interpreted that legislation correctly. As true when federal courts review federal agency adjudicatory decisions, federal courts reviewing federal agency rules do not simply ask whether the agency's interpretation was correct. Rather, they analyze the agency's interpretation using the *Chevron/Mead* doctrine.

An agency also regularly must interpret its own rules. After all, once an agency issues a rule, the rule doesn't just sit there on the books. Agency officials apply it. Members of the public rely on it. Ambiguities in the rule become evident and must be addressed. Thus, it is not unusual for an agency to issue a substantive legislative rule and later issue interpretive rules addressing questions that have arisen about the meaning of the earlier, legislative rule. When a federal court reviews a federal agency's interpretation of the agency's own rule, the court doesn't approach the task thinking there's a 50% chance the agency is right, and a 50% chance the agency is wrong. Instead, the court accords *Auer* deference to the agency's interpretation, meaning, roughly speaking, that the agency's interpretation will be upheld if reasonable.

Besides agency adjudication and agency rulemaking, many other types of agency action reflect the agency's interpretation of the agency legislation or agency rules. For example, agency investigative activities, such as the conduct of inspections, may require the agency to interpret statutory provisions granting investigative power.

In sum, the everyday work of agencies requires interpretation of the agency legislation and agency rules. And the everyday work of courts reviewing agency action requires review of those agency interpretations. The next sections explore when federal courts reviewing agency actions decide questions of law using the specialized principles of the *Chevron/Mead* doctrine and *Auer* deference, instead of using the de novo standard applicable to most other questions of law. You will see that the *Chevron/Mead* doctrine and *Auer* deference are judicial creations. You cannot find them anywhere in the text of the APA or the special review provisions under which judicial review occurs. Actually, if you looked only at the text of § 706 of the federal APA, which governs the scope of review in most cases, you might think from the following language that courts independently decide all questions of law:

---

5 U.S.C. § 706. Scope of review

To the extent necessary to decision and when presented, the reviewing court shall decide all relevant questions of law ... [and] interpret constitutional and statutory provisions ...

This sentence does not mean that courts decide all questions of law de novo. But that reality is apparent only when you dive beneath the surface of the statute to the case law on the federal courts' authority to review federal agency action. In the next section, we dive in.

Exercise: Identifying Standards of Judicial Review Applicable to Questions of Law

Please identify which of the three standards or doctrines of judicial review discussed above apply to the following questions of law.

1. The Federal Communications Commission has statutory authority to regulate "indecent" television broadcasts. 18 U.S.C. § 1464 (2012). The Commission has developed an indecency policy for identifying specific broadcasts that are indecent and, as such, subject to civil fines and other sanctions. A broadcast television company that has been fined because of a supposedly "indecent" broadcast brings an APA-type challenge arguing that the FCC's indecency policy violates the First Amendment.

2. The EPA has authority under the Clean Air Act to approve plans submitted by States for regulating air pollution emissions from "stationary source[s]." 42 U.S.C. § 7502(c)(6) (2012). Confusion about this statutory term has arisen. For example, is a plant that has multiple sources of pollution—e.g., multiple smokestacks—just one big "stationary source," or is each smoke stack in the plant a separate "stationary source"? To dispel the confusion, the EPA issues a legislative rule defining the term "stationary source." A company challenges EPA's rule in an APA-type challenge, arguing that the rule violates the Clean Air Act.

3. The U.S. Secretary of Labor has issued legislative rules to implement the federal minimum wage and overtime laws. The rules define when an employee is exempt from those laws under the statutory exemption for "bona fide executive, administrative, or professional employees." 29 U.S.C. § 213(a) (2012). The rules state that an employee falls within this statutory exemption when the employee is paid on a "salary basis." After the Secretary issues these legislative rules establishing the "salary-basis" test, employers and employees

have questions about the meaning of the test. To address those questions, the Secretary has issued interpretative rules explaining how the salary-basis test applies in various situations. An employer challenges one of those interpretative rules in an APA-type challenge, contending that the interpretative rule is not a valid interpretation of the legislative rules establishing the salary-basis test.

4. During a formal adjudication before the National Labor Relations Board, the ALJ discusses the case with someone outside the agency. On judicial review of the outcome of that adjudication, a party argues that the ALJ's discussion violated APA § 554(d)(1)'s ban on ex parte communications. The contents of the discussion are undisputed. The question is whether the discussion concerned a **"fact in issue"** within the meaning of § 554(d)(1).

B. Federal Agencies' Interpretation of Statutes They Administer

1. Historical Cases

We begin with two historical cases about how the federal courts should review a federal agency's interpretation of its legislation. We begin with these two cases for two reasons. First, they are famous cases that every well-educated administrative lawyer knows. Second, they help you understand current law. Indeed, the second case, *Skidmore v. Swift & Co.*, 323 U.S. 134 (1944), is still cited all the time.

a. Background on the *Hearst* Case

In the mid-twentieth century, newspaper companies used "newsboys" (and newsgirls) to distribute their newspapers in large cities. For the most part, newsboys and newsgirls exist today only in movies from that era, in which you will see them on street corners with large bundles of newspapers, shouting, "Extra! Extra! Read all about it!" The "newsboys" were in many cases adults, as was true of the workers at issue in the case you are about to read, which is known as the *Hearst* case: *National Labor Relations Board v. Hearst Publications, Inc.*, 322 U.S. 111 (1944).

In *Hearst*, a union (Union) sought to represent the newsboys at four Los Angeles newspapers. To that end, the Union asked the National Labor Relations Board to determine that the newsboys had a right to unionize under the National Labor Relations Act (also known as the Wagner Act). The Union made this request to the Board, as stated in the *Hearst* opinion, by filing petitions with the Board "for investigation and certification." *See* 29 U.S.C. § 159(c) (2012) (current statute prescribing investigation and certification processes).

The Union's request triggered a formal adjudication before the Board. *See id.* § 159(c)(1) (authorizing a hearing and requiring the Board to make a decision "upon the record of such hearing"). In that adjudication, the Board determined that the newsboys did have the right to unionize under the Act because they were "employees" as that term is used in the Act. The Board also determined what groups of newsboys constituted appropriate "bargaining units" to be represented by a union in collective bargaining with their newspaper employers. The Board ordered elections in which a majority of the employees in each bargaining unit selected the Union.

The newspapers refused to bargain with the Union. This is the common way for an employer to lay the foundation for a legal challenge to the Board's action. The newspapers' refusal led the Union to file a complaint with the Board charging the newspapers with committing an unfair labor practice, in violation of the Wagner Act. The Union's complaint led to a second formal adjudication before the Board, which ended in the Board's ordering the newspapers to bargain with the Union. *See* 29 U.S.C. § 160(b) & (c) (2012) (current statute on unfair labor practice proceedings). The newspapers petitioned a federal court of appeals for judicial review of the Board's order, in response to which the Board cross-petitioned the court for enforcement of the Board's order. *See id.* § 160(e) & (f) (current statute governing these kinds of petitions).

Then as now, the Act said that when a court reviewed a Board order, "[t]he findings of the Board with respect to questions of fact if supported by substantial evidence on the record considered as a whole shall be conclusive." *Id.* § 160(e). In *Hearst*, as the case came to the U.S. Supreme Court, the question was whether the newsboys were "employees" within the meaning of the National Labor Relations (i.e. Wagner) Act—and accordingly entitled by the Act to unionize. Before you read the opinion, please consider how to classify the question whether the newsboys were "employees" under the Act: pure question of law? pure question of fact? mixed question of law and fact?

b. The *Hearst* Opinion

National Labor Relations Board v. Hearst Publications, Inc.[1]

322 U.S. 111 (1944)

JUSTICE RUTLEDGE delivered the opinion of the Court.

These cases arise from the refusal of respondents, publishers of four Los Angeles daily newspapers, to bargain collectively with a union representing newsboys who distribute their papers on the streets of that city. Respondents' contention that they were not required to bargain because the newsboys are not their "employees" within the meaning of that term in the National Labor Relations Act, 49 Stat. 450, 29 U.S.C. § 152,[1] presents the important question which we granted certiorari to resolve.

---

1. Editor's note: You will find a red flag and red stop sign attached to this case in the Westlaw and LexisNexis databases, respectively. They signify that Congress legislatively "overruled" the Court's conclusion in this case by amending the statutory definition of "employee." *See NLRB v. United Ins. Co. of America*, 390 U.S. 254, 256 (1968). This congressional response does not affect the case's significance for administrative law.

1. [Court's footnote:] Section 2(3) of the Act [29 U.S.C. § 152] provides that "The term 'employee' shall include any employee, and shall not be limited to the employees of a particular employer, unless the Act explicitly states otherwise, and shall include any individual whose work has ceased as a consequence of, or in connection with, any current labor dispute or because of any unfair labor practice, and who has not obtained any other regular and substantially equivalent employment, but shall not include any individual employed as an agricultural laborer, or in the domestic service of any family or person at his home, or any individual employed by his parent or spouse."

The proceedings before the National Labor Relations Board were begun with the filing of four petitions for investigation and certification by Los Angeles Newsboys Local Industrial Union No. 75. Hearings were held in a consolidated proceeding after which the Board made findings of fact and concluded that the regular full time newsboys selling each paper were employees within the Act.... It designated appropriate units and ordered elections. At these the union was selected as their representative by majorities of the eligible newsboys. After the union was appropriately certified, the respondents refused to bargain with it. Thereupon [unfair labor practice] proceedings ... were instituted, a hearing was held and respondents were found to have violated [the Act by refusing to bargain with the Union.] ...

The findings of the Board disclose that ... [the newspapers'] papers are distributed to the ultimate consumer through a variety of channels, including independent dealers and newsstands often attached to drug, grocery or confectionery stores, carriers who make home deliveries, and newsboys who sell on the streets of the city and its suburbs. Only the last of these are involved in this case.

The newsboys work under varying terms and conditions. They may be "bootjackers," selling to the general public at places other than established corners, or they may sell at fixed "spots." They may sell only casually or part time, or full time; and they may be employed regularly and continuously or only temporarily. The units which the Board determined to be appropriate are composed of those who sell full time at established spots. Those vendors, misnamed boys, are generally mature men, dependent upon the proceeds of their sales for their sustenance, and frequently supporters of families....

Over-all circulation and distribution of the papers are under the general supervision of circulation managers. But for purposes of street distribution each paper has divided metropolitan Los Angeles into geographic districts. Each district is under the direct and close supervision of a district manager. His function in the mechanics of distribution is to supply the newsboys in his district with papers which he obtains from the publisher and to turn over to the publisher the receipts which he collects from their sales, either directly or with the assistance of "checkmen" or "main spot" boys. The latter, stationed at the important corners or "spots" in the district, are newsboys who, among other things, receive delivery of the papers, redistribute them to other newsboys stationed at less important corners, and collect receipts from their sales....

The newsboys' compensation consists in the difference between the prices at which they sell the papers and the prices they pay for them. The former are fixed by the publishers and the latter are fixed either by the publishers or ... by the district manager.... Not only is the "profit" per paper thus effectively fixed by the publisher, but substantial control of the newsboys' total "take home" can be effected through the ability to designate their sales areas and the power to determine the number of papers allocated to each....

In addition to effectively fixing the compensation, respondents in a variety of ways prescribe, if not the minutiae of daily activities, at least the broad terms and conditions of work. This is accomplished largely through the supervisory efforts of the district managers, who serve as the nexus between the publishers and the newsboys. The district managers assign "spots" or corners to which the newsboys are expected to confine their selling activities.... Hours of work on the spots are determined not simply by the impersonal pressures of the market, but to a real extent by explicit instructions from the district managers. Adherence to the prescribed hours is observed closely by the district managers or other supervisory agents of the publishers. Sanctions, varying in severity from reprimand to dismissal, are visited on the tardy and the delinquent. By similar supervisory controls minimum standards of diligence and good conduct while at work are sought to be enforced.... In this pattern of employment the Board found that the newsboys are an integral part of the publishers' distribution system and circulation organization. And the record discloses that the newsboys and checkmen feel they are employees of the papers; and respondents' supervisory employees, if not respondents themselves, regard them as such.

In addition to questioning the sufficiency of the evidence to sustain these findings, respondents point to a number of other attributes characterizing their relationship with the newsboys[17] and urge that on the entire record the latter cannot be considered their employees. They base this conclusion on the argument that by common law standards the extent of their control and direction of the newsboys' working activities creates no more than an "independent contractor" relationship and that common law standards determine the "employee" relationship under the Act....

I

The principal question is whether the newsboys are "employees." Because Congress did not explicitly define the term, respondents say its meaning must be determined by reference to common law standards. In their view "common law standards" are those the courts have applied in distinguishing between "employees" and "independent contractors" when working out various problems unrelated to the Wagner Act's purposes and provisions.

The argument assumes that there is some simple, uniform and easily applicable test which the courts have used, in dealing with such problems, to determine whether persons doing work for others fall in one class or the other. Unfortunately this is not true.... Few problems in the law have given greater variety of application and conflict in results than the cases arising in the borderland between what is clearly an employer-employee relationship and what is clearly one of independent, entrepreneurial dealing....

... [In light of the conflicting approaches that common-law jurisdictions have taken to distinguishing "employees" from "independent contractors," one option would be] to refer the decision of who are employees to local state law.... Congress obviously did not intend [this approach]....

Both the terms and the purposes of the statute, as well as the legislative history, show that Congress had in mind no such patchwork plan for securing freedom of employees' organization and of collective bargaining. The Wagner Act is federal legislation, administered by a national agency, intended to solve a national problem on a national scale....

II

Whether, given the intended national uniformity, the term "employee" includes such workers as these newsboys must be answered primarily from the history, terms and purposes of the legislation....

-----

17. E.g., that there is either no evidence in the record to show, or the record explicitly negatives, that respondents carry the newsboys on their payrolls, pay "salaries" to them, keep records of their sales or locations, or register them as "employees" with the Social Security Board, or that the newsboys are covered by workmen's compensation insurance or the California Compensation Act. Furthermore, it is urged the record shows that the newsboys all sell newspapers, periodicals and other items not furnished to them by their respective publishers, assume the risk for papers lost, stolen or destroyed, purchase and sell their "spots," hire assistants and relief men and make arrangements among themselves for the sale of competing or leftover papers.

The Act, as its first section states, was designed to avert the "substantial obstructions to the free flow of commerce" which result from "strikes and other forms of industrial strife or unrest" by eliminating the causes of that unrest. It is premised on explicit findings that strikes and industrial strife themselves result in large measure from the refusal of employers to bargain collectively and the inability of individual workers to bargain successfully for improvements in their "wages, hours, or other working conditions" with employers who are "organized in the corporate or other forms of ownership association."...

The mischief at which the Act is aimed and the remedies it offers are not confined exclusively to "employees" within the traditional legal distinctions separating them from "independent contractors." Myriad forms of service relationship, with infinite and subtle variations in the terms of employment, blanket the nation's economy. Some are within this Act, others beyond its coverage. Large numbers will fall clearly on one side or on the other, by whatever test may be applied. But intermediate there will be many, the incidents of whose employment partake in part of the one group, in part of the other, in varying proportions of weight....

Unless the common law tests are to be imported and made exclusively controlling, without regard to the statute's purposes, it cannot be irrelevant that the particular workers in these cases are subject, as a matter of economic fact, to the evils the statute was designed to eradicate and that the remedies it affords are appropriate for preventing them or curing their harmful effects in the special situation.... [W]hen the particular situation of employment combines these characteristics, so that the economic facts of the relation make it more nearly one of employment than of independent business enterprise with respect to the ends sought to be accomplished by the legislation, those characteristics may outweigh technical legal classification for purposes unrelated to the statute's objectives and bring the relation within its protections....

It is not necessary in this case to make a completely definitive limitation around the term "employee." That task has been assigned primarily to the agency created by Congress to administer the Act. Determination of "where all the conditions of the relation require protection" involves inquiries for the Board charged with this duty. Everyday experience in the administration of the statute gives it familiarity with the circumstances and backgrounds of employment relationships in various industries, with the abilities and needs of the workers for self organization and collective action, and with the adaptability of collective bargaining for the peaceful settlement of their disputes with their employers. The experience thus acquired must be brought frequently to bear on the question who is an employee under the Act. Resolving that question, like determining whether unfair labor practices have been committed, "belongs to the usual administrative routine" of the Board. *Gray v. Powell*, 314 U.S. 402, 411

In making that body's determinations as to the facts in these matters conclusive, if supported by evidence, Congress entrusted to it primarily the decision whether the evidence establishes the material facts. Hence in reviewing the Board's ultimate conclusions, it is not the court's function to substitute its own inferences of fact for the Board's, when the latter have support in the record. *Labor Board v. Nevada Copper Corp.*, 316 U.S. 105. Undoubtedly questions of statutory interpretation, especially when arising in the first instance in judicial proceedings, are for the courts to resolve, giving appropriate weight to the judgment of those whose special duty is to administer the questioned statute. *Norwegian Nitrogen Products Co. v. United States*, 288 U.S. 294. But where the question is one of specific application of a broad statutory term in a proceeding in which the agency administering the statute must determine it initially, the reviewing court's function is limited. Like the commissioner's determination under the Longshoremen's & Harbor

Workers' Act, that a man is not a "member of a crew" (*South Chicago Coal & Dock Co. v. Bassett*, 309 U.S. 251) or that he was injured "in the course of employment" (*Parker v. Motor Boat Sales*, 314 U.S. 244) and the Federal Communications Commission's determination that one company is under the "control" of another (*Rochester Telephone Corp. v. United States*, 307 U.S. 125), the Board's determination that specified persons are "employees" under this Act is to be accepted if it has "warrant in the record" and a reasonable basis in law.

In this case the Board found that the designated newsboys work continuously and regularly, rely upon their earnings for the support of themselves and their families, and have their total wages influenced in large measure by the publishers, who dictate their buying and selling prices, fix their markets and control their supply of papers. Their hours of work and their efforts on the job are supervised and to some extent prescribed by the publishers or their agents. Much of their sales equipment and advertising materials is furnished by the publishers with the intention that it be used for the publisher's benefit. Stating that "the primary consideration in the determination of the applicability of the statutory definition is whether effectuation of the declared policy and purposes of the Act comprehend securing to the individual the rights guaranteed and protection afforded by the Act," the Board concluded that the newsboys are employees. The record sustains the Board's findings and there is ample basis in the law for its conclusion.…

The judgments are reversed and the causes are remanded for further proceedings not inconsistent with this opinion. *Reversed.*

Mr. Justice Reed concurs in the result.…

Mr. Justice Roberts [dissenting]: …

I think it plain that newsboys are not "employees" of the respondents within the meaning and intent of the National Labor Relations Act. When Congress, in §2(3), said "The term 'employee' shall include any employee, …" it stated as clearly as language could do it that the provisions of the Act were to extend to those who, as a result of decades of tradition which had become part of the common understanding of our people, bear the named relationship. Clearly also Congress did not delegate to the National Labor Relations Board the function of defining the relationship of employment so as to promote what the Board understood to be the underlying purpose of the statute. The question who is an employee, so as to make the statute applicable to him, is a question of the meaning of the Act and, therefore, is a judicial and not an administrative question.…

c. The Significance of *Hearst*

Hearst is famous because it discusses how responsibility for interpreting an agency's statute should be allocated between a federal court and the federal agency that administers the statute. Roughly speaking, *Hearst* reserves to courts the determination of "macro" questions about the agency legislation—what we might call "pure" questions of law— while leaving to agencies the "micro" issue of how the agency legislation applies in individual situations. *See generally* John H. Reese, *Bursting the* Chevron *Bubble: Clarifying the Scope of Judicial Review in Troubled Times*, 73 Fordham L. Rev. 1103 (2004).

The Court in *Hearst* independently decided a broad legal question about the meaning of the term "employee" in the National Labor Relations Act: namely, whether the term "employee" incorporates the common law distinction between employees and independent contractors. The Court independently determined that the statutory term does not incorporate that common law distinction. Rather, the term's "applicability [to particular workers] is to be determined broadly, in doubtful situations, by underlying economic facts rather than technically and exclusively by previously established legal classifications." 322 U.S. at 129. By independently deciding this pure, macro question of law, the Court established boundaries for the meaning of the term, and in the process constrained the Board's authority to interpret the term when applying it in individual cases.

The Court found it unnecessary, however, "to make a completely definitive limitation around the term 'employee.'" *Id.* 130. Congress created the Board to determine how the term applied to particular workers in "myriad" situations. *Id.* at 126. Deference to the Board's determinations was not only mandated by Congress's assigning to the Board the responsibility for administering the statute. Deference was also warranted because, in carrying out its assigned responsibilities, the Board gained experience that "must be brought frequently to bear on the question who is an employee under the Act," a question the resolution of which "belongs to the usual administrative routine" of the Board. *Id.* As to questions of how the term applied in individual cases, therefore, the Court would uphold the Board's determination if the Board's determination "ha[d] warrant in the record and a reasonable basis in law." *Hearst*, 322 U.S. at 131 (internal quotation marks omitted). In other words, the Board's determination had to be warranted by evidence in the record and had to reflect a reasonable understanding of the law (as that law had been independently interpreted at the macro level by the Court).

The question of how the law applies to a particular set of circumstances — such as the question whether the newsboys working for four Los Angeles newspapers were "employees" under the Act — represents a legal determination, and in that sense is a "question of law." Yet it is not a "pure" a question of law. Instead, it is a mixed question of law and fact (also known as a question of "ultimate fact"). Whatever name you give to the question of the newsboys' status, the Board must interpret its legislation when determining that question, and the Court in *Hearst* promises deference to the agency's interpretation of its statute at this level. That is what makes *Hearst* famous. That is what prompts Justice Roberts' dissent.

The disagreement between the majority and Justice Roberts highlights a pervasive question in administrative law: What is the proper line between the courts (judicial branch) and the agencies (executive branch)? (Where should the knife of policy cut?) The federal courts have long considered it "emphatically the province and duty of the judicial department to say what the law is." *Marbury v. Madison*, 5 U.S. (1 Cranch) 137, 177 (1803). In this role as law declarers, federal courts are first among equals, relative to Congress and the Executive Branch. How is it consistent with this role to let agencies say what the law is as long as what they say is reasonable? Isn't this like letting the fox guard the hen house, as long as the fox flosses between meals? On the other hand, if one recognizes that Congress can delegate to administrative agencies the power to *make* law in legislative rules and formal adjudications that are subject to only limited review, what is wrong with giving agencies some leeway to *interpret* the law that Congress has assigned them to administer? These questions do not have easy answers, which is why they remain pervasive.

The majority in *Hearst* seemed to premise judicial deference to the agency's interpretation on two factors: (1) the nature of the question addressed by the agency's interpretation — involving a micro, law-application issue — and (2) the context in which the interpretation was rendered, an on-the-record adjudication by an agency to which Congress had delegated board authority to make labor policy in light of the realities of labor conditions.

The context was partly a matter of timing: Congress gave the Board the first whack at deciding the issue in its formal adjudication. On the one hand, the Court said, "[Q]uestions of statutory interpretation, especially when arising in the first instance in judicial proceedings, are for the courts to resolve, giving appropriate weight to the judgment of those whose special duty is to administer the questioned statute." *Hearst*, 322 U.S. at 130–131. On the other hand, "where the question is one of specific application of a broad statutory term in a proceeding in which the agency administering the statute must determine it initially, the reviewing court's function is limited." *Id.* at 131. Schematically, Diagram 32-1 depicts the situation in which the Court said deference is appropriate to agency applications of its statute in the exercise of quasi-judicial power:

Diagram 32-1. The Judicial Review Situation in *Hearst*

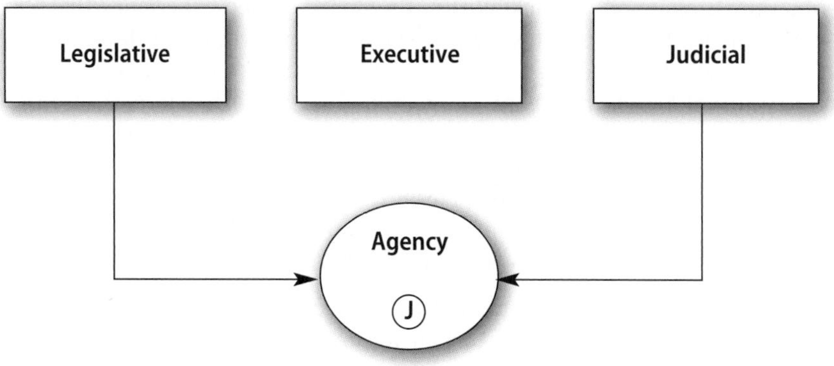

Hearst is still good law, though its precise formulation of the applicable standard of judicial review is generally cited only in cases involving formal adjudications by the National Labor Relations Board. *E.g.*, *Bath Marine Draftsmen's Ass'n v. Nat'l Labor Relations Bd.*, 475 F.3d 14, 28 (1st Cir. 2007). *Hearst* also has historical importance in establishing, more broadly, that courts should sometimes defer to a federal agency's statutory interpretation. Today, however, the Court has developed a different framework for analyzing agency interpretations of the statutes that they administer. The framework goes by somewhat different names. We will call it the "*Chevron/Mead* doctrine" after the principal cases establishing it. *Chevron U. S. A. Inc. v. Natural Resources Defense Council, Inc.*, 467 U.S. 837 (1984); *United States v. Mead Corp.*, 533 U.S. 218 (2001).

Overall, the *Chevron/Mead* doctrine *expands* the circumstances under which courts must defer to an agency's interpretation of the statute it administers. Under the *Chevron/Mead* doctrine, federal agencies continue to get deference when they *apply* broad terms in the agency legislation to particular situations in formal adjudications. Agencies also get deference in other situations, the most important of which is when agencies interpret the agency legislation in issuing a legislative rule through informal or formal rulemaking. Even so, *Hearst* is a direct ancestor of the *Chevron/Mead* and is studied in most or all law school courses on administrative law in the United States. That is why, although newsboys and newsgirls have largely disappeared from city streets, they live on, evoking warm feelings in the hearts of modern administrative lawyers who, like you, have studied the *Hearst* case. Now you, too, have "read all about it"!

d. Background on the *Skidmore* Case

The next case is *Skidmore v. Swift & Co.*, 323 U.S. 134 (1944). *Skidmore* involved interpretation of the Fair Labor Standards Act of 1938 (FLSA or Act). In 1944, as now, the

Act generally required employers to pay employees overtime pay (150% of their regular pay) when they worked more than 40 hours in a week. *See* 29 U.S.C. § 207(a)(1) (2012) (current statute). The Act also authorized employees to sue employers for violations of the Act. In those private lawsuits, employees could recover the wages they were due under the Act, plus liquidated damages and attorney's fees. Besides authorizing private actions, the Act authorized a federal official—the Administrator of the Wage and Hour Division of the U.S. Department of Labor—to sue employers for injunctions against violations of the Act. Thus, the Act was enforced through a combination of private lawsuits by employees and suits for injunctions by a federal official.

Although the Administrator had authority to enforce the Act by filing lawsuits, the Administrator had very limited power to promulgate legislative rules implementing the Act. The Administrator also lacked power to conduct formal adjudications against employers suspected of violating the Act. Instead, the Act left to the courts the task of deciding cases presenting questions of statutory interpretation. Lacking quasi-legislative or quasi-judicial power, the Administrator developed enforcement policy for the Fair Labor Standards Act as may any executive officer responsible for administering a statute: The Administrator announced those policies in interpretative bulletins and informal rulings that served to guide employers and employees. The Administrator also could advocate in court for an interpretation of the Act when suing employers directly or, as in *Skidmore*, when appearing as an *amicus curiae*. In sum, the Administrator interpreted the FLSA in exercising executive-type powers.

The Court in *Skidmore* addresses the weight that federal courts should give agency interpretations rendered in the exercise of executive power. *Skidmore* is good law today. *See, e.g., Kasten v. Saint-Gobain Performance Plastics Corp.*, 131 S.Ct. 1325, 1335 (2011).

e. The *Skidmore* Opinion

Please read *Skidmore* with these questions in mind:

1. What question of statutory interpretation does this case present?

2. What does the Court in this case and the companion case mentioned in this opinion (called *Armour*) decide about the meaning of the statute, as it bears on this case?

3. What does the Court say about the Administrator's interpretation of the Act?

Skidmore v. Swift & Co.

323 U.S. 134 (1944)

MR. JUSTICE JACKSON delivered the opinion of the Court.

Seven employees of the Swift and Company packing plant at Fort Worth, Texas, brought an action under the Fair Labor Standards Act to recover overtime, liquidated damages, and attorneys' fees, totalling approximately $77,000. The District Court rendered judgment denying this claim wholly, and the Circuit Court of Appeals for the Fifth Circuit affirmed.

It is not denied that the daytime employment of these persons was working time within the Act. Two were engaged in general fire-hall duties and maintenance of fire-fighting equipment of the Swift plant. The others operated elevators or acted as relief men in fire duties. They worked from 7:00 a.m. to 3:30 p.m., with a half-hour lunch period, five days a week. They were paid weekly salaries.

Under their oral agreement of employment, however, petitioners undertook to stay in the fire hall on the Company premises, or within hailing distance, three and a half to four nights a week. This involved no task except to answer alarms, either because of fire or because the sprinkler was set off for some other reason.... For each alarm answered the employees were paid in addition to their fixed compensation an agreed amount, fifty cents at first, and later sixty-four cents. The Company provided a brick fire hall equipped with steam heat and air-conditioned rooms. It provided sleeping quarters, a pool table, a domino table, and a radio. The men used their time in sleep or amusement as they saw fit, except that they were required to stay in or close by the fire hall and be ready to respond to alarms.... The trial court ... said ... as a "conclusion of law" that "the time plaintiffs spent in the fire hall subject to call to answer fire alarms does not constitute hours worked, for which overtime compensation is due them under the Fair Labor Standards Act, as interpreted by the Administrator and the Courts," and in its opinion observed, "of course we know pursuing such pleasurable occupations or performing such personal chores, does not constitute work." The Circuit Court of Appeals affirmed.

For reasons set forth in the *Armour* case decided herewith [*Armour & Co. v. Wantock*, 323 U.S. 126 (1944)], we hold that no principle of law found either in the statute or in Court decisions precludes waiting time from also being working time. We have not attempted to, and we cannot, lay down a legal formula to resolve cases so varied in their facts as are the many situations in which employment involves waiting time. Whether in a concrete case such time falls within or without the Act is a question of fact to be resolved by appropriate findings of the trial court. This involves scrutiny and construction of the agreements between the particular parties, appraisal of their practical construction of the working agreement by conduct, consideration of the nature of the service, and its relation to the waiting time, and all of the surrounding circumstances. Facts may show that the employee was engaged to wait, or they may show that he waited to be engaged. His compensation may cover both waiting and task, or only performance of the task itself. Living quarters may in some situations be furnished as a facility of the task and in another as a part of its compensation. The law does not impose an arrangement upon the parties. It imposes upon the courts the task of finding what the arrangement was.

We do not minimize the difficulty of such an inquiry where the arrangements of the parties have not contemplated the problem posed by the statute. But it does not differ in nature or in the standards to guide judgment from that which frequently confronts courts where they must find retrospectively the effect of contracts as to matters which the parties failed to anticipate or explicitly to provide for.

Congress did not utilize the services of an administrative agency to find facts and to determine in the first instance whether particular cases fall within or without the Act. Instead, it put this responsibility on the courts. But it did create the office of Administrator, impose upon him a variety of duties, endow him with powers to inform himself of conditions in industries and employments subject to the Act, and put on him the duties of bringing injunction actions to restrain violations. Pursuit of his duties has accumulated a considerable experience in the problems of ascertaining working time in employments involving periods of inactivity and a knowledge of the customs prevailing in reference to their solution. From these he is obliged to reach conclusions as to conduct without the law, so that he should seek injunctions to stop it, and that within the law, so that he has no call to interfere. He has set forth his views of the application of the Act under different circumstances in an interpretative bulletin and in informal rulings. They provide a practical guide to employers and employees as to how the office representing the public interest in its enforcement will seek to apply it. Wage and Hour Division, Interpretative Bulletin No. 13.

The Administrator thinks the problems presented by inactive duty require a flexible solution, rather than the all-in or all-out rules respectively urged by the parties in this case, and his Bulletin endeavors to suggest standards and examples to guide in particular situations. In some occupations, it says, periods of inactivity are not properly counted as working time even though the employee is subject to call. Examples are an operator of a small telephone exchange where the switchboard is in her home and she ordinarily gets several hours of uninterrupted sleep each night; or a pumper of a stripper well or watchman of a lumber camp during the off season, who may be on duty twenty-four hours a day but ordinarily "has a normal night's sleep, has ample time in which to eat his meals, and has a certain amount of time for relaxation and entirely private pursuits." Exclusion of all such hours the Administrator thinks may be justified. In general, the answer depends "upon the degree to which the employee is free to engage in personal activities during periods of idleness when he is subject to call and the number of consecutive hours that the employee is subject to call without being required to perform active work." "Hours worked are not limited to the time spent in active labor but include time given by the employee to the employer...."

The facts of this case do not fall within any of the specific examples given, but the conclusion of the Administrator, as expressed in the brief amicus curiae, is that the general tests which he has suggested point to the exclusion of sleeping and eating time of these employees from the workweek and the inclusion of all other on-call time ...

There is no statutory provision as to what, if any, deference courts should pay to the Administrator's conclusions. And, while we have given them notice, we have had no occasion to try to prescribe their influence. The rulings of this Administrator are not reached as a result of hearing adversary proceedings in which he finds facts from evidence and reaches conclusions of law from findings of fact. They are not, of course, conclusive, even in the cases with which they directly deal, much less in those to which they apply only by analogy. They do not constitute an interpretation of the Act or a standard for judging factual situations which binds a district court's processes, as an authoritative pronouncement of a higher court might do. But the Administrator's policies are made in pursuance of official duty, based upon more specialized experience and broader investigations and information than is likely to come to a judge in a particular case. They do determine the policy which will guide applications for enforcement by injunction on behalf of the Government. Good administration of the Act and good judicial administration alike require that the standards of public enforcement and those for determining private rights shall be at variance only where justified by very good reasons. The fact that the Administrator's policies and standards are not reached by trial in adversary form does not mean that they are not entitled to respect. This Court has long given considerable and in some cases decisive weight to Treasury Decisions and to interpretative regulations of the Treasury and of other bodies that were not of adversary origin.

We consider that the rulings, interpretations and opinions of the Administrator under this Act, while not controlling upon the courts by reason of their authority, do constitute a body of experience and informed judgment to which courts and litigants may properly resort for guidance. The weight of such a judgment in a particular case will depend upon the thoroughness evident in its consideration, the validity of its reasoning, its consistency with earlier and later pronouncements, and all those factors which give it power to persuade, if lacking power to control.

... [I]n this case, although the District Court referred to the Administrator's Bulletin, its evaluation and inquiry were apparently restricted by its notion that waiting time may not be work, an understanding of the law which we hold to be erroneous. Accordingly, the judgment is reversed and the cause remanded for further proceedings consistent herewith. *Reversed.*

f. The Significance of *Skidmore*

When we introduced the executive-type powers of agencies at the beginning of this book, we explained that executive powers include not only the power to *interpret* the law that the executive agency or official is responsible for administering but also the power to *advise* the public of that interpretation. The agency may advise the public on a wholesale basis, by publishing interpretative rules, or on a retail basis, by providing advice to individuals. In *Skidmore*, the Administrator did both. The Administrator published Interpretive Bulletin No. 13 with general guidance for determining whether "waiting time" was "work time." *See Skidmore*, 323 U.S. at 138 (citing Bulletin). In addition, the Administrator appeared as an amicus in the *Skidmore* case to advise the parties and the Court of the Administrator's interpretation of the FLSA as applied to Swift's employees. In both roles, the Administrator was exercising an executive power.

The Court reviewed the Administrator's interpretation indirectly, in litigation that did not challenge the Administrator's interpretation and that did not include the Administrator as a party. In other situations, courts review agency interpretations directly: typically in lawsuits by or actions against the agency, in which the court must review an agency action based on the agency's interpretation. Whether the court reviews an agency interpretation directly or indirectly, *Skidmore* addresses the weight or "respect" that courts should give statutory interpretations rendered by federal agencies or officials in the exercise of their executive power. The situation is depicted in Diagram 32-2.

Diagram 32-2. The Judicial Review Situation in *Skidmore*

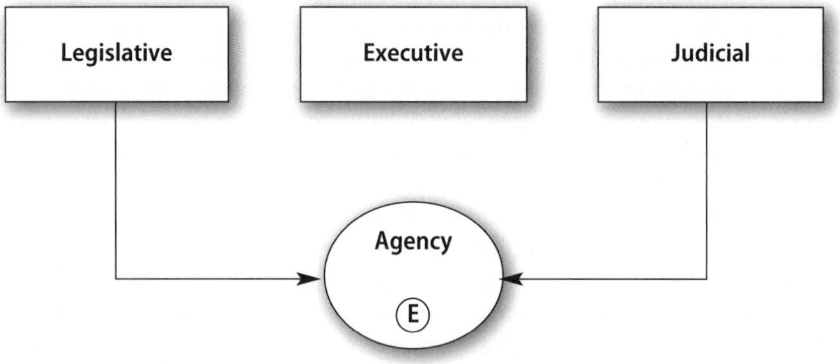

There is a difference between, on the one hand, the respect that the Court gave the Administrator's statutory interpretation in *Skidmore* and, on the other hand, the deference that the Court gave the National Labor Relations Board's statutory interpretation in *Hearst*. The difference stems from the different contexts in which the Administrator and Board rendered their interpretations. As the Court said in *Hearst*:

> Undoubtedly questions of statutory interpretation, especially when arising in the first instance in judicial proceedings, are for the courts to resolve, giving appropriate weight to the judgment of those whose special duty is to administer the questioned statute.... But where the question is one of specific application of a broad statutory term in a proceeding in which the agency administering the statute must determine it initially, the reviewing court's function is limited.... [T]he Board's determination that specified persons are "employees" under this Act is to be accepted if it has "warrant in the record" and a reasonable basis in law.

322 U.S. at 860–861. The first sentence of this passage describes the situation in *Skidmore*. The issue of whether Swift's employees were on "working time" when they spent evenings at the company's fire hall arose initially when those employees sued Swift in federal court. In that setting, the agency's view was entitled to "appropriate weight," depending on the considerations mentioned in *Skidmore*. The second and third sentences describe a situation in which the agency is exercising quasi-judicial power to make formal findings of fact on a formal record. These different contexts continue to influence the amount of deference that a court owes to an agency interpretation, as the Court has held in the modern leading case of *United States v. Mead*, 533 U.S. 218 (2001) (reproduced later in this chapter).

Reflecting the different contexts in which the agencies rendered their interpretations in *Skidmore* and *Hearst*, a court under *Skidmore* respects the agency's statutory interpretation if there are good reasons to do so. But the court ultimately makes its own decision about what the statute means. The court decides what the "right" answer is to the question of statutory interpretation. Under *Hearst*, in contrast, when a court reviews an agency's interpretation made in the course of taking action that has the force of law, as occurs in a formal adjudication under the National Labor Relations Act, the court simply determines whether the interpretation is one that is within the scope of the *agency's* interpretative authority—in other words, whether the interpretation has a "reasonable basis in law." In this effort, the court is not asking whether the agency's interpretation is right but, rather, whether it is reasonable.

In neither *Hearst* nor *Skidmore* did the Court abandon its duty to "say what the law is." In *Hearst*, the Court independently decided the "pure" question of law—namely whether the term "employee" in the National Labor Relations Act incorporated the common law distinction between employees and independent contractors. In *Skidmore*—or, to be precise, in the companion case of *Armour*—the Court also independently determined, as a pure question of law, that "no principle of law found either in the [FLSA] or in Court decisions [interpreting the FLSA categorically] precludes waiting time from also being working time." *Skidmore*, 323 U.S. at 137. *See generally* Nathaniel L. Nathanson, *Administrative Discretion in the Interpretation of Statutes*, 3 Vand. L. Rev. 470, 475–476, 481 (1950).

The Court's resolution of macro issues of law, even in situations (such as *Hearst*) where Congress has given an agency power to apply the law in particularized settings, reflects that Congress seldom gives agencies authority to determine such macro issues. Instead, Congress more often leaves to agencies more micro issues such as the case-specific question whether particular workers are employees and the highly technical, interstitial question of statutory interpretation posed in the leading modern case of *Chevron*. *See generally* John H. Reese, *Bursting the* Chevron *Bubble: Clarifying the Scope of Judicial Review in Troubled Times*, 73 Fordham L. Rev. 1103 (2004).

2. Modern Cases

Now we examine the two leading modern cases on how federal courts review a federal agency's interpretation of a statute that the agency administers.

a. Background on the *Chevron* Case

The next case is *Chevron U. S. A. Inc. v. Natural Resources Defense Council, Inc.*, 467 U.S. 837 (1984). *Chevron* is a famous administrative law case. To understand *Chevron*, it helps to understand the intricate regulatory scheme in which the case arose. To understand that scheme, some background may help in which we introduce the relevant laws and acronyms.

Chevron concerned federal legislation: The Clean Air Act Amendments of 1970, better known as the Clean Air Act. The Act sought to reduce air pollution through regulation by the U.S. Environmental Protection Agency (EPA) in coordination with the States.

Section 109 of the Act authorized the EPA to establish National Ambient Air Quality Standards (**NAAQSs**) for certain air pollutants. As their name suggested, NAAQSs were nationwide air quality standards; they weren't limits on specific polluters.

Section 110 of the Act required each State to submit for EPA approval a state implementation plan (**SIP**) that would enable the State to meet the NAAQSs by 1975. States had to include in their SIPs specific emission limits for *existing* sources of pollution (coal-fired power plants, etc.). Thus, States had the job of translating the NAAQSs into source-specific emission limits for existing sources.

Section 111 of the Act required the EPA (not the States) to prescribe limits on the amount of air pollution that various categories of *new* sources of pollution (e.g., steel mills built after a certain date) could emit. These limits for new sources were known as New Source Performance Standards (**NSPSs**).

In many parts of the country, particularly the most industrialized States, the NAAQSs were not achieved by 1975, as had been required in the 1970 Act. Partly in response to this failure, Congress enacted the Clean Air Act Amendments of 1977 (**1977 Amendments**).

The *Chevron* case concerns a provision in the 1977 Amendments addressed to those parts of the country that had not achieved the NAAQSs, which were known as **nonattainment areas**. (Areas that had achieved the NAAQSs, or where air quality data was not sufficient to determine achievement, were known as "**PSD areas**," because they were subject to statutory provisions requiring the "Prevention of Significant Deterioration" in air quality.)

As discussed in the *Chevron* opinion, § 172(b)(6) of the 1977 Amendments required each new SIP from a nonattainment State to require permits for the construction and operation of new or modified "stationary sources." The SIPs had to enforce stringent requirements for these permits, not least of which was that the proposed source would comply with the "lowest achievable emission rate."

Significantly, the 1977 Amendments did not define the term "stationary sourc[e]" as used in § 172(b)(6). The EPA issued a legislative rule addressing the term in October 1981. The EPA rule allowed States in nonattainment areas to adopt, in their new SIPs, what the Court in *Chevron* calls "a plantwide definition" of the term, reflecting what the Court calls "the bubble concept." At issue in *Chevron* is how a federal court should review the EPA's interpretation of § 172(b)(6) of the 1977 Amendments as allowing a "plantwide definition" under "the bubble concept." This interpretation, to repeat, was expressed in the EPA's October 1981 legislative rule prescribing requirements for SIPs from nonattainment States.

In the excerpt of *Chevron* below, we indicate by bracketed notations where the opinion in *Chevron* cites prior Court precedent. We do this because the opinion is unusual for the amount of precedent that it cites. The Court apparently considered its opinion firmly rooted in precedent, even though lower courts and academic commentators have treated *Chevron* as groundbreaking. *See* Thomas W. Merrill, *The Story of* Chevron: *The Making of an Accidental Landmark*, in Administrative Law Stories 402, 412–420 (Peter L. Strauss ed. 2005).

b. The *Chevron* Opinion

Please read *Chevron* with these questions in mind:

1. What two-step analysis does the Court say federal courts should use when reviewing an agency's construction of a statute that it administers?

2. What is the rationale for that analysis?

3. How does the Court apply that analysis to the agency interpretation at issue in this case?

Chevron U.S.A. Inc. v. Natural Resources Defense Council, Inc.
467 U.S. 837 (1984)

JUSTICE STEVENS delivered the opinion of the Court.

In the Clean Air Act Amendments of 1977, Congress enacted certain requirements applicable to States that had not achieved the national air quality standards established by the Environmental Protection Agency (EPA) pursuant to earlier legislation. The amended Clean Air Act required these "nonattainment" States to establish a permit program regulating "new or modified major stationary sources" of air pollution. Generally, a permit may not be issued for a new or modified major stationary source unless several stringent conditions are met.[1] The EPA regulation promulgated to implement this permit requirement allows a State to adopt a plantwide definition of the term "stationary source."[2] Under this definition, an existing plant that contains several pollution emitting devices may install or modify one piece of equipment without meeting the permit conditions if the alteration will not increase the total emissions from the plant. The question presented by these cases is whether EPA's decision to allow States to treat all of the pollution emitting devices within the same industrial grouping as though they were encased within a single "bubble" is based on a reasonable construction of the statutory term "stationary source."

I

The EPA regulations containing the plantwide definition of the term stationary source were promulgated on October 14, 1981. Respondents [Chevron U.S.A. Inc. and other companies] filed a timely petition for review in the United States Court of Appeals for the District of Columbia Circuit pursuant to 42 U.S.C. §7607(b)(1). The Court of

---

1. Section 172(b)(6), 42 U.S.C. §7502(b)(6), provides:
   "The plan provisions required by subsection (a) shall— ...
   "(6) require permits for the construction and operation of new or modified major stationary sources in accordance with section 173 (relating to permit requirements)." 91 Stat. 747.
2. "(i) 'Stationary source' means any building, structure, facility, or installation which emits or may emit any air pollutant subject to regulation under the Act.
   "(ii) 'Building, structure, facility, or installation' means all of the pollutant-emitting activities which belong to the same industrial grouping, are located on one or more contiguous or adjacent properties, and are under the control of the same person (or persons under common control) except the activities of any vessel." 40 CFR §§51.18(j)(1)(i) and (ii) (1983).

Appeals set aside the regulations.... [In addition to Chevron, the EPA sought and was granted Supreme Court review of the court of appeals decision setting aside the regulations.]

The basic legal error of the Court of Appeals was to adopt a static judicial definition of the term "stationary source" when it had decided that Congress itself had not commanded that definition....

II

When a court reviews an agency's construction of the statute which it administers, it is confronted with two questions. First, always, is the question whether Congress has directly spoken to the precise question at issue. If the intent of Congress is clear, that is the end of the matter; for the court, as well as the agency, must give effect to the unambiguously expressed intent of Congress.[9] If, however, the court determines Congress has not directly addressed the precise question at issue, the court does not simply impose its own construction on the statute,[10] as would be necessary in the absence of an administrative interpretation. Rather, if the statute is silent or ambiguous with respect to the specific issue, the question for the court is whether the agency's answer is based on a permissible construction of the statute.[11]

"The power of an administrative agency to administer a congressionally created ... program necessarily requires the formulation of policy and the making of rules to fill any gap left, implicitly or explicitly, by Congress." *Morton v. Ruiz*, 415 U.S. 199, 231 (1974). If Congress has explicitly left a gap for the agency to fill, there is an express delegation of authority to the agency to elucidate a specific provision of the statute by regulation. Such legislative regulations are given controlling weight unless they are arbitrary, capricious, or manifestly contrary to the statute. [Footnote citing earlier Court decisions omitted.] Sometimes the legislative delegation to an agency on a particular question is implicit rather than explicit. In such a case, a court may not substitute its own construction of a statutory provision for a reasonable interpretation made by the administrator of an agency. [Footnote citing earlier Court decisions is omitted.]

We have long recognized that considerable weight should be accorded to an executive department's construction of a statutory scheme it is entrusted to administer [Footnote citing earlier Court decisions is omitted.], and the principle of deference to administrative interpretations

> "has been consistently followed by this Court whenever decision as to the meaning or reach of a statute has involved reconciling conflicting policies, and a full understanding of the force of the statutory policy in the given situation has depended upon more than ordinary knowledge respecting the matters subjected to agency regulations. See, *e.g.*, ... *Labor Board v. Hearst Publications, Inc.*, 322 U.S. 111; ... *Securities & Exchange Comm'n v. Chenery Corp.*, 332 U.S. 194....

---

9. The judiciary is the final authority on issues of statutory construction and must reject administrative constructions which are contrary to clear congressional intent. See, e.g., [Citations to nine prior Court decisions are omitted.]. If a court, employing traditional tools of statutory construction, ascertains that Congress had an intention on the precise question at issue, that intention is the law and must be given effect.

10. See generally, R. Pound, The Spirit of the Common Law 174–175 (1921).

11. The court need not conclude that the agency construction was the only one it permissibly could have adopted to uphold the construction, or even the reading the court would have reached if the question initially had arisen in a judicial proceeding. [Citations to six prior Court decisions are omitted.]

... If this choice represents a reasonable accommodation of conflicting policies that were committed to the agency's care by the statute, we should not disturb it unless it appears from the statute or its legislative history that the accommodation is not one that Congress would have sanctioned." *United States v. Shimer*, 367 U.S. 374, 382, 383 (1961).

In light of these well-settled principles it is clear that the Court of Appeals misconceived the nature of its role in reviewing the regulations at issue. Once it determined, after its own examination of the legislation, that Congress did not actually have an intent regarding the applicability of the bubble concept to the permit program, the question before it was not whether in its view the concept is "inappropriate" in the general context of a program designed to improve air quality, but whether the Administrator's view that it is appropriate in the context of this particular program is a reasonable one. Based on the examination of the legislation and its history which follows, we agree with the Court of Appeals that Congress did not have a specific intention on the applicability of the bubble concept in these cases, and conclude that the EPA's use of that concept here is a reasonable policy choice for the agency to make.

III

... The Clean Air Amendments of 1970 ... sharply increased federal authority and responsibility in the continuing effort to combat air pollution, ... but continued to assign "primary responsibility for assuring air quality" to the several States, 84 Stat. 1678. Section 109 of the 1970 Amendments directed the EPA to promulgate National Ambient Air Quality Standards (NAAQS's) and § 110 directed the States to develop plans (SIP's) to implement the standards within specified deadlines. In addition, § 111 provided that major new sources of pollution would be required to conform to technology-based performance standards; the EPA was directed to publish a list of categories of sources of pollution and to establish new source performance standards (NSPS) for each. Section 111(e) prohibited the operation of any new source in violation of a performance standard....

Nonattainment

The 1970 legislation provided for the attainment of primary NAAQS's by 1975. In many areas of the country, particularly the most industrialized States, the statutory goals were not attained....

IV

The Clean Air Act Amendments of 1977 are a lengthy, detailed, technical, complex, and comprehensive response to a major social issue. A small portion of the statute—91 Stat. 745–751 (Part D of Title I of the amended Act, 42 U.S.C. §§ 7501–7508)—expressly deals with nonattainment areas. The focal point of this controversy is one phrase in that portion of the Amendments.

Basically, the statute required each State in a nonattainment area to prepare and obtain approval of a new SIP by July 1, 1979.... The deadline for attainment of the primary NAAQS's was extended..., but the SIP's were required to contain a number of provisions designed to achieve the goals as expeditiously as possible.

Most significantly for our purposes, the statute provided that each plan shall:

"(6) require permits for the construction and operation of new or modified major stationary sources in accordance with section 173...." Id., at 747.

Before issuing a permit, § 173 requires the state agency to determine that (1) there will be sufficient emissions reductions in the region to offset the emissions from the new source and also to allow for reasonable further progress toward attainment, or that the increased emissions will not exceed an allowance for growth established pursuant to § 172(b)(5); (2) the applicant must certify that his other sources in the State are in compliance with the SIP, (3) the agency must determine that the applicable SIP is otherwise being implemented, and (4) the proposed source complies with the lowest achievable emission rate (LAER).

The 1977 Amendments contain no specific reference to the "bubble concept." Nor do they contain a specific definition of the term "stationary source" ...

V

The legislative history of the portion of the 1977 Amendments dealing with nonattainment areas does not contain any specific comment on the "bubble concept" or the question whether a plantwide definition of a stationary source is permissible under the permit program....

VI

... [P]rior to the 1977 Amendments, the EPA had adhered to a plantwide definition of the term "source" under a NSPS program. After adoption of the 1977 Amendments, proposals for a plantwide definition were considered in at least three formal proceedings. [In those proceedings, EPA allowed States to use a plantwide definition in some circumstances.] ...

In August 1980, ... the EPA adopted a regulation that ... adopted a dual definition of "source" for nonattainment areas that required a permit whenever a change in either the entire plant, or one of its components, would result in a significant increase in emissions even if the increase was completely offset by reductions elsewhere in the plant. The EPA expressed the opinion that this interpretation was "more consistent with congressional intent" than the plantwide definition because it "would bring in more sources or modifications for review," 45 Fed. Reg. 52697 (1980), but its primary legal analysis was predicated on ... two Court of Appeals decisions.

In 1981 a new administration took office and initiated a "Government wide reexamination of regulatory burdens and complexities." 46 Fed. Reg. 16281. In the context of that review, the EPA ... concluded that the term should be given the same definition in both nonattainment areas and PSD areas.

In explaining its conclusion, the EPA first noted that the definitional issue was not squarely addressed in either the statute or its legislative history and therefore that the issue involved an agency "judgment as how to best carry out the Act." *Ibid.* It then set forth several reasons for concluding that the plantwide definition was more appropriate. It pointed out that the dual definition "can act as a disincentive to new investment and modernization by discouraging modifications to existing facilities" and "can actually retard progress in air pollution control by discouraging replacement of older, dirtier processes or pieces of equipment with new, cleaner ones." *Ibid.* Moreover, the new definition "would simplify EPA's rules by using the same definition of 'source' for PSD, nonattainment new source review and the construction moratorium. This reduces confusion and inconsistency." *Ibid.* Finally, the agency explained that additional requirements that remained in place would accomplish the fundamental purposes of achieving attainment with NAAQS's as expeditiously as possible. These conclusions were expressed in a proposed rulemaking in August 1981 that was formally promulgated in October....

VII

In this Court respondents expressly reject the basic rationale of the Court of Appeals' decision. That court viewed the statutory definition of the term "source" as sufficiently flexible to cover either a plantwide definition, a narrower definition covering each unit within a plant, or a dual definition that could apply to both the entire "bubble" and its components.... Respondents place a fundamentally different construction on the statute. They contend that the text of the Act requires the EPA to use a dual definition—if either a component of a plant, or the plant as a whole, emits over 100 tons of pollutant, it is a major stationary source. They thus contend that the ... 1981 rules which apply to nonattainment areas ... violate the statute.

Statutory Language

The definition of the term "stationary source" in § 111(a)(3) refers to "any building, structure, facility, or installation" which emits air pollution.... This definition is applicable only to the NSPS program by the express terms of the statute; the text of the statute does not make this definition applicable to the permit program. Petitioners therefore maintain that there is no statutory language even relevant to ascertaining the meaning of stationary source in the permit program aside from § 302(j), which defines the term "major stationary source." ... We disagree with petitioners on this point.

The definition in § 302(j) tells us what the word "major" means—a source must emit at least 100 tons of pollution to qualify—but it sheds virtually no light on the meaning of the term "stationary source." It does equate a source with a facility—a "major emitting facility" and a "major stationary source" are synonymous under § 302(j). The ordinary meaning of the term "facility" is some collection of integrated elements which has been designed and constructed to achieve some purpose. Moreover, it is certainly no affront to common English usage to take a reference to a major facility or a major source to connote an entire plant as opposed to its constituent parts. Basically, however, the language of § 302(j) simply does not compel any given interpretation of the term "source...."

We are not persuaded that parsing of general terms in the text of the statute will reveal an actual intent of Congress....

Legislative History

In addition, respondents argue that the legislative history and policies of the Act foreclose the plantwide definition, and that the EPA's interpretation is not entitled to deference because it represents a sharp break with prior interpretations of the Act.

... We find that the legislative history as a whole is silent on the precise issue before us. It is, however, consistent with the view that the EPA should have broad discretion in implementing the policies of the 1977 Amendments.

More importantly, that history plainly identifies the policy concerns that motivated the enactment; the plantwide definition is fully consistent with one of those concerns—the allowance of reasonable economic growth—and, whether or not we believe it most effectively implements the other, we must recognize that the EPA has advanced a reasonable explanation for its conclusion that the regulations serve the environmental objectives as well. Indeed, its reasoning is supported by the public record developed in the rulemaking process, as well as by certain private studies.

Our review of the EPA's varying interpretations of the word "source"—both before and after the 1977 Amendments—convinces us that the agency primarily responsible for administering this important legislation has consistently interpreted it flexibly—not in a sterile textual vacuum, but in the context of implementing policy decisions in a technical and complex arena. The fact that the agency has from time to time changed its interpretation of the term "source" does not, as respondents argue, lead us to conclude that no deference should be accorded the agency's interpretation of the statute. An initial agency interpretation is not instantly carved in stone. On the contrary, the agency, to engage in informed rule-making, must consider varying interpretations and the wisdom of its policy on a continuing basis. Moreover, the fact that the agency has adopted different definitions in different contexts adds force to the argument that the definition itself is flexible, particularly since Congress has never indicated any disapproval of a flexible reading of the statute....

Policy

The arguments over policy that are advanced in the parties' briefs create the impression that respondents are now waging in a judicial forum a specific policy battle which they ultimately lost in the agency and in the 32 jurisdictions opting for the bubble concept, but one which was never waged in the Congress. Such policy arguments are more properly addressed to legislators or administrators, not to judges.

In these cases the Administrator's interpretation represents a reasonable accommodation of manifestly competing interests and is entitled to deference: the regulatory scheme is technical and complex, the agency considered the matter in a detailed and reasoned fashion, and the decision involves reconciling conflicting policies. Congress intended to accommodate both interests, but did not do so itself on the level of specificity presented by these cases. Perhaps that body consciously desired the Administrator to strike the balance at this level, thinking that those with great expertise and charged with responsibility for administering the provision would be in a better position to do so; perhaps it simply did not consider the question at this level; and perhaps Congress was unable to forge a coalition on either side of the question, and those on each side decided to take their chances with the scheme devised by the agency. For judicial purposes, it matters not which of these things occurred.

Judges are not experts in the field, and are not part of either political branch of the Government. Courts must, in some cases, reconcile competing political interests, but not on the basis of the judges' personal policy preferences. In contrast, an agency to which Congress has delegated policy making responsibilities may, within the limits of that delegation, properly rely upon the incumbent administration's views of wise policy to inform its judgments. While agencies are not directly accountable to the people, the Chief Executive is, and it is entirely appropriate for this political branch of the Government to make such policy choices—resolving the competing interests which Congress itself either inadvertently did not resolve, or intentionally left to be resolved by the agency charged with the administration of the statute in light of everyday realities.

When a challenge to an agency construction of a statutory provision, fairly conceptualized, really centers on the wisdom of the agency's policy, rather than whether it is a reasonable choice within a "gap" left open by Congress, the challenge must fail. In such a case, federal judges—who have no constituency—have a duty to respect legitimate policy choices made by those who do. The responsibilities for assessing the wisdom of such policy choices and resolving the struggle between competing views of the public interest are not judicial ones: "Our Constitution vests such responsibilities in the political branches." *TVA v. Hill*, 437 U.S. 153, 195 (1978).

We hold that the EPA's definition of the term "source" is a permissible construction of the statute which seeks to accommodate progress in reducing air pollution with economic growth. "The Regulations which the Administrator has adopted provide what the agency could allowably view as ... [an] effective reconciliation of these twofold ends ..." *United*

States v. Shimer, 367 U.S., at 383.

The judgment of the Court of Appeals is reversed.

JUSTICE MARSHALL and JUSTICE REHNQUIST took no part in the consideration or decision of these cases.

JUSTICE O'CONNOR took no part in the decision of these cases.

Exercise: *Chevron* Revisited

1. The purpose of this question is to help you apply the *Chevron* analysis in a slightly different situation. Suppose that, instead of authorizing the bubble concept, EPA had adopted the "dual definition" for which the respondents in *Chevron* argued. Would that approach be upheld under *Chevron* analysis, as far as you can tell from the material included in the excerpt above?

2. The purpose of this question is to introduce the relationship among law, policy, and politics under *Chevron*. The Court says that "an agency to which Congress has delegated policy making responsibilities may, within the limits of that delegation, properly rely upon the incumbent administration's view of wise policy, to inform its judgment." *Chevron,* 467 U.S. at 865. The Court almost certainly made this statement with regard for the context in which EPA adopted the rule authorizing the bubble concept: EPA acted in the context of a "Government-wide reexamination of regulatory burdens and complexities," which was initiated by "a new administration" — under President Ronald Reagan — taking office in 1981, replacing the administration of President Jimmy Carter. *Id.* at 857–858. According to the Court, can electoral politics play a role in agency activity? If so, to what extent?

   This question has practical importance for administrative lawyers because politics *do* influence many agency actions, and so the question becomes to what extent political influence provides a ground for a successful judicial challenge to agency action.

---

c. The Significance of *Chevron*

Chevron describes a two-step analysis for federal court review of a federal agency's "construction of the statute which it administers." 467 U.S. at 842. When the *Chevron* "two-step" applies, the result, roughly speaking, is that a court will uphold an agency's reasonable interpretation of its statute. This result reflects what is called "*Chevron* deference."

The *Chevron* two-step analysis does not apply to *every* federal agency interpretation of the statute that the agency administers. Some such interpretations do not qualify for *Chevron* deference. In the later case of *United States v. Mead,* 533 U.S. 218 (2001), which we reproduce below, the Court held that a federal agency's interpretation qualifies for *Chevron* deference only "when it appears that Congress delegated authority to the agency generally to make rules carrying the force of law, and that the agency interpretation claiming deference was promulgated in the exercise of that authority." *Id.* at 226–227.

In *Chevron*, the agency interpreted its statute when promulgating a legislative rule. When the EPA Administrator issued the bubble rule, a provision in the Clean Air Act authorized the Administrator to "prescribe such regulations as are necessary to carry out his functions under this chapter." 42 U.S.C. § 7601(a)(1) (Supp. I 1977). The EPA issued the bubble rule under this provision. 46 Fed. Reg. 16,280, 16,282 (1981). Thus, *Chevron* involved judicial review of an agency interpreting its statute when exercising a delegation of quasi-legislative power:

Diagram 32-3. The Judicial Review Situation in *Chevron*

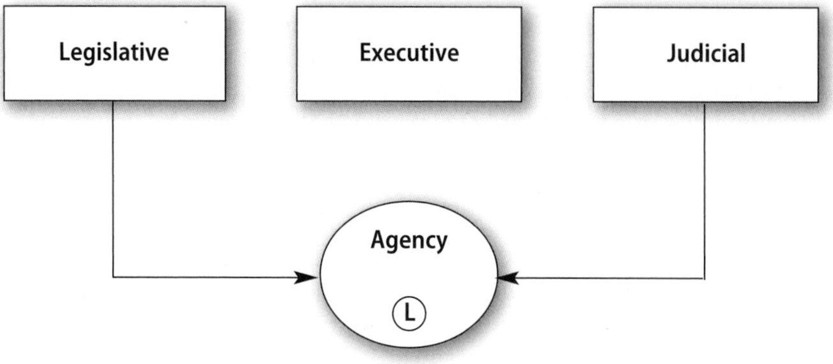

This context differs from (1) the context in which the agency interpreted its statute in *Hearst*, which occurred in formal adjudication exercising a delegation of quasi-judicial power, and from (2) the context in which the agency interpreted its statute in *Skidmore*, which occurred in the exercise of ordinary executive power.

Chevron, like *Hearst*, addresses the allocation of interpretive responsibility between the agency and the court. In *Chevron*, as in *Hearst*, the Court independently determined the boundaries of the agency's interpretive authority under its statute. Specifically, the Court in *Chevron* determined that the 1977 Clean Air Amendments did not preclude the bubble concept; the Court in *Hearst* determined that the National Labor Relations Act did not preclude the statutory term "employees" from including workers who would be independent contractors under the common law. In *Chevron*, as in *Hearst*, the Court deferred to the agency on interstitial (micro) issues of statutory interpretation: In *Chevron*, the agency got deference when interpreting "one phrase" in a "small portion" of a "lengthy, detailed, technical, complex and comprehensive" piece of legislation. 467 U.S. at 848–849. Similarly, in *Hearst*, the agency got deference in determining the micro issue of whether four newspapers' newsboys were "employees" within the meaning of the statute. 322 U.S. at 130–131.

In short, although *Chevron*, rather than *Hearst*, supplies the framework today for analyzing an agency's interpretation of its statute, *Hearst* is the forerunner of *Chevron* and is important for understanding it.

d. The *Mead* Opinion

Please read *United States v. Mead Corporation* with these questions in mind:

1. *Mead* concerns a tariff classification ruling by the U.S. Customs Service. Is that ruling a rule, an order, or something else, under the federal APA definitions of "**rule**" and "**order**"? 5 U.S.C. § 551(4) & (6) (2012).

2. What procedures did Customs use to make the tariff classification ruling? Did the procedures constitute informal rulemaking, formal rulemaking, or formal adjudication, as we discussed those procedures when studying agency activities under the federal APA?

3. Why doesn't the tariff classification ruling get *Chevron* deference?

United States v. Mead Corporation

533 U.S. 218 (2001)

JUSTICE SOUTER delivered the opinion of the Court.

The question is whether a tariff classification ruling by the United States Customs Service deserves judicial deference. The Federal Circuit rejected Customs's invocation of *Chevron U. S. A. Inc. v. Natural Resources Defense Council, Inc.*, 467 U.S. 837 (1984), in support of such a ruling, to which it gave no deference. We agree that a tariff classification has no claim to judicial deference under *Chevron*, there being no indication that Congress intended such a ruling to carry the force of law, but we hold that under *Skidmore v. Swift & Co.*, 323 U.S. 134 (1944), the ruling is eligible to claim respect according to its persuasiveness.

I

A

Imports are taxed under the Harmonized Tariff Schedule of the United States (HTSUS), 19 U.S.C. § 1202. Title 19 U.S.C. § 1500(b) provides that Customs "shall, under rules and regulations prescribed by the Secretary [of the Treasury] ... fix the final classification and rate of duty applicable to ... merchandise" under the HTSUS. Section 1502(a) provides that

> "the Secretary of the Treasury shall establish and promulgate such rules and regulations not inconsistent with the law (including regulations establishing procedures for the issuance of binding rulings prior to the entry of the merchandise concerned), and may disseminate such information as may be necessary to secure a just, impartial, and uniform appraisement of imported merchandise and the classification and assessment of duties thereon at the various ports of entry."

See also § 1624 (general delegation to Secretary to issue rules and regulations for the admission of goods).

The Secretary provides for tariff rulings before the entry of goods by regulations authorizing "ruling letters" setting tariff classifications for particular imports. 19 CFR § 177.8 (2000). A ruling letter

> "represents the official position of the Customs Service with respect to the particular transaction or issue described therein and is binding on all Customs Service personnel in accordance with the provisions of this section until modified or revoked. In the absence of a change of practice or other modification or revocation which affects the principle of the ruling set forth in the ruling letter, that principle may be cited as authority in the disposition of transactions involving the same circumstances." § 177.9(a).

After the transaction that gives it birth, a ruling letter is to "be applied only with respect to transactions involving articles identical to the sample submitted with the ruling request or to articles whose description is identical to the description set forth in the ruling letter." §177.9(b)(2). As a general matter, such a letter is "subject to modification or revocation without notice to any person, except the person to whom the letter was addressed," §177.9(c), and the regulations consequently provide that "no other person should rely on the ruling letter or assume that the principles of that ruling will be applied in connection with any transaction other than the one described in the letter," *ibid*. Since ruling letters respond to transactions of the moment, they are not subject to notice and comment before being issued, may be published but need only be made "available for public inspection," 19 U.S.C. §1625(a), and, at the time this action arose, could be modified without notice and comment under most circumstances, 19 CFR §177.10(c) (2000)....

Any of the 46 port of entry Customs offices may issue ruling letters, and so may the Customs Headquarters Office ...

B

Respondent, the Mead Corporation, imports "day planners," three ring binders with pages having room for notes of daily schedules and phone numbers and addresses, together with a calendar and suchlike. The tariff schedule on point falls under the HTSUS heading for "registers, account books, notebooks, order books, receipt books, letter pads, memorandum pads, diaries and similar articles," HTSUS subheading 4820.10, which comprises two subcategories. Items in the first, "diaries, notebooks and address books, bound; memorandum pads, letter pads and similar articles," were subject to a tariff of 4.0% at the time in controversy. 185 F.3d 1304, 1305 (C.A.Fed.1999) (citing subheading 4820.10.20). Objects in the second, covering "other" items, were free of duty. HTSUS subheading 4820.10.40....

Between 1989 and 1993, Customs repeatedly treated day planners under the "other" HTSUS subheading. In January 1993, however, Customs changed its position, and issued a Headquarters ruling letter classifying Mead's day planners as "Diaries..., bound" subject to tariff under subheading 4820.10.20. That letter was short on explanation, ... but after Mead's protest, Customs Headquarters issued a new letter, carefully reasoned but never published, reaching the same conclusion.... This letter considered two definitions of "diary" from the Oxford English Dictionary, the first covering a daily journal of the past day's events, the second a book including "'printed dates for daily memoranda and jottings; also ... calendars.... '" ... Customs concluded that "diary" was not confined to the first, in part because the broader definition reflects commercial usage and hence the "commercial identity of these items in the marketplace." As for the definition of "bound," Customs concluded that HTSUS was not referring to "bookbinding," but to a less exact sort of fastening described in the Harmonized Commodity Description and Coding System Explanatory Notes to Heading 4820, which spoke of binding by "'reinforcements or fittings of metal, plastics, etc.'"

Customs rejected Mead's further protest of the second Headquarters ruling letter, and Mead filed suit in the Court of International Trade (CIT). The CIT granted the Government's motion for summary judgment, adopting Customs's reasoning without saying anything about deference....

The Federal Circuit, however, reversed the CIT and held that Customs classification rulings should not get *Chevron* deference ... We granted certiorari, in order to consider the limits of *Chevron* deference owed to administrative practice in applying a statute. We hold that administrative implementation of a particular statutory provision qualifies for *Chevron* deference when it appears that Congress delegated authority to the agency generally to make rules carrying the force of law, and that the agency interpretation claiming deference was promulgated in the exercise of that authority. Delegation of such authority may be shown in a variety of ways, as by an agency's power to engage in adjudication or notice and comment rulemaking, or by some other indication of a comparable congressional intent. The Customs ruling at issue here fails to qualify, although the possibility that it deserves some deference under *Skidmore* leads us to vacate and remand.

II

A

When Congress has "explicitly left a gap for an agency to fill, there is an express delegation of authority to the agency to elucidate a specific provision of the statute by regulation," *Chevron*, 467 U.S. at 843–844, and any ensuing regulation is binding in the courts unless procedurally defective, arbitrary or capricious in substance, or manifestly contrary to the statute.[6] See *id.*, at 844; ... APA, 5 U.S.C. §§ 706(2)(A), (D). But whether or not they enjoy any express delegation of authority on a particular question, agencies charged with applying a statute necessarily make all sorts of interpretive choices, and while not all of those choices bind judges to follow them, they certainly may influence courts facing questions the agencies have already answered. "The well reasoned views of the agencies implementing a statute 'constitute a body of experience and informed judgment to which courts and litigants may properly resort for guidance,'" *Bragdon v. Abbott*, 524 U.S. 624, 642 (1998) (quoting *Skidmore*, 323 U.S. at 139–140), and "we have long recognized that considerable weight should be accorded to an executive department's construction of a statutory scheme it is entrusted to administer...." *Chevron*, *supra*, at 844 (footnote omitted).... The fair measure of deference to an agency administering its own statute has been understood to vary with circumstances, and courts have looked to the degree of the agency's care, its consistency, formality, and relative expertness, and to the persuasiveness of the agency's position, see *Skidmore*, *supra*, at 139–140....

Since 1984, we have identified a category of interpretive choices distinguished by an additional reason for judicial deference. This Court in *Chevron* recognized that Congress not only engages in express delegation of specific interpretive authority, but that "sometimes the legislative delegation to an agency on a particular question is implicit." 467 U.S. at 844. Congress, that is, may not have expressly delegated authority or responsibility to implement a particular provision or fill a particular gap. Yet it can still be apparent from the agency's generally conferred authority and other statutory circumstances that Congress would expect the agency to be able to speak with the force of law when it addresses ambiguity in the statute or fills a space in the enacted law, even one about which "Congress did not actually have an intent" as to a particular result. *Id.*, at 845. When circumstances implying such an expectation exist, a reviewing court has no business rejecting an agency's exercise of its generally conferred authority to resolve a particular statutory ambiguity simply because the agency's chosen resolution seems unwise, see *id.*, at 845–846, but is obliged to accept the agency's position if Congress has not previously spoken to the point at issue and the agency's interpretation is reasonable, see *id.*, at 842–845; cf. 5 U.S.C. § 706(2) (a reviewing court shall set aside agency action, findings, and conclusions found to be "arbitrary, capricious, an abuse of discretion, or otherwise not in accordance with law").

---

6. Assuming in each case, of course, that the agency's exercise of authority is constitutional, see 5 U.S.C. § 706(2)(B), and does not exceed its jurisdiction, see § 706(2)(C).

We have recognized a very good indicator of delegation meriting *Chevron* treatment in express congressional authorizations to engage in the process of rulemaking or adjudication that produces regulations or rulings for which deference is claimed. See, *e.g.*, *EEOC v. Arabian American Oil Co.*, 499 U.S. 244, 257 (1991) (no *Chevron* deference to agency guideline where congressional delegation did not include the power to "'promulgate rules or regulations'" (quoting *General Elec. Co. v. Gilbert*, 429 U.S. 125, 141 (1976)); see also *Christensen v. Harris County*, 529 U.S. 576, 596–597 (2000) (Breyer, J., dissenting) (where it is in doubt that Congress actually intended to delegate particular interpretive authority to an agency, *Chevron* is "inapplicable"). It is fair to assume generally that Congress contemplates administrative action with the effect of law when it provides for a relatively formal administrative procedure tending to foster the fairness and deliberation that should underlie a pronouncement of such force. Cf. *Smiley v. Citibank (South Dakota), N. A.*, 517 U.S. 735, 741 (1996) (APA notice and comment "designed to assure due deliberation"). Thus, the overwhelming number of our cases applying *Chevron* deference have reviewed the fruits of notice and comment rulemaking or formal adjudication. That said, and as significant as notice and comment is in pointing to *Chevron* authority, the want of that procedure here does not decide the case, for we have sometimes found reasons for *Chevron* deference even when no such administrative formality was required and none was afforded, see, *e.g.*, *NationsBank of N. C., N. A. v. Variable Annuity Life Ins. Co.*, 513 U.S. 251, 256–257, 263 (1995). The fact that the tariff classification here was not a product of such formal process does not alone, therefore, bar the application of *Chevron*.

There are, nonetheless, ample reasons to deny *Chevron* deference here. The authorization for classification rulings, and Customs's practice in making them, present a case far removed not only from notice and comment process, but from any other circumstances reasonably suggesting that Congress ever thought of classification rulings as deserving the deference claimed for them here.

B

No matter which angle we choose for viewing the Customs ruling letter in this case, it fails to qualify under *Chevron*. On the face of the statute, to begin with, the terms of the congressional delegation give no indication that Congress meant to delegate authority to Customs to issue classification rulings with the force of law. We are not, of course, here making any global statement about Customs's authority, for it is true that the general rulemaking power conferred on Customs, see 19 U.S.C. § 1624, authorizes some regulation with the force of law, or "legal norms," as we put it in *Haggar*, 526 U.S. at 391. It is true as well that Congress had classification rulings in mind when it explicitly authorized, in a parenthetical, the issuance of "regulations establishing procedures for the issuance of binding rulings prior to the entry of the merchandise concerned," 19 U.S.C. § 1502(a). The reference to binding classifications does not, however, bespeak the legislative type of activity that would naturally bind more than the parties to the ruling, once the goods classified are admitted into this country. And though the statute's direction to disseminate "information" necessary to "secure" uniformity, *ibid.*, seems to assume that a ruling may be precedent in later transactions, precedential value alone does not add up to *Chevron* entitlement; interpretive rules may sometimes function as precedents, see Strauss, The Rulemaking Continuum, 41 Duke L. J. 1463, 1472–1473 (1992), and they enjoy no *Chevron* status as a class. In any event, any precedential claim of a classification ruling is counterbalanced by the provision for independent review of Customs classifications by the CIT, see 28 U.S.C. §§ 2638–2640; the scheme for CIT review includes a provision that treats classification rulings on par with the Secretary's rulings on "valuation, rate of duty, marking, restricted merchandise, entry requirements, drawbacks, vessel repairs, or similar matters," § 1581(h); see § 2639(b). It is hard to imagine a congressional understanding more at odds with the *Chevron* regime.

It is difficult, in fact, to see in the agency practice itself any indication that Customs ever set out with a lawmaking pretense in mind when it undertook to make classifications like these. Customs does not generally engage in notice and comment practice when issuing them, and their treatment by the agency makes it clear that a letter's binding character as a ruling stops short of third parties; Customs has regarded a classification as conclusive only as between itself and the importer to whom it was issued, 19 CFR § 177.9(c) (2000), and even then only until Customs has given advance notice of intended change, §§ 177.9(a), (c). Other importers are in fact warned against assuming any right of detrimental reliance. § 177.9(c).

Indeed, to claim that classifications have legal force is to ignore the reality that 46 different Customs offices issue 10,000 to 15,000 of them each year ... Any suggestion that rulings intended to have the force of law are being churned out at a rate of 10,000 a year at an agency's 46 scattered offices is simply self refuting. Although the circumstances are less startling here, with a Headquarters letter in issue, none of the relevant statutes recognizes this category of rulings as separate or different from others ...

In sum, classification rulings are best treated like "interpretations contained in policy statements, agency manuals, and enforcement guidelines." *Christensen*, 529 U.S. at 587. They are beyond the *Chevron* pale.

C

To agree with the Court of Appeals that Customs ruling letters do not fall within *Chevron* is not, however, to place them outside the pale of any deference whatever. *Chevron* did nothing to eliminate *Skidmore*'s holding that an agency's interpretation may merit some deference whatever its form, given the "specialized experience and broader investigations and information" available to the agency, 323 U.S. at 139, and given the value of uniformity in its administrative and judicial understandings of what a national law requires, id., at 140....

There is room at least to raise a *Skidmore* claim here, where the regulatory scheme is highly detailed, and Customs can bring the benefit of specialized experience to bear on the subtle questions in this case: whether the daily planner with room for brief daily entries falls under "diaries," when diaries are grouped with "notebooks and address books, bound; memorandum pads, letter pads and similar articles," HTSUS subheading 4820.10.20; and whether a planner with a ring binding should qualify as "bound," when a binding may be typified by a book, but also may have "reinforcements or fittings of metal, plastics, etc." ... A classification ruling in this situation may therefore at least seek a respect proportional to its "power to persuade," *Skidmore, supra*, at 140.... Such a ruling may surely claim the merit of its writer's thoroughness, logic and expertness, its fit with prior interpretations, and any other sources of weight....

* * *

Since the *Skidmore* assessment called for here ought to be made in the first instance by the Court of Appeals for the Federal Circuit or the Court of International Trade, we go no further than to vacate the judgment and remand the case for further proceedings consistent with this opinion.

It is so ordered.

Justice Scalia, dissenting ...

e. The Significance of *Mead*

Mead clarifies or modifies *Chevron*. Specifically, *Mead* establishes two pre-conditions for an agency's statutory interpretation to "qualif[y] for *Chevron* deference." 533 U.S. at 226. Before we get into those pre-conditions, it is important to understand what the Court means in *Mead* when it talks about an agency interpretation "qualify[ing] for *Chevron* deference." When an agency interpretation "qualifies for *Chevron* deference," that just means that the interpretation should be analyzed under the two-step *Chevron* analysis; it doesn't mean the interpretation automatically gets deference. Under *Chevron* analysis, the agency interpretation may be rejected (at the first step) if it contradicts "the unambiguously expressed intent of Congress," *Chevron*, 467 U.S. at 843, or (at the second step) if it is unreasonable. Thus, an agency interpretation that survives *Mead*'s two pre-conditions is a finalist, but not yet a winner, in the bid for *Chevron* deference.

Exercise: The *Mead*/*Chevron* Gauntlet

Construct a flow chart, graphic organizer, or outline that depicts *Mead*'s two conditions for an agency interpretation to "qualify" for *Chevron* deference, followed by the two steps of the original *Chevron* analysis.

Mead suggests that the nature of the agency action may indicate whether the agency has, and has exercised, a delegation of authority to make rules carrying the force of law. Specifically, *Mead* implies that legislative rules made through notice-and-comment rulemaking usually fit that description and therefore qualify for *Chevron* deference. So do agency decisions made in formal adjudications (as well, presumably, as formal rulemaking). *See Mead*, 533 U.S. at 229–230.

Mead does not specifically address whether agency interpretations qualify for *Chevron* deference if they are (1) contained in non-legislative rules—e.g., interpretative rules— or (2) made in informal adjudications. The answer appears to be: Sometimes they will; other times they won't.

As to non-legislative rules:

Mead itself seems to involve a non-legislative rule. The Court says that tariff classification rulings "are best treated like interpretations contained in policy statements, agency manuals, and enforcement guidelines." *Mead*, 533 U.S. at 234. Policy statements, agency manuals, and enforcement guidelines are paradigms of non-legislative rules. The tariff classification ruling in *Mead*, like Interpretative Bulletin No. 13 in *Skidmore* and other non-legislative rules, reflects an agency's exercise of its inherent, executive power to interpret the law that it is responsible for administering. The non-legislative rule in *Mead* didn't get *Chevron* deference. But that does not mean that non-legislative rules will *never* qualify for *Chevron* deference.

On the contrary, a case after *Mead* suggests that non-legislative rules do sometimes qualify for *Chevron* deference. The case is *Barnhart v. Walton*, 535 U.S. 212 (2002). In *Walton*, the Court gave *Chevron* deference to an interpretation of the Social Security Act by the Social Security Administration (SSA). The interpretation was contained in a legislative rule that the SSA adopted through notice-and-comment rulemaking. You would think that the SSA interpretation would have qualified for *Chevron* deference because it was in a legislative rule adopted through notice-and-comment rulemaking. *Mead*, after all, said that a delegation of authority to make rules carrying the force of law can be shown "by an agency's power to engage in ... notice-and-comment rulemaking." 533 U.S. at 227. Instead, the Court in *Barnhart* cited the following reasons for giving the interpretation *Chevron* deference: "the interstitial nature of the legal question, the related expertise of the Agency, the importance of the question to administration of the statute, the complexity of that administration, and the careful consideration the Agency has given the question over a long period of time." *Walton*, 535 U.S. at 222.

Perhaps the Court in *Walton* cited all these factors because the SSA interpretation at issue actually pre-dated the legislative rule that codified it. The SSA interpretation originated in earlier, non-legislative interpretive material: a social security "ruling" and the "manual" that SSA gives to States that administer social security programs. *Walton*, 535 U.S. at 219–220. The *Walton* Court cited precedent in which the Court had given *Chevron* deference to an agency interpretation reached "though means less formal than 'notice and comment' rulemaking." *Walton*, 535 U.S. at 221–222. *Walton* thus supports *Chevron* deference for some non-legislative rules.

As for informal adjudications:

Walton cited with approval a case giving *Chevron* deference to an agency interpretation in an informal adjudication: *NationsBank v. Variable Annuity Life Insurance Co.*, 513 U.S. 251 (1995). In *NationsBank*, the Comptroller of the Currency granted a bank's application to sell annuities, holding that the sales would be "incidental" to "the business of banking," and thus fell within the federal statute allowing banks to engage in some non-banking activities. *Id.* at 255. The Comptroller did not have to hold a hearing before ruling on the bank's application; thus, the proceeding was an informal adjudication. *See id.* at 254 (citing 12 C.F.R. § 5.34 (1994)). Despite the informal nature of the adjudication, the Court gave *Chevron* deference to the Comptroller's interpretation of the banking statute. *Id.* at 257.

Walton suggests that the nature of the agency action is not the only factor relevant to whether an agency interpretation gets *Chevron* deference. *Walton* cites other factors, including the "interstitial nature" of the interpretative issue, as a factor favoring *Chevron* deference. The Court has cited this factor in other *Chevron* cases. *Long Island Care at Home, Ltd. v. Coke*, 551 U.S. 158, 165 (2007); *Zuni Pub. Sch. Dist. No. 89 v. Dep't of Educ.*, 550 U.S. 81, 90 (2007); *Household Credit Servs. v. Pfennig*, 541 U.S. 232, 244 (2004); *Barnhart v. Walton*, 535 U.S. 212, 222 (2002); *Negusie v. Holder*, 555 U.S. 511, 530 (2009) (Stevens, J., dissenting); *see also Ford Motor Credit Co. v. Milhollin*, 444 U.S. 555, 568 (1980) ("[J]udges ought to refrain from substituting their own interstitial lawmaking for that of [the agency], so long as the latter's lawmaking is not irrational."). Indeed, most cases in which the Court has given *Chevron* deference involve agency interpretation of what one scholar has called "micro-meaning" issues as distinguished from "macro-meaning" issues. John H. Reese, *Bursting the* Chevron *Bubble: Clarifying the Scope of Judicial Review in Troubled Times*, 73 Fordham L. Rev. 1103, 1109 (2004).

Having seen that an agency's interpretation in an informal adjudication may get *Chevron* deference, we can clear up some confusing language in the *Mead* opinion. *Mead* says that an agency interpretation can qualify for *Chevron* deference "when it appears that Congress delegated authority to the agency to make *rules* carrying the force of law." 533 U.S. at 226–227 (emphasis added). *Chevron* deference, however, is not limited to agency interpretations adopted in agency *rules*. Agency interpretations made in adjudications also may get *Chevron* deference. Therefore, the *Mead* reference to "*rules* carrying the force of law" really means "*rules and rulings* carrying the force of law."

To recap, *Mead* and cases after it say that a court should not always use *Chevron* analysis to review a federal agency's interpretation of a statute that the agency administers. The court should not use *Chevron* analysis unless the agency has interpreted its statute in the exercise of delegated authority to make rulings carrying the force of law. To determine whether the agency has exercised such authority, the court should consider the factors cited in *Walton*. Factors that seem to have particular weight are the nature of the agency action and the interstitial nature of the interpretive issue. Agency interpretations will almost always qualify for *Chevron* deference if they concern interstitial issues and are rendered in informal rulemaking, formal rulemaking, or formal adjudication. Things get iffy when the agency makes its interpretation in an informal adjudication or a non-legislative rule.

Exercise: Identifying When *Chevron* Applies and When *Mead* Applies

Please complete this chart by putting a check mark under the appropriate column.

Agency interpretation of agency legislation adopted in:	Usually *Chevron* deference	Usually *Skidmore* respect	It depends
Formal rulemaking			
Informal rulemaking			
Formal adjudication			
Informal adjudication			
Non-legislative rules			

Now please write a short explanation of what "It depends" on.

Many questions about the *Chevron/Mead* doctrine remain. One big question is: What is the legal authority for the doctrine? Two sources of law are *not* likely possibilities:

- The Court has never suggested that the *Chevron/Mead* doctrine is required by the U.S. Constitution.

- Although Section 706 of the APA is broadly applicable to federal court review of federal agency action, § 706 cannot be the source for the *Chevron/Mead* analysis. Section 706 did not apply in *Chevron*. Instead, judicial review was authorized in *Chevron* by a special review statute that comprehensively prescribed the scope of judicial review, thereby displacing § 706. *See Chevron*, 467 U.S. at 841 (noting that judicial review of EPA rule occurred under 42 U.S.C. § 7607(b)(1)); *see also* 42 U.S.C. § 7607(d)(1) & (d)(9) (Supp. I 1977) (providing that APA § 706 does not apply and providing alternative scope of review provision).

Here are possible sources:

- Although not required by the U.S. Constitution, maybe the *Chevron/Mead* doctrine represents a quasi-constitutional, prudential doctrine inspired by the separation of powers doctrine. On this theory, *Chevron* furthers separation of powers values by respecting Congress's statutory delegations to executive-branch agencies of the power to make law when interpreting ambiguous statutes.

- Whether judicial review is authorized by the federal APA or a special review statute, the statutory authority to conduct judicial review includes the power to determine whether and to what extent Congress has delegated interpretive authority to the agency.
- Finally, the *Chevron/Mead* doctrine may reflect the exercise of power to make federal common law — including the power to develop methods of federal statutory interpretation. *See Mead*, 533 U.S. at 230 (implying that *Chevron/Mead* doctrine is a canon of construction).

Whatever its source, the *Chevron/Mead* doctrine has become deeply entrenched in the federal law of judicial review of federal agency action.

C. Federal Agencies' Interpretation of Their Own Rules

The *Chevron/Mead* doctrine governs federal court review of a federal agency's interpretation of a *statute* that the agency administers. A different doctrine governs federal court review of a federal agency's interpretation of the agency's own *rules*. When a federal court reviews a federal agency's interpretation of that agency's own rules, the court applies what today is often called "*Auer* deference," after a 1997 case applying it: *Auer v. Robbins*, 519 U.S. 452, 461 (1997). You will also sometimes hear this doctrine called "*Seminole Rock* deference," after an earlier case applying it. *Bowles v. Seminole Rock & Sand Co.*, 325 U.S. 410, 413–414 (1945).

We explore *Auer* deference in four steps by discussing:

(1) when *Auer* deference applies

(2) rationales for *Auer* deference

(3) academic criticism of *Auer* deference

(4) limits on *Auer* deference

1. When *Auer* Deference Applies

At first, it can be hard to distinguish between, on the one hand, agency interpretations to which the *Chevron/Mead* doctrine applies and, on the other hand, agency interpretations to which *Auer* deference applies. The rule is simple: *Chevron/Mead* applies to agency interpretations of agency *legislation*, and *Auer* deference applies to agency interpretations of agency *rules*. Things get complicated, however, because some cases involve both sorts of interpretations. We illustrate the situation in which *Auer* deference applies by summarizing *Auer* itself.

- *Auer v. Robbins*, 519 U.S. 452 (1997)

St. Louis police sergeants and a lieutenant sued the St. Louis police commissioners for overtime pay allegedly due under the Fair Labor Standards Act (FLSA). The commissioners argued that the plaintiffs were exempt from the FLSA's overtime provisions. The FLSA exempts "bona fide executive, administrative, or professional employees." 29

U.S.C. §213(a)(1) (2012). The FLSA also authorizes the U.S. Secretary of Labor to promulgate legislative rules to "defin[e] and delimit[t]" that exemption. *Id.* Exercising that authority, the Secretary promulgated legislative rules providing that, to fall within the exemption, an employee had to be paid on a "salary basis." 29 C.F.R. §§ 541.(f), 541.2(e), 541.3(e) (1996). The rules defined "salary basis" to mean that the employees' pay was not "subject to reduction because of variations in the quality or quantity of work performed." *Id.* § 541.118(a). (Don't we all aspire to be paid on a salary basis, as so defined?)

As the case came to the U.S. Supreme Court, it presented two issues:

(1) Were the Secretary's salary-basis rules consistent with the FLSA?

(2) How did the Secretary's salary-basis rules apply to the plaintiffs in this case?

The first question concerned the Secretary's interpretation of the FLSA, as reflected in the salary-basis rules. The Court used the *Chevron/Mead* doctrine to analyze that question. The Court upheld the Secretary's interpretation.

Having upheld those legislative rules, the Court still had to decide how they applied to these plaintiffs. That was unclear because, in *theory*, the plaintiffs' pay was subject to reductions for disciplinary infractions—i.e., negative variations in "work quality"; in *practice*, however, reductions never occurred. The Secretary of Labor appeared before the Court as *amicus curiae* to explain his interpretation of how his salary-basis rules applied to the plaintiffs. The Court upheld the Secretary's interpretation. The Court said: "Because the salary-basis test is a creature of the Secretary's own regulations, his interpretation of it is, under our jurisprudence, controlling unless plainly erroneous or inconsistent with the regulation." *Auer*, 519 U.S. at 461 (internal quotation marks omitted). In short, the Court deferred to the Secretary's interpretation of his rules, under a standard that requires a court to uphold an agency's interpretation of its rule unless it is "plainly erroneous or inconsistent" with that rule.

Here are two recent cases in which the Court gave *Auer* deference to a federal agency's interpretation of the agency's own rules:

• *PLIVA, Inc. v. Mensing*, 131 S.Ct. 2567 (2011)

The Food and Drug Administration has authority under a federal statute to regulate the labeling of both generic drugs and their brand-name counterparts. The FDA regulations plainly state that, for the FDA to approve a generic drug, the generic drug's label must be identical to the label of its brand-name counterpart. A dispute arose, however, about whether the FDA regulations require a generic drug's label to *remain* identical to that of its brand-name counterpart after FDA approval of the generic drug. The plaintiff suing a generic drug maker argued that the FDA regulations allowed—indeed, required—a generic drug maker to change its drug label, even if the label of its brand-name counterpart was not first changed, when necessary to advise generic drug users of a previously unappreciated danger. The FDA interpreted its regulations to forbid such a labeling change. The Court gave *Auer* deference to the FDA's interpretation. *Id.* at 2575.

• *McCoy v. Chase Bank USA, N.A.*, 131 S.Ct. 871 (2011)

James McCoy sued his credit card company claiming the company violated the federal Truth in Lending Act and Regulation Z, the latter of which was issued by the Federal Reserve Board to implement the Act. Mr. McCoy claimed the violation occurred when the company raised the interest rate on his credit card without enough advance notice of the increase. Neither the statute nor Regulation Z addressed the issue clearly. The Court gave *Auer* deference to the Board's interpretation of Regulation Z. *Id.* at 880.

Auer deference requires a court to uphold an agency's reasonable interpretation of the agency's own rule even if the court would have interpreted the rule differently. *See Thomas Jefferson Univ. v. Shalala*, 512 U.S. 504, 512 (1994).

2. Rationale for *Auer* Deference

Auer deference rests on three justifications:

(1) When an agency makes a legislative rule, the agency acts like a legislature. Just as we try to interpret statutes to determine the legislative intent, we should try to interpret regulations to determine the agency's intent. The agency is the expert on what it intended, so its interpretation deserves weight.

(2) When a situation arises that the agency did not foresee when drafting its rule, the agency is in a good position to determine how the rule should be interpreted to address the unforeseen situation. The agency will have the expertise and experience to develop a workable interpretation.

(3) When Congress delegates to an agency the power to make legislative rules, Congress impliedly delegates to the agency the power to interpret those rules. Courts should respect the implicit delegation by deferring to the agency's interpretive authority.

See John F. Manning, *Constitutional Structure and Judicial Deference to Agency Interpretations of Agency Rules*, 96 Colum. L. Rev. 612, 629–631 (1996).

3. Criticisms of *Auer* Deference

In the article cited above, Professor Manning criticized *Auer* deference. Justice Scalia has endorsed this criticism. *Talk America, Inc. v. Mich. Bell Tel. Co.*, 131 S. Ct. at 2254, 2266 (2011)(Scalia, J., concurring). *Auer* does have downsides. The main problem with *Auer* is that it gives agencies an incentive to promulgate legislative rules that are vague, ambiguous mush, because that gives the agencies maximum interpretive freedom. And of course, unnecessarily vague, ambiguous rules disserve people affected by those rules, because the rules don't give adequate notice of their meaning.

4. Limits on *Auer* Deference

Reflecting limits on the justification for *Auer* deference, the Court will not give *Auer* deference to a federal agency's interpretation of its rules in three situations. Lower federal courts have put two more restrictions on *Auer* deference.

First, the Court will not give *Auer* deference to an agency interpretation of an *unambiguous* regulation. The Court encountered an unambiguous regulation in *Christensen v. Harris County*, 529 U.S. 576 (2000). The Court rejected an administrative interpretation of the regulation that conflicted with its plain text. *Id.* at 588. The Court reasoned that deferring to an agency interpretation that conflicted with an unambiguous regulation "would permit the agency, under the guise of interpreting a regulation, to create *de facto* a new regulation." *Id.*

Second, the Court will not give *Auer* deference to an agency interpretation of an agency rule that merely parrots a statute. The Court announced the anti-parroting limit on *Auer* deference in *Gonzales v. Oregon*, 546 U.S. 243 (2006). In that case, the U.S. Attorney General interpreted his regulation to bar doctors from prescribing drugs to help people kill themselves, even in Oregon, where physician-assisted suicide is allowed under state law. The Court refused to give *Auer* deference to the Attorney General's interpretation because the regulation did "little more than restate the terms of the statute itself." *Id.* at 257. The Court said, "[T]he existence of a parroting regulation does not change the fact that the question here is not the meaning of the regulation but the meaning of the statute." *Id.* The Court concluded, "An agency does not acquire special authority to interpret its own words when, instead of using its expertise and experience to formulate a regulation, it has elected merely to paraphrase the statutory language." *Id.* (The Court found other reasons not to give the Attorney General's interpretation *Chevron* deference as an interpretation of the underlying statute. *Id.* at 258–269.)

Third, the Court probably will not give *Auer* deference to an agency interpretation that the agency has cooked up to gain an advantage in litigation to which the agency is a party. In a 1988 case, the Court refused to defer to an agency interpretation of a *statute* when the agency announced that interpretation only after being sued. The Court said the agency's statutory interpretation was a "*post hoc* rationalization[n]" that "appear[ed] to be nothing more than [the] agency's convenient litigating position." *Bowen v. Georgetown Univ. Hosp.*, 488 U.S. 204, 474 (1988). In *Auer*, the Court suggested that the Court will likewise deny deference to an agency interpretation of the agency's own rule, if that interpretation appeared to be only "a '*post hoc* rationalization[n]' advanced by an agency seeking to defend past agency action against attack." *Auer*, 519 U.S. at 463 (quoting *Bowen v. Georgetown Hosp.*, 488 U.S. at 212). In contrast, the Court has given *Auer* deference to agency interpretations of the agency's rule when the agency presents the interpretation, for the first time, in litigation between private parties—where the agency is not itself a party to the lawsuit. *E.g., Talk America*, 131 S. Ct. at 2260–2261; *Long Island Care at Home, Ltd. v. Coke*, 551 U.S. 158, 171 (2007). In *Auer* itself, the Court deferred to an agency interpretation expressed in an *amicus* brief submitted in litigation between private parties. 519 U.S. at 461–462. This third limit on *Auer* deference thus appears to operate only when an agency renders its interpretation in the course of, and to gain advantage in, a lawsuit to which it is a party. In that situation, the Court may suspect the interpretation is more the work of the agency lawyers than the agency policy makers.

Lower federal courts of appeals have put two more limits on *Auer* deference.

As mentioned above, the Court in *Christensen* refused to defer to an agency interpretation of an unambiguous agency rule, reasoning that it would allow an agency "to create *de facto* a new [rule]." 529 U.S. at 588. Some lower courts have taken this reasoning one step further. They restrict a federal agency's power to *change* an interpretation of the agency's rule, *even if* the rule is ambiguous and *even if* the later interpretation reflects a reasonable interpretation of the rule. Specifically, if the agency wants to change an interpretation that the agency has held for a long time and on which people have relied, the agency can change that interpretation only by going through notice-and-comment rulemaking to amend the text of the actual rule. These courts impose this requirement in the belief that it is unfair for an agency to change a longstanding interpretation of a rule without giving the public adequate notice by using notice-and-comment procedures. These courts treat a longstanding interpretation as, in effect, melding with the rule that is being interpreted. *See, e.g., Shell Offshore, Inc. v. Babbitt*, 238 F.3d 622, 629 (5th Cir. 2001).

Lower federal courts also restrict federal agencies from using a change in their interpretation of a rule to impose unforeseeable punishment, such as a civil penalty, on someone. In one case, for example, the FCC relied on an unforeseeable interpretation of one of its regulations to refuse to renew a television broadcast license. *Trinity Broadcasting v, FCC*, 211 F.3d 618 (D.C. Cir. 2000). The court held that the FCC's interpretation was entitled to *Chevron* deference but, because the licensee could not have foreseen that interpretation, the FCC could not rely on the unforeseen interpretation to refuse to renew the license. Indeed, the court held that due process barred the FCC from applying its interpretation in this situation:

> Because due process requires that parties receive fair notice before being deprived of property, we have repeatedly held that in the absence of notice—for example, where the regulation is not sufficiently clear to warn a party about what is expected of it—an agency may not deprive a party of property by imposing civil or criminal liability. We thus ask whether by reviewing the regulations and other public statements issued by the agency, a regulated party acting in good faith would be able to identify, with ascertainable certainty, the standards with which the agency expects parties to conform.

Id. at 628 (brackets, internal quotation marks, and citations omitted); *see also United States v. Approximately 64,695 Pounds of Shark Fins*, 520 F.3d 976, 980 (9th Cir. 2008) (analogizing *Trinity Broadcasting* holding to U.S. Supreme Court precedent striking down laws as void for vagueness if they do not give reasonable notice of their requirements).

D. State Agencies' Interpretations of Statutes They Administer and of Their Own Rules

Courts in some, perhaps many, States give deference to state agencies' interpretations of the statutes they administer. *See generally* William R. Andersen, Chevron *in the States: An Assessment and a Proposal*, 58 Admin. L. Rev. 1017 (2006) (discussing results of research into state court decisions deferring to state agency interpretations of agency legislation). Similarly, some state courts give weight to state agencies' interpretation of their own rules.[2] The prevalence of specialized deference principles, however, is hard to pin down because the principles almost always have been developed by courts, rather than being codified in statutes or other source of law. As such, those principles are not always fully articulated or rationalized, and in any event may present a moving target, much like the principles of federal law that have developed into the *Chevron/Mead* doctrine.

---

2. *See, e.g., Hardesty v. Sacramento Metro. Air Quality Mg'mt Dist.*, 136 Cal. Rptr. 3d 132, 143 (Cal. App. 2011); *Women's & Children's Hosp. v. State Dep't of Health & Hosps.*, 2 So. 3d 397, 403 (La. 2009); *St. Otto's Home v. Minn. Dep't of Human Servs.*, 437 N.W.2d 35, 40 (Minn. 1989); *Clear Channel Outdoors v. Tenn. Dep't of Transp.*, 337 S.W.3d 801, 806–807 (Tenn. Ct. App. 2010).

The 2010 Model APA reflects the judicial origin of, and responsibility for, developing these principles. Section 508 specifies the grounds on which a court may set aside agency action. Those grounds include that "the agency erroneously interpreted the law." 2010 Model State APA § 508. Section 508 does not specify the standard of judicial review for agency interpretations of their own statutes. Indeed, the official comment on Section 508 explains that it "is not intended to preclude courts from according deference to agency interpretations of law, where such deference is appropriate." *Id.* Comment. More generally, the official comment indicates that standards of judicial review are best developed by courts, rather than by the legislature. *Id.* (citing William D. Araiza, *In Praise of a Skeletal APA*, 56 Admin. L. Rev. 979 (2004)).

When researching state case law, you cannot assume you will find judicial-review principles identical to those of the *Chevron/Mead* doctrine or *Auer*. Nor can you assume that the judicial-review principles applicable to one type of agency action, such as an agency's legislative rules, will apply to other types of agency action, such as agency advisory opinions. Judicial-review principles may depend on other factors, such as whether an agency's interpretation is informed by the agency's expertise in a specialized area. Before delving directly into the case law, you may wish to look for secondary sources on how that State's courts review the state agencies' interpretations of the statutes they administer and rules they issue. This is a topic that many people find fascinating and worth writing about.

Exercise: Specialized Review Standards in State Courts

Please select a State of your choice and research how courts of that State have answered these questions:

1. Should courts defer to an agency's interpretation of a statute it administers?
2. Should courts defer to an agency's interpretation of its own rules?

E. Chapter 32 Wrap Up and Look Ahead

From this chapter you learned that federal courts review de novo most questions of law that arise on review of federal agency action, but this de novo standard of review for questions of law has two main exceptions. Federal courts often give deference to a federal agency's interpretation of a statute that the agency administers and to a federal agency's interpretation of the agency's own rules. Some States have adopted similar doctrines of deference.

The next chapters turn to two standards of review that apply when courts review the factual basis for an agency's action: the "arbitrary and capricious" standard and the "substantial evidence" standard.

Chapter Problem Revisited

This problem was based on *Mayo Foundation for Medical Education & Research v. United States*, 131 S.Ct. 704 (2011). In *Mayo*, the Court used the *Chevron/Mead* doctrine to review the Treasury Department's interpretation of FICA. The Court upheld that interpretation as a reasonable rendering of ambiguous statutory language. As reflected in *Chevron*, the Treasury Department's change in interpretation does not weaken the deference due under *Chevron/Mead*.

Professional Development Reflection Question

Many lawyers who work for the government leave their government jobs and enter the private sector, using their government experience as a valuable credential and as a source of inside knowledge about "who to talk to" to "get things done." Indeed, once in the private sector, the lawyer may be highly effective because of relationships formed with former government colleagues. For that reason, service as a government lawyer can lead to a high-paying job in the private sector, reflecting a premium for that lawyer's government "connections."

A *New York Times* article gives a specific example. The article reports on developments after Congress enacted the Dodd-Frank Wall Street Reform and Consumer Protection Act in 2010. The Act authorized a range of federal agencies to issue tighter regulations for the financial industry, in an effort to prevent the sort of abuses that led to the Great Recession. The *Times* article reports:

> As the battle over toughened financial restrictions moves to a new front, the regulatory agencies that will create hundreds of new rules for the nation's banks will face a lobbying blitz from companies intent on softening the blow. And many of the lobbyists the regulators hear from will be their former colleagues.
>
> Nearly 150 lobbyists registered since last year used to work in the executive branch at financial agencies, from lawyers for the Securities and Exchange Commission to Federal Reserve bankers ...
>
> In addition, dozens of former lawyers for the government, who are not registered as lobbyists, are now scouring the financial regulations on behalf of corporate clients ...

Eric Lichtblau, *Ex-Regulators Lobby to Shape Overhaul*, N.Y. Times, July 28, 2010, at p. B1.

The Model Rules of Professional Conduct address this situation in Rule 1.11, entitled "Special Conflicts of Interest for Former and Current Government Officers and Employees." Rule 1.11's main restriction says a former government lawyer "shall not ... represent a client in connection with a matter in which the lawyer participated personally and substantially as a public officer or employee, unless the appropriate government agency gives its informed consent, confirmed in writing, to the representation." Rule 1.11(a)(2).

Do you think the Rule goes far enough (or too far) in restricting the ability of a former government lawyer to capitalize on the lawyer's prior government service? What's wrong with a lawyer cashing in on government experience?

Chapter 33

The "Substantial Evidence" Standard

Overview

The last chapter addressed how courts review questions of *law* that arise upon judicial review of agency action. Now we turn to how courts review questions of *fact* under a standard of review, the "substantial evidence" standard, that governs judicial review of the factual basis of certain agency actions.

The sections of this chapter address these subjects:

A. When Does the Substantial Evidence Standard Apply to Judicial Review of Federal Agency Action?

B. The Distinction between "Substantial Evidence" as a Standard of Judicial Review and "Substantial Evidence" as a Standard of Proof

C. What Does the Substantial Evidence Standard of Review Mean?

D. The "Substantial Evidence" Standard in the States

E. Chapter 33 Wrap Up and Look Ahead

Chapter Problem

Intake Memo

To: Pro Bono Attorney

From: Legal Intern

Re: Judicial Review of Immigration Case

You asked me to summarize the case in which the U.S. Court of Appeals for the Ninth Circuit has just appointed us to represent Jin Weng. As you know, Ms. Weng has filed in the Ninth Circuit a challenge to a decision by the Board of Immigration Appeals (BIA) denying her request for relief from removal. The major issue is whether we will be able to impugn the factual basis for the BIA's decision. The Ninth Circuit will review the factual basis for the BIA's decision under a "substantial evidence" standard, meaning that the Ninth Circuit will set aside the BIA's decision only if it is not supported by "substantial evidence." *See, e.g., Menendez-Donis v. Ashcroft*, 360 F.3d 915, 917–918 (8th Cir. 2004).

Ms. Weng is a twenty-three-year-old native of China. In March 2012, she was detained in Texas, near the U.S.-Mexico border, by U.S. immigration officials, who found her in the trunk of a car. Shortly after Ms. Weng's detention, an immigration official interviewed her using a Mandarin interpreter.

At the beginning of the interview, the official told Ms. Weng that she had to tell the truth about why she had come to the United States. Ms. Weng was also told that she should explain whether she feared harm if she was returned to China, and, if so, why she feared harm. The official gave Ms. Weng a written form that said:

> "Please feel comfortable telling me why you fear harm. U.S. law has strict rules to prevent the disclosure of what you tell me today about the reason why you fear harm. The information you tell me about the reasons for your fear will not be disclosed to your government, except in exceptional circumstances. The statements you make today may be used in deciding your claim and in any future immigration proceedings."

The Mandarin translator orally translated this form to Ms. Weng. The immigration officials then put her under oath and interviewed her about how and why she had come to the U.S.

In the interview, Ms. Weng said she left China because she was poor and could not find work because of her low social status. She said that when she was four years old her parents sent her away to live with her aunt. That was so her parents could try to have a boy for their second child without Chinese officials knowing that they had already had the one (and only) child permitted under China's "one-child policy." Ms. Weng stated that she opposed that policy.

After the interview, the Department of Homeland Security began a proceeding to remove Ms. Weng from the United States and return her to China. In response, Ms. Weng applied for three forms of relief from removal: asylum, withholding of removal, and protection under the Convention Against Torture.

In her written application for relief from removal, Ms. Weng asserted that Chinese officials had persecuted her for practicing the religion of Zun Wang. She explained that the government warned Ms. Weng and other Zun Wang followers in November 2011 that they must stop practicing their religion and, that same month, sent a notice to Ms. Weng's parents instructing them to force Ms. Weng to stop practicing that religion. Ms. Weng said that she continued practicing the Zun Wang religion despite the warnings. In early December 2011, five uniformed officers broke up a Zun Wang prayer meeting at which Ms. Weng was present; the officers arrested her and the other attendees. According to Ms. Weng, Chinese officials interrogated Ms. Weng for thirty minutes and slapped her. They kept her in jail for two days, until her parents bailed her out. Soon after that, her parents paid money to "snakeheads" to help Ms. Weng get into the United States.

In support of these assertions in her written application for relief, Ms. Weng submitted documentary evidence. The documentary evidence included U.S. State Department reports confirming that Chinese officials were persecuting followers of the Zun Wang religion. Ms. Weng also submitted: (1) affidavits from her sister and mother confirming her arrest at a prayer meeting in December 2011; (2) a purported copy of a notice posted in Ms. Weng's village that accused her of continuing to practice a banned religion and ordered her to report to authorities immediately or face "severe penalties." (3) Finally, she submitted a purported receipt confirming her parents' payment of bail to get her released from jail. The receipt stated that she had been arrested for "disturbing social order and promoting superstition."

At a hearing before an Immigration Judge (IJ), Ms. Weng explained that she did not mention religious persecution in her interview with U.S. immigration officials because she was scared that her statements would be reported to Chinese officials. Ms. Weng claimed that only after consulting a lawyer did she understand that her statements would not be reported to China.

After the hearing, the IJ denied Ms. Weng's application for relief from removal, and the IJ's decision was affirmed by the BIA, which adopted the IJ's opinion as its own. The IJ determined that Ms. Weng was not credible because she had not mentioned religious persecution in the sworn statements she made in her interview with U.S. immigration officials. The IJ disbelieved Ms. Weng's assertion that she feared during the interview that her statements would be reported to China. The IJ observed that this supposed fear did not prevent Ms. Weng from criticizing China's one-child policy. The IJ also reasoned that the "snakeheads" who helped Ms. Weng get into the United States presumably advised her that, if she wanted to stay in the United States, her best hope was to claim religious persecution. The IJ did not discuss Ms. Weng's documentary evidence.

After reading this memo, you have to formulate arguments for why the IJ's decision was not supported by substantial evidence and to advise Ms. Weng of the likelihood of success in challenging the IJ's decision in the Ninth Circuit.

A. When Does the Substantial Evidence Standard Apply to Judicial Review of Federal Agency Action?

The substantial evidence standard applies primarily to (1) judicial review under federal APA § 706 of agency decisions in formal rulemaking and formal adjudication; and (2) judicial review under special review statutes that prescribe the substantial evidence standard.

The substantial evidence standard in the federal APA comes from § 706(2)(E):

---

5 U.S.C. § 706. Scope of review

... The reviewing court shall— ...

(2) hold unlawful and set aside agency action, findings, and conclusions found to be— ...

(E) unsupported by substantial evidence in a case subject to sections 556 and 557 of this title or otherwise reviewed on the record of an agency hearing provided by statute....

Broken down, § 706(2)(E) makes the substantial evidence standard applicable to two categories of cases:

(1) "[C]ase[s] subject to sections 556 and 557," which will be either formal adjudications or formal rulemakings; and

(2) **"[C]ase[s] ... otherwise reviewed on the record of an agency hearing provided by statute,"** which will mostly be agency decisions made in on-the-record adjudications that are exempt from §§ 556 and 557 or that occur under statutes that do not trigger §§ 556 and 557. *See, e.g., Hoffman v. Solis*, 636 F.3d 262, 268 (6th Cir. 2011) (applying substantial evidence standard to review agency action under the **"otherwise reviewed"** clause of § 706(2)(E)); *Brand v. Miller*, 487 F.3d 862, 868 (Fed. Cir. 2007) (proceedings of Patent and Trademark Office are subject to substantial evidence standard even though they are not governed by §§ 556 and 557).

The second category of cases is rare.

In addition to § 706(2)(E), some special review statutes prescribe the substantial evidence standard. An example is the special review statute governing review of decisions by the National Labor Relations Board in unfair labor practice proceedings, which are formal adjudications. *See* 29 U.S.C. § 160(e) & (f) (2012). Moreover, some special review statutes applicable to rules made through hybrid rulemaking prescribe the substantial evidence standard, such as this statute governing Consumer Product Safety Commission rules:

---

15 U.S.C. § 2060. Judicial review of consumer product safety rules ...

(d) ... The consumer product safety rule shall not be affirmed unless the Commission's findings under sections 2058(f)(1) and 2058(f)(3) of this title are supported by substantial evidence on the record taken as a whole....

You will occasionally find special review provisions making the substantial evidence standard applicable to agency actions other than formal adjudications and hybrid rules. *See, e.g.,* 7 U.S.C. § 1636b (2012) (specialized judicial review provision for informal adjudications by Secretary of Agriculture to impose civil penalties for statutory violations). All in all, "substantial evidence" is a pretty popular standard for review of the factual basis for various agency actions.

Although the substantial evidence standard may apply to different types of agency action, most agency actions subject to the standard will be formal adjudications. That is why most case law on the standard concerns formal adjudications. Therefore, to simplify things, from now on we will generally speak of the substantial evidence standard as the standard governing judicial review of agency factfinding in formal adjudications.

B. The Distinction between "Substantial Evidence" as a Standard of Judicial Review and "Substantial Evidence" as a Standard of Proof

As used in § 706(2)(E) and special review statutes, the term "substantial evidence" establishes a standard of judicial review. But beware: The term "substantial evidence" also appears in *§ 556(d)* of the federal APA, where it serves, not as a standard of judicial review, but instead as the *standard of proof* in formal adjudications and formal rulemakings. To avoid confusion, this section emphasizes the distinction between the two roles that the term "substantial evidence" plays.

The meaning of "substantial evidence" as a standard of proof was addressed in *Steadman v. Securities & Exchange Commission*, 450 U.S. 91 (1981). In that case, the SEC conducted a formal adjudication against Charles Steadman, charging him with violating the federal securities laws in his management of mutual funds. The adjudication ended in an order that permanently barred Mr. Steadman from associating with any investment adviser. In his judicial challenge to that order, Mr. Steadman argued that the SEC erred by using a "preponderance of the evidence" standard to determine whether he committed the violations. Instead, he argued, the SEC should have decided whether the violations had been proven through "clear and convincing proof." *Id.* at 92–95.

The U.S. Supreme Court held that the SEC correctly used a preponderance-of-the-evidence standard of proof in the formal adjudication, because that standard was required by the following language in § 556 of the federal APA:

---

5 U.S.C. § 556. Hearings; ... burden of proof ...

(d) ... A sanction may not be imposed or rule or order issued except on consideration of the whole record or those parts thereof cited by a party and supported by and in accordance with the reliable, probative, and substantial evidence....

Specifically, the Court held that the preponderance standard was imposed by the phrase **"in accordance with ... substantial evidence."** The Court recognized that this language "is somewhat opaque concerning the precise standard of proof to be used." *Steadman*, 450 U.S. at 91. The legislative history, however, made clear that Congress intended "**substantial evidence**" in § 556(d) to mean a preponderance of the evidence.

"Substantial evidence" does *not* mean "a preponderance of the evidence" when used as a standard of judicial review. If it did, it would allow courts to determine independently whether the facts found by the agency were more likely than not to be true. But courts cannot do that. The Supreme Court has held that the substantial evidence standard of judicial review does not allow courts to re-weigh the evidence that the agency considered. The Court made this clear in *Universal Camera Corp. v. National Labor Relations Board*, 340 U.S. 474 (1951), which we excerpt in the next section. The Court said in *Universal Camera* that the substantial evidence standard of review does not allow a court to displace an agency's "choice between two fairly conflicting views" of the evidence, "even though the court would justifiably have made a different choice had the matter been before it *de novo*." *Id.* at 488. In short, the substantial evidence standard of judicial review is deferential; it gives the benefit of the doubt to the agency when reasonable minds could differ about a factual determination. *Allentown Mack Sales & Serv., Inc. v. NLRB*, 522 U.S. 359, 377 (1998) ("The 'substantial evidence' test ... gives the agency the benefit of the doubt, since it requires not the degree of evidence which satisfies the *court* that the requisite fact exists, but merely the degree which *could* satisfy a reasonable factfinder.") (emphasis in original).

From now on we focus on the meaning of substantial evidence as a standard of judicial review.

C. What Does the Substantial Evidence Standard of Review Mean?

In a nutshell, the substantial evidence standard of review requires a court to uphold an agency's finding of fact unless no reasonable trier of fact could have made that finding. Put another way, the court can set aside the agency's finding of fact only if a reasonable factfinder would have been compelled to reach a conclusion contrary to the agency's. *See, e.g., Immigration & Naturalization Serv. v. Elias-Zacarias*, 502 U.S. 478, 483–484 (1992). This is a deferential standard, the details and operation of which we explore in this section.

1. *Universal Camera Corp. v. National Labor Relations Board*

a. Background

The most famous case on the substantial evidence standard of review is *Universal Camera Corp. v. National Labor Relations Board*, 340 U.S. 474 (1951). To understand the Court's opinion in *Universal Camera* and its importance, you need background on the statutes and facts at issue in the case and its procedural history.

(i) Statutory Background

The National Labor Relations Board was created in 1935 by National Labor Relations Act, which was commonly known as the Wagner Act. *See* Pub. L. No. 198, ch. 372, 49 Stat. 449 (1935) (codified as amended at 29 U.S.C. § 153 (2012)). The Wagner Act authorized judicial review of the Board's decisions in the federal courts of appeals. The Wagner Act provision authorizing judicial review said in relevant part:

> The findings of the Board as to the facts, if supported by evidence, shall be conclusive.

§ 10(e), 49 Stat. 454.

The Wagner Act was amended in 1947 by the Labor Management Relations Act, commonly known as the Taft-Hartley Act. *See* Pub. L. No. 101, ch. 120, 61 Stat. 136 (1947). The Taft-Hartley Act amended the Wagner Act's judicial review provision to read in relevant part:

> The findings of the Board with respect to questions of fact if supported by substantial evidence on the record considered as a whole shall be conclusive.

61 Stat. 148. The current version of the statute is similar. *See* 29 U.S.C. § 160(e) & (f) (2012). The Court in *Universal Camera* addressed Taft-Hartley's additions of the term "substantial evidence" and the phrase "on the record considered as a whole."

The "substantial evidence" standard also appeared in the judicial review provision of the federal APA, which was enacted in 1946, the year before Taft-Hartley. The Court in *Universal Camera* confirmed that the term means the same thing in the APA and Taft-Hartley.

(ii) Facts and Procedural History

The *Universal Camera* case arose when the Universal Camera Corporation (Company) fired Imre Chairman from his job as supervisor of the maintenance employees. Mr. Chairman claimed that the Company fired him because of testimony that he had given at a hearing before the National Labor Relations Board. Specifically, Mr. Chairman had testified that the Board should recognize the Company's maintenance employees as an appropriate bargaining unit to be represented by a union. The Company opposed recognition of the maintenance employees as a separate bargaining unit, and several of the Company's officers testified against such recognition at the same hearing. The Company later claimed, however, that it did not fire Mr. Chairman for his testimony to the Board. Instead, the Company claimed that it fired Mr. Chairman because he was insubordinate to his superior, Mr. Weintraub. Mr. Chairman and Mr. Weintraub had gotten into an argument in which Mr. Chairman, with other employees present, accused Mr. Weintraub of being drunk. *See NLRB v. Universal Camera Corp.*, 179 F.2d 749, 750–751 (2nd Cir. 1950), *rev'd*, 340 U.S. 474 (1951).

The Board's prosecuting arm initiated a formal adjudication against the Company, charging the Company had violated the Wagner Act by firing Mr. Chairman for testifying before the Board in the prior proceeding on whether the maintenance workers could unionize. After a formal evidentiary hearing, the hearing examiner, who today would be called an "ALJ," found that the Board's prosecutors had not met their burden of proving by a preponderance of evidence that the Company had fired Mr. Chairman for previous Board testimony. On review of the examiner's decision, however, the Board reversed the hearing examiner's decision. The Board concluded that the Company *did* fire Mr. Chairman because of his previous Board testimony. The Board ordered the Company to reinstate Mr. Chairman with backpay, and the Board filed a petition in the U.S. Court of Appeals for enforcement of its order.

The Second Circuit granted enforcement of the Board's order. The court reviewed whether there was enough evidence to support the Board's determination that Mr. Chairman was fired because of his previous Board testimony. The court did not think that the Board had strong reasons to disagree with the examiner's finding on that issue. The court concluded, however, that it could not consider the Board's disagreement with the examiner's finding as a factor that weighed against the Board's decision. The court upheld the Board's decision even though the court found little factual support for the Board's decision. The court explained:

> If by special verdict a jury had made [the Board's findings] we should not reverse
> the verdict; and we understand our function in cases of this kind to be the same.
> Such a verdict would be within the bounds of rational entertainment.

NLRB v. Universal Camera Corp., 179 F.2d at 754. Thus, the court believed that the "substantial evidence" standard of review required the court to review the Board's findings of fact with a level of deference comparable to that owed by an appellate court to findings by a jury in a special verdict. This belief reflected the court's view that the Taft-Hartley Act did not require courts to give increased scrutiny to the Board's findings of fact. *Id.* at 752 ("We cannot agree that our review has been broadened.") (internal quotation marks omitted).

In the opinion you are about to read, the U.S. Supreme Court rejected the lower court's view that Taft-Hartley did not increase the scrutiny reviewing courts had to give to the Board's factfinding. More generally, the Court explained the modern meaning of the "substantial evidence" standard.

b. The *Universal Camera* Opinion

Universal Camera Corp. v.
National Labor Relations Board
340 U.S. 474 (1951)

JUSTICE FRANKFURTER delivered the opinion of the Court.

The essential issue raised by this case … is the effect of the Administrative Procedure Act and the legislation colloquially known as the Taft-Hartley Act on the duty of Courts of Appeals when called upon to review orders of the National Labor Relations Board.…

I

Want of certainty in judicial review of Labor Board decisions partly reflects the intractability of any formula to furnish definiteness of content for all the impalpable factors involved in judicial review. But in part doubts as to the nature of the reviewing power and uncertainties in its application derive from history …

The Wagner Act provided: "The findings of the Board as to the facts, if supported by evidence, shall be conclusive." This Court read "evidence" to mean "substantial evidence," and we said that "[s]ubstantial evidence is more than a mere scintilla. It means such relevant evidence as a reasonable mind might accept as adequate to support a conclusion." …

… [T]he inevitably variant applications of the standard to conflicting evidence soon brought contrariety of views and in due course bred criticism.… [In particular,] the phrasing of this Court's process of review readily lent itself to the notion that it was enough that the evidence supporting the Board's result was "substantial" when considered by itself.… [B]y imperceptible steps regard for the fact finding function of the Board led to the assumption that the requirements of the Wagner Act were met when the reviewing court could find in the record evidence which, when viewed in isolation, substantiated the Board's findings.…

Criticism of so contracted a reviewing power reinforced dissatisfaction felt in various quarters with the Board's administration of the Wagner Act in the years preceding the war.… Protests against "shocking injustices" and intimations of judicial "abdication" with which some courts granted enforcement of the Board's orders stimulated pressures for legislative relief from alleged administrative excesses.…

The strength of these pressures was reflected in the passage in 1940 of the Walter-Logan Bill. It was vetoed by President Roosevelt, partly because … of the investigation into the actual operation of the administrative process then being conducted by an experienced committee appointed by the Attorney General.…

The final report of the Attorney General's Committee was submitted in January, 1941. The majority [of the Committee] … recommended against legislation embodying a general scheme of judicial review.…

Three members of the Committee registered a dissent. Their view was that the "present system or lack of system of judicial review" led to inconsistency and uncertainty.… Their view led them to recommend that Congress enact principles of review applicable to all agencies not excepted by unique characteristics. One of these principles was expressed by the formula that judicial review could extend to "findings, inferences, or conclusions of fact unsupported, upon the whole record, by substantial evidence." … This evidence of the close relationship between the phrase and the criticism out of which it arose is important, for the substance of this formula for judicial review found its way into the statute books when Congress ... enacted the Administrative Procedure Act.

... [T]he legislative history of that Act ... expressed disapproval of the manner in which the courts were applying ... [the substantial evidence standard that the Court itself had first articulated] ...

Similar dissatisfaction with too restricted application of the "substantial evidence" test is reflected in the legislative history of the Taft-Hartley Act....

It is fair to say that in all this Congress expressed a mood. And it expressed its mood not merely by oratory but by legislation. As legislation that mood must be respected ...

... [W]e hold that the standard of proof specifically required of the Labor Board by the Taft-Hartley Act is the same as that to be exacted by courts reviewing every administrative action subject to the Administrative Procedure Act.

Whether or not it was ever permissible for courts to determine the substantiality of evidence supporting a Labor Board decision merely on the basis of evidence which in and of itself justified it, without taking into account contradictory evidence or evidence from which conflicting inferences could be drawn, the new legislation definitively precludes such a theory of review and bars its practice. The substantiality of evidence must take into account whatever in the record fairly detracts from its weight. This is clearly the significance of the requirement in both statutes that courts consider the whole record....

To be sure, the requirement for canvassing "the whole record" [was not intended] ... to negative the function of the Labor Board as one of those agencies presumably equipped or informed by experience to deal with a specialized field of knowledge, whose findings within that field carry the authority of an expertness which courts do not possess and therefore must respect. Nor does it mean that even as to matters not requiring expertise a court may displace the Board's choice between two fairly conflicting views, even though the court would justifiably have made a different choice had the matter been before it *de novo*. Congress has merely made it clear that a reviewing court is not barred from setting aside a Board decision when it cannot conscientiously find that the evidence supporting that decision is substantial, when viewed in the light that the record in its entirety furnishes, including the body of evidence opposed to the Board's view.

There remains, then, the question whether enactment of these two statutes has altered the scope of review other than to require that substantiality be determined in the light of all that the record relevantly presents....

Whatever changes were made by the Administrative Procedure and Taft-Hartley Acts are clearly within [an] area where precise definition is impossible. Retention of the familiar "substantial evidence" terminology indicates that no drastic reversal of attitude was intended.

... [Nonetheless,] [t]he legislative history of these Acts demonstrates a purpose to impose on courts a responsibility which has not always been recognized.... The adoption in these statutes of the judicially constructed "substantial evidence" test was a response to pressures for stricter and more uniform practice ...

We conclude, therefore, that the Administrative Procedure Act and the Taft-Hartley Act direct that courts must now assume more responsibility for the reasonableness and fairness of Labor Board decisions than some courts have shown in the past. Reviewing courts must be influenced by a feeling that they are not to abdicate the conventional judicial function. Congress has imposed on them responsibility for assuring that the

Board keeps within reasonable grounds. That responsibility is not less real because it is limited to enforcing the requirement that evidence appear substantial when viewed, on the record as a whole, by courts invested with the authority and enjoying the prestige of the Courts of Appeals. The Board's findings are entitled to respect; but they must nonetheless be set aside when the record before a Court of Appeals clearly precludes the Board's decision from being justified by a fair estimate of the worth of the testimony of witnesses or its informed judgment on matters within its special competence or both....

II ...

The decision of the Court of Appeals is assailed on two grounds. It is said (1) that the court erred in holding that it was barred from taking into account the report of the examiner on questions of fact insofar as that report was rejected by the Board, and (2) that the Board's order was not supported by substantial evidence on the record considered as a whole, even apart from the validity of the court's refusal to consider the rejected portions of the examiner's report.

... [I]t is clear from the court's opinion in this case that it in fact did consider the "record as a whole." ...

The first contention, however, raises serious questions to which we now turn.

III

The Court of Appeals deemed itself bound by the Board's rejection of the examiner's findings.... [The U.S. Supreme Court holds that in this respect the court of appeals erred.]

The Taft-Hartley Act provides that "The findings of the Board with respect to questions of fact if supported by substantial evidence on the record considered as a whole shall be conclusive." 61 Stat. 148.... Surely an examiner's report is as much a part of the record as the complaint or the testimony. According to the Administrative Procedure Act, "All decisions (including initial, recommended, or tentative decisions) shall become a part of the record...." § 8(b), 60 Stat. 242.... The similarity of the two statutes in language and purpose ... requires that the definition of "record" found in the Administrative Procedure Act be construed to be applicable as well to the term "record" as used in the Taft-Hartley Act.

It is therefore difficult to escape the conclusion that the plain language of the statutes directs a reviewing court to determine the substantiality of evidence on the record including the examiner's report. The conclusion is confirmed by the indications in the legislative history that enhancement of the status and function of the trial examiner was one of the important purposes of the movement for administrative reform....

We do not require that the examiner's findings be given more weight than in reason and in the light of judicial experience they deserve. The "substantial evidence" standard is not modified in any way when the Board and its examiner disagree. We intend only to recognize that evidence supporting a conclusion may be less substantial when an impartial, experienced examiner who has observed the witnesses and lived with the case has drawn conclusions different from the Board's than when he has reached the same conclusion. The findings of the examiner are to be considered along with the consistency and inherent probability of testimony. The significance of his report, of course, depends largely on the importance of credibility in the particular case....

We therefore remand the cause to the Court of Appeals....

Mr. Justice Black and Mr. Justice Douglas concur with parts I and II of this opinion but as to part III agree with the opinion of the court below....

c. The Significance of *Universal Camera*

The federal APA and the National Labor Relations Act prescribe the "substantial evidence" standard for judicial review of an agency's findings of fact in a formal adjudication. *Universal Camera* concerned application of the "substantial evidence" standard to the Board's determination of a pure question of fact: Why did Universal Camera fire Imre Chairman?

It is useful to compare *Universal Camera* with another case involving the National Labor Relations Act, which was presented in Chapter 32.B.1: *National Labor Relations Board v. Hearst Publications, Inc.*, 322 U.S. 111 (1944). The main issue in *Hearst* was whether four newspaper companies' "newsboys" were "employees" within the meaning of the National Labor Relations Act. That issue required the application of law (the Act's definition of "employee") to the facts of a particular case. It was a mixed question of law and fact. The Court in *Hearst* held that the Board's determination of that mixed question had to be upheld if it had "a warrant in the record and a reasonable basis in law." *Id.* at 131. That determination by the Board in the *Hearst* case differed from — and was subject to a different standard of judicial review than — the Board's determinations in *Hearst* of basic facts about the newsboys' working conditions. Those determinations of basic facts were the type of determination that would have been, and are today, subject to the "substantial evidence" standard of judicial review. *See id.* at 115–119. As a question of basic facts, the question "What were the newsboys' working conditions?" is comparable to the question in *Universal Camera* "What was the reason for Imre Chairman's firing?". Judicial review of the Board's determination of the latter question, like its determination of the former, was and is governed by the substantial evidence standard.

The Court in *Universal Camera* says three things about the "substantial evidence" standard:

(1) The substantial evidence standard requires courts to review agency decisions more closely than they did before. On the one hand, courts may not "displace the Board's choice between two fairly conflicting views, even though the court would justifiably have made a different choice had the matter been before it *de novo*." 340 U.S. at 488. On the other hand, Board findings must be "set aside when the record before a Court of Appeals clearly precludes the Board's decision from being justified by a fair estimate of the worth of the testimony of witnesses or its informed judgment on matters within its special competence or both." *Id.* at 490.

(2) Courts should apply the substantial evidence standard to the "whole record," by considering the evidence that supports the Board's factual determination as well as the evidence that weighs against it. 340 U.S. at 487–488.

(3) An ALJ's factual determination contrary to the agency's determination counts as record evidence that weighs against the agency's decision.

Today, these principles govern federal court review of federal agency factfinding not only under the APA and the National Labor Relations Act, but also under other review statutes that prescribe the "substantial evidence" standard. *See, e.g.*, 12 U.S.C. § 1848 (2012) (judicial review of orders of the Federal Reserve Board); 15 U.S.C. § 78y(a)(4) & (b)(4) (2012) (judicial review of orders and rules of SEC); 16 U.S.C. § 825*l*(b) (2012) (judicial review of decisions of Federal Energy Regulatory Commission); 42 U.S.C. § 405(g) (2012) (judicial review of any final decision of the Commissioner of Social Security).

As a practical matter, when an agency disagrees with the ALJ's findings of fact, the agency must justify its disagreement to the satisfaction of the reviewing court. That is particularly important—and can be particularly difficult—when the ALJ's decision rests directly on the credibility of witnesses, as distinguished from inferences drawn from the testimony and other evidence. As the Court said in *Universal Camera*, the significance of the ALJ's decision "depends largely on the importance of credibility in the particular case." 340 U.S. at 496. Some lower federal courts after *Universal Camera* have accordingly given "special scrutiny" to decisions by the Board that contradict ALJ findings based on witness credibility. *See, e.g., Slusher v. NLRB*, 432 F.3d 715, 727 (7th Cir. 2005). *But see NLRB v. Galicks, Inc.*, 2012 WL 678142 (6th Cir. 2012) (stating that the special-scrutiny concept should be "put ... out to pasture"). In any event, the lawyer must put on the strongest case possible before the ALJ.

2. *Allentown Mack Sales & Service, Inc. v. National Labor Relations Board*

The next case, like *Universal Camera*, addresses the "substantial evidence" standard. It also discusses other issues of judicial review of agency action.

a. The *Allentown Mack* Opinion

Please read the *Allentown Mack* opinion with these questions in mind:

1. What aspect of the Board's decision in this case does the Court review to determine whether it is "rational"—i.e., to ensure that it is not "arbitrary [or] capricious"?

2. What aspect of the Board's decision in this case does the Court review under the "substantial evidence" standard?

3. According to the Court in part IV of its opinion, why is it a problem if the Board is *articulating* one legal standard while, in reality, *applying* a different legal standard, to decide cases?

Allentown Mack Sales and Service, Inc. v. National Labor Relations Board
522 U.S. 359 (1998)

JUSTICE SCALIA delivered the opinion of the Court.

Under longstanding precedent of the National Labor Relations Board, an employer who believes that an incumbent union no longer enjoys the support of a majority of its employees has three options: to request a formal, Board-supervised election, to withdraw recognition from the union and refuse to bargain, or to conduct an internal poll of employee support for the union. The Board has held that the latter two are unfair labor practices unless the employer can show that it had a "good-faith reasonable doubt" about the union's majority support. We must decide whether the Board's standard for employer polling is rational and consistent with the National Labor Relations Act, and whether the Board's factual determinations in this case are supported by substantial evidence in the record.

I

Mack Trucks, Inc., had a factory branch in Allentown, Pennsylvania, whose service and parts employees were represented by Local Lodge 724 of the International Association of Machinists and Aerospace Workers, AFL-CIO (Local 724). Mack notified its Allentown managers in May 1990 that it intended to sell the branch, and several of those managers formed Allentown Mack Sales & Service, Inc., the petitioner here, which purchased the assets of the business on December 20, 1990, and began to operate it as an independent dealership. From December 21, 1990, to January 1, 1991, Allentown hired 32 of the original 45 Mack employees.

During the period before and immediately after the sale, a number of Mack employees made statements to the prospective owners of Allentown Mack Sales suggesting that the incumbent union had lost support among employees in the bargaining unit. In job interviews, eight employees made statements indicating, or at least arguably indicating, that they personally no longer supported the union. In addition, Ron Mohr, a member of the union's bargaining committee and shop steward for the Mack Trucks service department, told an Allentown manager that it was his feeling that the employees did not want a union, and that "with a new company, if a vote was taken, the Union would lose." 316 N.L.R.B. 1199, 1207 (1995). And Kermit Bloch, who worked for Mack Trucks as a mechanic on the night shift, told a manager that the entire night shift (then five or six employees) did not want the union.

On January 2, 1991, Local 724 asked Allentown Mack Sales to recognize it as the employees' collective-bargaining representative, and to begin negotiations for a contract. The new employer rejected that request by letter dated January 25, claiming a "good faith doubt as to support of the Union among the employees." *Id.*, at 1205. The letter also announced that Allentown had "arranged for an independent poll by secret ballot of its hourly employees to be conducted under guidelines prescribed by the National Labor Relations Board." *Ibid.* The poll, supervised by a Roman Catholic priest, was conducted on February 8, 1991; the union lost 19 to 13. Shortly thereafter, the union filed an unfair-labor-practice charge with the Board.

The Administrative Law Judge (ALJ) concluded that Allentown was a "successor" employer to Mack Trucks, Inc., and therefore inherited Mack's bargaining obligation and a presumption of continuing majority support for the union. *Id.*, at 1203. The ALJ held that Allentown's poll was conducted in compliance with the procedural standards enunciated by the Board..., but that it violated §§ 8(a)(1) and 8(a)(5) of the National Labor Relations Act (Act), ... 29 U.S.C. §§ 158(a)(1) and 158(a)(5), because Allentown did not have an "objective reasonable doubt" about the majority status of the union. The Board adopted the ALJ's findings and agreed with his conclusion that Allentown "had not demonstrated that it harbored a reasonable doubt, based on objective considerations, as to the incumbent Union's continued majority status after the transition." 316 N.L.R.B., at 1199. The Board ordered Allentown to recognize and bargain with Local 724.

On review in the Court of Appeals for the District of Columbia Circuit, Allentown challenged both the facial rationality of the Board's test for employer polling and the Board's application of that standard to the facts of this case. The court enforced the Board's bargaining order ...

II

Allentown challenges the Board's decision in this case on several grounds. First, it contends that because the Board's "reasonable doubt" standard for employer polls is the same as its standard for unilateral withdrawal of recognition and for employer initiation of a Board-supervised election (a so-called "Representation Management," or "RM" election), the Board irrationally permits employers to poll only when it would be unnecessary and legally pointless to do so. Second, Allentown argues that the record evidence clearly demonstrates that it had a good-faith reasonable doubt about the union's claim to majority support. Finally, it asserts that the Board has, *sub silentio* (and presumably in violation of law), abandoned the "reasonable doubt" prong of its polling standard, and recognizes an employer's "reasonable doubt" only if a majority of the unit employees renounce the union. In this Part of our opinion we address the first of these challenges; the other two, which are conceptually intertwined, will be addressed in Parts III and IV.

Courts must defer to the requirements imposed by the Board if they are "rational and consistent with the Act," *Fall River Dyeing & Finishing Corp. v. NLRB*, 482 U.S. 27, 42 (1987), and if the Board's "explication is not inadequate, irrational or arbitrary," *NLRB v. Erie Resistor Corp.*, 373 U.S. 221, 236 (1963). Allentown argues that it is irrational to require the same factual showing to justify a poll as to justify an outright withdrawal of recognition, because that leaves the employer with no legal incentive to poll. Under the Board's framework, the results of a poll can never supply an otherwise lacking "good-faith reasonable doubt" necessary to justify a withdrawal of recognition, since the employer must already have that same reasonable doubt before he is permitted to conduct a poll. Three Courts of Appeals have found that argument persuasive.

While the Board's adoption of a unitary standard for polling, RM elections, and withdrawals of recognition is in some respects a puzzling policy, we do not find it so irrational as to be "arbitrary [or] capricious" within the meaning of the Administrative Procedure Act, 5 U.S.C. §706. The Board believes that employer polling is potentially "disruptive" to established bargaining relationships and "unsettling" to employees, and so has chosen to limit severely the circumstances under which it may be conducted. The unitary standard reflects the Board's apparent conclusion that polling should be tolerated only when the employer might otherwise simply withdraw recognition and refuse to bargain.

It is true enough that this makes polling useless as a means of insulating a contemplated withdrawal of recognition against an unfair-labor-practice charge—but there is more to life (and even to business) than escaping unfair-labor-practice findings. An employer concerned with good employee relations might recognize that abrupt withdrawal of recognition—even from a union that no longer has majority support—will certainly antagonize union supporters, and perhaps even alienate employees who are on the fence. Preceding that action with a careful, unbiased poll can prevent these consequences. The "polls are useless" argument falsely assumes, moreover, that every employer will want to withdraw recognition as soon as he has enough evidence of lack of union support to defend against an unfair-labor-practice charge. It seems to us that an employer whose evidence met the "good-faith reasonable doubt" standard might nonetheless want to withdraw recognition only if he had conclusive evidence that the union in fact lacked majority support, lest he go through the time and expense of an (ultimately victorious) unfair-labor-practice suit for a benefit that will only last until the next election.... And finally, it is probably the case that, though the standard for conviction of an unfair labor practice with regard to polling is identical to the standard with regard to withdrawal of recognition, the chance that a charge will be filed is significantly less with regard to the polling, particularly if the union wins.

It must be acknowledged that the Board's avowed preference for RM elections over polls fits uncomfortably with its unitary standard; as the Court of Appeals pointed out, that preference should logically produce a more rigorous standard for polling. But there are other reasons why the standard for polling ought to be less rigorous than the standard for Board elections. For one thing, the consequences of an election are more severe: If the union loses an employer poll it can still request a Board election, but if the union loses a formal election it is barred from seeking another for a year. See 29 U.S.C. § 159(c)(3). If it would be rational for the Board to set the polling standard either higher or lower than the threshold for an RM election, then surely it is not irrational for the Board to split the difference.

III

The Board held Allentown guilty of an unfair labor practice in its conduct of the polling because it "ha[d] not demonstrated that it held a reasonable doubt, based on objective considerations, that the Union continued to enjoy the support of a majority of the bargaining unit employees." 316 N.L.R.B., at 1199. We must decide whether that conclusion is supported by substantial evidence on the record as a whole. *Fall River Dyeing, supra,* at 42; *Universal Camera Corp. v. NLRB,* 340 U.S. 474 (1951). Put differently, we must decide whether on this record it would have been possible for a reasonable jury to reach the Board's conclusion.

Before turning to that issue, we must clear up some semantic confusion. The Board asserted at argument that the word "doubt" may mean either "uncertainty" or "disbelief," and that its polling standard uses the word only in the latter sense. We cannot accept that linguistic revisionism. "Doubt" is precisely that sort of "disbelief" (failure to believe) which consists of an uncertainty rather than a belief in the opposite. If the subject at issue were the existence of God, for example, "doubt" would be the disbelief of the agnostic, not of the atheist. A doubt is an uncertain, tentative, or provisional disbelief....

The question presented for review, therefore, is whether, on the evidence presented to the Board, a reasonable jury could have found that Allentown lacked a genuine, reasonable uncertainty about whether Local 724 enjoyed the continuing support of a majority of unit employees. In our view, the answer is no. The Board's finding to the contrary rests on a refusal to credit probative circumstantial evidence, and on evidentiary demands that go beyond the substantive standard the Board purports to apply.

The Board adopted the ALJ's finding that 6 of Allentown's 32 employees had made "statements which could be used as objective considerations supporting a good-faith reasonable doubt as to continued majority status by the Union." 316 N.L.R.B., at 1207. (These included, for example, the statement of Rusty Hoffman that "he did not want to work in a union shop," and "would try to find another job if he had to work with the Union." *Id.,* at 1206.) The Board seemingly also accepted (though this is not essential to our analysis) the ALJ's willingness to assume that the statement of a seventh employee (to the effect that he "did not feel comfortable with the Union and thought it was a waste of $35 a month," *ibid.*) supported good-faith reasonable doubt of his support for the union — as in our view it unquestionably does. And it presumably accepted the ALJ's assessment that "7 of 32, or roughly 20 percent of the involved employees" was not alone sufficient to create "an objective reasonable doubt of union majority support," *id.,* at 1207. The Board did not specify how many express disavowals would have been enough to establish reasonable doubt, but the number must presumably be less than 16 (half of the bargaining unit), since that would establish reasonable certainty. Still, we would not say that 20% first-hand-confirmed opposition (even with no countering evidence of union support) is alone enough to require a conclusion of reasonable doubt. But there was much more.

For one thing, the ALJ and the Board totally disregarded the effect upon Allentown of the statement of an eighth employee, Dennis Marsh, who said that "he was not being represented for the $35 he was paying." *Ibid.* The ALJ, whose findings were adopted by the Board, said that this statement "seems more an expression of a desire for better representation than one for no representation at all." *Ibid.* It seems to us that it is, more accurately, simply an expression of dissatisfaction with the union's performance—which *could* reflect the speaker's desire that the union represent him more effectively, but *could also* reflect the speaker's desire to save his $35 and get rid of the union. The statement would assuredly engender an *uncertainty* whether the speaker supported the union, and so could not be entirely ignored.

But the most significant evidence excluded from consideration by the Board consisted of statements of two employees regarding not merely their own support of the union, but support among the work force in general. Kermit Bloch, who worked on the night shift, told an Allentown manager "the entire night shift did not want the Union." *Ibid.* The ALJ refused to credit this, because "Bloch did not testify and thus could not explain how he formed his opinion about the views of his fellow employees." *Ibid.* Unsubstantiated assertions that other employees do not support the union certainly do not establish *the fact of that disfavor* with the degree of reliability ordinarily demanded in legal proceedings. But under the Board's enunciated test for polling, it is not the fact of disfavor that is at issue (the poll itself is meant to establish that), but rather the existence of a reasonable uncertainty on the part of the employer regarding that fact. On that issue, absent some reason for the employer to know that Bloch had no basis for his information, or that Bloch was lying, reason demands that the statement be given considerable weight.

Another employee who gave information concerning overall support for the union was Ron Mohr, who told Allentown managers that "if a vote was taken, the Union would lose" and that "it was his feeling that the employees did not want a union." *Ibid.* The ALJ again objected irrelevantly that "there is no evidence with respect to how he gained this knowledge." *Id.*, at 1208. In addition, the Board held that Allentown "could not legitimately rely on [the statement] as a basis for doubting the Union's majority status," *id.*, at 1200, because Mohr was "referring to Mack's existing employee complement, not to the individuals who were later hired by [Allentown]," *ibid.* This basis for disregarding Mohr's statements is wholly irrational. Local 724 had never won an election, or even an informal poll, within the actual unit of 32 Allentown employees. Its claim to represent them rested entirely on the Board's presumption that the work force of a successor company has the same disposition regarding the union as did the work force of the predecessor company, if the majority of the new work force came from the old one. See *id.*, at 1197, n. 3. The Board cannot rationally adopt that presumption for purposes of imposing the duty to bargain, and adopt precisely the opposite presumption (i.e., contend that there is no relationship between the sentiments of the two work forces) for purposes of determining what evidence tends to establish a reasonable doubt regarding union support. Such irrationality is impermissible ...

It must be borne in mind that the issue here is not whether Mohr's statement clearly establishes a majority in opposition to the union, but whether it contributes to a reasonable uncertainty whether a majority in favor of the union existed. We think it surely does. Allentown would reasonably have given great credence to Mohr's assertion of lack of union support, since he was not hostile to the union, and was in a good position to assess antiunion sentiment. Mohr was a union shop steward for the service department, and a member of the union's bargaining committee; according to the ALJ, he "did not indicate personal dissatisfaction with the Union." 316 N.L.R.B., at 1208. It seems to us that Mohr's statement has undeniable and substantial probative value on the issue of "reasonable doubt."

Accepting the Board's apparent (and in our view inescapable) concession that Allentown received reliable information that 7 of the bargaining-unit employees did not support the union, the remaining 25 would have had to support the union by a margin of 17 to 8 — a ratio of more than 2 to 1 — if the union commanded majority support. The statements of Bloch and Mohr would cause anyone to doubt that degree of support, and neither the Board nor the ALJ discussed any evidence that Allentown should have weighed on the other side. The most pro-union statement cited in the ALJ's opinion was Ron Mohr's comment that he personally "could work with or without the Union," and "was there to do his job." *Id.*, at 1207. The Board cannot covertly transform its presumption of continuing majority support into a working assumption that all of a successor's employees support the union until proved otherwise. Giving fair weight to Allentown's circumstantial evidence, we think it quite impossible for a rational factfinder to avoid the conclusion that Allentown had reasonable, good-faith grounds to doubt — to be uncertain about — the union's retention of majority support.

IV

That conclusion would make this a fairly straightforward administrative-law case, except for the contention that the Board's factfinding here was not an aberration. Allentown asserts that, although "the Board continues to cite the words of the good faith doubt branch of its withdrawal of recognition standard," a systematic review of the Board's decisions will reveal that "it has in practice eliminated the good faith doubt branch in favor of a strict head count." ... That the current decision may conform to a long pattern is ... suggested by academic commentary. One scholar ... concluded:

> "[C]ircumstantial evidence, no matter how abundant, is rarely, if ever, enough to satisfy the good-faith doubt test. In practice, the Board deems the test satisfied only if the employer has proven that a majority of the bargaining unit has expressly repudiated the union.... Flynn, The Costs and Benefits of "Hiding the Ball": NLRB Policymaking and the Failure of Judicial Review, 75 B.U.L.Rev. 387, 394–395 (1995) (footnotes omitted).

Members of this Court have observed the same phenomenon....

It is certainly conceivable that an adjudicating agency might consistently require a particular substantive standard to be established by a quantity or character of evidence so far beyond what reason and logic would require as to make it apparent that the announced standard is not really the effective one.... The question arises, then, whether, if that should be the situation that obtains here, we ought to measure the evidentiary support for the Board's decision against the standards consistently applied rather than the standards recited. [The Court concludes that courts should review the Board's decisions against the standards recited.] ...

The Administrative Procedure Act ... establishes a scheme of "reasoned decisionmaking." *Motor Vehicle Mfrs. Assn. of United States, Inc. v. State Farm Mut. Automobile Ins. Co.*, 463 U.S. 29, 52 (1983). Not only must an agency's decreed result be within the scope of its lawful authority, but the process by which it reaches that result must be logical and rational. Courts enforce this principle with regularity when they set aside agency regulations which, though well within the agencies' scope of authority, are not supported by the reasons that the agencies adduce.... [A]djudication is subject to the requirement of reasoned decisionmaking as well. It is hard to imagine a more violent breach of that requirement than applying a rule of primary conduct or a standard of proof which is in fact different from the rule or standard formally announced. And the consistent repetition of that breach can hardly mend it.

... The evil of a decision that applies a standard other than the one it enunciates spreads in both directions, preventing both consistent application of the law by subordinate agency personnel (notably ALJ's), and effective review of the law by the courts....

... If revision of the Board's standard of proof can be achieved thus subtly and obliquely, it becomes a much more complicated enterprise for a court of appeals to determine whether substantial evidence supports the conclusion that the required standard has or has not been met.... An agency should not be able to impede judicial review, and indeed even political oversight, by disguising its policymaking as factfinding.

Because reasoned decisionmaking demands it, and because the systemic consequences of any other approach are unacceptable, the Board must be required to apply in fact the clearly understood legal standards that it enunciates in principle, such as good-faith reasonable doubt and preponderance of the evidence. Reviewing courts are entitled to take those standards to mean what they say, and to conduct substantial-evidence review on that basis....

We conclude that the Board's "reasonable doubt" test for employer polls is facially rational and consistent with the Act. But the Board's factual finding that Allentown Mack Sales lacked such a doubt is not supported by substantial evidence on the record as a whole. The judgment of the Court of Appeals for the District of Columbia Circuit is therefore reversed, and the case is remanded with instructions to deny enforcement....

CHIEF JUSTICE REHNQUIST, with whom JUSTICE O'CONNOR, JUSTICE KENNEDY, and JUSTICE THOMAS join, concurring in part and dissenting in part....

JUSTICE BREYER, with whom JUSTICE STEVENS, JUSTICE SOUTER, and JUSTICE GINSBURG join, concurring in part and dissenting in part....

---

b. The Significance of *Allentown Mack*

(i) The Court's Application of a Stringent Version of the "Substantial Evidence" Standard

Allentown Mack equates the substantial evidence standard to the standard trial judges use to decide whether to grant a judgment notwithstanding the verdict (also known as a judgment as a matter of law), which asks whether a reasonable factfinder could have reached the factual determination under review. This equation is consistent with history suggesting that the "substantial evidence" standard originated as a standard for judicial review of jury verdicts. See, e.g., Robert L. Stern, *Review of Findings of Administrators, Judges and Juries: A Comparative Analysis*, 58 Harv. L. Rev. 70, 72–75 (1944). The Court used the substantial evidence standard in *Allentown Mack* to review the Board's finding that an employer lacked a reasonable, good-faith doubt that the union lacked majority support. Under that standard, the Court reviewed the evidence before the Board quite closely—indeed, more closely than courts usually do when applying the substantial evidence standard.

Several factors seem to increase the scrutiny involved in the *Allentown Mack* Court's application of the "substantial evidence" standard. (1) The issue was not highly technical, as it is, for example, in some cases involving complex scientific evidence. (2) The Court was reviewing formal adjudication, a much more "comfortable" setting for appellate courts to review, because of its resemblance to trial court proceedings, than agency rulemaking. (3) The Board is a federal agency whose decisions often seem to get a stringent version of substantial evidence review, perhaps because the Board deals with factual issues that are familiar to courts. (4) The Court suspected that the Board was acting dishonestly by articulating one legal standard ("good-faith reasonable doubt" of continued majority support of the union) while actually applying a different legal standard (clear and cogent proof of an actual loss of majority support of the union). In any event, just like some types of coffee are stronger than others, some versions of the "substantial evidence" seem to involve closer judicial scrutiny than others.

In fact, courts often apply the "substantial evidence" standard more deferentially than the Court did in *Allentown Mack*. An example of a highly deferential version of the standard is illustrated by a case in which the D.C. Circuit reviewed an Occupational Safety and Health Administration (OSHA) rule under the "substantial evidence" standard prescribed in OSHA's organic act. The OSHA rule regulated vertical tandem lifts (VTLs). VTLs are machines that lift intermodal cargo containers — for example, from a cargo ship to a train. A trade association challenged the VTL rule, arguing that substantial evidence did not support OSHA's finding that VTLs pose a "significant risk" as required for OSHA regulation. In rejecting that challenge, the court wrote about "substantial evidence" review of agency rules:

> We have previously noted the "peculiar problem of reviewing the rules of agencies like OSHA" that arises from "applying the substantial evidence test to regulations which are essentially legislative and rooted in inferences from complex scientific and factual data." *United Steelworkers of Am. v. Marshall*, 647 F.2d 1189, 1206–07 (D.C.Cir.1980), *cert. denied*, 453 U.S. 913 (1981). In such a case, as this one is, our task is not to "second-guess an agency decision that falls within a zone of reasonableness" but rather to "ensure public accountability" by requiring the agency to identify the evidence upon which it relies, to explain its logic and the policies underlying its choices, to state candidly any assumptions on which it relies and to provide its reasons for rejecting contrary evidence and arguments. *Id.* (internal quotation marks omitted). OSHA has met that burden regarding its significant risk determination of VTLs.

Nat'l Maritime Safety Ass'n v. OHSA, 649 F.3d 743, 751–752 (D.C. Cir. 2011).

An earlier, well-known case likewise emphasized the difficulty of applying the substantial evidence standard to rulemaking that involved complex and often uncertain scientific data:

> [S]ome of the questions involved in the promulgation of these standards are on the frontiers of scientific knowledge, and consequently as to them, insufficient data is presently available to make a fully informed factual determination. Decisionmaking must in that circumstance depend to a greater degree upon policy judgments and less upon purely factual analysis....
>
> ... When the Secretary is obliged to make policy judgments where no factual certainties exist or where facts alone do not provide the answer, he should so state and go on to identify the considerations he found persuasive....

Indus. Union Dep't, AFL-CIO v. Hodgson, 499 F.2d 467, 474, 476 (D.C. Cir. 1974). In this early case, the court was suggesting that scrutiny of the rulemaking record for substantial evidence supporting the agency decision can only take you so far. At some point, scientific uncertainty requires the agency to make policy judgments, which a court must review using an approach more closely associated with review under the "arbitrary and capricious" standard that we introduce next and explore in the next chapter.

(ii) The Court's Application of the "Substantial Evidence" Standard to the Board's Factfinding While Using the "Arbitrary and Capricious" Standard to Review the Board's "Good-Faith Reasonable Doubt" Test

Allentown Mack illustrates the relationship between the "substantial evidence" standard of review and one function of the "arbitrary and capricious" standard of review. To express the relationship metaphorically, the substantial evidence standard was used to review the Board's determination that the Employer broke the speed limit; the arbitrary and capricious standard was used to review the rationality of the Board-created speed limit. (As discussed below, the arbitrary and capricious standard also governed the permissibility of the Board's apparently announcing one speed limit while enforcing a different one.)

In actuality, the Court in *Allentown Mack* uses the substantial evidence standard to review the Board's determination that an employer lacked "good-faith reasonable doubt" that a majority of its employees supported the union. (See Part III of the Court's opinion.) This is an example of a court using the substantial evidence standard to review an agency's findings of fact. The Board found that the facts did not support a good-faith reasonable doubt. True, the Board was also determining how a legal standard (the good faith reasonable doubt test) applied to the facts. But the dispute centered on the factual basis for the Board's decision. *See Allentown Mack*, 522 U.S. at 372 (referring to Board's "factfinding").

In contrast, the Court uses the arbitrary and capricious (A&C) standard to review the rationality of the Board's "good-faith reasonable doubt" test for polling employees. (See Part II of the Court's opinion.) Under the A&C standard, the Court holds that the test is rational, barely. This shows the A&C standard in its role as imposing a requirement of "reasoned decisionmaking." *Id.* at 374. As discussed in the next chapter, the A&C standard also serves a second role: as a default standard for reviewing the factual basis of agency actions that are not subject to the "substantial evidence" or "de novo" standards of review. In its role as the source of the reasoned decisionmaking requirement, the A&C standard applies to the process as well as the result of the agency's decision making. And it can invalidate agency action even if that agency action is within the agency's authority. *See id.* at 374.

(iii) The Court's Discussion of the Possibility That the Board Has Covertly Departed from the "Good-Faith Reasonable Doubt" Test

The Court discusses in Part IV of its opinion whether the Board is in practice demanding more or different proof from employers than is implied by the Board's stated "good-faith reasonable doubt" test. The Court says that if the Board is allowed to get away with covert departures from its stated legal standards, "it becomes a much more complicated enterprise for a court of appeals to determine whether substantial evidence supports the conclusion that the required standard has or has not been met." *Allentown Mack*, 522 U.S. at 376. Why?

The Court also says that covert departures by agencies from their stated standards are antithetical to the "scheme of reasoned decisionmaking" established by the APA. *Id.* at 374. As mentioned above, the precise source of the APA's "reasoned decisionmaking" requirement is the A&C standard in §706(2)(A). Notice that the Court applies the requirement twice in the *Allentown Mack* opinion. The Court uses it first in Part II of the opinion to review the rationality of the good-faith reasonable doubt test and again in Part IV to condemn covert agency departures from their stated standards. This gives you a sense of the breadth and versatility of the A&C standard and, we hope, whets your appetite for our exploration of the A&C standard in the next chapter.

D. The "Substantial Evidence" Standard in the States

You need only examine the model State APAs to appreciate the prevalence of the "substantial evidence" standard in the States. The 1961 Model State APA uses the standard in §15, which governs judicial review of agency decisions in contested cases, the state analog to formal adjudications under the APA. Section 15 authorizes judicial relief if an agency decision is "clearly erroneous in view of the reliable, probative, and substantial evidence on the whole record." 1961 Model State APA §15(g)(5). The 1981 Model Act authorizes judicial relief if an agency action "is based on a determination of fact ... that is not supported by evidence that is substantial when viewed in light of the whole record." 1981 Model APA §5-116(c)(7). Finally, the 2010 Model State APA authorizes judicial relief if "any agency determination of fact in a contested case is not supported by substantial evidence in the record as a whole." 2010 Model State APA §508(a)(3)(D). The "substantial evidence" thus has had staying power, though the term is elastic enough that it may mean different things in different States, and may even, as is true at the federal level, be applied even within a State to review some factual determinations by agencies more closely than others.

E. Chapter 33 Wrap Up and Look Ahead

This chapter has introduced you to the substantial evidence standard of judicial review. From this chapter, you have learned:

- In federal law, the substantial evidence standard applies primarily to review of the factual basis for agency decisions in formal adjudications subject to review under §706(2)(E) of the APA.

- The term "substantial evidence" is used for both a standard of judicial review and a standard of proof, and the term has different meanings in those two different settings.

- As a standard of judicial review, the "substantial evidence" requires a federal court to review the whole record, and to uphold a federal agency's factual determination unless no reasonable factfinder could have made that determination.

- Although you may encounter similar definitions of the "substantial evidence" standard in many different settings, in reality courts *apply* the standard somewhat differently depending on various factors. Furthermore, States do not have to define "substantial evidence" to have the same meaning as the federal courts have given it.

Now that you have substantial understanding of the substantial evidence standard, we turn in the next chapter to a different standard of review, which made a cameo appearance in this chapter: the "arbitrary and capricious" standard.

Chapter Problem Revisited

You have learned that the substantial evidence standard is deferential. Even so, arguments can be made that substantial evidence did not support the IJ's decision in this case. We hope you have identified some good arguments. Notice that the IJ discounted Ms. Weng's account based, not on her demeanor during her testimony, but on inferences drawn from her failure to mention religious persecution at the initial interview. Also, the IJ's decision did not address Ms. Weng's documentary evidence.

This chapter problem is based on *Weng v. Holder*, 593 F.3d 66 (1st Cir. 2010).

Professional Development Reflection Question

Pro bono service includes "participation in activities for improving the law, the legal system or the legal profession." Model Rule of Professional Conduct 6.1(b)(3). One area of the law that needs improvement is the subject of the chapter problem: the immigration system. Lawyers who specialize in immigration law develop expertise that can help improve this area of the law. Such improvement efforts often occur through organizations of lawyers, which can include bar associations and nonprofit organization such as the American Immigration Lawyers Association (AILA).

If your casebook author's experience is typical, law students may doubt they have any expertise useful for law reform efforts. In reality, you might be surprised how quickly your law school education gives you perspectives and insights that non-lawyers can't easily match. To prove the point, consider this question: Has your study of administrative law given you better insight into how the government works (or doesn't work) when it comes to administering laws like the immigration laws? Do you believe you have a more nuanced understanding of "all the moving parts" involved in administration of federal and state laws than you did before you began studying administrative law?

If you answer yes to these questions, imagine the depth of knowledge possessed by a lawyer who has specialized in immigration law for twenty years, and the important role that specialized knowledge could play in efforts to reform this area of law.

Chapter 34

The "Arbitrary and Capricious" Standard

Overview

Section 706(2)(A) of the federal APA and some special review statutes authorize federal courts to set aside agency action that is "arbitrary, capricious, [or] an abuse of discretion." *E.g.*, 5 U.S.C. § 706(2)(A) (2012); 42 U.S.C. § 7607(d)(9)(A) (2012). The "arbitrary and capricious" standard also appears in many state APAs. Because of its prevalence, it is an important standard of review for administrative lawyers to understand. This chapter examines the standard.

This chapter has four sections, which are entitled:

A. When Does the Arbitrary and Capricious Standard Apply?

B. What Does the Arbitrary and Capricious Standard Mean?

C. Leading Cases on the Arbitrary and Capricious Standard

D. Chapter 34 Wrap Up and Look Ahead

Chapter Problem

Email

To: New Associate

From: Junior Partner

Re: Preparation for Meeting with Client on New Matter

I need your help getting ready for a meeting with a client tomorrow about a new matter. Our client is the King Candy Company. King Candy has hired us to represent it in a rulemaking matter before the U.S. Department of Agriculture (USDA). The rulemaking will result in new nutritional criteria that school lunches will have to meet to receive federal funding. As you know, these federal funds make it possible for schools to give free lunches to poor children.

King Candy makes a ton of money selling fruit jerky (also known as "fruit leather") to schools that include them in their school lunches. King Candy has every reason to believe USDA's new nutritional criteria will require schools to serve real fruit instead of fruit jerky, because some health experts claim that real fruit is "healthier" than fruit jerky. King Candy wants us to prepare material for submission to USDA to prevent the new criteria from excluding fruit jerky. We expect the USDA to publish proposed new nutritional criteria any day now, so we will need to hit the ground running.

I need your help with long range planning. I suspect USDA will indeed propose excluding fruit jerky from the new criteria and that we will therefore have to bring a lawsuit challenging the exclusion if it is adopted in the final rule. I will give you the background statutes and regulations when we meet later today. For now, all you need to know is two things. First, the statutes give USDA broad discretion to formulate guidelines to ensure that federally subsidized school lunches are "nutritious." Second, the standards for judicial review of the new USDA regulations will be those supplied by the federal APA.

You can help me brainstorm data that we can develop, and arguments that we can make, to maximize our chances of ultimately proving that a decision to exclude fruit jerky would be arbitrary and capricious.

Let's meet at 4 pm today to discuss these issues. I hope you will be available tomorrow morning, so I can have you meet the client. Thank you.

A. When Does the Arbitrary and Capricious Standard Apply?

The arbitrary and capricious standard applies whenever a court reviews agency action under a statute authorizing review under that standard. This includes all federal agency actions reviewed under § 706(2)(A) of the federal APA, as well as federal agency actions reviewed under a special review statute prescribing the standard. To better understand the A&C standard's applicability, however, you have to recall from Chapter 33 that it serves two roles.

First, the A&C standard serves as a default standard for judicial review, under federal APA § 706, of the factual basis for agency action. The A&C standard serves this default role because of the limited applicability of the two standards in § 706 that specifically address questions of fact. Specifically, § 706(2)(E) authorizes review of the factual basis of some agency actions under a "substantial evidence" standard, and § 706(2)(F) authorizes review of the factual basis of some other agency actions under a "de novo" standard. Those two standards, however, generally do not apply to agency decisions in informal rulemaking and informal adjudication. Nor do they apply to rules made through hybrid rulemaking unless a special review statute prescribes the "substantial evidence" standard. For those types of agency action — namely, informal adjudication, informal rulemaking, and many rules made through hybrid rulemaking — the A&C standard fills the gap by supplying the standard for review of the factual basis for the agency's action. In this role, the A&C standard requires the agency's factual determinations to be reasonable.

Second, the A&C standard serves to impose on federal agencies a requirement of "reasoned decisionmaking." *E.g., Motor Vehicle Mfrs. Ass'n v. State Farm Mut. Auto. Ins. Co.*, 463 U.S. 29, 52 (1983). We explore the meaning of this reasoned-decisionmaking requirement later in this chapter. For now, the thing to understand is that, in its role as the source of a reasoned-decisionmaking requirement, the A&C standard applies in essentially all APA-type challenges to federal agency action. That is because essentially all APA-type actions are subject to §706(2)(A). Section 706(2)(A) applies not only to judicial challenges resting on the cause of action created by the APA. Section 706(2)(A) also applies to judicial challenges resting on causes of action supplied by special review statutes. *See Dickinson v. Zurko*, 527 U.S. 150, 154–155 (1999). Moreover, some special review statutes themselves prescribe the A&C standard for review of agency action. *E.g.*, 42 U.S.C. §7697(d)(9)(A) (2012) (special review statute for certain EPA rules imposing A&C standard). The near-universal applicability of the A&C standard is reflected in the Court's statement: "In all cases agency action must be set aside if the action was 'arbitrary, capricious, an abuse of discretion, or otherwise not in accordance with law.'" *Citizens to Preserve Overton Park, Inc. v. Volpe*, 401 U.S. 402, 416 (1971). It will be the rare APA-type challenge in which the A&C standard is not available as a potential ground for invalidating agency action.

In judicial review of a particular agency action, the A&C standard may serve one or both of the functions described above. The A&C standard served both functions in a leading case on the standard reproduced later in this chapter: *Citizens to Preserve Overton Park, Inc. v. Volpe*, 401 U.S. 402. That case involved a judicial challenge to a decision of the U.S. Secretary of Transportation to build a segment of an interstate highway through a city park. The federal APA supplied the cause of action for the judicial challenge, because no special review statute applied. This meant that the Secretary's decision was subject to the reasoned-decisionmaking requirement imposed by the A&C standard in §706(2)(A). In addition, the A&C standard governed review of the factual basis for the Secretary's decision because, as a decision made through informal adjudication, neither the "substantial evidence" standard" of §706(2)(E) nor the "de novo" standard of §706(2)(F) applied. Thus, the A&C standard required the Secretary's decision both to reflect reasoned decision making and to have a reasonable factual basis.

By comparison, the A&C standard in §706(2)(A) served only to impose a reasoned-decisionmaking requirement in the *Allentown Mack* case examined in Chapter 33. *See Allentown Mack Sales & Serv., Inc. v. NLRB*, 522 U.S. 359 (1998). *Allentown Mack* involved a judicial challenge to the NLRB's decision in a formal adjudication subject to APA §§556 and 557. The factual basis for the NLRB's decision was subject to the "substantial evidence" standard in a special review statute. Still, the A&C standard of §706(2)(A) also applied, by requiring the decision to reflect reasoned decision making. Specifically, the A&C standard authorized judicial review of the rationality of the Board's use of an "objective reasonable doubt" test for employer polling. *Allentown Mack* shows that, even when the A&C standard does not govern judicial review of the factual basis for an agency's decision, the A&C standard still ordinarily applies in an APA-type challenge.

The table on the next page attempts to show the applicability of the A&C standard to judicial review of federal agency actions in APA-type challenges in which the standards of review are governed solely by the APA—i.e., not modified by a special review statute.

In short, the A&C standard has near-universal application to judicial review of federal agency action. Depending on your cultural frame of reference, you can consider the A&C standard the Kilroy, the Zelig, the Forrest Gump, or the Waldo of administrative law; it shows up everywhere![1]

---

1. Kilroy was a fictional character from the World War II era who could be depended on to show up at every significant war event. Zelig and Forrest Gump were characters in movies who appeared

Table: Applicability of the "Arbitrary and Capricious" Standard

	judicial review of factual basis for agency action	judicial review of whether agency has engaged in reasoned decision making
formal adjudication	substantial evidence	arbitrary and capricious
formal rulemaking	substantial evidence	arbitrary and capricious
informal adjudication	arbitrary and capricious	arbitrary and capricious
informal rulemaking	arbitrary and capricious	arbitrary and capricious
other agency actions as to which standard for judicial review of factual basis is not specified but §706 applies (e.g., rules made through hybrid rule-manking)	arbitrary and capricious	arbitrary and capricious

B. What Does the Arbitrary and Capricious Standard Mean?

As discussed above, the A&C standard serves two functions: as a standard for judicial review of the factual basis for agency actions in some cases and as a standard for invalidating irrational agency action in nearly all cases. This does not tell you much about what the standard means, in either role. You will learn much about the meaning of the standard from the leading cases, which we set out in Section C of this chapter. Before we get to the cases, we will set out the basics.

In its role as the source of the "reasoned decision making" requirement, the A&C standard entails at least five requirements:

(1) The agency's reasoning process must be rational and comprehensible.

(2) The agency's decision should rest on consideration of all relevant factors.

(3) The agency's decision should not rest on consideration of irrelevant factors.

(4) There should be a clear, logical connection between the agency's factual determinations and its ultimate decision.

---

at significant historical events. Waldo is a character in a children's book series who shows up on every page of the book (but is hard to find).

(5) The agency action should be consistent with prior agency action—and thus the agency must treat similar situations similarly—unless the agency adequately explains why it has changed course.

By putting these requirements on agencies, the A&C standard gives courts power to prevent irrational agency decisionmaking, including agency abuses of discretion. That judicial power has particular importance because of (1) the awesome powers agencies have to determine legal rights and duties and (2) the many instances in which the laws directly limiting agency power leave agencies with great discretion.

As a standard for review of the factual basis for agency action, the A&C standard requires that an agency's factual determinations be reasonable. Lower federal courts have disagreed whether this "reasonableness" standard differs from the "substantial evidence" standard. In one famous case, a court described the A&C standard as identical to the substantial evidence standard. *Ass'n of Data Processing Serv. Orgs., Inc. v. Bd. of Governors of Fed. Reserve Sys.*, 745 F.2d 677 (D.C. Cir. 1984). The court recognized that the substantial evidence standard "has acquired a reputation for being more stringent" than the A&C standard. *Id.* at 685. The court reasoned, however, that the substantial evidence standard itself is not a demanding test; it is comparable to the amount of evidence required for a case to go to the jury rather than being resolved by a directed verdict. The court found it hard to imagine an agency's factual determination could fail the standard for a directed verdict and yet still be considered not "arbitrary and capricious." *Id.* at 683–684. Other courts, however, have concluded that the "substantial evidence" standard requires a reviewing court to take "[a] harder look" at the evidence supporting agency action than does the A&C standard. *E.g., Ala. Power Co. v. Occupational Safety & Health Admin.*, 89 F.3d 740 (11th Cir. 1996). Thus, courts do not agree on nuances, but they *do* tend to agree in understanding the A&C standard to require reasonable evidentiary support for an agency's factual determinations.

We will explore these requirements when we study the case law on the A&C standard, which we do next.

C. Leading Cases on the Arbitrary and Capricious Standard

In this section we study the two leading cases on the A&C standard. The first involves informal adjudication. The second involves an agency proceeding that the Court analogized to informal rulemaking.

1. *Citizens to Preserve Overton Park, Inc. v. Volpe*

a. The *Citizens to Preserve Overton Park* Opinion

Please read *Overton Park* with these questions in mind:

1. What agency action is before the Court? By way of review, why does that agency action constitute informal adjudication?

2. What agency-specific statutes govern the agency action before the Court? What are the competing interpretations of those statutes, as applied to that agency action?

Citizens to Preserve Overton Park, Inc. v. Volpe

401 U.S. 402 (1971)[2]

Opinion of the Court by MR. JUSTICE MARSHALL, announced by MR. JUSTICE STEWART.

The growing public concern about the quality of our natural environment has prompted Congress in recent years to enact legislation designed to curb the accelerating destruction of our country's natural beauty. We are concerned in this case with § 4 (f) of the Department of Transportation Act of 1966, as amended,[2] and § 18 (a) of the Federal-Aid Highway Act of 1968, 82 Stat. 823, 23 U.S.C. § 138 (1964 ed., Supp. V) (hereafter § 138).[3] These statutes prohibit the Secretary of Transportation from authorizing the use of federal funds to finance the construction of highways through public parks if a "feasible and prudent" alternative route exists. If no such route is available, the statutes allow him to approve construction through parks only if there has been "all possible planning to minimize harm" to the park.

Petitioners, private citizens as well as local and national conservation organizations, contend that the Secretary has violated these statutes by authorizing the expenditure of federal funds for the construction of a six-lane interstate highway through a public park in Memphis, Tennessee. Their claim was rejected by the District Court, which granted the Secretary's motion for summary judgment, and the Court of Appeals for the Sixth Circuit affirmed. After oral argument, this Court granted a stay that halted construction and, treating the application for the stay as a petition for certiorari, granted review. We now reverse the judgment below and remand for further proceedings in the District Court.

Overton Park is a 342-acre city park located near the center of Memphis. The park contains a zoo, a nine-hole municipal golf course, an outdoor theater, nature trails, a bridle path, an art academy, picnic areas, and 170 acres of forest. The proposed highway,

---

2. You will find a red flag and a red stop sign attached to *Overton Park* in the Westlaw and LexisNexis databases, respectively. They signify that the Court in *Overton Park* made a statement about the federal APA that the Court later repudiated. The Court in *Overton Park* said in a part of the opinion not included in our excerpt that the APA grants subject matter jurisdiction. 387 U.S. at 141. The Court later held in *Califano v. Sanders*, 430 U.S. 99, 105 (1977), that the APA does not grant subject matter jurisdiction. *Overton Park* is still good law for the judicial review analysis we reproduce here. We note that the holding in *Califano v. Sanders* likewise repudiated language in another famous, "red flagged" administrative law case, *Abbott Laboratories v. Gardner*, 387 U.S. 136 (1967), that we have excerpted in Chapter 30.

2. [Court's footnote:] "It is hereby declared to be the national policy that special effort should be made to preserve the natural beauty of the countryside and public park and recreation lands, wildlife and waterfowl refuges, and historic sites. The Secretary of Transportation shall cooperate and consult with the Secretaries of the Interior, Housing and Urban Development, and Agriculture, and with the States in developing transportation plans and programs that include measures to maintain or enhance the natural beauty of the lands traversed. After August 23, 1968, the Secretary shall not approve any program or project which requires the use of any publicly owned land from a public park, recreation area, or wildlife and waterfowl refuge of national, State, or local significance as determined by the Federal, State, or local officials having jurisdiction thereof, or any land from an historic site of national, State, or local significance as so determined by such officials unless (1) there is no feasible and prudent alternative to the use of such land, and (2) such program includes all possible planning to minimize harm to such park, recreational area, wildlife and waterfowl refuge, or historic site resulting from such use." 82 Stat. 824, 49 U.S.C. § 1653 (f) (1964 ed., Supp. V).

3. [Editor's note: The Court's footnote 3 reproduces the text of 23 U.S.C. § 138 (1964 ed., Supp. V), a statutory provision that is identical in relevant part to 49 U.S.C. § 1653(f) (1964 ed. Supp. V), which is the provision reproduced in the Court's footnote 2. Congress passed the duplicative provisions for reasons that don't matter for our purposes.]

which is to be a six-lane, high-speed, expressway, will sever the zoo from the rest of the park. Although the roadway will be depressed below ground level except where it crosses a small creek, 26 acres of the park will be destroyed. The highway is to be a segment of Interstate Highway I-40, part of the National System of Interstate and Defense Highways. I-40 will provide Memphis with a major east-west expressway which will allow easier access to downtown Memphis from the residential areas on the eastern edge of the city.

Although the route through the park was approved by the Bureau of Public Roads in 1956 and by the Federal Highway Administrator in 1966, the enactment of §4 (f) of the Department of Transportation Act prevented distribution of federal funds for the section of the highway designated to go through Overton Park until the Secretary of Transportation determined whether the requirements of §4 (f) had been met. Federal funding for the rest of the project was, however, available; and the [S]tate acquired a right of way on both sides of the park. In April 1968, the Secretary announced that he concurred in the judgment of local officials that I-40 should be built through the park. And in September 1969 the State acquired the right of way inside Overton Park from the city. Final approval for the project—the route as well as the design—was not announced until November 1969, after Congress had reiterated in §138 of the Federal-Aid Highway Act that highway construction through public parks was to be restricted. Neither announcement approving the route and design of I-40 was accompanied by a statement of the Secretary's factual findings. He did not indicate why he believed there were no feasible and prudent alternative routes or why design changes could not be made to reduce the harm to the park.

Petitioners contend that the Secretary's action is invalid without such formal findings and that the Secretary did not make an independent determination but merely relied on the judgment of the Memphis City Council. They also contend that it would be "feasible and prudent" to route I-40 around Overton Park either to the north or to the south. And they argue that if these alternative routes are not "feasible and prudent," the present plan does not include "all possible" methods for reducing harm to the park. Petitioners claim that I-40 could be built under the park by using either of two possible tunneling methods, and they claim that, at a minimum, by using advanced drainage techniques the expressway could be depressed below ground level along the entire route through the park including the section that crosses the small creek.

Respondents argue that it was unnecessary for the Secretary to make formal findings, and that he did, in fact, exercise his own independent judgment which was supported by the facts. In the District Court, respondents introduced affidavits, prepared specifically for this litigation, which indicated that the Secretary had made the decision and that the decision was supportable. These affidavits were contradicted by affidavits introduced by petitioners, who also sought to take the deposition of a former Federal Highway Administrator who had participated in the decision to route I-40 through Overton Park.

The District Court and the Court of Appeals found that formal findings by the Secretary were not necessary and refused to order the deposition of the former Federal Highway Administrator because those courts believed that probing of the mental processes of an administrative decision maker was prohibited. And, believing that the Secretary's authority was wide and reviewing courts' authority narrow in the approval of highway routes, the lower courts held that the affidavits contained no basis for a determination that the Secretary had exceeded his authority.

We agree that formal findings were not required. But we do not believe that in this case judicial review based solely on litigation affidavits was adequate.

A threshold question—whether petitioners are entitled to any judicial review—is easily answered. Section 701 of the Administrative Procedure Act, 5 U.S.C. §701 (1964 ed., Supp. V), provides that the action of "each authority of the Government of the United States," which includes the Department of Transportation, is subject to judicial review except where there is a statutory prohibition on review or where "agency action is committed to agency discretion by law." In this case, there is no indication that Congress sought to prohibit judicial review and there is most certainly no "showing of 'clear and convincing evidence' of a legislative intent" to restrict access to judicial review. *Abbott Laboratories v. Gardner*, 387 U.S. 136, 141 (1967), *Brownell v. We Shung*, 352 U.S. 180, 185 (1956).

Similarly, the Secretary's decision here does not fall within the exception for action "committed to agency discretion." This is a very narrow exception. The legislative history of the Administrative Procedure Act indicates that it is applicable in those rare instances where "statutes are drawn in such broad terms that in a given case there is no law to apply." S. Rep. No. 752, 79th Cong., 1st Sess., 26 (1945).

Section 4(f) of the Department of Transportation Act and §138 of the Federal-Aid Highway Act are clear and specific directives. Both the Department of Transportation Act and the Federal-Aid Highway Act provide that the Secretary "shall not approve any program or project" that requires the use of any public parkland "unless (1) there is no feasible and prudent alternative to the use of such land, and (2) such program includes all possible planning to minimize harm to such park...." 23 U.S.C. §138 (1964 ed., Supp. V); 49 U.S.C. §1653 (f) (1964 ed., Supp. V). This language is a plain and explicit bar to the use of federal funds for construction of highways through parks—only the most unusual situations are exempted.

Despite the clarity of the statutory language, respondents argue that the Secretary has wide discretion. They recognize that the requirement that there be no "feasible" alternative route admits of little administrative discretion. For this exemption to apply the Secretary must find that as a matter of sound engineering it would not be feasible to build the highway along any other route. Respondents argue, however, that the requirement that there be no other "prudent" route requires the Secretary to engage in a wide-ranging balancing of competing interests. They contend that the Secretary should weigh the detriment resulting from the destruction of parkland against the cost of other routes, safety considerations, and other factors, and determine on the basis of the importance that he attaches to these other factors whether, on balance, alternative feasible routes would be "prudent."

But no such wide-ranging endeavor was intended. It is obvious that in most cases considerations of cost, directness of route, and community disruption will indicate that parkland should be used for highway construction whenever possible. Although it may be necessary to transfer funds from one jurisdiction to another, there will always be a smaller outlay required from the public purse when parkland is used since the public already owns the land and there will be no need to pay for right of way. And since people do not live or work in parks, if a highway is built on parkland no one will have to leave his home or give up his business. Such factors are common to substantially all highway construction. Thus, if Congress intended these factors to be on an equal footing with preservation of parkland there would have been no need for the statutes.

Congress clearly did not intend that cost and disruption of the community were to be ignored by the Secretary. But the very existence of the statutes indicates that protection of parkland was to be given paramount importance. The few green havens that are public parks were not to be lost unless there were truly unusual factors present in a particular case or the cost or community disruption resulting from alternative routes reached extraordinary magnitudes. If the statutes are to have any meaning, the Secretary cannot approve the destruction of parkland unless he finds that alternative routes present unique problems.

Plainly, there is "law to apply" and thus the exemption for action "committed to agency discretion" is inapplicable. But the existence of judicial review is only the start: the standard for review must also be determined. For that we must look to § 706 of the Administrative Procedure Act, 5 U.S.C. § 706 (1964 ed., Supp. V), which provides that a "reviewing court shall ... hold unlawful and set aside agency action, findings, and conclusions found" not to meet six separate standards. In all cases agency action must be set aside if the action was "arbitrary, capricious, an abuse of discretion, or otherwise not in accordance with law" or if the action failed to meet statutory, procedural, or constitutional requirements. 5 U.S.C. §§ 706 (2) (A), (B), (C), (D) (1964 ed., Supp. V). In certain narrow, specifically limited situations, the agency action is to be set aside if the action was not supported by "substantial evidence." And in other equally narrow circumstances the reviewing court is to engage in a de novo review of the action and set it aside if it was "unwarranted by the facts." 5 U.S.C. §§ 706 (2) (E), (F) (1964 ed., Supp. V).

Petitioners argue that the Secretary's approval of the construction of I-40 through Overton Park is subject to one or the other of these latter two standards of limited applicability. First, they contend that the "substantial evidence" standard of § 706 (2) (E) must be applied. In the alternative, they claim that § 706 (2) (F) applies and that there must be a de novo review to determine if the Secretary's action was "unwarranted by the facts." Neither of these standards is, however, applicable....

Even though there is no *de novo* review in this case and the Secretary's approval of the route of I-40 does not have ultimately to meet the substantial evidence test, the generally applicable standards of § 706 require the reviewing court to engage in a substantial inquiry. Certainly, the Secretary's decision is entitled to a presumption of regularity. See, *e.g.*, *Pacific States Box & Basket Co. v. White*, 296 U.S. 176, 185 (1935). But that presumption is not to shield his action from a thorough, probing, in depth review.

The court is first required to decide whether the Secretary acted within the scope of his authority. This determination naturally begins with a delineation of the scope of the Secretary's authority and discretion. As has been shown, Congress has specified only a small range of choices that the Secretary can make. Also involved in this initial inquiry is a determination of whether on the facts the Secretary's decision can reasonably be said to be within that range. The reviewing court must consider whether the Secretary properly construed his authority to approve the use of parkland as limited to situations where there are no feasible alternative routes or where feasible alternative routes involve uniquely difficult problems. And the reviewing court must be able to find that the Secretary could have reasonably believed that in this case there are no feasible alternatives or that alternatives do involve unique problems.

Scrutiny of the facts does not end, however, with the determination that the Secretary has acted within the scope of his statutory authority. Section 706 (2)(A) requires a finding that the actual choice made was not "arbitrary, capricious, an abuse of discretion, or otherwise not in accordance with law." 5 U.S.C. § 706 (2)(A) (1964 ed., Supp. V). To make this finding the court must consider whether the decision was based on a consideration of the relevant factors and whether there has been a clear error of judgment.... Although this inquiry into the facts is to be searching and careful, the ultimate standard of review is a narrow one. The court is not empowered to substitute its judgment for that of the agency.

The final inquiry is whether the Secretary's action followed the necessary procedural requirements. Here the only procedural error alleged is the failure of the Secretary to make formal findings and state his reasons for allowing the highway to be built through the park.

Undoubtedly, review of the Secretary's action is hampered by his failure to make such findings, but the absence of formal findings does not necessarily require that the case be remanded to the Secretary. Neither the Department of Transportation Act nor the Federal-Aid Highway Act requires such formal findings. Moreover, the Administrative Procedure Act requirements that there be formal findings in certain rulemaking and adjudicatory proceedings do not apply to the Secretary's action here. See 5 U.S.C. §§ 553(a)(2), 554(a) (1964 ed., Supp. V). And, although formal findings may be required in some cases in the absence of statutory directives when the nature of the agency action is ambiguous, those situations are rare.... Plainly, there is no ambiguity here; the Secretary has approved the construction of I-40 through Overton Park and has approved a specific design for the project....

... Moreover, there is an administrative record that allows the full, prompt review of the Secretary's action that is sought without additional delay which would result from having a remand to the Secretary.

That administrative record is not, however, before us. The lower courts based their review on the litigation affidavits that were presented. These affidavits were merely *"post hoc"* rationalizations, *Burlington Truck Lines v. United States*, 371 U.S. 156, 168–169 (1962), which have traditionally been found to be an inadequate basis for review. *Burlington Truck Lines v. United States, supra; SEC v. Chenery Corp.*, 318 U.S. 80, 87 (1943). And they clearly do not constitute the "whole record" compiled by the agency: the basis for review required by § 706 of the Administrative Procedure Act.

Thus it is necessary to remand this case to the District Court for plenary review of the Secretary's decision. That review is to be based on the full administrative record that was before the Secretary at the time he made his decision. But since the bare record may not disclose the factors that were considered or the Secretary's construction of the evidence it may be necessary for the District Court to require some explanation in order to determine if the Secretary acted within the scope of his authority and if the Secretary's action was justifiable under the applicable standard.

The court may require the administrative officials who participated in the decision to give testimony explaining their action. Of course, such inquiry into the mental processes of administrative decisionmakers is usually to be avoided. *United States v. Morgan*, 313 U.S. 409, 422 (1941). And where there are administrative findings that were made at the same time as the decision, as was the case in *Morgan*, there must be a strong showing of bad faith or improper behavior before such inquiry may be made. But here there are no such formal findings and it may be that the only way there can be effective judicial review is by examining the decisionmakers themselves.

The District Court is not, however, required to make such an inquiry. It may be that the Secretary can prepare formal findings ... that will provide an adequate explanation for his action. Such an explanation will, to some extent, be a "post hoc rationalization" and thus must be viewed critically. If the District Court decides that additional explanation is necessary, that court should consider which method will prove the most expeditious so that full review may be had as soon as possible. Reversed and remanded.

Mr. Justice Douglas took no part in the consideration or decision of this case.

Separate opinion of Mr. Justice Black, with whom Mr. Justice Brennan joins....

Mr. Justice Blackmun.

I fully join the Court in its opinion and in its judgment. I merely wish to state the obvious: (1) The case comes to this Court as the end product of more than a decade of endeavor to solve the interstate highway problem at Memphis. (2) The administrative decisions under attack here are not those of a single Secretary; some were made by the present Secretary's predecessor and, before him, by the Department of Commerce's Bureau of Public Roads. (3) The 1966 Act and the 1968 Act have cut across former methods and here have imposed new standards and conditions upon a situation that already was largely developed....

b. The Significance of *Citizens to Preserve Overton Park*

Overton Park is one of the most important cases in modern U.S. administrative law. *Overton Park's* primary importance lies in its discussion of the "arbitrary and capricious" (A&C) standard of judicial review. *Overton Park* also has importance because of its discussion of the record for judicial review. Finally, *Overton Park* has great influence because of its discussion of the broader framework of judicial review into which the A&C standard fits.

(i) Arbitrary and Capricious

Overton Park establishes four things about the arbitrary and capricious (A&C) standard:

(1) The A&C standard in § 706(2)(A) governs judicial review of the factual basis for agency decisions in informal adjudications.

(2) The A&C standard also governs judicial review of the factual basis for other types of agency action — besides informal adjudication — that are reviewed under § 706 but that are not governed by either the "substantial evidence" standard in § 706(2)(E) or the de novo review under § 706(2)(F). Most importantly, this means that the A&C standard governs judicial review of the factual basis for agency rules made through informal rulemaking.

(3) In reviewing facts under the A&C standard, the court's "inquiry into the facts is to be searching and careful," though "[t]he court is not empowered to substitute its judgment for that of the agency." *Overton Park*, 401 U.S. at 416. Overall, the A&C standard requires the agency's factual determinations to be reasonable in light of the administrative record. For example, under the A&C standard "the reviewing court must be able to find that the Secretary could have reasonably believed that in this case there are no feasible alternatives or that alternatives do involve unique problems." *Id.* at 416.

(4) The A&C standard does more than supply the standard for judicial review of the factual basis of certain agency decisions. The A&C standard also requires courts to "consider whether the decision was based on a consideration of the relevant factors and whether there has been a clear error of judgment." *Id.* This involves judicial review of the overall rationality of the agency decision. In this role of requiring what the Court came to call "reasoned decisionmaking," the A&C standard applies to *all* agency actions subject to review under § 706, including agency actions the factual basis of which is subject to the substantial evidence or de novo standards. *See Overton Park*, 401 U.S. at 416 ("*In all cases* agency action must be set aside if the action was 'arbitrary, capricious, an abuse of

discretion, or otherwise not in accordance with law.") (emphasis added); *see also id.* at 415 (including the "arbitrary and capricious" standard among the "generally applicable standards of § 706").

These four principles apply whether the A&C standard governing review of a particular agency action comes from § 706(2)(A) of the federal APA or a special review statute. *See, e.g.,* 7 U.S.C. § 2(a)(1)(C)(v)(VI) (2012) (A&C standard in special review provision for actions of Commodity Futures Trading Commission); 15 U.S.C. § 78y(b)(4) (2012) (A&C standard in special review provision for rules promulgated by the Securities and Exchange Commission); 42 U.S.C. § 7607(d) (2012) (A&C standard in special review provision for EPA actions). Because of the prevalence of the A&C standard in the APA and other judicial review statutes, almost every federal agency action is subject to the A&C standard when reviewed in an APA-type challenge.

Exercise: The Arbitrary and Capricious Standard

Please review the excerpt of *Allentown Mack Sales and Service, Inc. v. National Labor Relations Board*, 522 U.S. 359 (1998), reproduced in Chapter 33, to see an example of a case in which the A&C standard applied to review of agency action that was also reviewed under the "substantial evidence" standard.

(ii) The Record for Judicial Review

Overton Park has importance not only for its discussion of the A&C standard but also for its discussion of the record for judicial review of informal agency action under § 706. *Overton Park* establishes that court should base review on "the full administrative record." 401 U.S. at 420. The Court based this requirement on § 706's language requiring the court to **"review the whole record or those parts of it cited by a party."** 5 U.S.C. § 706 (2006). The "administrative record" consists of all material on which the agency based its action.

Overton Park's requirement that the court review the administrative record was significant because informal rulemakings and informal adjudications like the one before the Court in *Overton Park* are not "on the record" — i.e., they are not "closed record" — proceedings. In other words, informal adjudication and informal rulemaking are not proceedings in which hard-and-fast rules determine what material should form the exclusive basis for the agency's decision and all participants in the proceeding have access to this material. The administrative record in *Overton Park*, for example, probably consisted of many tens of thousands of pages of documents of many different types. Those documents were not all located in Secretary Volpe's office (much less in a computer database). Instead, they were probably sitting in dozens of desks drawers, file cabinets, and boxes in various offices of the Department of Transportation building in Washington, D.C., as well as in local offices in Memphis. It would take a huge effort just to identify the relevant documents, and then they would have to be gathered and, presumably, organized for court review.

Overton Park changed the way federal agencies do business by requiring courts to review (and hence agencies to supply) the administrative record on which the agency based its decision. Today, federal agencies often begin compiling the administrative record for an informal proceeding when the proceeding begins. They use computer databases to create an electronic docket for these proceedings. This way, the work of creating the record will be almost finished if someone seeks judicial review of the agency action that results from the proceeding.

Although *Overton Park* referred to courts reviewing "the full administrative record," § 706 gives courts the less burdensome option of reviewing only **those parts of it cited by a party.**" 5 U.S.C. § 706 (2012). In addition, the Federal Rules of Appellate Procedure allow parties to designate parts of the administrative record for filing with the court, so that the court can focus on relevant portions. Fed. R. App. P. 17(b)(1)(A). The same can occur in federal district court proceedings by consent of the parties, with the court's approval. Ordinarily the lawyer challenging agency action will want to agree on a slimmed-down administrative record for court review that contains only the material relevant to the challenge; otherwise the court is all too likely to throw up its hands at the size of the record and simply uphold the agency action.

Overton Park identified two important situations, and there is a third, in which a court can hold evidentiary proceedings of its own, or order the agency to hold additional evidentiary proceedings, to supplement the administrative record.

(1) If the agency has not explained the action that is being judicially challenged, the court may require officials to testify in court or make affidavits to explain their actions. *Overton Park*, 401 U.S. at 420. The court can do this, however, only when, as in *Overton Park* itself, there is no "contemporaneous explanation of the agency decision." *Camp v. Pitts*, 411 U.S. 138, 143 (1973). If the agency has explained itself, but the court finds the explanation inadequate, the court should remand the case to the agency for further consideration (including, if necessary, a better explanation). *Id.*; *see also Fla. Power & Light Co. v. Lorion*, 470 U.S. 729, 744 (1985) ("[I]f the reviewing court simply cannot evaluate the challenged agency action on the basis of the record before it, the proper course, except in rare circumstances, is to remand to the agency for additional investigation or explanation.").

(2) Courts generally cannot "inquir[e] into the mental processes of administrative decisionmakers" but instead must take the agency's explanation for its decision at face value. *Overton Park*, 401 U.S. at 825 (citing *United States v. Morgan*, 313 U.S. 409, 422 (1941)). Courts can, however, hold evidentiary proceedings to look into the agency's decisionmaking process upon a "strong showing of bad faith or improper behavior." *Overton Park*, 401 U.S. at 420. It takes a very strong showing indeed, because courts do not allow their own decisionmaking processes to be probed and consider agencies entitled to the same respect. *See Morgan*, 313 U.S. at 422.

(3) Some judicial challenges to agency action depend on information outside the administrative record. In one case, for example, the plaintiffs argued that an agency failed to follow its procedural regulations in adjudicating plaintiffs' administrative case. The court of appeals upheld the district court's supplementing the administrative record with material necessary to consider plaintiffs' procedural challenge. *Esch v. Yeutter*, 876 F.2d 976, 991–993 (D.C. Cir. 1989). Another situation in which a court would consider evidence outside the administrative record is when an agency adopts a rule through notice-and-comment procedures without disclosing the technical basis for the proposed rule. If documents containing the technical basis come to light after the rulemaking proceeding has ended, the parties challenging the rule can submit the belatedly disclosed documents to the court, so the court can determine whether the documents

should have been disclosed them sooner. We reproduced in Chapter 12 a case presenting this situation: *American Radio Relay League, Inc. v. FCC*, 524 F.3d 227 (D.C. Cir. 2008). A third situation in which a reviewing court would consider additional evidence is in a case involving credible claims that the agency action was tainted by ex parte contacts. This situation was illustrated in the *PATCO* case that we summarized in Chapter 24. The court in the *PATCO* case remanded the case to the agency to have an ALJ hold an evidentiary hearing on asserted ex parte contacts between the agency and people outside the agency. *See Professional Air Traffic Controllers Organization (PATCO) v. Federal Labor Relations Authority*, 685 F.2d 547 (D.C. Cir. 1982) (discussed in Chapter 24.D.2).

Because *Overton Park* presented the first situation — "the bare [administrative] record [did] not disclose" the basis for the Secretary's decision, 401 U.S. at 420 — the Court remanded the case to the district court without deciding whether the Secretary's decision was arbitrary and capricious. This makes the Court's decision somewhat anticlimactic and no doubt left you wondering what happened afterwards.

Long story short: After the Supreme Court remanded the case to the district court, that court held a trial, which led to remand of the matter to the Secretary of Transportation. The Secretary decided that there was at least one feasible and prudent alternative to building I-40 through the park. But now the State of Tennessee sued the Secretary in federal court, challenging that determination, because Tennessee wanted I-40 built through the park. After more litigation, a congressional hearing, and several changes in administration, the idea of building I-40 through Overton Park was dropped. *See* Peter L. Strauss, Citizens to Preserve Overton Park v. Volpe — *of Politics and Law, Young Lawyers and the Highway Goliath* in Administrative Law Stories 288, 328–332 (Peter L. Strauss ed. 2006). Overton Park lives. *See* Citizens to Preserve Overton Park, http://www.overtonparkforever.org/.

(iii) *Overton Park* and *Chevron*

Overton Park is important mainly for its discussion of the A&C standard and the administrative record to which the standard applies. *Overton Park* also has importance, however, because of the Court's approach to interpreting agency legislation. The Court's approach in *Overton Park* (1971) provides a historical link between *Hearst* (1944) and *Chevron* (1984).

Overton Park presented two questions of statutory interpretation. One was a "macro" issue; it concerned the meaning, in general, of the statutory term "feasible and prudent alternative." The other was a "micro" issue; it concerned whether there were any alternatives to building I-40 through Overton Park that were "feasible and prudent." The Court independently determined the first, "macro" issue, while leaving the second, "micro" issue to be judged under a standard of reasonableness.

On the macro issue, the Court rejected the Secretary's view that, by including the word "prudent," Congress intended to permit the Secretary of Transportation to "engage in a wide-ranging balancing of competing interests." 401 U.S. at 411. The Court independently determined that the statute did not allow the Secretary to "approve the destruction of parkland unless he finds that alternative routes present unique problems." *Id.* at 413; *see id.* at 416 (statute allowed destruction of parkland where there were no feasible alternatives or where feasible alternatives involved "uniquely difficult problems"). Thus, the Court's "delineation of the scope of the Secretary's authority and discretion" was much narrower than the scope of authority and discretion for which the Secretary contended. *Id.* at

415–416. The Court independently determined that "Congress has specified only a small range of choices that the Secretary can make." *Id.* at 416.

On the micro issue, the Court said that a reviewing court had to determine whether the Secretary's decision "on the facts" of the Overton Park situation was "reasonably … within th[e] range" of choice that Congress gave him (as the Court interpreted Congress's intent). *Id.* 416. This is deferential judicial review of an agency's determination of a micro, law-application issue under its legislation.

The Court's approach in *Overton Park* resembles steps one and two of *Chevron* analysis. Under *Overton Park*, as under *Chevron* step one, the Court first independently examines the statute to determine the range of authority or discretion that the agency has. If, at this first step, the Court determines that the agency is reasonably within the range of its authority, the court proceeds—under both *Overton Park* and *Chevron* step two—to determine whether the agency's decision was reasonable. Thus, *Overton Park* foreshadows the *Chevron* doctrine. *See Mayo Found. for Med. Educ. & Res. v. United States*, 131 S. Ct. 704, 711 (2011) (if court determines under step one of *Chevron* that agency statute is ambiguous, under step two of *Chevron* court "may not disturb an agency rule unless it is arbitrary or capricious is substance, or manifestly contrary to the statute") (internal quotation marks omitted).

2. The *State Farm* Case

a. The *State Farm* Opinion

Please read *State Farm* with these questions in mind:

1. In this case, the State Farm Mutual Automobile Insurance Company is suing the U.S. Department of Transportation for rescinding an auto safety requirement. Why does State Farm care?

2. The Motor Vehicle Manufacturers Association intervened in State Farm's lawsuit to defend the Department of Transportation's rescission of the auto safety requirement. The Association is a trade association for car makers. Why do the car makers care?

3. According to the Court, when will an agency action ordinarily be arbitrary and capricious? How does the agency action in this case fit the Court's description of a typical arbitrary and capricious agency action?

Motor Vehicle Manufacturers Association of the United States, Inc. v. State Farm Mutual Automobile Insurance Co.

463 U.S. 29 (1983)

[Editor's summary: This case is about regulatory action under the National Traffic and Motor Vehicle Safety Act of 1966. At the time relevant to this case, the Act stated that "it is necessary to establish motor vehicle safety standards." 15 U.S.C. § 1381 (1976 & Supp. V 1982). According to the legislative history, Congress concluded that mandatory motor vehicle safety standards were necessary because "[t]he promotion of motor vehicle safety through voluntary standards [had] largely failed." S. Rep. No. 1301, 89th Cong., 2d Sess., 4 (1966). The Act authorized the Secretary of Transportation to establish the mandatory standards. The Act directed the Secretary, when creating the standards, to consider "relevant motor vehicle safety data," whether the proposed standard "is reasonable, practicable, and appropriate" for the particular type of motor vehicle, and the "extent to which such standards will contribute to carrying out the purposes" of the Act. 15 U.S.C. §§ 1392(f)(1), (3) & (4) (1976 & Supp. V 1982).

The Act further provided that the federal APA "shall apply to all orders establishing amending, or revoking a Federal motor vehicle safety standard under this [Act]." 15 U.S.C. § 1392(b) (1976 & Supp. V 1982).

This case specifically concerned the safety standard for occupant restraints—i.e., seatbelts or airbags. This safety standard was the subject of approximately sixty rulemaking notices between 1967 and 1981. In the 1967 safety standard, the Secretary simply required all cars to have seatbelts. Because of low seatbelt usage, however, the Department of Transportation began to consider "passive occupant restraint systems," including airbags and automatic seatbelts. In 1977, the National Highway Traffic Safety Administration (NHTSA)—the entity within the Transportation Department to which the Secretary had delegated authority to promulgate safety standards—estimated that passive restraints could prevent approximately 12,000 deaths and more than 100,000 serious injuries annually.

NHTSA formally proposed a standard requiring passive restraints in 1969. In 1972, NHTSA adopted a standard requiring cars manufactured beginning in late 1975 to be equipped with passive restraints for front seat occupants. This requirement was later suspended, however, and a modified version of the requirement—known as "Modified Standard 208"—provided for the phasing in of passive restraints during the model years 1982–1984. The two principal systems that would satisfy Modified Standard 208 were airbags and automatic seatbelts. The choice of which system to install was left to manufacturers.

In February 1981, after a new Administration came to power, the new Secretary of Transportation reopened the rulemaking proceeding. After receiving written comments and holding public hearings, NHTSA issued a final rule that rescinded the passive restraint requirement contained in Modified Standard 208.]

JUSTICE WHITE delivered the opinion of the Court....

II

In a statement explaining the rescission, NHTSA maintained that it was no longer able to find, as it had in 1977, that the automatic restraint requirement would produce significant safety benefits. This judgment reflected not a change of opinion on the effectiveness of the technology, but a change in plans by the automobile industry. In 1977, the agency had assumed that airbags would be installed in 60% of all new cars and automatic seatbelts in 40%. By 1981 it became apparent that automobile manufacturers planned to install the automatic seatbelts in approximately 99% of the new cars. For this reason, the lifesaving potential of airbags would not be realized. Moreover, it now appeared that the overwhelming majority of passive belts planned to be installed by manufacturers could be detached easily and left that way permanently. Passive belts, once detached, then required "the same type of affirmative action that is the stumbling block to obtaining high usage levels of manual belts." [46 Fed. Reg. 53421 (1981).] For this reason, the agency concluded that there was no longer a basis for reliably predicting that the Standard would lead to any significant increased usage of restraints at all.

In view of the possible minimal safety benefits, the automatic restraint requirement no longer was reasonable or practicable in the agency's view. The requirement would require approximately $1 billion to implement and the agency did not believe it would be reasonable to impose such substantial costs on manufacturers and consumers without more adequate assurance that sufficient safety benefits would accrue. In addition, NHTSA concluded that automatic restraints might have an adverse effect on the public's attitude toward safety. Given the high expense and limited benefits of detachable belts, NHTSA feared that many consumers would regard the Standard as an instance of ineffective regulation, adversely affecting the public's view of safety regulation and, in particular, "poisoning ... popular sentiment toward efforts to improve occupant restraint systems in the future." *Id.*, at 53424.

State Farm Mutual Automobile Insurance Co. and the National Association of Independent Insurers filed petitions for review of NHTSA's rescission of the passive restraint Standard. The United States Court of Appeals for the District of Columbia Circuit held that the agency's rescission of the passive restraint requirement was arbitrary and capricious....

III

... The agency's action in promulgating safety standards ... may be set aside if found to be "arbitrary, capricious, an abuse of discretion, or otherwise not in accordance with law." 5 U.S.C. § 706(2)(A); *Citizens to Preserve Overton Park v. Volpe*, 401 U.S. 402, 414 (1971); *Bowman Transportation, Inc. v. Arkansas Best Freight System, Inc.*, 419 U.S. 281 (1974). We believe that the rescission or modification of an occupant protection standard is subject to the same test. Section 103(b) of the Act, 15 U.S.C. § 1392(b), states that the procedural and judicial review provisions of the Administrative Procedure Act "shall apply to all orders establishing, amending, or revoking a Federal motor vehicle safety standard," and suggests no difference in the scope of judicial review depending upon the nature of the agency's action.

Petitioner Motor Vehicle Manufacturers Association (MVMA) disagrees, contending that the rescission of an agency rule should be judged by the same standard a court would use to judge an agency's refusal to promulgate a rule in the first place—a standard petitioner believes considerably narrower than the traditional arbitrary and capricious test. We reject this view. The Act expressly equates orders "revoking" and "establishing" safety standards; neither that Act nor the APA suggests that revocations are to be treated as refusals to promulgate standards. Petitioner's view would render meaningless Congress' authorization for judicial review of orders revoking safety rules. Moreover, the revocation of an extant regulation is substantially different than a failure to act. Revocation constitutes a reversal of the agency's former views as to the proper course. A "settled course of behavior embodies the agency's informed judgment that, by pursuing that course, it will carry out the policies committed to it by Congress. There is, then, at least a presumption that those policies will be carried out best if the settled rule is adhered to." *Atchison, T. & S.F.R. Co. v. Wichita Bd. of Trade*, 412 U.S. 800, 807–808 (1973). Accordingly, an agency changing its course by rescinding a rule is obligated to supply a reasoned analysis for the change beyond that which may be required when an agency does not act in the first instance.

In so holding, we fully recognize ... that an agency must be given ample latitude to "adapt their rules and policies to the demands of changing circumstances." *Permian Basin Area Rate Cases*, 390 U.S. 747, 784 (1968). But the forces of change do not always or necessarily point in the direction of deregulation. In the abstract, there is no more reason to presume that changing circumstances require the rescission of prior action, instead of a revision in or even the extension of current regulation. If Congress established a presumption from which judicial review should start, that presumption—contrary to petitioners' views—is not against safety regulation, but against changes in current policy that are not justified by the rulemaking record. . . .

The Department of Transportation accepts the applicability of the "arbitrary and capricious" standard. It argues that under this standard, a reviewing court may not set aside an agency rule that is rational, based on consideration of the relevant factors and within the scope of the authority delegated to the agency by the statute. We do not disagree with this formulation.[9] The scope of review under the "arbitrary and capricious" standard is narrow and a court is not to substitute its judgment for that of the agency. Nevertheless, the agency must examine the relevant data and articulate a satisfactory explanation for its action including a "rational connection between the facts found and the choice made." *Burlington Truck Lines, Inc. v. United States*, 371 U.S. 156, 168 (1962). In reviewing that explanation, we must "consider whether the decision was based on a consideration of the relevant factors and whether there has been a clear error of judgment." *Bowman Transportation, Inc. v. Arkansas Best Freight System, Inc., supra*, at 285; *Citizens to Preserve Overton Park v. Volpe, supra*, at 416. Normally, an agency rule would be arbitrary and capricious if the agency has relied on factors which Congress has not intended it to consider, entirely failed to consider an important aspect of the problem, offered an explanation for its decision that runs counter to the evidence before the agency, or is so implausible that it could not be ascribed to a difference in view or the product of agency expertise. . . . We will, however, "uphold a decision of less than ideal clarity if the agency's path may reasonably be discerned." *Bowman Transportation, Inc. v. Arkansas Best Freight System, Inc., supra*, at 286. For purposes of this case, it is also relevant that Congress required a record of the rulemaking proceedings to be compiled and submitted to a reviewing court, 15 U.S.C. § 1394, and intended that agency findings under the Motor Vehicle Safety Act would be supported by "substantial evidence on the record considered as a whole." S.Rep. No. 1301, 89th Cong., 2d Sess. p. 8 (1966); H.R.Rep. No. 1776, 89th Cong., 2d Sess. p. 21 (1966).

The ultimate question before us is whether NHTSA's rescission of the passive restraint requirement of Standard 208 was arbitrary and capricious. We conclude, as did the Court of Appeals, that it was. We also conclude, but for somewhat different reasons, that further consideration of the issue by the agency is therefore required. We deal separately with the rescission as it applies to airbags and as it applies to seatbelts.

A

The first and most obvious reason for finding the rescission arbitrary and capricious is that NHTSA apparently gave no consideration whatever to modifying the Standard to require that airbag technology be utilized. Standard 208 sought to achieve automatic crash protection by requiring automobile manufacturers to install either of two passive restraint devices: airbags or automatic seatbelts. There was no suggestion in the long rulemaking process that led to Standard 208 that if only one of these options were feasible, no passive restraint standard should be promulgated. . . . At that time, the passive belt approved by

---

9. The Department of Transportation suggests that the arbitrary and capricious standard requires no more than the minimum rationality a statute must bear in order to withstand analysis under the Due Process Clause. We do not view as equivalent the presumption of constitutionality afforded legislation drafted by Congress and the presumption of regularity afforded an agency in fulfilling its statutory mandate.

the agency could not be detached. Only later, at a manufacturer's behest, did the agency approve of the detachability feature—and only after assurances that the feature would not compromise the safety benefits of the restraint.

The agency has now determined that the detachable automatic belts will not attain anticipated safety benefits because so many individuals will detach the mechanism. Even if this conclusion were acceptable in its entirety ... standing alone it would not justify any more than an amendment of Standard 208 to disallow compliance by means of the one technology which will not provide effective passenger protection. It does not cast doubt on the need for a passive restraint standard or upon the efficacy of airbag technology. In its most recent rulemaking, the agency again acknowledged the lifesaving potential of the airbag....

Given the effectiveness ascribed to airbag technology by the agency, the mandate of the Act to achieve traffic safety would suggest that the logical response to the faults of detachable seatbelts would be to require the installation of airbags. At the very least this alternative way of achieving the objectives of the Act should have been addressed and adequate reasons given for its abandonment. But the agency not only did not require compliance through airbags, it also did not even consider the possibility in its 1981 rulemaking....

The automobile industry has opted for the passive belt over the airbag, but surely it is not enough that the regulated industry has eschewed a given safety device. For nearly a decade, the automobile industry waged the regulatory equivalent of war against the airbag and lost—the inflatable restraint was proved sufficiently effective. Now the automobile industry has decided to employ a seatbelt system which will not meet the safety objectives of Standard 208. This hardly constitutes cause to revoke the Standard itself. Indeed, the Act was necessary because the industry was not sufficiently responsive to safety concerns.... If, under the statute, the agency should not defer to the industry's failure to develop safer cars, which it surely should not do, *a fortiori* it may not revoke a safety standard which can be satisfied by current technology simply because the industry has opted for an ineffective seatbelt design....

Petitioners also invoke our decision *in Vermont Yankee Nuclear Power Corp. v. Natural Resources Defense Council, Inc.*, 435 U.S. 519 (1978).... In *Vermont Yankee*, we held that a court may not impose additional procedural requirements upon an agency. We do not require today any specific procedures which NHTSA must follow. Nor do we broadly require an agency to consider all policy alternatives in reaching decision.... But the airbag is more than a policy alternative to the passive restraint Standard; it is a technological alternative within the ambit of the existing Standard. We hold only that given the judgment made in 1977 that airbags are an effective and cost beneficial lifesaving technology, the mandatory passive restraint rule may not be abandoned without any consideration whatsoever of an airbags only requirement.

B

Although the issue is closer, we also find that the agency was too quick to dismiss the safety benefits of automatic seatbelts.... Rescission of the passive restraint requirement would not be arbitrary and capricious simply because there was no evidence in direct support of the agency's conclusion. It is not infrequent that the available data do not settle a regulatory issue, and the agency must then exercise its judgment in moving from the facts and probabilities on the record to a policy conclusion. Recognizing that policymaking in a complex society must account for uncertainty, however, does not imply that it is sufficient for an agency to merely recite the terms "substantial uncertainty" as a justification for its actions. As previously noted, the agency must explain the evidence which is available, and must offer a "rational connection between the facts found and the choice made" ... Generally, one aspect of that explanation would be a justification for rescinding the regulation before engaging in a search for further evidence.

In these cases, the agency's explanation for rescission of the passive restraint requirement is not sufficient to enable us to conclude that the rescission was the product of reasoned decisionmaking. To reach this conclusion, we do not upset the agency's view of the facts, but we do appreciate the limitations of this record in supporting the agency's decision. We start with the accepted ground that if used, seatbelts unquestionably would save many thousands of lives and would prevent tens of thousands of crippling injuries.... [T]he safety benefits of wearing seatbelts are not in doubt, and it is not challenged that were those benefits to accrue, the monetary costs of implementing the Standard would be easily justified. We move next to the fact that there is no direct evidence in support of the agency's finding that detachable automatic belts cannot be predicted to yield a substantial increase in usage. The empirical evidence on the record, consisting of surveys of drivers of automobiles equipped with passive belts, reveals more than a doubling of the usage rate experienced with manual belts. Much of the agency's rulemaking statement—and much of the controversy in this case—centers on the conclusions that should be drawn from these studies....

But accepting the agency's view of the field tests on passive restraints indicates only that there is no reliable real world experience that usage rates will substantially increase. To be sure, NHTSA opines that "it cannot reliably predict even a 5 percentage point increase as the minimum level of expected increased usage." But this and other statements that passive belts will not yield substantial increases in seatbelt usage apparently take no account of the critical difference between detachable automatic belts and current manual belts. A detached passive belt does require an affirmative act to reconnect it, but—unlike a manual seatbelt— the passive belt, once reattached, will continue to function automatically unless again disconnected. Thus, inertia—a factor which the agency's own studies have found significant in explaining the current low usage rates for seatbelts—works in favor of, not against, use of the protective device. Since 20% to 50% of motorists currently wear seatbelts on some occasions, there would seem to be grounds to believe that seatbelt use by occasional users will be substantially increased by the detachable passive belts. Whether this is in fact the case is a matter for the agency to decide, but it must bring its expertise to bear on the question....

The agency also failed to articulate a basis for not requiring nondetachable belts under Standard 208. It is argued that the concern of the agency with the easy detachability of the currently favored design would be readily solved by a continuous passive belt, which allows the occupant to "spool out" the belt and create the necessary slack for easy extrication from the vehicle. The agency did not separately consider the continuous belt option.... While the agency is entitled to change its view on the acceptability of continuous passive belts, it is obligated to explain its reasons for doing so ...

"An agency's view of what is in the public interest may change, either with or without a change in circumstances. But an agency changing its course must supply a reasoned analysis...." *Greater Boston Television Corp. v. FCC*, 143 U.S.App.D.C. 383, 394, 444 F.2d 841, 852 (1970) (footnote omitted), cert. denied, 403 U.S. 923 (1971). We do not accept all of the reasoning of the Court of Appeals but we do conclude that the agency has failed to supply the requisite "reasoned analysis" in this case. Accordingly, we vacate the judgment of the Court of Appeals and remand the cases to that court with directions to remand the matter to the NHTSA for further consideration consistent with this opinion.

Justice Rehnquist, with whom the Chief Justice, Justice Powell, and Justice O'-Connor join, concurring in part and dissenting in part....

I do not believe ... that NHTSA's view of detachable automatic seatbelts was arbitrary and capricious. The agency adequately explained its decision to rescind the standard insofar as it was satisfied by detachable belts....

The agency's changed view of the standard seems to be related to the election of a new President of a different political party. It is readily apparent that the responsible members of one administration may consider public resistance and uncertainties to be more important than do their counterparts in a previous administration. A change in administration brought about by the people casting their votes is a perfectly reasonable basis for an executive agency's reappraisal of the costs and benefits of its programs and regulations. As long as the agency remains within the bounds established by Congress, it is entitled to assess administrative records and evaluate priorities in light of the philosophy of the administration.

b. The Significance of *State Farm*

Events after the Court's decision in *State Farm* remind us that winning a court case against an agency, even in the U.S. Supreme Court, may not mean immediate victory. State Farm sued NHTSA because State Farm wanted NHTSA to require airbags in cars. The Court in *State Farm* held that NHTSA acted arbitrarily and capriciously when it rejected the airbag requirement. On remand from the Court's decision in *State Farm*, NHTSA came up with a new approach. NHTSA determined that mandatory seat belt laws would provide the safest alternative at least cost. Accordingly, NHTSA published a rule stating that car companies would not have to install "automatic occupant restraints" in all their cars if, within five years, two-thirds of the U.S. population was covered by state laws that mandated seat-belt use and met other NHTSA requirements. Most States eventually passed mandatory seat belt laws, but not by the deadline. NHTSA accordingly required car companies to install automatic restraints, and, as you know, now all new cars have airbags. So, State Farm did eventually get what it wanted, but only many years after it won its case in the U.S. Supreme Court. *See* Jerry L. Mashaw, *The Story of* Motor Vehicles Mfrs Ass'n of the US v. State Farm Mutual Automobile Ins. Co.: *Law, Science and Politics in the Administrative State* in Administrative Law Stories 381–385 (Peter L. Strauss ed. 2009).

State Farm, like *Overton Park*, is famous for its discussion of the arbitrary and capricious (A&C) standard. We will discuss three specific aspects of *State Farm*:

i.   *State Farm* discussed the meaning of the A&C standard and showed how it operates.

ii.   In the process of elaborating on and illustrating the A&C standard, *State Farm* highlighted the importance of identifying what "relevant factors" the agency must consider. 463 U.S. at 42, 43.

iii. *State Farm* addressed how to analyze an agency's change of course, which often arises in administrative law litigation.

(i) *State Farm*'s Elaboration and Illustration of the A&C Standard

You can best appreciate the significance of *State Farm* by comparing it to *Overton Park*. *Overton Park* discussed the A&C standard and established the standard's two functions,

(1) as a standard for review of the factual basis of certain agency actions and (2) as the source of a requirement of reasoned decision making. But the Court in *Overton Park* did not actually *apply* the A&C standard because the Court did not have the administrative record. In *State Farm*, the Court elaborated on the meaning of, and applied, the A&C standard in its role as the source of a requirement of "reasoned decisionmaking." 463 U.S. at 52. (The A&C standard did not function as a standard for review of the factual basis of the agency's decision in *State Farm*, because a special review statute instead prescribed the "substantial evidence" standard for review of agency factual determinations. *Id.* at 44.)

As elaborated and applied in *State Farm*, the A&C standard's requirement of reasoned decision making turns out to be pretty beefy. The Court said that a court must determine whether the agency decision "was based on a consideration of the relevant factors and whether there has been a clear error of judgment." *Id.* at 43. The Court also described when an agency rule will normally fail the standard:

> Normally, an agency rule would be arbitrary and capricious if the agency has relied on factors which Congress has not intended it to consider, entirely failed to consider an important aspect of the problem, offered an explanation for its decision that runs counter to the evidence before the agency, or is so implausible that it could not be ascribed to a difference in view or the product of agency expertise.

Id. at 43. The Court in later cases has used this same description when reviewing other kinds of agency action under the A&C standard to determine if the agency used reasoned decision making. *See, e.g., Nat'l Ass'n of Home Builders v. Defenders of Wildlife,* 551 U.S. 644, 658 (2007) (applying A&C standard to the EPA's decision transferring to Arizona authority to issue certain permits required by Clean Water Act). In addition, the Court in *State Farm* required the agency to "examine the relevant data and articulate a satisfactory explanation for its action including a rational connection between the facts found and the choice made." 463 U.S. at 43.

The Court in *State Farm* recognized that it was reading the A&C standard to allow for more intense judicial review than one might reasonably interpret § 706(2)(A) to require. In footnote 9, the Court acknowledged that it was requiring "more than the minimum rationality a statute must bear in order to withstand analysis under the Due Process Clause." *State Farm,* 463 U.S. at 43 n.9. This acknowledgement was significant because some of the Court's precedent and some lower federal court precedent suggested that judicial review under the A&C standard entailed no more than the "minimum rationality" standard associated with "rational basis" review of economic legislation challenged under the doctrine of substantive due process. *See Pacific States Box & Casket Co. v. White,* 296 U.S. 176, 186 (1935). By endorsing closer judicial review, *State Farm* has been described as "entrenching" the "hard look review" that many lower federal courts had developed before *State Farm.* Thomas J. Miles & Cass R. Sunstein, *The Real World of Arbitrariness Review,* 75 U. Chi. L. Rev. 761, 763 (2008). The concept of "hard look" originated as a demand by courts that *agencies* take a "hard look" at the problems before them, if their resolution of those problems were to survive judicial review under the A&C standard. *See, e.g., Greater Boston Television Corp. v. FCC,* 444 F.2d 841, 851(1st Cir. 1970). *State Farm* augmented the "hard look" concept, so that the concept required the *reviewing courts themselves,* in turn, to take a "hard look" at whether the agency took a hard look at the problem.

NHTSA failed the *State Farm* version of A&C review on two grounds: NHTSA failed to consider an important aspect of the problem by not considering making airbags mandatory. NHTSA also failed adequately to explain its rejection of automatic seatbelts. The Court in *State Farm* alluded to a third, possible flaw: NHTSA seemed influenced by the car makers' preference of automatic seatbelts over airbags. If NHTSA did cave in to the car makers, NHTSA would have relied on a factor (car maker preference) that Congress had not intended NHTSA to consider.

(ii) *State Farm*'s Focus on "[R]elevant [F]actors"

By requiring agencies to consider relevant factors (including relevant data) and to refrain from considering irrelevant factors, *State Farm* raises the question: What is relevant? We discussed this question initially in discussing the agency's duty in informal rulemaking to consider **"the relevant matter presented."** 5 U.S.C. §553(c). *See* Chapters 12.C.1. The main determinants of what is relevant are the agency legislation and applicable cross-cutting statutes. In *State Farm*, for example, the National Traffic and Motor Vehicle Safety Act of 1966 specified factors the Secretary was supposed to consider when establishing safety standards. The background of the legislation, which featured a failure of car companies to adopt safety standards voluntarily, implied that their preference for automatic seatbelts over airbags should have little or no relevance to the agency's choice of standards. When the agency legislation identifies relevant and irrelevant considerations, the legislation will ordinarily also identify, at least implicitly, the relevant data. For example, the Act in *State Farm* required NHTSA to examine scientific tests of safety equipment and surveys on how drivers would use it.

The Court discussed what is "relevant" for purposes of review under the A&C standard in a later case that we summarize and excerpt next.

Pension Benefit Guaranty Corp. v. The LTV Corp.
496 U.S. 633 (1990)

[Editor's summary: Many people save for retirement using pension plans maintained by their employers. People's pension plan benefits are protected by Title IV of the Employee Retirement Income Security Act (ERISA), a federal statute administered by a federal corporation, the Pension Benefit Guaranty Corporation (PBGC). One way Title IV of ERISA protects pension plan benefits is by authorizing the PBGC to terminate pension plans before they go belly up for lack of funding. When the PBGC terminates a pension plan, the PBGC becomes a trustee for the plan, essentially taking over the plan's administration.

After the PBGC terminates a pension plan, to the extent that the plan does not have enough money to pay vested pension benefits, the federal government makes up much of the shortfall with federal funds. In effect, Title IV provides pension-plan-benefits insurance. Title IV does not provide 100% insurance, however; it does not cover all pension plan benefits. Thus, termination of a pension plan inevitably causes some employees to lose some benefits to which they would have been entitled if the pension plan had stayed alive (and been adequately funded).

The PBGC terminated two pension plans for employees of The LTV Steel Corporation because those plans were woefully underfunded and LTV was on the brink of bankruptcy. After the PBGC terminated the plans, LTV did file for bankruptcy under Chapter 11. As part of its reorganization process, LTV worked out deals with the unions that represented LTV employees and retirees. The deals provided that LTV would pay employees and retirees some of the benefits they lost because of the plan terminations. These benefits would be paid on top of the benefits the retirees were getting (and the employees would get upon retirement) from the PBGC under the terminated plans. Remember, much of the benefits paid out by the PBGC under the terminated plans were federal insurance funds.

The PBGC objected to the deals that LTV made with the unions. The PBGC considered the deals abusive because they were using federal pension insurance funds to subsidize LTV's reorganization. The PBGC accordingly exercised its power under Title IV of ERISA to *restore* the terminated plans. Restoring the plans meant that the federal insurance fund spigot was turned off, and administration of the restored plans went back into private hands, with LTV on the hook for any funding deficiencies.

LTV sued the PBGC in federal court, claiming that the PBGC's restoration of the plans was arbitrary and capricious. The federal court of appeals held that the PBGC was an "agency" within the meaning of the federal APA, and that the restoration decision was subject to judicial review under § 706 of the APA. The court of appeals also concluded that the PBGC's restoration decision was arbitrary and capricious under § 706(2)(A). The court of appeals determined that the restoration decision in this case implicated important policies not only under ERISA but also under the Bankruptcy Code and federal labor laws. The court of appeals said that the PBGC had not adequately considered the policies under these non-ERISA bodies of law. "Rather," the court of appeals said, "PBGC focused inordinately on ERISA." 496 U.S. at 644 (quoting court of appeals' opinion). Thus, the court of appeals concluded, the PBGC had failed to consider all "relevant factors," as required for its decision not to be "arbitrary and capricious."

The U.S. Supreme Court rejected the court of appeal's broad view of "relevant factors." Here is the relevant part of the Court's opinion:]

JUSTICE BLACKMUN delivered the opinion of the Court....

The PBGC contends that the Court of Appeals misapplied the general rule that an agency must take into consideration all relevant factors, see *Citizens to Preserve Overton Park, Inc. v. Volpe*, 401 U.S. 402, 416 (1971), by requiring the agency explicitly to consider and discuss labor and bankruptcy law. We agree.

First, and most important, we do not think that the requirement imposed by the Court of Appeals upon the PBGC can be reconciled with the plain language of § 4047, under which the PBGC is operating in this case. This section gives the PBGC the power to restore terminated plans in any case in which the PBGC determines such action to be "appropriate and consistent with its duties *under this title* [i.e., Title IV of ERISA]" (emphasis added). The statute does not direct the PBGC to make restoration decisions that further the "public interest" generally, but rather empowers the agency to restore when restoration would further the interests that Title IV of ERISA is designed to protect. Given this specific and unambiguous statutory mandate, we do not think that the PBGC did or could focus "inordinately" on ERISA in making its restoration decision.

Even if Congress' directive to the PBGC had not been so clear, we are not entirely sure that the Court of Appeals' holding makes good sense as a general principle of administrative law. The PBGC points out problems that would arise if federal courts routinely were to require each agency to take explicit account of public policies that derive from federal statutes other than the agency's enabling Act. To begin with, there are numerous federal statutes that could be said to embody countless policies. If agency action may be disturbed whenever a reviewing court is able to point to an arguably relevant statutory policy that was not explicitly considered, then a very large number of agency decisions might be open to judicial invalidation.

The Court of Appeals' directive that the PBGC give effect to the "policies and goals" of other statutes, apart from what those statutes actually provide, is questionable for another reason as well. Because the PBGC can claim no expertise in the labor and bankruptcy areas, it may be ill equipped to undertake the difficult task of discerning and applying the "policies and goals" of those fields. This Court recently observed:

> "[N]o legislation pursues its purposes at all costs. Deciding what competing values will or will not be sacrificed to the achievement of a particular objective is the very essence of legislative choice — and it frustrates rather than effectuates legislative intent simplistically to assume that *whatever* furthers the statute's primary objective must be the law." *Rodriguez v. United States*, 480 U.S. 522, 525–526 (1987).

For these reasons, we believe the Court of Appeals erred in holding that the PBGC's restoration decision was arbitrary and capricious because the agency failed adequately to consider principles and policies of bankruptcy law and labor law. . . .

(iii) *State Farm*'s Discussion of Agency Changes in Course

Although the agency legislation is the main source of "relevant factors," agency legislation often gives the agency much discretion. The ERISA provision in *PBGC v. LTV Corp.*, for example, gave the PBGC discretion to determine whether restoration was an "appropriate" way of carrying out ERISA's purposes. Within statutory constraints, agencies can exercise their discretion so as to advance executive-branch policies. A federal agency's policies are shaped by the President and by the people whom the President appoints to head the agency. Policies change when Presidents change. In *Chevron*, the Court said there is nothing wrong with that:

> While agencies are not directly accountable to the people, the Chief Executive is, and it is entirely appropriate for this political branch of the Government to make such policy choices — resolving the competing interests which Congress itself either inadvertently did not resolve, or intentionally left to be resolved by the agency charged with the administration of the statute in light of everyday realities.

Chevron v. NRDC, 467 U.S. at 865–866. Notice this passage leaves room only for agency policy choices that Congress did not make.

The same change in Presidents that produced the "bubble concept" upheld in *Chevron* (1984) caused the safety-standard rescission invalidated in *State Farm* (1983). You might wonder whether the cases are consistent, given the different outcomes and the majority's failure in *State Farm* to acknowledge the role of politics, as had the majority in *Chevron*.

The two cases are compatible in result, if not in tone. The Court in *Chevron* determined that the bubble concept fell within the range of statutory authority available to EPA, and reasonably reconciled competing policies (the environment vs. the economy) that Congress itself sought to balance in the agency legislation. The Court in *State Farm* determined that NHTSA had not established the reasonableness of rescinding Standard 208 NHTSA, in light of the agency legislation's safety goals and the data on the apparent safety benefits of airbags and the possible safety benefits of automatic seatbelts.

Though the results in *Chevron* and *State Farm* are consistent, *State Farm* contains statements that in tone suggest more hostility to politically motivated changes in agency policy than the Court showed in *Chevron*. Specifically, the Court in *State Farm* said, "[T]he forces of change do not always or necessarily point in the direction of deregulation." 463 U.S. at 42. This seems like a dig against President Ronald Reagan, who took office in 1981 with a then-well-known pledge to reduce government regulation. More importantly, the Court in *State Farm* implied that when an agency changes its policy, it carries an extra burden of justification. The Court said:

> A "settled course of behavior embodies the agency's informed judgment that, by pursuing that course, it will carry out the policies committed to it by Congress. There is, then, at least a presumption that those policies will be carried out best if the settled rule is adhered to." *Atchison, T. & S.F.R. Co. v. Wichita Bd. of Trade*, 412 U.S. 800, 807–808 (1973). Accordingly, an agency changing its course by rescinding a rule is obligated to supply a reasoned analysis for the change beyond that which may be required when an agency does not act in the first instance.

State Farm, 463 U.S. at 42.

The Court rejected that implication in *Federal Communications Commission v. Fox Television Stations, Inc.*, 129 S. Ct. 1800 (2009). *FCC v. Fox Television* was about the FCC's statutory authority to punish television and radio broadcasts of "indecent … language." 18 U.S.C. § 1464 (2012). For about thirty years, the FCC followed a "fleeting expletives" policy, under which it did not punish a broadcaster for a broadcast that contained an isolated curse word or two. In 2004, the FCC changed its policy to a much stricter one: The FCC now reserved the discretion to punish a broadcaster for a broadcast that contained the words "shit" or "fuck," even if either word was used only once. The Court held that the FCC's change in policy was not arbitrary and capricious. In so holding, the Court rejected the argument that § 706(2)(A), as interpreted in *State* Farm, requires more searching judicial review when an agency changes its policy. The Court added this important qualification:

> To be sure, the requirement that an agency provide reasoned explanation for its action would ordinarily demand that it display awareness that it *is* changing position. An agency may not, for example, depart from a prior policy *sub silentio* or simply disregard rules that are still on the books. See *United States v. Nixon*, 418 U.S. 683, 696 (1974). And of course the agency must show that there are good reasons for the new policy. But it need not demonstrate to a court's satisfaction that the reasons for the new policy are *better* than the reasons for the old one; it suffices that the new policy is permissible under the statute, that there are good reasons for it, and that the agency *believes* it to be better, which the conscious change of course adequately indicates. This means that the agency need not always provide a more detailed justification than what would suffice for a new policy created on a blank slate. Sometimes it must—when, for example, its new policy rests upon factual findings that contradict those which underlay its prior policy; or when its prior policy has engendered serious reliance interests that must be taken into account. *Smiley v. Citibank (South Dakota), N. A.*, 517 U.S. 735, 742 (1996). It would be arbitrary or capricious to ignore such matters. In such cases it is not that further justification is demanded by the mere fact of policy change; but that a reasoned explanation is needed for disregarding facts and circumstances that underlay or were engendered by the prior policy.

FCC v. Fox Television, 129 S.Ct. at 1811.

D. Chapter 34 Wrap Up and Look Ahead

This chapter has introduced the arbitrary and capricious standard by examining where it comes from and what it means. Its direct origin is simple: It comes from judicial review statutes, including the federal APA (and many, if not most, state APAs). Its meaning is more complicated. In federal law, it serves two roles in APA-type challenges: (1) It supplies a default standard for review of the factual basis for certain agency actions; and (2) it imposes on almost all agency action a requirement of "reasoned decisionmaking," amounting to a requirement of rationality.

The next chapter ends our examination of the subject of "scope of judicial review." It examines special review situations in which federal courts articulate standards of review that differ from the A&C standard and the other standards of review we've discussed so far. The next chapter also discusses remedies available in APA-type challenges.

Chapter Problem Revisited

This chapter problem has two objectives. The first objective is to help you appreciate that planning for judicial review of agency action begins long before judicial review is sought, and even before the lawyer knows for sure that judicial review will be necessary. Thus, the chapter problem has you think about how to maximize the prospect for a successful judicial challenge to agency rules that have not been issued even in proposed form. The second objective is to give you a concrete example of an agency decision that is subject to judicial review under the arbitrary and capricious standard, and have you "reverse engineer" the standard by asking: How might a lawyer maximize the chance that an anticipated adverse agency decision will be found arbitrary and capricious?

There are some obvious arguments King Candy can make against excluding fruit jerky from school lunches. For one thing, if the company can show that a lot of kids don't eat the fresh fruit included with their lunch, but would eat fruit jerky, then King Candy has a strong argument that excluding fruit jerky would not ensure that kids were eating fresh fruit instead of fruit jerky; instead, they would lose the benefit of any fruit product in their lunch. King Candy probably already has data about the benefits of its product. You may have to develop additional data for specific use in the rulemaking proceeding.

As a newcomer to the issue, you may be able to bring fresh ideas to the problem. For example, is it possible to consider compromises: Might USDA be willing to allow fruit jerky to be used as a partial substitute for real fruit? Might King Candy be able to develop new products that are healthier alternatives to its traditional fruit jerky?

In addition to building the "affirmative" case for fruit jerky, you will want to prepare defensively for the unfavorable evidence that USDA and perhaps other participants in the rulemaking proceeding will use in support of excluding fruit jerky. What might this opposing evidence be? How can you impeach it?

The basic challenges are (1) to identify favorable evidence that courts will consider "relevant" for the agency to consider; (2) to make that evidence so compelling that the agency has a hard time adequately explaining why it rejects it; and (3) to shoot holes in unfavorable evidence, so that it becomes hard for USDA to rely on it to reach a decision unfavorable to the client (who is, after all, "King").

Who says rulemaking is a non-adversary proceeding?

Professional Development Reflection Questions

The chapter problem anticipates that the new associate will participate in the meeting that the junior partner has scheduled with the client. Many new attorneys wonder how to behave at such a meeting. Should you just keep your mouth shut and listen? Should you behave as the junior partner's equal, interjecting your opinion and asking the client questions, as appropriate? Should you try to avoid the meeting altogether?

Here is advice for that situation from one senior attorney:

> *Speaking at client meetings.* You see more young attorneys go up in flames in this situation than any other … Here are a few good rules:
>
> Speak only when spoken to. I always believed that you went into the meeting with the client seeing you as the bright, young (although expensive) attorney. It's easier than you think to change that opinion for the worse.
>
> There is no joke that you can tell that will be a guaranteed winner. Don't even think about taking the risk.
>
> Never correct the lead attorney no matter how wrong you think he or she is. It's more likely that you are wrong. Mention it after the meeting …
>
> Most of the time, you will be invited to attend a meeting to take notes and to observe and learn how to conduct a meeting. Do that.…
>
> If you are asked to summarize your research for a client, try to hit the main points and finish within a minute …
>
> The bottom line: talk with the lead attorney about what he or she wants you to do in the meeting.

Dennis Kennedy, *Twenty Lessons for Lawyers Starting Their Careers* (Mar. 2005), *available at* American Bar Association, Law Practice Today, http://apps.americanbar.org/lpm/lpt/articles/mgt03053.html (May 2012).

Do you find this advice helpful? What aspects of the advice, if any, do you think are most debatable?

Chapter 35

Specialized Review Situations; Judicial Remedies

Overview

This chapter has two pieces. The first piece identifies situations in which courts apply specialized standards of judicial review. These standards differ from those discussed in past chapters. The second piece examines judicial remedies in APA-type challenges.

The chapter's sections are entitled:

A. Specialized Review Situations

B. Remedies

C. Chapter 35 Wrap Up

Chapter Problem

This chapter problem differs from past chapter problems. Unlike past chapter problems, this chapter problem requires you to apply not just material that you will learn in this chapter—specifically, in Section A. This chapter problem also requires you to apply material that you learned in earlier chapters. Its purpose is to help you review and synthesize material on the scope of judicial review by organizing the material in a different way from the way we've presented it so far.

The outline below organizes agency action chronologically into three stages: (1) initiation of agency action; (2) the process (procedures) the agency uses to take action; and (3) the resulting agency action. Under each of these three stages are specific issues or agency actions that may be subject to judicial review. Your job is to identify the specific standard of review, principles of judicial review, or leading U.S. Supreme Court cases, or all three, that govern federal court review of the issues when they arise in the court's review of federal agency action. We have partly filled in this outline to get you started.

To reiterate two important points about this problem: The outline below is organized differently from the way we've presented the material to which it pertains. In addition, several of the issues discussed under stage (1) (initiation) have not been explored yet: They are explored in Section A of this chapter.

1. Agency decision on whether to initiate action

    A. Agency choice between rulemaking and adjudication: Abuse of discretion; *SEC v. Chenery; Storer Broadcasting*

    B. Agency refusal to undertake enforcement action: _____

    C.   Agency selection of target for enforcement action: _____

    D.   Agency denial of rulemaking petitions: _____

2.   Agency procedures for taking action

    A.   Compliance with constitutionally required procedures: _____

    B.   Compliance with statutorily required procedures

        1.   Procedures required by the agency legislation: *Chevron/Mead* doctrine

        2.   Procedures required by other legislation, including APA and other cross-cutting statutes: _____

    C.   Compliance with executive-branch material

        1.   The agency's own rules: *Auer deference*

        2.   Other executive-branch material: _____

3.   Resulting agency action

    A.   Compliance with constitution: De novo

    B.   Compliance with statutes

        1.   The agency legislation: _____

        2.   Other legislation: _____

    C.   Compliance with executive-branch material

        1.   The agency's own rules: _____

        2.   Other executive-branch material: _____

    D.   Factual basis for agency action (three possible standards of review)

        1.   _____

        2.   _____

        3.   _____

    E.   Reasoned Decision Making: _____

    F.   Other:

        1.   Agency choice of sanction: _____

        2.   Agency decision to reconsider, reopen, or rehear: _____

A. Specialized Review Situations

Federal courts have developed specialized standards of judicial review for certain agency actions or certain types of legal claims, five of which are discussed in this section:

(1) claims of selective enforcement

(2) agency choice of sanction

(3) agency denial of request to rehear, reconsider, or reopen prior decision

(4) agency denial of rulemaking petitions

(5) claim of unreasonable or unlawful agency delay

In each of these specialized review situations, the federal courts cite particular reasons for giving agencies particularly great respect. The reasons tend to concern either or both: (1) superior agency competence, relative to courts, to decide the matter; or (2) respect for Congress's decision to assign a matter to an administrative agency, a decision thought to compel particularly great judicial respect for some aspect of the agency's determinations of how best to carry out its assignment. The courts' specialized handling of these situations are probably best understood to reflect interpretive glosses on federal APA § 706 or the special review statute that authorizes judicial review in the particular case. In any event, you may find similar, specialized standards of review for similar situations in state law.

1. Claims of Selective Enforcement

Have you ever been driving on a highway where it seems almost everyone is breaking the speed limit (perhaps including you)? And have you ever seen a police officer pull one of those speeders over and wondered: Why did the officer pick that poor slob? It can be like watching a lion pounce on a random wildebeest on the Serengeti.

Like police officers, many agencies are responsible for enforcing laws regulating private conduct. Often, these agencies do not have resources to take enforcement action against every violator of those laws. So they must prioritize; they must pick and choose. Sometimes, the person picked out for enforcement action feels unfairly picked on and judicially challenges the agency's selection of that person. These challenges raise "selective enforcement" claims.

The agency legislation or other law may constrain an agency's selection of enforcement targets, and, if so, the agency must obey those constraints. To cite an obvious example, an agency cannot select enforcement targets using unconstitutional criteria, e.g., race. Aside from constitutional and occasional statutory restrictions, however, applicable laws usually give agencies broad discretion in determining whom to target for enforcement action. When so, the federal courts will not set aside a federal agency's selection of an enforcement target except for a "patent abuse of discretion."

The U.S. Supreme Court used the "patent abuse of discretion" standard in two cases involving the Federal Trade Commission. In each case, the FTC decided after a formal adjudication that a company had violated federal law. In each case, the FTC ordered the company to cease and desist its violations. When seeking judicial review of the cease-and-desist orders, each company asked the federal court to stay the cease-and-desist order until the FTC took enforcement action against all the *other* companies that were supposedly breaking the same laws that the targeted company had been found guilty of violating. The companies' argument in support of the stay took the classic form: "But other people are doing it! Why pick on us?"

The U.S. Supreme Court held that the companies should have first asked the FTC to stay its order, and that the FTC's decision on that request would be upheld unless it was a "patent abuse of discretion." *FTC v. Universal-Rundle*, 387 U.S. 244, 250 (1967); *Moog Industries v. FTC*, 355 U.S. 411, 414 (1958). The Court cited as one reason for the FTC's broad discretion that the FTC "alone is empowered to develop that enforcement policy best calculated to achieve the ends contemplated by Congress and to allocate its available funds and personnel in such a way as to execute its policy efficiently and economically." *Moog Industries*, 355 U.S. at 413 (quoted in *Universal-Rundle*, 387 U.S. at 251).

You may wonder how the "patent abuse of discretion" standard fits into § 706 or other statute governing the scope of review in a particular case presenting a selective-enforcement claim. The best answer is probably: The "patent abuse of discretion" standard is a judicially developed gloss on the statute governing the scope of review. For example, § 706(2)(A)'s term "arbitrary, capricious, [or] an abuse of discretion" as a ground for invalidating agency action can be interpreted to grant particularly broad discretion to agencies in their selection of enforcement targets. A respectable, if somewhat circular, rationale for the gloss is that Congress enacts judicial-review statutes against the background of judicially developed standards of judicial review and can be presumed to incorporate those standards unless the statute shows a contrary intent.

Exercise: Selective Enforcement

The Consumer Product Safety Commission started getting many consumer complaints about lawn chairs collapsing underneath their occupants and causing injury. Most complaints concerned chairs made by five different companies. CPSC decided to begin a formal adjudication against the smallest of the five companies, figuring that this "small fry" would lack the ability for a sustained legal challenge and would quickly settle on terms favorable to the CPSC, which CPSC could use as leverage to obtain favorable results against the other manufacturers. Is CPSC's selection of the most vulnerable wildebeest—excuse us, we mean the smallest company—as its initial enforcement target a "patent abuse of discretion"? Is it ethical? If not, how would you handle this situation if you were a lawyer for the CPSC?

---

2. Agency Choice of Sanction

Section 558(b) of the federal APA says, **"A sanction may not be imposed … except within jurisdiction delegated to the agency and as authorized by law."** The law authorizing an agency to impose a sanction typically takes the form of a statute, and typically gives the agency broad discretion in selecting the particular sanction for a particular violation.

For example, a federal statute authorizes a federal agency to assess a civil penalty of "not less than $5,000 and not more than $60,000" against a mining company that fails to report a mining accident. 30 U.S.C. § 820(a)(2) (2012). The statute does enumerate factors that the agency must consider when setting the penalty, such as the company's history of violations. *Id.* § 820(i). Even so, this leaves much room for agency discretion. If the agency issues a written decision discussing the statutory factors and then picks a number of, say, $45,000 for a particular failure to report a particular accident, how is a court to say the particular number chosen is too high? The same question arises for other agency decisions selecting other types of remedies for violations of the statutes and regulations the agency is responsible for enforcing.

The U.S. Supreme Court has suggested federal agencies deserve great respect in their selection of sanctions and other remedies for violations of the law. The Court has said, "The relation of remedy to policy is peculiarly a matter of administrative competence." *Butz v. Glover Livestock Comm'n Co.*, 411 U.S. 182, 185 (1973) (quoting *American Power*

Co. v. SEC, 329 U.S. 90, 112 (1946)). The lower federal courts have understood the Court's decisions to permit only "very limited judicial review" of an agency's determination of a sanction. *E.g., Woodard v. United States*, 725 F.2d 1072, 1077 (6th Cir. 1984). Some lower courts have said that, if the sanction is within legal limits, a court can set it aside only for a "gross abuse of discretion." *VanCook v. SEC*, 653 F.3d 130, 144 (2nd Cir. 2011).

What do you think? Is the "gross abuse of discretion" standard governing an agency's choice of sanction more deferential than the "patent abuse of discretion" governing an agency's selection of an enforcement target? In any event, the "gross abuse of discretion" standard is probably best understood as a gloss on § 706(2)(A)'s **"arbitrary, capricious, [or] an abuse of discretion"** standard or on whatever other statute governs the scope of review in a particular case.

Exercise: Agency Choice of Sanctions

The Securities and Exchange Commission has statutory authority to impose large civil penalties and other sanctions on people and companies who violate the federal securities laws. Suppose that, acting within that authority, the SEC permanently suspended a person from participating in the securities industry. Also suppose that person was able to show that the SEC had engaged in a long-standing pattern of slamming smaller, newer securities firms and their employees with more, and much harsher, sanctions than older, more well-established and well-connected firms and their employees. There is in fact some evidence that the SEC has left the larger, well-established firms alone because of personal connections between SEC officials and personnel in those firms. Given evidence of a "systematic pattern of disparate treatment, resulting in predictably disproportionately harsh sanctions," could a federal court find a "gross abuse of discretion"? *See D'Alessio v. SEC*, 380 F.3d 112, 124 (2nd Cir. 2004).

---

3. Agency Denial of Request to Rehear, Reconsider, or Reopen Prior Decision

The short of the matter is that judicial review of an agency's refusal to rehear, reconsider, or reopen a case is limited, if it is available at all. Before elaborating on that point, we briefly explain the procedural devices known variously as petitions for rehearing, reconsideration, or reopening.

To begin with the judicial context: Rehearing, reconsideration, and reopening are things that courts can do if convinced a prior court decision should be changed. The three types of revisiting a prior decision do differ in minor ways. When a court "rehears" a case, a "rehearing" will occur, though it may be either an oral hearing or just a new round of briefing. "Reconsideration" is similar to rehearing insofar as it involves a court taking a second look at a prior decision; but reconsideration may not entail a new hearing. "Reopening" refers to a court "reopening" a record for admission of new evidence; reopening may occur because of some later occurrence or belatedly discovered evidence that the court believes must be considered. Rather than differentiating the three ways an adjudicatory body may revisit a prior decision, from now on we use the term "rehear" as the general term for this revisiting process.

Agencies, too, may have power to rehear their prior decisions. But agencies, unlike courts, are not assumed to have inherent powers, so an agency's power to rehear must be traced at least implicitly to the agency legislation or other law that grants powers to the agency. Sometimes a statute will not only empower an agency to rehear a prior decision, but will *require* the agency to do so under certain circumstances. In addition to statutes addressing rehearing, many agencies issue procedural rules to prescribe procedures and time limits people must obey to request rehearing. Thus the administrative lawyer must identify and analyze the relevant statutes and rules when considering whether a petition for rehearing is required or advisable, and, if so, how to request it.

A request for rehearing is usually an optional remedy, and not required before seeking judicial review. It is usually optional because of the federal APA. Specifically, § 704 creates a broad right to judicial review of **"final"** agency action and continues: **"Except as otherwise expressly required by statute, agency action otherwise final is final for the purposes of this section whether or not there has been presented or determined an application for ... any form of reconsideration."** 5 U.S.C. § 704 (2012). "[R]econsideration" in this provision encompasses rehearing and reopening. As § 704's "exception" clause reflects, though, some federal statutes do expressly require a person to seek reconsideration (i.e., rehearing) before seeking judicial review. An example is the Natural Gas Act's provision authorizing judicial review of decisions of the Federal Energy Regulatory Commission. *See* 15 U.S.C. § 717r(a) & (b) (2012). But ordinarily the question whether to seek rehearing before seeking judicial review is a judgment call to be made by the attorney and client in consultation.

In making that judgment call, one factor to consider is the deadline for seeking judicial review. As discussed in Chapter 30.F, sometimes a special review statute tolls the statute of limitations for seeking judicial review of an agency's *original* decision until the agency has acted on a timely petition for rehearing. Suppose, however, that, because no tolling occurs or for some other reason, an agency denies a petition for rehearing after the deadline for seeking judicial review of its original decision has expired. Can the person who petitioned for rehearing get judicial review of the agency's denial of rehearing? In pondering that question, keep in mind that, by its nature, a petition for rehearing will claim that the agency's original decision should be changed. Thus, if a court reviews the agency's denial of rehearing, the court will usually end up having to review the agency's *original* decision. For this reason, if a person is allowed to seek judicial review of the denial of rehearing after the time for seeking judicial review of the original decision has expired, the person has in effect gotten an extension of the deadline for seeking judicial review of the *original* decision.

To avoid that result, the U.S. Supreme Court has laid down strict rules for federal court review of federal agencies' denial of rehearing. In *Interstate Commerce Commission v. Brotherhood of Locomotive Engineers*, 482 U.S. 270 (1987), the Court set out two rules, which make the availability of judicial review depend on the grounds for seeking rehearing:

1. When someone seeks rehearing on the ground that the federal agency's original decision was simply wrong—or, to use the jargon, reflected "material error"— the agency's denial of rehearing is not subject to judicial review at all. Judicial review is precluded because the agency's decision on rehearing is **"committed to agency discretion by law"** within the meaning of federal APA § 701(a)(2).

2. When someone seeks rehearing on the grounds of new facts; or newly discovered facts that couldn't reasonably have been discovered sooner; or other changed circumstances, the agency's denial of rehearing will be upheld unless the challenger can show "the clearest abuse of discretion."

ICC v. Brotherhood of Locomotive Engineers, 482 U.S. at 278–284. The Court devised the first rule mainly to avoid "a litigant's achieving … perpetual availability of review by the mere device of filing a suggestion that the agency has made a mistake and should consider the matter again." *Id.* at 281. The second rule came from the Court's precedent.

These rules have exceptions. For one thing, the Court made clear that these rules apply only in the absence of "some provision of law," such as a statute, altering them. *Id.* at 278. For example, some federal immigration statutes specifically address the reopening of removal proceedings, and case law interpreting those statutes establishes that courts can review certain cases in which the Board of Immigration Appeals had denied reopening. *See Kucana v. Holder*, 130 S.Ct. 827, 840 (2010). To cite another example, the federal statute governing judicial review of decisions by the Social Security Administration (SSA) has been interpreted generally to bar judicial review of SSA decisions refusing to reopen cases involving claims for SSA benefits, even when the rehearing petition asserts changed circumstances. *See Califano v. Sanders*, 430 U.S. 99 (1977). In addition to statutory exceptions to the rehearing rules laid down in *ICC v. Brotherhood of Locomotive Engineers*, a judicially developed exception might exist for rehearing petitions asserting constitutional claims. In *Califano v. Sanders*, the Court held that judicial review is not available for the SSA's denial of a petition to reopen, unless the denial is challenged on colorable constitutional grounds. 430 U.S. at 108–109. The Court's rationale for recognizing an exception for constitutional claims is applicable outside the SSA context: The Court refused to read the statutory provision limiting judicial review as taking the "extraordinary" step of foreclosing judicial review of colorable constitutional claims. *Id.* at 109.

The basic idea behind the law on agency rehearings is that an agency, like a court, should have a chance to revisit a prior decision. But this chance should not be used to circumvent limits on seeking judicial review of the prior decision.

Exercise: Agency Rehearing

To check your understanding of our discussion of agency rehearing, jot down examples of grounds that you'd think would justify reopening a decision by the Social Security Administration denying a claim for disability insurance benefits. Then check out the regulation that defines "good cause" for reopening such cases: 20 C.F.R. § 404.989 (2012).

---

4. Agency Denial of Rulemaking Petitions

Section 553(e) of the federal APA gives an **"interested person the right to petition for the issuance, amendment, or repeal of a rule."** When a federal agency denies such a rulemaking petition, § 555(e) generally requires the agency to give the petitioner **"a brief statement of the grounds for denial."** This statement facilitates judicial review of the denial.

In *Massachusetts v. EPA*, 549 U.S. 497 (2007), the Court held that a federal agency's denial of a petition for rulemaking is subject to judicial review. But, the Court added, "such review is 'extremely limited' and 'highly deferential.'" *Id.* at 527–528 (quoting *Nat'l Customs Brokers & Forwarders Ass'n of America v. United States*, 883 F.2d 93, 96 (D.C. Cir. 1989)). The Court conducted this highly deferential review under a special review statute that, like § 706 of the federal APA, authorized the reviewing court to set aside the agency's decision if it was "arbitrary, capricious, [or] an abuse of discretion." *Id.* at 528 (quoting 42 U.S.C. 7607(d)(9)). The Court effectively adopted an interpretive gloss requiring judicial review "at the high end of the range of levels of deference given to agency action under the 'arbitrary and capricious' standard." *Preminger v. Sec'y of Veterans Affairs*, 632 F.3d 1345, 1353 (Fed. Cir. 2011) (quoting *American Horse Protection Ass'n v. Lyng*, 812 F.2d 1, 4–5 (D.C. Cir. 1987)) (internal quotation marks omitted). We all should be lucky enough to get such deference from the reviewers of our actions.

But wait! *Massachusetts v. EPA* shows that even given extreme deference, an agency's denial of a rulemaking petition can be set aside if the denial rested on a mistaken understanding of the law or on a consideration that was not legally relevant. In that case, the EPA denied a petition to make rules limiting the emission of carbon dioxide and other "greenhouse gases" from new car engines. One reason the EPA denied the petition was the EPA's determination that it lacked statutory authority to issue the petitioned-for rules. *Massachusetts v. EPA*, 549 U.S. at 528. The Court held that this determination was wrong— so wrong that it did not deserve *Chevron* deference. *Id.* at 528–533. Another reason for the EPA's denial was its determination that issuing the rules would "conflict with other administration priorities." *Id.* at 528. The Court held that this determination was "divorced from the statutory text," which required the EPA to base its judgment, not on administration priorities, but instead on whether greenhouse gases from new car engines could "reasonably be anticipated to endanger public health or welfare." *Id.* at 533 (quoting 42 U.S.C. 7521(a)(1)). The Court remanded the case to the EPA to make the statutorily required determination about endangerment.

The disposition in *Massachusetts v. EPA* is typical in cases in which a court concludes that an agency has erroneously denied a rulemaking petition: The Court did not order the agency to undertake rulemaking. Rather, the Court remanded the matter for the agency to reconsider the petition unhindered by the errors that caused it to deny the petition originally. The only exception to this "remand for reconsideration in light of the court's opinion" disposition occurs when (1) a statute requires the agency to adopt the petitioned-for rules; and (2) the agency has missed the statutory deadline for issuing the rules or has unreasonably delayed issuing the rules. In that event, as discussed below, a court will more readily order the agency to undertake rulemaking.

In short, judicial review of an agency's denial of a rulemaking petition is extremely limited and deferential when no statute compels the rulemaking, but courts can still determine whether the agency properly understood the relevant law and considered all (and only) the relevant factors. All in all, judicial review reflects an agency-friendly version of the arbitrary and capricious standard.

5. Claim of Unreasonable or Unlawful Agency Delay

Section 706(1) of the federal APA authorizes a federal court to "**compel agency action unlawfully withheld or unreasonably delayed.**" Agency action is "**unlawfully withheld,**" for example, when an agency fails to meet a statutory deadline, such as a deadline for issuing rules on a particular subject. Agency action is "**unreasonably withheld,**" for example, when an agency is legally required to act on an application for benefits, and is under no specific legal deadline, but has delayed action so long that a court finds the delay unreasonable. *See Forest Guardians v. Babbitt*, 174 F.3d 1178, 1189 (10th Cir. 1999); *see also* 5 U.S.C. §555(b) (2012) (requiring agencies to resolve matters "within a reasonable time"). Either type of delay may be remedied under §706(1).

To get judicial review in an APA-type challenge, however, the plaintiff has to jump two big hurdles. First, the plaintiff must show the agency's delay constitutes "**agency action**" as defined in APA §551(13). We discussed the requirements for making that showing in Chapter 29's examination of the elements of the APA cause of action. Second, having shown that the delay qualifies as "**agency action**," the plaintiff must show also show that the delay is "*final* **agency action**," as required by APA §704 for a valid APA cause of action. We discussed the requirements for showing that agency delay is final in Chapter 30's examination of finality. The plaintiff who shows that agency delay is "**final agency action**" can get judicial review. The question remains: How does the plaintiff get judicial *relief*?

The D.C. Circuit addressed that question in *Telecommunications Research and Action Center v. FCC*, 750 F.2d 70 (D.C. Cir. 1984), which is commonly known as the "*TRAC* case."[1] The *TRAC* court listed six factors to consider in deciding whether to issue mandamus compelling an agency to take the delayed action:

> (1) the time agencies take to make decisions must be governed by a "rule of reason"; (2) where Congress has provided a timetable or other indication of the speed with which it expects the agency to proceed in the enabling statute, that statutory scheme may supply content for this rule of reason; (3) delays that might be reasonable in the sphere of economic regulation are less tolerable when human health and welfare are at stake; (4) the court should consider the effect of expediting delayed action on agency activities of a higher or competing priority; (5) the court should also take into account the nature and extent of the interests prejudiced by delay; and (6) the court need not find any impropriety lurking behind agency lassitude in order to hold that agency action is unreasonably delayed.

Id. at 79–80 (internal quotation marks omitted). The court has applied these factors in many later cases, but our objective is limited here to introducing the considerations one court found relevant in dealing with this specialized (yet all too common) situation of agency delay.

The question remains: What should a court do if the agency's delay has been unreasonable or unlawful? The answer is that the court has three choices. The court can choose not to do anything, which is a choice the court may make if the court believes the agency needs no prompting besides the lawsuit. *See TRAC*, 750 F.2d at 72. The court may order the agency to take action, but not set any specific deadline. *See Forest Guardians*, 174 F.3d at 1193. Finally, the court may order the agency to act by a certain deadline. See *Public Citizen Health Research Group v. Brock*, 823 F.2d 626, 629 (D.C. Cir. 1987); *Sierra Club v. Jackson*, 2011 WL 181097 (D.D.C. Jan. 20, 2011). Courts that use the third option often adopt a deadline the agency itself has proposed, recognizing that courts are in a poor position to set a realistic deadline by themselves. A court-ordered deadline, because of its specificity, can in theory lead to contempt sanctions if the agency violates the deadline. But even when an agency misses a court-ordered deadline, courts won't hold

---

1. We discussed the *TRAC* case in Chapter 28.A.1.b. There we discussed the court of appeals' holding that it had jurisdiction to review a claim that the FCC had unreasonably delayed entering a final order in a pending proceeding. The TRAC court held that the court, to protect its Hobbs Act jurisdiction to review final orders of the FCC, could review this claim of unreasonable FCC delay in issuing a final order.

agency officials in contempt as long as the officials show they are doing the best they can. *See Natural Resources Defense Council v. Train*, 510 F.2d 692, 713 (D.C. Cir. 1975) (discussing impossibility defense to contempt sanctions). You can't get blood from a turnip, and you can only get so much speed out of an overburdened, underfunded agency. You can best appreciate the situation of some of these agencies by picturing a sleep-deprived turtle.

Exercise: Judicial Relief for Agency Delay

Please review the *TRAC* factors quoted above and use them to construct a hypothetical "best case scenario" for getting judicial relief for an agency's delay in promulgating rules. You get to choose the subject matter of the rules, the agency, and the other background circumstances, unlike in practice!

B. Remedies

In this section we explore judicial remedies available before, during, and at the end of a judicial proceeding to review agency action. We also examine a potential barrier to a judicial remedy for agency error: namely, the harmless error rule. Finally, we touch on attorneys' fees.

1. Interim Relief

Interim relief means relief sought from a court before an agency has taken any action that is subject to judicial review. In one famous case, for example, a federal employee sought interim relief when her employing agency told her it was going to fire her. *Sampson v. Murray*, 415 U.S. 61 (1974). To cite another example, the Consumer Product Safety Commission (CPSC) can seek interim relief against a consumer product that poses an imminent hazard that must be addressed before the CPSC can complete an administrative proceeding to address the hazard. 15 U.S.C. § 2061 (2012). As these examples show, interim relief differs from relief sought *pending* judicial review, such as a preliminary injunction. A preliminary injunction or other relief pending judicial review is sought *after* an agency has taken an action that is subject to judicial review.

The availability of interim relief depends on whether a statute or other law authorizes it. The federal APA does not authorize interim relief. In contrast, some agency legislation authorizes interim relief, as shown by the provision in the CPSC's organic act cited in the last paragraph. *See also, e.g.*, 29 U.S.C. § 160(j) (2012) (authorizing National Labor Relations Board to go to federal court for "appropriate temporary relief or restraining order" pending an unfair labor practice proceeding before the Board). In addition, interim relief might be available from federal courts under the All Writs Act, which authorizes federal courts to "issue all writs necessary or appropriate in aid of their … jurisdictio[n] and agreeable to the usages and principles of law." 28 U.S.C. § 1651(a). In one case, for example, the Federal Trade Commission asked a federal court of appeals to enjoin a proposed merger until the FTC could complete its proceeding to determine the legality of the merger. *See FTC v. Dean Foods*, 384 U.S. 597 (1966). The U.S. Supreme Court held that the court of appeals had power to enjoin the proposed merger under the All Writs Act for the purpose of protecting the court's potential jurisdiction to review the FTC's final order on the proposed merger.

2. Relief Pending Judicial Review

a. Introduction

Once an agency has taken an action that is subject to judicial review, a person entitled to seek judicial review of that agency action usually will be entitled to seek judicial relief pending review. The most common type of relief is a stay of the agency action, which renders the action inoperative pending judicial review. Another common form of relief is a preliminary injunction. A person might seek a stay or other relief pending judicial review, for example, to suspend the operation of an agency order terminating a license or benefits or imposing some other sanction. Sometimes a stay or other relief pending review is necessary to prevent the judicial challenge to the agency action from becoming moot. *See, e.g., Norton v. Southern Utah Wilderness Alliance*, 542 U.S. 55, 68 (2004) (environmental organization's statutory challenge to manner in which Bureau of Land Management developed land use plans was rendered moot by completion and implementation of those plans).

As with the availability of interim relief, the availability of relief pending judicial review depends on the statute or other law authorizing such relief. In the federal court system, a court's authority to stay agency action ordinarily comes from one of three places: the APA; the agency legislation; or the courts' inherent authority, reflected in the All Writs Act. We will briefly discuss each source of stay authority separately, after which we will discuss preliminary injunctive relief, which is generally authorized by Federal Rule of Civil Procedure 65.

But regardless of the source of authority for a court to stay an agency action, a person usually cannot seek a stay from the court unless the person has first tried (and failed) to get the agency itself to stay its action. Federal agencies generally can stay their actions under § 705 of the federal APA:

---

5 U.S.C. § 705. Relief pending review

When an agency finds that justice so requires, it may postpone the effective date of action taken by it, pending judicial review....

As with other provisions of the federal APA, this provision in § 705 applies unless expressly modified or superseded by another statute. *See, e.g.,* 16 U.S.C. § 1855(f)(1)(A) (2012) (stays under § 705 not available in lawsuits challenging regulations issued under Magnuson-Stevens Fishery Conservation and Management Act of 1976). Like § 705 of the federal APA, state APAs may authorize state agencies to stay their actions pending judicial review. *See* 2010 Model State APA § 417 (authorizing agency to stay its decision in a contested case). As a practical matter, provisions authorizing agencies to stay their action pending judicial review create an administrative remedy that the federal courts and many state courts will require plaintiffs to exhaust before seeking stays from the court. And because the exhaustion-of-administrative-remedies doctrine requires *proper* exhaustion, the attorney seeking a stay from the agency on behalf of a client should always identify and comply with any agency rules for seeking a stay. *See, e.g.,* 12 C.F.R. § 1081.407(b) (2012) (procedures for seeking stay pending judicial review of certain orders of Bureau of Consumer Financial Protection). *But cf.* 2010 Model State APA § 504 (authorizing court to stay agency action pending review "regardless of whether the challenging party first sought a stay from the agency").

If the agency stays its action pending judicial review, you don't need to ask the court for a stay. On the other hand, if the agency denies a stay, you must go to court for it, and the court may defer to the agency's decision to deny the stay. *E.g., Moog Industries v. FTC,* 355 U.S. 411, 414 (1958). In any event, if the agency gives an explanation for denying the stay, you have to present that explanation to the court along with your cogent arguments about why the agency was wrong to deny the stay.

b. Federal APA

As discussed above, the first sentence of § 705 of the federal APA authorizes agencies to stay their actions pending judicial review. The second sentence of § 705 authorizes courts to stay agency actions pending judicial review:

---

5 U.S.C. § 705. Relief pending review

When an agency finds that justice so requires, it may postpone the effective date of action taken by it, pending judicial review. On such conditions as may be required and to the extent necessary to prevent irreparable injury, the reviewing court, including the court to which a case may be taken on appeal from or on application for certiorari or other writ to a reviewing court, may issue all necessary and appropriate process to postpone the effective date of an agency action or to preserve status or rights pending conclusion of the review proceedings.

We highlight three limits on courts' power to stay agency action under § 705.

First, the power granted by § 705 may be exercised only by a court that has power to review the agency action. This means that the agency action must be one that is subject to judicial review because it is either **"reviewable by statute"** or is **"final agency action for which there is no other adequate remedy in a court."** 5 U.S.C. § 704. (We discussed the meaning of the quoted phrases in Chapter 29.) In addition, the agency action must be reviewable by the particular court from which the stay is sought. In short the court's power to stay agency action under § 705 is incidental to that court's power to review that agency action.

Second, the court's power under § 705 is purely preservative. The court may postpone the effective date of the agency action or take other action to preserve the status quo or preserve rights threatened by the agency action. The court's power does not extend to granting affirmative types of relief pending review. For example, the court cannot order the agency to grant an initial license (though the court can postpone an agency order revoking an existing license). The court cannot order an initial award of benefits (though the court can postpone an agency order terminating existing benefits). *See* AGM 105. A person who wants affirmative relief pending judicial review must seek it under authority outside § 705.

Third, judicial relief under § 705 must be **"necessary to prevent irreparable injury."** This irreparable-injury requirement reflects a historic condition for equitable relief. Under § 705, as under traditional equity practice, a showing that relief is needed to prevent irreparable injury does not guarantee that the court will grant relief. The court must "balance the equities," including the interests of the agency, the interests of the public, and the likelihood that the person seeking the relief will prevail on the merits of the challenge to the agency action sought to be stayed. A showing of irreparable injury is thus necessary but not sufficient for a stay under § 705.

c. Special Review Provisions Addressing Stays

Special review statutes may address court-ordered stays pending judicial review, and thereby displace or supplement § 705 of the federal APA. For example, under § 705, the filing of a lawsuit seeking review of agency action does not, in and of itself, operate to stay the agency action pending judicial review. Many special review statutes simply confirm this general rule—i.e., that a request for judicial review doesn't automatically stay agency action. *See, e.g.,* 28 U.S.C. § 2349(b) (2012). Occasionally, however, a special review statute states, to the contrary, that an agency action covered by the provision *will* be automatically stayed pending judicial review. The following example concerns judicial review of orders that are issued under 15 U.S.C. § 80a-8(e) (2012), by the Securities and Exchange Commission and that suspend the registration of investment companies for misconduct.

---

15 U.S.C. § 80a-42. Court review of orders

(a) Any person or party aggrieved by an order issued by the Commission under this subchapter may obtain a review of such order in the United States court of appeals within any circuit wherein such person resides or has his principal place of business, or in the United States Court of Appeals for the District of Columbia, by filing in such court, within sixty days after the entry of such order, a written petition praying that the order of the Commission be modified or set aside in whole or in part....

(b) The commencement of proceedings under subsection (a) of this section to review an order of the Commission issued under section 80a-8(e) of this title shall operate as a stay of the Commission's order unless the court otherwise orders....

The suspension of an investment company's registration is a death sentence for the company, because unregistered investment companies can't buy or sell securities or conduct any other business in interstate commerce. *See id.* § 80a-7. What does this lead you to infer about the reason Congress provided for an automatic stay in this situation?

d. Federal Courts' Traditional Power to Stay Federal Agency Action Pending Review

The U.S. Supreme Court has indicated that federal courts have inherent power to stay federal agency orders pending judicial review. Two cases reflect that power.

- *Scripps-Howard Radio, Inc. v. Federal Communications Commission,* 316 U.S. 4 (1942)

In this classic administrative law case, the Court held that a federal court of appeals had power to stay an order of the FCC pending the court's review of that order. The Court described the rationale and source of the federal courts' power to enter stays as follows:

No court can make time stand still. The circumstances surrounding a controversy may change irrevocably during the pendency of an appeal, despite anything a court can do. But within these limits it is reasonable that an appellate court should be able to prevent irreparable injury to the parties or to the public resulting from the premature enforcement of a determination which may later be found

> to have been wrong. It has always been held, therefore, that, as part of its traditional equipment for the administration of justice, a federal court can stay the enforcement of a judgment pending the outcome of an appeal.

Id. at 9–10 (footnote omitted). By referring to the federal courts' "traditional equipment," the Court implied the power was inherent. Indeed, no statute expressly authorized the court of appeals to issue a stay in that case. In upholding the court of appeals' power to do so nonetheless, the Court cited the All Writs Act as recognizing, but not creating, the court's customary power to enter a stay to preserve the status quo pending judicial review. *Id.* at 10 n.4. In other words, the Court implied that the power would have existed even in the absence of the All Writs Act. *See In re McKenzie*, 180 U.S. 536, 551 (1901) (referring to power to grant stays as "inherent" power).

Scripps-Howard addressed a court's authority to issue a stay sought by someone who sought the stay at the same time as the party filed a statutorily authorized request for review of the agency action sought to be stayed. (In that case the authority came from a special review provision: § 402 of the Communications Act.) It matters that the stay was sought at the same time that judicial review was sought, because the All Writs Act is not a freestanding grant of subject matter jurisdiction. It just gives courts power "in aid of" jurisdiction conferred by another law. *See Syngenta Crop Protection, Inc. v. Henson*, 537 U.S. 28, 33 (2002). The broader point is that any inherent power that a federal court has to issue a stay inheres in — because it is justified by — the court's power to review the agency action sought to be stayed.

- *Nken v. Holder*, 556 U.S. 418 (2009)

The Court addressed the standard for staying an order of removal pending judicial review of that order. A federal statute says a federal court cannot "enjoin" the removal of an alien subject to a final removal order, "unless the alien shows by clear and convincing evidence that the entry or execution of such order is prohibited as a matter of law." 8 U.S.C. § 1252(f)(2). The Court held that this statute applies to *injunctions*, not *stays* pending judicial review. In so holding, the Court relied on precedent distinguishing injunctions from stays, as well as textual evidence in the statute indicating that Congress distinguished between these two procedural devices. In addition, the Court said, "Just like the Court in *Scripps-Howard*, we are loath to conclude that Congress would, without clearly expressing such a purpose, deprive the Court of Appeals of its customary power to stay orders under review." *Nken*, 556 U.S. at 433.

In the absence of a statute controlling the standard for granting a stay, the Court relied on the "traditional" test, which the Court "distilled" into four factors: "(1) whether the stay applicant has made a strong showing that he is likely to succeed on the merits; (2) whether the applicant will be irreparably injured absent a stay; (3) whether issuance of the stay will substantially injure the other parties interested in the proceeding; and (4) where the public interest lies." *Id.* at 434 (quoting *Hilton v. Braunskill*, 481 U.S. 770, 776 (1987), which cited the well-known case of *Virginia Petroleum Jobbers Ass'n v. Federal Power Comm'n*, 259 F.2d 921, 925 (D.C. Cir. 1958)). The Court in *Nken* discussed how those factors operate when a court decides whether to stay a removal order.

e. Preliminary Injunctive Relief

Sometimes a person needs more than a stay — the person needs a preliminary injunction — pending judicial review of agency action. The two forms of relief can be hard to distinguish. As the Court explained in *Nken v. Holder*:

A stay pending appeal certainly has some functional overlap with an injunction, particularly a preliminary one. Both can have the practical effect of preventing some action before the legality of that action has been conclusively determined. But a stay achieves this result by temporarily suspending the source of authority to act—the order or judgment in question—not by directing an actor's conduct.

556 U.S. at 428–429. The best way to illustrate a situation requiring a preliminary injunction, as distinguished from a stay, is to summarize one of the more recent cases in which the Court addressed the availability of preliminary injunctive relief against agency action, to which you should compare the cases discussed above involving stays:

- *Winter v. Natural Resources Defense Council*, 555 U.S. 7 (2008)

As part of its defense of U.S. waters, the U.S. Navy uses active sonar to detect submerged diesel-electric submarines. For the last forty years, the Navy has trained its personnel to use sonar technology in the waters of southern California, which are also used by marine mammals such as dolphins, sea lions, and whales. The Natural Resources Defense Council and other plaintiffs (collectively, NRDC) sued Navy officials in federal district court asserting that the Navy's sonar training exercises harmed marine mammals and violated several federal statutes. The NRDC got the district court to enter a preliminary injunction against the use of active sonar during training programs in the waters of southern California. The U.S. Court of Appeals for the Ninth Circuit affirmed the preliminary injunction.

The U.S. Supreme Court reversed and vacated the preliminary injunction. To begin, the Court stated the traditional standard for a preliminary injunction in federal court:

A plaintiff seeking a preliminary injunction must establish that he is likely to succeed on the merits, that he is likely to suffer irreparable harm in the absence of preliminary relief, that the balance of equities tips in his favor, and that an injunction is in the public interest.

Id. at 20. The Court then held that the lower courts misapplied this standard. For one thing, the Ninth Circuit erroneously required plaintiffs to demonstrate only a "possibility" of irreparable injury. Instead, a plaintiff must show that irreparable injury is *likely* in the absence of a preliminary injunction. *Id.* at 22. In addition, the Court held that even if the NRDC established the likelihood of irreparable injury, that likelihood was outweighed by "the public interest and the Navy's interest in effective, realistic training of its sailors." *Id.* at 23. The balance of interests weighed so strongly against the injunction that the Court found it unnecessary to assess NRDC's likelihood of succeeding on the merits. *Id.* 23–24.

Winter involved ongoing training exercises rather than a discrete adjudicatory order by an agency. The training exercises were not the sort of agency activity that a court could "stay." Only a preliminary injunction would do. *Winter* states and applies the traditional standard for preliminary injunctive relief in federal court. Of course, the standards for injunctive relief may be altered by statute and are likely to differ from State to State at least in minor ways.

3. Judicial Relief on a Final Judgment

a. Federal APA

We discussed earlier in this chapter the federal courts' power under § 706(1) to compel agency action unlawfully withheld or unreasonably delayed. Now we examine the courts' power under § 706(2) to **"hold unlawful and set aside"** agency action, findings, and conclusions on specified grounds. We address this question: Assuming a court finds one of those grounds, what exactly does it mean for the court to hold unlawful and set aside the agency action? The usual answer, in short, is that the court (1) identifies the flaw in the agency action; (2) "vacates"—i.e., nullifies—the agency action; and (3) remands the matter to the agency for further consideration in light of the court's decision. There is one significant exception to this usual vacate-and-remand disposition: Some lower federal courts sometimes will remand a flawed agency action to the agency without vacating the action, so that the action stays in effect while the agency figures out how to fix the flaw.

We will refer to the usual disposition using the Court's term for it: "the ordinary remand rule." *Gonzalez v. Thomas*, 547 U.S. 183, 187 (2006) (quoting *INS v. Orlando Ventura*, 537 U.S. 12, 18 (2002)). We will first explain the rule's practical significance for administrative lawyers and agencies. Then we will explain its rationale. Finally we discuss the "remand without vacating" exception that some courts apply to some invalid federal agency rules.

The ordinary remand rule makes a successful judicial challenge to agency action anti-climactic. This is because it seldom gives the challenger what the challenger ultimately wants from the agency. For example, if the challenger convinces a court to invalidate an agency's denial of the challenger's application for a license, the court does not itself grant the license or even order the agency to do so. Instead, the court remands the matter for the agency to reconsider the license application in light of the court's correction of whatever flaw caused the court to invalidate the agency's original denial of the license. Many successful challengers must feel a let-down when their lawyer tells them after a favorable judicial decision comes out: "Congratulations! We get to return to the agency and do it again!"

Worse still from the successful challenger's point of view, the agency on remand might again deny the license application. This option is often open to the agency, for example, if the flaw identified by the court was that the agency failed to follow proper procedures or that the agency's explanation for denying the license was inadequate or rested on a mistaken view of the law. A classic illustration of an agency "re-do" occurred in *SEC v. Chenery Corp.*, 332 U.S. 194 (1947). The Court initially held that the SEC erred when it refused to allow a company to reorganize in a way that enabled its management to retain control of the company. The Court determined that the SEC had based its refusal on a mistaken view of the judicially developed law of fiduciary duties. On remand, the SEC again refused to permit the reorganization scheme favored by the management, but this time the SEC grounded its refusal on its interpretation of statutory standards and its experience applying those statutory standards. The Court upheld the SEC's refusal on this new ground when the case went to the Court a second time.

The rationale for the ordinary remand rule concerns the differing roles of the court and the agency. A court can decide whether an agency has exercised its judgment properly, but a court cannot make that judgment for the agency. Congress has given the agency a job to do, subject to judicial oversight. A court gets authority from Congress to decide whether the agency has done its job right, but the court doesn't get authority to do the agency's job for it, even when the agency didn't get it right the first time.

The Court has explained this rationale in cases involving many different federal agencies and many different federal statutory schemes. The Court expressed the rationale this way in a case involving an alien's claim for asylum:

> Within broad limits the law entrusts the agency to make the basic asylum eligibility decision here in question. E.g., 8 U.S.C. § 1158(a); 8 U.S.C. § 1253(h)(1) (1994

ed.) ... In such circumstances a "judicial judgment cannot be made to do service for an administrative judgment." *SEC v. Chenery Corp.*, 318 U.S. 80, 88 (1943).

INS v. Orlando Ventura, 537 U.S. at 16. A useful summary of the rationale comes from a case involving the Federal Commission:

> [T]he guiding principle ... is that the function of the reviewing court ends when an error of law is laid bare. At that point the matter once more goes to the Commission for reconsideration.

Federal Power Comm'n v. Idaho Power Co., 344 U.S. 17, 20 (1952).

Courts usually vacate the flawed agency decision at the same time they remand it, but some federal courts claim equitable power to leave flawed federal agency rules intact pending remand. Illustrating this power is *Idaho Farm Bureau Federation v. Babbitt*, 58 F.3d 1392 (9th Cir. 1995). The court of appeals held that the Fish and Wildlife Service made a "significant procedural error" by failing to disclose some data to the public during a public comment period on a proposal of the Service. *Id.* at 1405. The proposal, which the Service ended up adopting, was to extend the protections of the Endangered Species Act to the Springs Snail. If the court vacated that extension, the Service wouldn't be able to protect the snail under the Act until after the Service went through the proper procedures. In the meantime, the snail might go extinct! To avoid that danger, and because there was a good chance that the Service would reach the same conclusion after allowing the public to comment in the undisclosed data, the court remanded the procedurally flawed decision to the Service without vacating that decision.

Although this result seems sensible, some judges and scholars criticize it. The critics say it violates § 706(2) of the APA, which requires a court to "set aside" flawed agency action. Critics also say a court can avoid results like the extinction of the Springs Snail by *staying* its decision invalidating an agency action to give the agency time to try to fix the flaw in its original action. *See, e.g., Comcast Corp. v. FCC*, 579 F.3d 1, 11–12 (D.C. Cir. 2009) (Randolph, J., concurring). One big difference between (1) remanding without vacating, on the one hand, and (2) staying the court's decision vacating agency action, on the other hand, is that, under the second approach, the agency bears the burden of justifying the stay. In contrast, courts don't expressly put any comparable burden on the agency when deciding whether to remand an agency rule without vacating it. Another big difference is that a court taking the second approach usually puts an expiration date on the stay of its decision vacating the agency action. This expiration date puts a deadline on the agency to fix the problem and convince the court that the problem is fixed and that the court can accordingly withdraw its decision vacating the action. Both differences cause agencies to prefer the remand-without-vacating approach.

In sum, courts in an APA-type challenge to agency action almost always vacate and remand the agency action if it is flawed, a disposition that may give the agency the opportunity on remand to do the same thing it did before. If this disposition does not illustrate the need to "win your case before the agency," we don't know what will.

Exercise: The Ordinary Remand Rule

The objective of this exercise is to have you project likely post-remand scenarios under the ordinary remand rule, depending on the type of flaw found by the reviewing court. Please jot down what the agency on remand might do in light of the court's grounds for vacating and remanding agency action.

1. The court holds that the agency action is arbitrary and capricious because the agency's explanation does not show the agency considered significant objections to its approach.

2. The court holds that the agency action is arbitrary and capricious because there was not enough evidence before the agency to support one of the agency's factual premises.

3. The court holds that the agency action regulating television broadcasters violates the First Amendment.

4. The court holds that the agency action exceeds the agency's statutory authority.

5. The court holds that the agency violated the federal APA's notice-and-comment procedures for rulemaking because the agency did not adequately disclose the technical data underlying the proposed rule that it published for public comment.

---

b. Special Review Statutes

A special review statute may or may not address judicial remedies. If it does not, the judicial remedies authorized by § 706 of the APA will control by default. Some special review provisions do address judicial remedies but authorize essentially the same remedies as are authorized under § 706. We focus on a third possibility: Some special review statutes authorize courts to *modify* an agency action, as an alternative to affirming it or vacating and remanding it.

When a special review provision authorizes modification, the authority usually applies to agency adjudicatory orders rather than agency rules. Perhaps that is because judicial modification of an agency rule would involve an exercise of quasi-legislative power that Congress doesn't think courts should have. In any event, the following provision illustrates the point. It comes from the special review statute for SEC actions. It authorizes modification of SEC orders, but not SEC rules.

---

15 U.S.C. § 78y. Court review of orders and rules

(a) Final Commission orders; persons aggrieved; petition; record; findings; affirmance, modification, enforcement, or setting aside of orders ...

(1) A person aggrieved by a final order of the Commission entered pursuant to this chapter may obtain review of the order in the United States Court of Appeals for the circuit in which he resides or has his principal place of business, or for the District of Columbia Circuit, by filing in such court, within sixty days after the entry of the order, a written petition requesting that the order be modified or set aside in whole or in part....

(3) On the filing of the petition, the court has jurisdiction, which becomes exclusive on the filing of the record, to affirm or modify and enforce or to set aside the order in whole or in part....

(b) Commission rules; persons adversely affected; petition; record; affirmance, enforcement, or setting aside of rules; findings; transfer of proceedings

(1) A person adversely affected by a rule of the Commission promulgated pursuant to section 78f, 78i(h)(2), 78k, 78k-1, 78o(c)(5) or (6), 78o-3, 78q, 78q-1, or 78s of this title may obtain review of this rule in the United States Court of Appeals for the circuit in which he resides or has his principal place of business or for the District of Columbia Circuit, by filing in such court, within sixty days after the promulgation of the rule, a written petition requesting that the rule be set aside....

(3) On the filing of the petition, the court has jurisdiction, which becomes exclusive on the filing of the materials set forth in paragraph (2) of this subsection, to affirm and enforce or to set aside the rule....

This statute seemingly empowers a court to modify an SEC order and then enforce it as modified. To take a simple example, if a court concluded that an SEC order imposing a $500,000 civil penalty was too high, the court could apparently reduce it to an appropriate amount — say $300,000 — and order the person against whom the penalty was entered to pay a penalty of $300,000. But despite the text of the statute, it doesn't work this way.

Federal court modification of federal agency action is generally forbidden under the case summarized next:

- *Federal Power Commission v. Idaho Power Co.*, 344 U.S. 17 (1952)

Idaho Power applied to the Federal Power Commission for a license to build a power plant with two transmission lines to carry power from the new plant to its existing power-transmission system. The federal government had its own power projects in the same locale, and the federal agencies that operated those projects asked that they be allowed to use the new transmission lines to carry some of the power that they generated. The Federal Power Commission agreed, and accordingly it granted the license to Idaho Power with one important set of conditions in paragraph (F) of the license: Under paragraph (F), Idaho Power had to allow the federal power projects to interconnect with the two new transmission lines that Idaho Power proposed to create; then Idaho Power had to allow federally generated power to be carried over its new transmission lines. Paragraph (F) promised the federal government would pay Idaho Power for carrying federally generated power.

Idaho Power didn't like the conditions in paragraph (F), so it challenged the Commission's order granting the license in the federal court of appeals. The court of appeals held that the Federal Power Commission lacked the (well ...) power to put these conditions in the license. Going further, the court of appeals entered a judgment ordering that the Commission's order granting the license "be, and it is hereby, modified by striking therefrom paragraph (F) thereof, and that the order of the Federal Power Commission ... as thus modified be ... affirmed." *Id.* at 20 (quoting court of appeals' judgment). The special review statute under which the court of appeals acted included the authority " 'to affirm, *modify*, or set aside' the order of the Commission 'in whole or in part.' " *Id.* (quoting review statute; emphasis added by your author).

The U.S. Supreme Court held that the court of appeals could not modify the Commission's order. Instead, the court of appeals should have remanded the matter to the Commission for the Commission to decide whether, lacking power to add paragraph (F), the Commission should either grant the license without the conditions set out in paragraph (F) or deny the license altogether. The Court explained:

When the court decided that the license should issue without the conditions, it usurped an administrative function. There doubtless may be situations where the provision excised from the administrative order is separable from the remaining parts or so minor as to make remand inappropriate. But the guiding principle, violated here, is that the function of the reviewing court ends when an error of law is laid bare. At that point the matter once more goes to the Commission for reconsideration. See *Federal Communications Commission v. Pottsville Broadcasting Co.*, 309 U.S. 134; *Federal Trade Commission v. Morton Salt Co.*, 334 U.S. 37.

The Court, it is true, has power "to affirm, modify, or set aside" the order of the Commission "in whole or in part." § 313(b). But that authority is not power to exercise an essentially administrative function. See *Ford Motor Co. v. National Labor Relations Board*, 305 U.S. 364, 373–374; *Jacob Siegel Co. v. Federal Trade Commission*, 327 U.S. 608.

Idaho Power, 344 U.S. at 20–21; *see also NLRB v. Food Store Employees Union, Local 347*, 417 U.S. 1, 8–9 (1974) (holding that court of appeals erred by modifying NLRB order without remanding).

Lower federal courts have read *Idaho Power* to allow them to modify an agency action only when the modification is minor. *See, e.g., Thompson v. U.S. Dep't of Labor*, 885 F.2d 551, 558 (9th Cir. 1989). This applies to the federal district courts as well as the federal courts of appeals. *See N.C. Fisheries Ass'n v Gutierrez*, 550 F.3d 16, 21 (D.C. Cir. 2008). And it applies, as *Idaho Power* itself shows, even when the special review statute authorizes modification of the agency action.

Though called "ordinary," the ordinary remand rule is rather extraordinary in its severely restrictive effect on special review statutes authorizing reviewing courts to modify agency action.

c. Nonstatutory Review

We discussed nonstatutory review in Chapter 29. There we said that nonstatutory remedies such as injunctions are most often sought today in suits seeking review under the APA or a special review statute. An example is provided by suits under federal APA § 706(1) to compel agency action unlawfully withheld or unreasonably delayed. In these suits some plaintiffs also seek a writ of mandamus compelling the agency to take action under 28 U.S.C. § 1361. Indeed, the relief available under § 706(1) closely resembles a writ of mandamus. The careful plaintiff's attorney ordinarily should seek relief under both § 706(1) and under the mandamus statute. The worst that can happen is that the court will find mandamus unavailable because there is an adequate remedy at law— namely, a remedy under § 706(1). *See Hollywood Mobile Estates Ltd. v. Seminole Tribe of Florida*, 641 F.3d 1259, 1268 (11th Cir. 2011).

Writs of mandamus and other nonmonetary, "nonstatutory" forms of relief such as declaratory judgments and injunctions can be obtained against federal agencies despite sovereign immunity. As discussed in Chapter 28, § 702 of the federal APA waives sovereign immunity from **"relief other than money damages."** Congress added this waiver in 1976 to eliminate the defense of sovereign immunity in *all* actions for nonmonetary relief against the government, including actions under the APA, actions under special review provisions, and actions for nonstatutory review. *See Michigan v. U.S. Army Corps of Eng'rs*, 667 F.3d 765, 775–776 (7th Cir. 2011).

The takeaway is that the remedies in suits seeking relief under the APA or a special review statute need not be limited to vacatur and remand of the agency action. If this is not adequate, you can seek additional, nonstatutory remedies.

4. Harmless Error

The last sentence of §706 of the federal APA instructs reviewing courts: "[D]ue account shall be taken of the rule of prejudicial error." That instruction codifies a judicially developed rule more commonly known by the name of prejudicial error's less evil twin: the rule of *harmless* error. The harmless error rule originated as a rule applicable when an appellate court reviews the decision of a trial court. Courts then began also applying the rule when they reviewed the actions of administrative agencies. In the latter application, the rule has been called "the administrative law ... harmless error rule." *Shinseki v. Sanders*, 556 U.S. 396, 406 (2009) (internal quotation marks omitted).

Because §706 merely codifies the judicially developed harmless error rule, administrative lawyers might encounter the rule in any judicial challenge to agency action, even ones not subject to §706. For example, the rule is part of many States' administrative law. Because of its prevalence, the rule deserves attention.

The U.S. Supreme Court discussed harmless error analysis in *Shinseki v. Sanders*, 556 U.S. 396 (2009). The Court said that the burden is usually on the person asserting error to show that the error harmed that person. The Court also explained how courts decide whether the person has met that burden:

> [T]he factors that inform a reviewing court's "harmless-error" determination are various, potentially involving, among other case-specific factors, an estimation of the likelihood that the result would have been different, an awareness of what body (jury, lower court, administrative agency) has the authority to reach that result, a consideration of the error's likely effects on the perceived fairness, integrity, or public reputation of judicial proceedings, and a hesitancy to generalize too broadly about particular kinds of errors when the specific factual circumstances in which the error arises may well make all the difference ...

Sanders, 556 U.S. at 411–412. The Court described the overall purpose of the harmless error rule as designed to prevent reviewing courts from invalidating trial court or agency actions for mere "technicalities." *Id.* at 407.

The Court in *Sanders* emphasized that it is hard to make generalizations about what kinds of errors are harmless. We will summarize one case in which a court found harmless error and one case in which a court found harmful (**"prejudicial"**) error. They may whet your appetite to do research to locate more examples.

- *City of Arlington, Texas v. Federal Communications Commission*, 668 F.3d 229 (5th Cir. 2012)

A federal statute restricts the authority of state and local governments to prevent cell phone towers from being erected within their borders. This federal statute is administered by the Federal Communications Commission (FCC).

The FCC received a petition for a declaratory ruling to clarify certain aspects of the statute, from a trade group of cell phone companies known as the CTIA. The FCC published public notice of CTIA's petition in the Federal Register. In that Federal Register notice, the FCC described the points of clarification that the CTIA sought. The FCC also invited public comment on the petition, in response to which the FCC got dozens of comments, including from Arlington and San Antonio, Texas. The FCC issued a Declaratory Ruling discussing issues raised by the public comments and addressing the points of clarification sought by the CTIA.

Arlington and San Antonio sought judicial review of the FCC's Declaratory Ruling. One of the Cities' challenges concerned the Declaratory Ruling's establishment of timelines within which state and local governments were supposed to act on applications to put up cell phone towers. If a state or local government violated the timelines in the Declaratory Ruling, the violation would presumptively violate the statute requiring state and local governments to act on applications within "a reasonable period of time." *Id.* at 235 (quoting statute; describing timelines). The Cities argued these timelines constituted **"rules"** within the meaning of the federal APA (5 U.S.C. § 551(4)), and that the FCC accordingly should have promulgated the timelines using the notice-and-comment rulemaking procedures of the APA, instead of establishing them in the adjudicatory proceeding on the CTIA's petition.

The court of appeals rejected this argument. In dicta, the court said the FCC might indeed have abused its discretion by using adjudication, rather than rulemaking, to establish the timelines. But if the FCC erred in its choice of adjudication, the error was harmless. The FCC gave public notice of the issues raised by the petition; the FCC gave the public a chance to comment; and the FCC considered all the relevant issues in its Declaratory Ruling. The court said, "[W]e are not aware of a single argument the [C]ities now present to this court that was not considered by the FCC in the agency proceedings below." *Id.* at 245. More generally, the procedure that the FCC used served the purposes that notice-and-comment rulemaking procedures are designed to serve, and "the citizens have not demonstrated that the FCC's approach here burdened them in any way," *Id.*

As the *City of Arlington* shows, agencies often use harmless-error arguments to avoid having their actions set aside for procedural errors, including violations of the APA's procedural requirements. In assessing the harmfulness of procedural errors, the courts disagree about what counts as "harm." Under the narrowest view, "harm" occurs only if a procedural error affects the *outcome* of an agency proceeding. Under a broader view, "harm" may arise even from errors that didn't affect the outcome, if the errors prevented the person asserting error from exercising important procedural rights such as the right to provide input. Under a still broader view, "harm" occurs—namely, harm to the rule of law—anytime an agency violates an important procedural requirement, and the harm is only compounded when a court excuses it. The different conceptions of harm make it important for the lawyer asserting procedural error to research the relevant case law in the jurisdiction and fully explain the effects of the procedural error. *See generally California Wilderness Coalition v. U.S. Dep't of Energy*, 631 F.3d 1072 (9th Cir. 2011) (majority and dissenting judges disagree on harmless error analysis, because of conflicting understanding of Court's decision in *Shinseki v. Sanders*).

- *American Radio Relay League, Inc. v. Federal Communications Commission*, 524 F.3d 227 (D.C. Cir. 2008)

The court in *American Radio Relay* held that the FCC violated its duty in an informal rulemaking under the federal APA to disclose the technical basis of a proposed rule. Specifically, the FCC failed to disclose unredacted reports of studies that the FCC conducted on a new type of internet technology—known as "Access BPL"—that uses electric power lines to supply internet service. The studies concerned the extent to which Access BPL technology interfered with radio communications. We excerpted the portion of the opinion discussing the FCC's violation in Chapter 12.

The FCC's final rules on Access BPL were challenged by an organization representing amateur radio operators, the American Radio Relay League. The League not only showed that the FCC erred by failing to disclose unredacted versions of its studies on Access BPL.

The League also "met its burden to demonstrate prejudice by showing that it has something useful to say regarding the unredacted studies." *Id.* at 237–238 (internal quotation marks and brackets omitted). The unredacted pages of the studies exposed potential weaknesses in the FCC's reasoning upon which the American Radio Relay League could fruitfully comment.

5. Attorneys' Fees

Under the "American rule," each party to a lawsuit pays his or her own attorneys' fees, and no one else's. The American rule has exceptions. Exceptions are created by statutes that authorize the winning party in certain kinds of lawsuits to recover all or part of his or her attorneys' fees and other costs of the lawsuit from the losing party. These are called "fee-shifting statutes."

Some fee-shifting statutes have particular relevance for administrative lawyers. Specifically, many citizen suit provisions in federal statutes authorize successful plaintiffs to recover some or all of their attorneys' fees and other costs from the defendant, which may include a federal agency. In addition to citizen suit provisions, a federal statute called the Equal Access to Justice Act (EAJA) authorizes people who win certain lawsuits with the federal government to recover attorneys' fees under certain circumstances. 28 U.S.C. § 2412 (2012). The EAJA even allows people to recover attorneys' fees incurred in some adversary agency adjudications with the federal government. 5 U.S.C. § 504 (2012).

You may be relieved to know that statutes seldom put the shoe on the other foot: Few statutes allow the *federal government* to recover *its* attorneys' fees from a losing private party. A rare statute that does so is in the Comprehensive Environmental Response, Compensation, and Liability Act, better known as the "Superfund law." It allows the government to recover "all costs of removal or remedial action" connected with cleaning up, or having responsible parties clean up, designated toxic waste sites. 42 U.S.C. § 9607(a)(4)(A) (2012). Lower federal courts have interpreted its broad language about recovery of clean-up costs to allow recovery of attorneys' fees. *See, e.g., United States v. Northernaire Plating Co.*, 685 F. Supp. 1410, 1418 (W.D. Mich. 1988), *aff'd*, 889 F.2d 1497 (6th Cir. 1989).

As you might guess, every fee-shifting statute has restrictions and ambiguities, as a result of which victory on the merits does not guarantee recovery of attorneys' fees. Even so, as an administrative lawyer your litigation planning and counseling of clients must account for the costs of litigation as well as the prospects for recovering some of those costs. You will thus have to become familiar with the applicable statutes and case law construing them.

C. Chapter 35 Wrap Up

This chapter began by exploring five situations for which courts have articulated specialized standards for judicial review of agency action.

(1) agency selection of target of enforcement action

(2) agency choice of sanction

(3) agency denial of request to rehear, reconsider, or reopen prior decision

(4) agency denial of rulemaking petitions

(5) claim of unreasonable or unlawful agency delay

All of these situations involve agency exercises of discretion. Courts review agency discretionary calls to ensure that agencies have acted within their statutory authority and haven't abused their discretion. At the same time, courts recognize that certain discretionary calls are ones that courts are not well equipped to review closely. For these discretionary judgments, courts may articulate unusually generous standards of review, which permit courts to set aside agency action only for "gross abuse of discretion" and similarly egregious abuses. In addition, the situation of unreasonable agency delay is heavily influenced by courts' recognition that many agencies lack resources to carry out all of their responsibilities as fully as might be ideal.

The second part of the chapter examined remedies available in proceedings for judicial review of agency action. Remedies may be available against an agency at three stages: (1) before judicial review is sought; (2) pending judicial review; and (3) at the conclusion of judicial review. In APA-type challenges, ordinarily the final relief is invalidation (vacatur) of agency action and a remand to the agency.

Chapter Problem Revisited

1. Agency decision on whether to initiate action

    A. Agency choice between rulemaking and adjudication: Usually, abuse of discretion; *SEC v. Chenery; Storer Broadcasting*

    B. Agency refusal to undertake enforcement action: Presumptively committed to agency discretion by law, and hence unreviewable except for constitutional challenges, under *Heckler v. Chaney*

    C. Agency selection of target for enforcement action: Review for a "patent abuse of discretion," under *FTC v. Universal-Rundle*; *Moog Industries v. FTC.*

    D. Agency denial of rulemaking petition: Highly deferential form of "arbitrary and capricious" review, under *Massachusetts v. EPA*

2. Agency procedures for taking action

    A. Compliance with constitutionally required procedures: De Novo

    B. Compliance with statutorily required procedures

        1. Procedures required by the agency legislation: *Chevron/Mead* doctrine

        2. Procedures required by other legislation, including APA and other cross-cutting statutes: De Novo

    C. Compliance with executive-branch material

        1. The agency's own procedural rules: *Auer deference*

        2. Other executive-branch material: De Novo

3. Resulting agency action

    A. Compliance with constitution: De novo

    B. Compliance with statutes

    1.   The agency legislation: *Chevron/Mead* doctrine

    2.   Other legislation: De Novo

  C. Compliance with executive-branch material

    1.   The agency's own rules: *Auer* deference

    2.   Other executive-branch material: De Novo

  D. Factual basis for agency action (three possible standards of review)

    1.   De Novo

    2.   Substantial Evidence

    3.   Arbitrary and Capricious

  E. Reasoned Decision Making: Arbitrary and Capricious

  F. Other:

    1.   Agency choice of sanction: In general, highly deferential review under abuse of discretion standard, *Butz v. Glover Livestock Comm'n Co.*, sometimes called "gross abuse of discretion"

    2.   Agency decision to reconsider, reopen, or rehear prior decision: In general, committed to agency discretion by law to the extent original decision is challenged only as involving material error; otherwise, generally standard of review is highly deferential under abuse of discretion standard. *Interstate Commerce Commission v. Brotherhood of Locomotive Engineers.*

Professional Development Reflection Questions

As you end your course on administrative law, you undoubtedly will review what you have learned to prepare for the final exam or other method of assessment your teacher plans to use. We invite you not only to review but also to *reflect* on what you've learned, and specifically to assess its significance for your professional path. In particular, please consider these questions:

1.   Have you found the course useful? If so, what aspect of the course do you think will be most useful to you in the future?

2.   Has the course developed or deepened an interest on your part in practicing in some area of administrative law? If so, what "next steps" can you realistically commit to that will help you pursue that interest?

Chapter 36

Farewell!

This farewell chapter is inspired by two ideas. First, we believe that as law students approach the end of a course and face final exams or some other form of final assessment, they worry about all that they *haven't* learned, without giving themselves enough credit for all that they *have* learned. And yet if you have gotten this far, you have learned a ton and for that we congratulate you! That brings us to the second idea behind this chapter, which is that, like Dr. Johnson, we believe people more often need "to be reminded than informed."[1] In that spirit, we briefly remind you of the main points of this book.

The main point of the book is that agencies have no inherent power. Most agencies are creatures of statute. Therefore, every agency action must rest on a valid grant of power (usually from a statute), and must comply with all valid limits on, and requirements for exercising, that power. Our legal system has several ways to ensure that agencies obey limits on their power. One way is that people harmed by agency action can invoke the courts' power to invalidate improper agency action. The courts' power includes authority to review agency action for abuses of power in matters as to which they have discretion.

To unpack this main point a bit:

From Part 1 you learned the fundamentals of administrative law. Those fundamentals include what agencies are, what they do, how they are created, what powers they typically have, and what limits on those powers exist. As to agency powers, their most distinctive feature is that they are commonly a blend of the powers traditionally associated with the three separate branches of government. Thus you learned about the quasi-legislative power that many agencies have to make legislative rules; agencies' executive powers, which include the power to interpret their legislation and advise the public of those interpretations through interpretative rules; and the quasi-judicial power to adjudicate cases. Besides learning about these powers, you got an overview of the types of law that potentially limit those powers — i.e., constitutional law, statutory law, etc. — and the way those limits are enforced — e.g., by the agency itself, by each of the three branches of government, and by people. You learned about, and began to practice, the key skills of identifying and analyzing the statutes relevant to an administrative law problem. You also got an introduction to a problem solving framework for analyzing most administrative law problems. Finally, you learned how federalism influences administrative law, including through the creation of programs of cooperative federalism.

---

1. The original had it, "Men more frequently require to be reminded than informed." Samuel Johnson, *The Rambler*, No. 2, §2, at 14 (Mar. 24, 1750), *available at* University of Virginia, Electronic Text Center, http://etext.lib.virginia.edu/toc/modeng/public/Joh1Ram.html. Samuel Johnson was a writer who lived in England in the 1700s. He wrote, among things, the periodical *The Rambler*, from which we have just quoted, and an influential dictionary of the English language. Dr. Johnson's fame rests in part on his biography, *The Life of Samuel Johnson, LL.D.*, written by James Boswell in 1791.

Part 2 had you explore agency rulemaking. First you learned the fundamental distinction between legislative and non-legislative rules. Next you learned how to determine when a statute grants an agency the power to make legislative rules. Then you learned how to use the problem solving framework introduced in Part 1 to identify, classify, and analyze limits on agency rulemaking power. Having learned that broad framework, you then focused on limits imposed on agency rulemaking power by agency legislation and the APA. While focusing on these statutory limits, you also learned that agency rules can put their own limits on an agency, including by elaborating on, and adding to, the statutorily required rulemaking procedures. Finally, you learned about the legal effects of a valid, published legislative rule. In connection with that final piece, you learned that valid federal legislative rules can preempt state law.

In Part 3, you explored agency adjudication. Initially, you learned to distinguish an agency's power to adjudicate a matter administratively, on the one hand, from an agency's power to go to court or to be taken to court, as a litigant. You learned that, in some agency adjudications (e.g., enforcement proceedings), one part of the agency may act as a prosecutor while another part of the agency acts as a judge. Having been introduced to agency adjudication, you learned how to determine whether a statute grants adjudicatory power. Then you learned how to use the problem solving framework introduced in Part 1 to identify, classify, and analyze limits on, and requirements for exercising, an agency's adjudicatory power. Next you learned about the legal effects of an agency adjudication, which includes the dauntingly named doctrines of administrative stare decisis and administrative res judicata. Finally, you explored an issue that straddles the rulemaking and adjudication powers—namely, an agency's choice between rulemaking and adjudication as means of carrying out its statutory responsibilities.

Part 4 steeped you in availability and scope of judicial review of agency action. First, you learned the main requirements for getting judicial review of agency action—e.g., finding a court with jurisdiction, identifying a cause of action, and bringing a timely challenge. Second, you learned what you get when you get judicial review of agency action in an APA-type challenge. This second subject introduced you to the standards of judicial review of agency action and the remedies available in an APA-type challenge to agency action.

We hope you have arrived at the end of this book with a better understanding of the central role that administrative agencies play in making and executing the law, and of the role that lawyers play in representing people with legal matters involving agencies, and representing the agencies themselves. We also hope that you have strengthened your statutory analysis skills; have learned about some types of legal material (e.g., executive orders, agency guidance documents) that used to be mysterious or utterly unknown to you; and have been exposed to some research strategies that may be useful in the future. Mostly, we hope that you have found the time and energy that you have put into learning administrative law worthwhile. Farewell!

Index

Page numbers followed by a "D" indicate pages with the indexed entry in a diagram. Page numbers followed by an "F" indicate pages with the indexed entry in a flowchart. Page numbers followed by "Fig." indicate pages with the indexed entry in a Figure. Page numbers followed by an "n" indicate pages with the indexed entry in a footnote. Finally, page numbers followed by a "T" indicate the indexed entry is in a table on that page. Case names and names of journal articles are in italic font. Titles of books are in small capitals. "APA" means "administrative procedure act."

F

O